THE GUINNESS
COMPLETE
GRAND
PRIX
WHO'S
WHO

THE GUINNESS COMPLETE

GRAND PRIX WHO'S WHO

STEVE SMALL

GUINNESS PUBLISHING

First published in 1994 by
GUINNESS PUBLISHING
33 London Road, Enfield
Middlesex, EN2 6DJ

Designed and typeset by Steve Small

A catalogue record for this book is available
from the British Library

Printed and bound in Great Britain by The Bath Press, Avon

ISBN: 0-85112-702-9

ACKNOWLEDGEMENTS

During the several years that it has taken for this project to come to fruition, there have been many friends and colleagues who have given their encouragement and assistance. I can truly say that without their help, this volume would not have been so complete.

There are two people who must be singled out for their sterling efforts on my behalf. Firstly, the late John Taylor, who was well known to serious followers of the sport for more than a decade as the statistical guru of the leading Grand Prix annual *Autocourse*. When I first discussed the idea for the book with him back in 1988, he willingly undertook the massive job of placing much of the contents of my folders onto a computer database, keeping his eagle eye out for the inevitable inaccuracies and omissions there and putting them to rights. Sadly, his early death from muscular dystrophy in 1991 means that he is not here to see the finished article in which he had played such a major part. More recently, I have been fortunate indeed to enlist the help of my friend, colleague and fellow Guinness author, Peter Lovering. His skills and patience have been stretched to the limit as, despite being put under tremendous pressure, he first brought some semblance of literacy to the biographical pieces, and then ran the rule over the massive bank of statistics, filtering out the remaining inconsistencies and errors with a diligence that could hardly be matched.

Apart from the aforementioned, my gratitude goes to the following for their help, enthusiasm and forbearance to a greater or lesser extent over the past five or so years: Kathy Ager, Jean-Luc Alexandre, Simon Arron, Jocelyne Bia, Jeff Bloxham, Liz Le Breton, Diana Burnett, Sallie Collins, Jane Doyle, Simon Duncan, Deirdre Fenney, Peter J Fox, George Greenfield, Soda Hayata, Alan Henry, Bryan Kennedy, Christine Lalla, Jo Mulroy, Doug Nye, Ivan Ponting, Richard Poulter, Charles Richards, David Roberts, Nigel Snowdon, Roger Swan and Steve Tee.

The author is also grateful for permission to reproduce photographs. The vast majority are from the amazing collection of LAT Photographic, Diana Burnett and Nigel Snowdon, with additional but telling contributions from The Ludvigsen Library, Autosport Photographic, Goddard Picture Library, Hulton Deutsch, MPS (Motoring Press Service, Japan) and Roger Swan.

Efforts have been made to trace copyright holders of all photographs used in this book. We apologise for any omissions, which are unintentional, and would be pleased to include an appropriate acknowledgement in any subsequent edition.

INTRODUCTION

The first seeds of *The Guinness Complete Grand Prix Who's Who* were sown in the mid-seventies, when I began piecing together records of Grand Prix drivers' careers, not just in Formula 1 but in all other types of racing as well. My files began to multiply at a disconcerting rate as trivial and minor, seemingly irrelevant, information about every driver was recorded. Even then I had in mind a volume of this sort, but not perhaps of this magnitude or detail.

As time passed I became increasingly aware of the need for such a book. There were few single sources of reference that enabled a reader to chart a driver's Grand Prix career, and even these were selective, usually concerning themselves merely with the upper strata who had scored championship points. It was this lack of completeness at even the most fundamental level that spurred me on. Through the eighties, with the huge upsurge of statistical works on sport in general, I genuinely believed that someone must be about to publish a book of this sort – but still nothing was forthcoming. So, as outlined in the acknowledgements, this project has taken shape over a span of some five years and the intial concept has not been fundamentally altered.

The *raison d'être* is the statistics, which comprise an entry for every driver who has started a World Championship Grand Prix since the inception of the drivers' championship in 1950, arranged alphabetically. Each driver's Grand Prix career is then set out in chronological order on a race-by-race basis. Here you will find: the placing, the race, the circuit, the entrant, the car and engine and a commentary. As this work is focused on the drivers, I have steered clear of the minefield that is individual chassis numbers; quite honestly, they have no place here, and would merely add to the clutter. What I have done, however, is to include additional lines where a driver competed in a different chassis/engine combination either in official practice or in the race itself, for example Alboreto in Austria in 1983 racing the Tyrrell 012, but practising in the 011 as well; or Arundell at Brands Hatch in 1966 driving two Lotus 33s, one with a BRM engine and the other a Climax. A late but hopefully worthwhile addition was the race numbers, which are now allocated for a whole season, but were not so in earlier days. A word of warning here. It was not uncommon for some Continental race organisers to change the numbers between practice and race, to try to defeat the wiles of pirate programme producers, so total accuracy here is next to impossible. The same applies to the comment column. Published reasons for retirements and so forth often proved to be contradictory, and teams were sometimes quite happy to give totally fictitious explanations of their cars' failures in an attempt to disguise any weaknesses. I have wherever possible followed the most generally held views, but out there someone probably knows different.

I have concerned myself solely with the core statistics as described; there are other authors whose books compare and analyse racing data, and I am happy to leave that field in their most capable hands. At the end of each driver's entry, however, I have included a line giving details of his total starts, wins, pole positions, fastest laps and points scored. The vexed question of starts should be addressed here. For when does a driver 'start' a Grand Prix? To my mind he does so *only* if he is on the grid when the flag drops or light goes green at the *final* start. Should a driver have failed to complete the parade lap, for instance (as was the case with Prost at Imola in 1990), he cannot truly be said to have started the race. In the case of restarted events such as the British GP in 1986, poor Jacques Laffite certainly did start the race, but this was declared null and void and he was not present to take the restart, which is the only one that counts. The different rules governing incidents of this sort over the years have led to inconsistencies that can probably never be resolved satisfactorily. I have decided wherever applicable to give two totals: the first, the true number of *actual* final race starts; and a second which includes any incidents of the kind outlined above. You pays yer money, you takes yer choice . . .

Although the statistics are the backbone of this work, on their own they tell only part of the story. As you will find, many drivers, particularly in recent times, have enjoyed Grand Prix careers of a length out of all proportion to their achievements, while there are literally dozens of other perhaps more worthy pilots over the years who maybe made only a minor mark and have been all but forgotten. This is due in part to the way motor racing has changed in the past forty years. In the fifties, it was possible for the amateur hopeful to participate in a Grand Prix and trundle round at the back of the field enjoying his big day as he rubbed shoulders with the greats. By the sixties, Formula 1 was the domain of the professional, but one could still compete quite usefully as an independent by purchasing a proprietary chassis and hope for the occasional placing, earning one's corn in the plethora of non-championship events that then abounded. By the seventies, the stakes had been raised, but the availability of the Ford-Cosworth engine still made it possible for those with enough talent and persistence to establish themselves. Since then the costs of producing a Grand Prix car, and the rule permitting only constructors who build their own machines to compete, have severely limited top Grand Prix opportunities to a select band who naturally dominate the scene.

In order to reflect the impact a driver has made not only on Grand Prix racing but also on motor racing as a whole, I have included biographies of virtually every racer to have made his mark on the sport – for those few whose records are generally of no great import, I have contented myself with providing the statistics alone. Therefore for the first time in one volume you will be able to read about both the great champions and also literally hundreds of other hopefuls who have rarely been profiled in the past. As you will find, these essays are not necessarily just blow-by-blow accounts chronicling the subject's Grand Prix career, which is already fully documented in the statistics, but attempt to paint a wider picture, encompassing early racing achievements, pivotal successes as well as the trials and tribulations and all too often the tragedy. Using the biographies as a signpost, the reader can add detail to the picture by studying the statistics. As an addendum, there is a section at the back which lists all the non-starters, those unlucky souls who tried in vain to make the grid for a championship Grand Prix.

The third, and by no means least important, facet of this volume is the hundreds of photographs which have been painstakingly assembled. Some have never been used before, and countless others only saw the light of day in the dim and distant past. Now, as never before, you can put a face to the names: from the fifties, very fast and debonair Argentinian Carlos Menditéguy, or the scholastic Rudi Fischer; from sun-drenched Kyalami in the sixties, locals such as Trevor Blokdyk, Sam Tingle and Doug Serrurier; from the land of the rising sun the complete Japanese racing quartet of the mid-seventies, Takahara, Takahashi, Hasemi and Hoshino. One of the great sources of satisfaction in attempting a project of these proportions has been the opportunity to unearth – and use – photographs of such glorious obscurities as Fred Wacker, Bernard Collomb, Xavier Perrot, Gus Hutchison, Torsten Palm and Alessandro Pesenti-Rossi. Now together at last, they have their place in motor racing literature!

At this point I would particularly like to thank the publishers, for they showed great faith in the idea from the start, and then gave me amazing freedom with which to work, a wonderful indulgence. They did not baulk when I told them of the massive increase in the number of pages that would be required to complete the task. I hope the end result meets their expectations.

Steve Small
Carshalton Beeches, Surrey
February 1994

THE
GRAND PRIX
DRIVERS

FROM ABECASSIS TO ZUNINO

**THE COMPLETE
GRAND PRIX CAREER RECORD
OF EVERY DRIVER TO HAVE STARTED
A WORLD CHAMPIONSHIP RACE
FROM 1950 TO 1993**

ABECASSIS, George (GB) b 21/3/1913 – d 21/3/1991

1951

	Race	Circuit	No	Entrant	Car/Engine	Comment
ret	SWISS GP	Bremgarten	12	HW Motors Ltd	2.0 HWM-Alta 4	magneto

1952

	Race	Circuit	No	Entrant	Car/Engine	Comment
ret	SWISS GP	Bremgarten	16	HW Motors Ltd	2.0 HWM-Alta 4	hub shaft failure-crashed

GP Starts: 2   GP Wins: 0   Pole positions: 0   Fastest laps: 0   Points: 0

ACHESON, Kenneth (GB) b 27/11/1957

1983

	Race	Circuit	No	Entrant	Car/Engine	Comment
dnq	BRITISH GP	Silverstone	17	RAM Automotive Team March	3.0 March-RAM 01-Cosworth V8	
dnq	GERMAN GP	Hockenheim	17	RAM Automotive Team March	3.0 March-RAM 01-Cosworth V8	
dnq	AUSTRIAN GP	Österreichring	17	RAM Automotive Team March	3.0 March-RAM 01-Cosworth V8	
dnq	DUTCH GP	Zandvoort	17	RAM Automotive Team March	3.0 March-RAM 01-Cosworth V8	
dnq	ITALIAN GP	Monza	17	RAM Automotive Team March	3.0 March-RAM 01-Cosworth V8	
dnq	EUROPEAN GP	Brands Hatch	17	RAM Automotive Team March	3.0 March-RAM 01-Cosworth V8	
12	SOUTH AFRICAN GP	Kyalami	17	RAM Automotive Team March	3.0 March-RAM 01-Cosworth V8	6 laps behind

1985

	Race	Circuit	No	Entrant	Car/Engine	Comment
ret	AUSTRIAN GP	Österreichring	10	Skoal Bandit Formula 1 Team	1.5 t/c RAM 03-Hart 4	engine
dnq	DUTCH GP	Zandvoort	10	Skoal Bandit Formula 1 Team	1.5 t/c RAM 03-Hart 4	
ret	ITALIAN GP	Monza	10	Skoal Bandit Formula 1 Team	1.5 t/c RAM 03-Hart 4	clutch

GP Starts: 3   GP Wins: 0   Pole positions: 0   Fastest laps: 0   Points: 0

ADAMICH, Andrea de (I) b 3/10/1941

1968

	Race	Circuit	No	Entrant	Car/Engine	Comment
ret	SOUTH AFRICAN GP	Kyalami	10	Scuderia Ferrari SpA SEFAC	3.0 Ferrari 312/67 V12	spun off on oil

1970

	Race	Circuit	No	Entrant	Car/Engine	Comment
dnq	SPANISH GP	Jarama	20	Bruce McLaren Motor Racing	3.0 McLaren M7D-Alfa Romeo V8	
dnq	MONACO GP	Monte Carlo	10	Bruce McLaren Motor Racing	3.0 McLaren M7D-Alfa Romeo V8	
dnq	DUTCH GP	Zandvoort	21	Bruce McLaren Motor Racing	3.0 McLaren M14D-Alfa Romeo V8	
nc	FRENCH GP	Clermont Ferrand	16	Bruce McLaren Motor Racing	3.0 McLaren M7D-Alfa Romeo V8	pit stops-water pipe/9 laps behind
dns	BRITISH GP	Brands Hatch	11	Bruce McLaren Motor Racing	3.0 McLaren M7D-Alfa Romeo V8	leaking fuel tank
dnq	GERMAN GP	Hockenheim	20	Bruce McLaren Motor Racing	3.0 McLaren M14D-Alfa Romeo V8	
12	AUSTRIAN GP	Österreichring	22	Bruce McLaren Motor Racing	3.0 McLaren M14D-Alfa Romeo V8	engine off song/3 laps behind
8/ret	ITALIAN GP	Monza	34	Bruce McLaren Motor Racing	3.0 McLaren M14D-Alfa Romeo V8	pit stop-tyres/fuel/7 laps behind
ret	CANADIAN GP	St Jovite	8	Bruce McLaren Motor Racing	3.0 McLaren M14D-Alfa Romeo V8	engine
dnq	US GP	Watkins Glen	10	Bruce McLaren Motor Racing	3.0 McLaren M14D-Alfa Romeo V8	

1971

	Race	Circuit	No	Entrant	Car/Engine	Comment
13	SOUTH AFRICAN GP	Kyalami	8	STP-March	3.0 March 711-Alfa Romeo V8	4 laps behind
ret	SPANISH GP	Montjuich Park	17	STP-March	3.0 March 711-Alfa Romeo V8	transmission
ret	FRENCH GP	Paul Ricard	19	STP-March	3.0 March 711-Alfa Romeo V8	
nc	BRITISH GP	Silverstone	19	STP-March	3.0 March 711-Alfa Romeo V8	pit stops-electrics/12 laps behind
ret	GERMAN GP	Nürburgring	16	STP-March	3.0 March 711-Alfa Romeo V8	fuel injection
ret	ITALIAN GP	Monza	23	STP-March	3.0 March 711-Alfa Romeo V8	engine
11	US GP	Watkins Glen	27	STP-March	3.0 March 711-Alfa Romeo V8	2 laps behind

1972

	Race	Circuit	No	Entrant	Car/Engine	Comment
ret	ARGENTINE GP	Buenos Aires	20	Ceramica Pagnossin Team Surtees	3.0 Surtees TS9A-Cosworth V8	fuel line
nc	SOUTH AFRICAN GP	Kyalami	18	Ceramica Pagnossin Team Surtees	3.0 Surtees TS9A-Cosworth V8	pit stop-brakes/10 laps behind
4	SPANISH GP	Jarama	26	Ceramica Pagnossin Team Surtees	3.0 Surtees TS9B-Cosworth V8	1 lap behind
7	MONACO GP	Monte Carlo	12	Ceramica Pagnossin Team Surtees	3.0 Surtees TS9B-Cosworth V8	3 laps behind
ret	BELGIAN GP	Nivelles	36	Ceramica Pagnossin Team Surtees	3.0 Surtees TS9B-Cosworth V8	engine
14	FRENCH GP	Clermont Ferrand	28	Ceramica Pagnossin Team Surtees	3.0 Surtees TS9B-Cosworth V8	pit stop-puncture/1 lap behind
ret	BRITISH GP	Brands Hatch	23	Ceramica Pagnossin Team Surtees	3.0 Surtees TS9B-Cosworth V8	spun off
13	GERMAN GP	Nürburgring	16	Ceramica Pagnossin Team Surtees	3.0 Surtees TS9B-Cosworth V8	pit stop-handling/1 lap behind
14	AUSTRIAN GP	Österreichring	11	Ceramica Pagnossin Team Surtees	3.0 Surtees TS9B-Cosworth V8	pit stop-engine/3 laps behind
ret	ITALIAN GP	Monza	9	Ceramica Pagnossin Team Surtees	3.0 Surtees TS9B-Cosworth V8	differential
ret	CANADIAN GP	Mosport Park	23	Ceramica Pagnossin Team Surtees	3.0 Surtees TS9B-Cosworth V8	gearbox
ret	US GP	Watkins Glen	25	Ceramica Pagnossin Team Surtees	3.0 Surtees TS9B-Cosworth V8	collision with Ganley

1973

	Race	Circuit	No	Entrant	Car/Engine	Comment
8	SOUTH AFRICAN GP	Kyalami	12	Ceramica Pagnossin Team Surtees	3.0 Surtees TS9B-Cosworth V8	2 laps behind
ret	SPANISH GP	Montjuich Park	21	Ceramica Pagnossin MRD	3.0 Brabham BT37-Cosworth V8	hub failure-accident
4	BELGIAN GP	Zolder	9	Ceramica Pagnossin MRD	3.0 Brabham BT37-Cosworth V8	1 lap behind
7	MONACO GP	Monte Carlo	9	Ceramica Pagnossin MRD	3.0 Brabham BT37-Cosworth V8	3 laps behind
ret	FRENCH GP	Paul Ricard	9	Ceramica Pagnossin MRD	3.0 Brabham BT37-Cosworth V8	driveshaft
ret/dns	BRITISH GP	Silverstone	9	Ceramica Pagnossin MRD	3.0 Brabham BT42-Cosworth V8	accident at first start-broken ankle

GP Starts: 29 (30)   GP Wins: 0   Pole positions: 0   Fastest laps: 0   Points: 6

GEORGE ABECASSIS

Having raced an Alta and an ERA before the war, Abecassis was involved in the development of the unsuccessful 1948 GP Alta before joining forces with John Heath to found the HW Motors team which ran their Alta-engined HWMs on a shoestring budget at home and abroad in the early fifties. In the main Abecassis concentrated on sports cars, driving for the works Aston Martin team between 1951 and '53 and enjoying success in national events with the potent Jaguar-engined HWM from 1953 until 1956, when the death of his partner Heath in the Mille Miglia saw George cease driving and ultimately wind down the Walton team's racing activities.

KENNETH ACHESON

Following a rapid and spectacularly successful rise from his 1976 Formula Ford debut through to F3 in 1980, Grovewood Award winner Acheson's progress – interrupted by a broken leg sustained in the F2 Pau GP in 1981 – finally ran up a cul-de-sac with his fruitless attempts to make an impression in Formula 1 with the uncompetitive RAM team. Although his subsequent career has lacked continuity, the quiet and talented Ulsterman has proved his ability in sports car racing, emerging as 1987 joint All-Japan champion in a Porsche 962. A works Sauber Mercedes driver in 1989, he finished third at Le Mans in 1991 in a factory Jaguar.

ANDREA de ADAMICH

With success in the 1965 Italian F3 championship and the 1966 European touring car series in an Alfa Romeo Giulia GTA behind him, de Adamich was given a works debut for Ferrari in the non-championship F1 Spanish GP at Jarama late in 1967 – finishing ninth after a puncture – but his Grand Prix career as a Ferrari driver faltered at the first hurdle with an accident at Kyalami in 1968 and came undone shortly afterwards when a crash in practice for the Race of Champions at Brands Hatch inflicted neck injuries which sidelined him for much of the season. Despite a victorious comeback with the works Ferrari Dino T166 which saw him win two races and the championship in the South American Formula 2 Temporada series, the Italian's big chance had gone.

Undaunted, he busied himself in the newly inaugurated F5000/FA series for Team Surtees on both sides of the Atlantic before returning to F1 in 1970, initially with backing from Alfa Romeo, racing their engine in a variety of 'third' works cars. A switch to Ford power made possible occasional good placings, but leg injuries sustained in the multiple accident caused by Jody Scheckter in the 1973 British Grand Prix brought his Formula 1 career to a premature end.

In parallel to his activities in Grand Prix racing, de Adamich was a works driver for Alfa Romeo in their successful T33 sports cars from 1970 to 1974, winning the Brands Hatch 1000 Km and the Watkins Glen 6 Hours in 1971. When his hectic racing schedule allowed, he also competed in Can-Am, touring cars and hill-climbs. Since his retirement in 1974 Andrea has returned to the Grand Prix scene as a respected motor sport journalist and TV commentator.

ADOLFF, Kurt (D) b 5/11/1921

1953

	Race	Circuit	No	Entrant	Car/Engine	Comment
ret	GERMAN GP	Nürburgring	34	Ecurie Espadon	2.0 Ferrari 166 V12	

GP Starts: 1   GP Wins: 0   Pole positions: 0   Fastest laps: 0   Points: 0

AHRENS Jnr, Kurt (D) b 19/4/1940

1966

	Race	Circuit	No	Entrant	Car/Engine	Comment
ret	GERMAN GP (F2)	Nürburgring	25	Caltex Racing Team	1.0 Brabham BT18-Cosworth 4	gearbox

1967

| ret | GERMAN GP (F2) | Nürburgring | 26 | Ron Harris Racing Team | 1.6 Protos-Cosworth 4 | split radiator |

1968

| 12 | GERMAN GP | Nürburgring | 17 | Caltex Racing Team | 3.0 Brabham BT24-Repco V8 | 3rd works car/1 lap behind |

1969

| 7* | GERMAN GP (F2) | Nürburgring | 20 | Ahrens Racing Team | 1.6 Brabham BT30-Cosworth 4 | * 3rd in F2 class/1 lap behind |

GP Starts: 4   GP Wins: 0   Pole positions: 0   Fastest laps: 0   Points: 0

ALBORETO, Michele (I) b 23/12/1956

1981

	Race	Circuit	No	Entrant	Car/Engine	Comment
ret	SAN MARINO GP	Imola	4	Team Tyrrell	3.0 Tyrrell 010-Cosworth V8	collision with Gabbiani
12	BELGIAN GP	Zolder	4	Team Tyrrell	3.0 Tyrrell 010-Cosworth V8	2 laps behind
ret	MONACO GP	Monte Carlo	4	Team Tyrrell	3.0 Tyrrell 010-Cosworth V8	spun-collision with Giacomelli
dnq	SPANISH GP	Jarama	4	Team Tyrrell	3.0 Tyrrell 010-Cosworth V8	
16	FRENCH GP	Dijon	4	Team Tyrrell	3.0 Tyrrell 010-Cosworth V8	3 laps behind
ret	BRITISH GP	Silverstone	4	Team Tyrrell	3.0 Tyrrell 010-Cosworth V8	clutch
dnq	GERMAN GP	Hockenheim	4	Team Tyrrell	3.0 Tyrrell 010-Cosworth V8	
ret	AUSTRIAN GP	Österreichring	4	Team Tyrrell	3.0 Tyrrell 010-Cosworth V8	engine
9/ret	DUTCH GP	Zandvoort	4	Team Tyrrell	3.0 Tyrrell 011-Cosworth V8	engine/-4 laps/dnq-reserve starter
ret	ITALIAN GP	Monza	4	Team Tyrrell	3.0 Tyrrell 011-Cosworth V8	hit Watson's wreckage
11	CANADIAN GP	Montreal	4	Team Tyrrell	3.0 Tyrrell 011-Cosworth V8	4 laps behind
nc	CAESARS PALACE GP	Las Vegas	4	Team Tyrrell	3.0 Tyrrell 011-Cosworth V8	electrical problems/8 laps behind

1982

7	SOUTH AFRICAN GP	Kyalami	3	Team Tyrrell	3.0 Tyrrell 011-Cosworth V8	1 lap behind
4*	BRAZILIAN GP	Rio	3	Team Tyrrell	3.0 Tyrrell 011-Cosworth V8	*1st & 2nd place cars disqualified
4*	US GP WEST	Long Beach	3	Team Tyrrell	3.0 Tyrrell 011-Cosworth V8	*3rd place car disqualified
3	SAN MARINO GP	Imola	3	Team Tyrrell	3.0 Tyrrell 011-Cosworth V8	
ret	BELGIAN GP	Zolder	3	Team Tyrrell	3.0 Tyrrell 011-Cosworth V8	engine
10/ret	MONACO GP	Monte Carlo	3	Team Tyrrell	3.0 Tyrrell 011-Cosworth V8	suspension/6 laps behind
ret	US GP (DETROIT)	Detroit	3	Team Tyrrell	3.0 Tyrrell 011-Cosworth V8	accident at chicane
ret	CANADIAN GP	Montreal	3	Team Tyrrell	3.0 Tyrrell 011-Cosworth V8	gearbox and fuel starvation
7	DUTCH GP	Zandvoort	3	Team Tyrrell	3.0 Tyrrell 011-Cosworth V8	1 lap behind
nc	BRITISH GP	Brands Hatch	3	Team Tyrrell	3.0 Tyrrell 011-Cosworth V8	handling problems/32 laps behind
6	FRENCH GP	Paul Ricard	3	Team Tyrrell	3.0 Tyrrell 011-Cosworth V8	
4	GERMAN GP	Hockenheim	3	Team Tyrrell	3.0 Tyrrell 011-Cosworth V8	1 lap behind
ret	AUSTRIAN GP	Österreichring	3	Team Tyrrell	3.0 Tyrrell 011-Cosworth V8	spun off
7	SWISS GP	Dijon	3	Team Tyrrell	3.0 Tyrrell 011-Cosworth V8	1 lap behind
5	ITALIAN GP	Monza	3	Team Tyrrell	3.0 Tyrrell 011-Cosworth V8	1 lap behind
1	CAESARS PALACE GP	Las Vegas	3	Team Tyrrell	3.0 Tyrrell 011-Cosworth V8	FL

1983

ret	BRAZILIAN GP	Rio	3	Benetton Tyrrell Team	3.0 Tyrrell 011-Cosworth V8	incident with Baldi-oil cooler
9	US GP WEST	Long Beach	3	Benetton Tyrrell Team	3.0 Tyrrell 011-Cosworth V8	collision with Jarier/2 laps behind
8	FRENCH GP	Paul Ricard	3	Benetton Tyrrell Team	3.0 Tyrrell 011-Cosworth V8	1 lap behind
ret	SAN MARINO GP	Imola	3	Benetton Tyrrell Team	3.0 Tyrrell 011-Cosworth V8	accident-collapsed suspension
ret	MONACO GP	Monte Carlo	3	Benetton Tyrrell Team	3.0 Tyrrell 011-Cosworth V8	collision with Mansell
14	BELGIAN GP	Spa	3	Benetton Tyrrell Team	3.0 Tyrrell 011-Cosworth V8	pit stop-gearbox/2 laps behind
1	US GP (DETROIT)	Detroit	3	Benetton Tyrrell Team	3.0 Tyrrell 011-Cosworth V8	
8	CANADIAN GP	Montreal	3	Benetton Tyrrell Team	3.0 Tyrrell 011-Cosworth V8	2 laps behind
13	BRITISH GP	Silverstone	3	Benetton Tyrrell Team	3.0 Tyrrell 011-Cosworth V8	2 laps behind
ret	GERMAN GP	Hockenheim	3	Benetton Tyrrell Team	3.0 Tyrrell 011-Cosworth V8	fuel pump drive
ret	AUSTRIAN GP	Österreichring	3	Benetton Tyrrell Team	3.0 Tyrrell 012-Cosworth V8	hit Johansson-spun off
dns	"	"	3		3.0 Tyrrell 011-Cosworth V8	qualified in this car
6	DUTCH GP	Zandvoort	3	Benetton Tyrrell Team	3.0 Tyrrell 012-Cosworth V8	pit stop-fuel/1 lap behind
ret	ITALIAN GP	Monza	3	Benetton Tyrrell Team	3.0 Tyrrell 012-Cosworth V8	clutch
ret	EUROPEAN GP	Brands Hatch	3	Benetton Tyrrell Team	3.0 Tyrrell 012-Cosworth V8	engine
ret	SOUTH AFRICAN GP	Kyalami	3	Benetton Tyrrell Team	3.0 Tyrrell 012-Cosworth V8	engine

1984

ret	BRAZILIAN GP	Rio	27	Scuderia Ferrari SpA SEFAC	1.5 t/c Ferrari 126C4 V6	brake caliper
11/ret	SOUTH AFRICAN GP	Kyalami	27	Scuderia Ferrari SpA SEFAC	1.5 t/c Ferrari 126C4 V6	ignition/11th place car disqualified
1	BELGIAN GP	Zolder	27	Scuderia Ferrari SpA SEFAC	1.5 t/c Ferrari 126C4 V6	Pole
ret	SAN MARINO GP	Imola	27	Scuderia Ferrari SpA SEFAC	1.5 t/c Ferrari 126C4 V6	exhaust
ret	FRENCH GP	Dijon	27	Scuderia Ferrari SpA SEFAC	1.5 t/c Ferrari 126C4 V6	engine

KURT AHRENS Jnr

Perhaps Germany's most promising young driver of the early sixties, Ahrens Jnr began racing in 1958, aged 18, driving an F3 Cooper. He was soon beating his father (a former 250 cc German speedway champion and accomplished national car racer), notching up a dozen wins by the end of 1959. After a rather barren 1960 season with a Formula Junior Cooper, Kurt made amends the following year, defeating Gerhard Mitter to win the German Formula Junior championship, a feat which he repeated in 1963 after returning from a six-month suspension imposed by the ONS for disputing the official result of a race the previous year.

The acquisition of a Brabham in 1965 provided him with the opportunity to race in both F3 and F2 but his outings in the latter category were restricted by his commitments at his father's garage and scrap metal business. Nevertheless he also found time to race the works Fiat-Abarth on occasion with success.

Backed by Caltex (who sponsored his only F1 ride in the German GP of that year), he enjoyed a full Formula 2 season in 1968, finishing second in the Eifelrennen and third at both Jarama and Hockenheim, relishing the chance to compete with Grand Prix stars such as Rindt and Stewart.

Having previously stated his dislike of long-distance racing, it is perhaps surprising that Ahrens chose to opt for this category in 1969, winning the Austrian GP with Jo Siffert in David Piper's Porsche 917. Racing a works Porsche, he proved a reliable partner for Vic Elford, the pair winning the Nürburgring 1000 Km in 1970, Kurt's final racing season before retirement.

MICHELE ALBORETO

A smooth and stylish driver without some of the more histrionic traits of his fellow countrymen, Alboreto's rise to the top was swift. Backed by Paolo Pavanello, he was runner-up in the 1979 Italian F3 championship and became the 1980 European F3 champion after a season-long battle with Thierry Boutsen. This led to a drive for the Minardi F2 team in 1981, which yielded an end-of-season win at Misano, but Michele had already leap-frogged this career stepping-stone by gaining a place in the Tyrrell team after an impressive Grand Prix debut at Imola which saw the curly-haired Italian smartly placed under a three-year contract.

The next two seasons were illuminated by wins at Las Vegas and Detroit but the normally aspirated Tyrrells were increasingly uncompetitive against the turbo onslaught and it was no great surprise when Alboreto took up the offer of a Ferrari drive for 1984. After a promising start and a victory at Zolder in the Belgian GP, the season disintegrated amid a plague of engine failures, but a strong finish to the year boded well for 1985, which was to be the high water-mark of his career. For much of the season he held off the challenge of Alain Prost's McLaren, but the team lost momentum and Michele saw his title chance blighted by mechanical failure. Although three more years were spent at Maranello, somehow things were never the same. The arrival of Gerhard Berger in 1987 pushed the Italian to the margins and he opted out of the political turmoil that was Ferrari to return to Tyrrell for 1989.

It was to be a brief reunion, with a splendid third in Mexico in the new Tyrrell 018 the highlight, before Michele split with the team after a sponsorship clash. Thereafter his career began a swift decline in a succession of uncompetitive cars which included the disastrously overweight Porsche-engined Footwork. An Indian summer in 1992 with some revitalised performances in the Footwork-Mugen restored his credibility, but the nadir of his Formula 1 career came with a move to the Lola Scuderia Italia team that could well have brought Alboreto's tenure in Grand Prix racing to an end.

6*	MONACO GP	Monte Carlo	27	Scuderia Ferrari SpA SEFAC	1.5 t/c Ferrari 126C4 V6	*3rd place car dsq/1 lap behind
ret	CANADIAN GP	Montreal	27	Scuderia Ferrari SpA SEFAC	1.5 t/c Ferrari 126C4 V6	engine
ret	US GP (DETROIT)	Detroit	27	Scuderia Ferrari SpA SEFAC	1.5 t/c Ferrari 126C4 V6	engine
ret	US GP (DALLAS)	Dallas	27	Scuderia Ferrari SpA SEFAC	1.5 t/c Ferrari 126C4 V6	hit wall
5	BRITISH GP	Brands Hatch	27	Scuderia Ferrari SpA SEFAC	1.5 t/c Ferrari 126C4 V6	1 lap behind
ret	GERMAN GP	Hockenheim	27	Scuderia Ferrari SpA SEFAC	1.5 t/c Ferrari 126C4 V6	misfire
3	AUSTRIAN GP	Österreichring	27	Scuderia Ferrari SpA SEFAC	1.5 t/c Ferrari 126C4 V6	
ret	DUTCH GP	Zandvoort	27	Scuderia Ferrari SpA SEFAC	1.5 t/c Ferrari 126C4 V6	engine
2	ITALIAN GP	Monza	27	Scuderia Ferrari SpA SEFAC	1.5 t/c Ferrari 126C4 V6	
2	EUROPEAN GP	Nürburgring	27	Scuderia Ferrari SpA SEFAC	1.5 t/c Ferrari 126C4 V6	FL (shared with Piquet)
4	PORTUGUESE GP	Estoril	27	Scuderia Ferrari SpA SEFAC	1.5 t/c Ferrari 126C4 V6	

1985

2	BRAZILIAN GP	Rio	27	Scuderia Ferrari SpA SEFAC	1.5 t/c Ferrari 156/85 V6	Pole
2	PORTUGUESE GP	Estoril	27	Scuderia Ferrari SpA SEFAC	1.5 t/c Ferrari 156/85 V6	
ret	SAN MARINO GP	Imola	27	Scuderia Ferrari SpA SEFAC	1.5 t/c Ferrari 156/85 V6	electrics/FL
2	MONACO GP	Monte Carlo	27	Scuderia Ferrari SpA SEFAC	1.5 t/c Ferrari 156/85 V6	FL
1	CANADIAN GP	Montreal	27	Scuderia Ferrari SpA SEFAC	1.5 t/c Ferrari 156/85 V6	
3	US GP (DETROIT)	Detroit	27	Scuderia Ferrari SpA SEFAC	1.5 t/c Ferrari 156/85 V6	
ret	FRENCH GP	Paul Ricard	27	Scuderia Ferrari SpA SEFAC	1.5 t/c Ferrari 156/85 V6	turbo
2	BRITISH GP	Silverstone	27	Scuderia Ferrari SpA SEFAC	1.5 t/c Ferrari 156/85 V6	1 lap behind
1	GERMAN GP	Nürburgring	27	Scuderia Ferrari SpA SEFAC	1.5 t/c Ferrari 156/85 V6	
3	AUSTRIAN GP	Österreichring	27	Scuderia Ferrari SpA SEFAC	1.5 t/c Ferrari 156/85 V6	
4	DUTCH GP	Zandvoort	27	Scuderia Ferrari SpA SEFAC	1.5 t/c Ferrari 156/85 V6	
13/ret	ITALIAN GP	Monza	27	Scuderia Ferrari SpA SEFAC	1.5 t/c Ferrari 156/85 V6	engine
ret	BELGIAN GP	Spa	27	Scuderia Ferrari SpA SEFAC	1.5 t/c Ferrari 156/85 V6	clutch
ret	EUROPEAN GP	Brands Hatch	27	Scuderia Ferrari SpA SEFAC	1.5 t/c Ferrari 156/85 V6	turbo
ret	SOUTH AFRICAN GP	Kyalami	27	Scuderia Ferrari SpA SEFAC	1.5 t/c Ferrari 156/85 V6	turbo
ret	AUSTRALIAN GP	Adelaide	27	Scuderia Ferrari SpA SEFAC	1.5 t/c Ferrari 156/85 V6	gear linkage

1986

ret	BRAZILIAN GP	Rio	27	Scuderia Ferrari SpA SEFAC	1.5 t/c Ferrari F1/86 V6	fuel pump
ret	SPANISH GP	Jerez	27	Scuderia Ferrari SpA SEFAC	1.5 t/c Ferrari F1/86 V6	wheel bearing
10/ret	SAN MARINO GP	Imola	27	Scuderia Ferrari SpA SEFAC	1.5 t/c Ferrari F1/86 V6	turbo/4 laps behind
ret	MONACO GP	Monte Carlo	27	Scuderia Ferrari SpA SEFAC	1.5 t/c Ferrari F1/86 V6	turbo
4	BELGIAN GP	Spa	27	Scuderia Ferrari SpA SEFAC	1.5 t/c Ferrari F1/86 V6	
8	CANADIAN GP	Montreal	27	Scuderia Ferrari SpA SEFAC	1.5 t/c Ferrari F1/86 V6	spin-Johansson/1 lap behind
4	US GP (DETROIT)	Detroit	27	Scuderia Ferrari SpA SEFAC	1.5 t/c Ferrari F1/86 V6	
8	FRENCH GP	Paul Ricard	27	Scuderia Ferrari SpA SEFAC	1.5 t/c Ferrari F1/86 V6	stalled on startline/2 laps behind
ret	BRITISH GP	Brands Hatch	27	Scuderia Ferrari SpA SEFAC	1.5 t/c Ferrari F1/86 V6	turbo
ret	GERMAN GP	Hockenheim	27	Scuderia Ferrari SpA SEFAC	1.5 t/c Ferrari F1/86 V6	transmission
ret	HUNGARIAN GP	Hungaroring	27	Scuderia Ferrari SpA SEFAC	1.5 t/c Ferrari F1/86 V6	hit Warwick
2	AUSTRIAN GP	Österreichring	27	Scuderia Ferrari SpA SEFAC	1.5 t/c Ferrari F1/86 V6	1 lap behind
ret	ITALIAN GP	Monza	27	Scuderia Ferrari SpA SEFAC	1.5 t/c Ferrari F1/86 V6	engine
5	PORTUGUESE GP	Estoril	27	Scuderia Ferrari SpA SEFAC	1.5 t/c Ferrari F1/86 V6	1 lap behind
ret	MEXICAN GP	Mexico City	27	Scuderia Ferrari SpA SEFAC	1.5 t/c Ferrari F1/86 V6	turbo
ret	AUSTRALIAN GP	Adelaide	27	Scuderia Ferrari SpA SEFAC	1.5 t/c Ferrari F1/86 V6	hit from behind on grid

1987

8/ret	BRAZILIAN GP	Rio	27	Scuderia Ferrari SpA SEFAC	1.5 t/c Ferrari F1/87 V6	spun off
3	SAN MARINO GP	Imola	27	Scuderia Ferrari SpA SEFAC	1.5 t/c Ferrari F1/87 V6	
ret	BELGIAN GP	Spa	27	Scuderia Ferrari SpA SEFAC	1.5 t/c Ferrari F1/87 V6	transmission
3	MONACO GP	Monte Carlo	27	Scuderia Ferrari SpA SEFAC	1.5 t/c Ferrari F1/87 V6	
ret	US GP (DETROIT)	Detroit	27	Scuderia Ferrari SpA SEFAC	1.5 t/c Ferrari F1/87 V6	gearbox
ret	FRENCH GP	Paul Ricard	27	Scuderia Ferrari SpA SEFAC	1.5 t/c Ferrari F1/87 V6	engine
ret	BRITISH GP	Silverstone	27	Scuderia Ferrari SpA SEFAC	1.5 t/c Ferrari F1/87 V6	suspension
ret	GERMAN GP	Hockenheim	27	Scuderia Ferrari SpA SEFAC	1.5 t/c Ferrari F1/87 V6	turbo
ret	HUNGARIAN GP	Hungaroring	27	Scuderia Ferrari SpA SEFAC	1.5 t/c Ferrari F1/87 V6	engine
ret	AUSTRIAN GP	Österreichring	27	Scuderia Ferrari SpA SEFAC	1.5 t/c Ferrari F1/87 V6	turbo/exhaust/started from pitlane
ret	ITALIAN GP	Monza	27	Scuderia Ferrari SpA SEFAC	1.5 t/c Ferrari F1/87 V6	turbo
ret	PORTUGUESE GP	Estoril	27	Scuderia Ferrari SpA SEFAC	1.5 t/c Ferrari F1/87 V6	gearbox
ret	SPANISH GP	Jerez	27	Scuderia Ferrari SpA SEFAC	1.5 t/c Ferrari F1/87 V6	engine/5 laps behind
ret	MEXICAN GP	Mexico City	27	Scuderia Ferrari SpA SEFAC	1.5 t/c Ferrari F1/87 V6	engine
4	JAPANESE GP	Suzuka	27	Scuderia Ferrari SpA SEFAC	1.5 t/c Ferrari F1/87 V6	
2*	AUSTRALIAN GP	Adelaide	27	Scuderia Ferrari SpA SEFAC	1.5 t/c Ferrari F1/87 V6	*2nd place car disqualified

1988

5	BRAZILIAN GP	Rio	27	Scuderia Ferrari SpA SEFAC	1.5 t/c Ferrari F1/87/88C V6	
18/ret	SAN MARINO GP	Imola	27	Scuderia Ferrari SpA SEFAC	1.5 t/c Ferrari F1/87/88C V6	engine/started at back of grid/-6 laps
3	MONACO GP	Monte Carlo	27	Scuderia Ferrari SpA SEFAC	1.5 t/c Ferrari F1/87/88C V6	
4	MEXICAN GP	Mexico City	27	Scuderia Ferrari SpA SEFAC	1.5 t/c Ferrari F1/87/88C V6	1 lap behind
ret	CANADIAN GP	Montreal	27	Scuderia Ferrari SpA SEFAC	1.5 t/c Ferrari F1/87/88C V6	engine
ret	US GP (DETROIT)	Detroit	27	Scuderia Ferrari SpA SEFAC	1.5 t/c Ferrari F1/87/88C V6	accident
3	FRENCH GP	Paul Ricard	27	Scuderia Ferrari SpA SEFAC	1.5 t/c Ferrari F1/87/88C V6	
17/ret	BRITISH GP	Silverstone	27	Scuderia Ferrari SpA SEFAC	1.5 t/c Ferrari F1/87/88C V6	out of fuel/3 laps behind
4	GERMAN GP	Hockenheim	27	Scuderia Ferrari SpA SEFAC	1.5 t/c Ferrari F1/87/88C V6	
ret	HUNGARIAN GP	Hungaroring	27	Scuderia Ferrari SpA SEFAC	1.5 t/c Ferrari F1/87/88C V6	engine cut out
ret	BELGIAN GP	Spa	27	Scuderia Ferrari SpA SEFAC	1.5 t/c Ferrari F1/87/88C V6	engine
2	ITALIAN GP	Monza	27	Scuderia Ferrari SpA SEFAC	1.5 t/c Ferrari F1/87/88C V6	FL
5	PORTUGUESE GP	Estoril	27	Scuderia Ferrari SpA SEFAC	1.5 t/c Ferrari F1/87/88C V6	
ret	SPANISH GP	Jerez	27	Scuderia Ferrari SpA SEFAC	1.5 t/c Ferrari F1/87/88C V6	engine
11	JAPANESE GP	Suzuka	27	Scuderia Ferrari SpA SEFAC	1.5 t/c Ferrari F1/87/88C V6	collision with Nannini/1 lap behind
ret	AUSTRALIAN GP	Adelaide	27	Scuderia Ferrari SpA SEFAC	1.5 t/c Ferrari F1/87/88C V6	collision with Caffi on lap 1

1989

10	BRAZILIAN GP	Rio	4	Tyrrell Racing Organisation	3.5 Tyrrell 017B-Cosworth V8	2 pit stops-gearbox/2 laps behind
dnq	SAN MARINO GP	Imola	4	Tyrrell Racing Organisation	3.5 Tyrrell 018-Cosworth V8	

dnq	" "	"	4	Tyrrell Racing Organisation	3.5 Tyrrell 017B-Cosworth V8	
5	MONACO GP	Monte Carlo	4	Tyrrell Racing Organisation	3.5 Tyrrell 018-Cosworth V8	2 laps behind
dns	" "	"	4	Tyrrell Racing Organisation	3.5 Tyrrell 017B-Cosworth V8	practice only
3	MEXICAN GP	Mexico City	4	Tyrrell Racing Organisation	3.5 Tyrrell 018-Cosworth V8	
ret	US GP (PHOENIX)	Phoenix	4	Tyrrell Racing Organisation	3.5 Tyrrell 018-Cosworth V8	gearbox
ret	CANADIAN GP	Montreal	4	Tyrrell Racing Organisation	3.5 Tyrrell 018-Cosworth V8	electrics
ret	GERMAN GP	Hockenheim	29	Equipe Larrousse	3.5 Lola LC89-Lamborghini V12	electrics
ret	HUNGARIAN GP	Hungaroring	29	Equipe Larrousse	3.5 Lola LC89-Lamborghini V12	engine
ret	BELGIAN GP	Spa	29	Equipe Larrousse	3.5 Lola LC89-Lamborghini V12	collision with Patrese
ret	ITALIAN GP	Monza	29	Equipe Larrousse	3.5 Lola LC89-Lamborghini V12	engine
11	PORTUGUESE GP	Estoril	29	Equipe Larrousse	3.5 Lola LC89-Lamborghini V12	pit stop-tyres/2 laps behind
dnpq	SPANISH GP	Jerez	29	Equipe Larrousse	3.5 Lola LC89-Lamborghini V12	
dnq	JAPANESE GP	Suzuka	29	Equipe Larrousse	3.5 Lola LC89-Lamborghini V12	
dnpq	AUSTRALIAN GP	Adelaide	29	Equipe Larrousse	3.5 Lola LC89-Lamborghini V12	

1990

10	US GP (PHOENIX)	Phoenix	9	Footwork Arrows Racing	3.5 Arrows A11B-Cosworth V8	2 laps behind
ret	BRAZILIAN GP	Interlagos	9	Footwork Arrows Racing	3.5 Arrows A11B-Cosworth V8	handling-suspension
dns	" "	"	9	Footwork Arrows Racing	3.5 Arrows A11-Cosworth V8	practice only
dnq	SAN MARINO GP	Imola	9	Footwork Arrows Racing	3.5 Arrows A11B-Cosworth V8	
dnq	MONACO GP	Monte Carlo	9	Footwork Arrows Racing	3.5 Arrows A11B-Cosworth V8	
ret	CANADIAN GP	Montreal	9	Footwork Arrows Racing	3.5 Arrows A11B-Cosworth V8	collision with Pirro
17	MEXICAN GP	Mexico City	9	Footwork Arrows Racing	3.5 Arrows A11B-Cosworth V8	power loss/3 laps behind
10	FRENCH GP	Paul Ricard	9	Footwork Arrows Racing	3.5 Arrows A11B-Cosworth V8	1 lap behind
ret	BRITISH GP	Silverstone	9	Footwork Arrows Racing	3.5 Arrows A11B-Cosworth V8	electrics
ret	GERMAN GP	Hockenheim	9	Footwork Arrows Racing	3.5 Arrows A11B-Cosworth V8	engine
12	HUNGARIAN GP	Hungaroring	9	Footwork Arrows Racing	3.5 Arrows A11B-Cosworth V8	pit stop-tyres/2 laps behind
13	BELGIAN GP	Spa	9	Footwork Arrows Racing	3.5 Arrows A11B-Cosworth V8	engine lost power/1 lap behind
12/ret	ITALIAN GP	Monza	9	Footwork Arrows Racing	3.5 Arrows A11B-Cosworth V8	spun off/3 laps behind
9	PORTUGUESE GP	Estoril	9	Footwork Arrows Racing	3.5 Arrows A11B-Cosworth V8	1 lap behind
10	SPANISH GP	Jerez	9	Footwork Arrows Racing	3.5 Arrows A11B-Cosworth V8	2 laps behind
ret	JAPANESE GP	Suzuka	9	Footwork Arrows Racing	3.5 Arrows A11B-Cosworth V8	engine
dnq	AUSTRALIAN GP	Adelaide	9	Footwork Arrows Racing	3.5 Arrows A11B-Cosworth V8	

1991

ret	US GP (PHOENIX)	Phoenix	9	Footwork Grand Prix International	3.5 Footwork A11C-Porsche V12	gearbox
dnq	BRAZILIAN GP	Interlagos	9	Footwork Grand Prix International	3.5 Footwork A11C-Porsche V12	
dnq	SAN MARINO GP	Imola	9	Footwork Grand Prix International	3.5 Footwork A11C-Porsche V12	
ret	MONACO GP	Monte Carlo	9	Footwork Grand Prix International	3.5 Footwork A12-Porsche V12	engine
ret	CANADIAN GP	Montreal	9	Footwork Grand Prix International	3.5 Footwork A12-Porsche V12	engine
ret	MEXICAN GP	Mexico City	9	Footwork Grand Prix International	3.5 Footwork A12-Porsche V12	oil pressure
ret	FRENCH GP	Magny Cours	9	Footwork Grand Prix International	3.5 Footwork A12-Cosworth V8	gearbox/transmission
ret	BRITISH GP	Silverstone	9	Footwork Grand Prix International	3.5 Footwork A12-Cosworth V8	gearbox
dnq	GERMAN GP	Hockenheim	9	Footwork Grand Prix International	3.5 Footwork A12-Cosworth V8	
dnq	HUNGARIAN GP	Hungaroring	9	Footwork Grand Prix International	3.5 Footwork A12-Cosworth V8	
dnpq	BELGIAN GP	Spa	9	Footwork Grand Prix International	3.5 Footwork A12-Cosworth V8	
dnq	ITALIAN GP	Monza	9	Footwork Grand Prix International	3.5 Footwork A12-Cosworth V8	
15	PORTUGUESE GP	Estoril	9	Footwork Grand Prix International	3.5 Footwork A12-Cosworth V8	3 laps behind
ret	SPANISH GP	Barcelona	9	Footwork Grand Prix International	3.5 Footwork A12-Cosworth V8	engine
dnq	JAPANESE GP	Suzuka	9	Footwork Grand Prix International	3.5 Footwork A12-Cosworth V8	
13	AUSTRALIAN GP	Adelaide	9	Footwork Grand Prix International	3.5 Footwork A12-Cosworth V8	wet race-stopped after 14 laps

1992

10	SOUTH AFRICAN GP	Kyalami	9	Footwork Grand Prix International	3.5 Footwork FA13-Mugen-Honda V10	gearbox
13	MEXICAN GP	Mexico City	9	Footwork Grand Prix International	3.5 Footwork FA13-Mugen-Honda V10	4 laps behind
6	BRAZILIAN GP	Interlagos	9	Footwork Grand Prix International	3.5 Footwork FA13-Mugen-Honda V10	1 lap behind
5	SPANISH GP	Barcelona	9	Footwork Grand Prix International	3.5 Footwork FA13-Mugen-Honda V10	1 lap behind
5	SAN MARINO GP	Imola	9	Footwork Grand Prix International	3.5 Footwork FA13-Mugen-Honda V10	1 lap behind
7	MONACO GP	Monte Carlo	9	Footwork Grand Prix International	3.5 Footwork FA13-Mugen-Honda V10	spin/1 lap behind
7	CANADIAN GP	Montreal	9	Footwork Grand Prix International	3.5 Footwork FA13-Mugen-Honda V10	1 lap behind
7*	FRENCH GP	Magny Cours	9	Footwork Grand Prix International	3.5 Footwork FA13-Mugen-Honda V10	*aggregate of two parts/-1 lap
7	BRITISH GP	Silverstone	9	Footwork Grand Prix International	3.5 Footwork FA13-Mugen-Honda V10	1 lap behind
9	GERMAN GP	Hockenheim	9	Footwork Grand Prix International	3.5 Footwork FA13-Mugen-Honda V10	1 lap behind
7	HUNGARIAN GP	Hungaroring	9	Footwork Grand Prix International	3.5 Footwork FA13-Mugen-Honda V10	spin/2 laps behind
ret	BELGIAN GP	Spa	9	Footwork Grand Prix International	3.5 Footwork FA13-Mugen-Honda V10	gearbox
7	ITALIAN GP	Monza	9	Footwork Grand Prix International	3.5 Footwork FA13-Mugen-Honda V10	1 lap behind
6	PORTUGUESE GP	Estoril	9	Footwork Grand Prix International	3.5 Footwork FA13-Mugen-Honda V10	1 lap behind
15	JAPANESE GP	Suzuka	9	Footwork Grand Prix International	3.5 Footwork FA13-Mugen-Honda V10	2 laps behind
ret	AUSTRALIAN GP	Adelaide	9	Footwork Grand Prix International	3.5 Footwork FA13-Mugen-Honda V10	accident on lap 1

1993

ret	SOUTH AFRICAN GP	Kyalami	21	BMS Scuderia Italia SpA	3.5 LolaT93/30 BMS-Ferrari V12	engine
11	BRAZILIAN GP	Interlagos	21	BMS Scuderia Italia SpA	3.5 LolaT93/30 BMS-Ferrari V12	3 laps behind
11	EUROPEAN GP	Donington	21	BMS Scuderia Italia SpA	3.5 LolaT93/30 BMS-Ferrari V12	6 laps behind
dnq	SAN MARINO GP	Imola	21	BMS Scuderia Italia SpA	3.5 LolaT93/30 BMS-Ferrari V12	
dnq	SPANISH GP	Barcelona	21	BMS Scuderia Italia SpA	3.5 LolaT93/30 BMS-Ferrari V12	
ret	MONACO GP	Monte Carlo	21	BMS Scuderia Italia SpA	3.5 LolaT93/30 BMS-Ferrari V12	gearbox
dnq	CANADIAN GP	Montreal	21	BMS Scuderia Italia SpA	3.5 LolaT93/30 BMS-Ferrari V12	
dnq	FRENCH GP	Magny Cours	21	BMS Scuderia Italia SpA	3.5 LolaT93/30 BMS-Ferrari V12	
dnq	BRITISH GP	Silverstone	21	BMS Scuderia Italia SpA	3.5 LolaT93/30 BMS-Ferrari V12	
16	GERMAN GP	Hockenheim	21	BMS Scuderia Italia SpA	3.5 LolaT93/30 BMS-Ferrari V12	no clutch/2 laps behind
ret	HUNGARIAN GP	Hungaroring	21	BMS Scuderia Italia SpA	3.5 LolaT93/30 BMS-Ferrari V12	overheating
14	BELGIAN GP	Spa	21	BMS Scuderia Italia SpA	3.5 LolaT93/30 BMS-Ferrari V12	car appalling-worst race of career!
ret	ITALIAN GP	Monza	21	BMS Scuderia Italia SpA	3.5 LolaT93/30 BMS-Ferrari V12	suspension failure
ret	PORTUGUESE GP	Estoril	21	BMS Scuderia Italia SpA	3.5 LolaT93/30 BMS-Ferrari V12	gearbox/accident

GP Starts: 178   GP Wins: 5   Pole positions: 2   Fastest laps: 5 (includes 1 shared)   Points: 185.5

JEAN ALESI

There are in any generation a handful of drivers whose talent and commitment set them apart and Jean Alesi is such a driver. The Frenchman, born in Avignon of Sicilian descent, displayed this early in his career when in 1986 he shook the established order in French F3. Running his own Dallara-Alfa, Alesi scored two race wins, three second places and three other top-three finishes to claim the runner-up spot behind champion Yannick Dalmas. That this was achieved without the benefit of major-sponsor backing – so prevalent in the series – was not lost on the ORECA team, who signed Jean to race for them in 1987. He duly took the team's fifth consecutive French F3 title, but only after a disastrous early season which eventually saw the troublesome Martini chassis replaced – at Jean's insistence – by a new Dallara 387, the switch allowing him to take six successive wins on his way to the crown.

Naturally Alesi moved into the Marlboro-backed ORECA F3000 team for the following season but the campaign proved to be a huge disappointment for all concerned, Jean being particularly unhappy at the lack of rapport on the engineering side. Marlboro's decision to back Lehto and Irvine for 1989 led to a switch to Eddie Jordan's team and the pair got on famously. Not only was the F3000 championship won – albeit narrowly from Erik Comas – but Alesi stepped into the Tyrrell vacated by Michele Alboreto to score a sensational fourth place in the French Grand Prix on his F1 debut. An 18-month contract was quickly signed and Alesi set about building a reputation as a fast and fearless racer intimidated by nobody – as Senna would find at Phoenix and Berger at Monaco in 1990 – but one sometimes running at the ragged edge and beyond, as at Monza, where he spun out early on in a fruitless attempt to match the pace of the McLarens.

Frank Williams decided he liked Jean's style and a contract was signed for him to race the Williams-Renault for 1991. However, after protracted negotiations it was announced he would be driving for Ferrari instead.

Initially he found the going tough, his relative lack of experience proving a handicap in a difficult team environment. There were drives of brilliance in 1992 – at Barcelona and Magny Cours, for example – but even more frustration in terms of solid results was to follow in 1993. Despite Ferrari's relative lack of success, Alesi has signed for a further two years at Maranello, but watching him, particularly in qualifying, as he wrings every last ounce from the Ferrari, leads one to wonder what he might have achieved had he elected to stick with Williams.

ALESI, Jean (F) b 11/6/1964

1989

	Race	Circuit	No	Entrant	Car/Engine	Comment
4	FRENCH GP	Paul Ricard	4	Tyrrell Racing Organisation	3.5 Tyrrell 018-Cosworth V8	
ret	BRITISH GP	Silverstone	4	Tyrrell Racing Organisation	3.5 Tyrrell 018-Cosworth V8	spun off
10	GERMAN GP	Hockenheim	4	Tyrrell Racing Organisation	3.5 Tyrrell 018-Cosworth V8	spin-pit stop-tyres/2 laps behind
9	HUNGARIAN GP	Hungaroring	4	Tyrrell Racing Organisation	3.5 Tyrrell 018-Cosworth V8	pit stop-tyres/1 lap behind
5	ITALIAN GP	Monza	4	Tyrrell Racing Organisation	3.5 Tyrrell 018-Cosworth V8	1 lap behind
4	SPANISH GP	Jerez	4	Tyrrell Racing Organisation	3.5 Tyrrell 018-Cosworth V8	pit stop-tyres/1 lap behind
ret	JAPANESE GP	Suzuka	4	Tyrrell Racing Organisation	3.5 Tyrrell 018-Cosworth V8	gearbox
ret	AUSTRALIAN GP	Adelaide	4	Tyrrell Racing Organisation	3.5 Tyrrell 018-Cosworth V8	electrics

1990

	Race	Circuit	No	Entrant	Car/Engine	Comment
2	US GP (PHOENIX)	Phoenix	4	Tyrrell Racing Organisation	3.5 Tyrrell 018-Cosworth V8	
7	BRAZILIAN GP	Interlagos	4	Tyrrell Racing Organisation	3.5 Tyrrell 018-Cosworth V8	collision, de Cesaris/1 lap behind
6	SAN MARINO GP	Imola	4	Tyrrell Racing Organisation	3.5 Tyrrell 019-Cosworth V8	incident with Piquet/1 lap behind
2	MONACO GP	Monte Carlo	4	Tyrrell Racing Organisation	3.5 Tyrrell 019-Cosworth V8	
dns	" " "	4	Tyrrell Racing Organisation	3.5 Tyrrell 018-Cosworth V8	practice only
ret	CANADIAN GP	Montreal	4	Tyrrell Racing Organisation	3.5 Tyrrell 019-Cosworth V8	spun off
7	MEXICAN GP	Mexico City	4	Tyrrell Racing Organisation	3.5 Tyrrell 019-Cosworth V8	misfire
ret	FRENCH GP	Paul Ricard	4	Tyrrell Racing Organisation	3.5 Tyrrell 019-Cosworth V8	differential
8	BRITISH GP	Silverstone	4	Tyrrell Racing Organisation	3.5 Tyrrell 019-Cosworth V8	pit stop-tyres/1 lap behind
ret	GERMAN GP	Hockenheim	4	Tyrrell Racing Organisation	3.5 Tyrrell 019-Cosworth V8	c.v. joint
ret	HUNGARIAN GP	Hungaroring	4	Tyrrell Racing Organisation	3.5 Tyrrell 019-Cosworth V8	collision with Martini
8	BELGIAN GP	Spa	4	Tyrrell Racing Organisation	3.5 Tyrrell 019-Cosworth V8	pit stop-tyres/1 lap behind
ret	ITALIAN GP	Monza	4	Tyrrell Racing Organisation	3.5 Tyrrell 019-Cosworth V8	spun off
8	PORTUGUESE GP	Estoril	4	Tyrrell Racing Organisation	3.5 Tyrrell 019-Cosworth V8	1 lap behind
ret	SPANISH GP	Jerez	4	Tyrrell Racing Organisation	3.5 Tyrrell 019-Cosworth V8	bumped by Berger-puncture
dns	JAPANESE GP	Suzuka	4	Tyrrell Racing Organisation	3.5 Tyrrell 019-Cosworth V8	neck injury in practice
8	AUSTRALIAN GP	Adelaide	4	Tyrrell Racing Organisation	3.5 Tyrrell 019-Cosworth V8	1 lap behind

1991

	Race	Circuit	No	Entrant	Car/Engine	Comment
12/ret	US GP (PHOENIX)	Phoenix	28	Scuderia Ferrari SpA	3.5 Fiat Ferrari 642/2 V12	gearbox/9 laps behind
6	BRAZILIAN GP	Interlagos	28	Scuderia Ferrari SpA	3.5 Fiat Ferrari 642/2 V12	
ret	SAN MARINO GP	Imola	28	Scuderia Ferrari SpA	3.5 Fiat Ferrari 642/2 V12	spun off
3	MONACO GP	Monte Carlo	28	Scuderia Ferrari SpA	3.5 Fiat Ferrari 642/2 V12	
ret	CANADIAN GP	Montreal	28	Scuderia Ferrari SpA	3.5 Fiat Ferrari 642/2 V12	engine
ret	MEXICAN GP	Mexico City	28	Scuderia Ferrari SpA	3.5 Fiat Ferrari 642/2 V12	clutch
4	FRENCH GP	Magny Cours	28	Scuderia Ferrari SpA	3.5 Fiat Ferrari 643 V12	
ret	BRITISH GP	Silverstone	28	Scuderia Ferrari SpA	3.5 Fiat Ferrari 643 V12	collision with Suzuki
3	GERMAN GP	Hockenheim	28	Scuderia Ferrari SpA	3.5 Fiat Ferrari 643 V12	ran without tyre change
5	HUNGARIAN GP	Hungaroring	28	Scuderia Ferrari SpA	3.5 Fiat Ferrari 643 V12	
ret	BELGIAN GP	Spa	28	Scuderia Ferrari SpA	3.5 Fiat Ferrari 643 V12	engine
ret	ITALIAN GP	Monza	28	Scuderia Ferrari SpA	3.5 Fiat Ferrari 643 V12	engine
3	PORTUGUESE GP	Estoril	28	Scuderia Ferrari SpA	3.5 Fiat Ferrari 643 V12	
4	SPANISH GP	Barcelona	28	Scuderia Ferrari SpA	3.5 Fiat Ferrari 643 V12	
ret	JAPANESE GP	Suzuka	28	Scuderia Ferrari SpA	3.5 Fiat Ferrari 643 V12	engine
ret	AUSTRALIAN GP	Adelaide	28	Scuderia Ferrari SpA	3.5 Fiat Ferrari 643 V12	collision with Larini

1992

	Race	Circuit	No	Entrant	Car/Engine	Comment
ret	SOUTH AFRICAN GP	Kyalami	27	Scuderia Ferrari SpA	3.5 Fiat Ferrari F92A V12	engine
ret	MEXICAN GP	Mexico City	27	Scuderia Ferrari SpA	3.5 Fiat Ferrari F92A V12	engine
4	BRAZILIAN GP	Interlagos	27	Scuderia Ferrari SpA	3.5 Fiat Ferrari F92A V12	1 lap behind
3	SPANISH GP	Barcelona	27	Scuderia Ferrari SpA	3.5 Fiat Ferrari F92A V12	
ret	SAN MARINO GP	Imola	27	Scuderia Ferrari SpA	3.5 Fiat Ferrari F92A V12	collision with Berger
ret	MONACO GP	Monte Carlo	27	Scuderia Ferrari SpA	3.5 Fiat Ferrari F92A V12	gearbox
3	CANADIAN GP	Montreal	27	Scuderia Ferrari SpA	3.5 Fiat Ferrari F92A V12	
ret	FRENCH GP	Magny Cours	27	Scuderia Ferrari SpA	3.5 Fiat Ferrari F92A V12	engine
ret	BRITISH GP	Silverstone	27	Scuderia Ferrari SpA	3.5 Fiat Ferrari F92A V12	fire extinguisher discharged
5	GERMAN GP	Hockenheim	27	Scuderia Ferrari SpA	3.5 Fiat Ferrari F92A V12	
ret	HUNGARIAN GP	Hungaroring	27	Scuderia Ferrari SpA	3.5 Fiat Ferrari F92A V12	spun off
ret	BELGIAN GP	Spa	27	Scuderia Ferrari SpA	3.5 Fiat Ferrari F92AT V12	spun off
ret	ITALIAN GP	Monza	27	Scuderia Ferrari SpA	3.5 Fiat Ferrari F92AT V12	fuel pressure
ret	PORTUGUESE GP	Estoril	27	Scuderia Ferrari SpA	3.5 Fiat Ferrari F92AT V12	spun off
5	JAPANESE GP	Suzuka	27	Scuderia Ferrari SpA	3.5 Fiat Ferrari F92AT V12	1 lap behind
4	AUSTRALIAN GP	Adelaide	27	Scuderia Ferrari SpA	3.5 Fiat Ferrari F92AT V12	1 lap behind

1993

	Race	Circuit	No	Entrant	Car/Engine	Comment
ret	SOUTH AFRICAN GP	Kyalami	27	Scuderia Ferrari SpA	3.5 Fiat Ferrari F93A V12	hydraulics
8	BRAZILIAN GP	Interlagos	27	Scuderia Ferrari SpA	3.5 Fiat Ferrari F93A V12	2 stop & go pens/1 lap behind
ret	EUROPEAN GP	Donington	27	Scuderia Ferrari SpA	3.5 Fiat Ferrari F93A V12	active system
ret	SAN MARINO GP	Imola	27	Scuderia Ferrari SpA	3.5 Fiat Ferrari F93A V12	clutch
ret	SPANISH GP	Barcelona	27	Scuderia Ferrari SpA	3.5 Fiat Ferrari F93A V12	engine
3	MONACO GP	Monte Carlo	27	Scuderia Ferrari SpA	3.5 Fiat Ferrari F93A V12	despite collision with Berger
ret	CANADIAN GP	Montreal	27	Scuderia Ferrari SpA	3.5 Fiat Ferrari F93A V12	engine
ret	FRENCH GP	Magny Cours	27	Scuderia Ferrari SpA	3.5 Fiat Ferrari F93A V12	engine
9	BRITISH GP	Silverstone	27	Scuderia Ferrari SpA	3.5 Fiat Ferrari F93A V12	1 lap behind
7	GERMAN GP	Hockenheim	27	Scuderia Ferrari SpA	3.5 Fiat Ferrari F93A V12	pit stop-loose bodywork
ret	HUNGARIAN GP	Hungaroring	27	Scuderia Ferrari SpA	3.5 Fiat Ferrari F93A V12	accident-collision with Fittipaldi
ret	BELGIAN GP	Spa	27	Scuderia Ferrari SpA	3.5 Fiat Ferrari F93A V12	suspension
2	ITALIAN GP	Monza	27	Scuderia Ferrari SpA	3.5 Fiat Ferrari F93A V12	
4	PORTUGUESE GP	Estoril	27	Scuderia Ferrari SpA	3.5 Fiat Ferrari F93A V12	led until first round of tyre stops
ret	JAPANESE GP	Suzuka	27	Scuderia Ferrari SpA	3.5 Fiat Ferrari F93A V12	electrics
4	AUSTRALIAN GP	Adelaide	27	Scuderia Ferrari SpA	3.5 Fiat Ferrari F93A V12	1 lap behind

GP Starts: 71   GP Wins: 0   Pole positions: 0   Fastest laps: 1   Points: 76

PHILIPPE ALLIOT

A late starter in racing, Philippe tried his hand at the Motul racing school in 1975 and did well enough to embark on a season in Formule Renault in 1976, abandoning his studies in political science in the process.

Alliot spent two seasons in the shadow of one Alain Prost before clinching the 1978 Formule Renault title in 1978. The next four seasons were devoted to climbing the ladder in F3. He was third in the French championship in 1979 and spent three seasons contesting the European championship (finishing fifth, third, then fifth again) before a season in F2 in 1983 where he was always quick but prone to error in the ORECA Martini. The highlight of his season came with his third place at Le Mans, sharing the Kremer Porsche with Mario and Michael Andretti.

Alliot moved up into the big league with the underpowered, underfinanced RAM-Hart but his two seasons with the team were littered with shunts and no points were scored. So it was back to ORECA and F3000 for 1986, Alliot taking his March to victory in the round at Spa, but then an opportunity to drive for Ligier arose after Laffite's accident at Brands Hatch. Philippe caused a stir by keeping pace with Arnoux and scored a point in Mexico – which was enough to interest Larrousse, for whom he raced for the next three seasons. He then returned to Ligier, where chassis of various appelations JS33, JS33B and JS33C were all subjected to a comprehensive crash-testing programme.

It was therefore surprising that he should have been invited to join Jean Todt's Peugeot sports car team for 1991-92. Paired with Mauro Baldi, he won three times (Suzuka '91, Donington and Magny Cours '92) as the French manufacturer trampled all over meagre oppositon and the sports car championship headed for extinction. Far from being an endangered species, a more self-confident Alliot then bounced back into Formula 1 for the third time at the age of 39, hoping to extend his career for several years to come.

ALLIOT, Philippe (F) b 27/7/1954

1984

	Race	Circuit	No	Entrant	Car/Engine	Comment
ret	BRAZILIAN GP	Rio	9	Skoal Bandit Formula 1 Team	1.5 t/c RAM 02-Hart 4	battery mounting
ret	SOUTH AFRICAN GP	Kyalami	9	Skoal Bandit Formula 1 Team	1.5 t/c RAM 02-Hart 4	water leak-engine
dnq	BELGIAN GP	Zolder	9	Skoal Bandit Formula 1 Team	1.5 t/c RAM 02-Hart 4	
ret	SAN MARINO GP	Imola	9	Skoal Bandit Formula 1 Team	1.5 t/c RAM 02-Hart 4	engine
ret	FRENCH GP	Dijon	9	Skoal Bandit Formula 1 Team	1.5 t/c RAM 02-Hart 4	electrics
dnq	MONACO GP	Monte Carlo	9	Skoal Bandit Formula 1 Team	1.5 t/c RAM 02-Hart 4	
10*	CANADIAN GP	Montreal	9	Skoal Bandit Formula 1 Team	1.5 t/c RAM 02-Hart 4	* 10th place car dsq/5 laps behind
ret	US GP (DETROIT)	Detroit	9	Skoal Bandit Formula 1 Team	1.5 t/c RAM 02-Hart 4	brakes-hit wall
dns	US GP (DALLAS)	Dallas	9	Skoal Bandit Formula 1 Team	1.5 t/c RAM 02-Hart 4	practice accident
ret	BRITISH GP	Brands Hatch	9	Skoal Bandit Formula 1 Team	1.5 t/c RAM 02-Hart 4	accident-Johansson & Cheever
ret	GERMAN GP	Hockenheim	9	Skoal Bandit Formula 1 Team	1.5 t/c RAM 02-Hart 4	overheating
11	AUSTRIAN GP	Österreichring	9	Skoal Bandit Formula 1 Team	1.5 t/c RAM 02-Hart 4	3 laps behind
10*	DUTCH GP	Zandvoort	9	Skoal Bandit Formula 1 Team	1.5 t/c RAM 02-Hart 4	* 8th & 9th cars dsqd/4 laps behind
ret	ITALIAN GP	Monza	9	Skoal Bandit Formula 1 Team	1.5 t/c RAM 02-Hart 4	electrics
ret	EUROPEAN GP	Nürburgring	9	Skoal Bandit Formula 1 Team	1.5 t/c RAM 02-Hart 4	turbo
ret	PORTUGUESE GP	Estoril	9	Skoal Bandit Formula 1 Team	1.5 t/c RAM 02-Hart 4	engine

1985

	Race	Circuit	No	Entrant	Car/Engine	Comment
9	BRAZILIAN GP	Rio	10	Skoal Bandit Formula 1 Team	1.5 t/c RAM 03-Hart 4	3 laps behind
ret	PORTUGUESE GP	Estoril	10	Skoal Bandit Formula 1 Team	1.5 t/c RAM 03-Hart 4	spun off
ret	SAN MARINO GP	Imola	10	Skoal Bandit Formula 1 Team	1.5 t/c RAM 03-Hart 4	engine
dnq	MONACO GP	Monte Carlo	10	Skoal Bandit Formula 1 Team	1.5 t/c RAM 03-Hart 4	
ret	CANADIAN GP	Montreal	10	Skoal Bandit Formula 1 Team	1.5 t/c RAM 03-Hart 4	accident
ret	US GP (DETROIT)	Detroit	10	Skoal Bandit Formula 1 Team	1.5 t/c RAM 03-Hart 4	accident with Brundle
ret	FRENCH GP	Paul Ricard	10	Skoal Bandit Formula 1 Team	1.5 t/c RAM 03-Hart 4	fuel pressure
ret	BRITISH GP	Silverstone	10	Skoal Bandit Formula 1 Team	1.5 t/c RAM 03-Hart 4	accident with Ghinzani
ret	GERMAN GP	Nürburgring	10	Skoal Bandit Formula 1 Team	1.5 t/c RAM 03-Hart 4	oil pressure
ret	AUSTRIAN GP	Österreichring	9	Skoal Bandit Formula 1 Team	1.5 t/c RAM 03-Hart 4	turbo
ret	DUTCH GP	Zandvoort	9	Skoal Bandit Formula 1 Team	1.5 t/c RAM 03-Hart 4	engine
ret	ITALIAN GP	Monza	9	Skoal Bandit Formula 1 Team	1.5 t/c RAM 03-Hart 4	turbo
ret	BELGIAN GP	Spa	9	Skoal Bandit Formula 1 Team	1.5 t/c RAM 03-Hart 4	accident
ret	EUROPEAN GP	Brands Hatch	9	Skoal Bandit Formula 1 Team	1.5 t/c RAM 03-Hart 4	engine

1986

	Race	Circuit	No	Entrant	Car/Engine	Comment
ret	GERMAN GP	Hockenheim	26	Equipe Ligier	1.5 t/c Ligier JS27-Renault V6	engine
9	HUNGARIAN GP	Hungaroring	26	Equipe Ligier	1.5 t/c Ligier JS27-Renault V6	3 laps behind
ret	AUSTRIAN GP	Österreichring	26	Equipe Ligier	1.5 t/c Ligier JS27-Renault V6	engine
ret	ITALIAN GP	Monza	26	Equipe Ligier	1.5 t/c Ligier JS27-Renault V6	engine
ret	PORTUGUESE GP	Estoril	26	Equipe Ligier	1.5 t/c Ligier JS27-Renault V6	engine
6	MEXICAN GP	Mexico City	26	Equipe Ligier	1.5 t/c Ligier JS27-Renault V6	1 lap behind
8	AUSTRALIAN GP	Adelaide	26	Equipe Ligier	1.5 t/c Ligier JS27-Renault V6	3 laps behind

1987

	Race	Circuit	No	Entrant	Car/Engine	Comment
10	SAN MARINO GP	Imola	30	Larrousse Calmels	3.5 Lola LC87-Cosworth V8	2nd non-turbo/3 laps behind
8	BELGIAN GP	Spa	30	Larrousse Calmels	3.5 Lola LC87-Cosworth V8	1st non-turbo/3 laps behind
ret	MONACO GP	Monte Carlo	30	Larrousse Calmels	3.5 Lola LC87-Cosworth V8	engine
ret	US GP (DETROIT)	Detroit	30	Larrousse Calmels	3.5 Lola LC87-Cosworth V8	collision with Arnoux
ret	FRENCH GP	Paul Ricard	30	Larrousse Calmels	3.5 Lola LC87-Cosworth V8	transmission
ret	BRITISH GP	Silverstone	30	Larrousse Calmels	3.5 Lola LC87-Cosworth V8	gearbox

6	GERMAN GP	Hockenheim	30	Larrousse Calmels	3.5 Lola LC87-Cosworth V8	*3rd non-turbo/2 laps behind*
ret	HUNGARIAN GP	Hungaroring	30	Larrousse Calmels	3.5 Lola LC87-Cosworth V8	*spun off*
12	AUSTRIAN GP	Österreichring	30	Larrousse Calmels	3.5 Lola LC87-Cosworth V8	*2nd non-turbo/3 laps behind*
ret	ITALIAN GP	Monza	30	Larrousse Calmels	3.5 Lola LC87-Cosworth V8	*spun off*
ret	PORTUGUESE GP	Estoril	30	Larrousse Calmels	3.5 Lola LC87-Cosworth V8	*fuel pump*
6	SPANISH GP	Jerez	30	Larrousse Calmels	3.5 Lola LC87-Cosworth V8	*1st non-turbo/1 lap behind*
6	MEXICAN GP	Mexico City	30	Larrousse Calmels	3.5 Lola LC87-Cosworth V8	*1st non-turbo/3 laps behind*
ret	JAPANESE GP	Suzuka	30	Larrousse Calmels	3.5 Lola LC87-Cosworth V8	*startline accident*
ret	AUSTRALIAN GP	Adelaide	30	Larrousse Calmels	3.5 Lola LC87-Cosworth V8	*electrics*

1988

ret	BRAZILIAN GP	Rio	30	Larrousse Calmels	3.5 Lola LC88-Cosworth V8	*broken suspension-spun off*
17	SAN MARINO GP	Imola	30	Larrousse Calmels	3.5 Lola LC88-Cosworth V8	*pit stop-puncture/3 laps behind*
ret	MONACO GP	Monte Carlo	30	Larrousse Calmels	3.5 Lola LC88-Cosworth V8	*collision with Patrese*
ret	MEXICAN GP	Mexico City	30	Larrousse Calmels	3.5 Lola LC88-Cosworth V8	*rear upright/started from back*
10/ret	CANADIAN GP	Montreal	30	Larrousse Calmels	3.5 Lola LC88-Cosworth V8	*engine cut out/3laps behind*
ret	US GP (DETROIT)	Detroit	30	Larrousse Calmels	3.5 Lola LC88-Cosworth V8	*gearbox*
ret	FRENCH GP	Paul Ricard	30	Larrousse Calmels	3.5 Lola LC88-Cosworth V8	*electrics*
14	BRITISH GP	Silverstone	30	Larrousse Calmels	3.5 Lola LC88-Cosworth V8	*2 laps behind*
ret	GERMAN GP	Hockenheim	30	Larrousse Calmels	3.5 Lola LC88-Cosworth V8	*spun off*
12	HUNGARIAN GP	Hungaroring	30	Larrousse Calmels	3.5 Lola LC88-Cosworth V8	*misfire/4 laps behind*
9*	BELGIAN GP	Spa	30	Larrousse Calmels	3.5 Lola LC88-Cosworth V8	**3rd & 4th cars dsqd/1 lap behind*
ret	ITALIAN GP	Monza	30	Larrousse Calmels	3.5 Lola LC88-Cosworth V8	*engine*
ret	PORTUGUESE GP	Estoril	30	Larrousse Calmels	3.5 Lola LC88-Cosworth V8	*engine*
14	SPANISH GP	Jerez	30	Larrousse Calmels	3.5 Lola LC88-Cosworth V8	*wheel problem/3 laps behind*
9	JAPANESE GP	Suzuka	30	Larrousse Calmels	3.5 Lola LC88-Cosworth V8	*1 lap behind*
10/ret	AUSTRALIAN GP	Adelaide	30	Larrousse Calmels	3.5 Lola LC88-Cosworth V8	*out of fuel7 laps behind*

1989

12	BRAZILIAN GP	Rio	30	Larrousse Calmels	3.5 Lola LC88B-Lamborghini V12	*3 laps behind*
ret	SAN MARINO GP	Imola	30	Equipe Larrousse	3.5 Lola LC89-Lamborghini V12	*engine-fuel injection*
ret	MONACO GP	Monte Carlo	30	Equipe Larrousse	3.5 Lola LC89-Lamborghini V12	*engine*
nc	MEXICAN GP	Mexico City	30	Equipe Larrousse	3.5 Lola LC89-Lamborghini V12	*p stops-acci damage-misfire/-41 laps*
ret	US GP (PHOENIX)	Phoenix	30	Equipe Larrousse	3.5 Lola LC89-Lamborghini V12	*spun off*
ret	CANADIAN GP	Montreal	30	Equipe Larrousse	3.5 Lola LC89-Lamborghini V12	*crashed*
ret	FRENCH GP	Paul Ricard	30	Equipe Larrousse	3.5 Lola LC89-Lamborghini V12	*engine*
ret	BRITISH GP	Silverstone	30	Equipe Larrousse	3.5 Lola LC89-Lamborghini V12	*engine*
ret	GERMAN GP	Hockenheim	30	Equipe Larrousse	3.5 Lola LC89-Lamborghini V12	*oil leak*
dnpq	HUNGARIAN GP	Hungaroring	30	Equipe Larrousse	3.5 Lola LC89-Lamborghini V12	
16/ret	BELGIAN GP	Spa	30	Equipe Larrousse	3.5 Lola LC89-Lamborghini V12	*engine-oil pressure/5 laps behind*
ret	ITALIAN GP	Monza	30	Equipe Larrousse	3.5 Lola LC89-Lamborghini V12	*throttle stuck-spun off*
9	PORTUGUESE GP	Estoril	30	Equipe Larrousse	3.5 Lola LC89-Lamborghini V12	*pit stop-tyres/1 lap behind*
6	SPANISH GP	Jerez	30	Equipe Larrousse	3.5 Lola LC89-Lamborghini V12	*pit stop-tyres/1 lap behind*
ret	JAPANESE GP	Suzuka	30	Equipe Larrousse	3.5 Lola LC89-Lamborghini V12	*engine*
ret	AUSTRALIAN GP	Adelaide	30	Equipe Larrousse	3.5 Lola LC89-Lamborghini V12	*collision with Berger*

1990

excl	US GP (PHOENIX)	Phoenix	26	Ligier Gitanes	3.5 Ligier JS33B-Cosworth V8	*dsq in practice-outside assistance*
12	BRAZILIAN GP	Interlagos	26	Ligier Gitanes	3.5 Ligier JS33B-Cosworth V8	*3 laps behind*
9	SAN MARINO GP	Imola	26	Ligier Gitanes	3.5 Ligier JS33B-Cosworth V8	*pit stop-tyres/1 lap behind*
dns	"	"	26	Ligier Gitanes	3.5 Ligier JS33-Cosworth V8	*practice only*
ret	MONACO GP	Monte Carlo	26	Ligier Gitanes	3.5 Ligier JS33B-Cosworth V8	*gearbox*
dns	"	"	26	Ligier Gitanes	3.5 Ligier JS33-Cosworth V8	*practice only*
ret	CANADIAN GP	Montreal	26	Ligier Gitanes	3.5 Ligier JS33B-Cosworth V8	*engine*
18	MEXICAN GP	Mexico City	26	Ligier Gitanes	3.5 Ligier JS33B-Cosworth V8	*pit stop-tyres/3 laps behind*
dns	"	"	26	Ligier Gitanes	3.5 Ligier JS33-Cosworth V8	*practice only*
9	FRENCH GP	Paul Ricard	26	Ligier Gitanes	3.5 Ligier JS33B-Cosworth V8	*pit stop-tyres/1 lap behind*
dns	"	"	26	Ligier Gitanes	3.5 Ligier JS33-Cosworth V8	*practice only*
13	BRITISH GP	Silverstone	26	Ligier Gitanes	3.5 Ligier JS33B-Cosworth V8	*3 laps behind*
dns	"	"	26	Ligier Gitanes	3.5 Ligier JS33C-Cosworth V8	*practice only*
dsq	GERMAN GP	Hockenheim	26	Ligier Gitanes	3.5 Ligier JS33B-Cosworth V8	*push start after startline accident*
dns	"	"	26	Ligier Gitanes	3.5 Ligier JS33C-Cosworth V8	*practice only*
14	HUNGARIAN GP	Hungaroring	26	Ligier Gitanes	3.5 Ligier JS33B-Cosworth V8	*pit stop/spin/3 laps behind*
dnq	BELGIAN GP	Spa	26	Ligier Gitanes	3.5 Ligier JS33B-Cosworth V8	
13	ITALIAN GP	Monza	26	Ligier Gitanes	3.5 Ligier JS33B-Cosworth V8	*3 laps behind*
ret	PORTUGUESE GP	Estoril	26	Ligier Gitanes	3.5 Ligier JS33B-Cosworth V8	*collision with Mansell*
ret	SPANISH GP	Jerez	26	Ligier Gitanes	3.5 Ligier JS33B-Cosworth V8	*spun off*
10	JAPANESE GP	Suzuka	26	Ligier Gitanes	3.5 Ligier JS33B-Cosworth V8	*1 lap behind*
11	AUSTRALIAN GP	Adelaide	26	Ligier Gitanes	3.5 Ligier JS33B-Cosworth V8	*3 laps behind*

1993

ret	SOUTH AFRICAN GP	Kyalami	19	Equipe Larrousse	3.5 Larrousse LH93-Lamborghini V12	*spun off*
7	BRAZILIAN GP	Interlagos	19	Equipe Larrousse	3.5 Larrousse LH93-Lamborghini V12	*1 lap behind*
ret	EUROPEAN GP	Donington	19	Equipe Larrousse	3.5 Larrousse LH93-Lamborghini V12	*accident-hit by de Cesaris*
5	SAN MARINO GP	Imola	19	Equipe Larrousse	3.5 Larrousse LH93-Lamborghini V12	*2 laps behind*
ret	SPANISH GP	Barcelona	19	Equipe Larrousse	3.5 Larrousse LH93-Lamborghini V12	*gearbox*
12	MONACO GP	Monte Carlo	19	Equipe Larrousse	3.5 Larrousse LH93-Lamborghini V12	*3 laps behind*
ret	CANADIAN GP	Montreal	19	Equipe Larrousse	3.5 Larrousse LH93-Lamborghini V12	*gearbox*
9	FRENCH GP	Magny Cours	19	Equipe Larrousse	3.5 Larrousse LH93-Lamborghini V12	*2 laps behind*
11	BRITISH GP	Silverstone	19	Equipe Larrousse	3.5 Larrousse LH93-Lamborghini V12	*2 laps behind*
12	GERMAN GP	Hockenheim	19	Equipe Larrousse	3.5 Larrousse LH93-Lamborghini V12	*lost clutch/1 lap behind*
8	HUNGARIAN GP	Hungaroring	19	Equipe Larrousse	3.5 Larrousse LH93-Lamborghini V12	*early spin/2 laps behind*
12	BELGIAN GP	Spa	19	Equipe Larrousse	3.5 Larrousse LH93-Lamborghini V12	*2 laps behind*
9	ITALIAN GP	Monza	19	Equipe Larrousse	3.5 Larrousse LH93-Lamborghini V12	*collision at start/2 laps behind*
10	PORTUGUESE GP	Estoril	19	Equipe Larrousse	3.5 Larrousse LH93-Lamborghini V12	*lost clutch/2 laps behind*

GP Starts: 107   GP Wins: 0   Pole positions: 0   Fastest laps: 0   Points: 7

CLIFF ALLISON

The son of a garage owner from Cumberland, Allison entered racing in 1952 with the little F3 Cooper-JAP and progressed steadily in the formula, finishing fourth in the 1955 championship. That year he also began racing the works Lotus XI sports cars for Colin Chapman, culminating in an Index of Performance win with the little 750 cc Lotus at Le Mans in 1957 – a season which also saw the Hornsey team move into single-seaters with their Lotus 12.

Ambitious plans were made for 1958 and Cliff led the team in their World Championship assault. He scored a fine fourth at Spa, finishing behind three cars which it transpired would not have survived a further lap, and put up a tremendous performance in the German Grand Prix when a burst radiator cost him a possible sensational win in the Lotus 16. His efforts did not go unnoticed, though, and on the recommendation of Mike Hawthorn Cliff was invited by Ferrari for tests at Modena and offered a works drive for 1959.

After a solid first season at Maranello his fortunes were to be mixed; 1960 began with success in Argentina, Cliff winning the 1000 Km for sports cars with Phil Hill and taking second place in the Grand Prix, but a practice crash at Monaco in which he was flung from the car and badly broke his arm curtailed his season. When fully recovered, he signed for the UDT Laystall team to race their Lotus 18 in 1961 and played himself back to form in the many non-championship races held that year, his results including a second place in the International Trophy, run to the 2.5 litre Inter-Continental Formula. For the Belgian Grand Prix, Cliff had to set a quicker practice time than team-mate Henry Taylor in order to claim the car for the race. Disaster struck when he crashed heavily and was thrown from the Lotus, sustaining serious leg injuries which prompted his retirement from racing.

CHRIS AMON

Chris Amon will always be best remembered as a notoriously unlucky driver who never managed to win a World Championship Grand Prix, for whenever he seemed poised to triumph dame fortune frowned and poor Chrissie was left to rue his unkind fate.

A New Zealand sheep farmer's son, Chris was racing a Maserati 250F by the age of 18, and he so impressed Reg Parnell in the 1962-63 winter series that he was invited to join the Parnell Grand Prix line-up at the tender age of 19. Amon learned quickly with the team, but the patron's untimely death was a big blow, and by 1965 Chris was spending most of his time with Bruce McLaren and his fledgling organisation, racing his big Elva sports cars. A proposed 1966 Grand Prix season with McLaren failed to get off the ground due to a lack of engines, so it was more sports car racing in Britain and in the Can-Am series, topped by a wonderful win for Ford at Le Mans with Bruce.

Amon's successful season was closely watched by Ferrari, who signed him for 1967. He got off to an encouraging start with wins in the Daytona 24 Hours and Monza 1000 Km, but then came turmoil. With Bandini killed, Parkes injured and Scarfiotti quitting, a huge burden fell on Chris's shoulders and he responded brilliantly with a string of great drives which continued into the following season, coming closest to a win in the 1968 British GP where he had a classic battle with Jo Siffert. The 1969 season started brightly, Chris taking a Dino 166 to the Tasman series and winning the championship, but the strain of the factory's huge racing programme was beginning to show, and F1 suffered most. Frustrated, Chris jumped ship to drive the new works March in 1970, winnng the International Trophy and taking a superb second to Rodriguez at Spa, but the team's limitations were soon apparent and, despite an excellent run of placings, he signed a big two-year deal with Matra for 1971-72. A splendid aggregate win in the non-title Argentine GP boded well only for luck to desert him at crucial times, most cruelly at Monza when he lost his visor, and then at Clermont Ferrand when nobody could live with him until a puncture intervened.

With Matra's withdrawal, Chris agreed a return to March for 1973 but a dis-agreement saw him sensationally sacked at the start of the year. It was to be the start of a downward Formula 1 spiral for the Kiwi, who became pro-gressively dispirited as he saw his efforts go to waste, first at Tecno and then disastrously in 1974 with his own Amon project. Even guest drives for Tyrrell and BRM failed to ignite the latent spark until, seemingly washed up, Chris accepted a drive in Mo Nunn's Ensign late in 1975. Suddenly there was a sense of purpose and in 1976 the old Amon was back, with a superb drive at Kyalami until a fuel problem halted his progress. The new MN176 was a cracking little chassis and Chris really flew, but unfortunately it was fragile and after a couple of very lucky escapes when things broke he decided to get out in one piece, finally quitting F1 for good after being T-boned in a practice collision at Mosport driving for Wolf. Although he raced briefly in Can-Am in 1977, Chris then married for the second time and returned to New Zealand to tend the family farm.

ALLISON, Cliff (GB) b 8/2/1932

1958

	Race	Circuit	No	Entrant	Car/Engine	Comment
6	MONACO GP	Monte Carlo	24	Team Lotus	2.0 Lotus 12-Climax 4	10 laps behind
6	DUTCH GP	Zandvoort	17	Team Lotus	2.2 Lotus 12-Climax 4	2 laps behind
4	BELGIAN GP	Spa	40	Team Lotus	2.2 Lotus 12-Climax 4	broken suspension
ret	FRENCH GP	Reims	26	Team Lotus	2.2 Lotus 12-Climax 4	engine
ret	BRITISH GP	Silverstone	17	Team Lotus	2.2 Lotus 12-Climax 4	oil pressure
ret	"	"	17	Team Lotus	2.2 Lotus 12-Climax 4	practice only
5/ret	GERMAN GP	Nürburgring	12	Team Lotus	2.0 Lotus 16-Climax 4	radiator/10th after 5 F2 cars/-2 laps
dns	PORTUGUESE GP	Oporto	18	Team Lotus	2.0 Lotus 16-Climax 4	practice accident
ret	"	"	18	Scuderia Centro Sud/Team Lotus	2.5 Maserati 250F 6	mechanical/borrowed car
7	ITALIAN GP	Monza	36	Team Lotus	1.5 Lotus 12-Climax 4	F2 car/9 laps behind
10	MOROCCAN GP	Casablanca	34	Team Lotus	2.0 Lotus 12-Climax 4	4 laps behind

1959

	Race	Circuit	No	Entrant	Car/Engine	Comment
ret	MONACO GP	Monte Carlo	52	Scuderia Ferrari	1.5 Ferrari Dino 156 V6	collided with von Trips & Halford
9	DUTCH GP	Zandvoort	16	Scuderia Ferrari	2.4 Ferrari Dino 246 V6	4 laps behind
ret	GERMAN GP	AVUS	17	Scuderia Ferrari	2.4 Ferrari Dino 246 V6	clutch in first heat
5	ITALIAN GP	Monza	34	Scuderia Ferrari	2.4 Ferrari Dino 246 V6	1 lap behind
ret	US GP	Sebring	3	Scuderia Ferrari	2.4 Ferrari Dino 246 V6	clutch

1960

	Race	Circuit	No	Entrant	Car/Engine	Comment
2	ARGENTINE GP	Buenos Aires	24	Scuderia Ferrari	2.4 Ferrari Dino 246 V6	
dns	MONACO GP	Monte Carlo	32	Scuderia Ferrari	2.4 Ferrari Dino 246 V6	accident at chicane-fractured arm

1961

	Race	Circuit	No	Entrant	Car/Engine	Comment
8	MONACO GP	Monte Carlo	32	UDT-Laystall Racing Team	1.5 Lotus 18-Climax 4	7 laps behind
dnq	BELGIAN GP	Spa	16	UDT-Laystall Racing Team	1.5 Lotus 18-Climax 4	crashed in practice-badly injured

GP Starts: 16   GP Wins: 0   Pole positions: 0   Fastest laps: 0   Points: 11

AMON, Chris (NZ) b 20/7/1943

1963

	Race	Circuit	No	Entrant	Car/Engine	Comment
dns	MONACO GP	Monte Carlo	15	Reg Parnell (Racing)	1.5 Lola 4A-Climax V8	car driven by Trintignant
ret	BELGIAN GP	Spa	21	Reg Parnell (Racing)	1.5 Lola 4A-Climax V8	oil leak
ret	DUTCH GP	Zandvoort	10	Reg Parnell (Racing)	1.5 Lola 4A-Climax V8	water pump
ret	"	"	10T	Reg Parnell (Racing)	1.5 Lotus 24-Climax V8	practice only
7	FRENCH GP	Reims	30	Reg Parnell (Racing)	1.5 Lola 4A-Climax V8	2 laps behind
7	BRITISH GP	Silverstone	19	Reg Parnell (Racing)	1.5 Lola 4A-Climax V8	2 laps behind
ret	GERMAN GP	Nürburgring	21	Reg Parnell (Racing)	1.5 Lola 4A-Climax V8	crashed-broken steering
dnq	ITALIAN GP	Monza	38	Reg Parnell (Racing)	1.5 Lola 4A-Climax V8	practice accident
ret	MEXICAN GP	Mexico City	18	Reg Parnell (Racing)	1.5 Lotus 24-BRM V8	gearbox

1964

	Race	Circuit	No	Entrant	Car/Engine	Comment
dnq	MONACO GP	Monte Carlo	17	Reg Parnell (Racing)	1.5 Lotus 25-BRM V8	
5	DUTCH GP	Zandvoort	10	Reg Parnell (Racing)	1.5 Lotus 25-BRM V8	1 lap behind
ret	BELGIAN GP	Spa	27	Reg Parnell (Racing)	1.5 Lotus 25-BRM V8	con-rod
10	FRENCH GP	Rouen	34	Reg Parnell (Racing)	1.5 Lotus 25-BRM V8	4 laps behind
ret	BRITISH GP	Brands Hatch	15	Reg Parnell (Racing)	1.5 Lotus 25-BRM V8	clutch
11/ret	GERMAN GP	Nürburgring	14	Reg Parnell (Racing)	1.5 Lotus 25-BRM V8	suspension/3laps behind
ret	AUSTRIAN GP	Zeltweg	16	Reg Parnell (Racing)	1.5 Lotus 25-BRM V8	engine
ret	US GP	Watkins Glen	15	Reg Parnell (Racing)	1.5 Lotus 25-BRM V8	starter motor bolt
ret	MEXICAN GP	Mexico City	15	Reg Parnell (Racing)	1.5 Lotus 25-BRM V8	gearbox

1965

	Race	Circuit	No	Entrant	Car/Engine	Comment
ret	FRENCH GP	Clermont Ferrand	24	Reg Parnell (Racing)	1.5 Lotus 25-BRM V8	fuel feed
dns	BRITISH GP	Silverstone	24	Ian Raby Racing	1.5 Brabham BT3-BRM V8	Raby drove car
ret	GERMAN GP	Nürburgring	19	Reg Parnell (Racing)	1.5 Lotus 25-BRM V8	electrics

1966

	Race	Circuit	No	Entrant	Car/Engine	Comment
8	FRENCH GP	Reims	8	Cooper Car Co	3.0 Cooper T81-Maserati V12	loose hub nut/4 laps behind
dnq	ITALIAN GP	Monza	32	Chris Amon	2.0 Brabham BT11-BRM V8	

1967

	Race	Circuit	No	Entrant	Car/Engine	Comment
3	MONACO GP	Monte Carlo	20	Scuderia Ferrari SpA SEFAC	3.0 Ferrari 312/67 V12	2 laps behind
4	DUTCH GP	Zandvoort	3	Scuderia Ferrari SpA SEFAC	3.0 Ferrari 312/67 V12	
3	BELGIAN GP	Spa	1	Scuderia Ferrari SpA SEFAC	3.0 Ferrari 312/67 V12	
ret	FRENCH GP	Le Mans	2	Scuderia Ferrari SpA SEFAC	3.0 Ferrari 312/67 V12	throttle cable
3	BRITISH GP	Silverstone	8	Scuderia Ferrari SpA SEFAC	3.0 Ferrari 312/67 V12	
3	GERMAN GP	Nürburgring	8	Scuderia Ferrari Spa SEFAC	3.0 Ferrari 312/67 V12	
6	CANADIAN GP	Mosport Park	20	Scuderia Ferrari SpA SEFAC	3.0 Ferrari 312/67 V12	3 laps behind
7	ITALIAN GP	Monza	2	Scuderia Ferrari SpA SEFAC	3.0 Ferrari 312/67 V12	pit stop-handling/4 laps behind
ret	US GP	Watkins Glen	9	Scuderia Ferrari SpA SEFAC	3.0 Ferrari 312/67 V12	engine
9	MEXICAN GP	Mexico City	9	Scuderia Ferrari SpA SEFAC	3.0 Ferrari 312/67 V12	fuel feed problem/3 laps behind

1968

	Race	Circuit	No	Entrant	Car/Engine	Comment
4	SOUTH AFRICAN GP	Kyalami	8	Scuderia Ferrari SpA SEFAC	3.0 Ferrari 312/67 V12	pit stop-fuel/2 laps behind
ret	SPANISH GP	Jarama	19	Scuderia Ferrari SpA SEFAC	3.0 Ferrari 312/67/68 V12	fuel pump/Pole
ret	BELGIAN GP	Spa	22	Scuderia Ferrari SpA SEFAC	3.0 Ferrari 312/67/68 V12	stone holed radiator/Pole
6	DUTCH GP	Zandvoort	9	Scuderia Ferrari SpA SEFAC	3.0 Ferrari 312/68 V12	pit stop-tyres/5 laps behind
10	FRENCH GP	Rouen	24	Scuderia Ferrari SpA SEFAC	3.0 Ferrari 312/68 V12	engine/tyres/5 laps behind
2	BRITISH GP	Brands Hatch	5	Scuderia Ferrari SpA SEFAC	3.0 Ferrari 312/68 V12	
ret	GERMAN GP	Nürburgring	8	Scuderia Ferrari SpA SEFAC	3.0 Ferrari 312/68 V12	spun off
ret	ITALIAN GP	Monza	9	Scuderia Ferrari SpA SEFAC	3.0 Ferrari 312/68 V12	spun off on oil
ret	CANADIAN GP	St Jovite	9	Scuderia Ferrari SpA SEFAC	3.0 Ferrari 312/68 V12	transmission

ret	US GP	Watkins Glen	6	Scuderia Ferrari SpA SEFAC	3.0 Ferrari 312/68 V12	*water pipe*
ret	MEXICAN GP	Mexico City	6	Scuderia Ferrari SpA SEFAC	3.0 Ferrari 312/68 V12	*water pump drive-overheating*

1969

ret	SOUTH AFRICAN GP	Kyalami	9	Scuderia Ferrari SpA SEFAC	3.0 Ferrari 312/69 V12	*engine*
ret	SPANISH GP	Montjuich Park	15	Scuderia Ferrari SpA SEFAC	3.0 Ferrari 312/69 V12	*engine while 1st*
ret	MONACO GP	Monte Carlo	11	Scuderia Ferrari SpA SEFAC	3.0 Ferrari 312/69 V12	*differential*
3	DUTCH GP	Zandvoort	8	Scuderia Ferrari SpA SEFAC	3.0 Ferrari 312/69 V12	
10/ret	FRENCH GP	Clermont Ferrand	6	Scuderia Ferrari SpA SEFAC	3.0 Ferrari 312/69 V12	*engine*
ret	BRITISH GP	Silverstone	11	Scuderia Ferrari SpA SEFAC	3.0 Ferrari 312/69 V12	*gearbox*

1970

ret	SOUTH AFRICAN GP	Kyalami	15	March Engineering	3.0 March 701-Cosworth V8	*overheating*
ret	SPANISH GP	Jarama	9	March Engineering	3.0 March 701-Cosworth V8	*engine*
ret	MONACO GP	Monte Carlo	28	March Engineering	3.0 March 701-Cosworth V8	*rear suspension bolt*
2	BELGIAN GP	Spa	10	March Engineering	3.0 March 701-Cosworth V8	*FL*
ret	DUTCH GP	Zandvoort	8	March Engineering	3.0 March 701-Cosworth V8	*clutch*
2	FRENCH GP	Clermont Ferrand	14	March Engineering	3.0 March 701-Cosworth V8	
5	BRITISH GP	Brands Hatch	16	March Engineering	3.0 March 701-Cosworth V8	*1 lap behind*
ret	GERMAN GP	Hockenheim	5	March Engineering	3.0 March 701-Cosworth V8	*engine*
8	AUSTRIAN GP	Österreichring	4	March Engineering	3.0 March 701-Cosworth V8	*1 lap behind*
7	ITALIAN GP	Monza	48	March Engineering	3.0 March 701-Cosworth V8	*1 lap behind*
3	CANADIAN GP	St Jovite	20	March Engineering	3.0 March 701-Cosworth V8	
5	US GP	Watkins Glen	12	March Engineering	3.0 March 701-Cosworth V8	*pit stop-tyres/1 lap behind*
4	MEXICAN GP	Mexico City	12	March Engineering	3.0 March 701-Cosworth V8	

1971

5	SOUTH AFRICAN GP	Kyalami	19	Equipe Matra Sports	3.0 Matra-Simca MS120B V12	*1 lap behind*
3	SPANISH GP	Montjuich Park	20	Equipe Matra Sports	3.0 Matra-Simca MS120B V12	
ret	MONACO GP	Monte Carlo	20	Equipe Matra Sports	3.0 Matra-Simca MS120B V12	*cwp*
ret	DUTCH GP	Zandvoort	20	Equipe Matra Sports	3.0 Matra-Simca MS120B V12	*spun off-damaged radiator*
5	FRENCH GP	Paul Ricard	20	Equipe Matra Sports	3.0 Matra-Simca MS120B V12	
ret	BRITISH GP	Silverstone	21	Equipe Matra Sports	3.0 Matra-Simca MS120B V12	*dropped valve*
ret	GERMAN GP	Nürburgring	10	Equipe Matra Sports	3.0 Matra-Simca MS120B V12	*spun, damaged suspension*
6	ITALIAN GP	Monza	12	Equipe Matra Sports	3.0 Matra-Simca MS120B V12	*lost visor while 1st/Pole*
10	CANADIAN GP	Mosport Park	20	Equipe Matra Sports	3.0 Matra-Simca MS120B V12	*3 laps behind*
12	US GP	Watkins Glen	11	Equipe Matra Sports	3.0 Matra-Simca MS120B V12	*pit stop-tyres/2 laps behind*

1972

dns	ARGENTINE GP	Buenos Aires	16	Equipe Matra	3.0 Matra-Simca MS120C V12	*gearbox on warm-up lap*
15	SOUTH AFRICAN GP	Kyalami	15	Equipe Matra	3.0 Matra-Simca MS120C V12	*2 pit stops-vibration/3 laps behind*
ret	SPANISH GP	Jarama	9	Equipe Matra	3.0 Matra-Simca MS120C V12	*gearbox*
6	MONACO GP	Monte Carlo	16	Equipe Matra	3.0 Matra-Simca MS120C V12	*4 pit stops-goggles/3 laps behind*
6	BELGIAN GP	Nivelles	5	Equipe Matra	3.0 Matra-Simca MS120C V12	*fuel stop lay 3rd/FL/1 lap behind*
3	FRENCH GP	Clermont Ferrand	9	Equipe Matra	3.0 Matra-Simca MS120D V12	*pit stop-puncture/Pole/FL*
4	BRITISH GP	Brands Hatch	17	Equipe Matra	3.0 Matra-Simca MS120C V12	*1 lap behind*
dns	"	" "	17	Equipe Matra	3.0 Matra-Simca MS120D V12	*practice only*
15	GERMAN GP	Nürburgring	8	Equipe Matra	3.0 Matra-Simca MS120D V12	*started from pitlane/1 lap behind*
5	AUSTRIAN GP	Österreichring	10	Equipe Matra	3.0 Matra-Simca MS120D V12	
dns	"	"	30T	Equipe Matra	3.0 Matra-Simca MS120C V12	*practice only*
ret	ITALIAN GP	Monza	20	Equipe Matra	3.0 Matra-Simca MS120D V12	*brakes-worn pads*
dns	"	"	20T	Equipe Matra	3.0 Matra-Simca MS120C V12	*practice only*
6	CANADIAN GP	Mosport Park	4	Equipe Matra	3.0 Matra-Simca MS120D V12	*1 lap behind*
15	US GP	Watkins Glen	18	Equipe Matra	3.0 Matra-Simca MS120D V12	*started from back of grid/-2 laps*

1973

6	BELGIAN GP	Zolder	22	Martini Racing Team	3.0 Tecno PA123 F12	*3 laps behind*
ret	MONACO GP	Monte Carlo	22	Martini Racing Team	3.0 Tecno PA123 F12	*overheating*
ret	BRITISH GP	Silverstone	22	Martini Racing Team	3.0 Tecno PA123 F12	*fuel pressure*
ret	DUTCH GP	Zandvoort	22	Martini Racing Team	3.0 Tecno PA123 F12	*fuel pressure*
dns	"	"	22T	Martini Racing Team	3.0 Tecno E731 F12	*practice only*
dns	AUSTRIAN GP	Österreichring	22	Martini Racing Team	3.0 Tecno PA123 F12	*no engine available*
dns	"	"	22T	Martini Racing Team	3.0 Tecno E731 F12	*no engine available*
10	CANADIAN GP	Mosport Park	29	Elf Team Tyrrell	3.0 Tyrrell 005-Cosworth V8	*pit stop-tyres/3 laps behind*
dns	US GP	Watkins Glen	29	Elf Team Tyrrell	3.0 Tyrrell 005-Cosworth V8	*withdrawn after Cevert's accident*

1974

ret	SPANISH GP	Jarama	30	Chris Amon Racing	3.0 Amon AF1-Cosworth V8	*brakeshaft*
dns	MONACO GP	Monte Carlo	30	Chris Amon Racing	3.0 Amon AF1-Cosworth V8	*withdrawn-hub failure*
dnq	GERMAN GP	Nürburgring	30	Chris Amon Racing	3.0 Amon AF1-Cosworth V8	*driver unwell*
dnq	ITALIAN GP	Monza	22	Chris Amon Racing	3.0 Amon AF1-Cosworth V8	
nc	CANADIAN GP	Mosport Park	15	Team Motul BRM	3.0 BRM P201 V12	*pit stop-misfire/10 laps behind*
9	US GP	Watkins Glen	15	Team Motul BRM	3.0 BRM P201 V12	*2 laps behind*

1975

12	AUSTRIAN GP	Österreichring	31	HB Bewaking Team Ensign	3.0 Ensign N175-Cosworth V8	*1 lap behind*
12	ITALIAN GP	Monza	32	HB Bewaking Team Ensign	3.0 Ensign N175-Cosworth V8	*misfire/4 laps behind*

1976

14	SOUTH AFRICAN GP	Kyalami	22	Team Ensign	3.0 Ensign N174-Cosworth V8	*pit stop-fuel/2 laps behind*
8	US GP WEST	Long Beach	22	Team Ensign	3.0 Ensign N174-Cosworth V8	*pit stop-brakes/2 laps behind*
5	SPANISH GP	Jarama	22	Team Ensign	3.0 Ensign N176-Cosworth V8	*1 lap behind*
ret	BELGIAN GP	Zolder	22	Team Ensign	3.0 Ensign N176-Cosworth V8	*lost wheel-crashed*
13	MONACO GP	Monte Carlo	22	Team Ensign	3.0 Ensign N176-Cosworth V8	*painful wrist/4 laps behind*
ret	SWEDISH GP	Anderstorp	22	Team Ensign	3.0 Ensign N176-Cosworth V8	*suspension failure-crashed*
ret	BRITISH GP	Brands Hatch	22	Team Ensign	3.0 Ensign N176-Cosworth V8	*water leak*
ret/dns	GERMAN GP	Nürburgring	22	Team Ensign	3.0 Ensign N176-Cosworth V8	*withdrawn after first start*
dns	CANADIAN GP	Mosport Park	21	Walter Wolf Racing	3.0 Williams FW05-Cosworth V8	*practice accident*

GP Starts: 95 (96)   GP Wins: 0   Pole positions: 5   Fastest laps: 3   Points: 83

BOB ANDERSON

This tough ex-motor cycle racer had tasted success before switching to four wheels at the relatively late age of 29 in 1961. A season was spent learning the ropes in Formula Junior before he bought the ex-Bowmaker Lola to have a crack at Formula 1 in 1963, competing in the many non-title races that abounded at the time. After a third place at Imola and a fourth at Syracuse, he won the Rome GP against fairly thin local opposition, quickly garnering the experience to compete full-time in the World Championship in 1964.

Making the absolute most of a minute budget, he frequently outdrove more vaunted competitors with his Brabham and was deservedly awarded the Wolfgang von Trips Trophy for the best private entrant. The days of the independent were already numbered but Bob – loyally supported by his French wife Marie-Edmée – ploughed on. His 1965 season was cut short after he wrote off his car in a practice accident at the Nürburgring, but this setback merely strengthened Anderson's resolve and he equipped his Brabham with an old Climax four-cylinder engine for the new 1966 3-litre formula.

Once again heroic performances gained placings which reflected the driver's skill and tenacity but as the Cosworth era dawned even Bob was facing the stark reality that the days of the impecunious privateer were over. Testing his ancient Brabham on a wet track at Silverstone in preparation for the 1967 Canadian GP, he crashed into a marshals' post, receiving severe throat and chest injuries. Poor Anderson had no chance of survival, and succumbed to his injuries in the ambulance on the way to hospital.

CONNY ANDERSSON

At 29, Andersson was a late starter and he became trapped in F3 from 1970 to 1976 by the lack of finance to move into higher spheres. He was particularly unlucky to be pipped by Patrese for the European championship in 1976 but his efforts gave him a one-off chance to drive a Surtees. Unwilling to face another year in F3, Conny had one last shot at F1 with the uncompetitive Stanley-BRM before calling it a day.

ANDERSON, Bob (GB) b 19/5/1931 – d 14/8/1967

1963

	Race	Circuit	No	Entrant	Car/Engine	Comment
12	BRITISH GP	Silverstone	22	DW Racing Enterprises	1.5 Lola 4-Climax V8	7 laps behind
12	ITALIAN GP	Monza	48	DW Racing Enterprises	1.5 Lola 4-Climax V8	7 laps behind

1964

	Race	Circuit	No	Entrant	Car/Engine	Comment
7/ret	MONACO GP	Monte Carlo	16	DW Racing Enterprises	1.5 Brabham BT11-Climax V8	gearbox mounting/14 laps behind
6	DUTCH GP	Zandvoort	34	DW Racing Enterprises	1.5 Brabham BT11-Climax V8	2 laps behind
dns	BELGIAN GP	Spa	18	DW Racing Enterprises	1.5 Brabham BT11-Climax V8	ignition problems
12	FRENCH GP	Rouen	19	DW Racing Enterprises	1.5 Brabham BT11-Climax V8	7 laps behind
7	BRITISH GP	Brands Hatch	19	DW Racing Enterprises	1.5 Brabham BT11-Climax V8	2 laps behind
ret	GERMAN GP	Nürburgring	16	DW Racing Enterprises	1.5 Brabham BT11-Climax V8	suspension
3	AUSTRIAN GP	Zeltweg	22	DW Racing Enterprises	1.5 Brabham BT11-Climax V8	3 laps behind
11	ITALIAN GP	Monza	22	DW Racing Enterprises	1.5 Brabham BT11-Climax V8	3 laps behind

1965

	Race	Circuit	No	Entrant	Car/Engine	Comment
nc	SOUTH AFRICAN GP	East London	14	DW Racing Enterprises	1.5 Brabham BT11-Climax V8	pit stops-brakes/35 laps behind
9	MONACO GP	Monte Carlo	9	DW Racing Enterprises	1.5 Brabham BT11-Climax V8	pit stops/15 laps behind
dns	BELGIAN GP	Spa	24	DW Racing Enterprises	1.5 Brabham BT11-Climax V8	withdrawn after practice
9/ret	FRENCH GP	Clermont Ferrand	30	DW Racing Enterprises	1.5 Brabham BT11-Climax V8	spun off/6 laps behind
ret	BRITISH GP	Silverstone	18	DW Racing Enterprises	1.5 Brabham BT11-Climax V8	gearbox
ret	DUTCH GP	Zandvoort	36	DW Racing Enterprises	1.5 Brabham BT11-Climax V8	engine-overheating
dns	GERMAN GP	Nürburgring	18	DW Racing Enterprises	1.5 Brabham BT11-Climax V8	practice accident

1966

	Race	Circuit	No	Entrant	Car/Engine	Comment
ret	MONACO GP	Monte Carlo	15	DW Racing Enterprises	2.7 Brabham BT11-Climax 4	engine
7/ret	FRENCH GP	Reims	36	DW Racing Enterprises	2.7 Brabham BT11-Climax 4	engine/4 laps behind
nc	BRITISH GP	Brands Hatch	21	DW Racing Enterprises	2.7 Brabham BT11-Climax 4	pit stops-battery/10 laps behind
ret	DUTCH GP	Zandvoort	34	DW Racing Enterprises	2.7 Brabham BT11-Climax 4	engine
ret	GERMAN GP	Nürburgring	19	DW Racing Enterprises	2.7 Brabham BT11-Climax 4	transmission
6	ITALIAN GP	Monza	40	DW Racing Enterprises	2.7 Brabham BT11-Climax 4	2 laps behind

1967

	Race	Circuit	No	Entrant	Car/Engine	Comment
5	SOUTH AFRICAN GP	Kyalami	14	DW Racing Enterprises	2.7 Brabham BT11-Climax 4	2 laps behind
dnq	MONACO GP	Monte Carlo	15	DW Racing Enterprises	2.7 Brabham BT11-Climax 4	
9	DUTCH GP	Zandvoort	21	DW Racing Enterprises	2.7 Brabham BT11-Climax 4	4 laps behind
8	BELGIAN GP	Spa	19	DW Racing Enterprises	2.7 Brabham BT11-Climax 4	2 laps behind
ret	FRENCH GP	Le Mans	17	DW Racing Enterprises	2.7 Brabham BT11-Climax 4	ignition
ret	BRITISH GP	Silverstone	19	DW Racing Enterprises	2.7 Brabham BT11-Climax 4	engine

GP Starts: 25   GP Wins: 0   Pole positions: 0   Fastest laps: 0   Points: 8

ANDERSSON, Conny (S) b 28/12/1939

1976

	Race	Circuit	No	Entrant	Car/Engine	Comment
ret	DUTCH GP	Zandvoort	18	Team Surtees	3.0 Surtees TS19-Cosworth V8	engine

1977

dnq	SPANISH GP	Jarama	35	Rotary Watches Stanley BRM	3.0 BRM P207 V12	
dnq	BELGIAN GP	Zolder	35	Rotary Watches Stanley BRM	3.0 BRM P207 V12	
dnq	SWEDISH GP	Anderstorp	35	Rotary Watches Stanley BRM	3.0 BRM P207 V12	
dnq	FRENCH GP	Dijon	35	Rotary Watches Stanley BRM	3.0 BRM P207 V12	

GP Starts: 1   GP Wins: 0   Pole positions: 0   Fastest laps: 0   Points: 0

MARIO ANDRETTI

Having arrived in the United States as the teenage son of poor Italian immigrants, Andretti has gone on to bcome one of America's greatest motor racing stars in a career which has spanned over thirty years – all of them spent racing competitively at the top level.

His interest in motor sport was kindled as a boy in his native Italy, and as soon as Mario was old enough to race seriously he set out with his twin brother Aldo on the US sprint and midget racing trail, finally winning the championship in 1964, the season which also saw his USAC debut. The following year he not only won the first of his four IndyCar titles but also took third place on his Indy 500 debut. He was champion again in 1966 and through until 1969 – when he won his only Indy 500 – Mario was the man to beat, even if luck was not always with him in terms of results.

Andretti had idolised Ascari in his youth and gladly accepted the chance to go Grand Prix racing with Lotus, causing a sensation by putting his car on pole at Watkins Glen. His clashing USAC commitments limited his F1 appearances – and chances of success – with both Lotus and March, but he shone in sports cars, winning at Sebring and Watkins Glen for Ferrari in 1970, before achieving a dream by signing to race for the Scuderia in F1 in 1971. His start could not have been better, Mario winning the South African GP followed by the Questor GP, but at this stage he was still splitting his season between IndyCar racing and his Ferrari F1 and sports car programme, the latter proving most successful in 1972, when he took four wins in the 312P with Ickx.

Mario concentrated on American racing in 1973-74, racing for Vel's Parnelli in F5000 and USAC events, and in late 1974 he debuted the team's Grand Prix contender. He campaigned the VPJ4 throughout 1975 (and briefly in 1976) before the team folded and then returned to a Lotus team in the doldrums. Together with Colin Chapman, he set about reviving the famous marque's fortunes and by the end of the 1976 season they were back in the winner's circle. Soon the team's 'ground-effect' type 78 and 79 cars were in the ascendancy, Mario winning the 1978 World Championship title after scoring six wins.

It was a different story in 1979 and 1980 as Lotus got it badly wrong, bogged down in a technical mire. Lured perhaps by sentiment as much as anything, Andretti joined Alfa Romeo in 1981, for what was to become another nightmare season, and in 1982 he undertook a full IndyCar schedule, his first for some years, before a brief Formula 1 swansong with Ferrari.

Mario won his last IndyCar crown to date in 1984 but, in the comforting surroundings of the Newman-Haas team, he remains capable of giving anyone a race to this day. At the end of 1993, Mario's Indy record was staggering. A record total of 391 starts, 52 wins and 66 pole positions are testimony to the enduring talent of this legendary figure.

ANDRETTI, Mario (USA) b 28/2/1940

	Race	Circuit	No	Entrant	Car/Engine	Comment
	1968					
	Race	*Circuit*	*No*	*Entrant*	*Car/Engine*	*Comment*
dns	ITALIAN GP	Monza	18	Gold Leaf Team Lotus	3.0 Lotus 49B-Cosworth V8	*raced in USA within 24 hours*
ret	US GP	Watkins Glen	12	Gold Leaf Team Lotus	3.0 Lotus 49B-Cosworth V8	*clutch/Pole*
	1969					
ret	SOUTH AFRICAN GP	Kyalami	3	Gold Leaf Team Lotus	3.0 Lotus 49B-Cosworth V8	*transmission*
ret	GERMAN GP	Nürburgring	3	Gold Leaf Team Lotus	3.0 Lotus 63-Cosworth V8 (4WD)	*accident-lost control*
ret	US GP	Watkins Glen	9	Gold Leaf Team Lotus	3.0 Lotus 63-Cosworth V8 (4WD)	*rear suspension damage*

1970

ret	SOUTH AFRICAN GP	Kyalami	8	STP Corporation	3.0 March 701-Cosworth V8	*overheating*
3	SPANISH GP	Jarama	18	STP Corporation	3.0 March 701-Cosworth V8	*only 5 finishers/1 lap behind*
ret	BRITISH GP	Brands Hatch	26	STP Corporation	3.0 March 701-Cosworth V8	*rear suspension*
ret	GERMAN GP	Hockenheim	11	STP Corporation	3.0 March 701-Cosworth V8	*gear selection*
ret	AUSTRIAN GP	Österreichring	5	STP Corporation	3.0 March 701-Cosworth V8	*accident-jammed throttle*

1971

1	SOUTH AFRICAN GP	Kyalami	6	Scuderai Ferrari SpA SEFAC	3.0 Ferrari 312B F12	*FL*
ret	SPANISH GP	Montjuich Park	6	Scuderia Ferrari SpA SEFAC	3.0 Ferrari 312B F12	*fuel pump*
dnq	MONACO GP	Monte Carlo	6	Scuderia Ferrari SpA SEFAC	3.0 Ferrari 312B F12	*missed the only dry session*
ret	DUTCH GP	Zandvoort	4	Scuderia Ferrari SpA SEFAC	3.0 Ferrari 312B F12	*fuel pump*
4	GERMAN GP	Nürburgring	5	Scuderia Ferrari SpA SEFAC	3.0 Ferrari 312B2 F12	
13	CANADIAN GP	Mosport Park	6	Scuderia Ferrari SpA SEFAC	3.0 Ferrari 312B2 F12	*pit stop-engine/4 laps behind*
dns	US GP	Watkins Glen	6	Scuderia Ferrari SpA SEFAC	3.0 Ferrari 312B2 F12	*practised-raced USAC race instead*

1972

ret	ARGENTINE GP	Buenos Aires	10	Scuderia Ferrari SpA SEFAC	3.0 Ferrari 312B2 F12	*engine misfire*
4	SOUTH AFRICAN GP	Kyalami	7	Scuderia Ferrari SpA SEFAC	3.0 Ferrari 312B2 F12	
ret	SPANISH GP	Jarama	7	Scuderia Ferrari SpA SEFAC	3.0 Ferrari 312B2 F12	*engine*
7	ITALIAN GP	Monza	3	Scuderia Ferrari SpA SEFAC	3.0 Ferrari 312B2 F12	*pit stop-wheel/1 lap behind*
6	US GP	Watkins Glen	9	Scuderia Ferrari SpA SEFAC	3.0 Ferrari 312B2 F12	*handling problems/1 lap behind*

1974

7	CANADIAN GP	Mosport Park	55	Vel's Parnelli Jones Racing	3.0 Parnelli VPJ4-Cosworth V8	*stalled at start/1 lap behind*
dsq	US GP	Watkins Glen	55	Vel's Parnelli Jones Racing	3.0 Parnelli VPJ4-Cosworth V8	*push start on grid*

1975

ret	ARGENTINE GP	Buenos Aires	27	Vel's Parnelli Jones Racing	3.0 Parneiil VPJ4-Cosworth V8	*driveshaft-c.v. joint*
7	BRAZILIAN GP	Interlagos	27	Vel's Parnelli Jones Racing	3.0 Parnelli VPJ4-Cosworth V8	
17/ret	SOUTH AFRICAN GP	Kyalami	27	Vel's Parnelli Jones Racing	3.0 Parnelli VPJ4-Cosworth V8	*driveshaft-c.v. joint/5 laps behind*
ret	SPANISH GP	Montjuich Park	27	Vel's Parnelli Jones Racing	3.0 Parnelli VPJ4-Cosworth V8	*suspension breakage-accident/FL*
ret	MONACO GP	Monte Carlo	27	Vel's Parnelli Jones Racing	3.0 Parnelli VPJ4-Cosworth V8	*broken oil line-fire*
4	SWEDISH GP	Anderstorp	27	Vel's Parnelli Jones Racing	3.0 Parnelli VPJ4-Cosworth V8	
5	FRENCH GP	Paul Ricard	27	Vel's Parnelli Jones Racing	3.0 Parnelli VPJ4-Cosworth V8	
12	BRITISH GP	Silverstone	27	Vel's Parnelli Jones Racing	3.0 Parnelli VPJ4-Cosworth V8	*collision, Jarier-pit stop/2 laps behind*
10/ret	GERMAN GP	Nürburgring	27	Vel's Parnelli Jones Racing	3.0 Parnelli VPJ4-Cosworth V8	*broken wheel/fuel leak/2 laps behind*
ret	AUSTRIAN GP	Österreichring	27	Vel's Parnelli Jones Racing	3.0 Parnelli VPJ4-Cosworth V8	*spun off*
ret	ITALIAN GP	Monza	27	Vel's Parnelli Jones Racing	3.0 Parnelli VPJ4-Cosworth V8	*multiple accident at chicane*
ret	US GP	Watkins Glen	27	Vel's Parnelli Jones Racing	3.0 Parnelli VPJ4-Cosworth V8	*suspension*

1976

ret	BRAZILIAN GP	Interlagos	6	John Player Team Lotus	3.0 Lotus 77-Cosworth V8	*collision with Peterson*
6	SOUTH AFRICAN GP	Kyalami	27	Vel's Parnelli Jones Racing	3.0 Parnelli VPJ4B-Cosworth V8	*1 lap behind*
ret	US GP WEST	Long Beach	27	Vel's Parnelli Jones Racing	3.0 Parnelli VPJ4B-Cosworth V8	*water leak*
ret	SPANISH GP	Jarama	5	John Player Team Lotus	3.0 Lotus 77-Cosworth V8	*gear selection*
ret	BELGIAN GP	Zolder	5	John Player Team Lotus	3.0 Lotus 77-Cosworth V8	*driveshaft*
ret	SWEDISH GP	Anderstorp	5	John Player Team Lotus	3.0 Lotus 77-Cosworth V8	*engine/FL*
5	FRENCH GP	Paul Ricard	5	John Player Team Lotus	3.0 Lotus 77-Cosworth V8	
ret	BRITISH GP	Brands Hatch	5	John Player Team Lotus	3.0 Lotus 77-Cosworth V8	*engine*
12	GERMAN GP	Nürburgring	5	John Player Team Lotus	3.0 Lotus 77-Cosworth V8	*pit stop-battery*
5	AUSTRIAN GP	Österreichring	5	John Player Team Lotus	3.0 Lotus 77-Cosworth V8	
3	DUTCH GP	Zandvoort	5	John Player Team Lotus	3.0 Lotus 77-Cosworth V8	
ret	ITALIAN GP	Monza	5	John Player Team Lotus	3.0 Lotus 77-Cosworth V8	*collision with Stuck*
3	CANADIAN GP	Mosport Park	5	John Player Team Lotus	3.0 Lotus 77-Cosworth V8	
ret	US GP EAST	Watkins Glen	5	John Player Team Lotus	3.0 Lotus 77-Cosworth V8	*hit kerb-damaged suspension*
1	JAPANESE GP	Mount Fuji	5	John Player Team Lotus	3.0 Lotus 77-Cosworth V8	*Pole*

1977

5/ret	ARGENTINE GP	Buenos Aires	5	John Player Team Lotus	3.0 Lotus 78-Cosworth V8	*rear wheel bearing/2 laps behind*
ret	BRAZILIAN GP	Interlagos	5	John Player Team Lotus	3.0 Lotus 78-Cosworth V8	*ignition*
ret	SOUTH AFRICAN GP	Kyalami	5	John Player Team Lotus	3.0 Lotus 78-Cosworth V8	*collision, Reutemann-suspension*
1	US GP WEST	Long Beach	5	John Player Team Lotus	3.0 Lotus 78-Cosworth V8	
1	SPANISH GP	Jarama	5	John Player Team Lotus	3.0 Lotus 78-Cosworth V8	*Pole*
5	MONACO GP	Monte Carlo	5	John Player Team Lotus	3.0 Lotus 78-Cosworth V8	
ret	BELGIAN GP	Zolder	5	John Player Team Lotus	3.0 Lotus 78-Cosworth V8	*hit Watson/Pole*
6	SWEDISH GP	Anderstorp	5	John Player Team Lotus	3.0 Lotus 78-Cosworth V8	*pit stop-fuel/Pole/FL*
1	FRENCH GP	Dijon	5	John Player Team Lotus	3.0 Lotus 78-Cosworth V8	*Pole/FL*
14/ret	BRITISH GP	Silverstone	5	John Player Team Lotus	3.0 Lotus 78-Cosworth V8	*engine/6 laps behind*
ret	GERMAN GP	Hockenheim	5	John Player Team Lotus	3.0 Lotus 78-Cosworth V8	*engine*
ret	AUSTRIAN GP	Österreichring	5	John Player Team Lotus	3.0 Lotus 78-Cosworth V8	*engine*
ret	DUTCH GP	Zandvoort	5	John Player Team Lotus	3.0 Lotus 78-Cosworth V8	*engine/Pole*
1	ITALIAN GP	Monza	5	John Player Team Lotus	3.0 Lotus 78-Cosworth V8	*FL*
2	US GP EAST	Watkins Glen	5	John Player Team Lotus	3.0 Lotus 78-Cosworth V8	
9/ret	CANADIAN GP	Mosport Park	5	John Player Team Lotus	3.0 Lotus 78-Cosworth V8	*engine/Pole/FL/3 laps behind*
ret	JAPANESE GP	Mount Fuji	5	John Player Team Lotus	3.0 Lotus 78-Cosworth V8	*collision with Laffite/Pole*

1978 World Champion Driver

1	ARGENTINE GP	Buenos Aires	5	John Player Team Lotus	3.0 Lotus 78-Cosworth V8	*Pole*
4	BRAZILIAN GP	Rio	5	John Player Team Lotus	3.0 Lotus 78-Cosworth V8	
7	SOUTH AFRICAN GP	Kyalami	5	John Player Team Lotus	3.0 Lotus 78-Cosworth V8	*pit stop-fuel/FL/1 lap behind*
2	US GP WEST	Long Beach	5	John Player Team Lotus	3.0 Lotus 78-Cosworth V8	
11	MONACO GP	Monte Carlo	5	John Player Team Lotus	3.0 Lotus 78-Cosworth V8	*pit stop-fuel gauge/6 laps behind*
1	BELGIAN GP	Zolder	5	John Player Team Lotus	3.0 Lotus 79-Cosworth V8	*Pole*
1	SPANISH GP	Jarama	5	John Player Team Lotus	3.0 Lotus 79-Cosworth V8	*Pole/FL*
ret	SWEDISH GP	Anderstorp	5	John Player Team Lotus	3.0 Lotus 79-Cosworth V8	*engine/Pole*
1	FRENCH GP	Paul Ricard	5	John Player Team Lotus	3.0 Lotus 79-Cosworth V8	

ret	BRITISH GP	Brands Hatch	5	John Player Team Lotus	3.0 Lotus 79-Cosworth V8	*engine*
1	GERMAN GP	Hockenheim	5	John Player Team Lotus	3.0 Lotus 79-Cosworth V8	*Pole*
ret/dns	AUSTRIAN GP	Österreichring	5	John Player Team Lotus	3.0 Lotus 79-Cosworth V8	*crashed/did not start 2nd part*
1	DUTCH GP	Zandvoort	5	John Player Team Lotus	3.0 Lotus 79-Cosworth V8	*Pole*
6*	ITALIAN GP	Monza	5	John Player Team Lotus	3.0 Lotus 79-Cosworth V8	* *1st but 1 min pen jump start/Pole/FL*
ret	US GP EAST	Watkins Glen	5	John Player Team Lotus	3.0 Lotus 79-Cosworth V8	*engine/Pole*
10	CANADIAN GP	Montreal	5	John Player Team Lotus	3.0 Lotus 79-Cosworth V8	*spin/1 lap behind*

1979

5	ARGENTINE GP	Buenos Aires	1	Martini Racing Team Lotus	3.0 Lotus 79-Cosworth V8	*1 lap behind*
ret	BRAZILIAN GP	Interlagos	1	Martini Racing Team Lotus	3.0 Lotus 79-Cosworth V8	*fuel leak-fire*
4	SOUTH AFRICAN GP	Kyalami	1	Martini Racing Team Lotus	3.0 Lotus 79-Cosworth V8	
4	US GP WEST	Long Beach	1	Martini Racing Team Lotus	3.0 Lotus 79-Cosworth V8	
3	SPANISH GP	Jarama	1	Martini Racing Team Lotus	3.0 Lotus 80-Cosworth V8	
ret	BELGIAN GP	Zolder	1	Martini Racing Team Lotus	3.0 Lotus 79-Cosworth V8	*brakes*
dns	"	"	1		3.0 Lotus 80-Cosworth V8	*practice only*
ret	MONACO GP	Monte Carlo	1	Martini Racing Team Lotus	3.0 Lotus 80-Cosworth V8	*rear suspension*
ret	FRENCH GP	Dijon	1	Martini Racing Team Lotus	3.0 Lotus 80-Cosworth V8	*brakes/suspension/flat tyre*
ret	BRITISH GP	Silverstone	1	Martini Racing Team Lotus	3.0 Lotus 79-Cosworth V8	*wheel bearing*
ret	GERMAN GP	Hockenheim	1	Martini Racing Team Lotus	3.0 Lotus 79-Cosworth V8	*driveshaft*
ret	AUSTRIAN GP	Österreichring	1	Martini Racing Team Lotus	3.0 Lotus 79-Cosworth V8	*clutch*
ret	DUTCH GP	Zandvoort	1	Martini Racing Team Lotus	3.0 Lotus 79-Cosworth V8	*rear suspension*
5	ITALIAN GP	Monza	1	Martini Racing Team Lotus	3.0 Lotus 79-Cosworth V8	
10/ret	CANADIAN GP	Montreal	1	Martini Racing Team Lotus	3.0 Lotus 79-Cosworth V8	*out of fuel/6 laps behind*
ret	US GP EAST	Watkins Glen	1	Martini Racing Team Lotus	3.0 Lotus 79-Cosworth V8	*gearbox*

1980

ret	ARGENTINE GP	Buenos Aires	11	Team Essex Lotus	3.0 Lotus 81-Cosworth V8	*fuel metering unit*
ret	BRAZILIAN GP	Interlagos	11	Team Essex Lotus	3.0 Lotus 81-Cosworth V8	*spun off*
12	SOUTH AFRICAN GP	Kyalami	11	Team Essex Lotus	3.0 Lotus 81-Cosworth V8	*broken exhaust/2 laps behind*
ret	US GP WEST	Long Beach	11	Team Essex Lotus	3.0 Lotus 81-Cosworth V8	*collision with Jarier*
ret	BELGIAN GP	Zolder	11	Team Essex Lotus	3.0 Lotus 81-Cosworth V8	*gear linkage*
7	MONACO GP	Monte Carlo	11	Team Essex Lotus	3.0 Lotus 81-Cosworth V8	*pit stop-gear linkage/3 laps behind*
ret	FRENCH GP	Paul Ricard	11	Team Essex Lotus	3.0 Lotus 81-Cosworth V8	*gearbox*
ret	BRITISH GP	Brands Hatch	11	Team Essex Lotus	3.0 Lotus 81-Cosworth V8	*engine*
7	GERMAN GP	Hockenheim	11	Team Essex Lotus	3.0 Lotus 81-Cosworth V8	
ret	AUSTRIAN GP	Österreichring	11	Team Essex Lotus	3.0 Lotus 81-Cosworth V8	*engine*
8/ret	DUTCH GP	Zandvoort	11	Team Essex Lotus	3.0 Lotus 81-Cosworth V8	*out of fuel/2 laps behind*
ret	ITALIAN GP	Imola	11	Team Essex Lotus	3.0 Lotus 81-Cosworth V8	*engine*
ret	CANADIAN GP	Montreal	11	Team Essex Lotus	3.0 Lotus 81-Cosworth V8	*engine*
6	US GP EAST	Watkins Glen	11	Team Essex Lotus	3.0 Lotus 81-Cosworth V8	*1 lap behind*

1981

4	US GP WEST	Long Beach	22	Marlboro Team Alfa Romeo	3.0 Alfa Romeo 179C V12	
ret	BRAZILIAN GP	Rio	22	Marlboro Team Alfa Romeo	3.0 Alfa Romeo 179C V12	*collision at start*
8	ARGENTINE GP	Buenos Aires	22	Marlboro Team Alfa Romeo	3.0 Alfa Romeo 179C V12	*1 lap behind*
ret	SAN MARINO GP	Imola	22	Marlboro Team Alfa Romeo	3.0 Alfa Romeo 179C V12	*gearbox*
10	BELGIAN GP	Zolder	22	Marlboro Team Alfa Romeo	3.0 Alfa Romeo 179C V12	*misfire/1 lap behind*
ret	MONACO GP	Monte Carlo	22	Marlboro Team Alfa Romeo	3.0 Alfa Romeo 179C V12	*hit by de Cesaris*
8	SPANISH GP	Jarama	22	Marlboro Team Alfa Romeo	3.0 Alfa Romeo 179C V12	*hit by Piquet*
8	FRENCH GP	Dijon	22	Marlboro Team Alfa Romeo	3.0 Alfa Romeo 179C V12	*1 lap behind*
ret	BRITISH GP	Silverstone	22	Marlboro Team Alfa Romeo	3.0 Alfa Romeo 179C V12	*throttle linkage*
9	GERMAN GP	Hockenheim	22	Marlboro Team Alfa Romeo	3.0 Alfa Romeo 179C V12	*1 lap behind*
ret	AUSTRIAN GP	Österreichring	22	Marlboro Team Alfa Romeo	3.0 Alfa Romeo 179C V12	*engine*
ret	DUTCH GP	Zandvoort	22	Marlboro Team Alfa Romeo	3.0 Alfa Romeo 179C V12	*tyre failure-crashed*
ret	ITALIAN GP	Monza	22	Marlboro Team Alfa Romeo	3.0 Alfa Romeo 179C V12	*engine*
7	CANADIAN GP	Montreal	22	Marlboro Team Alfa Romeo	3.0 Alfa Romeo 179C V12	*1 lap behind*
ret	CAESARS PALACE GP	Las Vegas	22	Marlboro Team Alfa Romeo	3.0 Alfa Romeo 179C V12	*rear suspension*

1982

ret	US GP WEST	Long Beach	5	TAG Williams Team	3.0 Williams FW07C-Cosworth V8	*accident damage*
3	ITALIAN GP	Monza	28	Scuderia Ferrari SpA SEFAC	1.5 t/c Ferrari 126C2 V6	*Pole*
ret	CAESARS PALACE GP	Las Vegas	28	Scuderia Ferrari SpA SEFAC	1.5 t/c Ferrari 126C2 V6	*rear suspension*

GP Starts: 128   GP Wins: 12   Pole positions: 18   Fastest laps: 10   Points: 180

ANDRETTI, Michael (USA) b 5/10/1962

	Race	Circuit	No	Entrant	Car/Engine	Comment

1993

ret	SOUTH AFRICAN GP	Kyalami	7	Marlboro McLaren	3.5 McLaren MP4/8-Ford HB V8	*accident-ran into Warwick*
ret	BRAZILIAN GP	Interlagos	7	Marlboro McLaren	3.5 McLaren MP4/8-Ford HB V8	*accident with Berger at start*
ret	EUROPEAN GP	Donington	7	Marlboro McLaren	3.5 McLaren MP4/8-Ford HB V8	*lap 1 collision Wendlinger-spun off*
ret	SAN MARINO GP	Imola	7	Marlboro McLaren	3.5 McLaren MP4/8-Ford HB V8	*spun off-brake trouble*
5	SPANISH GP	Barcelona	7	Marlboro McLaren	3.5 McLaren MP4/8-Ford HB V8	*1 lap behind*
8	MONACO GP	Monte Carlo	7	Marlboro McLaren	3.5 McLaren MP4/8-Ford HB V8	*early p stop new nose/2 laps behind*
14	CANADIAN GP	Montreal	7	Marlboro McLaren	3.5 McLaren MP4/8-Ford HB V8	*started late from pits/3 laps behind*
6	FRENCH GP	Magny Cours	7	Marlboro McLaren	3.5 McLaren MP4/8-Ford HB V8	*1 lap behind*
ret	BRITISH GP	Silverstone	7	Marlboro McLaren	3.5 McLaren MP4/8-Ford HB V8	*spun off first corner*
ret	GERMAN GP	Hockenheim	7	Marlboro McLaren	3.5 McLaren MP4/8-Ford HB V8	*collision, Berger-steering damage*
ret	HUNGARIAN GP	Hungaroring	7	Marlboro McLaren	3.5 McLaren MP4/8-Ford HB V8	*throttle failure*
8	BELGIAN GP	Spa	7	Marlboro McLaren	3.5 McLaren MP4/8-Ford HB V8	*stalled at pit stop/1 lap behind*
3	ITALIAN GP	Monza	7	Marlboro McLaren	3.5 McLaren MP4/8-Ford HB V8	*despite early spin/1 lap behind*

GP Starts: 13   GP Wins: 0   Pole positions: 0   Fastest laps: 0   Points: 7

MICHAEL ANDRETTI

Son of the legendary Mario, Michael followed his father into racing in 1980, first in Formula Ford and then Super Vee (winning the 1982 championship). He broke into Indy cars the following season, which also saw him partner his father at Le Mans, where the pair finished third in a Porsche with Philippe Alliot.

Michael was soon making a big impact on the IndyCar scene, scoring the first of 27 wins to date in 1986. From that year through to 1992 – aside from a lean year in 1988, when he was sixth overall – he always finished in the top three places in the points standings, and 1991 proved to be a record-breaking season, with Andretti's Newman-Haas Lola taking eight wins, accumulating a record 234 points and posting single-season earnings of $2,461,734.

With this pedigree, the former IndyCar champion arrived in the high-profile world of Formula 1 for the 1993 season with great expectations, only to be embroiled in a catalogue of collisions, spins and mechanical gremlins which seemed to sap his confidence visibly race by race.

A lack of testing mileage, the FIA's rationing of practice laps and his unfamiliarity with the circuits all told against the pleasant American, who was under pressure to produce results.

Just as crucial, perhaps, was the difficulty he and his wife Sandy experienced in coming to terms with the way of life in Europe, preferring to fly back to the States whenever possible. By September he had had enough. Having attained a little credibility by finishing third in the Italian GP, the younger Andretti ended his unhappy sojourn and headed home buoyed by the prospect of returning to the familiarity of the IndyCar circuit for 1994 with a new challenger from Reynard.

ANGELIS, Elio de (I) b 26/3/1958 – d 15/5/1986

1979

	Race	Circuit	No	Entrant	Car/Engine	Comment
7	ARGENTINE GP	Buenos Aires	18	Interscope Shadow Racing Team	3.0 Shadow DN9-Cosworth V8	*1 lap behind*
12	BRAZILIAN GP	Interlagos	18	Interscope Shadow Racing Team	3.0 Shadow DN9-Cosworth V8	*1 lap behind*
ret	SOUTH AFRICAN GP	Kyalami	18	Interscope Shadow Racing Team	3.0 Shadow DN9-Cosworth V8	*spun off*
7	US GP WEST	Long Beach	18	Interscope Shadow Racing Team	3.0 Shadow DN9-Cosworth V8	*2 laps behind*
ret	SPANISH GP	Jarama	18	Interscope Shadow Racing Team	3.0 Shadow DN9-Cosworth V8	*engine*
ret	BELGIAN GP	Zolder	18	Interscope Shadow Racing Team	3.0 Shadow DN9-Cosworth V8	*hit Giacomelli*
dnq	MONACO GP	Monte Carlo	18	Interscope Shadow Racing Team	3.0 Shadow DN9-Cosworth V8	
dnq/16	FRENCH GP	Dijon	18	Interscope Shadow Racing Team	3.0 Shadow DN9-Cosworth V8	*started as 1st reserve/5 laps behind*
12*	BRITISH GP	Silverstone	18	Interscope Shadow Racing Team	3.0 Shadow DN9-Cosworth V8	** 1m. pen-jump start/3 laps behind*
11	GERMAN GP	Hockenheim	18	Interscope Shadow Racing Team	3.0 Shadow DN9-Cosworth V8	*2 laps behind*
ret	AUSTRIAN GP	Österreichring	18	Interscope Shadow Racing Team	3.0 Shadow DN9-Cosworth V8	*engine*
ret	DUTCH GP	Zandvoort	18	Interscope Shadow Racing Team	3.0 Shadow DN9-Cosworth V8	*driveshaft*
ret	ITALIAN GP	Monza	18	Interscope Shadow Racing Team	3.0 Shadow DN9-Cosworth V8	*clutch*
ret	CANADIAN GP	Montreal	18	Interscope Shadow Racing Team	3.0 Shadow DN9-Cosworth V8	*broken rotor arm*
4	US GP EAST	Long Beach	18	Interscope Shadow Racing Team	3.0 Shadow DN9-Cosworth V8	

1980

	Race	Circuit	No	Entrant	Car/Engine	Comment
ret	ARGENTINE GP	Buenos Aires	12	Team Essex Lotus	3.0 Lotus 81-Cosworth V8	*suspension*
2	BRAZILIAN GP	Interlagos	12	Team Essex Lotus	3.0 Lotus 81-Cosworth V8	
ret	SOUTH AFRICAN GP	Kyalami	12	Team Essex Lotus	3.0 Lotus 81-Cosworth V8	*spun off*
ret	US GP WEST	Long Beach	12	Team Essex Lotus	3.0 Lotus 81-Cosworth V8	*multiple accident-broken foot*
10/ret	BELGIAN GP	Zolder	12	Team Essex Lotus	3.0 Lotus 81-Cosworth V8	*spun off/3 laps behind*
9/ret	MONACO GP	Monte Carlo	12	Team Essex Lotus	3.0 Lotus 81-Cosworth V8	*spun off into wall/8 laps behind*
ret	FRENCH GP	Paul Ricard	12	Team Essex Lotus	3.0 Lotus 81-Cosworth V8	*clutch*
ret	BRITISH GP	Brands Hatch	12	Team Essex Lotus	3.0 Lotus 81-Cosworth V8	*rear suspension*
16/ret	GERMAN GP	Hockenheim	12	Team Essex Lotus	3.0 Lotus 81-Cosworth V8	*wheel bearing/2 laps behind*
6	AUSTRIAN GP	Österreichring	12	Team Essex Lotus	3.0 Lotus 81-Cosworth V8	
ret	DUTCH GP	Zandvoort	12	Team Essex Lotus	3.0 Lotus 81-Cosworth V8	*collision with Pironi*
4	ITALIAN GP	Imola	12	Team Essex Lotus	3.0 Lotus 81-Cosworth V8	*1 lap behind*
10	CANADIAN GP	Montreal	12	Team Essex Lotus	3.0 Lotus 81-Cosworth V8	*damaged skirt/2 laps behind*
4	US GP EAST	Watkins Glen	12	Team Essex Lotus	3.0 Lotus 81-Cosworth V8	

1981

	Race	Circuit	No	Entrant	Car/Engine	Comment
ret	US GP WEST	Long Beach	11	Team Essex Lotus	3.0 Lotus 81-Cosworth V8	*hit wall*
5	BRAZILIAN GP	Rio	11	Team Essex Lotus	3.0 Lotus 81-Cosworth V8	
6	ARGENTINE GP	Buenos Aires	11	Team Essex Lotus	3.0 Lotus 81-Cosworth V8	*1 lap behind*
5	BELGIAN GP	Zolder	11	Team Essex Lotus	3.0 Lotus 81-Cosworth V8	
ret	MONACO GP	Monte Carlo	11	Team Essex Lotus	3.0 Lotus 87-Cosworth V8	*engine*
5	SPANISH GP	Jarama	11	John Player Team Lotus	3.0 Lotus 87-Cosworth V8	
6	FRENCH GP	Dijon	11	John Player Team Lotus	3.0 Lotus 87-Cosworth V8	*1 lap behind*
ret	BRITISH GP	Silverstone	11	John Player Team Lotus	3.0 Lotus 87-Cosworth V8	*retired after being black-flagged*
dns	"	"	11	John Player Team Lotus	3.0 Lotus 88B-Cosworth V8	*practice only*
7	GERMAN GP	Hockenheim	11	John Player Team Lotus	3.0 Lotus 87-Cosworth V8	*1 lap behind*
7	AUSTRIAN GP	Österreichring	11	John Player Team Lotus	3.0 Lotus 87-Cosworth V8	*1 lap behind*
5	DUTCH GP	Zandvoort	11	John Player Team Lotus	3.0 Lotus 87-Cosworth V8	*1 lap behind*
4	ITALIAN GP	Monza	11	John Player Team Lotus	3.0 Lotus 87-Cosworth V8	
6	CANADIAN GP	Montreal	11	John Player Team Lotus	3.0 Lotus 87-Cosworth V8	*1 lap behind*
ret	CAESARS PALACE GP	Las Vegas	11	John Player Team Lotus	3.0 Lotus 87-Cosworth V8	*water leak*

1982

	Race	Circuit	No	Entrant	Car/Engine	Comment
8	SOUTH AFRICAN GP	Kyalami	11	John Player Team Lotus	3.0 Lotus 87B-Cosworth V8	*1 lap behind*

	Race	Circuit	No	Entrant	Car/Engine	Comment
ret	BRAZILIAN GP	Rio	11	John Player Team Lotus	3.0 Lotus 91-Cosworth V8	hit by Baldi
5*	US GP WEST	Long Beach	11	John Player Team Lotus	3.0 Lotus 91-Cosworth V8	* 3rd place car dsq/1 lap behind
4*	BELGIAN GP	Zolder	11	John Player Team Lotus	3.0 Lotus 91-Cosworth V8	* 3rd place car dsq/2 laps behind
5	MONACO GP	Monte Carlo	11	John Player Team Lotus	3.0 Lotus 91-Cosworth V8	1 lap behind
ret	US GP (DETROIT)	Detroit	11	John Player Team Lotus	3.0 Lotus 91-Cosworth V8	gearbox
4	CANADIAN GP	Montreal	11	John Player Team Lotus	3.0 Lotus 91-Cosworth V8	1 lap behind
ret	DUTCH GP	Zandvoort	11	John Player Team Lotus	3.0 Lotus 91-Cosworth V8	handling
4	BRITISH GP	Brands Hatch	11	John Player Team Lotus	3.0 Lotus 91-Cosworth V8	
ret	FRENCH GP	Paul Ricard	11	John Player Team Lotus	3.0 Lotus 91-Cosworth V8	fuel pressure
ret	GERMAN GP	Hockenheim	11	John Player Team Lotus	3.0 Lotus 91-Cosworth V8	transmission
1	AUSTRIAN GP	Österreichring	11	John Player Team Lotus	3.0 Lotus 91-Cosworth V8	won by 0.050s from Rosberg
6	SWISS GP	Dijon	11	John Player Team Lotus	3.0 Lotus 91-Cosworth V8	1 lap behind
ret	ITALIAN GP	Monza	11	John Player Team Lotus	3.0 Lotus 91-Cosworth V8	handling/sticking throttle
ret	CAESARS PALACE GP	Las Vegas	11	John Player Team Lotus	3.0 Lotus 91-Cosworth V8	engine

1983

	Race	Circuit	No	Entrant	Car/Engine	Comment
dsq	BRAZILIAN GP	Rio	11	John Player Team Lotus	3.0 Lotus 91-Cosworth V8	dsq-did not practise in this car
dns	"		11	John Player Team Lotus	1.5 t/c Lotus 93T-Renault V6	turbo on warm-up lap-raced T91 car
ret	US GP WEST	Long Beach	11	John Player Team Lotus	1.5 t/c Lotus 93T-Renault V6	tyres
ret	FRENCH GP	Paul Ricard	11	John Player Team Lotus	1.5 t/c Lotus 93T-Renault V6	electrics
ret	SAN MARINO GP	Imola	11	John Player Team Lotus	1.5 t/c Lotus 93T-Renault V6	handling/driver gave up
ret	MONACO GP	Monte Carlo	11	John Player Team Lotus	1.5 t/c Lotus 93T-Renault V6	driveshaft
9	BELGIAN GP	Spa	11	John Player Team Lotus	1.5 t/c Lotus 93T-Renault V6	1 lap behind
ret	US GP (DETROIT)	Detroit	11	John Player Team Lotus	1.5 t/c Lotus 93T-Renault V6	transmission
ret	CANADIAN GP	Montreal	11	John Player Team Lotus	1.5 t/c Lotus 93T-Renault V6	throttle linkage
ret	BRITISH GP	Silverstone	11	John Player Team Lotus	1.5 t/c Lotus 94T-Renault V6	engine-turbo fire
ret	GERMAN GP	Hockenheim	11	John Player Team Lotus	1.5 t/c Lotus 94T-Renault V6	overheating
ret	AUSTRIAN GP	Österreichring	11	John Player Team Lotus	1.5 t/c Lotus 94T-Renault V6	spun, hit Giacomelli
dns	"		11	John Player Team Lotus	1.5 t/c Lotus 93T-Renault V6	practice only-qualifying car
ret	DUTCH GP	Zandvoort	11	John Player Team Lotus	1.5 t/c Lotus 94T-Renault V6	fuel metering unit
5	ITALIAN GP	Monza	11	John Player Team Lotus	1.5 t/c Lotus 94T-Renault V6	
ret	EUROPEAN GP	Brands Hatch	11	John Player Team Lotus	1.5 t/c Lotus 94T-Renault V6	engine/Pole
ret	SOUTH AFRICAN GP	Kyalami	11	John Player Team Lotus	1.5 t/c Lotus 94T-Renault V6	engine misfire

1984

	Race	Circuit	No	Entrant	Car/Engine	Comment
3	BRAZILIAN GP	Rio	11	John Player Team Lotus	1.5 t/c Lotus 95T-Renault V6	Pole
7	SOUTH AFRICAN GP	Kyalami	11	John Player Team Lotus	1.5 t/c Lotus 95T-Renault V6	pit stop-throttle cable/4 laps behind
5	BELGIAN GP	Zolder	11	John Player Team Lotus	1.5 t/c Lotus 95T-Renault V6	1 lap behind
3/ret	SAN MARINO GP	Imola	11	John Player Team Lotus	1.5 t/c Lotus 95T-Renault V6	out of fuel/1 lap behind
5	FRENCH GP	Dijon	11	John Player Team Lotus	1.5 t/c Lotus 95T-Renault V6	
5*	MONACO GP	Monte Carlo	11	John Player Team Lotus	1.5 t/c Lotus 95T-Renault V6	* 3rd place car disqualified
4	CANADIAN GP	Montreal	11	John Player Team Lotus	1.5 t/c Lotus 95T-Renault V6	1 lap behind
2*	US GP (DETROIT)	Detroit	11	John Player Team Lotus	1.5 t/c Lotus 95T-Renault V6	* 2nd place car disqualified
3	US GP (DALLAS)	Dallas	11	John Player Team Lotus	1.5 t/c Lotus 95T-Renault V6	1 lap behind
4	BRITISH GP	Brands Hatch	11	John Player Team Lotus	1.5 t/c Lotus 95T-Renault V6	1 lap behind
ret	GERMAN GP	Hockenheim	11	John Player Team Lotus	1.5 t/c Lotus 95T-Renault V6	turbo
ret	AUSTRIAN GP	Österreichring	11	John Player Team Lotus	1.5 t/c Lotus 95T-Renault V6	engine
4	DUTCH GP	Zandvoort	11	John Player Team Lotus	1.5 t/c Lotus 95T-Renault V6	1 lap behind
ret	ITALIAN GP	Monza	11	John Player Team Lotus	1.5 t/c Lotus 95T-Renault V6	gearbox
ret	EUROPEAN GP	Nürburgring	11	John Player Team Lotus	1.5 t/c Lotus 95T-Renault V6	turbo
5	PORTUGUESE GP	Estoril	11	John Player Team Lotus	1.5 t/c Lotus 95T-Renault V6	

1985

	Race	Circuit	No	Entrant	Car/Engine	Comment
3	BRAZILIAN GP	Rio	11	John Player Special Team Lotus	1.5 t/c Lotus 97T-Renault V6	1 lap behind
4	PORTUGUESE GP	Estoril	11	John Player Special Team Lotus	1.5 t/c Lotus 97T-Renault V6	1 lap behind
1	SAN MARINO GP	Imola	11	John Player Special Team Lotus	1.5 t/c Lotus 97T-Renault V6	
3	MONACO GP	Monte Carlo	11	John Player Special Team Lotus	1.5 t/c Lotus 97T-Renault V6	
5	CANADIAN GP	Montreal	11	John Player Special Team Lotus	1.5 t/c Lotus 97T-Renault V6	Pole
5	US GP (DETROIT)	Detroit	11	John Player Special Team Lotus	1.5 t/c Lotus 97T-Renault V6	
5	FRENCH GP	Paul Ricard	11	John Player Special Team Lotus	1.5 t/c Lotus 97T-Renault V6	
nc	BRITISH GP	Silverstone	11	John Player Special Team Lotus	1.5 t/c Lotus 97T-Renault V6	pit stop-engine/28 laps behind
ret	GERMAN GP	Hockenheim	11	John Player Special Team Lotus	1.5 t/c Lotus 97T-Renault V6	engine
5	AUSTRIAN GP	Österreichring	11	John Player Special Team Lotus	1.5 t/c Lotus 97T-Renault V6	
5	DUTCH GP	Zandvoort	11	John Player Special Team Lotus	1.5 t/c Lotus 97T-Renault V6	1 lap behind
6	ITALIAN GP	Monza	11	John Player Special Team Lotus	1.5 t/c Lotus 97T-Renault V6	1 lap behind
ret	BELGIAN GP	Spa	11	John Player Special Team Lotus	1.5 t/c Lotus 97T-Renault V6	turbo
5	EUROPEAN GP	Brands Hatch	11	John Player Special Team Lotus	1.5 t/c Lotus 97T-Renault V6	1 lap behind
ret	SOUTH AFRICAN GP	Kyalami	11	John Player Special Team Lotus	1.5 t/c Lotus 97T-Renault V6	engine
dsq*	AUSTRALIAN GP	Adelaide	11	John Player Special Team Lotus	1.5 t/c Lotus 97T-Renault V6	* excluded-changed grid position

1986

	Race	Circuit	No	Entrant	Car/Engine	Comment
8	BRAZILIAN GP	Rio	8	Motor Racing Developments	1.5 t/c Brabham BT55-BMW 4	lost wheel/3 laps behind
ret	SPANISH GP	Jerez	8	Motor Racing Developments	1.5 t/c Brabham BT55-BMW 4	gearbox
ret	SAN MARINO GP	Imola	8	Motor Racing Developments	1.5 t/c Brabham BT55-BMW 4	engine
ret	MONACO GP	Monte Carlo	8	Motor Racing Developments	1.5 t/c Brabham BT55-BMW 4	engine

GP Starts: 108   GP Wins: 2   Pole positions: 3   Fastest laps: 0   Points: 122

APICELLA, Marco (I) b 7/10/1965

1993

	Race	Circuit	No	Entrant	Car/Engine	Comment
ret	ITALIAN GP	Monza	15	Sasol Jordan	3.5 Jordan 193-Hart V10	collision-suspension damage lap 1

GP Starts: 1   GP Wins: 0   Pole positions: 0   Fastest laps: 0   Points: 0

ELIO de ANGELIS

From a wealthy background, Elio had a reputation as something of a cocky rich-kid when he stepped from karting into Italian F3 at the beginning of 1977. Winning his third-ever F3 race, de Angelis snatched the championship at the very last gasp from Piercarlo Ghinzani, and took an impressive seventh in the European series. After taking a controversial win in the 1978 Monaco F3 race, Elio moved up to Formula 2 but he endured a fairly barren year and, since he was not slow to show his feelings, was seen as something of a spoilt prima donna.

It may have been a considerable gamble, but at the age of just 20 the inexperienced de Angelis joined a Shadow team which was in steep decline. With the exuberance of youth and not a little skill, the young Roman extracted the very best from a poor car and his performances were not lost on Colin Chapman, who signed him for 1980. He made a great start for Lotus, taking a brilliant second place in Brazil, and – one or two silly incidents apart – soon settled down to become a most consistent points finisher over the next couple of seasons, the highlight of which was a hair's-breadth win over Keke Rosberg in the 1982 Austrian GP.

The following year was a transitional period for the team as they struggled to gain reliability from their Renault turbo-engined car, and results where thin on the ground. It was the reverse in 1984, though, as a string of excellent placings saw Elio leading the World Championship by mid-season, but in the end he had to settle for third place in the points table behind Lauda and Prost.

De Angelis had spent four seasons vying somewhat inconclusively for number one status with Nigel Mansell, but the arrival of Ayrton Senna in 1985 soon put the Roman in the shade, a lucky win at Imola following Prost's disqualification notwithstanding. Accepting the situation would not change in his favour, Elio joined Brabham in 1986 to race their radical but complicated 'low-line' BT55, but he managed just one finish, and that after losing a wheel, before a routine testing session at Paul Ricard in mid-May ended in catastrophe when the Brabham was thought to have suffered a component failure, crashing heavily at 180 mph. Elio's injuries were so severe he stood no chance of survival, dying in hospital a few hours later, and the entire motor racing world mourned the loss of a popular driver who had long since earned the respect of his peers.

MARCO APICELLA

This diminutive Italian was a contemporary of Caffi, Tarquini, Larini and Barbazza in the national F3 series in 1984-85. He was certainly quick but also somewhat erratic, sampling three different chassis in 1985 and taking a couple of wins at Misano. In 1986 he was teamed with Larini in Enzo Coloni's Dallaras and the young hot-shots dominated proceedings, with Apicella taking the runner-up slot.

If he felt something of a bridesmaid in that formula, it was as nothing to his experiences in the FIA F3000 championship, where he spent five seasons (1987-1991) as 'the man most likely to' searching in vain for a win before he joined the wave of Europeans invading the Japanese F3000 series in a bid to revive his career. Marco was a surprise choice for a one-off Jordan ride in the 1993 Italian GP, and his race was short lived, Apicella being eliminated in a first-lap mêlée.

RENÉ ARNOUX

Arnoux's early career was rich with promise. Winning the Shell Volant award set him on his way in Formule Renault, but René switched to Elf in 1974 when an opportunity arose to race their Formula 2 car, taking fourth place at Nogaro on his debut. In 1975 he competed in Formule Super Renault, winning the championship, before undertaking a full season of Formula 2 with an Elf-backed works Martini-Renault. He was the fastest man around and came agonisingly close to taking the championship, scoring three wins (at Pau, Enna and Estoril) and six fastest laps but eventually lost out to Jabouille. Resolved to iron out the errors which had cost him so dear in 1976, Arnoux was back the following season and again won three races (at Silverstone, Pau and Nogaro), deservedly taking the coveted title.

The little Martini team, which had enjoyed enviable success in the junior formulae for many years, ambitiously moved into Formula 1 for 1978 and Arnoux was naturally entrusted with their neat Cosworth-powered car, but the underfinanced project was doomed from the start, leaving the GP novice to scratch around for drives from mid-season. He did a couple of races for Surtees, who would dearly have loved to have got his hands on him earlier, for after running a string of second-raters here at last he could see gold. However, René was destined for greater things, joining Renault for 1979.

Teamed with his old rival Jabouille, the still shy newcomer began to assert himself from mid-season onwards, and looked a serious championship prospect at the start of 1980. Consecutive wins in Brazil and Argentina proved sadly illusory, but the game little Frenchman never gave up the struggle although his car repeatedly let him down. Unfortunately for Arnoux, his nemesis in the shape of Alain Prost joined the team for 1981, immediately pushing the unhappy incumbent to the margins. He bounced back in 1982 to something like his best, all but matching Prost's speed, but not his measured performances. When he won the French GP in defiance of team orders it seemed that a split was inevitable, and sure enough he moved to Ferrari for 1983. Driving in typically forceful style, Arnoux mounted a serious championship bid on the back of three mid-season wins, but eventually fell just short.

In 1984 his performances became increasingly inconsistent and, despite an absolutely brilliant drive at Dallas, there were times when he seemed totally uninterested. It was a situation that could not last and early in 1985 an 'amicable' separation was agreed. Joining Ligier for 1986, Arnoux showed brief flashes of his old form in the Renault-powered car, but when he voiced criticism in the press of the Alfa engine the team had arranged to use the following season, the Italian concern immediately terminated the project. The team was then obliged to adapt their new design to accept the Megatron engine, and suffered the inevitable consequences. Things got even worse in 1988 with the totally disastrous JS31, which was perhaps one of the most evil-handling machines of recent times.

Although no longer a contender, Arnoux blithely drove on as if he were, but by now the summit of his ambitions was a desperate search for the championship point or two that would keep his team out of the pre-qualifying trap. His ever-increasing lack of track manners and general cussedness caused mounting consternation among his fellow drivers and by the time he retired at the end of 1989, the halcyon days of the early eighties were all but forgotten.

ARNOUX, René (F) b 4/7/1948

1978

	Race	Circuit	No	Entrant	Car/Engine	Comment
dnq	SOUTH AFRICAN GP	Kyalami	31	Automobiles Martini	3.0 Martini MK23-Cosworth V8	
dnpq	MONACO GP	Monte Carlo	31	Automobiles Martini	3.0 Martini MK23-Cosworth V8	
9	BELGIAN GP	Zolder	31	Automobiles Martini	3.0 Martini MK23-Cosworth V8	2 laps behind
14	FRENCH GP	Paul Ricard	31	Automobiles Martini	3.0 Martini MK23-Cosworth V8	1 lap behind
dnp	BRITISH GP	Brands Hatch	31	Automobiles Martini	3.0 Martini MK23-Cosworth V8	on reserve list-no practice allowed
dnpq	GERMAN GP	Hockenheim	31	Automobiles Martini	3.0 Martini MK23-Cosworth V8	
9	AUSTRIAN GP	Österreichring	31	Automobiles Martini	3.0 Martini MK23-Cosworth V8	2 laps behind
ret	DUTCH GP	Zandvoort	31	Automobiles Martini	3.0 Martini MK23-Cosworth V8	rear wing mounting

9	US GP EAST	Watkins Glen	18	Team Surtees	3.0 Surtees TS20-Cosworth V8	*1 lap behind*
ret	CANADIAN GP	Montreal	18	Team Surtees	3.0 Surtees TS20-Cosworth V8	*oil pressure*

1979

dnq/ret	ARGENTINE GP	Buenos Aires	16	Equipe Renault Elf	1.5 t/c Renault RS01 V6	*dnq-started as 1st reserve/engine*
ret	BRAZILIAN GP	Interlagos	16	Equipe Renault Elf	1.5 t/c Renault RS01 V6	*spun off-could not restart*
ret	SOUTH AFRICAN GP	Kyalami	16	Equipe Renault Elf	1.5 t/c Renault RS01 V6	*burst tyre*
dns	US GP WEST	Long Beach	16	Equipe Renault Elf	1.5 t/c Renault RS01 V6	*withdrawn on race morning*
9	SPANISH GP	Jarama	16	Equipe Renault Elf	1.5 t/c Renault RS01 V6	*1 lap behind*
ret	BELGIAN GP	Zolder	16	Equipe Renault Elf	1.5 t/c Renault RS01 V6	*no turbo boost*
ret	MONACO GP	Monte Carlo	16	Equipe Renault Elf	1.5 t/c Renault RS10 V6	*accident-damaged suspension*
3	FRENCH GP	Dijon	16	Equipe Renault Elf	1.5 t/c Renault RS12 V6	*FL*
2	BRITISH GP	Silverstone	16	Equipe Renault Elf	1.5 t/c Renault RS12 V6	
ret	GERMAN GP	Hockenheim	16	Equipe Renault Elf	1.5 t/c Renault RS12 V6	*puncture*
6	AUSTRIAN GP	Österreichring	16	Equipe Renault Elf	1.5 t/c Renault RS12 V6	*pit stop-fuel/Pole/FL/1 lap behind*
ret	DUTCH GP	Zandvoort	16	Equipe Renault Elf	1.5 t/c Renault RS12 V6	*collision with Regazzoni/Pole*
ret	ITALIAN GP	Monza	16	Equipe Renault Elf	1.5 t/c Renault RS12 V6	*misfire*
ret	CANADIAN GP	Montreal	16	Equipe Renault Elf	1.5 t/c Renault RS12 V6	*accident with Stuck*
2	US GP EAST	Watkins Glen	16	Equipe Renault Elf	1.5 t/c Renault RS12 V6	

1980

ret	ARGENTINE GP	Buenos Aires	16	Equipe Renault Elf	1.5 t/c Renault RE21 V6	*suspension*
1	BRAZILIAN GP	Interlagos	16	Equipe Renault Elf	1.5 t/c Renault RE21 V6	*FL*
1	SOUTH AFRICAN GP	Kyalami	16	Equipe Renault Elf	1.5 t/c Renault RE21 V6	*FL*
9	US GP WEST	Long Beach	16	Equipe Renault Elf	1.5 t/c Renault RE24 V6	*brake problems/2 laps behind*
4	BELGIAN GP	Zolder	16	Equipe Renault Elf	1.5 t/c Renault RE24 V6	*1 lap behind*
ret	MONACO GP	Monte Carlo	16	Equipe Renault Elf	1.5 t/c Renault RE24 V6	*accident with Patrese*
5	FRENCH GP	Paul Ricard	16	Equipe Renault Elf	1.5 t/c Renault RE24 V6	
nc	BRITISH GP	Brands Hatch	16	Equipe Renault Elf	1.5 t/c Renault RE24 V6	*pit stop-brakes/9 laps behind*
ret	GERMAN GP	Hockenheim	16	Equipe Renault Elf	1.5 t/c Renault RE25 V6	*valve spring*
9	AUSTRIAN GP	Österreichring	16	Equipe Renault Elf	1.5 t/c Renault RE25 V6	*pit stops-tyres/Pole/FL/1 lap behind*
2	DUTCH GP	Zandvoort	16	Equipe Renault Elf	1.5 t/c Renault RE25 V6	*Pole/FL*
10	ITALIAN GP	Imola	16	Equipe Renault Elf	1.5 t/c Renault RE25 V6	*shock absorber/Pole/2 laps behind*
ret	CANADIAN GP	Montreal	16	Equipe Renault Elf	1.5 t/c Renault RE25 V6	*brakes/gearbox*
7	US GP EAST	Watkins Glen	16	Equipe Renault Elf	1.5 t/c Renault RE25 V6	*pit stop-tyres/1 lap behind*

1981

8	US GP WEST	Long Beach	16	Equipe Renault Elf	1.5 t/c Renault RE27B V6	*3 laps behind*
ret	BRAZILIAN GP	Rio	16	Equipe Renault Elf	1.5 t/c Renault RE27B V6	*start line collision*
5	ARGENTINE GP	Buenos Aires	16	Equipe Renault Elf	1.5 t/c Renault RE27B V6	
8	SAN MARINO GP	Imola	16	Equipe Renault Elf	1.5 t/c Renault RE27B V6	*1 lap behind*
dnq	BELGIAN GP	Zolder	16	Equipe Renault Elf	1.5 t/c Renault RE30 V6	
ret	MONACO GP	Monte Carlo	16	Equipe Renault Elf	1.5 t/c Renault RE30 V6	*spun off*
9	SPANISH GP	Jarama	16	Equipe Renault Elf	1.5 t/c Renault RE30 V6	
4	FRENCH GP	Dijon	16	Equipe Renault Elf	1.5 t/c Renault RE30 V6	
9/ret	BRITISH GP	Silverstone	16	Equipe Renault Elf	1.5 t/c Renault RE30 V6	*engine/Pole/FL/4 laps behind*
13	GERMAN GP	Hockenheim	16	Equipe Renault Elf	1.5 t/c Renault RE30 V6	*pit stop-split tyre/1 lap behind*
2	AUSTRIAN GP	Österreichring	16	Equipe Renault Elf	1.5 t/c Renault RE30 V6	*Pole*
ret	DUTCH GP	Zandvoort	16	Equipe Renault Elf	1.5 t/c Renault RE30 V6	*accident*
ret	ITALIAN GP	Monza	16	Equipe Renault Elf	1.5 t/c Renault RE30 V6	*crashed*
ret	CANADIAN GP	Montreal	16	Equipe Renault Elf	1.5 t/c Renault RE30 V6	*startline collision*
ret	CAESARS PALACE GP	Las Vegas	16	Equipe Renault Elf	1.5 t/c Renault RE30 V6	*electrics*

1982

3	SOUTH AFRICAN GP	Kyalami	16	Equipe Renault Elf	1.5 t/c Renault RE30B V6	*Pole*
ret	BRAZILIAN GP	Rio	16	Equipe Renault Elf	1.5 t/c Renault RE30B V6	*accident with Reutemann*
ret	US GP WEST	Long Beach	16	Equipe Renault Elf	1.5 t/c Renault RE30B V6	*hit by Giacomelli*
ret	SAN MARINO GP	Imola	16	Equipe Renault Elf	1.5 t/c Renault RE30B V6	*engine/Pole*
ret	BELGIAN GP	Zolder	16	Equipe Renault Elf	1.5 t/c Renault RE30B V6	*throttle linkage*
ret	MONACO GP	Monte Carlo	16	Equipe Renault Elf	1.5 t/c Renault RE30B V6	*spun off/Pole*
10	US GP (DETROIT)	Detroit	16	Equipe Renault Elf	1.5 t/c Renault RE30B V6	*3 laps behind*
ret	CANADIAN GP	Montreal	16	Equipe Renault Elf	1.5 t/c Renault RE30B V6	*spun off*
ret	DUTCH GP	Zandvoort	16	Equipe Renault Elf	1.5 t/c Renault RE30B V6	*suspension failure-crashed/Pole*
ret	BRITISH GP	Brands Hatch	16	Equipe Renault Elf	1.5 t/c Renault RE30B V6	*startline accident-hit by Patrese*
1	FRENCH GP	Paul Ricard	16	Equipe Renault Elf	1.5 t/c Renault RE30B V6	*Pole*
2	GERMAN GP	Hockenheim	16	Equipe Renault Elf	1.5 t/c Renault RE30B V6	
ret	AUSTRIAN GP	Österreichring	16	Equipe Renault Elf	1.5 t/c Renault RE30B V6	*turbo*
ret	SWISS GP	Dijon	16	Equipe Renault Elf	1.5 t/c Renault RE30B V6	*fuel injection/5 laps behind*
1	ITALIAN GP	Monza	16	Equipe Renault Elf	1.5 t/c Renault RE30B V6	*FL*
ret	CAESARS PALACE GP	Las Vegas	16	Equipe Renault Elf	1.5 t/c Renault RE30B V6	*engine*

1983

10*	BRAZILIAN GP	Rio	28	Scuderia Ferrari SpA SEFAC	1.5 t/c Ferrari 126C2/B V6	** 2nd place car disqualified/1 lap behind**
3	US GP WEST	Long Beach	28	Scuderia Ferrari SpA SEFAC	1.5 t/c Ferrari 126C2/B V6	
7	FRENCH GP	Paul Ricard	28	Scuderia Ferrari SpA SEFAC	1.5 t/c Ferrari 126C2/B V6	*1 lap behind*
3	SAN MARINO GP	Imola	28	Scuderia Ferrari SpA SEFAC	1.5 t/c Ferrari 126C2/B V6	*Pole/1 lap behind*
ret	MONACO GP	Monte Carlo	28	Scuderia Ferrari SpA SEFAC	1.5 t/c Ferrari 126C2/B V6	*hit barrier*
ret	BELGIAN GP	Spa	28	Scuderia Ferrari SpA SEFAC	1.5 t/c Ferrari 126C2/B V6	*engine*
ret	US GP (DETROIT)	Detroit	28	Scuderia Ferrari SpA SEFAC	1.5 t/c Ferrari 126C2/B V6	*electrics/Pole*
1	CANADIAN GP	Montreal	28	Scuderia Ferrari SpA SEFAC	1.5 t/c Ferrari 126C2/B V6	*Pole*
5	BRITISH GP	Silverstone	28	Scuderia Ferrari SpA SEFAC	1.5 t/c Ferrari 126C3 V6	*Pole*
1	GERMAN GP	Hockenheim	28	Scuderia Ferrari SpA SEFAC	1.5 t/c Ferrari 126C3 V6	*FL*
2	AUSTRIAN GP	Österreichring	28	Scuderia Ferrari SpA SEFAC	1.5 t/c Ferrari 126C3 V6	
1	DUTCH GP	Zandvoort	28	Scuderia Ferrari SpA SEFAC	1.5 t/c Ferrari 126C3 V6	*FL*
2	ITALIAN GP	Monza	28	Scuderia Ferrari SpA SEFAC	1.5 t/c Ferrari 126C3 V6	
9	EUROPEAN GP	Brands Hatch	28	Scuderia Ferrari SpA SEFAC	1.5 t/c Ferrari 126C3 V6	*spin/1 lap behind*
ret	SOUTH AFRICAN GP	Kyalami	28	Scuderia Ferrari SpA SEFAC	1.5 t/c Ferrari 126C3 V6	*engine*

1984

ret	BRAZILIAN GP	Rio	28	Scuderia Ferrari SpA SEFAC	1.5 t/c Ferrari 126C4 V6	battery
ret	SOUTH AFRICAN GP	Kyalami	28	Scuderia Ferrari SpA SEFAC	1.5 t/c Ferrari 126C4 V6	fuel injection
3	BELGIAN GP	Zolder	28	Scuderia Ferrari SpA SEFAC	1.5 t/c Ferrari 126C4 V6	FL
2	SAN MARINO GP	Imola	28	Scuderia Ferrari SpA SEFAC	1.5 t/c Ferrari 126C4 V6	
4	FRENCH GP	Dijon	28	Scuderia Ferrari SpA SEFAC	1.5 t/c Ferrari 126C4 V6	
3*	MONACO GP	Monte Carlo	28	Scuderia Ferrari SpA SEFAC	1.5 t/c Ferrari 126C4 V6	* 3rd place car disqualified
5	CANADIAN GP	Montreal	28	Scuderia Ferrari SpA SEFAC	1.5 t/c Ferrari 126C4 V6	pit stop-tyres/2 laps behind
ret	US GP (DETROIT)	Detroit	28	Scuderia Ferrari SpA SEFAC	1.5 t/c Ferrari 126C4 V6	spun off
2	US GP (DALLAS)	Dallas	28	Scuderia Ferrari SpA SEFAC	1.5 t/c Ferrari 126C4 V6	
6	BRITISH GP	Brands Hatch	28	Scuderia Ferrari SpA SEFAC	1.5 t/c Ferrari 126C4 V6	collision with de Cesaris/1 lap behind
6	GERMAN GP	Hockenheim	28	Scuderia Ferrari SpA SEFAC	1.5 t/c Ferrari 126C4 V6	pit stop-tyres/1 lap behind
7	AUSTRIAN GP	Österreichring	28	Scuderia Ferrari SpA SEFAC	1.5 t/c Ferrari 126C4 V6	pit stop-tyres/1 lap behind
11*/ret	DUTCH GP	Zandvoort	28	Scuderia Ferrari SpA SEFAC	1.5 t/c Ferrari 126C4 V6	electrics/FL/*8th & 9th place cars dsq
ret	ITALIAN GP	Monza	28	Scuderia Ferrari SpA SEFAC	1.5 t/c Ferrari 126C4 V6	gearbox
5	EUROPEAN GP	Nürburgring	28	Scuderia Ferrari SpA SEFAC	1.5 t/c Ferrari 126C4 V6	
9	PORTUGUESE GP	Estoril	28	Scuderia Ferrari SpA SEFAC	1.5 t/c Ferrari 126C4 V6	1 lap behind

1985

4	BRAZILIAN GP	Rio	28	Scuderia Ferrari SpA SEFAC	1.5 t/c Ferrari 156/85	1 lap behind

1986

4	BRAZILIAN GP	Rio	25	Equipe Ligier	1.5 t/c Ligier JS27-Renault V6	
ret	SPANISH GP	Jerez	25	Equipe Ligier	1.5 t/c Ligier JS27-Renault V6	driveshaft
ret	SAN MARINO GP	Imola	25	Equipe Ligier	1.5 t/c Ligier JS27-Renault V6	lost wheel
5	MONACO GP	Monte Carlo	25	Equipe Ligier	1.5 t/c Ligier JS27-Renault V6	1 lap behind
ret	BELGIAN GP	Spa	25	Equipe Ligier	1.5 t/c Ligier JS27-Renault V6	engine
6	CANADIAN GP	Montreal	25	Equipe Ligier	1.5 t/c Ligier JS27-Renault V6	1 lap behind
ret	US GP (DETROIT)	Detroit	25	Equipe Ligier	1.5 t/c Ligier JS27-Renault V6	hit wall & Boutsen-suspension
5	FRENCH GP	Paul Ricard	25	Equipe Ligier	1.5 t/c Ligier JS27-Renault V6	1 lap behind
4	BRITISH GP	Brands Hatch	25	Equipe Ligier	1.5 t/c Ligier JS27-Renault V6	2 laps behind
4	GERMAN GP	Hockenheim	25	Equipe Ligier	1.5 t/c Ligier JS27-Renault V6	
ret	HUNGARIAN GP	Hungaroring	25	Equipe Ligier	1.5 t/c Ligier JS27-Renault V6	engine
10	AUSTRIAN GP	Österreichring	25	Equipe Ligier	1.5 t/c Ligier JS27-Renault V6	pit stop-misfire/5 laps behind
ret	ITALIAN GP	Monza	25	Equipe Ligier	1.5 t/c Ligier JS27-Renault V6	gearbox
7	PORTUGUESE GP	Estoril	25	Equipe Ligier	1.5 t/c Ligier JS27-Renault V6	1 lap behind
15/ret	MEXICAN GP	Mexico City	25	Equipe Ligier	1.5 t/c Ligier JS27-Renault V6	engine/5 laps behind
7	AUSTRALIAN GP	Adelaide	25	Equipe Ligier	1.5 t/c Ligier JS27-Renault V6	pit stop-puncture/3 laps behind

1987

dns	SAN MARINO GP	Imola	25	Ligier Loto	1.5 t/c Ligier JS29B-Megatron 4	suspension in a.m. warm-up
6	BELGIAN GP	Spa	25	Ligier Loto	1.5 t/c Ligier JS29B-Megatron 4	2 laps behind
11	MONACO GP	Monte Carlo	25	Ligier Loto	1.5 t/c Ligier JS29B-Megatron 4	4 laps behind
10	US GP (DETROIT)	Detroit	25	Ligier Loto	1.5 t/c Ligier JS29B-Megatron 4	3 laps behind
ret	FRENCH GP	Paul Ricard	25	Ligier Loto	1.5 t/c Ligier JS29C-Megatron 4	broken exhaust
ret	BRITISH GP	Silverstone	25	Ligier Loto	1.5 t/c Ligier JS29C-Megatron 4	engine
ret	GERMAN GP	Hockenheim	25	Ligier Loto	1.5 t/c Ligier JS29C-Megatron 4	electrics
ret	HUNGARIAN GP	Hungaroring	25	Ligier Loto	1.5 t/c Ligier JS29C-Megatron 4	electrics
10	AUSTRIAN GP	Österreichring	25	Ligier Loto	1.5 t/c Ligier JS29C-Megatron 4	3 laps behind
10	ITALIAN GP	Monza	25	Ligier Loto	1.5 t/c Ligier JS29C-Megatron 4	2 laps behind
ret	PORTUGUESE GP	Estoril	25	Ligier Loto	1.5 t/c Ligier JS29C-Megatron 4	holed intercooler
ret	SPANISH GP	Jerez	25	Ligier Loto	1.5 t/c Ligier JS29C-Megatron 4	engine
ret	MEXICAN GP	Mexico City	25	Ligier Loto	1.5 t/c Ligier JS29C-Megatron 4	ignition
ret	JAPANESE GP	Suzuka	25	Ligier Loto	1.5 t/c Ligier JS29C-Megatron 4	out of fuel
ret	AUSTRALIAN GP	Adelaide	25	Ligier Loto	1.5 t/c Ligier JS29C-Megatron 4	electrics

1988

ret	BRAZILIAN GP	Rio	25	Ligier Loto	3.5 Ligier JS31-Judd V8	clutch
dnq	SAN MARINO GP	Imola	25	Ligier Loto	3.5 Ligier JS31-Judd V8	
ret	MONACO GP	Monte Carlo	25	Ligier Loto	3.5 Ligier JS31-Judd V8	started from pit lane/electrics
ret	MEXICAN GP	Mexico City	25	Ligier Loto	3.5 Ligier JS31-Judd V8	accident with Caffi
ret	CANADIAN GP	Montreal	25	Ligier Loto	3.5 Ligier JS31-Judd V8	gearbox
ret	US GP (DETROIT)	Detroit	25	Ligier Loto	3.5 Ligier JS31-Judd V8	engine
dnq	FRENCH GP	Paul Ricard	25	Ligier Loto	3.5 Ligier JS31-Judd V8	
18	BRITISH GP	Silverstone	25	Ligier Loto	3.5 Ligier JS31-Judd V8	3 laps behind
17	GERMAN GP	Hockenheim	25	Ligier Loto	3.5 Ligier JS31-Judd V8	3 laps behind
ret	HUNGARIAN GP	Hungaroring	25	Ligier Loto	3.5 Ligier JS31-Judd V8	engine
ret	BELGIAN GP	Spa	25	Ligier Loto	3.5 Ligier JS31-Judd V8	accident with de Cesaris
13	ITALIAN GP	Monza	25	Ligier Loto	3.5 Ligier JS31-Judd V8	2 laps behind
10	PORTUGUESE GP	Estoril	25	Ligier Loto	3.5 Ligier JS31-Judd V8	2 laps behind
ret	SPANISH GP	Jerez	25	Ligier Loto	3.5 Ligier JS31-Judd V8	throttle jammed closed
17	JAPANESE GP	Suzuka	25	Ligier Loto	3.5 Ligier JS31-Judd V8	pit stop-tyres/3 laps behind
ret	AUSTRALIAN GP	Adelaide	25	Ligier Loto	3.5 Ligier JS31-Judd V8	accident with Berger

1989

dnq	BRAZILIAN GP	Rio	25	Ligier Loto	3.5 Ligier JS33-Cosworth V8	
dnq	SAN MARINO GP	Imola	25	Ligier Loto	3.5 Ligier JS33-Cosworth V8	
12	MONACO GP	Monte Carlo	25	Ligier Loto	3.5 Ligier JS33-Cosworth V8	4 laps behind
14	MEXICAN GP	Mexico City	25	Ligier Loto	3.5 Ligier JS33-Cosworth V8	lost use of clutch/3 laps behind
dnq	US GP (PHOENIX)	Phoenix	25	Ligier Loto	3.5 Ligier JS33-Cosworth V8	
5	CANADIAN GP	Montreal	25	Ligier Loto	3.5 Ligier JS33-Cosworth V8	1 lap behind
ret	FRENCH GP	Paul Ricard	25	Ligier Loto	3.5 Ligier JS33-Cosworth V8	gearbox
dnq	BRITISH GP	Silverstone	25	Ligier Loto	3.5 Ligier JS33-Cosworth V8	
11	GERMAN GP	Hockenheim	25	Ligier Loto	3.5 Ligier JS33-Cosworth V8	gearbox problems/3 laps behind
dnq	HUNGARIAN GP	Hungaroring	25	Ligier Loto	3.5 Ligier JS33-Cosworth V8	
ret	BELGIAN GP	Spa	25	Ligier Loto	3.5 Ligier JS33-Cosworth V8	collision with Alliot

	Race	Circuit	No	Entrant	Car/Engine	Comment
9	ITALIAN GP	Monza	25	Ligier Loto	3.5 Ligier JS33-Cosworth V8	2 laps behind
13	PORTUGUESE GP	Estoril	25	Ligier Loto	3.5 Ligier JS33-Cosworth V8	2 laps behind
dnq	SPANISH GP	Jerez	25	Ligier Loto	3.5 Ligier JS33-Cosworth V8	
dnq	JAPANESE GP	Suzuka	25	Ligier Loto	3.5 Ligier JS33-Cosworth V8	
ret	AUSTRALIAN GP	Adelaide	25	Ligier Loto	3.5 Ligier JS33-Cosworth V8	collision with Cheever

GP Starts: 149   GP Wins: 7   Pole positions: 18   Fastest laps: 12   Points: 179

ARUNDELL, Peter (GB) b 8/11/1933

1963

	Race	Circuit	No	Entrant	Car/Engine	Comment
dns	FRENCH GP	Reims	22	Team Lotus	1.5 Lotus 25-Climax V8	practised but drove in FJ event

1964

3	MONACO GP	Monte Carlo	11	Team Lotus	1.5 Lotus 25-Climax V8	3 laps behind
3	DUTCH GP	Zandvoort	20	Team Lotus	1.5 Lotus 25-Climax V8	1 lap behind
9	BELGIAN GP	Spa	24	Team Lotus	1.5 Lotus 25-Climax V8	pit stop-water/4 laps behind
4	FRENCH GP	Rouen	4	Team Lotus	1.5 Lotus 25-Climax V8	

1966

dns	BELGIAN GP	Spa	11	Team Lotus	3.0 Lotus 43-BRM H16	engine in practice
ret	FRENCH GP	Reims	4	Team Lotus	3.0 Lotus 43-BRM H16	gearbox
ret	BRITISH GP	Brands Hatch	2	Team Lotus	2.0 Lotus 33-BRM V8	gear linkage
dns	"	"	1	Team Lotus	2.0 Lotus 33-Climax V8	practice only
ret	DUTCH GP	Zandvoort	8	Team Lotus	2.0 Lotus 33-BRM V8	ignition
8*	GERMAN GP	Nürburgring	2	Team Lotus	2.0 Lotus 33-BRM V8	* 12th after 4 F2 cars/1 lap behind
8/ret	ITALIAN GP	Monza	24	Team Lotus	2.0 Lotus 33-BRM V8	engine/5 laps behind
6	US GP	Watkins Glen	2	Team Lotus	2.0 Lotus 33-Climax V8	spin-pit stop/7 laps behind
dns	"	"	2	Team Lotus	3.0 Lotus 43-BRM H16	practice only
7	MEXICAN GP	Mexico City	2	Team Lotus	2.0 Lotus 33-BRM V8	4 laps behind

GP Starts: 11   GP Wins: 0   Pole positions: 0   Fastest laps: 0   Points: 12

PETER ARUNDELL

The sight of his vermilion-red helmet at the front of an F1 grid should have been a regular one during the mid-sixties, but sadly Grand Prix racing was to see the true Peter Arundell on only four occasions before a massive accident in a Formula 2 race at Reims effectively ended his aspirations to emulate his team-mate Jim Clark.

Arundell began his career with an MG TC in 1957 before racing a Lotus XI, and then a Lola sports car, soon becoming the fastest private practitioner behind the works entries. When Peter then won an end-of-season Junior race in the front-engined Elva-DKW, Colin Chapman was not slow to recognise the Essex man's potential and signed him for his Junior team in 1960, a season which saw him beat both his team-mates – Trevor Taylor and Jim Clark – on occasion. As number two to Taylor during 1961, Peter maintained his progress, highlighted by winning the Monaco Junior race, and for 1962 he rightfully assumed the team leadership, dominating proceedings with some brilliant displays, taking 18 wins from 25 starts, and easily claiming the BARC Junior championship.

In truth he should have been promoted to Formula 1 at this stage, and there would certainly have been a drive for him elsewhere had he chosen to seek it. Instead Peter waited patiently for his opportunity, knowing that a better prospect than a Lotus would be hard to find. So it was more Formula Junior in 1963, with occasional F1 outings merely confirming his talent. A superb drive into second place at the Solitude GP was matched in the Mediterranean GP at Enna.

Arundell's fully deserved promotion finally came in 1964, and the season began in tremendous style, his Grand Prix performances being backed by some equally impressive results in non-championship Formula 1 races. He was second in the News of the World Trophy at Goodwood and third at both the Aintree 200 and the Syracuse GP (shared with Spence). In the newly inaugurated Formula 2, Peter was just as impressive, taking third place at Pau, second in the Grovewood Trophy at Mallory Park and fourth in the London Trophy before the fateful Reims race, when his spinning Lotus was hit broadside by Ginther. The car was smashed into an earth bank and Arundell was hurled from the cockpit suffering a broken arm, thigh and collarbone and severe concussion.

His rehabilitation was long and slow, but Chapman promised him a place in the team when fit, and he reappeared at the South African GP on New Year's Day in 1966, to take third place in the Lotus 33. Once the season got under way, Peter seemed a shadow of his former self, though, to be fair, the machinery at his disposal hardly gave him a chance to shine. Racing the works Formula 2 car brought only a second place at the Eifelrennen, so when Graham Hill was signed for 1967 Arundell was released.

Really that was the end for Peter, though in 1968 he briefly raced Alan Mann's Escort before a short spell with the McNamara F3 and Formula Vee projects in 1969.

ALBERTO ASCARI

The son of a famous racing driver – his father, Antonio, was killed at Montlhéry when the young Ascari was just seven years old – it was perhaps inevitable that Alberto should also follow a career in the sport. After racing Bianchi motor cycles from 1937, he drove the very first Ferrari T815 sports car in the 1940 Mille Miglia with his cousin Minozzi, the pair leading their class before retirement.

The war soon brought racing to a halt in Italy, and it was 1947 before he was back in action. Second place in a little Cisitalia in a one-make race at Gezereh Island behind Cortese brought him to the fore, and he was soon impressing with his speed behind the wheel of a Maserati 4CLT. His first major success was in a sports car race at Modena that year, and he benefited greatly from the tutelage of team-mate Villoresi, whom he beat to win the 1948 San Remo GP. He was second to his mentor in the British GP and even drove once for rivals Alfa Romeo, finishing third in the French GP at Reims.

After winning the 1949 Buenos Aires GP for Maserati, both Ascari and Villoresi left for Ferrari, where Alberto was to enjoy spectacular success. In his first season he won the Swiss, Italian and Peron GPs in the T125. In 1950, Alfa were back in competition with their 158s and Ferrari concentrated mainly on Formula 2, winning a succession of races at Modena, Mons, Rome, Reims, Garda and the Nürburgring, while their T375 F1 car was being developed. He did, however, take a second at Monaco, and at season's end won the Penya Rhin GP at Barcelona in the new 4.5-litre car.

In 1951 Ascari won two Grands Prix as at last the might of Alfa was beaten, but the championship went to Fangio. With the change of formula restricting GP racing to 2-litre cars for 1952 and the Alfa team disbanded, Alberto was sitting pretty. His task in taking the championship was further eased by the absence of the injured Fangio, and missing the Swiss GP to compete at Indianapolis merely denied him the opportunity of a clean sweep, as the brilliant Italian swept to six championship victories, in addition to wins at Syracuse, Pau, Marseilles, Comminges and La Baule.

It was much the same in 1953 when he trampled on the opposition to take five more championship wins, adding victories at Pau and Bordeaux to his burgeoning tally. The run of success came to a halt with a move to Lancia for 1954 which left Ascari frustrated as the car was delayed until the end of that year. He did win the Mille Miglia in a Lancia sports car and was allowed to appear as a guest driver for both Maserati and Ferrari, putting in a brilliant drive at Monza against the works Mercedes.

With the Lancias *'au point'* at the start of 1955, Ascari led the Argentine GP until he lost control of the car on melting tar, won the non-championship Turin GP and Naples GP at Posillipo, and led at Pau before finishing fifth. At the Monaco GP Alberto famously crashed his car into the harbour, emerging with facial injuries, but four days later he turned up unexpectedly at Monza to test a Ferrari sports car in preparation for the forthcoming Supercortemaggiore race. For some inexplicable reason Ascari crashed the car, and he was thrown onto the track and killed instantly. While the Italian nation mourned the loss of its finest driver, Fangio is reported to have said: 'I have lost my greatest opponent.' Clearly this was true, but close scrutiny of their careers reveals that only rarely did they have the opportunity to race against each other in equally matched machinery.

PETER ASHDOWN

Although his sole Grand Prix appearance was in a Cooper, Peter's reputation was built as a Lotus man. Consistently high placings in the marque's early sports cars between 1955 and 1957 brought him a works drive, but a broken collarbone sustained in a crash at Rouen ended his season. On his return in 1959 Peter drove some sparkling races, the best of which saw him win the Auvernge Trophy in a Lotus XI at Clermont Ferrand, beating Behra's RS Porsche.

Though there were no further opportunities to compete in Grands Prix, Ashdown raced on until 1962, driving a Lola in Formula Junior, and his gift for handling small-capacity sports cars was underlined by class wins in the Nürburgring 1000 Km in both 1960 and 1962.

IAN ASHLEY

Ashley raced extensively in Formula Ford, F3 and F5000 from 1967 to 1975, often showing great speed but not always the ability to keep the car on the road.

His forays into Grand Prix racing with some of the formula's lesser lights ranged between the undistinguished and, on one occasion, when he was very fortunate to escape a lurid 170 mph practice crash in Canada in 1977 with no worse than broken ankles, the disastrous.

After a slow recovery Ian took up the same career as his father and became a pilot. The itch to go racing remained, however, and he has recently returned to the tracks, looking trim and fit, to contest the fiercely competitive BTCC series in a Vauxhall Cavalier.

ASCARI, Alberto (I) b 13/7/1918 – d 26/5/1955

1950

	Race	Circuit	No	Entrant	Car/Engine	Comment
2	MONACO GP	Monte Carlo	40	Scuderia Ferrari	1.5 s/c Ferrari 125F1 V12	1 lap behind
ret	SWISS GP	Bremgarten	18	Scuderia Ferrari	1.5 s/c Ferrari 125F1 V12	scavenger pump
5	BELGIAN GP	Spa	4	Scuderia Ferrari	3.3 Ferrari 125/275F1 V12	1 lap behind
dns	FRENCH GP	Reims	10	Scuderia Ferrari	1.5 s/c Ferrari 125F1 V12	car not fast enough-raced in F2 support
ret	ITALIAN GP	Monza	16	Scuderia Ferrari	4.5 Ferrari 375F1 V12	engine
2*	"	"	48	Scuderia Ferrari	4.5 Ferrari 375F1 V12	* took over Serafini's car

1951

	Race	Circuit	No	Entrant	Car/Engine	Comment
6	SWISS GP	Bremgarten	20	Scuderia Ferrari	4.5 Ferrari 375F1 V12	2 laps behind
2	BELGIAN GP	Spa	8	Scuderia Ferrari	4.5 Ferrari 375F1 V12	
ret	FRENCH GP	Reims	12	Scuderia Ferrari	4.5 Ferrari 375F1 V12	gearbox
2*	"	"	14	Scuderia Ferrari	4.5 Ferrari 375F1 V12	* took over Gonzalez's car
ret	BRITISH GP	Silverstone	11	Scuderia Ferrari	4.5 Ferrari 375F1 V12	gearbox
1	GERMAN GP	Nürburgring	71	Scuderia Ferrari	4.5 Ferrari 375F1 V12	Pole
1	ITALIAN GP	Monza	2	Scuderia Ferrari	4.5 Ferrari 375F1 V12	
4	SPANISH GP	Pedralbes	2	Scuderia Ferrari	4.5 Ferrari 375F1 V12	tyre problems/Pole/2 laps behind

1952 World Champion Driver

	Race	Circuit	No	Entrant	Car/Engine	Comment
1	BELGIAN GP	Spa	4	Scuderia Ferrari	2.0 Ferrari 500 4	Pole/FL
1	FRENCH GP	Rouen	8	Scuderia Ferrari	2.0 Ferrari 500 4	Pole/FL
1	BRITISH GP	Silverstone	15	Scuderia Ferrari	2.0 Ferrari 500 4	FL
1	GERMAN GP	Nürburgring	101	Scuderia Ferrari	2.0 Ferrari 500 4	Pole/FL
1	DUTCH GP	Zandvoort	2	Scuderia Ferrari	2.0 Ferrari 500 4	Pole/FL
1	ITALIAN GP	Monza	12	Scuderia Ferrari	2.0 Ferrari 500 4	Pole/FL (shared with Gonzalez)

1953 World Champion Driver

	Race	Circuit	No	Entrant	Car/Engine	Comment
1	ARGENTINE GP	Buenos Aires	10	Scuderia Ferrari	2.0 Ferrari 500 4	Pole/FL
1	DUTCH GP	Zandvoort	2	Scuderia Ferrari	2.0 Ferrari 500 4	Pole
1	BELGIAN GP	Spa	10	Scuderia Ferrari	2.0 Ferrari 500 4	
4	FRENCH GP	Reims	10	Scuderia Ferrari	2.0 Ferrari 500 4	Pole
1	BRITISH GP	Silverstone	5	Scuderia Ferrari	2.0 Ferrari 500 4	Pole/FL(shared with Gonzalez)
8*	GERMAN GP	Nürburgring	1	Scuderia Ferrari	2.0 Ferrari 500 4	lost wheel/*Villoresi took car/Pole/-1 lap
ret	"	"	4	Scuderia Ferrari	2.0 Ferrari 500 4	engine/took over Villoresi's car/FL
1	SWISS GP	Bremgarten	46	Scuderia Ferrari	2.0 Ferrari 500 4	FL
ret	ITALIAN GP	Monza	4	Scuderia Ferrari	2.0 Ferrari 500 4	collision with Marimón/Pole

1954

	Race	Circuit	No	Entrant	Car/Engine	Comment
ret	FRENCH GP	Reims	10	Officine Alfieri Maserati	2.5 Maserati 250F 6	engine
ret	BRITISH GP	Silverstone	31	Officine Alfieri Maserati	2.5 Maserati 250F 6	dropped valve/FL (shared)
ret	"	"	32	Officine Alfieri Maserati	2.5 Maserati 250F 6	took Villoresi's car/con rod
ret	ITALIAN GP	Monza	34	Scuderia Ferrari	2.5 Ferrari 625 4	engine
ret	SPANISH GP	Pedralbes	34	Scuderia Lancia	2.5 Lancia D50 V8	clutch/FL

1955

	Race	Circuit	No	Entrant	Car/Engine	Comment
ret	ARGENTINE GP	Buenos Aires	32	Scuderia Lancia	2.5 Lancia D50 V8	spun off on melting tar
ret	MONACO GP	Monte Carlo	26	Scuderia Lancia	2.5 Lancia D50 V8	crashed into harbour

GP Starts: 31   GP Wins: 13   Pole positions: 14   Fastest laps: 13   Points: 140.64

ASHDOWN, Peter (GB) b 16/10/1934

1959

	Race	Circuit	No	Entrant	Car/Engine	Comment
12	BRITISH GP (F2)	Aintree	52	Alan Brown Equipe	1.5 Cooper T45-Climax 4	3rd F2 car/6 laps behind

GP Starts: 1   GP Wins: 0   Pole positions: 0   Fastest laps: 0   Points: 0

ASHLEY, Ian (GB) b 26/10/1947

1974

	Race	Circuit	No	Entrant	Car/Engine	Comment
14	GERMAN GP	Nürburgring	32	Token Racing	3.0 Token RJ02-Cosworth V8	1 lap behind
nc	AUSTRIAN GP	Österreichring	35	Token Racing	3.0 Token RJ02-Cosworth V8	2 stops-wheel problems/8 laps behind
dnq	CANADIAN GP	Mosport Park	42	Chequered Flag/Richard Oaten	3.0 Brabham BT42-Cosworth V8	
dnq	US GP	Watkins Glen	42	Chequered Flag/Richard Oaten	3.0 Brabham BT42-Cosworth V8	

1975

	Race	Circuit	No	Entrant	Car/Engine	Comment
dns	GERMAN GP	Nürburgring	20	Frank Williams Racing Cars	3.0 Williams FW03-Cosworth V8	practice accident-leg injuries

1976

	Race	Circuit	No	Entrant	Car/Engine	Comment
ret	BRAZILIAN GP	Interlagos	14	Stanley BRM	3.0 BRM P201B V12	oil pump

1977

	Race	Circuit	No	Entrant	Car/Engine	Comment
dnq	AUSTRIAN GP	Österreichring	39	Hesketh Racing	3.0 Hesketh 308E-Cosworth V8	
dnq	DUTCH GP	Zandvoort	39	Hesketh Racing	3.0 Hesketh 308E-Cosworth V8	
dnq	ITALIAN GP	Monza	25	Hesketh Racing	3.0 Hesketh 308E-Cosworth V8	
17	US GP EAST	Watkins Glen	25	Hesketh Racing	3.0 Hesketh 308E-Cosworth V8	pit stop-wheel bearing/4 laps behind
dns	CANADIAN GP	Mosport Park	25	Hesketh Racing	3.0 Hesketh 308E-Cosworth V8	practice accident-serious injuries

GP Starts: 4   GP Wins: 0   Pole positions: 0   Fastest laps: 0   Points: 0

GERRY ASHMORE

From a motor racing family, Gerry cut his teeth on Jaguars before taking the bold step of racing a Lotus 18 in Formula 1 in 1961. His best result was second place in the Naples GP, well behind Baghetti's Ferrari, but he courted disaster on his next visit to Italy, crashing on the first lap of the Italian GP in an accident independent from the von Trips tragedy.

After a handful of races with the Lotus in 1962, he continued to make occasional appearances, such as in 1965 with the ex-David Prophet Lotus 30.

ASHMORE, Gerry (GB) b 25/7/1936

1961

	Race	Circuit	No	Entrant	Car/Engine	Comment
ret	BRITISH GP	Aintree	40	Gerry Ashmore	1.5 Lotus 18-Climax 4	ignition
16	GERMAN GP	Nürburgring	27	Gerry Ashmore	1.5 Lotus 18-Climax 4	2 laps behind
ret	ITALIAN GP	Monza	18	Gerry Ashmore	1.5 Lotus 18-Climax 4	accident

1962

dnq	ITALIAN GP	Monza	52	Gerry Ashmore	1.5 Lotus 18/21-Climax 4	

GP Starts: 3   GP Wins: 0   Pole positions: 0   Fastest laps: 0   Points: 0

ASTON, Bill (GB) b 29/3/1900 – d 4/3/1974

1952

	Race	Circuit	No	Entrant	Car/Engine	Comment
dns	BRITISH GP	Silverstone	2	W S Aston	2.0 Aston NB 41-Butterworth F4	too slow
ret	GERMAN GP	Nürburgring	114	W S Aston	2.0 Aston NB 41-Butterworth F4	oil pressure
dnq	ITALIAN GP	Monza	64	W S Aston	2.0 Aston NB 41-Butterworth F4	

GP Starts: 1   GP Wins: 0   Pole positions: 0   Fastest laps: 0   Points: 0

ATTWOOD, Richard (GB) b 4/4/1940

1964

	Race	Circuit	No	Entrant	Car/Engine	Comment
dns	BRITISH GP	Brands Hatch	21	Owen Racing Organisation	1.5 BRM P67 V8 4WD	car withdrawn

1965

ret	MONACO GP	Monte Carlo	15	Reg Parnell (Racing)	1.5 Lotus 25-BRM V8	lost wheel
14/ret	BELGIAN GP	Spa	23	Reg Parnell (Racing)	1.5 Lotus 25-BRM V8	spun off in rain, car destroyed/-6 laps
13	BRITISH GP	Silverstone	22	Reg Parnell (Racing)	1.5 Lotus 25-BRM V8	pit stops/17 laps behind
12	DUTCH GP	Zandvoort	34	Reg Parnell (Racing)	1.5 Lotus 25-BRM V8	3 laps behind
ret	GERMAN GP	Nürburgring	20	Reg Parnell (Racing)	1.5 Lotus 25-BRM V8	water hose
6	ITALIAN GP	Monza	40	Reg Parnell (Racing)	1.5 Lotus 25-BRM V8	1 lap behind
10	US GP	Watkins Glen	21	Reg Parnell (Racing)	1.5 Lotus 25-BRM V8	pit stop/9 laps behind
6	MEXICAN GP	Mexico City	21	Reg Parnell (Racing)	1.5 Lotus 25-BRM V8	1 lap behind

1967

10	CANADIAN GP	Mosport Park	8	Cooper Car Co	3.0 Cooper T81-Maserati V12	6 laps behind

1968

2	MONACO GP	Monte Carlo	15	Owen Racing Organisation	3.0 BRM P126 V12	FL
ret	BELGIAN GP	Spa	12	Owen Racing Organisation	3.0 BRM P126 V12	broken oil pipe
7	DUTCH GP	Zandvoort	16	Owen Racing Organisation	3.0 BRM P126 V12	5 laps behind
7	FRENCH GP	Rouen	22	Owen Racing Organisation	3.0 BRM P126 V12	pit stop-tyres/3 laps behind
ret	BRITISH GP	Brands Hatch	11	Owen Racing Organisation	3.0 BRM P126 V12	radiator holed by stone
14	GERMAN GP	Nürburgring	11	Owen Racing Organisation	3.0 BRM P126 V12	1 lap behind

1969

4	MONACO GP	Monte Carlo	2	Gold Leaf Team Lotus	3.0 Lotus 49B-Cosworth V8	
6*	GERMAN GP (F2)	Nürburgring	29	Frank Williams Racing Cars	1.6 Brabham BT30-Cosworth 4	* 2nd in F2 class/no points scored

GP Starts: 17   GP Wins: 0   Pole positions: 0   Fastest laps: 1   Points: 11

BADOER, Luca (I) b 25/1/1971

1993

	Race	Circuit	No	Entrant	Car/Engine	Comment
ret	SOUTH AFRICAN GP	Kyalami	22	BMS Scuderia Italia SpA	3.5 Lola T93/30 BMS-Ferrari V12	gearbox
12	BRAZILIAN GP	Interlagos	22	BMS Scuderia Italia SpA	3.5 Lola T93/30 BMS-Ferrari V12	p stop-new nose/3 laps behind
dnq	EUROPEAN GP	Donington	22	BMS Scuderia Italia SpA	3.5 Lola T93/30 BMS-Ferrari V12	
7	SAN MARINO GP	Imola	22	BMS Scuderia Italia SpA	3.5 Lola T93/30 BMS-Ferrari V12	3 laps behind
ret	SPANISH GP	Barcelona	22	BMS Scuderia Italia SpA	3.5 Lola T93/30 BMS-Ferrari V12	clutch
dnq	MONACO GP	Monte Carlo	22	BMS Scuderia Italia SpA	3.5 Lola T93/30 BMS-Ferrari V12	
15	CANADIAN GP	Montreal	22	BMS Scuderia Italia SpA	3.5 Lola T93/30 BMS-Ferrari V12	4 laps behind
ret	FRENCH GP	Magny Cours	22	BMS Scuderia Italia SpA	3.5 Lola T93/30 BMS-Ferrari V12	suspension
ret	BRITISH GP	Silverstone	22	BMS Scuderia Italia SpA	3.5 Lola T93/30 BMS-Ferrari V12	engine
ret	GERMAN GP	Hockenheim	22	BMS Scuderia Italia SpA	3.5 Lola T93/30 BMS-Ferrari V12	suspension
ret	HUNGARIAN GP	Hungaroring	22	BMS Scuderia Italia SpA	3.5 Lola T93/30 BMS-Ferrari V12	spun off
13	BELGIAN GP	Spa	22	BMS Scuderia Italia SpA	3.5 Lola T93/30 BMS-Ferrari V12	2 laps behind
10	ITALIAN GP	Monza	22	BMS Scuderia Italia SpA	3.5 Lola T93/30 BMS-Ferrari V12	2 laps behind
14	PORTUGUESE GP	Estoril	22	BMS Scuderia Italia SpA	3.5 Lola T93/30 BMS-Ferrari V12	3 laps behind

GP Starts: 12   GP Wins: 0   Pole positions: 0   Fastest laps: 0   Points: 0

RICHARD ATTWOOD

A trade-apprentice at Jaguar, Attwood made his competition debut in the 1960 season with a Triumph TR3, before joining the Midland Racing Partnership to race in Formula Junior, spending most of 1961 and 1962 at club level. In 1963, driving a Mk 5A Lola-Ford, Dickie shot to international prominence by winning the Monaco Formula Junior race, and his performances won him the first Grovewood award and the princely sum of £500.

In 1964 Attwood was given a couple of chances in the works BRM, taking fourth in the News of the World Trophy at Goodwood, but non-starting the 4WD P67 at the British GP. Racing in Formula 2 for MRP, he produced some excellent performances, most notably a win at Aspern in the Vienna GP, and second place – behind Clark – at Pau, plus further runner-up spots in the Eifelrennen and at Albi. His ability was being recognised more widely, and he became a founder member of the Ford sports-prototype team.

Joining Parnell Racing, Richard drove the team's none-too-quick Lotus 25-BRM sensibly to two points-scoring finishes, while in F2 he was again second at Pau, and won the Rome GP at Vallelunga. His sports car career was now taking off, and he began what was to be a long and successful partnership with David Piper, ending the season with a fantastic drive to win the Rand 9 Hours in Piper's Ferrari 365 P2.

Driving for BRM in the 1966 Tasman series, Attwood won the Gold Leaf Trophy race at Levin before another season of F2 and sports car events, which once again ended with a win at Kyalami in the Rand 9 Hours. Despite another successful Tasman interlude in New Zealand, where he took two second places and two thirds in four starts, Richard's only other single-seater drive in 1967 was a works Cooper outing at Mosport.

When Mike Spence was so tragically killed at Indianapolis, early in 1968, Attwood was signed to replace him at BRM. His debut for the team at Monaco was stunning, Dickie taking second place and fastest lap. Unfortunately subsequent performances were not so impressive and after the German GP he was released from his contract, returning to sports car racing. In 1969 he was called back to F1 to try and reprise his Monaco performance for Lotus when Rindt was recovering from injury, scoring a fine fourth place, while later in the season he took Frank Williams' F2 Brabham to sixth (and second in class) at the Nürburgring. It was also the season in which he raced a factory Porsche for the first time, sharing a 908 Spyder with Elford to take second place in the BOAC 500. In 1970 he scored his greatest triumph, winning Le Mans in a Porsche 917 with Hans Herrmann, and took second place with the German at the Nürburgring 1000 Km. In 1971, Attwood's final racing year, he drove the John Wyer/Gulf Porsche, winning the Österreichring 1000 Km with Rodriguez, and finishing second at Le Mans with Müller. Retiring at the end of the season for business reasons, Attwood was occasionally tempted back to the circuits in the eighties, mainly in historic sports car events, but also at Le Mans in 1984 when he raced a Nimrod.

LUCA BADOER

Badoer was regarded as something of a prodigy when, aged only 19, he made his mark in Italian Formula 3 by winning the final round of the 1990 season ahead of championship contenders Colciago and Zanardi.

Naturally all eyes were on the former Italian karting champion from Montebelluna the following season and, after a quiet start in the early rounds, Luca reeled off four wins in a row amid growing acrimony as rival teams questioned the legality of his car. In fact the last of these victories was wiped out due to the team running a non-scrutineered tyre and Badoer's season never recovered thereafter.

He had done enough, however, to move up to F3000 for 1992 and, at the wheel of the superbly engineered Team Crypton Reynard, Luca was a convincing champion, winning three of the early rounds and overcoming the effects of a nasty shunt at Spa to clinch the title with another victory at Nogaro.

The slightly built Badoer then found himself pitched into the big time with the newly formed Lola Scuderia Italia team for 1993. The season was a fiasco with the car floundering at the back of the grid and the only question to be answered at most of the early Grands Prix was which of the two unfortunate drivers – Luca or Michele Alboreto – would fail to qualify. With the team folding after the Portuguese GP, Badoer was left looking for a drive for 1994 and a winter test for Benetton raised serious doubts about his chances of finding one.

GIANCARLO BAGHETTI

Baghetti will for ever be known for his extraordinary feat of winning the very first championship Grand Prix that he entered. In searing heat at Reims in 1961, the young Italian showed remarkable racecraft and composure as he took the sole surviving Ferrari to victory over the works Porsche driven by Dan Gurney. It was no fluke, for some weeks earlier Baghetti had done exactly the same thing in his first Formula 1 race at Syracuse and he had then followed that up with another victory, though the field at the Naples GP was weak and Giancarlo had an easy win. No other driver has ever won his first three Formula 1 races and probably none ever will, so Baghetti's place in motor racing folklore is secure.

His racing career started with an Alfa Romeo in 1956 and, after a second place in the Mille Miglia Rally in 1958, driving an Alfa 1900TI, Baghetti turned to sports car and Formula Junior racing over the next two years. He took three wins in the FJ Dragada-Lancia, and was invited to join the Scuderia Sant Ambroeus team who were in turn members of FISA (Federazione Italiane Scuderie Automobilistiche), a body helping to promote young Italian racing talent, the ultimate aim being a place in the Ferrari Formula 1 team. Eventually Baghetti was chosen and, as related above, the early results were sensational, but his subsequent career never matched those dizzy heights. His next race, in the rain at Aintree, ended in a shunt, and Monza brought an engine failure, though he did set fastest lap. In 1962 the Ferrari team were left behind by the V8 opposition and, although Baghetti scored a few decent finishes in Grands Prix and a second place in the Mediterranean GP, he was now being overshadowed by his old Junior rival Bandini, though the pair shared a Ferrari 196 to take second place in the Targa Florio.

With Ferrari in a state of disarray by the end of the year, Baghetti made a disastrous move (with Phil Hill) to Carlo Chiti's breakaway ATS organisation for 1963, and there was to be no Grand Prix salvation when he joined the Centro Sud team with their elderly BRMs. His reputation got him the occasional Grand Prix ride thereafter, but he could still be found in sports cars. He finished second, with Guichet, in the 1966 Targa Florio in a works Ferrari, and was a regular in the European touring car championship with a Fiat Abarth. Surprisingly for one so famous, he was quite happy to drop down into the Italian F3 championship between 1967 and 1968, and he also took a Lancia Fulvia on the London-Sydney marathon but was forced to abandon the trip when his passport and all his documents were stolen in Bombay. Subsequently Giancarlo has become a photo-journalist.

BAGHETTI, Giancarlo (I) b 25/3/1934

1961

	Race	Circuit	No	Entrant	Car/Engine	Comment
1	FRENCH GP	Reims	50	FISA	1.5 Ferrari 156 V6	only driver to win first GP
ret	BRITISH GP	Aintree	58	Scuderia Sant Ambroeus	1.5 Ferrari 156 V6	crashed in rain
ret	ITALIAN GP	Monza	32	Scuderia Sant Ambroeus	1.5 Ferrari 156 V6	engine/FL

1962

	Race	Circuit	No	Entrant	Car/Engine	Comment
4	DUTCH GP	Zandvoort	2	Scuderia Ferrari SpA SEFAC	1.5 Ferrari 156 V6	1 lap behind
ret	BELGIAN GP	Spa	11	Scuderia Ferrari SpA SEFAC	1.5 Ferrari 156 V6	ignition
10	GERMAN GP	Nürburgring	2	Scuderia Ferrari SpA SEFAC	1.5 Ferrari 156 V6	
5	ITALIAN GP	Monza	2	Scuderia Ferrari SpA SEFAC	1.5 Ferrari 156 V6	

1963

	Race	Circuit	No	Entrant	Car/Engine	Comment
ret	BELGIAN GP	Spa	27	Automobili Tourismo Sport	1.5 ATS 100 V8	gearbox
ret	DUTCH GP	Zandvoort	26	Automobili Tourismo Sport	1.5 ATS 100 V8	ignition
15	ITALIAN GP	Monza	14	Automobili Tourismo Sport	1.5 ATS 100 V8	pit stops/23 laps behind

	Race	Circuit	No	Entrant	Car/Engine	Comment
ret	US GP	Watkins Glen	26	Automobili Tourismo Sport	1.5 ATS 100 V8	*oil pump*
ret	MEXICAN GP	Mexico City	26	Automobili Tourismo Sport	1.5 ATS 100 V8	*carburation*

1964

	Race	Circuit	No	Entrant	Car/Engine	Comment
10	DUTCH GP	Zandvoort	32	Scuderia Centro Sud	1.5 BRM P57 V8	*6 laps behind*
8	BELGIAN GP	Spa	6	Scuderia Centro Sud	1.5 BRM P57 V8	*1 lap behind*
12	BRITISH GP	Brands Hatch	18	Scuderia Centro Sud	1.5 BRM P57 V8	*4 laps behind*
ret	GERMAN GP	Nürburgring	18	Scuderia Centro Sud	1.5 BRM P57 V8	*throttle linkage*
7	AUSTRIAN GP	Zeltweg	18	Scuderia Centro Sud	1.5 BRM P57 V8	*7 laps behind*
8	ITALIAN GP	Monza	30	Scuderia Centro Sud	1.5 BRM P57 V8	*1 lap behind*

1965

	Race	Circuit	No	Entrant	Car/Engine	Comment
ret	ITALIAN GP	Monza	10	Brabham Racing Organisation	1.5 Brabham BT7-Climax V8	*cod rod*

1966

	Race	Circuit	No	Entrant	Car/Engine	Comment
nc	ITALIAN GP	Monza	44	Reg Parnell Racing Ltd	2.4 Ferrari Dino 246 V6	*loaned by works/pit stop/9 laps behind*
dns	"	"	44	Reg Parnell Racing Ltd	2.0 Lotus 25-BRM V8	*engine in practice*

1967

	Race	Circuit	No	Entrant	Car/Engine	Comment
ret	ITALIAN GP	Monza	24	Team Lotus	3.0 Lotus 49-Cosworth V8	*engine*

GP Starts: 21   GP Wins: 1   Pole positions: 0   Fastest laps: 1   Points: 14

BAILEY, Julian (GB) b 9/10/1961

1988

	Race	Circuit	No	Entrant	Car/Engine	Comment
dnq	BRAZILIAN GP	Rio	4	Tyrrell Racing Organisation	3.5 Tyrrell 017-Cosworth V8	
ret	SAN MARINO GP	Imola	4	Tyrrell Racing Organisation	3.5 Tyrrell 017-Cosworth V8	*gearbox*
dnq	MONACO GP	Monte Carlo	4	Tyrrell Racing Organisation	3.5 Tyrrell 017-Cosworth V8	
dnq	MEXICAN GP	Mexico City	4	Tyrrell Racing Organisation	3.5 Tyrrell 017-Cosworth V8	
ret	CANADIAN GP	Montreal	4	Tyrrell Racing Organisation	3.5 Tyrrell 017-Cosworth V8	*collision with Sala on lap 1*
9/ret	US GP (DETROIT)	Detroit	4	Tyrrell Racing Organisation	3.5 Tyrrell 017-Cosworth V8	*hit wall/4 laps behind*
dnq	FRENCH GP	Paul Ricard	4	Tyrrell Racing Organisation	3.5 Tyrrell 017-Cosworth V8	
16	BRITISH GP	Silverstone	4	Tyrrell Racing Organisation	3.5 Tyrrell 017-Cosworth V8	*2 laps behind*
dnq	GERMAN GP	Hockenheim	4	Tyrrell Racing Organisation	3.5 Tyrrell 017-Cosworth V8	
dnq	HUNGARIAN GP	Hungaroring	4	Tyrrell Racing Organisation	3.5 Tyrrell 017-Cosworth V8	
dnq	BELGIAN GP	Spa	4	Tyrrell Racing Organisation	3.5 Tyrrell 017-Cosworth V8	
12	ITALIAN GP	Monza	4	Tyrrell Racing Organisation	3.5 Tyrrell 017-Cosworth V8	*2 laps behind*
dnq	PORTUGUESE GP	Estoril	4	Tyrrell Racing Organisation	3.5 Tyrrell 017-Cosworth V8	
dnq	SPANISH GP	Jerez	4	Tyrrell Racing Organisation	3.5 Tyrrell 017-Cosworth V8	*incident with Patrese in practice*
14	JAPANESE GP	Suzuka	4	Tyrrell Racing Organisation	3.5 Tyrrell 017-Cosworth V8	*2 laps behind*
dnq	AUSTRALIAN GP	Adelaide	4	Tyrrell Racing Organisation	3.5 Tyrrell 017-Cosworth V8	

1991

	Race	Circuit	No	Entrant	Car/Engine	Comment
dnq	US GP (PHOENIX)	Phoenix	12	Team Lotus	3.5 Lotus 102B-Judd V8	
dnq	BRAZILIAN GP	Interlagos	12	Team Lotus	3.5 Lotus 102B-Judd V8	
6	SAN MARINO GP	Imola	12	Team Lotus	3.5 Lotus 102B-Judd V8	*3 laps behind*
dnq	MONACO GP	Monte Carlo	12	Team Lotus	3.5 Lotus 102B-Judd V8	

GP Starts: 7   GP Wins: 0   Pole positions: 0   Fastest laps: 0   Points: 1

JULIAN BAILEY

The determination with which Julian Bailey has pursued his career has enabled him to ride out innumerable financial crises as well as serious injuries sustained when a huge crash at Snetterton in 1980 left him with multiple fractures of his arm and leg. By the end of 1981 he was back in business and quicker than ever. Racing in FF1600 in 1982, Julian was involved in a season-long battle with Mauricio Gugelmin which saw him lose out in the RAC championship but gain some recompense by winning the prestigious Formula Ford Festival at Brands Hatch.

Julian's career then got bogged down with a number of seasons spent scratching around in less than competitive cars – notably in F3. But he plugged away waiting for the break which finally came his way with an end-of-season deal to race a Lola in Formula 3000. Bailey took to the category and, with backing from Cavendish Finance, embarked on a full F3000 season in 1987, with a superb win at Brands Hatch, his favourite circuit, providing the highlight. The credibility which this win brought him led to a seat at Tyrrell for 1988, but as luck would have it the 017 car fielded by the team that year was a poor one and his season was a complete wash-out.

After some excellent drives for the Nissan sports car team (including a third place at Donington in 1989), Julian scraped up enough cash to buy a ride with Lotus at the start of the 1991 season but, despite picking up a sixth place at Imola, he was dropped in favour of Johnny Herbert. Accepting that Formula 1 would for ever be out of his reach, he concentrated on forging a career in the British touring car championship, enjoying the chance to race a works Toyota in 1993 alongside Will Hoy.

MAURO BALDI

This Italian driver began racing in 1975 with a Renault 5, winning the Italian and European one-make championships and earning an F3 Ralt into the bargain. After finding his feet in 1978, Baldi was soon making his mark, finishing fourth in the 1979 European championship and third in the Italian series.

Victory in the Monaco F3 race in 1980 by the huge margin of 47 seconds was the platform from which Mauro began his domination of the formula. Armed with a March for the 1981 season, he trounced the opposition, recording eight wins and four second places in the 15-race European series.

By-passing Formula 2, he secured a drive with Arrows for 1982 and did well enough in a difficult car, but when the opportunity arose to rejoin his former boss Paolo Pavanello in the reconstructed Alfa Romeo team Mauro switched camps. However, the year disintegrated after political frictions had prompted the mid-season departure of designer Gérard Ducarouge. Unable to continue with the team for 1984 as a result of sponsor Benetton's preference for Patrese and Cheever, Mauro was left with no alternative but to race for the underfinanced Spirit outfit.

Meanwhile Baldi had taken the opportunity to race sports cars for Martini Lancia, winning at Spa in 1985, and he quickly became one of protoype racing's most successful exponents, forging his reputation with privateer Porsches, before becoming a key member of the Sauber-Mercedes and Peugeot factory teams.

BALDI, Mauro (I) b 31/1/1954

1982

	Race	Circuit	No	Entrant	Car/Engine	Comment
dnq	SOUTH AFRICAN GP	Kyalami	30	Arrows Racing Team	3.0 Arrows A4-Cosworth V8	
10*	BRAZILIAN GP	Rio	30	Arrows Racing Team	3.0 Arrows A4-Cosworth V8	* 1st & 2nd dsq/hit by de Angelis-6 laps
dnq	US GP WEST	Long Beach	30	Arrows Racing Team	3.0 Arrows A4-Cosworth V8	
nc	BELGIAN GP	Zolder	30	Arrows Racing Team	3.0 Arrows A4-Cosworth V8	long pit stop/19 laps behind
dnq	MONACO GP	Monte Carlo	30	Arrows Racing Team	3.0 Arrows A4-Cosworth V8	
ret	US GP (DETROIT)	Detroit	30	Arrows Racing Team	3.0 Arrows A4-Cosworth V8	hit Boesel
8	CANADIAN GP	Montreal	30	Arrows Racing Team	3.0 Arrows A4-Cosworth V8	2 laps behind
6	DUTCH GP	Zandvoort	30	Arrows Racing Team	3.0 Arrows A4-Cosworth V8	1 lap behind
9	BRITISH GP	Brands Hatch	30	Arrows Racing Team	3.0 Arrows A4-Cosworth V8	2 laps behind
ret	FRENCH GP	Paul Ricard	30	Arrows Racing Team	3.0 Arrows A4-Cosworth V8	accident with Mass
ret	GERMAN GP	Hockenheim	30	Arrows Racing Team	3.0 Arrows A4-Cosworth V8	misfire
6	AUSTRIAN GP	Österreichring	30	Arrows Racing Team	3.0 Arrows A4-Cosworth V8	1 lap behind
dnq	SWISS GP	Dijon	30	Arrows Racing Team	3.0 Arrows A4-Cosworth V8	
12	ITALIAN GP	Monza	30	Arrows Racing Team	3.0 Arrows A5-Cosworth V8	3 laps behind
11	CAESARS PALACE GP	Las Vegas	30	Arrows Racing Team	3.0 Arrows A4-Cosworth V8	3 laps behind

1983

	Race	Circuit	No	Entrant	Car/Engine	Comment
ret	BRAZILIAN GP	Rio	23	Marlboro Team Alfa Romeo	1.5 t/c Alfa Romeo 183T V8	collision damage
ret	US GP WEST	Long Beach	23	Marlboro Team Alfa Romeo	1.5 t/c Alfa Romeo 183T V8	accident
ret	FRENCH GP	Paul Ricard	23	Marlboro Team Alfa Romeo	1.5 t/c Alfa Romeo 183T V8	accident with Winkelhock
10/ret	SAN MARINO	Imola	23	Marlboro Team Alfa Romeo	1.5 t/c Alfa Romeo 183T V8	engine
6	MONACO GP	Monte Carlo	23	Marlboro Team Alfa Romeo	1.5 t/c Alfa Romeo 183T V8	2 laps behind
ret	BELGIAN GP	Spa	23	Marlboro Team Alfa Romeo	1.5 t/c Alfa Romeo 183T V8	throttle linkage
12	US GP (DETROIT)	Detroit	23	Marlboro Team Alfa Romeo	1.5 t/c Alfa Romeo 183T V8	4 laps behind
10*	CANADIAN GP	Montreal	23	Marlboro Team Alfa Romeo	1.5 t/c Alfa Romeo 183T V8	* 9th place car dsq/3 laps behind
7	BRITISH GP	Silverstone	23	Marlboro Team Alfa Romeo	1.5 t/c Alfa Romeo 183T V8	1 lap behind
ret	GERMAN GP	Hockenheim	23	Marlboro Team Alfa Romeo	1.5 t/c Alfa Romeo 183T V8	engine
ret	AUSTRIAN GP	Österreichring	23	Marlboro Team Alfa Romeo	1.5 t/c Alfa Romeo 183T V8	engine
5	DUTCH GP	Zandvoort	23	Marlboro Team Alfa Romeo	1.5 t/c Alfa Romeo 183T V8	
ret	ITALIAN GP	Monza	23	Marlboro Team Alfa Romeo	1.5 t/c Alfa Romeo 183T V8	turbo
ret	EUROPEAN GP	Brands Hatch	23	Marlboro Team Alfa Romeo	1.5 t/c Alfa Romeo 183T V8	clutch
ret	SOUTH AFRICAN GP	Kyalami	23	Marlboro Team Alfa Romeo	1.5 t/c Alfa Romeo 183T V8	engine

1984

	Race	Circuit	No	Entrant	Car/Engine	Comment
ret	BRAZILIAN GP	Rio	21	Spirit Racing	1.5 t/c Spirit 101-Hart 4	distributor
8	SOUTH AFRICAN GP	Kyalami	21	Spirit Racing	1.5 t/c Spirit 101-Hart 4	tyre vibration/4 laps behind
ret	BELGIAN GP	Zolder	21	Spirit Racing	1.5 t/c Spirit 101-Hart 4	suspension
8*	SAN MARINO GP	Imola	21	Spirit Racing	1.5 t/c Spirit 101-Hart 4	* 5th place car dsq/2 laps behind
ret	FRENCH GP	Dijon	21	Spirit Racing	1.5 t/c Spirit 101-Hart 4	engine
dnq	MONACO GP	Monte Carlo	21	Spirit Racing	1.5 t/c Spirit 101-Hart 4	
8	EUROPEAN GP	Nürburgring	21	Spirit Racing	1.5 t/c Spirit 101-Hart 4	2 laps behind
15	PORTUGUESE GP	Estoril	21	Spirit Racing	1.5 t/c Spirit 101-Hart 4	4 laps behind

1985

	Race	Circuit	No	Entrant	Car/Engine	Comment
ret	BRAZILIAN GP	Rio	21	Spirit Enterprises Ltd	1.5 t/c Spirit 101D-Hart 4	turbo/misfire
ret	PORTUGUESE GP	Estoril	21	Spirit Enterprises Ltd	1.5 t/c Spirit 101D-Hart 4	spun off
ret	SAN MARINO GP	Imola	21	Spirit Enterprises Ltd	1.5 t/c Spirit 101D-Hart 4	electrics

GP Starts: 36   GP Wins: 0   Pole positions: 0   Fastest laps: 0   Points: 5

BALSA, Marcel (F) 1/1/1909

1952

	Race	Circuit	No	Entrant	Car/Engine	Comment
ret	GERMAN GP	Nürburgring	110	Marcel Balsa	2.0 BMW Special 6	

GP Starts: 1   GP Wins: 0   Pole positions: 0   Fastest laps: 0   Points: 0

LORENZO BANDINI

With such a name, he just had to be an Italian racing driver, though as a personality he didn't fit the stereotype, being calm and possessed of an even temperament and a pleasant disposition. Bandini worked as a garage mechanic for a Signor Freedi, who was later to become his father-in-law, before setting up on his own in Milan. Dreaming of nothing but racing, he worked assiduously, until beginning his racing career tentatively with Fiats and later a Lancia Appia Zagato, in which he won his class in the 1958 Mille Miglia Rally. Later that year he bought a Volpini Formula Junior and finished third on aggregate on his debut in the Sicilian Gold Cup at Syracuse.

Bandini began the 1959 season with his own machine, but was quickly taken into the works Stanguellini team where he was soon a leading runner, winning the Liberty GP in Cuba at the beginning of 1960, and later taking the Pescara GP ahead of Denny Hulme. Already yearning for more powerful machinery, Lorenzo was fortunate to come under the wing of Signor Mimmo Dei, of the Scuderia Centro Sud, who put him into his Formula 1 Cooper for 1961. An early-season third place at the Pau GP was a splendid start, but Bandini was soon in the shadow of Giancarlo Baghetti, who had been given the FISA-backed Ferrari in preference to Lorenzo, and was about to enjoy his brief spell of fame. Much was made in the press of the rivalry between the two young Italians, but in fact there was no friction, as they were good friends. Bandini raced on in the Cooper without much success, but took a superb win in the sports car Pescara GP before the season was out.

In 1962 Bandini was invited to join the Ferrari team at last, but it was a season of disarray at Maranello, with drivers chosen for races on a seemingly *ad hoc* basis. Nevertheless he finished a cool third at the Monaco GP, and in non-title races he took fifth place at Pau and second at Naples and won the Mediterranean GP at Enna. Amazingly he was dropped from the F1 team in favour of Mairesse for 1963, so it was back to Centro Sud to race their newly acquired BRM, while continuing in the Ferrari sports car squad. After a second place in the Targa Florio, Bandini then shared a Ferrari 250P with Scarfiotti to win Le Mans and later took second in the Reims 12 Hours with Surtees. This success stood him in good stead, and after Mairesse was injured Lorenzo returned to the fold.

Largely due to the efforts of Surtees, the team were on their way back, and in 1964 Bandini was the Englishman's number two, accepting his position stoically and scoring his first, and only, Grand Prix victory at the bumpy Zeltweg airfield circuit, when more fancied runners failed. The final 1.5-litre season in 1965 was relatively uneventful and, though Bandini's position in the team remained the same, he was increasingly unhappy with the status quo and relationships with Surtees were becoming a little strained. In sports cars, Ferrari's programme was limited, but Lorenzo won the Targa Florio with Vaccarella. The friction in the team continued into 1966, and Bandini drove the 2.4-litre Dino into second place at Monaco, even though Surtees wanted to race the car. The situation could not last and when Surtees quit Maranello, Bandini suddenly found himself leading the team. A certain win in the French GP was lost when a throttle cable snapped, and Scarfiotti and Parkes took the honours at Monza when he encountered fuel feed problems.

The 1967 season started well with victories in the Daytona 24 Hours and Monza 1000 Km in a Ferrari 330P4 shared with newcomer Chris Amon, and then second place in the Race of Champions behind Gurney's Eagle. The next race in which he competed was his favourite, the Monaco Grand Prix. Qualifying second on the grid, Bandini led in the early stages before dropping behind Denny Hulme's Brabham. Late in the race, however, he made a charge in a bid for victory. On the 82nd lap he clipped the chicane entering the harbour front, rolling the Ferrari, which burst into flames upside down in the middle of the track. The rescue crew were terribly slow to react and the ill-fated driver, dreadfully burnt and injured, lay trapped for what seemed an eternity. Broken and charred, he was eventually dragged from the foam-covered wreck and rushed to hospital. There was no prospect of recovery for poor Bandini and, mercifully perhaps, he passed away after clinging on to life for three days.

BANDINI, Lorenzo (I) b 21/12/1935 – d 10/5/1967

1961

	Race	Circuit	No	Entrant	Car/Engine	Comment
ret	BELGIAN GP	Spa	46	Scuderia Centro Sud	1.5 Cooper T53-Maserati 4	engine
12	BRITISH GP	Aintree	60	Scuderia Centro Sud	1.5 Cooper T53-Maserati 4	4 laps behind
ret	GERMAN GP	Nürburgring	32	Scuderia Centro Sud	1.5 Cooper T53-Maserati 4	engine
8	ITALIAN GP	Monza	62	Scuderia Centro Sud	1.5 Cooper T53-Maserati 4	2 laps behind

1962

	Race	Circuit	No	Entrant	Car/Engine	Comment
3	MONACO GP	Monte Carlo	38	Scuderia Ferrari SpA SEFAC	1.5 Ferrari 156 V6	
ret	GERMAN GP	Nürburgring	4	Scuderia Ferrari SpA SEFAC	1.5 Ferrari 156 V6	accident
8	ITALIAN GP	Monza	62	Scuderia Ferrari SpA SEFAC	1.5 Ferrari 156 V6	2 laps behind

1963

	Race	Circuit	No	Entrant	Car/Engine	Comment
10	FRENCH GP	Reims	46	Scuderia Centro Sud	1.5 BRM P57 V8	8 laps behind
5	BRITISH GP	Silverstone	3	Scuderia Centro Sud	1.5 BRM P57 V8	1 lap behind
ret	GERMAN GP	Nürburgring	15	Scuderia Centro Sud	1.5 BRM P57 V8	collision with Ireland
ret	ITALIAN GP	Monza	2	Scuderia Ferrari SpA SEFAC	1.5 Ferrari 156 V6	gearbox
5	US GP	Watkins Glen	24	Scuderia Ferrari SpA SEFAC	1.5 Ferrari 156 V6	4 laps behind
ret	MEXICAN GP	Mexico City	24	Scuderia Ferrari SpA SEFAC	1.5 Ferrari 156 V6	ignition
5	SOUTH AFRICAN GP	East London	4	Scuderia Ferrari SpA SEFAC	1.5 Ferrari 156 V6	1 lap behind

1964

	Race	Circuit	No	Entrant	Car/Engine	Comment
ret	MONACO GP	Monte Carlo	20	Scuderia Ferrari SpA SEFAC	1.5 Ferrari 156 V6	gearbox
ret	DUTCH GP	Zandvoort	4	Scuderia Ferrari SpA SEFAC	1.5 Ferrari 158 V8	fuel injection pump
dns	"	"	4	Scuderia Ferrari SpA SEFAC	1.5 Ferrari 156 V6	practice only
ret	BELGIAN GP	Spa	11	Scuderia Ferrari SpA SEFAC	1.5 Ferrari 158 V8	no oil
9	FRENCH GP	Rouen	26	Scuderia Ferrari SpA SEFAC	1.5 Ferrari 158 V8	2 laps behind
5	BRITISH GP	Brands Hatch	8	Scuderia Ferrari SpA SEFAC	1.5 Ferrari 156 V6	2 laps behind
3	GERMAN GP	Nürburgring	8	Scuderia Ferrari SpA SEFAC	1.5 Ferrari 156 V6	
1	AUSTRIAN GP	Zeltweg	8	Scuderia Ferrari SpA SEFAC	1.5 Ferrari 156 V6	
3	ITALIAN GP	Monza	4	Scuderia Ferrari SpA SEFAC	1.5 Ferrari 158 V8	1 lap behind
dns	"	"	4	Scuderia Ferrari SpA SEFAC	1.5 Ferrari 156 V6	practice only
dns	"	"	4	Scuderia Ferrari Spa SEFAC	1.5 Ferrari 1512 F12	practice only
ret	US GP	Watkins Glen	8	North American Racing Team	1.5 Ferrari 1512 F12	engine
dns	"	"	8	North American Racing Team	1.5 Ferrari 156 V6	practice only
3	MEXICAN GP	Mexico City	8	North American Racing Team	1.5 Ferrari 1512 F12	

1965

	Race	Circuit	No	Entrant	Car/Engine	Comment
15/ret	SOUTH AFRICAN GP	East London	2	Scuderia Ferrari SpA SEFAC	1.5 Ferrari 1512 F12	ignition/18 laps behind
2	MONACO GP	Monte Carlo	17	Scuderia Ferrari SpA SEFAC	1.5 Ferrari 1512 F12	
9	BELGIAN GP	Spa	2	Scuderia Ferrari SpA SEFAC	1.5 Ferrari 1512 F12	2 laps behind
8/ret	FRENCH GP	Clermont Ferrand	4	Scuderia Ferrari SpA SEFAC	1.5 Ferrari 1512 F12	spun off/3 laps behind
ret	BRITISH GP	Silverstone	2	Scuderia Ferrari SpA SEFAC	1.5 Ferrari 158 V8	piston
9	DUTCH GP	Zandvoort	4	Scuderia Ferrari SpA SEFAC	1.5 Ferrari 158 V8	1 lap behind
6	GERMAN GP	Nürburgring	8	Scuderia Ferrari SpA SEFAC	1.5 Ferrari 158 V8	
4	ITALIAN GP	Monza	4	Scuderia Ferrari SpA SEFAC	1.5 Ferrari 1512 F12	
4	US GP	Watkins Glen	2	Scuderia Ferrari SpA SEFAC	1.5 Ferrari 1512 F12	1 lap behind
8	MEXICAN GP	Mexico City	2	Scuderia Ferrari SpA SEFAC	1.5 Ferrari 1512 F12	3 laps behind

1966

	Race	Circuit	No	Entrant	Car/Engine	Comment
2	MONACO GP	Monte Carlo	16	Scuderia Ferrari SpA SEFAC	2.4 Ferrari Dino 246 V6	FL
dns	"	" "	16T	Scuderia Ferrari SpA SEFAC	3.0 Ferrari 312/66 V12	practice only
3	BELGIAN GP	Spa	7	Scuderia Ferrari SpA SEFAC	2.4 Ferrari Dino 246 V6	1 lap behind
nc	FRENCH GP	Reims	20	Scuderia Ferrari SpA SEFAC	3.0 Ferrari 312/66 V12	broken-throttle cable/Pole/FL/-11 laps
6	DUTCH GP	Zandvoort	2	Scuderia Ferrari SpA SEFAC	3.0 Ferrari 312/66 V12	spin/3 laps behind
6	GERMAN GP	Nürburgring	9	Scuderia Ferrari SpA SEFAC	3.0 Ferrari 312/66 V12	
ret	ITALIAN GP	Monza	2	Scuderia Ferrari SpA SEFAC	3.0 Ferrari 312/66 V12	ignition
ret	US GP	Watkins Glen	9	Scuderia Ferrari SpA SEFAC	3.0 Ferrari 312/66 V12	engine

1967

	Race	Circuit	No	Entrant	Car/Engine	Comment
ret	MONACO GP	Monte Carlo	18	Scuderia Ferrari SpA SEFAC	3.0 Ferrari 312/67 V12	fatal accident-hit chicane exit

GP Starts: 42   GP Wins: 1   Pole positions: 1   Fastest laps: 2   Points: 58

BARBAZZA, Fabrizio (I) b 4/4/1963

	Race	Circuit	No	Entrant	Car/Engine	Comment
	1991					
dnq	SAN MARINO GP	Imola	18	Automobiles Gonfaronaise Sportive	3.5 AGS JH25-Cosworth DFR V8	
dnq	MONACO GP	Monaco	18	Automobiles Gonfaronaise Sportive	3.5 AGS JH25-Cosworth DFR V8	
dnq	CANADIAN GP	Montreal	18	Automobiles Gonfaronaise Sportive	3.5 AGS JH25-Cosworth DFR V8	
dnq	MEXICAN GP	Mexico City	18	Automobiles Gonfaronaise Sportive	3.5 AGS JH25-Cosworth DFR V8	
dnq	FRENCH GP	Magny Cours	18	Automobiles Gonfaronaise Sportive	3.5 AGS JH25B-Cosworth DFR V8	
dnq	BRITISH GP	Silverstone	18	Automobiles Gonfaronaise Sportive	3.5 AGS JH25B-Cosworth DFR V8	
dnpq	GERMAN GP	Hockenheim	18	Automobiles Gonfaronaise Sportive	3.5 AGS JH25B-Cosworth DFR V8	
dnpq	HUNGARIAN GP	Hungaroring	18	Automobiles Gonfaronaise Sportive	3.5 AGS JH25B-Cosworth DFR V8	
dnpq	BELGIAN GP	Spa	18	Automobiles Gonfaronaise Sportive	3.5 AGS JH25B-Cosworth DFR V8	
dnpq	ITALIAN GP	Monza	18	Automobiles Gonfaronaise Sportive	3.5 AGS JH25B-Cosworth DFR V8	
dnpq	PORTUGUESE GP	Estoril	18	Automobiles Gonfaronaise Sportive	3.5 AGS JH27-Cosworth DFR V8	
dnpq	SPANISH GP	Barcelona	18	Automobiles Gonfaronaise Sportive	3.5 AGS JH27-Cosworth DFR V8	
	1993					
ret	SOUTH AFRICAN GP	Kyalami	24	Minardi Team	3.5 Minardi M193-Ford HB V8	accident-hit by Suzuki
ret	BRAZILIAN GP	Interlagos	24	Minardi Team	3.5 Minardi M193-Ford HB V8	collision, Brundle on lap 1

6	EUROPEAN GP	Donington	24	Minardi Team		3.5 Minardi M193-Ford HB V8	2 laps behind
6	SAN MARINO GP	Imola	24	Minardi Team		3.5 Minardi M193-Ford HB V8	2 laps behind
ret	SPANISH GP	Barcelona	24	Minardi Team		3.5 Minardi M193-Ford HB V8	spun off
11	MONACO GP	Monte Carlo	24	Minardi Team		3.5 Minardi M193-Ford HB V8	steering after collision/3 laps behind
ret	CANADIAN GP	Montreal	24	Minardi Team		3.5 Minardi M193-Ford HB V8	gearbox
ret	FRENCH GP	Magny Cours	24	Minardi Team		3.5 Minardi M193-Ford HB V8	gearbox

GP Starts: 8   GP Wins: 0   Pole positions: 0   Fastest laps: 0   Points: 2

BARBER, John (GB)

1953

	Race	Circuit	No	Entrant	Car/Engine	Comment
8	ARGENTINE GP	Buenos Aires	22	Cooper Car Co	2.0 Cooper T23-Bristol 6	7 laps behind

GP Starts: 1   GP Wins: 0   Pole positions: 0   Fastest laps: 0   Points: 0

BARBER, Skip (USA) b 16/11/1936

1971

	Race	Circuit	No	Entrant	Car/Engine	Comment
dnq	MONACO GP	Monte Carlo	28	Gene Mason Racing	3.0 March 711-Cosworth V8	
nc	DUTCH GP	Zandvoort	22	Gene Mason Racing	3.0 March 711-Cosworth V8	10 laps behind
ret	CANADIAN GP	Mosport Park	33	Gene Mason Racing	3.0 March 711-Cosworth V8	oil pressure
nc	US GP	Watkins Glen	33	Gene Mason Racing	3.0 March 711-Cosworth V8	pit stop-gearbox/7 laps behind

1972

	Race	Circuit	No	Entrant	Car/Engine	Comment
nc	CANADIAN GP	Mosport Park	33	Gene Mason Racing	3.0 March 711-Cosworth V8	pit stops-dirt in throttle/56 laps behind
16	US GP	Watkins Glen	33	Gene Mason Racing	3.0 March 711-Cosworth V8	2 laps behind

GP Starts: 5   GP Wins: 0   Pole positions: 0   Fastest laps: 0   Points: 0

FABRIZIO BARBAZZA

Barbazza earned a reputation as a wild but fast driver in Italian F3, finishing third in the series with a Dallara-Alfa in 1985. Frustrated at the lack of opportunities in Europe, he then took the unusual step of moving across the Atlantic to contest the newly created American Racing Series, which he won. More succces was to follow in 1987. Filling a vacancy in Frank Arciero's IndyCar team, Fabrizio took a splendid third place at Indianapolis, earning the accolade of top rookie, and finished twelfth in the final points standings to claim the PPG Rookie of the Year Award.

Still intent on breaking into Grand Prix racing, Barbazza returned to Europe and scraped around in F3000 before finally securing an F1 drive in 1991, only to endure a dismal time fruitlessly attempting to qualify the AGS. Finding the finance to buy a seat in the Minardi team for 1993, Fabrizio confirmed that he has ability, gaining two valuable sixth places for the team before making way for Pierluigi Martini at mid-season.

SKIP BARBER

A late starter in racing, having competed in Formula Ford and FB in 1969-70 and become national champion, Barber was still relatively inexperienced when he headed to Europe in 1971 to buy a March 711 (to replace his 701, which had been written off in an early-season crash) which he intended to race in the US L & M F5000 series.

Before shipping the new car back, however, he tackled a few Grands Prix – 'keeping out of the way' – as well as the non-championship Jochen Rindt Memorial Trophy at Hockenheim, in which he managed a worthy sixth place.

Back in America, Barber enjoyed some success in Formula A with the car in 1972 before switching to GT machinery. Since his retirement from racing he has built up one of the world's leading racing schools and, in conjunction with Saab, instigated the very successful single-seater 'Pro Series'.

BARRICHELLO, Rubens (BR) b 23/5/1972

1993

	Race	Circuit	No	Entrant	Car/Engine	Comment
ret	SOUTH AFRICAN GP	Kyalami	14	Sasol Jordan	3.5 Jordan 193-Hart V10	gearbox
ret	BRAZILIAN GP	Interlagos	14	Sasol Jordan	3.5 Jordan 193-Hart V10	gearbox hydraulics
10/ret	EUROPEAN GP	Donington	14	Sasol Jordan	3.5 Jordan 193-Hart V10	fuel pressure/5 laps behind
ret	SAN MARINO GP	Imola	14	Sasol Jordan	3.5 Jordan 193-Hart V10	spun off
12	SPANISH GP	Barcelona	14	Sasol Jordan	3.5 Jordan 193-Hart V10	p stop-front wing flap/3 laps behind
9	MONACO GP	Monte Carlo	14	Sasol Jordan	3.5 Jordan 193-Hart V10	2 laps behind
ret	CANADIAN GP	Montreal	14	Sasol Jordan	3.5 Jordan 193-Hart V10	electrical
7	FRENCH GP	Magny Cours	14	Sasol Jordan	3.5 Jordan 193-Hart V10	fading brakes/1 lap behind
10	BRITISH GP	Silverstone	14	Sasol Jordan	3.5 Jordan 193-Hart V10	1 lap behind
ret	GERMAN GP	Hockenheim	14	Sasol Jordan	3.5 Jordan 193-Hart V10	wheel bearing failure
ret	HUNGARIAN GP	Hungaroring	14	Sasol Jordan	3.5 Jordan 193-Hart V10	collision-Suzuki lap 1/lost wheel
ret	BELGIAN GP	Spa	14	Sasol Jordan	3.5 Jordan 193-Hart V10	wheel bearing failure
ret	ITALIAN GP	Monza	14	Sasol Jordan	3.5 Jordan 193-Hart V10	collision-Lehto on lap 1
13	PORTUGUESE GP	Estoril	14	Sasol Jordan	3.5 Jordan 193-Hart V10	p stop-puncture/3 laps behind
5	JAPANESE GP	Suzuka	14	Sasol Jordan	3.5 Jordan 193-Hart V10	
11	AUSTRALIAN GP	Adelaide	14	Sasol Jordan	3.5 Jordan 193-Hart V10	3 laps behind

GP Starts: 16   GP Wins: 0   Pole positions: 0   Fastest laps: 0   Points: 2

BARILLA, Paolo (I) b 20/4/1961

1989

	Race	Circuit	No	Entrant	Car/Engine	Comment
ret	JAPANESE GP	Suzuka	23	Minardi SpA	3.5 Minardi M189-Cosworth V8	clutch at start

1990

ret	US GP (PHOENIX)	Phoenix	24	SCM Minardi Team	3.5 Minardi M189-Cosworth V8	driver cramp
ret	BRAZILIAN GP	Interlagos	24	SCM Minardi Team	3.5 Minardi M189-Cosworth V8	engine
11	SAN MARINO GP	Imola	24	SCM Minardi Team	3.5 Minardi M190-Cosworth V8	spin/2 laps behind
dns	"	"	24	SCM Minardi Team	3.5 Minardi M190-Cosworth V8	practice only
ret	MONACO GP	Monte Carlo	24	SCM Minardi Team	3.5 Minardi M190-Cosworth V8	gearbox
dnq	CANADIAN GP	Montreal	24	SCM Minardi Team	3.5 Minardi M190-Cosworth V8	
14	MEXICAN GP	Mexico City	24	SCM Minardi Team	3.5 Minardi M190-Cosworth V8	2 laps behind
dnq	FRENCH GP	Paul Ricard	24	SCM Minardi Team	3.5 Minardi M190-Cosworth V8	
12	BRITISH GP	Silverstone	24	SCM Minardi Team	3.5 Minardi M190-Cosworth V8	2 laps behind
dnq	GERMAN GP	Hockenheim	24	SCM Minardi Team	3.5 Minardi M190-Cosworth V8	
15	HUNGARIAN GP	Hungaroring	24	SCM Minardi Team	3.5 Minardi M190-Cosworth V8	3 laps behind
ret/dns	BELGIAN GP	Spa	24	SCM Minardi Team	3.5 Minardi M190-Cosworth V8	crashed at second aborted start
dnq	ITALIAN GP	Monza	24	SCM Minardi Team	3.5 Minardi M190-Cosworth V8	
dnq	PORTUGUESE GP	Estoril	24	SCM Minardi Team	3.5 Minardi M190-Cosworth V8	
dnq	SPANISH GP	Jerez	24	SCM Minardi Team	3.5 Minardi M190-Cosworth V8	

GP Starts: 9   GP Wins: 0   Pole positions: 0   Fastest laps: 0   Points: 0

BARTH, Edgar (D) b 26/11/1917 – d 20/5/1965

1953

	Race	Circuit	No	Entrant	Car/Engine	Comment
ret	GERMAN GP	Nürburgring	35	Rennkollektiv EMW	2.0 EMW 6	exhaust

1957

12	GERMAN GP (F2)	Nürburgring	21	Dr Ing F Porsche KG	1.5 Porsche 550RS F4 sports car	1st in F2 class/1 lap behind

1958

6	GERMAN GP (F2)	Nürburgring	21	Dr Ing F Porsche KG	1.5 Porsche RSK F4	2nd in F2 class/sports car

1960

7	ITALIAN GP (F2)	Monza	24	Dr Ing F Porsche KG	1.5 Porsche 718 RSK F4	3 laps behind

1964

ret	GERMAN GP	Nürburgring	12	Rob Walker Racing Team	1.5 Cooper T66-Climax V8	clutch

GP Starts: 4   GP Wins: 0   Pole positions: 0   Fastest laps: 0   Points: 0

BASSI, Giorgio (I) b 20/1/1934

1965

	Race	Circuit	No	Entrant	Car/Engine	Comment
ret	ITALIAN GP	Monza	52	Scuderia Centro Sud	1.5 BRM P57 V8	engine

GP Starts: 1   GP Wins: 0   Pole positions: 0   Fastest laps: 0   Points: 0

BAUER, Erwin (D) b 17/7/1912 – d 2/6/1958 (killed in Nürburgring 1000 Km, having missed the chequered flag and raced on)

1953

	Race	Circuit	No	Entrant	Car/Engine	Comment
ret	GERMAN GP	Nürburgring	32	Erwin Bauer	2.0 Veritas RS 6	

GP Starts: 1   GP Wins: 0   Pole positions: 0   Fastest laps: 0   Points: 0

RUBENS BARRICHELLO

Five times the Brazilian karting champion, Barrichello arrived in Europe as a shy 17-year-old at the beginning of 1990, having contested only 11 Formula Ford races in his native country.

He came to compete in the GM Lotus Euroseries – the first rung on the ladder to Formula 1 – with backing from Arisco (a Brazilian food conglomerate), which intended to take him all the way to the top. In the comfortable environment provided by Scuderia Salvati Draco, Rubens quickly became the season's front-runner, winning five rounds and the title.

This triumph earned him a seat in Dick Bennetts' West Surrey Racing F3 team for 1991. It was success again as Rubens came through late in the season to win the title when his main rival, David Coulthard, stumbled.

Already the subject of interest from Formula 1 teams, Barrichello took the next step up into F3000 and, despite the political and financial pressures that beset the Il Barone Rampante team, Rubens was a consistent finisher, achieving third place in the final standings. His seemingly inexorable climb to Grand Prix racing was complete when that great talent-spotter Eddie Jordan placed his faith in the 21-year-old to help wipe away the memories of a disastrous 1992 season.

A stunning drive in the rain-soaked European GP at Donington, which saw him as high as second place until fuel-pressure problems ended his race, no doubt reflected the benefit of traction control. However, he comfortably outpaced his more vaunted (if demotivated) team-mates Capelli and Boutsen, before the uncertainty regarding Rubens' real ability was increased by a succession of partners towards the end of the year. Certainly the arrival of Eddie Irvine at Suzuka helped lift the team – and Barrichello – to a new level of performance, and it will be interesting to see how this young man progresses in 1994, which will be a crucial term in his Grand Prix education.

PAOLO BARILLA

The wealthy scion of a family owning a famous Italian pasta company, Barilla first came to international prominence in 1983 with a privately entered Lancia LC2. After some excellent performances he was invited to join the works team the following season, taking second place at Kyalami, third at Monza and the Nürburgring and fourth at Silverstone.

Switching to the Joest Porsche team, he drove immaculately to win the 1985 Le Mans 24 Hours (with Ludwig and Winter) and the 1986 Mount Fuji 1000 Km (with Ghinzani). However, Paolo still yearned for success in single-seaters and spent two largely unsuccessful seasons in F3000 switching from team to team in search of a winning formula.

His friendship with Giancarlo Minardi provided him with the long-sought opportunity to race in Formula 1 but his performances in the Minardi were disappointing and he was replaced by Gianni Morbidelli before the 1990 season was out.

EDGAR BARTH

A distinguished pre-war motor cycle racer, Barth drove the EMW sports cars between 1953 and 1956 and, by winning his class in the 1956 Coupe de Paris at Montlhéry, he attracted the attention of the Porsche team. After a successful class-winning debut for Porsche at the 1957 Nürburgring 1000 Km, Edgar and his family defected from East Germany. He then became a mainstay of the company's Formula 2, sports and hill-climb programme. He won the Targa Florio outright in 1959 (with Seidel) and was European mountain champion in 1959, 1963 and 1964, by which time he was already suffering from the cancer to which he succumbed, at the age of 48, in May 1965.

His son, Jurgen, also represented the Porsche factory team, winning the Le Mans 24-hour race in 1977.

ELIE BAYOL

Bayol built a reputation as a very quick driver in René Bonnet's 750 cc Panhard during the 1951 season. For 1952 he ordered one of the latest OSCA F2 cars but, as this was not delivered until August, he was forced to make do in the meantime with a stripped sports model which he drove to good effect, finishing fourth at Pau, fifth at Marseilles and sixth at Modena. He then raced the F2 car during the 1953 season, the highlight of which was an aggregate win in the Circuit du Lac at Aix-les-Bains.

Accepting an invitation to join the Gordini team for 1954, Bayol made a fine debut, taking fifth place in the Argentine GP, and followed this with fourth at Pau and fifth at Bordeaux, where he blotted his copybook by ignoring repeated signals to pit and hand his car over to team leader Jean Behra. Gordini sacked him, but he was later forgiven and rejoined the team for 1955, only for his season to be curtailed after he sustained serious head injuries when he crashed the latest 3-litre Gordini in practice at Le Mans. Thankfully he made a full recovery and briefly reappeared on the circuits the following year, finishing sixth (with Pilette) at Monaco and in the Reims 12 Hours sports car race (with de Silva Ramos).

CAREL DE BEAUFORT

The last truly amateur driver to compete in Grand Prix racing on a regular basis, de Beaufort metamorphosed from the roly-poly dilettante of his early racing career into a much more serious and competent performer– without losing his perenially sunny disposition – to earn the respect of his peers.

De Beaufort began his racing career with production Porsche spyders in 1956 and was soon itching to pit himself against the stars of the day, racing his Porsche RSK sports car in the Formula 2 category of the 1957 German Grand Prix. He had to content himself, however, with occasional Grand Prix outings until the 1961 season, when he acquired the ex-Moss Rob Walker Porsche 718.

This car, with its four-cylinder engine, then saw extensive service over the next four seasons, the broad-shouldered Count – invariably driving in stockinged feet – battling nobly against more powerful fuel-injected cars. His orange-painted machine was entered in non-championship races the length and breadth of Europe, enjoying its greatest successes in 1963 with second place in both the Syracuse and Rome GPs and third in the Austrian GP at Zeltweg.

De Beaufort plugged away into the 1964 season with the by now veteran Porsche, but in practice for the German Grand Prix he crashed heavily, sustaining injuries from which there was no recovery and dying three days later in hospital in Düsseldorf.

DON BEAUMAN

A popular figure on the national scene, Beauman entered racing in 1950 with 500 cc Coopers before spending the 1953 season with the coveted pre-war TT Riley previously campaigned by his great chum Mike Hawthorn.

Supported by Sir Jeremy Boles, Beauman intensified his racing activities in 1954 with an F2 Connaught, winning Formula Libre events at Oulton Park and Brands Hatch as well as taking a class win in an Aston Martin at Zandvoort.

The 1955 season saw the London hotelier claim third place in the Glover Trophy at Goodwood and compete in the Le Mans 24-hour race in a works Jaguar. This shy and retiring figure, who had hopes of one day moving into Grand Prix racing, lost his life when he crashed his Connaught in the 1955 Leinster Trophy sports car race in Wicklow, Northern Ireland.

BAYOL, Elie (F) b 28/2/1914

1952

	Race	Circuit	No	Entrant	Car/Engine	Entrant
ret	ITALIAN GP	Monza	34	Elie Bayol	2.0 OSCA 20 6	gearbox

1953

ret	FRENCH GP	Reims	34	Elie Bayol	2.0 OSCA 20 6	mechanical
dns	SWISS GP	Berne	22	Elie Bayol	2.0 OSCA 20 6	
ret	ITALIAN GP	Monza	34	OSCA Automobili	2.0 OSCA 20 6	mechanical

1954

5	ARGENTINE GP	Buenos Aires	20	Equipe Gordini	2.5 Gordini Type 16 6	2 laps behind

1955

ret	ARGENTINE GP	Buenos Aires	38	Equipe Gordini	2.5 Gordini Type 16 6	engine
ret	MONACO GP	Monte Carlo	12	Equipe Gordini	2.5 Gordini Type 16 6	rear axle

1956

6*	MONACO GP	Monte Carlo	4	Equipe Gordini	2.5 Gordini Type 32 8	* Pilette took over/12 laps behind

GP Starts: 7   GP Wins: 0   Pole positions: 0   Fastest laps: 0   Points: 2

BEAUFORT, Carel Godin de (NL) b 10/4/1934 – d 3/8/1964

1957

	Race	Circuit	No	Entrant	Car/Engine	Comment
14	GERMAN GP (F2)	Nürburgring	27	Ecurie Maarsbergen	1.5 Porsche 550RS F4 sports car	3rd in F2 class/2 laps behind

1958

11	DUTCH GP	Zandvoort	18	Ecurie Maarsbergen	1.5 Porsche RSK F4 sports car	6 laps behind
ret	GERMAN GP (F2)	Nürburgring	18	Ecurie Maarsbergen	1.5 Porsche RSK F4 sports car	mechanical

1959

10	DUTCH GP	Zandvoort	15	Ecurie Maarsbergen	1.5 Porsche RSK F4 sports car	7 laps behind
9	FRENCH GP	Reims	42	Scuderia Ugolini	2.5 Maserati 250F 6	8th place car dsq/10 laps behind

1960

8	DUTCH GP	Zandvoort	20	Ecurie Maarsbergen	1.5 Cooper T51-Climax 4	F2 car/6 laps behind

1961

14	DUTCH GP	Zandvoort	8	Ecurie Maarsbergen	1.5 Porsche 718 F4	3 laps behind
11	BELGIAN GP	Spa	22	Ecurie Maarsbergen	1.5 Porsche 718 F4	2 laps behind
ret	FRENCH GP	Reims	14	Ecurie Maarsbergen	1.5 Porsche 718 F4	overheating
16	BRITISH GP	Aintree	56	Ecurie Maarsbergen	1.5 Porsche 718 F4	6 laps behind
14	GERMAN GP	Nürburgring	31	Ecurie Maarsbergen	1.5 Porsche 718 F4	1 lap behind
7	ITALIAN GP	Monza	74	Ecurie Maarsbergen	1.5 Porsche 718 F4	2 laps behind

1962

6	DUTCH GP	Zandvoort	14	Ecurie Maarsbergen	1.5 Porsche 718 F4	4 laps behind
dnq	MONACO GP	Monte Carlo	44	Ecurie Maarsbergen	1.5 Porsche 718 F4	
7	BELGIAN GP	Spa	7	Ecurie Maarsbergen	1.5 Porsche 718 F4	2 laps behind
6	FRENCH GP	Rouen	38	Ecurie Maarsbergen	1.5 Porsche 718 F4	3 laps behind
14	BRITISH GP	Aintree	54	Ecurie Maarsbergen	1.5 Porsche 718 F4	6 laps behind
13	GERMAN GP	Nürburgring	18	Ecurie Maarsbergen	1.5 Porsche 718 F4	
10	ITALIAN GP	Monza	32	Ecurie Maarsbergen	1.5 Porsche 718 F4	5 laps behind
ret	US GP	Watkins Glen	12	Ecurie Maarsbergen	1.5 Porsche 718 F4	hit guard rail
11/ret	SOUTH AFRICAN GP	East London	15	Ecurie Maarsbergen	1.5 Porsche 718 F4	fuel pump/12 laps behind

1963

6	BELGIAN GP	Spa	29	Ecurie Maarsbergen	1.5 Porsche 718 F4	2 laps behind
9	DUTCH GP	Zandvoort	32	Ecurie Maarsbergen	1.5 Porsche 718 F4	5 laps behind
10	BRITISH GP	Silverstone	23	Ecurie Maarsbergen	1.5 Porsche 718 F4	6 laps behind
ret	GERMAN GP	Nürburgring	17	Ecurie Maarsbergen	1.5 Porsche 718 F4	lost wheel
dnq	ITALIAN GP	Monza	28	Ecurie Maarsbergen	1.5 Porsche 718 F4	
6	US GP	Watkins Glen	12	Ecurie Maarsbergen	1.5 Porsche 718 F4	11 laps behind
10	MEXICAN GP	Mexico City	12	Ecurie Maarsbergen	1.5 Porsche 718 F4	7 laps behind
10	SOUTH AFRICAN GP	East London	14	Ecurie Maarsbergen	1.5 Porsche 718 F4	6 laps behind

1964

ret	DUTCH GP	Zandvoort	28	Ecurie Maarsbergen	1.5 Porsche 718 F4	valve
dns	GERMAN GP	Nürburgring	29	Ecurie Maarsbergen	1.5 Porsche 718 F4	fatal practice accident

GP Starts: 28   GP Wins: 0   Pole positions: 0   Fastest laps: 0   Points: 4

BEAUMAN, Don (GB) b 26/7/1928 – d 9/7/1955

1954

	Race	Circuit	No	Entrant	Car/Engine	Comment
11	BRITISH GP	Silverstone	25	Sir Jeremy Boles	2.0 Connaught A-Lea Francis 4	6 laps behind

GP Starts: 1   GP Wins: 0   Pole positions: 0   Fastest laps: 0   Points: 0

BECHEM, Gunther (D) b 21/12/1921

1953

	Race	Circuit	No	Entrant	Car/Engine	Comment
ret	GERMAN GP	Nürburgring	41	Gunther Bechem	2.0 AFM U8-BMW 6	

GP Starts: 1   GP Wins: 0   Pole positions: 0   Fastest laps: 0   Points: 0

JEAN BEHRA

How can a driver who never won a World Championship Grand Prix have left such a legacy? Even today those old enough to recall Behra remember the tiger, and those like me, too young to have seen him, are inspired by his mighty reputation and heroic deeds when, in the early fifties, he was cast as the perpetual underdog, battling for Gordini against the mighty works teams.

Behra took up the four-wheeled discipline after an immensely successful motor cycling career in which he was French champion three years running. Switching from his red bike to the French blue of Talbot, he placed sixth in the 1949 Coupe du Salon at Montlhéry, and then took part in the 1950 Monte Carlo Rally driving a Simca with Roger Loyer, another ex-motor cyclist who was later to race Gordinis. A month later Jean won a hill-climb in a borrowed Maserati four-cylinder, bringing him to the attention of Amédée Gordini. A drive in the 1950 Bol d'Or at St Germain convinced *le patron* that here was a nugget that could be polished, and Behra was signed for the 1951 season, beginning his serious motor racing career at the age of 30. He finished third in his first race at Les Sables d'Olonne, and then did the same at Cadours.

It was 1952, however, when Behra became a national hero for his deeds not in championship Grands Prix, though he did superbly well to finish third at Bremgarten and fifth at the Nürburgring – circuits for the skilled and brave – but at the non-championship Reims GP. With Ascari hitherto virtually unbeatable, there was some surprise when Behra shot into an early lead, and this became mild consternation as the light-blue car held off the Ferrari challenge for lap after lap. Then came frenzied hysteria as the T500 suffered an engine failure, leaving Jean to cruise to a historic victory, much to the delight of the delirious French public. There were post-race mutterings about an oversize engine, but the result stood and Behra was for ever taken to the hearts of his countrymen.

He stayed with Gordini to the end of the 1954 season, suffering the heartbreaking succession of maladies that inevitablty struck at the little underfinanced *équipe*, but when resullts were achieved the success was all the sweeter, as at Pau in 1954 when, after more than three hours' racing, Behra defeated the works Ferrari of Trintignant by a mere 60 yards.

After a test in a Maserati at Monza, where Ascari no less could only equal his time, Behra signed for the 1955 season and was immediately rewarded with non-championship wins at Pau and Bordeaux. Although he was out of luck in championship Grands Prix, Behra took sports car wins at Bari, Monza, the Nürburgring and Oporto in the 300TS, before a crash in the Tourist Trophy resulted in his ear being sliced off – Jean subsequently receiving a plastic replacement. For 1956 he was relegated to the number two slot with the arrival of Stirling Moss, but this did not dampen his spirit; he merely raised his game to enjoy his best-ever championship year, even if that much sought first Grand Prix win still eluded him.

In 1957 he was cast as number two to Fangio, but still had his moments, none more memorable than the British GP when he left them all – Fangio, Hawthorn, Moss and Collins – in his wake until his Maserati's clutch failed. Perversely in non-title events his luck would hold, and he won the Pau, Modena and Moroccan GPs for Maserati, and the Caen GP and the International Trophy for BRM.

The following season, driving for BRM in F1 and for Porsche in sports cars and Formula 2, Behra had little luck with the cars from Bourne but won sports car races at AVUS and Rouen and took the Formula 2 honours at AVUS and in the Coupe de Vitesse at Reims. An offer to drive for a Ferrari team now bereft of Hawthorn, Collins and Musso in 1959 was too good to turn down, and the signs were encouraging when he won the Aintree 200 and finished second in the Syracuse GP after a spirited batle with Moss ended in a spin. Two sports car races for the Scuderia yielded a second place at Sebring with Allison and a third in the Nürburgring 1000 Km with Brooks, while he finished second in the Auvergne Trophy at Clermont Ferrand in his own Porsche. In championship Grands Prix, a great drive at Reims ended with engine failure. On pulling his stricken Ferrari into the pits, the frustration was too much for the little Frenchman, who was involved in a scuffle with team manager Tavoni which ended with Behra being shown the door. Running his own Porsches, he was entered for both the Grand Prix and the sports car race at AVUS, but in the rain-soaked support race he was killed instantly when he lost control on the slippery banking, crashed and was flung out of the car into a flag pole.

BEHRA, Jean (F) b 16/2/1921 – d 1/8/1959

1952

	Race	Circuit	No	Entrant	Car/Engine	Comment
3	SWISS GP	Bremgarten	6	Equipe Gordini	2.0 Gordini Type 16 6	1 lap behind
ret	BELGIAN GP	Spa	16	Equipe Gordini	2.0 Gordini Type 16 6	hit Taruffi's spinning car
7	FRENCH GP	Rouen	4	Equipe Gordini	2.0 Gordini Type 16 6	6 laps behind
5	GERMAN GP	Nürburgring	108	Equipe Gordini	2.0 Gordini Type 16 6	1 lap behind
ret	DUTCH GP	Zandvoort	8	Equipe Gordini	2.0 Gordini Type 16 6	magneto drive
ret	ITALIAN GP	Monza	6	Equipe Gordini	2.0 Gordini Type 16 6	valve

1953

	Race	Circuit	No	Entrant	Car/Engine	Comment
6	ARGENTINE GP	Buenos Aires	30	Equipe Gordini	2.0 Gordini Type 16 6	3 laps behind
ret	BELGIAN GP	Spa	16	Equipe Gordini	2.0 Gordini Type 16 6	cylinder head gasket
10	FRENCH GP	Reims	2	Equipe Gordini	2.0 Gordini Type 16 6	5 laps behind
ret	BRITISH GP	Silverstone	30	Equipe Gordini	2.0 Gordini Type 16 6	fuel pump
ret	GERMAN GP	Nürburgring	9	Equipe Gordini	2.0 Gordini Type 16 6	gearbox
ret	SWISS GP	Bremgarten	6	Equipe Gordini	2.0 Gordini Type 16 6	oil pressure

1954

	Race	Circuit	No	Entrant	Car/Engine	Comment
dsq	ARGENTINE GP	Buenos Aires	18	Equipe Gordini	2.5 Gordini Type 16 6	outside assistance after spin
ret	BELGIAN GP	Spa	12	Equipe Gordini	2.5 Gordini Type 16 6	rear suspension
6	FRENCH GP	Reims	24	Equipe Gordini	2.5 Gordini Type 16 6	5 laps behind
ret	BRITISH GP	Silverstone	17	Equipe Gordini	2.5 Gordini Type 16 6	rear suspension/FL(shared)
10	GERMAN GP	Nürburgring	9	Equipe Gordini	2.5 Gordini Type 16 6	2 laps behind
ret	SWISS GP	Bremgarten	10	Equipe Gordini	2.5 Gordini Type 16 6	clutch
ret	ITALIAN GP	Monza	44	Equipe Gordin	2.5 Gordini Type 16 6	engine
ret	SPANISH GP	Pedralbes	46	Equipe Gordin	2.5 Gordini Type 16 6	brakes

1955

	Race	Circuit	No	Entrant	Car/Engine	Comment
ret	ARGENTINE GP	Buenos Aires	16	Officine Alfieri Maserati	2.5 Maserati 250F 6	accident
ret	"	" "	20	Officine Alfieri Maserati	2.5 Maserati 250F 6	mechanical/Mantovani/Musso c/drove
6*	"	" "	28	Officine Alfieri Maserati	2.5 Maserati 250F 6	* took over Schell's car/8 laps behind
3*	MONACO GP	Monte Carlo	34	Officine Alfieri Maserati	2.5 Maserati 250F 6	* Perdisa took over/1 lap behind
ret	"	" "	40	Officine Alfieri Maserati	2.5 Maserati 250F 6	took over Perdisa's car/spun off
ret	BELGIAN GP	Spa	20	Officine Alfieri Maserati	2.5 Maserati 250F 6	spun off
5*	"	"	24	Officine Alfieri Maserati	2.5 Maserati 250F 6	* took over Mieres' car/1 lap behind
6	DUTCH GP	Zandvoort	14	Officine Alfieri Maserati	2.5 Maserati 250F 6	3 laps behind
ret	BRITISH GP	Aintree	2	Officine Alfieri Maserati	2.5 Maserati 250F 6	oil pipe
4	ITALIAN GP	Monza	36	Officine Alfieri Maserati	2.5 Maserati 250F 6	

1956

	Race	Circuit	No	Entrant	Car/Engine	Comment
2	ARGENTINE GP	Buenos Aires	4	Officine Alfieri Maserati	2.5 Maserati 250F 6	
3	MONACO GP	Monte Carlo	30	Officine Alfieri Maserati	2.5 Maserati 250F 6	1 lap behind
7	BELGIAN GP	Spa	32	Officine Alfieri Maserati	2.5 Maserati 250F 6	engine problems/3 laps behind
3	FRENCH GP	Reims	4	Officine Alfieri Maserati	2.5 Maserati 250F 6	
3	BRITISH GP	Silverstone	8	Officine Alfieri Maserati	2.5 Maserati 250F 6	2 laps behind
3	GERMAN GP	Nürburgring	6	Officine Alfieri Maserati	2.5 Maserati 250F 6	
ret	ITALIAN GP	Monza	32	Officine Alfieri Maserati	2.5 Maserati 250F 6	magneto
ret	"	"	46	Officine Alfieri Maserati	2.5 Maserati 250F 6	steering/took over Maglioli's car

1957

	Race	Circuit	No	Entrant	Car/Engine	Comment
2	ARGENTINE GP	Buenos Aires	6	Officine Alfieri Maserati	2.5 Maserati 250F 6	
6	FRENCH GP	Rouen	4	Officine Alfieri Maserati	2.5 Maserati 250F 6	pit stop-engine/8 laps behind
ret	BRITISH GP	Aintree	4	Officine Alfieri Maserati	2.5 Maserati 250F 6	clutch when leading
6	GERMAN GP	Nürburgring	2	Officine Alfieri Maserati	2.5 Maserati 250F 6	
ret	PESCARA GP	Pescara	4	Officine Alfieri Maserati	2.5 Maserati 250F 6	oil pipe
ret	ITALIAN GP	Monza	6	Officine Alfieri Maserati	2.5 Maserati 250F V12	engine-overheating

1958

	Race	Circuit	No	Entrant	Car/Engine	Comment
5	ARGENTINE GP	Buenos Aires	4	Ken Kavanagh	2.5 Maserati 250F 6	2 laps behind
ret	MONACO GP	Monte Carlo	6	Owen Racing Organisation	2.5 BRM P25 4	brakes
3	DUTCH GP	Zandvoort	14	Owen Racing Organisation	2.5 BRM P25 4	
ret	BELGIAN GP	Spa	8	Owen Racing Organisation	2.5 BRM P25 4	oil pressure
ret	FRENCH GP	Reims	14	Owen Racing Organisation	2.5 BRM P25 4	fuel pump
ret	BRITISH GP	Silverstone	19	Owen Racing Organisation	2.5 BRM P25 4	puncture-hit hare
ret	GERMAN GP	Nürburgring	5	Owen Racing Organisation	2.5 BRM P25 4	suspension
4	PORTUGUESE GP	Oporto	8	Owen Racing Organisation	2.5 BRM P25 4	1 lap behind
ret	ITALIAN GP	Monza	8	Owen Racing Organisation	2.5 BRM P25 4	brakes/clutch
ret	MOROCCAN GP	Casablanca	14	Owen Racing Organisation	2.5 BRM P25 4	engine

1959

	Race	Circuit	No	Entrant	Car/Engine	Comment
ret	MONACO GP	Monte Carlo	46	Scuderia Ferrari	2.4 Ferrari Dino 246 V6	engine
5	DUTCH GP	Zandvoort	1	Scuderia Ferrari	2.4 Ferrari Dino 246 V6	1 lap behind
ret	FRENCH GP	Reims	30	Scuderia Ferrari	2.4 Ferrari Dino 246 V6	engine
dns	GERMAN GP	AVUS	12	Jean Behra	1.5 Behra-Porsche F4	fatal accident in support race

GP Starts: 52   GP Wins: 0   Pole positions: 0   Fastest laps: 1   Points: 53.14

BELL, Derek (GB) b 31/10/1941

1968

	Race	Circuit	No	Entrant	Car/Engine	Comment
ret	ITALIAN GP	Monza	7	Scuderia Ferrari SpA SEFAC	3.0 Ferrari 312/68 V12	fuel metering unit
ret	US GP	Watkins Glen	7	Scuderia Ferrari Spa SEFAC	3.0 Ferrari 312/68 V12	engine

1969

	Race	Circuit	No	Entrant	Car/Engine	Comment
ret	BRITISH GP	Silverstone	20	Bruce McLaren Motor Racing	3.0 McLaren M9A-Cosworth V8	rear suspension

1970

ret	BELGIAN GP	Spa	8	Tom Wheatcroft Racing	3.0 Brabham BT26A-Cosworth V8	gear linkage
6	US GP	Watkins Glen	18	Team Surtees	3.0 Surtees TS7-Cosworth V8	1 lap behind

1971

ret	BRITISH GP	Silverstone	25	Team Surtees	3.0 Surtees TS9-Cosworth V8	radius rod
dns	"	"	25	Team Surtees	3.0 Surtees TS7-Cosworth V8	practice only-qualified in this car

1972

dnq	FRENCH GP	Clermont Ferrand	21	Martini Racing Team	3.0 Tecno PA123 F12	chassis cracked
ret	GERMAN GP	Nürburgring	27	Martini Racing Team	3.0 Tecno PA123 F12	engine
dnq	ITALIAN GP	Monza	12	Martini Racing Team	3.0 Tecno PA123 F12	
dns	CANADIAN GP	Mosport Park	31	Martini Racing Team	3.0 Tecno PA123 F12	accident in a.m.warm-up
ret	US GP	Watkins Glen	31	Martini Racing Team	3.0 Tecno PA123 F12	engine

1974

dnq	BRITISH GP	Brands Hatch	39	Bang & Olufsen Team Surtees	3.0 Surtees TS16-Cosworth V8	
11	GERMAN GP	Nürburgring	18	Bang & Olufsen Team Surtees	3.0 Surtees TS16-Cosworth V8	
dnq	AUSTRIAN GP	Österreichring	18	Team Surtees	3.0 Surtees TS16-Cosworth V8	
dnq	ITALIAN GP	Monza	18	Team Surtees	3.0 Surtees TS16-Cosworth V8	
dnq	CANADIAN GP	Mosport Park	18	Team Surtees	3.0 Surtees TS16-Cosworth V8	

GP Starts: 9   GP Wins: 0   Pole positions: 0   Fastest laps: 0   Points: 1

DEREK BELL

It seems incomprehensible that a driver as talented as Derek Bell has only started in nine World Championship Grands Prix. He seemed to be jinxed when it came to Formula 1 – always in the wrong car at the wrong time – and eventually he was passed over in favour of younger talent.

Tentatively entering the sport with a Lotus Seven in 1964, Bell soon moved into Formula 3, initially with a Lotus which was run – with the support of his step-father 'Colonel Hender' – under the Church Farm Racing banner. It proved to be a character-building couple of years for Bell, who realised that he needed the help of wiser and more experienced heads if his career was to progress. He therefore decided to team up with Peter Westbury, which got his career onto a stable footing and brought results as well.

Despite a lack of funds, Bell and his step-father financed a season of Formula 2 in 1968 with a Brabham BT23, which brought him to the attention of Ferrari, who offered him a drive midway through the season. His debut for the Scuderia started badly with Derek in the midst of a huge pile-up in the F2 Monza Lottery GP. Fortunately he was exonerated from blame and looked set to win at Zandvoort until his gearbox failed. Bell tasted Grand Prix racing in the scarlet cars and enjoyed a trip down-under to contest the Tasman championship. Unfortunately for Derek, Ferrari withdrew from the bulk of their programme in mid-1969, leaving him without a drive apart from a one-off outing in the 4WD McLaren.

To the rescue came Tom Wheatcoft, who, after financing a disastrous foray to the Tasman series, sponsored Derek for a full Formula 2 season in 1970, Clay Regazzoni just pipping him to the title. He was also invited by Jacques Swaters to drive a Ferrari 512 in the Spa 1000 Km – a race which was to lay the foundations of his future sports car success – and scored his only World Championship point with an appearance for Team Surtees at Watkins Glen. For 1971 Derek was paired with Jo Siffert in the Gulf/John Wyer Porsche as the team took the sports car championship. Derek stayed with Gulf/Wyer through the next three years, proving his worth as a top-drawer sports car driver while his miscellaneous Grand Prix appearances with Tecno and Surtees proved forgettable.

The 1975 season brought the first of his five Le Mans victories with Jacky Ickx in the Gulf and a successful championship campaign for Alfa Romeo – winning three times with Pescarolo – in the T33. The next few seasons saw a globe-trotting Derek competing in F5000, G8, touring cars, Formula Atlantic, World Championship of Makes events, etc. before joining the Rothmans Porsche factory squad which was to dominate sports car racing in the eighties (Derek taking the drivers' championship – with Hans Stuck – in 1985 and 1986). Now approaching his 30th year in motor sport, Derek shows no sign of hanging up his gloves and helmet, enjoying the cut and thrust of racing in IMSA, where he was still a front-runner in 1993. With a Nissan GTP he took a splendid second place in the Sebring 12 Hours and finished fourth in the GTP championship standings.

STEFAN BELLOF

Thought by many to be the great lost talent of the eighties, Bellof's progress in motor sport was indeed sensational.

Already a karting champion many times in his native Germany, Stefan took the national Formula Ford title at the first attempt in 1980, adding the international German FF title the followiwing year, which saw his winning debut in Formula 3. Aboard a Ralt RT3 entered by ex-racer Bertram Schafer, Stefan won three races from just seven starts to finish third in the championship.

These exploits brought him to the attention of Willy Maurer, who, with help in the form of an engine deal from BMW's Dieter Stappert, made a place available for Stefan in his Formula 2 team for 1982. He won first time out at Silverstone in the rain after a battle with Frank Jelinski, following this up with a dominant win from pole position in round two at Hockenheim. Although he could not sustain this success, as various troubles blunted his challenge, he did record five fastest laps during the season.

He chose to continue in F2 with Maurer in 1983, but the focus of his attention shifted with the offer of a works Porsche drive. Paired with both the experienced Derek Bell and Jochen Mass, Stefan took the car by the scruff of the neck and, with his aggressive point-and-squirt driving style, began to demolish lap records (and on occasion the car itself). Championship wins were chalked up at Silverstone, Mount Fuji and Kyalami. Bellof continued this success with Rothmans Porsche in 1984, winning six rounds (Monza, the Nürburgring, Spa, Imola, Mount Fuji and Sandown Park) and the endurance drivers' championship. He also found time to win the six-round German endurance championship in a Brun-entered Porsche.

Having reportedly turned down an offer from ATS to enter Grands Prix in 1983, Stefan had no qualms about joining the Tyrrell team for the following season. Despite the lack of a turbo engine he was soon extracting the maximum from his car, and could well have won the rain-shortened Monaco GP if the race had been allowed to run longer. However, the punitive treatment meted out to the Tyrrell team after the Dutch GP brought an early end to his Formula 1 season and all his efforts were declared null and void.

His last season dawned with the prospect of waiting until mid-term for Renault turbo power, and a one-race suspension (Brazil) after a dispute with the team. Despite this Bellof still gave his all. It was such commitment, which some would say bordered on reckless-ness, which was to prove his undoing. He had switched to Walter Brun's team for sports car racing and at the Spa 1000 Km he attempted an audacious overtaking manoeuvre on former team-mate Jacky Ickx at Eau Rouge. Their Porsches collided and poor Stefan perished as his car was destroyed against the barriers.

BELLOF, Stefan (D) b 20/11/1957 – d 1/9/1985

1984

	Race	Circuit	No	Entrant	Car/Engine	Comment
ret/dsq	BRAZILIAN GP	Rio	4	Tyrrell Racing Organisation	3.0 Tyrrell 012-Cosworth V8	throttle cable/dsq after Dutch GP
ret/dsq	SOUTH AFRICAN GP	Kyalami	4	Tyrrell Racing Organisation	3.0 Tyrrell 012-Cosworth V8	broken hub/dsq after Dutch GP
6/dsq	BELGIAN GP	Zolder	4	Tyrrell Racing Organisation	3.0 Tyrrell 012-Cosworth V8	6th on road/dsq after Dutch GP
5/dsq	SAN MARINO GP	Imola	4	Tyrrell Racing Organisation	3.0 Tyrrell 012-Cosworth V8	5th on road/dsq after Dutch GP
ret/dsq	FRENCH GP	Dijon	4	Tyrrell Racing Organisation	3.0 Tyrrell 012-Cosworth V8	engine problems/dsq after Dutch GP
3/dsq	MONACO GP	Monte Carlo	4	Tyrrell Racing Organisation	3.0 Tyrrell 012-Cosworth V8	3rd on road/dsq after Dutch GP
ret/dsq	CANADIAN GP	Montreal	4	Tyrrell Racing Organisation	3.0 Tyrrell 012-Cosworth V8	driveshaft/dsq after Dutch GP
ret/dsq	US GP (DETROIT)	Detroit	4	Tyrrell Racing Organisation	3.0 Tyrrell 012-Cosworth V8	accident/dsq after Dutch GP
ret/dsq	US GP (DALLAS)	Dallas	4	Tyrrell Racing Organisation	3.0 Tyrrell 012-Cosworth V8	hit wall/dsq after Dutch GP
11/dsq	BRITISH GP	Brands Hatch	4	Tyrrell Racing Organisation	3.0 Tyrrell 012-Cosworth V8	11th on road/dsq after Dutch GP
dsq	AUSTRIAN GP	Österreichring	4	Tyrrell Racing Organisation	3.0 Tyrrell 012-Cosworth V8	excluded in practice/underweight
9/dsq	DUTCH GP	Zandvoort	4	Tyrrell Racing Organisation	3.0 Tyrrell 012-Cosworth V8	9th on road/dsq after Dutch GP

1985

	Race	Circuit	No	Entrant	Car/Engine	Comment
6	PORTUGUESE GP	Estoril	4	Tyrrell Racing Organisation	3.0 Tyrrell 012-Cosworth V8	2 laps behind
ret	SAN MARINO GP	Imola	4	Tyrrell Racing Organisation	3.0 Tyrrell 012-Cosworth V8	engine
dnq	MONACO GP	Monte Carlo	4	Tyrrell Racing Organisation	3.0 Tyrrell 012-Cosworth V8	
11	CANADIAN GP	Montreal	4	Tyrrell Racing Organisation	3.0 Tyrrell 012-Cosworth V8	2 laps behind
4	US GP (DETROIT)	Detroit	4	Tyrrell Racing Organisation	3.0 Tyrrell 012-Cosworth V8	
13	FRENCH GP	Paul Ricard	4	Tyrrell Racing Organisation	3.0 Tyrrell 012-Cosworth V8	3 laps behind
11	BRITISH GP	Silverstone	4	Tyrrell Racing Organisation	3.0 Tyrrell 012-Cosworth V8	6 laps behind
8	GERMAN GP	Nürburgring	3	Tyrrell Racing Organisation	1.5 t/c Tyrrell 014-Renault V6	1 lap behind
7/ret	AUSTRIAN GP	Österreichring	3	Tyrrell Racing Organisation	1.5 t/c Tyrrell 014-Renault V6	out of fuel/3 laps behind
ret	DUTCH GP	Zandvoort	4	Tyrrell Racing Organisation	1.5 t/c Tyrrell 014-Renault V6	engine

GP Starts: 20   GP Wins: 0   Pole positions: 0   Fastest laps: 0   Points: 4

PAUL BELMONDO

Being the son of one of France's most famous actors has probably done Belmondo no favours, but he has steadily plugged away at his chosen career, shrugging aside the jealous accusations that he is no more than a 'playboy racer'.

Certainly he was something of an enigma during his years in French Formula 3 between 1983 and 1986, the young Belmondo putting in some useful performances without being quite on the pace of each new batch of hot-shots as they leap-frogged over him on their way up.

Eventually, in 1987, he followed more stellar talents into F3000 and scored a fifth place at Pau with a GBDA Lola, but nothing concrete was achieved during the next three seasons save a single sixth place in the Le Mans round in 1990. A disastrous 1991 season with the Apomatox team's Reynard was hardly ideal preparation for his unexpected elevation to the Grand Prix ranks, but he settled into the second March in the first half of 1992 surprisingly well – ironically his best performances for the team were at Hockenheim and the Hungaroring, his last two races before his money ran out. Charged with bringing the car home in one piece at all costs, Paul's sensible approach helped to keep the team afloat financially, and even his greatest detractors would admit that he had done a sound job in difficult circumstances. Just as it seemed that Paul would join the ranks of ex-Formula 1 drivers, it was announced that he would be part of the new Pacific Grand Prix team for 1994.

TOM BELSO

Forever being fatuously described as 'The smiling Dane' ill served this hard-working driver. After many years of endeavour he eventually became Denmark's first racing driver to compete in a World Championship Grand Prix and, more importantly, proved himself a formidable competitor in the early seventies in Formula 5000.

Originally a mechanic, his meticulous preparation was rewarded by the chance to race the Volvo on which he had worked. Tom was a winner first time out and by 1969, driving a Ford Escort, he was the Scandinavian saloon car champion. This success led to a test and subsequent drive in Formula Ford with Hawke in 1970.

Encouraged by his progress, Belso sold his business interests and moved his family to England to compete in Formula Atlantic in 1971. He finished third in the championship with an old Brabham and then took the leap into Formula 2 for 1972. A fourth place at Albi was the best result in a season strewn with engine problems, but he caught the eye of Jackie Epstein, who signed him for his Shellsport F5000 team – for which he drove splendidly for three seasons. It was during this period that Frank Williams gave Tom his Grand Prix opportunities. Lack of finance curtailed his racing activities for 1976 but, irrepressible as ever, he was back for one more tilt at F5000 in 1977 with John Jordan's Lola.

JEAN-PIERRE BELTOISE

Like Behra, Beltoise was a French motor cycle champion, winning 11 championships between 1961 and 1964 while working for the René Bonnet team as a mechanic. He made his four-wheel debut at Le Mans in 1963, winning the Index of Performance, but a year later his career was nearly ended when a horrendous accident at Reims left him with burns and multiple injuries, the most serious of which was a left arm so badly broken that its movement was permanently restricted. Nevertheless he was back in 1965 racing the F3 Matra (the aerospace company having taken over the René Bonnet concern) and scored a great first win for the marque at Reims. His pre-eminence in this formula was later to be confirmed when he won the 1966 Monaco F3 race, and all four rounds of the Argentine Temporada series early in 1967. This success encouraged Matra to continue with their racing activities, and Beltoise was the spearhead of the team's Formula 2 programme from 1966, winning the F2 class of the German GP and later the European F2 championship for non-graded drivers in 1968 when he won rounds at Hockenheim, Jarama and Zandvoort.

Although he contested a number of Grands Prix in a ballasted F2 Matra, Beltoise had to wait until early 1968 to get his hands on the team's raucous V12-engined F1 car but was soon showing its potential with a brilliant second place and fastest lap at Zandvoort. In 1969 Beltoise was placed in Ken Tyrrell's team as number two to Stewart while development work was undertaken on the V12 project and scored seven point-scoring finishes, but the following season he raced the new Matra MS120-V12 and was unlucky not to win the French GP when a puncture robbed him of the lead. Although Jean-Pierre had done well enough on occasion, Matra signed Amon for 1971, frustrating the Frenchman's F1 aspirations, and it was not a happy season for Beltoise, who received a suspension when he was blamed for his involvement in the fatal accident that befell Giunti in the Buenos Aires 1000 Km.

In 1972 he moved to BRM, where he was soon to enjoy his day of days, winning the Monaco GP with a scintillating performance in pouring rain. A second place in the International Trophy and a win in the John Player Victory race at Brands Hatch merely disguised the team's imminent decline, but Beltoise was to stay on until 1974, with a fantastic drive into second place at Kyalami in the P201 the only highlight of his final season with the team. An established member of the Matra squad, Jean-Pierre enjoyed a tremendous year in sports car racing, winning four championship rounds (the Nürburgring, Watkins Glen, Paul Ricard and Brands Hatch) but at season's end he was looking for work on two fronts. With Matra out of endurance racing, Beltoise was forced to scratch around for drives and the prospect of an F1 return with Ligier in 1976 evaporated when the drive went to Laffite. Jean-Pierre was involved with both the Ligier and Inaltera sports car projects before successfully switching to French touring cars, in which he was to drive and gain much enjoyment for many, many years.

BELMONDO Paul (F) b 23/4/63

1992

	Race	Circuit	No	Entrant	Car/Engine	Comment
dnq	SOUTH AFRICAN GP	Kyalami	17	March F1	3.5 March CG911-Ilmor V10	
dnq	MEXICAN GP	Mexico City	17	March F1	3.5 March CG911-Ilmor V10	
dnq	BRAZILIAN GP	Interlagos	17	March F1	3.5 March CG911-Ilmor V10	
12	SPANISH GP	Barcelona	17	March F1	3.5 March CG911-Ilmor V10	4 laps behind
13	SAN MARINO GP	Imola	17	March F1	3.5 March CG911-Ilmor V10	3 laps behind
dnq	MONACO GP	Monte Carlo	17	March F1	3.5 March CG911-Ilmor V10	
14	CANADIAN GP	Montreal	17	March F1	3.5 March CG911-Ilmor V10	5 laps behind
dnq	FRENCH GP	Magny Cours	17	March F1	3.5 March CG911-Ilmor V10	
dnq	BRITISH GP	Silverstone	17	March F1	3.5 March CG911-Ilmor V10	
13	GERMAN GP	Hockenheim	17	March F1	3.5 March CG911-Ilmor V10	1 lap behind
9	HUNGARIAN GP	Hungaroring	17	March F1	3.5 March CG911-Ilmor V10	3 laps behind

GP Starts: 5   GP Wins: 0   Pole positions: 0   Fastest laps: 0   Points: 0

BELSO, Tom (DK) b 27/8/42

1973

	Race	Circuit	No	Entrant	Car/Engine	Comment
dns	SWEDISH GP	Anderstorp	26	Frank Williams Racing Cars	3.0 Iso Williams 1R-Cosworth V8	practice only-Ganley drove in race

1974

ret	SOUTH AFRICAN GP	Kyalami	21	Frank Williams Racing Cars	3.0 Iso Williams FW01-Cosworth V8	clutch slip
dnq	SPANISH GP	Jarama	21	Frank Williams Racing Cars	3.0 Iso Williams FW02-Cosworth V8	
8	SWEDISH GP	Anderstorp	21	Frank Williams Racing Cars	3.0 Iso Williams FW02-Cosworth V8	1 lap behind
dnq	BRITISH GP	Brands Hatch	21	Frank Williams Racing Cars	3.0 Iso Williams FW01-Cosworth V8	

GP Starts: 2   GP Wins: 0   Pole positions: 0   Fastest laps: 0   Points: 0

BELTOISE, Jean-Pierre (F) b 26/4/1937

1966

	Race	Circuit	No	Entrant	Car/Engine	Comment
8*	GERMAN GP (F2)	Nürburgring	34	Matra Sports	1.0 Matra MS5-Cosworth 4	* 1st in F2 class/1 lap behind

1967

dnq	MONACO GP	Monte Carlo	1	Matra Sports	1.6 Matra MS7-Cosworth 4	F2 car
7	US GP	Watkins Glen	22	Matra Sports	1.6 Matra MS7-Cosworth 4	F2 car/7 laps behind
7	MEXICAN GP	Mexico City	22	Matra Sports	1.6 Matra MS7-Cosworth 4	F2 car/2 laps behind

1968

6	SOUTH AFRICAN GP	Kyalami	21	Matra Sports	1.6 Matra MS7-Cosworth 4	ballasted F2 car/3 laps behind
5	SPANISH GP	Jarama	6	Matra International	3.0 Matra MS10-Cosworth V8	2 pit stops-oil leak/FL/9 laps behind
ret	MONACO GP	Monte Carlo	1	Matra Sports	3.0 Matra MS11 V12	hit chicane-damaged suspension
8	BELGIAN GP	Spa	10	Matra Sports	3.0 Matra MS11 V12	pit stop-fuel/3 laps behind
2	DUTCH GP	Zandvoort	17	Matra Sports	3.0 Matra MS11 V12	pit stop-sand in throttle slides/FL
9	FRENCH GP	Rouen	6	Matra Sports	3.0 Matra MS11 V12	pit stop-tyres/4 laps behind
ret	BRITISH GP	Brands Hatch	18	Matra Sports	3.0 Matra MS11 V12	oil pressure
ret	GERMAN GP	Nürburgring	12	Matra Sports	3.0 Matra MS11 V12	crashed
5	ITALIAN GP	Monza	6	Matra Sports	3.0 Matra MS11 V12	2 laps behind
ret	CANADIAN GP	St Jovite	18	Matra Sports	3.0 Matra MS11 V12	transmission
ret	US GP	Watkins Glen	21	Matra Sports	3.0 Matra MS11 V12	driveshaft
ret	MEXICAN GP	Mexico City	21	Matra Sports	3.0 Matra MS11 V12	rear suspension

1969

6	SOUTH AFRICAN GP	Kyalami	8	Matra International	3.0 Matra MS10-Cosworth V8	2 laps behind
3	SPANISH GP	Montjuich Park	8	Matra International	3.0 Matra MS80-Cosworth V8	2 pit stops-gear linkage/3 laps behind
ret	MONACO GP	Monte Carlo	8	Matra International	3.0 Matra MS80-Cosworth V8	universal joint
8	DUTCH GP	Zandvoort	5	Matra International	3.0 Matra MS80-Cosworth V8	3 laps behind
2	FRENCH GP	Clermont Ferrand	7	Matra International	3.0 Matra MS80-Cosworth V8	
9	BRITISH GP	Silverstone (30)	4	Matra International	3.0 Matra MS84-Cosworth V8	6 laps behind
dns	"	"	4	Matra International	3.0 Matra MS80-Cosworth V8	practice only/Stewart in race
12/ret	GERMAN GP	Nürburgring	8	Matra International	3.0 Matra MS80-Cosworth V8	front upright/6th F1 car/2 laps behind
3	ITALIAN GP	Monza	22	Matra International	3.0 Matra MS80-Cosworth V8	FL
4	CANADIAN GP	Mosport Park	18	Matra International	3.0 Matra MS80-Cosworth V8	1 lap behind
ret	US GP	Watkins Glen	4	Matra International	3.0 Matra MS80-Cosworth V8	engine
5	MEXICAN GP	Mexico City	4	Matra International	3.0 Matra MS80-Cosworth V8	

1970

4	SOUTH AFRICAN GP	Kyalami	3	Equipe Matra Elf	3.0 Matra-Simca MS120 V12	
ret	SPANISH GP	Jarama	4	Equipe Matra Elf	3.0 Matra-Simca MS120 V12	engine
ret	MONACO GP	Monte Carlo	8	Equipe Matra Elf	3.0 Matra-Simca MS120 V12	cwp
3	BELGIAN GP	Spa	25	Equipe Matra Elf	3.0 Matra-Simca MS120 V12	
5	DUTCH GP	Zandvoort	23	Equipe Matra Elf	3.0 Matra-Simca MS120 V12	1 lap behind
13/ret	FRENCH GP	Clermont Ferrand	21	Equipe Matra Elf	3.0 Matra-Simca MS120 V12	fuel pressure/3 laps behind
ret	BRITISH GP	Brands Hatch	7	Equipe Matra Elf	3.0 Matra-Simca MS120 V12	wheel problem
ret	GERMAN GP	Hockenheim	8	Equipe Matra Elf	3.0 Matra-Simca MS120 V12	front suspension
6	AUSTRIAN GP	Österreichring	19	Equipe Matra Elf	3.0 Matra-Simca MS120 V12	pit stop-fuel/1 lap behind
3	ITALIAN GP	Monza	40	Equipe Matra Elf	3.0 Matra-Simca MS120 V12	
8	CANADIAN GP	St Jovite	23	Equipe Matra Elf	3.0 Matra-Simca MS120 V12	5 laps behind
ret	US GP	Watkins Glen	6	Equipe Matra Elf	3.0 Matra-Simca MS120 V12	handling
5	MEXICAN GP	Mexico City	6	Equipe Matra Elf	3.0 Matra-Simca MS120 V12	

1971

6	SPANISH GP	Montjuich Park	21	Equipe Matra Sports	3.0 Matra-Simca MS120B V12	*1 lap behind*
ret	MONACO GP	Monte Carlo	21	Equipe Matra Sports	3.0 Matra-Simca MS120B V12	*cwp*
9	DUTCH GP	Zandvoort	21	Equipe Matra Sports	3.0 Matra-Simca MS120B V12	*5 laps behind*
7	FRENCH GP	Paul Ricard	21	Equipe Matra Sports	3.0 Matra-Simca MS120B V12	
7	BRITISH GP	Silverstone	22	Equipe Matra Sports	3.0 Matra-Simca MS120B V12	*2 laps behind*
ret	CANADIAN GP	Mosport Park	21	Equipe Matra Sports	3.0 Matra-Simca MS120B V12	*hit guard rail*
8	US GP	Watkins Glen	12	Equipe Matra Sports	3.0 Matra-Simca MS120B V12	*1 lap behind*

1972

ret	SOUTH AFRICAN GP	Kyalami	10	Marlboro BRM	3.0 BRM P160B V12	*engine*
ret	SPANISH GP	Jarama	19	Marlboro BRM	3.0 BRM P160B V12	*gear selection*
dns	"		19T	Marlboro BRM	3.0 BRM P180 V12	*practice only*
1	MONACO GP	Monte Carlo	17	Marlboro BRM	3.0 BRM P160B V12	*FL*
ret	BELGIAN GP	Nivelles	23	Marlboro BRM	3.0 BRM P160B V12	*overheating*
15	FRENCH GP	Clermont Ferrand	5T	Marlboro BRM	3.0 BRM P160B V12	*started from back/spin/-1 lap*
dns	"	"	5	Marlboro BRM	3.0 BRM P160C V12	*practice only*
11	BRITISH GP	Brands Hatch	11	Marlboro BRM	3.0 BRM P160C V12	*pit stop-puncture/6 laps behind*
dns	"	" "	43	Marlboro BRM	3.0 BRM P160B V12	*practice only*
9	GERMAN GP	Nürburgring	6	Marlboro BRM	3.0 BRM P160C V12	*black flagged when 5th*
8	AUSTRIAN GP	Österreichring	7	Marlboro BRM	3.0 BRM P160C V12	
8	ITALIAN GP	Monza	21	Marlboro BRM	3.0 BRM P180 V12	*1 lap behind*
ret	CANADIAN GP	Mosport Park	14	Marlboro BRM	3.0 BRM P180 V12	*oil cooler leak*
ret	US GP	Watkins Glen	17	Marlboro BRM	3.0 BRM P180 V12	*ignition rotor*

1973

ret	ARGENTINE GP	Buenos Aires	30	Marlboro BRM	3.0 BRM P160D V12	*engine*
ret	BRAZILIAN GP	Interlagos	15	Marlboro BRM	3.0 BRM P160D V12	*electrics-damaged by stone*
ret	SOUTH AFRICAN GP	Kyalami	16	Marlboro BRM	3.0 BRM P160D V12	*clutch slip*
5	SPANISH GP	Montjuich Park	15	Marlboro BRM	3.0 BRM P160D V12	*1 lap behind*
ret	BELGIAN GP	Zolder	20	Marlboro BRM	3.0 BRM P160E V12	*engine*
ret	MONACO GP	Monte Carlo	20	Marlboro BRM	3.0 BRM P160E V12	*hit kerb and Armco*
ret	SWEDISH GP	Anderstorp	20	Marlboro BRM	3.0 BRM P160E V12	*engine*
11	FRENCH GP	Paul Ricard	20	Marlboro BRM	3.0 BRM P160E V12	*1 lap behind*
ret/dns	BRITISH GP	Silverstone	20	Marlboro BRM	3.0 BRM P160E V12	*accident 1st start/did not restart*
5	DUTCH GP	Zandvoort	20	Marlboro BRM	3.0 BRM P160E V12	
ret	GERMAN GP	Nürburgring	20	Marlboro BRM	3.0 BRM P160E V12	*gearbox*
5	AUSTRIAN GP	Österreichring	20	Marlboro BRM	3.0 BRM P160E V12	
13	ITALIAN GP	Monza	20	Marlboro BRM	3.0 BRM P160E V12	*pit stop-puncture/1 lap behind*
4	CANADIAN GP	Mosport Park	20	Marlboro BRM	3.0 BRM P160E V12	
9	US GP	Watkins Glen	20	Marlboro BRM	3.0 BRM P160E V12	*pit stop/1 lap behind*

1974

5	ARGENTINE GP	Buenos Aires	14	Team Motul BRM	3.0 BRM P160E V12	
10	BRAZILIAN GP	Interlagos	14	Team Motul BRM	3.0 BRM P160E V12	*1 lap behind*
2	SOUTH AFRICAN GP	Kyalami	14	Team Motul BRM	3.0 BRM P201 V12	
ret	SPANISH GP	Jarama	14	Team Motul BRM	3.0 BRM P201 V12	*engine*
5	BELGIAN GP	Nivelles	14	Team Motul BRM	3.0 BRM P201 V12	
ret	MONACO GP	Monte Carlo	14	Team Motul BRM	3.0 BRM P201 V12	*collision with Hulme*
ret	SWEDISH GP	Anderstorp	14	Team Motul BRM	3.0 BRM P201 V12	*engine*
ret	DUTCH GP	Zandvoort	14	Team Motul BRM	3.0 BRM P201 V12	*gearbox*
10	FRENCH GP	Dijon	14	Team Motul BRM	3.0 BRM P201 V12	*1 lap behind*
12	BRITISH GP	Brands Hatch	14	Team Motul BRM	3.0 BRM P201 V12	*pit stop-tyres/3 laps behind*
ret	GERMAN GP	Nürburgring	14	Team Motul BRM	3.0 BRM P201 V12	*accessory drive belt*
ret	AUSTRIAN GP	Österreichring	14	Team Motul BRM	3.0 BRM P201 V12	*engine*
ret	ITALIAN GP	Monza	14	Team Motul BRM	3.0 BRM P201 V12	*electrics*
nc	CANADIAN GP	Mosport Park	14	Team Motul BRM	3.0 BRM P201 V12	*pit stops-handling/20 laps behind*
dns	US GP	Watkins Glen	14	Team Motul BRM	3.0 BRM P201 V12	*practice accident-broken bone in foot*

GP Starts: 86   GP Wins: 1   Pole positions: 0   Fastest laps: 4   Points: 77

BERG, Allen (CDN) b 1/8/1961

1986

	Race	Circuit	No	Entrant	Car/Engine	Comment
ret	US GP (DETROIT)	Detroit	8	Osella Squadra Corse	1.5 t/c Osella FA1F-Alfa Romeo V8	*electrics*
ret	FRENCH GP	Dijon	8	Osella Squadra Corse	1.5 t/c Osella FA1G-Alfa Romeo V8	*turbo*
ret/dns	BRITISH GP	Brands Hatch	8	Osella Squadra Corse	1.5 t/c Osella FA1H-Alfa Romeo V8	*accident in first start*
12	GERMAN GP	Hockenheim	8	Osella Squadra Corse	1.5 t/c Osella FA1F-Alfa Romeo V8	*4 laps behind*
ret	HUNGARIAN GP	Hungaroring	8	Osella Squadra Corse	1.5 t/c Osella FA1F-Alfa Romeo V8	*turbo*
ret	AUSTRIAN GP	Österreichring	8	Osella Squadra Corse	1.5 t/c Osella FA1F-Alfa Romeo V8	*electrics*
13	PORTUGUESE GP	Estoril	8	Osella Squadra Corse	1.5 t/c Osella FA1F-Alfa Romeo V8	*7 laps behind*
16	MEXICAN GP	Mexico City	8	Osella Squadra Corse	1.5 t/c Osella FA1F-Alfa Romeo V8	*7 laps behind*
nc	AUSTRALIAN GP	Adelaide	8	Osella Squadra Corse	1.5 t/c Osella FA1F-Alfa Romeo V8	*started from pits/21 laps behind*

GP Starts: 8   GP Wins: 0   Pole positions: 0   Fastest laps: 0   Points: 0

BERGER, Georges (B) b 14/9/1918 – d 23/8/1967

1953

	Race	Circuit	No	Entrant	Car/Engine	Comment
ret	BELGIAN GP	Spa	34	Georges Berger	1.5 Gordini Type 15 4	*engine*

1954

ret	BELGIAN GP	Spa	30	Georges Berger	1.5 Gordini Type 15 4	*engine-valve*

GP Starts: 2   GP Wins: 0   Pole positions: 0   Fastest laps: 0   Points: 0

ALLEN BERG

A stocky little Canadian driver, Berg emerged from the 1982 North American Formula Atlantic series by way of the winter Pacific championship (which he won for New Zealand ex-racer Graeme Lawrence in a Ralt) to contest the 1983 British F3 championship.

With no experience of F3 cars or, naturally, the circuits, he did a good job in this formative season, especially after switching to the Eddie Jordan Racing team. This was the year in which the Senna–Brundle axis dominated proceedings, but Allen was regularly leading the rest in pursuit of the star duo. Staying with EJR, hopes for success in 1984 were high, but a season of mishaps and frustrations saw him finish second in the standings to Johnny Dumfries.

This left Berg's career in something of a vacuum, and it was a considerable surprise when he scraped together sufficient finance to take over the unwieldy Osella in mid-1986 after Christian Danner had moved over to Arrows. This was a year without the pressures of having to qualify, so Allen was at least able get some experience and racing mileage under his belt.

Since then, Berg has been scratching round for rides, trying his hand at the German touring car championship with his own car in 1991.

GERHARD BERGER

Berger has been comfortably ensconced in the top echelon of the Grand Prix fraternity for many years now, and is highly regarded both for his one hundred per cent professionalism behind the wheel and his light-hearted demeanour off the track.

With a limited racing background firstly in Alfas and then in the German and European Formula 3 series, Berger had gained a reputation as a fast and safe driver who, above all, brought his car home to the finish when he breezed into the ATS team towards the end of 1984. His sixth place at Monza was sufficient indication that here was a rough diamond waiting to be polished, and a close-season accident which left him with broken vertebrae in his neck was not enough to prevent him from lining up at the start of the 1985 season in the Arrows-BMW team. At first Gerhard struggled somewhat alongside the quiet and talented Thierry Boutsen, but his aggressive driving style began to pay dividends in the second half of the season.

Benetton were running BMW engines in 1986 and Berger's connections with the German company helped him to a place in the team, but he was soon to prove the wisdom of his selection with some eye-catching drives, especially when the Pirelli tyres were working well. After disappointment in Austria came his first Grand Prix win in Mexico and, on the not too distant horizon, a contract with Ferrari for 1987. After a hesitant beginning, Gerhard's natural ebullience was quickly apparent, and after throwing away a victory in the Portuguese GP, he won the end-of-season Japanese and Australian races. In 1988 McLaren-Honda were utterly dominant, but Berger never gave up and a lucky win at Monza was just reward for perhaps his best-ever year. However, his final season at Maranello was distinctly low-key. Psychologically outgunned by Nigel Mansell, and striving to shake off the effects of a horrendous crash at Imola, he picked up a win at Estoril almost unnoticed before joining McLaren on a three-year contract to partner Ayrton Senna.

Initially it was a morale-sapping experience, as he struggled in his stellar team-mate's trail. He had difficulty fitting into the cockpit and was sometimes guilty of over-taxing his tyres, but gradually he got to grips with the situation at McLaren to become a perfect foil for Senna both on and off the track. Grand Prix wins came here and there; some were lucky and others well earned, with his final race for the team being perhaps his best, when his finely judged tactics brought him victory in the Australian GP.

Enticed by a reputedly massive retainer, Gerhard rejoined Ferrari for 1993, but endured a pretty torrid year adapting to 'active' suspension, which he obviously disliked. Worryingly, he was involved in a number of alarming on-track incidents and claimed but a single podium finish; 1994 will have to be a better season for the Austrian if he is to keep his hard-earned status as one of Grand Prix racing's premier drivers.

BERGER, Gerhard (A) b 27/8/1959

1984

	Race	Circuit	No	Entrant	Car/Engine	Comment
12/ret	AUSTRIAN GP	Österreichring	31	Team ATS	1.5 t/c ATS D7-BMW 4	gearbox/3 laps behind
6*	ITALIAN GP	Monza	31	Team ATS	1.5 t/c ATS D7-BMW 4	* not eligible for points/2 laps behind
ret	EUROPEAN GP	Nürburgring	31	Team ATS	1.5 t/c ATS D7-BMW 4	accident with Surer
13	PORTUGUESE GP	Estoril	31	Team ATS	1.5 t/c ATS D7-BMW 4	2 laps behind

1985

	Race	Circuit	No	Entrant	Car/Engine	Comment
ret	BRAZILIAN GP	Rio	17	Barclay Arrows BMW	1.5 t/c Arrows A8-BMW 4	suspension
ret	PORTUGUESE GP	Estoril	17	Barclay Arrows BMW	1.5 t/c Arrows A8-BMW 4	spun off
ret	SAN MARINO GP	Imola	17	Barclay Arrows BMW	1.5 t/c Arrows A8-BMW 4	electrics/engine
ret	MONACO GP	Monte Carlo	17	Barclay Arrows BMW	1.5 t/c Arrows A8-BMW 4	accident damage
13	CANADIAN GP	Montreal	17	Barclay Arrows BMW	1.5 t/c Arrows A8-BMW 4	3 laps behind
11	US GP (DETROIT)	Detroit	17	Barclay Arrows BMW	1.5 t/c Arrows A8-BMW 4	3 laps behind
ret	FRENCH GP	Paul Ricard	17	Barclay Arrows BMW	1.5 t/c Arrows A8-BMW 4	accident with Martini
8	BRITISH GP	Silverstone	17	Barclay Arrows BMW	1.5 t/c Arrows A8-BMW 4	2 laps behind
7	GERMAN GP	Nürburgring	17	Barclay Arrows BMW	1.5 t/c Arrows A8-BMW 4	1 lap behind
ret	AUSTRIAN GP	Österreichring	17	Barclay Arrows BMW	1.5 t/c Arrows A8-BMW 4	turbo
9	DUTCH GP	Zandvoort	17	Barcaly Arrows BMW	1.5 t/c Arrows A8-BMW 4	2 laps behind
ret	ITALIAN GP	Monza	17	Barclay Arrows BMW	1.5 t/c Arrows A8-BMW 4	engine
7	BELGIAN GP	Spa	17	Barclay Arrows BMW	1.5 t/c Arrows A8-BMW 4	1 lap behind
10	EUROPEAN GP	Brands Hatch	17	Barclay Arrows BMW	1.5 t/c Arrows A8-BMW 4	2 laps behind
5	SOUTH AFRICAN GP	Kyalami	17	Barclay Arrows BMW	1.5 t/c Arrows A8-BMW 4	1 lap behind
6	AUSTRALIAN GP	Adelaide	17	Barclay Arrows BMW	1.5 t/c Arrows A8-BMW 4	1 lap behind

1986

	Race	Circuit	No	Entrant	Car/Engine	Comment
6	BRAZILIAN GP	Rio	20	Benetton Formula Ltd	1.5 t/c Benetton B186-BMW 4	electrical problem/2 laps behind
6	SPANISH GP	Jerez	20	Benetton Formula Ltd	1.5 t/c Benetton B186-BMW 4	1 lap behind
3	SAN MARINO GP	Imola	20	Benetton Formula Ltd	1.5 t/c Benetton B186-BMW 4	1 lap behind
ret	MONACO GP	Monte Carlo	20	Benetton Formula Ltd	1.5 t/c Benetton B186-BMW 4	wheel drive pegs
10	BELGIAN GP	Spa	20	Benetton Formula Ltd	1.5 t/c Benetton B186-BMW 4	lost clutch/2 laps behind
ret	CANADIAN GP	Montreal	20	Benetton Formula Ltd	1.5 t/c Benetton B186-BMW 4	turbo
ret	US GP (DETROIT)	Detroit	20	Benetton Formula Ltd	1.5 t/c Benetton B186-BMW 4	engine cut out
ret	FRENCH GP	Paul Ricard	20	Benetton Formula Ltd	1.5 t/c Benetton B186-BMW 4	gearbox
ret	BRITISH GP	Brands Hatch	20	Benetton Formula Ltd	1.5 t/c Benetton B186-BMW 4	electrics
10	GERMAN GP	Hockenheim	20	Benetton Formula Ltd	1.5 t/c Benetton B186-BMW 4	2 laps behind
ret	HUNGARIAN GP	Hungaroring	20	Benetton Formula Ltd	1.5 t/c Benetton B186-BMW 4	fuel leak/transmission
7	AUSTRIAN GP	Österreichring	20	Benetton Formula Ltd	1.5 t/c Benetton B186-BMW 4	pit stop-battery/FL/3 laps behind
5	ITALIAN GP	Monza	20	Benetton Formula Ltd	1.5 t/c Benetton B186-BMW 4	1 lap behind
ret	PORTUGUESE GP	Estoril	20	Benetton Formula Ltd	1.5 t/c Benetton B186-BMW 4	spun off-incident with Johansson
1	MEXICAN GP	Mexico City	20	Benetton Formula Ltd	1.5 t/c Benetton B186-BMW 4	
ret	AUSTRALIAN GP	Adelaide	20	Benetton Formula Ltd	1.5 t/c Benetton B186-BMW 4	clutch/engine

1987

	Race	Circuit	No	Entrant	Car/Engine	Comment
4	BRAZILIAN GP	Rio	28	Scuderia Ferrari SpA SEFAC	1.5 t/c Ferrari F1/87 V6	
ret	SAN MARINO GP	Imola	28	Scuderia Ferrari SpA SEFAC	1.5 t/c Ferrari F1/87 V6	electrics
ret	BELGIAN GP	Spa	28	Scuderia Ferrari SpA SEFAC	1.5 t/c Ferrari F1/87 V6	turbo
4	MONACO GP	Monte Carlo	28	Scuderia Ferrari SpA SEFAC	1.5 t/c Ferrari F1/87 V6	1 lap behind
4	US GP (DETROIT)	Detroit	28	Scuderia Ferrari SpA SEFAC	1.5 t/c Ferrari F1/87 V6	
ret	FRENCH GP	Paul Ricard	28	Scuderia Ferrari SpA SEFAC	1.5 t/c Ferrari F1/87 V6	spun off-suspension
ret	BRITISH GP	Silverstone	28	Scuderia Ferrari SpA SEFAC	1.5 t/c Ferrari F1/87 V6	spun off
ret	GERMAN GP	Hockenheim	28	Scuderia Ferrari SpA SEFAC	1.5 t/c Ferrari F1/87 V6	turbo
ret	HUNGARIAN GP	Hungaroring	28	Scuderia Ferrari SpA SEFAC	1.5 t/c Ferrari F1/87 V6	differential
ret	AUSTRIAN GP	Österreichring	28	Scuderia Ferrari SpA SEFAC	1.5 t/c Ferrari F1/87 V6	turbo
4	ITALIAN GP	Monza	28	Scuderia Ferrari SpA SEFAC	1.5 t/c Ferrari F1/87 V6	
2	PORTUGUESE GP	Estoril	28	Scuderia Ferrari SpA SEFAC	1.5 t/c Ferrari F1/87 V6	spin when leading/Pole/FL
ret	SPANISH GP	Jerez	28	Scuderia Ferrari SpA SEFAC	1.5 t/c Ferrari F1/87 V6	smashed oil cooler/engine/FL
ret	MEXICAN GP	Mexico City	28	Scuderia Ferrari SpA SEFAC	1.5 t/c Ferrari F1/87 V6	engine
1	JAPANESE GP	Suzuka	28	Scuderia Ferrari SpA SEFAC	1.5 t/c Ferrari F1/87 V6	Pole
1	AUSTRALIAN GP	Adelaide	28	Scuderia Ferrari SpA SEFAC	1.5 t/c Ferrari F1/87 V6	Pole/FL

1988

	Race	Circuit	No	Entrant	Car/Engine	Comment
2	BRAZILIAN GP	Rio	28	Scuderia Ferrari SpA SEFAC	1.5 t/c Ferrari F1/87/88C V6	FL
5	SAN MARINO GP	Imola	28	Scuderia Ferrari SpA SEFAC	1.5 t/c Ferrari F1/87/88C V6	power loss-engine/1 lap behind
2	MONACO GP	Monte Carlo	28	Scuderia Ferrari SpA SEFAC	1.5 t/c Ferrari F1/87/88C V6	
3	MEXICAN GP	Mexico City	28	Scuderia Ferrari SpA SEFAC	1.5 t/c Ferrari F1/87/88C V6	
ret	CANADIAN GP	Montreal	28	Scuderia Ferrari SpA SEFAC	1.5 t/c Ferrari F1/87/88C V6	electrics/engine
ret	US GP (DETROIT)	Detroit	28	Scuderia Ferrari SpA SEFAC	1.5 t/c Ferrari F1/87/88C V6	puncture
4	FRENCH GP	Paul Ricard	28	Scuderia Ferrari SpA SEFAC	1.5 t/c Ferrari F1/87/88C V6	1 lap behind
9	BRITISH GP	Silverstone	28	Scuderia Ferrari SpA SEFAC	1.5 t/c Ferrari F1/87/88C V6	low on fuel/Pole/1 lap behind
3	GERMAN GP	Hockenheim	28	Scuderia Ferrari SpA SEFAC	1.5 t/c Ferrari F1/87/88C V6	
4	HUNGARIAN GP	Hungaroring	28	Scuderia Ferrari SpA SEFAC	1.5 t/c Ferrari F1/87/88C V6	
ret	BELGIAN GP	Spa	28	Scuderia Ferrari SpA SEFAC	1.5 t/c Ferrari F1/87/88C V6	electrics/FL
1	ITALIAN GP	Monza	28	Scuderia Ferrari SpA SEFAC	1.5 t/c Ferrari F1/87/88C V6	
ret	PORTUGUESE GP	Estoril	28	Scuderia Ferrari SpA SEFAC	1.5 t/c Ferrari F1/87/88C V6	spun off-fire extinguisher/FL
6	SPANISH GP	Jerez	28	Scuderia Ferrari SpA SEFAC	1.5 t/c Ferrari F1/87/88C V6	pit stop-tyres/low on fuel
4	JAPANESE GP	Suzuka	28	Scuderia Ferrari SpA SEFAC	1.5 t/c Ferrari F1/87/88C V6	
ret	AUSTRALIAN GP	Adelaide	28	Scuderia Ferrari SpA SEFAC	1.5 t/c Ferrari F1/87/88C V6	accident with Arnoux

1989

	Race	Circuit	No	Entrant	Car/Engine	Comment
ret	BRAZILIAN GP	Rio	28	Scuderia Ferrari SpA SEFAC	3.5 Ferrari 640 V12	collision with Senna
ret	SAN MARINO GP	Imola	28	Scuderia Ferrari SpA SEFAC	3.5 Ferrari 640 V12	car went straight on at Tamburello
ret	MEXICAN GP	Mexico City	28	Scuderia Ferrari SpA SEFAC	3.5 Ferrari 640 V12	transmission
ret	US GP (PHOENIX)	Phoenix	28	Scuderia Ferrari SpA SEFAC	3.5 Ferrari 640 V12	alternator
ret	CANADIAN GP	Montreal	28	Scuderia Ferrari SpA SEFAC	3.5 Ferrari 640 V12	gearbox

ret	FRENCH GP	Paul Ricard	28	Scuderia Ferrari SpA SEFAC	3.5 Ferrari 640 V12	oil leak
ret	BRITISH GP	Silverstone	28	Scuderia Ferrari SpA SEFAC	3.5 Ferrari 640 V12	gearbox
ret	GERMAN GP	Hockenheim	28	Scuderia Ferrari SpA SEFAC	3.5 Ferrari 640 V12	puncture-crashed
ret	HUNGARIAN GP	Hungaroring	28	Scuderia Ferrari SpA SEFAC	3.5 Ferrari 640 V12	gearbox
ret	BELGIAN GP	Spa	28	Scuderia Ferrari SpA SEFAC	3.5 Ferrari 640 V12	spun off
2	ITALIAN GP	Monza	28	Scuderia Ferrari SpA SEFAC	3.5 Ferrari 640 V12	
1	PORTUGUESE GP	Estoril	28	Scuderia Ferrari SpA SEFAC	3.5 Ferrari 640 V12	FL
2	SPANISH GP	Jerez	28	Scuderia Ferrari SpA SEFAC	3.5 Ferrari 640 V12	
ret	JAPANESE GP	Suzuka	28	Scuderia Ferrari SpA SEFAC	3.5 Ferrari 640 V12	gearbox electrics
ret	AUSTRALIAN GP	Adelaide	28	Scuderia Ferrari SpA SEFAC	3.5 Ferrari 640 V12	collision with Alliot

1990

ret	US GP (PHOENIX)	Phoenix	28	Honda Marlboro McLaren	3.5 McLaren MP4/5B-Honda V10	led-spun-pit stop/clutch/Pole/FL
2	BRAZILIAN GP	Interlagos	28	Honda Marlboro McLaren	3.5 McLaren MP4/5B-Honda V10	pit stop-tyres/FL
2	SAN MARINO GP	Imola	28	Honda Marlboro McLaren	3.5 McLaren MP4/5B-Honda V10	
3	MONACO GP	Monte Carlo	28	Honda Marlboro McLaren	3.5 McLaren MP4/5B-Honda V10	
4	CANADIAN GP	Montreal	28	Honda Marlboro McLaren	3.5 McLaren MP4/5B-Honda V10	1 min penalty-jumped start/FL
3	MEXICAN GP	Mexico City	28	Honda Marlboro McLaren	3.5 McLaren MP4/5B-Honda V10	pit stop-tyres/Pole
5	FRENCH GP	Paul Ricard	28	Honda Marlboro McLaren	3.5 McLaren MP4/5B-Honda V10	pit stop-tyres/lost 1st gear
14/ret	BRITISH GP	Silverstone	28	Honda Marlboro McLaren	3.5 McLaren MP4/5B-Honda V10	throttle cable/4 laps behind
3	GERMAN GP	Hockenheim	28	Honda Marlboro McLaren	3.5 McLaren MP4/5B-Honda V10	
16/ret	HUNGARIAN GP	Hungaroring	28	Honda Marlboro McLaren	3.5 McLaren MP4/5B-Honda V10	collision with Mansell/5 laps behind
3	BELGIAN GP	Spa	28	Honda Marlboro McLaren	3.5 McLaren MP4/5B-Honda V10	pit stop-tyres
3	ITALIAN GP	Monza	28	Honda Marlboro McLaren	3.5 McLaren MP4/5B-Honda V10	pit stop-tyres/brake problems
4	PORTUGUESE GP	Estoril	28	Honda Marlboro McLaren	3.5 McLaren MP4/5B-Honda V10	pit stop-tyres
ret	SPANISH GP	Jerez	28	Honda Marlboro McLaren	3.5 McLaren MP4/5B-Honda V10	collision with Boutsen
ret	JAPANESE GP	Suzuka	28	Honda Marlboro McLaren	3.5 McLaren MP4/5B-Honda V10	spun off
4	AUSTRALIAN GP	Adelaide	28	Honda Marlboro McLaren	3.5 McLaren MP4/5B-Honda V10	pit stop-tyres/cramp problems

1991

ret	US GP (PHOENIX)	Phoenix	2	Honda Marlboro McLaren	3.5 McLaren MP4/6-Honda V12	fuel pump
3	BRAZILIAN GP	Interlagos	2	Honda Marlboro McLaren	3.5 McLaren MP4/6-Honda V12	
2	SAN MARINO GP	Imola	2	Honda Marlboro McLaren	3.5 McLaren MP4/6-Honda V12	
ret	MONACO GP	Monte Carlo	2	Honda Marlboro McLaren	3.5 McLaren MP4/6-Honda V12	crashed
ret	CANADIAN GP	Montreal	2	Honda Marlboro McLaren	3.5 McLaren MP4/6-Honda V12	electrics
ret	MEXICAN GP	Mexico City	2	Honda Marlboro McLaren	3.5 McLaren MP4/6-Honda V12	engine-overheating
ret	FRENCH GP	Magny Cours	2	Honda Marlboro McLaren	3.5 McLaren MP4/6-Honda V12	engine
2	BRITISH GP	Silverstone	2	Honda Marlboro McLaren	3.5 McLaren MP4/6-Honda V12	wheel vibration/pit stop-tyres
4	GERMAN GP	Hockenheim	2	Honda Marlboro McLaren	3.5 McLaren MP4/6-Honda V12	
4	HUNGARIAN GP	Hungaroring	2	Honda Marlboro McLaren	3.5 McLaren MP4/6-Honda V12	
2	BELGIAN GP	Spa	2	Honda Marlboro McLaren	3.5 McLaren MP4/6-Honda V12	
4	ITALIAN GP	Monza	2	Honda Marlboro McLaren	3.5 McLaren MP4/6-Honda V12	
ret	PORTUGUESE GP	Estoril	2	Honda Marlboro McLaren	3.5 McLaren MP4/6-Honda V12	engine
ret	SPANISH GP	Jerez	2	Honda Marlboro McLaren	3.5 McLaren MP4/6-Honda V12	engine-valve/Pole
1	JAPANESE GP	Suzuka	2	Honda Marlboro McLaren	3.5 McLaren MP4/6-Honda V12	Pole
3	AUSTRALIAN GP	Adelaide	2	Honda Marlboro McLaren	3.5 McLaren MP4/6-Honda V12	race abandoned-half pts/FL

1992

5	SOUTH AFRICAN GP	Kyalami	2	Honda Marlboro McLaren	3.5 McLaren MP4/6B-Honda V12	
4	MEXICAN GP	Mexico City	2	Honda Marlboro McLaren	3.5 McLaren MP4/6B-Honda V12	FL
ret	BRAZILIAN GP	Interlagos	2	Honda Marlboro McLaren	3.5 McLaren MP4/7A-Honda V12	started from pit lane/overheating
dns	"	"	2	Honda Marlboro McLaren	3.5 McLaren MP4/6B-Honda V12	practice only
4	SPANISH GP	Barcelona	2	Honda Marlboro McLaren	3.5 McLaren MP4/7A-Honda V12	
ret	SAN MARINO GP	Imola	2	Honda Marlboro McLaren	3.5 McLaren MP4/7A-Honda V12	collision Alesi
ret	MONACO GP	Monte Carlo	2	Honda Marlboro McLaren	3.5 McLaren MP4/7A-Honda V12	gearbox
1	CANADIAN GP	Montreal	2	Honda Marlboro McLaren	3.5 McLaren MP4/7A-Honda V12	won despite gearbox problems/FL
ret	FRENCH GP	Magny Cours	2	Honda Marlboro McLaren	3.5 McLaren MP4/7A-Honda V12	engine
5	BRITISH GP	Silverstone	2	Honda Marlboro McLaren	3.5 McLaren MP4/7A-Honda V12	
ret	GERMAN GP	Hockenheim	2	Honda Marlboro McLaren	3.5 McLaren MP4/7A-Honda V12	2 pit stops/misfire
3	HUNGARIAN GP	Hungaroring	2	Honda Marlboro McLaren	3.5 McLaren MP4/7A-Honda V12	
ret	BELGIAN GP	Spa	2	Honda Marlboro McLaren	3.5 McLaren MP4/7A-Honda V12	transmission failure at start
4	ITALIAN GP	Monza	2	Honda Marlboro McLaren	3.5 McLaren MP4/7A-Honda V12	pit stop/tyres
2	PORTUGUESE GP	Estoril	2	Honda Marlboro McLaren	3.5 McLaren MP4/7A-Honda V12	touched by Patrese entering pits
2	JAPANESE GP	Suzuka	2	Honda Marlboro McLaren	3.5 McLaren MP4/7A-Honda V12	
1	AUSTRALIAN GP	Adelaide	2	Honda Marlboro McLaren	3.5 McLaren MP4/7A-Honda V12	tactical pit stop-tyres

1993

6/ret	SOUTH AFRICAN GP	Kyalami	28	Scuderia Ferrari SpA	3.5 Fiat Ferrari F93A V12	engine/3 laps behind
ret	BRAZILIAN GP	Interlagos	28	Scuderia Ferrari SpA	3.5 Fiat Ferrari F93A V12	taken off by Andretti-first corner
ret	EUROPEAN GP	Donington	28	Scuderia Ferrari SpA	3.5 Fiat Ferrari F93A V12	active system leakage
ret	SAN MARINO GP	Imola	28	Scuderia Ferrari SpA	3.5 Fiat Ferrari F93A V12	gearbox
6	SPANISH GP	Barcelona	28	Scuderia Ferrari SpA	3.5 Fiat Ferrari F93A V12	2 laps behind
14/ret	MONACO GP	Monte Carlo	28	Scuderia Ferrari SpA	3.5 Fiat Ferrari F93A V12	collision-Hill/8 laps behind
4	CANADIAN GP	Montreal	28	Scuderia Ferrari SpA	3.5 Fiat Ferrari F93A V12	1 lap behind
14	FRENCH GP	Magny Cours	28	Scuderia Ferrari SpA	3.5 Fiat Ferrari F93A V12	active system trouble/2 laps behind
ret	BRITISH GP	Silverstone	28	Scuderia Ferrari SpA	3.5 Fiat Ferrari F93A V12	active system
6	GERMAN GP	Hockenheim	28	Scuderia Ferrari SpA	3.5 Fiat Ferrari F93A V12	
3	HUNGARIAN GP	Hungaroring	28	Scuderia Ferrari SpA	3.5 Fiat Ferrari F93A V12	
10/ret	BELGIAN GP	Spa	28	Scuderia Ferrari SpA	3.5 Fiat Ferrari F93A V12	started from pits/collision-Brundle/-2 laps
ret	ITALIAN GP	Monza	28	Scuderia Ferrari SpA	3.5 Fiat Ferrari F93A V12	active system
ret	PORTUGUESE GP	Estoril	28	Scuderia Ferrari SpA	3.5 Fiat Ferrari F93A V12	active system-spun exiting pit lane
ret	JAPANESE GP	Suzuka	28	Scuderia Ferrari SpA	3.5 Fiat Ferrari F93A V12	engine/
5	AUSTRALIAN GP	Adelaide	28	Scuderia Ferrari SpA	3.5 Fiat Ferrari F93A V12	1 lap behind

GP Starts: 147   GP Wins: 8   Pole positions: 8   Fastest laps: 16   Points: 265

BERNARD, Eric (F) b 24/8/1964

1989

	Race	Circuit	No	Entrant	Car/Engine	Comment
11/ret	FRENCH GP	Paul Ricard	29	Equipe Larrousse	3.5 Lola LC89-Lamborghini V12	engine/3 laps behind
ret	BRITISH GP	Silverstone	29	Equipe Larrousse	3.5 Lola LC89-Lamborghini V12	engine

1990

	Race	Circuit	No	Entrant	Car/Engine	Comment
8	US GP (PHOENIX)	Phoenix	29	Espo Larrousse F1	3.5 Lola LC89-Lamborghini V12	spin/1 lap behind
ret	BRAZILIAN GP	Interlagos	29	Espo Larrousse F1	3.5 Lola LC89-Lamborghini V12	gearbox
13/ret	SAN MARINO GP	Imola	29	Espo Larrousse F1	3.5 Lola 90-Lamborghini V12	gearbox/5 laps behind
6	MONACO GP	Monte Carlo	29	Espo Larrousse F1	3.5 Lola 90-Lamborghini V12	2 laps behind
9	CANADIAN GP	Montreal	29	Espo Larrousse F1	3.5 Lola 90-Lamborghini V12	3 laps behind
ret	MEXICAN GP	Mexico City	29	Espo Larrousse F1	3.5 Lola 90-Lamborghini V12	spun off
8	FRENCH GP	Paul Ricard	29	Espo Larrousse F1	3.5 Lola 90-Lamborghini V12	pit stop-tyres/1 lap behind
4	BRITISH GP	Silverstone	29	Espo Larrousse F1	3.5 Lola 90-Lamborghini V12	
ret	GERMAN GP	Hockenheim	29	Espo Larrousse F1	3.5 Lola 90-Lamborghini V12	fuel pressure
6	HUNGARIAN GP	Hungaroring	29	Espo Larrousse F1	3.5 Lola 90-Lamborghini V12	brake problems
9	BELGIAN GP	Spa	29	Espo Larrousse F1	3.5 Lola 90-Lamborghini V12	long pit stop-tyres/1 lap behind
ret	ITALIAN GP	Monza	29	Espo Larrousse F1	3.5 Lola 90-Lamborghini V12	clutch
ret	PORTUGUESE GP	Estoril	29	Espo Larrousse F1	3.5 Lola 90-Lamborghini V12	gearbox
ret	SPANISH GP	Jerez	29	Espo Larrousse F1	3.5 Lola 90-Lamborghini V12	gearbox
ret	JAPANESE GP	Suzuka	29	Espo Larrousse F1	3.5 Lola 90-Lamborghini V12	engine
ret	AUSTRALIAN GP	Adelaide	29	Espo Larrousse F1	3.5 Lola 90-Lamborghini V12	gear selection

1991

	Race	Circuit	No	Entrant	Car/Engine	Comment
ret	US GP (PHOENIX)	Phoenix	29	Larrousse F1	3.5 Larrousse Lola L91-Cosworth V8	engine
ret	BRAZILIAN GP	Interlagos	29	Larrousse F1	3.5 Larrousse Lola L91-Cosworth V8	clutch
ret	SAN MARINO GP	Imola	29	Larrousse F1	3.5 Larrousse Lola L91-Cosworth V8	water leak
9	MONACO GP	Monte Carlo	29	Larrousse F1	3.5 Larrousse Lola L91-Cosworth V8	2 laps behind
ret	CANADIAN GP	Montreal	29	Larrousse F1	3.5 Larrousse Lola L91-Cosworth V8	gearbox
6	MEXICAN GP	Mexico City	29	Larrousse F1	3.5 Larrousse Lola L91-Cosworth V8	1 lap behind
ret	FRENCH GP	Magny Cours	29	Larrousse F1	3.5 Larrousse Lola L91-Cosworth V8	puncture
ret	BRITISH GP	Silverstone	29	Larrousse F1	3.5 Larrousse Lola L91-Cosworth V8	gearbox
ret	GERMAN GP	Hockenheim	29	Larrousse F1	3.5 Larrousse Lola L91-Cosworth V8	transmission
ret	HUNGARIAN GP	Hungaroring	29	Larrousse F1	3.5 Larrousse Lola L91-Cosworth V8	engine
ret	BELGIAN GP	Spa	29	Larrousse F1	3.5 Larrousse Lola L91-Cosworth V8	gearbox
ret	ITALIAN GP	Monza	29	Larrousse F1	3.5 Larrousse Lola L91-Cosworth V8	engine
dnq	PORTUGUESE GP	Estoril	29	Larrousse F1	3.5 Larrousse Lola L91-Cosworth V8	gearbox
ret	SPANISH GP	Barcelona	29	Larrousse F1	3.5 Larrousse Lola L91-Cosworth V8	collision with Boutsen-lap 1
dnp	JAPANESE GP	Suzuka	29	Larrousse F1	3.5 Larrousse Lola L91-Cosworth V8	free practice accident-broken leg

GP Starts: 31   GP Wins: 0   Pole positions: 0   Fastest laps: 0   Points: 6

BEUTTLER, Mike (GB) b 13/8/1940 – 29/12/1988

1971

	Race	Circuit	No	Entrant	Car/Engine	Comment
ret	BRITISH GP	Silverstone	6	Clarke-Mordaunt-Guthrie Racing	3.0 March 711-Cosworth V8	oil pressure
dsq	GERMAN GP	Nürburgring	28	Clarke-Mordaunt-Guthrie Racing	3.0 March 711-Cosworth V8	puncture-wrong entry to pits
nc	AUSTRIAN GP	Österreichring	27	Clarke-Mordaunt-Guthrie Racing	3.0 March 711-Cosworth V8	pit stop-engine/7 laps behind
ret	ITALIAN GP	Monza	24	Clarke-Mordaunt-Guthrie Racing	3.0 March 711-Cosworth V8	engine
nc	CANADIAN GP	Mosport Park	19	STP March	3.0 March 711-Cosworth V8	pit stop/8 laps behind

1972

	Race	Circuit	No	Entrant	Car/Engine	Comment
dnq	SPANISH GP	Jarama	23	Clarke-Mordaunt-Guthrie Racing	3.0 March 721G-Cosworth V8	
13	MONACO GP	Monte Carlo	5	Clarke-Mordaunt-Guthrie Racing	3.0 March 721G-Cosworth V8	4 laps behind
ret	BELGIAN GP	Nivelles	14	Clarke-Mordaunt-Guthrie Racing	3.0 March 721G-Cosworth V8	driveshaft
ret	FRENCH GP	Clermont Ferrand	15	Clarke-Mordaunt-Guthrie Racing	3.0 March 721G-Cosworth V8	out of fuel
13	BRITISH GP	Brands Hatch	31	Clarke-Mordaunt-Guthrie Racing	3.0 March 721G-Cosworth V8	7 laps behind
8	GERMAN GP	Nürburgring	28	Clarke-Mordaunt-Guthrie Racing	3.0 March 721G-Cosworth V8	
ret	AUSTRIAN GP	Österreichring	3	Clarke-Mordaunt-Guthrie Racing	3.0 March 721G-Cosworth V8	fuel metering unit
10	ITALIAN GP	Monza	16	Clarke-Mordaunt-Guthrie Racing	3.0 March 721G-Cosworth V8	1 lap behind
nc	CANADIAN GP	Mosport Park	27	Clarke-Mordaunt-Guthrie Racing	3.0 March 721G-Cosworth V8	spin-pit stop/21 laps behind
13	US GP	Watkins Glen	6	Clarke-Mordaunt-Guthrie Racing	3.0 March 721G-Cosworth V8	incident with Lauda/2 laps behind

1973

	Race	Circuit	No	Entrant	Car/Engine	Comment
10/ret	ARGENTINE GP	Buenos Aires	22	Clarke-Mordaunt-Guthrie-Durlacher	3.0 March 721G-Cosworth V8	radius rod/6 laps behind
ret	BRAZILIAN GP	Interlagos	12	Clarke-Mordaunt-Guthrie-Durlacher	3.0 March 721G-Cosworth V8	overheating
nc	SOUTH AFRICAN GP	Kyalami	24	Clarke-Mordaunt-Guthrie-Durlacher	3.0 March 721G-Cosworth V8	pit stops/14 laps behind
7	SPANISH GP	Montjuich Park	12	Clarke-Mordaunt-Guthrie-Durlacher	3.0 Montjuich 721G/731-Cosworth V8	1 lap behind
11/ret	BELGIAN GP	Zolder	15	Clarke-Mordaunt-Guthrie-Durlacher	3.0 March 721G/731-Cosworth V8	spun off/7 laps behind
ret	MONACO GP	Monte Carlo	15	Clarke-Mordaunt-Guthrie-Durlacher	3.0 March 721G/731-Cosworth V8	engine
8	SWEDISH GP	Anderstorp	15	Clarke-Mordaunt-Guthrie-Durlacher	3.0 March 721G/731-Cosworth V8	2 laps behind
11	BRITISH GP	Silverstone	15	Clarke-Mordaunt-Guthrie-Durlacher	3.0 March 721G/731-Cosworth V8	2 laps behind
ret	DUTCH GP	Zandvoort	15	Clarke-Mordaunt-Guthrie-Durlacher	3.0 March 721G/731-Cosworth V8	electrics
16	GERMAN GP	Nürburgring	15	Clarke-Mordaunt-Guthrie-Durlacher	3.0 March 721G/731-Cosworth V8	1 lap behind
ret	AUSTRIAN GP	Österreichring	15	Clarke-Mordaunt-Guthrie-Durlacher	3.0 March 721G/731-Cosworth V8	hit by Hailwood-broken oil cooler
ret	ITALIAN GP	Monza	15	Clarke-Mordaunt-Guthrie-Durlacher	3.0 March 721G/731-Cosworth V8	broken gear lever
ret	CANADIAN GP	Mosport Park	15	Clarke-Mordaunt-Guthrie-Durlacher	3.0 March 721G/731-Cosworth V8	engine
10	US GP	Watkins Glen	15	Clarke-Morduant-Guthrie-Durlacher	3.0 March 721G/731-Cosworth V8	1 lap behind

GP Starts: 28   GP Wins: 0   Pole positions: 0   Fastest laps: 0   Points: 0

ERIC BERNARD

A four-times French karting champion, Bernard showed immediate ability in a Winfield School competition (in which he beat Jean Alesi) and his prize was a season in Formule Renault. Fifth place in the 1984 championship formed the platform for a successful title bid the following season.

He had little money but decided to tackle the French F3 series. Running his own Martini-Alfa, Eric finished a creditable fifth, and armed with a Ralt for 1987 ran old rival Alesi and his mighty ORECA team very close as the pair dominated proceedings.

The backing of Winfield and Elf facilitated the step up into F3000 and after a false start with a works Ralt Bernard switched to Bromley Motorsport to kick-start his season. A fine second place in the final round at Dijon led to a place in the DAMS Lola team for 1989. He won at Jerez, but was out of luck elsewhere and, compounding this with some unforced errors, could only finish a disappointed third in the championship. The season had its compensations, though, a couple of drives for Larrousse in mid-season paving the way for a full-time ride in 1990, with a magnificent fourth place in the British Grand Prix the highlight of his first full season. The Larrousse team lost the use of Lamborghini engines in 1991, putting Eric into the also-ran category, and his season ended disastrously when he sustained a broken leg in a practice crash at the Japanese GP.

With the injury proving slow to heal, Bernard was sidelined for the following season but, not forgotten by his long-time sponsors Elf, he became the Ligier team's test driver in 1993. With a berth in the team's 1994 line-up likely to be earmarked for a French driver, Erik could be well placed to revive his F1 career.

MIKE BEUTTLER

Born in Cairo in 1943 of English parents while his father was serving in the Army, Mike became involved in the motor racing world immediately upon leaving school at the age of 16, assuming administrative duties with the Chequered Flag team. He had occasional chances to drive their front-engined Gemini car, but only when he struck out on his own – at the comparatively late age of 24 – with a Brabham F3 in club and Libre events did his racing career start in earnest.

With the backing of stockbroker colleagues Ralph Clarke and David Mordaunt – which was to be so vital to his progress to Formula 1 – Beuttler moved into F3 for 1969 with encouraging results given the calibre of opposition. Staying with the class for another season, Mike won three high-profile events, at Silverstone, Brands Hatch and Montlhéry, gaining third place in the Shellsport F3 championship and second place in that year's Grovewood Awards for his efforts.

For 1971 ambitious plans were laid to race a March 712. Alistair Guthrie joined the roster of backers and with the factory 'overseeing' his efforts, Mike undertook a full European F2 series. However, it was to prove a bitter disappointment, with the car beset by sundry maladies until the last round when he won the Madunina GP at Vallelunga. March had also helped him into Formula 1, without any great success.

It was the same recipe for 1972, with the addition of another backer – Jack Durlacher – to help pay the bills but no worthwhile results in Grands Prix. The most interesting aspect of the season, in fact, was the team's decision to adapt their 722 F2 car to accept the Cosworth engine. So much better was this machine's handling than the notorious 721X that the full-works cars were quickly consigned to history and Peterson and Lauda found themseves the beneficiaries.

Beuttler and his partners gave it one more shot in 1973, starting the season with the old car, but he was no more competitive when the new March 731 finally arrived. Mike called it quits and, after a single outing in the Brands Hatch 1000 Km in 1974, turned his back on racing and went into business. He later moved to San Francisco, where he died at the tragically young age of 45.

BIANCHI, Lucien (B) b 10/11/1934 – 30/3/1969

1959

	Race	Circuit	No	Entrant	Car/Engine	Comment
dnq	MONACO GP	Monte Carlo	10	Equipe Nationale Belge	1.5 Cooper T51-Climax 4	F2 car

1960

	Race	Circuit	No	Entrant	Car/Engine	Comment
6	BELGIAN GP	Spa	32	Equipe Nationale Belge	2.5 Cooper T45-Climax 4	pit stop-driveshaft/8 laps behind
ret	FRENCH GP	Reims	36	Fred Tuck Cars	2.5 Cooper T45-Climax 4	transmission
ret	BRITISH GP	Silverstone	24	Fred Tuck Cars	2.5 Cooper T45-Climax 4	engine

1961

	Race	Circuit	No	Entrant	Car/Engine	Comment
dnq	MONACO GP	Monte Carlo	10	Equipe Nationale Belge	1.5 Emeryson 1001-Maserati 4	
ret	BELGIAN GP	Spa	12	Equipe Nationale Belge	1.5 Lotus 18-Climax 4	hired Seidel's car/oil pipe
dns	"	"	12	Equipe Nationale Belge	1.5 Emeryson 1001-Maserati 4	car uncompetitive
ret	FRENCH GP	Reims	28	UDT Laystall Racing Team	1.5 Lotus 18/21-Climax 4	overheating/clutch
ret	BRITISH GP	Aintree	32	UDT Laystall Racing Team	1.5 Lotus 18/21-Climax 4	gearbox

1962

	Race	Circuit	No	Entrant	Car/Engine	Comment
9	BELGIAN GP	Spa	19	Equipe Nationale Belge	1.5 Lotus 18/21-Climax 4	3 laps behind
16	GERMAN GP	Nürburgring	21	Equipe Nationale Belge	1.5 ENB-Maserati 4	1 lap behind

1963

	Race	Circuit	No	Entrant	Car/Engine	Comment
ret	BELGIAN GP	Spa	22	Reg Parnell (Racing)	1.5 Lola 4-Climax V8	accident in rain

1965

	Race	Circuit	No	Entrant	Car/Engine	Comment
12	BELGIAN GP	Spa	27	Scuderia Centro Sud	1.5 BRM P57 V8	3 laps behind

1968

	Race	Circuit	No	Entrant	Car/Engine	Comment
3	MONACO GP	Monte Carlo	7	Cooper Car Co	3.0 Cooper T86B-BRM V12	4 laps behind
6	BELGIAN GP	Spa	15	Cooper Car Co	3.0 Cooper T86B-BRM V12	2 laps behind
ret	DUTCH GP	Zandvoort	14	Cooper Car Co	3.0 Cooper T86B-BRM V12	accident
ret	GERMAN GP	Nürburgring	19	Cooper Car Co	3.0 Cooper T86B-BRM V12	fuel leak
nc	CANADIAN GP	St Jovite	20	Cooper Car Co	3.0 Cooper T86B-BRM V12	pit stop-misfire/34 laps behind
ret	US GP	Watkins Glen	19	Cooper Car Co	3.0 Cooper T86B-BRM V12	clutch
ret	MEXICAN GP	Mexico City	19	Cooper Car Co	3.0 Cooper T86B-BRM V12	engine

GP Starts: 17   GP Wins: 0   Pole positions: 0   Fastest laps: 0   Points: 6

BIANCO, Gino (BR)

1952

	Race	Circuit	No	Entrant	Car/Engine	Comment
18	BRITISH GP	Silverstone	34	Escuderia Bandeirantes	2.0 Maserati A6GCM 6	8 laps behind
ret	GERMAN GP	Nürburgring	115	Escuderia Bandeirantes	2.0 Maserati A6GCM 6	
ret	DUTCH GP	Zandvoort	18	Escuderia Bandeirantes	2.0 Maserati A6GCM 6	rear axle
ret	ITALIAN GP	Monza	46	Escuderia Bandeirantes	2.0 Maserati A6GCM 6	mechanical

GP Starts: 4   GP Wins: 0   Pole positions: 0   Fastest laps: 0   Points: 0

BINDER, Hans (A) b 12/6/1948

1976

	Race	Circuit	No	Entrant	Car/Engine	Comment
ret	AUSTRIAN GP	Österreichring	22	Team Ensign	3.0 Ensign N176-Cosworth V8	throttle cable
ret	JAPANESE GP	Mount Fuji	21	Walter Wolf Racing	3.0 Williams FW05-Cosworth V8	wheel bearing

1977

	Race	Circuit	No	Entrant	Car/Engine	Comment
ret	ARGENTINE GP	Buenos Aires	18	Durex Team Surtees	3.0 Surtees TS19-Cosworth V8	damaged nose section
ret	BRAZILIAN GP	Interlagos	18	Durex Team Surtees	3.0 Surtees TS19-Cosworth V8	hit kerb-suspension damage
11	SOUTH AFRICAN GP	Kyalami	18	Durex Team Surtees	3.0 Surtees TS19-Cosworth V8	1 lap behind
11	US GP WEST	Long Beach	18	Durex Team Surtees	3.0 Surtees TS19-Cosworth V8	3 laps behind
9	SPANISH GP	Jarama	18	Durex Team Surtees	3.0 Surtees TS19-Cosworth V8	2 laps behind
ret	MONACO GP	Monte Carlo	18	Durex Team Surtees	3.0 Surtees TS19-Cosworth V8	fuel injection
12	AUSTRIAN GP	Österreichring	33	ATS Racing Team	3.0 Penske PC4-Cosworth V8	1 lap behind
8	DUTCH GP	Zandvoort	35	ATS Racing Team	3.0 Penske PC4-Cosworth V8	2 laps behind
dnq	ITALIAN GP	Monza	33	ATS Racing Team	3.0 Penske PC4-Cosworth V8	
11	US GP EAST	Watkins Glen	18	Durex Team Surtees	3.0 Surtees TS19-Cosworth V8	2 laps behind
ret	CANADIAN GP	Mosport Park	18	Durex Team Surtees	3.0 Surtees TS19-Cosworth V8	collision with Keegan
ret	JAPANESE GP	Mount Fuji	18	Durex Team Surtees	3.0 Surtees TS19-Cosworth V8	collision with Takahara

1978

	Race	Circuit	No	Entrant	Car/Engine	Comment
dnq	AUSTRIAN GP	Österreichring	10	ATS Racing Team	3.0 ATS HS1-Cosworth V8	

GP Starts: 13   GP Wins: 0   Pole positions: 0   Fastest laps: 0   Points: 0

BIONDETTI, Clemente (I) b 18/10/1898 – d 24/2/1955

1950

	Race	Circuit	No	Entrant	Car/Engine	Comment
ret	ITALIAN GP	Monza	22	Clemente Biondetti	3.4 Ferrari 166S-Jaguar 6	engine

GP Starts: 1   GP Wins: 0   Pole positions: 0   Fastest laps: 0   Points: 0

LUCIEN BIANCHI

Born in Italy, Lucien moved to Belgium as a child, when his father went to work as a racing mechanic for Johnny Claes. The young Bianchi nurtured hopes of a competition career, and in fact shared a Lancia with Claes in the 1955 Liège-Rome-Liège Rally, taking third place in what proved to be the terminally ill Claes' last event. Gradually Bianchi began to build his career in both sports cars and rallying, taking a class win with a Ferrari at Le Mans in 1957, and the first of three Tour de France rally wins (1957, 1958 and 1964).

Joining Equipe Nationale Belge, Lucien scored a third place at Pau in 1959, and a fourth the following year in the non-title South African GP, but the Belgian team was hardly front rank, and most of his success during this period was in sports cars, Bianchi winning the 1960 Paris 1000 Km with Gendebien in ENB's Ferrari, and the Sebring 12 Hours and the Angola GP in 1962.

Between 1963 and 1967, Formula 1 opportunities practically dried up, but Lucien busied himself in virtually every other form of competition – sports car and GT racing, Formula 2 (taking second on aggregate at Zolder in 1964) and Formula 3 as well as selected rallies. A reliable endurance racer, Bianchi became much in demand, driving works Porsches and Fords on occasion in addition to his regular seat in the Equipe Nationale Belge, while the 1967 season saw him try his hand at the Indianapolis 500. Having comfortably posted a good qualifying time, he flew back to race in the Nürburgring 1000 Km for Porsche, where an electrical failure on the last lap cost him the race win and dropped him to fourth place. Afterwards he was given the news that he had been 'bumped' from the grid at Indy.

Bianchi found a regular Grand Prix drive at last in 1968, albeit in the fading Cooper team, and scored points in his first two races. However, he enjoyed his best-ever sports car season, winning the Le Mans 24 Hours with Rodriguez and the Watkins Glen 6 Hours with Ickx for John Wyer, and taking the Circuit of Mugello in a works Alfa. At the end of the year Bianchi took part in the London-Sydney Marathon, and his Citroën was in a seemingly unassailable lead, less than 100 miles from the finish, when the car was involved in an accident with a non-competing vehicle while his co-driver Ogier was at the wheel, leaving Lucien with a broken ankle and shock.

Recovered from this crushing disappointment, Bianchi signed for Autodelta to race their Alfa T33s, but while practising at the Le Mans test weekend he lost control on the Mulsanne Straight. The car veered across the track into a telegraph pole, disintegrated and burst into flames, and the luckless Bianchi was killed instantly.

HANS BINDER

With promising performances in Formula Ford and the Polifac German F3 championship behind him, this protégé of Dr Helmut Marko entered Formula 2 in 1975 with a privately run March 752. He found the car a handful to drive and, although he finished second at the Salzburgring, an accident at Enna saw him switch to a works-loaned Chevron for the last four races.

Binder found himself in the same position the following season; after the first five races of the F2 campaign with the troubled Osella team brought no reward, a deal was struck with Fred Opert and Hans was back in a Chevron. Things improved rapidly, claiming fourth place in each of the final three races at Estoril, Nogaro and Hockenheim.

One-off drives for Ensign in Austria (replacing a disaffected Amon) and for Wolf in Japan (the injured Ickx and local driver Kuwashima) whetted his appetite for 1977. With Team Surtees providing the bread and ATS-Penske the jam in his season, it would be charitable to say his performances were somewhat lacklustre, and in Grand Prix terms he was redundant.

CLEMENTE BIONDETTI

Biondetti's racing career began in 1923 on motor cycles, the Italian turning to cars in 1927. After early success in a Talbot, he joined the Maserati factory team in 1931, finishing third in both the Rome and French GPs.

His reputation really grew with Alfa Romeo, Biondetti valiantly hanging on to a trio of Mercedes in the Tripoli GP of 1937 as the rest of the field surrendered, before the engine blew. 1938 saw the first of his wins in the Mille Miglia and he was at his peak as a driver as war broke out. Despite being 49 when racing resumed, Biondetti took a hat-trick of wins (1947-49) in his beloved Mille Miglia as well as emerging triumphant in the Tour of Sicily in both 1948 and 1949. His win in the rain-soaked 1947 race was quite brilliant. Minus two gears and suffering fuel-feed problems with his Alfa Romeo, the veteran Italian beat the legendary Nuvolari into second place. Eschewing the pure Ferrari sports cars which had brought him his other recent successes, Biondetti built a Ferrari-Jaguar hybrid which failed at the Italian GP in 1950 and disappointed elsewhere.

Not surprisingly he then returned to the trusty machines of the Prancing Horse, sharing Stagnoli's car to take third place in the 1952 Monaco Grand Prix, run that year for sports cars. The same year he was second in the Acerbo Cup, a 12-hour race at Pescara. For 1953 he raced the rival Lancia cars but returned to the fold in 1954 – his final season – marking his last appearance in the Mille Miglia with a fourth place. Clemente had known that he had been suffering from cancer for several years and felt that to continue racing any longer could endanger others. A year later he was dead.

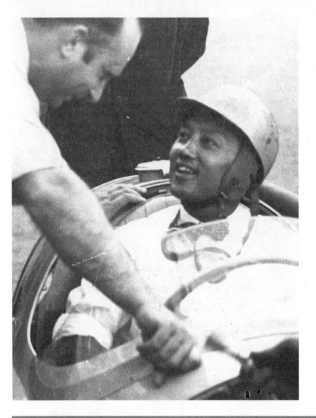

'B BIRA'

Prince Birabongse Bhanuban of Siam (now Thailand) was the true title of this aristocrat, who was educated at Eton and Cambridge before studying sculpture. In the mid-thirties he lived in London under the care of his cousin Prince Chula and, after 'Bira' had tried his hand with a Riley Imp and an MG Magnette, Chula gave him an ERA for his 21st birthday. Establishing the endearingly titled 'White Mouse Stable', 'Bira' won many races in a trio of ERAs in the immediate pre-war years, becoming one of the marque's most famous exponents. He also raced the ex-Whitney Straight Maserati and, less successfully, the ex-Seaman Delage, and his outstanding performances were rewarded with the BRDC Road Racing Gold Star in 1936, 1937 and 1938.

After the war 'Bira' was back in his ERA but soon switched to Maserati, winning the 1947 GP des Frontières at Chimay. He was to continue to race in partnership with Chula until the end of the 1948 season, but had meanwhile ventured out in an F2 Simca Gordini, winning a race at Skarpnack, Sweden.

Taking his Maserati San Remo into the Enrico Platé stable, 'Bira' had a busy year in 1949, which started with two fifths at Buenos Aires and a second to Fangio at Mar del Plata. He then returned to Europe and produced a run of excellent performances which brought second places at the Albi, French, San Remo and Rousillon Grands Prix, and third places in the Italian and Zandvoort GPs.

When the World Championship was inaugurated in 1950, 'Bira' managed a fourth place at Bremgarten but litle else, as the cars were really outclassed. The following year he put an OSCA V12 engine into the Maserati, winning only the five-lap Libre Richmond Trophy race at Goodwood. He continued to race the OSCA in Formula 1 races into 1952, but also handled the fast but fragile works Gordini. It was a frustrating time for the little prince, who seemed to lose interest after a long run of bad luck. Nevertheless he returned to the track occasionally in 1953 with the Connaught team until his own Maserati A6GCM was delivered late in the year. The acquisition of a true Maserati 250F early in 1954 seemed to whet 'Bira's' appetite for racing and, in non-championship races, he won at Chimay and took second places at Rouen and Pescara, while in the French GP at Reims he took his best championship placing for some years. Early in 1955 he scored his last win in the New Zealand GP at Ardmore, before returning to Europe to finish sixth at the Bordeaux GP and third in the International Trophy – his final race before his sudden decision to retire.

MICHAEL BLEEKEMOLEN

Bleekemolen was a Dutch Formula Super Vee and later Formula Ford driver who, due to his access to sponsorship money, found himself placed in a Grand Prix car in 1977 before he was really ready for the task. He was undeniably a quick driver in these lower formulae, but he needed much more experience to compete at Grand Prix level.

To this end Bleekemolen embarked on a full season of European Formula 3 for 1978, finishing fifth in the series, and then, again with the help of his F & S Properties backing, he joined ATS for another unsuccessful sortie into the world of Grands Prix. After that it was back to a diet of Formula 3, Michael plugging away for another three seasons with some good finishes but outright victory elusive.

HARRY BLANCHARD

Blanchard was invited to race his Porsche RSK sports car in the inaugural US GP at Sebring in order to make up the numbers. He was a regular on the late-fifties American road racing scene, his best result being third place in the 1959 Watkins Glen GP. However, Blanchard was fatally injured in the 1960 Buenos Aires 1000 Km when his Porsche crashed and overturned.

TREVOR BLOKDYK

A former South African speedway champion, Blokdyk went racing with a Cooper in 1961 and proved to be an extremely fast and fearless competitor. He first visited Europe in 1962, racing in Formula Junior, and did well (second at Nogaro and Caserta) until the money ran out. Trevor then returned home to contest the South African championships – and his only Grand Prix – in the ex-Love Cooper. Back in Europe in 1965 to race in F3, he was one of that season's stars until a massive crash at Albi hospitalised him for three months with pelvic and leg injuries. He made his comeback at Rouen in 1966, finishing sixth, and continued to race in F3 in 1968 and early 1969, before returning to compete in South Africa.

'BIRA, B' (Prince Birabongse) (T) b 15/7/1914 – d 23/12/1985

1950

	Race	Circuit	No	Entrant	Car/Engine	Comment
ret	BRITISH GP	Silverstone	21	Enrico Platé	1.5 s/c Maserati 4CLT/48 4	fuel feed
5	MONACO GP	Monte Carlo	50	Enrico Platé	1.5 s/c Maserati 4CLT/48 4	5 laps behind
4	SWISS GP	Bremgarten	30	Enrico Platé	1.5 s/c Maserati 4CLT/48 4	2 laps behind
ret	ITALIAN GP	Monza	30	Enrico Platé	1.5 s/c Maserati 4CLT/48 4	engine

1951

	Race	Circuit	No	Entrant	Car/Engine	Comment
ret	SPANISH GP	Pedralbes	18	'B Bira'	4.5 Maserati 4CLT/48-OSCA V12	engine

1952

	Race	Circuit	No	Entrant	Car/Engine	Comment
ret	SWISS GP	Bremgarten	10	Equipe Gordini	1.5 Gordini Type 15 4	engine
10	BELGIAN GP	Spa	20	Equipe Gordini	1.5 Gordini Type 15 4	4 laps behind
ret	FRENCH GP	Rouen	6	Equipe Gordini	2.0 Gordini Type 16 6	rear axle
11	BRITISH GP	Silverstone	26	Equipe Gordini	2.0 Gordini Type 16 6	4 laps behind

1953

	Race	Circuit	No	Entrant	Car/Engine	Comment
ret	FRENCH GP	Reims	42	Connaught Engineering	2.0 Connaught A-Lea Francis 4	transmission
7	BRITISH GP	Silverstone	10	Connaught Engineering	2.0 Connaught A-Lea Francis 4	8 laps behind
ret	GERMAN GP	Nürburgring	14	Connaught Engineering	2.0 Connaught A-Lea Francis 4	engine
11	ITALIAN GP	Monza	44	Scuderia Milan	2.0 Maserati A6GCM 6	8 laps behind

1954

	Race	Circuit	No	Entrant	Car/Engine	Comment
7	ARGENTINE GP	Buenos Aires	8	Officine Alfieri Maserati	2.5 Maserati A6GCM/250F 6	4 laps behind
6	BELGIAN GP	Spa	20	'B Bira'	2.5 Maserati 250F 6	1 lap behind
4	FRENCH GP	Reims	46	'B Bira'	2.5 Maserati 250F 6	1 lap behind
ret*	BRITISH GP	Silverstone	6	'B Bira'	2.5 Maserati 250F 6	* Flockhart took over-crashed
ret	GERMAN GP	Nürburgring	14	'B Bira'	2.5 Maserati 250F 6	steering
9	SPANISH GP	Pedralbes	18	'B Bira'	2.5 Maserati 250F 6	12 laps behind

GP Starts: 19   GP Wins: 0   Pole positions: 0   Fastest laps: 0   Points: 8

BIRGER, Pablo (RA) b 6/1/1924

1953

	Race	Circuit	No	Entrant	Car/Engine	Comment
ret	ARGENTINE GP	Buenos Aires	34	Equipe Gordini	1.5 Gordini Type 15 4	cwp

1955

	Race	Circuit	No	Entrant	Car/Engine	Comment
ret	ARGENTINE GP	Buenos Aires	40	Equipe Gordini	2.0 Gordini Type 16 6	spun, hit by Menditéguy

GP Starts: 2   GP Wins: 0   Pole positions: 0   Fastest laps: 0   Points: 0

BLANCHARD, Harry (USA) d 31/1/1960

1959

	Race	Circuit	No	Entrant	Car/Engine	Comment
7	US GP	Sebring	17	Blanchard Automobile Co	1.5 Porsche RSK F4	sports car/4 laps behind

GP Starts: 1   GP Wins: 0   Pole positions: 0   Fastest laps: 0   Points: 0

BLEEKEMOLEN, Michael (NL) b 2/10/1949

1977

	Race	Circuit	No	Entrant	Car/Engine	Comment
dnq	DUTCH GP	Zandvoort	32	RAM Racing/F & S Properties	3.0 March 761-Cosworth V8	

1978

	Race	Circuit	No	Entrant	Car/Engine	Comment
dnq	DUTCH GP	Zandvoort	10	F & S Properties/ATS Racing Team	3.0 ATS HS1-Cosworth V8	
dnq	ITALIAN GP	Monza	9	F & S Properties/ATS Racing Team	3.0 ATS HS1-Cosworth V8	
ret	US GP EAST	Watkins Glen	9	F & S Properties/ATS Racing Team	3.0 ATS HS1-Cosworth V8	oil pump leak
dnq	CANADIAN GP	Montreal	9	F & S Properties/ATS Racing Team	3.0 ATS HS1-Cosworth V8	

GP Starts: 1   GP Wins: 0   Pole positions: 0   Fastest laps: 0   Points: 0

BLOKDYK, Trevor (ZA) b 30/11/1935

1963

	Race	Circuit	No	Entrant	Car/Engine	Comment
12	SOUTH AFRICAN GP	East London	23	Scuderia Lupini	1.5 Cooper T51-Maserati 4	8 laps behind

1965

	Race	Circuit	No	Entrant	Car/Engine	Comment
dnq	SOUTH AFRICAN GP	East London	28	Trevor Blokdyk	1.5 Cooper T59-Ford 4	

GP Starts: 1   GP Wins: 0   Pole positions: 0   Fastest laps: 0   Points: 0

MARK BLUNDELL

Mark Blundell is typical of a generation of British drivers who have worked so hard to get into Formula 1 – a lot of talent, but not a lot of money. This former motocross rider had a quite remarkable first season in Formula Ford, winning 25 of his 70 races and receiving the 1984 Grovewood Award in recognition of this achievement.

The next two seasons were spent in FF1600 and FF2000, often in direct competition with the better-sponsored Bertrand Gachot, before Mark plunged straight into the F3000 championship for 1987 with an elderly Lola. Cracking drives in early-season races at Spa and Vallelunga brought him points-scoring finishes and seemed to vindicate his decision to miss out on the traditional stepping-stone of Formula 3, especially when he was offered the works Lola for the 1988 F3000 season. Second place in the opening round at Jerez showed promise, but the season then slid away in a mire of development tweaks that saw the car engineered out of competitiveness.

In some ways 1989 was a make-or-break year for Blundell in F3000. He moved to the Middlebridge team and all the ingredients for success seemed to be there, but his season was ragged and he failed to make the top ten in the final points standings. Nevertheless he must have shown something, because Nissan paired him with Julian Bailey in their rapid car to contest the endurance championship and Williams signed him as a test driver for 1990.

It was a year well spent as Mark familiarised himself with the intricacies of a Formula 1 car, but with no prospect of racing for the team in the immediate future he understandably accepted an offer to join Brabham-Yamaha for 1991. Paired with the experienced Martin Brundle, he was certainly not overshadowed, and scored his first championship point at Spa in the Belgian GP. However, the finances of the team were already parlous and Blundell was reluctantly shown the door in favour of 'paying guests' at season's end.

The 1992 season was again spent on the F1 bench, Mark acting as test driver for McLaren, but brought an unexpected highlight when, in a one-off appearance for Peugeot, he won the Le Mans 24 Hours with Derek Warwick and Yannick Dalmas. The well-funded but under-achieving Ligier team had changed hands and, despite much criticism in the French press, new owner Cyril de Rouvre hired both Mark and Martin Brundle to revive their fortunes in 1993. Mark's superb third place in the opening race, followed by a fifth next time out in Brazil, boded well, but as the season wore on question marks were raised as the number of spins and incidents mounted, and suddenly he was facing an anxious winter, hoping to land a drive in1994.

BLUNDELL, Mark (GB) b 8/4/1966

1991

	Race	Circuit	No	Entrant	Car/Engine	Comment
ret	US GP (PHOENIX)	Phoenix	7	Motor Racing Developments Ltd	3.5 Brabham BT59Y-Yamaha V12	spun off
ret	BRAZILIAN GP	Interlagos	7	Motor Racing Developments Ltd	3.5 Brabham BT59Y-Yamaha V12	engine
8	SAN MARINO GP	Imola	7	Motor Racing Developments Ltd	3.5 Brabham BT60Y-Yamaha V12	3 laps behind
ret	MONACO GP	Monte Carlo	7	Motor Racing Developments Ltd	3.5 Brabham BT60Y-Yamaha V12	crashed on Modena's oil
dnq	CANADIAN GP	Montreal	7	Motor Racing Developments Ltd	3.5 Brabham BT60Y-Yamaha V12	
ret	MEXICAN GP	Mexico City	7	Motor Racing Developments Ltd	3.5 Brabham BT60Y-Yamaha V12	engine
ret	FRENCH GP	Magny Cours	7	Motor Racing Developments Ltd	3.5 Brabham BT60Y-Yamaha V12	accident-slid into pit wall
ret	BRITISH GP	Silverstone	7	Motor Racing Developments Ltd	3.5 Brabham BT60Y-Yamaha V12	engine
12	GERMAN GP	Hockenheim	7	Motor Racing Developments Ltd	3.5 Brabham BT60Y-Yamaha V12	2 laps behind
ret	HUNGARIAN GP	Hungaroring	7	Motor Racing Developments Ltd	3.5 Brabham BT60Y-Yamaha V12	spun off-stalled
6	BELGIAN GP	Spa	7	Motor Racing Developments Ltd	3.5 Brabham BT60Y-Yamaha V12	
12	ITALIAN GP	Monza	7	Motor Racing Developments Ltd	3.5 Brabham BT60Y-Yamaha V12	1 lap behind
ret	PORTUGUESE GP	Estoril	7	Motor Racing Developments Ltd	3.5 Brabham BT60Y-Yamaha V12	rear suspension collapsed-spun off
ret	SPANISH GP	Barcelona	7	Motor Racing Developments Ltd	3.5 Brabham BT60Y-Yamaha V12	engine
dnpq	JAPANESE GP	Suzuka	7	Motor Racing Developments Ltd	3.5 Brabham BT60Y-Yamaha V12	
17	AUSTRALIAN GP	Adelaide	7	Motor Racing Developments Ltd	3.5 Brabham BT60Y-Yamaha V12	race abandoned after 14 laps

1993

	Race	Circuit	No	Entrant	Car/Engine	Comment
3	SOUTH AFRICAN GP	Kyalami	26	Ligier Gitanes Blondes	3.5 Ligier JS39-Renault V10	1 lap behind
5	BRAZILIAN GP	Interlagos	26	Ligier Gitanes Blondes	3.5 Ligier JS39-Renault V10	
ret	EUROPEAN GP	Donington	26	Ligier Gitanes Blondes	3.5 Ligier JS39-Renault V10	spun off
ret	SAN MARINO GP	Imola	26	Ligier Gitanes Blondes	3.5 Ligier JS39-Renault V10	spun off at first corner
7	SPANISH GP	Barcelona	26	Ligier Gitanes Blondes	3.5 Ligier JS39-Renault V10	2 laps behind
ret	MONACO GP	Monte Carlo	26	Ligier Gitanes Blondes	3.5 Ligier JS39-Renault V10	suspension
ret	CANADIAN GP	Montreal	26	Ligier Gitanes Blondes	3.5 Ligier JS39-Renault V10	spun off
ret	FRENCH GP	Magny Cours	26	Ligier Gitanes Blondes	3.5 Ligier JS39-Renault V10	collision-de Cesaris-spun off
7	BRITISH GP	Silverstone	26	Ligier Gitanes Blondes	3.5 Ligier JS39-Renault V10	spun/1 lap behind
3	GERMAN GP	Hockenheim	26	Ligier Gitanes Blondes	3.5 Ligier JS39-Renault V10	
7	HUNGARIAN GP	Hungaroring	26	Ligier Gitanes Blondes	3.5 Ligier JS39-Renault V10	gear selection problems/1 lap behind
11/ret	BELGIAN GP	Spa	26	Ligier Gitanes Blondes	3.5 Ligier JS39-Renault V10	taken off by Berger/2 laps behind
ret	ITALIAN GP	Monza	26	Ligier Gitanes Blondes	3.5 Ligier JS39-Renault V10	hit barrier-tyre damage
ret	PORTUGUESE GP	Estoril	26	Ligier Gitanes Blondes	3.5 Ligier JS39-Renault V10	collision-Wendlinger
7	JAPANESE GP	Suzuka	26	Ligier Gitanes Blondes	3.5 Ligier JS39-Renault V10	brake and gearbox troubles
9	AUSTRALIAN GP	Adelaide	26	Ligier Gitanes Blondes	3.5 Ligier JS39-Renault V10	2 laps behind

GP Starts: 30   GP Wins: 0   Pole positions: 0   Fastest laps: 0   Points: 11

BOESEL, Raul (BR) b 4/12/1957

1982

	Race	Circuit	No	Entrant	Car/Engine	Comment
15	SOUTH AFRICAN GP	Kyalami	18	March Grand Prix Team	3.0 March 821-Cosworth V8	5 laps behind
ret	BRAZILIAN GP	Rio	18	Rothmans March Grand Prix Team	3.0 March 821-Cosworth V8	puncture, spun off
9*	US GP WEST	Long Beach	18	Rothmans March Grand Prix Team	3.0 March 821-Cosworth V8	* 10th car dsq/5 laps behind
8	BELGIAN GP	Zolder	18	Rothmans March Grand Prix Team	3.0 March 821-Cosworth V8	4 laps behind
dnpq	MONACO GP	Monte Carlo	18	Rothmans March Grand Prix Team	3.0 March 821-Cosworth V8	
ret	US GP (DETROIT)	Detroit	18	Rothmans March Grand Prix Team	3.0 March 821-Cosworth V8	hit by Baldi

ret	CANADIAN GP	Montreal	18	Rothmans March Grand Prix Team	3.0 March 821-Cosworth V8	engine
ret	DUTCH GP	Zandvoort	18	Rothmans March Grand Prix Team	3.0 March 821-Cosworth V8	engine
dnq	BRITISH GP	Brands Hatch	18	Rothmans March Grand Prix Team	3.0 March 821-Cosworth V8	
dnq	FRENCH GP	Paul Ricard	18	Rothmans March Grand Prix Team	3.0 March 821-Cosworth V8	
ret	GERMAN GP	Hockenheim	18	Rothmans March Grand Prix Team	3.0 March 821-Cosworth V8	puncture
dnq	AUSTRIAN GP	Österreichring	18	Rothmans March Grand Prix Team	3.0 March 821-Cosworth V8	
ret	SWISS GP	Dijon	18	Rothmans March Grand Prix Team	3.0 March 821-Cosworth V8	gearbox oil leak
dnq	ITALIAN GP	Monza	18	Rothmans March Grand Prix Team	3.0 March 821-Cosworth V8	
13	CAESARS PALACE GP	Las Vegas	18	Rothmans March Grand Prix Team	3.0 March 821-Cosworth V8	6 laps behind

1983

ret	BRAZILIAN GP	Rio	26	Equipe Ligier Gitanes	3.0 Ligier JS21-Cosworth V8	electrics
7	US GP WEST	Long Beach	26	Equipe Ligier Gitanes	3.0 Ligier JS21-Cosworth V8	2 laps behind
ret	FRENCH GP	Paul Ricard	26	Equipe Ligier Gitanes	3.0 Ligier JS21-Cosworth V8	engine
9	SAN MARINO GP	Imola	26	Equipe Ligier Gitanes	3.0 Ligier JS21-Cosworth V8	2 laps behind
ret	MONACO GP	Monte Carlo	26	Equipe Ligier Gitanes	3.0 Ligier JS21-Cosworth V8	accident with Winkelhock
13	BELGIAN GP	Spa	26	Equipe Ligier Gitanes	3.0 Ligier JS21-Cosworth V8	1 lap behind
10	US GP (DETROIT)	Detroit	26	Equipe Ligier Gitanes	3.0 Ligier JS21-Cosworth V8	2 laps behind
ret	CANADIAN GP	Montreal	26	Equipe Ligier Gitanes	3.0 Ligier JS21-Cosworth V8	wheel bearing
ret	BRITISH GP	Silverstone	26	Equipe Ligier Gitanes	3.0 Ligier JS21-Cosworth V8	hydraulic suspension leak
ret	GERMAN GP	Hockenheim	26	Equipe Ligier Gitanes	3.0 Ligier JS21-Cosworth V8	engine
dnq	AUSTRIAN GP	Österreichring	26	Equipe Ligier Gitanes	3.0 Ligier JS21-Cosworth V8	
10	DUTCH GP	Zandvoort	26	Equipe Ligier Gitanes	3.0 Ligier JS21-Cosworth V8	2 laps behind
dnq	ITALIAN GP	Monza	26	Equipe Ligier Gitanes	3.0 Ligier JS21-Cosworth V8	
15	EUROPEAN GP	Brands Hatch	26	Equipe Ligier Gitanes	3.0 Ligier JS21-Cosworth V8	3 laps behind
nc	SOUTH AFRICAN GP	Kyalami	26	Equipe Ligier Gitanes	3.0 Ligier JS21-Cosworth V8	11 laps behind

GP Starts: 23   GP Wins: 0   Pole positions: 0   Fastest laps: 0   Points: 0

BONDURANT, Bob (USA) b 27/4/1933

1965

	Race	Circuit	No	Entrant	Car/Engine	Comment
9	US GP	Watkins Glen	24	North American Racing Team	1.5 Ferrari 158 V8	4 laps behind
ret	MEXICAN GP	Mexico City	22	Reg Parnell (Racing)	1.5 Lotus 33-Climax V8	rear suspension bolt

1966

4	MONACO GP	Monte Carlo	19	Team Chamaco Collect	2.0 BRM P261 V8	5 laps behind
ret	BELGIAN GP	Spa	8	Team Chamaco Collect	2.0 BRM P261 V8	spun off in rain
9	BRITISH GP	Brands Hatch	25	Team Chamaco Collect	2.0 BRM P261 V8	4 laps behind
ret	GERMAN GP	Nürburgring	14	Team Chamaco Collect	2.0 BRM P261 V8	engine
7	ITALIAN GP	Monza	48	Team Chamaco Collect	2.0 BRM P261 V8	3 laps behind
dsq	US GP	Watkins Glen	16	Anglo American Racers	2.7 Eagle T1G-Climax 4	pushstart
ret	MEXICAN GP	Mexico City	16	Anglo American Racers	3.0 Eagle T1G-Weslake V12	fuel feed
dns	"	" "	15	Anglo American Racers	2.7 Eagle T1G-Climax 4	practice only

GP Starts: 9   GP Wins: 0   Pole positions: 0   Fastest laps: 0   Points: 3

RAUL BOESEL

After karting and saloon car success, Boesel followed the well-trodden path of Brazilian hopefuls bound for Europe with the aim of becoming the next Fittipaldi.

Never having driven a single-seater and with no English, Raul sensibly bought himself a drive with van Diemen. Quickly learning from team-mates Moreno and Byrne, he finished runner-up in both Formula Ford championships in 1980, winning eight races. Opting for F3 for 1981, Boesel enjoyed a remarkably consistent season, finishing in the points in 16 of the 20 rounds, and winning three of them to take third place in the Marlboro championship.

Well-funded after his success, Raul took his sponsorship money into F1 with the RAM March team but it was to be a disastrous season. Things were not much better the following year, his F1 career effectively torpedoed as he struggled in a Ligier team then in decline.

Deciding to change course, he headed off to the States and found a ride with Dick Simon's IndyCar team in 1985 and '86. Just missing out on a couple of good seats for 1987, Boesel found himself a berth in the TWR Jaguar sports car team and enjoyed a highly successful season, the Brazilian winning the drivers' sports car title to raise his stature immensely.

Opting for a return to Indy cars, Raul has posed a consistent threat to the elite – 1993 proved to be his best season yet. That elusive first IndyCar win for Raul and Dick Simon could well happen in 1994.

BOB BONDURANT

Originally from Illinois, Bob later moved to the West Coast where he raced Triumphs and Corvettes with some success, though his big break came with the chance to race Carroll Shelby's hairy AC Cobra at Denver in 1963. A class win on his debut saw Bob signed full-time for 1964 as the Shelby team headed for Europe to contest the classic long-distance events. His best result was a fourth place at Le Mans (with Gurney) to win the GT class.

Bob had a hectic season in 1965, racing the Cobra and Ford GTs, in addition to a number of Formula 2 and Formula 3 outings. This led to an invitation to race the works Ferrari in place of the injured John Surtees at the season's end.

Back in Europe for 1966 Bob raced for Bernard White's private team – picking up a fourth place at Monaco – in tandem with a freelance season of sports car rides, sharing Ferarris with Rindt, Parkes and Gregory and bringing a works Porsche into fourth place in the Nürburgring 1000 Km.

His career seemed to be over after a huge accident at Watkins Glen in 1967 prevented him from racing but he made a successsful comeback in Can-Am in 1970 and '71. Thereafter he concentrated on his racing driver schools, but was occasionally tempted back behind the wheel in SCCA and NASCAR races.

FELICE BONETTO

Known as *'Il Pirata'* (the pirate), Bonetto was a fearless competitor who took no prisoners and was possessed of so much courage that some of his racing exploits placed him in the category of the foolhardy.

He was already well known in Italy in the late thirties through his exploits in his privately entered Alfa Romeo in the Mille Miglia, but did not come to the fore internationally until the late forties, first with Cisitalia and then with Ferrari, for whom he scored second places in the Mille Miglia and the Monza and Naples GPs in 1949.

The independently minded Felice campaigned the Maserati Milano and his own Alfa sports car to such effect that after winning the 1950 Oporto GP and leading the Mille Miglia in the Alfa, he was offered a works drive in 1951. He was very much the number three in the team, however, which did not go down too well, and he took the offer of a contract with Lancia to race their sports cars in 1952. This brought him perhaps his greatest triumph, in the Targa Florio.

Despite his age Bonetto was more active than ever in 1953. Undertaking a full season of Grands Prix for the first time with the Maserati works team and racing sports cars again for Lancia, he won the Portuguese GP in Lisbon and placed third in the Mille Miglia before competing in the gruelling Carrera Panamericana. He lay in second place to Taruffi when he was killed after skidding off the road and crashing into a lamp standard in the village of Silao.

JOAKIM BONNIER

From a comfortable background, this Swedish driver had built a mighty reputation as an ice-racer in the early fifties with an Alfa Romeo Disco Volante, which led to him being appointed a distributor for that marque in 1954. Moving into circuit racing the following year, Bonnier soon proved to be a front-runner in Scandinavia before venturing further afield in 1956 to race the GT Alfa, winning events at Aintree, AVUS and Castelfusano, and taking a class win at the Nürburgring 1000 Km with Mackay-Fraser. By now he had started to run Maserati sports cars, and in 1957 became involved with the works team, finishing third in the Swedish GP in a 300TS.

Although he had not really reached the front rank of drivers, Jo bought a Maserati 250F which he raced in the 1957-58 seasons with only moderate results, the best being second places at Syracuse and Caen against meagre opposition. At the tail-end of 1958 he joined BRM and soon became the first driver to win a championship Grand Prix for Bourne when he won the 1959 Dutch GP. He was to stay with BRM until the end of the 1960 season, but never came close to repeating his Zandvoort triumph, although he comfortably led the 1960 Argentine GP until the engine failed.

Having begun a successful association with Porsche in 1959, Bonnier took every opportunity to race for them again the following year, winning the Modena GP and taking a superb victory in the rain in the non-championship German GP in F2, and sharing the victorious RSK sports car with Herrmann in the the Targa Florio. With the Porsche team planning a Grand Prix assault in 1961, Bonnier – feeling his talents were being overlooked at BRM – joined Dan Gurney to race the silver cars. After a winter interlude which included taking a Yeoman Credit Cooper to victory in New Zealand at the Teretonga international and at Levin, the 1961 season started with a second place in Seidel's Lotus at Pau before Bonnier concentrated on his Porsche commitments. He made a promising beginning, with some good results in non-championship races, including second places at Solitude, Karlskoga and Modena and thirds at Syracuse and Zeltweg, but in Grands Prix things were much tougher, and he was increasingly overshadowed by Gurney, especially in 1962 when he endured a fairly depressing time with the new Porsche 804 flat-eight, with a second place at Solitude and a third at the Karlskoga GP his only worthwhile results.

With Porsche withdrawing from Formula 1, Bonnier joined Rob Walker in 1963 and raced his privately entered cars for the next three seasons. When the mood took him he could still be extremely quick, but by now he seemed more interested in his pivotal role as leader of the newly formed Grand Prix Drivers' Association. When Walker released him for 1966, Jo formed his own team, picking up occasional points racing a Cooper-Maserati and then a McLaren, as well as scrounging a few works drives, but he was really a shadow of his former self, especially in 1971, when he was very slow indeed.

If nothing else Bonnier still enjoyed the life of a racing driver, and while the best days of his Grand Prix career had long been in the past, he raced sports cars with great gusto. He shared a Chaparral with Phil Hill to win the Nürburgring 1000 Km in 1966 and raced his own and the Ecurie Filipinetti's Lola T70s with some minor success, but it was the acquisition of a 2-litre Lola in 1970 that seemingly re-awakened the racer that had for so long lain dormant. He won G5/6 races at both Silverstone and Jyllandsring and took the European 2-litre championship with some terrific drives.

Although just past 40, Bonnier's racing activities showed no sign of slackening in 1971, and his lacklustre Grand Prix performances were thrown into sharp relief by some more good results in the sports car categories, including a third in the Targa Florio with Attwood, second place in the Auvergne Trophy and an outright win in the Barcelona 1000 Km with Peterson. Retiring from Formula 1 at the end of the season, Bonnier raced on in a new Lola T280. However, at Le Mans in 1972 he was involved in a collision with a privateer Ferrari, and Jo's yellow Lola was launched over the barriers into the trees. The man who had spent so much time crusading for circuit safety over the years had become another victim among a whole generation of racers who paid the ultimate price.

BONETTO, Felice (I) b 9/6/1903 – d 21/11/1953

1950

	Race	Circuit	No	Entrant	Car/Engine	Comment
5	SWISS GP	Bremgarten	34	Scuderia Milano	1.5 s/c Maserati 4CLT/Milano 4	2 laps behind
ret	FRENCH GP	Reims	40	Scuderia Milano	1.5 s/c Maserati 4CLT/Milano 4	engine
dns	ITALIAN GP	Monza	52	Scuderia Milano	1.5 s/c Maserati 4CLT/Milano 4	

1951

	Race	Circuit	No	Entrant	Car/Engine	Comment
4	BRITISH GP	Silverstone	4	Alfa Romeo SpA	1.5 s/c Alfa Romeo 159A 8	3 laps behind
ret	GERMAN GP	Nürburgring	77	Alfa Romeo SpA	1.5 s/c Alfa Romeo 159A 8	supercharger
3*	ITALIAN GP	Monza	40	Alfa Romeo SpA	1.5 s/c Alfa Romeo 159A 8	* Farina took over/1 lap behind
5	SPANISH GP	Pedralbes	24	Alfa Romeo SpA	1.5 s/c Alfa Romeo 159M 8	2 laps behind

1952

	Race	Circuit	No	Entrant	Car/Engine	Comment
dsq	GERMAN GP	Nürburgring	105	Officine Alfieri Maserati	2.0 Maserati A6GCM 6	push start after spin
5	ITALIAN GP	Monza	22	Officine Alfieri Maserati	2.0 Maserati A6GCM 6	1 lap behind

1953

	Race	Circuit	No	Entrant	Car/Engine	Comment
ret	ARGENTINE GP	Buenos Aires	6	Officine Alfieri Maserati	2.0 Maserati A6GCM 6	transmission
3	DUTCH GP	Zandvoort	16	Officine Alfieri Maserati	2.0 Maserati A6GCM 6	Gonzalez took over/1 lap behind
ret	FRENCH GP	Reims	24	Officine Alfieri Maserati	2.0 Maserati A6GCM 6	engine
6	BRITISH GP	Silverstone	25	Officine Alfieri Maserati	2.0 Maserati A6GCM 6	9 laps behind
4	GERMAN GP	Nürburgring	7	Officine Alfieri Maserati	2.0 Maserati A6GCM 6	
ret*	SWISS GP	Bremgarten	30	Officine Alfieri Maserati	2.0 Maserati A6GCM 6	* Fangio took over/engine
4	"	"	32	Officine Alfieri Maserati	2.0 Maserati A6GCM 6	took Fangio's car/1 lap behind
ret	ITALIAN GP	Monza	52	Officine Alfieri Maserati	2.0 Maserati A6GCM 6	out of fuel/3 laps behind

GP Starts: 15   GP Wins: 0   Pole positions: 0   Fastest laps: 0   Points: 17.5

BONNIER, Joakim (S) b 31/11/1930 – d 11/6/1972

1956

	Race	Circuit	No	Entrant	Car/Engine	Comment
ret	ITALIAN GP	Monza	34	Officine Alfieri Maserati	2.5 Maserati 250F 6	took over Villoresi's car/engine

1957

	Race	Circuit	No	Entrant	Car/Engine	Comment
7	ARGENTINE GP	Buenos Aires	24	Scuderia Centro Sud	2.5 Maserati 250F 6	5 laps behind
ret	BRITISH GP	Aintree	28	Jo Bonnier	2.5 Maserati 250F 6	transmission
ret	PESCARA GP	Pescara	16	Scuderia Centro Sud	2.5 Maserati 250F 6	overheating
ret	ITALIAN GP	Monza	24	Scuderia Centro Sud	2.5 Maserati 250F 6	overheating

1958

	Race	Circuit	No	Entrant	Car/Engine	Comment
ret	MONACO GP	Monte Carlo	58	Jo Bonnier	2.5 Maserati 250F 6	accident
10	DUTCH GP	Zandvoort	11	Jo Bonnier	2.5 Maserati 250F 6	4 laps behind
9	BELGIAN GP	Spa	36	Jo Bonnier	2.5 Maserati 250F 6	2 laps behind
8	FRENCH GP	Reims	38	Giorgio Scarlatti	2.5 Maserati 250F 6	2 laps behind
ret	BRITISH GP	Silverstone	22	Jo Bonnier	2.5 Maserati 250F 6	gearbox
ret	GERMAN GP	Nürburgring	16	Scuderia Centro Sud	2.5 Maserati 250F 6	damage after collision with Brabham
ret	PORTUGUESE GP	Oporto	32	Jo Bonnier	2.5 Maserati 250F 6	unwell
ret	ITALIAN GP	Monza	12	Owen Racing Organisation	2.5 BRM P25 4	fire
4	MOROCCAN GP	Casablanca	18	Owen Racing Organisation	2.5 BRM P25 4	

1959

	Race	Circuit	No	Entrant	Car/Engine	Comment
ret	MONACO GP	Monte Carlo	18	Owen Racing Organisation	2.5 BRM P25 4	brakes
1	DUTCH GP	Zandvoort	7	Owen Racing Organisation	2.5 BRM P25 4	Pole
ret	FRENCH GP	Reims	4	Owen Racing Organisation	2.5 BRM P25 4	engine-head gasket
ret	BRITISH GP	Aintree	10	Owen Racing Organisation	2.5 BRM P25 4	throttle linkage
5 agg	GERMAN GP	AVUS	9	Owen Racing Organisation	2.5 BRM P25 4	7th heat 1/5th heat 2/2 laps behind
ret	PORTUGUESE GP	Monsanto	7	Owen Racing Organisation	2.5 BRM P25 4	fuel feed
8	ITALIAN GP	Monza	6	Owen Racing Organisation	2.5 BRM P25 4	2 laps behind
dns	"	"	6	Owen Racing Organisation	2.5 BRM P48 4	practice only

1960

	Race	Circuit	No	Entrant	Car/Engine	Comment
7	ARGENTINE GP	Buenos Aires	40	Owen Racing Organisation	2.5 BRM P25 4	1 lap behind
5	MONACO GP	Monte Carlo	2	Owen Racing Organisation	2.5 BRM P48 4	p stop-suspension/17 laps behind
ret	DUTCH GP	Zandvoort	14	Owen Racing Organisation	2.5 BRM P48 4	engine-spun off on own oil
ret	BELGIAN GP	Spa	6	Owen Racing Organisation	2.5 BRM P48 4	engine
ret	FRENCH GP	Reims	8	Owen Racing Organisation	2.5 BRM P48 4	engine
ret	BRITISH GP	Silverstone	6	Owen Racing Organisation	2.5 BRM P48 4	rear suspension
ret	PORTUGUESE GP	Oporto	20	Owen Racing Organisation	2.5 BRM P48 4	engine
5	US GP	Riverside	15	Owen Racing Organisation	2.5 BRM P48 4	1 lap behind

1961

	Race	Circuit	No	Entrant	Car/Engine	Comment
ret	MONACO GP	Monte Carlo	2	Porsche System Engineering	1.5 Porsche 787 F4	fuel injection
dns	"	" "	2	Porsche System Engineering	1.5 Porsche 718 F4	practice only
11	DUTCH GP	Zandvoort	6	Porsche System Engineering	1.5 Porsche 787 F4	2 laps behind
7	BELGIAN GP	Spa	18	Porsche System Engineering	1.5 Porsche 718 F4	
7	FRENCH GP	Reims	10	Porsche System Engineering	1.5 Porsche 718 F4	
5	BRITISH GP	Aintree	8	Porsche System Engineering	1.5 Porsche 718 F4	
ret	GERMAN GP	Nürburgring	8	Porsche System Engineering	1.5 Porsche 718 F4	engine
ret	ITALIAN GP	Monza	44	Porsche System Engineering	1.5 Porsche 718 F4	suspension
dns	"	"	44	Porsche System Engineering	1.5 Porsche 787 F4	practice only
6	US GP	Watkins Glen	11	Porsche System Engineering	1.5 Porsche 718 F4	2 laps behind

1962

	Race	Circuit	No	Entrant	Car/Engine	Comment
7	DUTCH GP	Zandvoort	11	Porsche System Engineering	1.5 Porsche 804 F8	5 laps behind

5	MONACO GP	Monte Carlo	2	Porsche System Engineering	1.5 Porsche 718 F4	*7 laps behind*
ret	FRENCH GP	Rouen	32	Porsche System Engineering	1.5 Porsche 804 F8	*fuel feed*
ret	BRITISH GP	Aintree	10	Porsche System Engineering	1.5 Porsche 804 F8	*cwp*
7	GERMAN GP	Nürburgring	8	Porsche System Engineering	1.5 Porsche 804 F8	
6	ITALIAN GP	Monza	8	Porsche System Engineering	1.5 Porsche 804 F8	*1 lap behind*
13	US GP	Watkins Glen	11	Porsche System Engineering	1.5 Porsche 804 F8	*pit stops/21 laps behind*
1963						
7	MONACO GP	Monte Carlo	11	R R C Walker Racing Team	1.5 Cooper T60-Climax V8	*6 laps behind*
5	BELGIAN GP	Spa	12	R R C Walker Racing Team	1.5 Cooper T60-Climax V8	*2 laps behind*
dns	"	"	12	R R C Walker Racing Team	1.5 Cooper T66-Climax V8	*practice only-oil leak engine*
11	DUTCH GP	Zandvoort	28	R R C Walker Racing Team	1.5 Cooper T60-Climax V8	*pit stop-gearbox/24 laps behind*
dns	"	"	28	R R C Walker Racing Team	1.5 Cooper T66-Climax V8	*practice only*
nc	FRENCH GP	Reims	44	R R C Walker Racing Team	1.5 Cooper T60-Climax V8	*pit stop/21 laps behind*
dns	"	"	44	R R C Walker Racing Team	1.5 Cooper T66-Climax V8	*practice only-engine problems*
ret	BRITISH GP	Silverstone	14	R R C Walker Racing Team	1.5 Cooper T66-Climax V8	*oil pressure*
6	GERMAN GP	Nürburgring	16	R R C Walker Racing Team	1.5 Cooper T66-Climax V8	*1 lap behind*
7	ITALIAN GP	Monza	58	R R C Walker Racing Team	1.5 Cooper T66-Climax V8	*pit stop-fuel/2 laps behind*
dns	"	"	58	R R C Walker Racing Team	1.5 Cooper T60-Climax V8	*practice only*
8	US GP	Watkins Glen	11	R R C Walker Racing Team	1.5 Cooper T66-Climax V8	*pit stops/25 laps behind*
5	MEXICAN GP	Mexico City	11	R R C Walker Racing Team	1.5 Cooper T66-Climax V8	*3 laps behind*
6	SOUTH AFRICAN GP	East London	12	R R C Walker Racing Team	1.5 Cooper T66-Climax V8	*2 laps behind*
1964						
5	MONACO GP	Monte Carlo	19	R R C Walker Racing Team	1.5 Cooper T66-Climax V8	*4 laps behind*
9	DUTCH GP	Zandvoort	26	R R C Walker Racing Team	1.5 Brabham BT11-BRM V8	*4 laps behind*
dns	"	"	26T	R R C Walker Racing Team	1.5 Cooper T66-Climax V8	*practice only*
ret	BELGIAN GP	Spa	16	R R C Walker Racing Team	1.5 Brabham BT11-BRM V8	*driver unwell*
dns	"	"	16	R R C Walker Racing Team	1.5 Cooper T66-Climax V8	*practice only*
ret	BRITISH GP	Brands Hatch	16	R R C Walker Racing Team	1.5 Brabham BT11-BRM V8	*brake pipe*
dns	"	"	16	R R C Walker Racing Team	1.5 Cooper T66-Climax V8	*practice only*
ret	GERMAN GP	Nürburgring	11	R R C Walker Racing Team	1.5 Brabham BT11-BRM V8	*electrics*
6	AUSTRIAN GP	Zeltweg	11	R R C Walker Racing Team	1.5 Brabham BT7-Climax V8	*4 laps behind*
12	ITALIAN GP	Monza	34	R R C Walker Racing Team	1.5 Brabham BT7-Climax V8	*alternator problems/4 laps behind*
ret	US GP	Watkins Glen	16	R R C Walker Racing Team	1.5 Brabham BT7-Climax V8	*stub axle*
ret	MEXICAN GP	Mexico City	16	R R C Walker Racing Team	1.5 Brabham BT7-Climax V8	*wishbone*
1965						
ret	SOUTH AFRICAN GP	East London	11	R R C Walker Racing Team	1.5 Brabham BT7-Climax V8	*clutch*
7	MONACO GP	Monte Carlo	12	R R C Walker Racing Team	1.5 Brabham BT7-Climax V8	*3 laps behind*
ret	BELGIAN GP	Spa	20	R R C Walker Racing Team	1.5 Brabham BT7-Climax V8	*ignition*
ret	FRENCH GP	Clermont Ferrand	34	R R C Walker Racing Team	1.5 Brabham BT7-Climax V8	*alternator drive*
7	BRITISH GP	Silverstone	15	R R C Walker Racing Team	1.5 Brabham BT7-Climax V8	*1 lap behind*
ret	DUTCH GP	Zandvoort	26	R R C Walker Racing Team	1.5 Brabham BT7-Climax V8	*valve spring*
7	GERMAN GP	Nürburgring	16	R R C Walker Racing Team	1.5 Brabham BT7-Climax V8	
7	ITALIAN GP	Monza	42	R R C Walker Racing Team	1.5 Brabham BT7-Climax V8	*2 laps behind*
8	US GP	Watkins Glen	15	R R C Walker Racing Team	1.5 Brabham BT7-Climax V8	*3 laps behind*
ret	MEXICAN GP	Mexico City	15	R R C Walker Racing Team	1.5 Brabham BT7-Climax V8	*broken wishbone*
1966						
nc	MONACO GP	Monte Carlo	18	Anglo-Suisse Racing Team	3.0 Cooper T81-Maserati V12	*pit stops/27 laps behind*
dns	"	" "	18T	Reg Parnell Racing Ltd	2.7 Lotus 25-Climax 4	*practice only*
ret	BELGIAN GP	Spa	20	Anglo-Suisse Racing Team	3.0 Cooper T81-Maserati V12	*spun off in rain*
nc	FRENCH GP	Reims	30	Brabham Racing Organisation	2.5 Brabham BT11-Climax 4	*16 laps behind*
dns	"	"	30	Anglo-Suisse Racing Team	3.0 Cooper T77-ATS V8	*practice only*
ret	BRITISH GP	Brands Hatch	23	Anglo-Suisse Racing Team	1.5 Brabham BT11-Climax V8	*engine*
7	DUTCH GP	Zandvoort	30	Anglo-Suisse Racing Team	3.0 Cooper T81-Maserati V12	*6 laps behind*
ret	GERMAN GP	Nürburgring	17	Anglo-Suisse Racing Team	3.0 Cooper T81-Maserati V12	*clutch*
ret	ITALIAN GP	Monza	38	Anglo-Suisse Racing Team	3.0 Cooper T81-Maserati V12	*throttle linkage*
nc	US GP	Watkins Glen	22	Anglo-Suisse Racing Team	3.0 Cooper T81-Maserati V12	*pit stops/51 laps behind*
6	MEXICAN GP	Mexico City	16	Anglo-Suisse Racing Team	3.0 Cooper T81-Maserati V12	*2 laps behind*
1967						
ret	SOUTH AFRICAN GP	Kyalami	15	Joakim Bonnier Racing Team	3.0 Cooper T81-Maserati V12	*engine*
ret	BELGIAN GP	Spa	39	Joakim Bonnier Racing Team	3.0 Cooper T81-Maserati V12	*fuel feed*
ret	BRITISH GP	Silverstone	23	Joakim Bonnier Racing Team	3.0 Cooper T81-Maserati V12	*engine*
5	GERMAN GP	Nürburgring	16	Joakim Bonnier Racing Team	3.0 Cooper T81-Maserati V12	*6th on road behind F2 car*
8	CANADIAN GP	Mosport Park	9	Joakim Bonnier Racing Team	3.0 Cooper T81-Maserati V12	*5 laps behind*
ret	ITALIAN GP	Monza	26	Joakim Bonnier Racing Team	3.0 Cooper T81-Maserati V12	*overheating*
6	US GP	Watkins Glen	16	Joakim Bonnier Racing Team	3.0 Cooper T81-Maserati V12	*pit stop-wheel/7 laps behind*
10	MEXICAN GP	Mexico City	16	Joakim Bonnier Racing Team	3.0 Cooper T81-Maserati V12	*4 laps behind*
1968						
ret	SOUTH AFRICAN GP	Kyalami	20	Joakim Bonnier Racing Team	3.0 Cooper T81-Maserati V12	*lost rear wheel*
dnq	MONACO GP	Monte Carlo	18	Joakim Bonnier Racing Team	3.0 McLaren M5A-BRM V12	
ret	BELGIAN GP	Spa	17	Joakim Bonnier Racing Team	3.0 McLaren M5A-BRM V12	*wheel stud*
8	DUTCH GP	Zandvoort	19	Joakim Bonnier Racing Team	3.0 McLaren M5A-BRM V12	*8 laps behind*
ret	BRITISH GP	Brands Hatch	23	Joakim Bonnier Racing Team	3.0 McLaren M5A-BRM V12	*engine*
6	ITALIAN GP	Monza	3	Joakim Bonnier Racing Team	3.0 McLaren M5A-BRM V12	*4 laps behind*
ret/dns	CANADIAN GP	St Jovite	22	Joakim Bonnier Racing Team	3.0 McLaren M5A-BRM V12	*car would not start on grid*
ret	US GP	Watkins Glen	17	Joakim Bonnier Racing Team	3.0 McLaren M5A-BRM V12	*ignition trouble/4 laps behind*
5	MEXICAN GP	Mexico City	17	Joakim Bonnier Racing Team	3.0 Honda RA301 V12	*drove works spare/1 lap behind*
dns	"	" "	17	Joakim Bonnier Racing Team	3.0 McLaren M5A-BRM V12	*engine in practice*
1969						
ret	BRITISH GP	Silverstone	18	Ecurie Bonnier/Gold Leaf Team Lotus	3.0 Lotus 63-Cosworth V8	*engine*
ret	GERMAN GP	Nürburgring	16	Ecurie Bonnier	3.0 Lotus 49B-Cosworth V8	*fuel leak*

	1970					
dnq	ITALIAN GP	Monza	38	Ecurie Bonnier	3.0 McLaren M7C-Cosworth V8	
ret	US GP	Watkins Glen	27	Ecurie Bonnier	3.0 McLaren M7C-Cosworth V8	water pipe
	1971					
ret	SOUTH AFRICAN GP	Kyalami	23	Ecurie Bonnier	3.0 McLaren M7C-Cosworth V8	suspension
dnq	GERMAN GP	Nürburgring	27	Ecurie Bonnier	3.0 McLaren M7C-Cosworth V8	
dns	AUSTRIAN GP	Österreichring	28	Ecurie Bonnier	3.0 McLaren M7C-Cosworth V8	fuel leak before start
10	ITALIAN GP	Monza	28	Ecurie Bonnier	3.0 McLaren M7C-Cosworth V8	4 laps behind
16/ret	US GP	Watkins Glen	29	Ecurie Bonnier	3.0 McLaren M7C-Cosworth V8	out of fuel/5 laps behind

GP Starts: 103 (104)   GP Wins: 1   Pole positions: 1   Fastest laps: 0   Points: 39

BONOMI, Roberto (RA) b 30/9/1919

	1960					
	Race	Circuit	No	Entrant	Car/Engine	Comment
11	ARGENTINE GP	Buenos Aires	4	Scuderia Centro Sud	2.5 Cooper T51-Maserati 4	4 laps behind

GP Starts: 1   GP Wins: 0   Pole positions: 0   Fastest laps: 0   Points: 0

SLIM BORGUDD

Tommy Borgudd began racing in Formula Ford and sports cars in his native Sweden between 1970 and 1973, but lack of finance forced him to fall back on his career as drummer (most famously with Abba).

It was 1978 before he could find sufficient backing to return to the tracks, but he was soon performing heroics in both the Swedish and European F3 series with an outdated Ralt. Particularly impressive were his efforts in the European championship in 1979 when he finished third overall behind the dazzling Prost and experienced Bleekemolen despite having to miss races due to lack of money as the season wore on.

A planned season in Formula 2 in 1980 was aborted when the finance was not forthcoming, but Slim occasionally competed in a March in F3 while working on a deal that saw him join the ATS team in Grands Prix for 1981.

Sixth place – and a championship point – in the British Grand Prix was the high spot in a difficult season. Borgudd then began the next campaign with the Tyrrell team, but his money soon ran out he was replaced by Brian Henton. That there is more to life than struggling at the back of the grid in Formula 1 has surely been proved by Slim, who has since carved out a hugely successful, enjoyable – and profitable! – career as truck racing World Champion.

BORGUDD, Slim (Tommy) (S) b 25/11/1946

	1981					
	Race	Circuit	No	Entrant	Car/Engine	Comment
13	SAN MARINO GP	Imola	10	Team ATS	3.0 ATS D4-Cosworth V8	pit stop-tyres/3 laps behind
dnq	BELGIAN GP	Zolder	10	Team ATS	3.0 ATS HGS1-Cosworth V8	
dnpq	MONACO GP	Monte Carlo	10	Team ATS	3.0 ATS D4-Cosworth V8	
dnq	SPANISH GP	Jarama	10	Team ATS	3.0 ATS HGS1-Cosworth V8	
dnq	FRENCH GP	Dijon	10	Team ATS	3.0 ATS HGS1-Cosworth V8	
6	BRITISH GP	Silverstone	10	Team ATS	3.0 ATS HGS1-Cosworth V8	1 lap behind
ret	GERMAN GP	Hockenheim	10	Team ATS	3.0 ATS HGS1-Cosworth V8	engine
ret	AUSTRIAN GP	Österreichring	10	Team ATS	3.0 ATS HGS1-Cosworth V8	brakes
10	DUTCH GP	Zandvoort	10	Team ATS	3.0 ATS HGS1-Cosworth V8	pit stop-tyres/4 laps behind
ret	ITALIAN GP	Monza	10	Team ATS	3.0 ATS HGS1-Cosworth V8	spun off
ret	CANADIAN GP	Montreal	10	Team ATS	3.0 ATS HGS1-Cosworth V8	spun off
dnq	CAESARS PALACE GP	Las Vegas	10	Team ATS	3.0 ATS HGS1-Cosworth V8	
	1982					
16	SOUTH AFRICAN GP	Kyalami	4	Team Tyrrell	3.0 Tyrrell 011-Cosworth V8	pit stop-tyres/5 laps behind
7*	BRAZILIAN GP	Rio	4	Team Tyrrell	3.0 Tyrrell 011-Cosworth V8	* 1st & 2nd cars dsq/2laps behind
10*	US GP WEST	Long Beach	4	Team Tyrrell	3.0 Tyrrell 011-Cosworth V8	*3rd car dsq/collision-Winkelhock/-7 laps

GP Starts: 10   GP Wins: 0   Pole positions: 0   Fastest laps: 0   Points: 1

BOTHA, Luki (ZA)

	1967					
	Race	Circuit	No	Entrant	Car/Engine	Comment
nc	SOUTH AFRICAN GP	Kyalami	20	Luki Botha	2.7 Brabham BT7-Climax 4	pit stop/20 laps behind

GP Starts: 1   GP Wins: 0   Pole positions: 0   Fastest laps: 0   Points: 0

THIERRY BOUTSEN

With no family racing background, Thierry went to the Pilette racing school where he soon became a star pupil and set out on a Formula Ford career. In 1978 the young Belgian raced a Crosslé in the Benelux countries, winning 15 of his 18 races, which brought him to the attention of his boyhood idol Jacky Ickx. With his help, Boutsen found a Formula 3 ride in 1979, but the season was fraught with troubles until a spectacular performance in the final round at Jarama, where he matched European champion Alain Prost. This one drive was enough to persuade the works Martini team to sign him in place of the little Frenchman, who was off to McLaren, and the new season began well, with three wins in the first four races, but when March launched their new wing car, a depressed Boutsen was powerless to prevent himself being overhauled by the determined Michele Alboreto.

Stepping up into Formula 2 with a works March in 1981, Boutsen was the surprise of the championship, winning races at the Nürburgring and Enna, and finishing runner-up once more, this time to Geoff Lees. Opting to race for Spirit in 1982 was something of a gamble which didn't quite come off, but his brilliant wins at the Nürburgring, Enna and especially Spa marked him down as an immediate Grand Prix prospect. Thierry's hopes of racing the Spirit F1 car in 1983 were dashed when Johansson got the nod but he managed to finance a ride with Arrows, with whom he was to stay for three more seasons, quietly but impressively getting on with the job in hand. The car was never really competitive, but Boutsen was always a contender for points, and when Benetton signed him it was a long-overdue promotion.

Results in his first season with Benetton, 1987, were a mite disappointing, with niggling mechanical problems restricting the team's progress, while in 1988 his position was somewhat eroded by the arrival of the gregarious Nannini, but Boutsen still finished third behind the dominant McLarens on four occasions.

Joining Williams with Renault power for 1989 offered Thierry his big chance, but though he did little wrong – indeed he took two brilliant wins in torrential rain at Montreal and Adelaide – it seemed that he didn't quite fit the bill at Didcot, rather unfairly being compared with Mansell. In 1990, already feeling under-appreciated at Williams, he scored an absolutely superb win in the Hungarian GP, proving he had nerves of steel by fending off Senna's late challenge, before he took the only feasible option open to him and signed a two-year deal with Ligier. Despite a massive budget, Ligier made a hash of things as usual, particularly in 1991 when Thierry just kept his head down hoping things would improve. In fact they did somewhat the following season, when Renault engines became available, but such was the strained atmosphere within the team that at the end of the year the Belgian was probably glad to be out of it. Without a drive for 1993, Thierry was soon called into the Jordan line-up, replacing the crestfallen Capelli. However, it was to be an undistinguished swansong, which came to a sad end when, in his farewell Formula 1 race at Spa, Boutsen retired on the first lap.

BOUTSEN, Thierry (B) b 13/7/1957

1983

	Race	Circuit	No	Entrant	Car/Engine	Comment
ret	BELGIAN GP	Spa	30	Arrows Racing Team	3.0 Arrows A6-Cosworth V8	rear suspension
7	US GP (DETROIT)	Detroit	30	Arrows Racing Team	3.0 Arrows A6-Cosworth V8	1 lap behind
7	CANADIAN GP	Montreal	30	Arrows Racing Team	3.0 Arrows A6-Cosworth V8	1 lap behind
15	BRITISH GP	Silverstone	30	Arrows Racing Team	3.0 Arrows A6-Cosworth V8	2 laps behind
9*	GERMAN GP	Hockenheim	30	Arrows Racing Team	3.0 Arrows A6-Cosworth V8	* 5th place car dsq/1 lap behind
13	AUSTRIAN GP	Österreichring	30	Arrows Racing Team	3.0 Arrows A6-Cosworth V8	pit stop-plugs/5 laps behind
14/ret	DUTCH GP	Zandvoort	30	Arrows Racing Team	3.0 Arrows A6-Cosworth V8	engine
ret	ITALIAN GP	Monza	30	Arrows Racing Team	3.0 Arrows A6-Cosworth V8	engine
11	EUROPEAN GP	Brands Hatch	30	Arrows Racing Team	3.0 Arrows A6-Cosworth V8	1 lap behind
9	SOUTH AFRICAN GP	Kyalami	30	Arrows Racing Team	3.0 Arrows A6-Cosworth V8	3 laps behind

1984

	Race	Circuit	No	Entrant	Car/Engine	Comment
6*	BRAZILIAN GP	Rio	18	Barclay Nordica Arrows BMW	3.0 Arrows A6-Cosworth V8	* 5th place car dsq/1 lap behind
12*	SOUTH AFRICAN GP	Kyalami	18	Barclay Nordica Arrows BMW	3.0 Arrows A6-Cosworth V8	* 11th place car dsq/5 laps behind
ret	BELGIAN GP	Zolder	18	Barclay Nordica Arrows BMW	1.5 t/c Arrows A7-BMW 4	misfire
5*	SAN MARINO GP	Imola	18	Barclay Nordica Arrows BMW	3.0 Arrows A6-Cosworth V8	* 5th place car dsq/1 lap behind
11	FRENCH GP	Dijon	18	Barclay Nordica Arrows BMW	1.5 t/c Arrows A7-BMW 4	2 laps behind
dnq	MONACO GP	Monte Carlo	18	Barclay Nordica Arrows BMW	1.5 t/c Arrows A7-BMW 4	
ret	CANADIAN GP	Montreal	18	Barclay Nordica Arrows BMW	1.5 t/c Arrows A7-BMW 4	engine
ret	US GP (DETROIT)	Detroit	18	Barclay Nordica Arrows BMW	1.5 t/c Arrows A7-BMW 4	engine
ret	US GP (DALLAS)	Dallas	18	Barclay Nordica Arrows BMW	1.5 t/c Arrows A7-BMW 4	hit wall
ret	BRITISH GP	Brands Hatch	18	Barclay Nordica Arrows BMW	1.5 t/c Arrows A7-BMW 4	electrics
ret	GERMAN GP	Hockenheim	18	Barclay Nordica Arrows BMW	1.5 t/c Arrows A7-BMW 4	oil pressure
5	AUSTRIAN GP	Österreichring	18	Barclay Nordica Arrows BMW	1.5 t/c Arrows A7-BMW 4	1 lap behind
ret	DUTCH GP	Zandvoort	18	Barclay Nordica Arrows BMW	1.5 t/c Arrows A7-BMW 4	accident with Arnoux
10	ITALIAN GP	Monza	18	Barclay Nordica Arrows BMW	1.5 t/c Arrows A7-BMW 4	2 pit stops/6 laps behind
9/ret	EUROPEAN GP	Nürburgring	18	Barclay Nordica Arrows BMW	1.5 t/c Arrows A7-BMW 4	electrics/3 laps behind
ret	PORTUGUESE GP	Estoril	18	Barclay Nordica Arrows BMW	1.5 t/c Arrows A7-BMW 4	driveshaft

1985

	Race	Circuit	No	Entrant	Car/Engine	Comment
11	BRAZILIAN GP	Rio	18	Barclay Arrows BMW	1.5 t/c Arrows A8-BMW 4	started late-fuel pressure/-4 laps
ret	PORTUGUESE GP	Estoril	18	Barclay Arrows BMW	1.5 t/c Arrows A8-BMW 4	
2	SAN MARINO GP	Imola	18	Barclay Arrows BMW	1.5 t/c Arrows A8-BMW 4	1 lap behind
9	MONACO GP	Monte Carlo	18	Barclay Arrows BMW	1.5 t/c Arrows A8-BMW 4	2 laps behind

9	CANADIAN GP	Montreal	18	Barclay Arrows BMW	1.5 t/c Arrows A8-BMW 4	2 laps behind
7	US GP (DETROIT)	Detroit	18	Barclay Arrows BMW	1.5 t/c Arrows A8-BMW 4	1 lap behind
9	FRENCH GP	Paul Ricard	18	Barclay Arrows BMW	1.5 t/c Arrows A8-BMW 4	1 lap behind
ret	BRITISH GP	Silverstone	18	Barclay Arrows BMW	1.5 t/c Arrows A8-BMW 4	spun off
4	GERMAN GP	Nürburgring	18	Barclay Arrows BMW	1.5 t/c Arrows A8-BMW 4	
8	AUSTRIAN GP	Österreichring	18	Barclay Arrows BMW	1.5 t/c Arrows A8-BMW 4	turbo boost probs/3 laps behind
ret	DUTCH GP	Zandvoort	18	Barclay Arrows BMW	1.5 t/c Arrows A8-BMW 4	suspension
9	ITALIAN GP	Monza	18	Barclay Arrows BMW	1.5 t/c Arrows A8-BMW 4	1 lap behind
10/ret	BELGIAN GP	Spa	18	Barclay Arrows BMW	1.5 t/c Arrows A8-BMW 4	gearbox/3 laps behind
6	EUROPEAN GP	Brands Hatch	18	Barclay Arrows BMW	1.5 t/c Arrows A8-BMW 4	2 laps behind
6	SOUTH AFRICAN GP	Kyalami	18	Barclay Arrows BMW	1.5 t/c Arrows A8-BMW 4	1 lap behind
ret	AUSTRALIAN GP	Adelaide	18	Barclay Arrows BMW	1.5 t/c Arrows A8-BMW 4	oil leak
1986						
ret	BRAZILIAN GP	Rio	18	Barclay Arrows BMW	1.5 t/c Arrows A8-BMW 4	broken exhaust
7	SPANISH GP	Jerez	18	Barclay Arrows BMW	1.5 t/c Arrows A8-BMW 4	4 laps behind
7	SAN MARINO GP	Imola	18	Barclay Arrows BMW	1.5 t/c Arrows A8-BMW 4	2 laps behind
8	MONACO GP	Monte Carlo	18	Barclay Arrows BMW	1.5 t/c Arrows A8-BMW 4	3 laps behind
ret	BELGIAN GP	Spa	18	Barclay Arrows BMW	1.5 t/c Arrows A8-BMW 4	electrics
ret	CANADIAN GP	Montreal	18	Barclay Arrows BMW	1.5 t/c Arrows A8-BMW 4	electrics
ret	US GP (DETROIT)	Detroit	18	Barclay Arrows BMW	1.5 t/c Arrows A8-BMW 4	accident-hit by Arnoux
nc	FRENCH GP	Paul Ricard	18	Barclay Arrows BMW	1.5 t/c Arrows A8-BMW 4	stops-bodywork/13 laps behind
nc	BRITISH GP	Brands Hatch	18	Barclay Arrows BMW	1.5 t/c Arrows A8-BMW 4	pit stop-electrics/13 laps behind
ret	GERMAN GP	Hockenheim	18	Barclay Arrows BMW	1.5 t/c Arrows A9-BMW 4	turbo
ret	HUNGARIAN GP	Hungaroring	18	Barclay Arrows BMW	1.5 t/c Arrows A9-BMW 4	electrics
dns	"	"	18	Barclay Arrows BMW	1.5 t/c Arrows A9-BMW 4	practice only
ret	AUSTRIAN GP	Österreichring	18	Barclay Arrows BMW	1.5 t/c Arrows A9-BMW 4	turbo
dns	"	"	18	Barclay Arrows BMW	1.5 t/c Arrows A9-BMW 4	practice only
7	ITALIAN GP	Monza	18	Barclay Arrows BMW	1.5 t/c Arrows A8-BMW 4	2 laps behind
10	PORTUGUESE GP	Estoril	18	Barclay Arrows BMW	1.5 t/c Arrows A8-BMW 4	3 laps behind
7	MEXICAN GP	Mexico City	18	Barclay Arrows BMW	1.5 t/c Arrows A8-BMW 4	2 laps behind
ret	AUSTRALIAN GP	Adelaide	18	Barclay Arrows BMW	1.5 t/c Arrows A8-BMW 4	throttle spring
1987						
5	BRAZILIAN GP	Rio	20	Benetton Formula Ltd	1.5 t/c Benetton B187-Cosworth V6	1 lap behind
ret	SAN MARINO GP	Imola	20	Benetton Formula Ltd	1.5 t/c Benetton B187-Cosworth V6	engine
ret	BELGIAN GP	Spa	20	Benetton Formula Ltd	1.5 t/c Benetton B187-Cosworth V6	driveshaft
ret	MONACO GP	Monte Carlo	20	Benetton Formula Ltd	1.5 t/c Benetton B187-Cosworth V6	driveshaft
ret	US GP (DETROIT)	Detroit	20	Benetton Formula Ltd	1.5 t/c Benetton B187-Cosworth V6	brake disc
ret	FRENCH GP	Paul Ricard	20	Benetton Formula Ltd	1.5 t/c Benetton B187-Cosworth V6	distributor drive
7	BRITISH GP	Silverstone	20	Benetton Formula Ltd	1.5 t/c Benetton B187-Cosworth V6	3 laps behind
ret	GERMAN GP	Hockenheim	20	Benetton Formula Ltd	1.5 t/c Benetton B187-Cosworth V6	engine
4	HUNGARIAN GP	Hungaroring	20	Benetton Formula Ltd	1.5 t/c Benetton B187-Cosworth V6	1 lap behind
4	AUSTRIAN GP	Österreichring	20	Benetton Formula Ltd	1.5 t/c Benetton B187-Cosworth V6	1 lap behind
5	ITALIAN GP	Monza	20	Benetton Formula Ltd	1.5 t/c Benetton B187-Cosworth V6	
14	PORTUGUESE GP	Estoril	20	Benetton Formula Ltd	1.5 t/c Benetton B187-Cosworth V6	pit stop-engine/6 laps behind
16/ret	SPANISH GP	Jerez	20	Benetton Formula Ltd	1.5 t/c Benetton B187-Cosworth V6	spun off-brakes
ret	MEXICAN GP	Mexico City	20	Benetton Formula Ltd	1.5 t/c Benetton B187-Cosworth V6	electrics
5	JAPANESE GP	Suzuka	20	Benetton Formula Ltd	1.5 t/c Benetton B187-Cosworth V6	
3*	AUSTRALIAN GP	Adelaide	20	Benetton Formula Ltd	1.5 t/c Benetton B187-Cosworth V6	* 2nd place car dsq/1 lap behind
1988						
7	BRAZILIAN GP	Rio	20	Benetton Formula Ltd	3.5 Benetton B188-Cosworth V8	1 lap behind
4	SAN MARINO GP	Imola	20	Benetton Formula Ltd	3.5 Benetton B188-Cosworth V8	fractured exhaust/1 lap behind
8	MONACO GP	Monte Carlo	20	Benetton Formula Ltd	3.5 Benetton B188-Cosworth V8	2 laps behind
8	MEXICAN GP	Mexico City	20	Benetton Formula Ltd	3.5 Benetton B188-Cosworth V8	handling problems/3 laps behind
3	CANADIAN GP	Montreal	20	Benetton Formula Ltd	3.5 Benetton B188-Cosworth V8	
3	US GP (DETROIT)	Detroit	20	Benetton Formula Ltd	3.5 Benetton B188-Cosworth V8	1 lap behind
ret	FRENCH GP	Paul Ricard	20	Benetton Formula Ltd	3.5 Benetton B188-Cosworth V8	electrics
ret	BRITISH GP	Silverstone	20	Benetton Formula Ltd	3.5 Benetton B188-Cosworth V8	driveshaft-c.v. joint
6	GERMAN GP	Hockenheim	20	Benetton Formula Ltd	3.5 Benetton B188-Cosworth V8	dry set up-wet race/1 lap behind
3	HUNGARIAN GP	Hungaroring	20	Benetton Formula Ltd	3.5 Benetton B188-Cosworth V8	
dsq*	BELGIAN GP	Spa	20	Benetton Formula Ltd	3.5 Benetton B188-Cosworth V8	* 3rd on the road/illegal fuel
6	ITALIAN GP	Monza	20	Benetton Formula Ltd	3.5 Benetton B188-Cosworth V8	misfire
3	PORTUGUESE GP	Estoril	20	Benetton Formula Ltd	3.5 Benetton B188-Cosworth V8	
9	SPANISH GP	Jerez	20	Benetton Formula Ltd	3.5 Benetton B188-Cosworth V8	pit stop-nose cone
3	JAPANESE GP	Suzuka	20	Benetton Formula Ltd	3.5 Benetton B188-Cosworth V8	
5	AUSTRALIAN GP	Adelaide	20	Benetton Formula Ltd	3.5 Benetton B188-Cosworth V8	spin/misfire/broken exhaust/-1 lap
1989						
ret	BRAZILIAN GP	Rio	5	Canon Williams Team	3.5 Williams FW12C-Renault V10	engine
4	SAN MARINO GP	Imola	5	Canon Williams Team	3.5 Williams FW12C-Renault V10	agg of 2 parts/understeer/clutch/-1 lap
10	MONACO GP	Monte Carlo	5	Canon Williams Team	3.5 Williams FW12C-Renault V10	pit stop-rear wing/3 laps behind
ret	MEXICAN GP	Mexico City	5	Canon Williams Team	3.5 Williams FW12C-Renault V10	electrics
6	US GP (PHOENIX)	Phoenix	5	Canon Williams Team	3.5 Williams FW12C-Renault V10	pit stop-puncture/1 lap behind
1	CANADIAN GP	Montreal	5	Canon Williams Team	3.5 Williams FW12C-Renault V10	
ret	FRENCH GP	Paul Ricard	5	Canon Williams Team	3.5 Williams FW12C-Renault V10	gearbox
10	BRITISH GP	Silverstone	5	Canon Williams Team	3.5 Williams FW12C-Renault V10	clutch problems/2 laps behind
ret	GERMAN GP	Hockenheim	5	Canon Williams Team	3.5 Williams FW12C-Renault V10	spun off after collision with Pirro
3	HUNGARIAN GP	Hungaroring	5	Canon Williams Team	3.5 Williams FW12C-Renault V10	
4	BELGIAN GP	Spa	5	Canon Williams Team	3.5 Williams FW12C-Renault V10	
3	ITALIAN GP	Monza	5	Canon Williams Team	3.5 Williams FW12C-Renault V10	
ret	PORTUGUESE GP	Estoril	5	Canon Williams Team	3.5 Williams FW13-Renault V10	overheating
ret	SPANISH GP	Jerez	5	Canon Williams Team	3.5 Williams FW13-Renault V10	fuel pressure-pump
3*	JAPANESE GP	Suzuka	5	Canon Williams Team	3.5 Williams FW13-Renault V10	* 1st place car disqualified
1	AUSTRALIAN GP	Adelaide	5	Canon Williams Team	3.5 Williams FW13-Renault V10	

1990

3	US GP (PHOENIX)	Phoenix	5	Canon Williams Renault	3.5 Williams FW13B-Renault V10	*engine cutting out*
5	BRAZILIAN GP	Interlagos	5	Canon Williams Renault	3.5 Williams FW13B-Renault V10	*long stop-tyres-nose/1 lap behind*
ret	SAN MARINO GP	Imola	5	Canon Williams Renault	3.5 Williams FW13B-Renault V10	*missed gear-engine*
4	MONACO GP	Monte Carlo	5	Canon Williams Renault	3.5 Williams FW13B-Renault V10	*throttle problems/1 lap behind*
ret	CANADIAN GP	Montreal	5	Canon Williams Renault	3.5 Williams FW13B-Renault V10	*spun and collided with Larini*
5	MEXICAN GP	Mexico City	5	Canon Williams Renault	3.5 Williams FW13B-Renault V10	*brake problems*
ret	FRENCH GP	Paul Ricard	5	Canon Williams Renault	3.5 Williams FW13B-Renault V10	*engine*
2	BRITISH GP	Silverstone	5	Canon Williams Renault	3.5 Williams FW13B-Renault V10	*blistered tyres*
6	GERMAN GP	Hockenheim	5	Canon Williams Renault	3.5 Williams FW13B-Renault V10	*FL*
1	HUNGARIAN GP	Hungaroring	5	Canon Williams Renault	3.5 Williams FW13B-Renault V10	*Pole*
ret	BELGIAN GP	Spa	5	Canon Williams Renault	3.5 Williams FW13B-Renault V10	*transmission*
ret	ITALIAN GP	Monza	5	Canon Williams Renault	3.5 Williams FW13B-Renault V10	*suspension*
ret	PORTUGUESE GP	Estoril	5	Canon Williams Renault	3.5 Williams FW13B-Renault V10	*gearbox*
4	SPANISH GP	Jerez	5	Canon Williams Renault	3.5 Williams FW13B-Renault V10	*collision with Berger*
5	JAPANESE GP	Suzuka	5	Canon Williams Renault	3.5 Williams FW13B-Renault V10	*long pit stop-tyres*
5	AUSTRALIAN GP	Adelaide	5	Canon Williams Renault	3.5 Williams FW13B-Renault V10	*pit stop-tyres*

1991

ret	US GP (PHOENIX)	Phoenix	25	Ligier Gitanes	3.5 Ligier JS35-Lamborghini V12	*electrics*
10	BRAZILIAN GP	Interlagos	25	Ligier Gitanes	3.5 Ligier JS35-Lamborghini V12	*3 laps behind*
7	SAN MARINO GP	Imola	25	Ligier Gitanes	3.5 Ligier JS35-Lamborghini V12	*cracked exhaust/3 laps behind*
7	MONACO GP	Monte Carlo	25	Ligier Gitanes	3.5 Ligier JS35-Lamborghini V12	*2 laps behind*
ret	CANADIAN GP	Montreal	25	Ligier Gitanes	3.5 Ligier JS35-Lamborghini V12	*engine*
8	MEXICAN GP	Mexico City	25	Ligier Gitanes	3.5 Ligier JS35-Lamborghini V12	*2 laps behind*
12	FRENCH GP	Magny Cours	25	Ligier Gitanes	3.5 Ligier JS35B-Lamborghini V12	*3 laps behind*
ret	BRITISH GP	Silverstone	25	Ligier Gitanes	3.5 Ligier JS35B-Lamborghini V12	*engine*
9	GERMAN GP	Hockenheim	25	Ligier Gitanes	3.5 Ligier JS35B-Lamborghini V12	*1 lap behind*
17/ret	HUNGARIAN GP	Hungaroring	25	Ligier Gitanes	3.5 Ligier JS35B-Lamborghini V12	*engine/6 laps behind*
11	BELGIAN GP	Spa	25	Ligier Gitanes	3.5 Ligier JS35B-Lamborghini V12	*1 lap behind*
ret	ITALIAN GP	Monza	25	Ligier Gitanes	3.5 Ligier JS35B-Lamborghini V12	*spun off on lap 1*
16	PORTUGUESE GP	Estoril	25	Ligier Gitanes	3.5 Ligier JS35B-Lamborghini V12	*3 laps behind*
ret	SPANISH GP	Barcelona	25	Ligier Gitanes	3.5 Ligier JS35B-Lamborghini V12	*spun off on lap 1*
9	JAPANESE GP	Suzuka	25	Ligier Gitanes	3.5 Ligier JS35B-Lamborghini V12	*1 lap behind*
ret	AUSTRALIAN GP	Adelaide	25	Ligier Gitanes	3.5 Ligier JS35B-Lamborghini V12	*collision with Nakajima*

1992

ret	SOUTH AFRICAN GP	Kyalami	25	Ligier Gitanes Blondes	3.5 Ligier JS37-Renault V10	*engine*
10	MEXICAN GP	Mexico City	25	Ligier Gitanes Blondes	3.5 Ligier JS37-Renault V10	*2 laps behind*
ret	BRAZILIAN GP	Interlagos	25	Ligier Gitanes Blondes	3.5 Ligier JS37-Renault V10	*collision with Comas*
ret	SPANISH GP	Barcelona	25	Ligier Gitanes Blondes	3.5 Ligier JS37-Renault V10	*engine*
ret	SAN MARINO GP	Imola	25	Ligier Gitanes Blondes	3.5 Ligier JS37-Renault V10	*fuel pump*
12	MONACO GP	Monte Carlo	25	Ligier Gitanes Blondes	3.5 Ligier JS37-Renault V10	*3 laps behind*
10	CANADIAN GP	Montreal	25	Ligier Gitanes Blondes	3.5 Ligier JS37-Renault V10	*2 laps behind*
ret	FRENCH GP	Magny Cours	25	Ligier Gitanes Blondes	3.5 Ligier JS37-Renault V10	*spun off*
10	BRITISH GP	Silverstone	25	Ligier Gitanes Blondes	3.5 Ligier JS37-Renault V10	*2 laps behind*
7	GERMAN GP	Hockenheim	25	Ligier Gitanes Blondes	3.5 Ligier JS37-Renault V10	*1 lap behind*
ret	HUNGARIAN GP	Hungaroring	25	Ligier Gitanes Blondes	3.5 Ligier JS37-Renault V10	*collision with Comas on lap 1*
ret	BELGIAN GP	Spa	25	Ligier Gitanes Blondes	3.5 Ligier JS37-Renault V10	*crashed at Blanchimont*
ret	ITALIAN GP	Monza	25	Ligier Gitanes Blondes	3.5 Ligier JS37-Renault V10	*electrics*
8	PORTUGUESE GP	Estoril	25	Ligier Gitanes Blondes	3.5 Ligier JS37-Renault V10	*2 laps behind*
ret	JAPANESE GP	Suzuka	25	Ligier Gitanes Blondes	3.5 Ligier JS37-Renault V10	*gearbox*
5	AUSTRALIAN GP	Adelaide	25	Ligier Gitanes Blondes	3.5 Ligier JS37-Renault V10	*1 lap behind*

1993

ret	EUROPEAN GP	Donington	15	Sasol Jordan	3.5 Jordan 193-Hart V10	*throttle problems*
ret	SAN MARINO GP	Imola	15	Sasol Jordan	3.5 Jordan 193-Hart V10	*gearbox hydraulic failure*
11	SPANISH GP	Barcelona	15	Sasol Jordan	3.5 Jordan 193-Hart V10	*throttle/fuel pressure/3 laps behind*
ret	MONACO GP	Monte Carlo	15	Sasol Jordan	3.5 Jordan 193-Hart V10	*suspension*
12	CANADIAN GP	Montreal	15	Sasol Jordan	3.5 Jordan 193-Hart V10	*2 laps behind*
11	FRENCH GP	Magny Cours	15	Sasol Jordan	3.5 Jordan 193-Hart V10	*2 laps behind*
ret	BRITISH GP	Silverstone	15	Sasol Jordan	3.5 Jordan 193-Hart V10	*wheel bearing*
13	GERMAN GP	Hockenheim	15	Sasol Jordan	3.5 Jordan 193-Hart V10	*ran without tyre change*
9	HUNGARIAN GP	Hungaroring	15	Sasol Jordan	3.5 Jordan 193-Hart V10	*2 laps behind*
ret	BELGIAN GP	Spa	15	Sasol Jordan	3.5 Jordan 193-Hart V10	*gearbox on lap 1*

GP Starts: 163   GP Wins: 3   Pole positions: 1   Fastest laps: 1   Points: 132

BRABHAM, David (AUS) b 5/9/1965

1990

	Race	Circuit	No	Entrant	Car/Engine	Comment
dnq	SAN MARINO GP	Imola	7	Motor Racing Developments	3.5 Brabham BT59-Judd V8	
ret	MONACO GP	Monte Carlo	7	Motor Racing Developments	3.5 Brabham BT59-Judd V8	*driveshaft-c.v. joint*
dnq	CANADIAN GP	Montreal	7	Motor Racing Developments	3.5 Brabham BT59-Judd V8	
ret	MEXICAN GP	Mexico City	7	Motor Racing Developments	3.5 Brabham BT59-Judd V8	*electrics*
15*	FRENCH GP	Paul Ricard	7	Motor Racing Developments	3.5 Brabham BT59-Judd V8	** 15th place car dsq/3 laps behind*
dnq	BRITISH GP	Silverstone	7	Motor Racing Developments	3.5 Brabham BT59-Judd V8	
ret	GERMAN GP	Hockenheim	7	Motor Racing Developments	3.5 Brabham BT59-Judd V8	*engine*
dnq	HUNGARIAN GP	Hungaroring	7	Motor Racing Developments	3.5 Brabham BT59-Judd V8	
ret	BELGIAN GP	Spa	7	Motor Racing Developments	3.5 Brabham BT59-Judd V8	*electrics*
dnq	ITALIAN GP	Monza	7	Motor Racing Developments	3.5 Brabham BT59-Judd V8	
ret	PORTUGUESE GP	Estoril	7	Motor Racing Developments	3.5 Brabham BT59-Judd V8	*gearbox*
dnq	SPANISH GP	Jerez	7	Motor Racing Developments	3.5 Brabham BT59-Judd V8	
ret	JAPANESE GP	Suzuka	7	Motor Racing Developments	3.5 Brabham BT59-Judd V8	*clutch*
ret	AUSTRALIAN GP	Adelaide	7	Motor Racing Developments	3.5 Brabham BT59-Judd V8	*spun off*

GP Starts: 8   GP Wins: 0   Pole positions: 0   Fastest laps: 0   Points: 0

DAVID BRABHAM

The youngest of the Brabham dynasty, David is the only one of the three brothers to have emulated his father in having started a World Championship Grand Prix. It is extremely unlikely that he will be able match the feats achieved by the legendary Sir Jack, but that should not reflect badly on David, who has thus far managed a worthy career without the aid of the massive finances needed for ultimate success.

A quick learner, David soon outgrew the Australian and New Zealand single-seater scene and headed first to the States to race in Formula Atlantic, then to England in 1988, initially to contest the Formula Vauxhall Lotus championship. This proved a backwards step but a switch to Class B of the Formula 3 series was an instant success, Brabham winning five times from just nine starts. Moving up to Class A with the Jewson-backed Bowman Ralt the following season, he had a season-long battle for the F3 championship with Allan McNish in 1989, which was only resolved in David's favour on appeal the following February. With a win in the prestigious Macau F3 race, Brabham seemed set for a year in F3000 with Middlebridge Racing, but this was to suddenly become a Grand Prix chance when they acquired the Brabham team and Gregor Foitek quit his seat after just two races of the 1990 season. He applied himself sensibly and did as much as a novice could in an uncompetitive car, but was not retained at season's end.

Turning to sports cars, David drove for TWR Jaguar in 1991 (winning at the Nürburgring with Warwick) and Toyota in 1992 while waiting for the opportunity to return to Grand Prix racing, which has finally presented itself with the ambitious but unproven Simtek team hiring him to lead their assault in 1994.

JACK BRABHAM

Much has been made of Sir Jack's achievement in becoming the only driver to win the World Championship in a car of his own make. But that is only part of the story, for he was also the man who was largely responsible for developing the rear-engined Cooper which was to change the face of Formula 1 for ever; went to Indianapolis in 1961 and shook the establishment; built not only his own Grand Prix challenger but also a succession of superb Formula 2 cars which allowed so many drivers to shine; and was competitive to the end of his long career. Bowing out at the age of 44 in 1970, he could still show the youngsters a trick or two!

Jack had spent a number of years in the cut and thrust of midget racing on the cinder tracks of his native Australia, winning four successive titles between 1948 and 1951, before switching to hill-climbs, taking the championship in 1953. That season Jack was bought a Cooper-Bristol which was christened the RedeX Special and began to clean up with it but, eager to progress, he came to England in 1955 and soon joined up with the Cooper team, making an early Grand Prix debut in the 'Bobtail' special. Although he drove a Maserati 250F in 1956, taking third places in the Aintree 200 and the Vanwall Trophy at Snetterton, Jack spent most of the season racing Cooper's 1500 cc sports car, while developing the Formula 2 car which he was to use to such great effect in 1957.

In 1958 Moss won the Argentine GP with Rob Walker's little Cooper, proving that the car could be a serious contender, and Jack persevered with the works machine, steadily honing the ground-breaking design on a race-by-race basis. He took occasional national wins, for example in the London Trophy and the Gold Cup, before the start of two golden years in 1959-60 when the Cooper proved, if not always unbeatable, at least very reliable, and Brabham won his first two championship titles, taking seven Grand Prix wins in the process. Other victories included the Brussels and Pau GPs in 1960, and the International Trophy in 1961, the year the team's fortunes began to slip.

In 1962 Jack branched out on his own, using a Lotus as a stop-gap while his first Brabham was completed. It was late in the season before the BT3 appeared but this simple spaceframe car was very effective, soon taking World Championship points and a second place in the non-title Mexican GP. For 1963, Jack signed Dan Gurney to drive for the team and with such a fine driver on board he sometimes took a back seat, but his delight on the occasions when he beat the lanky Californian was obvious. Although Jack did not manage a championship win with his Brabham in the 1.5-litre formula, he scored a number of non-title victories, including races at Solitude and Zeltweg in 1963, and the International Trophy and Aintree 200 in 1964. In addition, he was very successful during the winter trips down-under for the Tasman series and in the newly introduced Formula 2, where he took four firsts places and two seconds in seven 1964 starts.

Brabham's finest season was 1966, when he won four championship Grands Prix with the ultra-reliable Repco-engined car to secure his third title, in addition to the F1 International Trophy and Gold Cup races, and no fewer than ten Formula 2 events in the Brabham-Honda. For 1967 reliability paid dividends once more; Jack took a couple of wins but Denny Hulme won the title for Brabham before heading off to McLaren. The Repco success was a minor miracle which couldn't last, and it didn't, with the four-cam 1968 engine a disastrous failure that blighted the season. Brabham switched to Ford power for 1969 and signed Jacky Ickx, but still won the International Trophy and had another crack at Indianapolis which ended in retirement with ignition troubles. In 1970, Jack's final year, he was quickly out of the traps with a runaway victory in South Africa, before enduring the heartache of losing a win at Monaco on the last corner when pressured into a mistake by Rindt. He also led the British GP until running out of fuel on the last lap, with Rindt once again the beneficiary.

Upon his retirement Brabham sold up and walked away from racing to spend more time on his other business interests, but the sport would not let him go. His three sons, Geoff, Gary and David, all became successful drivers in their own right, and the 'old man' is often seen at the circuits, proffering his advice, no doubt, in his own inimitable and economical way.

BRABHAM, Jack (AUS) b 2/4/1926

1955

	Race	Circuit	No	Entrant	Car/Engine	Comment
ret	BRITISH GP	Aintree	40	Cooper Car Co	2.0 Cooper T40-Bristol 6	valve

1956

ret	BRITISH GP	Silverstone	30	Jack Brabham	2.5 Maserati 250F 6	engine

1957

6	MONACO GP	Monte Carlo	14	Cooper Car Co/R R C Walker	2.0 Cooper T43-Climax 4	out of fuel-pushed car home/-5 laps
ret	FRENCH GP	Rouen	22	Cooper Car Co	2.0 Cooper T43-Climax 4	hit straw bales
7	"	"	24	Cooper Car Co	1.5 Cooper T43-Climax 4	took over from MacDowel/-9 laps
ret	BRITISH GP	Aintree	34	R R C Walker	2.0 Cooper T43-Climax 4	clutch
ret	GERMAN GP (F2)	Nürburgring	24	Cooper Car Co	1.5 Cooper T43-Climax 4	transmission
7	PESCARA GP	Pescara	24	Cooper Car Co	1.5 Cooper T43-Climax 4	pit stop-fuel/2 laps behind

1958

4	MONACO GP	Monte Carlo	16	Cooper Car Co	2.2 Cooper T45-Climax 4	3 laps behind
8	DUTCH GP	Zandvoort	8	Cooper Car Co	2.0 Cooper T45-Climax 4	2 laps behind
ret	BELGIAN GP	Spa	22	Cooper Car Co	2.2 Cooper T45-Climax 4	overheating
6	FRENCH GP	Reims	22	Cooper Car Co	2.2 Cooper T45-Climax 4	1 lap behind
6	BRITISH GP	Silverstone	11	Cooper Car Co	2.0 Cooper T45-Climax 4	
ret	GERMAN GP (F2)	Nürburgring	24	Cooper Car Co	1.5 Cooper T45-Climax 4	accident
7	PORTUGUESE GP	Oporto	14	Cooper Car Co	2.2 Cooper T45-Climax 4	2 laps behind
ret	ITALIAN GP	Monza	4	Cooper Car Co	2.0 Cooper T45-Climax 4	collision with Gendebien-lap 1
11	MOROCCAN GP (F2)	Casablanca	50	Cooper Car Co	1.5 Cooper T45-Climax 4	1st in F2 class/4 laps behind

1959 World Champion Driver

1	MONACO GP	Monte Carlo	24	Cooper Car Co	2.5 Cooper T51-Climax 4	FL
2	DUTCH GP	Zandvoort	8	Cooper Car Co	2.5 Cooper T51-Climax 4	
3	FRENCH GP	Reims	8	Cooper Car Co	2.5 Cooper T51-Climax 4	
1	BRITISH GP	Aintree	12	Cooper Car Co	2.5 Cooper T51-Climax 4	Pole
ret	GERMAN GP	AVUS	1	Cooper Car Co	2.5 Cooper T51-Climax 4	clutch-heat 1
ret	PORTUGUESE GP	Monsanto	1	Cooper Car Co	2.5 Cooper T51-Climax 4	accident with Cabral/hit straw bales
3	ITALIAN GP	Monza	12	Cooper Car Co	2.5 Cooper T51-Climax 4	
4	US GP	Sebring	8	Cooper Car Co	2.5 Cooper T51-Climax 4	out of fuel/pushed over line
dns	"	"	8	Cooper Car Co	2.5 Cooper T45-Climax 4	practice only

1960 World Champion Driver

ret	ARGENTINE GP	Buenos Aires	18	Cooper Car Co	2.5 Cooper T51-Climax 4	engine
dsq	MONACO GP	Monte Carlo	8	Cooper Car Co	2.5 Cooper T53-Climax 4	outside assistance after spin
1	DUTCH GP	Zandvoort	11	Cooper Car Co	2.5 Cooper T53-Climax 4	
1	BELGIAN GP	Spa	2	Cooper Car Co	2.5 Cooper T53-Climax 4	Pole/FL (shared-Ireland & G Hill)
1	FRENCH GP	Reims	16	Cooper Car Co	2.5 Cooper T53-Climax 4	Pole/FL
1	BRITISH GP	Silverstone	1	Cooper Car Co	2.5 Cooper T53-Climax 4	Pole
1	PORTUGUESE GP	Oporto	2	Cooper Car Co	2.5 Cooper T53-Climax 4	
4	US GP	Riverside	3	Cooper Car Co	2.5 Cooper T53-Climax 4	FL/1 lap behind

1961

ret	MONACO GP	Monte Carlo	24	Cooper Car Co	1.5 Cooper T55-Climax 4	ignition
6	DUTCH GP	Zandvoort	10	Cooper Car Co	1.5 Cooper T55-Climax 4	
ret	BELGIAN GP	Spa	28	Cooper Car Co	1.5 Cooper T55-Climax 4	engine
ret	FRENCH GP	Reims	2	Cooper Car Co	1.5 Cooper T55-Climax 4	oil pressure
4	BRITISH GP	Aintree	12	Cooper Car Co	1.5 Cooper T55-Climax 4	
ret	GERMAN GP	Nürburgring	1	Cooper Car Co	1.5 Cooper T58-Climax V8	accident-throttle jammed
dns	"	"	1	Cooper Car Co	1.5 Cooper T55-Climax 4	practice only
ret	ITALIAN GP	Monza	10	Cooper Car Co	1.5 Cooper T58-Climax V8	overheating
dns	"	"	10	Cooper Car Co	1.5 Cooper T55-Climax 4	practice only
ret	US GP	Watkins Glen	1	Cooper Car Co	1.5 Cooper T58-Climax V8	overheating/FL
dns	"	" "	1	Cooper Car Co	1.5 Cooper T55-Climax 4	practice only

1962

ret	DUTCH GP	Zandvoort	8	Brabham Racing Organisation	1.5 Lotus 24-Climax V8	accident
8/ret	MONACO GP	Monte Carlo	22	Brabham Racing Organisation	1.5 Lotus 24-Climax V8	spin-suspension
6	BELGIAN GP	Spa	15	Brabham Racing Organisation	1.5 Lotus 24-Climax V8	2 laps behind
ret	FRENCH GP	Rouen	26	Brabham Racing Organisation	1.5 Lotus 24-Climax V8	rear suspension
5	BRITISH GP	Aintree	30	Brabham Racing Organisation	1.5 Lotus 24-Climax V8	1 lap behind
ret	GERMAN GP	Nürburgring	16	Brabham Racing Organisation	1.5 Brabham BT3-Climax V8	throttle linkage
4	US GP	Watkins Glen	17	Brabham Racing Organisation	1.5 Brabham BT3-Climax V8	1 lap behind
4	SOUTH AFRICAN GP	East London	10	Brabham Racing Organisation	1.5 Brabham BT3-Climax V8	

1963

9	MONACO GP	Monte Carlo	3	Brabham Racing Organisation	1.5 Lotus 25-Climax V8	borrowed works car/p stops/-23 laps
dns	"	" "	3	Brabham Racing Organisation	1.5 Brabham BT3-Climax V8	engine in practice
ret	BELGIAN GP	Spa	17	Brabham Racing Organisation	1.5 Brabham BT3-Climax V8	fuel injection pump
ret	DUTCH GP	Zandvoort	16	Brabham Racing Organisation	1.5 Brabham BT7-Climax V8	spin-chassis damage
4	FRENCH GP	Reims	6	Brabham Racing Organisation	1.5 Brabham BT7-Climax V8	
ret	BRITISH GP	Silverstone	8	Brabham Racing Organisation	1.5 Brabham BT7-Climax V8	engine
7	GERMAN GP	Nürburgring	9	Brabham Racing Organisation	1.5 Brabham BT7-Climax V8	pit stop/1 lap behind
5	ITALIAN GP	Monza	22	Brabham Racing Organisation	1.5 Brabham BT3-Climax V8	pit stop-fuel/2 laps behind
4	US GP	Watkins Glen	5	Brabham Racing Organisation	1.5 Brabham BT7-Climax V8	2 laps behind
2	MEXICAN GP	Mexico City	5	Brabham Racing Organisation	1.5 Brabham BT7-Climax V8	
13/ret	SOUTH AFRICAN GP	East London	8	Brabham Racing Organisation	1.5 Brabham BT7-Climax V8	spin-split fuel tank/15 laps behind

1964

ret	MONACO GP	Monte Carlo	5	Brabham Racing Organisation	1.5 Brabham BT7-Climax V8	fuel injection
ret	DUTCH GP	Zandvoort	14	Brabham Racing Organisation	1.5 Brabham BT7-Climax V8	ignition

3	BELGIAN GP	Spa	14	Brabham Racing Organisation	1.5 Brabham BT7-Climax V8	
3	FRENCH GP	Rouen	20	Brabham Racing Organisation	1.5 Brabham BT7-Climax V8	*FL*
4	BRITISH GP	Brands Hatch	5	Brabham Racing Organisation	1.5 Brabham BT7-Climax V8	*1 lap behind*
12/ret	GERMAN GP	Nürburgring	6	Brabham Racing Organisation	1.5 Brabham BT11-Climax V8	*cwp*
9	AUSTRIAN GP	Zeltweg	6	Brabham Racing Organisation	1.5 Brabham BT11-Climax V8	*pit stop-fuel feed problems/-29 laps*
ret	ITALIAN GP	Monza	14	Brabham Racing Organisation	1.5 Brabham BT11-Climax V8	*engine-con rod*
ret	US GP	Watkins Glen	5	Brabham Racing Organisation	1.5 Brabham BT11-Climax V8	*engine*
ret	MEXICAN GP	Mexico City	5	Brabham Racing Organisation	1.5 Brabham BT11-Climax V8	*electrics*

1965

8	SOUTH AFRICAN GP	East London	7	Brabham Racing Organisation	1.5 Brabham BT11-Climax V8	*pit stop-battery/4 laps behind*
ret	MONACO GP	Monte Carlo	1	Brabham Racing Organisation	1.5 Brabham BT11-Climax V8	*engine*
4	BELGIAN GP	Spa	14	Brabham Racing Organisation	1.5 Brabham BT11-Climax V8	*1 lap behind*
dns	BRITISH GP	Silverstone	7	Brabham Racing Organisation	1.5 Brabham BT11-Climax V8	*Gurney drove car*
5	GERMAN GP	Nürburgring	4	Brabham Racing Organisation	1.5 Brabham BT11-Climax V8	
3	US GP	Watkins Glen	7	Brabham Racing Organisation	1.5 Brabham BT11-Climax V8	
ret	MEXICAN GP	Mexico City	7	Brabham Racing Organisation	1.5 Brabham BT11-Climax V8	*oil leak*

1966 World Champion Driver

ret	MONACO GP	Monte Carlo	7	Brabham Racing Organisation	3.0 Brabham BT19-Repco V8	*gearbox*
4	BELGIAN GP	Spa	3	Brabham Racing Organisation	3.0 Brabham BT19-Repco V8	*2 laps behind*
1	FRENCH GP	Reims	12	Brabham Racing Organisation	3.0 Brabham BT19-Repco V8	
1	BRITISH GP	Brands Hatch	15	Brabham Racing Organisation	3.0 Brabham BT19-Repco V8	*Pole/FL*
1	DUTCH GP	Zandvoort	6	Brabham Racing Organisation	3.0 Brabham BT19-Repco V8	*Pole*
1	GERMAN GP	Nürburgring	3	Brabham Racing Organisation	3.0 Brabham BT19-Repco V8	
ret	ITALIAN GP	Monza	10	Brabham Racing Organisation	3.0 Brabham BT19-Repco V8	*oil leak*
dns	"		10T	Brabham Racing Organisation	3.0 Brabham BT20-Repco V8	*practice only*
ret	US GP	Watkins Glen	5	Brabham Racing Organisation	3.0 Brabham BT19-Repco V8	*engine/Pole*
dns	"	" "	6	Brabham Racing Organisation	3.0 Brabham BT20-Repco V8	*practice only*
2	MEXICAN GP	Mexico City	5	Brabham Racing Organisation	3.0 Brabham BT20-Repco V8	

1967

6	SOUTH AFRICAN GP	Kyalami	1	Brabham Racing Organisation	3.0 Brabham BT20-Repco V8	*p it stop-misfire/Pole/4 laps behind*
ret	MONACO GP	Monte Carlo	8	Brabham Racing Organisation	3.0 Brabham BT19-Repco V8	*engine/Pole*
2	DUTCH GP	Zandvoort	1	Brabham Racing Organisation	3.0 Brabham BT19-Repco V8	
dns	"	"	1		3.0 Brabham BT24-Repco V8	*practice only*
ret	BELGIAN GP	Spa	25	Brabham Racing Organisation	3.0 Brabham BT24-Repco V8	*engine*
1	FRENCH GP	Le Mans	3	Brabham Racing Organisation	3.0 Brabham BT24-Repco V8	
4	BRITISH GP	Silverstone	1	Brabham Racing Organisation	3.0 Brabham BT24-Repco V8	*wing mirrors fell off*
2	GERMAN GP	Nürburgring	1	Brabham Racing Organisation	3.0 Brabham BT24-Repco V8	
1	CANADIAN GP	Mosport Park	1	Brabham Racing Organisation	3.0 Brabham BT24-Repco V8	
2	ITALIAN GP	Monza	16	Brabham Racing Organisation	3.0 Brabham BT24-Repco V8	
5	US GP	Watkins Glen	1	Brabham Racing Organisation	3.0 Brabham BT24-Repco V8	*pit stop-puncture/4 laps behind*
2	MEXICAN GP	Mexico City	1	Brabham Racing Organisation	3.0 Brabham BT24-Repco V8	

1968

ret	SOUTH AFRICAN GP	Kyalami	2	Brabham Racing Organisation	3.0 Brabham BT24-Repco V8	*valve spring*
dns	SPANISH GP	Jarama	8	Brabham Racing Organisation	3.0 Brabham BT26-Repco V8	*engine in practice*
ret	MONACO GP	Monte Carlo	2	Brabham Racing Organisation	3.0 Brabham BT26-Repco V8	*rear radius arm*
ret	BELGIAN GP	Spa	18	Brabham Racing Organisation	3.0 Brabham BT26-Repco V8	*sticking throttle*
ret	DUTCH GP	Zandvoort	5	Brabham Racing Organisation	3.0 Brabham BT26-Repco V8	*spun off-could not restart*
ret	FRENCH GP	Rouen	4	Brabham Racing Organisation	3.0 Brabham BT26-Repco V8	*fuel pump*
ret	BRITISH GP	Brands Hatch	3	Brabham Racing Organisation	3.0 Brabham BT26-Repco V8	*camshaft*
5	GERMAN GP	Nürburgring	4	Brabham Racing Organisation	3.0 Brabham BT26-Repco V8	
ret	ITALIAN GP	Monza	10	Brabham Racing Organisation	3.0 Brabham BT26-Repco V8	*oil pressure*
ret	CANADIAN GP	St Jovite	5	Brabham Racing Organisation	3.0 Brabham BT26-Repco V8	*wishbone mounting*
ret	US GP	Watkins Glen	3	Brabham Racing Organisation	3.0 Brabham BT26-Repco V8	*cam follower*
ret	MEXICAN GP	Mexico City	3	Brabham Racing Organisation	3.0 Brabham BT26-Repco V8	*oil pressure*

1969

ret	SOUTH AFRICAN GP	Kyalami	14	Motor Racing Developments	3.0 Brabham BT26A-Cosworth V8	*lost rear wing/Pole*
ret	SPANISH GP	Montjuich Park	3	Motor Racing Developments	3.0 Brabham BT26A-Cosworth V8	*engine*
ret	MONACO GP	Monte Carlo	5	Motor Racing Developments	3.0 Brabham BT26A-Cosworth V8	*accident with Surtees*
6	DUTCH GP	Zandvoort	11	Motor Racing Developments	3.0 Brabham BT26A-Cosworth V8	
ret	ITALIAN GP	Monza	28	Motor Racing Developments	3.0 Brabham BT26A-Cosworth V8	*oil leak-loose fuel pump*
2	CANADIAN GP	Mosport Park	12	Motor Racing Developments	3.0 Brabham BT26A-Cosworth V8	*FL (shared with Ickx)*
4	US GP	Watkins Glen	8	Motor Racing Developments	3.0 Brabham BT26A-Cosworth V8	*pit stop-fuel/2 laps behind*
3	MEXICAN GP	Mexico City	8	Motor Racing Developments	3.0 Brabham BT26A-Cosworth V8	*engine problems/Pole*

1970

1	SOUTH AFRICAN GP	Kyalami	12	Motor Racing Developments	3.0 Brabham BT33-Cosworth V8	*FL*
ret	SPANISH GP	Jarama	7	Motor Racing Developments	3.0 Brabham BT33-Cosworth V8	*engine/Pole/FL*
2	MONACO GP	Monte Carlo	5	Motor Racing Developments	3.0 Brabham BT33-Cosworth V8	*lost lead in last corner accident*
ret	BELGIAN GP	Spa	18	Motor Racing Developments	3.0 Brabham BT33-Cosworth V8	*flywheel and clutch*
11	DUTCH GP	Zandvoort	18	Motor Racing Developments	3.0 Brabham BT33-Cosworth V8	*2 pit stops-punctures/4 laps behind*
3	FRENCH GP	Clermont Ferrand	23	Motor Racing Developments	3.0 Brabham BT33-Cosworth V8	*FL*
2	BRITISH GP	Brands Hatch	17	Motor Racing Developments	3.0 Brabham BT33-Cosworth V8	*lost lead on last lap-out of fuel/FL*
ret	GERMAN GP	Hockenheim	3	Motor Racing Developments	3.0 Brabham BT33-Cosworth V8	*split oil union*
13	AUSTRIAN GP	Österreichring	10	Motor Racing Developments	3.0 Brabham BT33-Cosworth V8	*pit stop-holed radiator/4 laps behind*
ret	ITALIAN GP	Monza	44	Motor Racing Developments	3.0 Brabham BT33-Cosworth V8	*accident when engine cut out*
ret	CANADIAN GP	St Jovite	11	Motor Racing Developments	3.0 Brabham BT33-Cosworth V8	*oil leak*
10	US GP	Watkins Glen	15	Motor Racing Developments	3.0 Brabham BT33-Cosworth V8	*3 laps behind*
10/ret	MEXICAN GP	Mexico City	15	Motor Racing Developments	3.0 Brabham BT33-Cosworth V8	*engine low oil pressure/-6 laps*

GP Starts: 126   GP Wins: 14   Pole positions: 13   Fastest laps: 12   Points: 261

BILL BRACK

Brack was a leading light on the Canadian motor racing scene from the late sixties through to the late seventies, and also made occasional racing forays abroad.

Initially concentrating on the Formula A and B series which were popular at the time, Brack raced mainly in Lotus cars, later switching to Chevron and March (with major STP backing) to contest Formula Atlantic events before stepping aside for the younger Jacques Villeneuve in 1979.

His Grand Prix appearances at the wheel of 'third' works cars yielded little in terms of results but added local interest for the spectators nevertheless.

VITTORIO BRAMBILLA

Vittorio began racing motor cycles as early as 1957, winning the 125 cc Italian championship before turning to karting. He temporarily forsook his racing activities to tend the cars of his elder brother Ernesto, before returning to two-wheel competition in 1968. The following year he burst upon the Italian national scene in his F3 Birel, and his forceful driving style soon found him dubbed 'the Monza Gorilla', partly due to his burly physique.

Still relatively unknown, he moved into Formula 2 in 1970 with a Brabham BT23, taking a second place at Salzburgring, and he was to spend another two years jumping between F2 and F3, gaining numerous successes in the latter category. It was the 1973 season which provided his big breakthrough. Vittorio had calmed his frenetic driving approach somewhat and, at the wheel of a well-sponsored March, he became a serious challenger for honours, looking particularly impressive as the season wore on and taking wins at Salzburgring and Albi.

Brambilla's sponsors, Beta Tools, were so delighted that they helped him secure a place in the March Grand Prix line-up for 1974. Joining the team two races into the season, he soon proved to be as quick as team-mate Stuck, but the propensity to crash was still there. The following year was to be his best; he was much more consistent, qualified well and raced his heart out. In Sweden he was stunningly fast in practice, and simply drove away from the field at the start until tyre trouble intervened, a driveshaft then failing. His moment came in Austria, however, when he scored the March factory team's first-ever championship Grand Prix win in pouring rain at the Österreichring. It made no difference to the exuberant Italian that he managed to dismantle the front of the car on the slowing-down lap – or that half-points were awarded as the race had been ended prematurely with the chequered flag rather than being stopped and then restarted as should have been the case. Max Mosley had read the rule book and nobody could argue against him!

Unfortunately 1976 saw a return to the bad habits of old as in an effort to stay on the pace Brambilla indulged in a spate of chassis-crunching which must have driven the factory to distraction, such was the replacement tally. He scored only one points finish, but claimed a second in the International Trophy and fourth in the Race of Champions. However, the situation was redressed in 1977 when Brambilla took his Beta money to Surtees as number one driver. He had a pretty good working relationship with his demanding employer, and an excellent reliabilty record, though the car was just not quick enough for anything like outright success.

Nevertheless the partnership continued into 1978, with the new TS20 a no more effective challenger than its predecessor. At Monza Vittorio was involved in the start crash which claimed the life of Peterson, suffering severe concussion which kept him out of the cockpit for almost a year, before Alfa Romeo (for whom he had won four rounds of the Worlds Sports Car Championship in 1977 with their T33) brought him back for the last three races of the season. He made two more appearances for them in 1980, but it was painfully obvious that his days as a Grand Prix driver were over, though he did race the Osella sports car in a few rounds of the World Championship of Makes, before phasing himself out completely in 1981.

BRACK, Bill (CDN) b 26/12/1935

1968

	Race	Circuit	No	Entrant	Car/Engine	Comment
ret	CANADIAN GP	St Jovite	27	Gold Leaf Team Lotus	3.0 Lotus 49B-Cosworth V8	driveshaft

1969

nc	CANADIAN GP	Mosport Park	16	Owen Racing Organisation	3.0 BRM P138 V12	10 laps behind

1972

ret	CANADIAN GP	Mosport Park	17	Marlboro BRM	3.0 BRM P180 V12	spun and stalled

GP Starts: 3   GP Wins: 0   Pole positions: 0   Fastest laps: 0   Points: 0

BRAMBILLA, Vittorio (I) b 11/11/1937

1974

	Race	Circuit	No	Entrant	Car/Engine	Comment
10	SOUTH AFRICAN GP	Kyalami	10	Beta Tools/March Engineering	3.0 March 741-Cosworth V8	1 lap behind
dns	SPANISH GP	Jarama	10	Beta Tools/March Engineering	3.0 March 741-Cosworth V8	accident in practice
9	BELGIAN GP	Nivelles	10	Beta Tools/March Engineering	3.0 March 741-Cosworth V8	2 laps behind
ret	MONACO GP	Monte Carlo	10	Beta Tools/March Engineering	3.0 March 741-Cosworth V8	multiple accident lap 1
10/ret	SWEDISH GP	Anderstorp	10	Beta Tools/March Engineering	3.0 March 741-Cosworth V8	engine/2 laps behind
10	DUTCH GP	Zandvoort	10	Beta Tools/March Engineering	3.0 March 741-Cosworth V8	3 laps behind
11	FRENCH GP	Dijon	10	Beta Tools/March Engineering	3.0 March 741-Cosworth V8	1 lap behind
ret	BRITISH GP	Brands Hatch	10	Beta Tools/March Engineering	3.0 March 741-Cosworth V8	fuel pressure
13	GERMAN GP	Nürburgring	10	Beta Tools/March Engineering	3.0 March 741-Cosworth V8	
6	AUSTRIAN GP	Österreichring	10	Beta Tools/March Engineering	3.0 March 741-Cosworth V8	
ret	ITALIAN GP	Monza	10	Beta Tools/March Engineering	3.0 March 741-Cosworth V8	crashed at chicane
dns	CANADIAN GP	Mosport Park	10	Beta Tools/March Engineering	3.0 March 741-Cosworth V8	accident in practice
ret	US GP	Watkins Glen	10	Beta Tools/March Engineering	3.0 March 741-Cosworth V8	fuel metering unit

1975

9	ARGENTINE GP	Buenos Aires	9	Beta Team March	3.0 March 741-Cosworth V8	1 lap behind
ret	BRAZILIAN GP	Interlagos	9	Beta Team March	3.0 March 741-Cosworth V8	engine
ret	SOUTH AFRICAN GP	Kyalami	9	Beta Team March	3.0 March 751-Cosworth V8	oil cooler leak
5*	SPANISH GP	Montjuich Park	9	Beta Team March	3.0 March 751-Cosworth V8	shortened race *half points only
ret	MONACO GP	Monte Carlo	9	Beta Team March	3.0 March 751-Cosworth V8	damage from accident with Pryce
ret	BELGIAN GP	Zolder	9	Beta Team March	3.0 March 751-Cosworth V8	brakes
ret	SWEDISH GP	Anderstorp	9	Beta Team March	3.0 March 751-Cosworth V8	driveshaft/Pole
ret	DUTCH GP	Zandvoort	9	Beta Team March	3.0 March 751-Cosworth V8	collision with Depailler at start
ret	FRENCH GP	Paul Ricard	9	Beta Team March	3.0 March 751-Cosworth V8	rear damper
6	BRITISH GP	Silverstone	9	Beta Team March	3.0 March 751-Cosworth V8	1 lap behind
ret	GERMAN GP	Nürburgring	9	Beta Team March	3.0 March 751-Cosworth V8	puncture-suspension damage
1*	AUSTRIAN GP	Österreichring	9	Beta Team March	3.0 March 751-Cosworth V8	rain shortened race-*half points/FL
ret	ITALIAN GP	Monza	9	Beta Team March	3.0 March 751-Cosworth V8	clutch
7	US GP	Watkins Glen	9	Beta Team March	3.0 March 751-Cosworth V8	

1976

ret	BRAZILIAN GP	Interlagos	9	Beta Team March	3.0 March 761-Cosworth V8	oil leak
8	SOUTH AFRICAN GP	Kyalami	9	Beta Team March	3.0 March 761-Cosworth V8	1 lap behind
ret	US GP WEST	Long Beach	9	Beta Team March	3.0 March 761-Cosworth V8	collision with Reutemann
ret	SPANISH GP	Jarama	9	Beta Team March	3.0 March 761-Cosworth V8	accident-damaged suspension
ret	BELGIAN GP	Zolder	9	Beta Team March	3.0 March 761-Cosworth V8	driveshaft
ret	MONACO GP	Monte Carlo	9	Beta Team March	3.0 March 761-Cosworth V8	suspension
10	SWEDISH GP	Anderstorp	9	Beta Team March	3.0 March 761-Cosworth V8	spin/1 lap behind
ret	FRENCH GP	Paul Ricard	9	Beta Team March	3.0 March 761-Cosworth V8	engine-oil pressure
ret	BRITISH GP	Brands Hatch	9	Beta Team March	3.0 March 761-Cosworth V8	collision with Peterson
ret/dns	GERMAN GP	Nürburgring	9	Beta Team March	3.0 March 761-Cosworth V8	brake failure-accident/did not restart
ret	AUSTRIAN GP	Österreichring	9	Beta Team March	3.0 March 761-Cosworth V8	collision with Fittipaldi
6	DUTCH GP	Zandvoort	9	Beta Team March	3.0 March 761-Cosworth V8	
7	ITALIAN GP	Monza	9	Beta Team March	3.0 March 761-Cosworth V8	
14	CANADIAN GP	Mosport Park	9	Beta Team March	3.0 March 761-Cosworth V8	1 lap behind
ret	US GP EAST	Watkins Glen	9	Beta Team March	3.0 March 761-Cosworth V8	burst tyre
ret	JAPANESE GP	Mount Fuji	9	Beta Team March	3.0 March 761-Cosworth V8	engine

1977

7/ret	ARGENTINE GP	Buenos Aires	19	Beta Team Surtees	3.0 Surtees TS19-Cosworth V8	fuel feed/5 laps behind
ret	BRAZILIAN GP	Interlagos	19	Beta Team Surtees	3.0 Surtees TS19-Cosworth V8	damaged radiator on kerb
7	SOUTH AFRICAN GP	Kyalami	19	Beta Team Surtees	3.0 Surtees TS19-Cosworth V8	
ret	US GP WEST	Long Beach	19	Beta Team Surtees	3.0 Surtees TS19-Cosworth V8	collision with Mass
ret	SPANISH GP	Jarama	19	Beta Team Surtees	3.0 Surtees TS19-Cosworth V8	collision with Regazzoni
8	MONACO GP	Monte Carlo	19	Beta Team Surtees	3.0 Surtees TS19-Cosworth V8	
4	BELGIAN GP	Zolder	19	Beta Team Surtees	3.0 Surtees TS19-Cosworth V8	
ret	SWEDISH GP	Anderstorp	19	Beta Team Surtees	3.0 Surtees TS19-Cosworth V8	engine
13	FRENCH GP	Dijon	19	Beta Team Surtees	3.0 Surtees TS19-Cosworth V8	pit stop-tyres/3 laps behind
8	BRITISH GP	Silverstone	19	Beta Team Surtees	3.0 Surtees TS19-Cosworth V8	pit stop-puncture/1 lap behind
5	GERMAN GP	Hockenheim	19	Beta Team Surtees	3.0 Surtees TS19-Cosworth V8	
15	AUSTRIAN GP	Österreichring	19	Beta Team Surtees	3.0 Surtees TS19-Cosworth V8	spin/2 laps behind
12/ret	DUTCH GP	Zandvoort	19	Beta Team Surtees	3.0 Surtees TS19-Cosworth V8	spun off
ret	ITALIAN GP	Monza	19	Beta Team Surtees	3.0 Surtees TS19-Cosworth V8	hit by Watson-damaged radiator
19	US GP EAST	Watkins Glen	19	Beta Team Surtees	3.0 Surtees TS19-Cosworth V8	pit stop-collision damage/-5 laps
6/ret	CANADIAN GP	Mosport Park	19	Beta Team Surtees	3.0 Surtees TS19-Cosworth V8	crashed on oil/2 laps behind
8	JAPANESE GP	Mount Fuji	19	Beta Team Surtees	3.0 Surtees TS19-Cosworth V8	2 p stops-plug leads/2 laps behind

1978

18	ARGENTINE GP	Buenos Aires	19	Beta Team Surtees	3.0 Surtees TS19-Cosworth V8	2 laps behind

	Race	Circuit	No	Entrant	Car/Engine	Comment
dnq	BRAZILIAN GP	Rio	19	Beta Team Surtees	3.0 Surtees TS19-Cosworth V8	
12	SOUTH AFRICAN GP	Kyalami	19	Beta Team Surtees	3.0 Surtees TS19-Cosworth V8	2 laps behind
ret	US GP WEST	Long Beach	19	Beta Team Surtees	3.0 Surtees TS19-Cosworth V8	cwp
dnq	MONACO GP	Monte Carlo	19	Beta Team Surtees	3.0 Surtees TS20-Cosworth V8	
dnq	" "	" "	19	Beta Team Surtees	3.0 Surtees TS19-Cosworth V8	
13/ret	BELGIAN GP	Zolder	19	Beta Team Surtees	3.0 Surtees TS20-Cosworth V8	engine
7	SPANISH GP	Jarama	19	Beta Team Surtees	3.0 Surtees TS20-Cosworth V8	1 lap behind
ret	SWEDISH GP	Anderstorp	19	Beta Team Surtees	3.0 Surtees TS20-Cosworth V8	collision with Pironi-hit barrier
17	FRENCH GP	Paul Ricard	19	Beta Team Surtees	3.0 Surtees TS20-Cosworth V8	spin/2 laps behind
9	BRITISH GP	Brands Hatch	19	Beta Team Surtees	3.0 Surtees TS20-Cosworth V8	1 lap behind
ret	GERMAN GP	Hockenheim	19	Beta Team Surtees	3.0 Surtees TS20-Cosworth V8	fuel vaporisation
6	AUSTRIAN GP	Österreichring	19	Beta Team Surtees	3.0 Surtees TS20-Cosworth V8	1 lap behind
dsq	DUTCH GP	Zandvoort	19	Beta Team Surtees	3.0 Surtees TS20-Cosworth V8	push start after spin
ret/dns	ITALIAN GP	Monza	19	Beta Team Surtees	3.0 Surtees TS20-Cosworth V8	accident in first start-head injuries

1979

	Race	Circuit	No	Entrant	Car/Engine	Comment
12	ITALIAN GP	Monza	36	Autodelta	3.0 Alfa Romeo 177 F12	1 lap behind
ret	CANADIAN GP	Montreal	36	Autodelta	3.0 Alfa Romeo 179 F12	fuel metering unit
dnq	US GP EAST	Watkins Glen	36	Autodelta	3.0 Alfa Romeo 179 F12	

1980

	Race	Circuit	No	Entrant	Car/Engine	Comment
ret	DUTCH GP	Zandvoort	22	Marlboro Team Alfa Romeo	3.0 Alfa Romeo 179 V12	accident with Lees
ret	ITALIAN GP	Imola	22	Marlboro Team Alfa Romeo	3.0 Alfa Romeo 179 V12	spun off

GP Starts: 74   GP Wins: 1   Pole positions: 1   Fastest laps: 1   Points: 15.5

BRANCA, Toni (Antonio) (CH) b 15/9/1916 – d 10/5/1955

1950

	Race	Circuit	No	Entrant	Car/Engine	Comment
11	SWISS GP	Bremgarten	40	Scuderia Achille Varzi	1.5 s/c Maserati 4CLT/48 4	7 laps behind
10	BELGIAN GP	Spa	30	Antonio Branca	1.5 s/c Maserati 4CLT/48 4	6 laps behind

1951

	Race	Circuit	No	Entrant	Car/Engine	Comment
ret	GERMAN GP	Nürburgring	92	Antonio Branca	1.5 s/c Maserati 4CLT/48 4	engine

GP Starts: 3   GP Wins: 0   Pole positions: 0   Fastest laps: 0   Points: 0

BRANDON, Eric (GB) b 18/7/1920 – d 8/8/1982

1952

	Race	Circuit	No	Entrant	Car/Engine	Comment
8	SWISS GP	Bremgarten	24	Ecurie Richmond	2.0 Cooper T20-Bristol 6	7 laps behind
9	BELGIAN GP	Spa	12	Ecurie Richmond	2.0 Cooper T20-Bristol 6	3 laps behind
20	BRITISH GP	Silverstone	10	Ecurie Richmond	2.0 Cooper T20-Bristol 6	9 laps behind
13	ITALIAN GP	Monza	36	Ecurie Richmond	2.0 Cooper T20-Bristol 6	7 laps behind

1954

	Race	Circuit	No	Entrant	Car/Engine	Comment
ret	BRITISH GP	Silverstone	30	Ecurie Richmond	2.0 Cooper T23-Bristol 6	

GP Starts: 4   GP Wins: 0   Pole positions: 0   Fastest laps: 0   Points: 0

BRIDGER, Tommy (GB) b 24/6/1934

1958

	Race	Circuit	No	Entrant	Car/Engine	Comment
ret	MOROCCAN GP (F2)	Casablanca	56	British Racing Partnership	1.5 Cooper T45-Climax 4	accident

GP Starts: 1   GP Wins: 0   Pole positions: 0   Fastest laps: 0   Points: 0

BRISE, Tony (GB) b 28/3/1952 – d 29/11/1975

1975

	Race	Circuit	No	Entrant	Car/Engine	Comment
7	SPANISH GP	Montjuich Park	21	Frank Williams Racing Cars	3.0 Williams FW03-Cosworth V8	hit by Pryce/2 laps behind
ret	BELGIAN GP	Zolder	23	Embassy Racing with Graham Hill	3.0 Hill GH1-Cosworth V8	engine
6	SWEDISH GP	Anderstorp	23	Embassy Racing with Graham Hill	3.0 Hill GH1-Cosworth V8	1 lap behind
7	DUTCH GP	Zandvoort	23	Embassy Racing with Graham Hill	3.0 Hill GH1-Cosworth V8	pit stop/1 lap behind
7	FRENCH GP	Paul Ricard	23	Embassy Racing with Graham Hill	3.0 Hill GH1-Cosworth V8	
15/ret	BRITISH GP	Silverstone	23	Embassy Racing with Graham Hill	3.0 Hill GH1-Cosworth V8	crashed in rainstorm/3 laps behind
ret	GERMAN GP	Nürburgring	23	Embassy Racing with Graham Hill	3.0 Hill GH1-Cosworth V8	crashed-suspension failure
15	AUSTRIAN GP	Österreichring	23	Embassy Racing with Graham Hill	3.0 Hill GH1-Cosworth V8	1 lap behind
ret	ITALIAN GP	Monza	23	Embassy Racing with Graham Hill	3.0 Hill GH1-Cosworth V8	multiple collision at chicane-lap 1
ret	US GP	Watkins Glen	23	Embassy Racing with Graham Hill	3.0 Hill GH1-Cosworth V8	collision with Henton

GP Starts: 10   GP Wins: 0   Pole positions: 0   Fastest laps: 0   Points: 1

BRISTOW, Chris (GB) b 2/12/1937 – d 19/6/60

1959

	Race	Circuit	No	Entrant	Car/Engine	Comment
10	BRITISH GP (F2)	Aintree	48	British Racing Partnership	1.5 Cooper T51-Borgward 4	1st in F2 class/5 laps behind

1960

	Race	Circuit	No	Entrant	Car/Engine	Comment
ret	MONACO GP	Monte Carlo	16	Yeoman Credit Racing Team	2.5 Cooper T51-Climax 4	gearbox
ret	DUTCH GP	Zandvoort	8	Yeoman Credit Racing Team	2.5 Cooper T51-Climax 4	engine
ret	BELGIAN GP	Spa	36	Yeoman Credit Racing Team	2.5 Cooper T51-Climax 4	fatal accident at Burnenville

GP Starts: 4   GP Wins: 0   Pole positions: 0   Fastest laps: 0   Points: 0

ERIC BRANDON

Brandon was a boyhood friend of John Cooper, who not unnaturally became involved in racing from the early days of the little Cooper 500 cc cars. By 1951 he was rightly regarded as one of the top drivers in the class, recording wins at home and abroad.

With Alan Brown he formed the Ecurie Richmond team, the pair running front-engined Cooper-Bristol cars to the Formula 2 rules in Grands Prix during 1952 and '53. Eric's best placing was a very distant fourth at a retirement-hit Syracuse GP in 1953.

Undaunted, Eric continued in his beloved F3, where he was always a front-runner, before moving into sports cars with the 1100 cc Halseylec-Climax which he raced in 1955 and early 1956.

TOMMY BRIDGER

Bridger first entered racing with a Cooper-JAP in 1953 and, once bitten by the bug, was back the following season, contesting minor events with a Kieft-Norton which he continued to race through 1955. Armed with a Cooper, he undertook a full season of F3 in both 1956 and 1957, enjoying some fantastic dices with 'the master', Jim Russell, usually emerging second best but dogging his rival's footsteps race in and race out.

For 1958 Tommy tried his hand at Formula 2, finishing second on aggregate in the minor Crystal Palace Trophy race, and eighth in the Coupe de Vitesse at Reims. His only Grand Prix appearance, in Morocco, ended in a crash from which he luckily emerged shaken but otherwise unharmed.

He returned to the circuits the following year, back in F3, winning four races in his faithful Cooper-Norton.

TONY BRISE

After Tony Brise had made his Grand Prix debut for Frank Williams and then been snapped up by Graham Hill to race for the Embassy Hill team, he was suddenly very hot property. Yet at the beginning of 1974, no one had been interested in securing the talents of the man who had just won the John Player F3 championship outright and, with Richard Robarts, was joint Lombard North Central champion. He lacked the necessary finance to secure a seat in the March team for a season of Formula 2 and, despite a second place in the F3 Monaco support race, was thus consigned to a season of racing in Formula Atlantic.

Having come from a motor sport family – his father John was a 500 cc and stock car racer – it was natural that young Tony would involve himself in some way. He started racing karts from the age of 8, eventually becoming joint British karting champion in 1969. By now keen to try his hand at Formula Ford, but without the resources, Brise contented himself with karting until, late in 1970, the opportunity finally arose to drive an Elden – not the best of chassis but at least it was a start. He raced the car in 1971 before replacing it with a more competitive Merlyn to finish his first full season as runner-up in the BOC Formula Ford championship.

Bernie Ecclestone had spotted Tony's talent and offered him a Brabham BT28 for 1972, but this car turned out to be uncompetitive and only when he switched to a GRD did his fortunes improve. Mike Warner of GRD was another who wasn't slow to see Brise's talent and he signed him for 1973 to replace poor Roger Williamson who was bound for F1 where he was destined to meet his terrible fate at Zandvoort. As described earlier Brise did the business, but only Teddy Savory was there to back him in 1974 with the Modus Atlantic drive.

Of Brise the Grand Prix driver, sadly, we were to see precious little, but at each of the ten Grands Prix Tony contested, be it in practice or the race itself, his brilliance was evident. His loss in the plane crash that also claimed the life of Graham Hill and four members of the Hill team was a devastating blow for all followers of British motor racing, who felt they had lost a future World Champion.

CHRIS BRISTOW

Many felt that Bristow had the ability to be a World Champion, while in the other camp his detractors maintained that he was too wild. Certainly he was very, very quick but sadly we would never find out just how much he could have achieved.

With the support of his father, Chris entered racing in 1956 at the wheel of an MG Special with which he scored an early win at Crystal Palace. Realising that he needed more competitive machinery than the special, he acquired an 1100 cc Cooper sports car for 1957 and won more than a dozen minor scratch and handicap events with it in a highly satisfying year.

For 1958 the Cooper was no longer eligible, so he purchased a very fast – but not so reliable – Elva, with which he traded places regularly with the more fashionable Lotus. His efforts brought him to the attention of the British Racing Partnership, who invited him to join them for 1959 to race their Formula 2 Cooper-Borgwards and Cooper-Monaco sports cars.

It was the John Davy Trophy at Brands Hatch that really brought him to the attention of the public, Bristow taking an aggregate win from Brabham, Salavadori and McLaren with a display of speed coupled with a maturity that belied his inexperience. For 1960 BRP – under the Yeoman Credit Racing Team banner – pinned their hopes on young Bristow and the experienced Harry Schell. When Schell was killed in practice for the International Trophy, Chris found himself leading the team, but in the Belgian Grand Prix at Spa, while dicing with the Ferrari of Willy Mairesse, he lost control of the Cooper, slid into some trackside fencing and was decapitated in a gruesome accident.

BROEKER, Peter (CDN) b 15/5/1929

1963

	Race	Circuit	No	Entrant	Car/Engine	Comment
7	US GP	Watkins Glen	21	Canadian Stebro Racing	1.5 Stebro 4-Ford 4	22 laps behind

GP Starts: 1   GP Wins: 0   Pole positions: 0   Fastest laps: 0   Points: 0

BROOKS, Tony (GB) b 25/2/1932

1956

	Race	Circuit	No	Entrant	Car/Engine	Comment
dns	MONACO GP	Monte Carlo	12	Owen Racing Organisation	2.5 BRM P25 4	valve problems in practice
ret	BRITISH GP	Silverstone	24	Owen Racing Organisation	2.5 BRM P25 4	crashed-throttle stuck open

1957

	Race	Circuit	No	Entrant	Car/Engine	Comment
2	MONACO GP	Monte Carlo	20	Vandervell Products	2.5 Vanwall 4	
1*	BRITISH GP	Aintree	20	Vandervell Products	2.5 Vanwall 4	* Moss took over
ret	"	"	18	Vandervell Products	2.5 Vanwall 4	took over Moss car/engine
9	GERMAN GP	Nürburgring	11	Vandervell Products	2.5 Vanwall 4	road holding problems/1 lap behind
ret	PESCARA GP	Pescara	28	Vandervell Products	2.5 Vanwall 4	engine
7	ITALIAN GP	Monza	22	Vandervell Products	2.5 Vanwall 4	pit stop-throttle/FL/5 laps behind

1958

	Race	Circuit	No	Entrant	Car/Engine	Comment
ret	MONACO GP	Monte Carlo	30	Vandervell Products	2.5 Vanwall 4	spark plug/Pole
ret	DUTCH GP	Zandvoort	2	Vandervell Products	2.5 Vanwall 4	rear axle
1	BELGIAN GP	Spa	4	Vandervell Products	2.5 Vanwall 4	
ret	FRENCH GP	Reims	10	Vandervell Products	2.5 Vanwall 4	gearbox
ret	"	"	12	Vandervell Products	2.5 Vanwall 4	engine/Lewis-Evans car
7	BRITISH GP	Silverstone	8	Vandervell Products	2.5 Vanwall 4	1 lap behind
1	GERMAN GP	Nürburgring	8	Vandervell Products	2.5 Vanwall 4	
ret	PORTUGUESE GP	Oporto	4	Vandervell Products	2.5 Vanwall 4	spun off
1	ITALIAN GP	Monza	28	Vandervell Products	2.5 Vanwall 4	
ret	MOROCCAN GP	Casablanca	10	Vandervell Products	2.5 Vanwall 4	engine

1959

	Race	Circuit	No	Entrant	Car/Engine	Comment
2	MONACO GP	Monte Carlo	50	Scuderia Ferrari	2.4 Ferrari Dino 246 V6	physically sick during race
ret	DUTCH GP	Zandvoort	2	Scuderia Ferrari	2.4 Ferrari Dino 246 V6	oil leak
1	FRENCH GP	Reims	24	Scuderia Ferrari	2.4 Ferrari Dino 246 V6	Pole
ret	BRITISH GP	Aintree	20	Vandervell Products	2.5 Vanwall 4	misfire
1	GERMAN GP	AVUS	4	Scuderia Ferrari	2.4 Ferrari Dino 246 V6	1st in both heats/Pole/FL (heat 1)
9	PORTUGUESE GP	Monsanto	14	Scuderia Ferrari	2.4 Ferrari Dino 246 V6	5 laps behind
ret	ITALIAN GP	Monza	30	Scuderia Ferrari	2.4 Ferrari Dino 246 V6	clutch at start
3	US GP	Sebring	2	Scuderia Ferrari	2.4 Ferrari Dino 246 V6	hit by von Trips-pit stop

1960

	Race	Circuit	No	Entrant	Car/Engine	Comment
4	MONACO GP	Monte Carlo	18	Yeoman Credit Racing Team	2.5 Cooper T51-Climax 4	1 lap behind
ret	DUTCH GP	Zandvoort	9	Yeoman Credit Racing Team	2.5 Cooper T51-Climax 4	gearbox
ret	BELGIAN GP	Spa	38	Yeoman Credit Racing Team	2.5 Cooper T51-Climax 4	gearbox
ret	FRENCH GP	Reims	14	Vandervell Products	2.5 Vanwall 4	transmission vibration
5	BRITISH GP	Silverstone	12	Yeoman Credit Racing Team	2.5 Cooper T51-Climax 4	1 lap behind
5	PORTUGUESE GP	Oporto	6	Yeoman Credit Racing Team	2.5 Cooper T51-Climax 4	6 laps behind
ret	US GP	Riverside	6	Yeoman Credit Racing Team	2.5 Cooper T51-Climax 4	spun off

1961

	Race	Circuit	No	Entrant	Car/Engine	Comment
ret	MONACO GP	Monte Carlo	16	Owen Racing Organisation	1.5 BRM P48/57-Climax 4	valve
9	DUTCH GP	Zandvoort	5	Owen Racing Organisation	1.5 BRM P48/57-Climax 4	1 lap behind
13	BELGIAN GP	Spa	38	Owen Racing Organisation	1.5 BRM P48/57-Climax 4	pit stop-6 laps behind
ret	FRENCH GP	Reims	24	Owen Racing Organisation	1.5 BRM P48/57-Climax 4	engine-overheating
9	BRITISH GP	Aintree	22	Owen Racing Organisation	1.5 BRM P48/57-Climax 4	FL
ret	GERMAN GP	Nürburgring	16	Owen Racing Organisation	1.5 BRM P48/57-Climax 4	engine
5	ITALIAN GP	Monza	26	Owen Racing Organisation	1.5 BRM P48/57-Climax 4	
3	US GP	Watkins Glen	5	Owen Racing Organisation	1.5 BRM P48/57-Climax 4	

GP Starts: 38   GP Wins: 6   Pole positions: 3   Fastest laps: 3   Points: 7

BROWN, Alan (GB) b 20/11/1919

1952

	Race	Circuit	No	Entrant	Car/Engine	Comment
5	SWISS GP	Bremgarten	26	Ecurie Richmond	2.0 Cooper T20-Bristol 6	3 laps behind
6	BELGIAN GP	Spa	10	Ecurie Richmond	2.0 Cooper T20-Bristol 6	2 laps behind
nc	BRITISH GP	Silverstone	11	Ecurie Richmond	2.0 Cooper T20-Bristol 6	16 laps behind
nc	ITALIAN GP	Monza	38	Ecurie Richmond	2.0 Cooper T20-Bristol 6	12 laps behind

1953

	Race	Circuit	No	Entrant	Car/Engine	Comment
9	ARGENTINE GP	Buenos Aires	20	Cooper Car Co	2.0 Cooper T20-Bristol 6	hit spectator/10 laps behind
ret	BRITISH GP	Silverstone	19	R J Chase	2.0 Cooper T23-Bristol 6	fan belt
ret	GERMAN GP	Nürburgring	38	Equipe Anglaise	2.0 Cooper T23-Bristol 6	misfire-crashed
nc	ITALIAN GP	Monza	46	Equipe Anglaise	2.0 Cooper T23-Bristol 6	10 laps behind

1954

	Race	Circuit	No	Entrant	Car/Engine	Comment
dns	BRITISH GP	Silverstone	27	Equipe Anglaise	2.0 Cooper T23-Bristol 6	

GP Starts: 8   GP Wins: 0   Pole positions: 0   Fastest laps: 0   Points: 2

TONY BROOKS

Tony Brooks was still a dental student with little front-line experience when he shot to international prominence on the back of an absolutely stunning win at the Syracuse GP in the works Connaught in 1955. In only his second-ever race abroad, the slightly built and reserved youngster trounced the works Maserati and Gordini cars, three times breaking the lap record, and setting a best race lap some five seconds faster than his qualifying time. It had all seemed so easy, yet this was the first Continental win by a British car and driver since Henry Segrave won at San Sebastian in 1924, so the excitement it generated was naturally immense. Little were we to know the flood gates were soon to be opened, and that for British teams and drivers this was just the start.

After racing a Healey in 1952, Tony switched to a Frazer Nash, competing mainly in club events during the next two seasons – successfully, but largely unnoticed. It was the middle of the 1955 season that really saw Brooks' career take a step forward. Having raced Aston Martin's DB3S at Le Mans and Goodwood (where he shared third place with Peter Collins), he drove Risely-Pritchard's F2 Connaught in the Daily Telegraph Trophy at Aintree, finishing fourth behind the Formula 1 cars of Hawthorn, Schell and Salvadori. A win in the F2 class of the Avon Trophy at Castle Combe immediately preceded his momentous Syracuse victory, which of course made Brooks a very hot property indeed.

Signed by BRM for the 1956 season, he took second place in the Aintree 200 after being hampered by brake trouble, and then – the team having withdrawn after practice at Monaco – he prepared for his first championship Grand Prix start at Silverstone. It was nearly his last; when the throttle stuck at Abbey Curve, the car somersaulted, throwing out the driver, who was lucky to escape with a fractured jaw.

Joining Vanwall for 1957, Brooks soon displayed the smooth style and masterful car control that was to bring him so much success in the next three seasons. After finishing second to Fangio, no less, at Monaco, his season was hampered by the effects of a crash at Le Mans, which accounted for him handing his car to Moss at Aintree, where the British pair shared a momentous victory in their home GP. The following season saw Vanwall and Ferrari wage a ferocious battle for supremacy, and although Hawthorn took the drivers' championship Moss, Brooks and Lewis-Evans ensured the constructors' title came to Britain. Tony's three victories at the classic circuits of Spa, the Nürburgring and Monza spoke for themselves. Here was a driver of true championship pedigree.

Unfortunately Tony Vandervell withdrew from racing at the end of the year, and Brooks joined Ferrari to drive their front-engined 246 Dino. He again put in some superb performances, finishing second at Monaco, despite physical sickness due to cockpit fumes, and giving wonderful demonstrations of high-speed artistry at Reims and AVUS. Ferrari did not enter his cars at Aintree, so Vandervell brought out one of his Vanwalls especially for Brooks, but he retired with ignition trouble. But for a clutch failure at the start of the Italian GP, Tony may have been able to take the championship from Brabham's fleet little Cooper, but it was not to be.

With increasing business interests and recently married to an Italian girl, Pina, Tony stayed in England during 1960, racing in a limited programme of events in the Yeoman Credit Cooper. Having seen many of his close friends and rivals perish in recent seasons, perhaps Brooks' appetite for racing had gone, or maybe the newer rear-engined cars were not to his taste, but certainly his performances in both 1960 and 1961, when he joined BRM, lacked the cutting edge of the late fifties. After finishing third in the US GP he quietly retired to develop his Weybridge garage business.

ALAN BROWN

Along with his friend and team-mate, Eric Brandon, Brown was a star of the 500 cc championships with his F3 Cooper, his personal highlight in this category being a win in the 1951 Luxembourg GP.

For 1952 he teamed up with Brandon to race the new F2 Cooper-Bristols under the Ecurie Richmond banner, but they were effectively works machines. Things started well when Brown scored two points on the car's Continental debut at Bremgarten and followed this with two sixths, at the Monza Autodrome GP and the Belgian GP at Spa, but it was steadily overtaken by more sophisticated machinery, encouraging Alan to look elsewhere for racing success. He gave the protoype Vanwall its debut at the 1954 International Trophy, and raced a Connaught at the same event a year later, but he concentrated on sports cars – Coopers and Connaughts from 1953 to 1955 and then a Jaguar D-Type in 1956, his last season of racing.

He then went on to became a well-known entrant for more than a deacade.

BROWN, Warwick (AUS) b 24/12/1949

1976

	Race	Circuit	No	Entrant	Car/Engine	Comment
14	US GP EAST	Watkins Glen	21	Walter Wolf Racing	3.0 Williams FW05-Cosworth V8	5 laps behind

GP Starts: 1   GP Wins: 0   Pole positions: 0   Fastest laps: 0   Points: 0

BRUDES von BRESLAU, Adolf (D) b 15/10/1899 – d 5/11/1986

1952

	Race	Circuit	No	Entrant	Car/Engine	Comment
ret	GERMAN GP	Nürburgring	126	Adolf Brudes	2.0 Veritas RS-BMW 6	engine

GP Starts: 1   GP Wins: 0   Pole positions: 0   Fastest laps: 0   Points: 0

WARWICK BROWN

A real tough nut – even by the standards of the Aussie school of hard knocks – Warwick had plenty of guts and not a little ability, but apart from a single Grand Prix appearance he had to content himself with a career outside top-flight racing.

Early promise in 1972 with an elderly McLaren encouraged Brown to buy a Lola T300 for the 1973 Tasman series, which ended in disaster with a massive crash at Surfers Paradise hospitalising him for three months with both legs broken. Unbowed, he limped back to compete in 1974, winning the final Tasman round at Adelaide and setting his sights on US F5000 later in the year. During a successful trip he competed in three races and took third place at Riverside.

He won the 1975 Tasman title before heading Stateside again where he was to compete very successfully, especially for the VDS team, in both F5000 and Can-Am until 1979.

ADOLF BRUDES

Brudes began his racing career on motor cycles before turning to four wheels. Just before Italy entered the Second World War in 1940, he took third place in the Coppa Brescia in a BMW.

After the cessation of hostilities he resumed his racing activities, occasionally taking the wheel of a Veritas – as in his appearance in the 1952 German GP – but mainly competing in a Borgward in events as diverse as the long-distance Buenos Aires 1000 Km, Le Mans 24 Hours and Carrera Panamericana and speed record attempts at AVUS.

MARTIN BRUNDLE

It must be more than a little galling for Brundle to see Ayrton Senna sweeping all before him in Grand Prix racing, for once they were very evenly matched in Formula 3. Martin may not have the innate talent of the Brazilian, but in the right car he would surely have won a Grand Prix at the very least.

Brundle entered the 1983 season on the back of a strong finish to his first year in F3 to pit himself against Senna, the latest Formula Ford hot-shot. Watching Senna simply disappear into the distance to win no fewer than nine races would have broken the resolve of a lesser man, but in the second half of the season Martin staged a comeback. Winning six races, he fell just short in the chase for the Marlboro F3 title, but had given his career prospects a massive boost.

Joining Tyrrell in 1984, he finished fifth in his first race, and the nimble Cosworth-powered car was later in its element at Detroit, where Martin took a brilliant second place. Then came two blows to his progress. A practice crash at Dallas left him with broken ankles, ending his season, and, to add insult to injury, Tyrrell's points were later expunged due to the team's technical mis-demeanours. Starting from scratch in 1985, Brundle waited patiently for the Renault turbo engine which by now was a long-overdue necessity for the team. Driving sensibly and displaying great car control, Brundle did what he could with the equipment at his disposal, showing the odd flash of naked aggression, no doubt due to the frustration of being so far off the pace.

Reasoning that any move would be beneficial, Brundle opted to join Zakspeed in 1987 but, a gutsy fifth at Imola notwithstanding, it turned out to be a big mistake. Now four seasons into his Grand Prix career and seemingly no further forward than when he came into Formula 1, Martin took the brave decision to join Jaguar for a season of sports car racing rather than just trail round at the tail-end of the Grand Prix pack. His courage was rewarded, the Norfolk man winning the World Sports Car drivers' title with wins at Jarama, Monza, Silverstone, Brands Hatch and Fuji. In tandem with this programme, he jetted back and forth across the Atlantic to compete for Jaguar in IMSA, sharing the winning car in the Daytona 24 Hours.

A one-off drive for Williams at Spa kept Brundle in the picture, and for 1989 he joined the Brabham team as a much more confident and puposeful performer, bringing the Judd-powered car into the points on three occasions. Unfortunately the team was already suffering from financial strictures and, tiring of the uncertainty over Brabham's plans, Martin went back to Jaguar for the 1990 season, the highlight of which was, of course, the team's Le Mans victory when Brundle shared the winning Jaguar with John Nielsen and Price Cobb. Tempted by a package which included a Yamaha engine, he rejoined Brabham for 1991, but spent a generally frustrating season watching the stop-start development of a quite promising car gradually tail away.

By the end of the year he was glad to be able to look forward to a really good drive at last. Joining his old Jaguar boss Tom Walkinshaw at Benetton, Brundle made a pretty disastrous start in the first four races, which in retrospect fatally damaged his long-term prospects with the team. From Imola onwards Martin scored points in every round bar Canada (a race which he could well have won), and it was very hard on him indeed when he was dropped in favour of Patrese. He moved to Ligier for 1993 and, after another tardy start to the season, helped bring about a welcome improvement in the team's fortunes, showing an application that had been sorely lacking. His reward would be the chance to carry on the good work in 1994.

BRUNDLE, Martin (GB) b 1/6/1959

1984

	Race	Circuit	No	Entrant	Car/Engine	Comment
dsq	BRAZILIAN GP	Rio	3	Tyrrell Racing Organisation	3.0 Tyrrell 012-Cosworth V8	5th on road/dsq after Dutch GP
dsq	SOUTH AFRICAN GP	Kyalami	3	Tyrrell Racing Organisation	3.0 Tyrrell 012-Cosworth V8	11th on road/dsq after Dutch GP
dsq	BELGIAN GP	Zolder	3	Tyrrell Racing Organisation	3.0 Tyrrell 012-Cosworth V8	lost wheel/dsq after Dutch GP
dsq	SAN MARINO GP	Imola	3	Tyrrell Racing Organisation	3.0 Tyrrell 012-Cosworth V8	11th on road/dsq after Dutch GP
dsq	FRENCH GP	Dijon	3	Tyrrell Racing Organisation	3.0 Tyrrell 012-Cosworth V8	12th on road/dsq after Dutch GP
dnq	MONACO GP	Monte Carlo	3	Tyrrell Racing Organisation	3.0 Tyrrell 012-Cosworth V8	accident in practice
dsq	CANADIAN GP	Montreal	3	Tyrrell Racing Organisation	3.0 Tyrrell 012-Cosworth V8	10th on road/dsq after Dutch GP
dsq	US GP (DETROIT)	Detroit	3	Tyrrell Racing Organisation	3.0 Tyrrell 012-Cosworth V8	2nd on road/dsq after Dutch GP
dnq	US GP (DALLAS)	Dallas	3	Tyrrell Racing Organisation	3.0 Tyrrell 012-Cosworth V8	injured in practice accident

1985

	Race	Circuit	No	Entrant	Car/Engine	Comment
8	BRAZILIAN GP	Rio	3	Tyrrell Racing Organisation	3.0 Tyrrell 012-Cosworth V8	3 laps behind
ret	PORTUGUESE GP	Estoril	3	Tyrrell Racing Organisation	3.0 Tyrrell 012-Cosworth V8	gear linkage
9	SAN MARINO GP	Imola	3	Tyrrell Racing Organisation	3.0 Tyrrell 012-Cosworth V8	4 laps behind
10	MONACO GP	Monte Carlo	3	Tyrrell Racing Organisation	3.0 Tyrrell 012-Cosworth V8	4 laps behind
12	CANADIAN GP	Montreal	3	Tyrrell Racing Organisation	3.0 Tyrrell 012-Cosworth V8	2 laps behind
ret	US GP (DETROIT)	Detroit	3	Tyrrell Racing Organisation	3.0 Tyrrell 012-Cosworth V8	accident with Alliot
ret	FRENCH GP	Paul Ricard	3	Tyrrell Racing Organisation	1.5 t/c Tyrrell 014-Renault V6	gearbox
7	BRITISH GP	Silverstone	3	Tyrrell Racing Organisation	1.5 t/c Tyrrell 014-Renault V6	started fom back of grid/-2 laps
10	GERMAN GP	Nürburgring	4	Tyrrell Racing Organisation	3.0 Tyrrell 012-Cosworth V8	4 laps behind
dnq	AUSTRIAN GP	Österreichring	4	Tyrrell Racing Organisation	3.0 Tyrrell 012-Cosworth V8	
7	DUTCH GP	Zandvoort	3	Tyrrell Racing Organisation	1.5 t/c Tyrrell 014-Renault V6	1 lap behind
8	ITALIAN GP	Monza	3	Tyrrell Racing Organisation	1.5 t/c Tyrrell 014-Renault V6	1 lap behind
13	BELGIAN GP	Spa	3	Tyrrell Racing Organisation	1.5 t/c Tyrrell 014-Renault V6	5 laps behind
ret	EUROPEAN GP	Brands Hatch	3	Tyrrell Racing Organisation	1.5 t/c Tyrrell 014-Renault V6	water pipe
7	SOUTH AFRICAN GP	Kyalami	3	Tyrrell Racing Organisation	1.5 t/c Tyrrell 014-Renault V6	2 laps behind
nc	AUSTRALIAN GP	Adelaide	3	Tyrrell Racing Organisation	1.5 t/c Tyrrell 014-Renault V6	pit stop-electrics/33 laps behind

1986

	Race	Circuit	No	Entrant	Car/Engine	Comment
5	BRAZILIAN GP	Rio	3	Data General Team Tyrrell	1.5 t/c Tyrrell 014-Renault V6	1 lap behind
dns	"	"	3	Data General Team Tyrrell	1.5 t/c Tyrrell 015-Renault V6	crashed in practice
ret	SPANISH GP	Jerez	3	Data General Team Tyrrell	1.5 t/c Tyrrell 015-Renault V6	engine-lost lubricant
8	SAN MARINO GP	Imola	3	Data General Team Tyrrell	1.5 t/c Tyrrell 014-Renault V6	crashed 015 in warm-up/-2 laps
ret	MONACO GP	Monte Carlo	3	Data General Team Tyrrell	1.5 t/c Tyrrell 015-Renault V6	accident with Tambay
ret	BELGIAN GP	Spa	3	Data General Team Tyrrell	1.5 t/c Tyrrell 015-Renault V6	gearbox
9	CANADIAN GP	Montreal	3	Data General Team Tyrrell	1.5 t/c Tyrrell 015-Renault V6	2 laps behind
ret	US GP (DETROIT)	Detroit	3	Data General Team Tyrrell	1.5 t/c Tyrrell 015-Renault V6	electrics
10	FRENCH GP	Paul Ricard	3	Data General Team Tyrrell	1.5 t/c Tyrrell 015-Renault V6	lost 4th gear/3 laps behind
5	BRITISH GP	Brands Hatch	3	Data General Team Tyrrell	1.5 t/c Tyrrell 015-Renault V6	3 laps behind
ret	GERMAN GP	Hockenheim	3	Data General Team Tyrrell	1.5 t/c Tyrrell 015-Renault V6	electrics
6	HUNGARIAN GP	Hungaroring	3	Data General Team Tyrrell	1.5 t/c Tyrrell 015-Renault V6	lost 4th gear/2 laps behind
ret	AUSTRIAN GP	Österreichring	3	Data General Team Tyrrell	1.5 t/c Tyrrell 015-Renault V6	turbo
10	ITALIAN GP	Monza	3	Data General Team Tyrrell	1.5 t/c Tyrrell 015-Renault V6	misfire/2 laps behind
ret	PORTUGUESE GP	Estoril	3	Data General Team Tyrrell	1.5 t/c Tyrrell 015-Renault V6	engine
11	MEXICAN GP	Mexico City	3	Data General Team Tyrrell	1.5 t/c Tyrrell 015-Renault V6	2 pit stops-tyres/3 laps behind
4	AUSTRALIAN GP	Adelaide	3	Data General Team Tyrrell	1.5 t/c Tyrrell 015-Renault V6	1 lap behind

1987

	Race	Circuit	No	Entrant	Car/Engine	Comment
ret	BRAZILIAN GP	Rio	9	West Zakspeed Racing	1.5 t/c Zakspeed 861 4	turbo
5	SAN MARINO GP	Imola	9	West Zakspeed Racing	1.5 t/c Zakspeed 871 4	2 laps behind
ret	BELGIAN GP	Spa	9	West Zakspeed Racing	1.5 t/c Zakspeed 871 4	engine
7	MONACO GP	Monte Carlo	9	West Zakspeed Racing	1.5 t/c Zakspeed 871 4	2 laps behind
ret	US GP (DETROIT)	Detroit	9	West Zakspeed Racing	1.5 t/c Zakspeed 871 4	turbo
ret	FRENCH GP	Paul Ricard	9	West Zakspeed Racing	1.5 t/c Zakspeed 871 4	lost rear wheel
nc	BRITISH GP	Silverstone	9	West Zakspeed Racing	1.5 t/c Zakspeed 871 4	pit stop-electrics/11 laps behind
nc	GERMAN GP	Hockenheim	9	West Zakspeed Racing	1.5 t/c Zakspeed 871 4	pit stops-electrics/10 laps behind
ret	HUNGARIAN GP	Hungaroring	9	West Zakspeed Racing	1.5 t/c Zakspeed 871 4	turbo
dsq	AUSTRIAN GP	Österreichring	9	West Zakspeed Racing	1.5 t/c Zakspeed 871 4	14th/dsq bodywork infringement
ret	ITALIAN GP	Monza	9	West Zakspeed Racing	1.5 t/c Zakspeed 871 4	gearbox
ret	PORTUGUESE GP	Estoril	9	West Zakspeed Racing	1.5 t/c Zakspeed 871 4	gearbox
11	SPANISH GP	Jerez	9	West Zakspeed Racing	1.5 t/c Zakspeed 871 4	2 laps behind
ret	MEXICAN GP	Mexico City	9	West Zakspeed Racing	1.5 t/c Zakspeed 871 4	turbo
ret	JAPANESE GP	Suzuka	9	West Zakspeed Racing	1.5 t/c Zakspeed 871 4	engine
ret	AUSTRALIAN GP	Adelaide	9	West Zakspeed Racing	1.5 t/c Zakspeed 871 4	turbo

1988

	Race	Circuit	No	Entrant	Car/Engine	Comment
7*	BELGIAN GP	Spa	5	Canon Williams Team	3.5 Williams FW12-Judd V8	*3rd & 4th cars dsq/1 lap behind

1989

	Race	Circuit	No	Entrant	Car/Engine	Comment
ret	BRAZILIAN GP	Rio	7	Motor Racing Developments	3.5 Brabham BT58-Judd V8	engine
ret	SAN MARINO GP	Imola	7	Motor Racing Developments	3.5 Brabham BT58-Judd V8	fuel pump
6	MONACO GP	Monte Carlo	7	Motor Racing Developments	3.5 Brabham BT58-Judd V8	pit stop when 3rd-battery/-2 laps
9	MEXICAN GP	Mexico City	7	Motor Racing Developments	3.5 Brabham BT58-Judd V8	1 lap behind
ret	US GP (PHOENIX)	Phoenix	7	Motor Racing Developments	3.5 Brabham BT58-Judd V8	brakes
dnpq	CANADIAN GP	Montreal	7	Motor Racing Developments	3.5 Brabham BT58-Judd V8	
dnpq	FRENCH GP	Paul Ricard	7	Motor Racing Developments	3.5 Brabham BT58-Judd V8	
ret	BRITISH GP	Silverstone	7	Motor Racing Developments	3.5 Brabham BT58-Judd V8	engine
8	GERMAN GP	Hockenheim	7	Motor Racing Developments	3.5 Brabham BT58-Judd V8	p stop-slow puncture/1 lap behind
12	HUNGARIAN GP	Hungaroring	7	Motor Racing Developments	3.5 Brabham BT58-Judd V8	hit Alesi and spun/2 laps behind
ret	BELGIAN GP	Spa	7	Motor Racing Developments	3.5 Brabham BT58-Judd V8	brakes
6	ITALIAN GP	Monza	7	Motor Racing Developments	3.5 Brabham BT58-Judd V8	1 lap behind
8	PORTUGUESE GP	Estoril	7	Motor Racing Developments	3.5 Brabham BT58-Judd V8	2 pit stops-tyres/1 lap behind
ret	SPANISH GP	Jerez	7	Motor Racing Developments	3.5 Brabham BT58-Judd V8	spun off

5*	JAPANESE GP	Suzuka	7	Motor Racing Developments	3.5 Brabham BT58-Judd V8	*1st place car dsq/1 lap behind
ret	AUSTRALIAN GP	Adelaide	7	Motor Racing Developments	3.5 Brabham BT58-Judd V8	hit by Senna in rain

1991

11	US GP (PHOENIX)	Phoenix	7	Motor Racing Developments Ltd	3.5 Brabham BT59Y-Yamaha V12	8 laps behind
12	BRAZILIAN GP	Interlagos	7	Motor Racing Developments Ltd	3.5 Brabham BT59Y-Yamaha V12	4 laps behind
11	SAN MARINO GP	Imola	7	Motor Racing Developments Ltd	3.5 Brabham BT60Y-Yamaha V12	4 laps behind
dsq	MONACO GP	Monte Carlo	7	Motor Racing Developments Ltd	3.5 Brabham BT60Y-Yamaha V12	missed weight check-Thurs practice
ret	CANADIAN GP	Montreal	7	Motor Racing Developments Ltd	3.5 Brabham BT60Y-Yamaha V12	engine
ret	MEXICAN GP	Mexico City	7	Motor Racing Developments Ltd	3.5 Brabham BT60Y-Yamaha V12	lost rear wheel
ret	FRENCH GP	Magny Cours	7	Motor Racing Developments Ltd	3.5 Brabham BT60Y-Yamaha V12	gearbox
ret	BRITISH GP	Silverstone	7	Motor Racing Developments Ltd	3.5 Brabham BT60Y-Yamaha V12	throttle cable
11	GERMAN GP	Hockenheim	7	Motor Racing Developments Ltd	3.5 Brabham BT60Y-Yamaha V12	2 laps behind
ret	HUNGARIAN GP	Hungaroring	7	Motor Racing Developments Ltd	3.5 Brabham BT60Y-Yamaha V12	foot cramp
9	BELGIAN GP	Spa	7	Motor Racing Developments Ltd	3.5 Brabham BT60Y-Yamaha V12	2 laps behind
13	ITALIAN GP	Monza	7	Motor Racing Developments Ltd	3.5 Brabham BT60Y-Yamaha V12	1 lap behind
12	PORTUGUESE GP	Estoril	7	Motor Racing Developments Ltd	3.5 Brabham BT60Y-Yamaha V12	2 laps behind
10	SPANISH GP	Barcelona	7	Motor Racing Developments Ltd	3.5 Brabham BT60Y-Yamaha V12	2 laps behind
5	JAPANESE GP	Suzuka	7	Motor Racing Developments Ltd	3.5 Brabham BT60Y-Yamaha V12	1 lap behind
dnq	AUSTRALIAN GP	Adelaide	7	Motor Racing Developments Ltd	3.5 Brabham BT60Y-Yamaha V12	

1992

ret	SOUTH AFRICAN GP	Kyalami	20	Camel Benetton Ford	3.5 Benetton B191B-Ford HB V8	spun-broke clutch restarting
ret	MEXICAN GP	Mexico City	20	Camel Benetton Ford	3.5 Benetton B191B-Ford HB V8	overheating
ret	BRAZILIAN GP	Interlagos	20	Camel Benetton Ford	3.5 Benetton B191B-Ford HB V8	collision with Alesi
ret	SPANISH GP	Barcelona	20	Camel Benetton Ford	3.5 Benetton B192-Ford HB V8	spun off
4	SAN MARINO GP	Imola	20	Camel Benetton Ford	3.5 Benetton B192-Ford HB V8	
5	MONACO GP	Monte Carlo	20	Camel Benetton Ford	3.5 Benetton B192-Ford HB V8	
ret	CANADIAN GP	Montreal	20	Camel Benetton Ford	3.5 Benetton B192-Ford HB V8	final drive
3	FRENCH GP	Magny Cours	20	Camel Benetton Ford	3.5 Benetton B192-Ford HB V8	
3	BRITISH GP	Silverstone	20	Camel Benetton Ford	3.5 Benetton B192-Ford HB V8	
4	GERMAN GP	Hockenheim	20	Camel Benetton Ford	3.5 Benetton B192-Ford HB V8	
5	HUNGARIAN GP	Hungaroring	20	Camel Benetton Ford	3.5 Benetton B192-Ford HB V8	
4	BELGIAN GP	Spa	20	Camel Benetton Ford	3.5 Benetton B192-Ford HB V8	
2	ITALIAN GP	Monza	20	Camel Benetton Ford	3.5 Benetton B192-Ford HB V8	
4	PORTUGUESE GP	Estoril	20	Camel Benetton Ford	3.5 Benetton B192-Ford HB V8	1 lap behind
3	JAPANESE GP	Suzuka	20	Camel Benetton Ford	3.5 Benetton B192-Ford HB V8	
3	AUSTRALIAN GP	Adelaide	20	Camel Benetton Ford	3.5 Benetton B192-Ford HB V8	

1993

ret	SOUTH AFRICAN GP	Kyalami	25	Ligier Gitanes Blondes	3.5 Ligier JS39-Renault V10	spun off on oil
ret	BRAZILIAN GP	Interlagos	25	Ligier Gitanes Blondes	3.5 Ligier JS39-Renault V10	collision, Barbazza lap 1-spun off
ret	EUROPEAN GP	Donington	25	Ligier Gitanes Blondes	3.5 Ligier JS39-Renault V10	spun off and stalled
3	SAN MARINO GP	Imola	25	Ligier Gitanes Blondes	3.5 Ligier JS39-Renault V10	1 lap behind
ret	SPANISH GP	Barcelona	25	Ligier Gitanes Blondes	3.5 Ligier JS39-Renault V10	puncture-spun off
6	MONACO GP	Monte Carlo	25	Ligier Gitanes Blondes	3.5 Ligier JS39-Renault V10	collision-p stop/2 laps behind
5	CANADIAN GP	Montreal	25	Ligier Gitanes Blondes	3.5 Ligier JS39-Renault V10	1 lap behind
5	FRENCH GP	Magny Cours	25	Ligier Gitanes Blondes	3.5 Ligier JS39-Renault V10	
14/ret	BRITISH GP	Silverstone	25	Ligier Gitanes Blondes	3.5 Ligier JS39-Renault V10	gearbox/6 laps behind
8	GERMAN GP	Hockenheim	25	Ligier Gitanes Blondes	3.5 Ligier JS39-Renault V10	stop & go pen/1 lap behind
5	HUNGARIAN GP	Hungaroring	25	Ligier Gitanes Blondes	3.5 Ligier JS39-Renault V10	collision-Berger/1 lap behind
7	BELGIAN GP	Spa	25	Ligier Gitanes Blondes	3.5 Ligier JS39-Renault V10	1 lap behind
ret	ITALIAN GP	Monza	25	Ligier Gitanes Blondes	3.5 Ligier JS39-Renault V10	taken off by Senna
6	PORTUGUESE GP	Estoril	25	Ligier Gitanes Blondes	3.5 Ligier JS39-Renault V10	1 lap behind
9/ret	JAPANESE GP	Suzuka	25	Ligier Gitanes Blondes	3.5 Ligier JS39-Renault V10	collision, Lehto-spun off/-2 laps
6	AUSTRALIAN GP	Adelaide	25	Ligier Gitanes Blondes	3.5 Ligier JS39-Renault V10	1 lap behind

GP Starts: 115   GP Wins: 0   Pole positions: 0   Fastest laps: 0   Points: 67

BUCCI, Clemar (RA) b 4/9/1920

1954

	Race	Circuit	No	Entrant	Car/Engine	Comment
ret	BRITISH GP	Silverstone	18	Equipe Gordini	2.5 Gordini Type 16 6	crashed
ret	GERMAN GP	Nürburgring	11	Equipe Gordini	2.5 Gordini Type 16 6	lost wheel
ret	SWISS GP	Bremgarten	12	Equipe Gordini	2.5 Gordini Type 16 6	fuel pump on grid
ret	ITALIAN GP	Monza	46	Equipe Gordini	2.5 Gordini Type 16 6	transmission

1955

ret	ARGENTINE GP	Buenos Aires	26	Officine Alfieri Maserati	2.5 Maserati 250F 6	fuel starvation/Schell/Menditéguy drove

GP Starts: 5   GP Wins: 0   Pole positions: 0   Fastest laps: 0   Points: 0

BUCKNUM, Ronnie (USA) b 5/4/1936 – d Apr 1992

1964

	Race	Circuit	No	Entrant	Car/Engine	Comment
ret	GERMAN GP	Nürburgring	20	Honda R & D Co	1.5 Honda RA271 V12	spun off
ret	ITALIAN GP	Monza	28	Honda R & D Co	1.5 Honda RA271 V12	brakes/engine oil leaks/overheating
ret	US GP	Watkins Glen	28	Honda R & D Co	1.5 Honda RA271 V12	engine-head gasket

1965

ret	MONACO GP	Monte Carlo	19	Honda R & D Co	1.5 Honda RA272 V12	gear linkage
ret	BELGIAN GP	Spa	11	Honda R & D Co	1.5 Honda RA272 V12	transmission
ret	FRENCH GP	Clermont Ferrand	28	Honda R & D Co	1.5 Honda RA272 V12	ignition
ret	ITALIAN GP	Monza	22	Honda R & D Co	1.5 Honda RA272 V12	engine
13	US GP	Watkins Glen	12	Honda R & D Co	1.5 Honda RA272 V12	pit stop/18 laps behind
5	MEXICAN GP	Mexico City	12	Honda R & D Co	1.5 Honda RA272 V12	1 lap behind

1966

ret	US GP	Watkins Glen	14	Honda R & D Co	3.0 Honda RA273 V12	*transmission*
8	MEXICAN GP	Mexico City	14	Honda R & D Co	3.0 Honda RA273 V12	*pit stop-fire/5 laps behind winner*

GP Starts: 11   GP Wins: 0   Pole positions: 0   Fastest laps: 0   Points: 2

RONNIE BUCKNUM

Although Bucknum had been competing in sports cars in America since 1957, his selection by Honda to spearhead their 1964 Grand Prix challenge was strange indeed. His lack of international racing pedigree had its attractions for the secretive Japanese, since Ronnie could test and race the car without raising undue attention or expectations, and the opposition would never really know just how well it was progressing in that first season. However, the novice did well just to survive a daunting debut at the Nürburgring which ended when the car suffered a steering failure.

Two more races were safely completed before the team signed the vastly more experienced Richie Ginther to head their 1965 challenge and embarked on a winter of testing at Suzuka, during which the unlucky Bucknum again suffered a steering failure, crashed and this time broke his leg. This set him back when the season began and he predictably played second fiddle to his team-mate, although he did score points with a fifth place in Mexico as Ginther swept aside the opposition to record Honda's first Grand Prix win.

If nothing else, everybody now knew who Ronnie Bucknum was and he was invited to join the Ford team for 1966, finishing third at Le Mans with Hutcherson. Honda still thought well of their man and once two of their 3-litre cars were available he returned for the end-of-season American races. Although this was his final bow in Grands Prix, in many ways Bucknum's career as a racing driver was really just beginning. After more sports cars in 1967, Ronnie went racing in Can-Am and USAC the following year, sensationally winning at Michigan in only his second oval race with an Eagle. Subsequently he raced sports and Trans-Am cars for Roger Penske and teamed up with Sam Posey in the NART Ferrari in long-distance events in the early seventies, by which time the Marine crew-cut had been replaced by collar-length hair and a beard! Bucknum, who was later to suffer from diabetes, died at the comparatively young age of 57 in April 1992.

IVOR BUEB

Bueb began his career in 1952 in 500 cc racing, though he did not taste success until he got his hands on a Cooper for the 1954 season. Ivor did so well that he was invited to join the works team the following year, racing the 1100 cc sports car in adddition to his F3 commitments. The high point of his season, though, was his win at Le Mans with Hawthorn in the D-Type Jaguar.

Bueb cheerfully continued to race anything and everything that came his way in next few seasons, winning the Reims 12 Hours for Jaguar (with Hamilton) in 1956 and repeating his Le Mans triumph with Hawthorn in 1957, a year which saw his Formula 1 debut for Connaught, Bueb claiming fifth at Syracuse and third at Pau in the ageing car.

Although opportunities at Grand Prix level were limited, Ivor maintained his busy racing schedule in 1958, campaigning his own Lotus 12 in F2 and driving for Ecurie Ecosse and Lister in sports cars. Teaming up with the ambitious BRP stable for 1959, Ivor was as competitive as ever with the team's Formula 2 Cooper-Borgward but disaster struck when he crashed fatally during the Auvergne Trophy race at Clermont Ferrand.

LUIS BUENO

Twice the Brazilian touring car champion, Bueno was a very talented driver who came to Britain in 1969 to race in Formula Ford courtesy of a Brazilian government scheme. He won five races and was well-placed elsewhere with a Merlyn, but opted to return to Brazil and continue in domestic racing in 1970.

Regarded as highly as Emerson Fittipaldi, Bueno felt that, at 32, he was too old to take up the offer of a full-time return to Europe in 1971, but he did compete in the inaugural non-championship Brazilian GP in a works March 721 in 1972, finishing sixth, and the World Championship race for Team Surtees a year later.

BUEB, Ivor (GB) b 6/6/1923 – d 1/8/1959

1957

	Race	Circuit	No	Entrant	Car/Engine	Comment
ret	MONACO GP	Monte Carlo	12	Connaught Engineering	2.5 Connaught B-Alta 4	*p stop exhaust/broken chassis*
nc	BRITISH GP	Aintree	32	Gilby Engineering	2.5 Maserati 250F 6	*19 laps behind*

1958

ret	BRITISH GP	Silverstone	15	B C Ecclestone	2.5 Connaught B-Alta 4	*gearbox oil pump*
11/ret	GERMAN GP (F2)	Nürburgring	12	Ecurie Demi Litre	1.5 Lotus 12-Climax 4	*oil pipe/6th in F2 class*

1959

dnq	MONACO GP	Monte Carlo	34	British Racing Partnership	1.5 Cooper T51-Climax 4	
13	BRITISH GP (F2)	Aintree	46	British Racing Partnership	1.5 Cooper T51-Borgward 4	*4th in F2 class/6 laps behind*

GP Starts: 5   GP Wins: 0   Pole positions: 0   Fastest laps: 0   Points: 0

BUENO, Luis Pereira (BR) b *circa* 1939

1973

	Race	Circuit	No	Entrant	Car/Engine	Comment
12	BRAZILIAN GP	Interlagos	23	Team Surtees	3.0 Surtees TS9B-Cosworth V8	*pit stop-electrics/4 laps behind*

GP Starts: 1   GP Wins: 0   Pole positions: 0   Fastest laps: 0   Points: 0

IAN BURGESS

Burgess caused quite stir when in 1951 he won the Eifelrennen 500 cc race in the pouring rain at the Nürburgring ahead of more seasoned practitioners Wharton and Whitehead.

Unfortunately he could not build on this triumph, and the next few seasons brought only moderate success.

It was only when he began working for the Cooper team at their Surbiton factory that his career started to prosper. Although employed in part to help run the Cooper's racing drivers school from Brands Hatch, Ian was cajoling the management into letting him race their new Formula 2 cars.

Fourth place in the 1957 Gold Cup at Oulton Park led to a season in Tommy Atkins' similar car for 1958. A brilliant start to the year saw Ian win at Crystal Palace and Snetterton and take fourth at both Montlhéry and Reims, until a broken leg sustained in a crash at AVUS curtailed his season.

He was back in 1959, driving for Atkins in F2 and also handling the Italian Scuderia Centro Sud team's Maserati-engined F1 Cooper, while a trip to New Zealand at the start of 1960 saw Ian win the Teretonga Trophy in Atkins' Cooper. For 1961 Burgess became involved with the American Camoradi Team, racing their Lotus 18 with only moderate success at minor events.

He concentrated on the plethora of non-championship races in 1962, driving a Cooper under the Anglo American Equipe banner. The season's highlight was an excellent drive to fourth at Solitude. For the 1963 season, his last in racing, Burgess joined the Scirocco team, bankrolled by wealthy American businessman Hugh Powell, but it proved to be a dismal and costly exercise for all concerned.

ROBERTO BUSSINELLO

Bussinello was an engineering graduate who began racing in 1958, also working as a development engineer and test driver for the de Tomaso team. He drove their F1 car on occasion, mainly in Italian events, taking fifth place in the Naples GP and fourth in the Coppa Italia of 1961.

In 1963 Bussinello moved to Alfa Romeo, again initially in a development role, but he was soon racing their lovely Giulietta GT car, finishing third in the 1964 Targa Florio and winning the Sandown Park 6-hour race at season's end. His handful of F1 sorties in the ageing Centro Sud BRM in 1965 yielded little, so it was back to Alfas and familiar territory for Roberto, who later acted as engineer to Muller's de Tomaso-Ford sports car in the early seventies.

BURGESS, Ian (GB) b 6/7/1930

1958

	Race	Circuit	No	Entrant	Car/Engine	Comment
ret	BRITISH GP	Silverstone	12	Cooper Car Co	2.0 Cooper T45-Climax 4	clutch
7	GERMAN GP (F2)	Nürburgring	26	High Efficiency Motors	1.5 Cooper T43-Climax 4	3rd in F2 class

1959

	Race	Circuit	No	Entrant	Car/Engine	Comment
ret	FRENCH GP	Reims	18	Scuderia Centro Sud	2.5 Cooper T51-Maserati 4	engine
ret	BRITISH GP	Aintree	22	Scuderia Centro Sud	2.5 Cooper T51-Maserati 4	gearbox
6	GERMAN GP	AVUS	18	Scuderia Centro Sud	2.5 Cooper T51-Maserati 4	9th heat 1/6th heat 2/2 laps behind
14	ITALIAN GP	Monza	42	Scuderia Centro Sud	2.5 Cooper T51-Maserati 4	5 laps behind

1960

	Race	Circuit	No	Entrant	Car/Engine	Comment
dnq	MONACO GP	Monte Carlo	42	Scuderia Centro Sud	2.5 Cooper T51-Maserati 4	
10	FRENCH GP	Reims	42	Scuderia Centro Sud	2.5 Cooper T51-Maserati 4	pit stop/14 laps behind
ret	BRITISH GP	Silverstone	17	Scuderia Centro Sud	2.5 Cooper T51-Maserati 4	engine
ret	US GP	Riverside	19	Scuderia Centro Sud	2.5 Cooper T51-Maserati 4	ignition

1961

	Race	Circuit	No	Entrant	Car/Engine	Comment
dns	DUTCH GP	Zandvoort	18	Camoradi International	1.5 Lotus 18-Climax 4	reserve entry (set qualifying time)
dnq	BELGIAN GP	Spa	50	Camoradi International	1.5 Lotus 18-Climax 4	
14	FRENCH GP	Reims	38	Camoradi International	1.5 Lotus 18-Climax 4	pit stop/10 laps behind
14	BRITISH GP	Aintree	44	Camoradi International	1.5 Lotus 18-Climax 4	6 laps behind
12	GERMAN GP	Nürburgring	30	Camoradi International	1.5 Cooper T53-Climax 4	1 lap behind

1962

	Race	Circuit	No	Entrant	Car/Engine	Comment
12	BRITISH GP	Aintree	36	Anglo American Equipe	1.5 Cooper T53-Climax 4	4 laps behind
11	GERMAN GP	Nürburgring	25	Anglo American Equipe	1.5 Cooper T53-Climax 4	
dnq	ITALIAN GP	Monza	62	Anglo American Equipe	1.5 Cooper T53-Climax 4	

1963

	Race	Circuit	No	Entrant	Car/Engine	Comment
ret	BRITISH GP	Silverstone	16	Scirocco-Powell (Racing Cars)	1.5 Scirocco 02-BRM V8	ignition
ret	GERMAN GP	Nürburgring	24	Scirocco-Powell (Racing Cars)	1.5 Scirocco 02-BRM V8	steering arm

GP Starts: 16   GP Wins: 0   Pole positions: 0   Fastest laps: 0   Points: 0

BUSSINELLO, Roberto (I) b 4/10/1927

1961

	Race	Circuit	No	Entrant	Car/Engine	Comment
ret	ITALIAN GP	Monza	54	Isobele de Tomaso	1.5 de Tomaso F1 004-Alfa Romeo 4	engine

1965

	Race	Circuit	No	Entrant	Car/Engine	Comment
dnq	GERMAN GP	Nürburgring	25	Scuderia Centro Sud	1.5 BRM P57 V8	
13/ret	ITALIAN GP	Monza	50	Scuderia Centro Sud	1.5 BRM P57 V8	oil pressure/16 laps behind

GP Starts: 2   GP Wins: 0   Pole positions: 0   Fastest laps: 0   Points: 0

BYRNE, Tommy (IRL) b 6/5/1958

1982

	Race	Circuit	No	Entrant	Car/Engine	Comment
dnq	GERMAN GP	Hockenheim	33	Theodore Racing Team	3.0 Theodore TY02-Cosworth V8	
ret	AUSTRIAN GP	Österreichring	33	Theodore Racing Team	3.0 Theodore TY02-Cosworth V8	*spun off*
dnq	SWISS GP	Dijon	33	Theodore Racing Team	3.0 Theodore TY02-Cosworth V8	
dnq	ITALIAN GP	Monza	33	Theodore Racing Team	3.0 Theodore TY02-Cosworth V8	
ret	CAESARS PALACE GP	Las Vegas	33	Theodore Racing Team	3.0 Theodore TY02-Cosworth V8	*spun off*

GP Starts: 2 GP Wins: 0 Pole positions: 0 Fastest laps: 0 Points: 0

CABIANCA, Giulio (I) b 19/2/1923 – d 15/6/1961

1958

	Race	Circuit	No	Entrant	Car/Engine	Comment
dnq	MONACO GP	Monte Carlo	52	OSCA Automobili	1.5 Osca 4	*F2 car*
ret	ITALIAN GP	Monza	22	Jo Bonnier	2.5 Maserati 250F 6	*engine*

1959

15	ITALIAN GP	Monza	28	Ottorino Volonterio	2.5 Maserati 250F 6	*pit stop/8 laps behind*

1960

4	ITALIAN GP	Monza	4	Scuderia Castellotti	2.5 Cooper T51-Ferrari 4	*2 laps behind*

GP Starts: 3 GP Wins: 0 Pole positions: 0 Fastest laps: 0 Points: 3

CABRAL, Mario Araujo (P) b 15/1/1934

1959

	Race	Circuit	No	Entrant	Car/Engine	Comment
10	PORTUGUESE GP	Monsanto	18	Scuderia Centro Sud	2.5 Cooper T51-Maserati 4	*4 laps behind*

1960

ret	PORTUGUESE GP	Oporto	32	Scuderia Centro Sud	2.5 Cooper T51-Maserati 4	*clutch/gearbox*

1963

ret	GERMAN GP	Nürburgring	22	Scuderia Centro Sud	1.5 Cooper T60-Climax V8	*gearbox*
dnq	ITALIAN GP	Monza	64	Scuderia Centro Sud	1.5 Cooper T60-Climax V8	

1964

ret	ITALIAN GP	Monza	50	Derrington-Francis Racing Team	1.5 ATS 100 V8	*ignition*

GP Starts: 4 GP Wins: 0 Pole positions: 0 Fastest laps: 0 Points: 0

TOMMY BYRNE

Tommy Byrne's rise to the top was so rapid he was pitched into Formula 1 before he had completed his first season in Formula 3. He felt the opportunity of racing the Theodore was too good to miss, but the car was uncompetitive and he was never given a second chance.

A sparkling Formula Ford debut in 1981 brought Byrne into the top Murray Taylor F3 team knowing he had to get results or else . . . And he did just that, taking seven wins and the Marlboro F3 title despite missing rounds while pursuing his Grand Prix adventure. Third place in the 1983 European F3 series led nowhere so Byrne headed off to America, where he has been successful but has remained marooned in the junior single-seaters classes.

GIULIO CABIANCA

A very experienced and reliable sports car driver, Cabianca spent most of the fifties pitting the works OSCA sports cars against more powerful opposition, regularly picking up class wins in classic events. He was seventh overall and first in class in the 1955 Targa Florio and after a superb drive repeated the feat in the 1957 Mille Miglia with Chiron (ninth overall). These performances led to his inclusion in the Ferrari sports car team for 1959 and 1960, when his best placing was fourth in the Targa Florio. He also took second place in the 1961 Mille Miglia in a Flammini Zagato.

With the F2 OSCA he finished third to Trintignant after taking an early lead in the 1958 Pau GP. Though his Grand Prix outings were few, he lay fifth in Bonnier's Maserati in the 1958 Italian GP before engine trouble, and scored points in the boycotted 1960 Italian GP for Scuderia Castellotti.

He lost his life testing one of the team's Coopers at Modena in 1961 when the throttle stuck open; the car ran through an open gateway into the street and crashed into a passing taxi, killing not only Cabianca but also the three unfortunate occupants of the passing cab.

MARIO CABRAL

Cabral was Portugal's outstanding driver of the late fifties, and acquitted himself well in his first two Grand Prix outings. He did not pursue a full-time racing career but appeared in the 1961 Pau GP, finishing in fourth place for Centro Sud, before National Service (as a paratrooper in Angola) took priority.

He managed to return to Formula 1 in 1963 with Centro Sud and made the grid for the 1964 Italian GP in the reworked but no less unsuccessful Derrington-Francis ATS. However, Mario was seriously injured when he crashed in the 1965 F2 Rouen GP, resulting in a three-year absence from the circuits.

On his return in 1968 Cabral raced a variety of sports cars through to 1975, including David Piper's Porsche 917, in which he finished second at Villa Real in 1971. In 1973 he hired a works March for the F2 Estoril GP and performed very creditably to finish eighth on aggregate.

ALEX CAFFI

Always the bridesmaid in Italian F3, Caffi was runner-up in both 1984 and 1985, when the lack of a Dallara chassis probably cost him the title, and third behind Coloni stars Larini and Apicella in 1986. Given a chance to race the unwieldy Osella at the Italian GP that season, Alex drove sensibly, kept out of the way and impressed everyone with his approach.

This led to a full season with the team in 1987. The car was totally uncompetitive, but Caffi plugged away uncomplainingly, quietly learning his trade. A move to the new Dallara team for 1988 brought some good performances in their neat little car, and the following season he seemed to be a star in the making, finishing fourth at Monaco and losing a potential good result at Phoenix when team-mate de Cesaris elbowed him into the wall.

In retrospect his move to the Arrows/Footwork team proved to be a complete disaster. The 1990 season was spent marking time and when the Porsche-engined car arrived it was hopelessly overweight and underpowered. Things took a further dive when Alex was involved in a road accident which resulted in a broken jaw, and the atmosphere was not helped when he threatened legal action to reclaim his seat at Hockenheim. A hot property barely two seasons earlier, Caffi's career was now on the skids, and after a brief flirtation with Andrea Moda he found himself languishing in the relative obscurity of the Italian touring car championship.

JOHN CAMPBELL-JONES

Campbell-Jones achieved some success in sports cars in 1958 before buying a Formula 2 Cooper to race at home and abroad. Usually to be found scratching around in minor F1 events, his 1961 season was cut short after a crash at Modena and his 1962 campaign in the Emeryson brought little but a distant fifth place on aggregate in the Brussels GP and sixth in the Aintree 200.

Under the wing of the Parnell stable in 1963, he still could not make much headway despite having a much better car, and was not seen on the circuits again except for a surprise appearance in the 1966 Gold Cup at Oulton Park in an old BRP-Climax.

ADRIAN CAMPOS

Without much of a track record to speak of (half a dozen F3000 races) during the previous season, Campos was a surprise choice for the second seat in the Minardi team for 1987. Though naturally overshadowed by team-mate Nannini, he did better than many would have expected given his lack of experience. He was joined by fellow countryman Luis Sala for 1988, but lost his seat to Pierluigi Martini after failing to qualify for three races in a row. Now contests the Spanish touring car championship, along with fellow outcast Sala.

CAFFI, Alex (I) b 18/3/1964

1986

	Race	Circuit	No	Entrant	Car/Engine	Comment
nc	ITALIAN GP	Monza	22	Osella Squadra Corse	1.5 t/c Osella FA1F-Alfa Romeo V8	6 laps behind

1987

	Race	Circuit	No	Entrant	Car/Engine	Comment
ret	BRAZILIAN GP	Rio	21	Osella Squadra Corse	1.5 t/c Osella FA1I-Alfa Romeo V8	exhaustion
12/ret	SAN MARINO GP	Imola	21	Osella Squadra Corse	1.5 t/c Osella FA1I-Alfa Romeo V8	out of fuel/5 laps behind
ret	BELGIAN GP	Spa	21	Osella Squadra Corse	1.5 t/c Osella FA1I-Alfa Romeo V8	engine
ret	MONACO GP	Monte Carlo	21	Osella Squadra Corse	1.5 t/c Osella FA1I-Alfa Romeo V8	electrics
ret	US GP (DETROIT)	Detroit	21	Osella Squadra Corse	1.5 t/c Osella FA1I-Alfa Romeo V8	gearbox
ret	FRENCH GP	Paul Ricard	21	Osella Squadra Corse	1.5 t/c Osella FA1I-Alfa Romeo V8	gearbox
ret	BRITISH GP	Silverstone	21	Osella Squadra Corse	1.5 t/c Osella FA1I-Alfa Romeo V8	engine
ret	GERMAN GP	Hockenheim	21	Osella Squadra Corse	1.5 t/c Osella FA1I-Alfa Romeo V8	engine
ret	HUNGARIAN GP	Hungaroring	21	Osella Squadra Corse	1.5 t/c Osella FA1I-Alfa Romeo V8	out of fuel
ret/dns	AUSTRIAN GP	Österreichring	21	Osella Squadra Corse	1.5 t/c Osella FA1I-Alfa Romeo V8	accident at 2nd start/electrics
ret	ITALIAN GP	Monza	21	Osella Squadra Corse	1.5 t/c Osella FA1I-Alfa Romeo V8	suspension
ret	PORTUGUESE GP	Estoril	21	Osella Squadra Corse	1.5 t/c Osella FA1I-Alfa Romeo V8	turbo
dnq	SPANISH GP	Jerez	21	Osella Squadra Corse	1.5 t/c Osella FA1I-Alfa Romeo V8	
ret	MEXICAN GP	Mexico City	21	Osella Squadra Corse	1.5 t/c Osella FA1I-Alfa Romeo V8	engine
ret	JAPANESE GP	Suzuka	21	Osella Squadra Corse	1.5 t/c Osella FA1I-Alfa Romeo V8	out of fuel
dnq	AUSTRALIAN GP	Adelaide	21	Osella Squadra Corse	1.5 t/c Osella FA1I-Alfa Romeo V8	

1988

	Race	Circuit	No	Entrant	Car/Engine	Comment
dnpq	BRAZILIAN GP	Rio	36	Scuderia Italia	3.5 Dallara 3087-Cosworth V8	F3000 car
ret	SAN MARINO GP	Imola	36	Scuderia Italia	3.5 Dallara F188-Cosworth V8	gearbox
ret	MONACO GP	Monte Carlo	36	Scuderia Italia	3.5 Dallara F188-Cosworth V8	hit by Capelli-spun off
ret	MEXICAN GP	Mexico City	36	Scuderia Italia	3.5 Dallara F188-Cosworth V8	brakes-accident
dnpq	CANADIAN GP	Montreal	36	Scuderia Italia	3.5 Dallara F188-Cosworth V8	
8	US GP (DETROIT)	Detroit	36	Scuderia Italia	3.5 Dallara F188-Cosworth V8	cracked exhaust/2 laps behind
12	FRENCH GP	Paul Ricard	36	Scuderia Italia	3.5 Dallara F188-Cosworth V8	p stop-puncture/fuel problems/-2 laps
11	BRITISH GP	Silverstone	36	Scuderia Italia	3.5 Dallara F188-Cosworth V8	1 lap behind
15	GERMAN GP	Hockenheim	36	Scuderia Italia	3.5 Dallara F188-Cosworth V8	pit stop-puncture/2 laps behind
ret	HUNGARIAN GP	Hungaroring	36	Scuderia Italia	3.5 Dallara F188-Cosworth V8	gearbox
8*	BELGIAN GP	Spa	36	Scuderia Italia	3.5 Dallara F188-Cosworth V8	*3rd & 4th cars dsq/1 lap behind
ret	ITALIAN GP	Monza	36	Scuderia Italia	3.5 Dallara F188-Cosworth V8	electrics
7	PORTUGUESE GP	Estoril	36	Scuderia Italia	3.5 Dallara F188-Cosworth V8	broken exhaust/1 lap behind
10	SPANISH GP	Jerez	36	Scuderia Italia	3.5 Dallara F188-Cosworth V8	broken exhaust/1 lap behind
ret	JAPANESE GP	Suzuka	36	Scuderia Italia	3.5 Dallara F188-Cosworth V8	spun off
ret	AUSTRALIAN GP	Adelaide	36	Scuderia Italia	3.5 Dallara F188-Cosworth V8	clutch

1989

	Race	Circuit	No	Entrant	Car/Engine	Comment
dnpq	BRAZILIAN GP	Rio	36	Scuderia Italia	3.5 Dallara F189-Cosworth V8	
7	SAN MARINO GP	Imola	36	Scuderia Italia	3.5 Dallara F189-Cosworth V8	pit stop-puncture1 lap behind
4	MONACO GP	Monte Carlo	36	Scuderia Italia	3.5 Dallara F189-Cosworth V8	agg of 2 parts/2 laps behind
13	MEXICAN GP	Mexico City	36	Scuderia Italia	3.5 Dallara F189-Cosworth V8	spun/tyre wear/2 laps behind
ret	US GP (PHOENIX)	Phoenix	36	Scuderia Italia	3.5 Dallara F189-Cosworth V8	hit by de Cesaris
6	CANADIAN GP	Montreal	36	Scuderia Italia	3.5 Dallara F189-Cosworth V8	2 pit stops-tyres/2 spins/-2 laps
ret	FRENCH GP	Paul Ricard	36	Scuderia Italia	3.5 Dallara F189-Cosworth V8	clutch
dnpq	BRITISH GP	Silverstone	36	Scuderia Italia	3.5 Dallara F189-Cosworth V8	

ret	GERMAN GP	Hockenheim	36	Scuderia Italia	3.5 Dallara F189-Cosworth V8	electrics
7	HUNGARIAN GP	Hungaroring	36	Scuderia Italia	3.5 Dallara F189-Cosworth V8	3rd on the grid
ret	BELGIAN GP	Spa	36	Scuderia Italia	3.5 Dallara F189-Cosworth V8	spun off
11/ret	ITALIAN GP	Monza	36	Scuderia Italia	3.5 Dallara F189-Cosworth V8	engine/6 laps behind
ret	PORTUGUESE GP	Estoril	36	Scuderia Italia	3.5 Dallara F189-Cosworth V8	collision with Piquet
ret	SPANISH GP	Jerez	36	Scuderia Italia	3.5 Dallara F189-Cosworth V8	engine
9	JAPANESE GP	Suzuka	36	Scuderia Italia	3.5 Dallara F189-Cosworth V8	1st place car dsq/1 lap behind
ret	AUSTRALIAN GP	Adelaide	36	Scuderia Italia	3.5 Dallara F189-Cosworth V8	spun off in rain

1990

ret	BRAZILIAN GP	Interlagos	21	Footwork Arrows Racing	3.5 Arrows A11B-Cosworth V8	driver exhaustion
dnq	SAN MARINO GP	Imola	21	Footwork Arrows Racing	3.5 Arrows A11B-Cosworth V8	
5	MONACO GP	Monte Carlo	21	Footwork Arrows Racing	3.5 Arrows A11B-Cosworth V8	tyre problems/2 laps behind
8	CANADIAN GP	Montreal	21	Footwork Arrows Racing	3.5 Arrows A11B-Cosworth V8	2 laps behind
dnq	MEXICAN GP	Mexico City	21	Footwork Arrows Racing	3.5 Arrows A11B-Cosworth V8	
ret	FRENCH GP	Paul Ricard	21	Footwork Arrows Racing	3.5 Arrows A11B-Cosworth V8	rear suspension
7	BRITISH GP	Silverstone	21	Footwork Arrows Racing	3.5 Arrows A11B-Cosworth V8	1 lap behind
9	GERMAN GP	Hockenheim	21	Footwork Arrows Racing	3.5 Arrows A11B-Cosworth V8	1 lap behind
9	HUNGARIAN GP	Hungaroring	21	Footwork Arrows Racing	3.5 Arrows A11B-Cosworth V8	rev limiter problems/1 lap behind
10	BELGIAN GP	Spa	21	Footwork Arrows Racing	3.5 Arrows A11B-Cosworth V8	oversteer problems/1 lap behind
9	ITALIAN GP	Monza	21	Footwork Arrows Racing	3.5 Arrows A11B-Cosworth V8	pit stop-tyres/2 laps behind
13/ret	PORTUGUESE GP	Estoril	21	Footwork Arrows Racing	3.5 Arrows A11B-Cosworth V8	collision with Suzuki/3 laps behind
9	JAPANESE GP	Suzuka	21	Footwork Arrows Racing	3.5 Arrows A11B-Cosworth V8	pit stop-tyres/1 lap behind
dnq	AUSTRALIAN GP	Adelaide	21	Footwork Arrows Racing	3.5 Arrows A11B-Cosworth V8	

1991

dnq	US GP (PHOENIX)	Phoenix	10	Footwork Grand Prix International	3.5 Footwork A11C-Porsche V12	
dnq	BRAZILIAN GP	Interlagos	10	Footwork Grand Prix International	3.5 Footwork A11C-Porsche V12	
dnq	SAN MARINO GP	Imola	10	Footwork Grand Prix International	3.5 Footwork FA12-Porsche V12	
dnq	MONACO GP	Monte Carlo	10	Footwork Grand Prix International	3.5 Footwork FA12-Porsche V12	accident in practice
dnpq	GERMAN GP	Hockenheim	10	Footwork Grand Prix International	3.5 Footwork FA12-Cosworth V8	
dnpq	HUNGARIAN GP	Hungaroring	10	Footwork Grand Prix International	3.5 Footwork FA12-Cosworth V8	
dnq	BELGIAN GP	Spa	10	Footwork Grand Prix International	3.5 Footwork FA12-Cosworth V8	
dnpq	ITALIAN GP	Monza	10	Footwork Grand Prix International	3.5 Footwork FA12-Cosworth V8	
dnpq	PORTUGUESE GP	Estoril	10	Footwork Grand Prix International	3.5 Footwork FA12-Cosworth V8	
dnpq	SPANISH GP	Barcelona	10	Footwork Grand Prix International	3.5 Footwork FA12-Cosworth V8	
10	JAPANESE GP	Suzuka	10	Footwork Grand Prix International	3.5 Footwork FA12-Cosworth V8	2 laps behind
15	AUSTRALIAN GP	Adelaide	10	Footwork Grand Prix International	3.5 Footwork FA12-Cosworth V8	rain shortened race/1 lap behind

1992

dnp	SOUTH AFRICAN GP	Kyalami	34	Andrea Moda Formula	3.5 Coloni C4B-Judd V10	car ineligible-team excluded
dnp	MEXICAN GP	Mexico City	34	Andrea Moda Formula	3.5 Moda S921-Judd V10	cars arrived late-entry withdrawn

GP Starts: 56   GP Wins: 0   Pole positions: 0   Fastest laps: 0   Points: 6

CAMPBELL-JONES, John (GB) b 21/1/1930

1962

	Race	Circuit	No	Entrant	Car/Engine	Comment
11	BELGIAN GP	Spa	4	Emeryson Cars	1.5 Lotus 18-Climax 4	borrowed car/pit stops/-16 laps
dns	"	"	4	Emeryson Cars	1.5 Emeryson 1006-Climax 4	practice only-broken gearbox

1963

13	BRITISH GP	Silverstone	24	Tim Parnell	1.5 Lola 4-Climax V8	pit stop/8 laps behind

GP Starts: 2   GP Wins: 0   Pole positions: 0   Fastest laps: 0   Points: 0

CAMPOS, Adrian (E) b 17/6/1960

1987

	Race	Circuit	No	Entrant	Car/Engine	Comment
dsq	BRAZILIAN GP	Rio	23	Minardi Team	1.5 t/c Minardi M/187-MM V6	incorrect starting procedure
ret	SAN MARINO GP	Imola	23	Minardi Team	1.5 t/c Minardi M/187-MM V6	gearbox
ret/dns	BELGIAN GP	Spa	23	Minardi Team	1.5 t/c Minardi M/187-MM V6	clutch at 1st start/did not restart
dns	MONACO GP	Monte Carlo	23	Minardi Team	1.5 t/c Minardi M/187-MM V6	accident in practice
ret	US GP (DETROIT)	Detroit	23	Minardi Team	1.5 t/c Minardi M/187-MM V6	hit by Nakajima
ret	FRENCH GP	Paul Ricard	23	Minardi Team	1.5 t/c Minardi M/187-MM V6	turbo
ret	BRITISH GP	Silverstone	23	Minardi Team	1.5 t/c Minardi M/187-MM V6	fuel pump
ret	GERMAN GP	Hockenheim	23	Minardi Team	1.5 t/c Minardi M/187-MM V6	engine
ret	HUNGARIAN GP	Hungaroring	23	Minardi Team	1.5 t/c Minardi M/187-MM V6	spun off
ret	AUSTRIAN GP	Österreichring	23	Minardi Team	1.5 t/c Minardi M/187-MM V6	electrics
ret	ITALIAN GP	Monza	23	Minardi Team	1.5 t/c Minardi M/187-MM V6	engine
ret	PORTUGUESE GP	Estoril	23	Minardi Team	1.5 t/c Minardi M/187-MM V6	holed intercooler/started from pit lane
14	SPANISH GP	Jerez	23	Minardi Team	1.5 t/c Minardi M/187-MM V6	4 laps behind
ret	MEXICAN GP	Mexico City	23	Minardi Team	1.5 t/c Minardi M/187-MM V6	engine
ret	JAPANESE GP	Suzuka	23	Minardi Team	1.5 t/c Minardi M/187-MM V6	engine
ret	AUSTRALIAN GP	Adelaide	23	Minardi Team	1.5 t/c Minardi M/187-MM V6	gearbox

1988

ret	BRAZILIAN GP	Rio	23	Lois Minardi Team	3.5 Minardi M188-Cosworth V8	rear wing mounting
16	SAN MARINO GP	Imola	23	Lois Minardi Team	3.5 Minardi M188-Cosworth V8	3 laps behind
dnq	MONACO GP	Monte Carlo	23	Lois Minardi Team	3.5 Minardi M188-Cosworth V8	
dnq	MEXICAN GP	Mexico City	23	Lois Minardi Team	3.5 Minardi M188-Cosworth V8	
dnq	CANADIAN GP	Montreal	23	Lois Minardi Team	3.5 Minardi M188-Cosworth V8	

GP Starts: 17   GP Wins: 0   Pole positions: 0   Fastest laps: 0   Points: 0

JOHN CANNON

A Canadian who had been born in Britain, Cannon in fact spent the early part of his career in California, where he began racing an Elva Courier in 1960. He drove a variety of powerful sports machines in the early 1960s before concentrating on the popular Can-Am series. Though his car was somewhat outdated, he put up a number of fine performances, none better than in the wet at Laguna Seca in 1968 when he lapped the field to score an amazing win. This success led to a drive in Formula A in 1969 and an opportunity to drive single-seaters at last. John won three rounds and finished fourth in the championship. The next year he took the SCCA Formula A title and then set about a completely new challenge, tackling the US GP in a BRM and the Questor GP in a March 701, as well as a full season in European F2, achieving moderate success. It was back to the USA and the L & M F5000 series for 1972, although he also drove in some British F5000 rounds and was right on the pace. Thereafter Cannon continued racing in the formula which had brought him so much success, spiced with occasional drives in USAC and Can-Am.

IVAN CAPELLI

The dividing line between success and failure in Grand Prix racing can be very narrow indeed, as the charming and popular Capelli has found to his cost. Having been generally perceived as being held back from the winner's circle only by the want of a top-flight car, the Italian's stock crashed with alarming rapidity when a golden opportunity with Ferrari turned sour.

Yet another ex-karting ace, Ivan went single-seater racing in 1982, taking sixth place in the Italian F3 championship. This brought him to the attention of Enzo Coloni, who quickly signed the Milanese to race his Ralt-Alfa. It was a stunning year for the team, with Capelli winning all but four of the series' 13 races to take the title by the staggering margin of 58 points. With Italy well and truly conquered, Coloni took his charge into the European arena, and once again Capelli triumphed, though much less decisively. His European F3 championship was tainted with allegations regarding the car's legality, and, as he acknowledged, he inherited a couple of lucky wins, including the prestigious Monaco race.

National Service then interrupted Ivan's racing progress, but when he entered the 1985 F3000 series at Vallelunga with a March, he immediately rolled it almost to the point of destruction. Despite the most meagre of budgets, Capelli and his team did an outstanding job and he won the Österreichring round to earn a couple of Grand Prix drives with Ken Tyrrell late in the season. Somewhat surprisingly, he was not on the F1 shopping list for 1986 and settled into another year of F3000 with the Genoa team, the mid-season arrival of Leyton House sponsorship giving the privateer outfit the boost it needed in its successsful championship quest. Capelli made another brief foray into Formula 1 with AGS, but long-term his future was to lie wrapped in the comforting folds of the turquoise-blue Leyton House March Racing Team. In a sense the team was Ivan's family; they believed in him and he reciprocated. Growing in stature, he had taken the car right to the front of the grid by the end of the 1988 season, and briefly led the Portuguese GP before taking a superb second place. This progress was temporarily halted in a disappointing year plagued by unreliability and the almost bewildering array of handling problems associated with the March CG891, but Capelli bounced back the following year, finishing second to Prost at Paul Ricard and looking a potential winner at Silverstone until retirement. Ivan's final year with the team was spent embroiled in development of the new Ilmor V10, and it has to be said that some of his performances were less than convincing. With the team's owner having been arrested over financial irregularities in Japan, the future looked bleak, and Capelli stood down for the two end-of-season races happy in the knowledge that he had a Ferrari contract in his pocket for 1992. However, it was to be a season of almost unmitigated misery for poor Ivan, who failed to come to grips with the Ferrari F92A, a car which missed the boat on just about every count.

Before the season was out, Capelli found himself cast aside in favour of test driver Nicola Larini and his options appeared limited. To everyone's surprise he was back on the grid at Kyalami with the Jordan team, reunited with his old boss from Leyton House/March, Ian Phillips. It was to be a brief and unhappy sojourn for the Italian, who crashed very heavily in South Africa and then failed to qualify at Interlagos before an amicable parting of the ways left a crushingly disappointed Capelli to ponder whether he had a Formula 1 future at all when he had not yet reached the age of thirty.

CANNON, John (CDN) b 21/6/1937

1971

	Race	Circuit	No	Entrant	Car/Engine	Comment
14	US GP	Watkins Glen	28	Yardley BRM	3.0 BRM P153 V12	3 laps behind

GP Starts: 1   GP Wins: 0   Pole positions: 0   Fastest laps: 0   Points: 0

CANTONI, Heitel (U)

1952

	Race	Circuit	No	Entrant	Car/Engine	Comment
ret	BRITISH GP	Silverstone	35	Escuderia Bandeirantes	2.0 Maserati A6GCM 6	brakes
ret	GERMAN GP	Nürburgring	116	Escuderia Bandeirantes	2.0 Maserati A6GCM 6	rear axle
11	ITALIAN GP	Monza	50	Escuderia Bandeirantes	2.0 Maserati A6GCM 6	5 laps behind

GP Starts: 3   GP Wins: 0   Pole positions: 0   Fastest laps: 0   Points: 0

CAPELLI, Ivan (I) b 24/5/1963

1985

	Race	Circuit	No	Entrant	Car/Engine	Comment
ret	EUROPEAN GP	Brands Hatch	4	Tyrrell Racing Organisation	1.5 t/c Tyrrell 014-Renault V6	accident
4	AUSTRALIAN GP	Adelaide	4	Tyrrell Racing Organisation	1.5 t/c Tyrrell 014-Renault V6	1 lap behind

1986

ret	ITALIAN GP	Monza	31	Jolly Club SpA	1.5 t/c AGS JH21C-MM V6	puncture
ret	PORTUGUESE GP	Estoril	31	Jolly Club SpA	1.5 t/c AGS JH21C-MM V6	transmission

1987

dns	BRAZILIAN GP	Rio	16	Leyton House March Racing Team	3.5 March 87P-Cosworth V8	no engine/F3000 car
ret	SAN MARINO GP	Imola	16	Leyton House March Racing Team	3.5 March 871-Cosworth V8	ignition
ret	BELGIAN GP	Spa	16	Leyton House March Racing Team	3.5 March 871-Cosworth V8	oil pressure
6	MONACO GP	Monte Carlo	16	Leyton House March Racing Team	3.5 March 871-Cosworth V8	2nd non-turbo/2 laps behind
ret	US GP (DETROIT)	Detroit	16	Leyton House March Racing Team	3.5 March 871-Cosworth V8	battery
ret	FRENCH GP	Paul Ricard	16	Leyton House March Racing Team	3.5 March 871-Cosworth V8	engine
ret	BRITISH GP	Silverstone	16	Leyton House March Racing Team	3.5 March 871-Cosworth V8	gearbox
ret	GERMAN GP	Hockenheim	16	Leyton House March Racing Team	3.5 March 871-Cosworth V8	started from pit lane/distributor
10	HUNGARIAN GP	Hungaroring	16	Leyton House March Racing Team	3.5 March 871-Cosworth V8	3rd non-turbo/2 laps behind
11	AUSTRIAN GP	Österreichring	16	Leyton House March Racing Team	3.5 March 871-Cosworth V8	1st non-turbo/3 laps behind
13	ITALIAN GP	Monza	16	Leyton House March Racing Team	3.5 March 871-Cosworth V8	2nd non-turbo/3 laps behind
9	PORTUGUESE GP	Estoril	16	Leyton House March Racing Team	3.5 March 871-Cosworth V8	1st non-turbo/3 laps behind
12	SPANISH GP	Jerez	16	Leyton House March Racing Team	3.5 March 871-Cosworth V8	3rd non-turbo/2 laps behind
ret	MEXICAN GP	Mexico City	16	Leyton House March Racing Team	3.5 March 871-Cosworth V8	engine
ret	JAPANESE GP	Suzuka	16	Leyton House March Racing Team	3.5 March 871-Cosworth V8	accident with Arnoux
ret	AUSTRALIAN GP	Adelaide	16	Leyton House March Racing Team	3.5 March 871-Cosworth V8	spun off

1988

ret	BRAZILIAN GP	Rio	16	Leyton House March Racing Team	3.5 March 881-Judd V8	started from pit lane/engine
ret	SAN MARINO GP	Imola	16	Leyton House March Racing Team	3.5 March 881-Judd V8	gearbox
10	MONACO GP	Monte Carlo	16	Leyton House March Racing Team	3.5 March 881-Judd V8	collision-Caffi-pit stop/6 laps behind
16	MEXICAN GP	Mexico City	16	Leyton House March Racing Team	3.5 March 881-Judd V8	pit stop-gearbox/6 laps behind
5	CANADIAN GP	Montreal	16	Leyton House March Racing Team	3.5 March 881-Judd V8	severe understeer/1 lap behind
dns	US GP (DETROIT)	Detroit	16	Leyton House March Racing Team	3.5 March 881-Judd V8	accident in practice
9	FRENCH GP	Paul Ricard	16	Leyton House March Racing Team	3.5 March 881-Judd V8	1 lap behind
ret	BRITISH GP	Silverstone	16	Leyton House March Racing Team	3.5 March 881-Judd V8	electrics
5	GERMAN GP	Hockenheim	16	Leyton House March Racing Team	3.5 March 881-Judd V8	
ret	HUNGARIAN GP	Hungaroring	16	Leyton House March Racing Team	3.5 March 881-Judd V8	
3*	BELGIAN GP	Spa	16	Leyton House March Racing Team	3.5 March 881-Judd V8	*3rd & 4th place cars disqualified
5	ITALIAN GP	Monza	16	Leyton House March Racing Team	3.5 March 881-Judd V8	
2	PORTUGUESE GP	Estoril	16	Leyton House March Racing Team	3.5 March 881-Judd V8	
ret	SPANISH GP	Jerez	16	Leyton House March Racing Team	3.5 March 881-Judd V8	engine
ret	JAPANESE GP	Suzuka	16	Leyton House March Racing Team	3.5 March 881-Judd V8	electrics
6	AUSTRALIAN GP	Adelaide	16	Leyton House March Racing Team	3.5 March 881-Judd V8	pit stop-puncture/gearbox/-1 lap

1989

ret	BRAZILIAN GP	Rio	16	Leyton House March Racing Team	3.5 March 881-Judd V8	suspension
ret	SAN MARINO GP	Imola	16	Leyton House March Racing Team	3.5 March 881-Judd V8	spun off
11/ret	MONACO GP	Monte Carlo	16	Leyton House March Racing Team	3.5 March CG891-Judd V8	engine/4 laps behind
dns	"	" "	16	Leyton House March Racing Team	3.5 March 881-Judd V8	practice only
ret	MEXICAN GP	Mexico City	16	Leyton House March Racing Team	3.5 March CG891-Judd V8	driveshaft-c.v. joint
dns	"	" "	16	Leyton House March Racing Team	3.5 March 881-Judd V8	practice only
ret	US GP (PHOENIX)	Phoenix	16	Leyton House March Racing Team	3.5 March CG891-Judd V8	transmission
dns	"	"	16	Leyton House March Racing Team	3.5 March 881-Judd V8	practice only
ret	CANADIAN GP	Montreal	16	Leyton House March Racing Team	3.5 March CG891-Judd V8	spun off
dns	"	"	16	Leyton House March Racing Team	3.5 March 881-Judd V8	practice only
ret	FRENCH GP	Paul Ricard	16	Leyton House March Racing Team	3.5 March CG891-Judd V8	electrics-engine
ret	BRITISH GP	Silverstone	16	Leyton House March Racing Team	3.5 March CG891-Judd V8	transmission
ret	GERMAN GP	Hockenheim	16	Leyton House March Racing Team	3.5 March CG891-Judd V8	engine
ret	HUNGARIAN GP	Hungaroring	16	Leyton House March Racing Team	3.5 March CG891-Judd V8	transmission
12	BELGIAN GP	Spa	16	Leyton House March Racing Team	3.5 March CG891-Judd V8	1 lap behind
ret	ITALIAN GP	Monza	16	Leyton House March Racing Team	3.5 March CG891-Judd V8	engine
ret	PORTUGUESE GP	Estoril	16	Leyton House March Racing Team	3.5 March CG891-Judd V8	misfire
ret	SPANISH GP	Jerez	16	Leyton House March Racing Team	3.5 March CG891-Judd V8	transmission
ret	JAPANESE GP	Suzuka	16	Leyton House March Racing Team	3.5 March CG891-Judd V8	suspension
ret	AUSTRALIAN GP	Adelaide	16	Leyton House March Racing Team	3.5 March CG891-Judd V8	holed radiator

1990

ret	US GP (PHOENIX)	Phoenix	16	Leyton House Racing	3.5 Leyton House CG901-Judd V8	electrics
dns	"	"	16	Leyton House Racing	3.5 March CG891-Judd V8	practice only
dnq	BRAZILIAN GP	Interlagos	16	Leyton House Racing	3.5 March CG891-Judd V8	
dnq	"	"	16	Leyton House Racing	3.5 March CG891-Judd V8	
ret	SAN MARINO GP	Imola	16	Leyton House Racing	3.5 Leyton House CG901-Judd V8	hit by Nakajima
ret	MONACO GP	Monte Carlo	16	Leyton House Racing	3.5 Leyton House CG901-Judd V8	brakes
10	CANADIAN GP	Montreal	16	Leyton House Racing	3.5 Leyton House CG901-Judd V8	handling problems/3 laps behind
dnq	MEXICAN GP	Mexico City	16	Leyton House Racing	3.5 Leyton House CG901-Judd V8	
2	FRENCH GP	Paul Ricard	16	Leyton House Racing	3.5 Leyton House CG901-Judd V8	
ret	BRITISH GP	Silverstone	16	Leyton House Racing	3.5 Leyton House CG901-Judd V8	fuel line when 3rd
7	GERMAN GP	Hockenheim	16	Leyton House Racing	3.5 Leyton House CG901-Judd V8	lost 4th gear/1 lap behind
ret	HUNGARIAN GP	Hungaroring	16	Leyton House Racing	3.5 Leyton House CG901-Judd V8	gearbox
7	BELGIAN GP	Spa	16	Leyton House Racing	3.5 Leyton House CG901-Judd V8	broken exhaust/1 lap behind
ret	ITALIAN GP	Monza	16	Leyton House Racing	3.5 Leyton House CG901-Judd V8	engine cut out
ret	PORTUGUESE GP	Estoril	16	Leyton House Racing	3.5 Leyton House CG901-Judd V8	engine
ret	SPANISH GP	Jerez	16	Leyton House Racing	3.5 Leyton House CG901-Judd V8	leg cramp
ret	JAPANESE GP	Suzuka	16	Leyton House Racing	3.5 Leyton House CG901-Judd V8	misfire
ret	AUSTRALIAN GP	Adelaide	16	Leyton House Racing	3.5 Leyton House CG901-Judd V8	sticking throttle

1991

ret	US GP (PHOENIX)	Phoenix	16	Leyton House Racing	3.5 Leyton House CG911-Ilmor V10	gearbox oil pump
ret	BRAZILIAN GP	Interlagos	16	Leyton House Racing	3.5 Leyton House CG911-Ilmor V10	engine
ret	SAN MARINO GP	Imola	16	Leyton House Racing	3.5 Leyton House CG911-Ilmor V10	spun off
ret	MONACO GP	Monte Carlo	16	Leyton House Racing	3.5 Leyton House CG911-Ilmor V10	leaking brake fluid
ret	CANADIAN GP	Montreal	16	Leyton House Racing	3.5 Leyton House CG911-Ilmor V10	engine
ret	MEXICAN GP	Mexico City	16	Leyton House Racing	3.5 Leyton House CG911-Ilmor V10	over-revved engine
ret	FRENCH GP	Magny Cours	16	Leyton House Racing	3.5 Leyton House CG911-Ilmor V10	spun avoiding Morbidelli
ret	BRITISH GP	Silverstone	16	Leyton House Racing	3.5 Leyton House CG911-Ilmor V10	selected wrong gear-spun off
ret	GERMAN GP	Hockenheim	16	Leyton House Racing	3.5 Leyton House CG911-Ilmor V10	engine-misfire
6	HUNGARIAN GP	Hungaroring	16	Leyton House Racing	3.5 Leyton House CG911-Ilmor V10	1 lap behind
ret	BELGIAN GP	Spa	16	Leyton House Racing	3.5 Leyton House CG911-Ilmor V10	engine
8	ITALIAN GP	Monza	16	Leyton House Racing	3.5 Leyton House CG911-Ilmor V10	
17/ret	PORTUGUESE GP	Estoril	16	Leyton House Racing	3.5 Leyton House CG911-Ilmor V10	broken nose cone when 5th
ret	SPANISH GP	Barcelona	16	Leyton House Racing	3.5 Leyton House CG911-Ilmor V10	collision with Pirro

1992

ret	SOUTH AFRICAN GP	Kyalami	28	Scuderia Ferrari SpA	3.5 Fiat Ferrari F92A V12	engine
ret	MEXICAN GP	Mexico City	28	Scuderia Ferrari SpA	3.5 Fiat Ferrari F92A V12	startline collision
5	BRAZILIAN GP	Interlagos	28	Scuderia Ferrari SpA	3.5 Fiat Ferrari F92A V12	pit stop-tyres/1 lap behind
10/ret	SPANISH GP	Barcelona	28	Scuderia Ferrari SpA	3.5 Fiat Ferrari F92A V12	spun off
ret	SAN MARINO GP	Imola	28	Scuderia Ferrari SpA	3.5 Fiat Ferrari F92A V12	spun off
ret	MONACO GP	Monte Carlo	28	Scuderia Ferrari SpA	3.5 Fiat Ferrari F92A V12	spun off-wedged car on Armco
ret	CANADIAN GP	Montreal	28	Scuderia Ferrari SpA	3.5 Fiat Ferrari F92A V12	crashed
ret	FRENCH GP	Magny Cours	28	Scuderia Ferrari SpA	3.5 Fiat Ferrari F92A V12	engine
9	BRITISH GP	Silverstone	28	Scuderia Ferrari SpA	3.5 Fiat Ferrari F92A V12	1 lap behind
ret	GERMAN GP	Hockenheim	28	Scuderia Ferrari SpA	3.5 Fiat Ferrari F92A V12	engine
6	HUNGARIAN GP	Hungaroring	28	Scuderia Ferrari SpA	3.5 Fiat Ferrari F92A V12	1 lap behind
ret	BELGIAN GP	Spa	28	Scuderia Ferrari SpA	3.5 Fiat Ferrari F92A V12	engine
ret	ITALIAN GP	Monza	28	Scuderia Ferrari SpA	3.5 Fiat Ferrari F92AT V12	spun off
ret	PORTUGUESE GP	Estoril	28	Scuderia Ferrari SpA	3.5 Fiat Ferrari F92AT V12	engine

1993

ret	SOUTH AFRICAN GP	Kyalami	15	Sasol Jordan	3.5 Jordan 193-Hart V10	crashed
dnq	BRAZILIAN GP	Interlagos	15	Sasol Jordan	3.5 Jordan 193-Hart V10	

GP Starts: 93   GP Wins: 0   Pole positions: 0   Fastest laps: 0   Points: 31

CARINI, Piero (I) b 6/3/1921 – d 30/5/1957

1952

	Race	Circuit	No	Entrant	Car/Engine	Comment
ret	FRENCH GP	Rouen	40	Scuderia Marzotto	2.0 Ferrari 166 V12	head gasket
ret	GERMAN GP	Nürburgring	104	Scuderia Marzotto	2.0 Ferrari 166 V12	brakes

1953

ret	ITALIAN GP	Monza	12	Scuderia Ferrari	2.0 Ferrari 553 4	mechanical

GP Starts: 3   GP Wins: 0   Pole positions: 0   Fastest laps: 0   Points: 0

CASTELLOTTI, Eugenio (I) b 10/10/1930 – d 14/3/1957

1955

	Race	Circuit	No	Entrant	Car/Engine	Comment
ret	ARGENTINE GP	Buenos Aires	36	Scuderia Lancia	2.5 Lancia D50 V8	crashed/Villoresi also drove
2	MONACO GP	Monte Carlo	30	Scuderia Lancia	2.5 Lancia D50 V8	pit stop-brakes
ret	BELGIAN GP	Spa	30	Scuderia Lancia	2.5 Lancia D50 V8	gearbox/Pole
5	DUTCH GP	Zandvoort	6	Scuderia Ferrari	2.5 Ferrari 555 4	3 laps behind
dns	"	"	6	Scuderia Ferrari	2.5 Ferrari 625 4	practice only
ret	BRITISH GP	Aintree	20	Scuderia Ferrari	2.5 Ferrari 625 4	transmission
6*	"	"	16	Scuderia Ferrari	2.5 Ferrari 625 4	* took Hawthorn's car/3 laps behind
3	ITALIAN GP	Monza	4	Scuderia Ferrari	2.5 Ferrari 555 4	

1956

ret	ARGENTINE GP	Buenos Aires	32	Scuderia Ferrari	2.5 Lancia-Ferrari D50 V8	gearbox
ret	MONACO GP	Monte Carlo	22	Scuderia Ferrari	2.5 Lancia-Ferrari D50 V8	clutch

4*	"	" "	20	Scuderia Ferrari	2.5 Lancia-Ferrari D50 V8	* took Fangio's car/6 laps behind
ret	BELGIAN GP	Spa	4	Scuderia Ferrari	2.5 Lancia-Ferrari D50 V8	transmission
2	FRENCH GP	Reims	12	Scuderia Ferrari	2.5 Lancia-Ferrari D50 V8	
10*	BRITISH GP	Silverstone	3	Scuderia Ferrari	2.5 Lancia-Ferrari D50 V8	*de Portago took over car
ret	GERMAN GP	Nürburgring	3	Scuderia Ferrari	2.5 Lancia-Ferrari D50 V8	magneto
ret	"		4	Scuderia Ferrari	2.5 Lancia-Ferrari D50 V8	accident-took Musso's car
ret	ITALIAN GP	Monza	24	Scuderia Ferrari	2.5 Lancia-Ferrari D50 V8	tyres-accident
8*	"	"	22	Scuderia Ferrari	2.5 Lancia-Ferrari D50 V8	*took Fangio's car/4 laps behind
	1957					
ret	ARGENTINE GP	Buenos Aires	14	Scuderia Ferrari	2.5 Lancia-Ferrari D50 V8	hub shaft-lost wheel

GP Starts: 14   GP Wins: 0   Pole positions: 1   Fastest laps: 0   Points: 19.5

PIERO CARINI

Carini came to prominence in 1950 when he finished third in the F2 Modena GP with a sports OSCA. This car proved fast but fragile in 1951, but he was invited to joined Scuderia Marzotto for 1952 to race their Ferrari Grand Prix and sports cars. He did well enough to be signed by the works for 1953 as in effect a 'junior team' driver, along with Umberto Maglioli. Carini was used only occasionally and therefore decided to move to Alfa Romeo to race their very successful touring cars, scoring class wins in the 1954 Mille Miglia, Tour of Sicily and Dolomite Cup.

In 1955 he ventured abroad to score sports car wins in a Ferrari at Dakar and Caracas, Venezuela, as well as taking a class win in the Targa Florio in an OSCA with Cabianca.

He was competing in a 1500 cc sports car race near St Etienne in 1957 when his Ferrari Testa Rossa inexplicably crossed the central barrier and ploughed head on into a similar competing car. Carini was killed instantly.

EUGENIO CASTELLOTTI

Castellotti was the archetypal Italian racing driver of the fifties: dashing, handsome, very fast, but wild and erratic. He often charged into the lead at the start of a race, only to be overhauled as his tyres gave out or the car cried enough in response to the punishing treatment to which it had been subjected.

Having been presented with a Ferrari sports car by a local benefactor in 1950 when aged only 20, Eugenio entered the spotlight in 1952 with a win in the Portuguese GP, third place in the Bari GP and second in the Monaco GP (held for sports cars that year), as well as a class win in the Circuit of Sicily. The following season saw him claim the first of his three Italian mountain championships, win the Messina 10 Hours in a Ferrari and finish third in the Carrera Panamericana in a Lancia.

Castellotti signed for Lancia for 1954, racing sports cars while waiting patiently for the chance to drive one of their much anticipated Grand Prix cars. In fact it was 1955 before he got his wish, making his Grand Prix debut at the Argentine GP, where he suffered from sun-stroke in the intense heat and finally crashed the car. Back in Europe, however, he made amends, finishing fourth in the Turin GP and second at Pau and – after Ascari had crashed his car into the harbour – Monaco. Days later Ascari was killed in a testing accident, and Castellotti led the team for one race, at Spa, before it was amalgamated with the Scuderia Ferrari, for whom he finished the season, taking third in the drivers' championship.

The 1956 season saw the Ferrari squad almost embarrassed by an over-supply of cars and drivers, which led to some friction within the team. This was particularly acute between Musso and Castellotti, the two Italians waging their own private duel in the Italian GP at Monza. Eugenio was by now at his peak, particularly in sports cars. A stunning win in atrocious conditions in the Mille Miglia made up in part for his disappointment the previous year when he destroyed his tyres racing too hard too early. Added to this was a victory in the Sebring 12 Hours and second in the Nürburgring 1000 Km (both with Fangio).

More sports car success lay ahead in 1957, Eugenio sharing the first and third cars in the Buenos Aires 1000 Km. On his return to Europe, he was recalled from a holiday to test the latest GP Ferrari at Modena. In wet conditions, the car crashed into a concrete barrier; 27-year-old Castellotti was hurled from the car and killed instantly.

JOHNNY CECOTTO

The son of an Italian immigrant, Cecotto began racing a 750 cc Honda motor cycle in 1972. Soon outgrowing domestic competition, the Venezuelan made a dramatic European debut, scoring a 250/350 cc double, and went on to take the 350 cc title in his first season, becoming the youngest-ever World Champion. More bike successes followed – at 20 he was the youngest winner of the famous Daytona 200 – but a crash early in 1977 put him out of contention for the season. He came back to win the F750 title in 1978, but as Kenny Roberts' star rose, Cecotto's appetite for bike racing waned.

He made an inconclusive F2 debut in 1980, taking part in just three races, but finally abandoned his bike career at the beginning of 1981. After a torrid first half of the season with Martini, Johnny changed teams and under the guiding influence of Markus Hotz knuckled down to the job, swiftly becoming a top-six regular and scoring points in the last four races of the season. A hoped-for Grand Prix opportunity for 1982 failed to materialise so Johnny remained in F2 with a works March. He lost the championship to his team-mate, Corrado Fabi, after the pair had finished the season level on points and Cecotto was forced to drop his worst score from his total. Nevertheless he had made the transition from two wheels to four brilliantly, and this time there was a seat for him in Formula 1.

His first Grand Prix season in the Theodore produced little save a welcome sixth place at Long Beach, so Cecotto moved to Toleman to partner F1 newcomer Ayrton Senna in 1984. He spent the first half of the season somewhat in the Brazilian's shadow, until a very heavy crash in practice for the British Grand Prix left him hospitalised with serious leg and ankle injuries. It was to be the end of his Formula 1 career.

Upon recovery he forged a successful new career in the flourishing touring car scene. Driving for BMW, he won the 1989 Italian championship, before moving into the German series where he has proved to be a constant thorn in the side of the works Mercedes.

ANDREA de CESARIS

De Cesaris has spent more than a decade trying to live down a reputation as a wild and erratic performer, who was only competing in the top echelon by virtue of his powerful sponsorship connections. As is usually the case, there was certainly more than a grain of truth in the snipings, though by the early nineties the *enfant terrible* had matured into a very professional performer.

A former world karting champion, Andrea was campaigning a Ralt run by Tiga's Tim Schenken in the 1978 British BP F3 championship at the age of 18. He continued in the formula the following year with Team Tiga's March, and though he won six rounds of the Vandervell series the silly mistakes which were to become a feature of his Formula 1 career were already apparent, spoiling his championship chances, and he finished second to Chico Serra at the season's end.

Joining Ron Dennis's Project Four outfit for the 1980 season, de Cesaris enjoyed a successful debut in the New Zealand Pacific series, winning both races at Pukekohe, before racing a March 802 in Formula 2. Though paired with Serra, it was the Italian who soon gained the upper hand and number one treatment in the team. His vast potential was there to be seen, and once a problematical tyre situation was eradicated Andrea looked a real prospect, winning the final race at Misano and a well-earned promotion to the McLaren team newly acquired by Dennis for 1981.

The season began badly when he crashed into Prost on the first lap at Long Beach, and roller-coastered downhill as the number of accidents mounted alarmingly. In most cases it would have been 'goodbye and thank you very much', but luckily for Andrea he was welcomed back by Alfa Romeo, for whom he had made his Grand Prix debut at the end of 1980. Although there were still many moments of desperation, in his two seasons with the team de Cesaris came up with some excellent performances, including a great drive at Spa in 1983, when he comfortably led the first half of the race before trouble hit. With the Alfa operation siphoned off to Pavanello's Euroracing in 1984, Andrea was found a place in the Ligier team, where all the bad traits and indiscipline which had been largely eradicated the previous year were soon to return. He was extremely lucky to emerge unharmed from a huge barrel-rolling crash in Austria in 1985, and after one more race Guy Ligier replaced him with Philippe Streiff.

Nothing if not a survivor, de Cesaris was back once more in 1986, this time leading the Minardi team, but it was to be an ucomfortable year in which he was overshadowed by team-mate Nannini despite first call on equipment. Team-hopping was an art at which de Cesaris was to become well-practised. Fetching up at Brabham in 1987, he proved the talent was still there, with excellent performances at Spa, Estoril, Jerez and Mexico, but so were the equally lacklustre displays. It was the same sweet and sour cocktail at Rial in 1988, with an impressive drive at Detroit, where he showed remarkable restraint to finish fourth. Andrea then had a two-year tenure at Dallara, where the Jekyll and Hyde character was ever more in evidence, with Mr Hyde playing the dominant role.

Just when it seemed that the game was up and de Cesaris's chequered Grand Prix career could go no further, he was a shock choice for Jordan for 1991. If the new team was a revelation then so was Andrea, who drove better than ever before, coming very close to a second place at Spa before his engine failed at the death. Though not retained by Jordan, his performances brought him to Tyrrell for 1992, where his racecraft and new-found maturity helped bring the team much-needed points on four occasions. Sadly, 1993 found the team in deep trouble despite the promise shown by a new Yamaha engine, and there was little sign of the de Cesaris we had seen in the previous two years.

After 14 seasons and close on 200 starts without a Grand Prix win, de Cesaris faces yet another reshuffle of the pack, which may at last find him on the discarded pile, but don't bet on it!

CAZE, Robert la (MA) b 26/2/1917

1958

	Race	Circuit	No	Entrant	Car/Engine	Comment
nc	MOROCCAN GP (F2)	Casablanca	58	Robert la Caze	1.5 Cooper T45-Climax 4	3rd in F2 class/5 laps behind

GP Starts: 1   GP Wins: 0   Pole positions: 0   Fastest laps: 0   Points: 0

CECOTTO, Johnny (YV) b 25/1/1956

1983

	Race	Circuit	No	Entrant	Car/Engine	Comment
14	BRAZILIAN GP	Rio	34	Theodore Racing Team	3.0 Theodore N183-Cosworth V8	3 laps behind
6	US GP WEST	Long Beach	34	Theodore Racing Team	3.0 Theodore N183-Cosworth V8	1 lap behind
11	FRENCH GP	Paul Ricard	34	Theodore Racing Team	3.0 Theodore N183-Cosworth V8	2 laps behind
ret	SAN MARINO GP	Imola	34	Theodore Racing Team	3.0 Theodore N183-Cosworth V8	accident damage
dpnq	MONACO GP	Monte Carlo	34	Theodore Racing Team	3.0 Theodore N183-Cosworth V8	
10	BELGIAN GP	Spa	34	Theodore Racing Team	3.0 Theodore N183-Cosworth V8	1 lap behind
ret	US GP (DETROIT)	Detroit	34	Theodore Racing Team	3.0 Theodore N183-Cosworth V8	gear linkage
ret	CANADIAN GP	Montreal	34	Theodore Racing Team	3.0 Theodore N183-Cosworth V8	cwp
dnq	BRITISH GP	Silverstone	34	Theodore Racing Team	3.0 Theodore N183-Cosworth V8	
11	GERMAN GP	Hockenheim	34	Theodore Racing Team	3.0 Theodore N183-Cosworth V8	1 lap behind
dnq	AUSTRIAN GP	Österreichring	34	Theodore Racing Team	3.0 Theodore N183-Cosworth V8	
dnq	DUTCH GP	Zandvoort	34	Theodore Racing Team	3.0 Theodore N183-Cosworth V8	
12	ITALIAN GP	Monza	34	Theodore Racing Team	3.0 Theodore N183-Cosworth V8	2 laps behind

1984

	Race	Circuit	No	Entrant	Car/Engine	Comment
ret	BRAZILIAN GP	Rio	20	Toleman Group Motorsport	1.5 t/c Toleman TG183B-Hart 4	turbo boost pressure
ret	SOUTH AFRICAN GP	Kyalami	20	Toleman Group Motorsport	1.5 t/c Toleman TG183B-Hart 4	tyre failure
ret	BELGIAN GP	Zolder	20	Toleman Group Motorsport	1.5 t/c Toleman TG183B-Hart 4	clutch
nc	SAN MARINO GP	Imola	20	Toleman Group Motorsport	1.5 t/c Toleman TG183B-Hart 4	pit stop/8 laps behind
ret	FRENCH GP	Dijon	20	Toleman Group Motorsport	1.5 t/c Toleman TG183B-Hart 4	turbo
ret	MONACO GP	Monte Carlo	20	Toleman Group Motorsport	1.5 t/c Toleman TG184-Hart 4	spun off
9	CANADIAN GP	Montreal	20	Toleman Group Motorsport	1.5 t/c Toleman TG184-Hart 4	2 laps behind
ret	US GP (DETROIT)	Detroit	20	Toleman Group Motorsport	1.5 t/c Toleman TG184-Hart 4	clutch
ret	US GP (DALLAS)	Dallas	20	Toleman Group Motorsport	1.5 t/c Toleman TG184-Hart 4	hit wall
dnq	BRITISH GP	Brands Hatch	20	Toleman Group Motorsport	1.5 t/c Toleman TG184-Hart 4	crashed in practice-hurt legs

GP Starts: 18   GP Wins: 0   Pole positions: 0   Fastest laps: 0   Points: 1

CESARIS, Andrea de (I) b 31/5/1959

1980

	Race	Circuit	No	Entrant	Car/Engine	Comment
ret	CANADIAN GP	Montreal	22	Marlboro Team Alfa Romeo	3.0 Alfa Romeo 179 V12	engine
ret	US GP EAST	Watkins Glen	22	Marlboro Team Alfa Romeo	3.0 Alfa Romeo 179 V12	collision with Daly

1981

	Race	Circuit	No	Entrant	Car/Engine	Comment
ret	US GP WEST	Long Beach	8	McLaren International	3.0 McLaren M29F-Cosworth V8	hit Prost
ret	BRAZILIAN GP	Rio	8	McLaren International	3.0 McLaren M29F-Cosworth V8	electrics
11	ARGENTINE GP	Buenos Aires	8	McLaren International	3.0 McLaren M29F-Cosworth V8	2 laps behind
6	SAN MARINO GP	Imola	8	McLaren International	3.0 McLaren M29F-Cosworth V8	
ret	BELGIAN GP	Zolder	8	McLaren International	3.0 McLaren M29F-Cosworth V8	gearbox
ret	MONACO GP	Monte Carlo	8	McLaren International	3.0 McLaren MP4-Cosworth V8	collision with Prost
ret	SPANISH GP	Jarama	8	McLaren International	3.0 McLaren MP4-Cosworth V8	accident
11	FRENCH GP	Dijon	8	McLaren International	3.0 McLaren MP4-Cosworth V8	2 laps behind
ret	BRITISH GP	Silverstone	8	McLaren International	3.0 McLaren MP4-Cosworth V8	accident with Villeneuve
ret	GERMAN GP	Hockenheim	8	McLaren International	3.0 McLaren MP4-Cosworth V8	spun off
8	AUSTRIAN GP	Österreichring	8	McLaren International	3.0 McLaren MP4-Cosworth V8	1 lap behind
dns	DUTCH GP	Zandvoort	8	McLaren International	3.0 McLaren MP4-Cosworth V8	withdrawn after practice accidents
7/ret	ITALIAN GP	Monza	8	McLaren International	3.0 McLaren MP4-Cosworth V8	puncture-accident
ret	CANADIAN GP	Montreal	8	McLaren International	3.0 McLaren MP4-Cosworth V8	spun off
12	CAESARS PALACE GP	Las Vegas	8	McLaren International	3.0 McLaren MP4-Cosworth V8	2 p stops-tyres-handling/-6 laps

1982

	Race	Circuit	No	Entrant	Car/Engine	Comment
13	SOUTH AFRICAN GP	Kyalami	22	Marlboro Team Alfa Romeo	3.0 Alfa Romeo 179D V12	4 laps behind
ret	BRAZILIAN GP	Rio	22	Marlboro Team Alfa Romeo	3.0 Alfa Romeo 182 V12	loose undertray
ret	US GP WEST	Long Beach	22	Marlboro Team Alfa Romeo	3.0 Alfa Romeo 182 V12	hit wall when 2nd/Pole
ret	SAN MARINO GP	Imola	22	Marlboro Team Alfa Romeo	3.0 Alfa Romeo 182 V12	fuel pump
ret	BELGIAN GP	Zolder	22	Marlboro Team Alfa Romeo	3.0 Alfa Romeo 182 V12	gear linkage
3/ret	MONACO GP	Monte Carlo	22	Marlboro Team Alfa Romeo	3.0 Alfa Romeo 182 V12	out of fuel on last lap
ret	US GP (DETROIT)	Detroit	22	Marlboro Team Alfa Romeo	3.0 Alfa Romeo 182 V12	transmission
6/ret	CANADIAN GP	Montreal	22	Marlboro Team Alfa Romeo	3.0 Alfa Romeo 182 V12	out of fuel when 3rd/2 laps behind
ret	DUTCH GP	Zandvoort	22	Marlboro Team Alfa Romeo	3.0 Alfa Romeo 182 V12	electrics
ret	BRITISH GP	Brands Hatch	22	Marlboro Team Alfa Romeo	3.0 Alfa Romeo 182 V12	electrics
ret	FRENCH GP	Paul Ricard	22	Marlboro Team Alfa Romeo	3.0 Alfa Romeo 182 V12	puncture-accident
ret	GERMAN GP	Hockenheim	22	Marlboro Team Alfa Romeo	3.0 Alfa Romeo 182 V12	hit by Watson-broken oil radiator
ret	AUSTRIAN GP	Österreichring	22	Marlboro Team Alfa Romeo	3.0 Alfa Romeo 182 V12	accident at start-Giacomelli & Daly
10	SWISS GP	Dijon	22	Marlboro Team Alfa Romeo	3.0 Alfa Romeo 182 V12	2 laps behind
10	ITALIAN GP	Monza	22	Marlboro Team Alfa Romeo	3.0 Alfa Romeo 182 V12	pit stop-ignition/2 laps behind
dns	"	"	22		1.5 t/c Alfa Romeo 182T V8	practice only
9	CAESARS PALACE GP	Las Vegas	22	Marlboro Team Alfa Romeo	3.0 Alfa Romeo 182 V12	3 laps behind

1983

	Race	Circuit	No	Entrant	Car/Engine	Comment
dns	BRAZILIAN GP	Rio	22	Marlboro Team Alfa Romeo	1.5 t/c Alfa Romeo 183T V8	missed weight check-excluded
ret	US GP WEST	Long Beach	22	Marlboro Team Alfa Romeo	1.5 t/c Alfa Romeo 183T V8	gearbox

12	FRENCH GP	Paul Ricard	22	Marlboro Team Alfa Romeo	1.5 t/c Alfa Romeo 183T V8	*pit stop-fuel-tyres/4 laps behind*
ret	SAN MARINO GP	Imola	22	Marlboro Team Alfa Romeo	1.5 t/c Alfa Romeo 183T V8	*distributor*
ret	MONACO GP	Monte Carlo	22	Marlboro Team Alfa Romeo	1.5 t/c Alfa Romeo 183T V8	*gearbox*
ret	BELGIAN GP	Spa	22	Marlboro Team Alfa Romeo	1.5 t/c Alfa Romeo 183T V8	*engine when 2nd/led race/FL*
ret	US GP (DETROIT)	Detroit	22	Marlboro Team Alfa Romeo	1.5 t/c Alfa Romeo 183T V8	*turbo*
ret	CANADIAN GP	Montreal	22	Marlboro Team Alfa Romeo	1.5 t/c Alfa Romeo 183T V8	*engine*
8	BRITISH GP	Silverstone	22	Marlboro Team Alfa Romeo	1.5 t/c Alfa Romeo 183T V8	*1 lap behind*
2	GERMAN GP	Hockenheim	22	Marlboro Team Alfa Romeo	1.5 t/c Alfa Romeo 183T V8	
ret	AUSTRIAN GP	Österreichring	22	Marlboro Team Alfa Romeo	1.5 t/c Alfa Romeo 183T V8	*out of fuel*
ret	DUTCH GP	Zandvoort	22	Marlboro Team Alfa Romeo	1.5 t/c Alfa Romeo 183T V8	*engine*
ret	ITALIAN GP	Monza	22	Marlboro Team Alfa Romeo	1.5 t/c Alfa Romeo 183T V8	*spun off*
4	EUROPEAN GP	Brands Hatch	22	Marlboro Team Alfa Romeo	1.5 t/c Alfa Romeo 183T V8	
2	SOUTH AFRICAN GP	Kyalami	22	Marlboro Team Alfa Romeo	1.5 t/c Alfa Romeo 183T V8	
1984						
ret	BRAZILIAN GP	Rio	26	Ligier Loto	1.5 t/c Ligier JS23-Renault V6	*startedspare from pit lane/gearbox*
5	SOUTH AFRICAN GP	Kyalami	26	Ligier Loto	1.5 t/c Ligier JS23-Renault V6	*2 laps behind*
ret	BELGIAN GP	Zolder	26	Ligier Loto	1.5 t/c Ligier JS23-Renault V6	*spun off*
6*/ret	SAN MARINO GP	Imola	26	Ligier Loto	1.5 t/c Ligier JS23-Renault V6	** 5th place car dsq/out of fuel*
10	FRENCH GP	Dijon	26	Ligier Loto	1.5 t/c Ligier JS23-Renault V6	*dnq-started as 1st reserve/-2 laps*
ret	MONACO GP	Monte Carlo	26	Ligier Loto	1.5 t/c Ligier JS23-Renault V6	*accident damage*
ret	CANADIAN GP	Montreal	26	Ligier Loto	1.5 t/c Ligier JS23-Renault V6	*brakes*
ret	US GP (DETROIT)	Detroit	26	Ligier Loto	1.5 t/c Ligier JS23-Renault V6	*overheating*
ret	US GP (DALLAS)	Dallas	26	Ligier Loto	1.5 t/c Ligier JS23-Renault V6	*hit wall*
10	BRITISH GP	Brands Hatch	26	Ligier Loto	1.5 t/c Ligier JS23-Renault V6	*3 laps behind*
7	GERMAN GP	Hockenheim	26	Ligier Loto	1.5 t/c Ligier JS23-Renault V6	*1 lap behind*
ret	AUSTRIAN GP	Österreichring	26	Ligier Loto	1.5 t/c Ligier JS23-Renault V6	*fuel injection*
ret	DUTCH GP	Zandvoort	26	Ligier Loto	1.5 t/c Ligier JS23-Renault V6	*engine*
ret	ITALIAN GP	Monza	26	Ligier Loto	1.5 t/c Ligier JS23-Renault V6	*engine*
7	EUROPEAN GP	Nürburgring	26	Ligier Loto	1.5 t/c Ligier JS23-Renault V6	*2 laps behind*
12	PORTUGUESE GP	Estoril	26	Ligier Loto	1.5 t/c Ligier JS23-Renault V6	*1 lap behind*
1985						
ret	BRAZILIAN GP	Rio	25	Equipe Ligier	1.5 t/c Ligier JS25-Renault V6	*hit Arnoux*
ret	PORTUGUESE GP	Estoril	25	Equipe Ligier	1.5 t/c Ligier JS25-Renault V6	*tyres/handling*
ret	SAN MARINO GP	Imola	25	Equipe Ligier	1.5 t/c Ligier JS25-Renault V6	*spun off*
4	MONACO GP	Monte Carlo	25	Equipe Ligier	1.5 t/c Ligier JS25-Renault V6	*1 lap behind*
14	CANADIAN GP	Montreal	25	Equipe Ligier Gitanes	1.5 t/c Ligier JS25-Renault V6	*spin-hit Winkelhock-pit stop/-3 laps*
10	US GP (DETROIT)	Detroit	25	Equipe Ligier Gitanes	1.5 t/c Ligier JS25-Renault V6	*2 laps behind*
ret	FRENCH GP	Paul Ricard	25	Equipe Ligier Gitanes	1.5 t/c Ligier JS25-Renault V6	*driveshaft*
ret	BRITISH GP	Silverstone	25	Equipe Ligier Gitanes	1.5 t/c Ligier JS25-Renault V6	*clutch*
ret	GERMAN GP	Nürburgring	25	Equipe Ligier Gitanes	1.5 t/c Ligier JS25-Renault V6	*hit by Laffite-broken steering arm*
ret	AUSTRIAN GP	Österreichring	25	Equipe Ligier Gitanes	1.5 t/c Ligier JS25-Renault V6	*accident-rolled car*
ret	DUTCH GP	Zandvoort	25	Equipe Ligier Gitanes	1.5 t/c Ligier JS25-Renault V6	*turbo*
1986						
ret	BRAZILIAN GP	Rio	23	Minardi Team	1.5 t/c Minardi M/185B-MM V6	*turbo*
ret	SPANISH GP	Jerez	23	Minardi Team	1.5 t/c Minardi M/185B-MM V6	*differential*
ret	SAN MARINO GP	Imola	23	Minardi Team	1.5 t/c Minardi M/185B-MM V6	*engine*
dnq	MONACO GP	Monte Carlo	23	Minardi Team	1.5 t/c Minardi M/185B-MM V6	
ret	BELGIAN GP	Spa	23	Minardi Team	1.5 t/c Minardi M1/85B-MM V6	*out of fuel*
ret	CANADIAN GP	Montreal	23	Minardi Team	1.5 t/c Minardi M/185B-MM V6	*gearbox*
ret	US GP (DETROIT)	Detroit	23	Minardi Team	1.5 t/c Minardi M/185B-MM V6	*gearbox*
ret	FRENCH GP	Paul Ricard	23	Minardi Team	1.5 t/c Minardi M/185B-MM V6	*turbo*
ret	BRITISH GP	Brands Hatch	23	Minardi Team	1.5 t/c Minardi M/185B-MM V6	*electrics*
ret	GERMAN GP	Hockenheim	23	Minardi Team	1.5 t/c Minardi M/185B-MM V6	*gearbox*
ret	HUNGARIAN GP	Hungaroring	23	Minardi Team	1.5 t/c Minardi M/186-MM V6	*engine*
ret	AUSTRIAN GP	Österreichring	23	Minardi Team	1.5 t/c Minardi M/186-MM V6	*clutch*
dns	"	"	23	Minardi Team	1.5 t/c Minardi M/185B-MM V6	*practice only*
ret	ITALIAN GP	Monza	23	Minardi Team	1.5 t/c Minardi M/186-MM V6	*engine*
ret	PORTUGUESE GP	Estoril	23	Minardi Team	1.5 t/c Minardi M/186-MM V6	*spun off*
8	MEXICAN GP	Mexico City	23	Minardi Team	1.5 t/c Minardi M/186-MM V6	*2 laps behind*
ret	AUSTRALIAN GP	Adelaide	23	Minardi Team	1.5 t/c Minardi M/186-MM V6	*fire extinguisher set off*
1987						
ret	BRAZILIAN GP	Rio	7	Motor Racing Developments Ltd	1.5 t/c Brabham BT56-BMW 4	*gearbox*
ret	SAN MARINO GP	Imola	7	Motor Racing Developments Ltd	1.5 t/c Brabham BT56-BMW 4	*started from pit lane/spun off*
3/ret	BELGIAN GP	Spa	7	Motor Racing Developments Ltd	1.5 t/c Brabham BT56-BMW 4	*out of fuel/1 lap behind*
ret	MONACO GP	Monte Carlo	7	Motor Racing Developments Ltd	1.5 t/c Brabham BT56-BMW 4	*suspension*
ret	US GP (DETROIT)	Detroit	7	Motor Racing Developments Ltd	1.5 t/c Brabham BT56-BMW 4	*gearbox*
ret	FRENCH GP	Paul Ricard	7	Motor Racing Developments Ltd	1.5 t/c Brabham BT56-BMW 4	*turbo*
ret	BRITISH GP	Silverstone	7	Motor Racing Developments Ltd	1.5 t/c Brabham BT56-BMW 4	*broken fuel line-fire*
ret	GERMAN GP	Hockenheim	7	Motor Racing Developments Ltd	1.5 t/c Brabham BT56-BMW 4	*engine*
ret	HUNGARIAN GP	Hungaroring	7	Motor Racing Developments Ltd	1.5 t/c Brabham BT56-BMW 4	*gearbox*
ret	AUSTRIAN GP	Österreichring	7	Motor Racing Developments Ltd	1.5 t/c Brabham BT56-BMW 4	*turbo*
ret	ITALIAN GP	Monza	7	Motor Racing Developments Ltd	1.5 t/c Brabham BT56-BMW 4	*suspension*
ret	PORTUGUESE GP	Estoril	7	Motor Racing Developments Ltd	1.5 t/c Brabham BT56-BMW 4	*engine*
ret	SPANISH GP	Jerez	7	Motor Racing Developments Ltd	1.5 t/c Brabham BT56-BMW 4	*gearbox*
ret	MEXICAN GP	Mexico City	7	Motor Racing Developments Ltd	1.5 t/c Brabham BT56-BMW 4	*incident with Senna*
ret	JAPANESE GP	Suzuka	7	Motor Racing Developments Ltd	1.5 t/c Brabham BT56-BMW 4	*turbo*
8*/ret	AUSTRALIAN GP	Adelaide	7	Motor Racing Developments Ltd	1.5 t/c Brabham BT56-BMW 4	** 2nd place car dsq/spun off/-4 laps*
1988						
ret	BRAZILIAN GP	Rio	22	Rial Racing	3.5 Rial ARC1-Cosworth V8	*engine*
ret	SAN MARINO GP	Imola	22	Rial Racing	3.5 Rial ARC1-Cosworth V8	*chassis*
ret	MONACO GP	Monte Carlo	22	Rial Racing	3.5 Rial ARC1-Cosworth V8	*oil pressure*
ret	MEXICAN GP	Mexico City	22	Rial Racing	3.5 Rial ARC1-Cosworth V8	*gearbox*

9/ret	CANADIAN GP	Montreal	22	Rial Racing	3.5 Rial ARC1-Cosworth V8	*out of fuel/3 laps behind*
4	US GP (DETROIT)	Detroit	22	Rial Racing	3.5 Rial ARC1-Cosworth V8	*1 lap behind*
10	FRENCH GP	Paul Ricard	22	Rial Racing	3.5 Rial ARC1-Cosworth V8	*p stop-tyres-wheel stuck/-2 laps*
ret	BRITISH GP	Silverstone	22	Rial Racing	3.5 Rial ARC1-Cosworth V8	*clutch*
13	GERMAN GP	Hockenheim	22	Rial Racing	3.5 Rial ARC1-Cosworth V8	*p stop-tyres/2 spins/2 laps behind*
ret	HUNGARIAN GP	Hungaroring	22	Rial Racing	3.5 Rial ARC1-Cosworth V8	*driveshaft-c.v. joint*
ret	BELGIAN GP	Spa	22	Rial Racing	3.5 Rial ARC1-Cosworth V8	*accident with Arnoux*
ret	ITALIAN GP	Monza	22	Rial Racing	3.5 Rial ARC1-Cosworth V8	*incident-Martini/front suspension*
ret	PORTUGUESE GP	Estoril	22	Rial Racing	3.5 Rial ARC1-Cosworth V8	*driveshaft*
ret	SPANISH GP	Jerez	22	Rial Racing	3.5 Rial ARC1-Cosworth V8	*engine*
ret	JAPANESE GP	Suzuka	22	Rial Racing	3.5 Rial ARC1-Cosworth V8	*overheating*
8/ret	AUSTRALIAN GP	Adelaide	22	Rial Racing	3.5 Rial ARC1-Cosworth V8	*out of fuel/5 laps behind*

1989

13/ret	BRAZILIAN GP	Rio	22	Scuderia Italia	3.5 Dallara F189-Cosworth V8	*engine/4 laps behind*
10	SAN MARINO GP	Imola	22	Scuderia Italia	3.5 Dallara F189-Cosworth V8	*spin/2 laps behind*
13	MONACO GP	Monte Carlo	22	Scuderia Italia	3.5 Dallara F189-Cosworth V8	*collision-Piquet-p stop/-4 laps*
ret	MEXICAN GP	Mexico City	22	Scuderia Italia	3.5 Dallara F189-Cosworth V8	*fuel pump*
ret	US GP (PHOENIX)	Phoenix	22	Scuderia Italia	3.5 Dallara F189-Cosworth V8	*fuel pump/5 laps behind*
3	CANADIAN GP	Montreal	22	Scuderia Italia	3.5 Dallara F189-Cosworth V8	
dnq	FRENCH GP	Paul Ricard	22	Scuderia Italia	3.5 Dallara F189-Cosworth V8	
ret	BRITISH GP	Silverstone	22	Scuderia Italia	3.5 Dallara F189-Cosworth V8	*engine*
7	GERMAN GP	Hockenheim	22	Scuderia Italia	3.5 Dallara F189-Cosworth V8	*1 lap behind*
ret	HUNGARIAN GP	Hungaroring	22	Scuderia Italia	3.5 Dallara F189-Cosworth V8	*clutch*
11	BELGIAN GP	Spa	22	Scuderia Italia	3.5 Dallara F189-Cosworth V8	*3 spins/1 lap behind*
ret	ITALIAN GP	Monza	22	Scuderia Italia	3.5 Dallara F189-Cosworth V8	*engine*
ret	PORTUGUESE GP	Estoril	22	Scuderia Italia	3.5 Dallara F189-Cosworth V8	*engine*
7	SPANISH GP	Jerez	22	Scuderia Italia	3.5 Dallara F189-Cosworth V8	*pit stop-tyres/1 lap behind*
10	JAPANESE GP	Suzuka	22	Scuderia Italia	3.5 Dallara F189-Cosworth V8	*collision-Pirro-p stop/2 laps behind*
ret	AUSTRALIAN GP	Adelaide	22	Scuderia Italia	3.5 Dallara F189-Cosworth V8	*spun off in rain*

1990

ret	US GP (PHOENIX)	Phoenix	22	Scuderia Italia	3.5 Dallara F190-Cosworth V8	*engine*
ret	BRAZILIAN GP	Interlagos	22	Scuderia Italia	3.5 Dallara F190-Cosworth V8	*collision with Alesi*
ret	SAN MARINO GP	Imola	22	Scuderia Italia	3.5 Dallara F190-Cosworth V8	*wheel hub*
ret	MONACO GP	Monte Carlo	22	Scuderia Italia	3.5 Dallara F190-Cosworth V8	*throttle linkage*
ret	CANADIAN GP	Montreal	22	Scuderia Italia	3.5 Dallara F190-Cosworth V8	*transmission*
13	MEXICAN GP	Mexico City	22	Scuderia Italia	3.5 Dallara F190-Cosworth V8	*1 lap behind*
dsq	FRENCH GP	Paul Ricard	22	Scuderia Italia	3.5 Dallara F190-Cosworth V8	*underweight/15th/2 laps behind*
ret	BRITISH GP	Silverstone	22	Scuderia Italia	3.5 Dallara F190-Cosworth V8	*gearbox*
dnq	GERMAN GP	Hockenheim	22	Scuderia Italia	3.5 Dallara F190-Cosworth V8	
ret	HUNGARIAN GP	Hungaroring	22	Scuderia Italia	3.5 Dallara F190-Cosworth V8	*engine*
ret	BELGIAN GP	Spa	22	Scuderia Italia	3.5 Dallara F190-Cosworth V8	*engine*
10	ITALIAN GP	Monza	22	Scuderia Italia	3.5 Dallara F190-Cosworth V8	*pit stop-tyres/2 laps behind*
ret	PORTUGUESE GP	Estoril	22	Scuderia Italia	3.5 Dallara F190-Cosworth V8	*sticking throttle*
ret	SPANISH GP	Jerez	22	Scuderia Italia	3.5 Dallara F190-Cosworth V8	*engine*
ret	JAPANESE GP	Suzuka	22	Scuderia Italia	3.5 Dallara F190-Cosworth V8	*spun off*
ret	AUSTRALIAN GP	Adelaide	22	Scuderia Italia	3.5 Dallara F190-Cosworth V8	*electrics*

1991

dnpq	US GP (PHOENIX)	Phoenix	33	Team 7UP Jordan	3.5 Jordan 191-Ford HB V8	
ret	BRAZILIAN GP	Interlagos	33	Team 7UP Jordan	3.5 Jordan 191-Ford HB V8	*engine cut out-spun off*
ret	SAN MARINO GP	Imola	33	Team 7UP Jordan	3.5 Jordan 191-Ford HB V8	*gear linkage*
ret	MONACO GP	Monte Carlo	33	Team 7UP Jordan	3.5 Jordan 191-Ford HB V8	*throttle cable*
4	CANADIAN GP	Montreal	33	Team 7UP Jordan	3.5 Jordan 191-Ford HB V8	
4/ret	MEXICAN GP	Mexico City	33	Team 7UP Jordan	3.5 Jordan 191-Ford HB V8	*throttle potentiometer/1 lap behind*
6	FRENCH GP	Magny Cours	33	Team 7UP Jordan	3.5 Jordan 191-Ford HB V8	*1 lap behind*
ret	BRITISH GP	Silverstone	33	Team 7UP Jordan	3.5 Jordan 191-Ford HB V8	*accident-suspension failure*
5	GERMAN GP	Hockenheim	33	Team 7UP Jordan	3.5 Jordan 191-Ford HB V8	
7	HUNGARIAN GP	Hungaroring	33	Team 7UP Jordan	3.5 Jordan 191-Ford HB V8	*1 lap behind*
13/ret	BELGIAN GP	Spa	33	Team 7UP Jordan	3.5 Jordan 191-Ford HB V8	*engine-overheating when 2nd*
7	ITALIAN GP	Monza	33	Team 7UP Jordan	3.5 Jordan 191-Ford HB V8	
8	PORTUGUESE GP	Estoril	33	Team 7UP Jordan	3.5 Jordan 191-Ford HB V8	*1 lap behind*
ret	SPANISH GP	Barcelona	33	Team 7UP Jordan	3.5 Jordan 191-Ford HB V8	*electrics*
ret	JAPANESE GP	Suzuka	33	Team 7UP Jordan	3.5 Jordan 191-Ford HB V8	*spun off*
8	AUSTRALIAN GP	Adelaide	33	Team 7UP Jordan	3.5 Jordan 191-Ford HB V8	*rain shortened race*

1992

ret	SOUTH AFRICAN GP	Kyalami	4	Tyrrell Racing Organisation	3.5 Tyrrell 020B-Ilmor V10	*engine*
5	MEXICAN GP	Mexico City	4	Tyrrell Racing Organisation	3.5 Tyrrell 020B-Ilmor V10	*1 lap behind*
ret	BRAZILIAN GP	Interlagos	4	Tyrrell Racing Organisation	3.5 Tyrrell 020B-Ilmor V10	*electrics*
ret	SPANISH GP	Barcelona	4	Tyrrell Racing Organisation	3.5 Tyrrell 020B-Ilmor V10	*oil pressure*
14/ret	SAN MARINO GP	Imola	4	Tyrrell Racing Organisation	3.5 Tyrrell 020B-Ilmor V10	*fuel pressure/5 laps behind*
ret	MONACO GP	Monte Carlo	4	Tyrrell Racing Organisation	3.5 Tyrrell 020B-Ilmor V10	*gearbox*
5	CANADIAN GP	Montreal	4	Tyrrell Racing Organisation	3.5 Tyrrell 020B-Ilmor V10	*1 lap behind*
ret	FRENCH GP	Magny Cours	4	Tyrrell Racing Organisation	3.5 Tyrrell 020B-Ilmor V10	*spun off*
ret	BRITISH GP	Silverstone	4	Tyrrell Racing Organisation	3.5 Tyrrell 020B-Ilmor V10	*suspension-spun off*
ret	GERMAN GP	Hockenheim	4	Tyrrell Racing Organisation	3.5 Tyrrell 020B-Ilmor V10	*engine*
8	HUNGARIAN GP	Hungaroring	4	Tyrrell Racing Organisation	3.5 Tyrrell 020B-Ilmor V10	*2 laps behind*
8	BELGIAN GP	Spa	4	Tyrrell Racing Organisation	3.5 Tyrrell 020B-Ilmor V10	*1 lap behind*
6	ITALIAN GP	Monza	4	Tyrrell Racing Organisation	3.5 Tyrrell 020B-Ilmor V10	*1 lap behind*
9	PORTUGUESE GP	Estoril	4	Tyrrell Racing Organisation	3.5 Tyrrell 020B-Ilmor V10	*2 laps behind*
4	JAPANESE GP	Suzuka	4	Tyrrell Racing Organisation	3.5 Tyrrell 020B-Ilmor V10	*1 lap behind*
ret	AUSTRALIAN GP	Adelaide	4	Tyrrell Racing Organisation	3.5 Tyrrell 020B-Ilmor V10	*fuel pressure-fire*

1993

ret	SOUTH AFRICAN GP	Kyalami	4	Tyrrell Racing Organisation	3.5 Tyrrell 020C-Yamaha V10	*transmission on grid at start*

ret	BRAZILIAN GP	Interlagos	4	Tyrrell Racing Organisation	3.5 Tyrrell 020C-Yamaha V10	engine-electrics
ret	EUROPEAN GP	Donington	4	Tyrrell Racing Organisation	3.5 Tyrrell 020C-Yamaha V10	gearbox
ret	SAN MARINO GP	Imola	4	Tyrrell Racing Organisation	3.5 Tyrrell 020C-Yamaha V10	gearbox
dsq	SPANISH GP	Barcelona	4	Tyrrell Racing Organisation	3.5 Tyrrell 020C-Yamaha V10	black-flagged-outside assistance
10	MONACO GP	Monte Carlo	4	Tyrrell Racing Organisation	3.5 Tyrrell 020C-Yamaha V10	2 laps behind
ret	CANADIAN GP	Montreal	4	Tyrrell Racing Organisation	3.5 Tyrrell 020C-Yamaha V10	active problems/spun off
15	FRENCH GP	Magny Cours	4	Tyrrell Racing Organisation	3.5 Tyrrell 020C-Yamaha V10	4 laps behind
nc	BRITISH GP	Silverstone	4	Tyrrell Racing Organisation	3.5 Tyrrell 021-Yamaha V10	p stops collision-Badoer/-16 laps
ret	GERMAN GP	Hockenheim	4	Tyrrell Racing Organisation	3.5 Tyrrell 021-Yamaha V10	gearbox
11	HUNGARIAN GP	Hungaroring	4	Tyrrell Racing Organisation	3.5 Tyrrell 021-Yamaha V10	p stop-transmission/5 laps behind
ret	BELGIAN GP	Spa	4	Tyrrell Racing Organisation	3.5 Tyrrell 021-Yamaha V10	engine
ret	ITALIAN GP	Monza	4	Tyrrell Racing Organisation	3.5 Tyrrell 021-Yamaha V10	oil pressure
12	PORTUGUESE GP	Estoril	4	Tyrrell Racing Organisation	3.5 Tyrrell 021-Yamaha V10	spin/water leak/3 laps behind
ret	JAPANESE GP	Suzuka	4	Tyrrell Racing Organisation	3.5 Tyrrell 021-Yamaha V10	collision-Gounon-puncture lap 1
13	AUSTRALIAN GP	Adelaide	4	Tyrrell Racing Organisation	3.5 Tyrrell 021-Yamaha V10	4 laps behind

GP Starts: 197   GP Wins: 0   Pole positions: 1   Fastest laps: 1   Points: 55

CEVERT, François (F)   b 25/2/1944 – d 6/10/1973

1969

	Race	Circuit	No	Entrant	Car/Engine	Comment
ret	GERMAN GP (F2)	Nürburgring	28	Tecno Racing	1.6 Tecno F2/69-Cosworth 4	gearbox

1970

ret	DUTCH GP	Zandvoort	6	Tyrrell Racing Organisation	3.0 March 701-Cosworth V8	engine
11	FRENCH GP	Clermont Ferrand	2	Tyrrell Racing Organisation	3.0 March 701-Cosworth V8	1 lap behind
7	BRITISH GP	Brands Hatch	2	Tyrrell Racing Organisation	3.0 March 701-Cosworth V8	1 lap behind
7	GERMAN GP	Hockenheim	23	Tyrrell Racing Organisation	3.0 March 701-Cosworth V8	1 lap behind
ret	AUSTRIAN GP	Österreichring	2	Tyrrell Racing Organisation	3.0 March 701-Cosworth V8	engine
6	ITALIAN GP	Monza	20	Tyrrell Racing Organisation	3.0 March 701-Cosworth V8	
9	CANADIAN GP	St Jovite	2	Tyrrell Racing Organisation	3.0 March 701-Cosworth V8	pit stop-shock absorber/-5 laps
ret	US GP	Watkins Glen	2	Tyrrell Racing Organisation	3.0 March 701-Cosworth V8	lost wheel
ret	MEXICAN GP	Mexico City	2	Tyrrell Racing Organisation	3.0 March 701-Cosworth V8	engine

1971

ret	SOUTH AFRICAN GP	Kyalami	10	Elf Team Tyrrel	3.0 Tyrrell 002-Cosworth V8	accident
7	SPANISH GP	Montjuich Park	12	Elf Team Tyrrell	3.0 Tyrrell 002-Cosworth V8	1 lap behind
ret	MONACO GP	Monte Carlo	12	Elf Team Tyrrell	3.0 Tyrrell 002-Cosworth V8	hit barrier/suspension-wheel
ret	DUTCH GP	Zandvoort	6	Elf Team Tyrrell	3.0 Tyrrell 002-Cosworth V8	spun off/collision with Galli
2	FRENCH GP	Paul Ricard	12	Elf Team Tyrrell	3.0 Tyrrell 002-Cosworth V8	
10	BRITISH GP	Silverstone	14	Elf Team Tyrrell	3.0 Tyrrell 002-Cosworth V8	pit stop-fuel pipe/3 laps behind
2	GERMAN GP	Nürburgring	3	Elf Team Tyrrell	3.0 Tyrrell 002-Cosworth V8	FL
ret	AUSTRIAN GP	Österreichring	12	Elf Team Tyrrell	3.0 Tyrrell 002-Cosworth V8	engine
3	ITALIAN GP	Monza	2	Elf Team Tyrrell	3.0 Tyrrell 002-Cosworth V8	
6	CANADIAN GP	Mosport Park	12	Elf Team Tyrrell	3.0 Tyrrell 002-Cosworth V8	2 laps behind
1	US GP	Watkins Glen	9	Elf Team Tyrrell	3.0 Tyrrell 002-Cosworth V8	

1972

ret	ARGENTINE GP	Buenos Aires	22	Elf Team Tyrrell	3.0 Tyrrell 002-Cosworth V8	transmission
9	SOUTH AFRICAN GP	Kyalami	2	Elf Team Tyrrell	3.0 Tyrrell 002-Cosworth V8	pit stop-ignition/1 lap behind
ret	SPANISH GP	Jarama	3	Elf Team Tyrrell	3.0 Tyrrell 002-Cosworth V8	ignition
18/ret	MONACO GP	Monte Carlo	2	Elf Team Tyrrell	3.0 Tyrrell 002-Cosworth V8	electrics/10 laps behind
2	BELGIAN GP	Nivelles	8	Elf Team Tyrrell	3.0 Tyrrell 002-Cosworth V8	
4	FRENCH GP	Clermont Ferrand	7	Elf Team Tyrrell	3.0 Tyrrell 002-Cosworth V8	
dns	"	"	7T/7	Elf Team Tyrrell	3.0 Tyrrell 005-Cosworth V8	practice only
ret	BRITISH GP	Brands Hatch	2	Elf Team Tyrrell	3.0 Tyrrell 002-Cosworth V8	spun off
10	GERMAN GP	Nürburgring	7	Elf Team Tyrrell	3.0 Tyrrell 002-Cosworth V8	pit stop-tyre
dns	"	"	7T	Elf Team Tyrrell	3.0 Tyrrell 004-Cosworth V8	practice only
9	AUSTRIAN GP	Österreichring	2	Elf Team Tyrrell	3.0 Tyrrell 002-Cosworth V8	1 lap behind
ret	ITALIAN GP	Monza	2	Elf Team Tyrrell	3.0 Tyrrell 002-Cosworth V8	engine
dns	"	"	1T	Elf Team Tyrrell	3.0 Tyrrell 004-Cosworth V8	practice only
ret	CANADIAN GP	Mosport Park	2	Elf Team Tyrrell	3.0 Tyrrell 006-Cosworth V8	gearbox
2	US GP	Watkins Glen	2	Elf Team Tyrrell	3.0 Tyrrell 006-Cosworth V8	

1973

2	ARGENTINE GP	Buenos Aires	8	Elf Team Tyrrell	3.0 Tyrrell 006-Cosworth V8	
10	BRAZILIAN GP	Interlagos	4	Elf Team Tyrrell	3.0 Tyrrell 006-Cosworth V8	pit stop-puncture/2 laps behind
nc	SOUTH AFRICAN GP	Kyalami	4	Elf Team Tyrrell	3.0 Tyrrell 005-Cosworth V8	3 pit stops-tyre-timing/-13 laps
dns	"	"	4	Elf Team Tyrrell	3.0 Tyrrell 006-Cosworth V8	practice only
2	SPANISH GP	Montjuich Park	4	Elf Team Tyrrell	3.0 Tyrrell 006-Cosworth V8	
2	BELGIAN GP	Zolder	6	Elf Team Tyrrell	3.0 Tyrrell 006-Cosworth V8	FL
4	MONACO GP	Monte Carlo	6	Elf Team Tyrrell	3.0 Tyrrell 006-Cosworth V8	1 lap behind
3	SWEDISH GP	Anderstorp	6	Elf Team Tyrrell	3.0 Tyrrell 006-Cosworth V8	
dns	"	"	6T	Elf Team Tyrrell	3.0 Tyrrell 005-Cosworth V8	practice only
2	FRENCH GP	Paul Ricard	6	Elf Team Tyrrell	3.0 Tyrrell 006-Cosworth V8	
5___	BRITISH GP	Silverstone	6	Elf Team Tyrrell	3.0 Tyrrell 006-Cosworth V8	
dns	"	"	43	Elf Team Tyrrell	3.0 Tyrrell 005-Cosworth V8	practice only
2	DUTCH GP	Zandvoort	6	Elf Team Tyrrell	3.0 Tyrrell 006-Cosworth V8	
2	GERMAN GP	Nürburgring	6	Elf Team Tyrrell	3.0 Tyrrell 006-Cosworth V8	
ret	AUSTRIAN GP	Österreichring	6	Elf Team Tyrrell	3.0 Tyrrell 006-Cosworth V8	collision with Merzario
dns	"	"	6T	Elf Team Tyrrell	3.0 Tyrrell 005-Cosworth V8	practice only
5	ITALIAN GP	Monza	6	Elf Team Tyrrell	3.0 Tyrrell 006-Cosworth V8	
dns	"	"	6T	Elf Team Tyrrell	3.0 Tyrrell 005-Cosworth V8	practice only
ret	CANADIAN GP	Mosport Park	6	Elf Team Tyrrell	3.0 Tyrrell 006-Cosworth V8	collision with Scheckter
dns	US GP	Watkins Glen	6	Elf Team Tyrrell	3.0 Tyrrell 006-Cosworth V8	fatal practice accident

GP Starts: 47   GP Wins: 1   Pole positions: 0   Fastest laps: 2   Points: 89

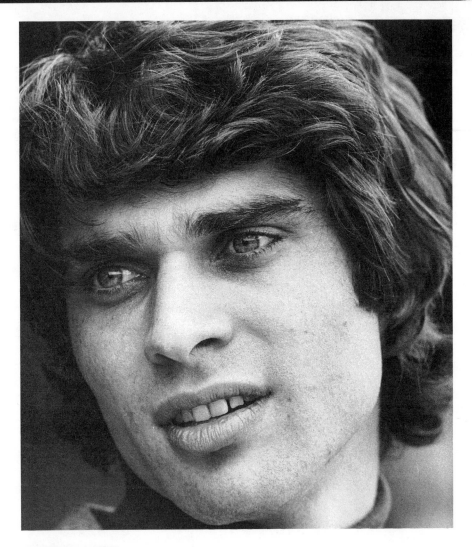

FRANÇOIS CEVERT

Cevert's immense natural talent had been nurtured and developed over a four-year period in the Tyrrell team. He had been given what amounted to a personal master-class in the art of Grand Prix racing by Jackie Stewart and learned so well that at the time of his shocking death at Watkins Glen in 1973 he was the finished article, ready to assume the mantle of a champion after his team leader's impending retirement.

A Volant Shell award had seen François begin his racing career in 1967 at the wheel of his prize, an F3 Alpine. The season was something of a disaster, with the old car proving very unreliable. Undismayed by this, he bought a Tecno for the following year and, after getting to grips with its inherent understeer, went on to take the French F3 championship. So impressed were the Italian manufacturers that they offered Cevert a place in their Formula 2 team for 1969, and despite his lack of experience he took third place in the championship and a win in the Tropheés de France meeting at Reims. François also made his Grand Prix debut in the car in the Formula 2 class of the German GP.

For 1970 he planned another season with Tecno as well as finally accepting an offer to drive for Matra in sports cars, which came via his brother-in-law Jean-Pierre Beltoise. But when Johnny Servoz-Gavin suddenly retired in mid-season, Cevert took over the Tyrrell drive and his perspective had suddenly changed. Playing himself in sensibly with the March 701, the Frenchman scored a satisfying sixth place at Monza, but he really blossomed in 1971 with the superb Tyrrell, taking two excellent second places behind his leader at Paul Ricard and the Nürburgring before posting his first (and only) Grand Prix win in the US GP.

The 1972 Formula 1 season was more difficult, perhaps not helped by Stewart's illness, and Cevert finished in the points on only three occasions. He also drove quite regularly in other formulae, dovetailing appearances in John Coombs' Elf-backed March in F2 with a full Can-Am programme (which saw a win at Donnybrooke) and a one-off drive at Le Mans, where he took a splendid second place for Matra with Howden Ganley. Tyrrell were back at their best in 1973. Stewart, already intending to retire after one last season, used all his considerable gifts to take a third World Championship with François right behind him, the apprentice having matured to the point that he could now be the faster man on occasion. Certainly it was felt that Cevert could have taken the German GP if he had so chosen, but in the event he had to be content with no fewer than five second-place finishes before that fateful day at Watkins Glen in October when, attempting to take pole position, he lost control of his car on a bumpy part of the track, the Tyrrell being hurled into the barriers with such ferocity that François stood no chance of survival. France's most likely World Champion was gone, and Ken Tyrrell had lost the man who could perhaps have kept his team at the pinnacle in the post-Stewart era.

EUGÈNE CHABOUD

With his friend Jean Trémoulet, Chaboud began racing late in 1936 with a Delahaye. The pair raced together until 1938 when, after winning the Le Mans 24-hour race, they went their separate ways.

Following the war, Chaboud was soon back racing, involved with Paul Vallée's Ecurie France team as sporting director and lead driver with his Delahaye 135S. In 1947 the team acquired a 1939 Talbot *monoplace* with which Eugène lost no time in winning races at Marseilles and Perpignan. The drive was then given to Louis Chiron, so Chaboud and Charles Pozzi left in disgust and set up their own team. Eugène emerged as French champion, and for 1948 they created Ecurie Leutitia, with Chaboud still racing his Delahaye. He took sixth place in the 1949 French GP, and was very unlucky at Le Mans when the car caught fire while leading the race by some nine miles and eventually had to be abandoned.

Chaboud's chance to race in more competitive machinery than the Delahaye came in 1950, when he was invited to drive a Lago-Talbot in place of the injured Martin. Sharing the car with Étancelin, he finished fifth in the French GP.

In the Le Mans 24 Hours of 1952, Chaboud lay sixth until, after the 22-hour mark, he crashed the Talbot. While lying under the overturned car waiting to be extricated, he had leisure to decide it was a good time to call it a day!

JAY CHAMBERLAIN

This SCCA sports car racer competed almost exclusively in Lotus cars, for which he was an early US distributor in the late fifties. He came to Europe in 1957 and finished ninth at Le Mans (with Mackay Fraser), winning the 750 cc class, and second in a sports car race at Rouen, before being seriously injured in a crash in the Reims 12 Hours. He recovered in time to return to Le Mans in 1958 but crashed at Mulsanne without harm. After racing a Formula Junior Lotus back in the States, Jay tried his hand at a Formula 1 season in Europe with a Lotus 18, his only result of any note being fifth in the minor Lavant Cup (for four-cylinder cars only) at Goodwood.

CHABOUD, Eugène (F) b 12/4/1907 – d 28/12/1983

1950

	Race	Circuit	No	Entrant	Car/Engine	Comment
ret	BELGIAN GP	Spa	20	Ecurie Leutitia	4.5 Lago-Talbot T26C 6	
dns	FRENCH GP	Reims	24	Ecurie Leutitia	4.5 Lago-Talbot T26C 6	
5*	"	"	16	Philippe Étancelin	4.5 Lago-Talbot T26C-DA 6	* took over Étancelin's car/-5 laps

1951

	Race	Circuit	No	Entrant	Car/Engine	Comment
8	FRENCH GP	Reims	44	Eugène Chaboud	4.5 Lago-Talbot T26C-GS 6	8 laps behind

GP Starts: 3   GP Wins: 0   Pole positions: 0   Fastest laps: 0   Points: 0

CHAMBERLAIN, Jay (USA)

1962

	Race	Circuit	No	Entrant	Car/Engine	Comment
15	BRITISH GP	Aintree	46	Ecurie Excelsior	1.5 Lotus 18-Climax 4	11 laps behind
dnq	GERMAN GP	Nürburgring	30	Ecurie Excelsior	1.5 Lotus 18-Climax 4	
dnq	ITALIAN GP	Monza	26	Ecurie Excelsior	1.5 Lotus 18-Climax 4	

GP Starts: 1   GP Wins: 0   Pole positions: 0   Fastest laps: 0   Points: 0

CHARLTON, Dave (ZA) b 27/10/1936

1965

	Race	Circuit	No	Entrant	Car/Engine	Comment
dnpq	SOUTH AFRICAN GP	East London	32	Ecurie Tomahawk	1.5 Lotus 20-Ford 4	

1967

	Race	Circuit	No	Entrant	Car/Engine	Comment
nc	SOUTH AFRICAN GP	Kyalami	19	Scuderia Scribante	2.7 Brabham BT11-Climax 4	17 laps behind

1968

	Race	Circuit	No	Entrant	Car/Engine	Comment
ret	SOUTH AFRICAN GP	Kyalami	22	Scuderia Scribante	3.0 Brabham BT11-Repco V8	crown wheel and pinion

1970

	Race	Circuit	No	Entrant	Car/Engine	Comment
12/ret	SOUTH AFRICAN GP	Kyalami	25	Scuderia Scribante	3.0 Lotus 49C-Cosworth V8	puncture/7 laps behind

1971

	Race	Circuit	No	Entrant	Car/Engine	Comment
ret	SOUTH AFRICAN GP	Kyalami	15	Motor Racing Developments	3.0 Brabham BT33-Cosworth V8	valve spring
dns	DUTCH GP	Zandvoort	12	Gold Leaf Team Lotus	3.0 Lotus 72D-Cosworth V8	car crashed by Walker in practice
ret	BRITISH GP	Silverstone	2	Gold Leaf Team Lotus	3.0 Lotus 72D-Cosworth V8	engine

1972

	Race	Circuit	No	Entrant	Car/Engine	Comment
ret	SOUTH AFRICAN GP	Kyalami	26	Scuderia Scribante-Lucky Strike	3.0 Lotus 72D-Cosworth V8	fuel pressure-seized fuel pump
dnq	FRENCH GP	Clermont Ferrand	29	Scuderia Scribante-Lucky Strike	3.0 Lotus 72D-Cosworth V8	
ret	BRITISH GP	Brands Hatch	29	Scuderia Scribante-Lucky Strike	3.0 Lotus 72D-Cosworth V8	gearbox
ret	GERMAN GP	Nürburgring	29	Scuderia Scribante-Lucky Strike	3.0 Lotus 72D-Cosworth V8	driver unwell

1973

	Race	Circuit	No	Entrant	Car/Engine	Comment
ret	SOUTH AFRICAN GP	Kyalami	25	Scuderia Scribante-Lucky Strike	3.0 Lotus 72D-Cosworth V8	spun, caused multiple accident

1974

	Race	Circuit	No	Entrant	Car/Engine	Comment
19	SOUTH AFRICAN GP	Kyalami	23	Scuderia Scribante-Lucky Strike	3.0 McLaren M23-Cosworth V8	p stop-collision-Robarts/-7 laps

1975

	Race	Circuit	No	Entrant	Car/Engine	Comment
14	SOUTH AFRICAN GP	Kyalami	31	Lucky Strike Racing	3.0 McLaren M23-Cosworth V8	2 laps behind

GP Starts: 11   GP Wins: 0   Pole positions: 0   Fastest laps: 0   Points: 0

DAVE CHARLTON

After club racing, Charlton moved into South Africa's major league in 1962, racing under the intriguingly titled Ecurie Tomahawk banner. Driving a four-cylinder-powered Lotus 20, he fared reasonably well on the local scene, but the car was not even good enough to qualify for practice in the 1965 Grand Prix.

The purchase of a Brabham BT11 brought him to the forefront in South Africa's national series, and helped ensure that he would be on the grid for the country's feature race as well. Building his reputation with Scuderia Scribante, Charlton was invited to England in early 1968 to test a works Cooper, also taking in the BOAC 500 in Sid Taylor's Lola T70.

In 1970 Dave purchased the ex-Bonnier Lotus 49C, which he used to devastating effect, cleaning up in the F1/FA series. This led to a deal to drive a works-run Brabham in the following year's Grand Prix, but more importantly secured lucrative sponsorship from Lucky Strike which allowed him to buy a Lotus 72 after his 49 was severely damaged in the 1971 Natal Winter Trophy. He raced the new car with great success, winning the 1972 series by a country mile to the chagrin of his great rival, John Love. Charlton blotted his copybook by spinning out of the 1973 Grand Prix and causing a multiple shunt, but success was to continue unabated when the Lotus was replaced by a McLaren M23. He comfortably won the 1974 series, but was extremely lucky to prevail over his new young challenger Ian Scheckter the following season – his consistency paid off and his six second places and one win were enough. The 1976 season was to see the beginning of the end of Charlton's domination. The championship was now run to Formula Atlantic rules and his Modus did not inspire quite the same awe among his competitors. By mid 1978 he had lost his long-time sponsorship deal and eventually forsook single-seaters for saloons, which he raced into the early eighties.

EDDIE CHEEVER

Eddie Cheever has enjoyed such a long innings in motor racing that it is perhaps easy to forget the startling impact he made on Formula 3 in 1975 when barely 18 years old, or the fact that two years later he had raced successfully for the Project Four team in Formula 2 (taking a superb win at Rouen in 1977) and the BMW Junior touring car team with their 320i in the German national series. The world was his oyster, or so it seemed, especially when a satisfactory test for Ferrari saw him lined up for a works F1 drive in 1978. But the best-laid plans don't always work out, and when Villeneuve was signed Eddie could see his chances of a regular ride were slim and backed away from the deal.

Cheever had his first stab at Grands Prix in 1978 when, after failing to qualify the hapless Theodore for the first two races, he switched to the Hesketh team, which at least enabled him to make the grid but had little else to recommend it. Then it was back to Formula 2 for the rest of the year and a series of morale-sapping incidents which seriously undermined his reputation, despite second-place finishes at Rouen and Enna.

Now no longer quite the hot property of just 12 months earlier, Eddie threw in his lot with Osella for another season of Formula 2 in 1979, and was to enjoy a happy year with the little Italian outfit, taking three wins (Silverstone, Pau and Zandvoort). When the team took the bold decision to enter Grand Prix racing the following year, naturally Cheever went with them. To say it was a character-building season would be an understatement, and Cheever certainly found out about life at the back of the grid. There was a little success to savour, however, for he joined the Lancia sports car team, winning a round of the World Championship of Makes at Mugello with Patrese, and taking second places at Brands Hatch and Watkins Glen with Alboreto.

A move to Tyrrell in 1981 found his career moving in the right direction, the American picking up points on no fewer than five occasions before being tempted to the Ligier team for 1982, where, when he managed to finish, it was usually in the points, including a second place at Detroit. Eddie was chosen to partner Alain Prost at Renault in 1983, a season which was to be his big opportunity to make the jump into the very front rank of driver talent. Although there were flashes of brilliance, he could not sustain them, and while he performed more than respectably, especially in qualifying, his performances were always judged against Prost's – a no-win situation. In the event, a switch to the Benetton Alfa team meant two seasons of disappointment and mechanical unreliability, but never did he ease his forceful driving style, or pay much attention to the subtle art of fuel economy. If the turbo engine lasted, all well and good; if not, then it was going out in a big way – and it usually did.

Out in the cold in 1986, save for a race for Lola at Detroit in place of the indisposed Tambay, Eddie drove the TWR Jaguar in endurance racing, winning at Silverstone and finishing well elsewhere, but the lure of Formula 1 was still great and he joined Arrows for three seasons during which his incredible enthusiasm sustained him through the frustrations of usually being no more than a midfield runner. There were occasional gems, such as his drive into third places at Monza in 1988 and Phoenix in 1989, where he hounded Patrese to the finish. But the down side was his increasing irritation with the team, which manifested itself on the track, particularly at Spa, where he was reprimanded for obstructive driving tactics.

Seeing no future in hanging on in Formula 1, Cheever joined the IndyCar trail from 1990, where in truth his form has been something of a disappointment considering the abundant skill he possesses. A chance to build a solid platform for success with Chip Ganassi's team came and went, despite a second place at Phoenix and a fourth at Indianapolis in 1992. At 37 – still no age for an IndyCar driver – Cheever was left to scratch around with second division teams, hoping for the big breakthrough that he still believed would come.

CHEEVER. Eddie (USA) b 10/1/1958

1978

	Race	Circuit	No	Entrant	Car/Engine	Comment
dnq	ARGENTINE GP	Buenos Aires	32	Theodore Racing	3.0 Theodore TR1-Cosworth V8	
dnq	BRAZILIAN GP	Rio	32	Theodore Racing	3.0 Theodore TR1-Cosworth V8	
ret	SOUTH AFRICAN GP	Kyalami	24	Olympus Cameras/Hesketh Racing	3.0 Hesketh 308E-Cosworth V8	*engine*

1980

dnq	ARGENTINE GP	Buenos Aires	31	Osella Squadra Corse	3.0 Osella FA1-Cosworth V8	
dnq	BRAZILIAN GP	Interlagos	31	Osella Squarda Corse	3.0 Osella FA1-Cosworth V8	
ret	SOUTH AFRICAN GP	Kyalami	31	Osella Squadra Corse	3.0 Osella FA1-Cosworth V8	*accident*
ret	US GP WEST	Long Beach	31	Osella Squadra Corse	3.0 Osella FA1-Cosworth V8	*driveshaft*
dnq	BELGIAN GP	Zolder	31	Osella Squadra Corse	3.0 Osella FA1-Cosworth V8	
dnq	MONACO GP	Monte Carlo	31	Osella Squadra Corse	3.0 Osella FA1-Cosworth V8	
ret	FRENCH GP	Paul Ricard	31	Osella Squadra Corse	3.0 Osella FA1-Cosworth V8	*engine*
ret	BRITISH GP	Brands Hatch	31	Osella Squadra Corse	3.0 Osella FA1-Cosworth V8	*rear suspension*
ret	GERMAN GP	Hockenheim	31	Osella Squadra Corse	3.0 Osella FA1-Cosworth V8	*gearbox*
ret	AUSTRIAN GP	Österreichring	31	Osella Squadra Corse	3.0 Osella FA1-Cosworth V8	*wheel bearing*
ret	DUTCH GP	Zandvoort	31	Osella Squadra Corse	3.0 Osella FA1-Cosworth V8	*engine*
12	ITALIAN GP	Imola	31	Osella Squadra Corse	3.0 Osella FA1-Cosworth V8	*3 laps behind*
ret	CANADIAN GP	Montreal	31	Osella Squadra Corse	3.0 Osella FA1-Cosworth V8	*fuel pressure*
ret	US GP EAST	Watkins Glen	31	Osella Squadra Corse	3.0 Osella FA1-Cosworth V8	*suspension*

1981

5	US GP WEST	Long Beach	3	Tyrrell Racing	3.0 Tyrrell 010-Cosworth V8	
nc	BRAZILIAN GP	Rio	3	Tyrrell Racing	3.0 Tyrrell 010-Cosworth V8	*2 p stops-collision damage/-13 laps*
ret	ARGENTINE GP	Buenos Aires	3	Tyrrell Racing	3.0 Tyrrell 010-Cosworth V8	*clutch*
ret	SAN MARINO GP	Imola	3	Tyrrell Racing	3.0 Tyrrell 010-Cosworth V8	*collision with Giacomelli*
6	BELGIAN GP	Zolder	3	Tyrrell Racing	3.0 Tyrrell 010-Cosworth V8	
5	MONACO GP	Monte Carlo	3	Tyrrell Racing	3.0 Tyrrell 010-Cosworth V8	*2 laps behind*
nc	SPANISH GP	Jarama	3	Tyrrell Racing	3.0 Tyrrell 010-Cosworth V8	*long pit stop/19 laps behind*
13	FRENCH GP	Dijon	3	Tyrrell Racing	3.0 Tyrrell 010-Cosworth V8	*3 laps behind*
4	BRITISH GP	Silverstone	3	Tyrrell Racing	3.0 Tyrrell 010-Cosworth V8	*1 lap behind*
5	GERMAN GP	Hockenheim	3	Tyrrell Racing	3.0 Tyrrell 011-Cosworth V8	
dnq	AUSTRIAN GP	Österreichring	3	Tyrrell Racing	3.0 Tyrrell 011-Cosworth V8	
dnq	"	"	3	Tyrrell Racing	3.0 Tyrrell 010-Cosworth V8	
ret	DUTCH GP	Zandvoort	3	Tyrrell Racing	3.0 Tyrrell 011-Cosworth V8	*suspension failure-accident*
ret	ITALIAN GP	Monza	3	Tyrrell Racing	3.0 Tyrrell 011-Cosworth V8	*spun off*
12/ret	CANADIAN GP	Montreal	3	Tyrrell Racing	3.0 Tyrrell 011-Cosworth V8	*engine/7 laps behind*
ret	CAESARS PALACE GP	Las Vegas	3	Tyrrell Racing	3.0 Tyrrell 011-Cosworth V8	*engine*

1982

ret	SOUTH AFRICAN GP	Kyalami	25	Equipe Talbot Gitanes	3.0 Ligier JS17-Matra V12	*misfire*
ret	BRAZILIAN GP	Rio	25	Equipe Talbot Gitanes	3.0 Ligier JS17-Matra V12	*water leak*
ret	US GP WEST	Long Beach	25	Equipe Talbot Gitanes	3.0 Ligier JS17B-Matra V12	*gearbox*
3	BELGIAN GP	Zolder	25	Equipe Talbot Gitanes	3.0 Ligier JS17-Matra V12	*3rd place car dsq/1 lap behind*
ret	MONACO GP	Monte Carlo	25	Equipe Talbot Gitanes	3.0 Ligier JS19-Matra V12	*engine*
2	US GP (DETROIT)	Detroit	25	Equipe Talbot Gitanes	3.0 Ligier JS17-Matra V12	
10/ret	CANADIAN GP	Montreal	25	Equipe Talbot Gitanes	3.0 Ligier JS17-Matra V12	*out of fuel*
dnq	DUTCH GP	Zandvoort	25	Equipe Talbot Gitanes	3.0 Ligier JS19-Matra V12	
ret	BRITISH GP	Brands Hatch	25	Equipe Talbot Gitanes	3.0 Ligier JS19-Matra V12	*engine*
16	FRENCH GP	Paul Ricard	25	Equipe Talbot Gitanes	3.0 Ligier JS19-Matra V12	*3 p stops-tyres-skirts/-5 laps*
ret	GERMAN GP	Hockenheim	25	Equipe Talbot Gitanes	3.0 Ligier JS19-Matra V12	*handling*
ret	AUSTRIAN GP	Österreichring	25	Equipe Talbot Gitanes	3.0 Ligier JS19-Matra V12	*engine*
nc	SWISS GP	Dijon	25	Equipe Talbot Gitanes	3.0 Ligier JS19-Matra V12	*2 pit stops-tyres/10 laps behind*
6	ITALIAN GP	Monza	25	Equipe Talbot Gitanes	3.0 Ligier JS19-Matra V12	*1 lap behind*
3	CAESARS PALACE GP	Las Vegas	25	Equipe Talbot Gitanes	3.0 Ligier JS19-Matra V12	

1983

ret	BRAZILIAN GP	Rio	16	Equipe Renault Elf	1.5 t/c Renault RE30C V6	*turbo*
ret	US GP WEST	Long Beach	16	Equipe Renault Elf	1.5 t/c Renault RE30C V6	*gearbox*
3	FRENCH GP	Paul Ricard	16	Equipe Renault Elf	1.5 t/c Renault RE40 V6	
ret	SAN MARINO GP	Imola	16	Equipe Renault Elf	1.5 t/c Renault RE40 V6	*turbo*
ret	MONACO GP	Monte Carlo	16	Equipe Renault Elf	1.5 t/c Renault RE40 V6	*engine cut out*
3	BELGIAN GP	Spa	16	Equipe Renault Elf	1.5 t/c Renault RE40 V6	
ret	US GP (DETROIT)	Detroit	16	Equipe Renault Elf	1.5 t/c Renault RE40 V6	*distributor*
2	CANADIAN GP	Montreal	16	Equipe Renault Elf	1.5 t/c Renault RE40 V6	
ret	BRITISH GP	Silverstone	16	Equipe Renault Elf	1.5 t/c Renault RE40 V6	*engine-head gasket*
ret	GERMAN GP	Hockenheim	16	Equipe Renault Elf	1.5 t/c Renault RE40 V6	*fuel injection pump*
4	AUSTRIAN GP	Österreichring	16	Equipe Renault Elf	1.5 t/c Renault RE40 V6	
ret	DUTCH GP	Zandvoort	16	Equipe Renault Elf	1.5 t/c Renault RE40 V6	*electrics*
3	ITALIAN GP	Monza	16	Equipe Renault Elf	1.5 t/c Renault RE40 V6	
10	EUROPEAN GP	Brands Hatch	16	Equipe Renault Elf	1.5 t/c Renault RE40 V6	*2 p stops-tyres-visor/1 lap behind*
6	SOUTH AFRICAN GP	Kyalami	16	Equipe Renault Elf	1.5 t/c Renault RE40 V6	*1 lap behind*

1984

4	BRAZILIAN GP	Rio	23	Benetton Team Alfa Romeo	1.5 t/c Alfa Romeo 184T V8	*1 lap behind*
ret	SOUTH AFRICAN GP	Kyalami	23	Benetton Team Alfa Romeo	1.5 t/c Alfa Romeo 184T V8	*radiator*
ret	BELGIAN GP	Zolder	23	Benetton Team Alfa Romeo	1.5 t/c Alfa Romeo 184T V8	*engine*
7*/ret	SAN MARINO GP	Imola	23	Benetton Team Alfa Romeo	1.5 t/c Alfa Romeo 184T V8	** 5th place car dsq/out of fuel/-2 laps*
ret	FRENCH GP	Dijon	23	Benetton Team Alfa Romeo	1.5 t/c Alfa Romeo 184T V8	*engine*
dnq	MONACO GP	Monte Carlo	23	Benetton Team Alfa Romeo	1.5 t/c Alfa Romeo 184T V8	
11*/ret	CANADIAN GP	Montreal	23	Benetton Team Alfa Romeo	1.5 t/c Alfa Romeo 184T V8	** 10th place car dsq/out of fuel/-7 laps*
ret	US GP (DETROIT)	Detroit	23	Benetton Team Alfa Romeo	1.5 t/c Alfa Romeo 184T V8	*engine*
ret	US GP (DALLAS)	Dallas	23	Benetton Team Alfa Romeo	1.5 t/c Alfa Romeo 184T V8	*hit wall*
ret	BRITISH GP	Brands Hatch	23	Benetton Team Alfa Romeo	1.5 t/c Alfa Romeo 184T V8	*accident damage*

ret	GERMAN GP	Hockenheim	23	Benetton Team Alfa Romeo	1.5 t/c Alfa Romeo 184T V8	*engine*
ret	AUSTRIAN GP	Österreichring	23	Benetton Team Alfa Romeo	1.5 t/c Alfa Romeo 184T V8	*engine*
13*/ret	DUTCH GP	Zandvoort	23	Benetton Team Alfa Romeo	1.5 t/c Alfa Romeo 184T V8	** 8th & 9th cars dsq/out of fuel/-6 laps*
9*/ret	ITALIAN GP	Monza	23	Benetton Team Alfa Romeo	1.5 t/c Alfa Romeo 184T V8	*out of fuel/6 laps behind*
ret	EUROPEAN GP	Nürburgring	23	Benetton Team Alfa Romeo	1.5 t/c Alfa Romeo 184T V8	*fuel pump*
17	PORTUGUESE GP	Estoril	23	Benetton Team Alfa Romeo	1.5 t/c Alfa Romeo 184T V8	*pit stop/6 laps behind*

1985

ret	BRAZILIAN GP	Rio	23	Benetton Team Alfa Romeo	1.5 t/c Alfa Romeo 185T V8	*engine*
ret	PORTUGUESE GP	Estoril	23	Benetton Team Alfa Romeo	1.5 t/c Alfa Romeo 185T V8	*started from pit lane/engine*
ret	SAN MARINO GP	Imola	23	Benetton Team Alfa Romeo	1.5 t/c Alfa Romeo 185T V8	*engine*
ret	MONACO GP	Monte Carlo	23	Benetton Team Alfa Romeo	1.5 t/c Alfa Romeo 185T V8	*alternator*
17	CANADIAN GP	Montreal	23	Benetton Team Alfa Romeo	1.5 t/c Alfa Romeo 185T V8	*pit stop-electrics/6 laps behind*
9	US GP (DETROIT)	Detroit	23	Benetton Team Alfa Romeo	1.5 t/c Alfa Romeo 185T V8	*pit stop-puncture/2 laps behind*
10	FRENCH GP	Paul Ricard	23	Benetton Team Alfa Romeo	1.5 t/c Alfa Romeo 185T V8	*1 lap behind*
ret	BRITISH GP	Silverstone	23	Benetton Team Alfa Romeo	1.5 t/c Alfa Romeo 185T V8	*turbo*
ret	GERMAN GP	Nürburgring	23	Benetton Team Alfa Romeo	1.5 t/c Alfa Romeo 184T V8	*turbo*
ret	AUSTRIAN GP	Österreichring	23	Benetton Team Alfa Romeo	1.5 t/c Alfa Romeo 184T V8	*turbo*
ret	DUTCH GP	Zandvoort	23	Benetton Team Alfa Romeo	1.5 t/c Alfa Romeo 184T V8	*turbo*
ret	ITALIAN GP	Monza	23	Benetton Team Alfa Romeo	1.5 t/c Alfa Romeo 184T V8	*engine*
ret	BELGIAN GP	Spa	23	Benetton Team Alfa Romeo	1.5 t/c Alfa Romeo 184T V8	*gearbox*
11	EUROPEAN GP	Brands Hatch	23	Benetton Team Alfa Romeo	1.5 t/c Alfa Romeo 184T V8	*2 laps behind*
ret	SOUTH AFRICAN GP	Kyalami	23	Benetton Team Alfa Romeo	1.5 t/c Alfa Romeo 184T V8	*collision with Ghinzani & Patrese*
ret	AUSTRALIAN GP	Adelaide	23	Benetton Team Alfa Romeo	1.5 t/c Alfa Romeo 184T V8	*engine*

1986

ret	US GP (DETROIT)	Detroit	16	Team Haas (USA) Ltd	1.5 t/c Lola THL2-Cosworth V6	*drive pegs*

1987

ret	BRAZILIAN GP	Rio	18	USF&G Arrows Megatron	1.5 t/c Arrows A10-Megatron 4	*engine*
ret	SAN MARINO GP	Imola	18	USF&G Arrows Megatron	1.5 t/c Arrows A10-Megatron 4	*engine*
4	BELGIAN GP	Spa	18	USF&G Arrows Megatron	1.5 t/c Arrows A10-Megatron 4	*1 lap behind*
ret	MONACO GP	Monte Carlo	18	USF&G Arrows Megatron	1.5 t/c Arrows A10-Megatron 4	*head gasket*
6/ret	US GP (DETROIT)	Detroit	18	USF&G Arrows Megatron	1.5 t/c Arrows A10-Megatron 4	*out of fuel/3 laps behind*
ret	FRENCH GP	Paul Ricard	18	USF&G Arrows Megatron	1.5 t/c Arrows A10-Megatron 4	*knocked off ingnition switch*
ret	BRITISH GP	Silverstone	18	USF&G Arrows Megatron	1.5 t/c Arrows A10-Megatron 4	*engine*
ret	GERMAN GP	Hockenheim	18	USF&G Arrows Megatron	1.5 t/c Arrows A10-Megatron 4	*throttle cable*
8	HUNGARIAN GP	Hungaroring	18	USF&G Arrows Megatron	1.5 t/c Arrows A10-Megatron 4	*hit Warwick-2 pit stops/-2 laps*
ret	AUSTRIAN GP	Österreichring	18	USF&G Arrows Megatron	1.5 t/c Arrows A10-Megatron 4	*puncture*
ret	ITALIAN GP	Monza	18	USF&G Arrows Megatron	1.5 t/c Arrows A10-Megatron 4	*driveshaft*
6	PORTUGUESE GP	Estoril	18	USF&G Arrows Megatron	1.5 t/c Arrows A10-Megatron 4	*2 laps behind*
8/ret	SPANISH GP	Jerez	18	USF&G Arrows Megatron	1.5 t/c Arrows A10-Megatron 4	*out of fuel*
4	MEXICAN GP	Mexico City	18	USF&G Arrows Megatron	1.5 t/c Arrows A10-Megatron 4	
9	JAPANESE GP	Suzuka	18	USF&G Arrows Megatron	1.5 t/c Arrows A10-Megatron 4	*1 lap behind*
ret	AUSTRALIAN GP	Adelaide	18	USF&G Arrows Megatron	1.5 t/c Arrows A10-Megatron 4	*engine*

1988

8	BRAZILIAN GP	Rio	18	USF&G Arrows Megatron	1.5 t/c Arrows A10B-Megatron 4	*1 lap behind*
7	SAN MARINO GP	Imola	18	USF&G Arrows Megatron	1.5 t/c Arrows A10B-Megatron 4	*1 lap behind*
ret	MONACO GP	Monte Carlo	18	USF&G Arrows Megatron	1.5 t/c Arrows A10B-Megatron 4	*electrics*
6	MEXICAN GP	Mexico City	18	USF&G Arrows Megatron	1.5 t/c Arrows A10B-Megatron 4	*1 lap behind*
ret	CANADIAN GP	Montreal	18	USF&G Arrows Megatron	1.5 t/c Arrows A10B-Megatron 4	*throttle return spring*
ret	US GP (DETROIT)	Detroit	18	USF&G Arrows Megatron	1.5 t/c Arrows A10B-Megatron 4	*engine*
11	FRENCH GP	Paul Ricard	18	USF&G Arrows Megatron	1.5 t/c Arrows A10B-Megatron 4	*handling/fuel problems/-2 laps*
7	BRITISH GP	Silverstone	18	USF&G Arrows Megatron	1.5 t/c Arrows A10B-Megatron 4	*1 lap behind*
10	GERMAN GP	Hockenheim	18	USF&G Arrows Megatron	1.5 t/c Arrows A10B-Megatron 4	*engine problems/1 lap behind*
ret	HUNGARIAN GP	Hungaroring	18	USF&G Arrows Megatron	1.5 t/c Arrows A10B-Megatron 4	*brakes*
6*	BELGIAN GP	Spa	18	USF&G Arrows Megatron	1.5 t/c Arrows A10B-Megatron 4	** 3rd & 4th cars dsq/1 lap behind*
3	ITALIAN GP	Monza	18	USF&G Arrows Megatron	1.5 t/c Arrows A10B-Megatron 4	
ret	PORTUGUESE GP	Estoril	18	USF&G Arrows Megatron	1.5 t/c Arrows A10B-Megatron 4	*turbo*
ret	SPANISH GP	Jerez	18	USF&G Arrows Megatron	1.5 t/c Arrows A10B-Megatron 4	*handling*
ret	JAPANESE GP	Suzuka	18	USF&G Arrows Megatron	1.5 t/c Arrows A10B-Megatron 4	*turbo*
ret	AUSTRALIAN GP	Adelaide	18	USF&G Arrows Megatron	1.5 t/c Arrows A10B-Megatron 4	*engine*

1989

ret	BRAZILIAN GP	Rio	10	USF&G Arrows	3.5 Arrows A11-Cosworth V8	*hit by Schneider*
9	SAN MARINO GP	Imola	10	USF&G Arrows	3.5 Arrows A11-Cosworth V8	*agg of 2 parts/broken exhaust/-2 laps*
7	MONACO GP	Monte Carlo	10	USF&G Arrows	3.5 Arrows A11-Cosworth V8	*spin/touched wheels-Arnoux/-2 laps*
7	MEXICAN GP	Mexico City	10	USF&G Arrows	3.5 Arrows A11-Cosworth V8	*1 lap behind*
3	US GP (PHOENIX)	Phoenix	10	USF&G Arrows	3.5 Arrows A11-Cosworth V8	*brakes fading at finish*
ret	CANADIAN GP	Montreal	10	USF&G Arrows	3.5 Arrows A11-Cosworth V8	*electrics-engine*
7	FRENCH GP	Paul Ricard	10	USF&G Arrows	3.5 Arrows A11-Cosworth V8	*1 lap behind*
dnq	BRITISH GP	Silverstone	10	USF&G Arrows	3.5 Arrows A11-Cosworth V8	
12/ret	GERMAN GP	Hockenheim	10	USF&G Arrows	3.5 Arrows A11-Cosworth V8	*fuel pick-up/5 laps behind*
5	HUNGARIAN GP	Hungaroring	10	USF&G Arrows	3.5 Arrows A11-Cosworth V8	*lost 4th place on last lap*
ret	BELGIAN GP	Spa	10	USF&G Arrows	3.5 Arrows A11-Cosworth V8	*lost wheel/warned for baulking*
dnq	ITALIAN GP	Monza	10	USF&G Arrows	3.5 Arrows A11-Cosworth V8	
ret	PORTUGUESE GP	Estoril	10	USF&G Arrows	3.5 Arrows A11-Cosworth V8	*engine cut out-crashed*
ret	SPANISH GP	Jerez	10	USF&G Arrows	3.5 Arrows A11-Cosworth V8	*engine*
8*	JAPANESE GP	Suzuka	10	USF&G Arrows	3.5 Arrows A11-Cosworth V8	** 1st place car dsq/1 lap behind*
ret	AUSTRALIAN GP	Adelaide	10	USF&G Arrows	3.5 Arrows A11-Cosworth V8	*spun off in rain*

GP Starts: 118   GP Wins: 0   Pole positions: 0   Fastest laps: 0   Points: 64

CHIESA, Andrea (CH) b 6/5/1964

1992

	Race	Circuit	No	Entrant	Car/Engine	Comment
dnq	SOUTH AFRICAN GP	Kyalami	14	Fondmetal	3.5 Fondmetal GR01-Ford HB V8	
ret	MEXICAN GP	Mexico City	14	Fondmetal	3.5 Fondmetal GR01-Ford HB V8	spun off
dnq	BRAZILIAN GP	Interlagos	14	Fondmetal	3.5 Fondmetal GR01-Ford HB V8	
ret	SPANISH GP	Barcelona	14	Fondmetal	3.5 Fondmetal GR01-Ford HB V8	spun off
dnq	SAN MARINO GP	Imola	14	Fondmetal	3.5 Fondmetal GR01-Ford HB V8	
dnq	MONACO GP	Monte Carlo	14	Fondmetal	3.5 Fondmetal GR01-Ford HB V8	
dnq	CANADIAN GP	Montreal	14	Fondmetal	3.5 Fondmetal GR01-Ford HB V8	
ret	FRENCH GP	Magny Cours	14	Fondmetal	3.5 Fondmetal GR02-Ford HB V8	collision with Gugelmin-lap 1
dnq	BRITISH GP	Silverstone	14	Fondmetal	3.5 Fondmetal GR02-Ford HB V8	
dnq	GERMAN GP	Hockenheim	14	Fondmetal	3.5 Fondmetal GR01-Ford HB V8	

GP Starts: 3   GP Wins: 0   Pole positions: 0   Fastest laps: 0   Points: 0

CHIMERI, Ettore (YV) b 1924 – d 27/2/1960 (killed practising for the Cuban Sports Car Grand Prix of 1960)

1960

	Race	Circuit	No	Entrant	Car/Engine	Comment
ret	ARGENTINE GP	Buenos Aires	44	Ettore Chimeri	2.5 Maserati 250F 6	electrics

GP Starts: 1   GP Wins: 0   Pole positions: 0   Fastest laps: 0   Points: 0

CHIRON, Louis (MC) b 3/8/1899 – d 22/6/1979

1950

	Race	Circuit	No	Entrant	Car/Engine	Comment
ret	BRITISH GP	Silverstone	19	Officine Alfieri Maserati	1.5 s/c Maserati 4CLT/48 4	oil leak/clutch
3	MONACO GP	Monte Carlo	48	Officine Alfieri Maserati	1.5 s/c Maserati 4CLT/48 4	2 laps behind
9	SWISS GP	Bremgarten	26	Officine Alfieri Maserati	1.5 s/c Maserati 4CLT/48 4	3 laps behind
ret	FRENCH GP	Reims	30	Officine Alfieri Maserati	1.5 s/c Maserati 4CLT/48 4	engine
ret	ITALIAN GP	Monza	6	Officine Alfieri Msaerati	1.5 s/c Maserati 4CLT/48 4	oil pressure

1951

	Race	Circuit	No	Entrant	Car/Engine	Comment
7	SWISS GP	Bremgarten	30	Enrico Platé	1.5 s/c Maserati 4CLT/48 4	2 laps behind
ret	BELGIAN GP	Spa	18	Ecurie Rosier	4.5 Lago-Talbot T26C 6	engine
6	FRENCH GP	Reims	42	Ecurie Rosier	4.5 Lago-Talbot T26C 6	6 laps behind
ret	BRITISH GP	Silverstone	23	Ecurie Rosier	4.5 Lago-Talbot T26C 6	brakes
ret	GERMAN GP	Nürburgring	28	Ecurie Rosier	4.5 Lago-Talbot T26C 6	ignition/engine
ret	ITALIAN GP	Monza	20	Ecurie Rosier	4.5 Lago-Talbot T26C 6	ignition
ret	SPANISH GP	Pedralbes	20	Ecurie Rosier	4.5 Lago-Talbot T26C 6	engine

1953

	Race	Circuit	No	Entrant	Car/Engine	Comment
nc	FRENCH GP	Reims	32	Louis Chiron	2.0 OSCA 20 6	17 laps behind
dns	SWISS GP	Bremgarten	12	Louis Chiron	2.0 OSCA 20 6	
10	ITALIAN GP	Monza	32	Louis Chiron	2.0 OSCA 20 6	8 laps behind

1955

	Race	Circuit	No	Entrant	Car/Engine	Comment
6	MONACO GP	Monte Carlo	32	Scuderia Lancia	2.5 Lancia D50 V8	5 laps behind

1956

	Race	Circuit	No	Entrant	Car/Engine	Comment
dns	MONACO GP	Monte Carlo	34	Scuderia Centro Sud	2.5 Maserati 250F 6	engine in practice

GP Starts: 15   GP Wins: 0   Pole positions: 0   Fastest laps: 0   Points: 4

CLAES, Johnny (B) b 11/8/1916 – d 3/2/1956

1950

	Race	Circuit	No	Entrant	Car/Engine	Comment
11	BRITISH GP	Silverstone	18	Ecurie Belge	4.5 Lago-Talbot T26C 6	6 laps behind
7	MONACO GP	Monte Carlo	6	Ecurie Belge	4.5 Lago-Talbot T26C 6	6 laps behind
10	SWISS GP	Bremgarten	4	Ecurie Belge	4.5 Lago-Talbot T26C 6	3 laps behind
8	BELGIAN GP	Spa	24	Ecurie Belge	4.5 Lago-Talbot T26C 6	3 laps behind
ret	FRENCH GP	Reims	42	Ecurie Belge	4.5 Lago-Talbot T26C 6	overheating
ret	ITALIAN GP	Monza	2	Ecurie Belge	4.5 Lago-Talbot T26C 6	overheating

1951

	Race	Circuit	No	Entrant	Car/Engine	Comment
nc	SWISS GP	Bremgarten	2	Ecurie Belge	4.5 Lago-Talbot T26C-DA 6	7 laps behind
7	BELGIAN GP	Spa	16	Ecurie Belge	4.5 Lago-Talbot T26C-DA 6	3 laps behind
ret	FRENCH GP	Reims	28	Ecurie Belge	4.5 Lago-Talbot T26C-DA 6	hit house
nc	BRITISH GP	Silverstone	25	Ecurie Belge	4.5 Lago-Talbot T26C-DA 6	10 laps behind
nc	GERMAN GP	Nürburgring	94	Ecurie Belge	4.5 Lago-Talbot T26C-DA 6	3 laps behind
ret	ITALIAN GP	Monza	26	Ecurie Belge	4.5 Lago-Talbot T26C-DA 6	ignition
ret	SPANISH GP	Pedralbes	36	Ecurie Belge	4.5 Lago-Talbot T26C-DA 6	hit straw bales

1952

	Race	Circuit	No	Entrant	Car/Engine	Comment
8	BELGIAN GP	Spa	18	Equipe Gordini	2.0 Gordini Type 16S 6	sports body/F2 engine/3 laps behind
ret	FRENCH GP	Rouen	32	Ecurie Belge	1.5 Gordini Type 15 4	engine
15	BRITISH GP	Silverstone	27	Ecurie Belge	1.5 Gordini Type 15 4	6 laps behind
ret	GERMAN GP	Nürburgring	113	HW Motors Ltd	2.0 HWM-Alta 4	rear axle bearing

1953

	Race	Circuit	No	Entrant	Car/Engine	Comment
nc	DUTCH GP	Zandvoort	30	Ecurie Belge	2.0 Connaught A-Lea Francis 4	38 laps behind
ret	BELGIAN GP	Spa	6	Officine Alfieri Maserati	2.0 Maserati A6GCM 6	Fangio took over & crashed

nc	FRENCH GP	Reims	48	Ecurie Belge	2.0 Connaught A-Lea Francis 4	*7 laps behind*
ret	GERMAN GP	Nürburgring	12	Ecurie Belge	2.0 Connaught A-Lea Francis 4	
ret	ITALIAN GP	Monza	26	Ecurie Belge	2.0 Connaught A-Lea Francis 4	*loose fuel line*
	1955					
dns	BELGIAN GP	Spa	38	Stirling Moss Ltd	2.5 Maserati 250F 6	*engine trouble in practice*
nc	DUTCH GP	Zandvoort	50	Equipe Nationale Belge	2.5 Ferrari 625 4	*22 laps behind*

GP Starts: 23   GP Wins: 0   Pole positions: 0   Fastest laps: 0   Points: 0

ANDREA CHIESA

A Swiss national born in Milan, Chiesa made a solid start in Italian F3 in 1986, but was hampered by problems with his VW engine. For 1987 he was well prepared, surging out of the blocks with three wins in the first four races, but his season then tailed off and Enrico Bertaggia pipped him to the title. Stepping up to F3000, Chiesa struggled in 1988, notching just a single point, but things improved the following year, Andrea winning at Enna and finishing second at Vallelunga to claim sixth place in the final points standings.

His third season in the formula, with Paul Stewart Racing, was much the same and he managed seventh in the final table, but his fourth, in 1991, was an utter disaster, Chiesa failing to score even a point with a competitive Reynard. But such are the vagaries of motor racing that when the Formula 1 team line-ups were confirmed for 1992, Andrea was confirmed at Fondmetal. He was out of his depth and his record of three starts (two spins, one collision) and seven dnqs tells the sorry tale. For Chiesa the F1 dream was over, but he briefly reappeared in 1993, racing in the opening round of the IndyCar series in Surfers Paradise, Australia.

LOUIS CHIRON

The bulk of Chiron's long motor racing story falls outside the scope of this book, but it is worthwhile outlining his pre-World Championship exploits, which began in the mid-twenties with a Bugatti, the make that was to be synonymous with the first part of his career. The 1928 season saw him victorious in the Rome, Marne, Spanish and Italian GPs, with victories in the German and Spanish GPs following in 1929. He also took a Delage to compete at Indianapolis, finishing a creditable seventh after a long tyre stop. More success came in 1930 as he added the European and Lyons GPs to his tally, and in 1931, still with the Bugatti, he took a brilliant win in the Monaco GP and shared a French GP triumph with Varzi.

Chiron was tempted away to Scuderia Ferrari for the 1933 season to race their Alfa Romeos, and remained with them until 1936, when the might of Mercedes and Auto Union had become virtually irresistible. He cut down his racing almost to the point of retirement in the immediate pre-war years, though he did find time to win the 1937 French GP in a sports Talbot.

As soon as was practicable after the war, Chiron was out in his Talbot once more. Outright success eluded him in 1946, but he won the 1947 French GP at Montlhéry, a victory he was to repeat at Reims two years later. In 1950 – the first season of the newly created World Championship – Chiron campaigned a 4CLT Maserati without success, except for a fine third place in his native Monte Carlo. After just one Grand Prix the following season, he abandoned the Maserati in favour of the trusty old Lago-Talbot, but the car was generally unreliable. The 1952 season started with near-disaster when he sustained serious burns when his Maserati-Platé caught fire at Syracuse. He did not compete for the rest of the season, but returned in 1953 at the wheel of the latest F2 OSCA which, though attractive, failed to live up to his expectations.

At the start of the 1954 season, Chiron was 54 years old, but he still had not had enough of winning, and he finally triumphed in the Monte Carlo Rally in a Lancia. Invited to handle a works Lancia in the 1955 Monaco GP, Chiron obliged with sixth place. When he finally retired, Prince Rainier asked him to run the Principality's two great events, which he did up until the 1979 Monaco GP, just a month before his death.

JOHNNY CLAES

A Belgian born in Fulham, London, whose mother was Scottish, Claes' first passion was jazz, but he became involved in motor racing after a chance visit to the 1947 French GP where his bilingualism allowed him to act as an interpreter to the English drivers. His Belgian father was wealthy, and when Johnny tried his hand at racing in 1948, a Talbot was duly ordered for him which saw much service in both 1949 and 1950. However, his first real success came at the wheel of an HWM in the 1950 GP des Frontières at Chimay, a race he was to win again the following season, this time in a Simca-Gordini.

With his Talbot effectively redundant following the adoption of Formula 2 regulations for Grands Prix, Claes secured drives with the Gordini, HWM and Connaught teams during the 1952 and 1953 seasons. Finding the competition tough at World Championship level, he tasted real success in the 1953 Liège-Rome-Liège Rally, which he won despite having to drive the car single-handed for 52 hours after his co-driver was taken ill.

By 1954 Johnny was a sick man and he raced little, though a visit to Le Mans with a Porsche saw him finsish 12th overall and take the 1500 cc class. He was more active in 1955, the highlight of his season being third place at Le Mans in the Ecurie Belgique Jaguar with Jacques Swaters. His last competitive event was to be the Liège-Rome-Liège Rally of that year, in which he took third place partnered by Lucien Bianchi. His health then deteriorated rapidly and, laid low by tuberculosis, he died in February 1956, aged just 39.

JIM CLARK

It really was a different era, the mid-sixties. There was no hype, the Grand Prix world was just a small close-knit community of rivals who were still friends, and the 'mega-buck' world of sponsorship was only just looming around the corner. Jim Clark's tragic death in a relatively meaningless Formula 2 race at Hockenheim on 7 April 1968 was a savage blow to everyone connected with the sport, which from that day seemed to change; suddenly it was more of a business. That Clark was not part of the new commercial order perversely seemed somehow fitting, yet in reality Clark was the supreme modern professional racing driver of his day, becoming a tax-exile to maximise his earnings, and employing a manager to run his farming affairs back home in Scotland.

It was this well-off agricultural environment that provided the background to his early motor racing activities – just minor rallies and trials to start with, before he graduated to the Porsche with which he began to make his name in 1958. Despite strong parental opposition, young Jimmy was soon racing for the Border Reivers in their Jaguar D-Type, a little Lotus Elite and the rather more potent Lister Jaguar with which he took 12 wins in the 1959 season. Clark agreed to drive for Aston Martin's Grand Prix team in 1960, but the project was delayed and he was released to Lotus for Formula 2 and Junior racing. However, once Colin Chapman had him under contract he lost no time in promoting him to the Grand Prix team, although the priority was the Junior championship, in which he tied for the title with Trevor Taylor. He was also committed to the Reivers sports car team, sharing the third-placed Aston Martin DBR 1 with Salvadori in the Le Mans 24 Hours, a race he disliked so much that he later refused to participate in it.

The 1961 season saw the introduction of the new 1.5-litre formula and Clark could concentrate fully on the championship Grands Prix and the proliferation of lesser meetings which were organised. He took his first F1 win at Pau, but the year saw little luck come the Scotsman's way, culminating in the tragic collision with von Trips' Ferrari at Monza in September, from which he was fortunate indeed to emerge shocked but unscathed. However, the end-of-season sunshine races in South Africa provided instant and welcome rehabilitation, with Jimmy winning the non-championship Rand, Natal and South African GPs.

For 1962 Chapman built the magnificent monocoque Lotus 25, which, propelled by the Climax V8 engine and driven by Jimmy, simply became the standard-setter for the next three years. Much is made of the heartbreaking failure at East London which cost Clark the championship, but that is harsh indeed on Graham Hill, who suffered equal bad luck earlier in the season, and fully deserved the crown. There were no hiccoughs in 1963, though, as Jimmy scorched to the title, winning no fewer than seven championship Grands Prix and non-title races at Pau, Imola, Silverstone, Kalskoga and Oulton Park. Lotus also made their first assault on USAC racing, with Clark shaking Indianapolis to its roots with the funny little rear-engined car and taking second place on its first appearance. To prove it was no fluke, later in the season he won the Milwaukee 200. The revolution had truly begun.

Jimmy was still indisputably the man to beat in 1964, but unreliability, particularly with the new Lotus 33, saw the title pass to Surtees at the very last gasp in Mexico. However, Clark had thrilled the fans as never before, particularly those in Britain who were also lucky enough to watch him three-wheeling the Lotus Ford Cortina with such abandon. Having seen the championship lost, Clark and Chapman were in no mood to face a repeat of their misfortunes in 1965 and after a highly successful winter Tasman series, which yielded five wins, their World Championship rivals were subjected to the full onslaught of the car's performance and Jimmy's brilliance. Leaving aside Monaco (which Clark skipped in order to win the Indy 500), he won the first six Grands Prix of the season to put the outcome of the championship beyond doubt by August.

The new 3-litre formula for once found Chapman without a ready answer, Team Lotus having to make do with 2-litre Climax engines until the BRM H16s became available. Clark was now in the unusual position of an underdog, which made for a fascinating year, illuminated by superb drives at Zandvoort, where he used all his powers to bring a sick car into third place, and at Watkins Glen, where he took the BRM H16 engine to its only championship victory. But, untypically, there were rare moments when he let his frustrations show, such as when he slid off in the wet at the Nürburgring.

The following year saw the advent of the Lotus 49-Cosworth V8 and Clark gave us the full repertoire of his bounteous gifts. That Denny Hulme won the championship seemed almost unimportant (yes, it really was different in those days!), for all eyes were on Clark. A crushing win on the car's debut in the Dutch GP, one of Grand Prix racing's greatest-ever drives at Monza when he made up almost a whole lap on the opposition only to run short of fuel on the last lap having regained the lead, and his skill in bringing the car home at Watkins Glen with the rear suspension broken and the wheel angled drunkenly as he crossed the finish line live fresh in the memory to this day. The 1968 season began in typical Clark fashion, with an unruffled win in the South African GP to take his tally of World Championship Grand Prix victories to 25, overhauling the legendary Fangio's then record total. Little did the world suspect that he would never compete in a Grand Prix again. For after another enjoyable trip down-under during which he won four Tasman races from seven starts, and a Formula 2 race at Barcelona, came Hockenheim . . .

More than 25 years have passed since Clark's death, but he stands as one of the truly great drivers of any era. On the track only Ayrton Senna in modern-day racing can compare, for both drivers set the benchmark for their peers with performances that were often truly extraordinary. It is a shame that, while the brilliance of the Brazilian in the eighties and nineties has been captured for posterity, such were the times that the magnificence of Jimmy's career went largely unrecorded on moving film. Indeed interviews are also exceedingly rare, and thus those too young to have seen him race will sadly have to make do with very much second best by way of the written word.

CLARK, Jim (GB) b 4/3/1936 – d 7/4/1968

1960

	Race	Circuit	No	Entrant	Car/Engine	Comment
ret	DUTCH GP	Zandvoort	6	Team Lotus	2.5 Lotus 18-Climax 4	transmission
5	BELGIAN GP	Spa	18	Team Lotus	2.5 Lotus 18-Climax 4	2 laps behind
5	FRENCH GP	Reims	24	Team Lotus	2.5 Lotus 18-Climax 4	1 lap behind
16	BRITISH GP	Silverstone	8	Team Lotus	2.5 Lotus 18-Climax 4	pit stop-suspension/7 laps behind
3	PORTUGUESE GP	Oporto	14	Team Lotus	2.5 Lotus 18-Climax 4	
16	US GP	Riverside	12	Team Lotus	2.5 Lotus 18-Climax 4	hit Surtees-pit stop/14 laps behind

1961

	Race	Circuit	No	Entrant	Car/Engine	Comment
10	MONACO GP	Monte Carlo	28	Team Lotus	1.5 Lotus 21-Climax 4	2 pit stops-plugs/11 laps behind
3	DUTCH GP	Zandvoort	15	Team Lotus	1.5 Lotus 21-Climax 4	FL
12	BELGIAN GP	Spa	34	Team Lotus	1.5 Lotus 21-Climax 4	2 p stops-gear change/6 laps behind
3	FRENCH GP	Reims	8	Team Lotus	1.5 Lotus 21-Climax 4	
ret	BRITISH GP	Aintree	18	Team Lotus	1.5 Lotus 21-Climax 4	oil leak
4	GERMAN GP	Nürburgring	14	Team Lotus	1.5 Lotus 21-Climax 4	
ret	ITALIAN GP	Monza	36	Team Lotus	1.5 Lotus 21-Climax 4	collision with von Trips
7	US GP	Watkins Glen	14	Team Lotus	1.5 Lotus 21-Climax 4	pit stop-clutch/14 laps behind

1962

	Race	Circuit	No	Entrant	Car/Engine	Comment
9	DUTCH GP	Zandvoort	4	Team Lotus	1.5 Lotus 25-Climax V8	pit stop-clutch/10 laps behind
dns	"	"	4	Team Lotus	1.5 Lotus 24-Climax V8	practice only
ret	MONACO GP	Monte Carlo	18	Team Lotus	1.5 Lotus 24-Climax V8	clutch/Pole/FL
dns	"	" "	18	Team Lotus	1.5 Lotus 24-Climax V8	practice only
1	BELGIAN GP	Spa	16	Team Lotus	1.5 Lotus 25-Climax V8	FL
dns	"	"	16	Team Lotus	1.5 Lotus 24-Climax V8	practice only
ret	FRENCH GP	Rouen	12	Team Lotus	1.5 Lotus 25-Climax V8	suspension/Pole
dns	"	"	12	Team Lotus	1.5 Lotus 24-Climax V8	practice only
1	BRITISH GP	Aintree	20	Team Lotus	1.5 Lotus 25-Climax V8	Pole/FL
dns	"	"	20	Team Lotus	1.5 Lotus 24-Climax V8	practice only
4	GERMAN GP	Nürburgring	5	Team Lotus	1.5 Lotus 25-Climax V8	stalled on grid-last away
ret	ITALIAN GP	Monza	20	Team Lotus	1.5 Lotus 25-Climax V8	transmission/Pole
1	US GP	Watkins Glen	8	Team Lotus	1.5 Lotus 25-Climax V8	Pole/FL
ret	SOUTH AFRICAN GP	East London	1	Team Lotus	1.5 Lotus 25-Climax V8	oil leak/Pole/FL

1963 World Champion Driver

	Race	Circuit	No	Entrant	Car/Engine	Comment
8/ret	MONACO GP	Monte Carlo	9	Team Lotus	1.5 Lotus 25-Climax V8	gear selection/Pole/22 laps behind
1	BELGIAN GP	Spa	1	Team Lotus	1.5 Lotus 25-Climax V8	FL
1	DUTCH GP	Zandvoort	6	Team Lotus	1.5 Lotus 25-Climax V8	Pole/FL
1	FRENCH GP	Reims	18	Team Lotus	1.5 Lotus 25-Climax V8	Pole/FL
dns	"	"	22	Team Lotus	1.5 Lotus 24-Climax V8	practice only
1	BRITISH GP	Silverstone	4	Team Lotus	1.5 Lotus 25-Climax V8	Pole
2	GERMAN GP	Nürburgring	3	Team Lotus	1.5 Lotus 25-Climax V8	engine on 7 cylinders/Pole
1	ITALIAN GP	Monza	8	Team Lotus	1.5 Lotus 25-Climax V8	FL
3	US GP	Watkins Glen	8	Team Lotus	1.5 Lotus 25-Climax V8	left on the grid-battery/1 lap behind/FL
1	MEXICAN GP	Mexico City	8	Team Lotus	1.5 Lotus 25-Climax V8	Pole/FL
1	SOUTH AFRICAN GP	East London	1	Team Lotus	1.5 Lotus 25-Climax V8	Pole

1964

	Race	Circuit	No	Entrant	Car/Engine	Comment
4/ret	MONACO GP	Monte Carlo	12	Team Lotus	1.5 Lotus 25-Climax V8	engine/Pole/4 laps behind
1	DUTCH GP	Zandvoort	18	Team Lotus	1.5 Lotus 25-Climax V8	FL
1	BELGIAN GP	Spa	23	Team Lotus	1.5 Lotus 25-Climax V8	
dns	"	"	2	Team Lotus	1.5 Lotus 33-Climax V8	practice only
ret	FRENCH GP	Rouen	2	Team Lotus	1.5 Lotus 25-Climax V8	engine/Pole
dns	"	"	2	Team Lotus	1.5 Lotus 33-Climax V8	practice only
1	BRITISH GP	Brands Hatch	1	Team Lotus	1.5 Lotus 25-Climax V8	Pole/FL
dns	"	" "	1	Team Lotus	1.5 Lotus 33-Climax V8	practice only
ret	GERMAN GP	Nürburgring	1	Team Lotus	1.5 Lotus 33-Climax V8	engine
ret	AUSTRIAN GP	Zeltweg	1	Team Lotus	1.5 Lotus 33-Climax V8	driveshaft
ret	ITALIAN GP	Monza	8	Team Lotus	1.5 Lotus 33-Climax V8	engine
dns	"	"	8	Team Lotus	1.5 Lotus 33-Climax V8	practice only
ret	US GP	Watkins Glen	1	Team Lotus	1.5 Lotus 25-Climax V8	fuel injection/Spence took car/Pole
7/ret	"	" "	2	Team Lotus	1.5 Lotus 33-Climax V8	fuel starvation/Spence's car/FL
5/ret	MEXICAN GP	Mexico City	1	Team Lotus	1.5 Lotus 33-Climax V8	engine-oil leak/Pole/FL/-1 lap
dns	"	" "	1	Team Lotus	1.5 Lotus 25-Climax V8	practice only

1965 World Champion Driver

	Race	Circuit	No	Entrant	Car/Engine	Comment
1	SOUTH AFRICAN GP	East London	5	Team Lotus	1.5 Lotus 33-Climax V8	Pole/FL
1	BELGIAN GP	Spa	17	Team Lotus	1.5 Lotus 33-Climax V8	FL
dns	"	"	17	Team Lotus	1.5 Lotus 25-Climax V8	practice only
1	FRENCH GP	Clermont Ferrand	6	Team Lotus	1.5 Lotus 25-Climax V8	Pole/FL
dns	"	" "	6	Team Lotus	1.5 Lotus 33-Climax V8	practice only
1	BRITISH GP	Silverstone	5	Team Lotus	1.5 Lotus 33-Climax V8	Pole
dns	"	"	77	Team Lotus	1.5 Lotus 25-Climax V8	practice only
1	DUTCH GP	Zandvoort	6	Team Lotus	1.5 Lotus 33-Climax V8	FL
1	GERMAN GP	Nürburgring	1	Team Lotus	1.5 Lotus 33-Climax V8	Pole/FL
10/ret	ITALIAN GP	Monza	24	Team Lotus	1.5 Lotus 33-Climax V8	fuel pump/Pole/FL/12 laps behind
dns	"	"	28	Team Lotus	1.5 Lotus 25-Climax V8	practice only
ret	US GP	Watkins Glen	5	Team Lotus	1.5 Lotus 33-Climax V8	engine
dns	"	" "	6	Team Lotus	1.5 Lotus 25-Climax V8	practice only
ret	MEXICAN GP	Mexico City	5	Team Lotus	1.5 Lotus 33-Climax V8	engine/Pole

1966

	Race	Circuit	No	Entrant	Car/Engine	Comment
ret	MONACO GP	Monte Carlo	4	Team Lotus	2.0 Lotus 33-Climax V8	suspension/Pole
ret	BELGIAN GP	Spa	10	Team Lotus	2.1 Lotus 33-Climax V8	engine

dns	FRENCH GP	Reims	2	Team Lotus	2.0 Lotus 33-Climax V8	hit in face by bird in practice
4	BRITISH GP	Brands Hatch	1	Team Lotus	2.0 Lotus 33-Climax V8	pit stop-brakes/1 lap behind
3	DUTCH GP	Zandvoort	6	Team Lotus	2.0 Lotus 33-Climax V8	2 pit stops-water/2 laps behind
dns	"	"	8	Team Lotus	2.0 Lotus 33-BRM V8	practice only
ret	GERMAN GP	Nürburgring	1	Team Lotus	2.0 Lotus 33-Climax V8	slid off road/Pole
ret	ITALIAN GP	Monza	20	Team Lotus	3.0 Lotus 43-BRM H16	gearbox
1	US GP	Watkins Glen	1	Team Lotus	3.0 Lotus 43-BRM H16	
dns	"	" "	1/2	Team Lotus	2.0 Lotus 33-Climax V8	practice only
ret	MEXICAN GP	Mexico City	1	Team Lotus	3.0 Lotus 43-BRM H16	gearbox

1967

ret	SOUTH AFRICAN GP	Kyalami	7	Team Lotus	3.0 Lotus 43-BRM H16	engine
ret	MONACO GP	Monte Carlo	12	Team Lotus	2.0 Lotus 33-Climax V8	shock absorber/FL
1	DUTCH GP	Zandvoort	5	Team Lotus	3.0 Lotus 49-Cosworth V8	FL
6	BELGIAN GP	Spa	21	Team Lotus	3.0 Lotus 49-Cosworth V8	pit stop-plugs/Pole/1 lap behind
ret	FRENCH GP	Le Mans	6	Team Lotus	3.0 Lotus 49-Cosworth V8	cwp
1	BRITISH GP	Silverstone	5	Team Lotus	3.0 Lotus 49-Cosworth V8	Pole
ret	GERMAN GP	Nürburgring	3	Team Lotus	3.0 Lotus 49-Cosworth V8	suspension/Pole
ret	CANADIAN GP	Mosport Park	3	Team Lotus	3.0 Lotus 49-Cosworth V8	wet ignition/Pole/FL
3	ITALIAN GP	Monza	20	Team Lotus	3.0 Lotus 49-Cosworth V8	out of fuel last lap when 1st/Pole/FL
1	US GP	Watkins Glen	5	Team Lotus	3.0 Lotus 49-Cosworth V8	despite rear suspension failure
1	MEXICAN GP	Mexico City	5	Team Lotus	3.0 Lotus 49-Cosworth V8	Pole/FL

1968

1	SOUTH AFRICAN GP	Kyalami	4	Team Lotus	3.0 Lotus 49-Cosworth V8	Pole/FL

GP Starts: 72   GP Wins: 25   Pole positions: 33   Fastest laps: 28   Points: 274

COLLINS, Peter (GB) b 8/11/1931 – d 3/8/1958

1952

	Race	Circuit	No	Entrant	Car/Engine	Comment
ret	SWISS GP	Bremgarten	18	HW Motors Ltd	2.0 HWM-Alta 4	halfshaft-spun off
ret	BELGIAN GP	Spa	26	HW Motors Ltd	2.0 HWM-Alta 4	driveshaft
6	FRENCH GP	Rouen	22	HW Motors Ltd	2.0 HWM-Alta 4	6 laps behind
ret	BRITISH GP	Silverstone	29	HW Motors Ltd	2.0 HWM-Alta 4	ignition/crankshaft
dnq	GERMAN GP	Nürburgring	111	HW Motors Ltd	2.0 HWM-Alta 4	insufficient practice laps
dnq	ITALIAN GP	Monza	54	HW Motors Ltd	2.0 HWM-Alta 4	

1953

8	DUTCH GP	Zandvoort	36	HW Motors Ltd	2.0 HWM-Alta 4	6 laps behind
ret	BELGIAN GP	Spa	26	HW Motors Ltd	2.0 HWM-Alta 4	clutch
nc	FRENCH GP	Reims	28	HW Motors Ltd	2.0 HWM-Alta 4	8 laps behind
ret	BRITISH GP	Silverstone	2	HW Motors Ltd	2.0 HWM-Alta 4	spun off

1954

ret	BRITISH GP	Silverstone	20	G A Vandervell	2.3 Vanwall 4	cylinder head gasket
7	ITALIAN GP	Monza	10	G A Vandervell	2.4 Vanwall 4	5 laps behind
dns	SPANISH GP	Pedralbes	42	G A Vandervell	2.4 Vanwall 4	practice accident

1955

ret	BRITISH GP	Aintree	42	Owen Racing Organisation	2.5 Maserati 250F 6	clutch
ret	ITALIAN GP	Monza	32	Officine Alfieri Maserati	2.5 Maserati 250F 6	rear suspension

1956

ret	ARGENTINE GP	Buenos Aires	36	Scuderia Ferrari	2.5 Lancia-Ferrari D50 V8	collision with Piotti
2*	MONACO GP	Monte Carlo	26	Scuderia Ferrari	2.5 Lancia-Ferrari D50 V8	* Fangio took over
1	BELGIAN GP	Spa	8	Scuderia Ferrari	2.5 Lancia-Ferrari D50 V8	
1	FRENCH GP	Reims	14	Scuderia Ferrari	2.5 Lancia-Ferrari D50 V8	†Pole-though Fangio set faster time
ret	BRITISH GP	Silverstone	2	Scuderia Ferrari	2.5 Lancia-Ferrari D50 V8	oil pressure
2*	"	"	4	Scuderia Ferrari	2.5 Lancia-Ferrari D50 V8	* took de Portago's car/-1 lap
ret	GERMAN GP	Nürburgring	2	Scuderia Ferrari	2.5 Lancia-Ferrari D50 V8	split fuel pipe
ret*	"	"	5	Scuderia Ferrari	2.5 Lancia-Ferrari D50 V8	* took de Portago's car/accident
2*	ITALIAN GP	Monza	26	Scuderia Ferrari	2.5 Lancia-Ferrari D50 V8	* Fangio took over

1957

ret	ARGENTINE GP	Buenos Aires	10	Scuderia Ferrari	2.5 Lancia-Ferrari D50 V8	clutch
6*	"	"	18	Scuderia Ferrari	2.5 Lancia-Ferrari D50 V8	* Perdisa & von Trips/2 laps behind
ret	MONACO GP	Monte Carlo	26	Scuderia Ferrari	2.5 Lancia-Ferrari D50 V8	accident with Moss & Hawthorn
dns	"	" "	26	Scuderia Ferrari	2.5 Lancia-Ferrari 801 V8	practice only
3	FRENCH GP	Rouen	12	Scuderia Ferrari	2.5 Lancia-Ferrari 801 V8	
ret	BRITISH GP	Aintree	12	Scuderia Ferrari	2.5 Lancia-Ferrari 801 V8	water leak-took Trintignant's car
4*	"	"	16	Scuderia Ferrari	2.5 Lancia-Ferrari 801 V8	*only 4 laps-no points awarded
3	GERMAN GP	Nürburgring	7	Scuderia Ferrari	2.5 Lancia-Ferrari 801 V8	
ret	ITALIAN GP	Monza	30	Scuderia Ferrari	2.5 Lancia-Ferrari 801 V8	engine

1958

ret	ARGENTINE GP	Buenos Aires	18	Scuderia Ferrari	2.4 Ferrari Dino 246 V6	rear axle on grid
3	MONACO GP	Monte Carlo	36	Scuderia Ferrari	2.4 Ferrari Dino 246 V6	
ret	DUTCH GP	Zandvoort	4	Scuderia Ferrari	2.4 Ferrari Dino 246 V6	gearbox seized-spun off
ret	BELGIAN GP	Spa	14	Scuderia Ferrari	2.4 Ferrari Dino 246 V6	overheating
5	FRENCH GP	Reims	42	Scuderia Ferrari	2.4 Ferrari Dino 246 V6	out of fuel last lap
1	BRITISH GP	Silverstone	1	Scuderia Ferrari	2.4 Ferrari Dino 246 V6	
ret	GERMAN GP	Nürburgring	2	Scuderia Ferrari	2.4 Ferrari Dino 246 V6	fatal accident

GP Starts: 32   GP Wins: 3   Pole positions: 1†   Fastest laps: 0   Points: 47

PETER COLLINS

Peter Collins' death at the Nürburgring in August 1958, just two weeks after his wonderful performance at the British Grand Prix at Silverstone, left the racing world shocked. For although he was indisputably one of the fastest men around, he was also regarded as being one of the safest.

Handsome and congenial, the young Collins graduated from the 500 cc school, driving Coopers and then the JBS-Norton in 1951, both on the circuits and in hill-climbs, winning his class with BTD at Prescott and Shelsley Walsh.

With Formula 2 effectively becoming the premier formula in 1952, John Heath of HWM signed the promising Collins to partner Moss and Macklin in a three-car team which roamed the Continent over the next two seasons. Peter proved to be extremely quick, but the cars were fragile and decent finishes were few and far between, though he managed a second place at Les Sables d'Olonne in 1952 and a third at the Eifelrennen the following year.

Collins' potential had been spotted by Aston Martin, who took him into their sports car squad with immediate results. Sharing a DB3 with Pat Griffiths, he won the 1952 BARC Goodwood 9 Hours and the 1953 Tourist Trophy, and he achieved many other good results (including second places at Le Mans in 1955 with Frère and in 1956 with Moss) in what was to be a very happy association with the team.

In 1954 Peter was recruited by Tony Vandervell to drive his Ferrari 'Thinwall Special', with which he was to delight British crowds in the popular Libre events of the day, winning at Snetterton and Goodwood. He was also one of the first to handle the new Vanwall special, but at this stage it was still very much in its infancy. Having found him a constant thorn in their flesh in Libre racing, BRM signed him for a full season in 1955, but in the event their programme was behind schedule, and he mainly raced the Owen team's Maserati 250F until the P25 was ready. Late in the year Collins ran the new car in the Gold Cup at Oulton Park where it proved staggeringly quick before he retired it, erroneously as it turned out, due to a lack of oil pressure.

Peter accepted the chance to join Ferrari in 1956 alongside the great Fangio with glee, and 'the Maestro' was to have a big influence on his racing. From then on he began to take a much more serious attitude to his craft, though thankfully he never lost his fun-loving, light-hearted spirit off the track. For a new boy at the Scuderia, he settled in very quickly. After handing his machine to Fangio at Monaco, Collins took Grand Prix wins in Belgium and France and then shared second place at Silverstone. Although he drew a blank at the Nürburgring, come the Italian GP at Monza he still had an outside chance of the championship. When Fangio was forced to retire his car early in the race, Peter was asked to hand his car over to the Argentinian at a pit stop and did so without hesitation, even though it meant the end of his own title bid. His actions were particularly appreciated by Enzo Ferrari, who had a special affection for the loyal Englishman from that moment on. However, the 1957 season was not one of the Scuderia's better ones, and Peter scored Formula 1 wins only in the relatively minor Syracuse and Naples Grands Prix, and third places in France and Germany, where Fangio put on such an unforgettable display.

The following season began promisingly for Collins with sports car victories in the Buenos Aires 1000 Km and the Sebring 12 Hours, driving with Phil Hill. Peter had already raced the new Ferrari Dino 246 at the tail-end of the previous year, finishing fourth in the Modena GP, and a win in the International Trophy race at Silverstone boded well for a Ferrari revival. Arriving at the Nürburgring for the German Grand Prix, Peter lay third in the championship standings behind Mike Hawthorn and Stirling Moss, but in the race, with Tony Brooks leading in the Vanwall and Peter in hot pursuit, it seems he made a simple but costly error of judgement, clipping a bank, which somer-saulted the car at over 100 mph over a hedge and down into a field. The luckless Collins was hurled from his machine, suffering severe head injuries from which he died soon after in hospital in Bonn, without regaining consciousness.

COLLOMB, Bernard (F) b 7/10/1930

1961

	Race	Circuit	No	Entrant	Car/Engine	Comment
ret	FRENCH GP	Reims	52	Bernard Collomb	1.5 Cooper T53-Climax 4	valve
nc	GERMAN GP	Nürburgring	38	Bernard Collomb	1.5 Cooper T53-Climax 4	4 laps behind

1962

	Race	Circuit	No	Entrant	Car/Engine	Comment
ret	GERMAN GP	Nürburgring	31	Bernard Collomb	1.5 Cooper T53-Climax 4	gearbox

1963

	Race	Circuit	No	Entrant	Car/Engine	Comment
dnq	MONACO GP	Monte Carlo	24	Bernard Collomb	1.5 Lotus 24-Climax V8	
10	GERMAN GP	Nürburgring	28	Bernard Collomb	1.5 Lotus 24-Climax V8	5 laps behind

1964

	Race	Circuit	No	Entrant	Car/Engine	Comment
dnq	MONACO GP	Monte Carlo	3	Bernard Collomb	1.5 Lotus 24-Climax V8	

GP Starts: 4   GP Wins: 0   Pole positions: 0   Fastest laps: 0   Points: 0

COMAS, Erik (F) b 28/9/1963

1991

	Race	Circuit	No	Entrant	Car/Engine	Comment
dnq	US GP (PHOENIX)	Phoenix	26	Ligier Gitanes	3.5 Ligier JS35-Lamborghini V12	
ret	BRAZILIAN GP	Interlagos	26	Ligier Gitanes	3.5 Ligier JS35-Lamborghini V12	spun off
10	SAN MARINO GP	Imola	26	Ligier Gitanes	3.5 Ligier JS35-Lamborghini V12	4 laps behind
10	MONACO GP	Monte Carlo	26	Ligier Gitanes	3.5 Ligier JS35-Lamborghini V12	2 laps behind
8	CANADIAN GP	Montreal	26	Ligier Gitanes	3.5 Ligier JS35-Lamborghini V12	1 lap behind
dnq	MEXICAN GP	Mexico City	26	Ligier Gitanes	3.5 Ligier JS35-Lamborghini V12	
11	FRENCH GP	Magny Cours	26	Ligier Gitanes	3.5 Ligier JS35B-Lamborghini V12	2 laps behind
dnq	BRITISH GP	Silverstone	26	Ligier Gitanes	3.5 Ligier JS35B-Lamborghini V12	
ret	GERMAN GP	Hockenheim	26	Ligier Gitanes	3.5 Ligier JS35B-Lamborghini V12	engine-oil pressure
10	HUNGARIAN GP	Hungaroring	26	Ligier Gitanes	3.5 Ligier JS35B-Lamborghini V12	2 laps behind
ret	BELGIAN GP	Spa	26	Ligier Gitanes	3.5 Ligier JS35B-Lamborghini V12	engine
11	ITALIAN GP	Monza	26	Ligier Gitanes	3.5 Ligier JS35B-Lamborghini V12	1 lap behind
11	PORTUGUESE GP	Estoril	26	Ligier Gitanes	3.5 Ligier JS35B-Lamborghini V12	1 lap behind
ret	SPANISH GP	Barcelona	26	Ligier Gitanes	3.5 Ligier JS35B-Lamborghini V12	electrics
ret	JAPANESE GP	Suzuka	26	Ligier Gitanes	3.5 Ligier JS35B-Lamborghini V12	alternator
18	AUSTRALIAN GP	Adelaide	26	Ligier Gitanes	3.5 Ligier JS35B-Lamborghini V12	rain shortened race/1 lap behind

1992

	Race	Circuit	No	Entrant	Car/Engine	Comment
9	SOUTH AFRICAN GP	Kyalami	26	Ligier Gitanes Blondes	3.5 Ligier JS37-Renault V10	lack of downforce/2 laps behind
ret	MEXICAN GP	Mexico City	26	Ligier Gitanes Blondes	3.5 Ligier JS37-Renault V10	engine
ret	BRAZILIAN GP	Interlagos	26	Ligier Gitanes Blondes	3.5 Ligier JS37-Renault V10	engine
ret	SPANISH GP	Barcelona	26	Ligier Gitanes Blondes	3.5 Ligier JS37-Renault V10	spun off
9	SAN MARINO GP	Imola	26	Ligier Gitanes Blondes	3.5 Ligier JS37-Renault V10	2 laps behind
10	MONACO GP	Monte Carlo	26	Ligier Gitanes Blondes	3.5 Ligier JS37-Renault V10	2 laps behind
6	CANADIAN GP	Montreal	26	Ligier Gitanes Blondes	3.5 Ligier JS37-Renault V10	1 lap behind
5	FRENCH GP	Magny Cours	26	Ligier Gitanes Blondes	3.5 Ligier JS37-Renault V10	1 lap behind
8	BRITISH GP	Silverstone	26	Ligier Gitanes Blondes	3.5 Ligier JS37-Renault V10	1 lap behind
6	GERMAN GP	Hockenheim	26	Ligier Gitanes Blondes	3.5 Ligier JS37-Renault V10	
ret	HUNGARIAN GP	Hungaroring	26	Ligier Gitanes Blondes	3.5 Ligier JS37-Renault V10	collision with Boutsen lap 1
dnp	BELGIAN GP	Spa	26	Ligier Gitanes Blondes	3.5 Ligier JS37-Renault V10	accident in untimed practice
ret	ITALIAN GP	Monza	26	Ligier Gitanes Blondes	3.5 Ligier JS37-Renault V10	spun off
ret	PORTUGUESE GP	Estoril	26	Ligier Gitanes Blondes	3.5 Ligier JS37-Renault V10	over-revved engine
ret	JAPANESE GP	Suzuka	26	Ligier Gitanes Blondes	3.5 Ligier JS37-Renault V10	engine
ret	AUSTRALIAN GP	Adelaide	26	Ligier Gitanes Blondes	3.5 Ligier JS37-Renault V10	over-revved engine

1993

	Race	Circuit	No	Entrant	Car/Engine	Comment
ret	SOUTH AFRICAN GP	Kyalami	20	Larrousse F1	3.5 Larrousse LH93-Lamborghini V12	engine
10	BRAZILIAN GP	Interlagos	20	Larrousse F1	3.5 Larrousse LH93-Lamborghini V12	stop & go pen/engine/2 laps behind
9	EUROPEAN GP	Donington	20	Larrousse F1	3.5 Larrousse LH93-Lamborghini V12	4 laps behind
ret	SAN MARINO GP	Imola	20	Larrousse F1	3.5 Larrousse LH93-Lamborghini V12	no oil pressure
9	SPANISH GP	Barcelona	20	Larrousse F1	3.5 Larrousse LH93-Lamborghini V12	2 laps behind
ret	MONACO GP	Monte Carlo	20	Larrousse F1	3.5 Larrousse LH93-Lamborghini V12	collision with Brundle
8	CANADIAN GP	Montreal	20	Larrousse F1	3.5 Larrousse LH93-Lamborghini V12	1 lap behind
16/ret	FRENCH GP	Magny Cours	20	Larrousse F1	3.5 Larrousse LH93-Lamborghini V12	gearbox/6 laps behind
ret	BRITISH GP	Silverstone	20	Larrousse F1	3.5 Larrousse LH93-Lamborghini V12	driveshaft at start
ret	GERMAN GP	Hockenheim	20	Larrousse F1	3.5 Larrousse LH93-Lamborghini V12	clutch at start
ret	HUNGARIAN GP	Hungaroring	20	Larrousse F1	3.5 Larrousse LH93-Lamborghini V12	oil leak
ret	BELGIAN GP	Spa	20	Larrousse F1	3.5 Larrousse LH93-Lamborghini V12	engine-oil pressure
6	ITALIAN GP	Monza	20	Larrousse F1	3.5 Larrousse LH93-Lamborghini V12	2 laps behind
11	PORTUGUESE GP	Estoril	20	Larrousse F1	3.5 Larrousse LH93-Lamborghini V12	3 laps behind
ret	JAPANESE GP	Suzuka	20	Larrousse F1	3.5 Larrousse LH93-Lamborghini V12	engine
12	AUSTRALIAN GP	Adelaide	20	Larrousse F1	3.5 Larrousse LH93-Lamborghini V12	3 laps behind

GP Starts: 44   GP Wins: 0   Pole positions: 0   Fastest laps: 0   Points: 5

COMOTTI, Gianfranco (I) b 24/7/1906 – d 10/5/1963

1950

	Race	Circuit	No	Entrant	Car/Engine	Comment
ret	ITALIAN GP	Monza	62	Scuderia Milano	1.5 s/c Maserati 4CLT/50-Speluzzi 4	

1952

	Race	Circuit	No	Entrant	Car/Engine	Comment
nc	FRENCH GP	Rouen	38	Scuderia Marzotto	2.0 Ferrari 166 V12	13 laps behind

GP Starts: 2   GP Wins: 0   Pole positions: 0   Fastest laps: 0   Points: 0

BERNARD COLLOMB

A former motor cycle racer from Nice, Collomb acquired a Cooper-Climax Formula 2 car which he raced briefly in 1960, embarking on a more ambitious programme of F1 races the following year. Fourth at Vienna and sixth at Naples were his best results in the car, which was replaced in mid-season by a new Cooper T53 with no discernible improvement in his results. Unfortunately this car was burnt out in practice for the 1962 Brussels GP, but Bernard reappeared in mid-1962 with another Cooper, achieving fifth place in the Mediterranean GP at Enna.

Collomb then bought himself a Lotus 24-Climax V8 for 1963, but he was ill-equipped to drive it to its full potential. It was given occasional unsuccessful outings in 1964 before being destroyed by fire on the way back to France from the 1965 Syracuse GP, where he had finished seventh. A Lotus 35 F2 car was then purchased which again saw little action after Collomb crashed it in the 1966 Barcelona F2 race. By the 1968 season he had wisely given up thoughts of success in single-seaters and could be found racing the little Alpine GT car.

ERIK COMAS

With Jean Alesi and Eric Bernard, Comas is one of a trio of French drivers whose careers have been closely intertwined asthey have made inexorable progress into Formula 1 along the French motor racing conveyor-belt.

A French karting champion in 1983, Erik was soon sampling cars, racing a Renault 5 previously driven by Alesi, with which he won the Volant Elf at Paul Ricard, then moving up to Formule Renault as number two to Bernard in 1985. Scoring consistently, he finished second on points to his team-mate but only fourth overall after his lowest scores had been discounted, but he made no mistake a year later.

This led to a seat in the Winfield team in the national Formula 3 series in 1987, but Comas found himself as number two to Bernard once more and was somewhat overshadowed, though he did finish sixth in the final placings. Erik also took the chance to compete in the French Superproduction category, and immensely enjoyed pitting himself against old hands such as Jabouille and Jarier in the powerful 400 bhp machines.

For 1988, he was chosen to lead the ORECA team, normally an absolute guarantee of success in French F3. Comas delivered, but only just, pipping Eric Cheli to the title after a fraught season spent developing the team's Dallara. However, the job was done and once again he followed Bernard on the upward path, joining him in the DAMS F3000 team for the 1989 season. After a slow start, Comas soon shone and by the season's end it was his turn to outshine his team-mate. Two wins at Le Mans and Dijon brought him level with Alesi at the top of the points standings, but Jean was champion by virtue of an extra win. Erik finished the job in 1990; still with DAMS, but now number one driver, he won four of the 11 rounds, and now he was ready for Formula 1.

On paper, a two-year contract with Ligier alongside the experienced Thierry Boutsen seemed to be ideal. The first season with the Lamborghini-engined car would allow Erik a chance to learn the ropes and the second, 1992, with Renault power, would put him in the front rank. The best-laid plans do not always work out, however, and with the team already split into factions, any potential assets it held had been dissipated, while Erik's working relationship with Boutsen was such that they were barely on speaking terms.

For the 1993 season he found refuge in the Larrousse team, making the best of a car run on very meagre resources. His sixth place at Monza was a fine achievement, but with the shortage of top seats in Formula 1 and a whole new generation of chargers knocking on the door, one wonders if Comas has missed his big chance to make it to the very top.

CONSTANTINE, George (USA) b 22/2/1918

1959

	Race	Circuit	No	Entrant	Car/Engine	Comment
ret	US GP	Sebring	16	Mike Taylor	2.5 Cooper T45-Climax 4	head gasket

GP Starts: 1   GP Wins: 0   Pole positions: 0   Fastest laps: 0   Points: 0

CORDTS, John (CDN) b 23/7/1935

1969

	Race	Circuit	No	Entrant	Car/Engine	Comment
ret	CANADIAN GP	Mosport Park	26	Paul Seitz	2.7 Brabham BT23B-Climax 4	oil leak

GP Starts: 1   GP Wins: 0   Pole positions: 0   Fastest laps: 0   Points: 0

COURAGE, Piers (GB) b 27/5/1942 – d 21/6/1970

1966

	Race	Circuit	No	Entrant	Car/Engine	Comment
ret	GERMAN GP (F2)	Nürburgring	32	Ron Harris-Team Lotus	1.0 Lotus 44-Cosworth 4	crashed

1967

	Race	Circuit	No	Entrant	Car/Engine	Comment
ret	SOUTH AFRICAN GP	Kyalami	16	Reg Parnell Racing Ltd	2.0 Lotus 25-BRM V8	oil pipe-engine
ret	MONACO GP	Monte Carlo	6	Reg Parnell Racing Ltd	2.1 BRM P261 V8	spun off-stalled
dns	BRITISH GP	Silverstone	6	Reg Parnell Racing Ltd	2.1 BRM P261 V8	Irwin drove car in race

1968

	Race	Circuit	No	Entrant	Car/Engine	Comment
ret	SPANISH GP	Jarama	5	Reg Parnell Racing Ltd	3.0 BRM P126 V12	fuel metering unit
ret	MONACO GP	Monte Carlo	16	Reg Parnell Racing Ltd	3.0 BRM P126 V12	rear sub-frame fracture
ret	BELGIAN GP	Spa	14	Reg Parnell Racing Ltd	3.0 BRM P126 V12	engine
ret	DUTCH GP	Zandvoort	20	Reg Parnell Racing Ltd	3.0 BRM P126 V12	accident
6	FRENCH GP	Rouen	36	Reg Parnell Racing Ltd	3.0 BRM P126 V12	pit stop-tyres/3 laps behind
8	BRITISH GP	Brands Hatch	20	Reg Parnell Racing Ltd	3.0 BRM P126 V12	pit stops-misfire/8 laps behind
8	GERMAN GP	Nürburgring	22	Reg Parnell Racing Ltd	3.0 BRM P126 V12	
4	ITALIAN GP	Monza	27	Reg Parnell Racing Ltd	3.0 BRM P126 V12	1 lap behind
ret	CANADIAN GP	St Jovite	24	Reg Parnell Racing Ltd	3.0 BRM P126 V12	transmission
7/ret	US GP	Watkins Glen	22	Reg Parnell Racing Ltd	3.0 BRM P126 V12	broken suspension bolt/-10 laps
ret	MEXICAN GP	Mexico City	22	Reg Parnell Racing Ltd	3.0 BRM P126 V12	overheating

1969

	Race	Circuit	No	Entrant	Car/Engine	Comment
ret	SPANISH GP	Montjuich Park	11	Frank Williams Racing Cars	3.0 Brabham BT26A-Cosworth V8	engine-valve spring
2	MONACO GP	Monte Carlo	16	Frank Williams Racing Cars	3.0 Brabham BT26A-Cosworth V8	
ret	DUTCH GP	Zandvoort	16	Frank Williams Racing Cars	3.0 Brabham BT26A-Cosworth V8	clutch
ret	FRENCH GP	Clermont Ferrand	9	Frank Williams Racing Cars	3.0 Brabham BT26A-Cosworth V8	nose cone mounting
5	BRITISH GP	Silverstone	16	Frank Williams Racing Cars	3.0 Brabham BT26A-Cosworth V8	1 lap behind
ret	GERMAN GP	Nürburgring	17	Frank Williams Racing Cars	3.0 Brabham BT26A-Cosworth V8	accident
5	ITALIAN GP	Monza	32	Frank Williams Racing Cars	3.0 Brabham BT26A-Cosworth V8	low fuel pressure
ret	CANADIAN GP	Mosport Park	21	Frank Williams Racing Cars	3.0 Brabham BT26A-Cosworth V8	fuel leak
2	US GP	Watkins Glen	18	Frank Williams Racing Cars	3.0 Brabham BT26A-Cosworth V8	
10	MEXICAN GP	Mexico City	18	Frank Williams Racing Cars	3.0 Brabham BT26A-Cosworth V8	spin-pit stop/4 laps behind

1970

	Race	Circuit	No	Entrant	Car/Engine	Comment
ret	SOUTH AFRICAN GP	Kyalami	22	Frank Williams Racing Cars	3.0 de Tomaso 505-Cosworth V8	suspension
dns	SPANISH GP	Jarama	12	Frank Williams Racing Cars	3.0 de Tomaso 505-Cosworth V8	accident in practice
nc	MONACO GP	Monte Carlo	24	Frank Williams Racing Cars	3.0 de Tomaso 505-Cosworth V8	pit stop-steering box/22 laps behind
ret	BELGIAN GP	Spa	7	Frank Williams Racing Cars	3.0 de Tomaso 505-Cosworth V8	low oil pressure
ret	DUTCH GP	Zandvoort	4	Frank Williams Racing Cars	3.0 de Tomaso 505-Cosworth V8	fatal accident

GP Starts: 28   GP Wins: 0   Pole positions: 0   Fastest laps: 0   Points: 20

CRAFT, Chris (GB) b 17/11/1939

1971

	Race	Circuit	No	Entrant	Car/Engine	Comment
dns	CANADIAN GP	Mosport Park	26	Ecurie Evergreen	3.0 Brabham BT33-Cosworth V8	engine
ret	US GP	Watkins Glen	24	Ecurie Evergreen	3.0 Brabham BT33-Cosworth V8	chunking tyres/rear suspension

GP Starts: 1   GP Wins: 0   Pole positions: 0   Fastest laps: 0   Points: 0

CRAWFORD, Jim (GB) b 13/2/1948

1975

	Race	Circuit	No	Entrant	Car/Engine	Comment
ret	BRITISH GP	Silverstone	6	John Player Team Lotus	3.0 Lotus 72E-Cosworth V8	spun off in rain
13	ITALIAN GP	Monza	6	John Player Team Lotus	3.0 Lotus 72E-Cosworth V8	6 laps behind

GP Starts: 2   GP Wins: 0   Pole positions: 0   Fastest laps: 0   Points: 0

CREUS, Antonio (RA)

1960

	Race	Circuit	No	Entrant	Car/Engine	Comment
ret	ARGENTINE GP	Buenos Aires	12	Antonio Creus	2.5 Maserati 250F 6	electrics

GP Starts: 1   GP Wins: 0   Pole positions: 0   Fastest laps: 0   Points: 0

GEORGE CONSTANTINE

A very successful driver in SCCA events, Constantine drove his production Jaguar XK120 in east coast races in the early 1950s. He then progressed to more powerful machinery, winning the 1956 Watkins Glen GP in a Jaguar D-Type. The 1959 season was his most successful, Constantine scoring many wins in an Aston Martin DBR2, including the Nassau Trophy, to earn the USSC Driver of the Year award with Walt Hansgen. It was not surprising, therefore, that he was one of the local attractions in the inaugural US Grand Prix at Sebring in a rented Cooper. His career continued into the early sixties, the veteran finishing fifth (and winning his class) in the 1962 Daytona 3 Hours.

PIERS COURAGE

Piers was the eldest son of the chairman of the Courage brewery group, but any thoughts that these connections were an asset to his motor racing aspirations were mistaken. His initial racing experience was gained regularly gyrating the Lotus Seven funded by his father, but after that Piers was on his own as far as finance was concerned. He teamed up with old pal Jonathan Williams in 1964 and the pair terrorised the circuits of Europe, initially with a Lotus 22. Entered under the grandiose Anglo-Swiss Racing Team banner, in reality Courage and Williams lived the sort hand-to-mouth existence that most privateers had to endure, but third place at Reims and second at Zandvoort in a Brabham encouraged Piers to contest a full F3 season in 1965.

Charles Lucas entered a pair of Brabhams for Piers and Frank Williams, and it proved to be a very successful campaign for Courage, with four wins in major events at Silverstone, Goodwood, Caserta and Reims. This led to an invitation to race the Lotus 41 F3 car for 1966, and although it was inferior to the rival Brabhams Piers still managed a string of wins, earning a ride in Ron Harris's works F2 Lotus in the German GP, where he blotted his copybook by crashing.

BRM signed both Courage and Chris Irwin for 1967, the idea being to run them under the Tim Parnell banner, grooming them for a drive in the works team in the future. It all went sour for Piers very quickly, however, all his good work being repeatedly undone by silly spins. After the Monaco GP, Parnell stuck with Irwin, but Piers had to content himself with a season of Formula 2 in John Coombs' McLaren. His speed was not in doubt and some excellent drives netted him fourth place in the non-graded drivers' championship, but – and it was a big but – the disturbing tendency to crash remained, with major shunts at Pau, Enna and Brands Hatch. Coombs advised him to quit, but Piers was determined to continue.

Early in 1968 he bought the McLaren from Coombs and took it down-under to contest the Tasman series. Pitted against the Lotuses of Clark and Hill, Amon's Ferrari and McLaren's BRM in the seven-race series, Piers was second, fourth, fifth, third, third and fifth before the final round at Longford. In pouring rain Courage simply outdrove the opposition – Clark included – to win the race, but more importantly finally established his credibility.

Turning down an offer to replace the late Jim Clark at Lotus, Piers instead chose to race for Tim Parnell in Grands Prix while teaming up with his old pal Frank Williams in Formula 2, and so successful was their partnership that it was decided to enter F1 with a Brabham in 1969. Aside from a shunt at the Nürburgring, things could hardly have gone better, Courage driving superbly for the fledgling outfit to take second place at Monaco and Watkins Glen. He was also still racing in Formula 2, scoring a win at Enna and five third places, while an invitation to join the Matra team for Le Mans saw Piers take fourth place with Beltoise.

For 1970 Williams took the brave and possibly foolhardy step of running the newly constructed de Tomaso-Ford in place of the proven Brabham. The early part of the season was inconclusive with only a third place in the International Trophy to show for their efforts. Meanwhile Piers busied himself in a hectic schedule of endurance events for Alfa Romeo, highlighted by a win with de Adamich in the Buenos Aires 1000 Km. By the time of the Dutch GP at Zandvoort in June, progress seemed to have been made with the de Tomaso, which was placed ninth on the grid, but in the race tragedy struck when Courage slid wide, ran up a bank and crashed. The red car rolled over and burst into flames, and the unfortunate Piers stood no chance.

CHRIS CRAFT

Chris began racing in a Ford Anglia in 1962 and soon built a reputation as one of Britain's foremost saloon car drivers, particularly with the Team Broadspeed Escort (1968-70). After F3 with a Tecno, he moved into sports cars, driving a Chevron in 1968, teaming up with Alain de Cadenet to race his Porsche 908 and McLaren M8C. It was this association that led to Craft's brief flirtation with Formula 1. It was to be merely a punctuation mark in a massive volume, for Chris continued to race sports and F5000 machines in the early seventies, then returned successfully to saloons (1976-79) with a Ford Capri. His career, which ran into hundreds of races, stretched into the eighties with the Dome sports car project.

JIM CRAWFORD

Crawford began his racing career as a mechanic who proved to be quicker in the car than his young charge, and this led to an offer from Derek Bennett to drive a works Chevron late in 1973. Jim built up his own car for 1974, just losing the Formula Atlantic title to John Nicholson. His performances earned him a testing contract with Lotus and a couple of Grand Prix outings in 1975, when he was again runner-up in the Atlantic series.

An expected Formula 2 drive in 1976 did not materialise and Crawford's career stalled. He spent 1978 in F3 and '79 back in Atlantic, before finding a ride in the Aurora AFX F1/F2 series in 1980, winning the F2 class in a Chevron. After putting together a full season in F2 in 1981 without much success, Jim decided to try his luck in the USA. It was a wise move, which was to revive and extend his career firstly into Can-Am in 1983 and '84 and then into IndyCar racing. He finished sixth at Indianapolis in 1988 and, but for an accident in which he sustained serious leg and foot injuries, he may have found a full-time ride, rather than employment just in the month of May.

CROOK, Anthony (GB) b 16/2/1920

	1952					
	Race	Circuit	No	Entrant	Car/Engine	Comment
nc	BRITISH GP	Silverstone	23	T A D Crook	2.0 Frazer Nash 421-Bristol 6	10 laps behind
	1953					
ret	BRITISH GP	Silverstone	22	T A D Crook	2.0 Cooper T20-Bristol 6	fuel feed on start line

GP Starts: 2   GP Wins: 0   Pole positions: 0   Fastest laps: 0   Points: 0

CHUCK DAIGH

Having started racing in the mid-fifties, Daigh campaigned a modified Mercury-Kurtis special until 1958, when he became involved with Lance Reventlow's plans to build the powerful Chevrolet-engined Scarab sports car. This proved to be very successful, with Daigh winning the Governor's Cup (beating Hansgen's Lister) and the Nassau Trophy, and defeating Phil Hill's Ferrari at Riverside.

Ambitiously, a front-engined F1 car was then commissioned by Reventlow, but by the time it appeared in 1960 it had been rendered almost obsolete by the rear-engined Cooper and Lotus cars. Chuck struggled manfully against the odds but the car was withdrawn after just three races, reappearing only on home soil at season's end. Daigh meanwhile had the chance to try a proper F1 car at the British GP when he drove a third works Cooper. Amazingly the Scarab raced again, being wheeled out for the Inter-Continental Formula in 1961. Chuck finished seventh in the International Trophy race, but after he crashed in practice for the British Empire Trophy – suffering a cracked pelvis – the car was seen no more.

Fortunately Daigh was seen again, racing one of Jim Hall's early Chaparrals at Sebring in 1962, and tasted victory at Mosport in 1963 when he won the Player's 200 sports car race in a Lotus 19.

YANNICK DALMAS

French F3 in the mid-eighties must have been bewildering. Potential World Champions were two a penny, as the conveyor-belt churned out hot-shots one after another: the Ferté brothers, Grouillard, Raphanel, Alesi, Bernard, Trollé, Comas – and Dalmas.

The reigning French Formule Renault champion, Yannick took the number two seat to Raphanel in the all-conquering ORECA F3 team for 1985 and duly finished second in the championship. Next year it was his turn to lead the team and he won six of the 11 races, impressing all watchers with his flair and speed.

Moving up to F3000 for 1987, his machinery did not always work as well as one would expect, but when things were right he flew. Victories at Pau and in the final round at Jarama brought him into a slightly disappointing fifth place in the championship, but for Dalmas it mattered little. He had already been given his Grand Prix chance by Larrousse in Mexico, and a fifth place in Australia at season's end made his place in the F1 team for 1988 a formality.

The year was a personal disaster. Early-season shunts blunted his confidence and then what appeared to be an ear problem that sidelined him towards the end of the season turned out to be a nasty bout of Legionnaires' disease.

He returned to the Larrousse équipe for 1989, but a string of non-qualifications led to him leaving the team in mid-season in favour of Alboreto. Taking up a seat at AGS merely hastened his depressing slide and, while he did manage to qualify the car on occasion in 1990, it must have been a great relief when Peugeot offered him the chance to re-establish his career with a place in their sports car team. Paired with Rosberg, he won two races (Magny Cours and Mexico City) and in 1992 he shared the World Sports Car Drivers' title with Derek Warwick after winning at Le Mans, Silverstone and Fuji, also finishing second at Monza and Donington.

With Peugeot competing only at Le Mans in 1993 (where Yannick finished second with Boutsen and Fabi), he drove a Peugeot 405 in the French Supertourisme series, and that is probably where his racing future now lies.

CROSSLEY, Geoffrey (GB) b 11/5/1921

1950

	Race	Circuit	No	Entrant	Car/Engine	Comment
ret	BRITISH GP	Silverstone	24	Geoffrey Crossley	1.5 s/c Alta GP 2 4	transmission
nc	BELGIAN GP	Spa	26	Geoffrey Crossley	1.5 s/c Alta GP 2 4	5 laps behind

GP Starts: 2   GP Wins: 0   Pole positions: 0   Fastest laps: 0   Points: 0

DAIGH, Chuck (USA) b 29/11/1923

1960

	Race	Circuit	No	Entrant	Car/Engine	Comment
dnq	MONACO GP	Monte Carlo	46	Reventlow Automobiles Inc	2.4 Scarab 4	
dns	DUTCH GP	Zandvoort	22	Reventlow Automobiles Inc	2.4 Scarab 4	dispute over start money
ret	BELGIAN GP	Spa	30	Reventlow Automobiles Inc	2.4 Scarab 4	engine
dns	FRENCH GP	Reims	26	Reventlow Automobiles Inc	2.4 Scarab 4	engine failure in practice
ret	BRITISH GP	Silverstone	3	Cooper Car Co	2.5 Cooper T51-Climax 4	engine-overheating
10	US GP	Riverside	23	Reventlow Automobiles Inc	2.4 Scarab 4	3 laps behind

GP Starts: 3   GP Wins: 0   Pole positions: 0   Fastest laps: 0   Points: 0

DALMAS, Yannick (F) b 28/7/1961

1987

	Race	Circuit	No	Entrant	Car/Engine	Comment
9	MEXICAN GP	Mexico City	29	Larrousse Calmels	3.5 Lola LC87-Cosworth V8	4th non-turbo/4 laps behind
14/ret	JAPANESE GP	Suzuka	29	Larrousse Calmels	3.5 Lola LC87-Cosworth V8	electrics/3rd non-turbo/-4 laps
5*	AUSTRALIAN GP	Adelaide	29	Larrousse Calmels	3.5 Lola LC87-Cosworth V8	2nd non-turbo/*not eligible for pts

1988

	Race	Circuit	No	Entrant	Car/Engine	Comment
ret	BRAZILIAN GP	Rio	29	Larrousse Calmels	3.5 Lola LC88-Cosworth V8	engine cut out
12	SAN MARINO GP	Imola	29	Larrousse Calmels	3.5 Lola LC88-Cosworth V8	broken front wing/2 laps behind
7	MONACO GP	Monte Carlo	29	Larrousse Calmels	3.5 Lola LC88-Cosworth V8	spin/1 lap behind
9	MEXICAN GP	Mexico City	29	Larrousse Calmels	3.5 Lola LC88-Cosworth V8	3 laps behind
dnq	CANADIAN GP	Montreal	29	Larrousse Calmels	3.5 Lola LC88-Cosworth V8	
7	US GP (DETROIT)	Detroit	29	Larrousse Calmels	3.5 Lola LC88-Cosworth V8	2 laps behind
13	FRENCH GP	Paul Ricard	29	Larrousse Calmels	3.5 Lola LC88-Cosworth V8	p stop-loose seat belts/-2 laps
13	BRITISH GP	Silverstone	29	Larrousse Calmels	3.5 Lola LC88-Cosworth V8	2 laps behind
ret	GERMAN GP	Hockenheim	29	Larrousse Calmels	3.5 Lola LC88-Cosworth V8	clutch
9	HUNGARIAN GP	Hungaroring	29	Larrousse Calmels	3.5 Lola LC88-Cosworth V8	collision with Sala/misfire/-3 laps
ret	BELGIAN GP	Spa	29	Larrousse Calmels	3.5 Lola LC88-Cosworth V8	engine
ret	ITALIAN GP	Monza	29	Larrousse Calmels	3.5 Lola LC88-Cosworth V8	holed oil tank
ret	PORTUGUESE GP	Estoril	29	Larrousse Calmels	3.5 Lola LC88-Cosworth V8	alternator belt
11	SPANISH GP	Jerez	29	Larrousse Calmels	3.5 Lola LC88-Cosworth V8	1 lap behind

1989

	Race	Circuit	No	Entrant	Car/Engine	Comment
dnq	BRAZILIAN GP	Rio	29	Larrousse Calmels Lola	3.5 Lola LC88B-Lamborghini V12	
dns	SAN MARINO GP	Imola	29	Equipe Larrousse	3.5 Lola LC89-Lamborghini V12	engine did not start on dummy grid
dnq	MONACO GP	Monte Carlo	29	Equipe Larrousse	3.5 Lola LC89-Lamborghini V12	
dnq	MEXICAN GP	Mexico City	29	Equipe Larrousse	3.5 Lola LC89-Lamborghini V12	
dnq	US GP (PHOENIX)	Phoenix	29	Equipe Larrousse	3.5 Lola LC89-Lamborghini V12	
dnq	CANADIAN GP	Montreal	29	Equipe Larrousse	3.5 Lola LC89-Lamborghini V12	
dnpq	BRITISH GP	Silverstone	41	Automobiles Gonfaronaise Sportive	3.5 AGS JH23B-Cosworth V8	
dnpq	GERMAN GP	Hockenheim	41	Automobiles Gonfaronaise Sportive	3.5 AGS JH23B-Cosworth V8	
dnpq	"	"	41	Automobiles Gonfaronaise Sportive	3.5 AGS JH24-Cosworth V8	
dnpq	HUNGARIAN GP	Hungaroring	41	Automobiles Gonfaronaise Sportive	3.5 AGS JH23B-Cosworth V8	
dnpq	BELGIAN GP	Spa	41	Automobiles Gonfaronaise Sportive	3.5 AGS JH24-Cosworth V8	
dnpq	ITALIAN GP	Monza	41	Automobiles Gonfaronaise Sportive	3.5 AGS JH24-Cosworth V8	
excl	PORTUGUESE GP	Estoril	41	Automobiles Gonfaronaise Sportive	3.5 AGS JH24-Cosworth V8	excluded/practised on wrong tyres
dnpq	SPANISH GP	Jerez	41	Automobiles Gonfaronaise Sportive	3.5 AGS JH24-Cosworth V8	
dnpq	JAPANESE GP	Suzuka	41	Automobiles Gonfaronaise Sportive	3.5 AGS JH24-Cosworth V8	
dnpq	AUSTRALIAN GP	Adelaide	41	Automobiles Gonfaronaise Sportive	3.5 AGS JH24-Cosworth V8	

1990

	Race	Circuit	No	Entrant	Car/Engine	Comment
dnpq	US GP (PHOENIX)	Phoenix	18	Automobiles Gonfaronaise Sportive	3.5 AGS JH24-Cosworth V8	
ret	BRAZILIAN GP	Interlagos	18	Automobiles Gonfaronaise Sportive	3.5 AGS JH24-Cosworth V8	front suspension
dnpq	MONACO GP	Monte Carlo	18	Automobiles Gonfaranaise Sportive	3.5 AGS JH25-Cosworth V8	
dnpq	CANADIAN GP	Montreal	18	Automobiles Gonfaronaise Sportive	3.5 AGS JH25-Cosworth V8	
dnpq	MEXICAN GP	Mexico City	18	Automobiles Gonfaronaise Sportive	3.5 AGS JH25-Cosworth V8	
17	FRENCH GP	Paul Ricard	18	Automobiles Gonfaronaise Sportive	3.5 AGS JH25-Cosworth V8	5 laps behind
dnpq	BRITISH GP	Silverstone	18	Automobiles Gonfaronaise Sportive	3.5 AGS JH25-Cosworth V8	
dnq	GERMAN GP	Hockenheim	18	Automobiles Gonfaronaise Sportive	3.5 AGS JH25-Cosworth V8	
dnq	HUNGARIAN GP	Hungaroring	18	Automobiles Gonfaronaise Sportive	3.5 AGS JH25-Cosworth V8	
dnq	BELGIAN GP	Spa	18	Automobiles Gonfaronaise Sportive	3.5 AGS JH25-Cosworth V8	
nc	ITALIAN GP	Monza	18	Automobiles Gonfaronaise Sportive	3.5 AGS JH25-Cosworth V8	pit stops/8 laps behind
ret	PORTUGUESE GP	Estoril	18	Automobiles Gonfaronaise Sportive	3.5 AGS JH25-Cosworth V8	driveshaft
9	SPANISH GP	Jerez	18	Automobiles Gonfaronaise Sportive	3.5 AGS JH25-Cosworth V8	1 lap behind
dnq	JAPANESE GP	Suzuka	18	Automobiles Gonfaronaise Sportive	3.5 AGS JH25-Cosworth V8	
dnq	AUSTRALIAN GP	Adelaide	18	Automobiles Gonfaronaise Sportive	3.5 AGS JH25-Cosworth V8	

GP Starts: 21   GP Wins: 0   Pole positions: 0   Fastest laps: 0   Points: 0

DEREK DALY

'Quick but accident prone' may be an unfair judgement on Derek Daly, but the likeable Irishman certainly had to endure more than his fair share of incidents during his Grand Prix career.

Early experience in the harum-scarum world of stock cars led Derek into Formula Ford in his native Ireland. In order to finance his efforts he went to Australia to work in the tin mines with his friend and fellow aspiring racer, David Kennedy, and earned enough to finance his season, winning the 1975 national championship. Then it was across the Irish Sea to try his luck in Formula Ford for 1976. It was a tough year for Daly, who was living out of a converted coach and perpetually strapped for cash, but it was all made worthwhile when he won the Formula Ford Festival at the end of the season.

Derek stepped up to Formula 3 for 1977 and, driving a Chevron, won the BP championship ahead of Nelson Piquet, while a one-off drive saw him finishing fifth on his Formula 2 debut at Estoril. So impressive was this performance that he got the seat for 1978, and offers also came in for Formula 1. He did a deal with Hesketh and made a sensational debut in the rain at the International Trophy race, leading all the big names until he spun off. Reality soon dawned, however, as he failed to qualify for the first three races and quit in disgust. Luckily Ensign needed a replacement for Ickx and Daly was back, scoring his first point in Canada. He was persuaded to stay on for 1979, but the revamped car was outclassed, and after Monaco Daly returned to his successful ICI Formula 2 ride. This left him available to step into the Tyrrell team, initially in place of the indisposed Jarier. A superb drive at Watkins Glen ended in Daly spinning out, but Tyrrell had seen enough to offer him a drive for 1980. It was again a story of hit and miss, the season yielding a pair of fourth places and a couple of huge shunts.

For 1981 he was forced to take a step backwards. The RAM March was not competitive, and the atmosphere in the team was tense, but he never gave up. Theodore then threw him a lifeline which put him back on the grid again in 1982, and with Reutemann's sudden decision to retire he found himself catapulted into the Williams team. It was a difficult season for Derek; he supported Rosberg with some classy drives, but found himself dumped at the end of the year.

Daly then took the decision to turn his back on F1 and try his luck in Indy cars. After a handful of rides in '83, and some promising performances early in 1984, his career was nearly ended by a huge crash at Michigan which badly smashed both his legs. After a long and painful recovery Derek made a tentative comeback to Indy cars late in 1986 and then raced in endurance events for Jaguar and in IMSA for Nissan before announcing his retirement in 1992.

CHRISTIAN DANNER

Christian got involved in motor sport by racing (and regularly crashing) a Renault 5 in Germany, and soon came to the attention of Manfred Cassani, who was looking for a young driver to promote. Danner was given a BMW M1 to race in the German G4 championship and a couple of ProCar GP support races, and did so well in these that BMW signed him on a three-year contract to race in the works March F2 team. With no single-seater experience, Christian struggled in 1981 – his first season – and he was usually overshadowed by the team's lead drivers, Boutsen, Corrado Fabi, Cecotto and Gabbiani, but by the end of 1983 he was not far off the pace, as witnessed by his pole position at the Nürburgring.

Unfortunately for Christian, BMW then pulled the plug on their F2 programme and at first he was left without a drive for 1984, eventually joining the Bob Sparshott team. That season was dominated by the Ralt-Hondas, but Danner was up there with the rest, and with a minimal budget he tackled the inaugural F3000 season in 1985 with the same team. This was to be the breakthrough year for Christian. Not the quickest driver but certainly the most consistent, he became the formula's first champion. This brought him a Grand Prix chance at Zakspeed, and then a contract with Osella for 1986, which was bought out in mid-season when Arrows needed a replacement for the badly injured Marc Surer.

Christian rejoined Zakspeed in 1987 and, paired with Martin Brundle, performed quite well given the equipment available. He was on the sidelines in 1988, but could have had the dubious privilege of a EuroBrun drive from mid-season had he not been too tall to fit into the car. The following season saw his final shot at F1, driving the Rial for Gunther Schmid. He scored a distant fourth at Phoenix, but finally quit as the team slid into oblivion. Since then Christian has competed in Japanese F3000, Indy cars and the GTCC, driving a BMW in 1991 and a works Alfa in 1993.

DALY, Derek (IRL) b 11/3/1953

1978

	Race	Circuit	No	Entrant	Car/Engine	Comment
dnpq	US GP WEST	Long Beach	24	Olympus Cameras with Hesketh	3.0 Hesketh 308E-Cosworth V8	
dnpq	MONACO GP	Monte Carlo	24	Olympus Cameras with Hesketh	3.0 Hesketh 308E-Cosworth V8	
dnq	BELGIAN GP	Zolder	24	Olympus Cameras with Hesketh	3.0 Hesketh 308E-Cosworth V8	
dnq	FRENCH GP	Paul Ricard	22	Team Tissot Ensign	3.0 Ensign N177-Cosworth V8	
ret	BRITISH GP	Brands Hatch	22	Team Tissot Ensign	3.0 Ensign N177-Cosworth V8	lost wheel-crashed
dsq	AUSTRIAN GP	Österreichring	22	Team Tissot Ensign	3.0 Ensign N177-Cosworth V8	outside assistance after spin
ret	DUTCH GP	Zandvoort	22	Team Tissot Ensign	3.0 Ensign N177-Cosworth V8	driveshaft
10	ITALIAN GP	Monza	22	Team Tissot Ensign	3.0 Ensign N177-Cosworth V8	
8	US GP EAST	Watkins Glen	22	Team Tissot Ensign	3.0 Ensign N177-Cosworth V8	1 lap behind
6	CANADIAN GP	Montreal	22	Team Tissot Ensign	3.0 Ensign N177-Cosworth V8	

1979

	Race	Circuit	No	Entrant	Car/Engine	Comment
11	ARGENTINE GP	Buenos Aires	22	Team Ensign	3.0 Ensign N177-Cosworth V8	2 laps behind
13	BRAZILIAN GP	Interlagos	22	Team Ensign	3.0 Ensign N177-Cosworth V8	1 lap behind
dnq	SOUTH AFRICAN GP	Kyalami	22	Team Ensign	3.0 Ensign N179-Cosworth V8	
ret	US GP WEST	Long Beach	22	Team Ensign	3.0 Ensign N179-Cosworth V8	collision with Rebaque
dnq	SPANISH GP	Jarama	22	Team Ensign	3.0 Ensign N177-Cosworth V8	
dnq	BELGIAN GP	Zolder	22	Team Ensign	3.0 Ensign N177-Cosworth V8	
dnq	MONACO GP	Monte Carlo	22	Team Ensign	3.0 Ensign N179-Cosworth V8	
8	AUSTRIAN GP	Österreichring	4	Candy Tyrrell Team	3.0 Tyrrell 009-Cosworth V8	1 lap behind
ret	CANADIAN GP	Montreal	33	Candy Tyrrell Team	3.0 Tyrrell 009-Cosworth V8	engine

ret	US GP EAST	Watkins Glen	33	Candy Tyrrell Team	3.0 Tyrrell 009-Cosworth V8	*spun off*

1980

4	ARGENTINE GP	Buenos Aires	4	Candy Tyrrell Team	3.0 Tyrrell 009-Cosworth V8	
14	BRAZILIAN GP	Interlagos	4	Candy Tyrrell Team	3.0 Tyrrell 009-Cosworth V8	*2 laps behind*
ret	SOUTH AFRICAN GP	Kyalami	4	Candy Tyrrell Team	3.0 Tyrrell 010-Cosworth V8	*puncture*
8	US GP WEST	Long Beach	4	Candy Tyrrell Team	3.0 Tyrrell 010-Cosworth V8	*1 lap behind*
9	BELGIAN GP	Zolder	4	Candy Tyrrell Team	3.0 Tyrrell 010-Cosworth V8	*2 laps behind*
ret	MONACO GP	Monte Carlo	4	Candy Tyrrell Team	3.0 Tyrrell 010-Cosworth V8	*multiple accident on lap 1*
11	FRENCH GP	Paul Ricard	4	Candy Tyrrell Team	3.0 Tyrrell 010-Cosworth V8	*2 laps behind*
4	BRITISH GP	Brands Hatch	4	Candy Tyrrell Team	3.0 Tyrrell 010-Cosworth V8	*1 lap behind*
10	GERMAN GP	Hockenheim	4	Candy Tyrrell Team	3.0 Tyrrell 010-Cosworth V8	*1 lap behind*
ret	AUSTRIAN GP	Österreichring	4	Candy Tyrrell Team	3.0 Tyrrell 010-Cosworth V8	*sheared brake disc-crashed*
ret	DUTCH GP	Zandvoort	4	Candy Tyrrell Team	3.0 Tyrrell 010-Cosworth V8	*broken disc brake-crashed*
ret	ITALIAN GP	Imola	4	Candy Tyrrell Team	3.0 Tyrrell 010-Cosworth V8	*spun off*
ret/dns	CANADIAN GP	Montreal	4	Candy Tyrrell Team	3.0 Tyrrell 010-Cosworth V8	*startline crash-did not restart*
ret	US GP EAST	Watkins Glen	4	Candy Tyrrell Team	3.0 Tyrrell 010-Cosworth V8	*hit by de Cesaris*

1981

dnq	US GP WEST	Long Beach	17	March Grand Prix Team	3.0 March 811-Cosworth V8	
dnq	BRAZILIAN GP	Rio	17	March Grand Prix Team	3.0 March 811-Cosworth V8	
dnq	ARGENTINE GP	Buenos Aires	17	March Grand Prix Team	3.0 March 811-Cosworth V8	
dnq	SAN MARINO GP	Imola	18	March Grand Prix Team	3.0 March 811-Cosworth V8	
dnq	BELGIAN GP	Zolder	18	March Grand Prix Team	3.0 March 811-Cosworth V8	*practice times disallowed*
dnpq	MONACO GP	Monte Carlo	18	March Grand Prix Team	3.0 March 811-Cosworth V8	
16	SPANISH GP	Jarama	17	March Grand Prix Team	3.0 March 811-Cosworth V8	*5 laps behind*
ret	FRENCH GP	Dijon	17	March Grand Prix Team	3.0 March 811-Cosworth V8	*engine*
7	BRITISH GP	Silverstone	17	March Grand Prix Team	3.0 March 811-Cosworth V8	*2 laps behind*
ret	GERMAN GP	Hockenheim	17	March Grand Prix Team	3.0 March 811-Cosworth V8	*steering tie rod*
11	AUSTRIAN GP	Österreichring	17	March Grand Prix Team	3.0 March 811-Cosworth V8	*6 laps behind*
ret	DUTCH GP	Zandvoort	17	March Grand Prix Team	3.0 March 811-Cosworth V8	*suspension*
ret	ITALIAN GP	Monza	17	March Grand Prix Team	3.0 March 811-Cosworth V8	*gearbox*
8	CANADIAN GP	Montreal	17	March Grand Prix Team	3.0 March 811-Cosworth V8	*2 laps behind*
dnq	CAESARS PALACE GP	Las Vegas	17	March Grand Prix Team	3.0 March 811-Cosworth V8	

1982

14	SOUTH AFRICAN GP	Kyalami	33	Theodore Racing Team	3.0 Theodore TY 01-Cosworth V8	*clutch/brake problems/-4 laps*
ret	BRAZILIAN GP	Rio	33	Theodore Racing Team	3.0 Theodore TY 01-Cosworth V8	*puncture-spun off*
ret	US GP WEST	Long Beach	33	Theodore Racing Team	3.0 Theodore TY 01-Cosworth V8	*ran off track-stalled*
ret	BELGIAN GP	Zolder	5	TAG Williams Team	3.0 Williams FW08-Cosworth V8	*missed braking point-ran off road*
6/ret	MONACO GP	Monte Carlo	5	TAG Williams Team	3.0 Williams FW08-Cosworth V8	*gearbox/accident damage/-2 laps*
5	US GP (DETROIT)	Detroit	5	TAG Williams Team	3.0 Williams FW08-Cosworth V8	
7/ret	CANADIAN GP	Montreal	5	TAG Williams Team	3.0 Williams FW08-Cosworth V8	*out of fuel/2 laps behind*
5	DUTCH GP	Zandvoort	5	TAG Williams Team	3.0 Williams FW08-Cosworth V8	*1 lap behind*
5	BRITISH GP	Brands Hatch	5	TAG Williams Team	3.0 Williams FW08-Cosworth V8	
7	FRENCH GP	Paul Ricard	5	TAG Williams Team	3.0 Williams FW08-Cosworth V8	*1 lap behind*
ret	GERMAN GP	Hockenheim	5	TAG Williams Team	3.0 Williams FW08-Cosworth V8	*engine*
ret	AUSTRIAN GP	Österreichring	5	TAG Williams Team	3.0 Williams FW08-Cosworth V8	*hit by de Cesaris*
9	SWISS GP	Dijon	5	TAG Williams Team	3.0 Williams FW08-Cosworth V8	*1 lap behind*
ret	ITALIAN GP	Monza	5	TAG Williams Team	3.0 Williams FW08-Cosworth V8	*hit by Guerrero-suspension*
6	CAESARS PALACE GP	Las Vegas	5	TAG Williams Team	3.0 Williams FW08-Cosworth V8	*1 lap behind*

GP Starts: 48 (49)   GP Wins: 0   Pole positions: 0   Fastest laps: 0   Points: 15

DANNER, Christian (D) b 4/4/1958

1985

	Race	Circuit	No	Entrant	Car/Engine	Comment
ret	BELGIAN GP	Spa	30	West Zakspeed Racing	1.5 t/c Zakspeed 841 4	*gearbox*
ret	EUROPEAN GP	Brands Hatch	30	West Zakspeed Racing	1.5 t/c Zakspeed 841 4	*engine*

1986

ret	BRAZILIAN GP	Rio	22	Osella Squadra Corse	1.5 t/c Osella FA1F-Alfa Romeo V8	*engine*
ret	SPANISH GP	Jerez	22	Osella Squadra Corse	1.5 t/c Osella FA1F-Alfa Romeo V8	*engine*
ret	SAN MARINO GP	Imola	22	Osella Squadra Corse	1.5 t/c Osella FA1F-Alfa Romeo V8	*electrics*
dnq	MONACO GP	Monte Carlo	22	Osella Squadra Corse	1.5 t/c Osella FA1F-Alfa Romeo V8	
ret	BELGIAN GP	Spa	22	Osella Squadra Corse	1.5 t/c Osella FA1F-Alfa Romeo V8	*started from pit lane/engine*
ret	CANADIAN GP	Montreal	22	Osella Squadra Corse	1.5 t/c Osella FA1F-Alfa Romeo V8	*turbo*
dnp	"	"	17	Barclay Arrows BMW	1.5 t/c Arrows A8-BMW 4	*contractual problems*
ret	US GP (DETROIT)	Detroit	17	Barclay Arrows BMW	1.5 t/c Arrows A8-BMW 4	*electrics*
11	FRENCH GP	Paul Ricard	17	Barclay Arrows BMW	1.5 t/c Arrows A8-BMW 4	*stalled on grid/4 laps behind*
ret/dns	BRITISH GP	Brands Hatch	17	Barclay Arrows BMW	1.5 t/c Arrows A8-BMW 4	*accident in first start/did not restart*
ret	GERMAN GP	Hockenheim	17	Barclay Arrows BMW	1.5 t/c Arrows A8-BMW 4	*turbo*
ret	HUNGARIAN GP	Hungaroring	17	Barclay Arrows BMW	1.5 t/c Arrows A9-BMW 4	*rear suspension*
dns	"	"	17	Barclay Arrows BMW	1.5 t/c Arrows A8-BMW 4	*practice only*
6	AUSTRIAN GP	Österreichring	17	Barclay Arrows BMW	1.5 t/c Arrows A8-BMW 4	*3 laps behind*
8	ITALIAN GP	Monza	17	Barclay Arrows BMW	1.5 t/c Arrows A8-BMW 4	*2 laps behind*
11	PORTUGUESE GP	Estoril	17	Barclay Arrows BMW	1.5 t/c Arrows A8-BMW 4	*3 laps behind*
9	MEXICAN GP	Mexico City	17	Barclay Arrows BMW	1.5 t/c Arrows A8-BMW 4	*2 laps behind*
ret	AUSTRALIAN GP	Adelaide	17	Barclay Arrows BMW	1.5 t/c Arrows A8-BMW 4	*engine*

1987

9	BRAZILIAN GP	Rio	10	West Zakspeed Racing	1.5 t/c Zakspeed 861 4	*3 laps behind*
7	SAN MARINO GP	Imola	10	West Zakspeed Racing	1.5 t/c Zakspeed 861 4	*2 laps behind*
ret	BELGIAN GP	Spa	10	West Zakspeed Racing	1.5 t/c Zakspeed 871 4	*spun off*
dns	MONACO GP	Monte Carlo	10	West Zakspeed Racing	1.5 t/c Zakspeed 871 4	*excluded-practice incident with Alboreto*

8	US GP (DETROIT)	Detroit	10	West Zakspeed Racing	1.5 t/c Zakspeed 871 4	*3 laps behind*
ret	FRENCH GP	Paul Ricard	10	West Zakspeed Racing	1.5 t/c Zakspeed 871 4	*engine*
ret	BRITISH GP	Silverstone	10	West Zakspeed Racing	1.5 t/c Zakspeed 871 4	*gearbox*
ret	GERMAN GP	Hockenheim	10	West Zakspeed Racing	1.5 t/c Zakspeed 871 4	*driveshaft*
ret	HUNGARIAN GP	Hungaroring	10	West Zakspeed Racing	1.5 t/c Zakspeed 871 4	*engine cut out*
9	AUSTRIAN GP	Österreichring	10	West Zakspeed Racing	1.5 t/c Zakspeed 871 4	*started from pit lane/3 laps behind*
9	ITALIAN GP	Monza	10	West Zakspeed Racing	1.5 t/c Zakspeed 871 4	*2 laps behind*
ret/dns	PORTUGUESE GP	Estoril	10	West Zakspeed Racing	1.5 t/c Zakspeed 871 4	*accident in first start*
ret	SPANISH GP	Jerez	10	West Zakspeed Racing	1.5 t/c Zakspeed 871 4	*gearbox*
ret	MEXICAN GP	Mexico City	10	West Zakspeed Racing	1.5 t/c Zakspeed 871 4	*hit Johansson*
ret	JAPANESE GP	Suzuka	10	West Zakspeed Racing	1.5 t/c Zakspeed 871 4	*accident*
7	AUSTRALIAN GP	Adelaide	10	West Zakspeed Racing	1.5 t/c Zakspeed 871 4	*2nd place car dsq/3 laps behind*
1989						
14/ret	BRAZILIAN GP	Rio	38	Rial Racing	3.5 Rial ARC2-Cosworth V8	*gearbox/5 laps behind*
dnq	SAN MARINO GP	Imola	38	Rial Racing	3.5 Rial ARC2-Cosworth V8	
dnq	MONACO GP	Monte Carlo	38	Rial Racing	3.5 Rial ARC2-Cosworth V8	
12	MEXICAN GP	Mexico City	38	Rial Racing	3.5 Rial ARC2-Cosworth V8	*2 laps behind*
4	US GP (PHOENIX)	Phoenix	38	Rial Racing	3.5 Rial ARC2-Cosworth V8	*1 lap behind*
8	CANADIAN GP	Montreal	38	Rial Racing	3.5 Rial ARC2-Cosworth V8	*3 laps behind*
dnq	FRENCH GP	Paul Ricard	38	Rial Racing	3.5 Rial ARC2-Cosworth V8	
dnq	BRITISH GP	Silverstone	38	Rial Racing	3.5 Rial ARC2-Cosworth V8	
dnq	GERMAN GP	Hockenheim	38	Rial Racing	3.5 Rial ARC2-Cosworth V8	
dnq	HUNGARIAN GP	Hungaroring	38	Rial Racing	3.5 Rial ARC2-Cosworth V8	
dnq	BELGIAN GP	Spa	38	Rial Racing	3.5 Rial ARC2-Cosworth V8	
dnq	ITALIAN GP	Monza	38	Rial Racing	3.5 Rial ARC2-Cosworth V8	
dnq	PORTUGUESE GP	Estoril	38	Rial Racing	3.5 Rial ARC2-Cosworth V8	

GP Starts: 34 (36)   GP Wins: 0   Pole positions: 0   Fastest laps: 0   Points: 4

COLIN DAVIS

Son of the legendary S C H 'Sammy' Davis, Colin began his career in 1954 with a Cooper Norton, using F3 as a good learning vehicle before switching to sports cars to pursue his intended aim of racing in long-distance events. Unusually for an Englishman with so much racing available in his homeland, Davis soon made Italy the centre of his activities, driving for de Tomaso, for Scuderia Centro Sud in Grands Prix and sports car races, and, from 1960, for Scuderia Serenissima. He was also a leading runner in Formula Junior, winning at Albi in 1959 and Pau in 1960 with a Taraschi.

His greatest success still lay ahead, though, Colin winning the 1964 Targa Florio in a works Porsche 904 GT with Pucci. This led to other races for the Stuttgart team, and he finished second in the 1965 Targa with Mitter and fourth at Le Mans in 1966 with Siffert.

PATRICK DEPAILLER

The archetypal wiry little Frenchman, a cigarette perpetually hanging from the corner of his mouth, Depailler was something of a free spirit – a throwback to an earlier age, who lived for the moment and raced accordingly.

Schooled in the French F3 championship, Patrick spent three seasons between 1967 and 1969 driving a works Alpine-Renault, but also had occasional races in the Alpine sports-prototype, taking a third place in the Monza 1000 Km of 1968. A switch to Formula 2 with the Elf-Pygmée team for 1970 proved something of a disaster, the final straw being a practice crash at Salzburgring from which he was lucky to escape with slight burns. Luckily he still had the faith of Elf, who backed him again the following year but this time in a Tecno. Apart from a sixth place at Pau little went right for Depailler at this level, but he was more than happy to race the works Alpine-Renault once more, becoming the 1971 French F3 champion.

By 1972 he was already 28 years of age and had left it quite late in motor racing terms if he was going to make the leap up into the big time. After winning the Monaco F3 race, it was third time lucky in his attempts to crack Formula 2, Patrick taking second places in the races at Pau, Enna and Albi. His performances in the Elf/John Coombs March 722 put him in the frame for a couple of rides with his old chum Ken Tyrrell. It was more of the same in 1973, when once again a win in F2 just seemed to elude him, poor Patrick having to settle for no fewer than four second places this time around, and even worse was to follow. A motor cycle accident left him with a broken leg and he was forced to miss the two drives in North America that Tyrrell had lined up for him.

Fortunately his leg was soon to mend, and he was in the Tyrrell team full-time in 1974 with Jody Scheckter as his team-mate. In a highly competitive year, he brought the Tyrrel home in the points on six occasions and took a pole in Sweden, the first time a Frenchman had achieved this feat in a World Championship race, while in Formula 2 he finally broke his long dry spell, winning four rounds, at Pau, Mugello, Hockenheim and Vallelunga.

Patrick stuck with Tyrrell to become Formula 1 racing's 'nearly-man' over the next three seasons, taking seven second places in Grands Prix (and another in the 1975 non-title Swiss GP) before an emotional triumph at Monaco in 1978. Lured to Ligier for the 1979 season, when the team were at their zenith, if only for a short spell, Patrick won the Spanish GP and lay equal third in the champi-onship when a mid-season hang-gliding accident sidelined him with serious leg injuries. Struggling back to fitness, he joined Alfa Romeo in 1980, shrugging aside the frustrations of developing the unreliable car. He was beginning to make real progress when, in a solitary test session at Hockenheim, something went wrong with the car, probably a suspension breakage, depositing the helpless driver into the Armco at massive speed. He stood no chance of survival. Depailler had lived life to the full, and even in darker moments, as he fought the pain of his injuries, it would not be long before a broad smile would emerge, crinkling his face with laughter lines. A fitting way to remember him.

DAPONTE, Jorge (RA) b 5/6/1923 – d 3/1963

1954

	Race	Circuit	No	Entrant	Car/Engine	Comment
ret	ARGENTINE GP	Buenos Aires	34	Jorge Daponte	2.5 Maserati A6GCM/250F 6	transmission
nc	ITALIAN GP	Monza	8	Jorge Daponte	2.5 Maserati A6GCM/250F 6	10 laps behind

GP Starts: 2   GP Wins: 0   Pole positions: 0   Fastest laps: 0   Points: 0

DAVIS, Colin (GB) b 29/7/1932

1959

	Race	Circuit	No	Entrant	Car/Engine	Comment
ret	FRENCH GP	Reims	20	Scuderia Centro Sud	2.5 Cooper T51-Maserati 4	oil pipe
11	ITALIAN GP	Monza	40	Scuderia Centro Sud	2.5 Cooper T51-Maserati 4	4 laps behind

GP Starts: 2   GP Wins: 0   Pole positions: 0   Fastest laps: 0   Points: 0

DEPAILLER, Patrick (F) b 9/8/1944 – d 1/8/1980

1972

	Race	Circuit	No	Entrant	Car/Engine	Comment
nc	FRENCH GP	Clermont Ferrand	8	Elf Team Tyrrell	3.0 Tyrrell 004-Cosworth V8	pit stops-suspension/5 laps behind
7	US GP	Watkins Glen	3	Elf Team Tyrrell	3.0 Tyrrell 004-Cosworth V8	1 lap behind

1974

	Race	Circuit	No	Entrant	Car/Engine	Comment
6	ARGENTINE GP	Buenos Aires	4	Elf Team Tyrrell	3.0 Tyrrell 005-Cosworth V8	
8	BRAZILIAN GP	Interlagos	4	Elf Team Tyrrell	3.0 Tyrrell 005-Cosworth V8	1 lap behind
4	SOUTH AFRICAN GP	Kyalami	4	Elf Team Tyrrell	3.0 Tyrrell 005-Cosworth V8	
8	SPANISH GP	Jarama	4	Elf Team Tyrrell	3.0 Tyrrell 006-Cosworth V8	3 laps behind
ret	BELGIAN GP	Nivelles	4	Elf Team Tyrrell	3.0 Tyrrell 007-Cosworth V8	brake strap
9	MONACO GP	Monte Carlo	4	Elf Team Tyrrell	3.0 Tyrrell 006-Cosworth V8	started from back of grid/-4 laps
dns	"	" "	4	Elf Team Tyrrell	3.0 Tyrrell 007-Cosworth V8	practised in this car
2	SWEDISH GP	Anderstorp	4	Elf Team Tyrrell	3.0 Tyrrell 007-Cosworth V8	Pole/FL
6	DUTCH GP	Zandvoort	4	Elf Team Tyrrell	3.0 Tyrrell 007-Cosworth V8	
8	FRENCH GP	Dijon	4	Elf Team Tyrrell	3.0 Tyrrell 006-Cosworth V8	1 lap behind
dns	"	"	4	Elf Team Tyrrell	3.0 Tyrrell 007-Cosworth V8	accident in practice
ret	BRITISH GP	Brands Hatch	4	Elf Team Tyrrell	3.0 Tyrrell 007-Cosworth V8	engine
ret	GERMAN GP	Nürburgring	4	Elf Team Tyrrell	3.0 Tyrrell 007-Cosworth V8	hit guard rail
ret	AUSTRIAN GP	Österreichring	4	Elf Team Tyrrell	3.0 Tyrrell 007-Cosworth V8	collision with Ickx
11	ITALIAN GP	Monza	4	Elf Team Tyrrell	3.0 Tyrrell 007-Cosworth V8	2 laps behind
5	CANADIAN GP	Mosport Park	4	Elf Team Tyrrell	3.0 Tyrrell 007-Cosworth V8	
6	US GP	Watkins Glen	4	Elf Team Tyrrell	3.0 Tyrrell 007-Cosworth V8	

1975

	Race	Circuit	No	Entrant	Car/Engine	Comment
5	ARGENTINE GP	Buenos Aires	4	Elf Team Tyrrell	3.0 Tyrrell 007-Cosworth V8	
ret	BRAZILIAN GP	Interlagos	4	Elf Team Tyrrell	3.0 Tyrrell 007-Cosworth V8	front suspension-crashed
3	SOUTH AFRICAN GP	Kyalami	4	Elf Team Tyrrell	3.0 Tyrrell 007-Cosworth V8	
ret	SPANISH GP	Montjuich Park	4	Elf Team Tyrrell	3.0 Tyrrell 007-Cosworth V8	multiple accident-lost wheel
5	MONACO GP	Monte Carlo	4	Elf Team Tyrrell	3.0 Tyrrell 007-Cosworth V8	FL
4	BELGIAN GP	Zolder	4	Elf Team Tyrrell	3.0 Tyrrell 007-Cosworth V8	
12	SWEDISH GP	Anderstorp	4	Elf Team Tyrrell	3.0 Tyrrell 007-Cosworth V8	2 laps behind
9	DUTCH GP	Zandvoort	4	Elf Team Tyrrell	3.0 Tyrrell 007-Cosworth V8	2 laps behind
6	FRENCH GP	Paul Ricard	4	Elf Team Tyrrell	3.0 Tyrrell 007-Cosworth V8	
9/ret	BRITISH GP	Silverstone	4	Elf Team Tyrrell	3.0 Tyrrell 007-Cosworth V8	spun off in rain/2 laps behind
9	GERMAN GP	Nürburgring	4	Elf Team Tyrrell	3.0 Tyrrell 007-Cosworth V8	pit stop-suspension/1 lap behind
11	AUSTRIAN GP	Österreichring	4	Elf Team Tyrrell	3.0 Tyrrell 007-Cosworth V8	1 lap behind
7	ITALIAN GP	Monza	4	Elf Team Tyrrell	3.0 Tyrrell 007-Cosworth V8	1 lap behind
ret	US GP	Watkins Glen	4	Elf Team Tyrrell	3.0 Tyrrell 007-Cosworth V8	collision with Pace

1976

	Race	Circuit	No	Entrant	Car/Engine	Comment
2	BRAZILIAN GP	Interlagos	4	Elf Team Tyrrell	3.0 Tyrrell 007-Cosworth V8	
9	SOUTH AFRICAN GP	Kyalami	4	Elf Team Tyrrell	3.0 Tyrrell 007-Cosworth V8	1 lap behind
3	US GP WEST	Long Beach	4	Elf Team Tyrrell	3.0 Tyrrell 007-Cosworth V8	
ret	SPANISH GP	Jarama	4	Elf Team Tyrrell	3.0 Tyrrell P34-Cosworth V8	brake failure-crashed
ret	BELGIAN GP	Zolder	4	Elf Team Tyrrell	3.0 Tyrrell P34-Cosworth V8	engine
3	MONACO GP	Monte Carlo	4	Elf Team Tyrrell	3.0 Tyrrell P34-Cosworth V8	
2	SWEDISH GP	Anderstorp	4	Elf Team Tyrrell	3.0 Tyrrell P34-Cosworth V8	
2	FRENCH GP	Paul Ricard	4	Elf Team Tyrrell	3.0 Tyrrell P34-Cosworth V8	
ret	BRITISH GP	Brands Hatch	4	Elf Team Tyrrell	3.0 Tyrrell P34-Cosworth V8	engine
ret	GERMAN GP	Nürburgring	4	Elf Team Tyrrell	3.0 Tyrrell P34-Cosworth V8	collision with Regazzoni
ret	AUSTRIAN GP	Österreichring	4	Elf Team Tyrrell	3.0 Tyrrell P34-Cosworth V8	suspension
7	DUTCH GP	Zandvoort	4	Elf Team Tyrrell	3.0 Tyrrell P34-Cosworth V8	
6	ITALIAN GP	Monza	4	Elf Team Tyrrell	3.0 Tyrrell P34-Cosworth V8	
2	CANADIAN GP	Mosport Park	4	Elf Team Tyrrell	3.0 Tyrrell P34-Cosworth V8	FL
ret	US GP EAST	Watkins Glen	4	Elf Team Tyrrell	3.0 Tyrrell P34-Cosworth V8	detached fuel line
2	JAPANESE GP	Mount Fuji	4	Elf Team Tyrrell	3.0 Tyrrell P34-Cosworth V8	1 lap behind

1977

	Race	Circuit	No	Entrant	Car/Engine	Comment
ret	ARGENTINE GP	Buenos Aires	4	Elf Team Tyrrell	3.0 Tyrrell P34B-Cosworth V8	engine-overheating
ret	BRAZILIAN GP	Interlagos	4	Elf Team Tyrrell	3.0 Tyrrell P34B-Cosworth V8	spun off
3	SOUTH AFRICAN GP	Kyalami	4	Elf Team Tyrrell	3.0 Tyrrell P34B-Cosworth V8	
4	US GP WEST	Long Beach	4	Elf Team Tyrrell	3.0 Tyrrell P34B-Cosworth V8	
ret	SPANISH GP	Jarama	4	Elf Team Tyrrell	3.0 Tyrrell P34B-Cosworth V8	engine
ret	MONACO GP	Monte Carlo	4	Elf Team Tyrrell	3.0 Tyrrell P34B-Cosworth V8	brakes/gearbox
dns	"	" "	4	Elf Team Tyrrell	3.0 Tyrrell 007-Cosworth V8	practice only

8	BELGIAN GP	Zolder	4	Elf Team Tyrrell	3.0 Tyrrell P34B-Cosworth V8	*1 lap behind*
4	SWEDISH GP	Anderstorp	4	Elf Team Tyrrell	3.0 Tyrrell P34B-Cosworth V8	
ret	FRENCH GP	Dijon	4	Elf Team Tyrrell	3.0 Tyrrell P34B-Cosworth V8	*collision with Stuck*
ret	BRITISH GP	Silverstone	4	Elf Team Tyrrell	3.0 Tyrrell P34B-Cosworth V8	*brake failure-crashed*
ret	GERMAN GP	Hockenheim	4	Elf Team Tyrrell	3.0 Tyrrell P34B-Cosworth V8	*engine*
13	AUSTRIAN GP	Österreichring	4	Elf Team Tyrrell	3.0 Tyrrell P34B-Cosworth V8	*1 lap behind*
ret	DUTCH GP	Zandvoort	4	Elf Team Tyrrell	3.0 Tyrrell P34B-Cosworth V8	*engine*
ret	ITALIAN GP	Monza	4	Elf Team Tyrrell	3.0 Tyrrell P34B-Cosworth V8	*engine*
14	US GP EAST	Watkins Glen	4	Elf Team Tyrrell	3.0 Tyrrell P34B-Cosworth V8	*3 laps behind*
2	CANADIAN GP	Mosport Park	4	Elf Team Tyrrell	3.0 Tyrrell P34B-Cosworth V8	
3	JAPANESE GP	Mount Fuji	4	Elf Team Tyrrell	3.0 Tyrrell P34B-Cosworth V8	
	1978					
3	ARGENTINE GP	Buenos Aires	4	Elf Team Tyrrell	3.0 Tyrrell 008-Cosworth V8	
ret	BRAZILIAN GP	Rio	4	Elf Team Tyrrell	3.0 Tyrrell 008-Cosworth V8	*hit kerb-damaged brake cylinder*
2	SOUTH AFRICAN GP	Kyalami	4	Elf Team Tyrrell	3.0 Tyrrell 008-Cosworth V8	*lost lead last lap-fuel pick up problem*
3	US GP WEST	Long Beach	4	Elf Team Tyrrell	3.0 Tyrrell 008-Cosworth V8	
1	MONACO GP	Monte Carlo	4	Elf Team Tyrrell	3.0 Tyrrell 008-Cosworth V8	
ret	BELGIAN GP	Zolder	4	Elf Team Tyrrell	3.0 Tyrrell 008-Cosworth V8	*gearbox*
ret	SPANISH GP	Jarama	4	Elf Team Tyrrell	3.0 Tyrrell 008-Cosworth V8	*engine*
ret	SWEDISH GP	Anderstorp	4	Elf Team Tyrrell	3.0 Tyrrell 008-Cosworth V8	*suspension-broken upright*
ret	FRENCH GP	Paul Ricard	4	Elf Team Tyrrell	3.0 Tyrrell 008-Cosworth V8	*engine*
4	BRITISH GP	Brands Hatch	4	Elf Team Tyrrell	3.0 Tyrrell 008-Cosworth V8	
ret	GERMAN GP	Hockenheim	4	Elf Team Tyrrell	3.0 Tyrrell 008-Cosworth V8	*accident with Tambay at start*
2	AUSTRIAN GP	Österreichring	4	Elf Team Tyrrell	3.0 Tyrrell 008-Cosworth V8	
ret	DUTCH GP	Zandvoort	4	Elf Team Tyrrell	3.0 Tyrrell 008-Cosworth V8	*engine*
11	ITALIAN GP	Monza	4	Elf Team Tyrrell	3.0 Tyrrell 008-Cosworth V8	
ret	US GP EAST	Watkins Glen	4	Elf Team Tyrrell	3.0 Tyrrell 008-Cosworth V8	*loose hub*
5	CANADIAN GP	Montreal	4	Elf Team Tyrrell	3.0 Tyrrell 008-Cosworth V8	
	1979					
4	ARGENTINE GP	Buenos Aires	25	Gitanes Ligier	3.0 Ligier JS11-Cosworth V8	*pit stop-misfire*
2	BRAZILIAN GP	Interlagos	25	Gitanes Ligier	3.0 Ligier JS11-Cosworth V8	
ret	SOUTH AFRICAN GP	Kyalami	25	Gitanes Ligier	3.0 Ligier JS11-Cosworth V8	*spun off*
5	US GP WEST	Long Beach	25	Gitanes Ligier	3.0 Ligier JS11-Cosworth V8	*lost 4th gear*
1	SPANISH GP	Jarama	25	Gitanes Ligier	3.0 Ligier JS11-Cosworth V8	
ret	BELGIAN GP	Zolder	25	Gitanes Ligier	3.0 Ligier JS11-Cosworth V8	*hit barrier*
5/ret	MONACO GP	Monte Carlo	25	Gitanes Ligier	3.0 Ligier JS11-Cosworth V8	*engine/FL/2 laps behind*
	1980					
ret	ARGENTINE GP	Buenos Aires	22	Marlboro Team Alfa Romeo	3.0 Alfa Romeo 179 V12	*engine*
ret	BRAZILIAN GP	Interlagos	22	Marlboro Team Alfa Romeo	3.0 Alfa Romeo 179 V12	*electrics*
nc	SOUTH AFRICAN GP	Kyalami	22	Marlboro Team Alfa Romeo	3.0 Alfa Romeo 179 V12	*pit stops-engine problems/-25 laps*
ret	US GP WEST	Long Beach	22	Marlboro Team Alfa Romeo	3.0 Alfa Romeo 179 V12	*suspension*
ret	BELGIAN GP	Zolder	22	Marlboro Team Alfa Romeo	3.0 Alfa Romeo 179 V12	*exhaust*
ret	MONACO GP	Monte Carlo	22	Marlboro Team Alfa Romeo	3.0 Alfa Romeo 179 V12	*engine*
ret	FRENCH GP	Paul Ricard	22	Marlboro Team Alfa Romeo	3.0 Alfa Romeo 179 V12	*handling*
ret	BRITISH GP	Brands Hatch	22	Marlboro Team Alfa Romeo	3.0 Alfa Romeo 179 V12	*engine*

GP Starts: 95   GP Wins: 2   Pole positions: 1   Fastest laps: 4   Points: 141

DOLHEM, José (F) b 26/4/1944 – d 16/4/1988

1974

	Race	Circuit	No	Entrant	Car/Engine	Comment
dnq	FRENCH GP	Dijon	18	Bang & Olufsen Team Surtees	3.0 Surtees TS16-Cosworth V8	
dnq	ITALIAN GP	Monza	18	Team Surtees	3.0 Surtees TS16-Cosworth V8	
ret	US GP	Watkins Glen	18	Team Surtees	3.0 Surtees TS16-Cosworth V8	*withdrawn after Koinigg's accident*

GP Starts: 1   GP Wins: 0   Pole positions: 0   Fastest laps: 0   Points: 0

DONNELLY, Martin (GB) b 26/3/1964

1989

	Race	Circuit	No	Entrant	Car/Engine	Comment
12	FRENCH GP	Paul Ricard	9	USF&G Arrows Team	3.5 Arrows A11-Cosworth V8	*started from pit lane/3 laps behind*
	1990					
dns	US GP (PHOENIX)	Phoenix	12	Camel Team Lotus	3.5 Lotus 102-Lamborghini V12	*gearbox failure on dummy grid*
ret	BRAZILIAN GP	Interlagos	12	Camel Team Lotus	3.5 Lotus 102-Lamborghini V12	*leg cramps-spun off*
8	SAN MARINO GP	Imola	12	Camel Team Lotus	3.5 Lotus 102-Lamborghini V12	*1 lap behind*
ret	MONACO GP	Monte Carlo	12	Camel Team Lotus	3.5 Lotus 102-Lamborghini V12	*gearbox*
ret	CANADIAN GP	Montreal	12	Camel Team Lotus	3.5 Lotus 102-Lamborghini V12	*engine*
8	MEXICAN GP	Mexico City	12	Camel Team Lotus	3.5 Lotus 102-Lamborghini V12	*tyre problems*
12	FRENCH GP	Paul Ricard	12	Camel Team Lotus	3.5 Lotus 102-Lamborghini V12	*handling problems/1 lap behind*
ret	BRITISH GP	Silverstone	12	Camel Team Lotus	3.5 Lotus 102-Lamborghini V12	*engine*
ret	GERMAN GP	Hockenheim	12	Camel Team Lotus	3.5 Lotus 102-Lamborghini V12	*clutch*
7	HUNGARIAN GP	Hungaroring	12	Camel Team Lotus	3.5 Lotus 102-Lamborghini V12	*1 lap behind*
12	BELGIAN GP	Spa	12	Camel Team Lotus	3.5 Lotus 102-Lamborghini V12	*std from pits/understeer/exhaust/-1 lap*
ret	ITALIAN GP	Monza	12	Camel Team Lotus	3.5 Lotus 102-Lamborghini V12	*engine*
ret	PORTUGUESE GP	Estoril	12	Camel Team Lotus	3.5 Lotus 102-Lamborghini V12	*alternator*
dns	SPANISH GP	Jerez	12	Camel Team Lotus	3.5 Lotus 102-Lamborghini V12	*practice accident/multiple injuries*

GP Starts: 13   GP Wins: 0   Pole positions: 0   Fastest laps: 0   Points: 0

JOSÉ DOLHEM

Dolhem dabbled with racing in 1964 at the wheel of a Lotus Seven, but it was not until he had completed his university studies in engineering and economics in 1969 that he returned to the sport, having won the prized Volant Shell award.

He was regarded as something of a playboy racer in his early days. Certainly his 1972 Formula 2 season with a March was undistinguished and his only F2 race the following year, the Rouen GP, where he drove for Team Surtees, he crashed on the warm-up lap after finishing third in his qualifying heat.

No doubt bringing much-needed finance, he raced for Surtees in both Grands Prix and Formula 2 in 1974, but his career was then interrupted by a neck injury sustained while skiing early in 1975. José continued to race in F2 – firstly with Fred Opert's Chevron in 1976 and later with Kauhsen and AGS cars – on and off without success until 1979. The half-brother of the late Didier Pironi, Dolhem lost his life in a private plane crash in April 1988.

MARTIN DONNELLY

A graduate of FF2000, Donnelly made an immediate impact on the Marlboro Formula 3 series in his first season in 1986, winning four races and finishing third overall in the rankings. A favourite for the title the following year, his chances were ruined by a disastrous early-season run, and only when he switched to the Cellnet Intersport team did things improve and Martin return to the winner's circle.

He remained in F3 for a third year in 1988, but in mid-season he jumped ship, much to Intersport's chagrin, to join Eddie Jordan's Q8 F3000 team. In just four races, the Ulsterman took two wins and two second places. Thing seemed set fair for a championship challenge in 1989, but after a win at Vallelunga had been wiped out he lost the initiative to new team-mate Jean Alesi, despite a victory at Brands Hatch. Meanwhile Donnelly had made a steady GP debut for Arrows, and signed to drive for Lotus in 1990. The car was not one of the best, but Martin impressed nevertheless, until disaster struck in practice for the Spanish GP. He was very fortunate to survive when his car disintegrated after impact with the barriers, the helpless driver being tossed onto the track still strapped to the seat and the remnants of the car, and only first-class medical help at track side saved his life.

Donnelly's rehabilitation was long and painful, but he was to make a miraculous recovery, although, sadly, it would not allow a return to the Grand Prix arena.

MARK DONOHUE

A graduate engineer, Mark merely dabbled with racing at first, but he was good enough to take a class of the SCCA production sports car championship in 1961 in an Elva Courier, then racing a Formula Junior Elva and a TVR before taking a championship double in 1965 with a Lotus 23 in SCCA class C and a Mustang in class B. By this time Donohue had been taken under the wing of Walt Hansgen, who was leading the works Ford Mk II sports car challenge in 1966. The pair shared second place at Sebring that year, Donohue's first major placing, but his mentor was tragically killed at the Le Mans testing in April, and Mark renewed an old association with Roger Penske, taking his Group 7 Lola-Chevrolet to a victory at Mosport in Can-Am before winning the 1967 and 1968 US Road Racing Championships.

Penske also entered Donohue in the Trans-Am championship in 1968, and Mark won ten of the 13 events to win the title easily, repeating the trick the following year with six wins from 12 starts. The 1969 season also saw Penske's first appearance at the Indy 500 as an entrant, Donohue qualifying fourth and finishing seventh to earn the 'Rookie of the Year' title. He was to finish second in the race in 1970 driving a Lola-Ford, and later on that season raced in Formula A, winning two of the three rounds he entered. Penske expanded his racing activities in 1971 and Mark faced a hectic schedule of Trans-Am (taking his third title), USAC (winning the Pocono 500 and the Michigan 200 in a McLaren) and sport car events, sharing a blue-painted Ferrari 512M with David Hobbs. However, his performance of the year was undoubtedly his Grand Prix debut at Mosport, Donohue taking a superb third place in Penske's McLaren M19A.

Grand Prix racing was just a diversion at this stage, for in 1972 Mark continued to race in USAC, duly winning the Indianapolis 500 in a Penske McLaren, and returned to Can-Am, where his title chances were ruined by a testing accident which saw him sidelined for a couple of months. He was back in 1973, however, and made no mistake this time round, taking six race victories and the championship in a Porsche 917. Mark announced his retirement at the end of the year, but was tempted back behind the wheel late in 1974 to apply his superb development expertise to the Penske Grand Prix challenger.

He was persuaded to race the car in 1975, but it was a disappointment to all concerned and Penske replaced it in mid-season with an 'off- the-shelf' March. Donohue was practising the car for the Austrian GP when a tyre is thought to have deflated, sending the March into catch fencing and over the Armco barrier. One marshal was killed and another seriously injured, but at first Mark, though dazed, was sitting up and talking. He seemed to have escaped relatively unharmed, but it was soon apparent that all was not well as he lapsed into unconsciousness and, despite brain surgery, he died three days later in Graz hospital.

DONOHUE, Mark (USA) b 18/3/1937 – d 19/8/1975

	1971					
	Race	Circuit	No	Entrant	Car/Engine	Comment
3	CANADIAN GP	Mosport Park	10	Penske-White Racing	3.0 McLaren M19A-Cosworth V8	
dns	US GP	Watkins Glen	31	Penske-White Racing	3.0 McLaren M19A-Cosworth V8	practised-raced USAC elsewhere
	1974					
12	CANADIAN GP	Mosport Park	66	Penske Cars	3.0 Penske PC1-Cosworth V8	2 laps behind
ret	US GP	Watkins Glen	66	Penske Cars	3.0 Penske PC1-Cosworth V8	rear suspension bracket
	1975					
7	ARGENTINE GP	Buenos Aires	28	Penske Cars	3.0 Penske PC1-Cosworth V8	1 lap behind
ret	BRAZILIAN GP	Interlagos	28	Penske Cars	3.0 Penske PC1-Cosworth V8	handling
8	SOUTH AFRICAN GP	Kyalami	28	Penske Cars	3.0 Penske PC1-Cosworth V8	1 lap behind
ret	SPANISH GP	Montjuich Park	28	Penske Cars	3.0 Penske PC1-Cosworth V8	spun off on Scheckter's oil
ret	MONACO GP	Monte Carlo	28	Penske Cars	3.0 Penske PC1-Cosworth V8	hit guard rail
11	BELGIAN GP	Zolder	28	Penske Cars	3.0 Penske PC1-Cosworth V8	handling problems/3 laps behind
5	SWEDISH GP	Anderstorp	28	Penske Cars	3.0 Penske PC1-Cosworth V8	
8	DUTCH GP	Zandvoort	28	Penske Cars	3.0 Penske PC1-Cosworth V8	1 lap behind
ret	FRENCH GP	Paul Ricard	28	Penske Cars	3.0 Penske PC1-Cosworth V8	driveshaft
5/ret	BRITISH GP	Silverstone	28	Penske Cars	3.0 March 751-Cosworth V8	spun off in rainstorm/1 lap behind
ret	GERMAN GP	Nürburgring	28	Penske Cars	3.0 March 751-Cosworth V8	puncture
dns	AUSTRIAN GP	Österreichring	28	Penske Cars	3.0 March 751-Cosworth V8	accident practice-died in hospital

GP Starts: 14   GP Wins: 0   Pole positions: 0   Fastest laps: 0   Points: 8

DOWNING, Ken (GB) b 5/12/1917

1952

	Race	Circuit	No	Entrant	Car/Engine	Comment
9	BRITISH GP	Silverstone	4	Connaught Engineering	2.0 Connaught A-Lea Francis 4	*3 laps behind*
ret	DUTCH GP	Zandvoort	22	Kenneth Downing	2.0 Connaught A-Lea Francis 4	*oil pressure*

GP Starts: 2   GP Wins: 0   Pole positions: 0   Fastest laps: 0   Points: 0

DRAKE, Bob (USA) b 12/1924

1960

	Race	Circuit	No	Entrant	Car/Engine	Comment
13	US GP	Riverside	20	Joe Lubin	2.5 Maserati 250F 6	*7 laps behind*

GP Starts: 1   GP Wins: 0   Pole positions: 0   Fastest laps: 0   Points: 0

DRIVER, Paddy (ZA) b 19/5/1934

1963

	Race	Circuit	No	Entrant	Car/Engine	Comment
dns	SOUTH AFRICAN GP	East London	6	Selby Auto Spares	1.5 Lotus 24-BRM V8	*practice accident*

1974

ret	SOUTH AFRICAN GP	Kyalami	30	Team Gunston	3.0 Lotus 72-Cosworth V8	*clutch slip*

GP Starts: 1   GP Wins: 0   Pole positions: 0   Fastest laps: 0   Points: 0

DROGO, Piero (YV) b 8/8/1926 – d 28/4/1973

1960

	Race	Circuit	No	Entrant	Car/Engine	Comment
8	ITALIAN GP	Monza	12	Scuderia Colonia	1.5 Cooper T43-Climax 4	*F2 car/5 laps behind*

GP Starts: 1   GP Wins: 0   Pole positions: 0   Fastest laps: 0   Points: 0

DUMFRIES, Johnny (GB) b 26/4/1958

1986

	Race	Circuit	No	Entrant	Car/Engine	Comment
9	BRAZILIAN GP	Rio	11	John Player Special Team Lotus	1.5 t/c Lotus 98T-Renault V6	*2 pit stops-misfire/3 laps behind*
ret	SPANISH GP	Jerez	11	John Player Special Team Lotus	1.5 t/c Lotus 98T-Renault V6	*gearbox*
ret	SAN MARINO GP	Imola	11	John Player Special Team Lotus	1.5 t/c Lotus 98T-Renault V6	*wheel bearing*
dnq	MONACO GP	Monte Carlo	11	John Player Special Team Lotus	1.5 t/c Lotus 98T-Renault V6	
ret	BELGIAN GP	Spa	11	John Player Special Team Lotus	1.5 t/c Lotus 98T-Renault V6	*spun off-holed radiator*
ret	CANADIAN GP	Montreal	11	John Player Special Team Lotus	1.5 t/c Lotus 98T-Renault V6	*accident with Johansson*
7	US GP (DETROIT)	Detroit	11	John Player Special Team Lotus	1.5 t/c Lotus 98T-Renault V6	*2 laps behind*
ret	FRENCH GP	Paul Ricard	11	John Player Special Team Lotus	1.5 t/c Lotus 98T-Renault V6	*engine*
7	BRITISH GP	Brands Hatch	11	John Player Special Team Lotus	1.5 t/c Lotus 98T-Renault V6	*3 laps behind*
ret	GERMAN GP	Hockenheim	11	John Player Special Team Lotus	1.5 t/c Lotus 98T-Renault V6	*holed water radiator*
5	HUNGARIAN GP	Hungaroring	11	John Player Special Team Lotus	1.5 t/c Lotus 98T-Renault V6	*2 laps behind*
ret	AUSTRIAN GP	Österreichring	11	John Player Special Team Lotus	1.5 t/c Lotus 98T-Renault V6	*engine*
ret	ITALIAN GP	Monza	11	John Player Special Team Lotus	1.5 t/c Lotus 98T-Renault V6	*gearbox*
9	PORTUGUESE GP	Estoril	11	John Player Special Team Lotus	1.5 t/c Lotus 98T-Renault V6	*2 laps behind*
ret	MEXICAN GP	Mexico City	11	John Player Special Team Lotus	1.5 t/c Lotus 98T-Renault V6	*electrics*
6	AUSTRALIAN GP	Adelaide	11	John Player Special Team Lotus	1.5 t/c Lotus 98T-Renault V6	*2 laps behind*

GP Starts: 15   GP Wins: 0   Pole positions: 0   Fastest laps: 0   Points: 3

EATON, George (CDN) b 12/11/1945

1969

	Race	Circuit	No	Entrant	Car/Engine	Comment
ret	US GP	Watkins Glen	22	Owen Racing Organisation	3.0 BRM P138 V12	*engine*
ret	MEXICAN GP	Mexico City	22	Owen Racing Organisation	3.0 BRM P138 V12	*gearbox*

1970

ret	SOUTH AFRICAN GP	Kyalami	21	Owen Racing Organisation	3.0 BRM P153 V12	*engine*
dnq	SPANISH GP	Jarama	21	Owen Racing Organisation	3.0 BRM P153 V12	
dnq	MONACO GP	Monte Carlo	15	Yardley Team BRM	3.0 BRM P153 V12	
ret	DUTCH GP	Zandvoort	3	Yardley Team BRM	3.0 BRM P153 V12	*oil tank*
12	FRENCH GP	Clermont Ferrand	4	Yardley Team BRM	3.0 BRM P153 V12	*pit stop-plug lead/2 laps behind*
ret	BRITISH GP	Brands Hatch	24	Yardley Team BRM	3.0 BRM P153 V12	*oil pressure*
11	AUSTRIAN GP	Österreichring	15	Yardley Team BRM	3.0 BRM P153 V12	*2 laps behind*
ret	ITALIAN GP	Monza	12	Yardley Team BRM	3.0 BRM P153 V12	*overheating*
10	CANADIAN GP	St Jovite	16	Yardley Team BRM	3.0 BRM P153 V12	*pit stop/5 laps behind*
ret	US GP	Watkins Glen	21	Yardley Team BRM	3.0 BRM P153 V12	*engine*

1971

15	CANADIAN GP	Mosport Park	28	Yardley Team BRM	3.0 BRM P160 V12	*collision-Peterson/5 laps behind*

GP Starts: 10   GP Wins: 0   Pole positions: 0   Fastest laps: 0   Points: 0

KEN DOWNING

A director of numerous companies, Downing was a supporter of the Connaught marque who also raced briefly in the early 1950s. He scored 17 wins in club events with his sports Connaught in 1951, before racing the A-Type model in 1953. Apart from a couple of Grand Prix appearances, he was seen little in major races, but did finish second in the GP of Chimay, being caught at the last gasp by Paul Frère's HWM in a thrilling finish.

After briefly racing an Aston Martin DB3S in 1953, Downing retired from the track, later emigrating to South Africa in 1955.

PADDY DRIVER

Driver flirted briefly with car racing in 1963 with a Lotus 20 Formula Junior car, but at that time he was still a top-notch motor cycle rider, having made his name on Nortons, and then the AJS/Matchless, on which he finished third in the 1965 500 cc championship.

His career on four wheels really began to take off in 1969 and from then on he enjoyed success in sports cars and single-seaters including a McLaren M10B-Chevrolet and a Team Gunston Lotus 72. Switching to saloon cars with a Mazda, Paddy was still racing in the eighties.

JOHNNY DUMFRIES

Looking at his record, it is clear Johnny Dumfries did little wrong and plenty right, yet his career petered out while those of many drivers with less ability have endured.

More formally known as the Earl of Dumfries, Johnny was determined to make it in his own right as a racing driver, and showed some promise and not a little speed when taken under the wing of Dave Morgan to race in Formula 3 in 1983. He landed a plum drive in the BP-backed Dave Price Racing team for 1984, and the season exceeded even his wildest expectations, Johnny winning the Marlboro F3 championship at home and nearly repeating the feat in the European series, achieving a magnificent total of 15 wins. His stock was justifiably high, and for 1985 he joined Onyx for a season in F3000, but a bright start soon faded and by mid-season he was out of work.

Luckily for Johnny, help was at hand in the form of Ayrton Senna, who declined to accept Derek Warwick as his new team-mate at Lotus, as he was entitled to under the terms of his contract. This gave Dumfries his big chance, but while he let no one down he was naturally very much the number two to Senna in all things. He did, however, score three points and handled himself pretty well. Politics of one sort had helped him into the team, and unfortunately the revolving door took him straight back out when an engine deal with Honda meant Satoru Nakajima would be Senna's partner in 1987. Johnny did some testing for Benetton and then went into endurance racing, with drives in both Porsches and Toyotas, but the unquestioned highlight was his win at Le Mans (with Lammers and Wallace) in 1988 in the TWR Jaguar.

GEORGE EATON

The affluent son of a Canadian family involved with a merchandising concern, George had the wherewithal to go racing, graduating to a McLaren M1C via a fearsome Cobra. After a few races late in 1967, Eaton ran the car in Can-Am the following season, his best finish being a very impressive third at Laguna Seca in the wet.

Ordering a new McLaren M12 for Can-Am and a McLaren M10 for Formula A, he was a front-runner in both series, which brought an invitation to race the works BRM in the final two Grands Prix of 1969. This contact led to a deal for Eaton to drive for BRM in F1 for the full season in 1970, as well as racing their P54 prototype in Can-Am. All in all, it proved to be a great disappointment for both parties, leaving George somewhat disillusioned. He raced for BRM once more in 1971, and also handled Ferrari sports cars at Sebring, Le Mans and Watkins Glen. But with success proving elusive, Eaton gradually lost interest, and after taking part in the 1972 Daytona 6-hour race he left the racing scene to pursue other interests.

GUY EDWARDS

Though not a front-rank driver, Edwards, intelligent and personable, had a talent for securing funding from sponsorship sources previously unconnected with motor sport, and with this backing he was able to rise from 2-litre sports cars via F5000 into Formula 1.

His first taste of Grands Prix ended bitterly, Guy losing his drive after a wrist injury had sidelined him from the Embassy Hill team. He then arranged sponsorship to drive for Hesketh in 1976, but the team was in decline, and results were poor, while one last stab in the hopeless Stanley-BRM is best forgotten. Perhaps realising his limitations, Edwards settled for a satisfying few seasons competing at national level and occasionally beyond, mainly racing Grand Prix machinery in the popular Aurora series, before retiring from driving to become a successful sponsorship consultant, a role which has made him a millionaire.

EDWARDS, Guy (GB) b 30/12/1942

1974

	Race	Circuit	No	Entrant	Car/Engine	Comment
11	ARGENTINE GP	Buenos Aires	27	Embassy Racing with Graham Hill	3.0 Lola T370-Cosworth V8	2 laps behind
ret	BRAZILIAN GP	Interlagos	27	Embassy Racing with Graham Hill	3.0 Lola T370-Cosworth V8	engine
dnq	SPANISH GP	Jarama	27	Embassy Racing with Graham Hill	3.0 Lola T370-Cosworth V8	
12	BELGIAN GP	Nivelles	27	Embassy Racing with Graham Hill	3.0 Lola T370-Cosworth V8	3 laps behind
8	MONACO GP	Monte Carlo	27	Embassy Racing with Graham Hill	3.0 Lola T370-Cosworth V8	3 laps behind
7	SWEDISH GP	Anderstorp	27	Embassy Racing with Graham Hill	3.0 Lola T370-Cosworth V8	1 lap behind
ret	DUTCH GP	Zandvoort	27	Embassy Racing with Graham Hill	3.0 Lola T370-Cosworth V8	fuel system
15	FRENCH GP	Dijon	27	Embassy Racing with Graham Hill	3.0 Lola T370-Cosworth V8	3 laps behind
dns	BRITISH GP	Brands Hatch	27	Embassy Racing with Graham Hill	3.0 Lola T370-Cosworth V8	withdrawn-injury from previous race
dnq	GERMAN GP	Nürburgring	27	Embassy Racing with Graham Hill	3.0 Lola T370-Cosworth V8	

1976

	Race	Circuit	No	Entrant	Car/Engine	Comment
dnq	BELGIAN GP	Zolder	25	Penthouse Rizla Racing with Hesketh	3.0 Hesketh 308D-Cosworth V8	
17	FRENCH GP	Paul Ricard	25	Penthouse Rizla Racing with Hesketh	3.0 Hesketh 308D-Cosworth V8	1 lap behind
ret	BRITISH GP	Brands Hatch	25	Penthouse Rizla Racing with Hesketh	3.0 Hesketh 308D-Cosworth V8	accident
15	GERMAN GP	Nürburgring	25	Penthouse Rizla Racing with Hesketh	3.0 Hesketh 308D-Cosworth V8	1 lap behind
dns	ITALIAN GP	Monza	25	Penthouse Rizla Racing with Hesketh	3.0 Hesketh 308D-Cosworth V8	withdrawn to allow Watson to race
20	CANADIAN GP	Mosport Park	25	Penthouse Rizla Racing with Hesketh	3.0 Hesketh 308D-Cosworth V8	5 laps behind

1977

	Race	Circuit	No	Entrant	Car/Engine	Comment
dnpq	BRITISH GP	Silverstone	35	Rotary Watches-Stanley BRM	3.0 BRM P207 V12	

GP Starts: 11   GP Wins: 0   Pole positions: 0   Fastest laps: 0   Points: 0

VIC ELFORD

Vic was a something of a star performer in every type of racing to which he turned his hand, and it is a great shame he was not seen in a competitive Grand Prix car earlier in his career, which was largely spent rallying, sprinkled with whatever circuit racing his limited finances would allow. He was a Ford works driver from 1964 until he switched to Porsche, Vic then winning the Group 3 title in 1967 and the Monte Carlo Rally in 1968. By now he had become an established member of the Porsche sports car team and produced some dazzling performances, winning the Daytona 24 Hours (after doing the lion's share of the driving), the Targa Florio – a truly epic performance – and the Nürburgring 1000 Km. Cooper, searching for a driver, offered Vic a chance at the French GP and he duly finished fourth first time out in the rain. He completed the season with them, but then the team folded.

For 1969 Elford continued with Porsche in sports car racing – taking time out to finish 11th in the Daytona 500 in a Dodge! – and drove for privateer Colin Crabbe in F1. Things looked promising until he was involved in Mario Andretti's accident at the German GP, his McLaren hitting debris from the American's car. Vic crashed badly and was lucky to escape with no worse than a broken arm and collarbone. The crash effectively spelt the end of his Grand Prix career, but he was soon back in the Porsche and driving as well as ever, winning the 1970 Nürburgring 1000 Km with Ahrens. Elford drove for BRM in the German GP of 1971, but was not really given a fair crack of the whip. He raced on, driving for Porsche and Alfa Romeo in endurance events, handling Chaparrals, McLarens and Shadows in Can-Am, and a Chevron in F2, and even won a Trans-Am race in a Camaro at Watkins Glen before finally retiring in 1974. He was team manager of the ATS F1 team in the second half of 1977.

PAUL EMERY

Paul Emery was one of those characters in life who was always chasing success, rarely found it, but had a hell of a good time along the way. He and his father were indefatigable builders of specials, based around whatever components were available at the time. Given the name Emeryson, these machines were always technically interesting in some respect, but the finance essential to their development was always lacking. Paul, a 500 cc racer of some note, developed an Emeryson-Alta in 1956, in which he finished second, to Moss no less, at Crystal Palace before racing it in the British Grand Prix. He was later to build the Emeryson F1 cars for ENB and Scirocco-Powell before jumping from project to project, most of which remained unrealised, eventually finding a niche building and driving oval-track midget racers.

HARALD ERTL

Ertl was a journalist/racer who competed in Formula Vee, Super Vee and F3 in Germany in the early seventies before moving on to the European touring car series, with victory in the 1973 Tourist Trophy with Derek Bell in a BMW the highlight.

He raised the finance to race in Formula 1 on and off for Hesketh between 1975 and 1977 and Ensign in 1978 but was never quite able to make the points – although he was desperately unlucky to lose sixth place at Hockenheim in 1978 when his engine failed – and was rarely more than a midfield runner in F2 during the same period. He had one more GP drive for ATS in 1980, but by then he was established as a leading light in the German G5 championship in BMW and Ford Capri turbos. A charming and popular figure around the circuits, Harald was killed in a light aeroplane crash in 1982 in which his wife and son were seriously injured.

ELFORD, Vic (GB) b 10/6/1935

1968

	Race	Circuit	No	Entrant	Car/Engine	Comment
4	FRENCH GP	Rouen	30	Cooper Car Co	3.0 Cooper T86B-BRM V12	*pit stop-tyres/2 laps behind*
ret	BRITISH GP	Brands Hatch	15	Cooper Car Co	3.0 Cooper T86B-BRM V12	*engine*
ret	GERMAN GP	Nürburgring	20	Cooper Car Co	3.0 Cooper T86B-BRM V12	*accident*
ret	ITALIAN GP	Monza	23	Cooper Car Co	3.0 Cooper T86B-BRM V12	*lost brakes-spun off*
5	CANADIAN GP	St Jovite	21	Cooper Car Co	3.0 Cooper T86B-BRM V12	*4 laps behind*
ret	US GP	Watkins Glen	18	Cooper Car Co	3.0 Cooper T86B-BRM V12	*camshaft*
8	MEXICAN GP	Mexico City	18	Cooper Car Co	3.0 Cooper T86B-BRM V12	*2 laps behind*

1969

	Race	Circuit	No	Entrant	Car/Engine	Comment
7	MONACO GP	Monte Carlo	12	Colin Crabbe-Antique Automobiles	3.0 Cooper T86-Maserati V12	*6 laps behind*
10	DUTCH GP	Zandvoort	18	Colin Crabbe-Antique Automobiles	3.0 McLaren M7A/B-Cosworth V8	*6 laps behind*
5	FRENCH GP	Clermont Ferrand	10	Colin Crabbe-Antique Automobiles	3.0 McLaren M7A/B-Cosworth V8	*1 lap behind*
6	BRITISH GP	Silverstone	19	Colin Crabbe-Antique Automobiles	3.0 McLaren M7A/B-Cosworth V8	*2 laps behind*
ret	GERMAN GP	Nürburgring	12	Colin Crabbe-Antique Automobiles	3.0 McLaren M7A/B-Cosworth V8	*hit debris from Andretti's crash-*

1971

	Race	Circuit	No	Entrant	Car/Engine	Comment
11	GERMAN GP	Nürburgring	22	Yardley Team BRM	3.0 BRM P160 V12	*pit stop-coil/1 lap behind*

GP Starts: 13   GP Wins: 0   Pole positions: 0   Fastest laps: 0   Points: 8

EMERY, Paul (GB) b 12/11/1916 – d 1992

1956

	Race	Circuit	No	Entrant	Car/Engine	Comment
ret	BRITISH GP	Silverstone	32	Emeryson Cars	2.5 Emeryson-Alta 4	*ignition*

1958

dnq	MONACO GP	Monte Carlo	14	B C Ecclestone	2.5 Connaught B-Alta 4	

GP Starts: 1   GP Wins: 0   Pole positions: 0   Fastest laps: 0   Points: 0

ENGLAND, Paul (AUS) b 28/3/1929

1957

	Race	Circuit	No	Entrant	Car/Engine	Comment
ret	GERMAN GP (F2)	Nürburgring	26	Ridgeway Managements	1.5 Cooper T41-Climax 4	*distributor*

GP Starts: 1   GP Wins: 0   Pole positions: 0   Fastest laps: 0   Points: 0

ERTL, Harald (A) b 31/8/1948 – d 7/4/1982

1975

	Race	Circuit	No	Entrant	Car/Engine	Comment
8	GERMAN GP	Nürburgring	25	Warsteiner Brewery	3.0 Hesketh 308-Cosworth V8	
ret	AUSTRIAN GP	Österreichring	32	Warsteiner Brewery	3.0 Hesketh 308-Cosworth V8	*electrics*
9	ITALIAN GP	Monza	34	Warsteiner Brewery	3.0 Hesketh 308-Cosworth V8	*1 lap behind*

1976

	Race	Circuit	No	Entrant	Car/Engine	Comment
15	SOUTH AFRICAN GP	Kyalami	24	Hesketh Racing	3.0 Hesketh 308D-Cosworth V8	*4 laps behind*
dnq	US GP WEST	Long Beach	24	Hesketh Racing	3.0 Hesketh 308D-Cosworth V8	
dnq	SPANISH GP	Jarama	24	Hesketh Racing	3.0 Hesketh 308D-Cosworth V8	
ret	BELGIAN GP	Zolder	24	Hesketh Racing	3.0 Hesketh 308D-Cosworth V8	*engine*
dnq	MONACO GP	Monte Carlo	24	Hesketh Racing	3.0 Hesketh 308D-Cosworth V8	
ret	SWEDISH GP	Anderstorp	24	Hesketh Racing	3.0 Hesketh 308D-Cosworth V8	*spun off-could not restart*
dnq/ret	FRENCH GP	Paul Ricard	24	Hesketh Racing	3.0 Hesketh 308D-Cosworth V8	*dnq but started illegally/driveshaft*
7*	BRITISH GP	Brands Hatch	24	Hesketh Racing	3.0 Hesketh 308D-Cosworth V8	** 1st place car dsq/3 laps behind*
ret/dns	GERMAN GP	Nürburgring	24	Hesketh Racing	3.0 Hesketh 308D-Cosworth V8	*crashed first start-did not restart*
8	AUSTRIAN GP	Österreichring	24	Hesketh Racing	3.0 Hesketh 308D-Cosworth V8	*1 lap behind*
ret	DUTCH GP	Zandvoort	24	Hesketh Racing	3.0 Hesketh 308D-Cosworth V8	*spun off-could not restart*
16/ret	ITALIAN GP	Monza	24	Hesketh Racing	3.0 Hesketh 308D-Cosworth V8	*driveshaft/3 laps behind*
dns	CANADIAN GP	Mosport Park	24	Hesketh Racing	3.0 Hesketh 308D-Cosworth V8	*practice accident with Amon*
13	US GP EAST	Watkins Glen	24	Hesketh Racing	3.0 Hesketh 308D-Cosworth V8	*hit Merzario-pit stop/5 laps behind*
8	JAPANESE GP	Mount Fuji	24	Hesketh Racing	3.0 Hesketh 308D-Cosworth V8	*1 lap behind*

1977

	Race	Circuit	No	Entrant	Car/Engine	Comment
ret	SPANISH GP	Jarama	25	Hesketh Racing	3.0 Hesketh 308E-Cosworth V8	*radiator*
dnq	MONACO GP	Monte Carlo	25	Hesketh Racing	3.0 Hesketh 308E-Cosworth V8	
9	BELGIAN GP	Zolder	25	Hesketh Racing	3.0 Hesketh 308E-Cosworth V8	*1 lap behind*
16	SWEDISH GP	Anderstorp	25	Hesketh Racing	3.0 Hesketh 308E-Cosworth V8	*4 laps behind*
dnq	FRENCH GP	Dijon	25	Hesketh Racing	3.0 Hesketh 308E-Cosworth V8	

1978

	Race	Circuit	No	Entrant	Car/Engine	Comment
11/ret	GERMAN GP	Hockenheim	23	Sachs Racing	3.0 Ensign N177-Cosworth V8	*engine/4 laps behind*
ret	AUSTRIAN GP	Österreichring	23	Sachs Racing	3.0 Ensign N177-Cosworth V8	*collision with Patrese at restart*
dnpq	DUTCH GP	Zandvoort	23	Sachs Racing	3.0 Ensign N177-Cosworth V8	
dnpq	ITALIAN GP	Monza	23	Sachs Racing	3.0 Ensign N177-Cosworth V8	
dnq	"	"	10	ATS Engineering	3.0 ATS HS1-Cosworth V8	

1980

dnq	GERMAN GP	Hockenheim	10	Team ATS	3.0 ATS D4-Cosworth V8	

GP Starts: 19 (18)   GP Wins: 0   Pole positions: 0   Fastest laps: 0   Points: 0

ESTEFANO, Nasif (RA) b 18/11/1932 – d 21/10/1973

1960

	Race	Circuit	No	Entrant	Car/Engine	Comment
14	ARGENTINE GP	Buenos Aires	10	Nasif Estefano	2.5 Maserati 250F 6	10 laps behind

1962

| dnq | ITALIAN GP | Monza | 34 | Scuderia de Tomaso | 1.5 de Tomaso F1-801 F8 | |

GP Starts: 1   GP Wins: 0   Pole positions: 0   Fastest laps: 0   Points: 0

ÉTANCELIN, Philippe (F) b 28/12/1896 – d 13/10/1981

1950

	Race	Circuit	No	Entrant	Car/Engine	Comment
8	BRITISH GP	Silverstone	16	Philippe Étancelin	4.5 Lago-Talbot T26C 6	5 laps behind
ret	MONACO GP	Monte Carlo	14	Philippe Étancelin	4.5 Lago-Talbot T26C 6	oil pipe
ret	SWISS GP	Bremgarten	42	Philippe Étancelin	4.5 Lago-Talbot T26C 6	gearbox
ret	BELGIAN GP	Spa	16	Automobiles Talbot-Darracq	4.5 Lago-Talbot T26C-DA 6	overheating
5*	FRENCH GP	Reims	16	Philippe Étancelin	4.5 Lago-Talbot T26C-DA 6	*Chaboud took over/5 laps behind
5	ITALIAN GP	Monza	24	Philippe Étancelin	4.5 Lago-Talbot T26C 6	5 laps behind

1951

10	SWISS GP	Bremgarten	4	Philippe Étancelin	4.5 Lago-Talbot T26C-DA 6	3 laps behind
ret	BELGIAN GP	Spa	20	Philippe Étancelin	4.5 Lago-Talbot T26C-DA 6	transmission
ret	FRENCH GP	Reims	38	Philippe Étancelin	4.5 Lago-Talbot T26C-DA 6	engine
ret	GERMAN GP	Nürburgring	86	Philippe Étancelin	4.5 Lago-Talbot T26C-DA 6	gearbox
8	SPANISH GP	Pedralbes	34	Philippe Étancelin	4.5 Lago-Talbot T26C-DA 6	7 laps behind

1952

| 8 | FRENCH GP | Rouen | 28 | Escuderia Bandeirantes | 2.0 Maserati A6GCM 6 | 6 laps behind |

GP Starts: 12   GP Wins: 0   Pole positions: 0   Fastest laps: 0   Points: 3

EVANS, Bob (GB) b 11/6/1947

1975

	Race	Circuit	No	Entrant	Car/Engine	Comment
15	SOUTH AFRICAN GP	Kyalami	14	Stanley BRM	3.0 BRM P201 V12	2 laps behind
ret	SPANISH GP	Montjuich Park	14	Stanley BRM	3.0 BRM P201 V12	ignition
dnq	MONACO GP	Monte Carlo	14	Stanley BRM	3.0 BRM P201 V12	
9	BELGIAN GP	Zolder	14	Stanley BRM	3.0 BRM P201 V12	2 laps behind
13	SWEDISH GP	Anderstorp	14	Stanley BRM	3.0 BRM P201 V12	2 laps behind
ret	DUTCH GP	Zandvoort	14	Stanley BRM	3.0 BRM P201 V12	gearbox
17	FRENCH GP	Paul Ricard	14	Stanley BRM	3.0 BRM P201 V12	2 laps behind
ret	AUSTRIAN GP	Österreichring	14	Stanley BRM	3.0 BRM P201 V12	engine
ret	ITALIAN GP	Monza	14	Stanley BRM	3.0 BRM P201 V12	engine-electrics

1976

10	SOUTH AFRICAN GP	Kyalami	5	John Player Team Lotus	3.0 Lotus 77-Cosworth V8	1 lap behind
dnq	US GP WEST	Long Beach	5	John Player Team Lotus	3.0 Lotus 77-Cosworth V8	
ret	BRITISH GP	Brands Hatch	32	RAM Racing	3.0 Brabham BT44B-Cosworth V8	gearbox

GP Starts: 10   GP Wins: 0   Pole positions: 0   Fastest laps: 0   Points: 0

FABI, Corrado (I) b 12/4/1961

1983

	Race	Circuit	No	Entrant	Car/Engine	Comment
ret	BRAZILIAN GP	Rio	31	Osella Squadra Corse	3.0 Osella FA1D-Cosworth V8	engine
dnq	US GP WEST	Long Beach	31	Osella Squadra Corse	3.0 Osella FA1D-Cosworth V8	
ret	FRENCH GP	Paul Ricard	31	Osella Squadra Corse	3.0 Osella FA1D-Cosworth V8	engine
ret	SAN MARINO GP	Imola	31	Osella Squadra Corse	3.0 Osella FA1D-Cosworth V8	spun off
dnq	MONACO GP	Monte Carlo	31	Osella Squadra Corse	3.0 Osella FA1D-Cosworth V8	
ret	BELGIAN GP	Spa	31	Osella Squadra Corse	3.0 Osella FA1D-Cosworth V8	rear suspension
dnq	US GP (DETROIT)	Detroit	31	Osella Squadra Corse	3.0 Osella FA1D-Cosworth V8	
ret	CANADIAN GP	Montreal	31	Osella Squadra Corse	3.0 Osella FA1D-Cosworth V8	engine
dnq	BRITISH GP	Silverstone	31	Osella Squadra Corse	3.0 Osella FA1E-Alfa Romeo V12	
dnq	GERMAN GP	Hockenheim	31	Osella Squadra Corse	3.0 Osella FA1E-Alfa Romeo V12	
10	AUSTRIAN GP	Österreichring	31	Osella Squadra Corse	3.0 Osella FA1E-Alfa Romeo V12	3 laps behind
11/ret	DUTCH GP	Zandvoort	31	Osella Squadra Corse	3.0 Osella FA1E-Alfa Romeo V12	engine
ret	ITALIAN GP	Monza	31	Osella Squadra Corse	3.0 Osella FA1E-Alfa Romeo V12	oil union
dnq	EUROPEAN GP	Brands Hatch	31	Osella Squadra Corse	3.0 Osella FA1E-Alfa Romeo V12	
ret	SOUTH AFRICAN GP	Kyalami	31	Osella Squadra Corse	3.0 Osella FA1E-Alfa Romeo V12	engine

1984

ret	MONACO GP	Monte Carlo	2	MRD International	1.5 t/c Brabham BT53-BMW 4	water in electrics/spun off
ret	CANADIAN GP	Montreal	2	MRD International	1.5 t/c Brabham BT53-BMW 4	lost turbo boost
7	US GP (DALLAS)	Dallas	2	MRD International	1.5 t/c Brabham BT53-BMW 4	3 laps behind

GP Starts: 12   GP Wins: 0   Pole positions: 0   Fastest laps: 0   Points: 0

NASIF ESTEFANO

An Argentinian who was highly regarded on his own shores, Estefano was tempted to Europe to race Alessandro de Tomaso's car in 1962. He raced this singularly unsuccessful machine briefly in a few non-championship races the following season before returning home. He was still active in the early seventies racing sports cars.

PHILIPPE ÉTANCELIN

Easily recognisable by the famous reversed cap that was to become his trademark, 'Phi Phi', as he was known to his friends, began racing in 1927, scoring a big win at Reims with his Bugatti in his first season. In 1929 he won at Reims once more, and claimed further victories at Antibes, Comminges and La Baule, while success continued into 1930 with wins at Pau and in the Algerian GP.

Late in 1931, Étancelin took the decision to order an Alfa Romeo, which he ran relatively successfully until rule changes for 1934 forced him to switch to a Maserati. He often finished second or third with this car over the next few seasons, outright successes mainly eluding him, though he did win at Pau in 1936, and had previously shared the 1934 Le Mans-winning car with Chinetti.

After the war, Étancelin took an Alfa Romeo to the first race in Paris , but it was 1948 before he could compete regularly after taking delivery of a Lago-Talbot. The car was raced to good effect in 1949, 'Phi Phi' winning the Paris GP and finishing second at Marseilles, Monza and Brno. In 1950 – the first season of the World Championship – Étancelin picked up a couple of fifth places, racing his now elderly Talbot on through the 1951 season and into the following year in the few F1 and Libre events for which it was still eligible.

By 1953 this hard trier had virtually retired from racing after finishing third with 'Levegh' in the Casablanca 3 Hours, but the Rouen GP of that year was a non-championship event, so the organisers, hoping to bolster the grid, invited Formula 1 cars to compete as well. 'Phi Phi' was a local man and could not resist the temptation to dust off his trusty Talbot and take up the challenge to the works Ferraris. To the immense delight of a partisan crowd he brought the car home in third place, thus finishing a wonderful career in splendid fashion.

BOB EVANS

Evans was one of many British drivers of the period who, having worked tremendously hard to reach Formula 1, had neither the machinery nor the opportunity to show what they could really do. He had begun his racing career in a Sprite before moving into Formula Ford and then F3 in 1971, but only after he had fortunately recovered from a broken neck sustained when he crashed while testing at Castle Combe.

It was F5000 that was to provide Bob with his big breakthrough. With a solid season in a Trojan under his belt, long-time supporter Alan McKechnie bought him a Lola T332 for 1974 and he duly swept to the Rothmans championship, picking up the first-place Grovewood Award in the process.

This led to an offer to drive for BRM in 1975. The car was well past its best and it was to Evans' credit that he plugged away so valiantly in the face of adversity. Things looked better for 1976 when Colin Chapman, impressed with his performances, gave Bob a testing contract – and three races, the best of which was the Race of Champions, when the car ran out fuel and fourth place was lost. Apart from a RAM drive in the British GP later that year, and a one-off outing to 11th place in the Hexagon Penske in the 1977 Race of Champions, that was that for Evans, who returned to the relative obscurity of the Aurora championship in a Surtees TS19 in 1978.

CORRADO FABI

Having started his racing career at the age of 12, raced a Formula 3 car before he was 18, and become a convincing European Formula 2 champion by the age of 21, Corrado Fabi was clearly a young man in a hurry – but where was he headed? Towards a brief Formula 1 careeer and racing oblivion, as it turned out, for today who remembers Teo's younger brother who promised so much a decade ago?

So swift was his rise to prominence (1979 – half a season in Italian F3; 1980 – third in the European F3 championship; 1981 – third in the European Formula 2 championship; 1982 – European Formula 2 champion) that it seemed certain he was a World Champion in the making. Then it was into Grands Prix, and a cold shower of reality, with the back-of-the-grid Osella team in 1983. Struggling to qualify must have been a culture shock for the easy-going Corrado, and after three races in a competitive car standing in for Teo at Brabham in 1984 no more was seen of the younger Fabi in Formula 1. Surely a great talent had been allowed to slip away.

FABI, Teo (I) b 9/3/1955

1982

	Race	Circuit	No	Entrant	Car/Engine	Comment
dnq	SOUTH AFRICAN GP	Kyalami	36	Candy Toleman Motorsport	1.5 t/c Toleman TG181B-Hart 4	no time recorded
dnq	BRAZILIAN GP	Rio	36	Candy Toleman Motorsport	1.5 t/c Toleman TG181B-Hart 4	
dnq	US GP WEST	Long Beach	36	Candy Toleman Motorsport	1.5 t/c Toleman TG181C-Hart 4	
nc	SAN MARINO GP	Imola	36	Toleman Group Motorsport	1.5 t/c Toleman TG181C-Hart 4	pit stop/8 laps behind
ret	BELGIAN GP	Zolder	35	Toleman Group Motorsport	1.5 t/c Toleman TG181C-Hart 4	brakes
dnpq	MONACO GP	Monte Carlo	36	Toleman Group Motorsport	1.5 t/c Toleman TG181C-Hart 4	
dnq	DUTCH GP	Zandvoort	36	Toleman Group Motorsport	1.5 t/c Toleman TG181C-Hart 4	
ret	BRITISH GP	Brands Hatch	36	Toleman Group Motorsport	1.5 t/c Toleman TG181C-Hart 4	startline accident
ret	FRENCH GP	Paul Ricard	36	Toleman Group Motorsport	1.5 t/c Toleman TG181C-Hart 4	oil pump drive
dnq	GERMAN GP	Hockenheim	36	Toleman Group Motorsport	1.5 t/c Toleman TG181C-Hart 4	
ret	AUSTRIAN GP	Österreichring	36	Toleman Group Motorsport	1.5 t/c Toleman TG181C-Hart 4	driveshaft
ret	SWISS GP	Dijon	36	Toleman Group Motorsport	1.5 t/c Toleman TG181C-Hart 4	misfire
ret	ITALIAN GP	Monza	36	Toleman Group Motorsport	1.5 t/c Toleman TG181C-Hart 4	engine cut out
dnq	CAESARS PALACE GP	Las Vegas	36	Toleman Group Motorsport	1.5 t/c Toleman TG181C-Hart 4	

1984

	Race	Circuit	No	Entrant	Car/Engine	Comment
ret	BRAZILIAN GP	Rio	2	MRD International	1.5 t/c Brabham BT53-BMW 4	turbo
ret	SOUTH AFRICAN GP	Kyalami	2	MRD International	1.5 t/c Brabham BT53-BMW 4	turbo compressor
ret	BELGIAN GP	Zolder	2	MRD International	1.5 t/c Brabham BT53-BMW 4	spun off
ret	SAN MARINO GP	Imola	2	MRD International	1.5 t/c Brabham BT53-BMW 4	turbo
9	FRENCH GP	Dijon	2	MRD International	1.5 t/c Brabham BT53-BMW 4	1 lap behind
3*	US GP (DETROIT)	Detroit	2	MRD International	1.5 t/c Brabham BT53-BMW 4	* 2nd place car disqualified
ret	BRITISH GP	Brands Hatch	2	MRD International	1.5 t/c Brabham BT53-BMW 4	electrics
ret	GERMAN GP	Hockenheim	2	MRD International	1.5 t/c Brabham BT53-BMW 4	lost turbo boost
4	AUSTRIAN GP	Österreichring	2	MRD International	1.5 t/c Brabham BT53-BMW 4	
5	DUTCH GP	Zandvoort	2	MRD International	1.5 t/c Brabham BT53-BMW 4	1 lap behind
ret	ITALIAN GP	Monza	2	MRD International	1.5 t/c Brabham BT53-BMW 4	engine/broken oil line
ret	EUROPEAN GP	Nürburgring	2	MRD International	1.5 t/c Brabham BT53-BMW 4	gearbox

1985

	Race	Circuit	No	Entrant	Car/Engine	Comment
ret	MONACO GP	Monte Carlo	19	Toleman Group Motorsport	1.5 t/c Toleman TG185-Hart 4	turbo
ret	CANADIAN GP	Montreal	19	Toleman Group Motorsport	1.5 t/c Toleman TG185-Hart 4	started from pit lane/turbo
ret	US GP (DETROIT)	Detroit	19	Toleman Group Motorsport	1.5 t/c Toleman TG185-Hart 4	clutch
14/ret	FRENCH GP	Paul Ricard	19	Toleman Group Motorsport	1.5 t/c Toleman TG185-Hart 4	fuel pressure/4 laps behind
ret	BRITISH GP	Silverstone	19	Toleman Group Motorsport	1.5 t/c Toleman TG185-Hart 4	cwp
ret	GERMAN GP	Nürburgring	19	Toleman Group Motorsport	1.5 t/c Toleman TG185-Hart 4	clutch/Pole
ret	AUSTRIAN GP	Österreichring	19	Toleman Group Motorsport	1.5 t/c Toleman TG185-Hart 4	electrics
ret	DUTCH GP	Zandvoort	19	Toleman Group Motorsport	1.5 t/c Toleman TG185-Hart 4	wheel bearing
12	ITALIAN GP	Monza	19	Toleman Group Motorsport	1.5 t/c Toleman TG185-Hart 4	2 pit stops-handling/4 laps behind
ret	BELGIAN GP	Spa	19	Toleman Group Motorsport	1.5 t/c Toleman TG185-Hart 4	throttle linkage
ret	EUROPEAN GP	Brands Hatch	19	Toleman Group Motorsport	1.5 t/c Toleman TG185-Hart 4	engine
ret	SOUTH AFRICAN GP	Kyalami	19	Toleman Group Motorsport	1.5 t/c Toleman TG185-Hart 4	engine
ret	AUSTRALIAN GP	Adelaide	19	Toleman Group Motorsport	1.5 t/c Toleman TG185-Hart 4	engine

1986

	Race	Circuit	No	Entrant	Car/Engine	Comment
10	BRAZILIAN GP	Rio	19	Benetton Formula Ltd	1.5 t/c Benetton B186-BMW 4	pit stop-electrics/5 laps behind
5	SPANISH GP	Jerez	19	Benetton Formula Ltd	1.5 t/c Benetton B186-BMW 4	hit Laffite-pit stop/1 lap behind
ret	SAN MARINO GP	Imola	19	Benetton Formula Ltd	1.5 t/c Benetton B186-BMW 4	engine
ret	MONACO GP	Monte Carlo	19	Benetton Formula Ltd	1.5 t/c Benetton B186-BMW 4	brakes
7	BELGIAN GP	Spa	19	Benetton Formula Ltd	1.5 t/c Benetton B186-BMW 4	collision with Tambay/1 lap behind
ret	CANADIAN GP	Montreal	19	Benetton Formula Ltd	1.5 t/c Benetton B186-BMW 4	battery
ret	US GP (DETROIT)	Detroit	19	Benetton Formula Ltd	1.5 t/c Benetton B186-BMW 4	gearbox
ret	FRENCH GP	Paul Ricard	19	Benetton Formula Ltd	1.5 t/c Benetton B186-BMW 4	engine misfire
ret	BRITISH GP	Brands Hatch	19	Benetton Formula Ltd	1.5 t/c Benetton B186-BMW 4	fuel system
ret	GERMAN GP	Hockenheim	19	Benetton Formula Ltd	1.5 t/c Benetton B186-BMW 4	accident at start
ret	HUNGARIAN GP	Hungaroring	19	Benetton Formula Ltd	1.5 t/c Benetton B186-BMW 4	transmission-spun off
ret	AUSTRIAN GP	Österreichring	19	Benetton Formula Ltd	1.5 t/c Benetton B186-BMW 4	engine/Pole
ret	ITALIAN GP	Monza	19	Benetton Formula Ltd	1.5 t/c Benetton B186-BMW 4	puncture/Pole/FL
8	PORTUGUESE GP	Estoril	19	Benetton Formula Ltd	1.5 t/c Benetton B186-BMW 4	2 laps behind
ret	MEXICAN GP	Mexico City	19	Benetton Formula Ltd	1.5 t/c Benetton B186-BMW 4	engine
10	AUSTRALIAN GP	Adelaide	19	Benetton Formula Ltd	1.5 t/c Benetton B186-BMW 4	2 pit stops-tyres/5 laps behind

1987

	Race	Circuit	No	Entrant	Car/Engine	Comment
ret	BRAZILIAN GP	Rio	19	Benetton Formula Ltd	1.5 t/c Benetton B187-Cosworth V6	turbo
ret	SAN MARINO GP	Imola	19	Benetton Formula Ltd	1.5 t/c Benetton B187-Cosworth V6	turbo/FL
ret	BELGIAN GP	Spa	19	Benetton Formula Ltd	1.5 t/c Benetton B187-Cosworth V6	engine/oil pump drive belt
8	MONACO GP	Monte Carlo	19	Benetton Formula Ltd	1.5 t/c Benetton B187-Cosworth V6	2 laps behind
ret	US GP (DETROIT)	Detroit	19	Benetton Formula Ltd	1.5 t/c Benetton B187-Cosworth V6	accident with Cheever
5/ret	FRENCH GP	Paul Ricard	19	Benetton Formula Ltd	1.5 t/c Benetton B187-Cosworth V6	driveshaft/3 laps behind
6	BRITISH GP	Silverstone	19	Benetton Formula Ltd	1.5 t/c Benetton B187-Cosworth V6	2 laps behind
ret	GERMAN GP	Hockenheim	19	Benetton Formula Ltd	1.5 t/c Benetton B187-Cosworth V6	engine
ret	HUNGARIAN GP	Hungaroring	19	Benetton Formula Ltd	1.5 t/c Benetton B187-Cosworth V6	gearbox
3	AUSTRIAN GP	Österreichring	19	Benetton Formula Ltd	1.5 t/c Benetton B187-Cosworth V6	1 lap behind
7	ITALIAN GP	Monza	19	Benetton Formula Ltd	1.5 t/c Benetton B187-Cosworth V6	1 lap behind
4/ret	PORTUGUESE GP	Estoril	19	Benetton Formula Ltd	1.5 t/c Benetton B187-Cosworth V6	out of fuel/1 lap behind
ret	SPANISH GP	Jerez	19	Benetton Formula Ltd	1.5 t/c Benetton B187-Cosworth V6	engine
5	MEXICAN GP	Mexico City	19	Benetton Formula Ltd	1.5 t/c Benetton B187-Cosworth V6	2 laps behind
ret	JAPANESE GP	Suzuka	19	Benetton Formula Ltd	1.5 t/c Benetton B187-Cosworth V6	engine
ret	AUSTRALIAN GP	Adelaide	19	Benetton Formula Ltd	1.5 t/c Benetton B187-Cosworth V6	brakes

GP Starts: 64   GP Wins: 0   Pole positions: 3   Fastest laps: 2   Points: 23

TEO FABI

Teo Fabi has been fortunate enough to have a foot in both the Formula 1 and IndyCar camps. However, sadly for the Italian, he seems not to have made the most of either opportunity.

The European karting champion of 1975, Teo began his rise to prominence with fourth place in the 1978 European F3 championship, followed by a trip down-under to win the New Zealand Formula Pacific series. This set up a season in Formula 2 for 1979 with a semi-works March, but Fabi took a while to find his feet and finished a disappointed tenth in the final standings.

With the backing of Robin Herd, who rated him very highly, Teo led the works March Formula 2 effort in 1980. The season was dominated by the Toleman pair of Henton and Warwick, but Fabi was third, and seemed certain to join the March F1 team for 1981 until the drive went to Derek Daly at the eleventh hour. Instead Teo opted for a season in Can-Am with the Paul Newman team's March 817 and won four races, but the more consistent Geoff Brabham took the title.

In 1982 the Toleman team gave Teo a Grand Prix opportunity that he was soon to regret taking. The year was a disaster and Fabi's stock in Europe was low, but help was at hand and, with Herd's backing, Teo got himself a ride in Indy cars for 1983. He put the Forsythe March on pole for the Indy 500 – only his second outing for the team – and led the race. He went on to score four wins that season and was undisputed Rookie of the Year. Teo then took on a punishing schedule for 1984, accepting an offer to continue in Indy cars while racing in F1 for Brabham whenever commitments allowed, and in the end he gave up the Indy ride to concentrate full-time on F1. Rejoining Toleman for 1985, he earned pole position at the Nürburgring, which indicated the car's potential, but reliability was elusive. After the take-over by Benetton, Fabi stayed on, and the 1986 BMW-powered car proved very fast, Teo taking two pole positions, but he was over-shadowed by his team-mate Berger and then, in 1987, by Boutsen.

Realising his chances of finding a top seat in F1 were slim, Fabi opted for a return to Indy cars in 1988 with the ambitious Porsche project but this was to prove fraught with many problems over its three-year span and yielded but a single win, in 1989. Teo then successfully turned to endurance racing with TWR Jaguar, winning the 1991 drivers' championship, mainly by dint of his consistent finishes. He had to be content with a place in the Toyota team at Le Mans the following year, but set up yet another return to Indy cars for 1993, although his season with the Pennzoil Hall/VDS team was to prove undistinguished.

PASCAL FABRE

Fabre seemed quite promising in his first season of Formula 2 in 1982 when paired with the very quick Philippe Streiff in the little AGS team, but he was forced to drop back into European F3 the following year and, despite a bright start, lack of finance forced his Martini off the grid before the season was out. Back in F2, he surprised many in 1984 with his speed in a March-BMW, winning at Hockenheim in mid-season only to depart from his team abruptly due to financial differences.

His plans for a Formula 3000 drive in 1985 fell through, and he had to settle for a single race at the end of the year before arranging a full season with a minimal budget in 1986. A winning start at Silverstone, followed by a second at Vallelunga, gave him an early-season lead which he was unable to maintain, Pascal finishing seventh in the championship table.

Prompted no doubt by his past links with the team, AGS chose Fabre to drive their F1 challenger in 1987. The car was slow, but he flogged away, usually bringing it to the finish, until he lost his ride to Roberto Moreno. Pascal then moved on to sports cars, most notably with the Cougar-Porsche.

FABRE, Pascal (F) b 9/1/1960

1987

	Race	Circuit	No	Entrant	Car/Engine	Comment
12	BRAZILIAN GP	Rio	14	Team El Charro AGS	3.5 AGS JH22-Cosworth V8	3rd non-turbo/6 laps behind
13	SAN MARINO GP	Imola	14	Team El Charro AGS	3.5 AGS JH22-Cosworth V8	3rd non-turbo/6 laps behind
10/ret	BELGIAN GP	Spa	14	Team El Charro AGS	3.5 AGS JH22-Cosworth V8	3rd non-turbo/electrics/-5 laps
13	MONACO GP	Monte Carlo	14	Team El Charro AGS	3.5 AGS JH22-Cosworth V8	3rd non-turbo/7 laps behind
12	US GP (DETROIT)	Detroit	14	Team El Charro AGS	3.5 AGS JH22-Cosworth V8	3rd non-turbo/5 laps behind
9	FRENCH GP	Paul Ricard	14	Team El Charro AGS	3.5 AGS JH22-Cosworth V8	3rd non-turbo/6 laps behind
9	BRITISH GP	Silverstone	14	Team El Charro AGS	3.5 AGS JH22-Cosworth V8	2nd non-turbo/6 laps behind
ret	GERMAN GP	Hockenheim	14	Team El Charro AGS	3.5 AGS JH22-Cosworth V8	engine
13	HUNGARIAN GP	Hungaroring	14	Team El Charro AGS	3.5 AGS JH22-Cosworth V8	4th non-turbo/5 laps behind
nc	AUSTRIAN GP	Österreichring	14	Team El Charro AGS	3.5 AGS JH22-Cosworth V8	started from pit lane/7 laps behind
dnq	ITALIAN GP	Monza	14	Team El Charro AGS	3.5 AGS JH22-Cosworth V8	
dnq	PORTUGUESE GP	Estoril	14	Team El Charro AGS	3.5 AGS JH22-Cosworth V8	
ret	SPANISH GP	Jerez	14	Team El Charro AGS	3.5 AGS JH22-Cosworth V8	clutch
dnq	MEXICAN GP	Mexico City	14	Team El Charro AGS	3.5 AGS JH22-Cosworth V8	

GP Starts: 11   GP Wins: 0   Pole positions: 0   Fastest laps: 0   Points: 0

FAGIOLI, Luigi (I) b 9/6/1898 – d 20/6/1952

1950

	Race	Circuit	No	Entrant	Car/Engine	Comment
2	BRITISH GP	Silverstone	3	Alfa Romeo SpA	1.5 s/c Alfa Romeo 158/50 8	
ret	MONACO GP	Monte Carlo	36	Alfa Romeo SpA	1.5 s/c Alfa Romeo 158/50 8	multiple accident on lap 1
2	SWISS GP	Bremgarten	12	Alfa Romeo SpA	1.5 s/c Alfa Romeo 158/50 8	
2	BELGIAN GP	Spa	12	Alfa Romeo SpA	1.5 s/c Alfa Romeo 158/50 8	
2	FRENCH GP	Reims	4	Alfa Romao SpA	1.5 s/c Alfa Romeo 158/50 8	
3	ITALIAN GP	Monza	36	Alfa Romeo SpA	1.5 s/c Alfa Romeo 158/50 8	

1951

	Race	Circuit	No	Entrant	Car/Engine	Comment
1*	FRENCH GP	Reims	8	Alfa Romeo SpA	1.5 s/c Alfa Romeo 159B 8	* Fangio took over car
11*	"	"	4	Alfa Romeo SpA	1.5 s/c Alfa Romeo 159B 8	* took Fangio's car/22 laps behind

GP Starts: 7   GP Wins: 1* *(shared)*   Pole positions: 0   Fastest laps: 0   Points: 32

FAIRMAN, Jack (GB) b 15/3/1913

1953

	Race	Circuit	No	Entrant	Car/Engine	Comment
ret	BRITISH GP	Silverstone	4	John Heath	2.0 HWM-Alta 4	clutch
nc	ITALIAN GP	Monza	20	Connaught Engineering	2.0 Connaught A-Lea Francis 4	15 laps behind

1955

	Race	Circuit	No	Entrant	Car/Engine	Comment
dns	BRITISH GP	Aintree	34	Connaught Engineering	2.5 Connaught B-Alta 4	engine problems

1956

	Race	Circuit	No	Entrant	Car/Engine	Comment
4	BRITISH GP	Silverstone	21	Connaught Engineering	2.5 Connaught B-Alta 4	3 laps behind
5	ITALIAN GP	Monza	6	Connaught Engineering	2.5 Connaught B-Alta 4	3 laps behind

1957

	Race	Circuit	No	Entrant	Car/Engine	Comment
ret	BRITISH GP	Aintree	24	Owen Racing Organisation	2.5 BRM P25 4	engine

1958

	Race	Circuit	No	Entrant	Car/Engine	Comment
ret	BRITISH GP	Silverstone	14	B C Ecclestone	2.5 Connaught B-Alta 4	engine
8	MOROCCAN GP	Casablanca	30	Cooper Car Co	2.0 Cooper T45-Climax 4	3 laps behind

1959

	Race	Circuit	No	Entrant	Car/Engine	Comment
ret	BRITISH GP	Aintree	26	High Efficiency Motors	2.5 Cooper T45-Climax 4	gearbox
ret	ITALIAN GP	Monza	22	High Efficiency Motors	2.5 Cooper T45-Maserati 4	engine

1960

	Race	Circuit	No	Entrant	Car/Engine	Comment
ret	BRITISH GP	Silverstone	23	C T Atkins	2.5 Cooper T51-Climax 4	fuel pump

1961

	Race	Circuit	No	Entrant	Car/Engine	Comment
dsq*	BRITISH GP	Aintree	26	R R C Walker Racing Team	1.5 Ferguson P99-Climax 4	Moss took over/*earlier push start
ret	ITALIAN GP	Monza	30	Fred Tuck	1.5 Cooper T45-Climax 4	engine

GP Starts: 12   GP Wins: 0   Pole positions: 0   Fastest laps: 0   Points: 5

LUIGI FAGIOLI

'The old Abruzzi robber', as he became affectionately known, Fagioli was one of Italy's greatest drivers and a true individualist, who often found himself at odds with those in authority. His career started in 1926, but he really shot to fame upon joining the Maserati team in 1930. Over the next three seasons he won occasionally but was often out of luck, which prompted him to join Ferrari's Alfa Romeo team in the second half of the 1933 season. Soon he had won the GPs of Pescara, Comminges, Marseilles and Italy, which brought an invitation to drive for Mercedes-Benz as number two driver in 1934.

In his first race, the Eifelrennen, irked at being told to stay behind the sister entry of von Brauchitsch, Fagioli showed his displeasure by parking his car out on the circuit and returning to the pits on foot. It was not to be the last time he would find himself in conflict with the team, but that did not stop him winning the Italian and Spanish GPs that year, and those at Monaco, AVUS and Barcelona the following season. He continued with the team for 1936 before moving to their great rivals Auto Union, but was forced to miss much of the season through illness, although he was fifth at Tripoli.

In fact Fagioli did not return to the Grand Prix arena until 1950, with the all-conquering Alfa Romeo team. His experience stood him in good stead and some cold and calculating performances brought him third place in the World Championship. He was retained for 1951 but at the French GP he was hauled from the car at a pit stop as he recovered from an early spin to allow Fangio to take over and complete the race, the Argentinian going on to win. This was the last straw for the proud Fagioli, and he never raced a GP car again.

Turning to his own OSCA, he won his class in the Mille Miglia, a feat which he repeated in 1952 at the wheel of a Lancia Aurelia tourer. More remarkable was the fact that he was third overall ahead of many pure sports racers. That year the Monaco GP was held for sports cars only, and during practice Fagioli lost control of his car in the tunnel and broadsided out into a stone balustrade. Thrown out, he was taken to hospital unconscious, with a broken arm and leg. Four days later he regained consciousness and seemed to be out of danger, but three weeks after the crash he relapsed – with a complete failure of the nervous system – and died, aged 54.

JACK FAIRMAN

Stong as an ox, and an extremely safe and reliable driver, Jack was ideally suited to long-distance sports car racing, in which raced with distinction for Bristol, Jaguar, Ecurie Ecosse and Aston Martin during the fifties. Fairman was also in great demand as a test driver and was instrumental in the development of the Connaught GP car, being rewarded with points finishes in two Grands Prix in 1956.

In an extremely long career which began immediately after the war and lasted into the early sixties, Jack could be found driving, at one time or another, just about every type of racing machine on the tracks of Britain, Europe and beyond.

JUAN MANUEL FANGIO

Fangio will always be 'the Maestro' and justifiably so. For all his phenomenal achievements in Grand Prix racing – five World Championships and 24 wins from just 51 starts – it was as much the way he conducted himself outside the cockpit which has created an aura that exists to this day.

His origins were humble. The son of an Italian immigrant family, he grew up in Argentina in a motoring environment, working in a garage from the age of 11 to supplement the family income. He saved everything he could towards the purchase of a Model T Ford, which he raced secretly before switching to a Ford V8 special and the real beginnings of his competition career. Supported by the people of his home town, Balcarce, he acquired a Chevrolet and won the 1940 Gran Premio del Norte, a 5,900 mile road race, scoring his first major success. Throughout the next seven years he raced in these marathons with a Chevrolet, often competing with 'Los Galvez' for the top honours.

When Varzi, Villoresi, Farina and Wimille were invited to appear in Libre events in 1948, Fangio was among their local opposition, and performed so well that he was sponsored for a brief trip to Europe in 1948 with Galvez, driving a Simca-Gordini at Reims before returning home with a Maserati 4CLT.

For 1949 he was back in Europe and, at the age of 38, enjoyed a staggering debut season, winning his first race at San Remo, and following it up with wins at Perpignan, Marseilles, Pau, Albi and Monza. This led to an invitation to join the Alfa Romeo team in 1950 and he eventually finished second in the World Championship to Farina, despite winning three of the six races. He also won at Pescara, Geneva and San Remo in the Alfa, and at Pau and Angoulême in a Maserati. After handling the pre-war Mercedes in the early-season Libre events back in Argentina, Fangio then took the first of his five titles in 1951, before Alfa withdrew from competition.

In 1952, the newly crowned champion started the year in imperious form on his home continent, winning six Libre events in Argentina, Brazil and Uruguay, before returning to Europe to drive for Maserati. However, he crashed at the Monza GP and was lucky to escape with his life, suffering concussion and a broken vertebra in his neck when he was thrown from the car. He convalesced in Balcarce for the rest of the season and had leisure to ponder the thin dividing line between glory and disaster, but it did not prevent him from undertaking an even bigger racing schedule in 1953. He drove Maserati's A6GCM to victory in the Italian and Modena GPs and also took the opportunity to return to his roots by winning the Carrera Panamericana road race in a works Lancia.

His stature was unrivalled and Mercedes-Benz made it their top priority to sign him when they re-entered racing in 1954. While the cars were being prepared, he continued to drive for Maserati, winning the first two races of the season before scoring another four wins in the silver machine. The combination of Fangio's sublime talent and German technology was overwhelming, and if the car lasted he generally won. Such was his mastery that it is thought he allowed team-mates Kling and Moss to takes victories at AVUS and Aintree respectively, though he has never admitted it. Despite being a relatively old man in Grand Prix terms by this stage, he had all the resources necessary to maintain his dominant position, his seemingly inexhaustible talents equal to the demands of any situation. If there was a corner that needed to be taken flat out, then Fangio would do it; his physical strength and stamina allowed him to cope with broiling heat or pouring rain; and his powers of concentration enabled him to annihilate the opposition when his car ran well, or nurse a sick machine to the chequered flag when lesser mortals would have given up.

Fangio also had the acumen to choose the best machinery available and then make the best possible use of it. Even an uncomfortable year at Scuderia Ferrari in 1956, where he could have been undermined by the young Italian pretenders, did not prevent him taking a fourth World Championship, but he moved back to Maserati for 1957 and, with the 250F in the final stages of its useful development, took his fifth and perhaps finest championship win, highlighted by one of Grand Prix racing's greatest-ever performances at the Nürburgring, where he overhauled Hawthorn and Collins to win a sensational German GP, having gambled that a pit stop for fresh tyres would pay off rather than run non-stop as did the Ferraris. His personal standards were such that at each track he set out to better his previous performances there. He was the World Champion and it was expected, but at the Italian GP even he could not defeat Stirling Moss, by now nearly his equal as a driver. With the advantage of driving one of the emerging Vanwalls, Moss repeated the win at Pescara, and the writing was on the wall for Fangio. With no wish to return to Ferrari and with Maserati winding down their operation, his thoughts were perhaps turning to retirement, but in the event he was to race on into 1958 as an independent, selecting his races. After a fourth place in the Argentine GP he took his final win in the Libre Buenos Aires GP. He was then tempted to Indianapolis to take part in the famous 500 and, despite being given a car which was far from new, duly passed his qualification tests, but he was unhappy with the machine. Perhaps fortuitously, he was forced to return home to deal with an urgent matter relating to his garage business and thus missed the race, which was marred by tragedy after a multiple crash on the first lap.

For Fangio there was to be just one more Grand Prix, and it was perhaps one of his best. Coming home fourth, he could have been lapped right at the finish by the winner Hawthorn, who chose to spare him this indignity. However, the spectators were unaware that Fangio had raced without the benefit of a clutch from early on. With the engine turning at 8,000 rpm, 'the Maestro' relied on his ears to judge when to change gear throughout the race in a remarkable display which showed his legendary empathy with his machinery. He went home to Balcarce never to return as a driver, deciding that the time was right for him to stop. Of course his presence has graced the circuits on many occasions since, and he holds a magnetic attraction for young and old alike, who recognise they are rubbing shoulders not only with a legendary racing driver, but also with a man of great sincerity and generosity of heart to whom the sport owes a great debt.

FANGIO, Juan Manuel (RA) b 24/6/1911

1950

	Race	Circuit	No	Entrant	Car/Engine	Comment
ret	BRITISH GP	Silverstone	1	Alfa Romeo SpA	1.5 s/c Alfa Romeo 158/50 8	oil pipe
1	MONACO GP	Monte Carlo	34	Alfa Romeo SpA	1.5 s/c Alfa Romeo 158/50 8	Pole/FL
ret	SWISS GP	Bremgarten	14	Alfa Romeo SpA	1.5 s/c Alfa Romeo 158/50 8	valve/Pole
1	BELGIAN GP	Spa	10	Alfa Romeo SpA	1.5 s/c Alfa Romeo 158/50 8	
1	FRENCH GP	Reims	6	Alfa Romeo SpA	1.5 s/c Alfa Romeo 158/50 8	Pole/FL
ret	ITALIAN GP	Monza	18	Alfa Romeo SpA	1.5 s/c Alfa Romeo 159A 8	gearbox/Pole/FL
ret	"	"	60	Alfa Romeo SpA	1.5 s/c Alfa Romeo 158/50 8	took Taruffi's car/engine

1951 World Champion Driver

1	SWISS GP	Bremgarten	24	Alfa Romeo SpA	1.5 s/c Alfa Romeo 159A 8	Pole/FL
9	BELGIAN GP	Spa	2	Alfa Romeo SpA	1.5 s/c Alfa Romeo 159B 8	jammed rear wheel in pits/Pole/FL
11*	FRENCH GP	Reims	4	Alfa Romeo SpA	1.5 s/c Alfa Romeo 159A 8	* Fagioli took over/Pole
1*	"	"	8	Alfa Romeo SpA	1.5 s/c Alfa Romeo 159A 8	* took over Fagioli's car/FL
2	BRITISH GP	Silverstone	2	Alfa Romeo SpA	1.5 s/c Alfa Romeo 159B 8	
2	GERMAN GP	Nürburgring	75	Alfa Romeo SpA	1.5 s/c Alfa Romeo 159B 8	FL
ret	ITALIAN GP	Monza	38	Alfa Romeo SpA	1.5 s/c Alfa Romeo 159M 8	engine/Pole
1	SPANISH GP	Pedralbes	22	Alfa Romeo SpA	1.5 s/c Alfa Romeo 159M 8	FL

1953

ret	ARGENTINE GP	Buenos Aires	2	Officine Alfieri Maserati	2.0 Maserati A6GCM 6	universal joint
ret	DUTCH GP	Zandvoort	12	Officine Alfieri Maserati	2.0 Maserati A6GCM 6	rear axle
ret	BELGIAN GP	Spa	4	Officine Alfieri Maserati	2.0 Maserati A6GCM 6	engine/Pole
ret	"	"	6	Officine Alfieri Maserati	2.0 Maserati A6GCM 6	took Claes' car/steering-accident
2	FRENCH GP	Reims	18	Officine Alfieri Maserati	2.0 Maserati A6GCM 6	FL
2	BRITISH GP	Silverstone	23	Officine Alfieri Maserati	2.0 Maserati A6GCM 6	
2	GERMAN GP	Nürburgring	5	Officine Alfieri Maserati	2.0 Maserati A6GCM 6	
4*	SWISS GP	Bremgarten	32	Officine Alfieri Maserati	2.0 Maserati A6GCM 6	Pole/*Bonetto took over/1 lap behind
ret	"	"	30	Officine Alfieri Maserati	2.0 Maserati A6GCM 6	* took over Bonetto's car/engine
1	ITALIAN GP	Monza	50	Officine Alfieri Maserati	2.0 Maserati A6GCM 6	FL

1954 World Champion Driver

1	ARGENTINE GP	Buenos Aires	2	Officine Alfieri Maserati	2.5 Maserati 250F 6	
1	BELGIAN GP	Spa	26	Officine Alfieri Maserati	2.5 Maserati 250F 6	Pole/FL
1	FRENCH GP	Reims	18	Daimler Benz AG	2.5 Mercedes-Benz W196 8	Pole
4	BRITISH GP	Silverstone	1	Daimler Benz AG	2.5 Mercedes-Benz W196 8	Pole/FL (shared)/1 lap behind
1	GERMAN GP	Nürburgring	18	Daimler Benz AG	2.5 Mercedes-Benz W196 8	Pole
1	SWISS GP	Bremgarten	4	Daimler Benz AG	2.5 Mercedes-Benz W196 8	FL
1	ITALIAN GP	Monza	16	Daimler Benz AG	2.5 Mercedes-Benz W196 8	Pole
3	SPANISH GP	Pedralbes	2	Daimler Benz AG	2.5 Mercedes-Benz W196 8	1 lap behind

1955 World Champion Driver

1	ARGENTINE GP	Buenos Aires	2	Daimler Benz AG	2.5 Mercedes-Benz W196 8	FL
ret	MONACO GP	Monte Carlo	2	Daimler Benz AG	2.5 Mercedes-Benz W196 8	rear axle/Pole/FL
1	BELGIAN GP	Spa	10	Daimler Benz AG	2.5 Mercedes-Benz W196 8	FL
1	DUTCH GP	Zandvoort	8	Daimler Benz AG	2.5 Mercedes-Benz W196 8	Pole
2	BRITISH GP	Aintree	10	Daimler Benz AG	2.5 Mercedes-Benz W196 8	
1	ITALIAN GP	Monza	18	Daimler Benz AG	2.5 Mercedes-Benz W196 8	Pole

1956 World Champion Driver

ret	ARGENTINE GP	Buenos Aires	30	Scuderia Ferrari	2.5 Lancia-Ferrari D50 V8	fuel pump/Pole
1*	"	" "	34	Scuderia Ferrari	2.5 Lancia-Ferrari D50 V8	*took over Musso's car/FL
4*	MONACO GP	Monte Carlo	20	Scuderia Ferrari	2.5 Lancia-Ferrari D50 V8	Pole/*Castellotti took over/-6 laps
2*	"	" "	26	Scuderia Ferrari	2.5 Lancia-Ferrari D50 V8	* took over Collins' car/FL
ret	BELGIAN GP	Spa	2	Scuderia Ferrari	2.5 Lancia-Ferrari D50 V8	transmission/Pole
4	FRENCH GP	Reims	10	Scuderia Ferrari	2.5 Lancia-Ferrari D50 V8	p stop-split fuel pipe/Pole/FL
1	BRITISH GP	Silverstone	1	Scuderia Ferrari	2.5 Lancia-Ferrari D50 V8	
1	GERMAN GP	Nürburgring	1	Scuderia Ferrari	2.5 Lancia-Ferrari D50 V8	Pole/FL
8*	ITALIAN GP	Monza	22	Scuderia Ferrari	2.5 Lancia-Ferrari D50 V8	Pole/*Castellotti took over/-4 laps
2*	"	"	26	Scuderia Ferrari	2.5 Lancia-Ferrari D50 V8	* took over Collins' car

1957 World Champion Driver

1	ARGENTINE GP	Buenos Aires	2	Officine Alfieri Maserati	2.5 Maserati 250F 6	
1	MONACO GP	Monte Carlo	32	Officine Alfieri Maserati	2.5 Maserati 250F 6	Pole/FL
dns	"	" "	32	Officine Alfieri Maserati	2.5 Maserati 250F V12	practice only
1	FRENCH GP	Rouen	2	Officine Alfieri Maserati	2.5 Maserati 250F 6	Pole
ret	BRITISH GP	Aintree	2	Officine Alfieri Maserati	2.5 Maserati 250F 6	engine
1	GERMAN GP	Nürburgring	1	Officine Alfieri Maserati	2.5 Maserati 250F 6	Pole/FL
2	PESCARA GP	Pescara	2	Officine Alfieri Maserati	2.5 Maserati 250F 6	Pole
dns	"	"	2	Officine Alfieri Maserati	2.5 Maserati 250F V12	practice only
2	ITALIAN GP	Monza	2	Officine Alfieri Maserati	2.5 Maserati 250F 6	
dns	"	"	2	Officine Alfieri Maserati	2.5 Maserati 250F V12	practice only

1958

4	ARGENTINE GP	Buenos Aires	2	Scuderia Sud Americana	2.5 Maserati 250F 6	Pole/FL
4	FRENCH GP	Reims	34	Juan Manuel Fangio	2.5 Maserati 250F 6	

GP Starts: 51   GP Wins: 24   Pole positions: 28   Fastest laps: 23   Points: 277.14

GIUSEPPE FARINA

Giuseppe 'Nino' Farina was very much his own man, a private person, who did not make any great attempts to mix and guarded his private life jealously. He even played down his achievement in becoming World Champion in 1950, refusing to get involved in the razzmatazz which followed.

By the time he won the title, he was one of the most senior campaigners still regularly active, having made his competition debut in the Aosta-St Bernard hill-climb as far back as 1932. It was a chastening experience for he crashed and ended up in hospital, but it was to be only the first of many accidents sustained in a long career by this tough, aristocratic Italian who seemed totally indestructible.

After driving a Maserati with little success, his first break came when he raced an Alfa Romeo under the tutelage of the great Nuvolari. At that time the red cars were outclassed by the mighty German machines and the young Farina often ran out of road in his desperate attempts to keep pace. He did, however, win the Naples GP in 1937 and was Italian champion in the years 1937-39, with further successes in the Alfa Romeo 158 at the Antwerp GP, Coppa Ciano and Prix de Berne. He also gave a fantastic display at the 1939 Swiss GP with the underpowered Alfa, leading many faster cars before giving way. Having won the Tripoli GP, Farina was probably reaching his peak when the war suspended all racing activity, but in 1946 he returned to immediate effect, winning the GP des Nations at Geneva. Enzo Ferrari had great regard for his ability, Farina excelling on fast courses with his imperious, upright, arms-at-length driving style.

In 1948 he drove an independent Maserati, winning at Monaco, Geneva and Mar del Plata, and he continued with the car into the following season, when he won the Lausanne GP and finished second in the International Trophy, but also drove for Ferrari, winning the Rosario GP in a Tipo 166.

When Alfa Romeo returned to action in 1950 Farina joined Fangio and Fagioli in the classic 158s and, keeping a cool head and showing tremendous courage, took the first-ever World Championship for drivers. In 1951 he remained with Alfa and won the Belgian GP, but was outshone by Fangio, and he was to find the same problem when he joined Ferrari the following year. With Ascari sweeping all before him, 'Nino' was left in his wake, picking up wins only in the minor GPs at Naples and Monza. He was none too happy to play second fiddle , but was generally unable to match the searing pace set by his team-mate, although he did take a brilliant win in the German GP after losing a wheel. When Ascari moved to Lancia for 1954, Farina sniffed another title chance after a bright start to the season which included a win in the Syracuse GP, but after crashing in the Mille Miglia he recovered only to be involved in a very nasty incident at Monza when his car caught fire, leaving the driver with badly burned legs.

He bravely returned in 1955, needing morphine to complete the Argentine GP, in which he shared two cars, and also took points at Monaco and Spa. His injuries caused him to announce his retirement at the end of the season, but he was soon back in a half-hearted attempt to qualify at Indianapolis, before yet another accident in practice at the Monza Supercortemaggiore race, which left him with a broken collarbone. Recovered once more, he returned to Indy, but after his car was crashed with fatal results by a young American, Keith Andrews, he lost interest and retired for good. It was ironic that after surviving so many racing accidents, Farina should lose his life in a road crash in 1966.

FARINA, Giuseppe (I) b 30/10/1906 – d 30/6/1966

	Race	Car	No	Entrant	Car/Engine	Comment
	1950 World Champion Driver					
1	BRITISH GP	Silverstone	2	Alfa Romeo SpA	1.5 s/c Alfa Romeo 158/50 8	Pole/FL
ret	MONACO GP	Monte Carlo	32	Alfa Romeo SpA	1.5 s/c Alfa Romeo 158/50 8	multiple accident–lap 1
1	SWISS GP	Bremgarten	16	Alfa Romeo SpA	1.5 s/c Alfa Romeo 158/50 8	FL
4	BELGIAN GP	Spa	8	Alfa Romeo SpA	1.5 s/c Alfa Romeo 158/50 8	long pit stop/Pole/FL
ret	FRENCH GP	Reims	2	Alfa Romeo SpA	1.5 s/c Alfa Romeo 158/50 8	fuel pump
1	ITALIAN GP	Monza	10	Alfa Romeo SpA	1.5 s/c Alfa Romeo 158/50 8	
	1951					
3	SWISS GP	Bremgarten	22	Alfa Romeo SpA	1.5 s/c Alfa Romeo 159A 8	
1	BELGIAN GP	Spa	4	Alfa Romeo SpA	1.5 s/c Alfa Romeo 159A 8	
5	FRENCH GP	Reims	2	Alfa Romeo SpA	1.5 s/c Alfa Romeo 159A 8	4 laps behind
ret	BRITISH GP	Silverstone	1	Alfa Romeo SpA	1.5 s/c Alfa Romeo 159B 8	slipping clutch/FL
ret	GERMAN GP	Nürburgring	76	Alfa Romeo SpA	1.5 s/c Alfa Romeo 159B 8	gearbox
ret	ITALIAN GP	Monza	34	Alfa Romeo SpA	1.5 s/c Alfa Romeo 159M 8	engine
3*	"	"	40	Alfa Romeo SpA	1.5 s/c Alfa Romeo 159A 8	*took Bonetto's car/FL/1 lap behind
3	SPANISH GP	Pedralbes	20	Alfa Romeo SpA	1.5 s/c Alfa Romeo 159M 8	
	1952					
ret	SWISS GP	Bremgarten	28	Scuderia Ferrari	2.0 Ferrari 500 4	magneto/Pole
ret	"	"	32	Scuderia Ferrari	2.0 Ferrari 500 4	took over Simon's car/magneto
2	BELGIAN GP	Spa	2	Scuderia Ferrari	2.0 Ferrari 500 4	
2	FRENCH GP	Rouen	10	Scuderia Ferrari	2.0 Ferrari 500 4	
6	BRITISH GP	Silverstone	16	Scuderia Ferrari	2.0 Ferrari 500 4	pit stop-plugs/Pole/3 laps behind
2	GERMAN GP	Nürburgring	102	Scuderia Ferrari	2.0 Ferrari 500 4	
2	DUTCH GP	Zandvoort	4	Scuderia Ferrari	2.0 Ferrari 500 4	
4	ITALIAN GP	Monza	10	Scuderia Ferrari	2.0 Ferrari 500 4	
	1953					
ret	ARGENTINE GP	Buenos Aires	12	Scuderia Ferrari	2.0 Ferrari 500 4	boy ran into path of car and killed
2	DUTCH GP	Zandvoort	6	Scuderia Ferrari	2.0 Ferrari 500 4	
ret	BELGIAN GP	Spa	12	Scuderia Ferrari	2.0 Ferrari 500 4	engine
5	FRENCH GP	Reims	14	Scuderia Ferrari	2.0 Ferrari 500 4	

3	BRITISH GP	Silverstone	6	Scuderia Ferrari	2.0 Ferrari 500 4	*2 laps behind*
1	GERMAN GP	Nürburgring	2	Scuderia Ferrari	2.0 Ferrari 500 4	
2	SWISS GP	Bremgarten	24	Scuderia Ferrari	2.0 Ferrari 500 4	
2	ITALIAN GP	Monza	6	Scuderia Ferrari	2.0 Ferrari 500 4	
	1954					
2	ARGENTINE GP	Buenos Aires	10	Scuderia Ferrari	2.5 Ferrari 625 4	*Pole*
ret	BELGIAN GP	Spa	4	Scuderia Ferrari	2.5 Ferrari 553 4	*ignition*
dns	"	"	4	Scuderia Ferrari	2.5 Ferrari 625 4	*practice only*
	1955					
3	ARGENTINE GP	Buenos Aires	10	Scuderia Ferrari	2.5 Ferrari 625/555 4	*Maglioli and Trintignant also/-2 laps*
2	"	" "	12	Scuderia Ferrari	2.5 Ferrari 625/555 4	*Gonzalez's car/Trintignant also*
4	MONACO GP	Monte Carlo	42	Scuderia Ferrari	2.5 Ferrari 625 4	*1 lap behind*
3	BELGIAN GP	Spa	2	Scuderia Ferrari	2.5 Ferrari 555 4	
dns	ITALIAN GP	Monza	2	Scuderia Ferrari	2.5 Lancia D50 V8	*withdrawn-tyre trouble in practice*

GP Starts: 33   GP Wins: 5   Pole positions: 5   Fastest laps: 5   Points: 127.33

MARIA-TERESA de FILIPPIS

Maria-Teresa made a little bit of Grand Prix history when she became the first woman to start a World Championship Grand Prix, having competed successfully for a number of years in Italian national sports car racing, first with a little OSCA and then, from 1955, with a more powerful Maserati.

With the help, initially, of Luigi Musso, she broke into Formula 1 in 1958, scoring a fifth place at Syracuse in a rather thin field, before tackling four Grands Prix in her Maserati 250F.

She was taken under the wing of Jean Behra for 1959, but after his death at AVUS she retired from racing. Today she retains a link with the sport through her involvement in the Société des Anciens Pilotes.

RUDI FISCHER

A restaurateur and highly proficient amateur racer and hill-climb expert, Fischer enjoyed great success with his own single-seater Ferraris in the early fifties, run under the Ecurie Espadon banner.

Encouraged by his form in a Simca in 1949, and a sixth place in the Prix de Berne, sharing an HWM with Moss, he acquired a V12 Ferrari for the 1951 season, which he drove to great effect, particularly in non-championship events, finishing second at Bordeaux, third at San Remo and Syracuse and fourth in the Dutch GP. That season he also won F2 events at AVUS, Aix-les-Bains and Angoulême and enjoyed success in hill-climbs.

For 1952 Rudi managed to buy one of the latest T500 Ferraris, and did justice to it by finishing second in the Swiss GP and third in the German GP at World Championship level, while victories at AVUS and in the Eifelrennen were the highlights of a productive programme of lesser races.

It was some surprise when this excellent and most underrated driver quit international racing at the end of the season, although he continued to make occasional appearances, mostly in hill-climbs, into the late fifties.

JOHN FITCH

With just two Grand Prix races recorded against his name, the uninitiated may be given the false impression that John Fitch was just another insignificant run-of-the-mill driver – far from it.

Born into a wealthy family, and with a motoring background courtesy of his step-father, Fitch served as a fighter pilot during World War II, and was held as a POW after being shot down. In poor physical condition upon his release, he did not turn to motor racing until 1949, but was soon a major name in SCCA circles. In March 1951, on his first racing trip overseas, he won the Peron Grand Prix, a sports car race in Buenos Aires, driving an Allard-Cadillac. This victory brought him to the attention of millionare racer and entrant Briggs Cunningham, who took him into his sports car team, which was attempting to win Le Mans and other long-distance events. John won the Sebring 12 Hours, and finished third in the Cunningham at Le Mans in 1953, a season which also saw him dip his toe into single-seater racing with HWM in the Italian GP and finish fourth at Aix-les-Bains in a Cooper-Bristol, attempt to qualify for Indianapolis, and take part in the Monte Carlo and Alpine Rallies . . .

Having impressed Neubauer during a test in a 300SL Mercedes in 1952, Fitch finally got the call from the great man and found himself in the factory sports car team for 1955, and reserve driver (not used) at a couple of Grands Prix. Unfortunately this was the year of the Le Mans disaster, and Fitch's co-driver 'Levegh' was a central figure in the tragedy. John did, however, have the satisfaction of sharing the winning Mercedes with Moss at Dundrod later in the year before the Stuttgart team withdrew from racing.

Fitch then returned to the States, initially to help Chevrolet's sports car effort, which limited his racing somewhat, but nothing was allowed to get in the way of his annual pilgrimage to Sebring which lasted until 1964 – by which time he was fully involved in the management of the Lime Rock circuit, which was used for both racing and the testing of road cars.

CHRISTIAN FITTIPALDI

With excellent backing from his Brazilian sponsors, and the guidance of his father Wilson, himself a former Grand Prix driver, Christian has so far done everything that could be expected of one so young.

With a single season in South American F3 behind him, he came to Britain to race in the 1990 F3 championship. Taking the number two seat to Häkkinen in the crack West Surrey Racing team, Fittipaldi finished fourth in the final standings with just one win at Donington. Moving up to F3000 for 1991 with Pacific Racing, young Christian was certainly fortunate to be in a Reynard chassis, but he held to his conviction that consistency would count and, when he had to, could show the pack a clean pair of heels, as he proved at Jerez and Nogaro. The championship was his, and he thus became the third Grand Prix driver to emerge from this remarkable family.

His first season with Minardi was interrupted when a practice crash at Magny Cours inflicted back injuries that put him out for a spell, but after a shaky return he bounced back in Japan to score his first championship point. Continuing with the underfinanced Minardi team in 1993, Fittipaldi started well but, with the car less and less competitive as the season progressed, the young Brazilian was stood down for the final two races to make room for the well-financed Gounon. Meanwhile Christian, his sponsors and advisers were busy trying to arrange a move to a bigger team for 1994.

FILIPPIS, Maria-Teresa de (I) b 11/11/1926

1958

	Race	Circuit	No	Entrant	Car/Engine	Comment
dnq	MONACO GP	Monte Carlo	44	Maria-Teresa de Filippis	2.5 Maserati 250F 6	
10	BELGIAN GP	Spa	26	Maria-Teresa de Filippis	2.5 Maserati 250F 6	2 laps behind
ret	PORTUGUESE GP	Oporto	30	Scuderia Centro Sud	2.5 Maserati 250F 6	mechanical
ret	ITALIAN GP	Monza	42	Maria-Teresa de Filippis	2.5 Maserati 250F 6	engine

1959

	Race	Circuit	No	Entrant	Car/Engine	Comment
dnq	MONACO GP	Monte Carlo	4	Dr Ing F Porsche KG	1.5 Behra-Porsche F4	F2 car

GP Starts: 3   GP Wins: 0   Pole positions: 0   Fastest laps: 0   Points: 0

FISCHER, Rudi (CH) b 19/5/1912 – d 30/12/1976

1951

	Race	Circuit	No	Entrant	Car/Engine	Comment
11	SWISS GP	Bremgarten	38	Ecurie Espadon	2.5 Ferrari 212 V12	3 laps behind
6	GERMAN GP	Nürburgring	91	Ecurie Espadon	2.5 Ferrari 212 V12	1 lap behind

1952

	Race	Circuit	No	Entrant	Car/Engine	Comment
2	SWISS GP	Bremgarten	42	Ecurie Espadon	2.0 Ferrari 500 4	
11*	FRENCH GP	Rouen	34	Ecurie Espadon	2.0 Ferrari 500 4	* Hirt took over/13 laps behind
13	BRITISH GP	Silverstone	19	Ecurie Espadon	2.0 Ferrari 500 4	5 laps behind
3	GERMAN GP	Nürburgring	117	Ecurie Espadon	2.0 Ferrari 500 4	
ret	ITALIAN GP	Monza	18	Ecurie Espadon	2.0 Ferrari 500 4	engine

GP Starts: 7   GP Wins: 0   Pole positions: 0   Fastest laps: 0   Points: 10

FISHER, Mike (CDN)

1967

	Race	Circuit	No	Entrant	Car/Engine	Comment
11	CANADIAN GP	Mosport Park	6	Mike Fisher	2.0 Lotus 33-BRM V8	pit stops-electrics/9 laps behind
dns	MEXICAN GP	Mexico City	10	Mike Fisher	2.0 Lotus 33-BRM V8	fuel metering unit on grid

GP Starts: 1   GP Wins: 0   Pole positions: 0   Fastest laps: 0   Points: 0

FITCH, John (USA) b 4/8/1917

1953

	Race	Circuit	No	Entrant	Car/Engine	Comment
ret	ITALIAN GP	Monza	18	HW Motors Ltd	2.0 HWM-Alta 4	engine

1955

	Race	Circuit	No	Entrant	Car/Engine	Comment
9	ITALIAN GP	Monza	40	Stirling Moss Ltd	2.5 Maserati 250F 6	4 laps behind

GP Starts: 2   GP Wins: 0   Pole positions: 0   Fastest laps: 0   Points: 0

FITTIPALDI, Christian (BR) b 18/1/1971

1992

	Race	Circuit	No	Entrant	Car/Engine	Comment
ret	SOUTH AFRICAN GP	Kyalami	23	Minardi Team	3.5 Minardi M191B-Lamborghini V12	electrics
ret	MEXICAN GP	Mexico City	23	Minardi Team	3.5 Minardi M191B-Lamborghini V12	spun off
ret	BRAZILIAN GP	Interlagos	23	Minardi Team	3.5 Minardi M191B-Lamborghini V12	gearbox
11	SPANISH GP	Barcelona	23	Minardi Team	3.5 Minardi M191B-Lamborghini V12	4 laps behind
ret	SAN MARINO GP	Imola	23	Minardi Team	3.5 Minardi M192-Lamborghini V12	transmission
8	MONACO GP	Monte Carlo	23	Minardi Team	3.5 Minardi M192-Lamborghini V12	1 lap behind
13	CANADIAN GP	Montreal	23	Minardi Team	3.5 Minardi M192-Lamborghini V12	4 laps behind
dnq	FRENCH GP	Magny Cours	23	Minardi Team	3.5 Minardi M192-Lamborghini V12	practice crash-injured back
dnq	BELGIAN GP	Spa	23	Minardi Team	3.5 Minardi M192-Lamborghini V12	
dnq	ITALIAN GP	Monza	23	Minardi Team	3.5 Minardi M192-Lamborghini V12	
12	PORTUGUESE GP	Estoril	23	Minardi Team	3.5 Minardi M192-Lamborghini V12	3 laps behind
6	JAPANESE GP	Suzuka	23	Minardi Team	3.5 Minardi M192-Lamborghini V12	1 lap behind
9	AUSTRALIAN GP	Adelaide	23	Minardi Team	3.5 Minardi M192-Lamborghini V12	2 laps behind

1993

	Race	Circuit	No	Entrant	Car/Engine	Comment
4	SOUTH AFRICAN GP	Kyalami	23	Minardi Team	3.5 Minardi M193-Ford HB V8	1 lap behind
ret	BRAZILIAN GP	Interlagos	23	Minardi Team	3.5 Minardi M193-Ford HB V8	spun off in rainstorm
7	EUROPEAN GP	Donington	23	Minardi Team	3.5 Minardi M193-Ford HB V8	3 laps behind
ret	SAN MARINO GP	Imola	23	Minardi Team	3.5 Minardi M193-Ford HB V8	damaged steering
8	SPANISH GP	Barcelona	23	Minardi Team	3.5 Minardi M193-Ford HB V8	2 laps behind
5	MONACO GP	Monte Carlo	23	Minardi Team	3.5 Minardi M193-Ford HB V8	2 laps behind
9	CANADIAN GP	Montreal	23	Minardi Team	3.5 Minardi M193-Ford HB V8	gearbox trouble/2 laps behind
8	FRENCH GP	Magny Cours	23	Minardi Team	3.5 Minardi M193-Ford HB V8	ran without stop/1 lap behind
12/ret	BRITISH GP	Silverstone	23	Minardi Team	3.5 Minardi M193-Ford HB V8	gearbox/2 laps behind
11	GERMAN GP	Hockenheim	23	Minardi Team	3.5 Minardi M193-Ford HB V8	ran without stop/1 lap behind
ret	HUNGARIAN GP	Hungaroring	23	Minardi Team	3.5 Minardi M193-Ford HB V8	collision-Alesi-suspension
ret	BELGIAN GP	Spa	23	Minardi Team	3.5 Minardi M193-Ford HB V8	accident
8	ITALIAN GP	Monza	23	Minardi Team	3.5 Minardi M193-Ford HB V8	ran into Martini at finish/-2 laps
9	PORTUGUESE GP	Estoril	23	Minardi Team	3.5 Minardi M193-Ford HB V8	ran without stop/2 laps behind

GP Starts: 24   GP Wins: 0   Pole positions: 0   Fastest laps: 0   Points: 6

EMERSON FITTIPALDI

Crowned the youngest-ever World Champion driver at 25 in 1972, Emerson Fittipaldi was one of the outstanding drivers of the seventies, but a spectacularly ill-judged career move at the end of 1975 turned him into a Grand Prix racing also-ran, before he came back from retirement to conquer IndyCar racing.

Success in Brazil led Fittipaldi to turn his sights to Europe. The sale of his Formula Vee car financed a three-month trip to England in 1969 and he quickly made his mark in a Formula Ford Merlyn. Emerson's talent was obvious and a move up to F3 in a Jim Russell Lotus 59 paid immediate dividends, the Brazilian winning a string of races, which gave him the confidence to move into Formula 2 with Mike Warner in 1970. An outright win eluded him, but he finished virtually every race in the top six, and Colin Chapman soon had his signature on a Lotus F1 contract.

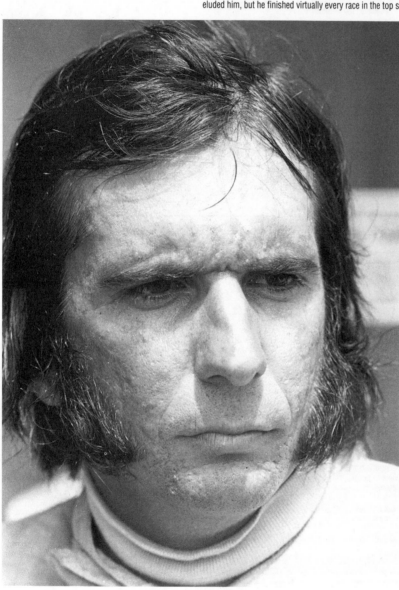

Fittipaldi was eased onto the Grand Prix scene with a Lotus 49C, but tragedy soon befell the team with the death of Jochen Rindt at Monza. Emerson was suddenly thrust into the spotlight upon the team's return at Watkins Glen, and he provided a great morale booster for Chapman by winning the race, albeit only after Rodriguez hit trouble late on. For 1971 Fittipaldi was given the number one seat, but lost momentum with a mid-season road accident. Nevertheless he did remarkably well in his first full Formula 1 season, and with the Lotus 72 finely honed, he became the man to beat the following year. Victories in the Race of Champions and International Trophy provided the springboard for a mid-season burst of scintillating form which saw him claim the World Championship.

Joined in the team by Ronnie Peterson for 1973, Emerson was quick straight out of the blocks with three wins in the first six Grands Prix, and a second title looked a formality, but his year then turned sour, particularly after a practice crash at Zandvoort left him with a niggling ankle injury. By the end of the season he was somewhat over-shadowed by Peterson and accepted a big-money offer from McLaren for 1974. It proved to be a wise decision, his smooth, unruffled driving and great tactical acumen bringing him his second World Championship in an evenly contested season. The following year yielded just one Grand Prix win at Silverstone, Emerson keeping his head in a rainstorm while those all around were spinning out. In the end Lauda's Ferrari had the legs of his McLaren, and he had to settle for second place in the championship.

Then came the bombshell. He was to join the Copersucar-Fittipaldi team established by his brother Wilson for 1976 to drive the outfit's well-funded but uncompetitive Brazilian-built challenger. From Olympian heights, Emerson soon found himself in a valley of despair as the project struggled on, occasionally breaking into the top six, but achieving little else. A magnificent race at Rio in 1978, when he finished a brilliant second to Reutemann's Ferrari, and an excellent third place at Long Beach in 1980 were but isolated reminders of former glories. At the end of that season Emerson switched from driving to management duties but the Fittipaldi team was finally forced to close its doors at the end of 1982.

Returning home to Brazil, he concentrated on the family orange growing and automobile accessory businesses, not missing racing in the slightest. A few races in super karts for fun in 1983 led to an invitation to take part in an IMSA race at Miami early in 1984 and he enjoyed himself so much that he was soon tempted to accept an IndyCar drive at Long Beach, finishing a remarkable fifth. The wheel-to-wheel racing ignited Emerson's lost passion for driving and he was soon to get a big break, joining the Patrick Racing team to replace the severely injured Chip Ganassi. With Fittipaldi as the focal point, the team steadily grew in stature, ultimate success arriving in 1989 when he not only won the PPG Indy Car World Series title but also took a famous last-gasp win in the Indy 500 after a coming-together with Al Unser Jnr on the penultimate lap.

'Emmo' joined Roger Penske's three-car team in 1990, and has since been one of the top guns in the IndyCar championship. In 1993 he won the Indy 500 for the second time with a beautifully judged performance and finished second to Nigel Mansell in the final points standings, proving that he still had plenty of racing mileage left even though he was approaching his 48th year.

FITTIPALDI, Emerson (BR) b 12/12/1946

1970

	Race	Circuit	No	Entrant	Car/Engine	Comment
8	BRITISH GP	Brands Hatch	28	Gold Leaf Team Lotus	3.0 Lotus 49C-Cosworth V8	2 laps behind
4	GERMAN GP	Hockenheim	17	Gold Leaf Team Lotus	3.0 Lotus 49C-Cosworth V8	
15	AUSTRIAN GP	Österreichring	8	Gold Leaf Team Lotus	3.0 Lotus 49C-Cosworth V8	pit stop-fuel/5 laps behind
dns	ITALIAN GP	Monza	26	Gold Leaf Team Lotus	3.0 Lotus 72C-Cosworth V8	withdrawn after Rindt's fatal accident
1	US GP	Watkins Glen	24	Gold Leaf Team Lotus	3.0 Lotus 72C-Cosworth V8	
ret	MEXICAN GP	Mexico City	24	Gold Leaf Team Lotus	3.0 Lotus 72C-Cosworth V8	engine

1971

	Race	Circuit	No	Entrant	Car/Engine	Comment
ret	SOUTH AFRICAN GP	Kyalami	2	Gold Leaf Team Lotus	3.0 Lotus 72C-Cosworth V8	engine
ret	SPANISH GP	Montjuich Park	2	Gold Leaf Team Lotus	3.0 Lotus 72C-Cosworth V8	rear suspension
5	MONACO GP	Monte Carlo	1	Gold Leaf Team Lotus	3.0 Lotus 72D-Cosworth V8	1 lap behind
3	FRENCH GP	Paul Ricard	1	Gold Leaf Team Lotus	3.0 Lotus 72D-Cosworth V8	
3	BRITISH GP	Silverstone	1	Gold Leaf Team Lotus	3.0 Lotus 72D-Cosworth V8	
ret	GERMAN GP	Nürburgring	8	Gold Leaf Team Lotus	3.0 Lotus 72D-Cosworth V8	oil leak
2	AUSTRIAN GP	Österreichring	2	Gold Leaf Team Lotus	3.0 Lotus 72D-Cosworth V8	
8	ITALIAN GP	Monza	5	World Wide Racing	Turbine Lotus 56B-Pratt & Witney	1 lap behind
7	CANADIAN GP	Mosport Park	2	Gold Leaf Team Lotus	3.0 Lotus 72D-Cosworth V8	2 laps behind
nc	US GP	Watkins Glen	2	Gold Leaf Team Lotus	3.0 Lotus 72D-Cosworth V8	pit stops-throttle/10 laps behind

1972 World Champion Driver

	Race	Circuit	No	Entrant	Car/Engine	Comment
ret	ARGENTINE GP	Buenos Aires	11	John Player Team Lotus	3.0 Lotus 72D-Cosworth V8	broken rear suspension
2	SOUTH AFRICAN GP	Kyalami	8	John Player Team Lotus	3.0 Lotus 72D-Cosworth V8	
1	SPANISH GP	Jarama	5	John Player Team Lotus	3.0 Lotus 72D-Cosworth V8	
3	MONACO GP	Monte Carlo	8	John Player Team Lotus	3.0 Lotus 72D-Cosworth V8	Pole/1 lap behind
1	BELGIAN GP	Nivelles	32	John Player Team Lotus	3.0 Lotus 72D-Cosworth V8	Pole
2	FRENCH GP	Clermont Ferrand	1	John Player Team Lotus	3.0 Lotus 72D-Cosworth V8	
1	BRITISH GP	Brands Hatch	8	John Player Team Lotus	3.0 Lotus 72D-Cosworth V8	
ret	GERMAN GP	Nürburgring	2	John Player Team Lotus	3.0 Lotus 72D-Cosworth V8	gearbox casing-oil fire
1	AUSTRIAN GP	Österreichring	31	John Player Team Lotus	3.0 Lotus 72D-Cosworth V8	Pole
1	ITALIAN GP	Monza	6	World Wide Racing	3.0 Lotus 72D-Cosworth V8	
11	CANADIAN GP	Mosport Park	5	John Player Team Lotus	3.0 Lotus 72D-Cosworth V8	pit stop-nose cone/gearbox/-2 laps
ret	US GP	Watkins Glen	10	John Player Team Lotus	3.0 Lotus 72D-Cosworth V8	shock absorber

1973

	Race	Circuit	No	Entrant	Car/Engine	Comment
1	ARGENTINE GP	Buenos Aires	2	John Player Team Lotus	3.0 Lotus 72D-Cosworth V8	FL
1	BRAZILIAN GP	Interlagos	1	John Player Team Lotus	3.0 Lotus 72D-Cosworth V8	FL (shared with Hulme)
3	SOUTH AFRICAN GP	Kyalami	1	John Player Team Lotus	3.0 Lotus 72D-Cosworth V8	FL
1	SPANISH GP	Montjuich Park	1	John Player Team Lotus	3.0 Lotus 72E-Cosworth V8	
3	BELGIAN GP	Zolder	1	John Player Team Lotus	3.0 Lotus 72E-Cosworth V8	
2	MONACO GP	Monte Carlo	1	John Player Team Lotus	3.0 Lotus 72E-Cosworth V8	FL
12/ret	SWEDISH GP	Anderstorp	1	John Player Team Lotus	3.0 Lotus 72E-Cosworth V8	transmission/4 laps behind
ret	FRENCH GP	Paul Ricard	1	John Player Team Lotus	3.0 Lotus 72E-Cosworth V8	accident with Scheckter
ret	BRITISH GP	Silverstone	1	John Player Team Lotus	3.0 Lotus 72E-Cosworth V8	transmission-c.v. joint
ret	DUTCH GP	Zandvoort	1	John Player Team Lotus	3.0 Lotus 72E-Cosworth V8	in pain after practice accident
6	GERMAN GP	Nürburgring	1	John Player Team Lotus	3.0 Lotus 72E-Cosworth V8	
11/ret	AUSTRIAN GP	Österreichring	1	John Player Team Lotus	3.0 Lotus 72E-Cosworth V8	fuel pipe/6 laps behind/Pole
2	ITALIAN GP	Monza	1	John Player Team Lotus	3.0 Lotus 72E-Cosworth V8	
2	CANADIAN GP	Mosport Park	1	John Player Team Lotus	3.0 Lotus 72E-Cosworth V8	FL
6	US GP	Watkins Glen	1	John Player Team Lotus	3.0 Lotus 72E-Cosworth V8	

1974 World Champion Driver

	Race	Circuit	No	Entrant	Car/Engine	Comment
10	ARGENTINE GP	Buenos Aires	5	Marlboro Team Texaco	3.0 McLaren M23-Cosworth V8	knocked off ignition/1 lap behind
1	BRAZILIAN GP	Interlagos	5	Marlboro Team Texaco	3.0 McLaren M23-Cosworth V8	Pole
7	SOUTH AFRICAN GP	Kyalami	5	Marlboro Team Texaco	3.0 McLaren M23-Cosworth V8	
3	SPANISH GP	Jarama	5	Marlboro Team Texaco	3.0 McLaren M23-Cosworth V8	1 lap behind
1	BELGIAN GP	Nivelles	5	Marlboro Team Texaco	3.0 McLaren M23-Cosworth V8	
5	MONACO GP	Monte Carlo	5	Marlboro Team Texaco	3.0 McLaren M23-Cosworth V8	1 lap behind
4	SWEDISH GP	Anderstorp	5	Marlboro Team Texaco	3.0 McLaren M23-Cosworth V8	
3	DUTCH GP	Zandvoort	5	Marlboro Team Texaco	3.0 McLaren M23-Cosworth V8	
ret	FRENCH GP	Dijon	5	Marlboro Team Texaco	3.0 McLaren M23-Cosworth V8	engine
2	BRITISH GP	Brands Hatch	5	Marlboro Team Texaco	3.0 McLaren M23-Cosworth V8	
ret	GERMAN GP	Nürburgring	5	Marlboro Team Texaco	3.0 McLaren M23-Cosworth V8	accident damage/collision with Hulme
ret	AUSTRIAN GP	Österreichring	5	Marlboro Team Texaco	3.0 McLaren M23-Cosworth V8	engine
2	ITALIAN GP	Monza	5	Marlboro Team Texaco	3.0 McLaren M23-Cosworth V8	
1	CANADIAN GP	Mosport Park	5	Marlboro Team Texaco	3.0 McLaren M23-Cosworth V8	Pole
4	US GP	Watkins Glen	5	Marlboro Team Texaco	3.0 McLaren M23-Cosworth V8	

1975

	Race	Circuit	No	Entrant	Car/Engine	Comment
1	ARGENTINE GP	Buenos Aires	1	Marlboro Team Texaco	3.0 McLaren M23-Cosworth V8	
2	BRAZILIAN GP	Interlagos	1	Marlboro Team Texaco	3.0 McLaren M23-Cosworth V8	
nc	SOUTH AFRICAN GP	Kyalami	1	Marlboro Team Texaco	3.0 McLaren M23-Cosworth V8	pit stop-misfire/13 laps behind
dns	SPANISH GP	Montjuich Park	1	Marlboro Team Texaco	3.0 McLaren M23-Cosworth V8	protest at poor safety of track
2	MONACO GP	Monte Carlo	1	Marlboro Team Texaco	3.0 McLaren M23-Cosworth V8	
7	BELGIAN GP	Zolder	1	Marlboro Team Texaco	3.0 McLaren M23-Cosworth V8	brake problems/1 lap behind
8	SWEDISH GP	Anderstorp	1	Marlboro Team Texaco	3.0 McLaren M23-Cosworth V8	handling problems/1 lap behind
ret	DUTCH GP	Zandvoort	1	Marlboro Team Texaco	3.0 McLaren M23-Cosworth V8	engine
4	FRENCH GP	Paul Ricard	1	Marlboro Team Texaco	3.0 McLaren M23-Cosworth V8	
1	BRITISH GP	Silverstone	1	Marlboro Team Texaco	3.0 McLaren M23-Cosworth V8	
ret	GERMAN GP	Nürburgring	1	Marlboro Team Texaco	3.0 McLaren M23-Cosworth V8	puncture rear suspension damage
9	AUSTRIAN GP	Österreichring	1	Marlboro Team Texaco	3.0 McLaren M23-Cosworth V8	1 lap behind
2	ITALIAN GP	Monza	1	Marlboro Team Texaco	3.0 McLaren M23-Cosworth V8	
2	US GP	Watkins Glen	1	Marlboro Team Texaco	3.0 McLaren M23-Cosworth V8	FL

1976

13	BRAZILIAN GP	Interlagos	30	Copersucar-Fittipaldi	3.0 Fittipaldi FD04-Cosworth V8	*misfire/3 laps behind*
17/ret	SOUTH AFRICAN GP	Kyalami	30	Copersucar-Fittipaldi	3.0 Fittipaldi FD04-Cosworth V8	*engine/4 laps behind*
6	US GP WEST	Long Beach	30	Copersucar-Fittipaldi	3.0 Fittipaldi FD04-Cosworth V8	*1 lap behind*
ret	SPANISH GP	Jarama	30	Copersucar-Fittipaldi	3.0 Fittipaldi FD04-Cosworth V8	*gear linkage*
dnq	BELGIAN GP	Zolder	30	Copersucar-Fittipaldi	3.0 Fittipaldi FD04-Cosworth V8	
6	MONACO GP	Monte Carlo	30	Copersucar-Fittipaldi	3.0 Fittipaldi FD04-Cosworth V8	*1 lap behind*
ret	SWEDISH GP	Anderstorp	30	Copersucar-Fittipaldi	3.0 Fittipaldi FD04-Cosworth V8	*handling*
ret	FRENCH GP	Paul Ricard	30	Copersucar-Fittipaldi	3.0 Fittipaldi FD04-Cosworth V8	*engine/oil pressure*
6*	BRITISH GP	Brands Hatch	30	Copersucar-Fittipaldi	3.0 Fittipaldi FD04-Cosworth V8	** 1st place car dsq/2 laps behind*
13	GERMAN GP	Nürburgring	30	Copersucar-Fittipaldi	3.0 Fittipaldi FD04-Cosworth V8	
ret	AUSTRIAN GP	Österreichring	30	Copersucar-Fittipaldi	3.0 Fittipaldi FD04-Cosworth V8	*collision with Brambilla*
ret	DUTCH GP	Zandvoort	30	Copersucar-Fittipaldi	3.0 Fittipaldi FD04-Cosworth V8	*electrics*
15	ITALIAN GP	Monza	30	Copersucar-Fittipaldi	3.0 Fittipaldi FD04-Cosworth V8	*2 laps behind*
ret	CANADIAN GP	Mosport Park	30	Copersucar-Fittipaldi	3.0 Fittipaldi FD04-Cosworth V8	*exhaust and rear wing bracket*
9	US GP EAST	Watkins Glen	30	Copersucar-Fittipaldi	3.0 Fittipaldi FD04-Cosworth V8	*2 laps behind*
ret	JAPANESE GP	Mount Fuji	30	Copersucar-Fittipaldi	3.0 Fittipaldi FD04-Cosworth V8	*withdrew-adverse weather conditions*

1977

4	ARGENTINE GP	Buenos Aires	28	Copersucar-Fittipaldi	3.0 Fittipaldi FD04-Cosworth V8	
4	BRAZILIAN GP	Interlagos	28	Copersucar-Fittipaldi	3.0 Fittipaldi FD04-Cosworth V8	*1 lap behind*
10	SOUTH AFRICAN GP	Kyalami	28	Copersucar-Fittipaldi	3.0 Fittipaldi FD04-Cosworth V8	
5	US GP WEST	Long Beach	28	Copersucar-Fittipaldi	3.0 Fittipaldi FD04-Cosworth V8	
14	SPANISH GP	Jarama	28	Copersucar-Fittipaldi	3.0 Fittipaldi FD04-Cosworth V8	*vibration/overheating/5 laps behind*
ret	MONACO GP	Monte Carlo	28	Copersucar-Fittipaldi	3.0 Fittipaldi FD04-Cosworth V8	*engine*
ret	BELGIAN GP	Zolder	28	Copersucar-Fittipaldi	3.0 Fittipaldi F5-Cosworth V8	*water in electrics*
18	SWEDISH GP	Anderstorp	28	Copersucar-Fittipaldi	3.0 Fittipaldi F5-Cosworth V8	*handling/6 laps behind*
dns	"	"	28	Copersucar-Fittipaldi	3.0 Fittipaldi F5-Cosworth V8	*accident in practice*
11	FRENCH GP	Dijon	28	Copersucar-Fittipaldi	3.0 Fittipaldi F5-Cosworth V8	*3 laps behind*
ret	BRITISH GP	Silverstone	28	Copersucar-Fittipaldi	3.0 Fittipaldi F5-Cosworth V8	*engine*
dnq	GERMAN GP	Hockenheim	28	Copersucar-Fittipaldi	3.0 Fittipaldi F5-Cosworth V8	
11	AUSTRIAN GP	Österreichring	28	Copersucar-Fittipaldi	3.0 Fittipaldi F5-Cosworth V8	*1 lap behind*
4	DUTCH GP	Zandvoort	28	Copersucar-Fittipaldi	3.0 Fittipaldi F5-Cosworth V8	*1 lap behind*
dnq	ITALIAN GP	Monza	28	Copersucar-Fittipaldi	3.0 Fittipaldi F5-Cosworth V8	
13	US GP EAST	Watkins Glen	28	Copersucar-Fittipaldi	3.0 Fittipaldi F5-Cosworth V8	*2 laps behind*
ret	CANADIAN GP	Mosport Park	28	Copersucar-Fittipaldi	3.0 Fittipaldi F5-Cosworth V8	*engine*

1978

9	ARGENTINE GP	Buenos Aires	14	Fittipaldi Automotive	3.0 Fittipaldi F5A-Cosworth V8	
2	BRAZILIAN GP	Rio	14	Fittipaldi Automotive	3.0 Fittipaldi F5A-Cosworth V8	
ret	SOUTH AFRICAN GP	Kyalami	14	Fittipaldi Automotive	3.0 Fittipaldi F5A-Cosworth V8	*driveshaft*
8	US GP WEST	Long Beach	14	Fittipaldi Automotive	3.0 Fittipaldi F5A-Cosworth V8	*1 lap behind*
9	MONACO GP	Monte Carlo	14	Fittipaldi Automotive	3.0 Fittipaldi F5A-Cosworth V8	*1 lap behind*
ret	BELGIAN GP	Zolder	14	Fittipaldi Automotive	3.0 Fittipaldi F5A-Cosworth V8	*collision with Ickx at start*
ret	SPANISH GP	Jarama	14	Fittipaldi Automotive	3.0 Fittipaldi F5A-Cosworth V8	*thottle linkage*
6	SWEDISH GP	Anderstorp	14	Fittipaldi Automotive	3.0 Fittipaldi F5A-Cosworth V8	*1 lap behind*
ret	FRENCH GP	Paul Ricard	14	Fittipaldi Automotive	3.0 Fittipaldi F5A-Cosworth V8	*rear suspension*
ret	BRITISH GP	Brands Hatch	14	Fittipaldi Automotive	3.0 Fittipaldi F5A-Cosworth V8	*engine*
4	GERMAN GP	Hockenheim	14	Fittipaldi Automotive	3.0 Fittipaldi F5A-Cosworth V8	
4	AUSTRIAN GP	Österreichring	14	Fittipaldi Automotive	3.0 Fittipaldi F5A-Cosworth V8	*1 lap behind*
5	DUTCH GP	Zandvoort	14	Fittipaldi Automotive	3.0 Fittipaldi F5A-Cosworth V8	
8	ITALIAN GP	Monza	14	Fittipaldi Automotive	3.0 Fittipaldi F5A-Cosworth V8	
5	US GP EAST	Watkins Glen	14	Fittipaldi Automotive	3.0 Fittipaldi F5A-Cosworth V8	
ret	CANADIAN GP	Montreal	14	Fittipaldi Automotive	3.0 Fittipaldi F5A-Cosworth V8	*collision with Stuck*

1979

6	ARGENTINE GP	Buenos Aires	14	Fittipaldi Automotive	3.0 Fittipaldi F5A-Cosworth V8	*1 lap behind*
11	BRAZILIAN GP	Interlagos	14	Fittipaldi Automotive	3.0 Fittipaldi F5A-Cosworth V8	*1 lap behind*
dns	"	"	14	Fittipaldi Automotive	3.0 Fittipaldi F6-Cosworth V8	*practice only*
13	SOUTH AFRICAN GP	Kyalami	14	Fittipaldi Automotive	3.0 Fittipaldi F6-Cosworth V8	*4 laps behind*
dns	"	"	14	Fittipaldi Automotive	3.0 Fittipaldi F6-Cosworth V8	*practice only*
ret	US GP WEST	Long Beach	14	Fittipaldi Automotive	3.0 Fittipaldi F5A-Cosworth V8	*driveshaft*
dns	"	"	14	Fittipaldi Automotive	3.0 Fittipaldi F6-Cosworth V8	*practice only*
11	SPANISH GP	Jarama	14	Fittipaldi Automotive	3.0 Fittipaldi F5A-Cosworth V8	*1 lap behind*
dns	"	"	14	Fittipaldi Automotive	3.0 Fittipaldi F6-Cosworth V8	*practice only*
9	BELGIAN GP	Zolder	14	Fittipaldi Automotive	3.0 Fittipaldi F5A-Cosworth V8	*2 laps behind*
ret	MONACO GP	Monte Carlo	14	Fittipaldi Automotive	3.0 Fittipaldi F5A-Cosworth V8	*engine*
ret	FRENCH GP	Paul Ricard	14	Fittipaldi Automotive	3.0 Fittipaldi F5A-Cosworth V8	*engine-oil loss*
ret	BRITISH GP	Silverstone	14	Fittipaldi Automotive	3.0 Fittipaldi F5A-Cosworth V8	*engine*
ret	GERMAN GP	Hockenheim	14	Fittipaldi Automotive	3.0 Fittipaldi F6A-Cosworth V8	*electrics*
ret	AUSTRIAN GP	Österreichring	14	Fittipaldi Automotive	3.0 Fittipaldi F6A-Cosworth V8	*brakes*
dns	"	"	14	Fittipaldi Automotive	3.0 Fittipaldi F5A-Cosworth V8	*practice only*
ret	DUTCH GP	Zandvoort	14	Fittipaldi Automotive	3.0 Fittipaldi F6A-Cosworth V8	*electrics*
dns	"	"	14	Fittipaldi Automotive	3.0 Fittipaldi F5A-Cosworth V8	*practice only*
8	ITALIAN GP	Monza	14	Fittipaldi Automotive	3.0 Fittipaldi F6A-Cosworth V8	*1 lap behind*
8	CANADIAN GP	Montreal	14	Fittipaldi Automotive	3.0 Fittipaldi F6A-Cosworth V8	*wheel bearing problem/5 laps behind*
7	US GP EAST	Watkins Glen	14	Fittipaldi Automotive	3.0 Fittipaldi F6A-Cosworth V8	*5 laps behind*

1980

nc	ARGENTINE GP	Buenos Aires	20	Skol Fittipaldi Team	3.0 Fittipaldi F7-Cosworth V8	*pit stops/16 laps behind*
15	BRAZILIAN GP	Interlagos	20	Skol Fittipaldi Team	3.0 Fittipaldi F7-Cosworth V8	*2 laps behind*
8	SOUTH AFRICAN GP	Kyalami	20	Skol Fittipaldi Team	3.0 Fittipaldi F7-Cosworth V8	*1 lap behind*
3	US GP WEST	Long Beach	20	Skol Fittipaldi Team	3.0 Fittipaldi F7-Cosworth V8	
ret	BELGIAN GP	Zolder	20	Skol Fittipaldi Team	3.0 Fittipaldi F7-Cosworth V8	*electrics*
6	MONACO GP	Monte Carlo	20	Skol Fittipaldi Team	3.0 Fittipaldi F7-Cosworth V8	*2 laps behind*
13/ret	FRENCH GP	Paul Ricard	20	Skol Fittipaldi Team	3.0 Fittipaldi F7-Cosworth V8	*engine*

12	BRITISH GP	Brands Hatch	20	Skol Fittipaldi Team	3.0 Fittipaldi F8-Cosworth V8	*4 laps behind*
ret	GERMAN GP	Hockenheim	20	Skol Fittipaldi Team	3.0 Fittipaldi F8-Cosworth V8	*broken skirt*
11	AUSTRIAN GP	Österreichring	20	Skol Fittipaldi Team	3.0 Fittipaldi F8-Cosworth V8	*1 lap behind*
ret	DUTCH GP	Zandvoort	20	Skol Fittipaldi Team	3.0 Fittipaldi F8-Cosworth V8	*brakes*
ret	ITALIAN GP	Imola	20	Skol Fittipaldi Team	3.0 Fittipaldi F8-Cosworth V8	*hit guard rail*
ret	CANADIAN GP	Montreal	20	Skol Fittipaldi Team	3.0 Fittipaldi F8-Cosworth V8	*gearbox*
ret	US GP EAST	Watkins Glen	20	Skol Fittipaldi Team	3.0 Fittipaldi F8-Cosworth V8	*rear suspension*

GP Starts: 144   GP Wins: 14   Pole positions: 6   Fastest laps: 6   Points: 281

WILSON FITTIPALDI

Wilson had to content himself with life as a racing driver for ever in the shadow of his brilliant younger brother, but that should not disguise the fact that he was a more than useful performer in his own right.

He made a brief and dispiriting trip to Europe in 1966 before returning home to Brazil, where he raced saloons, sports cars and Formula Fords, as well as acting as engineer for Emerson's Super Vee efforts. Wilson was back in Europe in 1970 to race in F3, and a good showing was enough to see him joining his brother in Formula 2 in 1971, driving first a Lotus 69, then a March. Given his lack of experience, he fared well, taking fourth on his debut at Hockenheim, second at Vallelunga and third again at Hockenheim at season's end. A deal was struck with Bernie Ecclestone to race a Brabham in Formula 1 in 1972, as effectively the third driver to Reutemann and Hill, but he did not enjoy the best of luck after a sixth place on his debut in the non-championship Brazilian GP. Things were better the following year, and his drive at Monaco was particularly impressive, Wilson holding third place in the BT42 when the fuel system failed. But at least he scored some points in Argentina and Germany, and took an aggregate win in Formula 2 at Misano.

Wilson was now set on developing a Grand Prix car of his own and much of 1974 was spent setting up the Copersucar-Fittipaldi team which made its debut in 1975. The car was not a success, and Wilson was a perpetual back-marker. At the end of the year came the shock announcement that Emerson would drive for the team in 1976, so the elder Fittipaldi happily retired to fill a management position in a project which was doomed to eventual failure.

FITTIPALDI, Wilson (BR) b 25/12/1943

1972

	Race	Circuit	No	Entrant	Car/Engine	Comment
7	SPANISH GP	Jarama	22	Motor Racing Developments	3.0 Brabham BT33-Cosworth V8	*2 laps behind*
9	MONACO GP	Monte Carlo	21	Motor Racing Developments	3.0 Brabham BT33-Cosworth V8	*3 laps behind*
ret	BELGIAN GP	Nivelles	18	Motor Racing Developments	3.0 Brabham BT34-Cosworth V8	*gearbox*
8	FRENCH GP	Clermont Ferrand	19	Motor Racing Developments	3.0 Brabham BT34-Cosworth V8	
12/ret	BRITISH GP	Brands Hatch	28	Motor Racing Developments	3.0 Brabham BT34-Cosworth V8	*suspension/2 laps behind*
7	GERMAN GP	Nürburgring	26	Motor Racing Developments	3.0 Brabham BT34-Cosworth V8	
ret	AUSTRIAN GP	Österreichring	28	Motor Racing Developments	3.0 Brabham BT34-Cosworth V8	*brake pipe*
ret	ITALIAN GP	Monza	29	Motor Racing Developments	3.0 Brabham BT34-Cosworth V8	*broken rear suspension*
ret	CANADIAN GP	Mosport Park	9	Motor Racing Developments	3.0 Brabham BT34-Cosworth V8	*gearbox*
ret	US GP	Watkins Glen	30	Motor Racing Developments	3.0 Brabham BT34-Cosworth V8	*engine*

1973

6	ARGENTINE GP	Buenos Aires	12	Motor Racing Developments	3.0 Brabham BT37-Cosworth V8	*1 lap behind*
ret	BRAZILIAN GP	Interlagos	18	Motor Racing Developments	3.0 Brabham BT37-Cosworth V8	*engine*
ret	SOUTH AFRICAN GP	Kyalami	19	Motor Racing Developments	3.0 Brabham BT37-Cosworth V8	*gear selection*
10	SPANISH GP	Montjuich Park	17	Motor Racing Developments	3.0 Brabham BT42-Cosworth V8	*pit stop-throttle cable/6 laps behind*
11/ret	BELGIAN GP	Zolder	11	Motor Racing Developments	3.0 Brabham BT42-Cosworth V8	*engine/brakes*
ret	MONACO GP	Monte Carlo	11	Motor Racing Developments	3.0 Brabham BT42-Cosworth V8	*split collector pot/7 laps behind*
ret	SWEDISH GP	Anderstorp	11	Motor Racing Developments	3.0 Brabham BT42-Cosworth V8	*accident on lap 1*
16/ret	FRENCH GP	Paul Ricard	11	Motor Racing Developments	3.0 Brabham BT42-Cosworth V8	*throttle linkage/4 laps behind*
ret	BRITISH GP	Silverstone	11	Motor Racing Developments	3.0 Brabham BT42-Cosworth V8	*oil pipe*
ret	DUTCH GP	Zandvoort	11	Motor Racing Developments	3.0 Brabham BT42-Cosworth V8	*spun off*
5	GERMAN GP	Nürburgring	11	Motor Racing Developments	3.0 Brabham BT42-Cosworth V8	
ret	AUSTRIAN GP	Österreichring	11	Motor Racing Developments	3.0 Brabham BT42-Cosworth V8	*fuel metering unit*
ret	ITALIAN GP	Monza	11	Motor Racing Developments	3.0 Brabham BT42-Cosworth V8	*brakes*
11	CANADIAN GP	Mosport Park	11	Motor Racing Developments	3.0 Brabham BT42-Cosworth V8	*3 laps behind*
nc	US GP	Watkins Glen	11	Motor Racing Developments	3.0 Brabham BT42-Cosworth V8	*pit stops-various/7 laps behind*

1975

ret	ARGENTINE GP	Buenos Aires	30	Copersucar-Fittipaldi	3.0 Fittipaldi FD01-Cosworth V8	*crashed*
13	BRAZILIAN GP	Interlagos	30	Copersucar-Fittipaldi	3.0 Fittipaldi FD02-Cosworth V8	*1 lap behind*
dnq	SOUTH AFRICAN GP	Kyalami	30	Copersucar-Fittipaldi	3.0 Fittipaldi FD02-Cosworth V8	
ret	SPANISH GP	Montjuich Park	30	Copersucar-Fittipaldi	3.0 Fittipaldi FD02-Cosworth V8	*protest at lack of safety of track*
dnq	MONACO GP	Monte Carlo	30	Copersucar-Fittipaldi	3.0 Fittipaldi FD02-Cosworth V8	
12	BELGIAN GP	Zolder	30	Copersucar-Fittipaldi	3.0 Fittipaldi FD02-Cosworth V8	*3 laps behind*
17	SWEDISH GP	Anderstorp	30	Copersucar-Fittipaldi	3.0 Fittipaldi FD02-Cosworth V8	*pit stop/6 laps behind*
11	DUTCH GP	Zandvoort	30	Copersucar-Fittipaldi	3.0 Fittipaldi FD03-Cosworth V8	*4 laps behind*
dns	"	"	30	Copersucar-Fittipaldi	3.0 Fittipaldi FD02-Cosworth V8	*practice only*
ret	FRENCH GP	Paul Ricard	30	Copersucar-Fittipaldi	3.0 Fittipaldi FD03-Cosworth V8	*engine*
19/ret	BRITISH GP	Silverstone	30	Copersucar-Fittipaldi	3.0 Fittipaldi FD03-Cosworth V8	*crashed in rain/6 laps behind*
ret	GERMAN GP	Nürburgring	30	Copersucar-Fittipaldi	3.0 Fittipaldi FD03-Cosworth V8	*engine*
dns	AUSTRIAN GP	Österreichring	30	Copersucar-Fittipaldi	3.0 Fittipaldi FD03-Cosworth V8	*practice accident-injured hand*
10	US GP	Watkins Glen	30	Copersucar-Fittipaldi	3.0 Fittipaldi FD03-Cosworth V8	*4 laps behind*

GP Starts: 36   GP Wins: 0   Pole positions: 0   Fastest laps: 0   Points: 3

FITZAU, Theo (D)

1953

	Race	Circuit	No	Entrant	Car/Engine	Comment
ret	GERMAN GP	Nürburgring	28	Helmut Niedermeyer	2.0 AFM U8-BMW 6	

GP Starts: 1   GP Wins: 0   Pole positions: 0   Fastest laps: 0   Points: 0

FLINTERMAN, Jan (NL) b 2/10/1919

1952

	Race	Circuit	No	Entrant	Car/Engine	Comment
ret	DUTCH GP	Zandvoort	20	Escuderia Bandeirantes	2.0 Maserati A6GCM 6	rear axle
9*	"	"	16	Escuderia Bandeirantes	2.0 Maserati A6GCM 6	*took Landi's car/7 laps behind

GP Starts: 1   GP Wins: 0   Pole positions: 0   Fastest laps: 0   Points: 0

FLOCKHART, Ron (GB) b 16/6/1923 – d 12/4/1962

1954

	Race	Circuit	No	Entrant	Car/Engine	Comment
ret	BRITISH GP	Silverstone	6	Prince Bira	2.5 Maserati 250F 6	took over Bira's car/crashed

1956

ret	BRITISH GP	Silverstone	25	Owen Racing Organisation	2.5 BRM P25 4	engine
3	ITALIAN GP	Monza	4	Connaught Engineering	2.5 Connaught B-Alta 4	1 lap behind

1957

ret	MONACO GP	Monte Carlo	6	Owen Racing Organisation	2.5 BRM P25 4	timing gear
ret	FRENCH GP	Rouen	26	Owen Racing Organisation	2.5 BRM P25 4	accident-suffered burns

1958

dnq	MONACO GP	Monte Carlo	22	R R C Walker Racing Team	2.0 Cooper T43-Climax 4	
ret	MOROCCAN GP	Casablanca	20	Owen Racing Organisation	2.5 BRM P25 4	camshaft

1959

ret	MONACO GP	Monte Carlo	20	Owen Racing Organisation	2.5 BRM P25 4	brake failure-spun off
6	FRENCH GP	Reims	44	Owen Racing Organisation	2.5 BRM P25 4	
ret	BRITISH GP	Aintree	42	Owen Racing Organisation	2.5 BRM P25 4	spun off
7	PORTUGUESE GP	Oporto	8	Owen Racing Organisation	2.5 BRM P25 4	3 laps behind
13	ITALIAN GP	Monza	4	Owen Racing Organisation	2.5 BRM P25 4	5 laps behind

1960

6	FRENCH GP	Reims	22	Team Lotus	2.5 Lotus 18-Climax 4	1 lap behind
ret	US GP	Riverside	4	Cooper Car Co	2.5 Cooper T51-Climax 4	brakes

GP Starts: 13   GP Wins: 0   Pole positions: 0   Fastest laps: 0   Points: 5

FOITEK, Gregor (CH) b 27/3/1965

1989

	Race	Circuit	No	Entrant	Car/Engine	Comment
dnq	BRAZILIAN GP	Rio	33	EuroBrun Racing	3.5 EuroBrun ER188B-Judd V8	
dnpq	SAN MARINO GP	Imola	33	EuroBrun Racing	3.5 EuroBrun ER188B-Judd V8	
dnpq	MONACO GP	Monte Carlo	33	EuroBrun Racing	3.5 EuroBrun ER188B-Judd V8	
dnpq	MEXICAN GP	Mexico City	33	EuroBrun Racing	3.5 EuroBrun ER188B-Judd V8	
dnpq	US GP (PHOENIX)	Phoenix	33	EuroBrun Racing	3.5 EuroBrun ER188B-Judd V8	
dnpq	CANADIAN GP	Montreal	33	EuroBrun Racing	3.5 EuroBrun ER188B-Judd V8	
dnpq	FRENCH GP	Paul Ricard	33	EuroBrun Racing	3.5 EuroBrun ER188B-Judd V8	
dnpq	BRITISH GP	Silverstone	33	EuroBrun Racing	3.5 EuroBrun ER188B-Judd V8	
dnpq	GERMAN GP	Hockenheim	33	EuroBrun Racing	3.5 EuroBrun ER189-Judd V8	
dnpq	"	"	33	EuroBrun Racing	3.5 EuroBrun ER188B-Judd V8	
dnpq	HUNGARIAN GP	Hungaroring	33	EuroBrun Racing	3.5 EuroBrun ER189-Judd V8	
dnpq	"	"	33	EuroBrun Racing	3.5 EuroBrun ER188B-Judd V8	
dnpq	BELGIAN GP	Spa	33	EuroBrun Racing	3.5 EuroBrun ER188B-Judd V8	
dnq	SPANISH GP	Jerez	38	Rial Racing	3.5 Rial ARC2-Cosworth V8	practice accident-rear wing collapsed

1990

ret	US GP (PHOENIX)	Phoenix	7	Motor Racing Developments	3.5 Brabham BT58-Judd V8	collision with Grouillard
ret	BRAZILIAN GP	Interlagos	7	Motor Racing Developments	3.5 Brabham BT58-Judd V8	gear selection
ret	SAN MARINO GP	Imola	35	Moneytron Onyx	3.5 Onyx ORE 1B-Cosworth V8	engine
7/ret	MONACO GP	Monte Carlo	35	Moneytron Onyx	3.5 Onyx ORE 1B-Cosworth V8	collision-Bernard/6 laps behind
ret	CANADIAN GP	Montreal	35	Moneytron Onyx	3.5 Onyx ORE 1B-Cosworth V8	over-revved engine
15	MEXICAN GP	Mexico City	35	Moneytron Onyx	3.5 Onyx ORE 1B-Cosworth V8	brake problems/2 laps behind
dnq	FRENCH GP	Paul Ricard	35	Moneytron Onyx	3.5 Onyx ORE 1B-Cosworth V8	
dnq	BRITISH GP	Silverstone	35	Monteverdi Onyx Formula One	3.5 Onyx ORE 1B-Cosworth V8	
ret	GERMAN GP	Hockenheim	35	Monteverdi Onyx Formula One	3.5 Monteverdi ORE 1B-Cosworth V8	spun off
dnq	HUNGARIAN GP	Hungaroring	35	Monteverdi Onyx Formula One	3.5 Monteverdi ORE 1B-Cosworth V8	

GP Starts: 7   GP Wins: 0   Pole positions: 0   Fastest laps: 0   Points: 0

RON FLOCKHART

Flockhart began by racing motor cycles, but in 1948 he switched to MG and JP-Vincent cars, before taking a serious step up with the purchase of an ERA D-Type in 1952. He enjoyed a fabulous 1953 season with the ex-Mays car, embarrassing many a newer machine in Formula Libre races. Naturally this brought him to the attention of BRM, who signed him up in 1954, initially to race in national Formula Libre events with the supercharged car. He also made his GP debut that season, taking over Bira's Maserati in the British GP before crashing.

In 1956 Ron was invited to race in sports cars for Ecurie Ecosse and won at Le Mans (with Sanderson) with their Jaguar E-Type, while he took full advantage of a last-minute opportunity to race for Connaught, finishing third in the Italian GP. The 1957 season saw him repeat his Le Mans success for Ecosse (this time with Bueb), but his luck with BRM was still out, an accident in the French GP leaving him with burns to arm and legs. The following year was marred by further injury after a crash at Rouen in a sports car race, but he was back in action for 1959 and won the Lady Wigram Trophy in New Zealand and the minor Silver City Trophy at Snetterton for BRM. Easily his best effort that year was to finish sixth in the French GP when a stone smashed his goggles and he drove on gamely to the finish with the use of virtually only one eye and a badly cut face.

After parting company with the Bourne concern, Flockhart raced for Alan Brown in Formula 2 in 1960, and finished second in the GP of Chimay behind Jack Lewis and fourth at Pau. Ron also drove a single Grand Prix for both Lotus and Cooper, but already his thoughts were turning towards his other passion, aviation. He had gained a pilot's licence back in 1948, and now set about breaking flying records. He raced less frequently in 1961, and after taking part in three races in New Zealand and Australia with his Lotus 18 early in 1962, Flockhart was killed when his aeroplane broke up in turbulence while he was in Australia practising for a London-to-Sydney record attempt.

GREGOR FOITEK

Winning that curious anomaly, the Swiss F3 championship, in 1986 in a Dallara meant little, and the wealthy Foitek's first season in F3000 the following year was to be a more searching test. A poor start and a string of DNQs was to some extent overcome by switching teams to GA Motorsport in mid-season, though it was 1988 before he tasted success with a superb win at Vallelunga. But then came a worrying number of incidents, culminating in the Johnny Herbert crash at Brands Hatch, when Gregor's Lola was launched into a terrifying series of barrel-rolls from which he was fortunate to escape with no more than a fractured wrist.

Moving into Grands Prix in 1989, he spent a fruitless time trying in vain to qualify the EuroBrun, and decided to quit while ahead when the rear wing fell off on his debut for Rial. Foitek took his money to Brabham at the start of 1990 and at least made a couple starts, but then he moved to the Onyx team, which was on the way to oblivion as a Swiss gentleman by the name of Monteverdi took control. All in all, it was a sorry mess and before long Foitek had disappeared from view.

GEORGE FOLLMER

Follmer was 39 when he first sampled life in Formula 1, thrown in at the deep end with the newly formed UOP Shadow team in 1973. At first things went well, but as the season wore on he slipped further down the grid, and by the end of the year his Grand Prix tenure was over.

He started racing in 1960, but it was 1964-65 before he began competing seriously, becoming USRRC champion in the under-2-litre class with six wins in nine races in a Lotus-Porsche sports car. This led to an invitation to race a works Porsche 904 in the 1966 Sebring 12-hour race, in which Follmer finished seventh with Kolb, winning the under-2-litre class. Still a part-time racer and full-time insurance broker, George financed his own Lola-Chevrolet for 1967 to race in USRRC events, but the car repeatedly broke down, and when Roger Penske offered him a Can-Am ride late in the season Follmer accepted, taking two third places and a sixth in his three races. The die was cast. Seeing how a serious team was run, George then embarked upon a professional racing career, competing successfully in USAC, Can-Am, Trans-Am and Formula A before his 1973 season with Shadow.

Following his sojourn in Formula 1, Follmer initially took a ride in NASCAR, but was soon tempted back into Can-Am by Shadow's Don Nichols. The next few seasons saw George on a regular diet of Can-Am, Trans-Am (winning the 1976 championship) and sports cars until his career was interrupted by a terrible practice crash at Laguna Seca in 1978 which left him with a broken leg and internal injuries. But despite still being in some pain from his leg injuries, he made a comeback in 1979 and continued racing into the early eighties in Trans-Am with a Chevrolet Camaro.

FOLLMER, George (USA) b 27/1/1934

1973

	Race	Circuit	No	Entrant	Car/Engine	Comment
6	SOUTH AFRICAN GP	Kyalami	23	UOP Shadow Racing Team	3.0 Shadow DN1-Cosworth V8	2 laps behind
3	SPANISH GP	Montjuich Park	20	UOP Shadow Racing Team	3.0 Shadow DN1-Cosworth V8	
ret	BELGIAN GP	Zolder	16	UOP Shadow Racing Team	3.0 Shadow DN1-Cosworth V8	stuck throttle slides
dns	MONACO GP	Monte Carlo	16	UOP Shadow Racing Team	3.0 Shadow DN1-Cosworth V8	collision with Merzario in practice
14	SWEDISH GP	Anderstorp	16	UOP Shadow Racing Team	3.0 Shadow DN1-Cosworth V8	6 laps behind
ret	FRENCH GP	Paul Ricard	16	UOP Shadow Racing Team	3.0 Shadow DN1-Cosworth V8	vapour lock
ret/dns	BRITISH GP	Silverstone	16	UOP Shadow Racing Team	3.0 Shadow DN1-Cosworth V8	accident in first start/did not restart
10	DUTCH GP	Zandvoort	16	UOP Shadow Racing Team	3.0 Shadow DN1-Cosworth V8	5 laps behind
ret	GERMAN GP	Nürburgring	16	UOP Shadow Racing Team	3.0 Shadow DN1-Cosworth V8	accident
ret	AUSTRIAN GP	Österreichring	16	UOP Shadow Racing Team	3.0 Shadow DN1-Cosworth V8	cwp
10	ITALIAN GP	Monza	16	UOP Shadow Racing Team	3.0 Shadow DN1-Cosworth V8	1 lap behind
17	CANADIAN GP	Mosport Park	16	UOP Shadow Racing Team	3.0 Shadow DN1-Cosworth V8	pit stop/7 laps behind
14	US GP	Watkins Glen	16	UOP Shadow Racing Team	3.0 Shadow DN1-Cosworth V8	2 laps behind

GP Starts: 11 (12)   GP Wins: 0   Pole positions: 0   Fastest laps: 0   Points: 5

FRANCO FORINI

Forini raced in European F3 before finding success in the Italian F3 series. Having finished third and fifth with his Dallara-Alfa in 1983 and '84, the Swiss driver switched to a VW-powered car in 1985 and emerged as a worthy champion ahead of Barbazza and Caffi. A largely moribund F3000 season in 1986 left Forini out of the picture, until a surprise call from Osella brought him briefly into the Grand Prix arena in 1987.

PHILIP FOTHERINGHAM-PARKER

A company director who raced intermittently in the immediate post-war years, Fotheringham-Parker's greatest success was second place with a Maserati in the 1949 Wakefield Trophy race at the Curragh. He raced the 4CLT in the 1951 British GP and also used it to win a very minor Formula 1 race at Winfield that year. In 1953 he raced with Sydney Allard at Le Mans, and took part in the 1954 Monte Carlo Rally in a Ford Zephyr.

PAUL FRÈRE

Paul Frère was a rarity in that he was not a full-time driver, preferring to maintain his profession as an international motoring journalist throughout a long and successful racing career.

He made his debut in the Spa 24 Hours, sharing an MG with Jacques Swaters, the pair finishing fourth in class, but it was not until 1952 that he raced in earnest. After winning a big production car race in an Oldsomobile at Spa, Frère picked up a last-minute drive with HWM in the GP des Frontières at Chimay. Left at the start, he overhauled Downing's Connaught right at the death to score a surprise win. HWM's John Heath immediately offered Paul a drive in the forthcoming Belgian GP and he delighted his entrant by bringing the car home in fifth place in pouring rain.

Frère raced for HWM again in 1953; his luck was out this time in Grands Prix, but he did finish a brilliant second in the rain in the Eifelrennen. For 1954 he accepted a few rides with Gordini in F1, and drove at Le Mans for the first time in an Aston Martin sports car.

The Sarthe classic was to become an important race in Frère's career. Second in the tragic 1955 race in an Aston, he was involved in a first-lap crash in a works Jaguar in 1956, finished fourth in 1957 and '58, second again in an Aston in 1959, and finally won in 1960 sharing a works Ferrari with Gendebien. This partnership incidentally was also victorious in the Reims 12 Hours of 1957.

Ferrari also gave Paul an opportunity to drive his Formula 1 cars, and he did not disappoint, taking fourth place in the 1955 Belgian GP and a quite magnificent second behind Peter Collins at Spa again in 1956. He made a return to single-seaters in 1960, his final season, winning the South African GP in an Equipe Nationale Belge Cooper, then showing his consistency and reliable driving skills on his return to Europe to take fifth places at Syracuse and Brussels and sixth at Pau.

BEPPE GABBIANI

After seven years in karting, this Italian rich kid decided to try his hand at F3 in 1977, immediately winning his first big race at Paul Ricard. Flushed with his success, Beppe was soon in Formula 2 and by the end of the 1978 season he had had a couple of GP drives with Surtees in place of the injured Brambilla.

Ghinzani's fortunes dipped in the first part of 1979, when he seemed to crash regularly in Formula 2 and a 'rent-a-drive' in a Shadow in a non-championship F1 race at Imola saw him non-start after an embarrassing practice period. But to be fair he was a quick driver, and he buckled down to rescue his season with second places in F2 at Mugello and Misano.

His next season in F2 with Maurer brought little success after a late start, and for 1981 he joined Osella for tilt at Grands Prix which found him out of his depth. The Italian's Grand Prix opportunities had undoubtedly come to soon, and he retrenched in 1982, returning to F2 with Maurer, where he faced a stern challenge from gifted team-mate Stefan Bellof. Given a real chance to demonstrate his class in 1983 with the top Onyx March team, Gabbiani started brilliantly, with four wins in the first five races, but the title eventually slipped from his grasp as the Ralt-Hondas of Palmer and Thackwell overwhelmed him. After this disappointment Gabbiani's front-line career dribbled away, occasional outings in F2 and F3000 offering little encouragement.

FORINI, Franco (CH) b 22/9/1958

1987

	Race	Circuit	No	Entrant	Car/Engine	Comment
ret	ITALIAN GP	Monza	22	Osella Squadra Corse	1.5 t/c Osella FA1I-Alfa Romeo V8	turbo
ret	PORTUGUESE GP	Estoril	22	Osella Squadra Corse	1.5 t/c Osella FA1I-Alfa Romeo V8	suspension
dnq	SPANISH GP	Jerez	22	Osella Squadra Corse	1.5 t/c Osella FA1I-Alfa Romeo V8	

GP Starts: 2   GP Wins: 0   Pole positions: 0   Fastest laps: 0   Points: 0

FOTHERINGHAM-PARKER, Philip (GB) b 22/9/1907 – d 15/10/1981

1951

	Race	Circuit	No	Entrant	Car/Engine	Comment
ret	BRITISH GP	Silverstone	17	Philip Fotheringham-Parker	1.5 s/c Maserati 4CL 4	oil pipe

GP Starts: 1   GP Wins: 0   Pole positions: 0   Fastest laps: 0   Points: 0

FRÈRE, Paul (B) b 30/1/1917

1952

	Race	Circuit	No	Entrant	Car/Engine	Comment
5	BELGIAN GP	Spa	28	HW Motors Ltd	2.0 HWM-Alta 4	2 laps behind
ret	GERMAN GP	Nürburgring	112	HW Motors Ltd	2.0 HWM-Alta 4	gearbox
ret	DUTCH GP	Zandvoort	14	Ecurie Belge	1.5 Gordini Type 15 4	clutch/gearbox

1953

	Race	Circuit	No	Entrant	Car/Engine	Comment
nc	BELGIAN GP	Spa	24	HW Motors Ltd	2.0 HWM-Alta 4	6 laps behind
ret	SWISS GP	Bremgarten	14	HW Motors Ltd	2.0 HWM-Alta 4	engine

1954

	Race	Circuit	No	Entrant	Car/Engine	Comment
ret	BELGIAN GP	Spa	16	Equipe Gordini	2.0 Gordini Type 16 6	rear axle
ret	FRENCH GP	Reims	28	Equipe Gordini	2.0 Gordini Type 16 6	rear axle
ret	GERMAN GP	Nürburgring	10	Equipe Gordini	2.0 Gordini Type 16 6	lost wheel

1955

	Race	Circuit	No	Entrant	Car/Engine	Comment
nc*	MONACO GP	Monte Carlo	48	Scuderia Ferrari	2.5 Ferrari 555 4	*took overTaruffi's car/-14 laps
4	BELGIAN GP	Spa	6	Scuderia Ferrari	2.5 Ferrari 555 4	

1956

	Race	Circuit	No	Entrant	Car/Engine	Comment
2	BELGIAN GP	Spa	6	Scuderia Ferrari	2.5 Lancia-Ferrari D50 V8	

GP Starts: 11   GP Wins: 0   Pole positions: 0   Fastest laps: 0   Points: 11

FRY, Joe (GB) d 29/7/1950 (Killed at Blandford hill-climb driving the Freikaiserwagen)

1950

	Race	Circuit	No	Entrant	Car/Engine	Comment
10*	BRITISH GP	Silverstone	10	Joe Fry	1.5 s/c Maserati 4CL 4	*Shawe-Taylor also drove

GP Starts: 1   GP Wins: 0   Pole positions: 0   Fastest laps: 0   Points: 0

GABBIANI, Beppe (I) b 2/1/1957

1978

	Race	Circuit	No	Entrant	Car/Engine	Comment
dnq	US GP EAST	Watkins Glen	19	Team Surtees	3.0 Surtees TS20-Cosworth V8	
dnq	CANADIAN GP	Montreal	19	Team Surtees	3.0 Surtees TS20-Cosworth V8	

1981

	Race	Circuit	No	Entrant	Car/Engine	Comment
ret	US GP WEST	Long Beach	32	Osella Squadra Corse	3.0 Osella FA1B-Cosworth V8	accident-broken front suspension
dnq	BRAZILIAN GP	Rio	32	Osella Squadra Corse	3.0 Osella FA1B-Cosworth V8	
dnq	ARGENTINE GP	Buenos Aires	32	Osella Squadra Corse	3.0 Osella FA1B-Cosworth V8	
ret	SAN MARINO GP	Imola	32	Osella Squadra Corse	3.0 Osella FA1B-Cosworth V8	collision with Alboreto
ret	BELGIAN GP	Zolder	32	Osella Squadra Corse	3.0 Osella FA1B-Cosworth V8	engine
dnq	MONACO GP	Monte Carlo	31	Osella Squadra Corse	3.0 Osella FA1B-Cosworth V8	
dnq	SPANISH GP	Jarama	31	Osella Squadra Corse	3.0 Osella FA1B-Cosworth V8	
dnq	FRENCH GP	Dijon	31	Osella Squadra Corse	3.0 Osella FA1B-Cosworth V8	
dnq	BRITISH GP	Silverstone	31	Osella Squadra Corse	3.0 Osella FA1B-Cosworth V8	
dnq	GERMAN GP	Hockenheim	31	Osella Squadra Corse	3.0 Osella FA1B-Cosworth V8	
dnq	AUSTRIAN GP	Österreichring	31	Osella Squadra Corse	3.0 Osella FA1B-Cosworth V8	
dnq	DUTCH GP	Zandvoort	31	Osella Squadra Corse	3.0 Osella FA1B-Cosworth V8	
dnq	ITALIAN GP	Monza	31	Osella Squadra Corse	3.0 Osella FA1B-Cosworth V8	
dnq	CANADIAN GP	Montreal	31	Osella Squadra Corse	3.0 Osella FA1B-Cosworth V8	
dnq	CAESARS PALACE GP	Las Vegas	31	Osella Squadra Corse	3.0 Osella FA1B-Cosworth V8	

GP Starts: 3   GP Wins: 0   Pole positions: 0   Fastest laps: 0   Points: 0

BERTRAND GACHOT

A very confident and determined driver, Gachot assiduously built his career to reach his goal of racing in a front-running Formula 1 team, only to throw it away with a moment of madness when an assault on a London taxi-driver after a traffic altercation left him facing imprisonment.

Brilliantly successful in Formula Ford, winning the major British 1600 title in 1985 and the 2000 crown the following year after a torrid battle with Mark Blundell, Bertrand graduated to the British F3 championship with West Surrey Racing for 1987 and emerged as runner-up after another no-holds barred battle, this time with Johnny Herbert.

A solid 1988 season in F3000 lacked only a win and he finished fifth overall, quickly tying up a deal to race for the newly formed Onyx Grand Prix team in 1989. It was not a happy season for Gachot who, having been overshadowed by the experienced Johansson, found himself replaced by J J Lehto. Taking his sponsorship money to Rial for a couple more unproductive outings, Gachot then plunged into a disastrous 1990 season with the Coloni-Subaru. Then came the big break with Eddie Jordan's fledgling F1 team, whose new Gary Anderson-designed car was a revelation. Suddenly Gachot was really racing and showing his undoubted talent – until his shock incarceration. His drive with Jordan was lost but, undaunted, he bounced back with the struggling Larrousse team. Bertrand's F1 career was on hold in 1993 – although he made a good IndyCar debut at Toronto – while he finalised plans to lead Pacific's proposed Grand Prix challenge in 1994.

PATRICK GAILLARD

A graduate of Formule Super Renault, Gaillard made his reputation in Formula 3 with a Chevron, finishing third in the 1978 European championship in a works B43 and winning rounds at Imola and the Nürburgring. He moved into Formula 2 for the 1979 season, but stepped into the Ensign seat vacated by Derek Daly at the French GP. The car was extremely difficult to handle, and Patrick, though very brave, qualified only twice in five races before he in turn was replaced by Marc Surer.

Gaillard made a brief return the following season to finish sixth in the infamous Spanish GP which was subsequently downgraded from championship status. He then picked up the odd Formula 2 ride before slipping from the limelight.

NANNI GALLI

Giovanni Galli was the son of a wealthy textile merchant, who began racing at the comparatively late age of 24. He had sensed that his family would be opposed to his early racing activities, and ran under the pseudonym 'Nanni', which stuck. He bought a Mini-Cooper with which he entered the 1965 Italian touring car championship and proceeded to take ten class wins in ten starts, before moving on to an Alfa Romeo GTA.

Galli began to forge a reputation in sports car racing in the factory Alfa Romeo T33 in 1967, though he had to wait until the following season for success, winning the Circuit of Mugello (with Bianchi and Vaccarella), and finishing second in both the Targa Florio and the Imola 500 Km (both with Giunti). He was to be a mainstay of the Autodelta sports car programme right through until 1972, with many placings in the top six.

In tandem with his long-distance activities, Galli moved into single-seaters, initially with Tecno in Formula 2. He then graduated to Grand Prix racing via an Alfa Romeo engine-supply deal, first at Monza in 1970 with McLaren, and then with March in 1971. For 1972, he became involved in the well-funded but unsuccessful Tecno F1 project, his best result being a third place in the poorly supported GP of the Italian Republic at Vallelunga. With Clay Regazzoni indisposed, Galli was invited to represent Ferrari in the French GP, but could finish no better than 13th.

For 1973, 'Nanni' joined Frank Williams to race his new Iso car, but after a handful of disappointing outings, he quit the team and announced his retirement, athough he was to return briefly in 1974 at the wheel of a works Abarth sports car.

GACHOT, Bertrand (F) b 23/12/1962

1989

	Race	Circuit	No	Entrant	Car/Engine	Comment
dnpq	BRAZILIAN GP	Rio	37	Moneytron Onyx	3.5 Onyx ORE 1-Cosworth V8	
dnpq	SAN MARINO GP	Imola	37	Moneytron Onyx	3.5 Onyx ORE 1-Cosworth V8	
dnpq	MONACO GP	Monte Carlo	37	Moneytron Onyx	3.5 Onyx ORE 1-Cosworth V8	
dnpq	MEXICAN GP	Mexico City	37	Moneytron Onyx	3.5 Onyx ORE 1-Cosworth V8	
dnpq	US GP (PHOENIX)	Phoenix	37	Moneytron Onyx	3.5 Onyx ORE 1-Cosworth V8	
dnpq	CANADIAN GP	Montreal	37	Moneytron Onyx	3.5 Onyx ORE 1-Cosworth V8	
13	FRENCH GP	Paul Ricard	37	Moneytron Onyx	3.5 Onyx ORE 1-Cosworth V8	pit stop-overheating battery/-4 laps
12	BRITISH GP	Silverstone	37	Moneytron Onyx	3.5 Onyx ORE 1-Cosworth V8	raced spare car/3 laps behind
dnq	GERMAN GP	Hockenheim	37	Moneytron Onyx	3.5 Onyx ORE 1-Cosworth V8	
ret	HUNGARIAN GP	Hungaroring	37	Moneytron Onyx	3.5 Onyx ORE 1-Cosworth V8	differential
ret	BELGIAN GP	Spa	37	Moneytron Onyx	3.5 Onyx ORE 1-Cosworth V8	wheel bearing-crashed
ret	ITALIAN GP	Monza	37	Moneytron Onyx	3.5 Onyx ORE 1-Cosworth V8	accident damage-holed radiator
dnq	JAPANESE GP	Suzuka	39	Rial Racing	3.5 Rial ARC2-Cosworth V8	
dnq	AUSTRALIAN GP	Adelaide	39	Rial Racing	3.5 Rial ARC2-Cosworth V8	

1990

	Race	Circuit	No	Entrant	Car/Engine	Comment
dnpq	US GP (PHOENIX)	Phoenix	31	Subaru Coloni Racing	3.5 Coloni C3B-Subaru F12	no time set
dnpq	BRAZILIAN GP	Interlagos	31	Subaru Coloni Racing	3.5 Coloni C3B-Subaru F12	
dnpq	SAN MARINO GP	Imola	31	Subaru Coloni Racing	3.5 Coloni C3B-Subaru F12	
dnpq	MONACO GP	Monte Carlo	31	Subaru Coloni Racing	3.5 Coloni C3B-Subaru F12	
dnpq	CANADIAN GP	Montreal	31	Subaru Coloni Racing	3.5 Coloni C3B-Subaru F12	
dnpq	MEXICAN GP	Mexico City	31	Subaru Coloni Racing	3.5 Coloni C3B-Subaru F12	
dnpq	FRENCH GP	Paul Ricard	31	Subaru Coloni Racing	3.5 Coloni C3B-Subaru F12	
dnpq	BRITISH GP	Silverstone	31	Subaru Coloni Racing	3.5 Coloni C3B-Subaru F12	
dnpq	GERMAN GP	Hockenheim	31	Subaru Coloni Racing	3.5 Coloni C3C-Cosworth V8	

dnpq	HUNGARIAN GP	Hungaroring	31	Subaru Coloni Racing	3.5 Coloni C3C-Cosworth V8	
dnq	BELGIAN GP	Spa	31	Subaru Coloni Racing	3.5 Coloni C3C-Cosworth V8	
dnq	ITALIAN GP	Monza	31	Subaru Coloni Racing	3.5 Coloni C3C-Cosworth V8	
dnq	PORTUGUESE GP	Estoril	31	Subaru Coloni Racing	3.5 Coloni C3C-Cosworth V8	
dnq	SPANISH GP	Jerez	31	Subaru Coloni Racing	3.5 Coloni C3C-Cosworth V8	
dnq	JAPANESE GP	Suzuka	31	Subaru Coloni Racing	3.5 Coloni C3C-Cosworth V8	
dnq	AUSTRALIAN GP	Adelaide	31	Subaru Coloni Racing	3.5 Coloni C3C-Cosworth V8	

1991

10/ret	US GP (PHOENIX)	Phoenix	32	Team 7UP Jordan	3.5 Jordan 191-Ford HB V8	engine/6 laps behind
13/ret	BRAZILIAN GP	Interlagos	32	Team 7UP Jordan	3.5 Jordan 191-Ford HB V8	fuel pick-up/8 laps behind
ret	SAN MARINO GP	Imola	32	Team 7UP Jordan	3.5 Jordan 191-Ford HB V8	damage after earlier spin
8	MONACO GP	Monte Carlo	32	Team 7UP Jordan	3.5 Jordan 191-Ford HB V8	2 laps behind
5	CANADIAN GP	Montreal	32	Team 7UP Jordan	3.5 Jordan 191-Ford HB V8	
ret	MEXICAN GP	Mexico City	32	Team 7UP Jordan	3.5 Jordan 191-Ford HB V8	spun off
ret	FRENCH GP	Magny Cours	32	Team 7UP Jordan	3.5 Jordan 191-Ford HB V8	spun off on first lap
6	BRITISH GP	Silverstone	32	Team 7UP Jordan	3.5 Jordan 191-Ford HB V8	1 lap behind
6	GERMAN GP	Hockenheim	32	Team 7UP Jordan	3.5 Jordan 191-Ford HB V8	
9	HUNGARIAN GP	Hungaroring	32	Team 7UP Jordan	3.5 Jordan 191-Ford HB V8	spin/FL/1 lap behind
dnq	AUSTRALIAN GP	Adelaide	29	Larrousse F1	3.5 Larrousse Lola L91-Cosworth V8	

1992

ret	SOUTH AFRICAN GP	Kyalami	29	Central Park Venturi Larrousse	Venturi LC92-Lamborghini V12	suspension damage
11	MEXICAN GP	Mexico City	29	Central Park Venturi Larrousse	Venturi LC92-Lamborghini V12	engine misfire/3 laps behind
ret	BRAZILIAN GP	Interlagos	29	Central Park Venturi Larrousse	Venturi LC92-Lamborghini V12	rear suspension
ret	SPANISH GP	Barcelona	29	Central Park Venturi Larrousse	Venturi LC92-Lamborghini V12	engine
ret	SAN MARINO GP	Imola	29	Central Park Venturi Larrousse	Venturi LC92-Lamborghini V12	spun off
6	MONACO GP	Monte Carlo	29	Central Park Venturi Larrousse	Venturi LC92-Lamborghini V12	1 lap behind
dsq	CANADIAN GP	Montreal	29	Central Park Venturi Larrousse	Venturi LC92-Lamborghini V12	shunted by Grouillard-dsq push start
ret	FRENCH GP	Magny Cours	29	Central Park Venturi Larrousse	Venturi LC92-Lamborghini V12	collision with Suzuki lap 1
ret	BRITISH GP	Silverstone	29	Central Park Venturi Larrousse	Venturi LC92-Lamborghini V12	rear wheel bearing
14	GERMAN GP	Hockenheim	29	Central Park Venturi Larrousse	Venturi LC92-Lamborghini V12	1 lap behind
ret	HUNGARIAN GP	Hungaroring	29	Central Park Venturi Larrousse	Venturi LC92-Lamborghini V12	collision with Suzuki
18/ret	BELGIAN GP	Spa	29	Central Park Venturi Larrousse	Venturi LC92-Lamborghini V12	spun off/4 laps behind
ret	ITALIAN GP	Monza	29	Central Park Venturi Larrousse	Venturi LC92-Lamborghini V12	engine
ret	PORTUGUESE GP	Estoril	29	Central Park Venturi Larrousse	Venturi LC92-Lamborghini V12	fuel pressure
ret	JAPANESE GP	Suzuka	29	Central Park Venturi Larrousse	Venturi LC92-Lamborghini V12	collision with team-mate Katayama
ret	AUSTRALIAN GP	Adelaide	29	Central Park Venturi Larrousse	Venturi LC92-Lamborghini V12	engine

GP Starts: 31   GP Wins: 0   Pole positions: 0   Fastest laps: 1   Points: 5

GAILLARD, Patrick (F) b 12/2/1952

1979

	Race	Circuit	No	Entrant	Car/Engine	Comment
dnq	FRENCH GP	Dijon	22	Team Ensign	3.0 Ensign N179-Cosworth V8	
13	BRITISH GP	Silverstone	22	Team Ensign	3.0 Ensign N179-Cosworth V8	3 laps behind
dnq	GERMAN GP	Hockenheim	22	Team Ensign	3.0 Ensign N179-Cosworth V8	
ret	AUSTRIAN GP	Österreichring	22	Team Ensign	3.0 Ensign N179-Cosworth V8	front suspension
dnq	DUTCH GP	Zandvoort	22	Team Ensign	3.0 Ensign N179-Cosworth V8	

GP Starts: 2   GP Wins: 0   Pole positions: 0   Fastest laps: 0   Points: 0

GALLI, Nanni (Giovanni) (I) b 2/10/1940

1970

	Race	Circuit	No	Entrant	Car/Engine	Comment
dnq	ITALIAN GP	Monza	36	Bruce McLaren Motor Racing	3.0 McLaren M7D-Alfa Romeo V8	

1971

dnq	MONACO GP	Monte Carlo	19	STP March	3.0 March 711-Alfa Romeo V8	
ret	DUTCH GP	Zandvoort	18	STP March	3.0 March 711-Alfa Romeo V8	spun off/incident with Cevert
dns	FRENCH GP	Paul Ricard	33	STP March	3.0 March 711-Cosworth V8	Soler-Roig drove car in race
11	BRITISH GP	Silverstone	20	STP March	3.0 March 711-Cosworth V8	3 laps behind
12	GERMAN GP	Nürburgring	17	STP March	3.0 March 711-Alfa Romeo V8	despite broken engine mounting/-2 laps
12	AUSTRIAN GP	Österreichring	19	STP March	3.0 March 711-Alfa Romeo V8	pit stop/3 laps behind
ret	ITALIAN GP	Monza	22	STP March	3.0 March 711-Cosworth V8	electrics
nc	CANADIAN GP	Mosport Park	18	STP March	3.0 March 711-Cosworth V8	7 laps behind
ret	US GP	Watkins Glen	26	STP March	3.0 March 711-Cosworth V8	steering and suspension

1972

ret	BELGIAN GP	Nivelles	22	Martini Racing Team	3.0 Tecno PA123 F12	spun-hit by Regazzoni-suspension
13	FRENCH GP	Clermont Ferrand	30	Scuderia Ferrari SpA SEFAC	3.0 Ferrari 312B2 F12	1 lap behind
ret	BRITISH GP	Brands Hatch	30	Martini Racing Team	3.0 Tecno PA123 F12	spun off
nc	AUSTRIAN GP	Österreichring	15	Martini Racing Team	3.0 Tecno PA123 F12	pit stops/9 laps behind
ret	ITALIAN GP	Monza	11	Martini Racing Team	3.0 Tecno PA123 F12	engine

1973

ret	ARGENTINE GP	Buenos Aires	36	Frank Williams Racing Cars	3.0 Williams FX3B-Cosworth V8	accessory belt to pumps
9	BRAZILIAN GP	Interlagos	20	Frank Williams Racing Cars	3.0 Williams FX3B-Cosworth V8	2 laps behind
11	SPANISH GP	Montjuich Park	24	Frank Williams Racing Cars	3.0 Williams 1R-Cosworth V8	pit stop/6 laps behind
ret	BELGIAN GP	Zolder	26	Frank Williams Racing Cars	3.0 Williams 1R-Cosworth V8	engine
ret	MONACO GP	Monte Carlo	26	Frank Williams Racing Cars	3.0 Williams 1R-Cosworth V8	driveshaft

GP Starts: 17   GP Wins: 0   Pole positions: 0   Fastest laps: 0   Points: 0

GALVEZ, Oscar (RA) b 17/8/1913 – d 16/12/1989

1953

	Race	Circuit	No	Entrant	Car/Engine	Comment
5	ARGENTINE GP	Buenos Aires	8	Officine Alfieri Maserati	2.0 Maserati A6GCM 6	1 lap behind

GP Starts: 1   GP Wins: 0   Pole positions: 0   Fastest laps: 0   Points: 0

GAMBLE, Fred (USA)

1960

	Race	Circuit	No	Entrant	Car/Engine	Comment
10	ITALIAN GP	Monza	28	Camoradi International	1.5 Behra-Porsche F4	F2 car/9 laps behind

GP Starts: 1   GP Wins: 0   Pole positions: 0   Fastest laps: 0   Points: 0

GANLEY, Howden (NZ) b 24/12/1941

1971

	Race	Circuit	No	Entrant	Car/Engine	Comment
ret	SOUTH AFRICAN GP	Kyalami	27	Yardley BRM	3.0 BRM P153 V12	driver unwell
10	SPANISH GP	Montjuich Park	16	Yardley BRM	3.0 BRM P153 V12	4 laps behind
dnq	MONACO GP	Monte Carlo	16	Yardley BRM	3.0 BRM P153 V12	
7	DUTCH GP	Zandvoort	10	Yardley BRM	3.0 BRM P153 V12	4 laps behind
10	FRENCH GP	Paul Ricard	16	Yardley BRM	3.0 BRM P153 V12	1 lap behind
8	BRITISH GP	Silverstone	17	Yardley BRM	3.0 BRM P153 V12	pit stop-puncture/2 laps behind
ret	GERMAN GP	Nürburgring	23	Yardley BRM	3.0 BRM P153 V12	engine
ret	AUSTRIAN GP	Österreichring	15	Yardley BRM	3.0 BRM P160 V12	ignition
5	ITALIAN GP	Monza	19	Yardley BRM	3.0 BRM P160 V12	
dns	CANADIAN GP	Mosport Park	16	Yardley BRM	3.0 BRM P160 V12	accident on warm-up lap
4	US GP	Watkins Glen	16	Yardley BRM	3.0 BRM P160 V12	

1972

	Race	Circuit	No	Entrant	Car/Engine	Comment
9	ARGENTINE GP	Buenos Aires	3	Marlboro BRM	3.0 BRM P160B V12	2 laps behind
nc	SOUTH AFRICAN GP	Kyalami	23	Marlboro BRM	3.0 BRM P160B V12	pit stop/9 laps behind
ret	SPANISH GP	Jarama	25	Marlboro BRM	3.0 BRM P160B V12	engine
ret	MONACO GP	Monte Carlo	19	Marlboro BRM	3.0 BRM P180 V12	collision with Hailwood-suspension
8	BELGIAN GP	Nivelles	25	Marlboro BRM	3.0 BRM P160B V12	2 laps behind
dns	FRENCH GP	Clermont Ferrand	23	Marlboro BRM	3.0 BRM P160B V12	car driven by Beltoise
4	GERMAN GP	Nürburgring	17	Marlboro BRM	3.0 BRM P160C V12	
6	AUSTRIAN GP	Österreichring	9	Marlboro BRM	3.0 BRM P160C V12	
11	ITALIAN GP	Monza	22	Marlboro BRM	3.0 BRM P160C V12	pit stop/3 laps behind
10	CANADIAN GP	Mosport Park	15	Marlboro BRM	3.0 BRM P160C V12	2 laps behind
ret	US GP	Watkins Glen	16	Marlboro BRM	3.0 BRM P160C V12	engine

1973

	Race	Circuit	No	Entrant	Car/Engine	Comment
nc	ARGENTINE GP	Buenos Aires	38	Frank Williams Racing Cars	3.0 Williams FX3B-Cosworth V8	pit stop/17 laps behind
7	BRAZILIAN GP	Interlagos	19	Frank Williams Racing Cars	3.0 Williams FX3B-Cosworth V8	1 lap behind
10	SOUTH AFRICAN GP	Kyalami	21	Frank Williams Racing Cars	3.0 Williams FX3B-Cosworth V8	pit stop-puncture/6 laps behind
ret	SPANISH GP	Montjuich Park	23	Frank Williams Racing Cars	3.0 Williams 1R-Cosworth V8	out of fuel
ret	BELGIAN GP	Zolder	25	Frank Williams Racing Cars	3.0 Williams 1R-Cosworth V8	throttle stuck/accident
ret	MONACO GP	Monte Carlo	25	Frank Williams Racing Cars	3.0 Williams 1R-Cosworth V8	driveshaft
11	SWEDISH GP	Anderstorp	25	Frank Willaims Racing Cars	3.0 Williams 1R-Cosworth V8	3 laps behind
14	FRENCH GP	Paul Ricard	25	Frank Williams Racing Cars	3.0 Williams 1R-Cosworth V8	3 laps behind
9	BRITISH GP	Silverstone	25	Frank Williams Racing Cars	3.0 Williams 1R-Cosworth V8	1 lap behind
9	DUTCH GP	Zandvoort	25	Frank Williams Racing Cars	3.0 Williams 1R-Cosworth V8	collision with Lauda-pit stop/-4 laps
dns	GERMAN GP	Nürburgring	25	Frank Williams Racing Cars	3.0 Williams 1R-Cosworth V8	practice accident
nc	AUSTRIAN GP	Österreichring	25	Frank Williams Racing Cars	3.0 Williams 1R-Cosworth V8	pit stop/10 laps behind
nc	ITALIAN GP	Monza	25	Frank Williams Racing Cars	3.0 Williams 1R-Cosworth V8	pit stops/11 laps behind
6	CANADIAN GP	Mosport Park	25	Frank Williams Racing Cars	3.0 Williams 1R-Cosworth V8	1 lap behind
12	US GP	Watkins Glen	25	Frank Williams Racing Cars	3.0 Williams 1R-Cosworth V8	pit stop/2 laps behind

1974

	Race	Circuit	No	Entrant	Car/Engine	Comment
8/ret	ARGENTINE GP	Buenos Aires	10	March Engineering	3.0 March 741-Cosworth V8	out of fuel/11 laps behind
ret	BRAZILIAN GP	Interlagos	10	March Engineering	3.0 March 741-Cosworth V8	ignition
dnq	BRITISH GP	Brands Hatch	25	Maki Engineering	3.0 Maki F101-Cosworth V8	
dnq	GERMAN GP	Nürburgring	25	Maki Engineering	3.0 Maki F101-Cosworth V8	injured in practice accident

GP Starts: 35   GP Wins: 0   Pole positions: 0   Fastest laps: 0   Points: 10

GARDNER, Frank (AUS) b 1/10/1930

1964

	Race	Circuit	No	Entrant	Car/Engine	Comment
ret	BRITISH GP	Brands Hatch	26	John Willment Automobiles	1.5 Brabham BT10-Ford 4	startline accident

1965

	Race	Circuit	No	Entrant	Car/Engine	Comment
12	SOUTH AFRICAN GP	East London	16	John Willment Automobiles	1.5 Brabham BT11-BRM V8	pit stop/10 laps behind
ret	MONACO GP	Monte Carlo	11	John Willment Automobiles	1.5 Brabham BT11-BRM V8	engine mounting
ret	BELGIAN GP	Spa	26	John Willment Automobiles	1.5 Brabham BT11-BRM V8	ignition
8	BRITISH GP	Silverstone	17	John Willment Automobiles	1.5 Brabham BT11-BRM V8	2 laps behind
11	DUTCH GP	Zandvoort	30	John Willment Automobiles	1.5 Brabham BT11-BRM V8	3 laps behind
ret	GERMAN GP	Nürburgring	21	John Willment Automobiles	1.5 Brabham BT11-BRM V8	gearbox
ret	ITALIAN GP	Monza	46	John Willment Automobiles	1.5 Brabham BT11-BRM V8	engine

1968

	Race	Circuit	No	Entrant	Car/Engine	Comment
dnq	ITALIAN GP	Monza	28	Bernard White Racing Ltd	3.0 BRM P261 V12	

GP Starts: 8   GP Wins: 0   Pole positions: 0   Fastest laps: 0   Points: 0

OSCAR GALVEZ

A great hidden talent, Galvez was the early rival and inspiration to Fangio back in their native Argentina both before and after the war. Oscar and his younger brother Juan set new standards of preparation and performance in the gruelling road races so popular there and they were usually seriously threatened only by 'the Maestro'.

His single-seater outings were usually limited to guesting for visiting teams, but he never let them down, as fifth place in his only Grand Prix, for Maserati, confirms.

In the absence of Fangio, 'Los Galvez' continued to dominate South American road racing in their Fords through the fifties and into the early sixties until disaster struck when Juan was killed in a crash early in 1963. Oscar raced on, but retired following a serious accident in 1964 to concentrate on managing the works-supported Ford team.

HOWDEN GANLEY

It took a long time for Ganley to realise his ambition to become a Grand Prix driver – which was fired by a visit as a youngster in his native New Zealand to the Grand Prix at Ardmore in 1955. He sailed for England in 1961 with just $50 in his pocket, and found employment as a mechanic preparing cars at a racing school. The urge to drive was occasionally satisfied over the next few years, but his engineering talent kept him well occupied (and paid), so his racing career was on hold.

It was 1967 before Howden embarked on a serious season of Formula 3 in his own shiny-new Brabham which had been financed by his engagement as crew chief for Skip Scott and Peter Revson in the 1966 Can-Am series. Howden plugged away in the formula for another two seasons, mixing it with the best, hoping for the big break which was to come in 1970.

Given the opportunity to compete in F5000, he finished runner-up to Peter Gethin in the championship with a private McLaren M10B, and this success brought an offer to join the BRM team for 1971 as a junior driver. It was a mixed first season, but Howden scored some points at Monza and Watkins Glen, and in non-championship races finished second in the Oulton Park Gold Cup, fourth in the Jochen Rindt Memorial at Hockenheim and fifth in the Race of Champions. Continuing with BRM for 1972, he did not enjoy the best of seasons, again being restricted in the main from using the latest chassis. The high spot of his year came in a different arena, with second place at Le Mans sharing a works Matra with Cevert.

For 1973 Howden threw in his lot with Frank Williams and the Iso-FX3, which was to be a severe disappointment for all concerned, with only a sixth place in Canada salvaging some pride. The season was redeemed a little by his inclusion in the Gulf/John Wyer sports car team for whom Ganley's best result was second in the Spa 1000 Km in the Mirage with Schuppan. At the beginning of 1974, Ganley was scratching for a drive, and after racing for March in the first two GPs, and taking fifth in the GP Presidente Medici – a Brazilian non-championship race – he unwisely accepted an offer to drive the mysterious F1 Maki, a Japanese dog with no pedigree. The car suffered a suspension failure in practice for the German GP and Howden was left with serious foot and ankle injuries which ended his Grand Prix career.

He returned to action in mid-1975 with a few sports car outings, but soon gave up driving to produce Formula Ford Tigas with fellow ex-racer Tim Schenken.

FRANK GARDNER

Frank is another driver whose brief Grand Prix career did no justice to his talent, for here was one of the world's toughest, most determined and professional drivers, who was destined to enjoy an immensely long and successful career outside the sphere of Formula 1.

A typical Australian all-round sportsman, boxer, swimmer and motor cycle ace, Frank took up car racing in 1956-57 when he won 23 out of 24 races in a C-Type Jaguar to become NSW sports car champion. Inevitably he headed for England and found employment not as a driver but as a mechanic, for Aston Martin, Jim Russell and, in 1962, Jack Brabham's newly formed team, working on the Formula Junior cars. He drove the Brabham a few times that year but turned down Jack's offer of a full-time ride for 1963 (taken instead by Denny Hulme), opting to join Ian Walker for a massively successful sports and Formula Junior programme.

This had established Gardner as a serious proposition, and he moved to John Willment's team in 1964 to drive in Formula 2, also handling his stable of powerful sports and saloon cars. Ambitiously, the team went into Formula 1 in 1965, but were just not up to it, though they did take an aggregate fourth place in the Race of Champions. Frank felt he had made a bit of a fool of himself, and gave Grand Prix racing a wide berth except for a couple of drives in 1968. He contested the Tasman series in a Brabham during this period, giving a good account of himself against the likes of Clark, Hill and Stewart, and did more Formula 2 in the MRP Lola and a works Brabham, but really established a niche in saloon cars, taking a string of championships from 1968 with Alan Mann's Escort and into the seventies with both the Ford Mustang and Chevrolet Camaro. In fact Gardner seemed to be racing virtually every weekend, as he was also contesting F5000 in the works Lola, taking the championship in both 1971 and '72, before suddenly quitting single-seaters after the Tasman series early in 1973 ('I drove like an old woman' was Frank's over-critical assessment, having won one round and taken three second places).

He continued to thunder on in the Camaro, until returning to his native land to race in the sports sedan championships, inevitably winning the title in 1976 and '77. Frank Gardner was truly a 'racing' driver in the very best sense of the word.

TONY GAZE

An ex-RAF pilot, Gaze was successful in his native Australia in the in immediate post-war years with a 1936 Alta before coming to Britain to try his hand. He initially raced one of Geoffrey Taylor's Altas, before buying one of John Heath's HWMs to race in Grands Prix during 1952. He was soon to turn his attention to sports car racing, an arena where he had more chance of success, racing his Maserati, HWM-Jaguar and Ferrari over the next few seasons both at home and abroad.

Gaze was something of a pioneering figure with his regular racing trips 'down-under' between 1954 and 1956, and was a prime mover in the development of Australian motor sport, helping to bring European-style circuit racing to that continent, thus encouraging greater international competition in the years that followed.

JO GARTNER

Much self-sacrifice and an iron determination to succeed against seemingly overwhelming odds kept Jo Gartner in motor racing when many drivers with lesser fibre would have fallen by the wayside.

From his early Formula 3 days (he was third in the 1978 European championship), Jo proved he had talent, but he was lacking finance and had to act as his own mechanic, running second-rate machinery for much of his Formula 2 career – though he did have his day, winning the Pau GP in 1983. Finding some backing, he got himself briefly into the Osella Grand Prix team in 1984, and even scored a fifth place for them at Monza but, against his expectations and much to his dismay, he was not retained for the following year. Gartner then switched to sports car and IMSA racing, which he enjoyed but saw as a means to get back into Formula 1. Sadly it was not to be, for he was killed instantly during the 1986 Le Mans 24 Hours when his Porsche crashed on the Mulsanne Straight in the middle of the night.

'GEKI' (Giacomo Russo)

Racing under the pseudonym 'Geki', this talented driver from Milan was a multiple Formula Junior champion in Italy during the early 1960s, graduating from the relatively primitive Stanguellini to a Lotus. He was always difficult to beat at Monza, and thus a local attraction come Grand Prix time each year; after hiring Rob Walker's car and failing to qualify in 1964, he was subsequently seen in a works Lotus.

After an abortive time with the Abarth F2 car in 1964, 'Geki' raced occasionally for the Alfa Romeo works team in sports cars and GTs during 1965-66, and was still competing successfully in Italian F3 with a Matra when he met his death at Caserta in 1967. Having been involved in a multiple pile-up, the Swiss driver, Fehr Beat, jumped from his stricken car and ran back along the track to warn the leading bunch – which included 'Geki', who was tragically unable to avoid striking and killing his unfortunate rival. The Italian's Matra then ploughed into a concrete wall and he perished when the car burst into flames.

GARTNER, Jo (A) b 24/1/1954 – d 1/6/1986

1984

	Race	Circuit	No	Entrant	Car/Engine	Comment
ret	SAN MARINO GP	Imola	30	Osella Squadra Corse	3.0 Osella FA1E-Alfa Romeo V12	engine
ret	BRITISH GP	Brands Hatch	30	Osella Squadra Corse	1.5 t/c Osella FA1F-Alfa Romeo V8	accident at start
ret	GERMAN GP	Nürburgring	30	Osella Squadra Corse	1.5 t/c Osella FA1F-Alfa Romeo V8	turbo
ret	AUSTRIAN GP	Österreichring	30	Osella Squadra Corse	1.5 t/c Osella FA1F-Alfa Romeo V8	engine
12*	DUTCH GP	Zandvoort	30	Osella Squadra Corse	1.5 t/c Osella FA1F-Alfa Romeo V8	* 8th & 9th cars dsq/5 laps behind
5	ITALIAN GP	Monza	30	Osella Squadra Corse	1.5 t/c Osella FA1F-Alfa Romeo V8	2 laps behind
ret	EUROPEAN GP	Nürburgring	30	Osella Squadra Corse	1.5 t/c Osella FA1F-Alfa Romeo V8	fuel feed
16/ret	PORTUGUESE GP	Estoril	30	Osella Squadra Corse	1.5 t/c Osella FA1F-Alfa Romeo V8	out of fuel/5 laps behind

GP Starts: 8   GP Wins: 0   Pole positions: 0   Fastest laps: 0   Points: 2

GAZE, Tony (AUS) b 3/3/1920

1952

	Race	Circuit	No	Entrant	Car/Engine	Comment
15	BELGIAN GP	Spa	42	Tony Gaze	2.0 HWM-Alta 4	6 laps behind
ret	BRITISH GP	Silverstone	28	Tony Gaze	2.0 HWM-Alta 4	gasket
ret	GERMAN GP	Nürburgring	120	Tony Gaze	2.0 HWM-Alta 4	suspension
dnq	ITALIAN GP	Monza	56	Tony Gaze	2.0 HWM-Alta 4	

GP Starts: 4   GP Wins: 0   Pole positions: 0   Fastest laps: 0   Points: 0

'GEKI' (RUSSO, Giacomo) (I) b 23/10/1937 – d 18/6/1967

1964

	Race	Circuit	No	Entrant	Car/Engine	Comment
dnq	ITALIAN GP	Monza	36	R R C Walker Racing Team	1.5 Brabham BT11-BRM V8	

1965

	Race	Circuit	No	Entrant	Car/Engine	Comment
ret	ITALIAN GP	Monza	28	Team Lotus	1.5 Lotus 25-Climax V8	gearbox oil seal

1966

	Race	Circuit	No	Entrant	Car/Engine	Comment
9	ITALIAN GP	Monza	(22) 20	Team Lotus	2.0 Lotus 33-Climax V8	5 laps behind

GP Starts: 2   GP Wins: 0   Pole positions: 0   Fastest laps: 0   Points: 0

GENDEBIEN, Olivier (B) b 12/1/1924

1956

	Race	Circuit	No	Entrant	Car/Engine	Comment
5	ARGENTINE GP	Buenos Aires	38	Scuderia Ferrari	2.5 Ferrari-Lancia 555/D50 V8	7 laps behind
ret	FRENCH GP	Reims	44	Scuderia Ferrari	2.5 Lancia-Ferrari D50 V8	clutch

1958

6	BELGIAN GP	Spa	20	Scuderia Ferrari	2.4 Ferrari-Dino 246 V6	1 lap behind
ret	ITALIAN GP	Monza	20	Scuderia Ferrari	2.4 Ferrari-Dino 246 V6	suspension
ret	MOROCCAN GP	Casablanca	2	Scuderia Ferrari	2.4 Ferrari-Dino 246 V6	spun, hit by Picard

1959

4	FRENCH GP	Reims	22	Scuderia Ferrari	2.4 Ferrari-Dino 246 V6	
6	ITALIAN GP	Monza	38	Scuderia Ferrari	2.4 Ferrari-Dino 246 V6	1 lap behind

1960

3	BELGIAN GP	Spa	34	Yeoman Credit Racing Team	2.5 Cooper T51-Climax 4	1 lap behind
2	FRENCH GP	Reims	44	Yeoman Credit Racing Team	2.5 Cooper T51-Climax 4	
9	BRITISH GP	Silverstone	14	Yeoman Credit Racing Team	2.5 Cooper T51-Climax 4	3 laps behind
7	PORTUGUESE GP	Oporto	8	Yeoman Credit Racing Team	2.5 Cooper T51-Climax 4	stuck in top gear/9 laps behind
12	US GP	Riverside	7	Yeoman Credit Racing Team	2.5 Cooper T51-Climax 4	pit stop/6 laps behind

1961

dnq	MONACO GP	Monte Carlo	12	Equipe Nationale Belge	1.5 Emeryson 1003-Maserati 4	
4	BELGIAN GP	Spa	8	Scuderia Ferrari SpA SEFAC	1.5 Ferrari 156 V6	
11*	US GP	Watkins Glen	21	UDT Laystall Racing Team	1.5 Lotus 18/21-Climax 4	*unwell-Gregory took over/-8 laps

GP Starts: 14   GP Wins: 0   Pole positions: 0   Fastest laps: 0   Points: 18

OLIVIER GENDEBIEN

A Belgian aristocrat, and former World War II paratrooper, Gendebien spent some four years in forestry in the Congo, where he met rally driver Charles Fraikin, who was lamenting the lack of a co-driver with whom to compete back in Europe.

Gendebien then returned and raced a Veritas in the GP des Frontières at Chimay, finishing sixth, before joining Fraikin, initially to rally a Jaguar, the pair staying together until 1955. By the time they split they had become known as 'the eternal bridesmaids' due to the number of times they had to be content with second place. Twice they just missed winning the Liège-Rome-Liège Rally but in 1955 it was third time lucky with a Mercedes 300SL. Without his partner, Olivier had great success, winning his class with a Plymouth in the Round Italy Rally, the Tulip Rally and the Northern Roads Rally in a Porsche, all in 1954.

Such was the impression made that he was offered a contract to drive a works Ferrari in sports car events and selected Grands Prix. His first race for the team nearly ended in disaster, when in late 1955 he crashed heavily in practice for the Tourist Trophy at Dundrod, suffering concussion. He was fit for the start of 1956 and, with virtually no single-seater experience behind him, finished fifth on his Grand Prix debut at the Argentine GP, followed by sixth in the Mendoza GP. The season also saw a splendid run of finishes in sports car races, including second places at Buenos Aires and in the Supercortemaggiore at Monza and thirds in the Nürburgring 1000 Km, Targa Florio and Le Mans.

That was to be the first of seven wonderful seasons that Gendebien spent in Ferrari's sports car team. He subsequently won the Reims 12 Hours in 1957 and '58, the Targa Florio in 1958, '61 and '62, Sebring in 1959, '60 and '61 and the Nürburgring 1000 Km in 1962, not forgetting his wonderful achievement of four wins at Le Mans in 1958, '60, '61 and '62, after the last of which he retired.

He was no slouch in a Grand Prix car either. His outings were generally infrequent, but whenever he raced a competitive machine he invariably brought it into the points, as a check on the statistics above will show. But it is inevitably as one of the greatest sports car drivers of any era that he will be best remembered.

GERARD, Bob (GB) b 19/1/1914 – d Jan 1990

1950

	Race	Circuit	No	Entrant	Car/Engine	Comment
6	BRITISH GP	Silverstone	12	Bob Gerard	1.5 s/c ERA B Type 6	*3 laps behind*
6	MONACO GP	Monte Carlo	26	Bob Gerard	1.5 s/c ERA B Type 6	*6 laps behind*

1951

11	BRITISH GP	Silverstone	8	Bob Gerard	1.5 s/c ERA B Type 6	*8 laps behind*

1953

11	FRENCH GP	Reims	38	Bob Gerard	2.0 Cooper T23-Bristol 6	*5 laps behind*
ret	BRITISH GP	Silverstone	17	Bob Gerard	2.0 Cooper T23-Bristol 6	*front suspension*

1954

10	BRITISH GP	Silverstone	29	Bob Gerard	2.0 Cooper T23-Bristol 6	*5 laps behind*

1956

nc	BRITISH GP	Silverstone	26	Bob Gerard	2.2 Cooper T23-Bristol 6	*13 laps behind*

1957

6	BRITISH GP	Aintree	38	Bob Gerard	2.2 Cooper BG43-Bristol 6	*8 laps behind*

GP Starts: 8   GP Wins: 0   Pole positions: 0   Fastest laps: 0   Points: 0

GERINI, Gerino (I)

1956

	Race	Circuit	No	Entrant	Car/Engine	Comment
4*	ARGENTINE GP	Buenos Aires	10	Officine Alfieri Maserati	2.5 Maserati 250F 6	**shared with Landi/6 laps behind*
10	ITALIAN GP	Monza	42	Scuderia Guastalla	2.5 Maserati 250F 6	*8 laps behind*

1958

dnq	MONACO GP	Monte Carlo	48	Scuderia Centro Sud	2.5 Maserati 250F 6	
9	FRENCH GP	Reims	32	Scuderia Centro Sud	2.5 Maserati 250F 6	*3 laps behind*
ret	BRITISH GP	Silverstone	6	Scuderia Centro Sud	2.5 Maserati 250F 6	*gearbox*
ret	ITALIAN GP	Monza	40	Scuderia Centro Sud	2.5 Maserati 250F 6	*mechanical*
nc	MOROCCAN GP	Casablanca	26	Scuderia Centro Sud	2.5 Maserati 250F 6	*12th behind 1 F2 car/5 laps behind*

GP Starts: 6   GP Wins: 0   Pole positions: 0   Fastest laps: 0   Points: 0

GETHIN, Peter (GB) b 21/2/1940

1970

	Race	Circuit	No	Entrant	Car/Engine	Comment
ret	DUTCH GP	Zandvoort	20	Bruce McLaren Motor Racing	3.0 McLaren M14A-Cosworth V8	*spun off*
ret	GERMAN GP	Hockenheim	24	Bruce McLaren Motor Racing	3.0 McLaren M14A-Cosworth V8	*engine*
10	AUSTRIAN GP	Österreichring	23	Bruce McLaren Motor Racing	3.0 McLaren M14A-Cosworth V8	*1 lap behind*
nc	ITALIAN GP	Monza	32	Bruce McLaren Motor Racing	3.0 McLaren M14A-Cosworth V8	*pit stops-various/8 laps behind*
6	CANADIAN GP	St Jovite	6	Bruce McLaren Motor Racing	3.0 McLaren M14A-Cosworth V8	*2 laps behind*
14	US GP	Watkins Glen	9	Bruce McLaren Motor Racing	3.0 McLaren M14A-Cosworth V8	*pit stop-tyres/8 laps behind*
ret	MEXICAN GP	Mexico City	9	Bruce McLaren Motor Racing	3.0 McLaren M14A-Cosworth V8	*engine*

1971

ret	SOUTH AFRICAN GP	Kyalami	12	Bruce McLaren Motor Racing	3.0 McLaren M14A-Cosworth V8	*loose fuel line*
8	SPANISH GP	Montjuich Park	10	Bruce McLaren Motor Racing	3.0 McLaren M14A-Cosworth V8	*2 laps behind*
ret	MONACO GP	Monte Carlo	10	Bruce McLaren Motor Racing	3.0 McLaren M14A-Cosworth V8	*hit chicane*
nc	DUTCH GP	Zandvoort	28	Bruce McLaren Motor Racing	3.0 McLaren M19A-Cosworth V8	*spin-pit stop/10 laps behind*
9	FRENCH GP	Paul Ricard	10	Bruce McLaren Motor Racing	3.0 McLaren M19A-Cosworth V8	*1 lap behind*
ret	BRITISH GP	Silverstone	10	Bruce McLaren Motor Racing	3.0 McLaren M19A-Cosworth V8	*oil pressure*
ret	GERMAN GP	Nürburgring	20	Bruce McLaren Motor Racing	3.0 McLaren M19A-Cosworth V8	*accident-damaged suspension*
10	AUSTRIAN GP	Österreichring	23	Yardley BRM	3.0 BRM P160 V12	*misfire/2 laps behind*
1	ITALIAN GP	Monza	18	Yardley BRM	3.0 BRM P160 V12	
14	CANADIAN GP	Mosport Park	15	Yardley BRM	3.0 BRM P160 V12	*5 laps behind*
9	US GP	Watkins Glen	15	Yardley BRM	3.0 BRM P160 V12	*broken valve spring/1 lap behind*

1972

ret	ARGENTINE GP	Buenos Aires	5	Marlboro BRM	3.0 BRM P160B V12	*accident-broken fuel line*
nc	SOUTH AFRICAN GP	Kyalami	11	Marlboro BRM	3.0 BRM P160B V12	*pit stops/14 laps behind*
ret	SPANISH GP	Jarama	8	Marlboro BRM	3.0 BRM P180 V12	*engine*
ret/dsq*	MONACO GP	Monte Carlo	18	Marlboro BRM	3.0 BRM P160B V12	*hit chicane/*reversed into pit lane*
ret	BELGIAN GP	Nivelles	24	Marlboro BRM	3.0 BRM P160B V12	*fuel pump-engine misfire*
dns	FRENCH GP	Clermont Ferrand	22	Marlboro BRM	3.0 BRM P160B V12	*crashed in practice*
ret	BRITISH GP	Brands Hatch	12	Marlboro BRM	3.0 BRM P160B V12	*engine*
13	AUSTRIAN GP	Österreichring	6	Marlboro BRM	3.0 BRM P160C V12	*pit stops/3 laps behind*
6	ITALIAN GP	Monza	23	Marlboro BRM	3.0 BRM P160C V12	
ret	CANADIAN GP	Mosport Park	16	Marlboro BRM	3.0 BRM P160C V12	*rear suspension mounting*
ret	US GP	Watkins Glen	14	Marlboro BRM	3.0 BRM P160C V12	*engine*

1973

ret	CANADIAN GP	Mosport Park	19	Marlboro BRM	3.0 BRM P160E V12	*accessory drive belt*

1974

ret	BRITISH GP	Brands Hatch	27	Embassy Racing with Graham Hill	3.0 Lola T370-Cosworth V8	*did not fit car/deflating tyre*

GP Starts: 30   GP Wins: 1   Pole positions: 0   Fastest laps: 0   Points: 11

BOB GERARD

Gerard enjoyed an extremely long and active career in motor racing, from his early days as a trialist with a Riley in 1933 through to the early 1970s as an entrant.

At first he was identified with the family Riley, but it was after the war that he really came into his own, with an ERA, winning the British Empire Trophy in 1947, '48 and '49, in addition to the 1949 Jersey Road Race. Bob also came close to winning that year's British Grand Prix, finishing second to de Graffenried.

As the fifties dawned, the old ERA was placed sixth in a couple of Grands Prix, but it was only really suitable for national races, so Gerard had to wait until 1953, when he acquired a Cooper-Bristol, to prove his worth. He drove it doggedly, frequently putting more powerful cars to shame and regularly scoring respectable placings in minor Formula 2 and Libre events until 1956.

Gerard made his final GP appearance in 1957 at the wheel of the unsuccessful rear-engined Cooper-BG-Bristol, just missing the points. From 1959 to 1961 he happily drove a Turner in club events, before retiring from active service to enter a Cooper for John Taylor, mainly in non-championship races, later running Formula 2 cars for Alan Rollinson, Mike Beckwith and Peter Gethin among others.

GERINO GERINI

This Italian driver raced Ferrari sports cars in the mid-fifties, before switching to rivals Maserati.

The 1956 season started promisingly, with a shared fourth place (with Landi) in the Argentine GP, plus a third at Naples and a fifth at Syracuse, but then nothing of note was achieved except a class win in the Maserati sports car at the Coppa Inter Europa at Monza.

In fact Gerini was not to reappear in Grands Prix until 1958, when, apart from a distant sixth place at Caen, he struggled to make an impression in the by now elderly 250F. He briefly reappeared in sports cars in 1960, when his Ferrari crashed out of the Nürburgring 1000 Km.

PETER GETHIN

It is perhaps unfair that Gethin should be best remembered for his sensational Grand Prix win at Monza in 1971, when he took his BRM to a wonderful victory by the margin of one-hundredth of a second in a four-car dash to the line, for in fact he enjoyed a splendid career which spanned some 15 years and encompassed almost every category of the sport.

After an early start in a Lotus Seven in 1962, Peter soon became one of the country's top club sports car drivers in his Lotus 23. He then moved into Formula 3 in 1965 with Charles Lucas, but his career really stood still until 1968 when he ran a full Formula 2 season with Frank Lythgoe, finishing strongly with a brilliant second at Albi and a third at Vallelunga after a Brabham had been acquired to replace a disappointing Chevron.

It was the introduction of F5000 in 1969 that really put Peter's career on the map. In a semi-works McLaren, he dominated the early part of the season with four straight wins and then defended his advantage grimly as his title lead was whittled away. The final round ended in anti-climax with a collision but the title went to Gethin, and he proved himself a more than worthy champion by retaining the title convincingly the following year. By this time he was closely involved with the McLaren Grand Prix effort; having made a promising debut to finish sixth in the Race of Champions, he was brought into the team after the sad loss of Bruce McLaren in a testing accident at Goodwood and also took over the vacant Can-Am drive, winning a round at Elkhart Lake.

Staying with the team for 1971, Peter inexplicably continued to struggle in Grands Prix, though he did finish second on aggregate in the International Trophy, but it was something of a surprise when he moved to BRM. Almost immediately he won at Monza and then repeated that triumph in the tragically shortened Victory Race at Brands Hatch, in which team-mate Jo Siffert perished.

Hopes were high for 1972, but Peter endured a thin time of it with BRM, though an equally low-key season in Formula 2 with Chevron did bring an unexpected win in the Pau GP. So it was back to F5000 at home and abroad, which yielded a shock win in the Race of Champions. Gethin made a couple more Grand Prix appearances, but concentrated on F5000 with Chevron and VDS, and also raced in the newly revived Can-Am series before retiring at the end of 1977. He later became involved with the March F2 team, looking after Beppe Gabbiani, and Toleman in F1.

PIERCARLO GHINZANI

'Better to be at the back in Formula 1 than not to be in Formula 1 at all,' said Piercarlo Ghinzani, and that's pretty well where he stayed in a Grand Prix career that was to span eight seasons, mostly at the tail-end of the grid.

It was all a long way from the start of his career when, after his 1970 debut in Italian Formula Ford, he began the slow climb up the motor racing ladder through Formula Italia to Formula 3 in 1973. His early days in Italian F3 were underfinanced, but he did finish second to Riccardo Patrese in 1976. Moving up to the European series in 1977, Piercarlo did extremely well to take the title, his phlegmatic approach being vital in a team that was beset by upheaval. The next step into Formula 2 with a March was a big disappointment, and this appeared to be a major blow to his aspirations.

Salvation was nigh. In 1981 he was called in as a last-minute replacement for Osella after Giorgio Francia's credentials failed to satisfy FISA, and he qualified for the Belgian GP. This was the start of what was to be a long association with the little team, his best result being a much-needed fifth place at Dallas in 1984. He did take a brief sabbatical in mid-1985 when a second Toleman was entered, but returned to the fold for 1986. In Grands Prix, results were understandably hard to find, but he had been successful in endurance events, winning the Fuji 1000 Km in a Porsche with Barilla.

In 1987, Ghinzani tried his luck in a Ligier team suddenly shorn of potential when an Alfa Romeo engine deal foundered as the season dawned, and then it was on to an equally fruitless sojourn at Zakspeed, before just one more season back in the Osella camp.

Ghinzani certainly had staying power; he started 96 Grands Prix, but more pointedly failed to qualify for another 31 – a real glutton for punishment!

GHINZANI, Piercarlo (I) b 16/1/1952

1981

	Race	Circuit	No	Entrant	Car/Engine	Comment
13	BELGIAN GP	Zolder	31	Osella Squadra Corse	3.0 Osella FA1B-Cosworth V8	spin-pit stop/4 laps behind
dnq	MONACO GP	Monte Carlo	32	Osella Squadra Corse	3.0 Osella FA1B-Cosworth V8	

1983

	Race	Circuit	No	Entrant	Car/Engine	Comment
dnq	BRAZILIAN GP	Rio	32	Osella Squadra Corse	3.0 Osella FA1D-Cosworth V8	
dnq	US GP WEST	Long Beach	32	Osella Squadra Corse	3.0 Osella FA1D-Cosworth V8	
dnq	FRENCH GP	Paul Ricard	32	Osella Squadra Corse	3.0 Osella FA1D-Cosworth V8	
dnq	SAN MARINO GP	Imola	32	Osella Squadra Corse	3.0 Osella FA1E-Alfa Romeo V12	
dnq	MONACO GP	Monte Carlo	32	Osella Squadra Corse	3.0 Osella FA1E-Alfa Romeo V12	
dnq	BELGIAN GP	Spa	32	Osella Squadra Corse	3.0 Osella FA1E-Alfa Romeo V12	
ret	US GP (DETROIT)	Detroit	32	Osella Squadra Corse	3.0 Osella FA1E-Alfa Romeo V12	overheating
dnq	CANADIAN GP	Montreal	32	Osella Squadra Corse	3.0 Osella FA1E-Alfa Romeo V12	
ret	BRITISH GP	Silverstone	32	Osella Squadra Corse	3.0 Osella FA1E-Alfa Romeo V12	fuel pressure
ret	GERMAN GP	Hockenheim	32	Osella Squadra Corse	3.0 Osella FA1E-Alfa Romeo V12	engine
11	AUSTRIAN GP	Österreichring	32	Osella Squadra Corse	3.0 Osella FA1E-Alfa Romeo V12	4 laps behind
dnq	DUTCH GP	Zandvoort	32	Osella Squadra Corse	3.0 Osella FA1E-Alfa Romeo V12	
ret	ITALIAN GP	Monza	32	Osella Squadra Corse	3.0 Osella FA1E-Alfa Romeo V12	gearbox
nc	EUROPEAN GP	Brands Hatch	32	Osella Squadra Corse	3.0 Osella FA1E-Alfa Romeo V12	3 pit stops-throttle/13 laps behind
ret	SOUTH AFRICAN GP	Kyalami	32	Osella Squadra Corse	3.0 Osella FA1E-Alfa Romeo V12	engine

1984

	Race	Circuit	No	Entrant	Car/Engine	Comment
ret	BRAZILIAN GP	Rio	24	Osella Squadra Corse	1.5 t/c Osella FA1F-Alfa Romeo V8	gearbox
dns	SOUTH AFRICAN GP	Kyalami	24	Osella Squadra Corse	1.5 t/c Osella FA1F-Alfa Romeo V8	accident in a.m. warm up
ret	BELGIAN GP	Zolder	24	Osella Squadra Corse	1.5 t/c Osella FA1F-Alfa Romeo V8	transmission
dnq	SAN MARINO GP	Imola	24	Osella Squadra Corse	1.5 t/c Osella FA1F-Alfa Romeo V8	
12*	FRENCH GP	Dijon	24	Osella Squadra Corse	1.5 t/c Osella FA1F-Alfa Romeo V8	* 12th place car dsq/5 laps behind
7*	MONACO GP	Monte Carlo	24	Osella Squadra Corse	1.5 t/c Osella FA1F-Alfa Romeo V8	* 3rd place car dsq/1 lap behind
ret	CANADIAN GP	Montreal	24	Osella Squadra Corse	1.5 t/c Osella FA1F-Alfa Romeo V8	gearbox
ret	US GP (DETROIT)	Detroit	24	Osella Squadra Corse	1.5 t/c Osella FA1F-Alfa Romeo V8	accident with Hesnault
5	US GP (DALLAS)	Dallas	24	Osella Squadra Corse	1.5 t/c Osella FA1F-Alfa Romeo V8	2 laps behind
9	BRITISH GP	Brands Hatch	24	Osella Squadra Corse	1.5 t/c Osella FA1F-Alfa Romeo V8	3 laps behind
ret	GERMAN GP	Hockenheim	24	Osella Squadra Corse	1.5 t/c Osella FA1F-Alfa Romeo V8	electrics
ret	AUSTRIAN GP	Österreichring	24	Osella Squadra Corse	1.5 t/c Osella FA1F-Alfa Romeo V8	gearbox
ret	DUTCH GP	Zandvoort	24	Osella Squadra Corse	1.5 t/c Osella FA1F-Alfa Romeo V8	fuel pump
7/ret	ITALIAN GP	Monza	24	Osella Squadra Corse	1.5 t/c Osella FA1F-Alfa Romeo V8	out of fuel/2 laps behind
ret	EUROPEAN GP	Nürburgring	24	Osella Squadra Corse	1.5 t/c Osella FA1F-Alfa Romeo V8	accident
ret	PORTUGUESE GP	Estoril	24	Osella Squadra Corse	1.5 t/c Osella FA1F-Alfa Romeo V8	engine

1985

	Race	Circuit	No	Entrant	Car/Engine	Comment
12	BRAZILIAN GP	Rio	24	Osella Squadra Corse	1.5 t/c Osella FA1G-Alfa Romeo V8	4 laps behind
9	PORTUGUESE GP	Estoril	24	Osella Squadra Corse	1.5 t/c Osella FA1F-Alfa Romeo V8	6 laps behind
nc	SAN MARINO GP	Imola	24	Osella Squadra Corse	1.5 t/c Osella FA1G-Alfa Romeo V8	pit stop-gearbox/14 laps behind

dnq	MONACO GP	Monte Carlo	24	Osella Squadra Corse	1.5 t/c Osella FA1G-Alfa Romeo V8	
ret	CANADIAN GP	Montreal	24	Osella Squadra Corse	1.5 t/c Osella FA1G-Alfa Romeo V8	engine
ret	US GP (DETROIT)	Detroit	24	Osella Squadra Corse	1.5 t/c Osella FA1G-Alfa Romeo V8	accident
15	FRENCH GP	Paul Ricard	24	Osella Squadra Corse	1.5 t/c Osella FA1G-Alfa Romeo V8	4 laps behind
ret	BRITISH GP	Silverstone	24	Osella Squadra Corse	1.5 t/c Osella FA1G-Alfa Romeo V8	accident damage-lap 1
ret/dns	AUSTRIAN GP	Österreichring	20	Toleman Group Motorsport	1.5 t/c Toleman TG185-Hart 4	engine in first start/did not restart
ret	DUTCH GP	Zandvoort	20	Toleman Group Motorsport	1.5 t/c Toleman TG185-Hart 4	engine
ret	ITALIAN GP	Monza	20	Toleman Group Motorsport	1.5 t/c Toleman TG185-Hart 4	stalled at start
ret	BELGIAN GP	Spa	20	Toleman Group Motorsport	1.5 t/c Toleman TG185-Hart 4	accident
ret	EUROPEAN GP	Brands Hatch	20	Toleman Group Motorsport	1.5 t/c Toleman TG185-Hart 4	engine
ret	SOUTH AFRICAN GP	Kyalami	20	Toleman Group Motorsport	1.5 t/c Toleman TG185-Hart 4	engine
ret	AUSTRALIAN GP	Adelaide	20	Toleman Group Motorsport	1.5 t/c Toleman TG185-Hart 4	clutch

1986

ret	BRAZILIAN GP	Rio	21	Osella Squadra Corse	1.5 t/c Osella FA1G-Alfa Romeo V8	engine
ret	SPANISH GP	Jerez	21	Osella Squadra Corse	1.5 t/c Osella FA1G-Alfa Romeo V8	engine
ret	SAN MARINO GP	Imola	21	Osella Squadra Corse	1.5 t/c Osella FA1G-Alfa Romeo V8	out of fuel
dnq	MONACO GP	Monte Carlo	21	Osella Squadra Corse	1.5 t/c Osella FA1G-Alfa Romeo V8	
ret	BELGIAN GP	Spa	21	Osella Squadra Corse	1.5 t/c Osella FA1G-Alfa Romeo V8	engine
ret	CANADIAN GP	Montreal	21	Osella Squadra Corse	1.5 t/c Osella FA1G-Alfa Romeo V8	gearbox
ret	US GP (DETROIT)	Detroit	21	Osella Squadra Corse	1.5 t/c Osella FA1G-Alfa Romeo V8	turbo
ret	FRENCH GP	Paul Ricard	21	Osella Squadra Corse	1.5 t/c Osella FA1H-Alfa Romeo V8	accident with Nannini
ret/dns	BRITISH GP	Brands Hatch	21	Osella Squadra Corse	1.5 t/c Osella FA1G-Alfa Romeo V8	accident in first start
ret	GERMAN GP	Hockenheim	21	Osella Squadra Corse	1.5 t/c Osella FA1G-Alfa Romeo V8	clutch
ret	HUNGARIAN GP	Hungaroring	21	Osella Squadra Corse	1.5 t/c Osella FA1G-Alfa Romeo V8	rear suspension
11	AUSTRIAN GP	Österreichring	21	Osella Squadra Corse	1.5 t/c Osella FA1G-Alfa Romeo V8	6 laps behind
ret	ITALIAN GP	Monza	21	Osella Squadra Corse	1.5 t/c Osella FA1G-Alfa Romeo V8	spun off-broken suspension
ret	PORTUGUESE GP	Estoril	21	Osella Squadra Corse	1.5 t/c Osella FA1G-Alfa Romeo V8	engine
ret	MEXICAN GP	Mexico City	21	Osella Squadra Corse	1.5 t/c Osella FA1G-Alfa Romeo V8	turbo
ret	AUSTRALIAN GP	Adelaide	21	Osella Squadra Corse	1.5 t/c Osella FA1G-Alfa Romeo V8	transmission

1987

ret	SAN MARINO GP	Imola	26	Ligier Loto	1.5 t/c Ligier JS29B-Megatron 4	withdrawn-handling problems
7/ret	BELGIAN GP	Spa	26	Ligier Loto	1.5 t/c Ligier JS29B-Megatron 4	out of fuel/3 laps behind
12	MONACO GP	Monte Carlo	26	Ligier Loto	1.5 t/c Ligier JS29B-Megatron 4	4 laps behind
nc	US GP (DETROIT)	Detroit	26	Ligier Loto	1.5 t/c Ligier JS29B-Megatron 4	pit stop/12 laps behind
ret	FRENCH GP	Paul Ricard	26	Ligier Loto	1.5 t/c Ligier JS29C-Megatron 4	engine
dns	BRITISH GP	Silverstone	26	Ligier Loto	1.5 t/c Ligier JS29C-Megatron 4	disqualified in practice
ret	GERMAN GP	Hockenheim	26	Ligier Loto	1.5 t/c Ligier JS29C-Megatron 4	engine
12	HUNGARIAN GP	Hungaroring	26	Ligier Loto	1.5 t/c Ligier JS29C-Megatron 4	bad oversteer/3 laps behind
8	AUSTRIAN GP	Österreichring	26	Ligier Loto	1.5 t/c Ligier JS29C-Megatron 4	2 laps behind
8	ITALIAN GP	Monza	26	Ligier Loto	1.5 t/c Ligier JS29C-Megatron 4	2 laps behind
ret	PORTUGUESE GP	Estoril	26	Ligier Loto	1.5 t/c Ligier JS29C-Megatron 4	clutch
ret	SPANISH GP	Jerez	26	Ligier Loto	1.5 t/c Ligier JS29C-Megatron 4	ignition
ret	MEXICAN GP	Mexico City	26	Ligier Loto	1.5 t/c Ligier JS29C-Megatron 4	overheating
13/ret	JAPANESE GP	Suzuka	26	Ligier Loto	1.5 t/c Ligier JS29C-Megatron 4	out of fuel
ret	AUSTRALIAN GP	Adelaide	26	Ligier Loto	1.5 t/c Ligier JS29C-Megatron 4	engine

1988

dnq	BRAZILIAN GP	Rio	9	West Zakspeed Racing	1.5 t/c Zakspeed 881 4	
ret	SAN MARINO GP	Imola	9	West Zakspeed Racing	1.5 t/c Zakspeed 881 4	electrics
ret	MONACO GP	Monte Carlo	9	West Zakspeed Racing	1.5 t/c Zakspeed 881 4	gearbox
15	MEXICAN GP	Mexico City	9	West Zakspeed Racing	1.5 t/c Zakspeed 881 4	spin-broken nose wing-p stop/-6 laps
14/ret	CANADIAN GP	Montreal	9	West Zakspeed Racing	1.5 t/c Zakspeed 881 4	engine
dnq	US GP (DETROIT)	Detroit	9	West Zakspeed Racing	1.5 t/c Zakspeed 881 4	
excl	FRENCH GP	Paul Ricard	9	West Zakspeed Racing	1.5 t/c Zakspeed 881 4	dsq for missing weight check
dnq	BRITISH GP	Silverstone	9	West Zakspeed Racing	1.5 t/c Zakspeed 881 4	
14	GERMAN GP	Hockenheim	9	West Zakspeed Racing	1.5 t/c Zakspeed 881 4	lost clutch/2 laps behind
dnq	HUNGARIAN GP	Hungaroring	9	West Zakspeed Racing	1.5 t/c Zakspeed 881 4	
ret	BELGIAN GP	Spa	9	West Zakspeed Racing	1.5 t/c Zakspeed 881 4	engine oil leak
ret	ITALIAN GP	Monza	9	West Zakspeed Racing	1.5 t/c Zakspeed 881 4	engine
dnq	PORTUGUESE GP	Estoril	9	West Zakspeed Racing	1.5 t/c Zakspeed 881 4	
dnq	SPANISH GP	Jerez	9	West Zakspeed Racing	1.5 t/c Zakspeed 881 4	
dnq	JAPANESE GP	Suzuka	9	West Zakspeed Racing	1.5 t/c Zakspeed 881 4	
ret	AUSTRALIAN GP	Adelaide	9	West Zakspeed Racing	1.5 t/c Zakspeed 881 4	fuel pump

1989

dnpq	BRAZILIAN GP	Rio	18	Osella Squadra Corse	3.5 Osella FA1M-Cosworth V8	
dnpq	SAN MARINO GP	Imola	18	Osella Squadra Corse	3.5 Osella FA1M-Cosworth V8	
dnpq	MONACO GP	Monte Carlo	18	Osella Squadra Corse	3.5 Osella FA1M-Cosworth V8	
excl	MEXICAN GP	Mexico City	18	Osella Squadra Corse	3.5 Osella FA1M-Cosworth V8	dsq for missing weight check
dnpq	US GP (PHOENIX)	Phoenix	18	Osella Squadra Corse	3.5 Osella FA1M-Cosworth V8	
dnpq	CANADIAN GP	Montreal	18	Osella Squadra Corse	3.5 Osella FA1M-Cosworth V8	
dnpq	FRENCH GP	Paul Ricard	18	Osella Squadra Corse	3.5 Osella FA1M-Cosworth V8	
dnpq	BRITISH GP	Silverstone	18	Osella Squadra Corse	3.5 Osella FA1M-Cosworth V8	
dnpq	GERMAN GP	Hockenheim	18	Osella Squadra Corse	3.5 Osella FA1M-Cosworth V8	
ret	HUNGARIAN GP	Hungaroring	18	Osella Squadra Corse	3.5 Osella FA1M-Cosworth V8	electrics
dnpq	BELGIAN GP	Spa	18	Osella Squadra Corse	3.5 Osella FA1M-Cosworth V8	
dnpq	ITALIAN GP	Monza	18	Osella Squadra Corse	3.5 Osella FA1M-Cosworth V8	
dnpq	PORTUGUESE GP	Estoril	18	Osella Squadra Corse	3.5 Osella FA1M-Cosworth V8	
ret	SPANISH GP	Jerez	18	Osella Squadra Corse	3.5 Osella FA1M-Cosworth V8	gearbox
dnpq	JAPANESE GP	Suzuka	18	Osella Squadra Corse	3.5 Osella FA1M-Cosworth V8	
ret	AUSTRALIAN GP	Adelaide	18	Osella Squadra Corse	3.5 Osella FA1M-Cosworth V8	car hit by Piquet in rain

GP Starts: 74 (76)   GP Wins: 0   Pole positions: 0   Fastest laps: 0   Points: 2

BRUNO GIACOMELLI

This ebullient Italian seemed to be well set for a successful Grand Prix career, but after he had been given some excellent early opportunities his star waned and was eventually reduced to a distant flicker.

Bruno came through Formula Italia to contest the 1976 BP Formula 3 championship in a March, and he did very well to run a close second to Rupert Keegan in his first season in the category. Benefiting from the close attentions of Robin Herd and the March factory, Giacomelli graduated to Formula 2 in 1977 and took three wins, but suffered through poor reliability. Enjoying substantial backing, he made his Grand Prix debut in a third works McLaren in selected races, but at this point he was still focusing on Formula 2. In 1978 he blitzed the opposition, winning eight of the 12 rounds in the works March to become the first Italian ever to win the title.

In 1979, Bruno joined the Alfa Romeo team for what was to be very much a learning year. The gloves were off in 1980 and at first he floundered, prone to silly errors which undid much good work. Then, after Depailler's death in a mid-season testing accident, he found himself leading the team, and rose to the challenge magnificently.

Maybe he lacked motivation, for while there were occasions during the next three seasons when his undoubted ability shone, too often he seemed uninterested and at odds with his machinery. Out of a Grand Prix drive from 1984, Giacomelli surfaced occasionally in IndyCar and sports car racing over the next few seasons to no great effect, so it was a considerable surprise when he was brought into the Life team in 1990 to replace the disenchanted Gary Brabham. The excercise was something of a joke, however, as Bruno rarely seemed to venture beyond the pit lane.

GIACOMELLI, Bruno (I) b 10/9/1952

	1977					
	Race	Circuit	No	Entrant	Car/Engine	Comment
ret	ITALIAN GP	Monza	14	Marlboro Team McLaren	3.0 McLaren M23-Cosworth V8	engine/spun off
	1978					
8	BELGIAN GP	Zolder	33	Marlboro Team McLaren	3.0 McLaren M26-Cosworth V8	1 lap behind
ret	FRENCH GP	Paul Ricard	33	Marlboro Team McLaren	3.0 McLaren M26-Cosworth V8	engine
7	BRITISH GP	Brands Hatch	33	Marlboro Team McLaren	3.0 McLaren M26-Cosworth V8	1 lap behind
ret	DUTCH GP	Zandvoort	33	Marlboro Team McLaren	3.0 McLaren M26-Cosworth V8	spun off-stalled
14	ITALIAN GP	Monza	33	Marlboro Team McLaren	3.0 McLaren M26-Cosworth V8	1 lap behind
	1979					
ret	BELGIAN GP	Zolder	35	Autodelta	3.0 Alfa Romeo 177 F12	hit by de Angelis
17	FRENCH GP	Dijon	35	Autodelta	3.0 Alfa Romeo 177 F12	pit stop/5 laps behind
ret	ITALIAN GP	Monza	35	Autodelta	3.0 Alfa Romeo 179 V12	spun off
dnp	CANADIAN GP	Montreal	35	Autodelta	3.0 Alfa Romeo 179 V12	had to pre qualify-entry withdrawn
ret	US GP EAST	Watkins Glen	35	Autodelta	3.0 Alfa Romeo 179 V12	spun avoiding Rosberg
	1980					
5	ARGENTINE GP	Buenos Aires	23	Marlboro Team Alfa Romeo	3.0 Alfa Romeo 179 V12	1 lap behind
13	BRAZILIAN GP	Interlagos	23	Marlboro Team Alfa Romeo	3.0 Alfa Romeo 179 V12	1 lap behind
ret	SOUTH AFRICAN GP	Kyalami	23	Marlboro Team Alfa Romeo	3.0 Alfa Romeo 179 V12	engine
ret	US GP WEST	Long Beach	23	Marlboro Team Alfa Romeo	3.0 Alfa Romeo 179 V12	collison with Jones
ret	BELGIAN GP	Zolder	23	Marlboro Team Alfa Romeo	3.0 Alfa Romeo 179 V12	suspension
ret	MONACO GP	Monte Carlo	23	Marlboro Team Alfa Romeo	3.0 Alfa Romeo 179 V12	multiple accident
ret	FRENCH GP	Paul Ricard	23	Marlboro Team Alfa Romeo	3.0 Alfa Romeo 179 V12	handling

	Race	Circuit	No	Entrant	Car/Engine	Comment
ret	BRITISH GP	Brands Hatch	23	Marlboro Team Alfa Romeo	3.0 Alfa Romeo 179 V12	spun off
5	GERMAN GP	Hockenheim	23	Marlboro Team Alfa Romeo	3.0 Alfa Romeo 179 V12	
ret	AUSTRIAN GP	Österreichring	23	Marlboro Team Alfa Romeo	3.0 Alfa Romeo 179 V12	rear suspension
ret	DUTCH GP	Zandvoort	23	Marlboro Team Alfa Romeo	3.0 Alfa Romeo 179 V12	damaged skirt
ret	ITALIAN GP	Imola	23	Marlboro Team Alfa Romeo	3.0 Alfa Romeo 179 V12	puncture-spun off
ret	CANADIAN GP	Montreal	23	Marlboro Team Alfa Romeo	3.0 Alfa Romeo 179 V12	damaged skirt
ret	US GP EAST	Watkins Glen	23	Marlboro Team Alfa Romeo	3.0 Alfa Romeo 179 V12	electrics/Pole

1981

	Race	Circuit	No	Entrant	Car/Engine	Comment
ret	US GP WEST	Long Beach	23	Marlboro Team Alfa Romeo	3.0 Alfa Romeo 179C V12	collision with Lammers
nc	BRAZILIAN GP	Rio	23	Marlboro Team Alfa Romeo	3.0 Alfa Romeo 179C V12	4 pit stops-electrics/22 laps behind
10/ret	ARGENTINE GP	Buenos Aires	23	Marlboro Team Alfa Romeo	3.0 Alfa Romeo 179C V12	out of fuel/2 laps behind
ret	SAN MARINO GP	Imola	23	Marlboro Team Alfa Romeo	3.0 Alfa Romeo 179C V12	collision with Cheever
9	BELGIAN GP	Zolder	23	Marlboro Team Alfa Romeo	3.0 Alfa Romeo 179C V12	
ret	MONACO GP	Monte Carlo	23	Marlboro Team Alfa Romeo	3.0 Alfa Romeo 179C V12	accident with Alboreto
10	SPANISH GP	Jarama	23	Marlboro Team Alfa Romeo	3.0 Alfa Romeo 179C V12	
15	FRENCH GP	Dijon	23	Marlboro Team Alfa Romeo	3.0 Alfa Romeo 179C V12	3 laps behind
ret	BRITISH GP	Silverstone	23	Marlboro Team Alfa Romeo	3.0 Alfa Romeo 179C V12	gearbox
15	GERMAN GP	Hockenheim	23	Marlboro Team Alfa Romeo	3.0 Alfa Romeo 179C V12	2 laps behind
ret	AUSTRIAN GP	Österreichring	23	Marlboro Team Alfa Romeo	3.0 Alfa Romeo 179C V12	engine fire
ret	DUTCH GP	Zandvoort	23	Marlboro Team Alfa Romeo	3.0 Alfa Romeo 179C V12	suspension-crashed
8	ITALIAN GP	Monza	23	Marlboro Team Alfa Romeo	3.0 Alfa Romeo 179C V12	2 laps behind
4	CANADIAN GP	Montreal	23	Marlboro Team Alfa Romeo	3.0 Alfa Romeo 179C V12	1 lap behind
3	CAESARS PALACE GP	Las Vegas	23	Marlboro Team Alfa Romeo	3.0 Alfa Romeo 179C V12	

1982

	Race	Circuit	No	Entrant	Car/Engine	Comment
11	SOUTH AFRICAN GP	Kyalami	23	Marlboro Team Alfa Romeo	3.0 Alfa Romeo 179D V12	3 laps behind
ret	BRAZILIAN GP	Rio	23	Marlboro Team Alfa Romeo	3.0 Alfa Romeo 182 V12	engine
ret	US GP WEST	Long Beach	23	Marlboro Team Alfa Romeo	3.0 Alfa Romeo 182 V12	accident with Arnoux
ret	SAN MARINO GP	Imola	23	Marlboro Team Alfa Romeo	3.0 Alfa Romeo 182 V12	engine
ret	BELGIAN GP	Zolder	23	Marlboro Team Alfa Romeo	3.0 Alfa Romeo 182 V12	startline accident
ret	MONACO GP	Monte Carlo	23	Marlboro Team Alfa Romeo	3.0 Alfa Romeo 182 V12	transmission
ret	US GP (DETROIT)	Detroit	23	Marlboro Team Alfa Romeo	3.0 Alfa Romeo 182 V12	collision with Watson-hit barrier
ret	CANADIAN GP	Montreal	23	Marlboro Team Alfa Romeo	3.0 Alfa Romeo 182 V12	accident with Mansell
11	DUTCH GP	Zandvoort	23	Marlboro Team Alfa Romeo	3.0 Alfa Romeo 182 V12	2 laps behind
7	BRITISH GP	Brands Hatch	23	Marlboro Team Alfa Romeo	3.0 Alfa Romeo 182 V12	1 lap behind
9	FRENCH GP	Paul Ricard	23	Marlboro Team Alfa Romeo	3.0 Alfa Romeo 182 V12	1 lap behind
5	GERMAN GP	Hockenheim	23	Marlboro Team Alfa Romeo	3.0 Alfa Romeo 182 V12	1 lap behind
ret	AUSTRIAN GP	Österreichring	23	Marlboro Team Alfa Romeo	3.0 Alfa Romeo 182 V12	hit by de Cesaris
12	SWISS GP	Dijon	23	Marlboro Team Alfa Romeo	3.0 Alfa Romeo 182 V12	2 laps behind
ret	ITALIAN GP	Monza	23	Marlboro Team Alfa Romeo	3.0 Alfa Romeo 182 V12	broken side pod
10	CAESARS PALACE GP	Las Vegas	23	Marlboro Team Alfa Romeo	3.0 Alfa Romeo 182 V12	3 laps behind

1983

	Race	Circuit	No	Entrant	Car/Engine	Comment
ret	BRAZILIAN GP	Rio	36	Candy Toleman Motorsport	1.5 t/c Toleman TG183B-Hart 4	spun off
ret	US GP WEST	Long Beach	36	Candy Toleman Motorsport	1.5 t/c Toleman TG183B-Hart 4	battery-could not restart at pit stop
13/ret	FRENCH GP	Paul Ricard	36	Candy Toleman Motorsport	1.5 t/c Toleman TG183B-Hart 4	gearbox/5 laps behind
ret	SAN MARINO GP	Imola	36	Candy Toleman Motorsport	1.5 t/c Toleman TG183B-Hart 4	rear suspension
dnq	MONACO GP	Monte Carlo	36	Candy Toleman Motorsport	1.5 t/c Toleman TG183B-Hart 4	
8	BELGIAN GP	Spa	36	Candy Toleman Motorsport	1.5 t/c Toleman TG183B-Hart 4	
9	US GP (DETROIT)	Detroit	36	Candy Toleman Motorsport	1.5 t/c Toleman TG183B-Hart 4	1 lap behind
nc	CANADIAN GP	Montreal	36	Candy Toleman Motorsport	1.5 t/c Toleman TG183B-Hart 4	2 pit stops/27 laps behind
ret	BRITISH GP	Silverstone	36	Candy Toleman Motorsport	1.5 t/c Toleman TG183B-Hart 4	turbo
ret	GERMAN GP	Hockenheim	36	Candy Toleman Motorsport	1.5 t/c Toleman TG183B-Hart 4	turbo
ret	AUSTRIAN GP	Österreichring	36	Candy Toleman Motorsport	1.5 t/c Toleman TG183B-Hart 4	accident damage
13	DUTCH GP	Zandvoort	36	Candy Toleman Motorsport	1.5 t/c Toleman TG183B-Hart 4	pit stop/4 laps behind
7	ITALIAN GP	Monza	36	Candy Toleman Motorsport	1.5 t/c Toleman TG183B-Hart 4	
6	EUROPEAN GP	Brands Hatch	36	Candy Toleman Motorsport	1.5 t/c Toleman TG183B-Hart 4	
ret	SOUTH AFRICAN GP	Kyalami	36	Candy Toleman Motorsport	1.5 t/c Toleman TG183B-Hart 4	turbo fire

1990

	Race	Circuit	No	Entrant	Car/Engine	Comment
dnpq	SAN MARINO GP	Imola	39	Life Racing Engines	3.5 Life L190 W12	
dnpq	MONACO GP	Monte Carlo	39	Life Racing Engines	3.5 Life L190 W12	
dnpq	CANADIAN GP	Montreal	39	Life Racing Engines	3.5 Life L190 W12	
dnpq	MEXICAN GP	Mexico City	39	Life Racing Engines	3.5 Life L190 W12	
dnpq	FRENCH GP	Paul Ricard	39	Life Racing Engines	3.5 Life L190 W12	no time recorded
dnpq	BRITISH GP	Silverstone	39	Life Racing Engines	3.5 Life L190 W12	
dnpq	GERMAN GP	Hockenheim	39	Life Racing Engines	3.5 Life L190 W12	
dnpq	HUNGARIAN GP	Hungaroring	39	Life Racing Engines	3.5 Life L190 W12	
dnpq	BELGIAN GP	Spa	39	Life Racing Engines	3.5 Life L190 W12	
dnpq	ITALIAN GP	Monza	39	Life Racing Engines	3.5 Life L190 W12	
dnpq	PORTUGUESE GP	Estoril	39	Life Racing Engines	3.5 Life-Judd V8	no time recorded
dnpq	SPANISH GP	Jerez	39	Life Racing Engines	3.5 Life-Judd V8	

GP Starts: 69   GP Wins: 0   Pole positions: 1   Fastest laps: 0   Points: 14

GIBSON, Dick (GB) b 16/4/1918

1957

	Race	Circuit	No	Entrant	Car/Engine	Comment
ret	GERMAN GP (F2)	Nürburgring	29	R Gibson	1.5 Cooper T43-Climax 4	suspension

1958

	Race	Circuit	No	Entrant	Car/Engine	Comment
ret	GERMAN GP (F2)	Nürburgring	19	R Gibson	1.5 Cooper T43-Climax 4	mechanical

GP Starts: 2   GP Wins: 0   Pole positions: 0   Fastest laps: 0   Points: 0

RICHIE GINTHER

Small and freckle-faced, Richie Ginther was always just outside the top echelon of Grand Prix talent but on his day he was more than capable of delivering the goods. In many ways he was the pefect number two driver, being conscientious, reliable and an extremely fine tester, with a rare mechanical sympathy born of his early days as a mechanic on both cars and aeroplanes during his National Service.

Although he had run an MG in 1951, it was two years later that he really became involved in serious competition when he shared Phil Hill's Ferrari in the Carrera Panamericana. The pair were lucky to emerge unscathed from a crash which wrote off the car, but returned the following year to take second place behind Maglioli's works entry.

Richie then found employment with Ferrari importer Johnnie von Neumann, who gave him plenty of drives over the next few seasons, Ginther making a big name for himself in West Coast racing and coming to the attention of Luigi Chinetti, who in turn entered him in his Ferraris, Richie's programme including a visit to Le Mans in 1957. Combining his job running the car agency with a racing career was becoming something of a strain, but after he shared a Ferrari sports car with von Trips to take second place in the Buenos Aires 1000 Km, Ginther was offered a four-race contract by the Scuderia. He quit his job and took the opportunity, moving to Italy with his wife. Although the sports car races yielded no success, his single-seater rides were a revelation. He was second in the Modena GP in the front-engined F2 car and made three Grand Prix starts, finishing an impressive sixth at Monaco in the rear-engined prototype, and second at Monza in the boycotted Italian GP. Quickly realising his tremendous engineering expertise, Ferrari gave Richie the role of chief development driver in addition to his racing duties. In 1961 the team virtually swept the board with their 'sharknose' 156 V6 car and Ginther really impressed with his spirited pursuit of Stirling Moss at Monaco. Surprisingly he found himself surplus to requirements at the end of the year but BRM were more than willing to bring him into the fold.

He made an ideal partner to Graham Hill, putting in much hard work as the Bourne team came good at last and won the World Championship. The 1963 season was his most successful and consistent, Ginther scoring points in every Grand Prix bar one to finish equal second with his team-mate in the championship behind runaway winner Jim Clark. Ginther stayed on for a third year in 1964, again proving his mechanical sympathy by finishing every Grand Prix.

It was all-change for 1965 as Ginther was hired to bring some much-needed experience to the still-fledgling Honda project. As the season wore on the car became a real threat, until Richie had his greatest moment when he won the Mexican Grand Prix at the last race of the year. It must have been galling for all concerned that it marked the end of the 1.5-litre formula, for Honda would have been a very tough act to beat in 1966 under the old rules. As it was they had to start again, and after filling in with a Cooper until the new car was ready towards the end of the season, Ginther was fortunate to escape a huge accident at Monza when a tyre failed. For 1967 Honda went with John Surtees and Richie joined up with Dan Gurney at Eagle. He lay second in the Race of Champions before retiring, but then surprisingly failed to qualify at Monaco. While practising for the Indianapolis 500 he suddenly decided that it was time to quit. Richie became involved in team management roles, for example running a Porsche 911 with Elliot Forbes-Robinson in 1971, before cutting his links with the sport and dropping out of the rat race to live in a camper in the desert. He returned to the circuits in 1977, invited to the German GP at Hockenheim by Goodyear to present the winner, Niki Lauda, with a prize to mark the tyre company's 100th win, though many would not have recognised him with his moustache and long hair replacing the once familiar crew-cut.

It was a frail and sick Ginther who arrived at Donington in 1989 to attend BRM's 40th anniversary celebrations, and it was with much sadness but little surprise that the racing world learned of his death after a heart attack just days later while holidaying in France.

YVES GIRAUD-CABANTOUS

Giraud-Cabantous began his long career back in 1925, and by 1927 he had won his first race, the GP des Frontières at Chimay in a Salmson. He was soon developing his own cars and in 1930 won the Bol d'Or 24-hour race in his own Caban, later successfully racing a Bugatti and a Delahaye, in which he finished second at Le Mans. After the war, Yves joined the Ecurie France team, emerging victorious at Chimay, Montlhéry, and San Remo in 1947, and winning the GP de Paris in 1948. He was also involved with the infamous CTA Arsenal project, before purchasing a Talbot which he was to race extensively over the next five seasons.

In 1950 he joined the official Talbot team and by finishing fourth in the British Grand Prix became the first French driver to score World Championship points. Financial difficulties saw the team disbanded, but Giraud-Cabantous continued on his own with the Talbot, finishing third at Albi in 1952, then joined the HWM team for a number of races in 1952-53. His 'steady-as-she-goes' approach by this time was perhaps understandable, but he did bring the car home to the finish regularly. In sports cars he was second sharing Rosier's Talbot in the Reims 12 Hours in 1953, his last full season. Yves made occasional appearances over the next few years, in the little VP and Giaur sports cars, before retiring in 1957 to concentrate fully on his transport business.

GINTHER, Richie (USA) b 5/8/1930 – d 28/9/1989

	1960					
	Race	Circuit	No	Entrant	Car/Engine	Comment
6	MONACO GP	Monte Carlo	34	Scuderia Ferrari	2.4 Ferrari-Dino 246P V6	rear-engined prototype/-30 laps
6	DUTCH GP	Zandvoort	3	Scuderia Ferrari	2.4 Ferrari-Dino 246 V6	1 lap behind
2	ITALIAN GP	Monza	18	Scuderia Ferrari	2.4 Ferrari-Dino 246 V6	
	1961					
2	MONACO GP	Monte Carlo	36	Scuderia Ferrari SpA SEFAC	1.5 Ferrari 156 V6	FL (shared with Moss)
5	DUTCH GP	Zandvoort	2	Scuderia Ferrari SpA SEFAC	1.5 Ferrari 156 V6	
3	BELGIAN GP	Spa	6	Scuderia Ferrari SpA SEFAC	1.5 Ferrari 156 V6	FL
15/ret	FRENCH GP	Reims	18	Scuderia Ferrari SpA SEFAC	1.5 Ferrari 156 V6	oil pressure/12 laps behind

3	BRITISH GP	Aintree	6	Scuderia Ferrari SpA SEFAC	1.5 Ferrari 156 V6	
8	GERMAN GP	Nürburgring	5	Scuderia Ferrari SpA SEFAC	1.5 Ferrari 156 V6	
ret	ITALIAN GP	Monza	6	Scuderia Ferrari SpA SEFAC	1.5 Ferrari 156 V6	*engine*

1962

ret	DUTCH GP	Monza	18	Owen Racing Organisation	1.5 BRM P48/57 V8	*pushed off by Trevor Taylor*
ret	MONACO GP	Monte Carlo	8	Owen Racing Organisation	1.5 BRM P48/57 V8	*throttle stuck-accident*
ret	" "	" "	8	Owen Racing Organisation	1.5 BRM P57 V8	*practice only*
ret	BELGIAN GP	Spa	2	Owen Racing Organisation	1.5 BRM P57 V8	*gearbox*
3	FRENCH GP	Rouen	10	Owen Racing Organisation	1.5 BRM P57 V8	*would not start on grid/2 laps behind*
13	BRITISH GP	Aintree	14	Owen Racing Organisation	1.5 BRM P57 V8	*5 laps behind*
8	GERMAN GP	Nürburgring	12	Owen Racing Organisation	1.5 BRM P57 V8	
2	ITALIAN GP	Monza	12	Owen Racing Organisation	1.5 BRM P57 V8	
ret	US GP	Watkins Glen	5	Owen Racing Organisation	1.5 BRM P57 V8	*engine*
7	SOUTH AFRICAN GP	East London	4	Owen Racing Organisation	1.5 BRM P57 V8	*4 laps behind*

1963

2	MONACO GP	Monte Carlo	5	Owen Racing Organisation	1.5 BRM P57 V8	
4	BELGIAN GP	Spa	8	Owen Racing Organisation	1.5 BRM P57 V8	*1 lap behind*
5	DUTCH GP	Zandvoort	14	Owen Racing Organisation	1.5 BRM P57 V8	*1 lap behind*
ret	FRENCH GP	Reims	4	Owen Racing Organisation	1.5 BRM P57 V8	*holed radiator*
4	BRITISH GP	Silverstone	2	Owen Racing Organisation	1.5 BRM P57 V8	*1 lap behind*
3	GERMAN GP	Nürburgring	2	Owen Racing Organisation	1.5 BRM P57 V8	
2	ITALIAN GP	Monza	10	Owen Racing Organisation	1.5 BRM P57 V8	
2	US GP	Watkins Glen	2	Owen Racing Organisation	1.5 BRM P57 V8	
3	MEXICAN GP	Mexico City	2	Owen Racing Organisation	1.5 BRM P57 V8	
ret	SOUTH AFRICAN GP	East London	6	Owen Racing Organisation	1.5 BRM P57 V8	*driveshaft*

1964

2	MONACO GP	Monte Carlo	7	Owen Racing Organisation	1.5 BRM P261 V8	*1 lap behind*
11	DUTCH GP	Zandvoort	8	Owen Racing Organisation	1.5 BRM P261 V8	*p stop-fuel vaporisation/16 laps behind*
4	BELGIAN GP	Spa	2	Owen Racing Organisation	1.5 BRM P261 V8	
5	FRENCH GP	Rouen	10	Owen Racing Organisation	1.5 BRM P261 V8	
8	BRITISH GP	Brands Hatch	4	Owen Racing Organisation	1.5 BRM P261 V8	*3 laps behind*
7	GERMAN GP	Nürburgring	4	Owen Racing Organisation	1.5 BRM P261 V8	*1 lap behind*
2	AUSTRIAN GP	Zeltweg	4	Owen Racing Organisation	1.5 BRM P261 V8	
4	ITALIAN GP	Monza	20	Owen Racing Organisation	1.5 BRM P261 V8	*1 lap behind*
4	US GP	Watkins Glen	4	Owen Racing Organisation	1.5 BRM P261 V8	*3 laps behind*
8	MEXICAN GP	Mexico City	4	Owen Racing Organisation	1.5 BRM P261 V8	*1 lap behind*

1965

ret	MONACO GP	Monte Carlo	20	Honda R & D Co	1.5 Honda RA272 V12	*driveshaft*
6	BELGIAN GP	Spa	10	Honda R & D Co	1.5 Honda RA272 V12	*1 lap behind*
ret	FRENCH GP	Clermont Ferrand	26	Honda R & D Co	1.5 Honda RA272 V12	*ignition*
ret	BRITISH GP	Silverstone	11	Honda R & D Co	1.5 Honda RA272 V12	*fuel injection*
6	DUTCH GP	Zandvoort	22	Honda R & D Co	1.5 Honda RA272 V12	*led race/1 lap behind*
14/ret	ITALIAN GP	Monza	20	Honda R & D Co	1.5 Honda RA272 V12	*ignition/19 laps behind*
7	US GP	Watkins Glen	11	Honda R & D Co	1.5 Honda RA272 V12	*2 laps behind*
1	MEXICAN GP	Mexico City (12) 11		Honda R & D Co	1.5 Honda RA272 V12	

1966

ret	MONACO GP	Monte Carlo	9	Cooper Car Co	3.0 Cooper T81-Maserati V12	*driveshaft*
5	BELGIAN GP	Spa	18	Cooper Car Co	3.0 Cooper T81-Maserati V12	*3 laps behind*
ret	ITALIAN GP	Monza	18	Honda Racing Team	3.0 Honda RA273 V12	*tyre threw tread-accident*
nc	US GP	Watkins Glen	12	Honda Racing Team	3.0 Honda RA273 V12	*pit stops-gearbox/27 laps behind*
4	MEXICAN GP	Mexico City	12	Honda Racing Team	3.0 Honda RA273 V12	*FL/1 lap behind*

1967

dnq	MONACO GP	Monte Carlo	22	Anglo American Racers	3.0 Eagle T1G-Weslake V12

GP Starts: 52   GP Wins: 1   Pole positions: 0   Fastest laps: 3   Points: 107

GIRAUD-CABANTOUS, Yves (F) b 8/10/1903 – d 31/3/1973

1950

	Race	Circuit	No	Entrant	Car/Engine	Comment
4	BRITISH GP	Silverstone	14	Automobiles Talbot-Darracq SA	4.5 Lago-Talbot T26C-DA 6	*2 laps behind*
ret	SWISS GP	Bremgarten	6	Automobiles Talbot-Darracq SA	4.5 Lago-Talbot T26C-DA 6	*crashed*
ret	BELGIAN GP	Spa	18	Automobiles Talbot-Darracq SA	4.5 Lago-Talbot T26C-DA 6	*engine*
nc	FRENCH GP	Reims	18	Automobiles Talbot-Darracq SA	4.5 Lago-Talbot T26C-DA 6	*12 laps behind*

1951

ret	SWISS GP	Bremgarten	6	Yves Giraud-Cabantous	4.5 Lago-Talbot T26C 6	*ignition*
5	BELGIAN GP	Spa	22	Yves Giraud-Cabantous	4.5 Lago-Talbot T26C 6	*2 laps behind*
7	FRENCH GP	Reims	46	Yves Giraud-Cabantous	4.5 Lago-Talbot T26C 6	*6 laps behind*
ret	GERMAN GP	Nürburgring	87	Yves Giraud-Cabantous	4.5 Lago-Talbot T26C 6	*crashed*
8	ITALIAN GP	Monza	24	Yves Giraud-Cabantous	4.5 Lago-Talbot T26C 6	*8 laps behind*
ret	SPANISH GP	Pedralbes	32	Yves Giraud-Cabantous	4.5 Lago-Talbot T26C 6	*hit dog on track/overheating*

1952

10	FRENCH GP	Rouen	24	HW Motors Ltd	2.0 HWM-Alta 4	*8 laps behind*

1953

nc	FRENCH GP	Reims	30	HW Motors Ltd	2.0 HWM-Alta 4	*10 laps behind*
nc	ITALIAN GP	Monza	16	HW Motors Ltd	2.0 HWM-Alta 4	*13 laps behind*

GP Starts: 13   GP Wins: 0   Pole positions: 0   Fastest laps: 0   Points: 3

GIUNTI, Ignazio (I) b 30/8/1941 – d 10/1/1971

1970

	Race	Circuit	No	Entrant	Car/Engine	Comment
4	BELGIAN GP	Spa	28	Scuderia Ferrari SpA SEFAC	3.0 Ferrari 312B F12	pit stop-oil leak
14	FRENCH GP	Clermont Ferrand	11	Scuderia Ferrari SpA SEFAC	3.0 Ferrari 312B F12	pit stop-throttle/3 laps behind
7	AUSTRIAN GP	Österreichring	14	Scuderia Ferrari SpA SEFAC	3.0 Ferrari 312B F12	pit stop-wheel change/1 lap behind
ret	ITALIAN GP	Monza	6	Scuderia Ferrari SpA SEFAC	3.0 Ferrari 312B F12	overheating

GP Starts: 4   GP Wins: 0   Pole positions: 0   Fastest laps: 0   Points: 3

GODIA-SALES, Francesco (E) b 21/3/1921 – d 1991

1951

	Race	Circuit	No	Entrant	Car/Engine	Comment
10	SPANISH GP	Pedralbes	44	Scuderia Milano	1.5 s/c Maserati 4CLT/48 4	10 laps behind

1954

6	SPANISH GP	Pedralbes	16	Officine Alfieri Maserati	2.5 Maserati 250F 6	4 laps behind

1956

ret	BELGIAN GP	Spa	36	Officine Alfieri Maserati	2.5 Maserati 250F 6	crashed
7	FRENCH GP	Reims	40	Officine Alfieri Maserati	2.5 Maserati 250F 6	4 laps behind
8	BRITISH GP	Silverstone	10	Officine Alfieri Maserati	2.5 Maserati 250F 6	7 laps behind
4	GERMAN GP	Nürburgring	20	Officine Alfieri Maserati	2.5 Maserati 250F 6	2 laps behind
4	ITALIAN GP	Monza	6	Officine Alfieri Maserati	2.5 Maserati 250F 6	1 lap behind

1957

ret	GERMAN GP	Nürburgring	18	Francesco Godia-Sales	2.5 Maserati 250F 6	steering
ret	PESCARA GP	Pescara	10	Francesco Godia-Sales	2.5 Maserati 250F 6	engine
9	ITALIAN GP	Monza	10	Francesco Godia-Sales	2.5 Maserati 250F 6	6 laps behind

1958

8	ARGENTINE GP	Buenos Aires	10	Francesco Godia-Sales	2.5 Maserati 250F 6	5 laps behind
dnq	MONACO GP	Monte Carlo	4	Francesco Godia-Sales	2.5 Maserati 250F 6	
ret	BELGIAN GP	Spa	38	Francesco Godia-Sales	2.5 Maserati 250F 6	engine
ret	FRENCH GP	Reims	40	Francesco Godia-Sales	2.5 Maserati 250F 6	crashed

GP Starts: 13   GP Wins: 0   Pole positions: 0   Fastest laps: 0   Points: 6

GOETHALS, Christian (B) b 4/8/1928

1958

	Race	Circuit	No	Entrant	Car/Engine	Comment
ret	GERMAN GP (F2)	Nürburgring	27	Ecurie Eperon d'Or	1.5 Cooper T43-Climax 4	fuel pump

GP Starts: 1   GP Wins: 0   Pole positions: 0   Fastest laps: 0   Points: 0

IGNAZIO GIUNTI

From a well-to-do Rome family, Giunti was racing from his teens, driving Alfas in hill-climbs and club events. He progressed to the works Alfa team in 1966, winning the touring car section of the European mountain-climb championship the following year. Giunti was a regular member of the Autodelta sports car team in 1968, taking second in the Targa Florio and fourth (and class win) at Le Mans with Galli, who was his regular partner through 1969.

For 1970, Ignazio was signed by Ferrari for their successful sports car programme, sharing the winning 512S in the Sebring 12 Hours, Targa Florio and Rand 9 Hours, also taking second place in the Monza 1000 Km and third in the Watkins Glen 6 Hours. Meanwhile Giunti made a very impressive Grand Prix debut to finish fourth at Spa, earning three more drives. Though Regazzoni had laid claim to the number two seat in F1, Giunti stayed with the team for 1971. In the season's first sports car race, the Buenos Aires 1000 Km, Ignazio, unsighted by another car, ploughed into the back of the Matra of Beltoise which had run out of fuel and was being pushed along the track by its driver. The Ferrari somersaulted some 200 yards down the track, exploding into flames, leaving poor Giunti no chance of survival. Sustaining 70 per cent burns and multiple injuries, he died in hospital some two hours later.

CHRISTIAN GOETHALS

This amateur Belgian driver raced a Porsche Spyder in minor Continental events from the mid-fifties. With his brother, he took second place at Reims in 1956 in the up-to-1500 cc sports car race and won the same class at Forez the following year. Goethals acquired an F2 Cooper for 1958, but gained little success, and soon returned to a Porsche RSK. In 1960 he finished fifth in the Buenos Aires 1000 Km and second in the GP de Spa, but after he crashed out of the Angola GP in Luanda later in the season, no more was seen of Goethals and his Porsche on the circuits.

FRANCESCO GODIA-SALES

This wealthy Spanish businessman could afford to indulge his passion whenever he pleased, though he was really only competing regularly between 1956 – when he initially became part of the Maserati works team on the understanding that his car could be taken if needed by a more senior driver – and 1958, when he entered the car himself after the factory's closure. Not one to risk his neck unduly, he gained placings in races of high attrition, as when he finished fourth in the German and Italian GPs of 1956.

Perhaps the most fascinating feature of his long but intermittent career – which spanned more than twenty years – was its variety: in 1949 he raced a vintage Delage to fourth place at Le Mans; he made his GP debut in a Maserati 4CLT in 1951; and by the time his racing days were drawing to a close in 1969, he was handling machines such as the Ford GT40 and Porsche 908 Spyder.

JOSÉ FROILAN GONZALEZ

Gonzalez was invariably tagged 'the Bull of the Pampas' by the press and the name perfectly described the vast bulk of this unlikely looking racing driver. However, he was called Pepe by his friends, who knew him as a kind-hearted, good-natured soul, despite his sometimes fearsome façade.

A surprisingly keen sportsman for one of his physique, Gonzalez was a fair soccer player, swimmer and cyclist before he was old enough to begin a competition career racing motor cycles and then production cars. He caught the eye in 1949 at the wheel of a Maserati four-cylinder found for him by Fangio and joined his compatriot in Europe in 1950, driving a Maserati without luck in the championship races but taking a second place in the Albi GP.

His breakthrough came in 1951 when he defeated the visiting Mercedes-Benz team in both the Libre races at Buenos Aires in a Ferrari 166, and he began his proper Grand Prix career as a works driver for Ferrari. His style, hunched over the wheel, hard on the throttle, sliding the car to the limits of the track – and beyond on many occasions, was far from pretty, but no one could argue with his speed, and he soon gained immortality by defeating the works Alfa Romeos in the 1951 British GP, becoming the first driver to win a World Championship Grand Prix for the Scuderia. Gonzalez also won the non-title Pescara GP before signing for Maserati for 1952, a season which saw him race in only one Grand Prix, although he also handled the brutish BRM V16, winning the Goodwood Trophy, and Vandervell's Thinwall Ferrari, in which he took the Richmond Trophy. He continued with Maserati as Fangio's team-mate in 1953, but was in the shadow of his great friend and rival before a crash in practice for a sports car race at Lisbon sidelined him for three months with a fractured vertebra.

Signed by Ferrari for 1954, Gonzalez enjoyed his finest season, taking his 625 to another glorious win for the team over the for once hapless Mercedes, as well as claiming wins in the non-title International Trophy and Bari and Bordeaux GPs. His year also saw four wins in sports cars, including Le Mans, where he shared the winning Ferrari with Trintignant, before a practice crash in the Tourist Trophy left him with an injured arm. He returned home to Argentina and, apart from a visit to his beloved Silverstone to race the Vanwall in 1956 which ended with driveshaft failure at the start, mainly restricted his racing to home territory. His guest appearances in his home Grands Prix showed there was still considerable fire in his belly and he duelled with Ascari's Lancia for the lead in 1955 before finishing second, but after the 1957 race he was content just to take part in his Chevrolet-engined Ferrari, turning his attention more to his motor business.

GONZALEZ, José Froilan (RA) b 5/10/1922

1950

	Race	Circuit	No	Entrant	Car/Engine	Comment
ret	MONACO GP	Monte Carlo	2	Scuderia Achille Varzi	1.5 s/c Maserati 4CLT/50 4	multiple accident/car on fire
ret	FRENCH GP	Reims	36	Scuderia Achille Varzi	1.5 s/c Maserati 4CLT/50 4	engine

1951

ret	SWISS GP	Bremgarten	42	José Froilan Gonzalez	4.5 Lago-Talbot T26-GS 6	oil pump
2*	FRENCH GP	Reims	14	Scuderia Ferrari	4.5 Ferrari 375F1 V12	* Ascari took over car
1	BRITISH GP	Silverstone	16	Scuderia Ferrari	4.5 Ferrari 375F1 V12	Pole
3	GERMAN GP	Nürburgring	2	Scuderia Ferrari	4.5 Ferrari 375F1 V12	
2	ITALIAN GP	Monza	20	Scuderia Ferrari	4.5 Ferrari 375F1 V12	
2	SPANISH GP	Pedralbes	24	Scuderia Ferrari	4.5 Ferrari 375F1 V12	

1952

2	ITALIAN GP	Monza	26	Officine Alfieri Maserati	2.0 Maserati A6GCM 6	FL (shared with Ascari)

1953

3	ARGENTINE GP	Buenos Aires	4	Officine Alfieri Maserati	2.0 Maserati A6GCM 6	1 lap behind
ret	DUTCH GP	Zandvoort	14	Officine Alfieri Maserati	2.0 Maserati A6GCM 6	rear axle
3*	"	"	16	Officine Alfieri Maserati	2.0 Maserati A6GCM 6	* took Bonetto's car/1 lap behind
ret	BELGIAN GP	Spa	2	Officine Alfieri Maserati	2.0 Maserati A6GCM 6	throttle/FL
3	FRENCH GP	Reims	20	Officine Alfieri Maserati	2.0 Maserati A6GCM 6	
4	BRITISH GP	Silverstone	24	Officine Alfieri Maserati	2.0 Maserati A6GCM 6	FL(shared)/oil leak/2 laps behind

1954

3	ARGENTINE GP	Buenos Aires	12	Scuderia Ferrari	2.5 Ferrari 625 4	FL
ret	BELGIAN GP	Spa	6	Scuderia Ferrari	2.5 Ferrari 553/555 4	engine-oil pipe
4*	"	"	10	Scuderia Ferrari	2.5 Ferrari 625 4	* took Hawthorn's car/1 lap behind
ret	FRENCH GP	Reims	2	Scuderia Ferrari	2.5 Ferrari 553/555 4	engine
1	BRITISH GP	Silverstone	9	Scuderia Ferrari	2.5 Ferrari 625/555 4	FL (shared)
2*	GERMAN GP	Nürburgring	1	Scuderia Ferrari	2.5 Ferrari 625/555 4	* Hawthorn took over car
2	SWISS GP	Bremgarten	20	Scuderia Ferrari	2.5 Ferrari 625/555 4	Pole
ret	ITALIAN GP	Monza	32	Scuderia Ferrari	2.5 Ferrari 555 4	gearbox/FL
3*	"	"	38	Scuderia Ferrari	2.5 Ferrari 625 4	* took Maglioli's car/2 laps behind

1955

2*	ARGENTINE GP	Buenos Aires	12	Scuderia Ferrari	2.5 Ferrari 625 4	* Farina/Trintignant also drove/Pole

1956

ret	ARGENTINE GP	Buenos Aires	12	Officine Alfieri Maserati	2.5 Maserati 250F 6	valve
ret	BRITISH GP	Silverstone	18	Vandervell Products Ltd	2.5 Vanwall 4	driveshaft on grid

1957

5*	ARGENTINE GP	Buenos Aires	20	Scuderia Ferrari	2.5 Lancia-Ferrari D50 V8	* shared with de Portago/2 laps behind

1960

10	ARGENTINE GP	Buenos Aires	32	Scuderia Ferrari	2.4 Ferrari-Dino 246 V6	3 laps behind

GP Starts: 26   GP Wins: 2   Pole positions: 3   Fastest laps: 6   Points: 77.64

GONZALEZ, Oscar (U)

1956

	Race	Circuit	No	Entrant	Car/Engine	Comment
6*	ARGENTINE GP	Buenos Aires	16	Alberto Uria	2.5 Maserati A6GCM/250F 6	* shared with Uria/10 laps behind

GP Starts: 1 GP Wins: 0 Pole positions: 0 Fastest laps: 0 Points: 0

GORDINI, Aldo (F) b 20/5/1921

1951

	Race	Circuit	No	Entrant	Car/Engine	Comment
ret	FRENCH GP	Reims	36	Equipe Gordini	1.5 s/c Gordini Type 11 4	valve gear

GP Starts: 1 GP Wins: 0 Pole positions: 0 Fastest laps: 0 Points: 0

GOULD, Horace (GB) b 20/9/1921 – d 4/11/1968

1954

	Race	Circuit	No	Entrant	Car/Engine	Comment
nc	BRITISH GP	Silverstone	28	Goulds' Garage (Bristol)	2.0 Cooper T23-Bristol 6	pit stops/46 laps behind

1955

	Race	Circuit	No	Entrant	Car/Engine	Comment
ret	DUTCH GP	Zandvoort	32	Goulds' Garage (Bristol)	2.5 Maserati 250F 6	crashed
ret	BRITISH GP	Aintree	48	Goulds' Garage (Bristol)	2.5 Maserati 250F 6	brakes
ret	ITALIAN GP	Monza	38	Officine Alfieri Maserati	2.5 Maserati 250F 6	suspension

1956

	Race	Circuit	No	Entrant	Car/Engine	Comment
8	MONACO GP	Monte Carlo	18	Goulds' Garage (Bristol)	2.5 Maserati 250F 6	15 laps behind
ret	BELGIAN GP	Spa	26	Goulds' Garage (Bristol)	2.5 Maserati 250F 6	gearbox
5	BRITISH GP	Silverstone	31	Goulds' Garage (Bristol)	2.5 Maserati 250F 6	4 laps behind
ret	GERMAN GP	Nürburgring	19	Goulds' Garage (Bristol)	2.5 Maserati 250F 6	oil pressure

1957

	Race	Circuit	No	Entrant	Car/Engine	Comment
ret	MONACO GP	Monte Carlo	22	H H Gould	2.5 Maserati 250F 6	crashed
ret	FRENCH GP	Rouen	30	H H Gould	2.5 Maserati 250F 6	rear axle
dns	BRITISH GP	Aintree	30	H H Gould	2.5 Maserati 250F 6	injured in practice accident
ret	GERMAN GP	Nürburgring	19	H H Gould	2.5 Maserati 250F 6	rear axle
ret	PESCARA GP	Pescara	18	H H Gould	2.5 Maserati 250F 6	crashed
10	ITALIAN GP	Monza	14	H H Gould	2.5 Maserati 250F 6	9 laps behind

1958

	Race	Circuit	No	Entrant	Car/Engine	Comment
9	ARGENTINE GP	Buenos Aires	12	H H Gould	2.5 Maserati 250F 6	9 laps behind
dnq	MONACO GP	Monte Carlo	42	Scuderia Centro Sud	2.5 Maserati 250F 6	loan car
dns	DUTCH GP	Zandvoort	12	H H Gould	2.5 Maserati 250F 6	Gregory drove in race

GP Starts: 14 GP Wins: 0 Pole positions: 0 Fastest laps: 0 Points: 2

GOUNON, Jean-Marc (F) b 1/1/1963

1993

	Race	Circuit	No	Entrant	Car/Engine	Comment
ret	JAPANESE GP	Suzuka	23	Minardi Team	3.5 Minardi 193-Ford HB V8	collision p stop/later called in by team
ret	AUSTRALIAN GP	Adelaide	23	Minardi Team	3.5 Minardi 193-Ford HB V8	spun off

GP Starts: 2 GP Wins: 0 Pole positions: 0 Fastest laps: 0 Points: 0

HORACE GOULD

In a period when fat Italians regularly occupied the cockpits of Formula 1 cars, to Horace Gould it seemed quite reasonable that a fat Bristolian should do the same. After all, he had spent a couple of seasons competing in a Cooper-Bristol – albeit usually in second-division races, with the notable exception of the 1954 British GP. So for 1955 he took himself off to Modena and bought a Maserati 250F, living a hand-to-mouth existence and scrounging parts from the factory to keep his machine on the grid.

Horace enjoyed a nomadic three seasons on the Continent, entering selected Grands Prix (his best result was fifth at Silverstone in 1956) and cannily entering his 'Maser' in non-championship races where starting money was good and the chances of decent placings were high. Horace finished third at Albi and fourth at Syracuse in 1955, second at Naples in 1956 and fourth, behind the three works Ferraris of Hawthorn, Collins and Musso, in the same race in 1957. Once the factory withdrew, it was really the end for Gould, who could no longer gain the assistance he needed to keep running the car. His last hurrah was a fourth place at Syracuse in 1958, though he was tempted back just one more time – to the boycotted 1960 Italian GP – where the old Maserati failed even to turn a wheel in practice due to crossed fuel-lines. Horace, who later helped his son in his racing activities, died of a sudden heart attack in 1968.

JEAN-MARC GOUNON

At the end of 1993, at the relatively late age of 30, this amiable Frenchman finally realised his ambition to race a Grand Prix car, buying a ride for the year's last two Grands Prix, having been patiently waiting for another opportunity following the March team's collapse before the start of the season.

After making an excellent debut to finish fourth overall in the 1988 French F3 championship, Gounon convincingly took the title a year later in the ORECA Reynard. He then became a stalwart on the F3000 scene from 1990 to 1992, making the best of things when he was in the right team, but maybe the wrong chassis (a Ralt in 1991 and a Lola in 1992). Jean-Marc proved he was capable of being blindingly quick when circumstances allowed and his wins at Pau and Vallelunga were just reward for his efforts.

His two drives for Minardi could lead to a full Grand Prix season in 1994, for he has access to the government fund set up in the wake of the ban on tobacco sponsorship introduced in France.

EMMANUEL de GRAFFENRIED

Although his racing activities began well before the Second World War in his native Switzerland, with both a 3-litre Alfa Romeo and a Type 6C Maserati, it was the immediate post-war years that saw 'Toulo '– as he was popularly known – at his zenith.

In 1946 he formed Team Autosport with former Mercedes driver Christian Kautz, the pair acquiring a new four-cylinder Maserati which de Graffenried brought into fifth place in the Prix de Geneva. He finished third in the car at Lausanne the following year, and drove splendidly to finish second to Farina in Geneva, and third in the Monaco GP behind Farina and Chiron in 1948, before his season was overshadowed by the death of Kautz in the Grand Prix de l'Europe at Bremgarten.

'Toulo' enjoyed his greatest triumph in 1949, winning the British Grand Prix in his latest San Remo-type 4CLT/48 Maserati, backing this up with second places in the Pau, Zandvoort and Swedish GPs and the Jersey Road Race in St Helier, as well as many other placings. He continued to race the car into the 1950 season but it was now a little long in the tooth. However, his performances were such that Alfa Romeo invited him to race for the team in the Grand Prix des Nations at Geneva, where he performed creditably to finish second to Fangio but only two seconds ahead of Taruffi after more than two hours' racing on this demanding street circuit.

Although de Graffenried was forced to continue racing his faithful Maserati in 1951, Alfa invited him to join their all-conquering team for three Grands Prix that year, where he again acquitted himself more than respectably. With the new Formula 2 rules in force for 1952, he drove Enrico Platé's Maseratis without achieving much success in the championship races, but picked up third places at Cadours and Aix-les-Bains.

Things were very different in 1953, however. Now at the wheel of the latest Maserati A6GCM model, he enjoyed some memorable races, winning the Syracuse GP, the Eifelrennen F2 race and the Lavant Cup at Goodwood. Installing a 2.5-litre engine in the car, de Graffenried raced it briefly in 1954, as well as competing in a Maserati sports car which he took to South America early in the season, winning the Circuit of Gavea race at Rio and the São Paulo GP. He raced little after this, having a few sports car outings in Ferraris and Maseratis before making a final Grand Prix appearance at Monza in 1956.

'Toulo' was not lost to the Grand Prix world, however, for he was closely involved with the sport and seen regularly at the circuits over the next three decades.

GRAFFENRIED, Baron Emmanuel de (CH) b 18/5/1914

1950

	Race	Circuit	No	Entrant	Car/Engine	Comment
ret	BRITISH GP	Silverstone	20	Emmanuel de Graffenried	1.5 s/c Maserati 4CLT/50 4	engine
ret	MONACO GP	Monte Carlo	52	Emmanuel de Graffenried	1.5 s/c Maserati 4CLT/50 4	multiple accident
6	SWISS GP	Bremgarten	32	Emmanuel de Graffenried	1.5 s/c Maserati 4CLT/50 4	2 laps behind
6	ITALIAN GP	Monza	38	Emmanuel de Graffenried	1.5 s/c Maserati 4CLT/50 4	8 laps behind

1951

	Race	Circuit	No	Entrant	Car/Engine	Comment
5	SWISS GP	Bremgarten	26	Alfa Romeo SpA	1.5 s/c Alfa Romeo 159A 8	2 laps behind
ret	FRENCH GP	Reims	18	Enrico Platé	1.5 s/c Maserati 4CLT/50 4	transmission
ret	GERMAN GP	Nürburgring	79	Enrico Platé	1.5 s/c Maserati 4CLT/50 4	engine
ret	ITALIAN GP	Monza	36	Alfa Romeo SpA	1.5 s/c Alfa Romeo 159M 8	supercharger drive
6	SPANISH GP	Pedralbes	26	Alfa Romeo SpA	1.5 s/c Alfa Romeo 159M 8	4 laps behind

1952

	Race	Circuit	No	Entrant	Car/Engine	Comment
6	SWISS GP	Bremgarten	38	Enrico Platé	2.0 Maserati 4CLT/Platé 4	4 laps behind
ret*	FRENCH GP	Rouen	16	Enrico Platé	2.0 Maserati 4CLT/Platé 4	*Schell took over/brakes
19	BRITISH GP	Silverstone	32	Enrico Platé	2.0 Maserati 4CLT/Platé 4	no practice/9 laps behind
dnq	ITALIAN GP	Monza	60	Enrico Platé	2.0 Maserati 4CLT/Platé 4	

1953

	Race	Circuit	No	Entrant	Car/Engine	Comment
5	DUTCH GP	Zandvoort	18	Emmanuel de Graffenried	2.0 Maserati A6GCM 6	2 laps behind
4	BELGIAN GP	Spa	30	Emmanuel de Graffenried	2.0 Maserati A6GCM 6	1 lap behind
7	FRENCH GP	Reims	46	Emmanuel de Graffenried	2.0 Maserati A6GCM 6	2 laps behind
ret	BRITISH GP	Silverstone	31	Emmanuel de Graffenried	2.0 Maserati A6GCM 6	clutch
5	GERMAN GP	Nürburgring	17	Emmanuel de Graffenried	2.0 Maserati A6GCM 6	1 lap behind
ret	SWISS GP	Bremgarten	42	Emmanuel de Graffenried	2.0 Maserati A6GCM 6	transmission
ret	ITALIAN GP	Monza	58	Emmanuel de Graffenried	2.0 Maserati A6GCM 6	engine

1954

	Race	Circuit	No	Entrant	Car/Engine	Comment
8	ARGENTINE GP	Buenos Aires	30	Emmanuel de Graffenried	2.5 Maserati A6GCM/250F 6	4 laps behind
ret*	BELGIAN GP	Spa	50	Emmanuel de Graffenried	2.5 Maserati A6GCM/250F 6	* camera car only-not 'racing'
ret*	SPANISH GP	Pedralbes	22	Emmanuel de Graffenried	2.5 Maserati A6GCM/250F 6	* Volonterio also drove/engine

1956

	Race	Circuit	No	Entrant	Car/Engine	Comment
7	ITALIAN GP	Monza	14	Scuderia Centro Sud	2.5 Maserati 250F 6	4 laps behind

GP Starts: 22   GP Wins: 0   Pole positions: 0   Fastest laps: 0   Points: 9

GREENE, Keith (GB) b 5/1/1938

1959

	Race	Circuit	No	Entrant	Car/Engine	Comment
dnq	BRITISH GP	Aintree	54	Gilby Engineering Co Ltd	2.5 Cooper T45-Climax 4	F2 car

1960

ret	BRITISH GP	Silverstone	22	Gilby Engineering Co Ltd	2.5 Cooper T45-Maserati 4	overheating

1961

15	BRITISH GP	Aintree	54	Gilby Engineering Co Ltd	1.5 Gilby-Climax 4	6 laps behind

1962

dns	BRITISH GP	Aintree	48	John Dalton	1.5 Lotus 18/21-Climax 4	practised only in Shelly's car
ret	GERMAN GP	Nürburgring	27	Gilby Engineering Co Ltd	1.5 Gilby-BRM V8	front suspension
dnq	ITALIAN GP	Monza	56	Gilby Engineering Co Ltd	1.5 Gilby-BRM V8	

GP Starts: 2   GP Wins: 0   Pole positions: 0   Fastest laps: 0   Points: 0

GREGORY, Masten (USA) b 29/2/1932 – d 8/11/1985

1957

	Race	Circuit	No	Entrant	Car/Engine	Comment
3	MONACO GP	Monte Carlo	2	Scuderia Centro Sud	2.5 Maserati 250F 6	2 laps behind
8	GERMAN GP	Nürburgring	16	Scuderia Centro Sud	2.5 Maserati 250F 6	1 lap behind
4	PESCARA GP	Pescara	14	Scuderia Centro Sud	2.5 Maserati 250F 6	
4	ITALIAN GP	Monza	26	Scuderia Centro Sud	2.5 Maserati 250F 6	3 laps behind

1958

ret	DUTCH GP	Zandvoort	12	H H Gould	2.5 Maserati 250F 6	fuel pump
ret	BELGIAN GP	Spa	30	Scuderia Centro Sud	2.5 Maserati 250F 6	engine
dsq	ITALIAN GP	Monza	32	Temple Buell	2.5 Maserati 250F 6	4th/Shelby co-drove without practice
6	MOROCCAN GP	Casablanca	22	Temple Buell	2.5 Maserati 250F 6	1 lap behind

1959

ret	MONACO GP	Monte Carlo	26	Cooper Car Co	2.5 Cooper T51-Climax 4	gearbox
3	DUTCH GP	Zandvoort	9	Cooper Car Co	2.5 Cooper T51-Climax 4	
ret	FRENCH GP	Reims	10	Cooper Car Co	2.5 Cooper T51-Climax 4	exhaustion
7	BRITISH GP	Aintree	14	Cooper Car Co	2.5 Cooper T51-Climax 4	overheating/2 laps behind
ret	GERMAN GP	AVUS	3	Cooper Car Co	2.5 Cooper T51-Climax 4	engine-heat 1
2	PORTUGUESE GP	Monsanto	2	Cooper Car Co	2.5 Cooper T51-Climax 4	1 lap behind

1960

12	ARGENTINE GP	Buenos Aires	2	Camoradi International	1.5 Porsche RSK F4 sports	4 laps behind
dnq	MONACO GP	Monte Carlo	40	Scuderia Centro Sud	2.5 Cooper T51-Maserati 4	
dns	DUTCH GP	Zandvoort	19	Scuderia Centro Sud	2.5 Cooper T51-Maserati 4	starting money dispute
9	FRENCH GP	Reims	40	Scuderia Centro Sud	2.5 Cooper T51-Maserati 4	pit stop/13 laps behind
14	BRITISH GP	Silverstone	16	Scuderia Centro Sud	2.5 Cooper T51-Maserati 4	6 laps behind
ret	PORTUGUESE GP	Oporto	30	Scuderia Centro Sud	2.5 Cooper T51-Maserati 4	gearbox

1961

dnq	MONACO GP	Monte Carlo	14	Camoradi International	1.5 Cooper T53-Climax 4	
dnq	DUTCH GP	Zandvoort	17	Camoradi International	1.5 Cooper T53-Climax 4	qualified-but on reserve list
10	BELGIAN GP	Spa	44	Camoradi International	1.5 Cooper T53-Climax 4	1 lap behind
12	FRENCH GP	Reims	36	Camoradi International	1.5 Cooper T53-Climax 4	pit stop/9 laps behind
11	BRITISH GP	Aintree	42	Camoradi International	1.5 Cooper T53-Climax 4	4 laps behind
ret	ITALIAN GP	Monza	22	UDT Laystall Racing Team	1.5 Lotus 18/21-Climax 4	rear suspension
ret	US GP	Watkins Glen	22	UDT Laystall Racing Team	1.5 Lotus 18/21-Climax 4	gear selection
11*	"	" "	21	UDT Laystall Racing Team	1.5 Lotus 18/21-Climax 4	* took Gendebien's car/8 laps behind

1962

ret	DUTCH GP	Zandvoort	10	UDT Laystall Racing Team	1.5 Lotus 18/21-Climax 4	driveshaft
dnq	MONACO GP	Monte Carlo	32	UDT Laystall Racing Team	1.5 Lotus 24-BRM V8	
ret	BELGIAN GP	Spa	21	UDT Laystall Racing Team	1.5 Lotus 24-BRM V8	withdrawn after Ireland's accident
dns	"	"	20	UDT Laystall Racing Team	1.5 Lotus 24-Climax V8	practised in Ireland's car
ret	FRENCH GP	Rouen	34	UDT Laystall Racing Team	1.5 Lotus 24-BRM V8	overheating
7	BRITISH GP	Aintree	34	UDT Laystall Racing Team	1.5 Lotus 24-Climax V8	1 lap behind
12	ITALIAN GP	Monza	38	UDT Laystall Racing Team	1.5 Lotus 24-BRM V8	2 p stops-overheating-gearbox/-9 laps
6	US GP	Watkins Glen	16	UDT Laystall Racing Team	1.5 Lotus 24-BRM V8	1 lap behind

1963

ret	FRENCH GP	Reims	48	Tim Parnell	1.5 Lotus 24-BRM V8	gearbox housing
11	BRITISH GP	Silverstone	21	Reg Parnell (Racing)	1.5 Lotus 24-BRM V8	7 laps behind
ret	ITALIAN GP	Monza	42	Tim Parnell	1.5 Lotus 24-BRM V8	engine
ret	US GP	Watkins Glen	17	Reg Parnell (Racing)	1.5 Lola 4A-Climax 4	engine
ret	MEXICAN GP	Mexico City	17	Reg Parnell (Racing)	1.5 Lola 4A-Climax 4	radius arm bolt

1965

ret	BELGIAN GP	Spa	29	Scuderia Centro Sud	1.5 BRM P57 V8	fuel pump
12	BRITISH GP	Silverstone	12	Scuderia Centro Sud	1.5 BRM P57 V8	pit stop/10 laps behind
8	GERMAN GP	Nürburgring	24	Scuderia Centro Sud	1.5 BRM P57 V8	1 lap behind
ret	ITALIAN GP	Monza	48	Scuderia Centro Sud	1.5 BRM P57 V8	gearbox

GP Starts: 38   GP Wins: 0   Pole positions: 0   Fastest laps: 0   Points: 21

KEITH GREENE

Growing up in the environment of his father Syd's Gilby Engineering concern, it was natural for young Keith to want to try his hand. Entered by his father in handicaps and similar events soon after his 18th birthday, Keith soon got to grips with a Cooper-Climax sports car, replacing this with a Lotus XI for the 1958 season.

It was 1959 which saw the start of his single-seater career and a splendid second place in the F2 Aintree 200. Greene continued with the Cooper until the 1961 season, when Gilby ambitiously built their own chassis for the 1.5-litre formula. It found no success at the very highest level, but did gain modest placings when fitted with a BRM V8 engine in 1962, Keith taking the car to third place in the Naples GP behind the works Ferraris of Mairesse and Bandini, and a trio of fourths at Brussels, Snetterton and Goodwood.

When the Formula 1 project was abandoned, Keith turned to sports and GT racing for the rest of the sixties, before taking on management roles with a whole roster of teams through the seventies and eighties.

MASTEN GREGORY

Although his father died when he was very young, Masten was born into a wealthy Kansas family, and much later, when his mother sold the family business, he came into a great deal of money, some of which he immediately invested in some potent sports cars to further his fledgling racing career.

In the early days he was 'hairy' but very fast, particularly when he received his Allard J2X and then the even more powerful C-Type Jaguar. His US exploits in this car led to an offer to drive in the 1954 Buenos Aires 1000 Km, and although his outing ended in retirement the trip was still worthwhile, for he purchased the race-winning 4.5-litre Ferrari, which he then brought over to Europe. In his first race, paired with the veteran Biondetti, Gregory finished fourth in the Reims 12 Hours, and the season was to be a fruitful one, with third place in the Portuguese GP, second in class at the Tourist Trophy and a win in the Nassau Trophy. More success followed in the next two seasons, before Masten took the plunge into Grand Prix racing with Scuderia Centro Sud in 1957. Having already shared the winning works Ferrari in the Argentine 1000 Km, Gregory took a brilliant third place on his Grand Prix debut at Monaco and later scored points at both Monza and Pescara. He stayed with the Maserati for 1958, but the car was past its best.

Masten then negotiated a works drive with Cooper as number three to Jack Brabham and Bruce McLaren for 1959, and despite his position in the team he gave some excellent performances, finishing third at Zandvoort and second at Monsanto, as well as producing a great drive at AVUS. However, after bailing out of his Tojeiro-Jaguar in the Tourist Trophy at Goodwood when the steering failed, Gregory sustained rib and shoulder injuries which caused him to miss the season's remaining Grands Prix and he found his services were not retained by Cooper for 1960. He was irked at this, to say the least, and returned to Scuderia Centro Sud to race their Maserati-engined Coopers, but enjoyed little luck.

In 1961 Masten became involved with the American Camoradi outfit, running a Cooper in F1 and a Maserati in sports car racing. He won the Nürburgring 1000 Km in the 'Birdcage' Maserati with Casner, but in mid-season moved over to the UDT-Laystall team to race the more competitive Lotus 18. He continued with the team in 1962, partnered by Innes Ireland, and gained a victory in the minor Kanonloppet F1 race at Karlskoga in the Lotus, and a win in the Player's 200 at Mosport with a Lotus 19 sports car, but achieved little else.

The next few seasons saw his Grand Prix career draw to a close with less and less competitive machinery, but there were compensations, including an unexpected triumph at Le Mans with Rindt in the NART Ferrari, which suddenly opened up a whole new career for Masten back in sports cars. Over the next five years (1966-71) he raced Ford GT40s, Ferrari P3s, Porsche 910s, Lola T70s and Alfa Romeo T33s among others before retiring after the 1972 Le Mans 24 Hours. A chain-smoker, he died suddenly after a heart attack in 1985, aged just 53.

GRIGNARD, Georges (F) b 25/7/1905 – d 7/12/1977

1951

	Race	Circuit	No	Entrant	Car/Engine	Comment
ret	SPANISH GP	Pedralbes	38	Georges Grignard	4.5 Lago-Talbot T26C-DA 6	overheating-engine

GP Starts: 1   GP Wins: 0   Pole positions: 0   Fastest laps: 0   Points: 0

GROUILLARD, Olivier (F) b 2/9/1958

1989

	Race	Circuit	No	Entrant	Car/Engine	Comment
9	BRAZILIAN GP	Rio	26	Ligier Loto	3.5 Ligier JS33-Cosworth V8	oil leak/1 lap behind
dsq	SAN MARINO GP	Imola	26	Ligier Loto	3.5 Ligier JS33-Cosworth V8	car worked on in pits between starts
ret	MONACO GP	Monte Carlo	26	Ligier Loto	3.5 Ligier JS33-Cosworth V8	gearbox
8	MEXICAN GP	Mexico City	26	Ligier Loto	3.5 Ligier JS33-Cosworth V8	lost clutch/1 lap behind
dnq	US GP (PHOENIX)	Phoenix	26	Ligier Loto	3.5 Ligier JS33-Cosworth V8	
dnq	CANADIAN GP	Montreal	26	Ligier Loto	3.5 Ligier JS33-Cosworth V8	
6	FRENCH GP	Paul Ricard	26	Ligier Loto	3.5 Ligier JS33-Cosworth V8	tyre and gearbox problems/-1 lap
7	BRITISH GP	Silverstone	26	Ligier Loto	3.5 Ligier JS33-Cosworth V8	1 lap behind
ret	GERMAN GP	Hockenheim	26	Ligier Loto	3.5 Ligier JS33-Cosworth V8	input shaft
dnq	HUNGARIAN GP	Hungaroring	26	Ligier Loto	3.5 Ligier JS33-Cosworth V8	
13	BELGIAN GP	Spa	26	Ligier Loto	3.5 Ligier JS33-Cosworth V8	1 lap behind
ret	ITALIAN GP	Monza	26	Ligier Loto	3.5 Ligier JS33-Cosworth V8	p stop gearbox/ret-exhaust
dnq	PORTUGUESE GP	Estoril	26	Ligier Loto	3.5 Ligier JS33-Cosworth V8	
ret	SPANISH GP	Jerez	26	Ligier Loto	3.5 Ligier JS33-Cosworth V8	engine trumpet
ret	JAPANESE GP	Suzuka	26	Ligier Loto	3.5 Ligier JS33-Cosworth V8	engine
ret	AUSTRALIAN GP	Adelaide	26	Ligier Loto	3.5 Ligier JS33-Cosworth V8	hit wall in rain

1990

	Race	Circuit	No	Entrant	Car/Engine	Comment
ret	US GP (PHOENIX)	Phoenix	14	Osella Squadra Corse	3.5 Osella FA1M-Cosworth V8	collision with Foitek
ret	BRAZILIAN GP	Interlagos	14	Osella Squadra Corse	3.5 Osella FA1M-Cosworth V8	collision with Alboreto
ret	SAN MARINO GP	Imola	14	Osella Squadra Corse	3.5 Osella FA1ME-Cosworth V8	wheelbearing
dnq	MONACO GP	Monte Carlo	14	Osella Squadra Corse	3.5 Osella FA1ME-Cosworth V8	
13	CANADIAN GP	Montreal	14	Osella Squadra Corse	3.5 Osella FA1ME-Cosworth V8	handling problems/4 laps behind
19	MEXICAN GP	Mexico City	14	Osella Squadra Corse	3.5 Osella FA1ME-Cosworth V8	gear selection problems/4 laps behind
dnpq	FRENCH GP	Paul Ricard	14	Osella Squadra Corse	3.5 Osella FA1ME-Cosworth V8	
dnq	BRITISH GP	Silverstone	14	Osella Squadra Corse	3.5 Osella FA1ME-Cosworth V8	
dnq	GERMAN GP	Hockenheim	14	Osella Squadra Corse	3.5 Osella FA1ME-Cosworth V8	
dnpq	HUNGARIAN GP	Hungaroring	14	Osella Squadra Corse	3.5 Osella FA1ME-Cosworth V8	
16	BELGIAN GP	Spa	14	Osella Squadra Corse	3.5 Osella FA1ME-Cosworth V8	pit stop-tyres/2 laps behind
ret	ITALIAN GP	Monza	14	Osella Squadra Corse	3.5 Osella FA1ME-Cosworth V8	wheel bearing
dnq	PORTUGUESE GP	Estoril	14	Osella Squadra Corse	3.5 Osella FA1ME-Cosworth V8	
ret	SPANISH GP	Jerez	14	Osella Squadra Corse	3.5 Osella FA1ME-Cosworth V8	wheel bearing
dnq	JAPANESE GP	Suzuka	14	Osella Squadra Corse	3.5 Osella FA1ME-Cosworth V8	
13	AUSTRALIAN GP	Adelaide	14	Osella Squadra Corse	3.5 Osella FA1ME-Cosworth V8	2 pit stops-tyres/handling/-7 laps

1991

	Race	Circuit	No	Entrant	Car/Engine	Comment
dnpq	US GP (PHOENIX)	Phoenix	14	Fondmetal F1 SpA	3.5 Fomet FA1M-E90-Cosworth V8	
dnpq	BRAZILIAN GP	Interlagos	14	Fondmetal F1 SpA	3.5 Fomet FA1M-E90-Cosworth V8	
dnpq	SAN MARINO GP	Imola	14	Fondmetal F1 SpA	3.5 Fomet F1-Cosworth V8	
dnpq	MONACO GP	Monte Carlo	14	Fondmetal F1 SpA	3.5 Fomet F1-Cosworth V8	
dnpq	CANADIAN GP	Montreal	14	Fondmetal F1 SpA	3.5 Fomet F1-Cosworth V8	
ret	MEXICAN GP	Mexico City	14	Fondmetal F1 SpA	3.5 Fomet F1-Cosworth V8	started from back of grid/oil line
ret	FRENCH GP	Magny Cours	14	Fondmetal F1 SpA	3.5 Fomet F1-Cosworth V8	oil leak
dnpq	BRITISH GP	Silverstone	14	Fondmetal F1 SpA	3.5 Fomet F1-Cosworth V8	
dnpq	GERMAN GP	Nürburgring	14	Fondmetal F1 SpA	3.5 Fomet F1-Cosworth V8	
dnq	HUNGARIAN GP	Hungaroring	14	Fondmetal F1 SpA	3.5 Fomet F1-Cosworth V8	
10	BELGIAN GP	Spa	14	Fondmetal F1 SpA	3.5 Fomet F1-Cosworth V8	1 lap behind
ret	ITALIAN GP	Monza	14	Fondmetal F1 SpA	3.5 Fomet F1-Cosworth V8	engine
dnpq	PORTUGUESE GP	Estoril	14	Fondmetal F1 SpA	3.5 Fomet F1-Cosworth V8	
dnpq	SPANISH GP	Barcelona	17	Automobiles Gonfaronaise Sportive	3.5 AGS JH27-Cosworth V8	

1992

	Race	Circuit	No	Entrant	Car/Engine	Comment
ret	SOUTH AFRICAN GP	Kyalami	3	Tyrrell Racing Organisation	Tyrrell 020B-Ilmor V10	clutch
ret	MEXICAN GP	Mexico City	3	Tyrrell Racing Organisation	Tyrrell 020B-Ilmor V10	engine
ret	BRAZILIAN GP	Interlagos	3	Tyrrell Racing Organisation	Tyrrell 020B-Ilmor V10	engine
ret	SPANISH GP	Barcelona	3	Tyrrell Racing Organisation	Tyrrell 020B-Ilmor V10	spun off
8	SAN MARINO GP	Imola	3	Tyrrell Racing Organisation	Tyrrell 020B-Ilmor V10	2 laps behind
ret	MONACO GP	Monte Carlo	3	Tyrrell Racing Organisation	Tyrrell 020B-Ilmor V10	gearbox
12	CANADIAN GP	Montreal	3	Tyrrell Racing Organisation	Tyrrell 020B-Ilmor V10	2 laps behind
11	FRENCH GP	Magny Cours	3	Tyrrell Racing Organisation	Tyrrell 020B-Ilmor V10	3 laps behind
11	BRITISH GP	Kyalami	3	Tyrrell Racing Organisation	Tyrrell 020B-Ilmor V10	2 laps behind
ret	GERMAN GP	Hockenheim	3	Tyrrell Racing Organisation	Tyrrell 020B-Ilmor V10	overheating
ret	HUNGARIAN GP	Hungaroring	3	Tyrrell Racing Organisation	Tyrrell 020B-Ilmor V10	collision with Wendlinger
ret	BELGIAN GP	Spa	3	Tyrrell Racing Organisation	Tyrrell 020B-Ilmor V10	spun off lap 1
ret	ITALIAN GP	Monza	3	Tyrrell Racing Organisation	Tyrrell 020B-Ilmor V10	engine
ret	PORTUGUESE GP	Estoril	3	Tyrrell Racing Organisation	Tyrrell 020B-Ilmor V10	gearbox
ret	JAPANESE GP	Suzuka	3	Tyrrell Racing Organisation	Tyrrell 020B-Ilmor V10	spun off
ret	AUSTRALIAN GP	Adelaide	3	Tyrrell Racing Organisation	Tyrrell 020B-Ilmor V10	spun-collision with Martini lap 1

GP Starts: 41   GP Wins: 0   Pole positions: 0   Fastest laps: 0   Points: 1

GUELFI, André (F) b 6/5/1919

1958

	Race	Circuit	No	Entrant	Car/Engine	Comment
15	MOROCCAN GP (F2)	Casablanca	48	André Guelfi	1.5 Cooper T45-Climax 4	4th in F2 class/5 laps behind

GP Starts: 1   GP Wins: 0   Pole positions: 0   Fastest laps: 0   Points: 0

GUERRA, Miguel Angel (RA) b 31/8/1953

1981

	Race	Circuit	No	Entrant	Car/Engine	Comment
dnq	US GP WEST	Long Beach	31	Osella Squadra Corse	3.0 Osella FA1B-Cosworth V8	
dnq	BRAZILIAN GP	Rio	31	Osella Squadra Corse	3.0 Osella FA1B-Cosworth V8	
dnq	ARGENTINE GP	Buenos Aires	31	Osella Squadra Corse	3.0 Osella FA1B-Cosworth V8	
ret	SAN MARINO GP	Imola	31	Osella Squadra Corse	3.0 Osella FA1B-Cosworth V8	spun/collision-Salazar/broken ankle

GP Starts: 1   GP Wins: 0   Pole positions: 0   Fastest laps: 0   Points: 0

GEORGES GRIGNARD

Grignard began his career in rallying in the twenties, taking part in the Monte Carlo Rallies of 1928 and '29, and raced intermittently during the following deacade while building up his garage business. After the war he reappeared in a Delahaye which he raced for much of 1946. Georges then joined the Ecurie Vallée team for 1947 but, having disposed of the Delahaye, found himself virtually sidelined until late 1948, when he finally took delivery of a long-awaited Talbot. Once wedded to his beloved car, Grignard raced it extensively over the next few seasons, his best placings being third at Pau in 1949, and sixth at Rouen in 1953.

Not a particularly quick driver, he nevertheless possessed mechanical sympathy and continued to compete, mainly in sports cars, until 1955, after which he retired to his garage business. He was still not finished with the Talbot marque, however, for in 1959 he took the opportunity to buy up all the liquidated stock, subsequently acting as a supplier to collectors around the world.

OLIVIER GROUILLARD

Even from his earliest days in French Formula 3 Grouillard had developed something of a reputation as a wild and uncompromising performer. After finishing fourth in the 1983 series, he graduated to the all-conqering Marlboro-backed ORECA team the following year and swept to the title as was the established custom for the chosen incumbent, though it was a close-run thing, Grouillard edging out his rival Frédéric Delavallade by just two points, 108 to 106.

Rustling up enough budget for half a season in F3000 with ORECA in 1985, Grouillard made a good impression, coming close to a win at Enna. It was much the same the following year, when he was able to take part in only four races; he could have won at Mugello but made a mistake and ended up in fourth place. Back with ORECA again in 1987 he showed speed, but was rather overshadowed by team-mate Dalmas, who was on a rather quicker path to Formula 1. But Olivier was nothing if not persistent, and for 1988 he got himself into the well-funded GBDA team, running works-backed Lolas. He finished runner-up to Roberto Moreno, winning two races and putting in some superb performances.

At last Grouillard found himself in Formula 1 with Ligier, but after a bright start relationships between the tempestuous youngster and his volcanic proprietor broke down and the driver was forced to seek alternative employment with Osella. The next two seasons were spent trying to qualify for races above all else, and after the briefest of flirtations with the almost exstinct AGS team the future looked bleak.

Once again Grouillard dug himself out of a corner, finding the cash to join the underfinanced Tyrrell team. Freed from the perils of qualifying, he had a car that at the very least he could go racing with, but Olivier was overwhelmingly overshadowed by team-mate Andrea de Cesaris and succeeded only in attracting criticism for his bad track manners when being lapped.

For 1993 Groiullard took himself off to the States for a full season of IndyCar racing but failed completely to make a worthwhile impression, finishing 28th in the final points standings.

MIGUEL ANGEL GUERRA

The unfortunate Argentinian must be in the running for the unwanted tag of having one of the shortest Grand Prix careers on record, for he was barely a third of a lap into his debut, the 1981 San Marino Grand Prix, when he was pushed off the track and into the wall, sustaining a broken ankle and wrist in the process.

He had three seasons in Formula 2 behind him: the first, in 1978, saw a few outings in a Chevron; the next, in a March, yielded his best finish (third place at Hockenheim); and he then endured a disappointing year with the troublesome Minardi.

Guerra recovered from his Imola crash to reappear briefly in Formula 2 at the end of the 1981 season in the Adriatic GP at Misano, finishing a distant 13th.

ROBERTO GUERRERO

This personable Colombian driver could have made a good career for himself in Formula 1 had he not chosen to move into IndyCar racing at the end of 1983 when no suitable F1 drive was available for, on his speedy passage to the top, Roberto had already displayed genuine talent. Joint second in the British F3 series in the unfashionable Argo, and an immediate winner at Thruxton in his first Formula 2 season, Guerrero's fine performances caught the eye of Mo Nunn, who gave him the Ensign drive for 1982. Roberto did extremely well in difficult circumstances, as he did in his second season following the team's merger with Theodore.

So it was off to the States, and stardom, Guerrero finishing second in the 1984 Indy 500, and winning two races in 1987, at Phoenix and Mid-Ohio, before a crash while testing at Indy left him in a coma for 17 days. He made a full recovery but his career never quite recovered its earlier momentum, and he became bogged down in the largely disappointing Alfa Romeo Indy programme until he joined Kenny Bernstein's team in mid-1991. Roberto took pole at Indy in 1992 but crashed on the warm-up lap and spent the rest of the campaign on the sidelines. He then signed with Bernstein for a full season in 1993, but after a generally lacklustre year he lost his ride with three races remaining.

MAURICIO GUGELMIN

Presentable, articulate and displaying a mature approach to racing from his early days, Mauricio had a great deal of skill as well. A Formula Ford champion in 1981 in his native Brazil, Gugelmin followed his friend and ex-karting rival Ayrton Senna to Europe, initially taking the same route to the top – FF1600 and FF2000, then Formula 3 with West Surrey Racing in 1985. Fast, safe and above all consistent, Mauricio took the title, and rounded off the season, and his F3 career, with a win in the prestigious Macau GP.

Gugelmin moved into F3000 with West Surrey Racing for 1986, enduring a frustrating year fraught with problems, but his fortunes improved the following season. Now running a works Ralt-Honda with fellow Brazilian Roberto Moreno, he won the opening round at Silverstone, but a spate of mid-season non-finishes left him fourth in the points at the season's end.

Mauricio then joined the Leyton House March team and was happy to remain with them for four seasons in which he experienced the highs (third place in Brazil in 1989) and lows (a run of non-qualifications in 1990 when the car's sensitive chassis proved nearly impossible to set up) of F1. By the end of 1991 the whole organisation was crumbling after 18 months of internal dissent and personnel changes, and Gugelmin took his leave to join his old mentor Ian Phillips at Jordan. The year was a debacle for the team as they struggled with the Yamaha engine, but Mauricio earned their respect by never giving less than his best.

Without a drive for 1993, Gugelmin made his IndyCar debut in the last three races of the season, and while he enjoyed little success he showed enough promise to suggest he could be making a serious return in the future.

GUERRERO, Roberto (COL) b 16/11/1958

1982

	Race	Circuit	No	Entrant	Car/Entrant	Comment
dnp	SOUTH AFRICAN GP	Kyalami	14	Ensign Racing	3.0 Ensign N180B-Cosworth V8	withdrawn due drivers' strike
dnq	BRAZILIAN GP	Rio	14	Ensign Racing	3.0 Ensign N181-Cosworth V8	
ret	US GP WEST	Long Beach	14	Ensign Racing	3.0 Ensign N181-Cosworth V8	hit wall
dnq	BELGIAN GP	Zolder	14	Ensign Racing	3.0 Ensign N181-Cosworth V8	
dnq	MONACO GP	Monte Carlo	14	Ensign Racing	3.0 Ensign N181-Cosworth V8	
ret	US GP (DETROIT)	Detroit	14	Ensign Racing	3.0 Ensign N181-Cosworth V8	accident with de Angelis
ret	CANADIAN GP	Montreal	14	Ensign Racing	3.0 Ensign N181-Cosworth V8	clutch
dnq	DUTCH GP	Zandvoort	14	Ensign Racing	3.0 Ensign N181-Cosworth V8	
ret	BRITISH GP	Brands Hatch	14	Ensign Racing	3.0 Ensign N181-Cosworth V8	engine
dnq	FRENCH GP	Paul Ricard	14	Ensign Racing	3.0 Ensign N181-Cosworth V8	
8	GERMAN GP	Hockenheim	14	Ensign Racing	3.0 Ensign N181-Cosworth V8	1 lap behind
ret	AUSTRIAN GP	Österreichring	14	Ensign Racing	3.0 Ensign N181-Cosworth V8	driveshaft
ret	SWISS GP	Dijon	14	Ensign Racing	3.0 Ensign N181-Cosworth V8	engine
nc	ITALIAN GP	Monza	14	Ensign Racing	3.0 Ensign N181-Cosworth V8	hit Daly-pit stop/12 laps behind
dns	CAESARS PALACE GP	Las Vegas	14	Ensign Racing	3.0 Ensign N181-Cosworth V8	engine in warm-up

1983

	Race	Circuit	No	Entrant	Car/Entrant	Comment
nc	BRAZILIAN GP	Rio	33	Theodore Racing Team	3.0 Theodore N183-Cosworth V8	pit stop/10 laps behind
ret	US GP WEST	Long Beach	33	Theodore Racing Team	3.0 Theodore N183-Cosworth V8	gearbox
ret	FRENCH GP	Paul Ricard	33	Theodore Racing Team	3.0 Theodore N183-Cosworth V8	engine
ret	SAN MARINO GP	Imola	33	Theodore Racing Team	3.0 Theodore N183-Cosworth V8	incident with Sullivan
dnpq	MONACO GP	Monte Carlo	33	Theodore Racing Team	3.0 Theodore N183-Cosworth V8	
ret	BELGIAN GP	Spa	33	Theodore Racing Team	3.0 Theodore N183-Cosworth V8	engine
nc	US GP (DETROIT)	Detroit	33	Theodore Racing Team	3.0 Theodore N183-Cosworth V8	pit stop/22 laps behind
ret	CANADIAN GP	Montreal	33	Theodore Racing Team	3.0 Theodore N183-Cosworth V8	engine
16	BRITISH GP	Silverstone	33	Theodore Racing Team	3.0 Theodore N183-Cosworth V8	3 laps behind
ret	GERMAN GP	Hockenheim	33	Theodore Racing Team	3.0 Theodore N183-Cosworth V8	engine
ret	AUSTRIAN GP	Österreichring	33	Theodore Racing Team	3.0 Theodore N183-Cosworth V8	gearbox
12	DUTCH GP	Zandvoort	33	Theodore Racing Team	3.0 Theodore N183-Cosworth V8	incident-Jarier-pit stop/4 laps behind
13	ITALIAN GP	Monza	33	Theodore Racing Team	3.0 Theodore N183-Cosworth V8	2 laps behind
12	EUROPEAN GP	Brands Hatch	33	Theodore Racing Team	3.0 Theodore N183-Cosworth V8	1 lap behind

GP Starts: 21   GP Wins: 0   Pole positions: 0   Fastest laps: 0   Points: 0

GUGELMIN, Mauricio (BR) b 20/4/1963

1988

	Race	Circuit	No	Entrant	Car/Engine	Comment
ret	BRAZILIAN GP	Rio	15	Leyton House March Racing Team	3.5 March 881-Judd V8	transmission on lap 1
15	SAN MARINO GP	Imola	15	Leyton House March Racing Team	3.5 March 881-Judd V8	fuel pick-up problems/2 laps behind
ret	MONACO GP	Monte Carlo	15	Leyton House March Racing Team	3.5 March 881-Judd V8	electrics-engine/started from pit lane
ret	MEXICAN GP	Mexico City	15	Leyton House March Racing Team	3.5 March 881-Judd V8	electrical short-circuit

ret	CANADIAN GP	Montreal	15	Leyton House March Racing Team	3.5 March 881-Judd V8	gearbox
ret	US GP (DETROIT)	Detroit	15	Leyton House March Racing Team	3.5 March 881-Judd V8	engine
8	FRENCH GP	Paul Ricard	15	Leyton House March Racing Team	3.5 March 881-Judd V8	lost clutch/1 lap behind
4	BRITISH GP	Silverstone	15	Leyton House March Racing Team	3.5 March 881-Judd V8	
8	GERMAN GP	Hockenheim	15	Leyton House March Racing Team	3.5 March 881-Judd V8	1 lap behind
5	HUNGARIAN GP	Hungaroring	15	Leyton House March Racing Team	3.5 March 881-Judd V8	1 lap behind
ret	BELGIAN GP	Spa	15	Leyton House March Racing Team	3.5 March 881-Judd V8	clutch-spun off
8	ITALIAN GP	Monza	15	Leyton House March Racing Team	3.5 March 881-Judd V8	engine down on power
ret	PORTUGUESE GP	Estoril	15	Leyton House March Racing Team	3.5 March 881-Judd V8	engine
7	SPANISH GP	Jerez	15	Leyton House March Racing Team	3.5 March 881-Judd V8	
10	JAPANESE GP	Suzuka	15	Leyton House March Racing Team	3.5 March 881-Judd V8	clutch problems/1 lap behind
ret	AUSTRALIAN GP	Adelaide	15	Leyton House March Racing Team	3.5 March 881-Judd V8	hit by Nakajima

1989

3	BRAZILIAN GP	Rio	15	Leyton House March Racing Team	3.5 March 881-Judd V8	2 pit stops-tyres
ret	SAN MARINO GP	Imola	15	Leyton House March Racing Team	3.5 March 881-Judd V8	clutch/puncture/ret gearbox
ret	MONACO GP	Monte Carlo	15	Leyton House March Racing Team	3.5 March CG891-Judd V8	engine
dnq	MEXICAN GP	Mexico City	15	Leyton House March Racing Team	3.5 March CG891-Judd V8	
dsq	US GP (PHOENIX)	Phoenix	15	Leyton House March Racing Team	3.5 March CG891-Judd V8	topped up brake fluid during race
ret	CANADIAN GP	Montreal	15	Leyton House March Racing Team	3.5 March CG891-Judd V8	electrics
nc	FRENCH GP	Paul Ricard	15	Leyton House March Racing Team	3.5 March CG891-Judd V8	crashed-first start/pit stop-misfire/FL
ret	BRITISH GP	Silverstone	15	Leyton House March Racing Team	3.5 March CG891-Judd V8	started from pit lane/gearbox
ret	GERMAN GP	Hockenheim	15	Leyton House March Racing Team	3.5 March CG891-Judd V8	gearbox
ret	HUNGARIAN GP	Hungaroring	15	Leyton House March Racing Team	3.5 March CG891-Judd V8	electrics
7	BELGIAN GP	Spa	15	Leyton House March Racing Team	3.5 March CG891-Judd V8	1 lap behind
ret	ITALIAN GP	Monza	15	Leyton House March Racing Team	3.5 March CG891-Judd V8	throttle problems
10	PORTUGUESE GP	Estoril	15	Leyton House March Racing Team	3.5 March CG891-Judd V8	pit stop-tyres-stalled/2 laps behind
ret	SPANISH GP	Jerez	15	Leyton House March Racing Team	3.5 March CG891-Judd V8	hit by Sala
7*	JAPANESE GP	Suzuka	15	Leyton House March Racing Team	3.5 March CG891-Judd V8	* 1st place car dsq/1 lap behind
7	AUSTRALIAN GP	Adelaide	15	Leyton House March Racing Team	3.5 March CG891-Judd V8	4 laps behind

1990

14	US GP (PHOENIX)	Phoenix	15	Leyton House March Racing Team	3.5 Leyton House CG901-Judd V8	pit stop-tyres/vibration/6 laps behind
dns	" "	"	15	Leyton House March Racing Team	3.5 March CG891-Judd V8	practice only
dnq	BRAZILIAN GP	Interlagos	15	Leyton House March Racing Team	3.5 Leyton House CG901-Judd V8	
ret	SAN MARINO GP	Imola	15	Leyton House March Racing Team	3.5 Leyton House CG901-Judd V8	misfire-electrics
dnq	MONACO GP	Monte Carlo	15	Leyton House March Racing Team	3.5 Leyton House CG901-Judd V8	
dnq	CANADIAN GP	Montreal	15	Leyton House March Racing Team	3.5 Leyton House CG901-Judd V8	
dnq	MEXICAN GP	Mexico City	15	Leyton House March Racing Team	3.5 Leyton House CG901-Judd V8	
ret	FRENCH GP	Paul Ricard	15	Leyton House March Racing Team	3.5 Leyton House CG901-Judd V8	engine when 4th
dns	BRITISH GP	Silverstone	15	Leyton House March Racing Team	3.5 Leyton House CG901-Judd V8	fuel pump on dummy grid
ret	GERMAN GP	Hockenheim	15	Leyton House March Racing Team	3.5 Leyton House CG901-Judd V8	engine
8	HUNGARIAN GP	Hungaroring	15	Leyton House March Racing Team	3.5 Leyton House CG901-Judd V8	brake problems-spin/1 lap behind
6	BELGIAN GP	Spa	15	Leyton House March Racing Team	3.5 Leyton House CG901-Judd V8	clutch problems
ret	ITALIAN GP	Monza	15	Leyton House March Racing Team	3.5 Leyton House CG901-Judd V8	clutch
12	PORTUGUESE GP	Estoril	15	Leyton House March Racing Team	3.5 Leyton House CG901-Judd V8	feeling unwell/2 laps behind
8	SPANISH GP	Jerez	15	Leyton House March Racing Team	3.5 Leyton House CG901-Judd V8	pit stop-tyres/clutch problems/-1 lap
ret	JAPANESE GP	Suzuka	15	Leyton House March Racing Team	3.5 Leyton House CG901-Judd V8	engine cut out
ret	AUSTRALIAN GP	Adelaide	15	Leyton House March Racing Team	3.5 Leyton House CG901-Judd V8	rear brakes

1991

ret	US GP (PHOENIX)	Phoenix	15	Leyton House Racing	3.5 Leyton House CG911-Ilmor V10	gearbox
ret	BRAZILIAN GP	Interlagos	15	Leyton House Racing	3.5 Leyton House CG911-Ilmor V10	driver unwell, withdrew
12/ret	SAN MARINO	Phoenix	15	Leyton House Racing	3.5 Leyton House CG911-Ilmor V10	engine/6 laps behind
ret	MONACO GP	Monte Carlo	15	Leyton House Racing	3.5 Leyton House CG911-Ilmor V10	throttle cable
ret	CANADIAN GP	Montreal	15	Leyton House Racing	3.5 Leyton House CG911-Ilmor V10	engine
ret	MEXICAN GP	Mexico City	15	Leyton House Racing	3.5 Leyton House CG911-Ilmor V10	engine
7	FRENCH GP	Magny Cours	15	Leyton House Racing	3.5 Leyton House CG911-Ilmor V10	2 laps behind
ret	BRITISH GP	Silverstone	15	Leyton House Racing	3.5 Leyton House CG911-Ilmor V10	chassis vibration numbed leg
ret	GERMAN GP	Phoenix	15	Leyton House Racing '	3.5 Leyton House CG911-Ilmor V10	gearbox
11	HUNGARIAN GP	Hungaroring	15	Leyton House Racing	3.5 Leyton House CG911-Ilmor V10	2 laps behind
ret	BELGIAN GP	Spa	15	Leyton House Racing•	3.5 Leyton House CG911-Ilmor V10	engine
15	ITALIAN GP	Monza	15	Leyton House Racing	3.5 Leyton House CG911-Ilmor V10	no clutch/foot injury/4 laps behind
7	PORTUGUESE GP	Estoril	15	Leyton House Racing	3.5 Leyton House CG911-Ilmor V10	1 lap behind
7	SPANISH GP	Barcelona	15	Leyton House Racing	3.5 Leyton House CG911-Ilmor V10	1 lap behind
8	JAPANESE GP	Suzuka	15	Leyton House Racing	3.5 Leyton House CG911-Ilmor V10	1 lap behind
14/ret	AUSTRALIAN GP	Adelaide	15	Leyton House Racing	3.5 Leyton House CG911-Ilmor V10	crashed into pit lane entrance

1992

11	SOUTH AFRICAN GP	Kyalami	33	Sasol Jordan Yamaha	3.5 Jordan 192-Yamaha V12	2 laps behind
ret	MEXICAN GP	Mexico City	33	Sasol Jordan Yamaha	3.5 Jordan 192-Yamaha V12	engine lap 1
ret	BRAZILIAN GP	Interlagos	33	Sasol Jordan Yamaha	3.5 Jordan 192-Yamaha V12	gearbox
ret	SPANISH GP	Barcelona	33	Sasol Jordan Yamaha	3.5 Jordan 192-Yamaha V12	spun off
7	SAN MARINO GP	Imola	33	Sasol Jordan Yamaha	3.5 Jordan 192-Yamaha V12	2 laps behind
ret	MONACO GP	Monte Carlo	33	Sasol Jordan Yamaha	3.5 Jordan 192-Yamaha V12	transmission
ret	CANADIAN GP	Montreal	33	Sasol Jordan Yamaha	3.5 Jordan 192-Yamaha V12	transmission
ret	FRENCH GP	Magny Cours	33	Sasol Jordan Yamaha	3.5 Jordan 192-Yamaha V12	multiple collision-lap 1
ret	BRITISH GP	Silverstone	33	Sasol Jordan Yamaha	3.5 Jordan 192-Yamaha V12	engine
15	GERMAN GP	Nürburgring	33	Sasol Jordan Yamaha	3.5 Jordan 192-Yamaha V12	2 laps behind
10	HUNGARIAN GP	Hungaroring	33	Sasol Jordan Yamaha	3.5 Jordan 192-Yamaha V12	4 laps behind
14	BELGIAN GP	Spa	33	Sasol Jordan Yamaha	3.5 Jordan 192-Yamaha V12	2 laps behind
ret	ITALIAN GP	Monza	33	Sasol Jordan Yamaha	3.5 Jordan 192-Yamaha V12	transmission
ret	PORTUGUESE GP	Estoril	33	Sasol Jordan Yamaha	3.5 Jordan 192-Yamaha V12	electrics
ret	JAPANESE GP	Suzuka	33	Sasol Jordan Yamaha	3.5 Jordan 192-Yamaha V12	crashed
ret	AUSTRALIAN GP	Adelaide	33	Sasol Jordan Yamaha	3.5 Jordan 192-Yamaha V12	brake problem-crashed

GP Starts: 74   GP Wins: 0   Pole positions: 0   Fastest laps: 1   Points: 10

DAN GURNEY

Some drivers seem to exude a natural warmth, and by their demeanour both on and off the track firmly entrench themselves in the hearts of motor racing fans across the globe. Dan Gurney comes into this category. Standing at Paddock Bend at the start of the 1968 British Grand Prix, I remember spontaneously cheering loudly with the rest as he set off in grim but hopeless pursuit of the field, Lady Luck having left him stranded on the line. This minor moment serves to underline how universally popular the tall American was and still is to this day, not only for his many fine achievements but also for his stature as one of the sport's least affected and most enthusiastic participants.

The son of an opera singer, Gurney revelled in the environment of his Riverside youth, taking little interest in his studies, but enjoying the illicit drag racing around the local strips. After National Service he began his competition career in 1955 with a Triumph TR2, before building his reputation with a Porsche. By 1957 Dan was running a Ferrari entered by Frank Arciero, and was so successful that Luigi Chinetti arranged for him to race at Le Mans and Reims in 1958. In both races his co-driver crashed the car, but Dan had shown sufficient promise to be offered a test with Ferrari late that year.

Signing a contract with the wily Commendatore for the 1959 season which bound him tightly, Gurney soon proved to be a major asset, particularly after the acrimonious departure of Behra, scoring points in three of his four Grands Prix. The strictures of Maranello were such that Dan decided to join BRM for 1960, but it was an unhappy year with the car woefully unreliable – made even worse by a freak accident at Zandvoort in which a small boy was killed when Dan's brakes failed and the car crashed. Joining Porsche for 1961, Gurney found that the four-cylinder car was reliable (he finished all but one of his 14 Formula 1 races) but not quite capable of winning. He stayed on for 1962 and gained some reward with the flat-eight car, winning his first Grand Prix at Rouen and then the non-title race at Solitude. This was to be the pinnacle of Porsche's achievements as a manufacturer in Formula 1, as they withdrew at the season's end, leaving Dan to join Jack Brabham as the team's number one driver for Formula 1, but free to continue his sports and USAC programme which had begun so promisingly in 1962. Again it was so near yet so far in Grands Prix as Gurney repeatedly challenged Jim Clark *et al* over the next three seasons but was almost invariably frustrated by niggling problems which restricted him to just two victories. It seems ironic that after his departure to build his own Eagle racers the Brabham should have come good and won the World Championship for the next two seasons.

Gurney's Anglo American Racers car looked superb in its dark-blue livery, but stood no chance of success until its punchless four-cylinder Climax engine was replaced by the complex but potent Weslake unit. By 1967 this was a truly competitive proposition and Dan took victories in the Race of Champions and the Belgian GP before the onslaught of Cosworth power eventually overwhelmed the project. June of that year was kind to Dan, who also shared a Ford GT40 with A J Foyt to win the Le Mans 24 Hours. By now Gurney was extending his efforts to Can-Am and USAC, and after winning the Rex Mays 100 at Riverside in 1967 he finished second in the Indianapolis 500 the following season as well as winning at Mosport and Riverside again.

Formula 1 seemed a thing of the past in 1969 as Dan developed his USAC programme, finishing second at Indy yet again but winning at Donnybrooke. The following year he won at Sears Point and was third at Indy, before stepping into the breach at McLaren following Bruce's tragic death in a testing accident at Goodwood. After being away Dan never really found the pace in Formula 1, but he won two of the three Can-Am rounds he contested before problems over conflicting oil contracts pecipitated his departure from the team. Realising that perhaps his best days were now behind him, he retired from racing, his place in the USAC team being filled by Bobby Unser, who was to bring Eagle so much success in the seventies. Happily Dan was not tempted to return full-time, but he couldn't resist a one-off NASCAR outing in 1980 at his home track of Riverside, where he lay a superb third before gearbox trouble.

Gurney continued to enter his Eagles in USAC and had the satisfaction of winning Indy at last, as a constructor if not as a driver, with Gordon Johncock and Bobby Unser scoring victories in 1973 and 1975 respectively. Dan eventually withdrew from IndyCar racing, concentrating successfully on IMSA with the backing of Toyota in the early nineties. At the time of writing, plans are afoot for the AAR team to return to the IndyCar arena with Toyota in 1995.

GURNEY, Dan (USA) b 13/4/1931

1959

	Race	Circuit	No	Entrant	Car/Engine	Comment
ret	FRENCH GP	Reims	28	Scuderia Ferrari	2.4 Ferrari Dino 246 V6	*radiator*
2	GERMAN GP	AVUS	6	Scuderia Ferrari	2.4 Ferrari Dino 246 V6	*2nd heat 1/3rd heat 2*
3	PORTUGUESE GP	Monsanto	16	Scuderia Ferrari	2.4 Ferrari Dino 246 V6	*1 lap behind*
4	ITALIAN GP	Monza	36	Scuderia Ferrari	2.4 Ferrari Dino 246 V6	

1960

	Race	Circuit	No	Entrant	Car/Engine	Comment
10/ret	MONACO GP	Monte Carlo	4	Owen Racing Organisation	2.5 BRM P48 4	*suspension/52 laps behind*
ret	DUTCH GP	Zandvoort	15	Owen Racing Organisation	2.5 BRM P48 4	*brake failure-accident*
ret	BELGIAN GP	Spa	8	Owen Racing Organisation	2.5 BRM P48 4	*engine*
ret	FRENCH GP	Reims	10	Owen Racing Organisation	2.5 BRM P48 4	*engine*
10	BRITISH GP	Silverstone	5	Owen Racing Organisation	2.5 BRM P48 4	*pit stop/3 laps behind*
ret	PORTUGUESE GP	Oporto	24	Owen Racing Organisation	2.5 BRM P48 4	*engine*
ret	US GP	Riverside	16	Owen Racing Organisation	2.5 BRM P48 4	*overheating*

1961

	Race	Circuit	No	Entrant	Car/Engine	Comment
5	MONACO GP	Monte Carlo	4	Porsche System Engineering	1.5 Porsche 718 F4	*2 laps behind*
10	DUTCH GP	Zandvoort	7	Porsche System Engineering	1.5 Porsche 787 F4	*1 lap behind*
6	BELGIAN GP	Spa	20	Porsche System Engineering	1.5 Porsche 718 F4	
2	FRENCH GP	Reims	12	Porsche System Engineering	1.5 Porsche 718 F4	
7	BRITISH GP	Aintree	10	Porsche System Engineering	1.5 Porsche 718 F4	*1 lap behind*
7	GERMAN GP	Nürburgring	9	Porsche System Engineering	1.5 Porsche 718 F4	
2	ITALIAN GP	Monza	46	Porsche System Engineering	1.5 Porsche 718 F4	
dns	"	"	46	Porsche System Engineering	1.5 Porsche 788 F4	*practice only*
2	US GP	Watkins Glen	12	Porsche System Engineering	1.5 Porsche 718 F4	

1962

ret	DUTCH GP	Zandvoort	12	Porsche System Engineering	1.5 Porsche 804 F8	gearbox
ret	MONACO GP	Monte Carlo	4	Porsche System Engineering	1.5 Porsche 804 F8	first corner accident
dns	BELGIAN GP	Spa	23	Autosport Team Wolfgang Seidel	1.5 Lotus 24-BRM V8	car unraceworthy
1	FRENCH GP	Rouen	30	Porsche System Engineering	1.5 Porsche 804 F8	
9	BRITISH GP	Aintree	8	Porsche System Engineering	1.5 Porsche 804 F8	2 laps behind
3	GERMAN GP	Nürburgring	7	Porsche System Engineering	1.5 Porsche 804 F8	Pole
13/ret	ITALIAN GP	Monza	16	Porsche System Engineering	1.5 Porsche 804 F8	cwp/20 laps behind
5	US GP	Watkins Glen	10	Porsche System Engineering	1.5 Porsche 804 F8	1 lap behind

1963

ret	MONACO GP	Monte Carlo	4	Brabham Racing Organisation	1.5 Brabham BT7-Climax V8	cwp
3	BELGIAN GP	Spa	18	Brabham Racing Organisation	1.5 Brabham BT7-Climax V8	1 lap behind
2	DUTCH GP	Zandvoort	18	Brabham Racing Organisation	1.5 Brabham BT7-Climax V8	1 lap behind
5	FRENCH GP	Reims	8	Brabham Racing Organisation	1.5 Brabham BT7-Climax V8	
ret	BRITISH GP	Silverstone	9	Brabham Racing Organisation	1.5 Brabham BT7-Climax V8	engine
ret	GERMAN GP	Nürburgring	10	Brabham Racing Organisation	1.5 Brabham BT7-Climax V8	gearbox
14/ret	ITALIAN GP	Monza	24	Brabham Racing Organisation	1.5 Brabham BT7-Climax V8	fuel feed
ret	US GP	Watkins Glen	6	Brabham Racing Organisation	1.5 Brabham BT7-Climax V8	cracked chassis
6	MEXICAN GP	Mexico City	6	Brabham Racing Organisation	1.5 Brabham BT7-Climax V8	fuel starvation/3 laps behind
2	SOUTH AFRICAN GP	East London	9	Brabham Racing Organisation	1.5 Brabham BT7-Climax V8	FL

1964

ret	MONACO GP	Monte Carlo	6	Brabham Racing Organisation	1.5 Brabham BT7-Climax V8	gearbox
ret	DUTCH GP	Zandvoort	16	Brabham Racing Organisation	1.5 Brabham BT7-Climax V8	steering wheel/Pole
6/ret	BELGIAN GP	Spa	15	Brabham Racing Organisation	1.5 Brabham BT7-Climax V8	out of fuel last lap/Pole/FL
1	FRENCH GP	Rouen	22	Brabham Racing Organisation	1.5 Brabham BT7-Climax V8	
13	BRITISH GP	Brands Hatch	6	Brabham Racing Organisation	1.5 Brabham BT7-Climax V8	pit stop-ignition/5 laps behind
10	GERMAN GP	Nürburgring	5	Brabham Racing Organisation	1.5 Brabham BT7-Climax V8	2 pit stops-overheating/1 lap behind
ret	AUSTRIAN GP	Zeltweg	5	Brabham Racing Organisation	1.5 Brabham BT7-Climax V8	front suspension/FL
10	ITALIAN GP	Monza	16	Brabham Racing Organisation	1.5 Brabham BT7-Climax V8	pit stop-alternator/3 laps behind
ret	US GP	Watkins Glen	6	Brabham Racing Organisation	1.5 Brabham BT7-Climax V8	oil pressure-engine
1	MEXICAN GP	Mexico City	6	Brabham Racing Organisation	1.5 Brabham BT7-Climax V8	

1965

ret	SOUTH AFRICAN GP	East London	8	Brabham Racing Organisation	1.5 Brabham BT11-Climax V8	ignition
10	BELGIAN GP	Spa	15	Brabham Racing Organisation	1.5 Brabham BT11-Climax V8	pit stop-wet ignition/2 laps behind
ret	FRENCH GP	Clermont Ferrand	14	Brabham Racing Organisation	1.5 Brabham BT11-Climax V8	engine
6	BRITISH GP	Silverstone	7	Brabham Racing Organisation	1.5 Brabham BT11-Climax V8	drove Brabham's car/1 lap behind
3	DUTCH GP	Zandvoort	16	Brabham Racing Organisation	1.5 Brabham BT11-Climax V8	
3	GERMAN GP	Nürburgring	5	Brabham Racing Organisation	1.5 Brabham BT11-Climax V8	
3	ITALIAN GP	Monza	12	Brabham Racing Organisation	1.5 Brabham BT11-Climax V8	
2	US GP	Watkins Glen	8	Brabham Racing Organisation	1.5 Brabham BT11-Climax V8	
2	MEXICAN GP	Mexico City	8	Brabham Racing Organisation	1.5 Brabham BT11-Climax V8	FL

1966

nc	BELGIAN GP	Spa	27	Anglo American Racers	2.7 Eagle T1G-Climax 4	pit stop-tyres/5 laps behind
5	FRENCH GP	Reims	26	Anglo American Racers	2.7 Eagle T1G-Climax 4	3 laps behind
ret	BRITISH GP	Brands Hatch	16	Anglo American Racers	2.7 Eagle T1G-Climax 4	engine
ret	DUTCH GP	Zandvoort	10	Anglo American Racers	2.7 Eagle T1G-Climax 4	engine
7	GERMAN GP	Nürburgring	12	Anglo American Racers	2.7 Eagle T1G-Climax 4	1 lap behind
ret	ITALIAN GP	Monza	30	Anglo American Racers	3.0 Eagle T1G-Weslake V12	oil temperature
dns	"	"	34	Anglo American Racers	2.7 Eagle T1G-Climax 4	practice only
ret	US GP	Watkins Glen	15	Anglo American Racers	3.0 Eagle T1G-Weslake V12	clutch slip
5	MEXICAN GP	Mexico City	(16)15	Anglo American Racers	2.7 Eagle T1G-Climax 4	1 lap behind
dns	"	" "	15	Anglo American Racers	3.0 Eagle T1G-Weslake V12	practice only

1967

ret	SOUTH AFRICAN GP	Kyalami	9	Anglo American Racers	2.7 Eagle T1G-Climax 4	wishbone mounting
ret	MONACO GP	Monte Carlo	23	Anglo American Racers	3.0 Eagle T1G-Weslake V12	fuel pump drive
ret	DUTCH GP	Zandvoort	15	Anglo American Racers	3.0 Eagle T1G-Weslake V12	fuel injection
1	BELGIAN GP	Spa	36	Anglo American Racers	3.0 Eagle T1G-Weslake V12	FL
ret	FRENCH GP	Le Mans	9	Anglo American Racers	3.0 Eagle T1G-Weslake V12	fuel line
ret	BRITISH GP	Silverstone	7	Anglo American Racers	3.0 Eagle T1G-Weslake V12	clutch
ret	GERMAN GP	Nürburgring	9	Anglo American Racers	3.0 Eagle T1G-Weslake V12	driveshaft when 1st/FL
3	CANADIAN GP	Mosport Park	10	Anglo American Racers	3.0 Eagle T1G-Weslake V12	1 lap behind
ret	ITALIAN GP	Monza	8	Anglo American Racers	3.0 Eagle T1G-Weslake V12	engine
ret	US GP	Watkins Glen	11	Anglo American Racers	3.0 Eagle T1G-Weslake V12	suspension
ret	MEXICAN GP	Mexico City	11	Anglo American Racers	3.0 Eagle T1G-Weslake V12	damaged radiator

1968

ret	SOUTH AFRICAN GP	Kyalami	6	Anglo American Racers	3.0 Eagle T1G-Weslake V12	oil leak/overheating
ret	MONACO GP	Monte Carlo	19	Anglo American Racers	3.0 Eagle T1G-Weslake V12	ignition
ret	DUTCH GP	Zandvoort	18	Motor Racing Developments	3.0 Brabham BT24-Repco V8	sand in throttle slides
ret	BRITISH GP	Brands Hatch	24	Anglo American Racers	3.0 Eagle T1G-Weslake V12	fuel pump
9	GERMAN GP	Nürburgring	14	Anglo American Racers	3.0 Eagle T1G-Weslake V12	pit stop-cut tyre
ret	ITALIAN GP	Monza	21	Anglo American Racers	3.0 Eagle T1G-Weslake V12	oil pressure
ret	CANADIAN GP	St Jovite	11	Anglo American Racers	3.0 McLaren M7A-Cosworth V8	overheating-oil pressure
4	US GP	Watkins Glen	14	Anglo American Racers	3.0 McLaren M7A-Cosworth V8	1 lap behind
ret	MEXICAN GP	Mexico City	14	Anglo American Racers	3.0 McLaren M7A-Cosworth V8	rear suspension

1970

ret	DUTCH GP	Zandvoort	32	Bruce McLaren Motor Racing	3.0 McLaren M14A-Cosworth V8	timing gear
6	FRENCH GP	Clermont Ferrand	17	Bruce McLaren Motor Racing	3.0 McLaren M14A-Cosworth V8	
ret	BRITISH GP	Brands Hatch	10	Bruce McLaren Motor Racing	3.0 McLaren M14A-Cosworth V8	engine-overheating

GP Starts: 86   GP Wins: 4   Pole positions: 3   Fastest laps: 6   Points: 133

HUBERT HAHNE

With only a very few exceptions Hahne's racing career was spent racing cars made or powered by BMW. He built his reputation in 1964-66, racing the works BMW 1800Ti touring cars in the European championship. A fine second place in the F2 class in the 1966 German GP in a Matra then pointed Hahne in the direction of single-seaters and he became the non-graded works driver in the Lola-BMW for 1967 and a couple of races in 1968, when he returned to BMW tourers and also had the occasional Ford ride.

For 1969, Hubert was back with BMW's own F2 car, taking two second places at Hockenheim and a fourth in the Eifelrenen, although the season was marred by the death of Gerhard Mitter in practice for the German Grand Prix. He continued in F2 with BMW in 1970, winning the Rhine Cup race at Hockenheim, but had little other success. Taking delivery of a March 701 for the German Grand Prix at Hockenheim, he naturally expected to do well at his favourite circuit and there was much consternation when he failed to qualify the car. A disgruntled Hahne threatened legal action, contending that the car was delivered in an unraceworthy condition, but after this had been disproved by Ronnie Peterson in a subsequent test Hahne announced his retirement from racing.

MIKE HAILWOOD

Despite being the son of a brash millionaire, Mike Hailwood was totally without affectation and truly one of racing's 'nice guys'. He lived life to the full, but was nevertheless a dedicated sportsman who was undoubtedly one of motor cycle racing's greatest-ever exponents – many consider him the greatest of them all – and a fine all-round racing driver who missed out on ultimate success but still left a not inconsiderable mark on the four-wheeled sport.

By the age of 18 he was already a British motor cycle champion in four classes, winning his first World Championship in 1961. During the next six seasons Mike took a further eight World Championships in the 500 cc, 350 cc and 250 cc classes. His first taste of four-wheeled competition came in 1963, and with a couple of Junior races satisfactorily completed he joined the Reg Parnell team briefly in preparation for a full season the following year. He scored a World Championship point at Monaco in 1964 but felt uncomfortable in the Formula 1 environment, perhaps frustrated at being an also-ran in one category and the top dog in the other. He did a few more races for Parnell in 1965 before concentrating almost exclusively on bikes once more, though he did enjoy some winter sunshine racing sports cars, winning the 1966 Dickie Dale 3 Hours with David Hobbs in Bernard White's GT40.

With Honda having pulled out of Grand Prix motor cycle racing at the end of 1967, the sport was heading for a period of essentially privateer participation, so Mike turned to cars once again from the beginning of 1969. The newly inaugurated F5000 series provided an ideal base to rebuild his career, and in tandem he began a successful sports car programme, mainly for John Wyer, finishing third at Le Mans in 1969. In 1971 he joined forces with John Surtees to race his F5000 car, and benefited greatly from his guidance, taking second place in the series behind Frank Gardner. Late in the year, Surtees put Mike into his Formula 1 team for the Italian GP with startling results. In a great drive, Hailwood jousted for the lead in the four-car bunch which slipstreamed around the Monza circuit before finishing fourth.

Full of confidence, he lined up a massive programme with Surtees for 1972, undertaking the F2 Brazilian Torneio and F5000 Tasman series before the season proper had even started. A second place in the Race of Champions boded well for Formula 1, but Mike's luck was definitely out. In South Africa he put in an astounding drive to pressure Stewart before his suspension broke and at Monza he knew he had the opposition covered before the airbox blew off his Surtees. No one deserved a Grand Prix win more that year, but it was not to be. There was, however, the compensation of taking the European Formula 2 championship for Surtees with some excellent performances.

Unfortunately the progress made was not built upon in 1973, when unreliability beset the team to the extent that Mike failed to finish a single race in the points. In fact his season was best remembered for a typical act of bravery when he rescued Clay Regazzoni from his blazing car in South Africa to earn the George Medal. His only success came in endurance racing, when he shared the John Wyer Mirage with Derek Bell to win the Spa 1000 Km.

Frustrated at his lack of success at Surtees, Hailwood switched to McLaren in 1974, running a third works car in Yardley livery. Suddenly he was back in the frame, always running competitively until an accident at the German Grand Prix left him with such a badly broken leg that it was to spell the end of his Grand Prix career.

He announced his retirement in 1975, but after a couple of years kicking his heels 'Mike the Bike' was back. In a sensational return to the Isle of Man TT races in 1978, he won the Formula 1 race on a Ducati and in 1979 he was back again to smash the lap record and take the Senior TT on his Suzuki. There were no more comebacks, however, for in 1981 Mike lost his life in a tragic road accident when his car ran into a lorry executing an illegal U-turn across a dual carriageway after he had nipped out for a fish and chip family supper. The entire world of racing, on both two wheels and four, were united in their grief at the loss of one of motor sport's most popular and genuine sons.

HAHNE, Hubert (D) b 28/3/1935

1966

	Race	Circuit	No	Entrant	Car/Engine	Comment
9*	GERMAN GP (F2)	Nürburgring	26	Tyrrell Racing Organisation	1.0 Matra MS5-BRM 4	* 2nd in F2 class/1 lap behind

1967

ret	GERMAN GP	Nürburgring	17	Bayerische Motoren Werke	2.0 Lola T100-BMW 4	suspension

1968

10	GERMAN GP	Nürburgring	18	Bayerische Motoren Werke	2.0 Lola T108-BMW 4	

1969

dns	GERMAN GP (F2)	Nürburgring	23	Bayerische Motoren Werke	1.6 BMW T269-BMW 4	withdrawn after Mitter's accident

1970

dnq	GERMAN GP	Hockenheim	26	Hubert Hahne	3.0 March 701-Cosworth V8	

GP Starts: 3   GP Wins: 0   Pole positions: 0   Fastest laps: 0   Points: 0

HAILWOOD, Mike (GB) b 2/4/1940 – d 23/3/1981

1963

	Race	Circuit	No	Entrant	Car/Engine	Comment
8	BRITISH GP	Silverstone	20	Reg Parnell (Racing)	1.5 Lotus 24-Climax V8	4 laps behind
10	ITALIAN GP	Monza	40	Reg Parnell (Racing)	1.5 Lola 4-Climax V8	4 laps behind

1964

6	MONACO GP	Monte Carlo	18	Reg Parnell (Racing)	1.5 Lotus 25-BRM V8	4 laps behind
12/ret	DUTCH GP	Zandvoort	12	Reg Parnell (Racing)	1.5 Lotus 25-BRM V8	cwp
8	FRENCH GP	Rouen	6	Reg Parnell (Racing)	1.5 Lotus 25-BRM V8	1 lap behind
ret	BRITISH GP	Brands Hatch	14	Reg Parnell (Racing)	1.5 Lotus 25-BRM V8	oil pipe
ret	GERMAN GP	Nürburgring	15	Reg Parnell (Racing)	1.5 Lotus 25-BRM V8	engine
8	AUSTRIAN GP	Zeltweg	17	Reg Parnell (Racing)	1.5 Lotus 25-BRM V8	pit stop-suspension/10 laps behind
ret	ITALIAN GP	Monza	40	Reg Parnell (Racing)	1.5 Lotus 25-BRM V8	engine
8/ret	US GP	Watkins Glen	14	Reg Parnell (Racing)	1.5 Lotus 25-BRM V8	oil pipe/9 laps behind
ret	MEXICAN GP	Mexico City	14	Reg Parnell (Racing)	1.5 Lotus 25-BRM V8	overheating

1965

ret	MONACO GP	Monte Carlo	16	Reg Parnell (Racing)	1.5 Lotus 25-BRM V8	gearbox

1971

4	ITALIAN GP	Monza	9	Team Surtees	3.0 Surtees TS9-Cosworth V8	0.18 sec behind winner Gethin
15/ret	US GP	Watkins Glen	20	Team Surtees	3.0 Surtees TS9-Cosworth V8	spun on oil-hit barrier

1972

ret	SOUTH AFRICAN GP	Kyalami	17	Brooke Bond Oxo/Rob Walker/Team Surtees	3.0 Surtees TS9B-Cosworth V8	suspension when 2nd/FL
ret	SPANISH GP	Jarama	15	Brooke Bond Oxo/Rob Walker/Team Surtees	3.0 Surtees TS9B-Cosworth V8	master switch solenoid
ret	MONACO GP	Monte Carlo	11	Brooke Bond Oxo/Rob Walker/Team Surtees	3.0 Surtees TS9B-Cosworth V8	hit by Ganley
4	BELGIAN GP	Nivelles	34	Brooke Bond Oxo/Rob Walker/Team Surtees	3.0 Surtees TS9B-Cosworth V8	
6	FRENCH GP	Clermont Ferrand	26	Brooke Bond Oxo/Rob Walker/Team Surtees	3.0 Surtees TS9B-Cosworth V8	
ret	BRITISH GP	Brands Hatch	21	Brooke Bond Oxo/Rob Walker/Team Surtees	3.0 Surtees TS9B-Cosworth V8	gearbox
ret	GERMAN GP	Nürburgring	14	Brooke Bond Oxo/Rob Walker/Team Surtees	3.0 Surtees TS9B-Cosworth V8	suspension
4	AUSTRIAN GP	Österreichring	25	Brooke Bond Oxo/Rob Walker/Team Surtees	3.0 Surtees TS9B-Cosworth V8	
2	ITALIAN GP	Monza	10	Brooke Bond Oxo/Rob Walker/Team Surtees	3.0 Surtees TS9B-Cosworth V8	
17/ret	US GP	Watkins Glen	23	Brooke Bond Oxo/Rob Walker/Team Surtees	3.0 Surtees TS9B-Cosworth V8	collision with Beuttler/3 laps behind
dns	" " "	24T	Brooke Bond Oxo/Rob Walker/Team Surtees	3.0 Surtees TS14-Cosworth V8	practice only

1973

ret	ARGENTINE GP	Buenos Aires	26	Brooke Bond Oxo/Rob Walker/Team Surtees	3.0 Surtees TS14A-Cosworth V8	driveshaft
ret	BRAZILIAN GP	Interlagos	5	Brooke Bond Oxo/Rob Walker/Team Surtees	3.0 Surtees TS14A-Cosworth V8	gearbox
ret	SOUTH AFRICAN GP	Kyalami	10	Brooke Bond Oxo/Rob Walker/Team Surtees	3.0 Surtees TS14A-Cosworth V8	accident/saved Regazzoni
ret	SPANISH GP	Montjuich Park	9	Brooke Bond Oxo/Rob Walker/Team Surtees	3.0 Surtees TS14A-Cosworth V8	oil pipe
ret	BELGIAN GP	Zolder	23	Brooke Bond Oxo/Rob Walker/Team Surtees	3.0 Surtees TS14A-Cosworth V8	spun off
8	MONACO GP	Monte Carlo	26	Brooke Bond Oxo/Rob Walker/Team Surtees	3.0 Surtees TS14A-Cosworth V8	pit stop-puncture/3 laps behind
ret	SWEDISH GP	Anderstorp	26	Brooke Bond Oxo/Rob Walker/Team Surtees	3.0 Surtees TS14A-Cosworth V8	vibration caused by tyres
ret	FRENCH GP	Paul Ricard	26	Brooke Bond Oxo/Rob Walker/Team Surtees	3.0 Surtees TS14A-Cosworth V8	engine
ret	BRITISH GP	Silverstone	26	Brooke Bond Oxo/Rob Walker/Team Surtees	3.0 Surtees TS14A-Cosworth V8	accident-1st start/did not restart
ret	DUTCH GP	Zandvoort	26	Brooke Bond Oxo/Rob Walker/Team Surtees	3.0 Surtees TS14A-Cosworth V8	electrics
14	GERMAN GP	Nürburgring	26	Brooke Bond Oxo/Rob Walker/Team Surtees	3.0 Surtees TS14A-Cosworth V8	1 lap behind
10	AUSTRIAN GP	Österreichring	26	Brooke Bond Oxo/Rob Walker/Team Surtees	3.0 Surtees TS14A-Cosworth V8	pit stop-puncture/5 laps behind
7	ITALIAN GP	Monza	26	Brooke Bond Oxo/Rob Walker/Team Surtees	3.0 Surtees TS14A-Cosworth V8	
9	CANADIAN GP	Mosport Park	26	Brooke Bond Oxo/Rob Walker/Team Surtees	3.0 Surtees TS14A-Cosworth V8	2 laps behind
ret	US GP	Watkins Glen	26	Brooke Bond Oxo/Rob Walker/Team Surtees	3.0 Surtees TS14A-Cosworth V8	broken suspension

1974

4	ARGENTINE GP	Buenos Aires	33	Yardley Team McLaren	3.0 McLaren M23-Cosworth V8	
5	BRAZILIAN GP	Interlagos	33	Yardley Team McLaren	3.0 McLaren M23-Cosworth V8	1 lap behind
3	SOUTH AFRICAN GP	Kyalami	33	Yardley Team McLaren	3.0 McLaren M23-Cosworth V8	
9	SPANISH GP	Jarama	33	Yardley Team McLaren	3.0 McLaren M23-Cosworth V8	3 laps behind
7	BELGIAN GP	Nivelles	33	Yardley Team McLaren	3.0 McLaren M23-Cosworth V8	fuel starvation/1 lap behind
ret	MONACO GP	Monte Carlo	33	Yardley Team McLaren	3.0 McLaren M23-Cosworth V8	accident
ret	SWEDISH GP	Anderstorp	33	Yardley Team McLaren	3.0 McLaren M23-Cosworth V8	fuel line
4	DUTCH GP	Zandvoort	33	Yardley Team McLaren	3.0 McLaren M23-Cosworth V8	
7	FRENCH GP	Dijon	33	Yardley Team McLaren	3.0 McLaren M23-Cosworth V8	1 lap behind
ret	BRITISH GP	Brands Hatch	33	Yardley Team McLaren	3.0 McLaren M23-Cosworth V8	spun off-could not restart
15/ret	GERMAN GP	Nürburgring	33	Yardley Team McLaren	3.0 McLaren M23-Cosworth V8	accident-leg injuries/2 laps behind

GP Starts: 50   GP Wins: 0   Pole positions: 0   Fastest laps: 1   Points: 29

MIKA HÄKKINEN

Mika has always seemed bound for great things. With the benefit of long-term sponsorship and the guiding hand of Keke Rosberg, he has negotiated the slippery slope to the top in very short short order, and still shown the patience to bide his time when necessary.

A multiple karting champion in his native Finland, winner of three 1600 FF titles in 1987, and GM Vauxhall Lotus Series champion in 1988, Häkkinen had a pretty impressive C.V. to take into the 1989 Formula 3 season. Initially things went wrong. Having opted to stay with the Dragon team that had served him so well in 1988, he found himself way off the pace, but he persevered and when he switched to the WSR team for the prestigious Cellnet F3 race at the end of the season he promptly won it.

A deal was then concluded for 1990 and Mika never looked back, winning a total of 12 races at home and abroad. He took the British F3 championship, and before the year was out had a Formula 1 seat with Lotus. In his first season in Grand Prix racing, the confident young Finn impressed everyone with his car-control in a chassis that was never a match for the best, scoring points in only his third race. The following season, with a much better car, the team on the up and Ford HB engines, Mika firmly established himself in the top echelon, extracting the very maximum from the sleek Lotus 107.

Now came an unexpected chance that Häkkinen wisely grabbed. With Senna prevaricating over his contract at McLaren, Ron Dennis lost little time in signing Mika as cover in case the Brazilian should carry out his threat not to race. In the end Senna contested the full season, and Mika was left sitting on the sidelines, waiting patiently for his opportunity, which finally came when Michael Andretti headed back home. In his first race in Portugal, Mika out-qualified his master, and lay third until he ran wide and into the barrier. In his next race, in Japan, he was more circumspect, settling for a career-best third place in wildly fluctuating weather and track conditions.

For 1994, Häkkinen stands on the threshold of even greater success, leading the McLaren assault with Peugeot engines, and a first Grand Prix win at least must be a pretty safe bet.

BRUCE HALFORD

Despite limited experience gained with a Cooper-Bristol in 1956, Halford purchased the ex-Bira Maserati 250F but tasted success only in minor F1 races, his best placing being third at Caen in both 1957 and '58. By the following season, however, the car was long in the tooth and he turned to a Lister-Jaguar and a year of national sports car racing – which must certainly have sharpened up his driving, for he was a much improved performer when he returned to single-seaters in 1959 with a new Lotus 16, though his best result was a third in the Silver City Trophy race at Snetterton, guesting for the BRM team.

In 1960 Halford handled a Cooper with only moderate success, thereafter scaling down his racing activities.

With the new-found popularity of historic racing in the late seventies, Bruce returned to the circuits at the wheel of an immaculate Lotus 16 and enjoyed himself immensely in the friendly but fiercely competitive atmosphere.

JIM HALL

It is a pity that Jim Hall decided not to extend his season-long Grand Prix career and returned to the States, for he was undoubtedly a talented driver and could have gone much further in this sphere had he chosen to. As it was, Formula 1's loss was sports car racing's gain, for he would then set about building and racing a succession of just about the most exciting sports cars ever seen.

A multi-millionare teenager after the death of his parents in an air crash, Hall soon became involved with racing and exotic cars, teaming up with Carroll Shelby to run a Texas Maserati dealership until he went into the oil business in 1958, continuing to race in SCCA events.

Hall made an impressive GP debut at Riverside in 1960, lying fifth until last-lap gremlins intervened. This encouraged him to race a Lotus in 1961 and '62 – without success, although he finished fourth in the non-championship 1962 Mexican GP. His 1963 season with BRP was quite encouraging, Jim twice finishing in the points in GPs and taking fourth place in the Glover Trophy and sixth in the Lombank Trophy and at Solitude.

With the Formula 1 bug out of his system, Hall set about completing the task he and Hap Sharp had first undertaken in 1962, namely building an advanced automatic-transmission sports car. Immersed in the Chaparral's innovative design, Jim continued to drive, regularly clocking up wins and placings, and in 1965 the car dominated USRRC sports car racing in North America. From 1966, he concentrated his driving activities on Can-Am, generally leaving the long-distance programme to Hill, Bonnier and Spence until rule changes forced his Chaparral 2F out.

However, in the 1968 Stardust GP at Las Vegas, his Can-Am car ran into the back of a McLaren driven by Lothar Motschenbacher. The Chaparral flipped and was demolished, and Hall lay in hospital for nine weeks with multiple injuries. Apart from a couple of Trans-Am races in 1970, his racing career was over, but he continued to be involved with the sport throughout the seventies, collaborating with Carl Haas in F5000 before making a successful move to IndyCar racing, where his team is still competing.

HÄKKINEN, Mika (SF) b 28/9/1968

	Race	Circuit	No	Entrant	Car/Engine	Comment
	1991					
ret	US GP (PHOENIX)	Phoenix	11	Team Lotus	3.5 Lotus 102B-Judd V8	*engine*
9	BRAZILIAN GP	Interlagos	11	Team Lotus	3.5 Lotus 102B-Judd V8	*3 laps behind*
5	SAN MARINO GP	Imola	11	Team Lotus	3.5 Lotus 102B-Judd V8	*3 laps behind*
ret	MONACO GP	Monte Carlo	11	Team Lotus	3.5 Lotus 102B-Judd V8	*oil leak/caught fire*

ret	CANADIAN GP	Phoenix	11	Team Lotus	3.5 Lotus 102B-Judd V8	*spun off*
9	MEXICAN GP	Mexico City	11	Team Lotus	3.5 Lotus 102B-Judd V8	*2 laps behind*
dnq	FRENCH GP	Magny Cours	11	Team Lotus	3.5 Lotus 102B-Judd V8	
12	BRITISH GP	Silverstone	11	Team Lotus	3.5 Lotus 102B-Judd V8	*2 laps behind*
ret	GERMAN GP	Hockenheim	11	Team Lotus	3.5 Lotus 102B-Judd V8	*engine*
14	HUNGARIAN GP	Hungaroring	11	Team Lotus	3.5 Lotus 102B-Judd V8	*3 laps behind*
ret	BELGIAN GP	Spa	11	Team Lotus	3.5 Lotus 102B-Judd V8	*engine*
14	ITALIAN GP	Monza	11	Team Lotus	3.5 Lotus 102B-Judd V8	*4 laps behind*
14	PORTUGUESE GP	Estoril	11	Team Lotus	3.5 Lotus 102B-Judd V8	*3 laps behind*
ret	SPANISH GP	Barcelona	11	Team Lotus	3.5 Lotus 102B-Judd V8	*spun off*
ret	JAPANESE GP	Suzuka	11	Team Lotus	3.5 Lotus 102B-Judd V8	*spun off*
19	AUSTRALIAN GP	Adelaide	11	Team Lotus	3.5 Lotus 102B-Judd V8	*1 lap behind/race stopped 14 laps*

1992

9	SOUTH AFRICAN GP	Kyalami	11	Team Lotus	3.5 Lotus102D-Ford HB V8	*2 laps behind*
6	MEXICAN GP	Mexico City	11	Team Lotus	3.5 Lotus102D-Ford HB V8	*1 lap behind*
10	BRAZILIAN GP	Interlagos	11	Team Lotus	3.5 Lotus102D-Ford HB V8	*4 laps behind*
ret	SPANISH GP	Barcelona	11	Team Lotus	3.5 Lotus102D-Ford HB V8	*spun off*
dnq	SAN MARINO GP	Imola	11	Team Lotus	3.5 Lotus102D-Ford HB V8	
ret	MONACO GP	Monte Carlo	11	Team Lotus	3.5 Lotus107-Ford HB V8	*clutch*
dns	"	" "	11	Team Lotus	3.5 Lotus107-Ford HB V8	*practice only*
ret	CANADIAN GP	Montreal	11	Team Lotus	3.5 Lotus107-Ford HB V8	*gearbox*
4*	FRENCH GP	Magny Cours	11	Team Lotus	3.5 Lotus107-Ford HB V8	** aggregate of two parts/1 lap behind*
6	BRITISH GP	Silverstone	11	Team Lotus	3.5 Lotus107-Ford HB V8	
ret	GERMAN GP	Hockenheim	11	Team Lotus	3.5 Lotus107-Ford HB V8	*engine*
4	HUNGARIAN GP	Hungaroring	11	Team Lotus	3.5 Lotus107-Ford HB V8	
6	BELGIAN GP	Spa	11	Team Lotus	3.5 Lotus107-Ford HB V8	
ret	ITALIAN GP	Monza	11	Team Lotus	3.5 Lotus107-Ford HB V8	*electrics*
5	PORTUGUESE GP	Estoril	11	Team Lotus	3.5 Lotus107-Ford HB V8	*1 lap behind*
ret	JAPANESE GP	Suzuka	11	Team Lotus	3.5 Lotus107-Ford HB V8	*engine*
7	AUSTRALIAN GP	Adelaide	11	Team Lotus	3.5 Lotus107-Ford HB V8	*1 lap behind*

1993

ret	PORTUGUESE GP	Estoril	7	Marlboro McLaren	3.5 McLaren MP4/8-Ford HB V8	*accident-crashed into barrier*
3	JAPANESE GP	Suzuka	7	Marlboro McLaren	3.5 McLaren MP4/8-Ford HB V8	
ret	AUSTRALIAN GP	Adelaide	7	Marlboro McLaren	3.5 McLaren MP4/8-Ford HB V8	*brakes*

GP Starts: 33   GP Wins: 0   Pole positions: 0   Fastest laps: 0   Points: 17

HALFORD, Bruce (GB) b 18/5/1931

1956

	Race	Circuit	No	Entrant	Car/Engine	Comment
ret	BRITISH GP	Silverstone	29	Bruce Halford	2.5 Maserati 250F 6	*engine*
dsq	GERMAN GP	Nürburgring	21	Bruce Halford	2.5 Maserati 250F 6	*push start after a spin*
ret	ITALIAN GP	Monza	48	Bruce Halford	2.5 Maserati 250F 6	*engine*

1957

11	GERMAN GP	Nürburgring	15	Bruce Halford	2.5 Maserati 250F 6	*1 lap behind*
ret	PESCARA GP	Pescara	20	Bruce Halford	2.5 Maserati 250F 6	*differential*
ret	ITALIAN GP	Monza	16	Bruce Halford	2.5 Maserati 250F 6	*engine*

1959

ret	MONACO GP	Monte Carlo	44	John Fisher	1.5 Lotus 16-Climax 4	*accident with Allison and von Trips*

1960

dnq	MONACO GP	Monte Carlo	12	Fred Tuck Cars	2.5 Cooper T51-Climax 4	
8/ret	FRENCH GP	Reims	48	Yeoman Credit Racing Team	2.5 Cooper T51-Climax 4	*engine*

GP Starts: 8   GP Wins: 0   Pole positions: 0   Fastest laps: 0   Points: 0

HALL, Jim (USA) b 23/7/1935

1960

	Race	Circuit	No	Entrant	Car/Engine	Comment
7	US GP	Riverside	24	Jim Hall	2.5 Lotus 18-Climax 4	*2 laps behind*

1961

ret	US GP	Watkins Glen	17	Jim Hall	1.5 Lotus 18/21-Climax 4	*fuel leak*

1962

dns	US GP	Watkins Glen	25	Jim Hall	1.5 Lotus 21-Climax 4	*dropped valve on grid*

1963

ret	MONACO GP	Monte Carlo	12	British Racing Partnership	1.5 Lotus 24-BRM V8	*gearbox*
ret	BELGIAN GP	Spa	5	British Racing Partnership	1.5 Lotus 24-BRM V8	*accident in rain*
8	DUTCH GP	Zandvoort	42	British Racing Partnership	1.5 Lotus 24-BRM V8	*3 laps behind*
11	FRENCH GP	Reims	34	British Racing Partnership	1.5 Lotus 24-BRM V8	*pit stop/8 laps behind*
6	BRITISH GP	Silverstone	12	British Racing Partnership	1.5 Lotus 24-BRM V8	*2 laps behind*
5	GERMAN GP	Nürburgring	20	British Racing Partnership	1.5 Lotus 24-BRM V8	*1 lap behind*
8	ITALIAN GP	Monza	30	British Racing Partnership	1.5 Lotus 24-BRM V8	*2 laps behind*
10/ret	US GP	Watkins Glen	16	British Racing Partnership	1.5 Lotus 24-BRM V8	*gearbox*
8	MEXICAN GP	Mexico City	16	British Racing Partnership	1.5 Lotus 24-BRM V8	*4 laps behind*

GP Starts: 11   GP Wins: 0   Pole positions: 0   Fastest laps: 0   Points: 0

HAMILTON, Duncan (GB) b 30/4/1920

1951

	Race	Circuit	No	Entrant	Car/Engine	Comment
12	BRITISH GP	Silverstone	18	Duncan Hamilton	4.5 Lago-Talbot T26C 6	9 laps behind
ret	GERMAN GP	Nürburgring	88	Duncan Hamilton	4.5 Lago-Talbot T26C 6	oil pressure

1952

ret	BRITISH GP	Silverstone	30	HW Motors Ltd	2.0 HWM-Alta 4	engine
7	DUTCH GP	Zandvoort	28	HW Motors Ltd	2.0 HWM-Alta 4	5 laps behind

1953

ret	BRITISH GP	Silverstone	3	HW Motors Ltd	2.0 HWM-Alta 4	clutch

GP Starts: 5 GP Wins: 0 Pole positions: 0 Fastest laps: 0 Points: 0

HAMPSHIRE, David (GB) b 29/12/1917 – d 1990

1950

	Race	Circuit	No	Entrant	Car/Engine	Comment
9	BRITISH GP	Silverstone	6	Scuderia Ambrosiana	1.5 s/c Maserati 4CLT/48 4	6 laps behind
ret	FRENCH GP	Reims	34	Scuderia Ambrosiana	1.5 s/c Maserati 4CLT/48 4	engine

GP Starts: 2 GP Wins: 0 Pole positions: 0 Fastest laps: 0 Points: 0

HANSGEN, Walt (USA) b 28/10/1919 – d 7/4/1966

1961

	Race	Circuit	No	Entrant	Car/Engine	Comment
ret	US GP	Watkins Glen	60	Momo Corporation	1.5 Cooper T53-Climax 4	accident

1964

5	US GP	Watkins Glen	17	Team Lotus	1.5 Lotus 33-Climax V8	3 laps behind

GP Starts: 2 GP Wins: 0 Pole positions: 0 Fastest laps: 0 Points: 2

HARRIS, Mike (ZA) b 25/5/1939

1962

	Race	Circuit	No	Entrant	Car/Engine	Comment
ret	SOUTH AFRICAN GP	East London	22	Mike Harris	1.5 Cooper T53-Alfa Romeo 4	big end bearings

GP Starts: 1 GP Wins: 0 Pole positions: 0 Fastest laps: 0 Points: 0

HARRISON, Cuth (GB) b 6/7/1906 – d 22/1/1981

1950

	Race	Circuit	No	Entrant	Car/Engine	Comment
7	BRITISH GP	Silverstone	11	Cuth Harrison	1.5 s/c ERA B Type 6	3 laps behind
ret	MONACO GP	Monte Carlo	24	Cuth Harrison	1.5 s/c ERA B Type 6	multiple accident
ret	ITALIAN GP	Monza	32	Cuth Harrison	1.5 s/c ERA B Type 6	engine

GP Starts: 3 GP Wins: 0 Pole positions: 0 Fastest laps: 0 Points: 0

HART, Brian (GB) b 7/9/1936

1967

	Race	Circuit	No	Entrant	Car/Engine	Comment
12	GERMAN GP (F2)	Nürburgring	25	Ron Harris	1.6 Protos-Cosworth 4	4th in F2 class/3 laps behind

GP Starts: 1 GP Wins: 0 Pole positions: 0 Fastest laps: 0 Points: 0

HASEMI, Masahiro (J) b 13/11/1945

1976

	Race	Circuit	No	Entrant	Car/Engine	Comment
11	JAPANESE GP	Mount Fuji	51	Kojima Engineering	3.0 Kojima KE007-Cosworth V8	pit stop-tyres/FL/7 laps behind

GP Starts: 1 GP Wins: 0 Pole positions: 0 Fastest laps: 1 Points: 0

HAWKINS, Paul (AUS) b 12/10/1937 – d 26/5/1969

1965

	Race	Circuit	No	Entrant	Car/Engine	Comment
9	SOUTH AFRICAN GP	East London	18	John Willment Automobiles	1.5 Brabham BT10-Ford 4	4 laps behind
10/ret	MONACO GP	Monte Carlo	10	DW Racing Enterprises	1.5 Lotus 33-Climax V8	crashed into harbour/21 laps behind
ret	GERMAN GP	Nürburgring	22	DW Racing Enterprises	1.5 Lotus 33-Climax V8	oil pipe

GP Starts: 3 GP Wins: 0 Pole positions: 0 Fastest laps: 0 Points: 0

WALT HANSGEN

One of the greatest American sports car drivers of the 1950s, Hansgen built a mighty reputation with his own Jaguar XK120, before racing a D-Type for Briggs Cunningham from 1956. In 1958 he visited Britain to take delivery of a Lister-Jaguar, which he raced briefly before returning home to campaign the car with great success.

In the early 1960s Walt undertook occasional single-seater drives, earning fifth place at Watkins Glen in 1964 in a Lotus with a steady drive, and finishing 12th at Indianapolis the same year.

But it was in sports cars that Hansgen really shone, taking victories in a wide variety of machines including a Cooper-Monaco, before racing John Mecom's stable of cars which boasted a Ferrari 250LM, a Lotus 19, a Scarab Chevrolet and a Lola T70.

Hansgen began 1966 sharing the Ford MkII with his protégé Mark Donohue, taking third at Daytona and second at Sebring, but he was killed when he crashed the car in the Le Mans 24 Hours test weekend in April 1966.

DUNCAN HAMILTON

A larger-than-life character, this former RAF pilot manged to get hold of a Lago-Talbot which he raced during the 1951 season and later in Libre events, before having a handful of outings in an HWM.

However, his greatest moments came in sports car racing with a Jaguar D-Type. He won Le Mans in 1953, the Coupe de Paris in '54 and '56 and the 1956 Reims 12 Hours as well as taking many excellent placings elsewhere.

After the death of his close friend Mike Hawthorn in 1959, Duncan immediately retired from racing to concentrate on his successful garage business.

CUTH HARRISON

T C (Cuth) Harrison was an extremely enthusiastic amateur driver who raced an ERA C-Type – mainly in national events, where his duels with Bob Gerard were lively indeed, but also occasionally on the Continent, finishing sixth in the 1949 Italian GP. The 1950 season, his last with the car, brought no success in Grands Prix, but he did finish second in the British Empire Trophy in the Isle of Man, before concentrating on his garage business in Sheffield and returning to trials with an 1172 cc Harford, with which he was the 1952 RAC champion.

BRIAN HART

For the past two decades, Brian has been designing and building racing engines for Formula 2 and then Formula 1, with the Toleman, RAM and Jordan teams among his customers, but long before that he had enjoyed a worthy career as a driver. Between in 1958 and 1963, Hart scored numerous wins in Formula Junior and sports car events with Lotus and Terrier chassis, taking third place in the Grovewood Awards for 1963.

Moving up to Formula 2, Brian gained an almost immediate victory in the Pergusa GP, driving a Ron Harris-entered Lotus, and although he stepped back into Formula 3 in 1966, he was to become an F2 mainstay, mostly racing for Bob Gerard, for whom he won the 1969 Rhine Cup race at Hockenheim after a great drive. As his flourishing engine business grew, Hart inevitably found less time to go racing and he eventually retired at the end of 1971.

MASAHIRO HASEMI

A former motocross rider, Hasemi turned to cars with a Nissan Bluebird, and has since earned a reputation as one of Japan's finest drivers, having been a multiple champion in touring cars, Formula 2, Formula Pacific and elsewhere.

He caused a stir with the locally built Kojima on his only GP appearance in 1976. Benefiting from special Dunlop wet-weather tyres, Hasemi set fastest lap in the pouring rain before they – and his challenge – faded.

He has often been seen outside Japan as a member of the Nissan sports-prototype team, competing regularly at Le Mans.

PAUL HAWKINS

'Hawkeye' was another of those tough Aussies who came to Britain in the early sixties with no money, but plenty of determination to further their racing career and the willingness to graft ceaselessly to achieve their goal.

He found employment in the Healey factory in 1960, with an opportunity to race their Sprites. This led to two happy seasons with Ian Walker's sports car and Formula Junior team, before he was tempted to join John Willment in 1964 to race all sorts of cars, taking an aggregate second place in the Rand GP and winning the Rhodesian GP in an F2 Brabham, the same car that he used to make his GP debut in South Africa in 1965.

Back in Europe, Paul had an unproductive time in Dickie Stoop's Lotus 33, which he spectacularly crashed into the harbour at Monaco, but he won the F2 Eifelrennen in an Alexis. Apart from a few F1 races with Tim Parnell early in 1966, Hawkins turned his attention to sports cars, which offered him a better opportunity to show his talent. Racing his own Ford GT40, he achieved numerous excellent wins and countless placings during 1967 and '68, with his trips to South Africa proving particularly fruitful, and was also in demand by the top sports car teams of the period as a freelance, winning the 1967 Targa Florio for Porche and the 1967 Paris 1000 Km and the 1968 Monza 1000Km for John Wyer.

With his Lola T70 run from the factory, 'Hawkeye' embarked on a season of sports car racing in 1969 and it was a terrible loss for the sport when this no-nonsense character lost his life after crashing into a tree during the Tourist Trophy race at Oulton Park.

MIKE HAWTHORN

Blond and debonair, Hawthorn was in the vanguard of the new wave of English talent which came to the fore in Grand Prix racing in the early fifties, and to himfell the signal honour of becoming Great Britain's first-ever World Champion driver.

His rise was meteoric, Mike winning a championship Grand Prix barely two years after his circuit racing debut in a Riley in 1951. During that first full season he won the Leinster Trophy and the Ulster Handicap as well as the Brooklands Memorial Trophy for his consistent successes throughout the year at Goodwood, and for 1952 he took delivery of one of the new Cooper-Bristols, which had been purchased for him by a family friend, Bob Chase. The team would be run by his father Leslie. The season started well with F2 and Libre wins at the Goodwood Easter meeting before he headed for the Continent and fourth place on his Grand Prix debut at Spa. Certainly the car was quite useful, but Mike coaxed far, far more from it than anyone else with his uninhibited driving.

A minor meeting at Boreham saw a fantastic display of his ability. In pouring rain he left the great Villoresi floundering in his 4.5-litre Ferrari until the track dried and the little Cooper was overhauled. The Italian went back to Italy to report to Ferrari that he had unearthed a new British star. Arriving at Modena for the late-season Grand Prix, Mike was invited to drive for the Scuderia in 1953, and had plenty of time to consider the offer as he crashed the Cooper in practice and found himself hospitalised. He duly joined Ferrari's star-studded line up and wisely took thing easy to begin with, watching and learning from his more experienced team-mates.

It was to be a magnificent first season for the Englishman abroad, and he finished every championship Grand Prix bar one in the points, the highlight being a glorious victory, over Fangio no less, in the French GP at Reims after a wheel-to-wheel battle to the flag. Beyond the World Championship, Hawthorn won the International Trophy and the Ulster Trophy at Dundrod, while in sports cars he took the Spa 24 Hours with Farina, his achievements earning him a BRDC Gold Star. The 1954 season began badly when he crashed at Syracuse and received serious burns to his arms and legs, and there was then a furore over his exemption from National Service due to a kidney ailment, followed by the death of his father in road accident. Mike decided that it would be impossible to run the family garage business if he stayed at Maranello so, after signing off with a win at Pedralbes, he looked forward to racing for Vanwall in 1955, but the new car needed development and Mike was seriously unimpressed with the disarray of Vandervell's organisation. Even in victory he was followed by controversy, for when he won the Le Mans 24 Hours for Jaguar with Ivor Bueb he found the finger of blame pointed towards him as the unwitting instigator of the tragedy which killed more than eighty people. Some semblance of order was restored with an end-of-season return to Ferrari by way of the Lancia team which they had just taken over, and a splendid drive for Jaguar in the Tourist Trophy.

His desire to honour his contract with the sports car team for 1956 meant Mike had to join BRM for Formula 1, and the cars' unreliability restricted him to just a handful of outings. Hawthorn decided that for success he must drive for an Italian team, and he was welcomed back to Ferrari to drive alongside his great mate Peter Collins. The atmosphere, so strained in 1956, was completely changed with Mike's return and soon he was back to his consistent best. The magnificent Fangio bestrode the 1957 season in his Maserati, but when the Argentinian retired early in 1958 the title was there to be taken. Ironically the threat to Ferrari came from Vanwall, who had been so shambolic during Mike's brief tenure as a driver. He paced himself brilliantly, taking risks when necessary but making sure that he finished at all costs. The death of Collins in the German GP hit him very hard and, with Musso and Lewis-Evans also having lost their lives that year, Hawthorn, newly crowned as World Champion, announced his retirement.

Mike was planning both marriage and an expansion of his garage business when, on a rainy January morning in 1959, he lost control of his potent Jaguar near Guildford and was killed instantly when it wrapped itself around a tree.

BOY HAYJE

A former saloon car racer and Dutch Formula Ford champion, and a protégé of Toine Hezemans, Boy raced the ex-James Hunt March 731 in F5000 in 1975 without realising much by way of results, and thus switched to Formula 3 in 1976, a year which saw him make a promising GP debut at Zandvoort.

With backing from his loyal sponsors, Hayje secured a seat in the RAM March team for 1977, a move which was to prove disastrous for all concerned, the Dutchman departing abruptly following his non-qualification at his home Grand Prix. He then took his backing to Fred Opert in Formula 2 for 1978, again with little reward.

Thereafter Hayje perhaps found his true level and success came his way at last, racing in the European Renault 5 turbo championship.

HAWTHORN, Mike (GB) b 10/4/1929 – d 22/1/1959

1952

	Race	Circuit	No	Entrant	Car/Engine	Comment
4	BELGIAN GP	Spa	8	L D Hawthorn	2.0 Cooper T20-Bristol 6	2 pit stops-fuel leak/1 lap behind
ret	FRENCH GP	Rouen	42	A H M Bryde	2.0 Cooper T20-Bristol 6	ignition
3	BRITISH GP	Silverstone	9	L D Hawthorn	2.0 Cooper T20-Bristol 6	2 laps behind
4	DUTCH GP	Zandvoort	32	L D Hawthorn	2.0 Cooper T20-Bristol 6	2 laps behind
nc	ITALIAN GP	Monza	42	L D Hawthorn	2.0 Cooper T20-Bristol 6	long pit stop-magneto/38 laps behind

1953

	Race	Circuit	No	Entrant	Car/Engine	Comment
4	ARGENTINE GP	Buenos Aires	16	Scuderia Ferrari	2.0 Ferrari 500 4	1 lap behind
4	DUTCH GP	Zandvoort	8	Scuderia Ferrari	2.0 Ferrari 500 4	1 lap behind
6	BELGIAN GP	Spa	14	Scuderia Ferrari	2.0 Ferrari 500 4	1 lap behind
1	FRENCH GP	Reims	16	Scuderia Ferrari	2.0 Ferrari 500 4	
5	BRITISH GP	Silverstone	8	Scuderia Ferrari	2.0 Ferrari 500 4	spin-pit stop/3 laps behind
3	GERMAN GP	Nürburgring	3	Scuderia Ferrari	2.0 Ferrari 500 4	
3	SWISS GP	Bremgarten	26	Scuderia Ferrari	2.0 Ferrari 500 4	
4	ITALIAN GP	Monza	8	Scuderia Ferrari	2.0 Ferrari 500 4	1 lap behind

1954

	Race	Circuit	No	Entrant	Car/Engine	Comment
dsq	ARGENTINE GP	Buenos Aires	14	Scuderia Ferrari	2.5 Ferrari 625 4	push start after spin
4*	BELGIAN GP	Spa	10	Scuderia Ferrari	2.5 Ferrari 625 4	exhaust fumes/*Gonzalez took over
ret	FRENCH GP	Reims	6	Scuderia Ferrari	2.5 Ferrari 553/555 4	engine
2	BRITISH GP	Silverstone	11	Scuderia Ferrari	2.5 Ferrari 625/555 4	FL
ret	GERMAN GP	Nürburgring	3	Scuderia Ferrari	2.5 Ferrari 625/555 4	engine
2*	"	"	1	Scuderia Ferrari	2.5 Ferrari 625/555 4	*took over Gonzalez's car
ret	SWISS GP	Bremgarten	22	Scuderia Ferrari	2.5 Ferrari 625/555 4	fuel pump
2	ITALIAN GP	Monza	40	Scuderia Ferrari	2.5 Ferrari 625/555 4	1 lap behind
1	SPANISH GP	Pedralbes	38	Scuderia Ferrari	2.5 Ferrari 553 4	

1955

	Race	Circuit	No	Entrant	Car/Engine	Comment
ret	MONACO GP	Monte Carlo	18	Vandervell Products Ltd	2.5 Vanwall 4	throttle linkage
ret	BELGIAN GP	Spa	40	Vandervell Products Ltd	2.5 Vanwall 4	gearbox
7	DUTCH GP	Zandvoort	2	Scuderia Ferrari	2.5 Ferrari 555 4	pit stop/3 laps behind
dns	"	"	2	Scuderia Ferrari	2.5 Ferrari 625 4	practice only
6*	BRITISH GP	Aintree	16	Scuderia Ferrari	2.5 Ferrari 625/555 4	* unwell-Castellotti took over/-3 laps
ret	ITALIAN GP	Monza	6	Scuderia Ferrari	2.5 Ferrari 555 4	gearbox mounting
dns	"	"	T	Scuderia Ferrari	2.5 Lancia D50 V8	practice only-did not fit well in car

1956

	Race	Circuit	No	Entrant	Car/Engine	Comment
3	ARGENTINE GP	Buenos Aires	14	Owen Racing Organisation	2.5 Maserati 250F 6	2 laps behind
dns	MONACO GP	Monte Carlo	10	Owen Racing Organisation	2.5 BRM P25 4	engine problems in practice
10*	FRENCH GP	Reims	24	Vandervell Products Ltd	2.5 Vanwall 4	* Schell took over/5 laps behind
ret	BRITISH GP	Silverstone	23	Owen Racing Organisation	2.5 BRM P25 4	oil leak

1957

	Race	Circuit	No	Entrant	Car/Engine	Comment
ret	ARGENTINE GP	Buenos Aires	16	Scuderia Ferrari	2.5 Lancia-Ferrari D50A V8	clutch
ret	MONACO GP	Monte Carlo	28	Scuderia Ferrari	2.5 Lancia-Ferrari D50A V8	accident with Moss and Collins
7/ret	"	"	24	Scuderia Ferrari	2.5 Lancia-Ferrari 801 V8	shared with Trips/engine/-5 laps
4	FRENCH GP	Rouen	14	Scuderia Ferrari	2.5 Lancia-Ferrari D50A V8	1 lap behind
3	BRITISH GP	Aintree	10	Scuderia Ferrari	2.5 Lancia-Ferrari 801 V8	
2	GERMAN GP	Nürburgring	8	Scuderia Ferrari	2.5 Lancia-Ferrari 801 V8	
6	ITALIAN GP	Monza	34	Scuderia Ferrari	2.5 Lancia-Ferrari 801 V8	pit stop-oil pipe/4 laps behind

1958 World Champion Driver

	Race	Circuit	No	Entrant	Car/Engine	Comment
3	ARGENTINE GP	Buenos Aires	20	Scuderia Ferrari	2.4 Ferrari Dino 246 V6	
ret	MONACO GP	Monte Carlo	38	Scuderia Ferrari	2.4 Ferrari Dino 246 V6	fuel pump/FL
5	DUTCH GP	Zandvoort	5	Scuderia Ferrari	2.4 Ferrari Dino 246 V6	1 lap behind
2	BELGIAN GP	Spa	16	Scuderia Ferrari	2.4 Ferrari Dino 246 V6	Pole/FL
1	FRENCH GP	Reims	4	Scuderia Ferrari	2.4 Ferrari Dino 246 V6	Pole/FL
2	BRITISH GP	Silverstone	2	Scuderia Ferrari	2.4 Ferrari Dino 246 V6	FL
ret	GERMAN GP	Nürburgring	3	Scuderia Ferrari	2.4 Ferrari Dino 246 V6	clutch/Pole
2	PORTUGUESE GP	Oporto	22	Scuderia Ferrari	2.4 Ferrari Dino 246 V6	FL
2	ITALIAN GP	Monza	14	Scuderia Ferrari	2.4 Ferrari Dino 246 V6	
2	MOROCCAN GP	Casablanca	6	Scuderia Ferrari	2.4 Ferrari Dino 246 V6	Pole

GP Starts: 45   GP Wins: 3   Pole positions: 4   Fastest laps: 6   Points: 127.64

HAYJE, Boy (NL) b 3/5/1949

1976

	Race	Circuit	No	Entrant	Car/Engine	Comment
ret	DUTCH GP	Zandvoort	39	F & S Properties	3.0 Penske PC3-Cosworth V8	driveshaft

1977

	Race	Circuit	No	Entrant	Car/Engine	Comment
ret	SOUTH AFRICAN GP	Kyalami	33	RAM Racing/F & S Properties	3.0 March 761-Cosworth V8	gearbox
dnq	SPANISH GP	Jarama	33	RAM Racing/F & S Properties	3.0 March 761-Cosworth V8	
dnq	MONACO GP	Monte Carlo	33	RAM Racing/F & S Properties	3.0 March 761-Cosworth V8	
nc	BELGIAN GP	Zolder	33	RAM Racing/F & S Properties	3.0 March 761-Cosworth V8	7 laps behind
dnq	SWEDISH GP	Anderstorp	33	RAM Racing/F & S Properties	3.0 March 761-Cosworth V8	
dnq	DUTCH GP	Zandvoort	33	RAM Racing/F & S Properties	3.0 March 761-Cosworth V8	

GP Starts: 3   GP Wins: 0   Pole positions: 0   Fastest laps: 0   Points: 0

HEEKS, Willi (D) b 13/2/1922

	1952					
	Race	Circuit	No	Entrant	Car/Engine	Comment
ret	GERMAN GP	Nürburgring	123	Willi Heeks	2.0 AFM U8-BMW 6	
	1953					
ret	GERMAN GP	Nürburgring	23	Willi Heeks	2.0 Veritas Meteor 6	

GP Starts: 2   GP Wins: 0   Pole positions: 0   Fastest laps: 0   Points: 0

HELFRICH, Theo (D) b 13/5/1913 – d 29/4/1978

	1952					
	Race	Circuit	No	Entrant	Car/Engine	Comment
ret	GERMAN GP	Nürburgring	122	Theo Helfrich	2.0 Veritas RS 6	
	1953					
12	GERMAN GP	Nürburgring	24	Theo Helfrich	2.0 Veritas RS 6	1 lap behind
	1954					
ret	GERMAN GP	Nürburgring	22	Hans Klenk	2.0 Klenk Meteor-BMW 6	engine

GP Starts: 3   GP Wins: 0   Pole positions: 0   Fastest laps: 0   Points: 0

BRIAN HENTON

Career setbacks that would have seen a less determined character throw in the towel only seemed to encourage this tough, no-nonsense driver to get stuck in once more and prove his critics wrong. With three seasons of Formula Vee and Super Vee racing behind him, Brian took the plunge into F3 – initially with his own GRD before a move into the works March F3 team for 1974 really put him on the map. Easily winning the Lombard and Forward Trust championships, he graduated to Formula 2 and a brief salutary stint with Lotus. This was followed by an abortive 1976 season after a planned drive with Tom Wheatcroft foundered after just one race, and Henton had to start all over again.

His patriotic private F1 March got him back on the F1 grid, but he soon ran out of funds, so it was back to Formula 2 for 1978, Brian enjoying some success in his own car, and 1979, when he finished a close second to Marc Surer in the championship, winning at Mugello and Misano. With BP and Toleman behind him, Henton made no mistake the following year, taking the title and re-establishing himself as a serious proposition once more.

Brian had certainly earned his move back into Grands Prix with Toleman, but the season was another major disappointment, the underdeveloped car beset by turbo problems. Henton could have been sunk without trace, but he managed to find a seat for 1982, first with Arrows, deputising for the injured Surer, and then at Tyrrell in place of the Williams-bound Daly. He did a solid job, nearly making the points, and was credited with fastest lap at Brands Hatch, but it was not enough for Tyrrell to retain him. A one-off drive into fourth place for Theodore in the 1983 Race of Champions rounded off a career which eventually failed to meet Henton's expectations, but it wasn't for want of trying.

JOHNNY HERBERT

Perhaps Britain's most talented young prospect of the eighties, Johnny Herbert has established himself as one of the best of a group of young Grand Prix pretenders waiting for their first Grand Prix win, yet one wonders if the horrific crash at Brands Hatch in 1988 which interrupted his meteoric rise somehow robbed his career of an impetus which might otherwise have seen him a regular winner by now.

Racing in karts from the age of ten, Herbert worked his way through the classes, taking numerous championships on the way, before graduating to FF1600, winning the prestigious Brands Hatch Formula Ford Festival in 1985. Johnny's path then crossed that of Eddie Jordan, who took him into Formula 3 in 1987. Herbert won the title and a Benetton test, which led to an option to drive for the team in 1989, so it was a season of F3000 next, which started brilliantly with a win at Jerez, followed by a number of highly competititive drives before that fateful Brands accident.

Johnny had the goal of reaching the grid in Brazil to make his debut for Benetton, and after months of painful rehabilitation he not only drove in Rio, but brought the car into fourth place. But as the year progressed it became clear that he was still handicapped by his injuries, and he was summarily replaced by the less talented Pirro. Now came a period when Johnny had to step down into Japanese F3000, take the occasional F1 ride, and wait for another chance (an unexpected victory at Le Mans with Mazda in 1991 providing a highlight). Luckily his old mentor at Benetton, Peter Collins, was now busy reviving the fortunes of Lotus, and Herbert was very much the man he wanted for the job. Brought back into the team full time early in 1991, Herbert has shown he has the talent to win but, unfortunately, not yet the car. Such are the vagaries of motor racing that Damon Hill, his old sparring partner in F3, is now regarded as Britain's top driver, a position that Herbert will be hoping to challenge in 1994, as he begins yet another season with Lotus.

HENTON, Brian (GB) b 19/9/1946

1975

	Race	Circuit	No	Entrant	Car/Engine	Comment
16/ret	BRITISH GP	Silverstone	15	John Player Team Lotus	3.0 Lotus 72E-Cosworth V8	crashed in rainstorm/3 laps behind
dns	AUSTRIAN GP	Österreichring	6	John Player Team Lotus	3.0 Lotus 72E-Cosworth V8	accident in practice
nc	US GP	Watkins Glen	6	John Player Team Lotus	3.0 Lotus 72E-Cosworth V8	pit stop/10 laps behind

1977

	Race	Circuit	No	Entrant	Car/Engine	Comment
10	US GP WEST	Long Beach	10	Team Rothmans International	3.0 March 761B-Cosworth V8	3 laps behind
dnq	SPANISH GP	Jarama	38	British Formula One Racing Team	3.0 March 761B-Cosworth V8	
dnq	BRITISH GP	Silverstone	38	British Formula One Racing Team	3.0 March 761B-Cosworth V8	
dnq	AUSTRIAN GP	Österreichring	38	British Formula One Racing Team	3.0 March 761B-Cosworth V8	
dsq	DUTCH GP	Zandvoort	38	HB Bewaking Alarm Systems	3.0 Boro/Ensign N175-Cosworth V8	push start after spin
dnq	ITALIAN GP	Monza	38	HB Bewaking Alarm Systems	3.0 Boro/Ensign N175-Cosworth V8	

1978

	Race	Circuit	No	Entrant	Car/Engine	Comment
dns	AUSTRIAN GP	Österreichring	18	Team Surtees	3.0 Surtees TS20-Cosworth V8	tried Keegan's car in practice

1981

	Race	Circuit	No	Entrant	Car/Engine	Comment
dnq	SAN MARINO GP	Imola	35	Candy Toleman Motorsport	1.5 t/c Toleman TG181-Hart 4	
dnq	BELGIAN GP	Zolder	35	Candy Toleman Motorsport	1.5 t/c Toleman TG181-Hart 4	
dnpq	MONACO GP	Monte Carlo	35	Candy Toleman Motorsport	1.5 t/c Toleman TG181-Hart 4	
dnq	SPANISH GP	Jarama	35	Candy Toleman Motorsport	1.5 t/c Toleman TG181-Hart 4	
dnq	FRENCH GP	Dijon	35	Candy Toleman Motorsport	1.5 t/c Toleman TG181-Hart 4	
dnq	BRITISH GP	Silverstone	35	Candy Toleman Motorsport	1.5 t/c Toleman TG181-Hart 4	
dnq	GERMAN GP	Hockenheim	35	Candy Toleman Motorsport	1.5 t/c Toleman TG181-Hart 4	
dnq	AUSTRIAN GP	Österreichring	35	Candy Toleman Motorsport	1.5 t/c Toleman TG181-Hart 4	
dnq	DUTCH GP	Zandvoort	35	Candy Toleman Motorsport	1.5 t/c Toleman TG181-Hart 4	
10	ITALIAN GP	Monza	35	Candy Toleman Motorsport	1.5 t/c Toleman TG181-Hart 4	3 laps behind
dnq	CANADIAN GP	Montreal	35	Candy Toleman Motorsport	1.5 t/c Toleman TG181-Hart 4	
dnq	CAESARS PALACE GP	Las Vegas	35	Candy Toleman Motorsport	1.5 t/c Toleman TG181-Hart 4	

1982

	Race	Circuit	No	Entrant	Car/Engine	Comment
dnq	SOUTH AFRICAN GP	Kyalami	29	Arrows Racing Team	3.0 Arrows A4-Cosworth V8	
dnq	BRAZILIAN GP	Rio	29	Arrows Racing Team	3.0 Arrows A4-Cosworth V8	
ret	US GP WEST	Long Beach	29	Arrows Racing Team	3.0 Arrows A4-Cosworth V8	accident
ret	SAN MARINO GP	Imola	4	Team Tyrrell	3.0 Tyrrell 011-Cosworth V8	clutch
ret	BELGIAN GP	Zolder	4	Team Tyrrell	3.0 Tyrrell 011-Cosworth V8	engine
8	MONACO GP	Monte Carlo	4	Team Tyrrell	3.0 Tyrrell 011-Cosworth V8	pit stop-puncture/4 laps behind
9	US GP (DETROIT)	Detroit	4	Team Tyrrell	3.0 Tyrrell 011-Cosworth V8	pit stop/2 laps behind
nc	CANADIAN GP	Montreal	4	Team Tyrrell	3.0 Tyrrell 011-Cosworth V8	hit barrier-pit stop/11 laps behind
ret	DUTCH GP	Zandvoort	4	Team Tyrrell	3.0 Tyrrell 011-Cosworth V8	throttle linkage
8	BRITISH GP	Brands Hatch	4	Team Tyrrell	3.0 Tyrrell 011-Cosworth V8	pit stop-tyres/FL/1 lap behind
10	FRENCH GP	Paul Ricard	4	Team Tyrrell	3.0 Tyrrell 011-Cosworth V8	1 lap behind
7	GERMAN GP	Hockenheim	4	Team Tyrrell	3.0 Tyrrell 011-Cosworth V8	1 lap behind
ret	AUSTRIAN GP	Österreichring	4	Team Tyrrell	3.0 Tyrrell 011-Cosworth V8	engine
11	SWISS GP	Dijon	4	Team Tyrrell	3.0 Tyrrell 011-Cosworth V8	2 laps behind
ret	ITALIAN GP	Monza	4	Team Tyrrell	3.0 Tyrrell 011-Cosworth V8	spun off-collision with Daly
8	CAESARS PALACE GP	Las Vegas	4	Team Tyrrell	3.0 Tyrrell 011-Cosworth V8	1 lap behind

GP Starts: 19   GP Wins: 0   Pole positions: 0   Fastest laps: 1   Points: 0

HERBERT, Johnny (GB) b 25/6/1964

1989

	Race	Circuit	No	Entrant	Car/Engine	Comment
4	BRAZILIAN GP	Rio	20	Benetton Formula	3.5 Benetton B188-Cosworth V8	
11	SAN MARINO GP	Imola	20	Benetton Formula	3.5 Benetton B188-Cosworth V8	spin/2 laps behind
14	MONACO GP	Monte Carlo	20	Benetton Formula	3.5 Benetton B188-Cosworth V8	hit Arnoux-p stop-new wing/-4 laps
15	MEXICAN GP	Mexico City	20	Benetton Formula	3.5 Benetton B188-Cosworth V8	2 pit stops-gearbox-tyres/-3 laps
5	US GP (PHOENIX)	Phoenix	20	Benetton Formula	3.5 Benetton B188-Cosworth V8	lost 4th gear/1 lap behind
dnq	CANADIAN GP	Montreal	20	Benetton Formula	3.5 Benetton B188-Cosworth V8	
ret	BELGIAN GP	Spa	4	Tyrrell Racing Organisation	3.5 Tyrrell 018-Cosworth V8	spun off-hit barrier
dnq	PORTUGUESE GP	Estoril	4	Tyrrell Racing Organisation	3.5 Tyrrell 018-Cosworth V8	

1990

	Race	Circuit	No	Entrant	Car/Engine	Comment
ret	JAPANESE GP	Suzuka	12	Camel Team Lotus	3.5 Lotus 102-Lamborghini V12	engine
ret	AUSTRALIAN GP	Adelaide	12	Camel Team Lotus	3.5 Lotus 102-Lamborghini V12	clutch

1991

	Race	Circuit	No	Entrant	Car/Engine	Comment
dnq	CANADIAN GP	Montreal	12	Team Lotus	3.5 Lotus 102B-Judd V8	engine
10	MEXICAN GP	Mexico City	12	Team Lotus	3.5 Lotus 102B-Judd V8	2 laps behind
10	FRENCH GP	Magny Cours	12	Team Lotus	3.5 Lotus 102B-Judd V8	left at start-gears/2 laps behind
14/ret	BRITISH GP	Silverstone	12	Team Lotus	3.5 Lotus 102B-Judd V8	engine/4 laps behind
7	BELGIAN GP	Spa	12	Team Lotus	3.5 Lotus 102B-Judd V8	
ret	PORTUGUESE GP	Estoril	12	Team Lotus	3.5 Lotus 102B-Judd V8	engine/gearbox
ret	JAPANESE GP	Suzuka	12	Team Lotus	3.5 Lotus 102B-Judd V8	engine cut out
11	AUSTRALIAN GP	Adelaide	12	Team Lotus	3.5 Lotus 102B-Judd V8	race stopped at 14 laps

1992

	Race	Circuit	No	Entrant	Car/Engine	Comment
6	SOUTH AFRICAN GP	Kyalami	12	Team Lotus	3.5 Lotus 102D-Ford HB V8	1 lap behind
7	MEXICAN GP	Mexico City	12	Team Lotus	3.5 Lotus 102D-Ford HB V8	1 lap behind
ret	BRAZILIAN GP	Interlagos	12	Team Lotus	3.5 Lotus 102D-Ford HB V8	taken off by Boutsen and Comas
ret	SPANISH GP	Barcelona	12	Team Lotus	3.5 Lotus 102D-Ford HB V8	spun off
ret	SAN MARINO GP	Imola	12	Team Lotus	3.5 Lotus 107-Ford HB V8	gearbox
ret	MONACO GP	Monte Carlo	12	Team Lotus	3.5 Lotus 107-Ford HB V8	handling-slid into barriers

ret	CANADIAN GP	Montreal	12	Team Lotus	3.5 Lotus 107-Ford HB V8	clutch
6*	FRENCH GP	Magny Cours	12	Team Lotus	3.5 Lotus 107-Ford HB V8	*aggregate of two parts/1 lap behind
ret	BRITISH GP	Silverstone	12	Team Lotus	3.5 Lotus 107-Ford HB V8	gearbox
ret	GERMAN GP	Hockenheim	12	Team Lotus	3.5 Lotus 107-Ford HB V8	engine cut out
ret	HUNGARIAN GP	Hungaroring	12	Team Lotus	3.5 Lotus 107-Ford HB V8	spun off avoiding Comas/Boutsen
13/ret	BELGIAN GP	Spa	12	Team Lotus	3.5 Lotus 107-Ford HB V8	engine/2 laps behind
ret	ITALIAN GP	Monza	12	Team Lotus	3.5 Lotus 107-Ford HB V8	engine
ret	PORTUGUESE GP	Estoril	12	Team Lotus	3.5 Lotus 107-Ford HB V8	collision-bent steering arm
ret	JAPANESE GP	Suzuka	12	Team Lotus	3.5 Lotus 107-Ford HB V8	gearbox
13	AUSTRALIAN GP	Adelaide	12	Team Lotus	3.5 Lotus 107-Ford HB V8	p stop-nose & track rod/-4 laps
1993						
ret	SOUTH AFRICAN GP	Kyalami	12	Team Lotus	3.5 Lotus 107B-Ford HB V8	fuel pressure
4	BRAZILIAN GP	Interlagos	12	Team Lotus	3.5 Lotus 107B-Ford HB V8	
4	EUROPEAN GP	Donington	12	Team Lotus	3.5 Lotus 107B-Ford HB V8	1 lap behind
8/ret	SAN MARINO GP	Imola	12	Team Lotus	3.5 Lotus 107B-Ford HB V8	engine
ret	SPANISH GP	Barcelona	12	Team Lotus	3.5 Lotus 107B-Ford HB V8	started from back/active failure
ret	MONACO GP	Monte Carlo	12	Team Lotus	3.5 Lotus 107B-Ford HB V8	gearbox failed-crashed
10	CANADIAN GP	Montreal	12	Team Lotus	3.5 Lotus 107B-Ford HB V8	lack of grip/2 laps behind
ret	FRENCH GP	Magny Cours	12	Team Lotus	3.5 Lotus 107B-Ford HB V8	spun off
4	BRITISH GP	Silverstone	12	Team Lotus	3.5 Lotus 107B-Ford HB V8	
10	GERMAN GP	Hockenheim	12	Team Lotus	3.5 Lotus 107B-Ford HB V8	actuator problem/1 lap behind
ret	HUNGARIAN GP	Hungaroring	12	Team Lotus	3.5 Lotus 107B-Ford HB V8	spun and stalled
5	BELGIAN GP	Spa	12	Team Lotus	3.5 Lotus 107B-Ford HB V8	1 lap behind
ret	ITALIAN GP	Monza	12	Team Lotus	3.5 Lotus 107B-Ford HB V8	crashed at Parabolica
ret	PORTUGUESE GP	Estoril	12	Team Lotus	3.5 Lotus 107B-Ford HB V8	crashed
11	JAPANESE GP	Suzuka	12	Team Lotus	3.5 Lotus 107B-Ford HB V8	2 laps behind
ret	AUSTRALIAN GP	Adelaide	12	Team Lotus	3.5 Lotus 107B-Ford HB V8	hydraulics

GP Starts: 47   GP Wins: 0   Pole positions: 0   Fastest laps: 0   Points: 18

HANS HERRMANN

Young Herrmann displayed considerable promise in a Veritas and a Porsche, which earned him a golden opportunity to race for Mercedes-Benz on their return to Grand Prix and sports car racing in 1954. Although naturally somewhat overshadowed by Fangio, Moss and Kling, he scored good finishes at Bremgarten and Monza before a practice accident at Monte Carlo left him in hospital with cracked vertebrae and broken ribs.

With Mercedes' withdrawal from racing after the Le Mans tragedy, Herrmann, now fully recovered, joined Porsche for 1956 and would become a mainstay of the works team. His subsequent Grand Prix appearances were generally restricted to less-than-competitive machinery, and he caused a stir only with his spectacular crash in the 1959 German GP at AVUS, when he was thrown from his BRM, fortunately without serious injury.

He enjoyed some excellent drives in Formula 2 for Porsche in the early sixties, but found real success throughout the decade in sports cars, winning the Sebring 12 Hours (1960 and 1968), the Daytona 24 Hours (1968), the Targa Florio (1960), and the Paris 1000 Km (1968) before bowing out on a high note, retiring from racing after winning the 1970 Le Mans 24-hour race in a Porsche 917 with Richard Attwood.

FRANÇOIS HESNAULT

It was some surprise when Hesnault was drafted into the Ligier team in 1984, for his credentials showed only a single second-place finish in a round of the previous year's European F3 championship. However, the Frenchman acquitted himself respectably enough, sometimes proving more than a match for his team-mate Andrea de Cesaris, particularly at Dijon.

A move to Brabham in 1985 proved a big let-down, with a shaken Hesnault leaving the team after being lucky to escape injury in a massive testing accident at Paul Ricard. He did, however, reappear later in the season, at the wheel of a Renault which was acting as a camera car in the German Grand Prix.

HERRMANN, Hans (D) b 23/2/1938

1953

	Race	Circuit	No	Entrant	Car/Engine	Comment
9	GERMAN GP	Nürburgring	31	Hans Herrmann	2.0 Veritas Meteor 6	1 lap behind

1954

	Race	Circuit	No	Entrant	Car/Engine	Comment
ret	FRENCH GP	Reims	22	Daimler Benz AG	2.5 Mercedes Benz W196 8	engine/FL
ret	GERMAN GP	Nürburgring	20	Daimler Benz AG	2.5 Mercedes Benz W196 8	fuel pipe
3	SWISS GP	Bremgarten	6	Daimler Benz AG	2.5 Mercedes Benz W196 8	1 lap behind
4	ITALIAN GP	Monza	12	Daimler Benz AG	2.5 Mercedes Benz W196 8	pit stop-plugs/3 laps behind
ret	SPANISH GP	Pedralbes	6	Daimler Benz AG	2.5 Mercedes Benz W196 8	fuel injection pump

1955

	Race	Circuit	No	Entrant	Car/Engine	Comment
4*	ARGENTINE GP	Buenos Aires	8	Daimler Benz AG	2.5 Mercedes Benz W196 8	* Moss and Kling co-drove/-2 laps
dns	MONACO GP	Monte Carlo	4	Daimler Benz AG	2.5 Mercedes Benz W196 8	practice accident-internal injuries

1957

	Race	Circuit	No	Entrant	Car/Engine	Comment
dnq	MONACO GP	Monte Carlo	40	Officine Alfieri Maserati	2.5 Maserati 250F 6	
ret	GERMAN GP	Nürburgring	17	Scuderia Centro Sud	2.5 Maserati 250F 6	broken chassis

1958

	Race	Circuit	No	Entrant	Car/Engine	Comment
ret	GERMAN GP	Nürburgring	17	Scuderia Centro Sud	2.5 Maserati 250F 6	engine
ret	ITALIAN GP	Monza	24	Jo Bonnier	2.5 Maserati 250F 6	engine
9	MOROCCAN GP	Casablanca	38	Jo Bonnier	2.5 Maserati 250F 6	3 laps behind

1959

	Race	Circuit	No	Entrant	Car/Engine	Comment
ret	BRITISH GP	Aintree	24	Scuderia Centro Sud	2.5 Cooper T51-Maserati 4	gearbox
ret	GERMAN GP	AVUS	11	British Racing Partnership	2.5 BRM P25 4	8 heat 1/crashed heat 2

1960

	Race	Circuit	No	Entrant	Car/Engine	Comment
6	ITALIAN GP	Monza	26	Porsche System Engineering	1.5 Porsche 718 F4	F2 car/3 laps behind

1961

	Race	Circuit	No	Entrant	Car/Engine	Comment
9	MONACO GP	Monte Carlo	6	Porsche System Engineering	1.5 Porsche 718 F4	pit stop/9 laps behind
15	DUTCH GP	Zandvoort	9	Ecurie Maarsbergen	1.5 Porsche 718 F4	3 laps behind
13	GERMAN GP	Nürburgring	11	Porsche System Engineering	1.5 Porsche 718 F4	1 lap behind

1966

	Race	Circuit	No	Entrant	Car/Engine	Comment
11*	GERMAN GP (F2)	Nürburgring	28	Roy Winkelmann Racing/Hans Herrmann	1.0 Brabham BT18-Cosworth 4	* 4th in F2 class/1 lap behind

1969

	Race	Circuit	No	Entrant	Car/Engine	Comment
dns	GERMAN GP (F2)	Nürburgring	21	Roy Winkelmann Racing	1.6 Lotus 59B-Cosworth 4	withdrawn after Mitter's accident

GP Starts: 18   GP Wins: 0   Pole positions: 0   Fastest laps: 1   Points: 10

HESNAULT, François (F) b 30/12/1956

1984

	Race	Circuit	No	Entrant	Car/Engine	Comment
ret	BRAZILIAN GP	Rio	25	Ligier Loto	1.5 t/c Ligier JS23-Renault V6	overheating
10	SOUTH AFRICAN GP	Kyalami	25	Ligier Loto	1.5 t/c Ligier JS23-Renault V6	hit by Brundle/4 laps behind
ret	BELGIAN GP	Zolder	25	Ligier Loto	1.5 t/c Ligier JS23-Renault V6	radiator
ret	SAN MARINO GP	Imola	25	Ligier Loto	1.5 t/c Ligier JS23-Renault V6	hit by Laffite
dns	FRENCH GP	Dijon	25	Ligier Loto	1.5 t/c Ligier JS23-Renault V6	w/drawn to allow de Cesaris to start
ret	MONACO GP	Monte Carlo	25	Ligier Loto	1.5 t/c Ligier JS23-Renault V6	water in the electrics
ret	CANADIAN GP	Montreal	25	Ligier Loto	1.5 t/c Ligier JS23-Renault V6	turbo
ret	US GP (DETROIT)	Detroit	25	Ligier Loto	1.5 t/c Ligier JS23-Renault V6	accident with Ghinzani
ret	US GP (DALLAS)	Dallas	25	Ligier Loto	1.5 t/c Ligier JS23-Renault V6	hit wall-lap 1
ret	BRITISH GP	Brands Hatch	25	Ligier Loto	1.5 t/c Ligier JS23-Renault V6	electrics
8	GERMAN GP	Hockenheim	25	Ligier Loto	1.5 t/c Ligier JS23-Renault V6	1 lap behind
8	AUSTRIAN GP	Österreichring	25	Ligier Loto	1.5 t/c Ligier JS23-Renault V6	2 laps behind
7	DUTCH GP	Zandvoort	25	Ligier Loto	1.5 t/c Ligier JS23-Renault V6	2 laps behind
ret	ITALIAN GP	Monza	25	Ligier Loto	1.5 t/c Ligier JS23-Renault V6	spun off
10	EUROPEAN GP	Nürburgring	25	Ligier Loto	1.5 t/c Ligier JS23-Renault V6	3 laps behind
ret	PORTUGUESE GP	Estoril	25	Ligier Loto	1.5 t/c Ligier JS23-Renault V6	electrics

1985

	Race	Circuit	No	Entrant	Car/Engine	Comment
ret	BRAZILIAN GP	Rio	8	Motor Racing Developments	1.5 t/c Brabham BT54-BMW 4	accident
ret	PORTUGUESE GP	Estoril	8	Motor Racing Developments	1.5 t/c Brabham BT54-BMW 4	electrics
ret	SAN MARINO GP	Imola	8	Motor Racing Developments	1.5 t/c Brabham BT54-BMW 4	engine
dnq	MONACO GP	Monte Carlo	8	Motor Racing Developments	1.5 t/c Brabham BT54-BMW 4	
ret	GERMAN GP	Nürburgring	14	Equipe Renault Elf	1.5 t/c Renault RE60 V6	clutch

GP Starts: 19   GP Wins: 0   Pole positions: 0   Fastest laps: 0   Points: 0

HEYER, Hans (D) b 16/3/1943

1977

	Race	Circuit	No	Entrant	Car/Engine	Comment
dnq/ret	GERMAN GP	Hockenheim	35	ATS Racing Team	3.0 Penske PC4-Cosworth V8	dnq-started anyway/gear linkage

GP Starts: 1   GP Wins: 0   Pole positions: 0   Fastest laps: 0   Points: 0

DAMON HILL

Damon has earned his success the hard way, for just like his father he has had to work his way up to the top with plenty of determination but little in the way of the financial help which is such a crucial element in modern-day racing. Sadly, of course, his illustrious father has not been able to offer him the benefit of his experience, but it is to Damon's great credit that, once he had decided on a career in motor sport, he progressed entirely on his own merits.

In fact, at first he was more interested in bikes than cars and made his competition debut on two wheels, which led him into a job as a despatch rider while he worked on his fledgling career. After a brief taste of Formula Ford at the end of 1983, Hill found himself drawn into the world of motor racing and, with the help of Brands Hatch supremo John Webb in the form of free tuition and a little promotion, he went racing seriously in 1985, enjoying a very competitive year of Formula Ford. His elevation to F3 for 1986 with Murray Taylor Racing may have been a little premature, but he finished ninth in the championship and then proved himself in the formula during a two-year spell at Intersport, winning splendidly at Zandvoort and Spa in 1987 and taking two more victories in 1988, including the prestigious Grand Prix support race at Silverstone.

Damon then moved up to F3000 for 1989 and gave a good account of himself in the troubled Footwork before switching to Middlebridge the following year, when luck was not on his side in terms of results but more importantly he established himself as a genuine racer, capable of beating anyone in the field. A third year of F3000 in 1991 should have brought some real success at last but his Lola was no match for the Reynards and his first win remained elusive. There was, however, the consolation of a Williams testing contract, and the following year his work for the team helped ensure that the damage to his reputation arising from a calamitous half-season with Brabham, when he managed to qualify only twice, was merely superficial. So impressed was Patrick Head with his contribution that he was to be Damon's strongest advocate when the chance of a Grand Prix drive with the team in 1993 arose.

The way he handled his first year in a top team was exemplary in every respect. Unfazed by a couple of early gaffes at Kyalami and Imola, Hill pushed team leader Alain Prost harder and harder as the season wore on, while remaining acutely aware of the delicate political situation within the team. The fact that he won three Grands Prix was a bonus, his drive at Spa when he withstood severe pressure from Schumacher demonstrating that he has the stuff of which real winners are made. In 1994 he faces his biggest test: to come to terms with the arrival of Ayrton Senna, and to prove that he can be a winner again.

HILL, Damon (GB) b 17/9/1960

	1992					
dnq	SPANISH GP	Barcelona	8	Motor Racing Developments Ltd	3.5 Brabham BT60B-Judd V10	
dnq	SAN MARINO GP	Imola	8	Motor Racing Developments Ltd	3.5 Brabham BT60B-Judd V10	
dnq	MONACO GP	Monte Carlo	8	Motor Racing Developments Ltd	3.5 Brabham BT60B-Judd V10	
dnq	CANADIAN GP	Montreal	8	Motor Racing Developments Ltd	3.5 Brabham BT60B-Judd V10	
dnq	FRENCH GP	Magny Cours	8	Motor Racing Developments Ltd	3.5 Brabham BT60B-Judd V10	
16	BRITISH GP	Silverstone	8	Motor Racing Developments Ltd	3.5 Brabham BT60B-Judd V10	4 laps behind
dnq	GERMAN GP	Hockenheim	8	Motor Racing Developments Ltd	3.5 Brabham BT60B-Judd V10	
11	HUNGARIAN GP	Hungaroring	8	Motor Racing Developments Ltd	3.5 Brabham BT60B-Judd V10	4 laps behind
	1993					
ret	SOUTH AFRICAN GP	Kyalami	0	Canon Williams Team	3.5 Williams FW15C-Renault V10	accident with Zanardi
2	BRAZILIAN GP	Interlagos	0	Canon Williams Team	3.5 Williams FW15C-Renault V10	
2	EUROPEAN GP	Donington	0	Canon Williams Team	3.5 Williams FW15C-Renault V10	
ret	SAN MARINO GP	Imola	0	Canon Williams Team	3.5 Williams FW15C-Renault V10	spun off
ret	SPANISH GP	Barcelona	0	Canon Williams Team	3.5 Williams FW15C-Renault V10	engine
2	MONACO GP	Monte Carlo	0	Canon Williams Team	3.5 Williams FW15C-Renault V10	despite collision with Berger
3	CANADIAN GP	Montreal	0	Canon Williams Team	3.5 Williams FW15C-Renault V10	
2	FRENCH GP	Magny Cours	0	Canon Williams Team	3.5 Williams FW15C-Renault V10	
ret	BRITISH GP	Silverstone	0	Canon Williams Team	3.5 Williams FW15C-Renault V10	engine/FL
15/ret	GERMAN GP	Hockenheim	0	Canon Williams Team	3.5 Williams FW15C-Renault V10	blown tyre when leading/-2 laps
1	HUNGARIAN GP	Hungaroring	0	Canon Williams Team	3.5 Williams FW15C-Renault V10	
1	BELGIAN GP	Spa	0	Canon Williams Team	3.5 Williams FW15C-Renault V10	
1	ITALIAN GP	Monza	0	Canon Williams Team	3.5 Williams FW15C-Renault V10	FL
3	PORTUGUESE GP	Estoril	0	Canon Williams Team	3.5 Williams FW15C-Renault V10	started from back of grid/Pole/FL
4	JAPANESE GP	Suzuka	0	Canon Williams Team	3.5 Williams FW15C-Renault V10	pit stop-puncture
3	AUSTRALIAN GP	Adelaide	0	Canon Williams Team	3.5 Williams FW15C-Renault V10	

GP Starts: 18   GP Wins: 3   Pole positions: 2   Fastest laps: 4   Points: 69

HILL, Graham (GB) b 15/2/1939 – d 29/11/1975

	1958					
	Race	Circuit	No	Entrant	Car/Engine	Comment
ret	MONACO GP	Monte Carlo	26	Team Lotus	2.0 Lotus 12-Climax 4	halfshaft-lost wheel
ret	DUTCH GP	Zandvoort	16	Team Lotus	2.0 Lotus 12-Climax 4	overheating
ret	BELGIAN GP	Spa	42	Team Lotus	2.0 Lotus 12-Climax 4	engine
ret	FRENCH GP	Reims	24	Team Lotus	2.0 Lotus 16-Climax 4	overheating
ret	BRITISH GP	Silverstone	16	Team Lotus	2.0 Lotus 16-Climax 4	overheating-oil pressure
ret	GERMAN GP (F2)	Nürburgring	25	Team Lotus	1.5 Lotus 16-Climax 4	oil pipe
ret	PORTUGUESE GP	Oporto	20	Team Lotus	2.2 Lotus 16-Climax 4	spun off
5*	ITALIAN GP	Monza	38	Team Lotus	2.2 Lotus 16-Climax 4	* 5th car dsq/p stop-misfire/-8 laps
16	MOROCCAN GP	Casablanca	32	Team Lotus	2.0 Lotus 16-Climax 4	behind 4 F2 cars/7 laps behind
	1959					
ret	MONACO GP	Monte Carlo	40	Team Lotus	2.5 Lotus 16-Climax 4	fire
7	DUTCH GP	Zandvoort	14	Team Lotus	2.5 Lotus 16-Climax 4	pit stop-smoke in car/2 laps behind
ret	FRENCH GP	Reims	32	Team Lotus	2.5 Lotus 16-Climax 4	radiator
9	BRITISH GP	Aintree	28	Team Lotus	2.5 Lotus 16-Climax 4	spin/5 laps behind
ret	GERMAN GP	AVUS	16	Team Lotus	2.5 Lotus 16-Climax 4	gearbox
ret	PORTUGUESE GP	Monsanto	11	Team Lotus	2.5 Lotus 16-Climax 4	spun-hit by Phil Hill
ret	ITALIAN GP	Monza	18	Team Lotus	2.5 Lotus 16-Climax 4	clutch
	1960					
ret	ARGENTINE GP	Buenos Aires	42	Owen Racing Organisation	2.5 BRM P25 4	overheating
7/ret	MONACO GP	Monte Carlo	6	Owen Racing Organisation	2.5 BRM P48 4	spun off

GRAHAM HILL

Universally popular, Graham captured the public's imagination like no other racing driver of the period. Ordinary people, particularly those who had only a passing interest in the sport, took to this suave but somehow homely character, who could charm and amuse in a way which, say, the reserved Clark, opinionated Surtees or rather earnest Stewart could not – due in part, perhaps, to the fact that he had started his career from nothing and shown unbelievable single-mindedness and much courage, not to mention an appetite for hard work, to reach the very top of his profession.

The early days were spent scrounging drives in return for his services as a mechanic, before he began racing regularly in 1956 in Lotus and Cooper sports cars. In fact, he was working as a mechanic for Colin Chapman, who didn't consider him that seriously as a driver until he had proved himself elsewhere. When Lotus entered Grand Prix racing in 1958, Graham was back as a driver, making his debut at Monaco, where a wheel fell off. His two seasons with the fragile Lotus 16 were largely unsuccessful, the cars suffering all sorts of failures.

For 1960 he joined BRM, who had won a Grand Prix and were theoretically better placed to further his career. He missed the chance of his first Grand Prix win at Silverstone that year when, having taken the lead from Jack Brabham, a slight error brought a heavy penalty when he spun into retirement. If outright victory was still elusive, then at least he was now finishing races, and consolidating his position as a fine all-rounder by driving for Porsche in Formula 2 and sports cars, taking third and a class win in the Buenos Aires 1000 Km with Bonnier. After another barren year in 1961 when the British four-cylinder cars were outclassed by Ferrari, it was win or bust for the BRM team with the threat of closure if success was not achieved in 1962. Armed with the new V8-engined car, Graham responded brilliantly by winning the Dutch GP, and then, after losing seemingly certain triumphs in both the Monaco and French GPs, he took the BRM to three more victories to claim a thoroughly deserved first World Championship.

The next three seasons saw some magnificent racing with Hill battling it out for supremacy with Clark, Surtees, Gurney *et al*, and coming very close to a second title in Mexico City in 1964, where an accidental collision with Bandini cost him his chance. However, the championship seemed to be of less importance in those days, each race carrying more weight in its own right. Memorably he took a hat-trick of wins in both the Monaco and US GPs, but there were many great drives which brought only podium finishes, such was the level of competition.

Graham was certainly one of the most active drivers of the period, and every weekend he seemed to be flying somewhere to race, handling a bewildering array of machinery from Seattle to Kyalami, or Karlskoga to Pukekohe. Driving Ferrari sports and GT cars for Maranello Concessionaires, he won the 1963 and 1964 Tourist Trophy races and the 1964 Reims 12 Hours and Paris 1000 Km, as well as taking second place at Le Mans the same year – all co-driving with Bonnier. Graham was unable to add to his tally of Grand Prix wins during the first year of the 3-litre formula in 1966, but he scored a contentious victory after a confused finish at the Indianapolis 500.

It was a great surprise when Hill moved camps in 1967, joining Jim Clark at Lotus, to race the new Ford-Cosworth-engined Lotus 49. Its potential was enormous, and Graham was back in the hunt, but he had to endure a string of disappointments as his car fell prey to niggling maladies. Everything changed on 7 April 1968, when the team was devastated by the death of Jim Clark at Hockenheim. Graham helped restore morale by immediately winning the next two races in Spain and Monaco, and as the season wore on he resisted the challenges of Stewart and Hulme to take his second championship. Joined by Jochen Rindt in 1969, Hill won his fifth Monaco GP, but was soon overshadowed by the Austrian and the season ended in near-disaster when he was thrown from his Lotus at Watkins Glen when a tyre deflated, suffering badly broken legs.

Now aged 40, many believed it was time for him to retire, but Graham was no quitter and sheer bloody-mindedness saw him back in the cockpit of Rob Walker's Lotus at Kyalami despite still being almost unable to walk. Surprisingly he managed some points finishes early on and drove superbly in the Race of Champions to take fourth place despite gearbox trouble, but with Walker's Lotus 72 late in arriving the season petered out. Moving to Brabham for 1971, Hill won the International Trophy in the new 'lobster-claw' BT34, but had a thin time of it elsewhere. In Formula 2 he led the smart Rondel team, winning a thrilling race at Thruxton from Ronnie Peterson to show there was life in the old dog yet, but in truth a slow decline had already set in. His second season at Brabham was thoroughly lacklustre, and the year was illuminated only by his victory in the Le Mans 24 Hours for Matra with Pescarolo, Graham thus completing the unique achievement of winning the World Championship, the Indy 500 and the Sarthe classic.

With no prospect of a decent works drive in Grands Prix, Hill took the logical step of setting up his own team, showing some spirit with the difficult-to-handle Shadow in 1973 but getting nowhere fast in the reliable but heavy Lola the following year. In 1975 Graham took the decision to build his own car, but after failing to qualify at Monaco he remained out of the cockpit until announcing his retirement at the British GP meeting. Of course, by this time Graham had taken on Tony Brise, and felt he had in his charge a future champion. However, returning from a test session with the team's latest car at Paul Ricard in late November, Hill, piloting his own plane, clipped the tree tops in dense fog over Arkley golf course while approaching Elstree airfield and crashed. Not only did one of motor racing's great figures perish, so too did poor Brise and four other team members.

3	DUTCH GP	Zandvoort	16	Owen Racing Organisation	2.5 BRM P48 4	
ret	BELGIAN GP	Spa	10	Owen Racing Organisation	2.5 BRM P48 4	*engine*
ret	FRENCH GP	Reims	12	Owen Racing Organisation	2.5 BRM P48 4	*stalled on grid-hit by Trintignant*
ret	BRITISH GP	Silverstone	4	Owen Racing Organisation	2.5 BRM P48 4	*spun off when 1st/FL*
ret	PORTUGUESE GP	Oporto	22	Owen Racing Organisation	2.5 BRM P48 4	*gearbox*
ret	US GP	Riverside	17	Owen Racing Organisation	2.5 BRM P48 4	*gearbox*

1961

ret	MONACO GP	Monte Carlo	18	Owen Racing Organisation	1.5 BRM P48/57-Climax 4	*fuel pump*
8	DUTCH GP	Zandvoort	4	Owen Racing Organisation	1.5 BRM P48/57-Climax 4	
ret	BELGIAN GP	Spa	36	Owen Racing Organisation	1.5 BRM P48/57-Climax 4	*oil leak*
6	FRENCH GP	Reims	22	Owen Racing Organisation	1.5 BRM P48/57-Climax 4	
ret	BRITISH GP	Aintree	20	Owen Racing Organisation	1.5 BRM P48/57-Climax 4	*engine*
ret	GERMAN GP	Nürburgring	17	Owen Racing Organisation	1.5 BRM P48/57-Climax 4	*accident*
ret	ITALIAN GP	Monza	24	Owen Racing Organisation	1.5 BRM P48/57-Climax 4	*engine*
dns	"	"	24	Owen Racing Organisation	1.5 BRM P57 V8	*practice only*
5	US GP	Watkins Glen	4	Owen Racing Organisation	1.5 BRM P48/57-Climax 4	*1 lap behind*

1962 World Champion Driver

1	DUTCH GP	Zandvoort	17	Owen Racing Organisation	1.5 BRM P57 V8	
6/ret	MONACO GP	Monte Carlo	10	Owen Racing Organisation	1.5 BRM P57 V8	*engine/8 laps behind*
2	BELGIAN GP	Spa	1	Owen Racing Organisation	1.5 BRM P57 V8	*Pole*
9	FRENCH GP	Rouen	8	Owen Racing Organisation	1.5 BRM P57 V8	*pit stop-fuel injection/FL/-10 laps*
4	BRITISH GP	Aintree	12	Owen Racing Organisation	1.5 BRM P57 V8	
1	GERMAN GP	Nürburgring	11	Owen Racing Organisation	1.5 BRM P57 V8	*FL*
1	ITALIAN GP	Monza	14	Owen Racing Organisation	1.5 BRM P57 V8	*FL*
2	US GP	Watkins Glen	4	Owen Racing Organisation	1.5 BRM P57 V8	
1	SOUTH AFRICAN GP	East London	3	Owen Racing Organisation	1.5 BRM P57 V8	

1963

1	MONACO GP	Monte Carlo	6	Owen Racing Organisation	1.5 BRM P57 V8	
ret	BELGIAN GP	Spa	7	Owen Racing Organisation	1.5 BRM P57 V8	*gearbox/Pole*
ret	DUTCH GP	Zandvoort	12	Owen Racing Organisation	1.5 BRM P57 V8	*overheating*
ret	"	"	12	Owen Racing Organisation	1.5 BRM P61 V8	*practice only*
3*	FRENCH GP	Reims	2	Owen Racing Organisation	1.5 BRM P61 V8	** incl 1 min penalty for push start*
ret	"	"	2	Owen Racing Organisation	1.5 BRM P57 V8	*practice only*
3	BRITISH GP	Silverstone	1	Owen Racing Organisation	1.5 BRM P57 V8	*out of fuel last lap when 2nd*
ret	GERMAN GP	Nürburgring	1	Owen Racing Organisation	1.5 BRM P57 V8	*gearbox*
ret	"	"	1	Owen Racing Organisation	1.5 BRM P61 V8	*practice only*
ret	ITALIAN GP	Monza	12	Owen Racing Organisation	1.5 BRM P61 V8	*clutch*
ret	"	"	12	Owen Racing Organisation	1.5 BRM P57 V8	*practice only*
1	US GP	Watkins Glen	1	Owen Racing Organisation	1.5 BRM P57 V8	*Pole*
4	MEXICAN GP	Mexico City	1	Owen Racing Organisation	1.5 BRM P57 V8	*1 lap behind*
3	SOUTH AFRICAN GP	East London	5	Owen Racing Organisation	1.5 BRM P57 V8	*1 lap behind*

1964

1	MONACO GP	Monte Carlo	8	Owen Racing Organisation	1.5 BRM P261 V8	*FL*
4	DUTCH GP	Zandvoort	6	Owen Racing Organisation	1.5 BRM P261 V8	*1 lap behind*
5/ret	BELGIAN GP	Spa	1	Owen Racing Organisation	1.5 BRM P261 V8	*out of fuel last lap*
2	FRENCH GP	Rouen	8	Owen Racing Organisation	1.5 BRM P261 V8	
2	BRITISH GP	Brands Hatch	3	Owen Racing Organisation	1.5 BRM P261 V8	
2	GERMAN GP	Nürburgring	3	Owen Racing Organisation	1.5 BRM P261 V8	
ret	AUSTRIAN GP	Zeltweg	3	Owen Racing Organisation	1.5 BRM P261 V8	*distributor drive/Pole*
ret	ITALIAN GP	Monza	18	Owen Racing Organisation	1.5 BRM P261 V8	*clutch on startline*
1	US GP	Watkins Glen	3	Owen Racing Organisation	1.5 BRM P261 V8	
11	MEXICAN GP	Mexico City	3	Owen Racing Organisation	1.5 BRM P261 V8	*hit by Bandini when 2nd/-2 laps*

1965

3	SOUTH AFRICAN GP	East London	3	Owen Racing Organisation	1.5 BRM P261 V8	
1	MONACO GP	Monte Carlo	3	Owen Racing Organisation	1.5 BRM P261 V8	*Pole/FL*
5	BELGIAN GP	Spa	7	Owen Racing Organisation	1.5 BRM P261 V8	*Pole/1 lap behind*
5	FRENCH GP	Clermont Ferrand	10	Owen Racing Organisation	1.5 BRM P261 V8	*1 lap behind*
2	BRITISH GP	Silverstone	3	Owen Racing Organisation	1.5 BRM P261 V8	*FL*
4	DUTCH GP	Zandvoort	10	Owen Racing Organisation	1.5 BRM P261 V8	*Pole*
2	GERMAN GP	Nürburgring	9	Owen Racing Organisation	1.5 BRM P261 V8	
2	ITALIAN GP	Monza	30	Owen Racing Organisation	1.5 BRM P261 V8	
1	US GP	Watkins Glen	3	Owen Racing Organisation	1.5 BRM P261 V8	*Pole/FL*
ret	MEXICAN GP	Mexico City	3	Owen Racing Organisation	1.5 BRM P261 V8	*engine*

1966

3	MONACO GP	Monte Carlo	11	Owen Racing Organisation	2.0 BRM P261 V8	*1 lap behind*
dns	"	"	11T	Owen Racing Organisation	3.0 BRM P83 H16	*practice only*
ret	BELGIAN GP	Spa	14	Owen Racing Organisation	2.0 BRM P261 V8	*spun off in rainstorm*
ret	FRENCH GP	Reims	16	Owen Racing Organisation	2.0 BRM P261 V8	*engine*
dns	"	"	T2	Owen Racing Organisation	3.0 BRM P83 H16	*practice only*
3	BRITISH GP	Brands Hatch	3	Owen Racing Organisation	2.0 BRM P261 V8	*1 lap behind*
2	DUTCH GP	Zandvoort	12	Owen Racing Organisation	2.0 BRM P261 V8	*1 lap behind*
4	GERMAN GP	Nürburgring	5	Owen Racing Organisation	2.0 BRM P261 V8	
ret	ITALIAN GP	Monza	26	Owen Racing Organisation	3.0 BRM P83 H16	*engine-camshaft*
dns	"	"	26	Owen Racing Organisation	2.0 BRM P261 V8	*practice only*
ret	US GP	Watkins Glen	3	Owen Racing Organisation	3.0 BRM P83 H16	*cwp*
ret	MEXICAN GP	Mexico City	3	Owen Racing Organisation	3.0 BRM P83 H16	*engine*

1967

ret	SOUTH AFRICAN GP	Kyalami	8	Team Lotus	3.0 Lotus 43-BRM H16	*hit kerb*
2	MONACO GP	Monte Carlo	14	Team Lotus	2.1 Lotus 33-BRM V8	*1 lap behind*
ret	DUTCH GP	Zandvoort	6	Team Lotus	3.0 Lotus 49-Cosworth V8	*timing gears/Pole*

ret	BELGIAN GP	Spa	22	Team Lotus	3.0 Lotus 49-Cosworth V8	*gearbox*
ret	FRENCH GP	Le Mans	7	Team Lotus	3.0 Lotus 49-Cosworth V8	*gearbox/Pole/FL*
ret	BRITISH GP	Silverstone	6	Team Lotus	3.0 Lotus 49-Cosworth V8	*engine*
ret	GERMAN GP	Nürburgring	4	Team Lotus	3.0 Lotus 49-Cosworth V8	*suspension mounting*
4	CANADIAN GP	Mosport Park	4	Team Lotus	3.0 Lotus 49-Cosworth V8	*2 laps behind*
ret	ITALIAN GP	Monza	22	Team Lotus	3.0 Lotus 49-Cosworth V8	*engine*
2	US GP	Watkins Glen	6	Team Lotus	3.0 Lotus 49-Cosworth V8	*gearbox problems/Pole/FL*
ret	MEXICAN GP	Mexico City	6	Team Lotus	3.0 Lotus 49-Cosworth V8	*driveshaft-u-joint*

1968 World Champion Driver

2	SOUTH AFRICAN GP	Kyalami	5	Team Lotus	3.0 Lotus 49-Cosworth V8	
1	SPANISH GP	Jarama	10	Gold Leaf Team Lotus	3.0 Lotus 49-Cosworth V8	
1	MONACO GP	Monte Carlo	9	Gold Leaf Team Lotus	3.0 Lotus 49B-Cosworth V8	*Pole*
ret	BELGIAN GP	Spa	1	Gold Leaf Team Lotus	3.0 Lotus 49B-Cosworth V8	*driveshaft-u-joint*
9/ret	DUTCH GP	Zandvoort	3	Gold Leaf Team Lotus	3.0 Lotus 49B-Cosworth V8	*spun off/9 laps behind*
ret	FRENCH GP	Rouen	12	Gold Leaf Team Lotus	3.0 Lotus 49B-Cosworth V8	*driveshaft*
ret	BRITISH GP	Brands Hatch	8	Gold Leaf Team Lotus	3.0 Lotus 49B-Cosworth V8	*driveshaft-u-joint/Pole*
2	GERMAN GP	Nürburgring	3	Gold Leaf Team Lotus	3.0 Lotus 49B-Cosworth V8	
ret	ITALIAN GP	Monza	16	Gold Leaf Team Lotus	3.0 Lotus 49B-Cosworth V8	*lost wheel*
4	CANADIAN GP	St Jovite	3	Gold Leaf Team Lotus	3.0 Lotus 49B-Cosworth V8	*pit stop-vibration/4 laps behind*
2	US GP	Watkins Glen	10	Gold Leaf Team Lotus	3.0 Lotus 49B-Cosworth V8	
1	MEXICAN GP	Mexico City	10	Gold Leaf Team Lotus	3.0 Lotus 49B-Cosworth V8	

1969

2	SOUTH AFRICAN GP	Kyalami	1	Gold Leaf Team Lotus	3.0 Lotus 49B-Cosworth V8	
ret	SPANISH GP	Montjuich Park	1	Gold Leaf Team Lotus	3.0 Lotus 49B-Cosworth V8	*rear wing collapsed-crashed*
1	MONACO GP	Monte Carlo	1	Gold Leaf Team Lotus	3.0 Lotus 49B-Cosworth V8	
7	DUTCH GP	Zandvoort	1	Gold Leaf Team Lotus	3.0 Lotus 49B-Cosworth V8	*pit stop-handling/2 laps behind*
dns	"	"	1T	Gold Leaf Team Lotus	3.0 Lotus 63-Cosworth V8	*practice only*
6	FRENCH GP	Clermont Ferrand	1	Gold Leaf Team Lotus	3.0 Lotus 49B-Cosworth V8	*1 lap behind*
7	BRITISH GP	Silverstone	1	Gold Leaf Team Lotus	3.0 Lotus 49B-Cosworth V8	*pit stop-fuel/2 laps behind*
dns	"	"	1	Gold Leaf Team Lotus	3.0 Lotus 63-Cosworth V8	*practice only*
dns	"	"	9	Motor Racing Developments	3.0 Brabham BT26A-Cosworth V8	*practice only*
4	GERMAN GP	Nürburgring	1	Gold Leaf Team Lotus	3.0 Lotus 49B-Cosworth V8	
9/ret	ITALIAN GP	Monza	2	Gold Leaf Team Lotus	3.0 Lotus 49B-Cosworth V8	*driveshaft/5 laps behind*
ret	CANADIAN GP	Mosport Park	1	Gold Leaf Team Lotus	3.0 Lotus 49B-Cosworth V8	*engine*
ret	US GP	Watkins Glen	1	Gold Leaf Team Lotus	3.0 Lotus 49B-Cosworth V8	*puncture-thrown out-broken legs*

1970

6	SOUTH AFRICAN GP	Kyalami	11	Rob Walker Racing Team	3.0 Lotus 49C-Cosworth V8	*1 lap behind*
4	SPANISH GP	Jarama	6	Rob Walker Racing Team	3.0 Lotus 49C-Cosworth V8	*1 lap behind*
5	MONACO GP	Monte Carlo	1	Brooke Bond Oxo Racing/Rob Walker	3.0 Lotus 49C-Cosworth V8	*practice shunt-raced GLTL car/-1 lap*
ret	BELGIAN GP	Spa	23	Brooke Bond Oxo Racing/Rob Walker	3.0 Lotus 49C-Cosworth V8	*engine*
nc	DUTCH GP	Zandvoort	15	Brooke Bond Oxo Racing/Rob Walker	3.0 Lotus 49C-Cosworth V8	*pit stop-handling/9 laps behind*
10	FRENCH GP	Clermont Ferrand	8	Brooke Bond Oxo Racing/Rob Walker	3.0 Lotus 49C-Cosworth V8	*1 lap behind*
6	BRITISH GP	Brands Hatch	14	Brooke Bond Oxo Racing/Rob Walker	3.0 Lotus 49C-Cosworth V8	*1 lap behind*
ret	GERMAN GP	Hockenheim	9	Brooke Bond Oxo Racing/Rob Walker	3.0 Lotus 49C-Cosworth V8	*engine*
dns	ITALIAN GP	Monza	28	Brooke Bond Oxo Racing/Rob Walker	3.0 Lotus 72C-Cosworth V8	*withdrawn after Rindt's accident*
nc	CANADIAN GP	St Jovite	9	Brooke Bond Oxo Racing/Rob Walker	3.0 Lotus 72C-Cosworth V8	*pit stop-gearbox/13 laps behind*
ret	US GP	Watkins Glen	14	Brooke Bond Oxo Racing/Rob Walker	3.0 Lotus 72C-Cosworth V8	*clutch*
ret	MEXICAN GP	Mexico City	14	Brooke Bond Oxo Racing/Rob Walker	3.0 Lotus 72C-Cosworth V8	*overheating*

1971

9	SOUTH AFRICAN GP	Kyalami	14	Motor Racing Developments	3.0 Brabham BT33-Cosworth V8	*pit stop-rear wing/2 laps behind*
ret	SPANISH GP	Montjuich Park	7	Motor Racing Developments	3.0 Brabham BT34-Cosworth V8	*steering*
ret	MONACO GP	Monte Carlo	7	Motor Racing Developments	3.0 Brabham BT34-Cosworth V8	*hit wall at Tabac*
10	DUTCH GP	Zandvoort	24	Motor Racing Developments	3.0 Brabham BT34-Cosworth V8	*5 laps behind*
ret	FRENCH GP	Paul Ricard	7	Motor Racing Developments	3.0 Brabham BT34-Cosworth V8	*oil pressure*
ret	BRITISH GP	Silverstone	7	Motor Racing Developments	3.0 Brabham BT34-Cosworth V8	*hit by Oliver on grid*
9	GERMAN GP	Nürburgring	24	Motor Racing Developments	3.0 Brabham BT34-Cosworth V8	*left on grid*
5	AUSTRIAN GP	Österreichring	7	Motor Racing Developments	3.0 Brabham BT34-Cosworth V8	
11/ret	ITALIAN GP	Monza	10	Motor Racing Developments	3.0 Brabham BT34-Cosworth V8	*gearbox/7 laps behind*
ret	CANADIAN GP	Mosport Park	37	Motor Racing Developments	3.0 Brabham BT34-Cosworth V8	*spun off*
7	US GP	Watkins Glen	22	Motor Racing Developments	3.0 Brabham BT34-Cosworth V8	*1 lap behind*

1972

ret	ARGENTINE GP	Buenos Aires	1	Motor Racing Developments	3.0 Brabham BT33-Cosworth V8	*fuel pump/tyre problems*
6	SOUTH AFRICAN GP	Kyalami	19	Motor Racing Developments	3.0 Brabham BT33-Cosworth V8	*1 lap behind*
10	SPANISH GP	Jarama	18	Motor Racing Developments	3.0 Brabham BT37-Cosworth V8	*spin/4 laps behind*
12	MONACO GP	Monte Carlo	20	Motor Racing Developments	3.0 Brabham BT37-Cosworth V8	*4 laps behind*
ret	BELGIAN GP	Nivelles	17	Motor Racing Developments	3.0 Brabham BT37-Cosworth V8	*rear upright*
10	FRENCH GP	Clermont Ferrand	18	Motor Racing Developments	3.0 Brabham BT37-Cosworth V8	*hit by Beltoise*
ret	BRITISH GP	Brands Hatch	26	Motor Racing Developments	3.0 Brabham BT37-Cosworth V8	*spun off at Paddock*
6	GERMAN GP	Nürburgring	11	Motor Racing Developments	3.0 Brabham BT37-Cosworth V8	
ret	AUSTRIAN GP	Österreichring	16	Motor Racing Developments	3.0 Brabham BT37-Cosworth V8	*fuel metering unit*
5	ITALIAN GP	Monza	28	Motor Racing Developments	3.0 Brabham BT37-Cosworth V8	*brake problems*
8	CANADIAN GP	Mosport Park	7	Motor Racing Developments	3.0 Brabham BT37-Cosworth V8	*1 lap behind*
11	US GP	Watkins Glen	28	Motor Racing Developments	3.0 Brabham BT37-Cosworth V8	*spin/2 laps behind*

1973

ret	SPANISH GP	Montjuich Park	25	Embassy Racing	3.0 Shadow DN1-Cosworth V8	*brakes*
9	BELGIAN GP	Zolder	12	Embassy Racing	3.0 Shadow DN1-Cosworth V8	*pit stop-plug lead/5 laps behind*
ret	MONACO GP	Monte Carlo	12	Embassy Racing	3.0 Shadow DN1-Cosworth V8	*rear suspension*
ret	SWEDISH GP	Anderstorp	12	Embassy Racing	3.0 Shadow DN1-Cosworth V8	*ignition*
10	FRENCH GP	Paul Ricard	12	Embassy Racing	3.0 Shadow DN1-Cosworth V8	*1 lap behind*
ret	BRITISH GP	Silverstone	12	Embassy Racing	3.0 Shadow DN1-Cosworth V8	*steering rack*
nc	DUTCH GP	Zandvoort	12	Embassy Racing	3.0 Shadow DN1-Cosworth V8	*4 pit stops-water/16 laps behind*

13	GERMAN GP	Nürburgring	12	Embassy Racing	3.0 Shadow DN1-Cosworth V8	
ret	AUSTRIAN GP	Österreichring	12	Embassy Racing	3.0 Shadow DN1-Cosworth V8	*rear suspension mounting*
14	ITALIAN GP	Monza	12	Embassy Racing	3.0 Shadow DN1-Cosworth V8	*1 lap behind*
16	CANADIAN GP	Mosport Park	12	Embassy Racing	3.0 Shadow DN1-Cosworth V8	*4 pit stops-various/7 laps behind*
13	US GP	Watkins Glen	12	Embassy Racing	3.0 Shadow DN1-Cosworth V8	*pit stop-puncture/2 laps behind*

1974

ret	ARGENTINE GP	Buenos Aires	26	Embassy Racing with Graham Hill	3.0 Lola T370-Cosworth V8	*engine*
11	BRAZILIAN GP	Interlagos	26	Embassy Racing with Graham Hill	3.0 Lola T370-Cosworth V8	*1 lap behind*
12	SOUTH AFRICAN GP	Kyalami	26	Embassy Racing with Graham Hill	3.0 Lola T370-Cosworth V8	*1 lap behind*
ret	SPANISH GP	Jarama	26	Embassy Racing with Graham Hill	3.0 Lola T370-Cosworth V8	*engine*
8	BELGIAN GP	Nivelles	26	Embassy Racing with Graham Hill	3.0 Lola T370-Cosworth V8	*2 laps behind*
7	MONACO GP	Monte Carlo	26	Embassy Racing with Graham Hill	3.0 Lola T370-Cosworth V8	*2 laps behind*
6	SWEDISH GP	Anderstorp	26	Embassy Racing with Graham Hill	3.0 Lola T370-Cosworth V8	*1 lap behind*
ret	DUTCH GP	Zandvoort	26	Embassy Racing with Graham Hill	3.0 Lola T370-Cosworth V8	*loose clutch housing bolts*
13	FRENCH GP	Dijon	26	Embassy Racing with Graham Hill	3.0 Lola T370-Cosworth V8	*2 laps behind*
13	BRITISH GP	Brands Hatch	26	Embassy Racing with Graham Hill	3.0 Lola T370-Cosworth V8	*2 p stops-punctures/6 laps behind*
9	GERMAN GP	Nürburgring	26	Embassy Racing with Graham Hill	3.0 Lola T370-Cosworth V8	
12	AUSTRIAN GP	Österreichring	26	Embassy Racing with Graham Hill	3.0 Lola T370-Cosworth V8	*pit stop-tyres/6 laps behind*
8	ITALIAN GP	Monza	26	Embassy Racing with Graham Hill	3.0 Lola T370-Cosworth V8	*1 lap behind*
14	CANADIAN GP	Mosport Park	26	Embassy Racing with Graham Hill	3.0 Lola T370-Cosworth V8	*3 laps behind*
8	US GP	Watkins Glen	26	Embassy Racing with Graham Hill	3.0 Lola T370-Cosworth V8	*1 lap behind*

1975

10	ARGENTINE GP	Buenos Aires	22	Embassy Racing with Graham Hill	3.0 Lola T370-Cosworth V8	*1 lap behind*
12	BRAZILIAN GP	Interlagos	22	Embassy Racing with Graham Hill	3.0 Lola T370-Cosworth V8	*1 lap behind*
dns	SOUTH AFRICAN GP	Kyalami	22	Embassy Racing with Graham Hill	3.0 Lola T370-Cosworth V8	*practice accident-car damaged*
dnq	MONACO GP	Monte Carlo	23	Embassy Racing with Graham Hill	3.0 Hill GH1-Cosworth V8	
dnq	" "	" "	22	Embassy Racing with Graham Hill	3.0 Lola T370-Cosworth V8	

GP Starts: 176   GP Wins: 14   Pole positions: 13   Fastest laps: 10   Points: 289

HILL, Phil (USA) b 20/4/1927

1958

	Race	Circuit	No	Entrant	Car/Engine	Comment
7	FRENCH GP	Reims	36	Joakim Bonnier	2.5 Maserati 250F 6	*1 lap behind*
9	GERMAN GP (F2)	Nürburgring	23	Scuderia Ferrari	1.5 Ferrari Dino 156 V6	*5th in F2 class*
3	ITALIAN GP	Monza	18	Scuderia Ferrari	2.4 Ferrari Dino 246 V6	*FL*
3	MOROCCAN GP	Casablanca	4	Scuderia Ferrari	2.4 Ferrari Dino 246 V6	

1959

4	MONACO GP	Monte Carlo	48	Scuderia Ferrari	2.4 Ferrari Dino 246 V6	*3 spins-p stop-wheels/3 laps behind*
6	DUTCH GP	Zandvoort	3	Scuderia Ferrari	2.4 Ferrari Dino 246 V6	*2 laps behind*
2	FRENCH GP	Reims	26	Scuderia Ferrari	2.4 Ferrari Dino 246 V6	
3	GERMAN GP	AVUS	5	Scuderia Ferrari	2.4 Ferrari Dino 246 V6	*agg-3rd heat 1/2nd heat 2/FL heat 2*
ret	PORTUGUESE GP	Monsanto	15	Scuderia Ferrari	2.4 Ferrari Dino 246 V6	*hit a spinning Graham Hill*
2	ITALIAN GP	Monza	32	Scuderia Ferrari	2.4 Ferrari Dino 246 V6	*FL*
ret	US GP	Sebring	5	Scuderia Ferrari	2.4 Ferrari Dino 246 V6	*clutch*

1960

8	ARGENTINE GP	Buenos Aires	26	Scuderia Ferrari	2.4 Ferrari Dino 246 V6	*3 laps behind*
3	MONACO GP	Monte Carlo	26	Scuderia Ferrari	2.4 Ferrari Dino 246 V6	
ret	DUTCH GP	Zandvoort	1	Scuderia Ferrari	2.4 Ferrari Dino 246 V6	*engine*
4	BELGIAN GP	Spa	24	Scuderia Ferrari	2.4 Ferrari Dino 246 V6	*pit stop-fuel leak/FL (shared)/-1 lap*
12/ret	FRENCH GP	Reims	2	Scuderia Ferrari	2.4 Ferrari Dino 246 V6	*transmission*
7	BRITISH GP	Silverstone	10	Scuderia Ferrari	2.4 Ferrari Dino 246 V6	*2 laps behind*
ret	PORTUGUESE GP	Oporto	26	Scuderia Ferrari	2.4 Ferrari Dino 246 V6	*hit straw bales*
1	ITALIAN GP	Monza	20	Scuderia Ferrari	2.4 Ferrari Dino 246 V6	*Pole/FL*
6	US GP	Riverside	9	Yeoman Credit Racing Team	2.5 Cooper T51-Climax 4	*1 lap behind*

1961 World Champion Driver

3	MONACO GP	Monte Carlo	38	Scuderia Ferrari SpA SEFAC	1.5 Ferrari 156 V6	
2	DUTCH GP	Zandvoort	1	Scuderia Ferrari SpA SEFAC	1.5 Ferrari 156 V6	*Pole*
1	BELGIAN GP	Spa	4	Scuderia Ferrari SpA SEFAC	1.5 Ferrari 156 V6	*Pole*
9	FRENCH GP	Reims	16	Scuderia Ferrari SpA SEFAC	1.5 Ferrari 156 V6	*spin/Pole/FL/2 laps behind*
2	BRITISH GP	Aintree	2	Scuderia Ferrari SpA SEFAC	1.5 Ferrari 156 V6	*Pole*
3	GERMAN GP	Nürburgring	4	Scuderia Ferrari SpA SEFAC	1.5 Ferrari 156 V6	*Pole/FL*
1	ITALIAN GP	Monza	2	Scuderia Ferrari SpA SEFAC	1.5 Ferrari 156 V6	

1962

3	DUTCH GP	Zandvoort	1	Scuderia Ferrari SpA SEFAC	1.5 Ferrari 156 V6	
2	MONACO GP	Monte Carlo	36	Scuderia Ferrari SpA SEFAC	1.5 Ferrari 156 V6	
3	BELGIAN GP	Spa	9	Scuderia Ferrari SpA SEFAC	1.5 Ferrari 156 V6	
ret	BRITISH GP	Aintree	2	Scuderia Ferrari SpA SEFAC	1.5 Ferrari 156 V6	*ignition*
ret	GERMAN GP	Nürburgring	1	Scuderia Ferrari SpA SEFAC	1.5 Ferrari 156 V6	*shock absorbers*
11	ITALIAN GP	Monza	10	Scuderia Ferrari SpA SEFAC	1.5 Ferrari 156 V6	*pit stop-tyres/5 laps behind*
dns	US GP	Watkins Glen	11	Porsche System Engineering	1.5 Porsche 804 F8	*practice only*

1963

ret	BELGIAN GP	Spa	26	Automobili Tourisimo Sport	1.5 ATS 100 V8	*gearbox*
ret	DUTCH GP	Zandvoort	24	Automobili Tourisimo Sport	1.5 ATS 100 V8	*rear hub*
nc	FRENCH GP	Reims	42	Ecurie Filipinetti	1.5 Lotus 24-BRM V8	*1 min pen/p stops/-19 laps*
11	ITALIAN GP	Monza	16	Automobili Tourisimo Sport	1.5 ATS 100 V8	*pit stops-various/7 laps behind*
ret	US GP	Watkins Glen	25	Automobili Tourisimo Sport	1.5 ATS 100 V8	*oil pump*
ret	MEXICAN GP	Mexico City	25	Automobili Tourisimo Sport	1.5 ATS 100 V8	*rear suspension*

1964

9/ret	MONACO GP	Monte Carlo	9	Cooper Car Co		1.5 Cooper T73-Climax V8	*rear suspension*
8	DUTCH GP	Zandvoort	22	Cooper Car Co		1.5 Cooper T73-Climax V8	*4 laps behind*
ret	BELGIAN GP	Spa	21	Cooper Car Co		1.5 Cooper T73-Climax V8	*engine*
7	FRENCH GP	Rouen	14	Cooper Car Co		1.5 Cooper T73-Climax V8	*1 lap behind*
6	BRITISH GP	Brands Hatch	10	Cooper Car Co		1.5 Cooper T73-Climax V8	*2 laps behind*
ret	GERMAN GP	Nürburgring	10	Cooper Car Co		1.5 Cooper T73-Climax V8	*engine*
ret	AUSTRIAN GP	Zeltweg	10	Cooper Car Co		1.5 Cooper T66-Climax V8	*accident-car written off*
dns	"	"	10	Cooper Car Co		1.5 Cooper T73-Climax V8	*accident in practice*
ret	US GP	Watkins Glen	10	Cooper Car Co		1.5 Cooper T73-Climax V8	*ignition*
9/ret	MEXICAN GP	Mexico City	10	Cooper Car Co		1.5 Cooper T73-Climax V8	*engine/2 laps behind*

1966

dns	MONACO GP	Monte Carlo	20	Phil Hill		1.5 Lotus 33-Climax V8	*camera car-not competing*
dns	BELGIAN GP	Spa	28	Phil Hill		4.7 McLaren-Ford V8	*camera car-not competing*
dnq	ITALIAN GP	Monza	34	Anglo American Racers		2.7 Eagle TG101-Climax 4	

GP Starts: 48   GP Wins: 3   Pole positions: 6   Fastest laps: 6   Points: 98

PHIL HILL

Phil Hill is always remembered as the man who became America's first World Champion when he took the crown driving a Ferrari in 1961, yet that season he won only two Grands Prix and they were his only victories in small-capacity racing cars. In a long career he was overwhelmingly more effective and successful in big, powerful sports machines.

After business studies on the west coast, Phil decided he preferred working on cars to the office life and by 1950 he was racing an MG TC, which was duly replaced by a succession of machines all of which were hard-earned by the sweat of his brow. In 1952 he got a big break with a drive in Alan Guiberson's Ferrari, taking sixth place in the Carrera Panamericana, but the following year he fared badly and briefly considered retirement. He was persuaded to continue, however, and second place in the 1954 Carrera was a marvellous morale-booster. His career then took off in a big way Stateside, Phil winning the 1955 SCCA championship, and after he had finished second in the 1956 Buenos Aires 1000 Km he was given a contract to drive sports cars for the Scuderia. He won the Swedish GP and the Messina 5 Hours that season in works cars, and added more good results the following year, including a win in the Venezuelan GP at Caracas with Peter Collins.

By 1958 Phil was itching to get his hands on a Grand Prix car, but Ferrari seemed unwilling to give him the opportunity he craved, save for a little practice at the Libre Buenos Aires GP. Enzo felt he was best suited to sports cars, and Hill proved as much when he won at Buenos Aires and Sebring and then put in a brilliant drive in the wet to win Le Mans with Gendebien. However, by now his need to race in Formula 1 bordered on the obsessional and he hired Bonnier's Maserati to give himself a debut at the French GP. Perhaps Ferrari took the hint because come the German GP Hill was handed the team's F2 car, and then at Monza he was entrusted with the real thing – a Ferrari 246 – taking third and fastest lap. By backing off at the finish of the Moroccan GP to allow Hawthorn to move into second place and thus take the championship, Phil did his standing no harm and he became a full-time Grand Prix team member thereafter. He spent 1959 learning the art of Grand Prix driving, sometimes proving a little ragged in his approach and indulging in some hairy moments, but taking fourth place in the championship nevertheless. By 1960 the big front-engined cars were almost on the point of obsolescence, but Hill gave the dinosaurs one last hurrah by winning the rather hollow Italian GP held on Monza's banked circuit which was boycotted by the British teams.

The following season was to be his finest. In addition to winning the Sebring 12 Hours and Le Mans for the second time with Gendebien, he took the little 'shark-nose' Ferrari to victory at Spa and Monza to be crowned as World Champion in the saddest of circumstances following the terrible death of his team-mate and championship rival Wolfgang von Trips. Things progress quickly in Formula 1, however, and in 1962 Ferrari were totally eclipsed, leaving Phil with a few placings but no hope of defending his title. He was still regarded as one the finest exponents of sports car racing, however, and confirmed it by winning Le Mans for the third time with Gendebien, as well as the Nürburgring 1000 Km.

Such was the disharmony at Maranello that year that Phil joined what was effectively a breakaway group to race the ATS in 1963. To say it was a disastrous move would be an understatement, and it effectively destroyed his Grand Prix career. Initially left without a drive, he was called into the Cooper team following the tragic loss of Tim Mayer at Longford, but it was an unhappy liaison, with Phil's confidence hitting rock bottom at Zeltweg where he wrote off two cars. This resulted in the ignominy of his being dropped for Monza, but he was reinstated for the final two races.

Save for a drive in Gurney's Eagle at Monza in 1966, his Grand Prix career was done, but he still had something left. He had been a key member of the Ford works sports car effort in 1964-65, but a move to Jim Hall's Chaparral team gave the twilight of his career a final glow. In 1966 he won the Nürburgring 1000 Km with Bonnier, and a Can-Am round at Laguna Seca, and in his final season he took a memorable victory at Brands Hatch sharing the Chaparral 2F with Mike Spence. After this last win he drifted into contented retirement, restoring vintage cars and keeping in touch with the sport in a commentary role.

HIRT, Peter (CH) b 30/3/1910

1951

	Race	Circuit	No	Entrant	Car/Engine	Comment
ret	SWISS GP	Bremgarten	52	Peter Hirt	2.0 Veritas Meteor 6	fuel pump-lap 1

1952

7	SWISS GP	Bremgarten	44	Ecurie Espadon	2.0 Ferrari 166 V12	6 laps behind
11*	FRENCH GP	Rouen	34	Ecurie Espadon	2.0 Ferrari 166 V12	* shared Fischer's car/13 laps behind
ret	BRITISH GP	Silverstone	20	Ecurie Espadon	2.0 Ferrari 166 V12	brakes

1953

ret	SWISS GP	Bremgarten	38	Ecurie Espadon	2.0 Ferrari 500 4	water pump

GP Starts: 5   GP Wins: 0   Pole positions: 0   Fastest laps: 0   Points: 0

DAVID HOBBS

With only the occasional foray into Grand Prix racing, Hobbs forged a very satisfying career for himself over three decades, starting in the early 1960s with Lotus and Jaguar sports cars before graduating to Formula Junior, Formula 2 and then 'big-banger' sports cars with the Lola T70 in 1965.

His first Formula 1 break came with Bernard White's BRM, in which he finished third in the 1966 Syracuse GP, and this led to a season of F2 with Team Surtees in 1967, before he fully established himself in the top league of sports car racing with the John Wyer team in 1968 by winning the Monza 1000 Km in a Ford GT40.

The advent of F5000/Formula A in 1969 was to provide a profitable furrow for David to plough over the next few seasons, particularly with Carl Hogan's Lola in the States, where he was to base himself more and more. In 1974 he finished fifth in the Indianapolis 500 with a McLaren, and later in the season he deputised for the injured Mike Hailwood in a couple of Grands Prix. The sheer variety of cars that Hobbs has driven throughout a career that has encompassed F1, F2, endurance, Can-Am, F5000, touring cars, IMSA and much more is simply bewildering. Into the nineties David still raced occasionally, but he now concentrates on his role as a TV commentator for CBS in America, which he performs with all the characteristic professionalism one would expect from this seasoned racer.

INGO HOFFMANN

Hoffmann was a talented driver whose career was laid waste by a disastrous spell in the Fittipaldi brothers' Copersucar team.

A top Super Vee and saloon car driver in his native Brazil, Ingo came to Britain in 1975 and contested the Formula 3 series in a March, before his move into Grands Prix with Fittipaldi. With the team beset by all sorts of problems, Hoffman's difficulties were inevitably very much secondary to those of the team leader and after just two races of the 1977 season the second car was withdrawn, leaving the unhappy Ingo to concentrate on a programme of Formula 2 for Project Four with a Ralt. Although outright success eluded him in this class, he proved to be a very quick and tough competitor, and produced some great performances – particularly in 1978, his last in Europe, in the Project Four March. It is a shame that a second chance did not come the Brazilian's way.

HOBBS, David (GB) b 9/6/1939

1967

	Race	Circuit	No	Entrant	Car/Engine	Comment
8	BRITISH GP	Silverstone	20	Bernard White Racing	2.0 BRM P261 V8	3 laps behind
10	GERMAN GP (F2)	Nürburgring	27	Lola Cars Ltd	1.6 Lola T100-BMW 4	3rd in F2 class/2 laps behind
9	CANADIAN GP	Mosport Park	12	Bernard White Racing	2.0 BRM P261 V8	5 laps behind

1968

ret	ITALIAN GP	Monza	15	Honda Racing	3.0 Honda RA301 V12	engine

1971

10	US GP	Watkins Glen	31	Penske White Racing	3.0 McLaren M19A-Cosworth V8	stood in for Donohue/1 lap behind

1974

7	AUSTRIAN GP	Österreichring	33	Yardley Team McLaren	3.0 McLaren M23-Cosworth V8	1 lap behind
9	ITALIAN GP	Monza	33	Yardley Team McLaren	3.0 McLaren M23-Cosworth V8	1 lap behind

GP Starts: 7   GP Wins: 0   Pole positions: 0   Fastest laps: 0   Points: 0

HOFFMANN, Ingo (BR) b 18/2/1953

1976

	Race	Circuit	No	Entrant	Car/Engine	Comment
11	BRAZILIAN GP	Interlagos	31	Copersucar-Fittipaldi	3.0 Fittipaldi FD03-Cosworth V8	1 lap behind
dnq	US GP WEST	Long Beach	31	Copersucar-Fittipaldi	3.0 Fittipaldi FD04-Cosworth V8	
dnq	SPANISH GP	Jarama	31	Copersucar-Fittipaldi	3.0 Fittipaldi FD04-Cosworth V8	
dnq	FRENCH GP	Paul Ricard	31	Copersucar-Fittipaldi	3.0 Fittipaldi FD04-Cosworth V8	

1977

ret	ARGENTINE GP	Buenos Aires	29	Copersucar-Fittipaldi	3.0 Fittipaldi FD04-Cosworth V8	engine
7	BRAZILIAN GP	Interlagos	29	Copersucar-Fittipaldi	3.0 Fittipaldi FD04-Cosworth V8	2 laps behind

GP Starts: 3   GP Wins: 0   Pole positions: 0   Fastest laps: 0   Points: 0

HOSHINO, Kazuyoshi (J) b 1/7/1947

1976

	Race	Circuit	No	Entrant	Car/Engine	Comment
ret	JAPANESE GP	Mount Fuji	52	Heros Racing	3.0 Tyrrell 007-Cosworth V8	used up tyres-no more available

1977

11	JAPANESE GP	Mount Fuji	52	Heros Racing	3.0 Kojima KE009-Cosworth V8	2 laps behind

GP Starts: 2   GP Wins: 0   Pole positions: 0   Fastest laps: 0   Points: 0

KAZUYOSHI HOSHINO

His remarkable performance in the rain-sodden 1976 Japanese GP with a private Tyrrell on Bridgestone tyres confirmed Hoshino as one of Japan's leading racers. He was a works Nissan driver as far back as 1969, and since then he has swept the board in many forms of domestic racing, being four-times Formula 2 champion as well as a multiple Grand Champion. He remains very competitive, and the 1993 season saw the veteran snatch the Japanese F3000 title from the grasp of a clutch of young and hungry European drivers at the wheel of a Lola. He has also been a regular member of the Nissan sports car team, winning the Daytona 24 Hours in 1992 with his compatriots Masahiro Hasemi and Toshio Suzuki.

DENNY HULME

If there can be such a thing as an unfashionable World Champion, then that is what Denny Hulme was. Self-effacing to the point of anonymity in his public persona, he eschewed the glamorous trappings that Grand Prix racing had to offer, but in fact he was no shrinking violet and his inner determination was second to none, born of many years working as a humble mechanic.

After making an impact on the local scene, he came to Europe in 1960 with George Lawton on the 'New Zealand Driver to Europe' scheme, racing a Cooper in Formula 2 and Formula Junior around the Continent. Unfortunately poor Lawton was soon killed at Roskilde Ring but Hulme carried on before returning home to contest his local series early in 1961. He was soon back in Europe, carving out a reputation for himself in Ken Tyrrell's Cooper and the works Brabham, replacing the retired Gavin Youl.

While still working as a mechanic at Brabham, Hulme took over the leadership of the Junior team in 1963, winning seven of the 14 races he entered. Although top-flight chances were limited, Jack was shrewd enough to realise the young New Zealander's potential and took him down to the 1964 Tasman series, where he won at Levin and finished second in the New Zealand GP. Supporting his boss in the Formula 2 championship that year, Denny won two races, at Clermont Ferrand and Zolder, with plenty of other good placings besides. In 1965 Brabham had the problem of running himself, Gurney and Hulme, so he shuffled the pack to ensure that Hulme was well prepared for the 3-litre formula, and Denny backed 'Black Jack' superbly in 1966 as his mentor enjoyed an Indian summer and took the championship. As well as having another successful Formula 2 season, Denny also raced sports cars, taking second place at Le Mans with Ken Miles in a Ford GT40, and winning the Tourist Trophy and Martini International in Sid Taylor's Lola.

In 1967 it was Hulme's turn to take the spotlight. His wins in the Monaco and German GPs were the outstanding performances, but he scored points in all but two races to edge out his boss and claim the drivers' crown for himself. Typically thinking ahead, Denny had already decided to join forces with fellow 'Kiwi' Bruce McLaren in 1968, and he started the year in the team's new bright-orange livery. An early-season win in the International Trophy and then third to Bruce in the Race of Champions indicated things were on the right track, and sure enough Hulme's consistent approach put him in with an outside title chance after wins at Monza and Mont Tremblant. In the end his efforts fell short, but as a team McLaren had established themselves as a front-line outfit in both Formula 1 and Can-Am, which proved a lucrative sideline for both driver and constructor. Hulme took the Can-Am title that year, but this success could have been a double-edged sword, for the 1969 Grand Prix season only provided Denny with an end-of-season win in Mexico.

The following season should have been a real breakthrough year for the team, but instead it saw catastrophe as McLaren was killed in a testing accident, and Hulme was involved in a practice crash at Indy which left him with nasty burns to hands and feet. That the team recovered so well from Bruce's loss was a great credit to Denny, who hid his own devastation and gave the team a new sense of purpose by winning the Can-Am championship for the second time. From then on the tough New Zealander's approach became more circumspect. If he could sniff the scent of victory then he would really get stuck in, as we saw at Kyalami in 1972 and Sweden in 1973, but generally he drove within his limits. He was always a factor, even in his final season in 1974 when he pounced to claim a win in Argentina after a patient race. But after he had been on the scene of Peter Revson's fatal accident at Kyalami, he was generally content to let younger lions risk their necks before unobtrusively easing himself into a retirement of sorts.

Though Formula 1 was in the past, the lure of competition was too strong, and from 1978 he raced touring cars and trucks as and when the fancy took him with all the grit and determination he showed in his heyday. He was competing in the Bathurst 1000 Km in October 1992 when suddenly he pulled his BMW M3 over and parked neatly on the grass alongside the Armco barrier. For a while nothing happened, and when marshals arrived they found Denny dead, still strapped into the car, having apparently suffered a heart attack at the early age of 57

HULME, Denny (NZ) b 18/6/1936 – d 4/10/1992

1965

	Race	Circuit	No	Entrant	Car/Engine	Comment
8	MONACO GP	Monte Carlo	2	Brabham Racing Organisation	1.5 Brabham BT7-Climax V8	pit stop/8 laps behind
4	FRENCH GP	Clermont Ferrand	16	Brabham Racing Organisation	1.5 Brabham BT11-Climax V8	
ret	BRITISH GP	Silverstone	14	Brabham Racing Organisation	1.5 Brabham BT7-Climax V8	alternator belt
5	DUTCH GP	Zandvoort	14	Brabham Racing Organisation	1.5 Brabham BT11-Climax V8	1 lap behind
ret	GERMAN GP	Nürburgring	6	Brabham Racing Organisation	1.5 Brabham BT7-Climax V8	fuel leak
ret	ITALIAN GP	Monza	14	Brabham Racing Organisation	1.5 Brabham BT11-Climax V8	suspension

1966

ret	MONACO GP	Monte Carlo	8	Brabham Racing Organisation	2.5 Brabham BT11-Climax 4	*driveshaft*
ret	BELGIAN GP	Spa	4	Brabham Racing Organisation	2.5 Brabham BT11-Climax 4	*collision with Siffert*
3	FRENCH GP	Reims	14	Brabham Racing Organisation	3.0 Brabham BT20-Repco V8	*out of fuel last lap/2 laps behind*
dns	"	"	12	Brabham Racing Organisation	3.0 Brabham BT19-Repco V8	*practice only*
2	BRITISH GP	Brands Hatch	6	Brabham Racing Organisation	3.0 Brabham BT20-Repco V8	
ret	DUTCH GP	Zandvoort	18	Brabham Racing Organisation	3.0 Brabham BT20-Repco V8	*ignition/FL*
ret	GERMAN GP	Nürburgring	4	Brabham Racing Organisation	3.0 Brabham BT20-Repco V8	*ignition*
3	ITALIAN GP	Monza	12	Brabham Racing Organisation	3.0 Brabham BT20-Repco V8	
ret	US GP	Watkins Glen	6	Brabham Racing Organisation	3.0 Brabham BT20-Repco V8	*oil pressure*
3	MEXICAN GP	Mexico City	6	Brabham Racing Organisation	3.0 Brabham BT20-Repco V8	*1 lap behind*

1967 World Champion Driver

4	SOUTH AFRICAN GP	Kyalami	2	Brabham Racing Organisation	3.0 Brabham BT20-Repco V8	*2 p stops-brakes/FL/2 laps behind*
1	MONACO GP	Monte Carlo	9	Brabham Racing Organisation	3.0 Brabham BT20-Repco V8	
3	DUTCH GP	Zandvoort	2	Brabham Racing Organisation	3.0 Brabham BT20-Repco V8	
ret	BELGIAN GP	Spa	26	Brabham Racing Organisation	3.0 Brabham BT19-Repco V8	*engine*
2	FRENCH GP	Le Mans	4	Brabham Racing Organisation	3.0 Brabham BT24-Repco V8	
2	BRITISH GP	Silverstone	2	Brabham Racing Organisation	3.0 Brabham BT24-Repco V8	*FL*
1	GERMAN GP	Nürburgring	2	Brabham Racing Organisation	3.0 Brabham BT24-Repco V8	
2	CANADIAN GP	Mosport Park	2	Brabham Racing Organisation	3.0 Brabham BT24-Repco V8	
ret	ITALIAN GP	Monza	18	Brabham Racing Organisation	3.0 Brabham BT24-Repco V8	*engine*
3	US GP	Watkins Glen	2	Brabham Racing Organisation	3.0 Brabham BT24-Repco V8	*1 lap behind*
3	MEXICAN GP	Mexico City	2	Brabham Racing Organisation	3.0 Brabham BT24-Repco V8	*1 lap behind*

1968

5	SOUTH AFRICAN GP	Kyalami	1	Bruce McLaren Motor Racing	3.0 McLaren M5A-BRM V12	*2 laps behind*
2	SPANISH GP	Jarama	1	Bruce McLaren Motor Racing	3.0 McLaren M7A-Cosworth V8	
5	MONACO GP	Monte Carlo	12	Bruce McLaren Motor Racing	3.0 McLaren M7A-Cosworth V8	*long pit stop-driveshaft/7 laps behind*
ret	BELGIAN GP	Spa	6	Bruce McLaren Motor Racing	3.0 McLaren M7A-Cosworth V8	*driveshaft*
ret	DUTCH GP	Zandvoort	1	Bruce McLaren Motor Racing	3.0 McLaren M7A-Cosworth V8	*damp ignition*
5	FRENCH GP	Rouen	8	Bruce McLaren Motor Racing	3.0 McLaren M7A-Cosworth V8	*2 laps behind*
4	BRITISH GP	Brands Hatch	1	Bruce McLaren Motor Racing	3.0 McLaren M7A-Cosworth V8	*1 lap behind*
7	GERMAN GP	Nürburgring	1	Bruce McLaren Motor Racing	3.0 McLaren M7A-Cosworth V8	
1	ITALIAN GP	Monza	1	Bruce McLaren Motor Racing	3.0 McLaren M7A-Cosworth V8	
1	CANADIAN GP	St Jovite	1	Bruce McLaren Motor Racing	3.0 McLaren M7A-Cosworth V8	
ret	US GP	Watkins Glen	1	Bruce McLaren Motor Racing	3.0 McLaren M7A-Cosworth V8	*spun off*
ret	MEXICAN GP	Mexico City	1	Bruce McLaren Motor Racing	3.0 McLaren M7A-Cosworth V8	*suspension collapsed-crashed*

1969

3	SOUTH AFRICAN GP	Kyalami	5	Bruce McLaren Motor Racing	3.0 McLaren M7A-Cosworth V8	
4	SPANISH GP	Montjuich Park	5	Bruce McLaren Motor Racing	3.0 McLaren M7A-Cosworth V8	*pit stop-handling/3 laps behind*
6	MONACO GP	Monte Carlo	3	Bruce McLaren Motor Racing	3.0 McLaren M7A-Cosworth V8	*unwell/2 laps behind*
4	DUTCH GP	Zandvoort	7	Bruce McLaren Motor Racing	3.0 McLaren M7A-Cosworth V8	
8	FRENCH GP	Clermont Ferrand	4	Bruce McLaren Motor Racing	3.0 McLaren M7A-Cosworth V8	*brake problems/3 laps behind*
ret	BRITISH GP	Silverstone	5	Bruce McLaren Motor Racing	3.0 McLaren M7A-Cosworth V8	*engine*
ret	GERMAN GP	Nürburgring	9	Bruce McLaren Motor Racing	3.0 McLaren M7A-Cosworth V8	*transmission*
7	ITALIAN GP	Monza	16	Bruce McLaren Motor Racing	3.0 McLaren M7A-Cosworth V8	*brake problems/2 laps behind*
ret	CANADIAN GP	Mosport Park	5	Bruce McLaren Motor Racing	3.0 McLaren M7A-Cosworth V8	*distributor*
ret	US GP	Watkins Glen	5	Bruce McLaren Motor Racing	3.0 McLaren M7A-Cosworth V8	*gear selection*
1	MEXICAN GP	Mexico City	5	Bruce McLaren Motor Racing	3.0 McLaren M7A-Cosworth V8	

1970

2	SOUTH AFRICAN GP	Kyalami	6	Bruce McLaren Motor Racing	3.0 McLaren M14A-Cosworth V8	
ret	SPANISH GP	Jarama	4	Bruce McLaren Motor Racing	3.0 McLaren M14A-Cosworth V8	*rotor arm shaft*
4	MONACO GP	Monte Carlo	11	Bruce McLaren Motor Racing	3.0 McLaren M14A-Cosworth V8	
4	FRENCH GP	Clermont Ferrand	19	Bruce McLaren Motor Racing	3.0 McLaren M14D-Cosworth V8	
3	BRITISH GP	Brands Hatch	9	Bruce McLaren Motor Racing	3.0 McLaren M14D-Cosworth V8	
3	GERMAN GP	Hockenheim	4	Bruce McLaren Motor Racing	3.0 McLaren M14A-Cosworth V8	
ret	AUSTRIAN GP	Österreichring	21	Bruce McLaren Motor Racing	3.0 McLaren M14A-Cosworth V8	*engine*
4	ITALIAN GP	Monza	30	Bruce McLaren Motor Racing	3.0 McLaren M14A-Cosworth V8	
ret	CANADIAN GP	St Jovite	5	Bruce McLaren Motor Racing	3.0 McLaren M14A-Cosworth V8	*flywheel*
7	US GP	Watkins Glen	8	Bruce McLaren Motor Racing	3.0 McLaren M14A-Cosworth V8	*2 laps behind*
3	MEXICAN GP	Mexico City	8	Bruce McLaren Motor Racing	3.0 McLaren M14A-Cosworth V8	

1971

6	SOUTH AFRICAN GP	Kyalami	11	Bruce McLaren Motor Racing	3.0 McLaren M19A-Cosworth V8	*suspension problems/1 lap behind*
5	SPANISH GP	Montjuich Park	9	Bruce McLaren Motor Racing	3.0 McLaren M19A-Cosworth V8	
4	MONACO GP	Monte Carlo	9	Bruce McLaren Motor Racing	3.0 McLaren M19A-Cosworth V8	
12	DUTCH GP	Zandvoort	26	Bruce McLaren Motor Racing	3.0 McLaren M19A-Cosworth V8	*7 laps behind*
ret	FRENCH GP	Paul Ricard	9	Bruce McLaren Motor Racing	3.0 McLaren M19A-Cosworth V8	*ignition*
ret	BRITISH GP	Silverstone	9	Bruce McLaren Motor Racing	3.0 McLaren M19A-Cosworth V8	*engine*
ret	GERMAN GP	Nürburgring	18	Bruce McLaren Motor Racing	3.0 McLaren M19A-Cosworth V8	*fuel leak*
ret	AUSTRIAN GP	Österreichring	9	Bruce McLaren Motor Racing	3.0 McLaren M19A-Cosworth V8	*engine*
4	CANADIAN GP	Mosport Park	9	Bruce McLaren Motor Racing	3.0 McLaren M19A-Cosworth V8	*FL/1 lap behind*
ret	US GP	Watkins Glen	7	Bruce McLaren Motor Racing	3.0 McLaren M19A-Cosworth V8	*spun off on oil*

1972

2	ARGENTINE GP	Buenos Aires	17	Yardley Team McLaren	3.0 McLaren M19A-Cosworth V8	
1	SOUTH AFRICAN GP	Kyalami	12	Yardley Team McLaren	3.0 McLaren M19A-Cosworth V8	
ret	SPANISH GP	Jarama	11	Yardley Team McLaren	3.0 McLaren M19A-Cosworth V8	*gearbox*
dns	"	"	11	Yardley Team McLaren	3.0 McLaren M19C-Cosworth V8	*practice only*
15	MONACO GP	Monte Carlo	14	Yardley Team McLaren	3.0 McLaren M19C-Cosworth V8	*hit guard rail/6 laps behind*
dns	"	"	14T	Yardley Team McLaren	3.0 McLaren M19C-Cosworth V8	*practice only*
3	BELGIAN GP	Nivelles	9	Yardley Team McLaren	3.0 McLaren M19C-Cosworth V8	
dns	"	"	9T	Yardley Team McLaren	3.0 McLaren M19A-Cosworth V8	*practice only-not timed*
7	FRENCH GP	Clermont Ferrand	2	Yardley Team McLaren	3.0 McLaren M19C-Cosworth V8	*pit stop-puncture*

dns	"	" "	2T	Yardley Team McLaren	3.0 McLaren M19A-Cosworth V8	*practice only*
5	BRITISH GP	Brands Hatch	18	Yardley Team McLaren	3.0 McLaren M19C-Cosworth V8	*1 lap behind*
ret	GERMAN GP	Nürburgring	3	Yardley Team McLaren	3.0 McLaren M19C-Cosworth V8	*engine*
2	AUSTRIAN GP	Österreichring	12	Yardley Team McLaren	3.0 McLaren M19C-Cosworth V8	*FL*
dns	"	"	12T	Yardley Team McLaren	3.0 McLaren M19A-Cosworth V8	*practice only*
3	ITALIAN GP	Monza	14	Yardley Team McLaren	3.0 McLaren M19C-Cosworth V8	
dns	"	"	14T	Yardley Team McLaren	3.0 McLaren M19A-Cosworth V8	*practice only*
3	CANADIAN GP	Mosport Park	18	Yardley Team McLaren	3.0 McLaren M19C-Cosworth V8	
dns	"	"	18T	Yardley Team McLaren	3.0 McLaren M19A-Cosworth V8	*practice only*
3	US GP	Watkins Glen	19	Yardley Team McLaren	3.0 McLaren M19C-Cosworth V8	

1973

5	ARGENTINE GP	Buenos Aires	14	Yardley Team McLaren	3.0 McLaren M19C-Cosworth V8	*1 lap behind*
3	BRAZILIAN GP	Interlagos	7	Yardley Team McLaren	3.0 McLaren M19C-Cosworth V8	*FL*
5	SOUTH AFRICAN GP	Kyalami	5	Yardley Team McLaren	3.0 McLaren M23-Cosworth V8	*p stop-puncture/Pole/2 laps behind*
6	SPANISH GP	Montjuich Park	5	Yardley Team McLaren	3.0 McLaren M23-Cosworth V8	*pit stop-wheel/1 lap behind*
7	BELGIAN GP	Zolder	7	Yardley Team McLaren	3.0 McLaren M23-Cosworth V8	*spin-pit stop/3 laps behind*
6	MONACO GP	Monte Carlo	14	Yardley Team McLaren	3.0 McLaren M23-Cosworth V8	*pit stop-gear linkage/2 laps behind*
1	SWEDISH GP	Anderstorp	14	Yardley Team McLaren	3.0 McLaren M23-Cosworth V8	*FL*
8	FRENCH GP	Paul Ricard	14	Yardley Team McLaren	3.0 McLaren M23-Cosworth V8	*pit stop-tyre/FL*
3	BRITISH GP	Silverstone	14	Yardley Team McLaren	3.0 McLaren M23-Cosworth V8	
ret	DUTCH GP	Zandvoort	14	Yardley Team McLaren	3.0 McLaren M23-Cosworth V8	*engine*
12	GERMAN GP	Nürburgring	14	Yardley Team McLaren	3.0 McLaren M23-Cosworth V8	*pit stop-exhaust*
8	AUSTRIAN GP	Österreichring	14	Yardley Team McLaren	3.0 McLaren M23-Cosworth V8	*3 pit stops-plugs/1 lap behind*
15	ITALIAN GP	Monza	14	Yardley Team McLaren	3.0 McLaren M23-Cosworth V8	*spin-pit stop/2 laps behind*
13	CANADIAN GP	Mosport Park	14	Yardley Team McLaren	3.0 McLaren M23-Cosworth V8	*pit stop-puncture/5 laps behind*
4	US GP	Watkins Glen	14	Yardley Team McLaren	3.0 McLaren M23-Cosworth V8	

1974

1	ARGENTINE GP	Buenos Aires	6	Marlboro Team Texaco	3.0 McLaren M23-Cosworth V8	
12	BRAZILIAN GP	Interlagos	6	Marlboro Team Texaco	3.0 McLaren M23-Cosworth V8	*pit stop-front tyres/1 lap behind*
9	SOUTH AFRICAN GP	Kyalami	6	Marlboro Team Texaco	3.0 McLaren M23-Cosworth V8	*1 lap behind*
6	SPANISH GP	Jarama	56	Marlboro Team Texaco	3.0 McLaren M23-Cosworth V8	*pit stop-suspension/2 laps behind*
6	BELGIAN GP	Nivelles	6	Marlboro Team Texaco	3.0 McLaren M23-Cosworth V8	*FL*
ret	MONACO GP	Monte Carlo	6	Marlboro Team Texaco	3.0 McLaren M23-Cosworth V8	*collision with Beltoise*
ret	SWEDISH GP	Anderstorp	6	Marlboro Team Texaco	3.0 McLaren M23-Cosworth V8	*suspension*
ret	DUTCH GP	Zandvoort	6	Marlboro Team Texaco	3.0 McLaren M23-Cosworth V8	*ignition*
6	FRENCH GP	Dijon	6	Marlboro Team Texaco	3.0 McLaren M23-Cosworth V8	
7	BRITISH GP	Brands Hatch	6	Marlboro Team Texaco	3.0 McLaren M23-Cosworth V8	*1 lap behind*
ret	GERMAN GP	Nürburgring	6	Marlboro Team Texaco	3.0 McLaren M23-Cosworth V8	*accident on starting grid*
dsq	"	"	5T	Marlboro Team Texaco	3.0 McLaren M23-Cosworth V8	*restarted from pits in spare car*
2	AUSTRIAN GP	Österreichring	6	Marlboro Team Texaco	3.0 McLaren M23-Cosworth V8	
6	ITALIAN GP	Monza	6	Marlboro Team Texaco	3.0 McLaren M23-Cosworth V8	*1 lap behind*
6	CANADIAN GP	Mosport Park	6	Marlboro Team Texaco	3.0 McLaren M23-Cosworth V8	*1 lap behind*
ret	US GP	Watkins Glen	6	Marlboro Team Texaco	3.0 McLaren M23-Cosworth V8	*engine*

GP Starts: 112   GP Wins: 8   Pole positions: 1   Fastest laps: 9   Points: 248

HUNT, James (GB) b 29/8/1947 – d 15/6/1993

1973

	Race	Circuit	No	Entrant	Car/Engine	Comment
9/ret	MONACO GP	Monte Carlo	27	Hesketh Racing	3.0 March 731-Cosworth V8	*engine/5 laps behind*
6	FRENCH GP	Paul Ricard	27	Hesketh Racing	3.0 March 731-Cosworth V8	
4	BRITISH GP	Silverstone	27	Hesketh Racing	3.0 March 731-Cosworth V8	*FL*
3	DUTCH GP	Zandvoort	27	Hesketh Racing	3.0 March 731-Cosworth V8	
ret	AUSTRIAN GP	Österreichring	27	Hesketh Racing	3.0 March 731-Cosworth V8	*fuel metering unit*
dns	ITALIAN GP	Monza	27	Hesketh Racing	3.0 March 731-Cosworth V8	*car damaged in practice accident*
7	CANADIAN GP	Mosport Park	27	Hesketh Racing	3.0 March 731-Cosworth V8	*pit stop-tyres/2 laps behind*
2	US GP	Watkins Glen	27	Hesketh Racing	3.0 March 731-Cosworth V8	*FL*

1974

ret	ARGENTINE GP	Buenos Aires	24	Hesketh Racing	3.0 March 731-Cosworth V8	*overheating*
9	BRAZILIAN GP	Interlagos	24	Hesketh Racing	3.0 March 731-Cosworth V8	*1 lap behind*
ret	SOUTH AFRICAN GP	Kyalami	24	Hesketh Racing	3.0 Hesketh 308-Cosworth V8	*c.v. joint*
10	SPANISH GP	Jarama	24	Hesketh Racing	3.0 Hesketh 308-Cosworth V8	*pit stop-tyres/brakes/-3 laps*
ret	BELGIAN GP	Nivelles	24	Hesketh Racing	3.0 Hesketh 308-Cosworth V8	*rear suspension*
ret	MONACO GP	Monte Carlo	24	Hesketh Racing	3.0 Hesketh 308-Cosworth V8	*driveshaft*
3	SWEDISH GP	Anderstorp	24	Hesketh Racing	3.0 Hesketh 308-Cosworth V8	
ret	DUTCH GP	Zandvoort	24	Hesketh Racing	3.0 Hesketh 308-Cosworth V8	*collision with Pryce*
ret	FRENCH GP	Dijon	24	Hesketh Racing	3.0 Hesketh 308-Cosworth V8	*collision with Pryce*
ret	BRITISH GP	Brands Hatch	24	Hesketh Racing	3.0 Hesketh 308-Cosworth V8	*rear suspension-spun off*
ret	GERMAN GP	Nürburgring	24	Hesketh Racing	3.0 Hesketh 308-Cosworth V8	*transmission*
3	AUSTRIAN GP	Österreichring	24	Hesketh Racing	3.0 Hesketh 308-Cosworth V8	*pit stop-tyre*
ret	ITALIAN GP	Monza	24	Hesketh Racing	3.0 Hesketh 308-Cosworth V8	*engine*
4	CANADIAN GP	Mosport Park	24	Hesketh Racing	3.0 Hesketh 308-Cosworth V8	
3	US GP	Watkins Glen	24	Hesketh Racing	3.0 Hesketh 308-Cosworth V8	*fuel problems*

1975

2	ARGENTINE GP	Buenos Aires	24	Hesketh Racing	3.0 Hesketh 308-Cosworth V8	*FL*
6	BRAZILIAN GP	Interlagos	24	Hesketh Racing	3.0 Hesketh 308-Cosworth V8	
ret	SOUTH AFRICAN GP	Kyalami	24	Hesketh Racing	3.0 Hesketh 308-Cosworth V8	*fuel metering unit*
ret	SPANISH GP	Montjuich Park	24	Hesketh Racing	3.0 Hesketh 308-Cosworth V8	*spun off*
ret	MONACO GP	Monte Carlo	24	Hesketh Racing	3.0 Hesketh 308-Cosworth V8	*hit guard rail*
ret	BELGIAN GP	Zolder	24	Hesketh Racing	3.0 Hesketh 308-Cosworth V8	*gear linkage*
ret	SWEDISH GP	Anderstorp	24	Hesketh Racing	3.0 Hesketh 308-Cosworth V8	*brake pipe leakage*

1	DUTCH GP	Zandvoort	24	Hesketh Racing	3.0 Hesketh 308-Cosworth V8	*pit stop-tyres*
2	FRENCH GP	Paul Ricard	24	Hesketh Racing	3.0 Hesketh 308-Cosworth V8	
4/ret	BRITISH GP	Silverstone	24	Hesketh Racing	3.0 Hesketh 308-Cosworth V8	*spun off in rainstorm/1 lap behind*
ret	GERMAN GP	Nürburgring	24	Hesketh Racing	3.0 Hesketh 308-Cosworth V8	*rear hub*
2	AUSTRIAN GP	Österreichring	24	Hesketh Racing	3.0 Hesketh 308-Cosworth V8	
5	ITALIAN GP	Monza	24	Hesketh Racing	3.0 Hesketh 308C-Cosworth V8	
4	US GP	Watkins Glen	24	Hesketh Racing	3.0 Hesketh 308C-Cosworth V8	
dns	"	" "	24	Hesketh Racing	3.0 Hesketh 308-Cosworth V8	*practice only*

1976 World Champion Driver

ret	BRAZILIAN GP	Interlagos	11	Marlboro Team McLaren	3.0 McLaren M23-Cosworth V8	*stuck throttle-crashed/Pole*
2	SOUTH AFRICAN GP	Kyalami	11	Marlboro Team McLaren	3.0 McLaren M23-Cosworth V8	*Pole*
ret	US GP WEST	Long Beach	11	Marlboro Team McLaren	3.0 McLaren M23-Cosworth V8	*collision with Depailler*
1	SPANISH GP	Jarama	11	Marlboro Team McLaren	3.0 McLaren M23-Cosworth V8	*disqualified but reinstated/Pole*
ret	BELGIAN GP	Zolder	11	Marlboro Team McLaren	3.0 McLaren M23-Cosworth V8	*transmission*
ret	MONACO GP	Monte Carlo	11	Marlboro Team McLaren	3.0 McLaren M23-Cosworth V8	*engine*
5	SWEDISH GP	Anderstorp	11	Marlboro Team McLaren	3.0 McLaren M23-Cosworth V8	
1	FRENCH GP	Paul Ricard	11	Marlboro Team McLaren	3.0 McLaren M23-Cosworth V8	*Pole*
dsq	BRITISH GP	Brands Hatch	11	Marlboro Team McLaren	3.0 McLaren M23-Cosworth V8	*used spare car in restart/1st on road*
1	GERMAN GP	Nürburgring	11	Marlboro Team McLaren	3.0 McLaren M23-Cosworth V8	*race restarted/Pole*
4	AUSTRIAN GP	Österreichring	11	Marlboro Team McLaren	3.0 McLaren M23-Cosworth V8	*Pole/FL*
1	DUTCH GP	Zandvoort	11	Marlboro Team McLaren	3.0 McLaren M23-Cosworth V8	
ret	ITALIAN GP	Monza	11	Marlboro Team McLaren	3.0 McLaren M23-Cosworth V8	*ran off circuit-stuck in sand*
1	CANADIAN GP	Mosport Park	11	Marlboro Team McLaren	3.0 McLaren M23-Cosworth V8	*Pole*
1	US GP EAST	Watkins Glen	11	Marlboro Team McLaren	3.0 McLaren M23-Cosworth V8	*Pole/FL*
3	JAPANESE GP	Mount Fuji	11	Marlboro Team McLaren	3.0 McLaren M23-Cosworth V8	*pit stop-tyre/1 lap behind*

1977

ret	ARGENTINE GP	Buenos Aires	1	Marlboro Team McLaren	3.0 McLaren M23-Cosworth V8	*suspension mounting/Pole/FL*
2	BRAZILIAN GP	Interlagos	1	Marlboro Team McLaren	3.0 McLaren M23-Cosworth V8	*Pole/FL*
4	SOUTH AFRICAN GP	Kyalami	1	Marlboro Team McLaren	3.0 McLaren M23-Cosworth V8	*Pole*
7	US GP WEST	Long Beach	1	Marlboro Team McLaren	3.0 McLaren M23-Cosworth V8	*hit Watson-pit stop/1 lap behind*
ret	SPANISH GP	Jarama	1	Marlboro Team McLaren	3.0 McLaren M26-Cosworth V8	*engine*
ret	MONACO GP	Monte Carlo	1	Marlboro Team McLaren	3.0 McLaren M23-Cosworth V8	*engine*
7	BELGIAN GP	Zolder	1	Marlboro Team McLaren	3.0 McLaren M26-Cosworth V8	*1 lap behind*
dns	"	"	1	Marlboro Team McLaren	3.0 McLaren M23-Cosworth V8	*practice only*
12	SWEDISH GP	Anderstorp	1	Marlboro Team McLaren	3.0 McLaren M26-Cosworth V8	*1 lap behind*
3	FRENCH GP	Dijon	1	Marlboro Team McLaren	3.0 McLaren M26-Cosworth V8	
1	BRITISH GP	Silverstone	1	Marlboro Team McLaren	3.0 McLaren M26-Cosworth V8	*Pole/FL*
ret	GERMAN GP	Hockenheim	1	Marlboro Team McLaren	3.0 McLaren M26-Cosworth V8	*fuel pump*
ret	AUSTRIAN GP	Österreichring	1	Marlboro Team McLaren	3.0 McLaren M26-Cosworth V8	*engine*
ret	DUTCH GP	Zandvoort	1	Marlboro Team McLaren	3.0 McLaren M26-Cosworth V8	*collision with Andretti*
ret	ITALIAN GP	Monza	1	Marlboro Team McLaren	3.0 McLaren M26-Cosworth V8	*spun off/Pole*
1	US GP EAST	Watkins Glen	1	Marlboro Team McLaren	3.0 McLaren M26-Cosworth V8	*Pole*
ret	CANADIAN GP	Mosport Park	1	Marlboro Team McLaren	3.0 McLaren M26-Cosworth V8	*hit Mass*
1	JAPANESE GP	Mount Fuji	1	Marlboro Team McLaren	3.0 McLaren M26-Cosworth V8	

1978

4	ARGENTINE GP	Buenos Aires	7	Marlboro Team McLaren	3.0 McLaren M26-Cosworth V8	*FL*
ret	BRAZILIAN GP	Rio	7	Marlboro Team McLaren	3.0 McLaren M26-Cosworth V8	*spun off*
ret	SOUTH AFRICAN GP	Kyalami	7	Marlboro Team McLaren	3.0 McLaren M26-Cosworth V8	*engine*
ret	US GP WEST	Long Beach	7	Marlboro Team McLaren	3.0 McLaren M26-Cosworth V8	*spun off-damaged suspension*
ret	MONACO GP	Monte Carlo	7	Marlboro Team McLaren	3.0 McLaren M26-Cosworth V8	*anti-roll bar*
ret	BELGIAN GP	Zolder	7	Marlboro Team McLaren	3.0 McLaren M26-Cosworth V8	*startline collision with Patrese*
6	SPANISH GP	Jarama	7	Marlboro Team McLaren	3.0 McLaren M26-Cosworth V8	*pit stop-tyres/1 lap behind*
8	SWEDISH GP	Anderstorp	7	Marlboro Team McLaren	3.0 McLaren M26-Cosworth V8	*1 lap behind*
3	FRENCH GP	Paul Ricard	7	Marlboro Team McLaren	3.0 McLaren M26-Cosworth V8	*unwell*
ret	BRITISH GP	Brands Hatch	7	Marlboro Team McLaren	3.0 McLaren M26-Cosworth V8	*spun off*
dns	"	" "	7	Marlboro Team McLaren	3.0 McLaren M26E-Cosworth V8	*practice only*
dsq	GERMAN GP	Hockenheim	7	Marlboro Team McLaren	3.0 McLaren M26-Cosworth V8	*took short cut to pits*
ret	AUSTRIAN GP	Österreichring	7	Marlboro Team McLaren	3.0 McLaren M26-Cosworth V8	*collision with Daly*
10	DUTCH GP	Zandvoort	7	Marlboro Team McLaren	3.0 McLaren M26-Cosworth V8	*handling problems/1 lap behind*
ret	ITALIAN GP	Monza	7	Marlboro Team McLaren	3.0 McLaren M26-Cosworth V8	*distributor*
7	US GP EAST	Watkins Glen	7	Marlboro Team McLaren	3.0 McLaren M26-Cosworth V8	*1 lap behind*
ret	CANADIAN GP	Montreal	7	Marlboro Team McLaren	3.0 McLaren M26-Cosworth V8	*spun off*

1979

ret	ARGENTINE GP	Buenos Aires	20	Olympus Cameras Wolf Racing	3.0 Wolf WR7-Cosworth V8	*electrics*
ret	BRAZILIAN GP	Interlagos	20	Olympus Cameras Wolf Racing	3.0 Wolf WR7-Cosworth V8	*loose steering rack*
8	SOUTH AFRICAN GP	Kyalami	20	Olympus Cameras Wolf Racing	3.0 Wolf WR7-Cosworth V8	*1 lap behind*
ret	US GP WEST	Long Beach	20	Olympus Cameras Wolf Racing	3.0 Wolf WR8-Cosworth V8	*driveshaft*
ret	SPANISH GP	Jarama	20	Olympus Cameras Wolf Racing	3.0 Wolf WR7-Cosworth V8	*brakes*
dns	"	"	20	Olympus Cameras Wolf Racing	3.0 Wolf WR7-Cosworth V8	*practice only*
ret	BELGIAN GP	Zolder	20	Olympus Cameras Wolf Racing	3.0 Wolf WR8-Cosworth V8	*spun off*
dns	"	"	20	Olympus Cameras Wolf Racing	3.0 Wolf WR7-Cosworth V8	*practice only*
ret	MONACO GP	Monte Carlo	20	Olympus Cameras Wolf Racing	3.0 Wolf WR7-Cosworth V8	*c.v. joint*

GP Starts: 92   GP Wins: 10   Pole positions: 14   Fastest laps: 8   Points: 179

HUTCHISON, Gus (USA) b 26/4/1937

1970

	Race	Circuit	No	Entrant	Car/Engine	Comment
ret	US GP	Watkins Glen	31	Gus Hutchison	3.0 Brabham BT26A-Cosworth V8	*loose supplementary fuel tank*

GP Starts: 1   GP Wins: 0   Pole positions: 0   Fastest laps: 0   Points: 0

JAMES HUNT

Some drivers are cut out for the big stage, and undoubtedly James Hunt was a prime example. Here was a man who, having been quick but not at all convincing in his early career, took to Grand Prix racing like the proverbial 'duck to water', confounding his critics who had given him the unkind but not entirely inappropriate nickname of 'Hunt the Shunt'.

Though the son of a Surrey stockbroker, James had to finance his early racing career largely from his own pocket, stacking the shelves in his local Sainsbury's in order to race his Mini before moving into Formula Ford in 1968 with an Alexis and then a Merlyn Mk 11A in 1969. Midway through the season James moved up to F3 with a Brabham BT21B, but found the competition hot, gaining success only in Libre events at Brands Hatch.

It was during the 1970 season, when he was equipped with a Lotus 59, that people began to sit up and take notice, and not only because of his wins at Rouen and Zolder, for late in the season he was involved in a last-corner collision with Dave Morgan which saw the irate James exact pugilistic retribution on the spot. His penchant for attracting controversy followed him into the 1971 season, which was littered with accidents and mechanical gremlins, but once again he proved beyond doubt that when trouble stayed away he was a serious contender. March certainly thought so as they signed him for their STP-backed works car in 1972, but the team fell apart and as luck would have it James joined forces with Lord Hesketh's Dastle F3 team. Almost immediately Hesketh took the plunge into Formula 2 and Hunt placed the team's car on the front row at Salzburgring in his first race. After a really good drive he was forced to pull out with engine trouble, but crucially James had proved to himself that he was good enough. In the next race he gave a superb display at Oulton Park to finish third and there was now no stopping the upward momentum of 'young Master James'.

Third place in the 1973 Race of Champions with a hired Surtees convinced Lord Hesketh that Hunt had the talent for the big time, and James proved his faith was not misplaced, putting in some sensational performances once the team had acquired a March 731, with his drives at Zandvoort and Watkins Glen, where he dogged the Lotus of Ronnie Peterson, standing out. The Hesketh bandwagon was really gathering pace by now, and in 1974 the team launched their own car, which proved an immediate success, with Hunt winning the International Trophy before embarking on an up-and-down Grand Prix season which was marred by trivial mechanical failures and some misjudgements on the part of the driver, but contained some race-performance gems, such as in Austria where he drove from 18th after a pit stop to third at the finish. His reputation was such that Dan Gurney invited him over to the States to drive his Eagle in US F5000 for three races, his best result being a second at the Monterey GP. He also sampled sports cars, taking fourth at the Nürburgring 750 Km with Schuppan and Bell in John Wyer's Gulf-Ford.

That Hunt was a top-drawer racer was finally confirmed in 1975 when he drove the Hesketh to a magnificent win in the Dutch GP, defeating Lauda's Ferrari. To prove it was no fluke, Hunt took three second places that year before the financial burden of running the team independently became too great for its aristocratic patron. Briefly James looked to be without a drive for 1976, but with Fittipaldi's sudden defection to his family's Copersucar-backed project, Hunt found himself installed alongside Jochen Mass at McLaren. It was to be a season of high drama, controversy and courage, which saw James and his great pal Niki Lauda fight it out for the championship in a fashion which captured the imagination of the world at large and wassurely instrumental in increasing the sport's popularity during subsequent years. James soon asserted his number one status in the team by claiming pole in Brazil and then winning the Race of Champions and International Trophy. His first Grand Prix win for McLaren was contentious, Hunt being re-instated after a post-race disqualification in Spain, but a victory in France kept him in touch, and then came the famous British GP at Brands. Hunt, having been taken out by Regazzoni in a first-corner mêlée, won the restarted race but was then disqualified. His championship chances seemed over, but after Lauda's fiery accident at the Nürburgring James had an outside chance. By the time the Austrian had bravely returned to the cockpit, Hunt had made inroads into his points lead, and once on a roll he proved difficult to resist with two brilliant wins in Canada and the US. The showdown in Japan was hyped more intensely than anything ever seen before, and while his rival withdrew Hunt stayed out on a flooded track to take third place and the coveted championship.

James was now a public figure way beyond the confines of the sport, and perhaps this began to affect his racing. In 1977 he still put in some superb performances to win at Silverstone, Watkins Glen and Fuj, but his refusal to appear on the rostrum at the final race showed the more petulant side to his nature. The ground-effect Lotus was by this time in the ascendancy and McLaren were slow to follow this route, which left Hunt struggling in 1978, though it has to be said the driver's apparent lack of motivation certainly didn't help matters. Feeling a move would be beneficial for all concerned, Hunt switched to Walter Wolf for one final season in 1979, but the car proved difficult to handle and James seemed generally disinclined to give his all when there was little chance of outright success. Abruptly, and with no regrets, he quit the cockpit after the Monaco GP.

Another career was soon to open up for the extremely articulate and self-opinioned Hunt. He joined Murray Walker in the BBC's commentary booth to form a wonderful partnership and would enliven many a dreary race with his astute and pithy comments. By the early nineties, despite well-publicised money worries, Hunt's roller-coaster personal life had at last become settled, and it was a great shock when he died in 1993 after a massive heart attack at the tragically early age of 45.

GUS HUTCHISON

An amateur racer from Dallas, Hutchison was the US Formula B champion in 1967, with a Lotus 41B, winning each of the first seven races he entered. Late in 1969, he bought the ex-Jacky Ickx Brabham BT26 for a successful 1970 season of SCCA Continental racing and also took the car to Watkins Glen for that year's US GP.

Gus was then a regular competitor in the early seventies in the L & M F5000 series with both Lola and March chassis.

JACKY ICKX

Here was a prodigy with the brio of Rindt and the controlled circumspection of Stewart, absolutely brilliant in the wet and endowed with such natural driving gifts that surely the World Championship would be a formality. In the end it was not to be, as his mercurial powers became diluted in a succession of less and less competitive cars.

The son of a famous motor racing journalist, Jacky was three times Belgium's motor cycle trials champion before moving to cars, and quickly became the man to beat in his Lotus Cortina, taking his national saloon car championship in 1965. Though only 21, Ickx was pitched straight into a season of Formula 2 in 1966 under the guidance of Ken Tyrrell, who could see his vast potential. It was at the following year's German GP that the young Jacky caused a sensation by qualifying the little Matra third fastest in practice, and though he had to start with the other Formula 2 cars at the back of the grid, he soon carved his way through the field to fourth place before his suspension broke. Now a hot property, he guested for Cooper at Monza to score his first championship point, before signing for Ferrari in 1968.

His first great win was not long in coming, Ickx showing sublime control in the wet to win at Rouen, and his consistent placings left him with an outside championship chance until a practice crash in Canada scuppered his hopes. By this time he was already regarded as one of the world's very best sports car drivers; racing for John Wyer, he had already won the Spa 1000 Km twice in addition to victories at Brands, Watkins Glen and Kyalami, and so anxious were Gulf to keep their prize asset that they arranged for Jacky to join Brabham for 1969. In the light of Ferrari's plight that year, it was a smart move with Ickx reaching the heights of his considerable brilliance by defeating Jackie Stewart in the German GP. Another win followed in Canada, but Ickx had to be content with the runner-up spot in the championship that year. Meanwhile the wisdom of Gulf's decision was demonstrated when Jacky took a sensational last-gasp victory at Le Mans over Herrmann's Porsche.

In 1970 he rejoined Ferrari to race in both Formula 1 and sports car events, but once again he was the nearly-man, just failing to overhaul the late Jochen Rindt's points total after winning three Grands Prix. Apart from a non-title win in the Rindt Memorial race at Hockenheim, and yet another masterful display in the wet at Zandvoort, the following Grand Prix season was not as competitive as Ickx would have hoped, while in 1972 Ferrari were still a potent force, but not consistent enough. Jacky predictably took another superb win at the Nürburgring, as well as chalking up brilliant victories in the team's sports cars, races at Daytona, Sebring, Brands Hatch, the Österreichring and Watkins Glen all surrendering to the Belgian that year alone.

With Ferrari falling into one of their periodical troughs in 1973, Ickx's patience ran out by mid-season and he quit the team, freelancing for McLaren and Williams before joining Ronnie Peterson at Lotus for 1974. Apart from a memorable win in the Race of Champions, it was a disastrous move, the bewildered Belgian switching back and forth between the almost undriveable new Lotus 76 and the by now venerable 72E. Things got even worse in 1975, with Ickx and Lotus parting company in mid-season. By now his Formula 1 career was in the balance and a move to the Wolf-Williams team at the beginning of 1976 tipped him into the also-ran category. A brief spell at Ensign, ironically replacing Chris Amon, showed the spark was there, but a nasty crash at Watkins Glen convinced him his highly successful sports car career was a better bet.

Jacky completed a remarkable hat-trick of Le Mans wins between 1975 and 1977, and won a string of rounds of the World Championship of Makes in the Martini Porsche partnered by Jochen Mass. In 1979 Ickx was back in the Grand Prix world, replacing the injured Depailler at Ligier, but sadly it was not a successful return, the finesse of his driving style not suited to the ground-effect cars of the time. Racing in Can-Am for Jim Hall, Ickx took the 1979 title, before concentrating almost exclusively on endurance racing in the eighties. After taking a fifth Le Mans win in 1981, he became a key member of the Rothmans Porsche team the following season and won the drivers' World Championship, scoring a record sixth win at Le Mans in addition to victories at Spa, Fuji and Brands Hatch. Jacky continued to race successfully through to the end of the 1985 season, when he took honourable retirement, hailed not only as one of the all-time greats of sports car racing but also, by those who remembered his halcyon days, as one of Grand Prix racing's most brilliant talents.

ICKX, Jacky (B) b 1/1/1945

1966

	Race	Circuit	No	Entrant	Car/Engine	Comment
ret	GERMAN GP (F2)	Nürburgring	27	Ken Tyrrell Racing	1.0 Matra MS5-Cosworth 4	transmission

1967

	Race	Circuit	No	Entrant	Car/Engine	Comment
ret	GERMAN GP (F2)	Nürburgring	29	Ken Tyrrell Racing	1.6 Matra MS7-Cosworth 4	suspension (FL-F2 class)
6	ITALIAN GP	Monza	32	Cooper Car Co	3.0 Cooper T81B-Maserati V12	puncture on last lap/2 laps behind
ret	US GP	Watkins Glen	21	Cooper Car Co	3.0 Cooper T81B-Maserati V12	overheating

1968

	Race	Circuit	No	Entrant	Car/Engine	Comment
ret	SOUTH AFRICAN GP	Kyalami	9	Scuderia Ferrari SpA SEFAC	3.0 Ferrari 312/67 V12	oil tank/driver exhausted
ret	SPANISH GP	Jarama	21	Scuderia Ferrari SpA SEFAC	3.0 Ferrari 312/67/68 V12	ignition
3	BELGIAN GP	Spa	23	Scuderia Ferrari SpA SEFAC	3.0 Ferrari 312/67/68 V12	
4	DUTCH GP	Zandvoort	10	Scuderia Ferrari SpA SEFAC	3.0 Ferrari 312/68 V12	2 laps behind
1	FRENCH GP	Rouen	26	Scuderia Ferrari SpA SEFAC	3.0 Ferrari 312/68 V12	
3	BRITISH GP	Brands Hatch	6	Scuderia Ferrari SpA SEFAC	3.0 Ferrari 312/68 V12	1 lap behind
4	GERMAN GP	Nürburgring	9	Scuderia Ferrari SpA SEFAC	3.0 Ferrari 312/68 V12	pit stops-visor/Pole
3	ITALIAN GP	Monza	8	Scuderia Ferrari SpA SEFAC	3.0 Ferrari 312/68 V12	
dns	CANADIAN GP	St Jovite	10	Scuderia Ferrari SpA SEFAC	3.0 Ferrari 312/68 V12	accident in practice-broken leg
ret	MEXICAN GP	Mexico City	7	Scuderia Ferrari SpA SEFAC	3.0 Ferrari 312/68 V12	ignition

1969

	Race	Circuit	No	Entrant	Car/Engine	Comment
ret	SOUTH AFRICAN GP	Kyalami	15	Motor Racing Developments	3.0 Brabham BT26A-Cosworth V8	starter solenoid after pit stop
6/ret	SPANISH GP	Montjuich Park	4	Motor Racing Developments	3.0 Brabham BT26A-Cosworth V8	rear suspension/7 laps behind
ret	MONACO GP	Monte Carlo	6	Motor Racing Developments	3.0 Brabham BT26A-Cosworth V8	rear suspension

5	DUTCH GP	Zandvoort	12	Motor Racing Developments	3.0 Brabham BT26A-Cosworth V8	
3	FRENCH GP	Clermont Ferrand	11	Motor Racing Developments	3.0 Brabham BT26A-Cosworth V8	
2	BRITISH GP	Silverstone	7	Motor Racing Developments	3.0 Brabham BT26A-Cosworth V8	*out of fuel last lap/1 lap behind*
1	GERMAN GP	Nürburgring	6	Motor Racing Developments	3.0 Brabham BT26A-Cosworth V8	*Pole/FL*
10/ret	ITALIAN GP	Monza	26	Motor Racing Developments	3.0 Brabham BT26A-Cosworth V8	*oil pressure/6 laps behind*
1	CANADIAN GP	Mosport Park	11	Motor Racing Developments	3.0 Brabham BT26A-Cosworth V8	*Pole/FL (shared with Brabham)*
ret	US GP	Watkins Glen	7	Motor Racing Developments	3.0 Brabham BT26A-Cosworth V8	*engine*
2	MEXICAN GP	Mexico City	7	Motor Racing Developments	3.0 Brabham BT26A-Cosworth V8	*FL*

1970

ret	SOUTH AFRICAN GP	Kyalami	17	Scuderia Ferrari SpA SEFAC	3.0 Ferrari 312B F12	*engine*
ret	SPANISH GP	Jarama	2	Scuderia Ferrari SpA SEFAC	3.0 Ferrari 312B F12	*collision with Oliver-burns*
ret	MONACO GP	Monte Carlo	26	Scuderia Ferrari SpA SEFAC	3.0 Ferrari 312B F12	*driveshaft*
8	BELGIAN GP	Spa	27	Scuderia Ferrari SpA SEFAC	3.0 Ferrari 312B F12	*pit stop-fuel leak/2 laps behind*
3	DUTCH GP	Zandvoort	25	Scuderia Ferrari SpA SEFAC	3.0 Ferrari 312B F12	*pit stop-puncture/FL/1 lap behind*
ret	FRENCH GP	Clermont Ferrand	10	Scuderia Ferrari SpA SEFAC	3.0 Ferrari 312B F12	*engine/Pole*
ret	BRITISH GP	Brands Hatch	3	Scuderia Ferrari SpA SEFAC	3.0 Ferrari 312B F12	*differential*
2	GERMAN GP	Hockenheim	10	Scuderia Ferrari SpA SEFAC	3.0 Ferrari 312B F12	*Pole/FL*
1	AUSTRIAN GP	Österreichring	12	Scuderia Ferrari SpA SEFAC	3.0 Ferrari 312B F12	*FL (shared with Regazzoni)*
ret	ITALIAN GP	Monza	2	Scuderia Ferrari SpA SEFAC	3.0 Ferrari 312B F12	*clutch/Pole*
1	CANADIAN GP	St Jovite	18	Scuderia Ferrari SpA SEFAC	3.0 Ferrari 312B F12	
4	US GP	Watkins Glen	3	Scuderia Ferrari SpA SEFAC	3.0 Ferrari 312B F12	*pit stop-fuel leak//Pole/FL/-1 lap*
1	MEXICAN GP	Mexico City	3	Scuderia Ferrari SpA SEFAC	3.0 Ferrari 312B F12	*FL*

1971

8	SOUTH AFRICAN GP	Kyalami	4	Scuderia Ferrari SpA SEFAC	3.0 Ferrari 312B F12	*1 lap behind*
2	SPANISH GP	Montjuich Park	4	Scuderia Ferrari SpA SEFAC	3.0 Ferrari 312B F12	*Pole/FL*
3	MONACO GP	Monte Carlo	4	Scuderia Ferrari SpA SEFAC	3.0 Ferrari 312B2 F12	
1	DUTCH GP	Zandvoort	2	Scuderia Ferrari SpA SEFAC	3.0 Ferrari 312B2 F12	*wet race/Pole/FL*
ret	FRENCH GP	Paul Ricard	4	Scuderia Ferrari SpA SEFAC	3.0 Ferrari 312B2 F12	*engine*
ret	BRITISH GP	Silverstone	4	Scuderia Ferrari SpA SEFAC	3.0 Ferrari 312B2 F12	*engine*
ret	GERMAN GP	Nürburgring	4	Scuderia Ferrari SpA SEFAC	3.0 Ferrari 312B2 F12	*spun off*
ret	AUSTRIAN GP	Österreichring	4	Scuderia Ferrari SpA SEFAC	3.0 Ferrari 312B2 F12	*electrics-plug leads*
ret	ITALIAN GP	Monza	3	Scuderia Ferrari SpA SEFAC	3.0 Ferrari 312B F12	*engine damper*
dns	"	"	3	Scuderia Ferrari SpA SEFAC	3.0 Ferrari 312B2 F12	*practice only*
8	CANADIAN GP	Mosport Park	4	Scuderia Ferrari SpA SEFAC	3.0 Ferrari 312B2 F12	*2 laps behind*
ret	US GP	Watkins Glen	4	Scuderia Ferrari SpA SEFAC	3.0 Ferrari 312B F12	*alternator fell off/FL*
dns	"	" "	4	Scuderia Ferrari SpA SEFAC	3.0 Ferrari 312B2 F12	*practice only*

1972

3	ARGENTINE GP	Buenos Aires	8	Scuderia Ferrari SpA SEFAC	3.0 Ferrari 312B2 F12	
8	SOUTH AFRICAN GP	Kyalami	5	Scuderia Ferrari SpA SEFAC	3.0 Ferrari 312B2 F12	*1 lap behind*
2	SPANISH GP	Jarama	4	Scuderia Ferrari SpA SEFAC	3.0 Ferrari 312B2 F12	*Pole/FL*
2	MONACO GP	Monte Carlo	6	Scuderia Ferrari SpA SEFAC	3.0 Ferrari 312B2 F12	
ret	BELGIAN GP	Nivelles	29	Scuderia Ferrari SpA SEFAC	3.0 Ferrari 312B2 F12	*fuel injection*
11	FRENCH GP	Clermont Ferrand	3	Scuderia Ferrari SpA SEFAC	3.0 Ferrari 312B2 F12	*1 lap behind*
ret	BRITISH GP	Brands Hatch	5	Scuderia Ferrari SpA SEFAC	3.0 Ferrari 312B2 F12	*oil pressure/led race/Pole*
1	GERMAN GP	Nürburgring	4	Scuderia Ferrari SpA SEFAC	3.0 Ferrari 312B2 F12	*Pole/FL*
ret	AUSTRIAN GP	Österreichring	18	Scuderia Ferrari SpA SEFAC	3.0 Ferrari 312B2 F12	*fuel pressure*
ret	ITALIAN GP	Monza	4	Scuderia Ferrari SpA SEFAC	3.0 Ferrari 312B2 F12	*electrics/Pole/FL*
12	CANADIAN GP	Mosport Park	10	Scuderia Ferrari SpA SEFAC	3.0 Ferrari 312B2 F12	*pit stop-puncture/4 laps behind*
5	US GP	Watkins Glen	7	Scuderia Ferrari SpA SEFAC	3.0 Ferrari 312B2 F12	

1973

4	ARGENTINE GP	Buenos Aires	18	Scuderia Ferrari SpA SEFAC	3.0 Ferrari 312B2 F12	
5	BRAZILIAN GP	Interlagos	9	Scuderia Ferrari SpA SEFAC	3.0 Ferrari 312B2 F12	*pit stop-puncture/1 lap behind*
ret	SOUTH AFRICAN GP	Kyalami	8	Scuderia Ferrari SpA SEFAC	3.0 Ferrari 312B2 F12	*accident with Regazzoni & Hailwood*
12	SPANISH GP	Montjuich Park	7	Scuderia Ferrari SpA SEFAC	3.0 Ferrari 312B3 F12	*pit stop-brakes/6 laps behind*
ret	BELGIAN GP	Zolder	3	Scuderia Ferrari SpA SEFAC	3.0 Ferrari 312B3 F12	*oil pump*
ret	MONACO GP	Monte Carlo	3	Scuderia Ferrari SpA SEFAC	3.0 Ferrari 312B3 F12	*driveshaft*
6	SWEDISH GP	Anderstorp	3	Scuderia Ferrari SpA SEFAC	3.0 Ferrari 312B3 F12	*1 lap behind*
5	FRENCH GP	Paul Ricard	3	Scuderia Ferrari SpA SEFAC	3.0 Ferrari 312B3 F12	
8	BRITISH GP	Silverstone	3	Scuderia Ferrari SpA SEFAC	3.0 Ferrari 312B3 F12	
3	GERMAN GP	Nürburgring	30	Yardley Team McLaren	3.0 McLaren M23-Cosworth V8	
8	ITALIAN GP	Monza	3	Scuderia Ferrari SpA SEFAC	3.0 Ferrari 312B3 F12	*clipped chicane/1 lap behind*
7	US GP	Watkins Glen	26	Frank Williams Racing Cars	3.0 Williams 1R-Cosworth V8	*1 lap behind*

1974

ret	ARGENTINE GP	Buenos Aires	2	John Player Team Lotus	3.0 Lotus 72E-Cosworth V8	*transmission*
3	BRAZILIAN GP	Interlagos	2	John Player Team Lotus	3.0 Lotus 72E-Cosworth V8	*1 lap behind*
ret	SOUTH AFRICAN GP	Kyalami	2	John Player Team Lotus	3.0 Lotus 76-Cosworth V8	*brake balance/hit by Peterson*
ret	SPANISH GP	Jarama	2	John Player Team Lotus	3.0 Lotus 76-Cosworth V8	*leaking brake fluid*
ret	BELGIAN GP	Nivelles	2	John Player Team Lotus	3.0 Lotus 76-Cosworth V8	*brakes*
ret	MONACO GP	Monte Carlo	2	John Player Team Lotus	3.0 Lotus 72E-Cosworth V8	*gearbox*
dns	"	" "	2T	John Player Team Lotus	3.0 Lotus 76-Cosworth V8	*practice only*
ret	SWEDISH GP	Anderstorp	2	John Player Team Lotus	3.0 Lotus 76-Cosworth V8	*oil pressure*
11	DUTCH GP	Zandvoort	2	John Player Team Lotus	3.0 Lotus 72E-Cosworth V8	*pit stop-loose wheel/4 laps behind*
dns	"	"	2T	John Player Team Lotus	3.0 Lotus 76-Cosworth V8	*practice only*
5	FRENCH GP	Dijon	2	John Player Team Lotus	3.0 Lotus 72E-Cosworth V8	
3	BRITISH GP	Brands Hatch	2	John Player Team Lotus	3.0 Lotus 72E-Cosworth V8	
5	GERMAN GP	Nürburgring	2	John Player Team Lotus	3.0 Lotus 72E-Cosworth V8	
ret	AUSTRIAN GP	Österreichring	2	John Player Team Lotus	3.0 Lotus 76-Cosworth V8	*collision with Depailler*
dns	"	"	2T	John Player Team Lotus	3.0 Lotus 72E-Cosworth V8	*practice only*
ret	ITALIAN GP	Monza	2	John Player Team Lotus	3.0 Lotus 76-Cosworth V8	*throttle linkage*
13	CANADIAN GP	Mosport Park	2	John Player Team Lotus	3.0 Lotus 72E-Cosworth V8	*2 laps behind*
dns	"	" "	2T	John Player Team Lotus	3.0 Lotus 76-Cosworth V8	*practice only*
ret	US GP	Watkins Glen	2	John Player Team Lotus	3.0 Lotus 72E-Cosworth V8	*hit guard rail*

1975

8	ARGENTINE GP	Buenos Aires	6	John Player Team Lotus	3.0 Lotus 72E-Cosworth V8	*1 lap behind*
9	BRAZILIAN GP	Interlagos	6	John Player Team Lotus	3.0 Lotus 72E-Cosworth V8	
12	SOUTH AFRICAN GP	Kyalami	6	John Player Team Lotus	3.0 Lotus 72E-Cosworth V8	*2 laps behind*
2*	SPANISH GP	Montjuich Park	6	John Player Team Lotus	3.0 Lotus 72E-Cosworth V8	*shortened race/half points only*
8	MONACO GP	Monte Carlo	6	John Player Team Lotus	3.0 Lotus 72E-Cosworth V8	*1 lap behind*
ret	BELGIAN GP	Zolder	6	John Player Team Lotus	3.0 Lotus 72E-Cosworth V8	*brake shaft*
15	SWEDISH GP	Anderstorp	6	John Player Team Lotus	3.0 Lotus 72E-Cosworth V8	*3 laps behind*
ret	DUTCH GP	Zandvoort	6	John Player Team Lotus	3.0 Lotus 72E-Cosworth V8	*engine*
ret	FRENCH GP	Paul Ricard	6	John Player Team Lotus	3.0 Lotus 72E-Cosworth V8	*brake shaft*

1976

8	BRAZILIAN GP	Interlagos	20	Frank Williams Racing Cars	3.0 Williams FW05-Cosworth V8	*1 lap behind*
16	SOUTH AFRICAN GP	Kyalami	20	Frank Williams Racing Cars	3.0 Williams FW05-Cosworth V8	*pit stop/5 laps behind*
dnq	US GP WEST	Long Beach	20	Frank Williams Racing Cars	3.0 Williams FW05-Cosworth V8	
7	SPANISH GP	Jarama	20	Walter Wolf Racing	3.0 Williams FW05-Cosworth V8	*1 lap behind*
dnq	BELGIAN GP	Zolder	20	Walter Wolf Racing	3.0 Williams FW05-Cosworth V8	
dnq	MONACO GP	Monte Carlo	20	Walter Wolf Racing	3.0 Williams FW05-Cosworth V8	
10	FRENCH GP	Paul Ricard	20	Walter Wolf Racing	3.0 Williams FW05-Cosworth V8	*1 lap behind*
dnq	BRITISH GP	Silverstone	20	Walter Wolf Racing	3.0 Williams FW05-Cosworth V8	
ret	DUTCH GP	Zandvoort	22	Team Ensign	3.0 Ensign N176-Cosworth V8	*electrics*
10	ITALIAN GP	Monza	22	Team Ensign	3.0 Ensign N176-Cosworth V8	
13	CANADIAN GP	Mosport Park	22	Team Ensign	3.0 Ensign N176-Cosworth V8	*1 lap behind*
ret	US GP EAST	Watkins Glen	22	Team Ensign	3.0 Ensign N176-Cosworth V8	*accident-broken ankle/burns*

1977

10	MONACO GP	Monte Carlo	22	Team Tissot Ensign with Castrol	3.0 Ensign N177-Cosworth V8	*1 lap behind*

1978

ret	MONACO GP	Monte Carlo	22	Team Tissot Ensign	3.0 Ensign N177-Cosworth V8	*brakes*
12	BELGIAN GP	Zolder	22	Team Tissot Ensign	3.0 Ensign N177-Cosworth V8	*multiple accident-pit stop/-6 laps*
ret	SPANISH GP	Jarama	22	Team Tissot Ensign	3.0 Ensign N177-Cosworth V8	*engine*
dnq	SWEDISH GP	Anderstorp	22	Team Tissot Ensign	3.0 Ensign N177-Cosworth V8	

1979

ret	FRENCH GP	Dijon	25	Ligier Gitanes	3.0 Ligier JS11-Cosworth V8	*engine*
6	BRITISH GP	Silverstone	25	Ligier Gitanes	3.0 Ligier JS11-Cosworth V8	*1 lap behind*
ret	GERMAN GP	Hockenheim	25	Ligier Gitanes	3.0 Ligier JS11-Cosworth V8	*burst tyre*
ret	AUSTRIAN GP	Österreichring	25	Ligier Gitanes	3.0 Ligier JS11-Cosworth V8	*engine*
5	DUTCH GP	Zandvoort	25	Ligier Gitanes	3.0 Ligier JS11-Cosworth V8	*1 lap behind*
ret	ITALIAN GP	Monza	25	Ligier Gitanes	3.0 Ligier JS11-Cosworth V8	*engine*
ret	CANADIAN GP	Montreal	25	Ligier Gitanes	3.0 Ligier JS11-Cosworth V8	*gearbox*
ret	US GP EAST	Watkins Glen	25	Ligier Gitanes	3.0 Ligier JS11-Cosworth V8	*spun off*

GP Starts: 116   GP Wins: 8   Pole positions: 13   Fastest laps: 14   Points: 181

IGLESIAS, Jesus (RA) b 22/2/1922

1955

	Race	Circuit	No	Entrant	Car/Engine	Comment
ret	ARGENTINE GP	Buenos Aires	42	Equipe Gordini	2.5 Gordini Type 16 6	*transmission/exhaustion*

GP Starts: 1   GP Wins: 0   Pole positions: 0   Fastest laps: 0   Points: 0

IRELAND, Innes (GB) b 12/6/1930 – d 22/10/1993

1959

	Race	Circuit	No	Entrant	Car/Engine	Comment
4	DUTCH GP	Zandvoort	12	Team Lotus	2.5 Lotus 16-Climax 4	*1 lap behind*
ret	FRENCH GP	Reims	34	Team Lotus	2.5 Lotus 16-Climax 4	*front hub bearing*
ret	GERMAN GP	AVUS	15	Team Lotus	2.5 Lotus 16-Climax 4	*gear selection/cwp-heat 1*
ret	PORTUGUESE GP	Monsanto	12	Team Lotus	2.5 Lotus 16-Climax 4	*gearbox*
ret	ITALIAN GP	Monza	20	Team Lotus	2.5 Lotus 16-Climax 4	*brakes*
5	US GP	Sebring	10	Team Lotus	2.5 Lotus 16-Climax 4	*3 laps behind*

1960

6	ARGENTINE GP	Buenos Aires	20	Team Lotus	2.5 Lotus 18-Climax 4	*gear linkage problems-spin/-1 lap*
9	MONACO GP	Monte Carlo	22	Team Lotus	2.5 Lotus 18-Climax 4	*long p stop-engine/44 laps behind*
2	DUTCH GP	Zandvoort	4	Team Lotus	2.5 Lotus 18-Climax 4	
ret	BELGIAN GP	Spa	14	Team Lotus	2.5 Lotus 18-Climax 4	*spun off/FL(shared-P Hill & Brabham)*
7	FRENCH GP	Reims	20	Team Lotus	2.5 Lotus 18-Climax 4	*pit stop-suspension/7 laps behind*
3	BRITISH GP	Silverstone	7	Team Lotus	2.5 Lotus 18-Climax 4	
6	PORTUGUESE GP	Oporto	16	Team Lotus	2.5 Lotus 18-Climax 4	*p stop-fuel feed problems/-7 laps*
2	US GP	Riverside	10	Team Lotus	2.5 Lotus 18-Climax 4	

1961

dns	MONACO GP	Monte Carlo	30	Team Lotus	1.5 Lotus 21-Climax 4	*accident in practice*
ret	BELGIAN GP	Spa	32	Team Lotus	1.5 Lotus 21-Climax 4	*engine*
4	FRENCH GP	Reims	6	Team Lotus	1.5 Lotus 21-Climax 4	
10	BRITISH GP	Aintree	16	Team Lotus	1.5 Lotus 21-Climax 4	*despite spin/3 laps behind*
ret	GERMAN GP	Nürburgring	15	Team Lotus	1.5 Lotus 21-Climax 4	*fire*
ret	ITALIAN GP	Monza	38	Team Lotus	1.5 Lotus 18/21-Climax 4	*chassis frame*
dns	"	"	38	Team Lotus	1.5 Lotus 21-Climax 4	*practice only/car to Moss for race*
1	US GP	Watkins Glen	15	Team Lotus	1.5 Lotus 21-Climax 4	

1962

ret	DUTCH GP	Zandvoort	9	UDT Laystall Racing Team	1.5 Lotus 24-Climax V8	*overturned*
ret	MONACO GP	Monte Carlo	34	UDT Laystall Racing Team	1.5 Lotus 24-Climax V8	*fuel pump*

dns	"	"	"	34	UDT Laystall Racing Team	1.5 Lotus 18-Climax V8	*practice only*

Result	Race	Circuit	No.	Team	Car	Notes
dns	"	" "	34	UDT Laystall Racing Team	1.5 Lotus 18-Climax V8	*practice only*
ret	BELGIAN GP	Spa	20	UDT Laystall Racing Team	1.5 Lotus 24-BRM V8	*rear suspension*
dns	"	"	21	UDT Laystall Racing Team	1.5 Lotus 24-Climax V8	*practice only*
ret	FRENCH GP	Rouen	36	UDT Laystall Racing Team	1.5 Lotus 24-Climax V8	*puncture*
16	BRITISH GP	Aintree	32	UDT Laystall Racing Team	1.5 Lotus 24-Climax V8	*gear selection on grid/-14 laps*
ret	ITALIAN GP	Monza	40	UDT Laystall Racing Team	1.5 Lotus 24-Climax V8	*front suspension*
8	US GP	Watkins Glen	15	UDT Laystall Racing Team	1.5 Lotus 24-Climax V8	*pit stop/4 laps behind*
5	SOUTH AFRICAN GP	East London	11	UDT Laystall Racing Team	1.5 Lotus 24-Climax V8	*1 lap behind*
1963						
ret	MONACO GP	Monte Carlo	14	British Racing Partnership	1.5 Lotus 24-BRM V8	*accident*
ret	BELGIAN GP	Spa	4	British Racing Partnership	1.5 BRP 1-BRM V8	*gear selection*
dns	"	"	4	British Racing Partnership	1.5 Lotus 24-BRM V8	*practice only*
4	DUTCH GP	Zandvoort	30	British Racing Partnership	1.5 BRP 1-BRM V8	*1 lap behind*
dns	"	"	30	British Racing Partnership	1.5 Lotus 24-BRM V8	*practice only*
9	FRENCH GP	Reims	32	British Racing Partnership	1.5 BRP 1-BRM V8	*pit stop-gearbox/4 laps behind*
dsq	BRITISH GP	Silverstone	11	British Racing Partnership	1.5 BRP 1-BRM V8	*ignition at pit stop-push start*
dns	"	"	11	British Racing Partnership	1.5 Lotus 24-BRM V8	*practice only*
ret	GERMAN GP	Nürburgring	14	British Racing Partnership	1.5 Lotus 24-BRM V8	*collision with Bandini*
dns	"	"	14	British Racing Partnership	1.5 BRP 1-BRM V8	*accident in practice*
4/ret	ITALIAN GP	Monza	32	British Racing Partnership	1.5 BRP 1-BRM V8	*engine*
1964						
dns	MONACO GP	Monte Carlo	14	British Racing Partnership	1.5 Lotus 24-BRM V8	*practice accident*
10	BELGIAN GP	Spa	3	British Racing Partnership	1.5 BRP 1-BRM V8	*pit stop/4 laps behind*
ret	FRENCH GP	Rouen	16	British Racing Partnership	1.5 BRP 1-BRM V8	*accident*
10	BRITISH GP	Brands Hatch	11	British Racing Partnership	1.5 BRP 2-BRM V8	*engine problems/3 laps behind*
5	AUSTRIAN GP	Zeltweg	14	British Racing Partnership	1.5 BRP 2-BRM V8	*pit stop-engine/3 laps behind*
5	ITALIAN GP	Monza	46	British Racing Partnership	1.5 BRP 2-BRM V8	*fuel feed problems/1 lap behind*
ret	US GP	Watkins Glen	11	British Racing Partnership	1.5 BRP 2-BRM V8	*gear lever*
12	MEXICAN GP	Mexico City	11	British Racing Partnership	1.5 BRP 2-BRM V8	*pit stop/4 laps behind*
1965						
13	BELGIAN GP	Spa	22	Reg Parnell (Racing)	1.5 Lotus 25-BRM V8	*pit stop/5 laps behind*
ret	FRENCH GP	Clermont Ferrand	22	Reg Parnell (Racing)	1.5 Lotus 25-BRM V8	*gearbox*
ret	BRITISH GP	Silverstone	23	Reg Parnell (Racing)	1.5 Lotus 25-BRM V8	*engine*
10	DUTCH GP	Zandvoort	38	Reg Parnell (Racing)	1.5 Lotus 25-BRM V8	*2 laps behind*
9	ITALIAN GP	Monza	38	Reg Parnell (Racing)	1.5 Lotus 25-BRM V8	*2 laps behind*
ret	US GP	Watkins Glen	22	Reg Parnell (Racing)	1.5 Lotus 25-BRM V8	*unwell with flu*
dns	MEXICAN GP	Mexico City	22	Reg Parnell (Racing)	1.5 Lotus 25-BRM V8	*dropped by team-late for practice*
1966						
ret	US GP	Watkins Glen	10	Bernard White Racing	2.0 BRM P261 V8	*flat battery*
ret	MEXICAN GP	Mexico City	10	Bernard White Racing	2.0 BRM P261 V8	*gearbox*

GP Starts: 50   GP Wins: 1   Pole positions: 0   Fastest laps: 1   Points: 47

INNES IRELAND

It was all-change; the front-engined cars were out, as was the casual racing attire and devil-may-care attitude, but Innes carried the spirit of a fast-disappearing age into the sixties and in career terms it was to cost him dear.

The son of a veterinary surgeon, he showed no inclination to follow the same path and instead took up an engineering apprenticeship. After dabbling in racing between 1952 and 1955, a period which saw him complete his National Service as a paratrooper, Innes really got his racing career into gear with a Lotus XI in 1956. He began to build his reputation in 1957 and 1958, racing both his own car and the Ecurie Ecosse Jaguar D-Type. A class win in the Lotus at the Reims 12 Hours impressed Colin Chapman sufficiently for him to sign Innes for the 1959 season, and he took a fourth place in the International Trophy before making an impressive Grand Prix debut at Zandvoort. The cars were very unreliable, and little else was achieved until the 1960 season when the new rear-engined Lotus 18 proved sensationally quick. On its debut in Argentina, Ireland led comfortably until the gear linkage broke, and then at home he stormed to victory in the Glover Trophy at Goodwood, ahead of Moss, and the International Trophy, putting Brabham in his place. Although a Grand Prix victory was not to be his that season, Innes enjoyed a fabulous year, for in addition to the wins previously mentioned he took the Lombank Trophy and recorded some excellent placings as well as Formula 2 wins at Goodwood and Oulton Park.

The 1961 season started badly for Innes with a heavy crash at Monaco when he selected the wrong gear, but despite a fractured kneecap he was soon back in his stride, producing a splendid performance to win the Solitude GP, followed by a win in the Flugplatzrennen at Zeltweg. His great moment arrived at the end of the season

when he won the US GP after a text book drive. Much to his chagrin, Ireland was then released from his contract by Chapman, who had decided that youngsters Jim Clark and Trevor Taylor would race for him in 1962. It was effectively the end of Innes' front-line career. Joining the UDT-Laystall team, he found success in sports cars, winning the Tourist Trophy in a 250 GTO, but endured a largely frustrating time in single-seaters. He won the Crystal Palace Trophy in 1962 and the following season (the team having been renamed BRP) he enjoyed a respectable early-season run in non-championship events with both a Lotus 24 and the team's own BRP chassis, winning the Glover Trophy and finishing third at Snetterton, second at Aintree, fourth at Silverstone and third at Solitude, before an accident at Seattle left him with a dislocated hip.

In 1964 Innes plugged away with the disappointing BRP, claiming a victory in the Daily Mirror Trophy at Snetterton, but the team closed its doors at the end of the year, leaving Ireland to find a berth in the Parnell Racing team for 1965. His off-track popularity was as high as ever, but sadly he was by then less reliable as a driver. Appearing late for a practice session in Mexico saw him dismissed on the spot, but Tim Parnell must have forgiven him as he raced for the team again in the 1966 South African GP! Innes then found employment racing sports cars, sharing a Ford GT40 with Amon to take fifth place in the Spa 1000 Km. He drew down the curtain on his single-seater career late in 1966 when he joined Bernard White's suitably 'happy-go-lucky' *équipe* and took fourth place in the Gold Cup at Oulton Park, before his last two Grand Prix appearances in the US and Mexico. His hell-raising lifestyle had not fitted in with the new professionalism of the age, but this unique character, who could both charm and outrage in short order, continued to be happily associated with the sport in both journalistic and organisational capacities on and off until his death from cancer in 1993.

EDDIE IRVINE

Rarely can a Grand Prix debut have brought so much controversy. As Eddie Irvine shone in the wet in the Jordan-Hart, battling with Damon Hill for fourth place, he first balked and then had the temerity to repass the race leader, Ayrton Senna, who was attempting to lap him; late on in the race he punted Derek Warwick off to claim sixth place and a championship point; and then he suffered a physical and verbal assault from the irate Brazilian after the race.

It certainly moved the self-assured Ulsterman to centre stage, if only for a weekend. Eddie's early career had promised a great deal, particularly in 1990 when he was a front-runner in Formula 3000, winning at Hockenheim for Eddie Jordan and finishing third in the championship. Irvine has subsequently raced for Toyota at Le Mans, but he has concentrated on the Japanese F3000 series and was very unfortunate to lose the 1993 championship after scoring more points than the veteran, Kazuyoshi Hoshino. Eddie has signed for a full season of Grand Prix racing in 1994, so we will be able to see if Suzuka was a flash in the pan, or the arrival of a potential star who had been previously overlooked.

CHRIS IRWIN

An outstanding prospect, Irwin made an immediate impression in his first full Formula 3 season in 1964, taking third in the Grovewood Awards. Further success in F3 with the Chequered Flag Merlyn brought him a works Formula 2 drive for that marque in 1965. He then gained a works drive for Brabham in 1966, concentrating on F3 but occasionally racing in F2, and scoring a fine third place in the Albi GP. Given an old four-cylinder-engined Brabham, Chris finished seventh on his GP debut at Brands Hatch, impressing Tim Parnell, who signed him along with Piers Courage to share the semi-works BRM for 1967.

In fact, Courage made a tardy start to the season, while Irwin, after scoring a fourth at Sandown Park and a third at Longford in the Tasman series, followed by sixth place in the Race of Champions and fourth at Syracuse in Parnell's old Lotus 25-BRM, took his chance with some solid and sensible drives in both the 2-litre car and the heavy and unreliable H16, which he took to fifth in the French GP.

Chris had also joined up with John Surtees to race the works Lola in Formula 2, winning the 1968 Eifelrennen race at the Nürburgring and finishing third at Zolder, before a return to the 'Ring in Alan Mann's Ford PL3 sports car ended in a catastrophic practice crash. Poor Chris received very serious head injuries, from which he eventually made a recovery, but he never raced again.

JEAN-PIERRE JABOUILLE

Success was a long time coming for this popular Frenchman who, while never one to take the eye, certainly knew how to put the machinery at his disposal to the best use.

With no previous experience, Jean-Pierre competed in the R8 Renault Gordini series in 1966 and won a few races, earning an invitation to drive in French F3 in a team with the more seasoned Philippe Vidal. The F3 scene was very competitive, but Jabouille made his mark in 1968 when he ran and maintained his own car, keeping out of trouble and earning enough prize money from one race to make it to the next. The series that year was dominated by Cevert, but Jean-Pierre won five races to finish runner-up and gain an end-of-year Formula 2 ride with Matra at Hockenheim.

Alpine offered him a contract for 1969 as number two to Depailler, and he stayed with the team as a test and development driver over the next few seasons, his rather fragmented racing programme doing little to further his ambitions. Threre were outings for Pygmée in F2 in 1970 and for Elf-Tecno the following season, when he finished second at Pau, and Jabouille also tried his hand at sports cars, taking a splendid second place in the Paris 1000 Km in a Ferrari 512S. The Frenchman's career seemed to be stuck in something of a rut in 1972 when he received decidedly 'second best' treatment in the Elf/John Coombs team, and made his feelings known. When he was given a March 722, things improved and he took second place at Mantorp Park. His lot was much the same in 1973, when much of his time was given over to the development of the Alpine A440 sports car, but he was loaned to Matra for Le Mans, sharing the third-placed car with Jaussaud.

In 1974 Jabouille made a couple of unsuccessful attempts to qualify for a Grand Prix with Williams and Surtees, but concentrated on the same mix as the year before, only this time with more success. In Formula 2 he won his first race at Hockenheim and, racing the Alpine, he finished runner-up in the European 2-litre series. Seconded to Matra for Le Mans again, he finished third once more, this time with Migault. Determined to improve upon his somewhat patchy record of success in Formula 2, Jabouille took the brave step of constructing his own chassis for 1975 with the support of Elf. He lost out to his great chum Laffite in the championship but, thanks to his connections with Elf, he at least had the consolation of a decent Grand Prix opportunity, qualifying the Tyrrell for the French GP. It was a popular triumph when Jean-Pierre finally clinched the Formula 2 title in 1976 with three wins, and no one begrudged the Parisian his hard-earned triumph.

This goal achieved, Jabouille then undertook the development work on the F1 Renault turbo project, accepting the early disappointments with equanimity as failure heaped upon failure over the first two seasons until the glorious moment for France and Renault when the car finally came good – fittingly at Dijon – in 1979. Although overshadowed by the sparkling Arnoux in 1980, Jean-Pierre took a shrewd and well-judged win at the Österreichring before a crash in Montreal after a suspension failure left him with badly broken legs. Having already agreed to join Ligier for 1981, he made it back into the cockpit for the start of the season, but it soon became painfully obvious that he was far from fit and, with his leg injuries slow to heal, he decided to retire in mid-season.

Missing the thrill of competition, Jean-Pierre was soon back on the circuits, racing in the French Supertourisme series. His vast engineering and development experience later made a valuable contribution to Peugeot's successful sports car racing programme, and in 1993 he shared the third-placed car at Le Mans, before succeeding Jean Todt at the head of the French company's motor sport division as they prepared to enter Grand Prix racing with McLaren in 1994.

IRVINE, Eddie (GB) b 10/11/1965

1993

	Race	Circuit	No	Entrant	Car/Engine	Comment
6	JAPANESE GP	Suzuka	15	Team Sasol Jordan	3.5 Jordan 193-Hart V10	delayed Senna/collision-Warwick
ret	AUSTRALIAN GP	Adelaide	15	Team Sasol Jordan	3.5 Jordan 193-Hart V10	suspension damage after spin

GP Starts: 2   GP Wins: 0   Pole positions: 0   Fastest laps: 0   Points: 1

IRWIN, Chris (GB) b 27/6/1942

1966

	Race	Circuit	No	Entrant	Car/Engine	Comment
7	BRITISH GP	Brands Hatch	7	Brabham Racing Organisation	2.7 Brabham BT22-Climax 4	2 laps behind

1967

	Race	Circuit	No	Entrant	Car/Engine	Comment
7	DUTCH GP	Zandvoort	18	Reg Parnell Motor Racing	2.0 Lotus 25-BRM V8	2 laps behind
ret	BELGIAN GP	Spa	17	Reg Parnell Motor Racing	2.0 BRM P261 V8	engine
5/ret	FRENCH GP	Le Mans	15	Reg Parnell Motor Racing	3.0 BRM P83 H16	engine/4 laps behind
dns	"	" "	15	Reg Parnell Motor Racing	2.0 BRM P261 V8	practice only/Stewart in race
7	BRITISH GP	Silverstone	15	Reg Parnell Motor Racing	2.0 BRM P261 V8	3 laps behind
dns	"	"	15	Reg Parnell Motor Racing	3.0 BRM P83 H16	practice only/Stewart in race
7	GERMAN GP	Nürburgring	18	Reg Parnell Motor Racing	3.0 BRM P83 H16	p stop-gearbox/9th on road/-2 laps
ret	CANADIAN GP	Mosport Park	17	Reg Parnell Motor Racing	3.0 BRM P83 H16	spun off
ret	ITALIAN GP	Monza	38	Reg Parnell Motor Racing	3.0 BRM P83 H16	injection pump drive
ret	US GP	Watkins Glen	17	Reg Parnell Motor Racing	3.0 BRM P83 H16	engine
ret	MEXICAN GP	Mexico City	17	Reg Parnell Motor Racing	3.0 BRM P83 H16	low oil pressure

GP Starts: 10   GP Wins: 1   Pole positions: 0   Fastest laps: 0   Points: 2

JABOUILLE, Jean-Pierre (F) b 1/10/1942

1974

	Race	Circuit	No	Entrant	Car/Engine	Comment
dnq	FRENCH GP	Dijon	21	Frank Williams Racing Cars	3.0 Williams FW01-Cosworth V8	
dnq	AUSTRIAN GP	Österreichring	19	Team Surtees	3.0 Surtees TS16-Cosworth V8	

1975

	Race	Circuit	No	Entrant	Car/Engine	Comment
12	FRENCH GP	Paul Ricard	15	Elf Team Tyrrell	3.0 Tyrrell 007-Cosworth V8	

1977

	Race	Circuit	No	Entrant	Car/Engine	Comment
ret	BRITISH GP	Silverstone	15	Equipe Renault Elf	1.5 t/c Renault RS01 V6	turbo
ret	DUTCH GP	Zandvoort	15	Equipe Renault Elf	1.5 t/c Renault RS01 V6	rear suspension
ret	ITALIAN GP	Monza	15	Equipe Renault Elf	1.5 t/c Renault RS01 V6	engine
ret	US GP EAST	Watkins Glen	15	Equipe Renault Elf	1.5 t/c Renault RS01 V6	alternator
dnq	CANADIAN GP	Mosport Park	15	Equipe Renault Elf	1.5 t/c Renault RS01 V6	

1978

	Race	Circuit	No	Entrant	Car/Engine	Comment
ret	SOUTH AFRICAN GP	Kyalami	15	Equipe Renault Elf	1.5 t/c Renault RS01 V6	engine
ret	US GP WEST	Long Beach	15	Equipe Renault Elf	1.5 t/c Renault RS01 V6	turbo
10	MONACO GP	Monte Carlo	15	Equipe Renault Elf	1.5 t/c Renault RS01 V6	brake problem/4 laps behind
nc	BELGIAN GP	Zolder	15	Equipe Renault Elf	1.5 t/c Renault RS01 V6	3 pit stops-brakes/14 laps behind
13	SPANISH GP	Jarama	15	Equipe Renault Elf	1.5 t/c Renault RS01 V6	4 laps behind
ret	SWEDISH GP	Anderstorp	15	Equipe Renault Elf	1.5 t/c Renault RS01 V6	engine
ret	FRENCH GP	Paul Ricard	15	Equipe Renault Elf	1.5 t/c Renault RS01 V6	engine
ret	BRITISH GP	Brands Hatch	15	Equipe Renault Elf	1.5 t/c Renault RS01 V6	engine
ret	GERMAN GP	Hockenheim	15	Equipe Renault Elf	1.5 t/c Renault RS01 V6	engine
ret	AUSTRIAN GP	Österreichring	15	Equipe Renault Elf	1.5 t/c Renault RS01 V6	gearbox
ret	DUTCH GP	Zandvoort	15	Equipe Renault Elf	1.5 t/c Renault RS01 V6	engine
ret	ITALIAN GP	Monza	15	Equipe Renault Elf	1.5 t/c Renault RS01 V6	engine
4	US GP EAST	Watkins Glen	15	Equipe Renault Elf	1.5 t/c Renault RS01 V6	
12	CANADIAN GP	Montreal	15	Equipe Renault Elf	1.5 t/c Renault RS01 V6	pit stop/5 laps behind

1979

	Race	Circuit	No	Entrant	Car/Engine	Comment
ret	ARGENTINE GP	Buenos Aires	15	Equipe Renault Elf	1.5 t/c Renault RS01 V6	engine
10	BRAZILIAN GP	Interlagos	15	Equipe Renault Elf	1.5 t/c Renault RS01 V6	stalled on grid/1 lap behind
ret	SOUTH AFRICAN GP	Kyalami	15	Equipe Renault Elf	1.5 t/c Renault RS01 V6	engine/Pole
dns	US GP WEST	Long Beach	15	Equipe Renault Elf	1.5 t/c Renault RS01 V6	practice accident-injured arm
ret	SPANISH GP	Jarama	15	Equipe Renault Elf	1.5 t/c Renault RS10 V6	turbo
ret	BELGIAN GP	Zolder	15	Equipe Renault Elf	1.5 t/c Renault RS10 V6	turbo
nc	MONACO GP	Monte Carlo	15	Equipe Renault Elf	1.5 t/c Renault RS10 V6	pit stops-engine/8 laps behind
1	FRENCH GP	Dijon	15	Equipe Renault Elf	1.5 t/c Renault RS11 V6	Pole
ret	BRITISH GP	Silverstone	15	Equipe Renault Elf	1.5 t/c Renault RS11 V6	engine
ret	GERMAN GP	Hockenheim	15	Equipe Renault Elf	1.5 t/c Renault RS11 V6	spun off/Pole
ret	AUSTRIAN GP	Österreichring	15	Equipe Renault Elf	1.5 t/c Renault RS11 V6	clutch/gearbox
ret	DUTCH GP	Zandvoort	15	Equipe Renault Elf	1.5 t/c Renault RS11 V6	clutch
14/ret	ITALIAN GP	Monza	15	Equipe Renault Elf	1.5 t/c Renault RS11 V6	engine/Pole
ret	CANADIAN GP	Montreal	15	Equipe Renault Elf	1.5 t/c Renault RS14 V6	brakes
ret	US GP EAST	Watkins Glen	15	Equipe Renault Elf	1.5 t/c Renault RS14 V6	camshaft belt

1980

	Race	Circuit	No	Entrant	Car/Engine	Comment
ret	ARGENTINE GP	Buenos Aires	15	Equipe Renault Elf	1.5 t/c Renault RS22 V6	gearbox
ret	BRAZILIAN GP	Interlagos	15	Equipe Renault Elf	1.5 t/c Renault RS22 V6	turbo/Pole
ret	SOUTH AFRICAN GP	Kyalami	15	Equipe Renault Elf	1.5 t/c Renault RS23 V6	puncture/Pole
10	US GP WEST	Long Beach	15	Equipe Renault Elf	1.5 t/c Renault RS23 V6	pit stop-brakes/9 laps behind
ret	BELGIAN GP	Zolder	15	Equipe Renault Elf	1.5 t/c Renault RS23 V6	clutch

	Race	Circuit	No	Entrant	Car/Engine	Comment
ret	MONACO GP	Monte Carlo	15	Equipe Renault Elf	1.5 t/c Renault RS23 V6	gearbox
ret	FRENCH GP	Paul Ricard	15	Equipe Renault Elf	1.5 t/c Renault RS23 V6	transmission
ret	BRITISH GP	Brands Hatch	15	Equipe Renault Elf	1.5 t/c Renault RS23 V6	engine
ret	GERMAN GP	Hockenheim	15	Equipe Renault Elf	1.5 t/c Renault RS23 V6	engine
1	AUSTRIAN GP	Österreichring	15	Equipe Renault Elf	1.5 t/c Renault RS23 V6	
ret	DUTCH GP	Zandvoort	15	Equipe Renault Elf	1.5 t/c Renault RS23 V6	handling/differential
ret	ITALIAN GP	Imola	15	Equipe Renault Elf	1.5 t/c Renault RS23 V6	gearbox
ret	CANADIAN GP	Montreal	15	Equipe Renault Elf	1.5 t/c Renault RS23 V6	suspension failure-accident
1981						
dns	BRAZILIAN GP	Rio	25	Equipe Talbot Gitanes	3.0 Ligier JS17-Matra V12	withdrawn in practice/Jarier drove
dnq	ARGENTINE GP	Buenos Aires	25	Equipe Talbot Gitanes	3.0 Ligier JS17-Matra V12	
nc	SAN MARINO GP	Imola	25	Equipe Talbot Gitanes	3.0 Ligier JS17-Matra V12	pit stops-engine/15 laps behind
ret	BELGIAN GP	Zolder	25	Equipe Talbot Gitanes	3.0 Ligier JS17-Matra V12	transmission
dnq	MONACO GP	Monte Carlo	25	Equipe Talbot Gitanes	3.0 Ligier JS17-Matra V12	
ret	SPANISH GP	Jarama	25	Equipe Talbot Gitanes	3.0 Ligier JS17-Matra V12	brakes

GP Starts: 49   GP Wins: 2   Pole positions: 6   Fastest laps: 1   Points: 21

JAMES, John (GB) b 10/5/1914

	Race	Circuit	No	Entrant	Car/Engine	Comment
1951						
ret	BRITISH GP	Silverstone	26	John James	1.5 s/c Maserati 4CLT/48 4	radiator

GP Starts: 1   GP Wins: 0   Pole positions: 0   Fastest laps: 0   Points: 0

JEAN-PIERRE JARIER

Jarier had his few fleeting moments in Grand Prix racing when nobody could live with him, but this inconsistent Frenchman ultimately flattered to deceive and the once bright promise soon faded.

After impressing in saloons and Formula France, Jean-Pierre graduated to the highly competitive French F3 series, finishing third in the championship in 1970 with a Tecno before making an assault on the European Formula 2 championship in 1971. He took the Shell Arnold team's March to a couple of third-place finishes at Albi and Vallelunga, and had his first taste of Grand Prix racing when the team hired the ex-Hubert Hahne March 701 for the Italian GP, bringing the car home in a steady 12th place.

Unfortunately his career took a step backwards the following year when the Shell Arnold team ran out of funds just after Jarier had taken third place at Monza in the Lottery GP. The wealthy José Dolhem took over the ride, so it was back to the harum-scarum world of Formula 3, but then came his big break. Signed to lead the March Formula 2 team, Jean-Pierre also found himself promoted to Formula 1 after Chris Amon was sensationally dismissed before the start of the 1973 season. In Grands Prix he was not surprisingly a little overwhelmed but was nevertheless unlucky not to score the occasional point here and there, but in Formula 2 it was a different story as he stormed to the European championship with eight victories in 13 rounds.

Now in demand, Jarier signed for Shadow in 1974 as number two to Peter Revson, but the American was soon tragically killed at Kyalami, leaving the burden of leading the team on the young Frenchman's shoulders. He responded with much courage, taking third place in the International Trophy and then the Monaco GP. He was also a key member of the Matra sports car team that year, sharing the winning car at Spa (with Ickx), the Nürburgring, Watkins Glen, Paul Ricard and Brands Hatch (all with Beltoise).

The following season started sensationally for Jarier. On pole in Argentina, he was unlucky to strip his clutch, and was then leading in Brazil by the proverbial country mile until a metering unit failed. This dominance was not to last, however, and his season disintegrated in a series of spins and crashes while team-mate Tom Pryce was busy asserting himself. Jarier gathered his resources for 1976. In the Brazilian GP, he lay a splendid second and was closing on the leader, Lauda, when he unluckily crashed out on James Hunt's oil. Things were never the same after that as the moody Frenchman became increasingly disenchanted with life at Shadow, who dropped him at the end of the season.

He hoped for a drive at Ligier in 1977, but in the event found himself in the ATS team running the Penske. A sixth place on his debut boded well, but the car was never really more than a midfield runner and Jarier failed to score any further points. By the end of the season he was briefly back at Shadow, and then had a one-off outing with Ligier. Meanwhile Alfa Romeo, remembering his superb sports car displays with Matra, had invited Jean-Pierre to drive their T33 cars at Dijon and Paul Ricard, and he won both races with Merzario, while he also raced a Mirage-Renault at Le Mans that year, taking second place with Vern Schuppan.

Jarier was back with ATS in 1978, but achieved little, quitting the team in mid-season. However, his whole career was suddenly revived at the end of the year when he took over the Lotus seat left vacant by the death of Ronnie Peterson. At Watkins Glen he set fastest lap and was in third place until he ran out of fuel near the end, and then in Montreal 'Jumper' put the Lotus on pole and fairly streaked away from the field until a small oil leak in a brake pipe ended his dominance. Ken Tyrrell, looking for a replacement for the Ligier-bound Depailler, gave Jarier the chance to build on his swiftly restored credibility. His two seasons with the team yielded ten points-scoring finishes, but the cars were not world beaters nor did Jarier seem totally involved once he realised there was nothing to aim for.

Early in 1981 he deputised for the still injury-troubled Jabouille at Ligier, before taking the only drive available at Osella. He stayed on for 1982, but apart from a splendid fourth place for the little team at Imola he lost interest badly as the year wore on. He was in the last-chance saloon the following season; he had finally secured a place in the Ligier line-up, but unfortunately the car was not quite the competitive proposition he had dreamed of racing in previous years. On the one occasion a victory was possible, Jarier made a hash of things, running into the back of Rosberg when well placed. After a decade in Grand Prix racing, he faced the fact that he was no longer in demand and quietly slipped out of single-seater racing, contenting himself in the French Supertourisme series for many years.

JARIER, Jean-Pierre (F) b 10/7/1946

1971

	Race	Circuit	No	Entrant	Car/Engine	Comment
12	ITALIAN GP	Monza	26	Shell Arnold	3.0 March 701-Cosworth V8	*pit stops-brakes/8 laps behind*

1973

	Race	Circuit	No	Entrant	Car/Engine	Comment
ret	ARGENTINE GP	Buenos Aires	24	STP March Racing Team	3.0 March 721G-Cosworth V8	*gear linkage*
ret	BRAZILIAN GP	Interlagos	11	STP March Racing Team	3.0 March 721G-Cosworth V8	*gearbox*
nc	SOUTH AFRICAN GP	Kyalami	14	STP March Racing Team	3.0 March 721G-Cosworth V8	*13 laps behind*
ret	BELGIAN GP	Zolder	14	STP March Racing Team	3.0 March 721G-Cosworth V8	*accident*
ret	MONACO GP	Monte Carlo	14	STP March Racing Team	3.0 March 721G-Cosworth V8	*gearbox*
ret	SWEDISH GP	Anderstorp	14	STP March Racing Team	3.0 March 721G-Cosworth V8	*throttle cable*
ret	FRENCH GP	Paul Ricard	14	STP March Racing Team	3.0 March 721G-Cosworth V8	*driveshaft*
ret	AUSTRIAN GP	Österreichring	18	March Racing Team	3.0 March 731-Cosworth V8	*engine*
nc	CANADIAN GP	Mosport Park	18	March Racing Team	3.0 March 731-Cosworth V8	*spun off/gearbox/9 laps behind*
11/ret	US GP	Watkins Glen	18	March Racing Team	3.0 March 731-Cosworth V8	*accident/2 laps behind*

1974

	Race	Circuit	No	Entrant	Car/Engine	Comment
ret	ARGENTINE GP	Buenos Aires	17	UOP Shadow Racing Team	3.0 Shadow DN1-Cosworth V8	*collision with Revson*
ret	BRAZILIAN GP	Interlagos	17	UOP Shadow Racing Team	3.0 Shadow DN1-Cosworth V8	*brakes*
nc	SPANISH GP	Jarama	17	UOP Shadow Racing Team	3.0 Shadow DN3-Cosworth V8	*hit by Merzario-pit stop/11 laps behind*
13	BELGIAN GP	Nivelles	17	UOP Shadow Racing Team	3.0 Shadow DN3-Cosworth V8	*3 laps behind*
3	MONACO GP	Monte Carlo	17	UOP Shadow Racing Team	3.0 Shadow DN3-Cosworth V8	
5	SWEDISH GP	Anderstorp	17	UOP Shadow Racing Team	3.0 Shadow DN3-Cosworth V8	
ret	DUTCH GP	Zandvoort	17	UOP Shadow Racing Team	3.0 Shadow DN3-Cosworth V8	*clutch*
12	FRENCH GP	Dijon	17	UOP Shadow Racing Team	3.0 Shadow DN3-Cosworth V8	*1 lap behind*
ret	BRITISH GP	Brands Hatch	17	UOP Shadow Racing Team	3.0 Shadow DN3-Cosworth V8	*suspension*
8	GERMAN GP	Nürburgring	17	UOP Shadow Racing Team	3.0 Shadow DN3-Cosworth V8	
8	AUSTRIAN GP	Österreichring	17	UOP Shadow Racing Team	3.0 Shadow DN3-Cosworth V8	*fuel problems-pit stop/2 laps behind*
ret	ITALIAN GP	Monza	17	UOP Shadow Racing Team	3.0 Shadow DN3-Cosworth V8	*engine*
ret	CANADIAN GP	Mosport Park	17	UOP Shadow Racing Team	3.0 Shadow DN3-Cosworth V8	*driveshaft*
10	US GP	Watkins Glen	17	UOP Shadow Racing Team	3.0 Shadow DN3-Cosworth V8	*2 laps behind*

1975

	Race	Circuit	No	Entrant	Car/Engine	Comment
dns	ARGENTINE GP	Buenos Aires	17	UOP Shadow Racing Team	3.0 Shadow DN5-Cosworth V8	*cwp in warm-up/Pole*
ret	BRAZILIAN GP	Interlagos	17	UOP Shadow Racing Team	3.0 Shadow DN5-Cosworth V8	*fuel metering unit/Pole/FL*
ret	SOUTH AFRICAN GP	Kyalami	17	UOP Shadow Racing Team	3.0 Shadow DN5-Cosworth V8	*engine*
4*	SPANISH GP	Montjuich Park	17	UOP Shadow Racing Team	3.0 Shadow DN5-Cosworth V8	*shortened race-half points/-1 lap*
ret	MONACO GP	Monte Carlo	17	UOP Shadow Racing Team	3.0 Shadow DN5-Cosworth V8	*spun-hit barrier on lap 1*
ret	BELGIAN GP	Zolder	17	UOP Shadow Racing Team	3.0 Shadow DN5-Cosworth V8	*spun off*
ret	SWEDISH GP	Anderstorp	17	UOP Shadow Racing Team	3.0 Shadow DN5-Cosworth V8	*engine*
ret	DUTCH GP	Zandvoort	17	UOP Shadow Racing Team	3.0 Shadow DN5-Cosworth V8	*puncture-spun off*
8	FRENCH GP	Paul Ricard	17	UOP Shadow Racing Team	3.0 Shadow DN5-Cosworth V8	
14/ret	BRITISH GP	Silverstone	17	UOP Shadow Racing Team	3.0 Shadow DN5-Cosworth V8	*spun off/3 laps behind*
ret	GERMAN GP	Nürburgring	17	UOP Shadow Racing Team	3.0 Shadow DN5-Cosworth V8	*puncture*
ret	AUSTRIAN GP	Österreichring	17	UOP Shadow Racing Team	3.0 Shadow DN7-Matra V12	*fuel injection*
ret	ITALIAN GP	Monza	17	UOP Shadow Racing Team	3.0 Shadow DN7-Matra V12	*fuel pump*
ret	US GP	Watkins Glen	17	UOP Shadow Racing Team	3.0 Shadow DN5-Cosworth V8	*wheel bearing*
dns	" " "		17	UOP Shadow Racing Team	3.0 Shadow DN5-Matra V12	*practice only*

1976

	Race	Circuit	No	Entrant	Car/Engine	Comment
ret	BRAZILIAN GP	Interlagos	17	Shadow Racing Team	3.0 Shadow DN5-Cosworth V8	*spun off on Hunt's oil/FL*
ret	SOUTH AFRICAN GP	Kyalami	17	Shadow Racing Team	3.0 Shadow DN5-Cosworth V8	*radiator/engine*
7	US GP WEST	Long Beach	17	Shadow Racing Team	3.0 Shadow DN5-Cosworth V8	*1 lap behind*
ret	SPANISH GP	Jarama	17	Shadow Racing Team	3.0 Shadow DN5-Cosworth V8	*electrics*
9	BELGIAN GP	Zolder	17	Shadow Racing Team	3.0 Shadow DN5-Cosworth V8	*1 lap behind*
8	MONACO GP	Monte Carlo	17	Shadow Racing Team	3.0 Shadow DN5-Cosworth V8	*2 laps behind*
12	SWEDISH GP	Anderstorp	17	Shadow Racing Team	3.0 Shadow DN5-Cosworth V8	*1 lap behind*
12	FRENCH GP	Paul Ricard	17	Shadow Racing Team	3.0 Shadow DN5-Cosworth V8	*1 lap behind*
9	BRITISH GP	Brands Hatch	17	Shadow Racing Team	3.0 Shadow DN5-Cosworth V8	*pit stop/6 laps behind*
11	GERMAN GP	Nürburgring	17	Shadow Racing with Tabatip	3.0 Shadow DN5-Cosworth V8	
ret	AUSTRIAN GP	Österreichring	17	Shadow Racing with Tabatip	3.0 Shadow DN5-Cosworth V8	*fuel pump*
10	DUTCH GP	Zandvoort	17	Shadow Racing Team	3.0 Shadow DN5-Cosworth V8	*1 lap behind*
19	ITALIAN GP	Monza	17	Shadow Racing Team	3.0 Shadow DN5-Cosworth V8	*pit stop/5 laps behind*
18	CANADIAN GP	Mosport Park	17	Shadow Racing Team	3.0 Shadow DN5-Cosworth V8	*3 laps behind*
10	US GP EAST	Watkins Glen	17	Shadow Racing Team	3.0 Shadow DN5-Cosworth V8	*2 laps behind*
10	JAPANESE GP	Mount Fuji	17	Shadow Racing Team	3.0 Shadow DN5-Cosworth V8	*4 laps behind*

1977

	Race	Circuit	No	Entrant	Car/Engine	Comment
6	US GP WEST	Long Beach	34	ATS Racing Team	3.0 Penske PC4-Cosworth V8	*1 lap behind*
dnq	SPANISH GP	Jarama	34	ATS Racing Team	3.0 Penske PC4-Cosworth V8	*unwell*
11	MONACO GP	Monte Carlo	34	ATS Racing Team	3.0 Penske PC4-Cosworth V8	*pit stop/2 laps behind*
11	BELGIAN GP	Zolder	34	ATS Racing Team	3.0 Penske PC4-Cosworth V8	*2 laps behind*
8	SWEDISH GP	Anderstorp	34	ATS Racing Team	3.0 Penske PC4-Cosworth V8	
ret	FRENCH GP	Dijon	34	ATS Racing Team	3.0 Penske PC4-Cosworth V8	*gearbox problem-spun off*
9	BRITISH GP	Silverstone	34	ATS Racing Team	3.0 Penske PC4-Cosworth V8	*1 lap behind*
ret	GERMAN GP	Hockenheim	34	ATS Racing Team	3.0 Penske PC4-Cosworth V8	*damage from startline accident*
14	AUSTRIAN GP	Österreichring	34	ATS Racing Team	3.0 Penske PC4-Cosworth V8	*pit stop/2 laps behind*
ret	DUTCH GP	Zandvoort	34	ATS Racing Team	3.0 Penske PC4-Cosworth V8	*engine*
ret	ITALIAN GP	Monza	34	ATS Racing Team	3.0 Penske PC4-Cosworth V8	*engine*
9	US GP EAST	Watkins Glen	16	Shadow Racing Team	3.0 Shadow DN8-Cosworth V8	*1 lap behind*
ret	JAPANESE GP	Mount Fuji	27	Ligier Gitanes	3.0 Ligier JS7-Matra V12	*engine*

1978

	Race	Circuit	No	Entrant	Car/Engine	Comment
12	ARGENTINE GP	Buenos Aires	10	ATS Racing Team	3.0 Ligier JS7-Matra V12	*engine*
dns	BRAZILIAN GP	Rio	10	ATS Racing Team	3.0 ATS HS1-Cosworth V8	*car driven by Mass*

8	SOUTH AFRICAN GP	Kyalami	10	ATS Racing Team	3.0 ATS HS1-Cosworth V8	*1 lap behind*
11	US GP WEST	Long Beach	10	ATS Racing Team	3.0 ATS HS1-Cosworth V8	*pit stop-hit Brambilla/5 laps behind*
dnq	MONACO GP	Monte Carlo	10	ATS Racing Team	3.0 ATS HS1-Cosworth V8	
dnq	GERMAN GP	Hockenheim	10	ATS Racing Team	3.0 ATS HS1-Cosworth V8	
15/ret	US GP EAST	Watkins Glen	55	John Player Team Lotus	3.0 Lotus 79-Cosworth V8	*out of fuel/FL/4 laps behind*
ret	CANADIAN GP	Montreal	55	John Player Team Lotus	3.0 Lotus 79-Cosworth V8	*oil leak/Pole*

1979

ret	ARGENTINE GP	Buenos Aires	4	Team Tyrrell	3.0 Tyrrell 009-Cosworth V8	*engine*
dns	BRAZILIAN GP	Interlagos	4	Team Tyrrell	3.0 Tyrrell 009-Cosworth V8	*electrics on warm-up*
3	SOUTH AFRICAN GP	Kyalami	4	Team Tyrrell	3.0 Tyrrell 009-Cosworth V8	
6	US GP WEST	Long Beach	4	Team Tyrrell	3.0 Tyrrell 009-Cosworth V8	*pit stop-tyres/1 lap behind*
5	SPANISH GP	Jarama	4	Team Tyrrell	3.0 Tyrrell 009-Cosworth V8	
11	BELGIAN GP	Zolder	4	Candy Team Tyrrell	3.0 Tyrrell 009-Cosworth V8	*pit stops-skirts/3 laps behind*
ret	MONACO GP	Monte Carlo	4	Candy Team Tyrrell	3.0 Tyrrell 009-Cosworth V8	*broken rear upright*
5	FRENCH GP	Dijon	4	Candy Team Tyrrell	3.0 Tyrrell 009-Cosworth V8	
3	BRITISH GP	Silverstone	4	Candy Team Tyrrell	3.0 Tyrrell 009-Cosworth V8	*1 lap behind*
ret	DUTCH GP	Zandvoort	4	Candy Team Tyrrell	3.0 Tyrrell 009-Cosworth V8	*jammed throttle-spun off*
6	ITALIAN GP	Monza	4	Candy Team Tyrrell	3.0 Tyrrell 009-Cosworth V8	
ret	CANADIAN GP	Montreal	4	Candy Team Tyrrell	3.0 Tyrrell 009-Cosworth V8	*engine*
ret	US GP EAST	Watkins Glen	4	Candy Team Tyrrell	3.0 Tyrrell 009-Cosworth V8	*collision with Daly-spun off*

1980

ret	ARGENTINE GP	Buenos Aires	3	Candy Team Tyrrell	3.0 Tyrrell 009-Cosworth V8	*accident damage*
12	BRAZILIAN GP	Interlagos	3	Candy Team Tyrrell	3.0 Tyrrell 009-Cosworth V8	*1 lap behind*
7	SOUTH AFRICAN GP	Kyalami	3	Candy Team Tyrrell	3.0 Tyrrell 010-Cosworth V8	*1 lap behind*
ret	US GP WEST	Long Beach	3	Candy Team Tyrrell	3.0 Tyrrell 010-Cosworth V8	*multiple collision*
5	BELGIAN GP	Zolder	3	Candy Team Tyrrell	3.0 Tyrrell 010-Cosworth V8	*1 lap behind*
ret	MONACO GP	Monte Carlo	3	Candy Team Tyrrell	3.0 Tyrrell 010-Cosworth V8	*multiple collision lap 1*
14	FRENCH GP	Paul Ricard	3	Candy Team Tyrrell	3.0 Tyrrell 010-Cosworth V8	*2 pit stops-side pod/4 laps behind*
5	BRITISH GP	Brands Hatch	3	Candy Team Tyrrell	3.0 Tyrrell 010-Cosworth V8	*1 lap behind*
15	GERMAN GP	Hockenheim	3	Candy Team Tyrrell	3.0 Tyrrell 010-Cosworth V8	*1 lap behind*
ret	AUSTRIAN GP	Österreichring	3	Candy Team Tyrrell	3.0 Tyrrell 010-Cosworth V8	*engine*
5	DUTCH GP	Zandvoort	3	Candy Team Tyrrell	3.0 Tyrrell 010-Cosworth V8	
ret	ITALIAN GP	Imola	3	Candy Team Tyrrell	3.0 Tyrrell 010-Cosworth V8	*brakes*
7	CANADIAN GP	Montreal	3	Candy Team Tyrrell	3.0 Tyrrell 010-Cosworth V8	*1 lap behind*
nc	US GP EAST	Watkins Glen	3	Candy Team Tyrrell	3.0 Tyrrell 010-Cosworth V8	*pit stops/19 laps behind*

1981

ret	US GP WEST	Long Beach	25	Equipe Talbot Gitanes	3.0 Ligier JS17-Matra V12	*fuel pump*
7	BRAZILIAN GP	Rio	25	Equipe Talbot Gitanes	3.0 Ligier JS17-Matra V12	
8	BRITISH GP	Silverstone	32	Osella Squadra Corse	3.0 Osella FA1B-Cosworth V8	*pit stop/3 laps behind*
8	GERMAN GP	Hockenheim	32	Osella Squadra Corse	3.0 Osella FA1B-Cosworth V8	*1 lap behind*
10	AUSTRIAN GP	Österreichring	32	Osella Squadra Corse	3.0 Osella FA1B-Cosworth V8	*2 laps behind*
ret	DUTCH GP	Zandvoort	32	Osella Squadra Corse	3.0 Osella FA1B-Cosworth V8	*gearbox*
9	ITALIAN GP	Monza	32	Osella Squadra Corse	3.0 Osella FA1C-Cosworth V8	*2 laps behind*
ret	CANADIAN GP	Montreal	32	Osella Squadra Corse	3.0 Osella FA1C-Cosworth V8	*collision with Rebaque*
ret	CAESARS PALACE GP	Las Vegas	32	Osella Squadra Corse	3.0 Osella FA1C-Cosworth V8	*transmission*

1982

ret	SOUTH AFRICAN GP	Kyalami	31	Osella Squadra Corse	3.0 Osella FA1C-Cosworth V8	*spun avoiding Mansell-lap 1*
9*	BRAZILIAN GP	Rio	31	Osella Squadra Corse	3.0 Osella FA1C-Cosworth V8	** 1st & 2nd place dsq/3 laps behind*
ret	US GP WEST	Long Beach	31	Osella Squadra Corse	3.0 Osella FA1C-Cosworth V8	*engine*
4	SAN MARINO GP	Imola	31	Osella Squadra Corse	3.0 Osella FA1C-Cosworth V8	*1 lap behind*
ret	BELGIAN GP	Zolder	31	Osella Squadra Corse	3.0 Osella FA1C-Cosworth V8	*broken rear wing*
dnq	MONACO GP	Monte Carlo	31	Osella Squadra Corse	3.0 Osella FA1C-Cosworth V8	
ret	US GP (DETROIT)	Detroit	31	Osella Squadra Corse	3.0 Osella FA1C-Cosworth V8	*electrics*
dns	CANADIAN GP	Montreal	31	Osella Squadra Corse	3.0 Osella FA1C-Cosworth V8	*withdrawn after Paletti's accident*
14	DUTCH GP	Zandvoort	31	Osella Squadra Corse	3.0 Osella FA1C-Cosworth V8	*pit stop/3 laps behind*
ret	BRITISH GP	Brands Hatch	31	Osella Squadra Corse	3.0 Osella FA1C-Cosworth V8	*accident with Serra*
ret	FRENCH GP	Paul Ricard	31	Osella Squadra Corse	3.0 Osella FA1C-Cosworth V8	*driveshaft*
ret	GERMAN GP	Hockenheim	31	Osella Squadra Corse	3.0 Osella FA1C-Cosworth V8	*steering*
dnq	AUSTRIAN GP	Österreichring	31	Osella Squadra Corse	3.0 Osella FA1C-Cosworth V8	
ret	SWISS GP	Dijon	31	Osella Squadra Corse	3.0 Osella FA1C-Cosworth V8	*engine*
ret	ITALIAN GP	Monza	31	Osella Squadra Corse	3.0 Osella FA1C-Cosworth V8	*lost rear wheel-accident*
dnq	CAESARS PALACE GP	Las Vegas	31	Osella Squadra Corse	3.0 Osella FA1C-Cosworth V8	*accident in practice*

1983

ret	BRAZILIAN GP	Rio	25	Equipe Ligier Gitanes	3.0 Ligier JS21-Cosworth V8	*rear suspension*
ret	US GP WEST	Long Beach	25	Equipe Ligier Gitanes	3.0 Ligier JS21-Cosworth V8	*accident with Rosberg*
9	FRENCH GP	Paul Ricard	25	Equipe Ligier Gitanes	3.0 Ligier JS21-Cosworth V8	*1 lap behind*
ret	SAN MARINO GP	Imola	25	Equipe Ligier Gitanes	3.0 Ligier JS21-Cosworth V8	*holed radiator*
ret	MONACO GP	Monte Carlo	25	Equipe Ligier Gitanes	3.0 Ligier JS21-Cosworth V8	*hydraulic suspension pump*
ret	BELGIAN GP	Spa	25	Equipe Ligier Gitanes	3.0 Ligier JS21-Cosworth V8	*accident with Watson*
ret	US GP (DETROIT)	Detroit	25	Equipe Ligier Gitanes	3.0 Ligier JS21-Cosworth V8	*seized wheel nut*
ret	CANADIAN GP	Montreal	25	Equipe Ligier Gitanes	3.0 Ligier JS21-Cosworth V8	*gearbox*
10	BRITISH GP	Silverstone	25	Equipe Ligier Gitanes	3.0 Ligier JS21-Cosworth V8	*pit stop-tyres/2 laps behind*
8	GERMAN GP	Hockenheim	25	Equipe Ligier Gitanes	3.0 Ligier JS21-Cosworth V8	*pit stop-tyres/1 lap behind*
7	AUSTRIAN GP	Österreichring	25	Equipe Ligier Gitanes	3.0 Ligier JS21-Cosworth V8	*pit stop-tyres/2 laps behind*
ret	DUTCH GP	Zandvoort	25	Equipe Ligier Gitanes	3.0 Ligier JS21-Cosworth V8	*suspension*
9	ITALIAN GP	Monza	25	Equipe Ligier Gitanes	3.0 Ligier JS21-Cosworth V8	*1 lap behind*
dns	EUROPEAN GP	Brands Hatch	25	Equipe Ligier Gitanes	3.0 Ligier JS21-Cosworth V8	*transmission on grid*
10	SOUTH AFRICAN GP	Kyalami	25	Equipe Ligier Gitanes	3.0 Ligier JS21-Cosworth V8	*4 laps behind*

GP Starts: 136   GP Wins: 0   Pole positions: 3   Fastest laps: 3   Points: 31.5

STEFAN JOHANSSON

Bright, bubbly and immensely likeable, Stefan Johansson had gathered together all the credentials required to take him to the top of Grand Prix racing. Somehow, though, it never quite happened for him despite golden opportunities with two front-running teams.

Stefan's father raced Mini-Coopers, and the youngster was soon competing in karts before moving up the Swedish racing ladder in various third-hand single-seaters which he frequently had to drive above and beyond their limit to gain a modicum of success. He first hit the headlines in 1976 when still a complete novice by managing to shunt current Formula 3 big-shot Riccardo Patrese out of a European championship round. Stefan's F3 progress stuttered on over the next few seasons, with eyebrows raised over his wild and sometimes not so wonderful driving, but he eventually began to make some solid progress before having to return home when his money ran out.

It was in 1979 that things started to fall into place, for after a poor start to his British F3 championship campaign with a Chevron, a switch to March chassis seemed to work wonders and Stefan was on the pace thereafter. Then came a quite unexpected chance with the Shadow team at the beginning of 1980. In retrospect Stefan shouldn't have taken up the offer for his reputation inevitably suffered when he failed to qualify in Argentina and Brazil, but at least he was able to come back to a seat in the top Project Four F3 team and went on to win the Vandervell championship after a great tussle with Kenneth Acheson. Understandably on a high, he moved into Formula 2 with a Toleman and finished fourth in the final standings, gaining victories at Hockenheim and Mantorp Park. Joining the Spirit-Honda team for 1982, Johansson looked a good bet for championship honours, but it wasn't to be his year as bad luck seemed to dog his heels throughout the season.

Stefan moved into Formula 1 with Spirit and Honda in 1983, and by general consensus the Swede did a fine job with a far from sorted machine, but he found himself out of work when Honda abandoned the project to move to Williams. Johansson decided to drive anything and everything in 1984, travelling the globe to race in an effort to prove his worth, and it worked. Tyrrell called him in to replace the injured Brundle before political problems forced the team's withdrawal, and then Toleman gave him an opportunity and were sufficiently impressed to make plans to run him in 1985. In the event the team were unable to obtain tyres, which in truth worked in Stefan's favour, for he was available to take over from Arnoux at Ferrari just one race into the 1985 season. This was his main chance and he grabbed it with some gutsy race performances, bringing the car home regularly to earn a contract for 1986. His second season was fraught with endless technical problems, but the ever-smiling Swede plugged away, and he was lucky enough to be given a second top-line chance with McLaren in 1987. Again some of his races were excellent, but too often he qualified poorly, leaving himself much to do to retrieve the siuation once the racing started. The decision to bring Ayrton Senna in to partner Alain Prost for 1988 saw Johansson seeking employment elsewhere and he could hardly have found a worse berth than Ligier. The season was a write-off and things looked little better in 1989 with the new Onyx outfit, but to Stefan's credit he helped to establish the team's credibility with a terrific third place in Portugal. Just to show there is no such thing as loyalty in Grand Prix racing, poor Johansson was dumped just two races into the 1990 season in favour of the well-financed Foitek.

Desperate to stay in Formula 1, Stefan signed to drive for AGS in 1991, but when the team changed hands he found himself redundant once more, and a few outings for Footwork in place of the injured Caffi did him no favours as the team were in the midst of a crisis not of their own making with the ill-fated Porsche engine. Subsequently Johansson has found an excellent niche for himself in IndyCar racing with Tony Bettenhausen's team. Running a competitive Penske chassis has given him the chance to shine on a number of occasions, and his future looks bright if he can bring in a few more concrete results.

JOHANSSON, Stefan (S) b 8/9/1956

1980

	Race	Circuit	No	Entrant	Car/Engine	Comment
dnq	ARGENTINE GP	Buenos Aires	17	Shadow Cars	3.0 Shadow DN11-Cosworth V8	
dnq	BRAZILIAN GP	Interlagos	17	Shadow Cars	3.0 Shadow DN11-Cosworth V8	

1983

	Race	Circuit	No	Entrant	Car/Engine	Comment
ret	BRITISH GP	Silverstone	40	Spirit Racing	1.5 t/c Spirit 201-Honda V6	*fuel pump belt*
ret	GERMAN GP	Hockenheim	40	Spirit Racing	1.5 t/c Spirit 201-Honda V6	*engine*
12	AUSTRIAN GP	Österreichring	40	Spirit Racing	1.5 t/c Spirit 201-Honda V6	*2 pit stops-hit by Alboreto/-5 laps*
7	DUTCH GP	Zandvoort	40	Spirit Racing	1.5 t/c Spirit 201-Honda V6	*pit stop-tyres/2 laps behind*
ret	ITALIAN GP	Monza	40	Spirit Racing	1.5 t/c Spirit 201-Honda V6	*distributor*
14	EUROPEAN GP	Brands Hatch	40	Spirit Racing	1.5 t/c Spirit 201-Honda V6	*pit stop-tyres/2 laps behind*

1984

	Race	Circuit	No	Entrant	Car/Engine	Comment
dsq*	BRITISH GP	Brands Hatch	3	Tyrrell Racing Organisation	3.0 Tyrrell 012-Cosworth V8	*accident damage/*dsq after Dutch GP*
dsq*	GERMAN GP	Hockenheim	3	Tyrrell Racing Organisation	3.0 Tyrrell 012-Cosworth V8	*9th on road/*dsq after Dutch GP*
dnq	AUSTRIAN GP	Österreichring	3	Tyrrell Racing Organisation	3.0 Tyrrell 012-Cosworth V8	
dsq*	DUTCH GP	Zandvoort	3	Tyrrell Racing Organisation	3.0 Tyrrell 012-Cosworth V8	*8th on road/*dsq after Dutch GP*
4	ITALIAN GP	Monza	19	Toleman Group Motorsport	1.5 t/c Toleman TG184-Hart 4	*2 laps behind*
ret	EUROPEAN GP	Nürburgring	20	Toleman Group Motorsport	1.5 t/c Toleman TG184-Hart 4	*overheating*
11	PORTUGESE GP	Estoril	20	Toleman Group Motorsport	1.5 t/c Toleman TG184-Hart 4	*1 lap behind*

1985

	Race	Circuit	No	Entrant	Car/Engine	Comment
7	BRAZILIAN GP	Rio	4	Tyrrell Racing Organisation	3.0 Tyrrell 012-Cosworth V8	*pit stop-tyres/3 laps behind*
8	PORTUGESE GP	Estoril	28	Scuderia Ferrari SpA SEFAC	1.5 t/c Ferrari 156/85 V6	*pit stop-brakes/5 laps behind*
6/ret	SAN MARINO GP	Imola	28	Scuderia Ferrari SpA SEFAC	1.5 t/c Ferrari 156/85 V6	*out of fuel/3 laps behind*
ret	MONACO GP	Monte Carlo	28	Scuderia Ferrari SpA SEFAC	1.5 t/c Ferrari 156/85 V6	*accident damage*
2	CANADIAN GP	Montreal	28	Scuderia Ferrari SpA SEFAC	1.5 t/c Ferrari 156/85 V6	
2	US GP (DETROIT)	Detroit	28	Scuderia Ferrari SpA SEFAC	1.5 t/c Ferrari 156/85 V6	
4	FRENCH GP	Paul Ricard	28	Scuderia Ferrari SpA SEFAC	1.5 t/c Ferrari 156/85 V6	
ret	BRITISH GP	Silverstone	28	Scuderia Ferrari SpA SEFAC	1.5 t/c Ferrari 156/85 V6	*hit spinning Tambay*
9	GERMAN GP	Nürburgring	28	Scuderia Ferrari SpA SEFAC	1.5 t/c Ferrari 156/85 V6	*p stop-tyre-hit by Alboreto/-1 lap*
4	AUSTRIAN GP	Österreichring	28	Scuderia Ferrari SpA SEFAC	1.5 t/c Ferrari 156/85 V6	
ret	DUTCH GP	Zandvoort	28	Scuderia Ferrari SpA SEFAC	1.5 t/c Ferrari 156/85 V6	*engine*
5/ret	ITALIAN GP	Monza	28	Scuderia Ferrari SpA SEFAC	1.5 t/c Ferrari 156/85 V6	*out of fuel/1 lap behind*
ret	BELGIAN GP	Spa	28	Scuderia Ferrari SpA SEFAC	1.5 t/c Ferrari 156/85 V6	*engine-spun off*
ret	EUROPEAN GP	Brands Hatch	28	Scuderia Ferrari SpA SEFAC	1.5 t/c Ferrari 156/85 V6	*electrics*
4	SOUTH AFRICAN GP	Kyalami	28	Scuderia Ferrari SpA SEFAC	1.5 t/c Ferrari 156/85 V6	*pit stop-tyres/1 lap behind*
5	AUSTRALIAN GP	Adelaide	28	Scuderia Ferrari SpA SEFAC	1.5 t/c Ferrari 156/85 V6	*pit stop-tyres/1 lap behind*

1986

ret	BRAZILIAN GP	Rio	28	Scuderia Ferrari SpA SEFAC	1.5 t/c Ferrari F1/86 V6	brakes-spun off
ret	SPANISH GP	Jerez	28	Scuderia Ferrari SpA SEFAC	1.5 t/c Ferrari F1/86 V6	brakes-accident
4	SAN MARINO GP	Imola	28	Scuderia Ferrari SpA SEFAC	1.5 t/c Ferrari F1/86 V6	pit stop-brakes/1 lap behind
10	MONACO GP	Monte Carlo	28	Scuderia Ferrari SpA SEFAC	1.5 t/c Ferrari F1/86 V6	handling problems/3 laps behind
3	BELGIAN GP	Spa	28	Scuderia Ferrari SpA SEFAC	1.5 t/c Ferrari F1/86 V6	
ret	CANADIAN GP	Montreal	28	Scuderia Ferrari SpA SEFAC	1.5 t/c Ferrari F1/86 V6	accident with Dumfries
ret	US GP (DETROIT)	Detroit	28	Scuderia Ferrari SpA SEFAC	1.5 t/c Ferrari F1/86 V6	electrics
ret	FRENCH GP	Paul Ricard	28	Scuderia Ferrari SpA SEFAC	1.5 t/c Ferrari F1/86 V6	turbo
ret	BRITISH GP	Brands Hatch	28	Scuderia Ferrari SpA SEFAC	1.5 t/c Ferrari F1/86 V6	engine
11/ret	GERMAN GP	Hockenheim	28	Scuderia Ferrari SpA SEFAC	1.5 t/c Ferrari F1/86 V6	broken rear wing/3 laps behind
4	HUNGARIAN GP	Hungaroring	28	Scuderia Ferrari SpA SEFAC	1.5 t/c Ferrari F1/86 V6	2 pit stops-tyres/1 lap behind
3	AUSTRIAN GP	Österreichring	28	Scuderia Ferrari SpA SEFAC	1.5 t/c Ferrari F1/86 V6	2 pit stops-tyres/wing/2 laps behind
3	ITALIAN GP	Monza	28	Scuderia Ferrari SpA SEFAC	1.5 t/c Ferrari F1/86 V6	
6	PORTUGESE GP	Estoril	28	Scuderia Ferrari SpA SEFAC	1.5 t/c Ferrari F1/86 V6	hit by Berger/1 lap behind
12/ret	MEXICAN GP	Mexico City	28	Scuderia Ferrari SpA SEFAC	1.5 t/c Ferrari F1/86 V6	turbo/4 laps behind
3	AUSTRALIAN GP	Adelaide	28	Scuderia Ferrari SpA SEFAC	1.5 t/c Ferrari F1/86 V6	1 lap behind

1987

3	BRAZILIAN GP	Rio	2	Marlboro McLaren International	1.5 t/c McLaren MP4/3-TAG V6	
4	SAN MARINO GP	Imola	2	Marlboro McLaren International	1.5 t/c McLaren MP4/3-TAG V6	
2	BELGIAN GP	Spa	2	Marlboro McLaren International	1.5 t/c McLaren MP4/3-TAG V6	
ret	MONACO GP	Monte Carlo	2	Marlboro McLaren International	1.5 t/c McLaren MP4/3-TAG V6	engine
7	US GP (DETROIT)	Detroit	2	Marlboro McLaren International	1.5 t/c McLaren MP4/3-TAG V6	pit stop-electrics/3 laps behind
8/ret	FRENCH GP	Paul Ricard	2	Marlboro McLaren International	1.5 t/c McLaren MP4/3-TAG V6	alternator belt/6 laps behind
ret	BRITISH GP	Silverstone	2	Marlboro McLaren International	1.5 t/c McLaren MP4/3-TAG V6	engine
2	GERMAN GP	Hockenheim	2	Marlboro McLaren International	1.5 t/c McLaren MP4/3-TAG V6	finished on 3 wheels
ret	HUNGARIAN GP	Hungaroring	2	Marlboro McLaren International	1.5 t/c McLaren MP4/3-TAG V6	transmission
7	AUSTRIAN GP	Österreichring	2	Marlboro McLaren International	1.5 t/c McLaren MP4/3-TAG V6	pit stop-puncture-loose wheel/-2 laps
6	ITALIAN GP	Monza	2	Marlboro McLaren International	1.5 t/c McLaren MP4/3-TAG V6	
5	PORTUGUESE GP	Estoril	2	Marlboro McLaren International	1.5 t/c McLaren MP4/3-TAG V6	1 lap behind
3	SPANISH GP	Jerez	2	Marlboro McLaren International	1.5 t/c McLaren MP4/3-TAG V6	
ret	MEXICAN GP	Mexico City	2	Marlboro McLaren International	1.5 t/c McLaren MP4/3-TAG V6	spun off
3	JAPANESE GP	Suzuka	2	Marlboro McLaren International	1.5 t/c McLaren MP4/3-TAG V6	
ret	AUSTRALIAN GP	Adelaide	2	Marlboro McLaren International	1.5 t/c McLaren MP4/3-TAG V6	brakes

1988

9	BRAZILIAN GP	Rio	26	Ligier Loto	3.5 Ligier JS31-Judd V8	3 laps behind
dnq	SAN MARINO GP	Imola	26	Ligier Loto	3.5 Ligier JS31-Judd V8	
ret	MONACO GP	Monte Carlo	26	Ligier Loto	3.5 Ligier JS31-Judd V8	electrics
10	MEXICAN GP	Mexico City	26	Ligier Loto	3.5 Ligier JS31-Judd V8	4 laps behind
ret	CANADIAN GP	Montreal	26	Ligier Loto	3.5 Ligier JS31-Judd V8	engine
ret	US GP (DETROIT)	Detroit	26	Ligier Loto	3.5 Ligier JS31-Judd V8	engine
dnq	FRENCH GP	Paul Ricard	26	Ligier Loto	3.5 Ligier JS31-Judd V8	
dnq	BRITISH GP	Silverstone	26	Ligier Loto	3.5 Ligier JS31-Judd V8	
dnq	GERMAN GP	Hockenheim	26	Ligier Loto	3.5 Ligier JS31-Judd V8	
ret	HUNGARIAN GP	Hungaroring	26	Ligier Loto	3.5 Ligier JS31-Judd V8	stuck throttle
11/ret	BELGIAN GP	Spa	26	Ligier Loto	3.5 Ligier JS31-Judd V8	driveshaft/3rd & 4th place dsq/-4 laps
dnq	ITALIAN GP	Monza	26	Ligier Loto	3.5 Ligier JS31-Judd V8	
ret	PORTUGUESE GP	Estoril	26	Ligier Loto	3.5 Ligier JS31-Judd V8	engine
ret	SPANISH GP	Jerez	26	Ligier Loto	3.5 Ligier JS31-Judd V8	lost wheel
dnq	JAPANESE GP	Suzuka	26	Ligier Loto	3.5 Ligier JS31-Judd V8	
9/ret	AUSTRALIAN GP	Adelaide	26	Ligier Loto	3.5 Ligier JS31-Judd V8	out of fuel/6 laps behind

1989

dnpq	BRAZILIAN GP	Rio	36	Moneytron Onyx	3.5 Onyx ORE 1-Cosworth V8	
dnpq	SAN MARINO GP	Imola	36	Moneytron Onyx	3.5 Onyx ORE 1-Cosworth V8	
dnpq	MONACO GP	Monte Carlo	36	Moneytron Onyx	3.5 Onyx ORE 1-Cosworth V8	
ret	MEXICAN GP	Mexico City	36	Moneytron Onyx	3.5 Onyx ORE 1-Cosworth V8	transmission
ret	US GP (PHOENIX)	Phoenix	36	Moneytron Onyx	3.5 Onyx ORE 1-Cosworth V8	puncture-suspension damage
dsq	CANADIAN GP	Montreal	36	Moneytron Onyx	3.5 Onyx ORE 1-Cosworth V8	trailing air gun/ignored black flag
5	FRENCH GP	Paul Ricard	36	Moneytron Onyx	3.5 Onyx ORE 1-Cosworth V8	throttle linkage problems/-1 lap
dnpq	BRITISH GP	Silverstone	36	Moneytron Onyx	3.5 Onyx ORE 1-Cosworth V8	
ret	GERMAN GP	Hockenheim	36	Moneytron Onyx	3.5 Onyx ORE 1-Cosworth V8	rear wheel bearing
ret	HUNGARIAN GP	Hungaroring	36	Moneytron Onyx	3.5 Onyx ORE 1-Cosworth V8	gear selection
8	BELGIAN GP	Spa	36	Moneytron Onyx	3.5 Onyx ORE 1-Cosworth V8	1 lap behind
dnpq	ITALIAN GP	Monza	36	Moneytron Onyx	3.5 Onyx ORE 1-Cosworth V8	
3	PORTUGUESE GP	Estoril	36	Moneytron Onyx	3.5 Onyx ORE 1-Cosworth V8	
dnpq	SPANISH GP	Jerez	36	Moneytron Onyx	3.5 Onyx ORE 1-Cosworth V8	
dnpq	JAPANESE GP	Suzuka	36	Moneytron Onyx	3.5 Onyx ORE 1-Cosworth V8	
dnpq	AUSTRALIAN GP	Adelaide	36	Moneytron Onyx	3.5 Onyx ORE 1-Cosworth V8	

1990

dnq	US GP (PHOENIX)	Phoenix	35	Moneytron Onyx Formula One	3.5 Onyx ORE 1-Cosworth V8	
dnq	BRAZILIAN GP	Interlagos	35	Moneytron Onyx Formula One	3.5 Onyx ORE 1-Cosworth V8	

1991

dnq	US GP (PHOENIX)	Phoenix	18	Automobiles Gonfaronaise Sportive	3.5 AGS JH25-Cosworth V8	
dnq	BRAZILIAN GP	Interlagos	18	Automobiles Gonfaronaise Sportive	3.5 AGS JH25-Cosworth V8	
ret	CANADIAN GP	Montreal	10	Footwork Grand Prix International	3.5 Footwork FA12-Porsche V12	engine
dnq	MEXICAN GP	Mexico City	10	Footwork Grand Prix International	3.5 Footwork FA12-Porsche V12	
dnq	FRENCH GP	Magny Cours	10	Footwork Grand Prix International	3.5 Footwork FA12-Cosworth V8	
dnq	BRITISH GP	Silverstone	10	Footwork Grand Prix International	3.5 Footwork FA12-Cosworth V8	

GP Starts: 79   GP Wins: 0   Pole positions: 0   Fastest laps: 0   Points: 88

LESLIE JOHNSON

Having raced an ERA E-Type in the immediate post-war years, taking part in the 1950 British GP, Johnson later became the chairman of the once illustrious marque, but his driving successes were achieved at the wheel of rival cars, such as a Jaguar and the Frazer-Nash in which he finished third at Le Mans with Tommy Wisdom in 1952. Johnson collapsed with serious heart problems during the 1954 Monte Carlo Rally and it was partly as a result of this condition that he died in 1959.

BRUCE JOHNSTONE

Having finished runner-up in the 1961 South African championship in his Cooper-Alfa, and also raced for the Yeoman Credit team, Johnstone came to Europe briefly in 1962 and drove for Ian Walker, winning the up-to-1.5 litre class in the Nürburgring 1000 Km with Peter Ashdown in a Lotus 23, and taking fifth in the Vanwall Trophy at Snetterton with Walker's Formula Junior Lotus. He also drove a BRM in the Gold Cup race at Oulton Park, finishing fourth, and took the same car to ninth place in his only GP appearance later that year.

JOHNSON, Leslie (GB) d 8/6/1959

1950

	Race	Circuit	No	Entrant	Car/Engine	Comment
ret	BRITISH GP	Silverstone	8	T A S O Mathieson	1.5 s/c ERA E type 6	supercharger

GP Starts: 1   GP Wins: 0   Pole positions: 0   Fastest laps: 0   Points: 0

JOHNSTONE, Bruce (ZA) b 30/1/1937

1962

	Race	Circuit	No	Entrant	Car/engine	Comment
9	SOUTH AFRICAN GP	East London	5	Bruce Johnstone	1.5 BRM P48/57 V8	6 laps behind

GP Starts: 1   GP Wins: 0   Pole positions: 0   Fastest laps: 0   Points: 0

JONES, Alan (AUS) b 2/11/1946

1975

	Race	Circuit	No	Entrant	Car/Engine	Comment
ret	SPANISH GP	Montjuich Park	25	Custom Made Harry Stiller Racing	3.0 Hesketh 308-Cosworth V8	hit by Donohue
ret	MONACO GP	Monte Carlo	26	Custom Made Harry Stiller Racing	3.0 Hesketh 308-Cosworth V8	lost wheel
ret	BELGIAN GP	Zolder	26	Custom Made Harry Stiller Racing	3.0 Hesketh 308-Cosworth V8	avoiding Mass/Watson-hit by Laffite
11	SWEDISH GP	Anderstorp	26	Custom Made Harry Stiller Racing	3.0 Hesketh 308-Cosworth V8	2 laps behind
13	DUTCH GP	Zandvoort	22	Embassy Racing with Graham Hill	3.0 Hill GH1-Cosworth V8	pit stop-tyres/5 laps behind
16	FRENCH GP	Paul Ricard	22	Embassy Racing with Graham Hill	3.0 Hill GH1-Cosworth V8	spin-pit stop/1 lap behind
10	BRITISH GP	Silverstone	22	Embassy Racing with Graham Hill	3.0 Hill GH1-Cosworth V8	2 pit stops-tyres/2 laps behind
5	GERMAN GP	Nürburgring	22	Embassy Racing with Graham Hill	3.0 Hill GH1-Cosworth V8	

1976

	Race	Circuit	No	Entrant	Car/Engine	Comment
nc	US GP WEST	Long Beach	19	Durex Team Surtees	3.0 Surtees TS19-Cosworth V8	2 pit stops/10 laps behind
9	SPANISH GP	Jarama	19	Durex Team Surtees	3.0 Surtees TS19-Cosworth V8	1 lap behind
5	BELGIAN GP	Zolder	19	Durex Team Surtees	3.0 Surtees TS19-Cosworth V8	1 lap behind
ret	MONACO GP	Monte Carlo	19	Durex Team Surtees	3.0 Surtees TS19-Cosworth V8	collision with Reutemann
13	SWEDISH GP	Anderstorp	19	Durex Team Surtees	3.0 Surtees TS19-Cosworth V8	1 lap behind
ret	FRENCH GP	Paul Ricard	19	Durex Team Surtees	3.0 Surtees TS19-Cosworth V8	rear anti-roll bar
5	BRITISH GP	Brands Hatch	19	Durex Team Surtees	3.0 Surtees TS19-Cosworth V8	1 lap behind
10	GERMAN GP	Nürburgring	19	Durex Team Surtees	3.0 Surtees TS19-Cosworth V8	
ret	AUSTRIAN GP	Österreichring	19	Durex Team Surtees	3.0 Surtees TS19-Cosworth V8	engine cut out-crashed
8	DUTCH GP	Zandvoort	19	Durex Team Surtees	3.0 Surtees TS19-Cosworth V8	1 lap behind
12	ITALIAN GP	Monza	19	Durex Team Surtees	3.0 Surtees TS19-Cosworth V8	pit stop-thought race stopped/-1 lap
16	CANADIAN GP	Mosport Park	19	Durex Team Surtees	3.0 Surtees TS19-Cosworth V8	pit stop/2 laps behind
8	US GP EAST	Watkins Glen	19	Durex Team Surtees	3.0 Surtees TS19-Cosworth V8	1 lap behind
4	JAPANESE GP	Mount Fuji	19	Durex/Theodore Team Surtees	3.0 Surtees TS19-Cosworth V8	1 lap behind

1977

	Race	Circuit	No	Entrant	Car/Engine	Comment
ret	US GP WEST	Long Beach	17	Shadow Racing Team	3.0 Shadow DN8-Cosworth V8	gearbox
ret	SPANISH GP	Jarama	17	Shadow Racing Team	3.0 Shadow DN8-Cosworth V8	collision with Peterson
6	MONACO GP	Monte Carlo	17	Shadow Racing Team	3.0 Shadow DN8-Cosworth V8	
5	BELGIAN GP	Zolder	17	Shadow Racing Team	3.0 Shadow DN8-Cosworth V8	
17	SWEDISH GP	Anderstorp	17	Shadow Racing Team	3.0 Shadow DN8-Cosworth V8	2 pit stops-ignition/5 laps behind
ret	FRENCH GP	Dijon	17	Shadow Racing Team	3.0 Shadow DN8-Cosworth V8	driveshaft
7	BRITISH GP	Silverstone	17	Shadow Racing Team	3.0 Shadow DN8-Cosworth V8	1 lap behind
ret	GERMAN GP	Hockenheim	17	Shadow Racing Team	3.0 Shadow DN8-Cosworth V8	startline accident
1	AUSTRIAN GP	Österreichring	17	Shadow Racing Team	3.0 Shadow DN8-Cosworth V8	
ret	DUTCH GP	Zandvoort	17	Shadow Racing Team	3.0 Shadow DN8-Cosworth V8	engine
3	ITALIAN GP	Monza	17	Shadow Racing Team	3.0 Shadow DN8-Cosworth V8	
ret	US GP EAST	Watkins Glen	17	Shadow Racing Team	3.0 Shadow DN8-Cosworth V8	accident with Peterson
4	CANADIAN GP	Mosport Park	17	Shadow Racing Team	3.0 Shadow DN8-Cosworth V8	
4	JAPANESE GP	Mount Fuji	17	Shadow Racing Team	3.0 Shadow DN8-Cosworth V8	

1978

ret	ARGENTINE GP	Buenos Aires	27	Williams Grand Prix Engineering	3.0 Williams FW06-Cosworth V8	*fuel vapour lock*
11	BRAZILIAN GP	Rio	27	Williams Grand Prix Engineering	3.0 Williams FW06-Cosworth V8	*3 pit stops-tyres/5 laps behind*
4	SOUTH AFRICAN GP	Kyalami	27	Williams Grand Prix Engineering	3.0 Williams FW06-Cosworth V8	
7	US GP WEST	Long Beach	27	Williams Grand Prix Engineering	3.0 Williams FW06-Cosworth V8	*broken front wings/1 lap behind/FL*
ret	MONACO GP	Monte Carlo	27	Williams Grand Prix Engineering	3.0 Williams FW06-Cosworth V8	*gearbox*
10	BELGIAN GP	Zolder	27	Williams Grand Prix Engineering	3.0 Williams FW06-Cosworth V8	*2 pit stops-tyres/2 laps behind*
8	SPANISH GP	Jarama	27	Williams Grand Prix Engineering	3.0 Williams FW06-Cosworth V8	*1 lap behind*
ret	SWEDISH GP	Anderstorp	27	Williams Grand Prix Engineering	3.0 Williams FW06-Cosworth V8	*front wheel bearing seized*
5	FRENCH GP	Paul Ricard	27	Williams Grand Prix Engineering	3.0 Williams FW06-Cosworth V8	
ret	BRITISH GP	Brands Hatch	27	Williams Grand Prix Engineering	3.0 Williams FW06-Cosworth V8	*driveshaft*
ret	GERMAN GP	Hockenheim	27	Williams Grand Prix Engineering	3.0 Williams FW06-Cosworth V8	*fuel vaporisation*
ret	AUSTRIAN GP	Österreichring	27	Williams Grand Prix Engineering	3.0 Williams FW06-Cosworth V8	*accident*
ret	DUTCH GP	Zandvoort	27	Williams Grand Prix Engineering	3.0 Williams FW06-Cosworth V8	*broken throttle cable*
13	ITALIAN GP	Monza	27	Williams Grand Prix Engineering	3.0 Williams FW06-Cosworth V8	*pit stop-tyre/1 lap behind*
2	US GP EAST	Watkins Glen	27	Williams Grand Prix Engineering	3.0 Williams FW06-Cosworth V8	
9	CANADIAN GP	Montreal	27	Williams Grand Prix Engineering	3.0 Williams FW06-Cosworth V8	*handling problems/FL*

1979

9	ARGENTINE GP	Buenos Aires	27	Albilad-Saudia Racing Team	3.0 Williams FW06-Cosworth V8	*pit stop-tyres/2 laps behind*
ret	BRAZILIAN GP	Interlagos	27	Albilad-Saudia Racing Team	3.0 Williams FW06-Cosworth V8	*fuel pressure*
ret	SOUTH AFRICAN GP	Kyalami	27	Albilad-Saudia Racing Team	3.0 Williams FW06-Cosworth V8	*rear suspension*
3	US GP WEST	Long Beach	27	Albilad-Saudia Racing Team	3.0 Williams FW06-Cosworth V8	
ret	SPANISH GP	Jarama	27	Albilad-Saudia Racing Team	3.0 Williams FW07-Cosworth V8	*gear selection*
ret	BELGIAN GP	Zolder	27	Albilad-Saudia Racing Team	3.0 Williams FW07-Cosworth V8	*electrics*
ret	MONACO GP	Monte Carlo	27	Albilad-Saudia Racing Team	3.0 Williams FW07-Cosworth V8	*hit guard rail*
4	FRENCH GP	Dijon	27	Albilad-Saudia Racing Team	3.0 Williams FW07-Cosworth V8	
ret	BRITISH GP	Silverstone	27	Albilad-Saudia Racing Team	3.0 Williams FW07-Cosworth V8	*water pump when 1st/Pole*
1	GERMAN GP	Hockenheim	27	Albilad-Saudia Racing Team	3.0 Williams FW07-Cosworth V8	
1	AUSTRIAN GP	Österreichring	27	Albilad-Saudia Racing Team	3.0 Williams FW07-Cosworth V8	
1	DUTCH GP	Zandvoort	27	Albilad-Saudia Racing Team	3.0 Williams FW07-Cosworth V8	
9	ITALIAN GP	Monza	27	Albilad-Saudia Racing Team	3.0 Williams FW07-Cosworth V8	*pit stop-battery/1 lap behind*
1	CANADIAN GP	Montreal	27	Albilad-Saudia Racing Team	3.0 Williams FW07-Cosworth V8	*Pole/FL*
ret	US GP EAST	Watkins Glen	27	Albilad-Saudia Racing Team	3.0 Williams FW07-Cosworth V8	*lost rear wheel/Pole*

1980 World Champion Driver

1	ARGENTINE GP	Buenos Aires	27	Albilad-Williams Racing Team	3.0 Williams FW07-Cosworth V8	*Pole/FL*
3	BRAZILIAN GP	Interlagos	27	Albilad-Williams Racing Team	3.0 Williams FW07B-Cosworth V8	
ret	SOUTH AFRICAN GP	Kyalami	27	Albilad-Williams Racing Team	3.0 Williams FW07B-Cosworth V8	*gearbox*
ret	US GP WEST	Long Beach	27	Albilad-Williams Racing Team	3.0 Williams FW07B-Cosworth V8	*collision with Giacomelli*
2	BELGIAN GP	Zolder	27	Albilad-Williams Racing Team	3.0 Williams FW07B-Cosworth V8	*Pole*
ret	MONACO GP	Monte Carlo	27	Albilad-Williams Racing Team	3.0 Williams FW07B-Cosworth V8	*differential*
1	FRENCH GP	Paul Ricard	27	Albilad-Williams Racing Team	3.0 Williams FW07B-Cosworth V8	*FL*
1	BRITISH GP	Brands Hatch	27	Albilad-Williams Racing Team	3.0 Williams FW07B-Cosworth V8	
3	GERMAN GP	Hockenheim	27	Albilad-Williams Racing Team	3.0 Williams FW07B-Cosworth V8	*pit stop-puncture/Pole/FL*
2	AUSTRIAN GP	Österreichring	27	Albilad-Williams Racing Team	3.0 Williams FW07B-Cosworth V8	
11	DUTCH GP	Zandvoort	27	Albilad-Williams Racing Team	3.0 Williams FW07B-Cosworth V8	*ran off road-pit stop/3 laps behind*
2	ITALIAN GP	Imola	27	Albilad-Williams Racing Team	3.0 Williams FW07B-Cosworth V8	*FL*
1	CANADIAN GP	Montreal	27	Albilad-Williams Racing Team	3.0 Williams FW07B-Cosworth V8	
1	US GP EAST	Watkins Glen	27	Albilad-Williams Racing Team	3.0 Williams FW07B-Cosworth V8	*FL*

1981

1	US GP WEST	Long Beach	1	Albilad-Williams Racing Team	3.0 Williams FW07C-Cosworth V8	*FL*
2	BRAZILIAN GP	Rio	1	Albilad-Williams Racing Team	3.0 Williams FW07C-Cosworth V8	
4	ARGENTINE GP	Buenos Aires	1	Albilad-Williams Racing Team	3.0 Williams FW07C-Cosworth V8	*down on power engine*
12	SAN MARINO GP	Imola	1	Albilad-Williams Racing Team	3.0 Williams FW07C-Cosworth V8	*pit stop-front wing/2 laps behind*
ret	BELGIAN GP	Zolder	1	Albilad-Williams Racing Team	3.0 Williams FW07C-Cosworth V8	*accident*
2	MONACO GP	Monte Carlo	1	Albilad-Williams Racing Team	3.0 Williams FW07C-Cosworth V8	*pit stop when 1st-fuel starvation/FL*
7	SPANISH GP	Jarama	1	TAG Williams Team	3.0 Williams FW07C-Cosworth V8	*went off when leading/FL*
17	FRENCH GP	Dijon	1	TAG Williams Team	3.0 Williams FW07C-Cosworth V8	*3 pit stops-steering/tyres/-4 laps*
ret	BRITISH GP	Silverstone	1	TAG Williams Team	3.0 Williams FW07C-Cosworth V8	*went off avoiding Villeneuve*
11	GERMAN GP	Hockenheim	1	TAG Williams Team	3.0 Williams FW07C-Cosworth V8	*p stop-fuel starvation/1 lap behind/FL*
4	AUSTRIAN GP	Österreichring	1	TAG Williams Team	3.0 Williams FW07C-Cosworth V8	
3	DUTCH GP	Zandvoort	1	TAG Williams Team	3.0 Williams FW07C-Cosworth V8	*FL*
2	ITALIAN GP	Monza	1	TAG Williams Team	3.0 Williams FW07C-Cosworth V8	
ret	CANADIAN GP	Montreal	1	TAG Williams Team	3.0 Williams FW07C-Cosworth V8	*handling*
1	CAESARS PALACE GP	Las Vegas	1	TAG Williams Team	3.0 Williams FW07C-Cosworth V8	

1983

ret	US GP WEST	Long Beach	30	Arrows Racing Team	3.0 Arrows A6-Cosworth V8	*driver discomfort*

1985

ret	ITALIAN GP	Monza	33	Team Haas (USA) Ltd	1.5 t/c Lola THL1-Hart 4	*distributor*
ret	EUROPEAN GP	Brands Hatch	33	Team Haas (USA) Ltd	1.5 t/c Lola THL1-Hart 4	*holed water radiator*
dns	SOUTH AFRICAN GP	Kyalami	33	Team Haas (USA) Ltd	1.5 t/c Lola THL1-Hart 4	*unwell*
ret	AUSTRALIAN GP	Adelaide	33	Team Haas (USA) Ltd	1.5 t/c Lola THL1-Hart 4	*electrics*

1986

ret	BRAZILIAN GP	Rio	15	Team Haas (USA) Ltd	1.5 t/c Lola THL1-Hart 4	*distributor rotor arm*
ret	SPANISH GP	Jerez	15	Team Haas (USA) Ltd	1.5 t/c Lola THL1-Hart 4	*accident with Palmer-lap 1*
ret	SAN MARINO GP	Imola	15	Team Haas (USA) Ltd	1.5 t/c Lola THL2-Cosworth V6	*overheating*
ret	MONACO GP	Monte Carlo	15	Team Haas (USA) Ltd	1.5 t/c Lola THL2-Cosworth V6	*incident with Streiff*
11/ret	BELGIAN GP	Spa	15	Team Haas (USA) Ltd	1.5 t/c Lola THL2-Cosworth V6	*out of fuel/3 laps behind*
10	CANADIAN GP	Montreal	15	Team Haas (USA) Ltd	1.5 t/c Lola THL2-Cosworth V6	*2 pit stops-tyres/3 laps behind*
ret	US GP (DETROIT)	Detroit	15	Team Haas (USA) Ltd	1.5 t/c Lola THL2-Cosworth V6	*drive pegs*
ret	FRENCH GP	Paul Ricard	15	Team Haas (USA) Ltd	1.5 t/c Lola THL2-Cosworth V6	*accident*
ret	BRITISH GP	Brands Hatch	15	Team Haas (USA) Ltd	1.5 t/c Lola THL2-Cosworth V6	*throttle linkage*

9	GERMAN GP	Hockenheim	15	Team Haas (USA) Ltd	1.5 t/c Lola THL2-Cosworth V6	*started from back of grid/-2 laps*
ret	HUNGARIAN GP	Hungaroring	15	Team Haas (USA) Ltd	1.5 t/c Lola THL2-Cosworth V6	*differential*
4	AUSTRIAN GP	Österreichring	15	Team Haas (USA) Ltd	1.5 t/c Lola THL2-Cosworth V6	*slipping clutch/2 laps behind*
6	ITALIAN GP	Monza	15	Team Haas (USA) Ltd	1.5 t/c Lola THL2-Cosworth V6	*2 p stops-tyres-balance weight/-2 laps*
ret	PORTUGESE GP	Estoril	15	Team Haas (USA) Ltd	1.5 t/c Lola THL2-Cosworth V6	*brakes-spun off*
ret	MEXICAN GP	Mexico City	15	Team Haas (USA) Ltd	1.5 t/c Lola THL2-Cosworth V6	*started from back of grid/tyres*
ret	AUSTRALIAN GP	Adelaide	15	Team Haas (USA) Ltd	1.5 t/c Lola THL2-Cosworth V6	*engine*

GP Starts: 116   GP Wins: 12   Pole positions: 6   Fastest laps: 13   Points: 206

ALAN JONES

Tough and downright bloody-minded Alan Jones may have been, but once he had established himself in the Williams team there were few to argue with the Australian's methods. Endowed with immense physical strength and bucket loads of bravery, he became perhaps the 'ground-effect' era's most skilled practitioner with a driving style that appeared brutal at times, but certainly brought results.

The son of Stan Jones, a famous fifties Australian racer, young Alan left school to work in his father's Holden dealership, racing a Mini and then an old Cooper before coming to England in 1967 only to find that even a Formula Ford drive was out of his reach. Undaunted, he was back in 1970 with fellow racing aspirant Brian McGuire and the Aussie pair set about running a couple of F3 Brabhams financed by buying and selling second-hand cars. Money was tight, with Alan and his wife Beverley living a hand-to-mouth existence to pay for the racing programme, but by 1973 Jones had a foot on the ladder to the top with a DART-entered GRD, taking second place in the John Player championship. Then came a setback as the team folded, leaving Alan with no drive for 1974 until one Harry Stiller came to the rescue. He ran the Australian in Formula Atlantic, and then at the end of the year Jones made a big impression in a one-off F5000 drive for John MacDonald.

Alan stepped up to Formula 1 in 1975 with Stiller's Hesketh, but the team managed only three Grands Prix before its owner packed his bags and went abroad for tax reasons, leaving Alan high and dry. Graham Hill then invited him to join the Embassy team in place of the injured Rolf Stommelen, and he brought the car into fifth place at the Nürburgring before the German was fit to resume. Fortunately, MacDonald found Jones a seat in his RAM F5000 car while he continued to look for a Formula 1 ride. After a sensational drive to second place in the 1976 Race of Champions at the wheel of a Surtees Alan was placed under contract for the season, but relationships soon became strained between team boss and driver, with Jones more interested in his US F5000 programme with Theodore, which brought wins at Mosport and Watkins Glen. He ended the season with fourth place at Mount Fuji, but without the prospect of a Grand Prix ride after a complete breakdown of communications with Surtees.

Then in 1977 tragedy worked in his favour. When Tom Pryce was killed in South Africa Alan took over the vacant seat at Shadow and seized the opportunity brilliantly, winning in Austria and scoring points finishes with some aggressive drives. Frank Williams, rebuilding his team in the wake of the Walter Wolf fiasco, saw Jones as just the sort of pragmatic charger he needed for 1978 and, at the wheel of Patrick Head's no-nonsense machine, the Aussie regularly put himself in among the leaders, often dogging the omnipotent Lotus 79s. Eleventh place in the championship was in no way a reflection of the team's competitiveness that year, but Alan had the satisfaction of also making his mark in Can-Am, taking the title in the Haas/Hall Lola T333.

The following season marked the true blossoming of Alan Jones the racing driver. The new ground-effect Williams FW07 proved that the imitator had leapfrogged the innovator, and in Alan's hands the car was simply stunning. A spate of retirements in the first half of the year torpedoed his title hopes, but four wins from five starts gave a fair indication of his late-season dominance. Nothing was left to chance in 1980 as Jones squeezed every ounce of potential from the car. He never once eased up, and certainly took no prisoners, but the title was won with crushing dominance. There was no let-up in 1981 either, as he headed towards self-imposed retirement; he still raced as if that first Grand Prix win had not yet been achieved, finishing on a high note with a lights-to-flag win at Caesars Palace.

Perhaps the story should have ended there. But after racing Porsches back in Australia, and despite a broken leg sustained in a riding accident, Jones was tempted back in 1983. In his all-too-brief spell with Arrows, he took third in the Race of Champions, and then raced at Long Beach, before pulling out when he was unable to agree a contract.

The terms offered by Haas Lola proved sufficiently tempting to bring him back to the Grand Prix arena late in 1985. Both technically and administratively, the project was something of a fiasco, leaving Alan to pick his way through the 1986 season with no more than occasional glimpses of his racing past. Wisely there were no further attempts to extend his Grand Prix career, Jones preferring to keep his hand in 'down-under' in touring cars.

KARCH, Oswald (D)

1953

	Race	Circuit	No	Entrant	Car/Engine	Comment
ret	GERMAN GP	Nürburgring	26	Oswald Karch	2.0 Veritas RS 6	

GP Starts: 1   GP Wins: 0   Pole positions: 0   Fastest laps: 0   Points: 0

KATAYAMA, Ukyo (J) b 29/5/1963

1992

	Race	Circuit	No	Entrant	Car/Engine	Comment
12	SOUTH AFRICAN GP	Kyalami	30	Central Park Venturi Larrousse	3.5 Venturi LC92-Lamborghini V12	4 laps behind
12	MEXICAN GP	Mexico City	30	Central Park Venturi Larrousse	3.5 Venturi LC92-Lamborghini V12	4 laps behind
9	BRAZILIAN GP	Interlagos	30	Central Park Venturi Larrousse	3.5 Venturi LC92-Lamborghini V12	3 laps behind
dnq	SPANISH GP	Barcelona	30	Central Park Venturi Larrousse	3.5 Venturi LC92-Lamborghini V12	
ret	SAN MARINO GP	Imola	30	Central Park Venturi Larrousse	3.5 Venturi LC92-Lamborghini V12	spun off
dnpq	MONACO GP	Monte Carlo	30	Central Park Venturi Larrousse	3.5 Venturi LC92-Lamborghini V12	
ret	CANADIAN GP	Montreal	30	Central Park Venturi Larrousse	3.5 Venturi LC92-Lamborghini V12	engine
ret	FRENCH GP	Magny Cours	30	Central Park Venturi Larrousse	3.5 Venturi LC92-Lamborghini V12	engine
ret	BRITISH GP	Silverstone	30	Central Park Venturi Larrousse	3.5 Venturi LC92-Lamborghini V12	gear linkage
ret	GERMAN GP	Hockenheim	30	Central Park Venturi Larrousse	3.5 Venturi LC92-Lamborghini V12	accident
ret	HUNGARIAN GP	Hungaroring	30	Central Park Venturi Larrousse	3.5 Venturi LC92-Lamborghini V12	engine
17	BELGIAN GP	Spa	30	Central Park Venturi Larrousse	3.5 Venturi LC92-Lamborghini V12	2 laps behind
9/ret	ITALIAN GP	Monza	30	Central Park Venturi Larrousse	3.5 Venturi LC92-Lamborghini V12	transmission-spun off/-3 laps
ret	PORTUGUESE GP	Estoril	30	Central Park Venturi Larrousse	3.5 Venturi LC92-Lamborghini V12	spun off
11	JAPANESE GP	Suzuka	30	Central Park Venturi Larrousse	3.5 Venturi LC92-Lamborghini V12	1 lap behind
ret	AUSTRALIAN GP	Adelaide	30	Central Park Venturi Larrousse	3.5 Venturi LC92-Lamborghini V12	differential

1993

	Race	Circuit	No	Entrant	Car/Engine	Comment
ret	SOUTH AFRICAN GP	Kyalami	3	Tyrrell Racing Organisation	3.5 Tyrrell 020C-Yamaha V10	transmission
ret	BRAZILIAN GP	Interlagos	3	Tyrrell Racing Organisation	3.5 Tyrrell 020C-Yamaha V10	crashed in rainstorm
ret	EUROPEAN GP	Donington	3	Tyrrell Racing Organisation	3.5 Tyrrell 020C-Yamaha V10	clutch failure
ret	SAN MARINO GP	Imola	3	Tyrrell Racing Organisation	3.5 Tyrrell 020C-Yamaha V10	engine-water leak
ret	SPANISH GP	Barcelona	3	Tyrrell Racing Organisation	3.5 Tyrrell 020C-Yamaha V10	spun off
ret	MONACO GP	Monte Carlo	3	Tyrrell Racing Organisation	3.5 Tyrrell 020C-Yamaha V10	oil leak
17	CANADIAN GP	Montreal	3	Tyrrell Racing Organisation	3.5 Tyrrell 020C-Yamaha V10	spin-p stop/suspension/-5 laps
ret	FRENCH GP	Magny Cours	3	Tyrrell Racing Organisation	3.5 Tyrrell 020C-Yamaha V10	engine
13	BRITISH GP	Silverstone	3	Tyrrell Racing Organisation	3.5 Tyrrell 020C-Yamaha V10	
dns	"	"	3	Tyrrell Racing Organisation	3.5 Tyrrell 021-Yamaha V10	practice only
ret	GERMAN GP	Hockenheim	3	Tyrrell Racing Organisation	3.5 Tyrrell 021-Yamaha V10	spun off
10	HUNGARIAN GP	Hungaroring	3	Tyrrell Racing Organisation	3.5 Tyrrell 021-Yamaha V10	4 laps behind
15	BELGIAN GP	Spa	3	Tyrrell Racing Organisation	3.5 Tyrrell 021-Yamaha V10	4 laps behind
14	ITALIAN GP	Monza	3	Tyrrell Racing Organisation	3.5 Tyrrell 021-Yamaha V10	suspension/puncture/6 laps behind
dns	"	"	3	Tyrrell Racing Organisation	3.5 Tyrrell 020C-Yamaha V10	practice only
ret	PORTUGUESE GP	Estoril	3	Tyrrell Racing Organisation	3.5 Tyrrell 021-Yamaha V10	crashed
ret	JAPANESE GP	Suzuka	3	Tyrrell Racing Organisation	3.5 Tyrrell 021-Yamaha V10	engine
ret	AUSTRALIAN GP	Adelaide	3	Tyrrell Racing Organisation	3.5 Tyrrell 021-Yamaha V10	crashed

GP Starts: 30   GP Wins: 0   Pole positions: 0   Fastest laps: 0   Points: 0

KEEGAN, Rupert (GB) b 26/2/1955

1977

	Race	Circuit	No	Entrant	Car/Engine	Comment
ret	SPANISH GP	Jarama	24	Penthouse Rizla Racing	3.0 Hesketh 308E-Cosworth V8	missed gearchange-accident
12	MONACO GP	Monte Carlo	24	Penthouse Rizla Racing	3.0 Hesketh 308E-Cosworth V8	broken anti-roll bar/3 laps behind
ret	BELGIAN GP	Zolder	24	Penthouse Rizla Racing	3.0 Hesketh 308E-Cosworth V8	spun off
13	SWEDISH GP	Anderstorp	24	Penthouse Rizla Racing	3.0 Hesketh 308E-Cosworth V8	handling problems/1 lap behind
10	FRENCH GP	Dijon	24	Penthouse Rizla Racing	3.0 Hesketh 308E-Cosworth V8	2 laps behind
ret	BRITISH GP	Silverstone	24	Penthouse Rizla Racing	3.0 Hesketh 308E-Cosworth V8	collision with Merzario-lost wheel
ret	GERMAN GP	Hockenheim	24	Penthouse Rizla Racing	3.0 Hesketh 308E-Cosworth V8	accident-hit Ribeiro
7	AUSTRIAN GP	Österreichring	24	Penthouse Rizla Racing	3.0 Hesketh 308E-Cosworth V8	2 spins/1 lap behind
ret	DUTCH GP	Zandvoort	24	Penthouse Rizla Racing	3.0 Hesketh 308E-Cosworth V8	accident
9	ITALIAN GP	Monza	24	Penthouse Rizla Racing	3.0 Hesketh 308E-Cosworth V8	pit stop/4 laps behind
8	US GP EAST	Watkins Glen	24	Penthouse Rizla Racing	3.0 Hesketh 308E-Cosworth V8	1 lap behind
ret	CANADIAN GP	Mosport Park	24	Penthouse Rizla Racing	3.0 Hesketh 308E-Cosworth V8	hit Binder

1978

	Race	Circuit	No	Entrant	Car/Engine	Comment
ret	ARGENTINE GP	Buenos Aires	18	Durex Team Surtees	3.0 Surtees TS19-Cosworth V8	overheating
ret	BRAZILIAN GP	Rio	18	Durex Team Surtees	3.0 Surtees TS19-Cosworth V8	accident
ret	SOUTH AFRICAN GP	Kyalami	18	Durex Team Surtees	3.0 Surtees TS19-Cosworth V8	oil line-engine
dns	US GP WEST	Long Beach	18	Durex Team Surtees	3.0 Surtees TS19-Cosworth V8	practice accident
ret	MONACO GP	Monte Carlo	18	Durex Team Surtees	3.0 Surtees TS19-Cosworth V8	transmission
ret	"	"	18	Durex Team Surtees	3.0 Surtees TS20-Cosworth V8	practice only
dnq	BELGIAN GP	Zolder	18	Durex Team Surtees	3.0 Surtees TS20-Cosworth V8	
11	SPANISH GP	Jarama	18	Durex Team Surtees	3.0 Surtees TS20-Cosworth V8	2 laps behind
dnq	SWEDISH GP	Anderstorp	18	Durex Team Surtees	3.0 Surtees TS20-Cosworth V8	
ret	FRENCH GP	Paul Ricard	18	Durex Team Surtees	3.0 Surtees TS20-Cosworth V8	engine
dnq	BRITISH GP	Brands Hatch	18	Durex Team Surtees	3.0 Surtees TS20-Cosworth V8	
dnq	"	"	18	Durex Team Surtees	3.0 Surtees TS19-Cosworth V8	
dnq	GERMAN GP	Hockenheim	18	Durex Team Surtees	3.0 Surtees TS20-Cosworth V8	
dnq	AUSTRIAN GP	Österreichring	18	Durex Team Surtees	3.0 Surtees TS20-Cosworth V8	
dns	DUTCH GP	Zandvoort	18	Durex Team Surtees	3.0 Surtees TS20-Cosworth V8	accident in pre-race warm-up-injured

1980

			No	Entrant	Car/Engine	Comment
11	BRITISH GP	Brands Hatch	50	RAM/Williams Grand Prix Engineering	3.0 Williams FW07-Cosworth V8	pit stop/3 laps behind
dnq	GERMAN GP	Hockenheim	50	RAM/Penthouse Rizla Racing	3.0 Williams FW07B-Cosworth V8	
15	AUSTRIAN GP	Österreichring	50	RAM/Penthouse Rizla Racing	3.0 Williams FW07B-Cosworth V8	2 laps behind
dnq	DUTCH GP	Zandvoort	50	RAM/Penthouse Rizla Racing	3.0 Williams FW07B-Cosworth V8	
11	ITALIAN GP	Imola	50	RAM/Penthouse Rizla Racing	3.0 Williams FW07B-Cosworth V8	2 laps behind
dnq	CANADIAN GP	Montreal	50	RAM/Penthouse Rizla Racing	3.0 Williams FW07B-Cosworth V8	
9	US GP EAST	Watkins Glen	50	RAM/Penthouse Rizla Racing	3.0 Williams FW07B-Cosworth V8	2 laps behind

1982

			No	Entrant	Car/Engine	Comment
dnq	GERMAN GP	Hockenheim	17	Rothmans March Grand Prix Team	3.0 March 821-Cosworth V8	
ret	AUSTRIAN GP	Österreichring	17	Rothmans March Grand Prix Team	3.0 March 821-Cosworth V8	bent steering arm
ret	SWISS GP	Dijon	17	Rothmans March Grand Prix Team	3.0 March 821-Cosworth V8	spun off
dnq	ITALIAN GP	Monza	17	Rothmans March Grand Prix Team	3.0 March 821-Cosworth V8	
12	CAESARS PALACE GP	Las Vegas	17	Rothmans March Grand Prix Team	3.0 March 821-Cosworth V8	3 laps behind

GP Starts: 25   GP Wins: 0   Pole positions: 0   Fastest laps: 0   Points: 0

KEIZAN, Eddie (ZA) b 12/9/1944

1973

	Race	Circuit	No	Entrant	Car/Engine	Comment
nc	SOUTH AFRICAN GP	Kyalami	26	Blignaut-Lucky Strike Racing	3.0 Tyrrell 004-Cosworth V8	2 pit stops/12 laps behind

1974

14	SOUTH AFRICAN GP	Kyalami	32	Blignaut-Embassy Racing SA	3.0 Tyrrell 004-Cosworth V8	2 laps behind

1975

13	SOUTH AFRICAN GP	Kyalami	33	Team Gunston	3.0 Lotus 72-Cosworth V8	2 laps behind

GP Starts: 3   GP Wins: 0   Pole positions: 0   Fastest laps: 0   Points: 0

UKYO KATAYAMA

This diminutive Japanese driver first ventured to Europe some time before he entered Grand Prix racing with Larrousse in 1992, for he tried his hand at Formule Renault in France in 1986 and the French Formula 3 series in 1987 after winning junior single-seater championships at home in 1983-84. From 1988 he concentrated on racing in his national F3000 series, finally becoming champion in 1991, though he did come over to drive the uncompetitive Footwork briefly at the beginning of 1989.

Given his F1 opportunity, Katayama was certainly committed, but his lack of strength and stamina seemed to count against him. With the faith of his sponsors, Cabin, intact, Ukyo moved to Tyrrell with Yamaha engines for 1993. Sadly the season was not a happy one, with the promise of the new V10 being compromised by the shortcomings of the chassis, and poor Katayama was involved in a seemingly endless catalogue of spins in a desperate attempt to make up for its failings.

RUPERT KEEGAN

The much hyped Keegan did possess talent, but perhaps not quite as much as he and his father, backer and number-one fan Mike believed.

Starting his career with a win first time out in a Ford Escort Mexico, Keegan soon moved into Formula Ford, where he was quick but erratic. A successful end to the 1974 season encouraged him to move into Formula 3 the following year with the ex-Henton March 743, but the season was punctuated with crashes, including a very nasty one at Thruxton.

Things changed dramatically in 1976, with a more consistent Rupert winning nine rounds of the BP championship and the title to line up a seat in the Hesketh Grand Prix team for 1977. The car was awful but Keegan emerged with great credit, qualifying for every race in which he was entered, only to jump out of the frying pan and into the fire by joining the ailing Surtees team in 1978.

Left with no alternatives, Rupert drove an Arrows in the 1979 Aurora F1 series, winning five rounds and the championship, but his return to the Grand Prix arena in 1980 with the RAM Williams brought little reward, and the same could be said of his final shot in the Rothmans March at the end of 1982. After a spell in endurance racing and a brief flirtation with Indy cars, Keegan quit to pursue an entrepreneurial business career.

EDDIE KEIZAN

Eddie raced saloons in his native South Africa from the late sixties, winning the championship twice, then switched to sports cars with a Lola T212 in 1971. It was the purchase of a F5000 Surtees in 1972 which put him on the map as national champion in that class. He then raced a Tyrrell 004 and a Lotus 72 in the domestic series, and naturally the local Grands Prix as well. With his thriving business interests taking up more of his time, Eddie moved into the South African touring car championship with a BMW, winning the title twice more, and crowned his career by scoring a great victory in the Wynn's 1000 at Kyalami in 1979, when he was forced to drive for most of the race after his co-driver, Helmut Kelleners, was taken ill, to defeat such luminaries as Watson, Mass, Surer and Stuck.

He did not race again for ten years, but occasionally dons his overalls to drive a BMW in South African endurance events.

KELLY, Joe (IRL) b 13/3/1913

1950

	Race	Circuit	No	Entrant	Car/Engine	Comment
nc	BRITISH GP	Silverstone	23	Joe Kelly	1.5 s/c Alta GP 4	pit stops/23 laps behind

1951

	Race	Circuit	No	Entrant	Car/Engine	Comment
nc	BRITISH GP	Silverstone	5	Joe Kelly	1.5 s/c Alta GP 4	pit stops/15 laps behind

GP Starts: 2   GP Wins: 0   Pole positions: 0   Fastest laps: 0   Points: 0

KESSEL, Loris (CH) b 1/4/1950

1976

	Race	Circuit	No	Entrant	Car/Engine	Comment
dnq	SPANISH GP	Jarama	32	RAM Racing	3.0 Brabham BT44B-Cosworth V8	
12	BELGIAN GP	Zolder	32	RAM Racing	3.0 Brabham BT44B-Cosworth V8	pit stop/7 laps behind
ret	SWEDISH GP	Anderstorp	32	RAM Racing	3.0 Brabham BT44B-Cosworth V8	accident
dnq	FRENCH GP	Paul Ricard	32	RAM Racing	3.0 Brabham BT44B-Cosworth V8	
nc	AUSTRIAN GP	Österreichring	32	RAM Racing	3.0 Brabham BT44B-Cosworth V8	pit stop-fuel union/10 laps behind

1977

	Race	Circuit	No	Entrant	Car/Engine	Comment
dnq	ITALIAN GP	Monza	41	Jolly Club of Switzerland	3.0 Williams FW03-Cosworth V8	crashed in practice

GP Starts: 3   GP Wins: 0   Pole positions: 0   Fastest laps: 0   Points: 0

KINNUNEN, Leo (SF) b 5/8/1943

1974

	Race	Circuit	No	Entrant	Car/Engine	Comment
dnq	BELGIAN GP	Nivelles	44	AAW Racing Team	3.0 Surtees TS16-Cosworth V8	
ret	SWEDISH GP	Anderstorp	23	AAW Racing Team	3.0 Surtees TS16-Cosworth V8	electrics
dnq	FRENCH GP	Dijon	23	AAW Racing Team	3.0 Surtees TS16-Cosworth V8	
dnq	BRITISH GP	Brands Hatch	43	AAW Racing Team	3.0 Surtees TS16-Cosworth V8	
dnq	AUSTRIAN GP	Österreichring	43	AAW Racing Team	3.0 Surtees TS16-Cosworth V8	
dnq	ITALIAN GP	Monza	23	AAW Racing Team	3.0 Surtees TS16-Cosworth V8	

GP Starts: 1   GP Wins: 0   Pole positions: 0   Fastest laps: 0   Points: 0

KLENK, Hans (D) b 18/10/1919

1952

	Race	Circuit	No	Entrant	Car/Engine	Comment
nc	GERMAN GP	Nürburgring	123	Hans Klenk	2.0 Veritas Meteor 6	4 laps behind

GP Starts: 1   GP Wins: 0   Pole positions: 0   Fastest laps: 0   Points: 0

KLERK, Peter de (ZA) b 16/3/1936

1963

	Race	Circuit	No	Entrant	Car/Engine	Comment
ret	SOUTH AFRICAN GP	East London	18	Otelle Nucci	1.5 Alfa Romeo Special 4	gearbox

1965

	Race	Circuit	No	Entrant	Car/Engine	Comment
10	SOUTH AFRICAN GP	East London	20	Otelle Nucci	1.5 Alfa Romeo Special 4	6 laps behind

1969

	Race	Circuit	No	Entrant	Car/Engine	Comment
nc	SOUTH AFRICAN GP	Kyalami	19	Jack Holme	3.0 Brabham BT20-Repco V8	pit stop-clutch/7 laps behind

1970

	Race	Circuit	No	Entrant	Car/Engine	Comment
nc	SOUTH AFRICAN GP	Kyalami	24	Team Gunston	3.0 Brabham BT26A-Cosworth V8	pit stop/13 laps behind

GP Starts: 4   GP Wins: 0   Pole positions: 0   Fastest laps: 0   Points: 0

KLING, Karl (D) b 16/9/1910

1954

	Race	Circuit	No	Entrant	Car/Engine	Comment
2	FRENCH GP	Reims	20	Daimler Benz AG	2.5 Mercedes-Benz W196 8	
7	BRITISH GP	Silverstone	2	Daimler Benz AG	2.5 Mercedes-Benz W196 8	3 laps behind
4	GERMAN GP	Nürburgring	19	Daimler Benz AG	2.5 Mercedes-Benz W196 8	led race until suspension problems/FL
ret	SWISS GP	Bremgarten	8	Daimler Benz AG	2.5 Mercedes-Benz W196 8	injector pump drive
ret	ITALIAN GP	Monza	14	Daimler Benz AG	2.5 Mercedes-Benz W196 8	radius rod-crashed
5	SPANISH GP	Pedralbes	4	Daimler Benz AG	2.5 Mercedes-Benz W196 8	1 lap behind

1955

	Race	Circuit	No	Entrant	Car/Engine	Comment
ret	ARGENTINE GP	Buenos Aires	4	Daimler Benz AG	2.5 Mercedes-Benz W196 8	crashed
4*	" "	" "	8	Daimler Benz AG	2.5 Mercedes-Benz W196 8	* Moss & Herrmann co-drove/-2 laps
ret	BELGIAN GP	Spa	12	Daimler Benz AG	2.5 Mercedes-Benz W196 8	oil pipe
ret	DUTCH GP	Zandvoort	12	Daimler Benz AG	2.5 Mercedes-Benz W196 8	spun off
3	BRITISH GP	Aintree	14	Daimler Benz AG	2.5 Mercedes-Benz W196 8\	
ret	ITALIAN GP	Monza	20	Daimler Benz AG	2.5 Mercedes-Benz W196 8	gearbox

GP Starts: 11   GP Wins: 0   Pole positions: 0   Fastest laps: 1   Points: 17

LORIS KESSEL

A Swiss garage owner and former Alfa saloon racer, Kessel graduated from Formula 3 with no great record of success outside his native championship. A season of Formula 2 with a March in 1975 saw him briefly lead the opening race at Estoril and score a couple of fourth places at Hockenheim, but little else.

His undistinguished spell in the RAM F1 team in 1976 ended in legal acrimony, then followed a brief flirtation with the Apollon. Thereafter he made occasional appearances in F3 until 1981, when he returned to Formula 2 without success. However, in 1993, after many years out of the spotlight, he was to be found in the Porsche 962C that finished seventh in the Le Mans 24 Hours.

LEO KINNUNEN

Kinnunen raced successfully for a number of seasons in his native Finland with Volvos, Porsches and an F3 Titan before being plucked from this relative obscurity to partner Pedro Rodriguez in the Gulf/Wyer sports car team for 1970, the pair winning at Daytona, Brands Hatch, Monza and Watkins Glen.

Between 1971 and '73, Leo swept the board in Interserie racing with a Porsche 917 Spyder entered by AAW-Finland, who also backed his unhappy Grand Prix season in 1974. After this debacle, Kinnunen returned to sports car and GT racing, competing in Porsches for the rest of the decade.

PETER de KLERK

An extremely accomplished driver whose long and rewarding career was spent almost exclusively in his native South Africa, de Klerk started racing in the early 1960s, initially with an Alfa special before he laid hands on a Brabham. Always the bridesmaid, Peter seemed to finish second on numerous occasions before temporarily abandoning single-seaters at the end of 1965.

In 1967 he drove a Lola-Aston Martin at Le Mans, resuming his career in late 1968 and continuing to race into the early seventies.

HELMUTH KOINIGG

A protégé of Helmut Marko, Koinigg spent the bulk of his short career trapped, albeit successfully, in Formula Vee and Super Vee, with only occasional outings in Formula Ford offering a glimpse of his talent.

Without the backing to race in Formula 2, Koinigg found himself in the Ford Cologne team, also handling Martini Racing's Porsche before raising the finance to hire a private Brabham for the 1974 Austrian GP. He did well enough to interest Surtees, who signed him up, but in only his second race for the team, at Watkins Glen, the young Austrian inexplicably crashed heavily into the Armco and was killed instantly.

KARL KLING

Kling drove production cars in hill-climbs and trials as an amateur before the war but his racing career did not really start in earnest until 1947, when he scored a victory at Hockenheim with a BMW.

The next two seasons saw him crowned German sports car champion in the 2-litre class with the potent Veritas. In 1950, he raced the Veritas-Meteor in Formula 2, winning races at Grenzlandring and Solitude, and the Eifelrennen at the Nürburgring, which led to an invitation to help develop the pre-war Mercedes, which raced again at the start of 1951 in South America, taking second place in the Eva Peron Cup.

Leading the Mercedes 300SL sports car attack in 1952, Kling missed out at Le Mans, but made up for it elsewhere, winning the Carrera Panamericana and the Prix de Berne, and taking second in the Mille Miglia. After a short stay with Alfa Romeo in 1953, Kling was back in the silver cars the following season, but very much in the shadow of Fangio – although the Argentinian, allegedly, allowed him to take the Berlin GP at AVUS.

Relegated in the pecking order in 1955 by the arrival of Stirling Moss, Karl did not enjoy much success in Grands Prix, but took third place at Aintree, behind the star duo, and shared the second-placed Mercedes sports car with Fangio in both the Tourist Trophy and the Targa Florio, before retiring to take up a management position within the company following their withdrawal from racing at the end of the 1955 season.

KLODWIG, Ernst (D) b 23/5/1903

	1952				
	Race	Circuit	No Entrant	Car/Engine	Comment
nc	GERMAN GP	Nürburgring	135 Ernst Klodwig	2.0 BMW-Eigenbau 6	
	1953				
nc	GERMAN GP	Nürburgring	37 Ernst Klodwig	2.0 BMW-Eigenbau 6	3 laps behind

GP Starts: 2   GP Wins: 0   Pole positions: 0   Fastest laps: 0   Points: 0

KOINIGG, Helmuth (A) b 3/11/1948 – d 6/10/1974

	1974				
	Race	Circuit	No Entrant	Car/Engine	Comment
dnq	AUSTRIAN GP	Österreichring	32 Scuderia Finotto	3.0 Brabham BT42-Cosworth V8	
10	CANADIAN GP	Mosport Park	19 Team Surtees	3.0 Surtees TS16-Cosworth V8	2 laps behind
ret	US GP	Watkins Glen	19 Team Surtees	3.0 Surtees TS16-Cosworth V8	fatal accident

GP Starts: 2   GP Wins: 0   Pole positions: 0   Fastest laps: 0   Points: 0

KRAUSE, Rudolf (D) b 30/3/1907

1952

	Race	Circuit	No	Entrant	Car/Engine	Comment
ret	GERMAN GP	Nürburgring	136	Rudolf Krause	2.0 BMW-Greifzu 6	
	1953					
14	GERMAN GP	Nürburgring	36	Dora Greifzu	2.0 BMW-Eigenbau 6	2 laps behind

GP Starts: 2   GP Wins: 0   Pole positions: 0   Fastest laps: 0   Points: 0

JACQUES LAFFITE

The smiling countenance of Jacques Laffite brightened the Grand Prix scene for more than a decade, during which he was a consistent performer who really excelled only when his car was absolutely on the pace – but then he simply flew.

His introduction to the sport was as a mechanic to Jean-Pierre Jabouille during his 1968 F3 season. Jacques resolved to race himself and started in Formula France before hitting the French F3 trail in the early seventies. In 1973 he won the French F3 championship in his Martini, and came close to taking the British John Player title as well, his splendid season including big wins in the prestigious Monaco and Pau GPs. With backing from BP France, Laffite moved into Formula 2 in 1974 with a March-BMW, soon establishing himself among the front-runners and winning a round at Salzburgring. Having tried a number of drivers during the first half of the season, Frank Williams decided on Jacques for the German GP, and although his race ended in a shunt he had impressed more than the previous incumbents and settled in for the next season and a half. In 1975 Williams were very much in the doldrums, but Laffite profited from others' misfortune to provide the team with a much-needed second place in Germany. In Formula 2 meanwhile, racing an Elf-backed Martini, Jacques clocked up six victories, edging out Jabouille to secure the European title, and he also took the Kauhsen/Autodelta Alfa T33 to victory at Dijon, Monza and the Nürburgring.

Ousting the originally nominated driver, Jean-Pierre Beltoise, Laffite joined Guy Ligier's debutant Ligier-Matra team for 1976 and quickly became a favourite son at Vichy, working hard to bring the car to a competitive pitch. He was rewarded with a win at Anderstorp in 1977, but it soon became clear that Cosworth power was a necessity for sustained success. At the beginning of 1979, now partnered by Depailler, Jacques flashed to victory in the opening two Grands Prix, but the dominance could not be sustained, as development brought more questions than answers. He took another win at Hockenheim the following season, but plans were already afoot to return to Matra power in 1981 under the Talbot banner. The team enjoyed a remarkably consistent season, and a strong run saw Laffite take two wins and make a late bid for the title before finishing fourth just behind Piquet, Reutemann and Jones. The promise evaporated in 1982, however, and Jacques managed only two points-scoring finishes all year, prompting his return to Williams on a two-year deal to drive alongside Keke Rosberg.

His year began soundly, but the Cosworth car became less and less competitive and Laffite suffered the late-season embarrassment of non-qualification at Monza and Brands Hatch. Things picked up in 1984, but with Rosberg extracting the very maximum from the car, the Frenchman's efforts seemed pedestrian by comparison. Despite rumours of retirement, Jacques returned to Ligier and rediscovered some of his form of old, enough at least to ensure that his beaming smile appeared on the rostrum from time to time. Perhaps spurred by the arrival of Arnoux, Laffite produced some sparkling displays in 1986, even leading the Detroit race briefly. Then came a multiple shunt at the start at Brands Hatch which left the unlucky Jacques trapped in his car with both legs broken. His Grand Prix career was over, but he was to return to the circuits, enjoying the cut and thrust of the French touring car series over the next few seasons.

LAFFITE, Jacques (F) b 21/11/1943

1974

	Race	Circuit	No	Entrant	Car/Engine	Comment
ret	GERMAN GP	Nürburgring	21	Frank Williams Racing Cars	3.0 Williams FW02-Cosworth V8	accident damage
nc	AUSTRIAN GP	Österreichring	21	Frank Williams Racing Cars	3.0 Williams FW02-Cosworth V8	wheel damage on grid/17 laps behind
ret	ITALIAN GP	Monza	21	Frank Williams Racing Cars	3.0 Williams FW02-Cosworth V8	engine
15/ret	CANADIAN GP	Mosport Park	21	Frank Williams Racing Cars	3.0 Williams FW02-Cosworth V8	puncture/6 laps behind
ret	US GP	Watkins Glen	21	Frank Williams Racing Cars	3.0 Williams FW02-Cosworth V8	rear wheel
	1975					
ret	ARGENTINE GP	Buenos Aires	21	Frank Williams Racing Cars	3.0 Williams FW02-Cosworth V8	gearbox
11	BRAZILIAN GP	Interlagos	21	Frank Williams Racing Cars	3.0 Williams FW02-Cosworth V8	1 lap behind
nc	SOUTH AFRICAN GP	Kyalami	21	Frank Williams Racing Cars	3.0 Williams FW02-Cosworth V8	pit stop/9 laps behind
dnq	MONACO GP	Monte Carlo	21	Frank Williams Racing Cars	3.0 Williams FW04-Cosworth V8	
ret	BELGIAN GP	Zolder	21	Frank Williams Racing Cars	3.0 Williams FW04-Cosworth V8	gearbox
ret	DUTCH GP	Zandvoort	21	Frank Williams Racing Cars	3.0 Williams FW04-Cosworth V8	engine
11	FRENCH GP	Paul Ricard	21	Frank Williams Racing Cars	3.0 Williams FW04-Cosworth V8	
ret	BRITISH GP	Silverstone	21	Frank Williams Racing Cars	3.0 Williams FW04-Cosworth V8	gearbox
2	GERMAN GP	Nürburgring	21	Frank Williams Racing Cars	3.0 Williams FW04-Cosworth V8	
ret	AUSTRIAN GP	Österreichring	21	Frank Williams Racing Cars	3.0 Williams FW04-Cosworth V8	handling
ret	ITALIAN GP	Monza	21	Frank Williams Racing Cars	3.0 Williams FW04-Cosworth V8	gearbox
dns	US GP	Watkins Glen	21	Frank Williams Racing Cars	3.0 Williams FW04-Cosworth V8	unwell-petrol in eyes
	1976					
ret	BRAZILIAN GP	Interlagos	26	Ligier Gitanes	3.0 Ligier JS5-Matra V12	gear linkage
ret	SOUTH AFRICAN GP	Kyalami	26	Ligier Gitanes	3.0 Ligier JS5-Matra V12	engine

4	US GP WEST	Long Beach	26	Ligier Gitanes	3.0 Ligier JS5-Matra V12	
12	SPANISH GP	Jarama	26	Ligier Gitanes	3.0 Ligier JS5-Matra V12	*reinstated after dsq/3 laps behind*
3	BELGIAN GP	Zolder	26	Ligier Gitanes	3.0 Ligier JS5-Matra V12	
12/ret	MONACO GP	Monte Carlo	26	Ligier Gitanes	3.0 Ligier JS5-Matra V12	*collision with Mass/3 laps behind*
4	SWEDISH GP	Anderstorp	26	Ligier Gitanes	3.0 Ligier JS5-Matra V12	
14	FRENCH GP	Paul Ricard	26	Ligier Gitanes	3.0 Ligier JS5-Matra V12	*1 lap behind*
ret/dsq	BRITISH GP	Brands Hatch	26	Ligier Gitanes	3.0 Ligier JS5-Matra V12	*suspension/dsq spare car in restart*
ret/dns	GERMAN GP	Nürburgring	26	Ligier Gitanes	3.0 Ligier JS5-Matra V12	*gearbox-1st start/did not restart*
2	AUSTRIAN GP	Österreichring	26	Ligier Gitanes	3.0 Ligier JS5-Matra V12	
ret	DUTCH GP	Zandvoort	26	Ligier Gitanes	3.0 Ligier JS5-Matra V12	*oil pressure*
3	ITALIAN GP	Monza	26	Ligier Gitanes	3.0 Ligier JS5-Matra V12	*Pole*
ret	CANADIAN GP	Mosport Park	26	Ligier Gitanes	3.0 Ligier JS5-Matra V12	*oil pressure*
ret	US GP EAST	Watkins Glen	26	Ligier Gitanes	3.0 Ligier JS5-Matra V12	*burst tyre-suspension damage*
7	JAPANESE GP	Mount Fuji	26	Ligier Gitanes	3.0 Ligier JS5-Matra V12	*1 lap behind*

1977

nc	ARGENTINE GP	Buenos Aires	26	Ligier Gitanes	3.0 Ligier JS7-Matra V12	*3 pit stops-misfire/16 laps behind*
ret	BRAZILIAN GP	Interlagos	26	Ligier Gitanes	3.0 Ligier JS7-Matra V12	*accident*
ret	SOUTH AFRICAN GP	Kyalami	26	Ligier Gitanes	3.0 Ligier JS7-Matra V12	*hit by Pryce's crashing car*
9/ret	US GP WEST	Long Beach	26	Ligier Gitanes	3.0 Ligier JS7-Matra V12	*electrics/2 laps behind*
7	SPANISH GP	Jarama	26	Ligier Gitanes	3.0 Ligier JS7-Matra V12	*pit stop-loose wheel/1 lap behind/FL*
7	MONACO GP	Monte Carlo	26	Ligier Gitanes	3.0 Ligier JS7-Matra V12	
ret	BELGIAN GP	Zolder	26	Ligier Gitanes	3.0 Ligier JS7-Matra V12	*engine*
1	SWEDISH GP	Anderstorp	26	Ligier Gitanes	3.0 Ligier JS7-Matra V12	
8	FRENCH GP	Dijon	26	Ligier Gitanes	3.0 Ligier JS7-Matra V12	*collision-Stuck-pit stop/2 laps behind*
6	BRITISH GP	Silverstone	26	Ligier Gitanes	3.0 Ligier JS7-Matra V12	*1 lap behind*
ret	GERMAN GP	Hockenheim	26	Ligier Gitanes	3.0 Ligier JS7-Matra V12	*engine*
ret	AUSTRIAN GP	Österreichring	26	Ligier Gitaness	3.0 Ligier JS7-Matra V12	*oil leak*
2	DUTCH GP	Zandvoort	26	Ligier Gitaness	3.0 Ligier JS7-Matra V12	
8	ITALIAN GP	Monza	26	Ligier Gitanes	3.0 Ligier JS7-Matra V12	*pit stop-overheating/2 laps behind*
7	US GP EAST	Watkins Glen	26	Ligier Gitanes	3.0 Ligier JS7-Matra V12	*1 lap behind*
ret	CANADIAN GP	Mosport Park	26	Ligier Gitanes	3.0 Ligier JS7-Matra V12	*driveshaft*
5/ret	JAPANESE GP	Mount Fuji	26	Ligier Gitanes	3.0 Ligier JS7-Matra V12	*out of fuel/1 lap behind*

1978

16/ret	ARGENTINE GP	Buenos Aires	26	Ligier Gitanes	3.0 Ligier JS7-Matra V12	*engine/2 laps behind*
9	BRAZILIAN GP	Rio	26	Ligier Gitanes	3.0 Ligier JS7-Matra V12	*pit stop-tyres/2 laps behind*
5	SOUTH AFRICAN GP	Kyalami	26	Ligier Gitanes	3.0 Ligier JS7/9-Matra V12	
dns	" "	"	26	Ligier Gitanes	3.0 Ligier JS7-Matra V12	*practice only*
5	US GP WEST	Long Beach	26	Ligier Gitanes	3.0 Ligier JS7-Matra V12	
dns	" "	" "	26	Ligier Gitaness	3.0 Ligier JS7/9-Matra V12	*practice only*
ret	MONACO GP	Monte Carlo	26	Ligier Gitanes	3.0 Ligier JS9-Matra V12	*gearbox*
dns	"	" "	26	Ligier Gitanes	3.0 Ligier JS7-Matra V12	*practice only*
5/ret	BELGIAN GP	Zolder	26	Ligier Gitanes	3.0 Ligier JS7/9-Matra V12	*hit by Reutemann/1 lap behind*
3	SPANISH GP	Jarama	26	Ligier Gitanes	3.0 Ligier JS9-Matra V12	
dns	"	"	26	Ligier Gitanes	3.0 Ligier JS7/9-Matra V12	*practice only*
7	SWEDISH GP	Anderstorp	26	Ligier Gitanes	3.0 Ligier JS9-Matra V12	*1 lap behind*
dns	"	"	26	Ligier Gitanes	3.0 Ligier JS7/9-Matra V12	*practice only*
7	FRENCH GP	Paul Ricard	26	Ligier Gitanes	3.0 Ligier JS7/9-Matra V12	
10	BRITISH GP	Brands Hatch	26	Ligier Gitanes	3.0 Ligier JS7/9-Matra V12	*2 pit stops-tyres/3 laps behind*
3	GERMAN GP	Hockenheim	26	Ligier Gitanes	3.0 Ligier JS9-Matra V12	
5	AUSTRIAN GP	Österreichring	26	Ligier Gitanes	3.0 Ligier JS9-Matra V12	*1 lap behind*
8	DUTCH GP	Zandvoort	26	Ligier Gitanes	3.0 Ligier JS9-Matra V12	*1 lap behind*
4	ITALIAN GP	Monza	26	Ligier Gitanes	3.0 Ligier JS9-Matra V12	
11	US GP EAST	Watkins Glen	26	Ligier Gitanes	3.0 Ligier JS9-Matra V12	*pit stop-tyre/1 lap behind*
ret	CANADIAN GP	Montreal	26	Ligier Gitanes	3.0 Ligier JS9-Matra V12	*transmission*

1979

1	ARGENTINE GP	Buenos Aires	26	Ligier Gitanes	3.0 Ligier JS11-Cosworth V8	*Pole/FL*
1	BRAZILIAN GP	Rio	26	Ligier Gitanes	3.0 Ligier JS11-Cosworth V8	*Pole/FL*
ret	SOUTH AFRICAN GP	Kyalami	26	Ligier Gitanes	3.0 Ligier JS11-Cosworth V8	*puncture-spun off*
ret	US GP WEST	Long Beach	26	Ligier Gitanes	3.0 Ligier JS11-Cosworth V8	*started from pit lane/brakes*
ret	SPANISH GP	Jarama	26	Ligier Gitanes	3.0 Ligier JS11-Cosworth V8	*engine/Pole*
2	BELGIAN GP	Zolder	26	Ligier Gitanes	3.0 Ligier JS11-Cosworth V8	*Pole*
ret	MONACO GP	Monte Carlo	26	Ligier Gitanes	3.0 Ligier JS11-Cosworth V8	*gearbox*
8	FRENCH GP	Dijon	26	Ligier Gitanes	3.0 Ligier JS11-Cosworth V8	*1 lap behind*
ret	BRITISH GP	Silverstone	26	Ligier Gitanes	3.0 Ligier JS11-Cosworth V8	*engine*
3	GERMAN GP	Hockenheim	26	Ligier Gitanes	3.0 Ligier JS11-Cosworth V8	
3	AUSTRIAN GP	Österreichring	26	Ligier Gitanes	3.0 Ligier JS11-Cosworth V8	
3	DUTCH GP	Zandvoort	26	Ligier Gitanes	3.0 Ligier JS11-Cosworth V8	
ret	ITALIAN GP	Monza	26	Ligier Gitanes	3.0 Ligier JS11-Cosworth V8	*engine*
ret	CANADIAN GP	Montreal	26	Ligier Gitanes	3.0 Ligier JS11-Cosworth V8	*engine*
ret	US GP EAST	Watkins Glen	26	Ligier Gitanes	3.0 Ligier JS11-Cosworth V8	*spun off*

1980

ret	ARGENTINE GP	Buenos Aires	26	Equipe Ligier Gitanes	3.0 Ligier JS11/15-Cosworth V8	*engine*
ret	BRAZILIAN GP	Interlagos	26	Equipe Ligier Gitanes	3.0 Ligier JS11/15-Cosworth V8	*electrics*
2	SOUTH AFRICAN GP	Kyalami	26	Equipe Ligier Gitanes	3.0 Ligier JS11/15-Cosworth V8	
ret	US GP WEST	Long Beach	26	Equipe Ligier Gitanes	3.0 Ligier JS11/15-Cosworth V8	*puncture*
11	BELGIAN GP	Zolder	26	Equipe Ligier Gitanes	3.0 Ligier JS11/15-Cosworth V8	*pit stop-engine/4 laps behind/FL*
2	MONACO GP	Monte Carlo	26	Equipe Ligier Gitanes	3.0 Ligier JS11/15-Cosworth V8	
3	FRENCH GP	Paul Ricard	26	Equipe Ligier Gitanes	3.0 Ligier JS11/15-Cosworth V8	*Pole*
ret	BRITISH GP	Brands Hatch	26	Equipe Ligier Gitanes	3.0 Ligier JS11/15-Cosworth V8	*wheel/tyre failure-crashed*
1	GERMAN GP	Hockenheim	26	Equipe Ligier Gitanes	3.0 Ligier JS11/15-Cosworth V8	
4	AUSTRIAN GP	Österreichring	26	Equipe Ligier Gitanes	3.0 Ligier JS11/15-Cosworth V8	
3	DUTCH GP	Zandvoort	26	Equipe Ligier Gitanes	3.0 Ligier JS11/15-Cosworth V8	
9	ITALIAN GP	Imola	26	Equipe Ligier Gitanes	3.0 Ligier JS11/15-Cosworth V8	*1 lap behind*

8/ret	CANADIAN GP	Montreal	26	Equipe Ligier Gitanes	3.0 Ligier JS11/15-Cosworth V8	*out of fuel/2 laps behind*
5	US GP EAST	Watkins Glen	26	Equipe Ligier Gitanes	3.0 Ligier JS11/15-Cosworth V8	*1 lap behind*

1981

ret	US GP WEST	Long Beach	26	Equipe Talbot Gitanes	3.0 Ligier JS17-Matra V12	*collision with Cheever*
6	BRAZILIAN GP	Rio	26	Equipe Talbot Gitanes	3.0 Ligier JS17-Matra V12	
ret	ARGENTINE GP	Buenos Aires	26	Equipe Talbot Gitanes	3.0 Ligier JS17-Matra V12	*vibration/handling*
ret	SAN MARINO GP	Imola	26	Equipe Talbot Gitanes	3.0 Ligier JS17-Matra V12	*accident with Arnoux*
2	BELGIAN GP	Zolder	26	Equipe Talbot Gitanes	3.0 Ligier JS17-Matra V12	
3	MONACO GP	Monte Carlo	26	Equipe Talbot Gitanes	3.0 Ligier JS17-Matra V12	
2	SPANISH GP	Jarama	26	Equipe Talbot Gitanes	3.0 Ligier JS17-Matra V12	*Pole*
ret	FRENCH GP	Dijon	26	Equipe Talbot Gitanes	3.0 Ligier JS17-Matra V12	*front suspension*
3	BRITISH GP	Silverstone	26	Equipe Talbot Gitanes	3.0 Ligier JS17-Matra V12	*1 lap behind*
3	GERMAN GP	Hockenheim	26	Equipe Talbot Gitanes	3.0 Ligier JS17-Matra V12	
1	AUSTRIAN GP	Österreichring	26	Equipe Talbot Gitanes	3.0 Ligier JS17-Matra V12	*FL*
ret	DUTCH GP	Zandvoort	26	Equipe Talbot Gitanes	3.0 Ligier JS17-Matra V12	*collision with Reutemann*
ret	ITALIAN GP	Monza	26	Equipe Talbot Gitanes	3.0 Ligier JS17-Matra V12	*puncture*
1	CANADIAN GP	Montreal	26	Equipe Talbot Gitanes	3.0 Ligier JS17-Matra V12	
6	CAESARS PALACE GP	Las Vegas	26	Equipe Talbot Gitanes	3.0 Ligier JS17-Matra V12	*pit stop-tyres*

1982

ret	SOUTH AFRICAN GP	Kyalami	26	Equipe Talbot Gitanes	3.0 Ligier JS17-Matra V12	*misfire*
ret	BRAZILIAN GP	Rio	26	Equipe Talbot Gitanes	3.0 Ligier JS17-Matra V12	*handling/misfire*
ret	US GP WEST	Long Beach	26	Equipe Talbot Gitanes	3.0 Ligier JS17B-Matra V12	*ran off track and stalled*
9	BELGIAN GP	Zolder	26	Equipe Talbot Gitanes	3.0 Ligier JS17-Matra V12	*pit stop-tyres/4 laps behind*
ret	MONACO GP	Monte Carlo	26	Equipe Talbot Gitanes	3.0 Ligier JS19-Matra V12	*handling*
6	US GP (DETROIT)	Detroit	26	Equipe Talbot Gitanes	3.0 Ligier JS17-Matra V12	*1 lap behind*
ret	CANADIAN GP	Montreal	26	Equipe Talbot Gitanes	3.0 Ligier JS17-Matra V12	*handling*
ret	DUTCH GP	Zandvoort	26	Equipe Talbot Gitanes	3.0 Ligier JS19-Matra V12	*handling*
ret	BRITISH GP	Brands Hatch	26	Equipe Talbot Gitanes	3.0 Ligier JS19-Matra V12	*gearbox*
14	FRENCH GP	Paul Ricard	26	Equipe Talbot Gitanes	3.0 Ligier JS19-Matra V12	*3 p stops-handling-tyres/-3 laps*
ret	GERMAN GP	Hockenheim	26	Equipe Talbot Gitanes	3.0 Ligier JS19-Matra V12	*handling*
3	AUSTRIAN GP	Österreichring	26	Equipe Talbot Gitanes	3.0 Ligier JS19-Matra V12	*1 lap behind*
ret	SWISS GP	Dijon	26	Equipe Talbot Gitanes	3.0 Ligier JS19-Matra V12	*skirts/handling*
ret	ITALIAN GP	Monza	26	Equipe Talbot Gitanes	3.0 Ligier JS19-Matra V12	*gearbox*
ret	CAESARS PALACE GP	Las Vegas	26	Equipe Talbot Gitanes	3.0 Ligier JS19-Matra V12	*ignition*

1983

4	BRAZILIAN GP	Rio	2	TAG Williams Team	3.0 Williams FW08C-Cosworth V8	
4	US GP WEST	Long Beach	2	TAG Williams Team	3.0 Williams FW08C-Cosworth V8	*1 lap behind*
6	FRENCH GP	Paul Ricard	2	TAG Williams Team	3.0 Williams FW08C-Cosworth V8	*pit stop-fuel/1 lap behind*
7	SAN MARINO GP	Imola	2	TAG Williams Team	3.0 Williams FW08C-Cosworth V8	*pit stop-fuel/1 lap behind*
ret	MONACO GP	Monte Carlo	2	TAG Williams Team	3.0 Williams FW08C-Cosworth V8	*gearbox*
6	BELGIAN GP	Spa	2	TAG Williams Team	3.0 Williams FW08C-Cosworth V8	
5	US GP (DETROIT)	Detroit	2	TAG Williams Team	3.0 Williams FW08C-Cosworth V8	
ret	CANADIAN GP	Montreal	2	TAG Williams Team	3.0 Williams FW08C-Cosworth V8	*gearbox*
12	BRITISH GP	Silverstone	2	TAG Williams Team	3.0 Williams FW08C-Cosworth V8	*pit stop-fuel/2 laps behind*
6	GERMAN GP	Hockenheim	2	TAG Williams Team	3.0 Williams FW08C-Cosworth V8	*1 lap behind*
ret	AUSTRIAN GP	Österreichring	2	TAG Williams Team	3.0 Williams FW08C-Cosworth V8	*collision-Ghinzani and Surer*
ret	DUTCH GP	Zandvoort	2	TAG Williams Team	3.0 Williams FW08C-Cosworth V8	*tyres*
dnq	ITALIAN GP	Monza	2	TAG Williams Team	3.0 Williams FW08C-Cosworth V8	
dnq	EUROPEAN GP	Brands Hatch	2	TAG Williams Team	3.0 Williams FW08C-Cosworth V8	
ret	SOUTH AFRICAN GP	Kyalami	2	TAG Williams Team	1.5 t/c Williams FW09-Honda V6	*spun off*

1984

ret	BRAZILIAN GP	Rio	5	Williams Grand Prix Engineering	1.5 t/c Williams FW09-Honda V6	*electrics*
ret	SOUTH AFRICAN GP	Kyalami	5	Williams Grand Prix Engineering	1.5 t/c Williams FW09-Honda V6	*c.v. joint*
ret	BELGIAN GP	Zolder	5	Williams Grand Prix Engineering	1.5 t/c Williams FW09-Honda V6	*electrics*
ret	SAN MARINO GP	Imola	5	Williams Grand Prix Engineering	1.5 t/c Williams FW09-Honda V6	*engine*
8	FRENCH GP	Dijon	5	Williams Grand Prix Engineering	1.5 t/c Williams FW09-Honda V6	*1 lap behind*
8	MONACO GP	Monte Carlo	5	Williams Grand Prix Engineering	1.5 t/c Williams FW09-Honda V6	*3rd place car dsq/1 lap behind*
ret	CANADIAN GP	Montreal	5	Williams Grand Prix Engineering	1.5 t/c Williams FW09-Honda V6	*lost turbo boost*
5	US GP (DETROIT)	Detroit	5	Williams Grand Prix Engineering	1.5 t/c Williams FW09-Honda V6	*2nd place car dsq/1 lap behind*
4	US GP (DALLAS)	Dallas	5	Williams Grand Prix Engineering	1.5 t/c Williams FW09-Honda V6	*2 laps behind*
ret	BRITISH GP	Brands Hatch	5	Williams Grand Prix Engineering	1.5 t/c Williams FW09B-Honda V6	*water pump*
ret	GERMAN GP	Hockenheim	5	Williams Grand Prix Engineering	1.5 t/c Williams FW09B-Honda V6	*engine*
ret	AUSTRIAN GP	Österreichring	5	Williams Grand Prix Engineering	1.5 t/c Williams FW09B-Honda V6	*engine*
ret	DUTCH GP	Zandvoort	5	Williams Grand Prix Engineering	1.5 t/c Williams FW09B-Honda V6	*engine*
ret	ITALIAN GP	Monza	5	Williams Grand Prix Engineering	1.5 t/c Williams FW09B-Honda V6	*turbo*
ret	EUROPEAN GP	Nürburgring	5	Williams Grand Prix Engineering	1.5 t/c Williams FW09B-Honda V6	*engine*
14	PORTUGUESE GP	Estoril	5	Williams Grand Prix Engineering	1.5 t/c Williams FW09B-Honda V6	*2 pit stops-bodywork/3 laps behind*

1985

6	BRAZILIAN GP	Rio	26	Equipe Ligier	1.5 t/c Ligier JS25-Renault V6	*hit de Cesaris-pit stop/2 laps behind*
ret	PORTUGUESE GP	Estoril	26	Equipe Ligier	1.5 t/c Ligier JS25-Renault V6	*tyres/handling*
ret	SAN MARINO GP	Imola	26	Equipe Ligier	1.5 t/c Ligier JS25-Renault V6	*turbo*
6	MONACO GP	Monte Carlo	26	Equipe Ligier	1.5 t/c Ligier JS25-Renault V6	*spin/1 lap behind*
8	CANADIAN GP	Montreal	26	Equipe Ligier Gitanes	1.5 t/c Ligier JS25-Renault V6	*1 min pen-jumped start/-1 lap*
12	US GP (DETROIT)	Detroit	26	Equipe Ligier Gitanes	1.5 t/c Ligier JS25-Renault V6	*pit stop/5 laps behind*
ret	FRENCH GP	Paul Ricard	26	Equipe Ligier Gitanes	1.5 t/c Ligier JS25-Renault V6	*turbo*
3	BRITISH GP	Silverstone	26	Equipe Ligier Gitanes	1.5 t/c Ligier JS25-Renault V6	*1 lap behind*
3	GERMAN GP	Nürburgring	26	Equipe Ligier Gitanes	1.5 t/c Ligier JS25-Renault V6	
ret	AUSTRIAN GP	Österreichring	26	Equipe Ligier Gitanes	1.5 t/c Ligier JS25-Renault V6	*lost wheel-crashed*
ret	DUTCH GP	Zandvoort	26	Equipe Ligier Gitanes	1.5 t/c Ligier JS25-Renault V6	*electrics*
ret	ITALIAN GP	Monza	26	Equipe Ligier Gitanes	1.5 t/c Ligier JS25-Renault V6	*engine*
ret	BELGIAN GP	Spa	26	Equipe Ligier Gitanes	1.5 t/c Ligier JS25-Renault V6	*hit barrier/5 laps behind*
ret	EUROPEAN GP	Brands Hatch	26	Equipe Ligier Gitanes	1.5 t/c Ligier JS25-Renault V6	*engine/FL*

| 2 | AUSTRALIAN GP | Adelaide | 26 | Equipe Ligier Gitanes | 1.5 t/c Ligier JS25-Renault V6 | |

1986

3	BRAZILIAN GP	Rio	26	Equipe Ligier	1.5 t/c Ligier JS27-Renault V6	
ret	SPANISH GP	Jerez	26	Equipe Ligier	1.5 t/c Ligier JS27-Renault V6	driveshaft
ret	SAN MARINO GP	Imola	26	Equipe Ligier	1.5 t/c Ligier JS27-Renault V6	transmission
6	MONACO GP	Monte Carlo	26	Equipe Ligier	1.5 t/c Ligier JS27-Renault V6	started from back of grid/-1 lap
5	BELGIAN GP	Spa	26	Equipe Ligier	1.5 t/c Ligier JS27-Renault V6	
7	CANADIAN GP	Montreal	26	Equipe Ligier	1.5 t/c Ligier JS27-Renault V6	1 lap behind
2	US GP (DETROIT)	Detroit	26	Equipe Ligier	1.5 t/c Ligier JS27-Renault V6	
6	FRENCH GP	Paul Ricard	26	Equipe Ligier	1.5 t/c Ligier JS27-Renault V6	2 pit stops-tyres/1 lap behind
ret/dns	BRITISH GP	Brands Hatch	26	Equipe Ligier	1.5 t/c Ligier JS27-Renault V6	accident in 1st start/did not restart

GP Starts: 174 (176)   GP Wins: 6   Pole positions: 7   Fastest laps: 6   Points: 228

JAN LAMMERS

With a career stretching back twenty years, Lammers has tried his hand at most forms of racing since his early success as the Dutch Group 1 saloon car champion. Progressing through the single-seater formulae, the pint-sized Dutchman took the 1978 European F3 championship by the narrowest of margins with a Ralt, earning a chance with the restructured Shadow team alongside Elio de Angelis for 1979. The cars were not competitive, and Lammers found little more joy during his associations with ATS, Ensign and Theodore over the next two seasons, although he startled the Formula 1 fraternity at Long Beach in 1980 by qualifying his car fourth on the grid.

After his Grand Prix career had fizzled out, Jan enjoyed a productive spell in the Richard Lloyd Porsche sports car team before a having crack at IndyCar racing late in 1985 .However, he found his greatest success in the TWR Jaguar team, partnering John Watson to three wins (Jarama, Monza and Mount Fuji) in 1987, and winning Le Mans in 1988 with Dumfries and Wallace. He also won the Daytona 24-hour race for Jaguar twice (1988 and '90). After racing in Japanese F3000 in 1991, Lammers joined the Toyota sports car team for 1992, and made an unexpected return to F1 at the end of the year with March. Plans for a full Grand Prix season in 1993 came to nought when the financially bereft Bicester team was finally forced to close its doors.

LAMMERS, Jan (NL) b 2/6/1956

1979

	Race	Circuit	No	Entrant	Car/Engine	Comment
ret	ARGENTINE GP	Buenos Aires	17	Samson Shadow Racing Team	3.0 Shadow DN9-Cosworth V8	transmission
14	BRAZILIAN GP	Interlagos	17	Samson Shadow Racing Team	3.0 Shadow DN9-Cosworth V8	1 lap behind
ret	SOUTH AFRICAN GP	Kyalami	17	Samson Shadow Racing Team	3.0 Shadow DN9-Cosworth V8	collision with Rebaque
ret	US GP WEST	Long Beach	17	Samson Shadow Racing Team	3.0 Shadow DN9-Cosworth V8	collision with Pironi-bent suspension
12	SPANISH GP	Jarama	17	Samson Shadow Racing Team	3.0 Shadow DN9-Cosworth V8	2 laps behind
10	BELGIAN GP	Zolder	17	Samson Shadow Racing Team	3.0 Shadow DN9-Cosworth V8	2 laps behind
dnq	MONACO GP	Monte Carlo	17	Samson Shadow Racing Team	3.0 Shadow DN9-Cosworth V8	
18	FRENCH GP	Dijon	17	Samson Shadow Racing Team	3.0 Shadow DN9-Cosworth V8	pit stop/7 laps behind
11	BRITISH GP	Silverstone	17	Samson Shadow Racing Team	3.0 Shadow DN9-Cosworth V8	3 laps behind
10	GERMAN GP	Hockenheim	17	Samson Shadow Racing Team	3.0 Shadow DN9-Cosworth V8	1 lap behind
ret	AUSTRIAN GP	Österreichring	17	Samson Shadow Racing Team	3.0 Shadow DN9-Cosworth V8	crashed
ret	DUTCH GP	Zandvoort	17	Samson Shadow Racing Team	3.0 Shadow DN9-Cosworth V8	gearbox
dnq	ITALIAN GP	Monza	17	Samson Shadow Racing Team	3.0 Shadow DN9-Cosworth V8	
9	CANADIAN GP	Montreal	17	Samson Shadow Racing Team	3.0 Shadow DN9-Cosworth V8	5 laps behind
dnq	US GP EAST	Watkins Glen	17	Samson Shadow Racing Team	3.0 Shadow DN9-Cosworth V8	

1980

dnq	ARGENTINE GP	Buenos Aires	10	Team ATS	3.0 ATS D3-Cosworth V8	
dnq	BRAZILIAN GP	Interlagos	10	Team ATS	3.0 ATS D3-Cosworth V8	
dnq	SOUTH AFRICAN GP	Kyalami	9	Team ATS	3.0 ATS D3-Cosworth V8	replaced injured Surer
12/ret	US GP WEST	Long Beach	9	Team ATS	3.0 ATS D4-Cosworth V8	driveshaft-lap 1
ret	BELGIAN GP	Zolder	9	Team ATS	3.0 ATS D4-Cosworth V8	engine/8 laps behind
10	MONACO GP	Monte Carlo	9	Team ATS	3.0 ATS D4-Cosworth V8	hit Patrese-pit stop/12 laps behind
dnq	FRENCH GP	Paul Ricard	14	Unipart Racing Team	3.0 Ensign N180-Cosworth V8	
dnq	BRITISH GP	Brands Hatch	14	Unipart Racing Team	3.0 Ensign N180-Cosworth V8	
14	GERMAN GP	Hockenheim	14	Unipart Racing Team	3.0 Ensign N180-Cosworth V8	1 lap behind
dnq	AUSTRIAN GP	Österreichring	14	Unipart Racing Team	3.0 Ensign N180-Cosworth V8	
dnq	DUTCH GP	Zandvoort	14	Unipart Racing Team	3.0 Ensign N180-Cosworth V8	
dnq	ITALIAN GP	Imola	14	Unipart Racing Team	3.0 Ensign N180-Cosworth V8	
12	CANADIAN GP	Montreal	14	Unipart Racing Team	3.0 Ensign N180-Cosworth V8	4 laps behind
dnq/ret	US GP EAST	Watkins Glen	14	Unipart Racing Team	3.0 Ensign N180-Cosworth V8	1st reserve/steering mounting

1981

ret	US GP WEST	Long Beach	9	Team ATS	3.0 ATS D4-Cosworth V8	collision with Giacomelli
dnq	BRAZILIAN GP	Rio	9	Team ATS	3.0 ATS D4-Cosworth V8	
12	ARGENTINE GP	Buenos Aires	9	Team ATS	3.0 ATS D4-Cosworth V8	pit stop/2 laps behind
dnq	SAN MARINO GP	Imola	9	Team ATS	3.0 ATS D4-Cosworth V8	

1982

dnq	BELGIAN GP	Zolder	33	Theodore Racing Team	3.0 Theodore TY02-Cosworth V8	
dnq	MONACO GP	Monte Carlo	33	Theodore Racing Team	3.0 Theodore TY02-Cosworth V8	
dns	US GP (DETROIT)	Detroit	33	Theodore Racing Team	3.0 Theodore TY02-Cosworth V8	injured in unofficial practice
ret	DUTCH GP	Zandvoort	33	Theodore Racing Team	3.0 Theodore TY02-Cosworth V8	engine
dnq	BRITISH GP	Brands Hatch	33	Theodore Racing Team	3.0 Theodore TY02-Cosworth V8	
dnq	FRENCH GP	Paul Ricard	33	Theodore Racing Team	3.0 Theodore TY02-Cosworth V8	

1992

| ret | JAPANESE GP | Suzuka | 16 | March F1 | 3.5 March CG911-Ilmor V10 | clutch |
| 12 | AUSTRALIAN GP | Adelaide | 16 | March F1 | 3.5 March CG911-Ilmor V10 | 3 laps behind |

GP Starts: 23   GP Wins: 0   Pole positions: 0   Fastest laps: 0   Points: 0

PEDRO LAMY

A former motocrosser and karting champion, Lamy won the Portuguese FF1600 title in 1989 then graduated to the GM Lotus Euroseries, which he won in 1991. He really shot to prominence by dominating the 1992 German F3 championship, winning 11 races, and furthered his reputation as a very quick – but sometimes erratic – driver with his performances in F3000 in 1993.

Brought into the Lotus team at Monza to replace the unfit Zanardi, Lamy had a tough baptism but, with the backing of Portuguese sponsors, has secured a full-time ride with the team for 1994.

CHICO LANDI

Landi was the first Brazilian ace to try his luck in Europe, making the move in the late forties after building up a fine record with his Alfa Romeo. He won the Bari GP in a Ferrari in 1948, and raced spasmodically in Grands Prix and other events over the next few seasons. His best single-seater result was a second place in the Albi GP with a Ferrari T375 in 1952, a season which also saw him gain a string of fine placings at home. Landi raced on into the late fifties, before retiring to become a leading figure in the administration of Brazilian motor sport.

HERMANN LANG

One of the true stars of pre-war racing, Lang had been a motor cycling champion in 1930 and 1931 before he joined Mercedes in 1933, initially working in the experimental department and then, in 1934, as Fagioli's mechanic. Given his chance to race the following season, young Lang immediately tamed the fearsome silver beasts and became a full team member in 1937, celebrating with wins at Tripoli and AVUS. He was to add six more major victories to his tally before the war interrupted his career when he was undoubtedly at his peak.

Hermann was immediately back in action when peace returned, and rejoined the Mercedes team for their South American trip in February 1951, finishing second in the Peron Cup and third in the Eva Peron Cup. He then raced the team's 300SL cars in 1952, winning Le Mans (with Fritz Riess) and the Nürburgring sports car race, and scoring second places in the Prix de Berne and the Carrera Panamericana. In 1953 Lang made a surprise return to Grands Prix, replacing the injured Gonzalez in the Maserati team at Spa and taking fifth place. When Mercedes returned to GP racing in 1954, he was invited to drive in the German Grand Prix, but his race ended in disappointment when he spun off while challenging team-mate Kling for second place. He retired from competition immediately after this race, but for many years continued to demonstrate the famous cars which had brought him so much success early in his racing days.

LAMY, Pedro (P) b 20/3/1972

1951

	Race	Circuit	No	Entrant	Car/Engine	Comment
ret	ITALIAN GP	Monza	11	Team Lotus	3.5 Lotus 107B-Ford HB V8	engine
ret	PORTUGUESE GP	Estoril	11	Team Lotus	3.5 Lotus 107B-Ford HB V8	accident
13/ret	JAPANESE GP	Suzuka	11	Team Lotus	3.5 Lotus 107B-Ford HB V8	accident
ret	AUSTRALIAN GP	Adelaide	11	Team Lotus	3.5 Lotus 107B-Ford HB V8	collision-Katayama on lap 1

GP Starts: 4   GP Wins: 0   Pole positions: 0   Fastest laps: 0   Points: 0

LANDI, Chico (Francisco) (BR) b 14/7/1907 – d 7/6/1989

1951

	Race	Circuit	No	Entrant	Car/Engine	Comment
ret	ITALIAN GP	Monza	12	Francisco Landi	4.5 Ferrari 375F1/50 V12	transmission-lap 1
	1952					
9*	DUTCH GP	Zandvoort	16	Escuderia Bandeirantes	2.0 Maserati A6GCM 6	* Flinterman took over/7 laps behind
8	ITALIAN GP	Monza	48	Escuderia Bandeirantes	2.0 Maserati A6GCM 6	4 laps behind
	1953					
ret	SWISS GP	Bremgarten	4	Escuderia Bandeirantes	2.0 Maserati A6GCM 6	gearbox
ret	ITALIAN GP	Monza	42	Scuderia Milano	2.0 Maserati A6GCM 6	engine
	1956					
4*	ARGENTINE GP	Buenos Aires	10	Officine Alfieri Maserati	2.5 Maserati 250F 6	* Gerini took over/6 laps behind

GP Starts: 6   GP Wins: 0   Pole positions: 0   Fastest laps: 0   Points: 1.5

LANG, Hermann (D) b 6/4/1909 – d 19/10/1987

1953

	Race	Circuit	No	Entrant	Car/Engine	Comment
5	SWISS GP	Bremgarten	34	Officine Alfieri Maserati	2.0 Maserati A6GCM 6	stood in for Gonzalez/3 laps behind
	1954					
ret	GERMAN GP	Nürburgring	21	Daimler Benz AG	2.5 Mercedes-Benz W196 8	spun off

GP Starts: 2   GP Wins: 0   Pole positions: 0   Fastest laps: 0   Points: 2

LARINI, Nicola (I) b 19/3/1954

1987

	Race	Circuit	No	Entrant	Car/Engine	Comment
dnq	ITALIAN GP	Monza	32	Enzo Coloni Racing Car System	3.5 Coloni FC187-Cosworth V8	
ret	SPANISH GP	Jerez	32	Enzo Coloni Racing Car System	3.5 Coloni FC187-Cosworth V8	suspension

1988

	Race	Circuit	No	Entrant	Car/Engine	Comment
dnq	BRAZILIAN GP	Rio	21	Osella Squadra Corse	1.5 t/c Osella FA1I-Alfa Romeo V8	
excl	SAN MARINO GP	Imola	21	Osella Squadra Corse	1.5 t/c Osella FA1L-Alfa Romeo V8	failed to pass scrutineering
9	MONACO GP	Monte Carlo	21	Osella Squadra Corse	1.5 t/c Osella FA1L-Alfa Romeo V8	3 laps behind
dnq	MEXICAN GP	Mexico City	21	Osella Squadra Corse	1.5 t/c Osella FA1L-Alfa Romeo V8	
dnq	CANADIAN GP	Montreal	21	Osella Squadra Corse	1.5 t/c Osella FA1L-Alfa Romeo V8	
ret	US GP (DETROIT)	Detroit	21	Osella Squadra Corse	1.5 t/c Osella FA1L-Alfa Romeo V8	engine
ret	FRENCH GP	Paul Ricard	21	Osella Squadra Corse	1.5 t/c Osella FA1L-Alfa Romeo V8	driveshaft
19/ret	BRITISH GP	Silverstone	21	Osella Squadra Corse	1.5 t/c Osella FA1L-Alfa Romeo V8	out of fuel/5 laps behind
ret	GERMAN GP	Hockenheim	21	Osella Squadra Corse	1.5 t/c Osella FA1L-Alfa Romeo V8	started from pit lane/turbo pipe
dnpq	HUNGARIAN GP	Hungaroring	21	Osella Squadra Corse	1.5 t/c Osella FA1L-Alfa Romeo V8	
ret	BELGIAN GP	Spa	21	Osella Squadra Corse	1.5 t/c Osella FA1L-Alfa Romeo V8	electrics
ret	ITALIAN GP	Monza	21	Osella Squadra Corse	1.5 t/c Osella FA1L-Alfa Romeo V8	engine
12	PORTUGUESE GP	Estoril	21	Osella Squadra Corse	1.5 t/c Osella FA1L-Alfa Romeo V8	pit stop-steering/fuel/7 laps behind
ret	SPANISH GP	Jerez	21	Osella Squadra Corse	1.5 t/c Osella FA1L-Alfa Romeo V8	suspension
ret	JAPANESE GP	Suzuka	21	Osella Squadra Corse	1.5 t/c Osella FA1L-Alfa Romeo V8	lost wheel
dnpq	AUSTRALIAN GP	Adelaide	21	Osella Squadra Corse	1.5 t/c Osella FA1L-Alfa Romeo V8	

1989

	Race	Circuit	No	Entrant	Car/Engine	Comment
dsq	BRAZILIAN GP	Rio	17	Osella Squadra Corse	3.5 Osella FA1M-Cosworth V8	started from wrong grid position
12/ret	SAN MARINO GP	Imola	17	Osella Squadra Corse	3.5 Osella FA1M-Cosworth V8	broken hub-crashed/6 laps behind
dnpq	MONACO GP	Monte Carlo	17	Osella Squadra Corse	3.5 Osella FA1M-Cosworth V8	
dnpq	MEXICAN GP	Mexico City	17	Osella Squadra Corse	3.5 Osella FA1M-Cosworth V8	
dnpq	US GP (PHOENIX)	Phoenix	17	Osella Squadra Corse	3.5 Osella FA1M-Cosworth V8	
ret	CANADIAN GP	Montreal	17	Osella Squadra Corse	3.5 Osella FA1M-Cosworth V8	electrics
dnpq	FRENCH GP	Paul Ricard	17	Osella Squadra Corse	3.5 Osella FA1M-Cosworth V8	
ret	BRITISH GP	Silverstone	17	Osella Squadra Corse	3.5 Osella FA1M-Cosworth V8	handling
dnpq	GERMAN GP	Hockenheim	17	Osella Squadra Corse	3.5 Osella FA1M-Cosworth V8	
dnpq	HUNGARIAN GP	Hungaroring	17	Osella Squadra Corse	3.5 Osella FA1M-Cosworth V8	
dnpq	BELGIAN GP	Spa	17	Osella Squadra Corse	3.5 Osella FA1M-Cosworth V8	
ret	ITALIAN GP	Monza	17	Osella Squadra Corse	3.5 Osella FA1M-Cosworth V8	gearbox
excl	PORTUGUESE GP	Estoril	17	Osella Squadra Corse	3.5 Osella FA1M-Cosworth V8	excld from race-missed weight check
ret	SPANISH GP	Jerez	17	Osella Squadra Corse	3.5 Osella FA1M-Cosworth V8	suspension-crashed
ret	JAPANESE GP	Suzuka	17	Osella Squadra Corse	3.5 Osella FA1M-Cosworth V8	brakes
ret/tdns	AUSTRALIAN GP	Adelaide	17	Osella Squadra Corse	3.5 Osella FA1M-Cosworth V8	electrics on the grid at 2nd start

1990

	Race	Circuit	No	Entrant	Car/Engine	Comment
ret	US GP (PHOENIX)	Phoenix	25	Ligier Gitanes	3.5 Ligier JS33B-Cosworth V8	stuck throttle
11	BRAZILIAN GP	Interlagos	25	Ligier Gitanes	3.5 Ligier JS33B-Cosworth V8	pit stop-tyres/3 laps behind
10	SAN MARINO GP	Imola	25	Ligier Gitanes	3.5 Ligier JS33B-Cosworth V8	gearbox problems/2 laps behind
ret	MONACO GP	Monte Carlo	25	Ligier Gitanes	3.5 Ligier JS33B-Cosworth V8	gearbox
ret	CANADIAN GP	Montreal	25	Ligier Gitanes	3.5 Ligier JS33B-Cosworth V8	hit by Boutsen
16	MEXICAN GP	Mexico City	25	Ligier Gitanes	3.5 Ligier JS33B-Cosworth V8	2 laps behind
14	FRENCH GP	Paul Ricard	25	Ligier Gitanes	3.5 Ligier JS33B-Cosworth V8	brake problems/2 laps behind
10	BRITISH GP	Silverstone	25	Ligier Gitanes	3.5 Ligier JS33B-Cosworth V8	2 laps behind
10	GERMAN GP	Hockenheim	25	Ligier Gitanes	3.5 Ligier JS33B-Cosworth V8	2 pit stops-tyres/2 laps behind
11	HUNGARIAN GP	Hungaroring	25	Ligier Gitanes	3.5 Ligier JS33B-Cosworth V8	1 lap behind
14	BELGIAN GP	Spa	25	Ligier Gitanes	3.5 Ligier JS33B-Cosworth V8	2 pit stops-handling-tyres/-2 laps
11	ITALIAN GP	Monza	25	Ligier Gitanes	3.5 Ligier JS33B-Cosworth V8	2 laps behind
10	PORTUGUESE GP	Estoril	25	Ligier Gitanes	3.5 Ligier JS33B-Cosworth V8	pit stop-tyres/2 laps behind
7	SPANISH GP	Jerez	25	Ligier Gitanes	3.5 Ligier JS33B-Cosworth V8	1 lap behind
7	JAPANESE GP	Suzuka	25	Ligier Gitanes	3.5 Ligier JS33B-Cosworth V8	pit stop-tyres/1 lap behind
10	AUSTRALIAN GP	Adelaide	25	Ligier Gitanes	3.5 Ligier JS33B-Cosworth V8	2 laps behind

1991

	Race	Circuit	No	Entrant	Car/Engine	Comment
7	US GP (PHOENIX)	Phoenix	34	Modena Team SpA	3.5 Modena Lambo 291-Lamborghini V12	3 laps behind
dnpq	BRAZILIAN GP	Interlagos	34	Modena Team SpA	3.5 Modena Lambo 291-Lamborghini V12	
dnpq	SAN MARINO GP	Imola	34	Modena Team SpA	3.5 Modena Lambo 291-Lamborghini V12	
dnpq	MONACO GP	Monte Carlo	34	Modena Team SpA	3.5 Modena Lambo 291-Lamborghini V12	
dnpq	CANADIAN GP	Montreal	34	Modena Team SpA	3.5 Modena Lambo 291-Lamborghini V12	
dsq	MEXICAN GP	Mexico City	34	Modena Team SpA	3.5 Modena Lambo 291-Lamborghini V12	dsq-rear wing height infringement
dnpq	FRENCH GP	Paul Ricard	34	Modena Team SpA	3.5 Modena Lambo 291-Lamborghini V12	
dnpq	BRITISH GP	Silverstone	34	Modena Team SpA	3.5 Modena Lambo 291-Lamborghini V12	
ret	GERMAN GP	Hockenheim	34	Modena Team SpA	3.5 Modena Lambo 291-Lamborghini V12	spun off avoiding Blundell-lap 1
16	HUNGARIAN GP	Hungaroring	34	Modena Team SpA	3.5 Modena Lambo 291-Lamborghini V12	3 laps behind
dnq	BELGIAN GP	Spa	34	Modena Team SpA	3.5 Modena Lambo 291-Lamborghini V12	
16	ITALIAN GP	Monza	34	Modena Team SpA	3.5 Modena Lambo 291-Lamborghini V12	5 laps behind
dnq	PORTUGUESE GP	Estoril	34	Modena Team SpA	3.5 Modena Lambo 291-Lamborghini V12	
dnq	SPANISH GP	Barcelona	34	Modena Team SpA	3.5 Modena Lambo 291-Lamborghini V12	
dnq	JAPANESE GP	Suzuka	34	Modena Team SpA	3.5 Modena Lambo 291-Lamborghini V12	
ret	AUSTRALIAN GP	Adelaide	34	Modena Team SpA	3.5 Modena Lambo 291-Lamborghini V12	collision with Alesi

1992

	Race	Circuit	No	Entrant	Car/Engine	Comment
12	JAPANESE GP	Suzuka	28	Scuderia Ferrari SpA	3.5 Fiat Ferrari F9200 V12	left at start/active car/1 lap behind
12	AUSTRALIAN GP	Adelaide	28	Scuderia Ferrari SpA	3.5 Fiat Ferrari F9200 V12	again left at start-clutch/2 laps behind

GP Starts: 41 (42)   GP Wins: 0   Pole positions: 0   Fastest laps: 0   Points: 0

NICOLA LARINI

The talented little Italian is yet another example of a driver who, having achieved success in the junior formulae, reached Formula 1, only to make up the numbers at the back of the grid.

Taken under the wing of Enzo Coloni, Larini upstaged his team leader Marco Apicella to win the 1986 Italian F3 championship in a Dallara before briefly moving into Formula 3000 with the rival Forti Corse team.

Coloni then gave him his Grand Prix debut at the end of 1987, before he joined Osella for a couple of character-building seasons where he never gave less than 100 per cent. After an unhappy season with Ligier in 1990, Nicola threw in his lot with the ambitious but ill-starred Modena team, which soon foundered. Given a testing contract by Ferrari to develop their active suspension system, Larini re-established his reputation as a class driver by winning the 1992 Italian touring car championship for Alfa Romeo. His stock was to rise even higher in 1993 when he took the Alfa into the high-profile German series, regularly destroying the opposition with some brilliant drives to take that title as well.

OSCAR LARRAURI

Having raced in Argentinian F3 from 1979, 'Poppy' Larrauri found the going tough when he made the move to Europe until he secured the top drive in the Pavanello Euroracing F3 team for 1982. He then showed his mettle, winning seven races and the European championship. Unfortunately his aspirations were soon blunted by an unhappy Formula 2 liaison with Minardi, which left him out in the cold.

Larrauri then began a long and rewarding association with Walter Brun, racing the Swiss entrant's Porsche sports cars through to the early nineties, the high spot being a win at Jerez in 1986. However Brun's over-ambitious move into Formula 1 was a different story which found 'Poppy' struggling to qualify uncompetitive machinery.

GÉRARD LARROUSSE

After a distinguished career in rallying in the sixties with Alpine and Porsche cars, Gérard made the transition to circuit racing with ease, sharing the second-place Porsche with Herrmann at Le Mans in 1969. Over the next few seasons, Larrousse built up a fine reputation in endurance racing, winning the 1971 Sebring 12 Hours and the Nürburgring 1000 Km for Porsche, before enjoying two fabulously successful years with Matra in 1973 and 1974 during which, partnered by Pescarolo, Gérard won Le Mans twice and added further victories at Vallelunga, Dijon, the Österreichring, Watkins Glen, Imola and Kyalami. In 1974, he was also the European 2-litre champion in an Alpine-Renault and briefly sampled the ambience of Formula 1, but had a miserable time with the poorly prepared rent-a-drive Finotto Brabham.

In 1975 he undertook a season of Formula 2 with the Elf, winning the Jim Clark Trophy at Hockenheim on aggregate, in addition to a sports car programme for Renault. At the end of the season he was appointed competitions manager at Renault, overseeing the development of their Formula 1 turbo car, and later moved to Ligier before establishing his own team, which has been competing on minimal budgets and supported by a motley collection of sponsors since 1987.

LARRAURI, Oscar (RA) b 19/8/1954

1988

	Race	Circuit	No	Entrant	Car/Engine	Comment
dns	BRAZILIAN GP	Rio	32	EuroBrun Racing	3.5 EuroBrun ER188-Cosworth V8	electrical problems on parade lap
dnq	SAN MARINO GP	Imola	32	EuroBrun Racing	3.5 EuroBrun ER188-Cosworth V8	
ret	MONACO GP	Monte Carlo	32	EuroBrun Racing	3.5 EuroBrun ER188-Cosworth V8	accident
13	MEXICAN GP	Mexico City	32	EuroBrun Racing	3.5 EuroBrun ER188-Cosworth V8	handling/battery problems/~4 laps
ret	CANADIAN GP	Montreal	32	EuroBrun Racing	3.5 EuroBrun ER188-Cosworth V8	accident
ret	US GP (DETROIT)	Detroit	32	EuroBrun Racing	3.5 EuroBrun ER188-Cosworth V8	gearbox
ret	FRENCH GP	Paul Ricard	32	EuroBrun Racing	3.5 EuroBrun ER188-Cosworth V8	clutch
dnq	BRITISH GP	Silverstone	32	EuroBrun Racing	3.5 EuroBrun ER188-Cosworth V8	
16	GERMAN GP	Hockenheim	32	EuroBrun Racing	3.5 EuroBrun ER188-Cosworth V8	2 laps behind
dnq	HUNGARIAN GP	Hungaroring	32	EuroBrun Racing	3.5 EuroBrun ER188-Cosworth V8	
dnpq	BELGIAN GP	Spa	32	EuroBrun Racing	3.5 EuroBrun ER188-Cosworth V8	
dnpq	ITALIAN GP	Monza	32	EuroBrun Racing	3.5 EuroBrun ER188-Cosworth V8	
dnpq	PORTUGUESE GP	Estoril	32	EuroBrun Racing	3.5 EuroBrun ER188-Cosworth V8	
dnq	SPANISH GP	Jerez	32	EuroBrun Racing	3.5 EuroBrun ER188-Cosworth V8	
dnq	JAPANESE GP	Suzuka	32	EuroBrun Racing	3.5 EuroBrun ER188-Cosworth V8	
ret	AUSTRALIAN GP	Adelaide	32	EuroBrun Racing	3.5 EuroBrun ER188-Cosworth V8	driveshaft-spun off

1989

	Race	Circuit	No	Entrant	Car/Engine	Comment
dnpq	ITALIAN GP	Monza	33	EuroBrun Racing	3.5 EuroBrun ER189-Judd V8	
dnpq	"	"	33	EuroBrun Racing	3.5 EuroBrun ER188B-Judd V8	
dnpq	PORTUGUESE GP	Estoril	33	EuroBrun Racing	3.5 EuroBrun ER189-Judd V8	
dnpq	"	"	33	EuroBrun Racing	3.5 EuroBrun ER188B-Judd V8	
dnpq	SPANISH GP	Jerez	33	EuroBrun Racing	3.5 EuroBrun ER189-Judd V8	
dnpq	"	"	33	EuroBrun Racing	3.5 EuroBrun ER188B-Judd V8	
dnpq	JAPANESE GP	Suzuka	33	EuroBrun Racing	3.5 EuroBrun ER189-Judd V8	
dnpq	AUSTRALIAN GP	Adelaide	33	EuroBrun Racing	3.5 EuroBrun ER189-Judd V8	

GP Starts: 7 (8)   GP Wins: 0   Pole positions: 0   Fastest laps: 0   Points: 0

LARROUSSE, Gérard (F) b 23/5/1940

1974

	Race	Circuit	No	Entrant	Car/Engine	Comment
ret	BELGIAN GP	Nivelles	43	Scuderia Finotto	3.0 Brabham BT42-Cosworth V8	chunking tyres
dnq	FRENCH GP	Dijon	43	Scuderia Finotto	3.0 Brabham BT42-Cosworth V8	

GP Starts: 1   GP Wins: 0   Pole positions: 0   Fastest laps: 0   Points: 0

NIKI LAUDA

There are some who try to buck the system but usually fail, and others who play the game and manipulate it to their own ends. Niki Lauda managed to do both, with the adroitness of his off-track political and business manoeuvrings being matched only by that of his driving and racecraft, which saw him win three world titles.

After a couple of seasons in which he struggled to make an impression in Formula 3 and sports cars, with a Porsche 908, Lauda took a bank loan to finance a season of Formula 2 in a semi-works March and a one-off drive in his home GP in 1971. Although his results were hardly inspiring there were fleeting glimpses of his talent. Already the quiet self-confidence was there, as was the inner determination to overcome every setback, and he effectively mortgaged himself to the hilt to buy a seat in the works March team alongside Ronnie Peterson for 1972. To say the F1 season was disastrous is almost an understatement, and the dreadful 721X proved absolutely hopeless. Fortunately the F2 March 722 was competitive, at least allowing Niki to compete with his peers. His win in the spring John Player F2 race at Oulton Park was one indication of his potential, his ability to closely match Peterson's testing

times another, but March discarded him right at the end of the year, and he virtually saved his career by joining BRM for 1973 in a pay-as-you-race deal which he knew it would be difficult to honour.

When Lauda managed to overshadow his team-mates in the early races, took his first championship points at Zolder and held third place in the Monaco GP, he was able to put his contract problems behind him, but only by locking himself into a three-year deal. There were a few successful touring car races for BMW which proved quite lucrative, but most important was the fact that he had been targeted by Ferrari for 1974. Contract or not, there was no way Louis Stanley was going to stop Niki heading for Maranello, and the young Austrian wriggled his way out of the deal. Displaying typical pragmatism, he set about his new task at Ferrari with a huge programme of testing and constant development which paid immediate dividends. There were a couple of wins and four second places, but a mid-season dip in form cost him his title chance.

For a driver in his first year with a front-line team he had performed admirably, but Lauda was privately convinced that in 1975 the title would be his, and once the transverse-gearbox car was introduced there was no stopping him. Nine pole positions and five Grand Prix wins (complemented by victory in the International Trophy) saw the Austrian sweep to his first championship, and 1976 showed every sign of going the same way until the fiery crash at the Nürburgring which so nearly took his life. Though badly burned around the head, Niki returned to defend his title just weeks later and the fact that he ultimately failed to retain his crown was largely irrelevant, despite the dreadful treatment the

Italian press meted out to him after his decision to pull out of the Japanese GP. Even at Ferrari there were doubters who thought he had lost his bottle, however, and Reutemann was brought into the team, much to Lauda's annoyance.

Inwardly Niki must have relished the challenge, and with a perfect blend of aggression and circumspection he all but humiliated his new team-mate the following season to prove to the hierarchy that he was still the boss. A second title was duly won and, with a characteristic lack of sentiment, Lauda then announced that he was moving to Brabham. His two years with the team brought only limited success, Niki winning the Swedish GP in the notorious fan car and the Italian GP in 1978, and the non-title Dino Ferrari Trophy at Imola the following season. At Montreal that year, he tried the new Cosworth BT49 in practice and made the shock decision to retire then and there.

He stayed away for two years, during which he built up his airline business, before being tempted back in 1982. Perhaps it was his ego, the money, or maybe just the challenge of proving the inevitable doubters wrong. One thing was for sure: once he had demonstrated to himself that the speed was still there, he wasn't going to mess around. There was a job to be done in developing John Barnard's innovative McLaren MP4 and Niki was just the man to do it. True, there were occasional lapses and lacklustre performances in the Cosworth car, but once his attention turned to the TAG turbo-powered machine at the end of 1983 Lauda was fully focused. He needed to be for 1984, when he was joined by Alain Prost. Using all his experience, the wily Lauda hung on to the Frenchman's tail and eventually took his third World Championship by the narrowest of margins after a fabulous year. His final season perhaps went according to expectation, as the still hungry Prost forced the pace, while Niki was happy to adopt a more tactical approach. Unfortunately the season was blighted by unreliability, but at Zandvoort we saw Lauda the racer one last time, as he kept his number 1 McLaren in front of Prost's sister-car in a Formula 3-style battle to the finish. This time Niki stayed retired, but in 1992 he was invited to act as a consultant to Ferrari as they attempted to recapture the glory days which had been gone for so long.

LAUDA, Niki (A) b 22/2/1949

	1971					
	Race	Circuit	No	Entrant	Car/Engine	Comment
ret	AUSTRIAN GP	Österreichring	26	STP March Racing Team	3.0 March 711-Cosworth V8	*handling*
	1972					
11	ARGENTINE GP	Buenos Aires	15	STP March Racing Team	3.0 March 721-Cosworth V8	*2 laps behind*
7	SOUTH AFRICAN GP	Kyalami	4	STP March Racing Team	3.0 March 721-Cosworth V8	*1 lap behind*
ret	SPANISH GP	Jarama	24	STP March Racing Team	3.0 March 721X-Cosworth V8	*sticking throttle*
16	MONACO GP	Monte Carlo	4	STP March Racing Team	3.0 March 721X-Cosworth V8	*p stop-wheel/fuel leak/-6 laps*
12	BELGIAN GP	Nivelles	12	STP March Racing Team	3.0 March 721X-Cosworth V8	*handling problems/3 laps behind*
dns	"	"	14	Clarke-Mordaunt-Guthrie Racing	3.0 March 721G-Cosworth V8	*practice only*
ret	FRENCH GP	Clermont Ferrand	14	STP March Racing Team	3.0 March 721G-Cosworth V8	*loose driveshaft*
9	BRITISH GP	Brands Hatch	4	STP March Racing Team	3.0 March 721G-Cosworth V8	*3 laps behind*
ret	GERMAN GP	Nürburgring	23	STP March Racing Team	3.0 March 721G-Cosworth V8	*split oil tank*
10	AUSTRIAN GP	Österreichring	4	STP March Racing Team	3.0 March 721G-Cosworth V8	*1 lap behind*
13	ITALIAN GP	Monza	18	STP March Racing Team	3.0 March 721G-Cosworth V8	*p stop-throttle slides/5 laps behind*
dsq	CANADIAN GP	Mosport Park	26	STP March Racing Team	3.0 March 721G-Cosworth V8	*outside assistance on track*
nc	US GP	Watkins Glen	26	STP March Racing Team	3.0 March 721G-Cosworth V8	*p stop-fuel pressure/10 laps behind*

1973

Result	GP	Circuit	No.	Team	Engine	Notes
ret	ARGENTINE GP	Buenos Aires	34	Marlboro BRM	3.0 BRM P160C V12	oil pressure
8	BRAZILIAN GP	Interlagos	16	Marlboro BRM	3.0 BRM P160C V12	stopped-electrics/2 laps behind
ret	SOUTH AFRICAN GP	Kyalami	17	Marlboro BRM	3.0 BRM P160D V12	engine
ret	SPANISH GP	Montjuich Park	16	Marlboro BRM	3.0 BRM P160E V12	tyres
5	BELGIAN GP	Zolder	21	Marlboro BRM	3.0 BRM P160E V12	pit stop-fuel/1 lap behind
ret	MONACO GP	Monte Carlo	21	Marlboro BRM	3.0 BRM P160E V12	gearbox
13	SWEDISH GP	Anderstorp	21	Marlboro BRM	3.0 BRM P160E V12	pit stop-engine/5 laps behind
9	FRENCH GP	Paul Ricard	21	Marlboro BRM	3.0 BRM P160E V12	
12	BRITISH GP	Silverstone	21	Marlboro BRM	3.0 BRM P160E V12	pit stop-tyres/4 laps behind
ret	DUTCH GP	Zandvoort	21	Marlboro BRM	3.0 BRM P160E V12	tyres/fuel pump
ret	GERMAN GP	Nürburgring	21	Marlboro BRM	3.0 BRM P160E V12	crashed-fractured wrist
dns	AUSTRIAN GP	Österreichring	21	Marlboro BRM	3.0 BRM P160E V12	problems with German GP injury
ret	ITALIAN GP	Monza	21	Marlboro BRM	3.0 BRM P160E V12	tyre failure-accident
ret	CANADIAN GP	Mosport Park	21	Marlboro BRM	3.0 BRM P160E V12	transmission
ret	US GP	Watkins Glen	21	Marlboro BRM	3.0 BRM P160E V12	fuel pump

1974

Result	GP	Circuit	No.	Team	Engine	Notes
2	ARGENTINE GP	Buenos Aires	12	Scuderia Ferrari SpA SEFAC	3.0 Ferrari 312B3 F12	
ret	BRAZILIAN GP	Interlagos	12	Scuderia Ferrari SpA SEFAC	3.0 Ferrari 312B3 F12	broken wing stay
16/ret	SOUTH AFRICAN GP	Kyalami	12	Scuderia Ferrari SpA SEFAC	3.0 Ferrari 312B3 F12	ignition/4 laps behind/Pole
1	SPANISH GP	Jarama	12	Scuderia Ferrari SpA SEFAC	3.0 Ferrari 312B3 F12	Pole/FL
2	BELGIAN GP	Nivelles	12	Scuderia Ferrari SpA SEFAC	3.0 Ferrari 312B3 F12	
ret	MONACO GP	Monte Carlo	12	Scuderia Ferrari SpA SEFAC	3.0 Ferrari 312B3 F12	ignition/Pole
ret	SWEDISH GP	Anderstorp	12	Scuderia Ferrari SpA SEFAC	3.0 Ferrari 312B3 F12	transmission
1	DUTCH GP	Zandvoort	12	Scuderia Ferrari SpA SEFAC	3.0 Ferrari 312B3 F12	Pole
2	FRENCH GP	Dijon	12	Scuderia Ferrari SpA SEFAC	3.0 Ferrari 312B3 F12	Pole
5	BRITISH GP	Brands Hatch	12	Scuderia Ferrari SpA SEFAC	3.0 Ferrari 312B3 F12	trapped in pits/-1 lap/Pole/FL
ret	GERMAN GP	Nürburgring	12	Scuderia Ferrari SpA SEFAC	3.0 Ferrari 312B3 F12	hit Scheckter/Pole
ret	AUSTRIAN GP	Österreichring	12	Scuderia Ferrari SpA SEFAC	3.0 Ferrari 312B3 F12	engine/Pole
ret	ITALIAN GP	Monza	12	Scuderia Ferrari SpA SEFAC	3.0 Ferrari 312B3 F12	engine/Pole
ret	CANADIAN GP	Mosport Park	12	Scuderia Ferrari SpA SEFAC	3.0 Ferrari 312B3 F12	hit barrier when 1st/FL
ret	US GP	Watkins Glen	12	Scuderia Ferrari SpA SEFAC	3.0 Ferrari 312B3 F12	front suspension

1975 World Champion Driver

Result	GP	Circuit	No.	Team	Engine	Notes
6	ARGENTINE GP	Buenos Aires	12	Scuderia Ferrari SpA SEFAC	3.0 Ferrari 312B3 F12	
5	BRAZILIAN GP	Interlagos	12	Scuderia Ferrari SpA SEFAC	3.0 Ferrari 312B3 F12	
5	SOUTH AFRICAN GP	Kyalami	12	Scuderia Ferrari SpA SEFAC	3.0 Ferrari 312T F12	
dns	"	"	12	Scuderia Ferrari SpA SEFAC	3.0 Ferrari 312B3 F12	practice only
ret	SPANISH GP	Montjuich Park	12	Scuderia Ferrari SpA SEFAC	3.0 Ferrari 312T F12	hit by Andretti/Pole
1	MONACO GP	Monte Carlo	12	Scuderia Ferrari SpA SEFAC	3.0 Ferrari 312T F12	Pole
1	BELGIAN GP	Zolder	12	Scuderia Ferrari SpA SEFAC	3.0 Ferrari 312T F12	Pole
1	SWEDISH GP	Anderstorp	12	Scuderia Ferrari SpA SEFAC	3.0 Ferrari 312T F12	FL
2	DUTCH GP	Zandvoort	12	Scuderia Ferrari SpA SEFAC	3.0 Ferrari 312T F12	Pole/FL
1	FRENCH GP	Paul Ricard	12	Scuderia Ferrari SpA SEFAC	3.0 Ferrari 312T F12	Pole
8	BRITISH GP	Silverstone	12	Scuderia Ferrari SpA SEFAC	3.0 Ferrari 312T F12	2 laps behind
3	GERMAN GP	Nürburgring	12	Scuderia Ferrari SpA SEFAC	3.0 Ferrari 312T F12	pit stops-tyre problems/Pole
6	AUSTRIAN GP	Österreichring	12	Scuderia Ferrari SpA SEFAC	3.0 Ferrari 312T F12	Pole
3	ITALIAN GP	Monza	12	Scuderia Ferrari SpA SEFAC	3.0 Ferrari 312T F12	Pole
1	US GP	Watkins Glen	12	Scuderia Ferrari SpA SEFAC	3.0 Ferrari 312T F12	Pole

1976

Result	GP	Circuit	No.	Team	Engine	Notes
1	BRAZILIAN GP	Interlagos	1	Scuderia Ferrari SpA SEFAC	3.0 Ferrari 312T F12	
1	SOUTH AFRICAN GP	Kyalami	1	Scuderia Ferrari SpA SEFAC	3.0 Ferrari 312T F12	FL
2	US GP WEST	Long Beach	1	Scuderia Ferrari SpA SEFAC	3.0 Ferrari 312T F12	
2	SPANISH GP	Jarama	1	Scuderia Ferrari SpA SEFAC	3.0 Ferrari 312T2 F12	
1	BELGIAN GP	Zolder	1	Scuderia Ferrari SpA SEFAC	3.0 Ferrari 312T2 F12	Pole/FL
dns	"	"	1	Scuderia Ferrari SpA SEFAC	3.0 Ferrari 312T F12	practice only
1	MONACO GP	Monte Carlo	1	Scuderia Ferrari SpA SEFAC	3.0 Ferrari 312T2 F12	Pole
3	SWEDISH GP	Anderstorp	1	Scuderia Ferrari SpA SEFAC	3.0 Ferrari 312T2 F12	
ret	FRENCH GP	Paul Ricard	1	Scuderia Ferrari SpA SEFAC	3.0 Ferrari 312T2 F12	engine/FL
1*	BRITISH GP	Brands Hatch	1	Scuderia Ferrari SpA SEFAC	3.0 Ferrari 312T2 F12	* 1st place car dsq/Pole/FL
ret/dns	GERMAN GP	Nürburgring	1	Scuderia Ferrari SpA SEFAC	3.0 Ferrari 312T2 F12	accident in first start-badly burnt
4	ITALIAN GP	Monza	1	Scuderia Ferrari SpA SEFAC	3.0 Ferrari 312T2 F12	
8	CANADIAN GP	Mosport Park	1	Scuderia Ferrari SpA SEFAC	3.0 Ferrari 312T2 F12	
3	US GP EAST	Watkins Glen	1	Scuderia Ferrari SpA SEFAC	3.0 Ferrari 312T2 F12	
ret	JAPANESE GP	Mount Fuji	1	Scuderia Ferrari SpA SEFAC	3.0 Ferrari 312T2 F12	withdrew-lap 3 due to conditions

1977 World Champion Driver

Result	GP	Circuit	No.	Team	Engine	Notes
ret	ARGENTINE GP	Buenos Aires	11	Scuderia Ferrari SpA SEFAC	3.0 Ferrari 312T2 F12	fuel metering unit
3	BRAZILIAN GP	Interlagos	11	Scuderia Ferrari SpA SEFAC	3.0 Ferrari 312T2 F12	
1	SOUTH AFRICAN GP	Kyalami	11	Scuderia Ferrari SpA SEFAC	3.0 Ferrari 312T2 F12	
2	US GP WEST	Long Beach	11	Scuderia Ferrari SpA SEFAC	3.0 Ferrari 312T2 F12	Pole/FL
dns	SPANISH GP	Jarama	11	Scuderia Ferrari SpA SEFAC	3.0 Ferrari 312T2 F12	broken rib in Sun a.m. warm-up
2	MONACO GP	Monte Carlo	11	Scuderia Ferrari SpA SEFAC	3.0 Ferrari 312T2 F12	
2	BELGIAN GP	Zolder	11	Scuderia Ferrari SpA SEFAC	3.0 Ferrari 312T2 F12	
ret	SWEDISH GP	Anderstorp	11	Scuderia Ferrari SpA SEFAC	3.0 Ferrari 312T2 F12	handling
5	FRENCH GP	Dijon	11	Scuderia Ferrari SpA SEFAC	3.0 Ferrari 312T2 F12	
2	BRITISH GP	Silverstone	11	Scuderia Ferrari SpA SEFAC	3.0 Ferrari 312T2 F12	
1	GERMAN GP	Hockenheim	11	Scuderia Ferrari SpA SEFAC	3.0 Ferrari 312T2 F12	FL
2	AUSTRIAN GP	Österreichring	11	Scuderia Ferrari SpA SEFAC	3.0 Ferrari 312T2 F12	Pole
1	DUTCH GP	Zandvoort	11	Scuderia Ferrari SpA SEFAC	3.0 Ferrari 312T2 F12	FL
2	ITALIAN GP	Monza	11	Scuderia Ferrari SpA SEFAC	3.0 Ferrari 312T2 F12	
4	US GP EAST	Watkins Glen	11	Scuderia Ferrari SpA SEFAC	3.0 Ferrari 312T2 F12	

1978

Result	GP	Circuit	No.	Team	Engine	Notes
2	ARGENTINE GP	Buenos Aires	1	Parmalat Racing Team	3.0 Brabham BT45C-Alfa Romeo F12	

3	BRAZILIAN GP	Rio	1	Parmalat Racing Team	3.0 Brabham BT45C-Alfa Romeo F12	
ret	SOUTH AFRICAN GP	Kyalami	1	Parmalat Racing Team	3.0 Brabham BT46-Alfa Romeo F12	*engine/Pole*
ret	US GP WEST	Long Beach	1	Parmalat Racing Team	3.0 Brabham BT46-Alfa Romeo F12	*ignition*
2	MONACO GP	Monte Carlo	1	Parmalat Racing Team	3.0 Brabham BT46-Alfa Romeo F12	*FL*
ret	BELGIAN GP	Zolder	1	Parmalat Racing Team	3.0 Brabham BT46-Alfa Romeo F12	*hit by Scheckter at start*
ret	SPANISH GP	Jarama	1	Parmalat Racing Team	3.0 Brabham BT46-Alfa Romeo F12	*engine*
1	SWEDISH GP	Anderstorp	1	Parmalat Racing Team	3.0 Brabham BT46B-Alfa Romeo F12	*fan car/FL*
ret	FRENCH GP	Paul Ricard	1	Parmalat Racing Team	3.0 Brabham BT46-Alfa Romeo F12	*engine*
2	BRITISH GP	Brands Hatch	1	Parmalat Racing Team	3.0 Brabham BT46-Alfa Romeo F12	*FL*
ret	GERMAN GP	Hockenheim	1	Parmalat Racing Team	3.0 Brabham BT46-Alfa Romeo F12	*engine*
dns	"	"	1	Parmalat Racing Team	3.0 Brabham BT46C-Alfa Romeo F12	*practice only*
ret	AUSTRIAN GP	Österreichring	1	Parmalat Racing Team	3.0 Brabham BT46-Alfa Romeo F12	*crashed*
3	DUTCH GP	Zandvoort	1	Parmalat Racing Team	3.0 Brabham BT46-Alfa Romeo F12	*FL*
1*	ITALIAN GP	Monza	1	Parmalat Racing Team	3.0 Brabham BT46-Alfa Romeo F12	** 1st & 2nd place cars penalised 1 min*
ret	US GP EAST	Watkins Glen	1	Parmalat Racing Team	3.0 Brabham BT46-Alfa Romeo F12	*engine*
ret	CANADIAN GP	Montreal	1	Parmalat Racing Team	3.0 Brabham BT46-Alfa Romeo F12	*brakes-accident*

1979

ret	ARGENTINE GP	Buenos Aires	5	Parmalat Racing Team	3.0 Brabham BT48-Alfa Romeo V12	*fuel pressure*
dns	"	"	5	Parmalat Racing Team	3.0 Brabham BT46-Alfa Romeo F12	*practice only*
ret	BRAZILIAN GP	Interlagos	5	Parmalat Racing Team	3.0 Brabham BT48-Alfa Romeo V12	*gear linkage*
6	SOUTH AFRICAN GP	Kyalami	5	Parmalat Racing Team	3.0 Brabham BT48-Alfa Romeo V12	*pit stop-tyres/1 lap behind*
ret	US GP WEST	Long Beach	5	Parmalat Racing Team	3.0 Brabham BT48-Alfa Romeo V12	*collision with Tambay*
ret	SPANISH GP	Jarama	5	Parmalat Racing Team	3.0 Brabham BT48-Alfa Romeo V12	*water leak*
ret	BELGIAN GP	Zolder	5	Parmalat Racing Team	3.0 Brabham BT48-Alfa Romeo V12	*engine*
ret	MONACO GP	Monte Carlo	5	Parmalat Racing Team	3.0 Brabham BT48-Alfa Romeo V12	*accident with Pironi*
ret	FRENCH GP	Dijon	5	Parmalat Racing Team	3.0 Brabham BT48-Alfa Romeo V12	*spun off-could not restart*
ret	BRITISH GP	Silverstone	5	Parmalat Racing Team	3.0 Brabham BT48-Alfa Romeo V12	*brakes*
ret	GERMAN GP	Hockenheim	5	Parmalat Racing Team	3.0 Brabham BT48-Alfa Romeo V12	*engine*
ret	AUSTRIAN GP	Österreichring	5	Parmalat Racing Team	3.0 Brabham BT48-Alfa Romeo V12	*oil leak*
ret	DUTCH GP	Zandvoort	5	Parmalat Racing Team	3.0 Brabham BT48-Alfa Romeo V12	*withdrew-wrist injury*
4	ITALIAN GP	Monza	5	Parmalat Racing Team	3.0 Brabham BT48-Alfa Romeo V12	
dns	CANADIAN GP	Montreal	5	Parmalat Racing Team	3.0 Brabham BT49-Cosworth V8	*quit after a.m. practice*

1982

4	SOUTH AFRICAN GP	Kyalami	8	Marlboro McLaren International	3.0 McLaren MP4-Cosworth V8	
ret	BRAZILIAN GP	Rio	8	Marlboro McLaren International	3.0 McLaren MP4B-Cosworth V8	*hit by Reutemann*
1	US GP WEST	Long Beach	8	Marlboro McLaren International	3.0 McLaren MP4B-Cosworth V8	*FL*
dsq	BELGIAN GP	Zolder	8	Marlboro McLaren International	3.0 McLaren MP4B-Cosworth V8	*3rd on road/car underweight*
ret	MONACO GP	Monte Carlo	8	Marlboro McLaren International	3.0 McLaren MP4B-Cosworth V8	*engine*
ret	US GP (DETROIT)	Detroit	8	Marlboro McLaren International	3.0 McLaren MP4B-Cosworth V8	*hit Rosberg*
ret	CANADIAN GP	Montreal	8	Marlboro McLaren International	3.0 McLaren MP4B-Cosworth V8	*clutch*
4	DUTCH GP	Zandvoort	8	Marlboro McLaren International	3.0 McLaren MP4B-Cosworth V8	
1	BRITISH GP	Brands Hatch	8	Marlboro McLaren International	3.0 McLaren MP4B-Cosworth V8	
8	FRENCH GP	Paul Ricard	8	Marlboro McLaren International	3.0 McLaren MP4B-Cosworth V8	*pit stop-tyres/1 lap behind*
dns	GERMAN GP	Hockenheim	8	Marlboro McLaren International	3.0 McLaren MP4B-Cosworth V8	*hurt wrist in practice*
5	AUSTRIAN GP	Österreichring	8	Marlboro McLaren International	3.0 McLaren MP4B-Cosworth V8	*1 lap behind*
3	SWISS GP	Dijon	8	Marlboro McLaren International	3.0 McLaren MP4B-Cosworth V8	
ret	ITALIAN GP	Monza	8	Marlboro McLaren International	3.0 McLaren MP4B-Cosworth V8	*handling/brakes*
ret	CAESARS PALACE GP	Las Vegas	8	Marlboro McLaren International	3.0 McLaren MP4B-Cosworth V8	*engine*

1983

3	BRAZILIAN GP	Rio	8	Marlboro McLaren International	3.0 McLaren MP4/1C-Cosworth V8	
2	US GP WEST	Long Beach	8	Marlboro McLaren International	3.0 McLaren MP4/1C-Cosworth V8	*FL*
ret	FRENCH GP	Paul Ricard	8	Marlboro McLaren International	3.0 McLaren MP4/1C-Cosworth V8	*wheel bearing*
ret	SAN MARINO GP	Imola	8	Marlboro McLaren International	3.0 McLaren MP4/1C-Cosworth V8	*hit barrier*
dnq	MONACO GP	Monte Carlo	8	Marlboro McLaren International	3.0 McLaren MP4/1C-Cosworth V8	
ret	BELGIAN GP	Spa	8	Marlboro McLaren International	3.0 McLaren MP4/1C-Cosworth V8	*engine*
ret	US GP (DETROIT)	Detroit	8	Marlboro McLaren International	3.0 McLaren MP4/1C-Cosworth V8	*shock absorber*
ret	CANADIAN GP	Montreal	8	Marlboro McLaren International	3.0 McLaren MP4/1C-Cosworth V8	*spun off-could not restart*
6	BRITISH GP	Silverstone	8	Marlboro McLaren International	3.0 McLaren MP4/1C-Cosworth V8	*pit stop-tyres/1 lap behind*
dsq	GERMAN GP	Hockenheim	8	Marlboro McLaren International	3.0 McLaren MP4/1C-Cosworth V8	*5th on road/reversed into pits*
6	AUSTRIAN GP	Österreichring	8	Marlboro McLaren International	3.0 McLaren MP4/1C-Cosworth V8	*pit stop-tyres/2 laps behind*
ret	DUTCH GP	Zandvoort	8	Marlboro McLaren International	1.5 t/c McLaren MP4/1E-TAG V6	*brakes*
ret	ITALIAN GP	Monza	8	Marlboro McLaren International	1.5 t/c McLaren MP4/1E-TAG V6	*electrics*
ret	EUROPEAN GP	Brands Hatch	8	Marlboro McLaren International	1.5 t/c McLaren MP4/1E-TAG V6	*engine*
11/ret	SOUTH AFRICAN GP	Kyalami	8	Marlboro McLaren International	1.5 t/c McLaren MP4/1E-TAG V6	*electrics/6 laps behind*

1984 World Champion Driver

ret	BRAZILIAN GP	Rio	8	Marlboro McLaren International	1.5 t/c McLaren MP4/2-TAG V6	*electrics*
1	SOUTH AFRICAN GP	Kyalami	8	Marlboro McLaren International	1.5 t/c McLaren MP4/2-TAG V6	
ret	BELGIAN GP	Zolder	8	Marlboro McLaren International	1.5 t/c McLaren MP4/2-TAG V6	*water pump*
ret	SAN MARINO GP	Imola	8	Marlboro McLaren International	1.5 t/c McLaren MP4/2-TAG V6	*engine*
1	FRENCH GP	Dijon	8	Marlboro McLaren International	1.5 t/c McLaren MP4/2-TAG V6	
ret	MONACO GP	Monte Carlo	8	Marlboro McLaren International	1.5 t/c McLaren MP4/2-TAG V6	*spun off*
2	CANADIAN GP	Montreal	8	Marlboro McLaren International	1.5 t/c McLaren MP4/2-TAG V6	
ret	US GP (DETROIT)	Detroit	8	Marlboro McLaren International	1.5 t/c McLaren MP4/2-TAG V6	*electrics*
ret	US GP (DALLAS)	Dallas	8	Marlboro McLaren International	1.5 t/c McLaren MP4/2-TAG V6	*hit wall/FL*
1	BRITISH GP	Brands Hatch	8	Marlboro McLaren International	1.5 t/c McLaren MP4/2-TAG V6	*FL*
2	GERMAN GP	Hockenheim	8	Marlboro McLaren International	1.5 t/c McLaren MP4/2-TAG V6	
1	AUSTRIAN GP	Österreichring	8	Marlboro McLaren International	1.5 t/c McLaren MP4/2-TAG V6	*FL*
2	DUTCH GP	Zandvoort	8	Marlboro McLaren International	1.5 t/c McLaren MP4/2-TAG V6	
1	ITALIAN GP	Monza	8	Marlboro McLaren International	1.5 t/c McLaren MP4/2-TAG V6	*FL*
4	EUROPEAN GP	Nürburgring	8	Marlboro McLaren International	1.5 t/c McLaren MP4/2-TAG V6	
2	PORTUGESE GP	Estoril	8	Marlboro McLaren International	1.5 t/c McLaren MP4/2-TAG V6	*FL*

1985

ret	BRAZILIAN GP	Rio	1	Marlboro McLaren International	1.5 t/c McLaren MP4/2B-TAG V6	*fuel metering unit*
ret	PORTUGUESE GP	Estoril	1	Marlboro McLaren International	1.5 t/c McLaren MP4/2B-TAG V6	*engine*
4	SAN MARINO GP	Imola	1	Marlboro McLaren International	1.5 t/c McLaren MP4/2B-TAG V6	*gearbox problems/1 lap behind*
ret	MONACO GP	Monte Carlo	1	Marlboro McLaren International	1.5 t/c McLaren MP4/2B-TAG V6	*spun off-could not restart*
ret	CANADIAN GP	Montreal	1	Marlboro McLaren International	1.5 t/c McLaren MP4/2B-TAG V6	*engine*
ret	US GP (DETROIT)	Detroit	1	Marlboro McLaren International	1.5 t/c McLaren MP4/2B-TAG V6	*brakes*
ret	FRENCH GP	Paul Ricard	1	Marlboro McLaren International	1.5 t/c McLaren MP4/2B-TAG V6	*gearbox*
ret	BRITISH GP	Silverstone	1	Marlboro McLaren International	1.5 t/c McLaren MP4/2B-TAG V6	*electrics*
5	GERMAN GP	Nürburgring	1	Marlboro McLaren International	1.5 t/c McLaren MP4/2B-TAG V6	*pit stop-loose wheel/FL*
ret	AUSTRIAN GP	Österreichring	1	Marlboro McLaren International	1.5 t/c McLaren MP4/2B-TAG V6	*engine*
1	DUTCH GP	Zandvoort	1	Marlboro McLaren International	1.5 t/c McLaren MP4/2B-TAG V6	
ret	ITALIAN GP	Monza	1	Marlboro McLaren International	1.5 t/c McLaren MP4/2B-TAG V6	*transmission*
dns	BELGIAN GP	Spa	1	Marlboro McLaren International	1.5 t/c McLaren MP4/2B-TAG V6	*injured wrist in practice accident*
ret	SOUTH AFRICAN GP	Kyalami	1	Marlboro McLaren International	1.5 t/c McLaren MP4/2B-TAG V6	*turbo*
ret	AUSTRALIAN GP	Adelaide	1	Marlboro McLaren International	1.5 t/c McLaren MP4/2B-TAG V6	*brake problem-hit wall*

GP Starts: 170 (171)   GP Wins: 25   Pole positions: 24   Fastest laps: 25   Points: 420.5

CHRIS LAWRENCE

A club driver from the late fifties in MGs and particularly Morgans, with which he clocked up some modest triumphs, Lawrence ran a London engine-tuning business, and became involved in the ill-fated Deep-Sanderson sports car project of 1963-64.

With the introduction of the 3-litre formula in 1966, Chris raced a shoestring Cooper-Ferrari special, with which took to 5th place in that year's Gold Cup race at Oulton Park. Following the project's demise in 1967, he resurfaced briefly in sports car racing, then worked in France designing road cars, before returning to his beloved Morgans in the early seventies, running a tuning company specialising in that marque.

NEVILLE LEDERLE

Rightly regarded as one of his country's outstanding prospects, Lederle made an immediate impression on South African racing with his Lotus 18 late in 1961. This promise was confirmed the following year, when he finished sixth in the South African GP to score a point in what was to be his only Grand Prix start. This achievement proved to be a double-edged sword, however, for he was classed as a graded driver and was therefore not eligible to score points in Formula Junior or national races outside South Africa.

Neville stayed at home in 1963, dominating his domestic series with a string of wins in his Lotus 21, until a practice accident at the Rand 9 Hours sports car race left him sidelined with a broken leg. He missed that year's Grand Prix and also the 1964 Springbok series, after his injury proved very slow to heal. This, coupled with increasing business commitments, prompted Lederle's retirement, though he did bring the old Lotus out for the end-of-season Rand Grand Prix and the South African GP in January 1965, where, as fastest non-qualifier, he just failed to make the grid.

MICHEL LECLÈRE

A runner-up in the 1972 Formule Renault series, Leclère won the French Formula 3 championship for Alpine the following year.

Michel's career seemed to be taking shape well during 1974-75 when he was a front-runner in Formula 2 and won races at Rouen, Zolder and Silverstone, earning an F1 chance with Tyrrell and a contract with Wolf-Williams for 1976. In the event, the car was awful and the team despondent, and poor Leclère was jettisoned in mid-season, returning to Formula 2 with Elf-Renault and finishing fourth in the championship.

His career never really recovered after a disastrous F2 season with Kauhsen in 1977 destroyed his chances of a Formula 1 comeback. Thereafter he scratched about with only occasional sports car and single-seater outings before quitting for good.

GEOFF LEES

A professional racing driver in the truest sense of the word, Lees never really had the Formula 1 opportunities that his talent demanded, but he has nevertheless enjoyed continued success in virtually every other type of racing he has tried. A Formula Ford champion in the mid-seventies, Geoff soon moved into F3 with a works Chevron, then tackled the Aurora F1 series and Can-Am, and won the Macau GP twice, while taking the occasional Grand Prix chances that came his way.

In 1981 he won the European Formula 2 championship with the Ralt-Honda, but even this could not bring Lees the big chance he had hoped for, and he eventually turned his back on Europe. Since 1983 he has lived in Japan, marrying a local girl, and carved out a fine career, most recently as leader of the TOM'S Toyota sports car team.

LAURENT, Roger (B) b 21/2/1913

1952

	Race	Circuit	No	Entrant	Car/Engine	Comment
12	BELGIAN GP	Spa	30	HW Motors Ltd	2.0 HWM-Alta 4	4 laps behind
6	GERMAN GP	Nürburgring	119	Ecurie Francorchamps	2.0 Ferrari 500 4	2 laps behind

GP Starts: 2   GP Wins: 0   Pole positions: 0   Fastest laps: 0   Points: 0

LAWRENCE, Chris (GB) b 27/7/1933

1966

	Race	Circuit	No	Entrant	Car/Engine	Comment
11	BRITISH GP	Brands Hatch	24	J A Pearce Engineering Ltd	2.9 Cooper T73-Ferrari V12	7 laps behind
ret	GERMAN GP	Nürburgring	20	J A Pearce Engineering Ltd	2.9 Cooper T73-Ferrari V12	engine

GP Starts: 2   GP Wins: 0   Pole positions: 0   Fastest laps: 0   Points: 0

LECLÈRE, Michel (F) b 18/3/1947

1975

	Race	Circuit	No	Entrant	Car/Engine	Comment
ret	US GP	Watkins Glen	15	Elf Team Tyrrell	3.0 Tyrrell 007-Cosworth V8	engine

1976

	Race	Circuit	No	Entrant	Car/Engine	Comment
13	SOUTH AFRICAN GP	Kyalami	21	Frank Williams Racing Cars	3.0 Williams FW05-Cosworth V8	2 laps behind
dnq	US GP WEST	Long Beach	21	Frank Williams Racing Cars	3.0 Williams FW05-Cosworth V8	
10	SPANISH GP	Jarama	21	Walter Wolf Racing	3.0 Williams FW05-Cosworth V8	2 laps behind
11	BELGIAN GP	Zolder	21	Walter Wolf Racing	3.0 Williams FW05-Cosworth V8	2 laps behind
11	MONACO GP	Monte Carlo	21	Walter Wolf Racing	3.0 Williams FW05-Cosworth V8	2 laps behind
ret	SWEDISH GP	Anderstorp	21	Walter Wolf Racing	3.0 Williams FW05-Cosworth V8	engine
13	FRENCH GP	Paul Ricard	21	Walter Wolf Racing	3.0 Williams FW05-Cosworth V8	1 lap behind

GP Starts: 7   GP Wins: 0   Pole positions: 0   Fastest laps: 0   Points: 0

LEDERLE, Neville (ZA) b 25/9/1939

1962

	Race	Circuit	No	Entrant	Car/Engine	Comment
6	SOUTH AFRICAN GP	East London	20	Neville Lederle	1.5 Lotus 21-Climax 4	4 laps behind

1965

dnq	SOUTH AFRICAN GP	East London	23	Scuderia Scribante	1.5 Lotus 21-Climax 4	

GP Starts: 1   GP Wins: 0   Pole positions: 0   Fastest laps: 0   Points: 1

LEES, Geoff (GB) b 1/5/1951

1978

	Race	Circuit	No	Entrant	Car/Engine	Comment
dnq	BRITISH GP	Brands Hatch	23	Mario Deliotti Racing	3.0 Ensign N175-Cosworth V8	

1979

7	GERMAN GP	Hockenheim	4	Candy Tyrrell Team	3.0 Tyrrell 009-Cosworth V8	1 lap behind

1980

13/ret	SOUTH AFRICAN GP	Kyalami	17	Shadow Cars	3.0 Shadow DN11-Cosworth V8	suspension failure/8 laps behind
dnq	US GP WEST	Long Beach	17	Shadow Cars	3.0 Shadow DN11-Cosworth V8	withdrawn after 1st practice
dnq	BELGIAN GP	Zolder	17	Shadow Cars	3.0 Shadow DN12-Cosworth V8	
dnq	MONACO GP	Monte Carlo	17	Shadow Cars	3.0 Shadow DN12-Cosworth V8	
ret	SPANISH GP	Jarama	17	Shadow Cars	3.0 Shadow DN12-Cosworth V8	broken rear suspension
dnq	FRENCH GP	Paul Ricard	17	Shadow Cars	3.0 Shadow DN12-Cosworth V8	
ret	DUTCH GP	Zandvoort	41	Unipart Racing Team	3.0 Ensign N180-Cosworth V8	accident with Brambilla
dnq	ITALIAN GP	Imola	41	Unipart Racing Team	3.0 Ensign N180-Cosworth V8	
dnq	US GP EAST	Watkins Glen	51	RAM/Theodore/Rainbow Jeans Racing	3.0 Williams FW07B-Cosworth V8	

1982

ret/dns	CANADIAN GP	Montreal	33	Theodore Racing Team	3.0 Theodore TY02-Cosworth V8	startline accident/did not restart
12	FRENCH GP	Paul Ricard	12	John Player Team Lotus	3.0 Lotus 91-Cosworth V8	pit stop-puncture/2 laps behind

GP Starts: 5   GP Wins: 0   Pole positions: 0   Fastest laps: 0   Points: 0

LEGAT, Arthur (B) b 1/11/1898 – d 23/2/1960

1952

	Race	Circuit	No	Entrant	Car/Engine	Comment
nc	BELGIAN GP	Spa	38	Arthur Legat	2.0 Veritas Meteor 6	5 laps behind

1953

ret	BELGIAN GP	Spa	36	Arthur Legat	2.0 Veritas Meteor 6	transmission

GP Starts: 2   GP Wins: 0   Pole positions: 0   Fastest laps: 0   Points: 0

LEHTO J J (Jyrki Jarvilehto) (SF) b 31/1/1966

1989

	Race	Circuit	No	Entrant	Car/Engine	Comment
dnpq	PORTUGUESE GP	Estoril	37	Moneytron Onyx	3.5 Onyx ORE 1-Cosworth V8	
ret	SPANISH GP	Jerez	37	Moneytron Onyx	3.5 Onyx ORE 1-Cosworth V8	gearbox
dnpq	JAPANESE GP	Suzuka	37	Moneytron Onyx	3.5 Onyx ORE 1-Cosworth V8	
ret	AUSTRALIAN GP	Adelaide	37	Moneytron Onyx	3.5 Onyx ORE 1-Cosworth V8	engine

1990

	Race	Circuit	No	Entrant	Car/Engine	Comment
dnq	US GP (PHOENIX)	Phoenix	36	Moneytron Onyx Formula One	3.5 Onyx ORE 1-Cosworth V8	no time recorded
dnq	BRAZILIAN GP	Interlagos	36	Moneytron Onyx Formula One	3.5 Onyx ORE 1-Cosworth V8	
12	SAN MARINO GP	Imola	36	Moneytron Onyx Formula One	3.5 Onyx ORE 1B-Cosworth V8	engine problems/2 laps behind
ret	MONACO GP	Monte Carlo	36	Moneytron Onyx Formula One	3.5 Onyx ORE 1B-Cosworth V8	gearbox
ret	CANADIAN GP	Montreal	36	Moneytron Onyx Formula One	3.5 Onyx ORE 1B-Cosworth V8	engine
ret	MEXICAN GP	Mexico City	36	Moneytron Onyx Formula One	3.5 Onyx ORE 1B-Cosworth V8	engine
dnq	FRENCH GP	Paul Ricard	36	Moneytron Onyx Formula One	3.5 Onyx ORE 1B-Cosworth V8	
dnq	BRITISH GP	Silverstone	36	Monteverdi Onyx Formula One	3.5 Onyx ORE 1B-Cosworth V8	
nc	GERMAN GP	Hockenheim	36	Monteverdi Onyx Formula One	3.5 Monteverdi ORE 1B-Cosworth V8	misfire/bodywork problems/-6 laps
dnq	HUNGARIAN GP	Hungaroring	36	Monteverdi Onyx Formula One	3.5 Monteverdi ORE 1B-Cosworth V8	

1991

	Race	Circuit	No	Entrant	Car/Engine	Comment
ret	US GP (PHOENIX)	Phoenix	22	Scuderia Italia SpA	3.5 BMS Dallara 191-Judd V10	clutch
ret	BRAZILIAN GP	Interlagos	22	Scuderia Italia SpA	3.5 BMS Dallara 191-Judd V10	alternator
3	SAN MARINO GP	Imola	22	Scuderia Italia SpA	3.5 BMS Dallara 191-Judd V10	1 lap behind
11	MONACO GP	Monte Carlo	22	Scuderia Italia SpA	3.5 BMS Dallara 191-Judd V10	3 laps behind
ret	CANADIAN GP	Montreal	22	Scuderia Italia SpA	3.5 BMS Dallara 191-Judd V10	engine
ret	MEXICAN GP	Mexico City	22	Scuderia Italia SpA	3.5 BMS Dallara 191-Judd V10	engine
ret	FRENCH GP	Magny Cours	22	Scuderia Italia SpA	3.5 BMS Dallara 191-Judd V10	puncture
13	BRITISH GP	Silverstone	22	Scuderia Italia SpA	3.5 BMS Dallara 191-Judd V10	3 laps behind
ret	GERMAN GP	Hockenheim	22	Scuderia Italia SpA	3.5 BMS Dallara 191-Judd V10	engine
ret	HUNGARIAN GP	Hungaroring	22	Scuderia Italia SpA	3.5 BMS Dallara 191-Judd V10	engine
ret	BELGIAN GP	Spa	22	Scuderia Italia SpA	3.5 BMS Dallara 191-Judd V10	engine
ret	ITALIAN GP	Monza	22	Scuderia Italia SpA	3.5 BMS Dallara 191-Judd V10	puncture
ret	PORTUGUESE GP	Estoril	22	Scuderia Italia SpA	3.5 BMS Dallara 191-Judd V10	gear linkage
8	SPANISH GP	Barcelona	22	Scuderia Italia SpA	3.5 BMS Dallara 191-Judd V10	1 lap behind
ret	JAPANESE GP	Suzuka	22	Scuderia Italia SpA	3.5 BMS Dallara 191-Judd V10	spun avoiding de Cesaris
12	AUSTRALIAN GP	Phoenix	22	Scuderia Italia SpA	3.5 BMS Dallara 191-Judd V10	rain shortened race

1992

	Race	Circuit	No	Entrant	Car/Engine	Comment
ret	SOUTH AFRICAN GP	Kyalami	22	Scuderia Italia SpA	3.5 BMS Dallara 192-Ferrari V12	final drive
8	MEXICAN GP	Mexico City	22	Scuderia Italia SpA	3.5 BMS Dallara 192-Ferrari V12	1 lap behind
8	BRAZILIAN GP	Interlagos	22	Scuderia Italia SpA	3.5 BMS Dallara 192-Ferrari V12	2 laps behind
ret	SPANISH GP	Barcelona	22	Scuderia Italia SpA	3.5 BMS Dallara 192-Ferrari V12	spun off
11/ret	SAN MARINO GP	Imola	22	Scuderia Italia SpA	3.5 BMS Dallara 192-Ferrari V12	engine cut out/3 laps behind
9	MONACO GP	Monte Carlo	22	Scuderia Italia SpA	3.5 BMS Dallara 192-Ferrari V12	2 laps behind
9	CANADIAN GP	Montreal	22	Scuderia Italia SpA	3.5 BMS Dallara 192-Ferrari V12	1 lap behind
9*	FRENCH GP	Magny Cours	22	Scuderia Italia SpA	3.5 BMS Dallara 192-Ferrari V12	*agg of 2 parts/2 laps behind
13	BRITISH GP	Silverstone	22	Scuderia Italia SpA	3.5 BMS Dallara 192-Ferrari V12	2 laps behind
10	GERMAN GP	Hockenheim	22	Scuderia Italia SpA	3.5 BMS Dallara 192-Ferrari V12	1 lap behind
dnq	HUNGARIAN GP	Hungaroring	22	Scuderia Italia SpA	3.5 BMS Dallara 192-Ferrari V12	
7	BELGIAN GP	Spa	22	Scuderia Italia SpA	3.5 BMS Dallara 192-Ferrari V12	1 lap behind
11/ret	ITALIAN GP	Monza	22	Scuderia Italia SpA	3.5 BMS Dallara 192-Ferrari V12	electrics-engine/6 laps behind
ret	PORTUGUESE GP	Estoril	22	Scuderia Italia SpA	3.5 BMS Dallara 192-Ferrari V12	accident damage
9	JAPANESE GP	Suzuka	22	Scuderia Italia SpA	3.5 BMS Dallara 192-Ferrari V12	1 lap behind
ret	AUSTRALIAN GP	Phoenix	22	Scuderia Italia SpA	3.5 BMS Dallara 192-Ferrari V12	gearbox

1993

	Race	Circuit	No	Entrant	Car/Engine	Comment
5	SOUTH AFRICAN GP	Kyalami	30	Sauber	3.5 Sauber C12-Ilmor V10	3 laps behind
ret	BRAZILIAN GP	Interlagos	30	Sauber	3.5 Sauber C12-Ilmor V10	electrics
ret	EUROPEAN GP	Donington	30	Sauber	3.5 Sauber C12-Ilmor V10	started in spare from pit lane/handling
4/ret	SAN MARINO GP	Imola	30	Sauber	3.5 Sauber C12-Ilmor V10	engine/2 laps behind
ret	SPANISH GP	Barcelona	30	Sauber	3.5 Sauber C12-Ilmor V10	engine
ret	MONACO GP	Monte Carlo	30	Sauber	3.5 Sauber C12-Ilmor V10	collision with Wendlinger
7	CANADIAN GP	Montreal	30	Sauber	3.5 Sauber C12-Ilmor V10	lost 2nd & 3rd gears/1 lap behind
ret	FRENCH GP	Magny Cours	30	Sauber	3.5 Sauber C12-Ilmor V10	gearbox
8	BRITISH GP	Silverstone	30	Sauber	3.5 Sauber C12-Ilmor V10	1 lap behind
ret	GERMAN GP	Hockenheim	30	Sauber	3.5 Sauber C12-Ilmor V10	stuck throttle-spun out
ret	HUNGARIAN GP	Hungaroring	30	Sauber	3.5 Sauber C12-Ilmor V10	engine
9	BELGIAN GP	Spa	30	Sauber	3.5 Sauber C12-Ilmor V10	understeer/1 lap behind
ret	ITALIAN GP	Monza	30	Sauber	3.5 Sauber C12-Ilmor V10	started-back of grid/accident on lap 1
7	PORTUGUESE GP	Estoril	30	Sauber	3.5 Sauber C12-Ilmor V10	stop & go pen/2 laps behind
8	JAPANESE GP	Suzuka	30	Sauber	3.5 Sauber C12-Ilmor V10	collision Brundle/1 lap behind
ret	AUSTRALIAN GP	Phoenix	30	Sauber	3.5 Sauber C12-Ilmor V10	accident-ran over kerb

GP Starts: 54   GP Wins: 0   Pole positions: 0   Fastest laps: 0   Points: 9

LENNEP, Gijs van (NL) b 16/3/1942

1971

	Race	Circuit	No	Entrant	Car/Engine	Comment
8	DUTCH GP	Zandvoort	30	Stichting Autoraces Nederland	3.0 Surtees TS7-Cosworth V8	5 laps behind
dns	US GP	Watkins Glen	19	Team Surtees	3.0 Surtees TS9-Cosworth V8	Posey drove car

1973

	Race	Circuit	No	Entrant	Car/Engine	Comment
6	DUTCH GP	Zandvoort	26	Frank Williams Racing Cars	3.0 Williams 1R-Cosworth V8	2 laps behind
9	AUSTRIAN GP	Österreichring	26	Frank Williams Racing Cars	3.0 Williams 1R-Cosworth V8	2 laps behind

ret	ITALIAN GP	Monza	26	Frank Williams Racing Cars	3.0 Williams 1R-Cosworth V8	*overheating*
	1974					
14	BELGIAN GP	Nivelles	21	Frank Williams Racing Cars	3.0 Williams FW02-Cosworth V8	*3 laps behind*
dnq	DUTCH GP	Zandvoort	21	Frank Williams Racing Cars	3.0 Williams FW01-Cosworth V8	
	1975					
10	DUTCH GP	Zandvoort	31	HB Bewaking Tean Ensign	3.0 Ensign N174-Cosworth V8	*pit stop-tyres/4 laps behind*
15	FRENCH GP	Paul Ricard	31	HB Bewaking Team Ensign	3.0 Ensign N175-Cosworth V8	*1 lap behind*
6	GERMAN GP	Nürburgring	19	HB Bewaking Team Ensign	3.0 Ensign N175-Cosworth V8	

GP Starts: 8   GP Wins: 0   Pole positions: 0   Fastest laps: 0   Points: 2

LEONI, Lamberto (I)   b 24/5/1953

	1977					
	Race	*Circuit*	*No*	*Entrant*	*Car/Engine*	*Comment*
dnq	ITALIAN GP	Monza	18	Team Surtees	3.0 Surtees TS19-Cosworth V8	
	1978					
ret	ARGENTINE GP	Buenos Aires	23	Team Tissot Ensign	3.0 Ensign N177-Cosworth V8	*engine*
dns	BRAZILIAN GP	Rio	23	Team Tissot Ensign	3.0 Ensign N177-Cosworth V8	*driveshaft on warm-up*
dnq	SOUTH AFRICAN GP	Kyalami	22	Team Tissot Ensign	3.0 Ensign N177-Cosworth V8	
dnq	US GP WEST	Long Beach	22	Team Tissot Ensign	3.0 Ensign N177-Cosworth V8	

GP Starts: 1   GP Wins: 0   Pole positions: 0   Fastest laps: 0   Points: 0

J J LEHTO

Involved in motor sport since taking up karting at the age of six, J J built up a tremendous record in the junior formulae, winning the Scandinavian FF1600 championship in 1986 before coming to England in 1987 to take the British and European FF2000 titles.

His career carefully nurtured and guided by the shrewd hands of Keke Rosberg, Lehto moved into Fomula 3 in 1988 with the Pacific Racing team that had brought him his FF2000 success. After a devastating start to the season he cruised to yet another championship, with a total of eight wins and only a late-season charge from Gary Brabham by way of serious competition.

Lehto and Pacific found things tougher in F3000, however, with the Finn finding only modest success before replacing the out-of-favour Bertrand Gachot at Onyx late in 1989. The following season was largely wasted as the once promising little team fell into the hands of Monteverdi and folded after the Hungarian GP. Then followed a two-year deal with Dallara, which began brightly with a podium finish at Imola in 1991 but eventually proved dispiriting as the team struggled to make the best of its Ferrari engines.

By this time Lehto's career had not produced the success widely expected but he joined the Sauber team for 1993, only for early promise to evaporate when internal politics divided the team into two camps. He now stands at the crossroads, a drive with Benetton offering a real chance of glory, but should he fail to take this chance, it is unlikely he will have a better one in the future.

LAMBERTO LEONI

A Fomula Italia champion, Leoni proved to be quick in Italian F3 without gaining the necessary solid results. Racing in Formula 2 in 1977, he unexpectedly won the Adriatic GP on aggregate in his Ferrari-engined Chevron after a dismal start to the season in a Ralt. After failing to qualify his rented works Surtees at Monza in '77, Leoni joined Ensign for the following year, but only made the grid once in four outings and swiftly departed the team.

From then on his career stuttered on with occasional outings in Formula 2, seemingly with the aim of keeping his licence intact, but he then tackled F3000 more seriously and enjoyed some success before being sidelined after a massive shunt at the Österreichring in 1986.

Forming his own FIRST F3000 team, Lamberto returned more determined than ever in 1987, enjoying a consistent final season before retiring to concentrate on management duties, initially guiding the fortunes of Marco Apicella.

GIJS van LENNEP

A much respected driver, Gijs always gave a good account of himself whenever his occasional Grand Prix opportunities arose, and scored a point for both Williams and Ensign when their cars were hardly at their most competitive.

Beginning in Formula Vee in 1965, van Lennep soon took up sports car racing to such effect that he was in the Porsche factory team in 1967, taking third place with Elford in the Circuit of Mugello. After concentrating Formula 3 in 1968, Gijs returned to sports cars and was awarded the Porsche Cup for the best private entrant in 1970.

The 1971 season found him much in demand. He won the Le Mans 24 Hours with Helmut Marko for Martini Porsche and the Paris 1000 Kmfor Gulf/Wyer, and took second place in the Targa Florio for Alfa Romeo, as well as hiring a Surtees to make his GP debut.

Adding F5000 to his already hectic schedule, van Lennep won the 1972 Rothmans title in a Surtees, and enjoyed continued sports car success with Martini Racing, winning the 1973 Targa Florio with Herbert Muller and the 1976 Le Mans with Jacky Ickx, after which he announced his retirement.

LESTON, Les (GB) b 16/12/1920

1956

	Race	Circuit	No	Entrant	Car/Engine	Comment
ret	ITALIAN GP	Monza	2	Connaught Engineering	2.5 Connaught-Alta B Type 4	torsion bar

1957

dnq	MONACO GP	Monte Carlo	16	Cooper Car Co	1.5 Cooper T43-Climax 4	
ret	BRITISH GP	Aintree	26	Owen Racing Organisation	2.5 BRM P25 4	engine

GP Starts: 2 GP Wins: 0 Pole positions: 0 Fastest laps: 0 Points: 0

'LEVEGH, Pierre' (Pierre Bouillon) (F) b 22/12/1905 – d 11/6/1955

1950

	Race	Circuit	No	Entrant	Car/Engine	Comment
7	BELGIAN GP	Spa	22	'Pierre Levegh'	4.5 Lago-Talbot T26C 6	2 laps behind
ret	FRENCH GP	Reims	22	'Pierre Levegh'	4.5 Lago-Talbot T26C 6	engine
ret	ITALIAN GP	Monza	56	'Pierre Levegh'	4.5 Lago-Talbot T26C 6	

1951

8	BELGIAN GP	Spa	26	'Pierre Levegh'	4.5 Lago-Talbot T26C 6	4 laps behind
9	GERMAN GP	Nürburgring	90	'Pierre Levegh'	4.5 Lago-Talbot T26C 6	2 laps behind
ret	ITALIAN GP	Monza	22	'Pierre Levegh'	4.5 Lago-Talbot T26C 6	engine

GP Starts: 6 GP Wins: 0 Pole positions: 0 Fastest laps: 0 Points: 0

LEWIS, Jack (GB) b 1/11/1936

1961

	Race	Circuit	No	Entrant	Car/Engine	Comment
9	BELGIAN GP	Spa	40	H & L Motors	1.5 Cooper T53-Climax 4	1 lap behind
ret	FRENCH GP	Reims	44	H & L Motors	1.5 Cooper T53-Climax 4	overheating
ret	BRITISH GP	Aintree	46	H & L Motors	1.5 Cooper T53-Climax 4	steering
9	GERMAN GP	Nürburgring	28	H & L Motors	1.5 Cooper T53-Climax 4	
4	ITALIAN GP	Monza	60	H & L Motors	1.5 Cooper T53-Climax 4	

1962

8	DUTCH GP	Zandvoort	21	Ecurie Galloise	1.5 Cooper T53-Climax 4	pit stop/10 laps behind
dnq	MONACO GP	Monte Carlo	24	Ecurie Galloise	1.5 BRM P48/57 V8	despite being faster than 3 starters
ret	FRENCH GP	Rouen	42	Ecurie Galloise	1.5 Cooper T53-Climax 4	brakes-hit Graham Hill
10	BRITISH GP	Aintree	42	Ecurie Galloise	1.5 Cooper T53-Climax 4	3 laps behind
ret	GERMAN GP	Nürburgring	20	Ecurie Galloise	1.5 Cooper T53-Climax 4	front shock absober

GP Starts: 9 GP Wins: 0 Pole positions: 0 Fastest laps: 0 Points: 3

LEWIS-EVANS, Stuart (GB) b 20/4/1930 – d 25/10/1958

1957

	Race	Circuit	No	Entrant	Car/Engine	Comment
4	MONACO GP	Monte Carlo	10	Connaught Engineering	2.5 Connaught-Alta B Type 4	3 laps behind
ret	FRENCH GP	Rouen	18	Vandervell Products Ltd	2.5 Vanwall 4	steering
7	BRITISH GP	Aintree	22	Vandervell Products Ltd	2.5 Vanwall 4	pit stop-throttle/8 laps behind
ret	GERMAN GP	Nürburgring	12	Vandervell Products Ltd	2.5 Vanwall 4	gearbox
5	PESCARA GP	Pescara	30	Vandervell Products Ltd	2.5 Vanwall 4	pit stop-tyres/1 lap behind
ret	ITALIAN GP	Monza	20	Vandervall Products Ltd	2.5 Vanwall 4	overheating/Pole

1958

ret	MONACO GP	Monte Carlo	32	Vandervell Products Ltd	2.5 Vanwall 4	overheating/steering
ret	DUTCH GP	Zandvoort	3	Vandervell Products Ltd	2.5 Vanwall 4	engine/Pole
3	BELGIAN GP	Spa	6	Vandervell Products Ltd	2.5 Vanwall 4	
ret*	FRENCH GP	Reims	12	Vandervell Products Ltd	2.5 Vanwall 4	engine/*Brooks took over car
4	BRITISH GP	Silverstone	9	Vandervell Products Ltd	2.5 Vanwall 4	
3	PORTUGESE GP	Oporto	6	Vandervell Products Ltd	2.5 Vanwall 4	1 lap behind
ret	ITALIAN GP	Monza	30	Vandervell Products Ltd	2.5 Vanwall 4	overheating
ret	MOROCCAN GP	Casablanca	12	Vandervell Products Ltd	2.5 Vanwall 4	engine-crashed-fatal burns

GP Starts: 14 GP Wins: 0 Pole positions: 2 Fastest laps: 0 Points: 16

LIGIER, Guy (F) b 12/7/1930

1966

	Race	Circuit	No	Entrant	Car/Engine	Comment
nc	MONACO GP	Monte Carlo	21	Guy Ligier	3.0 Cooper T81-Maserati V12	pit stop/25 laps behind
nc	BELGIAN GP	Spa	22	Guy Ligier	3.0 Cooper T81-Maserati V12	4 laps behind
nc	FRENCH GP	Reims	42	Guy Ligier	3.0 Cooper T81-Maserati V12	6 laps behind
10	BRITISH GP	Brands Hatch	19	Guy Ligier	3.0 Cooper T81-Maserati V12	5 laps behind
9	DUTCH GP	Zandvoort	36	Guy Ligier	3.0 Cooper T81-Maserati V12	6 laps behind
dns	GERMAN GP	Nürburgring	18	Guy Ligier	3.0 Cooper T81-Maserati V12	accident in practice-broken knee

1967

10	BELGIAN GP	Spa	32	Guy Ligier	3.0 Cooper T81-Maserati V12	3 laps behind
7	FRENCH GP	Le Mans	16	Guy Ligier	3.0 Cooper T81-Maserati V12	pit stop/12 laps behind
10	BRITISH GP	Silverstone	18	Guy Ligier	3.0 Brabham BT20-Repco V8	4 laps behind
6	GERMAN GP	Nürburgring	15	Guy Ligier	3.0 Brabham BT20-Repco V8	1 lap behind
ret	ITALIAN GP	Monza	12	Guy Ligier	3.0 Brabham BT20-Repco V8	engine
ret	US GP	Watkins Glen	19	Guy Ligier	3.0 Brabham BT20-Repco V8	camshaft
11	MEXICAN GP	Mexico City	19	Guy Ligier	3.0 Brabham BT20-Repco V8	4 laps behind

GP Starts: 12 GP Wins: 0 Pole positions: 2 Fastest laps: 0 Points: 1

LES LESTON

A star of the exciting 500 cc Formula 3 racing of the early fifties, Leston scored an early British win on the Continent in 1952, winning the Luxembourg GP. A runner-up in 1952 and '53, he finally claimed the crown in 1954 at the wheel of a works Cooper before concentrating on sports car racing, enjoying a successful 1955 season in Peter Bell's Connaught.

Les mainly raced John Willment's Cooper sports in 1956, but handled a Connaught in the Italian GP and took third place in the Richmond Trophy with the same car. In 1957 he raced a Formula 2 Cooper in national events, drove for BRM in the British GP and took sixth place in the Nürburgring 1000 Km for Aston Martin, but after escaping with a shaking from a massive crash at Caen in 1958 when his F2 Lotus seized, Les concentrated on his expanding racewear business. He did not desert the circuits, though, having great fun in the early sixties in his red Lotus Elite with the famous 'DAD 10' plate.

'PIERRE LEVEGH'

Ultimately a tragic figure, 'Levegh' was given the name of his uncle, a racer in the early part of the century. From before the war, he became obsessed with the Le Mans 24-hour race, waiting patiently for an opportunity to take part in this classic and finally achieving his ambition as relief driver in the Talbot team in 1938. After the war he raced a Delage, taking second at Pau in 1947 before acquiring a Talbot in 1949, which he raced in Grands Prix in 1950 and '51.

He finished fourth at Le Mans in a works Talbot in 1951, but was dissatisfied with the car's performance, and resolved to return the following year in his own car, which was specially prepared at huge expense by 'Levegh' himself. His investment was very nearly rewarded when he drove the car single-handedly for more than 22 hours, only to lose a massive lead when he missed a gearchange and damaged the engine.

His dream of victory seemed over, but in 1955 Neubauer, remembering his exploits, offered him a drive in the works Mercedes. By some strange premonition, 'Levegh' had voiced his unease at the narrowness of the straight in front of the pits, and it was his misfortune to be involved in a collision at this point that catapulted his car into the crowd, killing the Frenchman and 80 others in the worst disaster in motor racing history.

JACK LEWIS

Now an almost forgotten figure in motor racing, Jack Lewis showed plenty of natural talent but perhaps not the necessary resilience to overcome the setbacks that are a part of any sport.

In 1958 he purchased the ex-Bueb F3 Cooper and won three races in his first season, which encouraged him to move into Formula 2 in 1959 with a Cooper. Despite setting the fastest practice time for the Pau GP (ahead of Brabham and Trintignant) and taking third in the Aintree 200, Lewis was frustrated by organisers' general reluctance to accept his entry, and returned to the tracks in 1960 well prepared to prove himself a serious competitor. He did just that, winning the Autocar F2 British championship, as well as races at Chimay and Montlhéry.

For 1961 he set out on the Grand Prix trail with a Cooper, setting 12th-fastest practice time on his debut at Spa, and fighting off Tony Brooks' late challenge to take fourth place in the Italian GP. Given 'grade A driver' status, Lewis then bought a BRM 48/57 for 1962, which he took to third in the Pau GP, but he failed to qualify at Monaco and was so dissatisfied with the car that it was returned to the factory.

Back in his Cooper, Lewis seemed to lose heart, feeling his reputation had suffered after the BRM episode, and it was a despondent Welshman who slipped into retirement at the age of just 27.

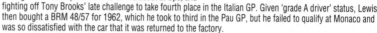

STUART LEWIS-EVANS

With his father 'Pop' a noted Formula 3 racer in his own right, it was no surprise when Stuart followed in his footsteps, and from 1951 he was one of the formula's leading exponents. He spent five seasons in this cut-and-thrust environment before Connaught gave him a chance to race at the end of 1956.

Encouraging early-season performances in the Connaught, including victory the Richmond Trophy at Goodwood and fourth place in the Monaco Grand Prix, then took Stuart into the Vanwall team for the rest of 1957. Some of his drives were brilliant, for example at Naples, where he led Hawthorn, and Reims, where he finished third. In World Championship races he displayed a rare blend of speed and finesse, but had only a fifth at Pescara to show for his efforts.

Although a slight, frail figure, Lewis-Evans embarked on a daunting racing programme in 1958, competing successfully in Formula 2 for BRP and in sports cars for Aston Martin, in addition to driving for Vanwall in Grands Prix. He played a crucial part in gaining the constructors' championship for the team but, in what should have been a glorious finale to the year in Morocco, Lewis-Evans' car crashed in flames after its transmission had locked. The poor driver was extricated from the wreckage suffering from terrible burns and, despite being flown back to England for expert attention, he succumbed some six days later.

GUY LIGIER

This uncompromising character came late onto the motor racing scene after a distinguished rugby career. A close friend and business partner of Jo Schlesser, he began racing in 1963 with a Porsche Carrera, then moving into endurance racing with a Porsche 904GT. Ligier competed in Formula 2 in 1964 and gained some minor success in a Brabham BT10, with fifth in the Pergusa GP and sixth places at both Albi and Montlhéry. In 1965 he raced a Ford GT, winning the sports and GT race at Albi, but achieving little of note elsewhere.

Taking delivery of a Cooper-Maserati, he joined the Grand Prix circus in 1966, but his season ended early, Ligier sustaining a smashed knee-cap after crashing in practice for the German GP. Undaunted, he returned in 1967, eventually replacing the Cooper with a more competitive Brabham, scoring his only championship point at the Nürburgring. He did record a major success in sports cars that year, however, winning the Reims 12 Hours in a Ford GT40 with Schlesser.

In 1968 Ligier returned to Formula 2 but, disillusioned after Schlesser's death at Rouen, he quit in mid-season, only to return the following year with the ex-Alan Mann Escort, before building a prototype sports car which he successfully debuted in 1970. This sports car programme eventually led to a Formula 1 machine being built for 1976 and, though the team have often failed to make the most of their resouces, the light blue cars have been been a constant presence on the grid ever since, even after Ligier sold most of his shareholding in 1992-93.

LIPPI, Roberto (I) b 17/10/1926

1961

	Race	Circuit	No	Entrant	Car/Engine	Comment
ret	ITALIAN GP	Monza	52	Scuderia Settecolli	1.5 de Tomaso 002-Osca 4	engine

1962

| dnq | ITALIAN GP | Monza | 50 | Scuderia Settecolli | 1.5 de Tomaso 002-Osca 4 | |

1963

| dnq | ITALIAN GP | Monza | 44 | Scuderia Settecolli | 1.5 de Tomaso 002-Ferrari V6 | |

GP Starts: 1   GP Wins: 0   Pole positions: 0   Fastest laps: 0   Points: 0

LOF, Andre van der (NL) b 23/8/1919

1952

	Race	Circuit	No	Entrant	Car/Engine	Comment
nc	DUTCH GP	Zandvoort	30	HW Motors Ltd	2.0 HWM-Alta 4	pit stop/20 laps behind

GP Starts: 1   GP Wins: 0   Pole positions: 0   Fastest laps: 0   Points: 0

LOMBARDI, Lella (I) b 26/3/1943 – d Mar 1992

1974

	Race	Circuit	No	Entrant	Car/Engine	Comment
dnq	BRITISH GP	Brands Hatch	208	Allied Polymer Group	3.0 Brabham BT42-Cosworth V8	

1975

ret	SOUTH AFRICAN GP	Kyalami	10	March Engineering	3.0 March 741-Cosworth V8	engine
6*	SPANISH GP	Montjuich Park	10	Lavazza March	3.0 March 751-Cosworth V8	*half points shortened race/-1 lap
dnq	MONACO GO	Monte Carlo	10	Lavazza March	3.0 March 751-Cosworth V8	
ret	BELGIAN GP	Zolder	10	Lavazza March	3.0 March 751-Cosworth V8	engine
ret	SWEDISH GP	Anderstorp	10	Lavazza March	3.0 March 751-Cosworth V8	fuel metering unit
14	DUTCH GP	Zandvoort	10	Lavazza March	3.0 March 751-Cosworth V8	pit stop-tyres/5 laps behind
18	FRENCH GP	Paul Ricard	10	Lavazza March	3.0 March 751-Cosworth V8	pit stop-handling/4 laps behind
ret	BRITISH GP	Silverstone	10	Lavazza March	3.0 March 751-Cosworth V8	ignition
7	GERMAN GP	Nürburgring	10	Lavazza March	3.0 March 751-Cosworth V8	
17	AUSTRIAN GP	Österreichring	10	Lavazza March	3.0 March 751-Cosworth V8	3 laps behind
ret	ITALIAN GP	Monza	10	Lavazza March	3.0 March 751-Cosworth V8	brake failure-crashed
dns	US GP	Watkins Glen	20	Frank Williams Racing Cars	3.0 Williams FW04-Cosworth V8	ignition in warm up

1976

14	BRAZILIAN GP	Interlagos	10	Lavazza March	3.0 March 761-Cosworth V8	pit stop-engine/4 laps behind
dnq	BRITISH GP	Brands Hatch	33	RAM Racing with Lavazza	3.0 Brabham BT44B-Cosworth V8	
dns	GERMAN GP	Nürburgring	33	RAM Racing with Lavazza	3.0 Brabham BT44B-Cosworth V8	legal wrangle-car impounded by police
12	AUSTRIAN GP	Österreichring	33	RAM Racing with Lavazza	3.0 Brabham BT44B-Cosworth V8	4 laps behind

GP Starts: 12   GP Wins: 0   Pole positions: 0   Fastest laps: 0   Points: 0.5

LOOF, Ernst (D) b 4/7/1907 – d 3/3/1956

1953

	Race	Circuit	No	Entrant	Car/Engine	Comment
ret	GERMAN GP	Nürburgring	30	Ernst Loof	2.0 Veritas Meteor 6	fuel pump

GP Starts: 1   GP Wins: 0   Pole positions: 0   Fastest laps: 0   Points: 0

LOUVEAU, Henri (F) b 25/1/1910

1950

	Race	Circuit	No	Entrant	Car/Engine	Comment
ret	ITALIAN GP	Monza	64	Ecurie Louis Rosier	4.5 Lago-Talbot T26C-GS 6	

1951

| ret | SWISS GP | Bremgarten | 10 | Ecurie Louis Rosier | 4.5 Lago-Talbot T26C 6 | hit telgraph pole/broken leg |

GP Starts: 2   GP Wins: 0   Pole positions: 0   Fastest laps: 0   Points: 0

LOVE, John (RSR) b 7/12/1924

1962

	Race	Circuit	No	Entrant	Car/Engine	Comment
8	SOUTH AFRICAN GP	East London	18	John Love	1.5 Cooper T55-Climax 4	4 laps behind

1963

| 9 | SOUTH AFRICAN GP | East London | 19 | John Love | 1.5 Cooper T55-Climax 4 | 5 laps behind |

1964

| dnq | ITALIAN GP | Monza | 24 | Cooper Car Co | 1.5 Cooper T73-Climax V8 | engine seized in practice |

1965

| ret | SOUTH AFRICAN GP | East London | 17 | John Love | 1.5 Cooper T55-Climax 4 | driveshaft |

1967

| 2 | SOUTH AFRICAN GP | Kyalami | 17 | John Love | 2.7 Cooper T75-Climax 4 | pit stop-fuel when in lead |

	1968					
9	SOUTH AFRICAN GP	Kyalami	17	Team Gunston	3.0 Brabham BT20-Repco V8	*5 laps behind*
	1969					
ret	SOUTH AFRICAN GP	Kyalami	16	Team Gunston	3.0 Lotus 49-Cosworth V8	*ignition*
	1970					
8	SOUTH AFRICAN GP	Kyalami	23	Team Gunston	3.0 Lotus 49-Cosworth V8	*2 laps behind*
	1971					
ret	SOUTH AFRICAN GP	Kyalami	24	Team Peco/Gunston	3.0 March 701-Cosworth V8	*differential*
	1972					
16/ret	SOUTH AFRICAN GP	Kyalami	27	Team Gunston	3.0 Surtees TS9-Cosworth V8	*puncture-spun off/6 laps behind*

GP Starts: 9   GP Wins: 0   Pole positions: 0   Fastest laps: 0   Points: 6

LELLA LOMBARDI

In 1975 Lella became the first and thus far the only woman to have finished in the top six in a Grand Prix (albeit one which was shortened and thus only counted for half-points).

Always harbouring an ambition to go racing, she drove in Formula Monza and F3 with Lotus and Brabham cars, before winning the Italian Ford Mexico championship in 1973.

In 1974 she was signed to race the Shellsport-Luxembourg Lola in F5000 and silenced her critics by finishing fourth in the final standings. This led to a full F1 season with March in 1975, with the result in Spain the high point, although she did extremely well to finish seventh in the German GP. Her hopes of continuing with March in 1976 were dashed when she lost her backing after the first race of the season, and her brief flirtation with the RAM team was predictably fruitless.

Although squeezed out of Formula 1, Lella continued her career, mainly in sports cars, through into the early eighties. She was to enjoy some excellent results in the Osella prototype with Giorgio Francia, the pair winning the Ignazio Giunti Trophy at Vallelunga in 1979, and the Ore di Mugello in 1981, a year which also saw them finish second in the Monza 1000 Km.

It was with great sadness that the motor racing world learned of her tragically early death, at the age of 48, from cancer in March 1992.

ERNST LOOF

Loof was eight times a German motor cycle champion between 1930 and 1938 and worked for BMW, building the sports car which von Hanstein used to win the 1000 Miles of Brescia before the war. However, it is as designer and engineer of the splendid Veritas machines of the late forties and early fifties that he is best remembered. He seldom took the wheel, but did appear in the 1953 German GP, the marque's last season in top-flight competition.

Loof rallied a BMW in 1954, but by then he had begun to develop cancer, and he died after a long illness in 1956.

JOHN LOVE

John Love was well known in Europe, having ventured to England in 1961 to race Ken Tyrrell's Formula Junior Cooper along with Tony Maggs. Although in his late thirties, Love was back for more in 1962, driving the works Mini-Cooper with spectacular success as well as competing in Formula Junior, but his season was cut short by an accident at Albi in which he sustained a badly broken arm. Business interests kept him at home from then onwards, apart from an abortive trip to the 1964 Italian GP, when his works Cooper was ill prepared.

The first of Love's six South African championships came in 1964, and it was a tally that was only halted by a determined rival in Dave Charlton, with whom he had some ding-dong battles over the years. Success generally eluded John in the local World Championship Grands Prix, though, with the exception of the 1967 event, when only a late pit stop for fuel prevented him taking what would have been a fairy-tale victory.

In addition to his single-seater exploits in South Africa, Love also regularly raced sports cars with distinction in the Springbok series of the late sixties and early seventies.

LOVELY, Pete (USA) b 11/4/1926

1959

	Race	Circuit	No	Entrant	Car/Engine	Comment
dnq	MONACO GP	Monte Carlo	42	Team Lotus	2.5 Lotus 16-Climax 4	

1960

11	US GP	Riverside	25	Fred Armbruster	2.4 Cooper T45-Ferrari 4	6 laps behind

1969

7	CANADIAN GP	Mosport Park	25	Pete Lovely Volkswagen Inc	3.0 Lotus 49B-Cosworth V8	9 laps behind
ret	US GP	Watkins Glen	21	Pete Lovely Volkswagen Inc	3.0 Lotus 49B-Cosworth V8	driveshaft
9	MEXICAN GP	Mexico City	21	Pete Lovely Volkswagen Inc	3.0 Lotus 49B-Cosworth V8	3 laps behind

1970

dnq	DUTCH GP	Zandvoort	31	Pete Lovely Volkswagen Inc	3.0 Lotus 49B-Cosworth V8	
dns	FRENCH GP	Clermont Ferrand	35	Pete Lovely Volkswagen Inc	3.0 Lotus 49B-Cosworth V8	
10	BRITISH GP	Brands Hatch	29	Pete Lovely Volkswagen Inc	3.0 Lotus 49B-Cosworth V8	pit stop-tyres/11 laps behind
dnq	US GP	Watkins Glen	28	Pete Lovely Volkswagen Inc	3.0 Lotus 49B-Cosworth V8	

1971

nc	CANADIAN GP	Mosport Park	35	Pete Lovely Volkswagen Inc	3.0 Lotus 49/69-Cosworth V8	pit stop-fuel/9 laps behind
21	US GP	Watkins Glen	30	Pete Lovely Volkswagen Inc	3.0 Lotus 49/69-Cosworth V8	pit stop-fuel/10 laps behind

GP Starts: 7   GP Wins: 0   Pole positions: 0   Fastest laps: 0   Points: 0

LOYER, Roger (F) b 5/8/1907 – d 24/3/1988

1954

	Race	Circuit	No	Entrant	Car/Engine	Comment
ret	ARGENTINE GP	Buenos Aires	22	Equipe Gordini	2.5 Gordini Type 16 6	lack of oil

GP Starts: 1   GP Wins: 0   Pole positions: 0   Fastest laps: 0   Points: 0

LUCAS, Jean (F) b 25/4/1917

1955

	Race	Circuit	No	Entrant	Car/Engine	Comment
ret	ITALIAN GP	Monza	24	Equipe Gordini	2.5 Gordini Type 32 8	subbed for Manzon/engine
ret	"	"	22	Equipe Gordini	2.5 Gordini Type 16 6	practice only

GP Starts: 1   GP Wins: 0   Pole positions: 0   Fastest laps: 0   Points: 0

LUNGER, Brett (USA) b 14/11/1945

1975

	Race	Circuit	No	Entrant	Car/Engine	Comment
13	AUSTRIAN GP	Österreichring	25	Hesketh Racing	3.0 Hesketh 308-Cosworth V8	1 lap behind
10	ITALIAN GP	Monza	25	Hesketh Racing	3.0 Hesketh 308-Cosworth V8	2 laps behind
ret	US GP	Watkins Glen	25	Hesketh Racing	3.0 Hesketh 308-Cosworth V8	missed gearchange-crashed

1976

11	SOUTH AFRICAN GP	Kyalami	18	Team Surtees	3.0 Surtees TS19-Cosworth V8	1 lap behind
dnq	US GP WEST	Long Beach	18	Team Surtees	3.0 Surtees TS19-Cosworth V8	
dnq	SPANISH GP	Jarama	18	Team Surtees	3.0 Surtees TS19-Cosworth V8	
ret	BELGIAN GP	Zolder	18	Team Surtees	3.0 Surtees TS19-Cosworth V8	electrics
15	SWEDISH GP	Anderstorp	18	Team Surtees	3.0 Surtees TS19-Cosworth V8	2 laps behind
16	FRENCH GP	Paul Ricard	18	Team Surtees	3.0 Surtees TS19-Cosworth V8	1 lap behind
ret	BRITISH GP	Brands Hatch	18	Team Surtees	3.0 Surtees TS19-Cosworth V8	gearbox
ret/dns	GERMAN GP	Nürburgring	18	Team Surtees	3.0 Surtees TS19-Cosworth V8	in Lauda's accident/did not restart
10/ret	AUSTRIAN GP	Österreichring	18	Team Surtees	3.0 Surtees TS19-Cosworth V8	brake failure-crashed/3 laps behind
14	ITALIAN GP	Monza	18	Team Surtees	3.0 Surtees TS19-Cosworth V8	pit stop-thought race stopped/-2 laps
15	CANADIAN GP	Mosport Park	18	Team Surtees	3.0 Surtees TS19-Cosworth V8	2 laps behind
11	US GP EAST	Watkins Glen	18	Team Surtees	3.0 Surtees TS19-Cosworth V8	2 laps behind

1977

14	SOUTH AFRICAN GP	Kyalami	30	Chesterfield Racing	3.0 March 761-Cosworth V8	2 laps behind
ret	US GP WEST	Long Beach	30	Chesterfield Racing	3.0 March 761-Cosworth V8	collision with Reutemann
10	SPANISH GP	Jarama	30	Chesterfield Racing	3.0 March 761-Cosworth V8	3 laps behind
dns	BELGIAN GP	Zolder	30	Chesterfield Racing	3.0 McLaren M23-Cosworth V8	car not ready after engine change
11	SWEDISH GP	Anderstorp	30	Chesterfield Racing	3.0 McLaren M23-Cosworth V8	1 lap behind
dnq	FRENCH GP	Dijon	30	Chesterfield Racing	3.0 McLaren M23-Cosworth V8	
13	BRITISH GP	Silverstone	30	Chesterfield Racing	3.0 McLaren M23-Cosworth V8	pit stop/4 laps behind
ret	GERMAN GP	Hockenheim	30	Chesterfield Racing	3.0 McLaren M23-Cosworth V8	damage from startline accident
10	AUSTRIAN GP	Österreichring	30	Chesterfield Racing	3.0 McLaren M23-Cosworth V8	1 lap behind
9	DUTCH GP	Zandvoort	30	Chesterfield Racing	3.0 McLaren M23-Cosworth V8	2 laps behind
ret	ITALIAN GP	Monza	30	Chesterfield Racing	3.0 McLaren M23-Cosworth V8	engine
10	US GP EAST	Watkins Glen	30	Chesterfield Racing	3.0 McLaren M23-Cosworth V8	2 laps behind
11/ret	CANADIAN GP	Mosport Park	30	Chesterfield Racing	3.0 McLaren M23-Cosworth V8	engine/4 laps behind

1978

13	ARGENTINE GP	Buenos Aires	30	Liggett Group/B & S Fabrications	3.0 McLaren M23-Cosworth V8	1 lap behind
ret	BRAZILIAN GP	Rio	30	Liggett Group/B & S Fabrications	3.0 McLaren M23-Cosworth V8	overheating
11	SOUTH AFRICAN GP	Kyalami	30	Liggett Group/B & S Fabrications	3.0 McLaren M23-Cosworth V8	2 laps behind
dnq	US GP WEST	Long Beach	30	Liggett Group/B & S Fabrications	3.0 McLaren M23-Cosworth V8	
dnpq	MONACO GP	Monte Carlo	30	Liggett Group/B & S Fabrications	3.0 McLaren M26-Cosworth V8	

			No	Entrant	Car/Engine	Comment
7	BELGIAN GP	Zolder	30	Liggett Group/B & S Fabrications	3.0 McLaren M26-Cosworth V8	1 lap behind
dnq	SPANISH GP	Jarama	30	Liggett Group/B & S Fabrications	3.0 McLaren M26-Cosworth V8	
dnq	"	"	30	Liggett Group/B & S Fabrications	3.0 McLaren M23-Cosworth V8	
dnq	SWEDISH GP	Anderstorp	30	Liggett Group/B & S Fabrications	3.0 McLaren M26-Cosworth V8	
dnq	"	"	30	Liggett Group/B & S Fabrications	3.0 McLaren M23-Cosworth V8	
ret	FRENCH GP	Paul Ricard	30	Liggett Group/B & S Fabrications	3.0 McLaren M26-Cosworth V8	engine
dns	"	"	30	Liggett Group/B & S Fabrications	3.0 McLaren M23-Cosworth V8	practice only
8	BRITISH GP	Brands Hatch	30	Liggett Group/B & S Fabrications	3.0 McLaren M26-Cosworth V8	1 lap behind
dnpq	GERMAN GP	Hockenheim	30	Liggett Group/B & S Fabrications	3.0 McLaren M26-Cosworth V8	
8	AUSTRIAN GP	Österreichring	30	Liggett Group/B & S Fabrications	3.0 McLaren M26-Cosworth V8	pit stop-tyres/2 laps behind
ret	DUTCH GP	Zandvoort	30	Liggett Group/B & S Fabrications	3.0 McLaren M26-Cosworth V8	engine
ret/dns	ITALIAN GP	Monza	30	Liggett Group/B & S Fabrications	3.0 McLaren M26-Cosworth V8	startline accident/did not restart
13	US G P EAST	Watkins Glen	23	Team Tissot Ensign	3.0 Ensign N177-Cosworth V8	1 lap behind

GP Starts: 32 (34)   GP Wins: 0   Pole positions: 0   Fastest laps: 0   Points: 0

McALPINE, Ken (GB) b 21/9/1920

1952

	Race	Circuit	No	Entrant	Car/Engine	Comment
16	BRITISH GP	Silverstone	3	Connaught Engineering	2.0 Connaught-Lea Francis A Type 4	6 laps behind
ret	ITALIAN GP	Monza	28	Connaught Engineering	2.0 Connaught-Lea Francis A Type 4	rear suspension
	1953					
ret	DUTCH GP	Zandvoort	28	Connaught Engineering	2.0 Connaught-Lea Francis A Type 4	engine
ret	BRITISH GP	Silverstone	11	Connaught Engineering	2.0 Connaught-Lea Francis A Type 4	split hose on startline
13	GERMAN GP	Nürburgring	16	Connaught Engineering	2.0 Connaught-Lea Francis A Type 4	2 laps behind
nc	ITALIAN GP	Monza	24	Connaught Engineering	2.0 Connaught-Lea Francis A Type 4	pit stops/24 laps behind
	1955					
ret	BRITISH GP	Aintree	32	Connaught Engineering	2.5 Connaught-Alta B Type 4	oil pressure

GP Starts: 7   GP Wins: 0   Pole positions: 0   Fastest laps: 0   Points: 0

PETE LOVELY

An SCCA sports car champion of 1955, Lovely came to Europe in the late fifties to race briefly for Lotus. With Ireland, he took a class win in the 1958 Reims 12 Hours, but a hoped-for Grand Prix debut at Monaco in 1959 came to nought when he failed to qualify, Pete returning disenchanted to the States. He did make a Grand Prix start the following season with an elderly Cooper, however.

Throughout the sixties his racing took a back seat to his thriving VW garage business in Seattle but, itching to get back behind the wheel, he then bought a Lotus 49, competing at a sedate pace in World Championship Grands Prix between 1969 and 1971.

JEAN LUCAS

Turning to racing after beginning his career in rallies, Jean recorded his best results behind the wheel of sports cars, winning at Spa in 1949 and Montlhéry the following year in Luigi Chinetti's Ferrari. In 1953 Lucas joined Gordini as team manager and occasional driver, though he was still to be seen racing his own Ferrari under the Los Amigos banner in North African events such as those held at Agadir and Marrakesh which were popular at the time. It was only when urgent business matters called Manzon away from the Monza circuit that Lucas stood in to make his solitary World Championship appearance.

In 1956 he took an old Ferrari 625 to fifth place in the Caen GP, and in 1957 he finished second in the F2 Coupe de Vitesse at Reims in Alan Brown's Cooper. He also took third place in his Los Amigos Jaguar D-Type at Le Mans that year, but driving du Puy's Maserati 250F in the end-of-season Moroccan GP he overturned the car and was badly injured. Realising that he would not be able to race again to his fullest abilities, he threw himself into administrative roles within the sport as well as co-founding the magazine *Sport-Auto* with Gérard Crombac in 1962, moving on to other publishing projects when his interest in motor sport had waned.

BRETT LUNGER

An heir to the DuPont family, Lunger began racing in 1965 with a Corvette, later graduating to Can-Am with a Caldwell-Chevrolet, but by his own admission he did not really know how to race properly, and it was more for fun than anything else.

His career then went on hold while he went to Vietnam with the Marines, only resuming in 1971 when he took part in the L & M F5000 series, finishing third in the championship. For 1972 Brett came to Europe to race in Formula 2 as well with a works-supported March 722, but could not match his Stateside success.

Lunger stayed in F5000 on both sides of the Atlantic until 1975, when he finally got a taste of Grand Prix racing with Hesketh, contesting three races in a second car alongside James Hunt. During the next three seasons the personable American, armed with a sizeable budget, plugged away without any real signs of making a breakthrough, even though he had decent cars at his disposal, including McLaren M23 and M26 machines run by B & S Fabrications.

Eventually falling out with his team at the end of 1978, Brett enjoyed a one-off ride with Ensign – his last Grand Prix appearance – after which he briefly drove in sports car events.

KEN McALPINE

A former hill-climber and speed-triallist, the wealthy McAlpine, a member of the civil engineering family, became a major benefactor of the Connaught team, racing their Formula 2 A-Type car in selected Grands Prix between 1952 and 1955. His best results were achieved in the less rarefied atmosphere of Libre events, Ken taking third place in the 1954 Glover Trophy. He enjoyed some success with the team's sports car during this period and finished second in the British Empire Trophy in 1955, his final racing season before retiring to concentrate on his business interests.

MacDOWEL, Mike (GB) b 13/9/1932

1957

	Race	Circuit	No	Entrant	Car/Engine	Comment
7*	FRENCH GP	Rouen	28	Cooper Car Co	1.5 Cooper T43-Climax 4	* Brabham took over/9 laps behind

GP Starts: 1   GP Wins: 0   Pole positions: 0   Fastest laps: 0   Points: 0

MACKAY-FRASER, Herbert (USA) b 23/6/1937 – d 14/7/1957

1957

	Race	Circuit	No	Entrant	Car/Engine	Comment
ret	FRENCH GP	Rouen	28	Owen Racing Organisation	2.5 BRM P25 4	overheating

GP Starts: 1   GP Wins: 0   Pole positions: 0   Fastest laps: 0   Points: 0

MACKLIN, Lance (GB) b 2/9/1919

1952

	Race	Circuit	No	Entrant	Car/Engine	Comment
ret	SWISS GP	Bremgarten	20	HW Motors Ltd	2.0 HWM-Alta 4	withdrawn/suspension problems
11	BELGIAN GP	Spa	24	HW Motors Ltd	2.0 HWM-Alta 4	4 laps behind
9	FRENCH GP	Rouen	20	HW Motors Ltd	2.0 HWM-Alta 4	6 laps behind
16	BRITISH GP	Silverstone	31	HW Motors Ltd	2.0 HWM-Alta 4	6 laps behind
8	DUTCH GP	Zandvoort	26	HW Motors Ltd	2.0 HWM-Alta 4	6 laps behind
dnq	ITALIAN GP	Monza	52	HW Motors Ltd	2.0 HWM-Alta 4	

1953

	Race	Circuit	No	Entrant	Car/Engine	Comment
ret	DUTCH GP	Zandvoort	38	HW Motors Ltd	2.0 HWM-Alta 4	throttle
ret	BELGIAN GP	Spa	22	HW Motors Ltd	2.0 HWM-Alta 4	engine
ret	FRENCH GP	Reims	26	HW Motors Ltd	2.0 HWM-Alta 4	clutch
ret	BRITISH GP	Silverstone	1	HW Motors Ltd	2.0 HWM-Alta 4	clutch housing
ret	SWISS GP	Bremgarten	16	HW Motors Ltd	2.0 HWM-Alta 4	engine
ret	ITALIAN GP	Monza	14	HW Motors Ltd	2.0 HWM-Alta 4	engine

1954

	Race	Circuit	No	Entrant	Car/Engine	Comment
ret	FRENCH GP	Reims	32	HW Motors Ltd	2.0 HWM-Alta 4	engine

1955

	Race	Circuit	No	Entrant	Car/Engine	Comment
dnq	MONACO GP	Monte Carlo	22	Stirling Moss Ltd	2.5 Maserati 250F 6	
8	BRITISH GP	Aintree	46	Stirling Moss Ltd	2.5 Maserati 250F 6	11 laps behind

GP Starts: 13   GP Wins: 0   Pole positions: 0   Fastest laps: 0   Points: 0

MIKE MacDOWEL

MacDowel was a keen amateur racer who made a name for himself in the 1172 cc Lotus sports car in 1955 with ten wins and five second places, and this success earned him a place in the Cooper works team for 1956 with their latest sports model.

His only Grand Prix appearance came in 1957 at the French GP, when his car was taken over in mid-race by Jack Brabham, but later in the year he finished second in the Prix de Paris at Montlhéry.

After a lengthy period away from racing, he returned to action on the hill-climb scene in 1968, winning the RAC championships in 1973 and '74 in his potent 5-litre Repco-engined Brabham BT36X. Though past the age of 60, Mike, looking extremely fit and trim, was still competing in hill-climbs in the early 1990s.

HERBERT MACKAY-FRASER

Originally from Connecticut, Mackay-Fraser tried his hand at ranching in Wyoming before moving to California, where his motor racing career took off, Herbert racing an XK120 Jaguar around the state. He then relocated again to Rio de Janeiro, where he competed in national events with a Ferrari 750 Monza, but it was always his ambition to race in Europe and in June 1955 he brought his Ferrari across to compete under the 'Kangaroo Stable' banner.

Settling in London, he soon integrated himself into the British motor racing scene, driving for Colin Chapman's fledgling sports car team at home and taking in a number of races on the Continent in his own Ferrari and Bonnier's Maserati during 1956. However, he really made a name for himself in the Reims 12-hour race, which he led superbly in Bueb's Lotus until engine troubles intervened.

In 1957 he continued his successful association with Lotus, and made an impressive debut for BRM in the French Grand Prix, which augured well for the future. But sadly a week later he was dead, after crashing his Lotus in the Coupe de Vitesse at Reims.

LANCE MACKLIN

A polished and extremely stylish driver, Macklin spent the bulk of his career driving for John Heath's underfinanced HWM team, and his Grand Prix career suffered through the cars' lack of reliability.

Early experience with an Invicta, and then a Maserati, led to him joining HWM for 1950 and he immediately made his mark with a second place at Naples and a third at Mettet and Perigueux. The minor Continental races provided a happy hunting ground for the team at this time with good starting and prize money on offer. Macklin continued to pick up many good places over the next few seasons, highlighted by a superb win in the 1952 International Trophy at Silverstone.

Lance also raced occasionally for Aston Martin, finishing third at Le Mans in 1951, but four years later he became involved in the catastrophic accident at the Sarthe that claimed so many lives when 'Levegh's Mercedes was launched off the back of his Healey and wreckage flew into the crowd. Macklin survived unhurt and raced on, but after a narrow escape in the Tourist Trophy at Dundrod, when he crashed to avoid a multiple accident in which two drivers were killed and another seriously injured, he decided to call it a day.

BRUCE McLAREN

Of all the many motor racing fatalities of the era, the death of Bruce McLaren was perhaps the most shocking. By general consensus the safest driver in the sport, his fatal accident while testing his Can-Am McLaren at Goodwood in 1970 was greeted at the time with utter disbelief.

Arriving in Europe virtually unknown, but with the endorsement of Jack Brabham, on a scholarship from the New Zealand Grand Prix Association in March 1958, McLaren's early career was sensational. In Formula 2 with a works Cooper, he took a class win and fifth overall in the German Grand Prix and, showing a maturity beyond his years, mixed it with seasoned competitors on unfamiliar tracks to such good effect that he finished runner-up in the Autocar F2 championship. Promoted to the F1 works team with Brabham in 1959, Bruce was completely unfazed in the top flight and at the end of the season became the youngest-ever GP winner (at 22) when he won the US GP at Sebring. The 1960 season opened with another triumph, this time in Argentina, but the rest of the year saw him content to understudy Brabham as he headed towards a second successive title. There is no doubt that Bruce learned much from his mentor, who moved on at the end of 1961 to build his own cars. Unfortunately, Cooper's fortunes now began to decline, although McLaren picked up a fortunate win at Monaco and also won the non-title Reims GP. During this period Bruce was happy to spend the winter months back home competing in the Tasman series which provided him with a number of wins. In 1964 he was forced to enter his own cars down-under and thus Bruce McLaren Motor Racing was born. That year also saw a great ambition fulfilled when he won the New Zealand GP at his eighth attempt. Tragedy struck with the death of Tim Mayer, whom Bruce had taken under his wing, but the young American's elder brother Teddy stayed on to become a pillar of the new team which slowly took shape over the next two seasons. Initially the programme centred on the Cooper Zerex Special sports car, later developments of which were to lead towards the team's successful Can-Am cars, which formed the basis of McLaren's emergence as a constructor. Meanwhile Bruce plugged away faithfully at Cooper to the end of the 1965 season, but his various freelance activities, which included racing for Ford in endurance events, had grown to such an extent that the final break was inevitable.

He introduced the white Formula 1 McLaren in 1966, but his season was hampered by the lack of a suitable engine, and the demands of a sports car programme with the McLaren Elva Oldsmobile which by this time was really taking off in North America. However, the highlight of the year for Bruce was winning the Le Mans 24 Hours for Ford with Chris Amon. The pace of expansion continued in 1967, when McLaren was totally involved in F1, now with BRM power. However, this was still an interim unit – indeed, Bruce was glad to race Dan Gurney's second Eagle for a spell after Ginther's sudden retirement rather than use his own machine. A Formula 2 version of the car appeared for the first time which Bruce drove when sports car and F1 commitments permitted. In addition, he shared the victorious Ford Mk II with Andretti at the Sebring 12 Hours, and also won rounds of the growing Can-Am series at Monterey and Riverside on his way to the title.

Clearly the task of heading the team and developing and driving the cars was becoming too much for Bruce to handle on his own, and he tempted Denny Hulme from Brabham for 1968 to take some of the weight off his shoulders. It was a move that showed his wisdom, for he was quite prepared to play second fiddle to the new World Champion, though when the mood took him McLaren the racer, for so long closeted, was allowed to re-emerge, as at Brands Hatch where he unleashed a stunning performance to win the Race of Champions in the bright-tangerine M7A. Onlookers that day were tempted to wonder just what reservoirs of talent lay untapped. Shortly afterwards he took his final Grand Prix win at Spa, but it was Hulme who led the team's title challenge for the rest of the season. However, it was the ever-consistent Bruce who enjoyed the upper hand in 1969, finishing third in the championship behind Stewart and Ickx. He also took the Can-Am title for the second time, dominating the series with six outright victories and three second places.

Though there were hints of impending retirement, Bruce carried on racing into 1970, with plans afoot to tackle Indianapolis after the success of the Can-Am cars. In due course a McLaren would win the Indy 500, but sadly the team's founder and inspiration was not around to see the success. He perished on a sunny June afternoon when a piece of bodywork flew from the car, sending it out of control. Poor Bruce was killed instantly when the car careered into a disused marshals' post.

Mention the name McLaren in the 1990s and most people will immediately think of the wonderful red and white cars which have now achieved more Grand Prix wins than even Ferrari. But Ron Dennis can surely testify that all those lucky enough to have either met the remarkable New Zealander or seen him in action will also never forget the man with the silver helmet in the tangerine car who began it all some three decades ago.

McLAREN, Bruce (NZ) b 30/8/1937 – d 2/7/1970

1958

	Race	Circuit	No	Entrant	Car/Engine	Comment
5	GERMAN GP (F2)	Nürburgring	20	Cooper Car Co	1.5 Cooper T45-Climax 4	1st in F2 class
12	MOROCCAN GP (F2)	Casablanca	52	Cooper Car Co	1.5 Cooper T45-Climax 4	1st in F2 class

1959

	Race	Circuit	No	Entrant	Car/Engine	Comment
5	MONACO GP	Monte Carlo	22	Cooper Car Co	1.5 Cooper T45-Climax 4	2nd in F2 class/5 laps behind
5	FRENCH GP	Reims	12	Cooper Car Co	2.2 Cooper T51-Climax 4	
3	BRITISH GP	Aintree	16	Cooper Car Co	2.5 Cooper T51-Climax 4	FL (shared with Moss)
ret	GERMAN GP	AVUS	2	Cooper Car Co	2.5 Cooper T51-Climax 4	4th in heat 1/clutch heat 2

ret	PORTUGUESE GP	Monsanto	3	Cooper Car Co	2.5 Cooper T51-Climax 4	clutch
ret	ITALIAN GP	Monza	8	Cooper Car Co	2.5 Cooper T51-Climax 4	engine
1	US GP	Sebring	9	Cooper Car Co	2.5 Cooper T51-Climax 4	

1960

1	ARGENTINE GP	Buenos Aires	16	Cooper Car Co	2.5 Cooper T51-Climax 4	
2	MONACO GP	Monte Carlo	10	Cooper Car Co	2.5 Cooper T53-Climax 4	FL
ret	DUTCH GP	Zandvoort	12	Cooper Car Co	2.5 Cooper T53-Climax 4	driveshaft
2	BELGIAN GP	Spa	4	Cooper Car Co	2.5 Cooper T53-Climax 4	
3	FRENCH GP	Reims	18	Cooper Car Co	2.5 Cooper T53-Climax 4	
4	BRITISH GP	Silverstone	2	Cooper Car Co	2.5 Cooper T53-Climax 4	1 lap behind
2	PORTUGUESE GP	Oporto	4	Cooper Car Co	2.5 Cooper T53-Climax 4	
3	US GP	Riverside	3	Cooper Car Co	2.5 Cooper T53-Climax 4	

1961

6	MONACO GP	Monte Carlo	26	Cooper Car Co	1.5 Cooper T55-Climax 4	5 laps behind
12	DUTCH GP	Zandvoort	11	Cooper Car Co	1.5 Cooper T55-Climax 4	2 laps behind
ret	BELGIAN GP	Spa	30	Cooper Car Co	1.5 Cooper T55-Climax 4	ignition
5	FRENCH GP	Reims	4	Cooper Car Co	1.5 Cooper T55-Climax 4	
8	BRITISH GP	Aintree	14	Cooper Car Co	1.5 Cooper T55-Climax 4	1 lap behind
6	GERMAN GP	Nürburgring	2	Cooper Car Co	1.5 Cooper T55-Climax 4	
3	ITALIAN GP	Monza	12	Cooper Car Co	1.5 Cooper T55-Climax 4	
4	US GP	Watkins Glen	2	Cooper Car Co	1.5 Cooper T55-Climax 4	

1962

ret	DUTCH GP	Zandvoort	6	Cooper Car Co	1.5 Cooper T60-Climax V8	gearbox/FL
1	MONACO GP	Monte Carlo	14	Cooper Car Co	1.5 Cooper T60-Climax V8	
ret	BELGIAN GP	Spa	25	Cooper Car Co	1.5 Cooper T60-Climax V8	oil pressure
4	FRENCH GP	Rouen	22	Cooper Car Co	1.5 Cooper T60-Climax V8	pit stop/3 laps behind
3	BRITISH GP	Aintree	16	Cooper Car Co	1.5 Cooper T60-Climax V8	
5	GERMAN GP	Nürburgring	9	Cooper Car Co	1.5 Cooper T60-Climax V8	
3	ITALIAN GP	Monza	28	Cooper Car Co	1.5 Cooper T60-Climax V8	
3	US GP	Watkins Glen	21	Cooper Car Co	1.5 Cooper T60-Climax V8	1 lap behind
2	SOUTH AFRICAN GP	East London	8	Cooper Car Co	1.5 Cooper T60-Climax V8	

1963

3	MONACO GP	Monte Carlo	7	Cooper Car Co	1.5 Cooper T66-Climax V8	
2	BELGIAN GP	Spa	14	Cooper Car Co	1.5 Cooper T66-Climax V8	
ret	DUTCH GP	Zandvoort	20	Cooper Car Co	1.5 Cooper T66-Climax V8	gearbox
12/ret	FRENCH GP	Reims	10	Cooper Car Co	1.5 Cooper T66-Climax V8	ignition/11 laps behind
ret	BRITISH GP	Silverstone	6	Cooper Car Co	1.5 Cooper T66-Climax V8	engine
ret	GERMAN GP	Nürburgring	5	Cooper Car Co	1.5 Cooper T66-Climax V8	car failure-crashed
3	ITALIAN GP	Monza	18	Cooper Car Co	1.5 Cooper T66-Climax V8	1 lap behind
11/ret	US GP	Watkins Glen	3	Cooper Car Co	1.5 Cooper T66-Climax V8	fuel pump/36 laps behind
ret	MEXICAN GP	Mexico City	3	Cooper Car Co	1.5 Cooper T66-Climax V8	engine
4	SOUTH AFRICAN GP	East London	10	Cooper Car Co	1.5 Cooper T66-Climax V8	1 lap behind

1964

ret	MONACO GP	Monte Carlo	10	Cooper Car Co	1.5 Cooper T66-Climax V8	oil leak-main bearing
dns	"	" "	10	Cooper Car Co	1.5 Cooper T73-Climax V8	practice only
7	DUTCH GP	Zandvoort	24	Cooper Car Co	1.5 Cooper T73-Climax V8	2 laps behind
2	BELGIAN GP	Spa	20	Cooper Car Co	1.5 Cooper T73-Climax V8	
6	FRENCH GP	Rouen	12	Cooper Car Co	1.5 Cooper T73-Climax V8	1 lap behind
ret	BRITISH GP	Brands Hatch	9	Cooper Car Co	1.5 Cooper T73-Climax V8	gearbox
ret	GERMAN GP	Nürburgring	9	Cooper Car Co	1.5 Cooper T73-Climax V8	engine
ret	AUSTRIAN GP	Zeltweg	9	Cooper Car Co	1.5 Cooper T73-Climax V8	engine
2	ITALIAN GP	Monza	26	Cooper Car Co	1.5 Cooper T73-Climax V8	
ret	US GP	Watkins Glen	9	Cooper Car Co	1.5 Cooper T73-Climax V8	engine
7	MEXICAN GP	Mexico City	9	Cooper Car Co	1.5 Cooper T73-Climax V8	1 lap behind

1965

5	SOUTH AFRICAN GP	East London	9	Cooper Car Co	1.5 Cooper T77-Climax V8	1 lap behind
5	MONACO GP	Monte Carlo	7	Cooper Car Co	1.5 Cooper T77-Climax V8	2 laps behind
3	BELGIAN GP	Spa	4	Cooper Car Co	1.5 Cooper T77-Climax V8	1 lap behind
ret	FRENCH GP	Clermont Ferrand	18	Cooper Car Co	1.5 Cooper T77-Climax V8	steering
10	BRITISH GP	Silverstone	9	Cooper Car Co	1.5 Cooper T77-Climax V8	3 laps behind
ret	DUTCH GP	Zandvoort	18	Cooper Car Co	1.5 Cooper T77-Climax V8	transmission
ret	GERMAN GP	Nürburgring	11	Cooper Car Co	1.5 Cooper T77-Climax V8	gear selection
5	ITALIAN GP	Monza	16	Cooper Car Co	1.5 Cooper T77-Climax V8	1 lap behind
ret	US GP	Watkins Glen	9	Cooper Car Co	1.5 Cooper T77-Climax V8	no oil pressure
ret	MEXICAN GP	Mexico City	9	Cooper Car Co	1.5 Cooper T77-Climax V8	gear selection

1966

ret	MONACO GP	Monte Carlo	2	Bruce McLaren Motor Racing	3.0 McLaren M2B-Ford V8	oil leak
dns	BELGIAN GP	Spa	24	Bruce McLaren Motor Racing	3.0 McLaren M2B-Serenissima V8	bearings in practice
6	BRITISH GP	Brands Hatch	14	Bruce McLaren Motor Racing	3.0 McLaren M2B-Serenissima V8	2 laps behind
dns	DUTCH GP	Zandvoort	20	Bruce McLaren Motor Racing	3.0 McLaren M2B-Serenissima V8	engine in practice
5	US GP	Watkins Glen	17	Bruce McLaren Motor Racing	3.0 McLaren M2B-Ford V8	3 laps behind
ret	MEXICAN GP	Mexico City	17	Bruce McLaren Motor Racing	3.0 McLaren M2B-Ford V8	engine

1967

4	MONACO GP	Monte Carlo	16	Bruce McLaren Motor Racing	2.1 McLaren M4B-BRM V8	pit stop-battery/3 laps behind
ret	DUTCH GP	Zandvoort	17	Bruce McLaren Motor Racing	2.1 McLaren M4B-BRM V8	spun off
ret	FRENCH GP	Le Mans	8	Anglo American Racers	3.0 Eagle TG102-Weslake V12	ignition drive
ret	BRITISH GP	Silverstone	10	Anglo American Racers	3.0 Eagle TG102-Weslake V12	engine
ret	GERMAN GP	Nürburgring	10	Anglo American Racers	3.0 Eagle TG102-Weslake V12	oil pipe leak
7	CANADIAN GP	Mosport Park	19	Bruce McLaren Motor Racing	3.0 McLaren M5A-BRM V12	pit stop-battery/4 laps behind
ret	ITALIAN GP	Monza	4	Bruce McLaren Motor Racing	3.0 McLaren M5A-BRM V12	engine

	Race	Circuit	No	Entrant	Car/Engine	Comment
ret	US GP	Watkins Glen	14	Bruce McLaren Motor Racing	3.0 McLaren M5A-BRM V12	water pipe
13/ret	MEXICAN GP	Mexico City	14	Bruce McLaren Motor Racing	3.0 McLaren M5A-BRM V12	oil pressure/21 laps behind
1968						
ret	SPANISH GP	Jarama	2	Bruce McLaren Motor Racing	3.0 McLaren M7A-Cosworth V8	oil loss
ret	MONACO GP	Monte Carlo	14	Bruce McLaren Motor Racing	3.0 McLaren M7A-Cosworth V8	spun off
1	BELGIAN GP	Spa	5	Bruce McLaren Motor Racing	3.0 McLaren M7A-Cosworth V8	
ret	DUTCH GP	Zandvoort	2	Bruce McLaren Motor Racing	3.0 McLaren M7A-Cosworth V8	crashed
8	FRENCH GP	Rouen	10	Bruce McLaren Motor Racing	3.0 McLaren M7A-Cosworth V8	pit stop-tyres/4 laps behind
7	BRITISH GP	Brands Hatch	7	Bruce McLaren Motor Racing	3.0 McLaren M7A-Cosworth V8	3 laps behind
13	GERMAN GP	Nürburgring	2	Bruce McLaren Motor Racing	3.0 McLaren M7A-Cosworth V8	1 lap behind
ret	ITALIAN GP	Monza	2	Bruce McLaren Motor Racing	3.0 McLaren M7A-Cosworth V8	oil loss
2	CANADIAN GP	St Jovite	2	Bruce McLaren Motor Racing	3.0 McLaren M7A-Cosworth V8	1 lap behind
6	US GP	Watkins Glen	2	Bruce McLaren Motor Racing	3.0 McLaren M7A-Cosworth V8	pit stop-fuel/5 laps behind
2	MEXICAN GP	Mexico City	2	Bruce McLaren Motor Racing	3.0 McLaren M7A-Cosworth V8	
1969						
5	SOUTH AFRICAN GP	Kyalami	6	Bruce McLaren Motor Racing	3.0 McLaren M7A-Cosworth V8	1 lap behind
2	SPANISH GP	Montjuich Park	6	Bruce McLaren Motor Racing	3.0 McLaren M7C-Cosworth V8	2 laps behind
5	MONACO GP	Monte Carlo	4	Bruce McLaren Motor Racing	3.0 McLaren M7C-Cosworth V8	1 lap behind
ret	DUTCH GP	Zandvoort	6	Bruce McLaren Motor Racing	3.0 McLaren M7C-Cosworth V8	front stub axle
4	FRENCH GP	Clermont Ferrand	5	Bruce McLaren Motor Racing	3.0 McLaren M7C-Cosworth V8	1 lap behind
3	BRITISH GP	Silverstone	6	Bruce McLaren Motor Racing	3.0 McLaren M7C-Cosworth V8	1 lap behind
3	GERMAN GP	Nürburgring	10	Bruce McLaren Motor Racing	3.0 McLaren M7C-Cosworth V8	
4	ITALIAN GP	Monza	18	Bruce McLaren Motor Racing	3.0 McLaren M7C-Cosworth V8	
5	CANADIAN GP	Mosport Park	4	Bruce McLaren Motor Racing	3.0 McLaren M7C-Cosworth V8	3 laps behind
dns	US GP	Watkins Glen	6	Bruce McLaren Motor Racing	3.0 McLaren M7C-Cosworth V8	engine in warm up
ret	MEXICAN GP	Mexico City	6	Bruce McLaren Motor Racing	3.0 McLaren M7C-Cosworth V8	fuel system
1970						
ret	SOUTH AFRICAN GP	Kyalami	5	Bruce McLaren Motor Racing	3.0 McLaren M14A-Cosworth V8	engine
2	SPANISH GP	Jarama	11	Bruce McLaren Motor Racing	3.0 McLaren M14A-Cosworth V8	1 lap behind
ret	MONACO GP	Monte Carlo	12	Bruce McLaren Motor Racing	3.0 McLaren M14A-Cosworth V8	hit chicane-damaged suspension

GP Starts: 103   GP Wins: 4   Pole positions: 0   Fastest laps: 3   Points: 196.5

McRAE, Graham (NZ) b 5/3/1940

	Race	Circuit	No	Entrant	Car/Engine	Comment
1973						
ret	BRITISH GP	Silverstone	26	Frank Williams Racing Cars	3.0 Williams 1R-Cosworth V8	sticking throttle

GP Starts: 1   GP Wins: 0   Pole positions: 0   Fastest laps: 0   Points: 0

MAGEE, Damien (GB) b 17/11/1945

	Race	Circuit	No	Entrant	Car/Engine	Comment
1975						
14	SWEDISH GP	Anderstorp	20	Frank Williams Racing Cars	3.0 Williams FW03-Cosworth V8	2 laps behind
1976						
dnq	FRENCH GP	Paul Ricard	33	RAM Racing	3.0 Brabham BT44B-Cosworth V8	

GP Starts: 1   GP Wins: 0   Pole positions: 0   Fastest laps: 0   Points: 0

GRAHAM McRAE

Although the sum total of McRae's Grand Prix career was one lap in Frank Williams' Iso car in the 1973 British GP, 'Cassius', as he was popularly known, nevertheless enjoyed a long racing career, mainly in F5000 single-seaters, winning the 1972 US L & M series in his modified Leda.

McRae built his own chassis in the late sixties and came to Europe to race in Formula 2 in 1969 with the ex-Courage Brabham. He soon switched to F5000, with a McLaren M10-Chevrolet, which launched him on his path to success as both driver and constructor.

Although his form tailed off towards the mid-seventies, McRae continued to race in Can-Am up until the early eighties with a modified version of his GM3 F5000 car.

DAMIEN MAGEE

An Ulsterman who showed potential in the junior formulae from his early days, Magee always seemed to be scratching round for a decent ride. With no substantial backing to speak of, he was forced to drive any sort of car he could get his hands on. Never less than 100 per cent committed, no sooner would poor Magee get a car going well than it seemed to be sold from under him.

Damien's only Grand Prix start came at very short notice in 1975 when he replaced Merzario in Sweden for Williams, though he did try to qualify the RAM-Brabham the following year at Paul Ricard. However, Magee had a regular drive at last for 1976 and 1977, in the Shellsport G8 series.

TONY MAGGS

With only a handful of races in an Austin Healey in South Africa behind him, Maggs came to Engand in 1959 to gain experience and his talent was quickly recognised, Tony soon progressing to a Formula 2 Cooper. He returned in 1960 to race a variety of machines, finishing third in the Vanwall Trophy in a Cooper, and doing well in the Formula Junior Gemini.

His big break came in 1961, when Ken Tyrrell signed him for a season of Formula Junior with his Cooper, young Tony winning eight races and sharing the European FJ title with Jo Siffert. He also made a steady start in Grand Prix racing with Louise Bryden-Brown's Lotus 18, impressing the Cooper team, who signed him as number two to Bruce McLaren. Always consistent, Maggs scored some fine placings over the next two seasons in a team that was slowly losing its competitive edge, but he was not retained for 1964 and joined up with Centro Sud to race their elderly BRM cars, even getting among the points on two occasions. With no real F1 prospects in sight, Maggs undertook a programme of Formula 2 in an MRP Lola and sports cars in David Piper's Ferrari GTO, the pair winning the Rand 9 Hours at Kyalami.

After handling Parnell's Lotus in the 1965 South African GP, Maggs raced abroad for the last time, taking second place in the Rome GP and fourth at both Oulton Park and Pau in MRP's F2 Lola, and third place in the Sebring 12 Hours with Piper in his Ferrari 250LM. Tony had planned to race the Surtees Lola in Formula 2, but when he crashed his Brabham in a national race at Pietermaritzburg a small boy who was standing in a prohibited area was unfortunately hit and killed, and an upset Maggs immediately retired from racing to concentrate on farming.

UMBERTO MAGLIOLI

A most accomplished sports car driver for nearly two decades, the pipe-smoking Maglioli found his Grand Prix opportunities severely limited, given his position as a junior Ferrari driver. He had made his reputation as national production car champion in 1952 with Lancia, then winning the 1953 Targa Florio and the Carrera Panamericana in 1954 in the marque's cars. Despite success at Maranello in hill-climbs and sports car races which included victories in the Pescara 12 Hours, Buenos Aires 1000 Km and Circuit of Mugello, Umberto joined Maserati for 1956, again racing only occasionally in Grands Prix, but he also began the start of a long and fruitful association with Porsche by winning the Targa Florio with Trips.

A practice crash at Salzburg in 1957 sidelined him with leg injuries but he bounced back in 1959, winning the Sebring 12 Hours with Hans Herrmann. Little success came Maglioli's way in the early sixties, but a return to the Ferrari sports car team in 1963 saw him take third place at Le Mans and in the Nürburgring 1000 Km, follwed by another win at Sebring in 1964.

Throughout the rest of the decade he continued to race a variety of potent machines, including a Ford GT40 and the works Porsche 907, with which, paired with Vic Elford, he won the Targa Florio in 1968, his last major victory.

GUY MAIRESSE

A tough and independent character with a big heart, Mairesse built up a long-distance haulage business from modest beginnings as a lorry driver before the war. He became interested in the sport after Paul Vallée invited him to the 1946 Coupe du Salon purely as a spectator. After winning the 1947 Lyons-Charbonnières Rally, Guy then bought a Delahaye from Vallée for 1948 which he took to victory at Chimay.

Joining his great friend's Ecurie France team for 1949 to race the Lago-Talbot, Mairesse took fourth at Pau and fifth at Albi, and in 1950, teamed with Meyrat, he finished second at Le Mans in a Talbot *'monoplace'*. On the Vallée team's demise, he bought the Le Mans car and a Talbot T26C, which he raced in only a couple of Grands Prix in 1951 due to his increasing business commitments.

At the start of 1952, Mairesse sold his cars but still appeared occasionally in machines provided by others, and it was while practising for the Coupe de Paris at Montlhéry in 1954 that he lost his life, swerving to avoid a slower car and crashing into a concrete wall.

WILLY MAIRESSE

Mairesse drove with a grim determination and frequently came unstuck, suffering a whole series of lurid accidents which burnt and battered his small frame but never dented his fearless approach.

He sprang to prominence in 1956 when he took his second-hand Mercedes 300SL to victory in the Liège-Rome-Liège Rally, beating the favourite, Olivier Gendebien, in the process, which sparked a bitter competition rivalry between the two Belgians. In 1957 Willy over-reached himself, wrecking a series of expensive cars, and he was lucky that Jacques Swaters rescued him from probable obscurity by furnishing him with a Ferrari Berlinetta for 1958 which he took to second place in the Reims 12 Hours. Mairesse clashed with Gendebien once more in the 1959 Tour de France, defeating his rival on a number of timed stages but missing out on overall victory. Ferrari took an interest in the little man, however, and offered him a drive in the 1960 Targa Florio. He finished fourth and was immediately taken into the works team for both F1 and sports cars. Late in the year he scored the first of two successive Tour de France victories in a Ferrari 250GT, but only after Gendebien of all people had helped to manhandle the Mairesse car from a ditch. This gutsy display from Willy made him Ferrari's blue-eyed boy of the moment and he was retained in the sports car team for 1961, taking a number of GT victories and second place at Le Mans with Parkes. After buying a couple of GP rides at Spa and Reims, Mairesse blew another Ferrari F1 chance by crashing at the Nürburgring, but another win in the Tour de France may have kept him employed in 1962, Willy accepting the role of test driver vacated by Ginther, who had moved to BRM.

The season started with wins in the Brussels and Naples GPs, before more success with victory in theTarga Florio. At the Belgian GP, though, Mairesse was involved in a lurid high-speed accident with Trevor Taylor, receiving burns which kept him out until a comeback at Monza which netted fourth place. He survived the Ferrari clear-out to partner Surtees in 1963, but his erratic performances culminated in a needless accident at the German GP when he wrote off the car and put himself out of racing for the remainder of the season. His Ferrari career finally at an end, Mairesse was still a more than useful sports car driver, and joined the Equipe Nationale Belge, winning the 1964 Angola GP in their Ferrari GTO and the Spa 500 Km in 1965. His last major win came the following year when he shared a Filipinetti Porsche Carrera with Herbert Müller to win the Targa Florio. His accident-prone career finally came to an end at the 1968 Le Mans 24 Hours when a door flew open on his Ford GT40, causing him to crash heavily, Mairesse suffering severe head injuries which left him unconscious for two weeks. He never fully recovered and after a year spent in poor health, and with no prospect of a return to racing, he committed suicide by taking an overdose of sleeping pills in an Ostend hotel room.

MAGGS, Tony (ZA) b 9/2/1937

1961

	Race	Circuit	No	Entrant	Car/Engine	Comment
13	BRITISH GP	Aintree	50	Louise Bryden-Brown	1.5 Lotus 18-Climax 4	6 laps behind
11	GERMAN GP	Nürburgring	33	Louise Bryden-Brown	1.5 Lotus 18-Climax 4	1 lap behind

1962

	Race	Circuit	No	Entrant	Car/Engine	Comment
5	DUTCH GP	Zandvoort	7	Cooper Car Co	1.5 Cooper T55-Climax 4	2 laps behind
ret	MONACO GP	Monte Carlo	16	Cooper Car Co	1.5 Cooper T55-Climax 4	gearbox
ret	BELGIAN GP	Spa	26	Cooper Car Co	1.5 Cooper T60-Climax V8	gearbox
2	FRENCH GP	Rouen	24	Cooper Car Co	1.5 Cooper T60-Cliamx V8	1 lap behind
6	BRITISH GP	Aintree	18	Cooper Car Co	1.5 Cooper T60-Climax V8	1 lap behind
9	GERMAN GP	Nürburgring	10	Cooper Car Co	1.5 Cooper T55-Climax 4	
dns	"	"	10	Cooper Car Co	1.5 Cooper T60-Climax V8	accident in practice
7	ITALIAN GP	Monza	30	Cooper Car Co	1.5 Cooper T60-Climax V8	1 lap behind
7	US GP	Watkins Glen	22	Cooper Car Co	1.5 Cooper T60-Climax V8	3 laps behind
3	SOUTH AFRCAN GP	East London	9	Cooper Car Co	1.5 Cooper T60-Climax V8	

1963

	Race	Circuit	No	Entrant	Car/Engine	Comment
5	MONACO GP	Monte Carlo	8	Cooper Car Co	1.5 Cooper T66-Climax V8	2 laps behind
7/ret	BELGIAN GP	Spa	15	Cooper Car Co	1.5 Cooper T66-Climax V8	accident in rain/5 laps behind
ret	DUTCH GP	Zandvoort	22	Cooper Car Co	1.5 Cooper T66-Climax V8	overheating
2	FRENCH GP	Reims	12	Cooper Car Co	1.5 Cooper T66-Climax V8	
9	BRITISH GP	Silverstone	7	Cooper Car Co	1.5 Cooper T66-Climax V8	4 laps behind
ret	GERMAN GP	Nürburgring	6	Cooper Car Co	1.5 Cooper T66-Climax V8	camshaft
6	ITALIAN GP	Monza	20	Cooper Car Co	1.5 Cooper T66-Climax V8	2 laps behind
ret	US GP	Watkins Glen	4	Cooper Car Co	1.5 Cooper T66-Climax V8	ignition
ret	MEXICAN GP	Mexico City	4	Cooper Car Co	1.5 Cooper T66-Climax V8	engine
7	SOUTH AFRICAN GP	East London	11	Cooper Car Co	1.5 Cooper T66-Climax V8	3 laps behind

1964

	Race	Circuit	No	Entrant	Car/Engine	Comment
dns	DUTCH GP	Zandvoort	30	Scuderia Centro Sud	1.5 BRM P57 V8	accident in practice
dns	BELGIAN GP	Spa	7	Scuderia Centro Sud	1.5 BRM P57 V8	engine failure in practice
ret	BRITISH GP	Brands Hatch	17	Scuderia Centro Sud	1.5 BRM P57 V8	gearbox
6	GERMAN GP	Nürburgring	26	Scuderia Centro Sud	1.5 BRM P57 V8	1 lap behind
4	AUSTRIAN GP	Zeltweg	19	Scuderia Centro Sud	1.5 BRM P57 V8	3 laps behind

1965

	Race	Circuit	No	Entrant	Car/Engine	Comment
11	SOUTH AFRICAN GP	East London	15	Reg Parnell (Racing)	1.5 Lotus 25-BRM V8	8 laps behind

GP Starts: 25   GP Wins: 0   Pole positions: 0   Fastest laps: 0   Points: 26

MAGLIOLI, Umberto (I) b 5/6/1928

1953

	Race	Circuit	No	Entrant	Car/Engine	Comment
8	ITALIAN GP	Monza	10	Scuderia Ferrari	2.0 Ferrari 553 4	5 laps behind

1954

	Race	Circuit	No	Entrant	Car/Engine	Comment
9	ARGENTINE GP	Buenos Aires	16	Scuderia Ferrari	2.5 Ferrari 625 4	5 laps behind
7	SWISS GP	Bremgarten	24	Scuderia Ferrari	2.5 Ferrari 555 4	5 laps behind
3*	ITALIAN GP	Monza	38	Scuderia Ferrari	2.5 Ferrari 625 4	* Gonzalez took over/2 laps behind

1955

	Race	Circuit	No	Entrant	Car/Engine	Comment
3*	ARGENTINE GP	Buenos Aires	10	Scuderia Ferrari	2.5 Ferrari 625 4	*shared Farina/Trintignant/-2 laps
6	ITALIAN GP	Monza	12	Scuderia Ferrari	2.5 Ferrari 555 4	1 lap behind

1956

	Race	Circuit	No	Entrant	Car/Engine	Comment
ret	BRITISH GP	Silverstone	12	Scuderia Guastalla	2.5 Maserati 250F 6	gearbox
ret	GERMAN GP	Nürburgring	8	Officine Alfieri Maserati	2.5 Maserati 250F 6	steering
ret*	ITALIAN GP	Monza	46	Officine Alfieri Maserati	2.5 Maserati 250F 6	* Behra took over/steering

1957

	Race	Circuit	No	Entrant	Car/Engine	Comment
ret	GERMAN GP (F2)	Nürburgring	20	Dr Ing F Porsche KG	1.5 Porsche 550RS F4	stub axle

GP Starts: 10   GP Wins: 0   Pole positions: 0   Fastest laps: 0   Points: 3.33

MAIRESSE, Guy (F) b 10/8/1910 – d 24/4/1954

1950

	Race	Circuit	No	Entrant	Car/Engine	Comment
ret	ITALIAN GP	Monza	40	Guy Mairesse	4.5 Lago-Talbot T26C 6	

1951

	Race	Circuit	No	Entrant	Car/Engine	Comment
nc	SWISS GP	Bremgarten	40	Ecurie Belgique	4.5 Lago-Talbot T26C 6	11 laps behind
nc	FRENCH GP	Reims	48	Ecurie Belgique	4.5 Lago-Talbot T26C 6	11 laps behind

GP Starts: 3   GP Wins: 0   Pole positions: 0   Fastest laps: 0   Points: 0

MAIRESSE, Willy (B) b 1/10/1928 – d 2/9/1969

1960

	Race	Circuit	No	Entrant	Car/Engine	Comment
ret	BELGIAN GP	Spa	22	Scuderia Ferrari	2.4 Ferrari Dino 246 V6	transmission
ret	FRENCH GP	Reims	6	Scuderia Ferrari	2.4 Ferrari Dino 246 V6	transmission
3	ITALIAN GP	Monza	16	Scuderia Ferrari	2.4 Ferrari Dino 246 V6	gearbox problems/1 lap behind

1961						
ret	BELGIAN GP	Spa	10	Equipe Nationale Belge	1.5 Lotus 18-Climax 4	*ignition/hiredTony Marsh's car*
dns	"	"	10	Equipe Nationale Belge	1.5 Emeryson 1003-Maserati 4	*car too slow*
ret	FRENCH GP	Reims	48	Team Lotus	1.5 Lotus 21-Climax 4	*3rd works car/engine*
ret	GERMAN GP	Nürburgring	6	Scuderia Ferrari SpA SEFAC	1.5 Ferrari 156 V6	*crashed*
1962						
7/ret	MONACO GP	Monte Carlo	40	Scuderia Ferrari SpA SEFAC	1.5 Ferrari 156 V6	*oil pressure/10 laps behind*
ret	BELGIAN GP	Spa	10	Scuderia Ferrari SpA SEFAC	1.5 Ferrari 156 V6	*huge accident with T Taylor*
4	ITALIAN GP	Monza	8	Scuderia Ferrari SpA SEFAC	1.5 Ferrari 156 V6	
1963						
ret	MONACO GP	Monte Carlo	20	Scuderia Ferrari SpA SEFAC	1.5 Ferrari 156 V6	*transmission*
ret	BELGIAN GP	Spa	10	Scuderia Ferrari SpA SEFAC	1.5 Ferrari 156 V6	*engine*
ret	GERMAN GP	Nürburgring	8	Scuderia Ferrari SpA SEFAC	1.5 Ferrari 156 V6	*crashed*
1965						
dns	BELGIAN GP	Spa	28	Scuderia Centro Sud	1.5 BRM P57 V8	*did only one lap*

GP Starts: 12   GP Wins: 0   Pole positions: 0   Fastest laps: 0   Points: 7

NIGEL MANSELL

If you look at it objectively, there are two Nigel Mansells. One belongs to the motor racing press, who see him as the whingeing, ungracious, 'chip-on-the-shoulder Brit' who courts success and disaster in equal measure but is actually a bloody brilliant racing driver, good for endless column inches and therefore a lucrative source of income. The second Mansell belongs to the 'man in the street', who doesn't give a damn about the scribblings of the journalists, but is content merely to revel in the many scintillating displays served up by one of the most brave, committed and entertaining drivers of the age, a man who still retains the common touch even if he is a superstar. In truth, of course, Mansell is a mixture of all these things, it really just depends on your perspective. I prefer to concentrate on the latter persona, for his remarkable deeds in a racing car are of primary concern in a book of this nature.

Mansell's story is well chronicled, but his dogged refusal to give up when the early part of his career seemed to be leading nowhere marked him down as a potential champion, even if his results in Formula 3 at the time indicated otherwise. The man most responsible for helping Nigel's career over that crucial first hurdle was none other than Colin Chapman, who knew a 'good-un' when he saw one and placed him in the Lotus team as a test driver. When given his Grand Prix debut in Austria, Mansell endured acute discomfort from petrol which leaked into his cockpit to tough it out until the engine failed, and this was the stuff that Lotus needed as they slipped from their pedestal in the early eighties. Certainly there were still rough edges, and Mansell made plenty of mistakes, but there were virtues. He absolutely gave his all, in contrast to team-mate de Angelis who could lose heart when his car was not performing. When Chapman died of a sudden heart attack in December 1992, it was a crushing blow to Nigel, not least because he had lost his greatest believer. His level of competitiveness was raised when the team received their new Renault turbo-powered, Gérard Ducarouge-designed car midway through the following season, as he demonstrated in the European GP at Brands Hatch, but he endured a generally unhappy time in 1984. A probable win in the rain at Monaco was thrown away when he slithered into the Armco and there were many at that stage who doubted if he would ever win a Grand Prix.

His move to Williams in 1985 changed everything. Soon coming to terms with Keke Rosberg, Nigel broke his duck at last, and continued his new-found form into the 1986 season, putting new team-mate Nelson Piquet in the shade with a series of brilliant drives to take five Grand Prix wins. The championship seemed to be there for the taking but a gaffe in the penultimate round in Mexico when he failed to put the car into gear on the grid was to cost him dear. Now under pressure at the final race in Adelaide, poor Nigel had the race covered and the championship within his grasp until a tyre failure sent him crashing out. Undaunted, he predictably bounced back in 1987, this time clocking up six wins in the Williams-Honda, but a practice crash at Suzuka handed the title to team-mate Piquet. The Williams team then lost their Honda engines to McLaren, and Nigel was forced to spend a year in purgatory with the Judd-powered car, though in the rain at Silverstone he drove quite brilliantly into second place.

Accepting a massive offer from Maranello, Mansell entered Ferrari folklore with a first-time-out win in Brazil, and carried the fight to McLaren with captivating brio. His win in Hungary after a stunning bit of opportunism in traffic was the highlight of a brilliant season which was soured somewhat after a skirmish with Senna in Portugal led to his supension from the Spanish GP a week later. Greater disenchantment was to follow in 1990, when Alain Prost joined the Ferrari payroll. The little Frenchman hi-jacked the team's attentions with four early-season wins, prompting Mansell to announce his retirement. An offer from Williams to return to Didcot in 1991 was enough to persuade him to continue, and it was a decision he was not to regret. Driving as well as ever before, Mansell's slow start to the season eventually counted against him, for despite a mid-season burst of five wins, punctuated by a heart-breaking pit-stop fiasco in Portugal, Nigel was unable to overhaul Senna in the race for the title.

In 1992 Nigel finally got the job done. With what was undeniably the best car, he fairly scorched away with the championship, taking five straight wins at the start of the season. Apart from an ill-judged clash with Senna in Canada, he hardly put a foot wrong and thoroughly earned his World Championship. Sadly relations with Williams had deteriorated to the point that an agreement could not be reached for Mansell to continue in 1993 and, with the parties seemingly unable to find a compromise, he headed off to the States and a new life in IndyCar racing with the Newman-Haas Lola. Proving all the doubters wrong, Nigel not only won the PPG Cup at his first attempt but – a crash at Phoenix apart – made light of the black art of racing on ovals to such effect that he was almost omnipotent. Mansell was very unlucky to miss out on a first-time win in the Indy 500 at the last gasp when a full-course yellow saw him outfumbled by the wily Fittipaldi. Perhaps more importantly, however, Nigel had found a new environment into which he settled happily, and this undoubtedly showed in his contented demeanour.

MANSELL, Nigel (GB) b 8/8/1953

1980

	Race	Circuit	No	Entrant	Car/Engine	Comment
ret	AUSTRIAN GP	Österreichring	43	Team Essex Lotus	3.0 Lotus 81B-Cosworth V8	engine
ret	DUTCH GP	Zandvoort	43	Team Essex Lotus	3.0 Lotus 81B-Cosworth V8	brake failure-spun off
dnq	ITALIAN GP	Imola	43	Team Essex Lotus	3.0 Lotus 81-Cosworth V8	

1981

	Race	Circuit	No	Entrant	Car/Engine	Comment
ret	US GP WEST	Long Beach	12	Team Essex Lotus	3.0 Lotus 81-Cosworth V8	hit wall
11	BRAZILIAN GP	Rio	12	Team Essex Lotus	3.0 Lotus 81-Cosworth V8	1 lap behind
ret	ARGENTINE GP	Buenos Aires	12	Team Essex Lotus	3.0 Lotus 81-Cosworth V8	engine
3	BELGIAN GP	Zolder	12	Team Essex Lotus	3.0 Lotus 81-Cosworth V8	
ret	MONACO GP	Monte Carlo	12	Team Essex Lotus	3.0 Lotus 87-Cosworth V8	rear suspension
6	SPANISH GP	Jarama	12	John Player Team Lotus	3.0 Lotus 87-Cosworth V8	
7	FRENCH GP	Dijon	12	John Player Team Lotus	3.0 Lotus 87-Cosworth V8	1 lap behind
dnq	BRITISH GP	Silverstone	12	John Player Team Lotus	3.0 Lotus 87-Cosworth V8	
dns	"	"	12	John Player Team Lotus	3.0 Lotus 88B-Cosworth V8	disqualified during practice
ret	GERMAN GP	Hockenheim	12	John Player Team Lotus	3.0 Lotus 87-Cosworth V8	fuel leak
ret	AUSTRIAN GP	Österreichring	12	John Player Team Lotus	3.0 Lotus 87-Cosworth V8	engine
ret	DUTCH GP	Zandvoort	12	John Player Team Lotus	3.0 Lotus 87-Cosworth V8	electrics
ret	ITALIAN GP	Monza	12	John Player Team Lotus	3.0 Lotus 87-Cosworth V8	handling
ret	CANADIAN GP	Montreal	12	John Player Team Lotus	3.0 Lotus 87-Cosworth V8	accident with Prost
4	CAESARS PALACE GP	Las Vegas	12	John Player Team Lotus	3.0 Lotus 87-Cosworth V8	

1982

	Race	Circuit	No	Entrant	Car/Engine	Comment
ret	SOUTH AFRICAN GP	Kyalami	12	John Player Team Lotus	3.0 Lotus 87B-Cosworth V8	electrics
3*	BRAZILIAN GP	Rio	12	John Player Team Lotus	3.0 Lotus 91-Cosworth V8	* 1st and 2nd place cars dsq
7	US GP WEST	Long Beach	12	John Player Team Lotus	3.0 Lotus 91-Cosworth V8	3 laps behind
ret	BELGIAN GP	Zolder	12	John Player Team Lotus	3.0 Lotus 91-Cosworth V8	clutch
4	MONACO GP	Monte Carlo	12	John Player Team Lotus	3.0 Lotus 91-Cosworth V8	1 lap behind
ret	US GP (DETROIT)	Detroit	12	John Player Team Lotus	3.0 Lotus 91-Cosworth V8	engine
ret	CANADIAN GP	Montreal	12	John Player Team Lotus	3.0 Lotus 91-Cosworth V8	accident with Giacomelli
ret	BRITISH GP	Brands Hatch	12	John Player Team Lotus	3.0 Lotus 91-Cosworth V8	handling and driver discomfort
9	GERMAN GP	Hockenheim	12	John Player Team Lotus	3.0 Lotus 91-Cosworth V8	pit stop-in pain/2 laps behind
ret	AUSTRIAN GP	Österreichring	12	John Player Team Lotus	3.0 Lotus 91-Cosworth V8	engine
8	SWISS GP	Dijon	12	John Player Team Lotus	3.0 Lotus 91-Cosworth V8	1 lap behind
7	ITALIAN GP	Monza	12	John Player Team Lotus	3.0 Lotus 91-Cosworth V8	1 lap behind
ret	CAESARS PALACE GP	Las Vegas	12	John Player Team Lotus	3.0 Lotus 91-Cosworth V8	accident with Baldi

1983

	Race	Circuit	No	Entrant	Car/Engine	Comment
12	BRAZILIAN GP	Rio	12	John Player Team Lotus	3.0 Lotus 92-Cosworth V8	pit stop-tyres/2 laps behind
12	US GP WEST	Long Beach	12	John Player Team Lotus	3.0 Lotus 92-Cosworth V8	3 pit stops-tyres/handling/-3 laps
ret	FRENCH GP	Paul Ricard	12	John Player Team Lotus	3.0 Lotus 92-Cosworth V8	handling/driver discomfort
12/ret	SAN MARINO GP	Imola	12	John Player Team Lotus	3.0 Lotus 92-Cosworth V8	broken rear wing-spun off/-4 laps
ret	MONACO GP	Monte Carlo	12	John Player Team Lotus	3.0 Lotus 92-Cosworth V8	accident with Alboreto
ret	BELGIAN GP	Spa	12	John Player Team Lotus	3.0 Lotus 92-Cosworth V8	gearbox
6	US GP (DETROIT)	Detroit	12	John Player Team Lotus	3.0 Lotus 92-Cosworth V8	1 lap behind
ret	CANADIAN GP	Montreal	12	John Player Team Lotus	3.0 Lotus 92-Cosworth V8	handling/tyres
4	BRITISH GP	Silverstone	12	John Player Team Lotus	1.5 t/c Lotus 94T-Renault V6	pit stop-fuel
4	"	"	12		1.5 t/c Lotus 93T-Renault V6	practice only/grid time in this car
ret	GERMAN GP	Hockenheim	12		1.5 t/c Lotus 94T-Renault V6	engine
dns	"	"	12		1.5 t/c Lotus 93T-Renault V6	practice only/grid time in this car
5	AUSTRIAN GP	Österreichring	12		1.5 t/c Lotus 94T-Renault V6	pit stop-fuel/1 lap behind
ret	DUTCH GP	Zandvoort	12		1.5 t/c Lotus 94T-Renault V6	spun off
8	ITALIAN GP	Monza	12		1.5 t/c Lotus 94T-Renault V6	
3	EUROPEAN GP	Brands Hatch	12		1.5 t/c Lotus 94T-Renault V6	FL
nc	SOUTH AFRICAN GP	Kyalami	12	John Player Team Lotus	1.5 t/c Lotus 94T-Renault V6	3 p stops-gear linkage/tyres/-9 laps

1984

	Race	Circuit	No	Entrant	Car/Engine	Comment
ret	BRAZILIAN GP	Rio	12	John Player Team Lotus	1.5 t/c Lotus 95T-Renault V6	slid off track
ret	SOUTH AFRICAN GP	Kyalami	12	John Player Team Lotus	1.5 t/c Lotus 95T-Renault V6	turbo inlet duct
ret	BELGIAN GP	Zolder	12	John Player Team Lotus	1.5 t/c Lotus 95T-Renault V6	clutch
ret	SAN MARINO GP	Imola	12	John Player Team Lotus	1.5 t/c Lotus 95T-Renault V6	brake failure-crashed
3	FRENCH GP	Dijon	12	John Player Team Lotus	1.5 t/c Lotus 95T-Renault V6	
ret	MONACO GP	Monte Carlo	12	John Player Team Lotus	1.5 t/c Lotus 95T-Renault V6	hit barrier when leading
6	CANADIAN GP	Montreal	12	John Player Team Lotus	1.5 t/c Lotus 95T-Renault V6	gearbox problems/2 laps behind
ret	US GP (DETROIT)	Detroit	12	John Player Team Lotus	1.5 t/c Lotus 95T-Renault V6	gearbox
6/ret	US GP (DALLAS)	Dallas	12	John Player Team Lotus	1.5 t/c Lotus 95T-Renault V6	gearbox/Pole/3 laps behind
ret	BRITISH GP	Brands Hatch	12	John Player Team Lotus	1.5 t/c Lotus 95T-Renault V6	gearbox
4	GERMAN GP	Hockenheim	12	John Player Team Lotus	1.5 t/c Lotus 95T-Renault V6	
ret	AUSTRIAN GP	Österreichring	12	John Player Team Lotus	1.5 t/c Lotus 95T-Renault V6	engine
3	DUTCH GP	Zandvoort	12	John Player Team Lotus	1.5 t/c Lotus 95T-Renault V6	
ret	ITALIAN GP	Monza	12	John Player Team Lotus	1.5 t/c Lotus 95T-Renault V6	spun off
ret	EUROPEAN GP	Nürburgring	12	John Player Team Lotus	1.5 t/c Lotus 95T-Renault V6	engine
ret	PORTUGUESE GP	Estoril	12	John Player Team Lotus	1.5 t/c Lotus 95T-Renault V6	lost brake fluid-spun off

1985

	Race	Circuit	No	Entrant	Car/Engine	Comment
ret	BRAZILIAN GP	Rio	5	Canon Williams Honda Team	1.5 t/c Williams FW10-Honda V6	broken exhaust/accident damage
5	PORTUGUESE GP	Estoril	5	Canon Williams Honda Team	1.5 t/c Williams FW10-Honda V6	started from pit lane/2 laps behind
5	SAN MARINO GP	Imola	5	Canon Williams Honda Team	1.5 t/c Williams FW10-Honda V6	gearbox problems/2 laps behind
7	MONACO GP	Monte Carlo	5	Canon Williams Honda Team	1.5 t/c Williams FW10-Honda V6	brake problems/1 lap behind
6	CANADIAN GP	Montreal	5	Canon Williams Honda Team	1.5 t/c Williams FW10-Honda V6	
ret	US GP (DETROIT)	Detroit	5	Canon Williams Honda Team	1.5 t/c Williams FW10-Honda V6	brake problems-crashed
dns	FRENCH GP	Paul Ricard	5	Canon Williams Honda Team	1.5 t/c Williams FW10-Honda V6	accident in practice
ret	BRITISH GP	Silverstone	5	Canon Williams Honda Team	1.5 t/c Williams FW10-Honda V6	clutch

6	GERMAN GP	Nürburgring	5	Canon Williams Honda Team	1.5 t/c Williams FW10-Honda V6	
ret	AUSTRIAN GP	Österreichring	5	Canon Williams Honda Team	1.5 t/c Williams FW10-Honda V6	*engine*
6	DUTCH GP	Zandvoort	5	Canon Williams Honda Team	1.5 t/c Williams FW10-Honda V6	*pit stop-tyres/1 lap behind*
11/ret	ITALIAN GP	Monza	5	Canon Williams Honda Team	1.5 t/c Williams FW10-Honda V6	*engine/FL/4 laps behind*
2	BELGIAN GP	Spa	5	Canon Williams Honda Team	1.5 t/c Williams FW10-Honda V6	
1	EUROPEAN GP	Brands Hatch	5	Canon Williams Honda Team	1.5 t/c Williams FW10-Honda V6	
1	SOUTH AFRICAN GP	Kyalami	5	Canon Williams Honda Team	1.5 t/c Williams FW10-Honda V6	*Pole*
ret	AUSTRALIAN GP	Adelaide	5	Canon Williams Honda Team	1.5 t/c Williams FW10-Honda V6	*transmission*

1986

ret	BRAZILIAN GP	Rio	5	Canon Williams Honda Team	1.5 t/c Williams FW11-Honda V6	*accident with Senna-lap 1*
2	SPANISH GP	Jerez	5	Canon Williams Honda Team	1.5 t/c Williams FW11-Honda V6	*FL*
ret	SAN MARINO	Imola	5	Canon Williams Honda Team	1.5 t/c Williams FW11-Honda V6	*engine*
4	MONACO GP	Monte Carlo	5	Canon Williams Honda Team	1.5 t/c Williams FW11-Honda V6	
1	BELGIAN GP	Spa	5	Canon Williams Honda Team	1.5 t/c Williams FW11-Honda V6	
1	CANADIAN GP	Montreal	5	Canon Williams Honda Team	1.5 t/c Williams FW11-Honda V6	*Pole*
5	US GP (DETROIT)	Detroit	5	Canon Williams Honda Team	1.5 t/c Williams FW11-Honda V6	*pit stop-tyres/1 lap behind*
1	FRENCH GP	Paul Ricard	5	Canon Williams Honda Team	1.5 t/c Williams FW11-Honda V6	*FL*
1	BRITISH GP	Brands Hatch	5	Canon Williams Honda Team	1.5 t/c Williams FW11-Honda V6	*FL*
3	GERMAN GP	Hockenheim	5	Canon Williams Honda Team	1.5 t/c Williams FW11-Honda V6	
3	HUNGARIAN GP	Hungaroring	5	Canon Williams Honda Team	1.5 t/c Williams FW11-Honda V6	*pit stop-tyres/handling/-1 lap*
ret	AUSTRIAN GP	Österreichring	5	Canon Williams Honda Team	1.5 t/c Williams FW11-Honda V6	*driveshaft-c.v.joint*
2	ITALIAN GP	Monza	5	Canon Williams Honda Team	1.5 t/c Williams FW11-Honda V6	
1	PORTUGUESE GP	Estoril	5	Canon Williams Honda Team	1.5 t/c Williams FW11-Honda V6	*FL*
5	MEXICAN GP	Mexico City	5	Canon Williams Honda Team	1.5 t/c Williams FW11-Honda V6	*last away/pit stop-tyres/-1 lap*
ret	AUSTRALIAN GP	Adelaide	5	Canon Williams Honda Team	1.5 t/c Williams FW11-Honda V6	*tyre failure-crashed/Pole*

1987

6	BRAZILIAN GP	Rio	5	Canon Williams Honda Team	1.5 t/c Williams FW11B-Honda V6	*p stop-paper in radiator/-1 lap/Pole*
1	SAN MARINO GP	Imola	5	Canon Williams Honda Team	1.5 t/c Williams FW11B-Honda V6	
ret	BELGIAN GP	Spa	5	Canon Williams Honda Team	1.5 t/c Williams FW11B-Honda V6	*collision damage-Senna/Pole*
ret	MONACO GP	Monte Carlo	5	Canon Williams Honda Team	1.5 t/c Williams FW11B-Honda V6	*wastegate pipe/Pole*
5	US GP (DETROIT)	Detroit	5	Canon Williams Honda Team	1.5 t/c Williams FW11B-Honda V6	*p stop-tyres-wheel stuck/-1 lap/Pole*
1	FRENCH GP	Paul Ricard	5	Canon Williams Honda Team	1.5 t/c Williams FW11B-Honda V6	*Pole*
1	BRITISH GP	Silverstone	5	Canon Williams Honda Team	1.5 t/c Williams FW11B-Honda V6	*FL*
ret	GERMAN GP	Hockenheim	5	Canon Williams Honda Team	1.5 t/c Williams FW11B-Honda V6	*engine/Pole/FL*
14/ret	HUNGARIAN GP	Hungaroring	5	Canon Williams Honda Team	1.5 t/c Williams FW11B-Honda V6	*lost wheel nut/6 laps behind/Pole*
1	AUSTRIAN GP	Österreichring	5	Canon Williams Honda Team	1.5 t/c Williams FW11B-Honda V6	*FL*
3	ITALIAN GP	Monza	5	Canon Williams Honda Team	1.5 t/c Williams FW11B-Honda V6	
ret	PORTUGUESE GP	Estoril	5	Canon Williams Honda Team	1.5 t/c Williams FW11B-Honda V6	*electrics*
1	SPANISH GP	Jerez	5	Canon Williams Honda Team	1.5 t/c Williams FW11B-Honda V6	
1	MEXICAN GP	Mexico City	5	Canon Williams Honda Team	1.5 t/c Williams FW11B-Honda V6	*Pole*
dns	JAPANESE GP	Suzuka	5	Canon Williams Honda Team	1.5 t/c Williams FW11B-Honda V6	*practice accident/hurt back*

1988

ret	BRAZILIAN GP	Rio	5	Canon Williams Team	3.5 Williams FW12-Judd V8	*overheating/electrics*
ret	SAN MARINO GP	Imola	5	Canon Williams Team	3.5 Williams FW12-Judd V8	*engine/electrics*
ret	MONACO GP	Monte Carlo	5	Canon Williams Team	3.5 Williams FW12-Judd V8	*accident with Alboreto*
ret	MEXICAN GP	Mexico City	5	Canon Williams Team	3.5 Williams FW12-Judd V8	*engine*
ret	CANADIAN GP	Montreal	5	Canon Williams Team	3.5 Williams FW12-Judd V8	*engine*
ret	US GP (DETROIT)	Detroit	5	Canon Williams Team	3.5 Williams FW12-Judd V8	*electrics*
ret	FRENCH GP	Paul Ricard	5	Canon Williams Team	3.5 Williams FW12-Judd V8	*suspension*
2	BRITISH GP	Silverstone	5	Canon Williams Team	3.5 Williams FW12-Judd V8	*FL*
ret	GERMAN GP	Hockenheim	5	Canon Williams Team	3.5 Williams FW12-Judd V8	*spun off*
ret	HUNGARIAN GP	Hungaroring	5	Canon Williams Team	3.5 Williams FW12-Judd V8	*driver exhaustion*
ret	PORTUGUESE GP	Estoril	5	Canon Williams Team	3.5 Williams FW12-Judd V8	*spun off*
2	SPANISH GP	Jerez	5	Canon Williams Team	3.5 Williams FW12-Judd V8	
ret	JAPANESE GP	Suzuka	5	Canon Williams Team	3.5 Williams FW12-Judd V8	*spun off-hit Piquet*
ret	AUSTRALIAN GP	Adelaide	5	Canon Williams Team	3.5 Williams FW12-Judd V8	*brakes-spun off*

1989

1	BRAZILIAN GP	Rio	27	Scuderia Ferrari SpA SEFAC	3.5 Ferrari 640 V12	
ret	SAN MARINO GP	Imola	27	Scuderia Ferrari SpA SEFAC	3.5 Ferrari 640 V12	*gearbox*
ret	MONACO GP	Monte Carlo	27	Scuderia Ferrari SpA SEFAC	3.5 Ferrari 640 V12	*gear selection*
ret	MEXICAN GP	Mexico City	27	Scuderia Ferrari SpA SEFAC	3.5 Ferrari 640 V12	*gearbox/FL*
ret	US GP (PHOENIX)	Phoenix	27	Scuderia Ferrari SpA SEFAC	3.5 Ferrari 640 V12	*alternator*
dsq	CANADIAN GP	Montreal	27	Scuderia Ferrari SpA SEFAC	3.5 Ferrari 640 V12	*started from pit lane before start*
2	FRENCH GP	Paul Ricard	27	Scuderia Ferrari SpA SEFAC	3.5 Ferrari 640 V12	
2	BRITISH GP	Silverstone	27	Scuderia Ferrari SpA SEFAC	3.5 Ferrari 640 V12	*FL*
3	GERMAN GP	Hockenheim	27	Scuderia Ferrari SpA SEFAC	3.5 Ferrari 640 V12	
1	HUNGARIAN GP	Hungaroring	27	Scuderia Ferrari SpA SEFAC	3.5 Ferrari 640 V12	*FL*
3	BELGIAN GP	Spa	27	Scuderia Ferrari SpA SEFAC	3.5 Ferrari 640 V12	
ret	ITALIAN GP	Monza	27	Scuderia Ferrari SpA SEFAC	3.5 Ferrari 640 V12	*gearbox*
dsq/ret	PORTUGUESE GP	Estoril	27	Scuderia Ferrari SpA SEFAC	3.5 Ferrari 640 V12	*reversed in pits/collision-Senna*
ret	JAPANESE GP	Suzuka	27	Scuderia Ferrari SpA SEFAC	3.5 Ferrari 640 V12	*engine*
ret	AUSTRALIAN GP	Adelaide	27	Scuderia Ferrari SpA SEFAC	3.5 Ferrari 640 V12	*spun off in rain*

1990

ret	US GP (PHOENIX)	Phoenix	2	Scuderia Ferrari SpA SEFAC	3.5 Ferrari 641 V12	*engine*
4	BRAZILIAN GP	Interlagos	2	Scuderia Ferrari SpA SEFAC	3.5 Ferrari 641 V12	*pit stop-tyres-anti-roll bar*
ret	SAN MARINO GP	Imola	2	Scuderia Ferrari SpA SEFAC	3.5 Ferrari 641/2 V12	*engine*
ret	MONACO GP	Monte Carlo	2	Scuderia Ferrari SpA SEFAC	3.5 Ferrari 641/2 V12	*battery*
3	CANADIAN GP	Montreal	2	Scuderia Ferrari SpA SEFAC	3.5 Ferrari 641/2 V12	
2	MEXICAN GP	Mexico City	2	Scuderia Ferrari SpA SEFAC	3.5 Ferrari 641/2 V12	
18/ret	FRENCH GP	Paul Ricard	2	Scuderia Ferrari SpA SEFAC	3.5 Ferrari 641/2 V12	*engine/Pole/FL/8 laps behind*
ret	BRITISH GP	Silverstone	2	Scuderia Ferrari SpA SEFAC	3.5 Ferrari 641/2 V12	*gearbox/Pole/FL*
ret	GERMAN GP	Hockenheim	2	Scuderia Ferrari SpA SEFAC	3.5 Ferrari 641/2 V12	*undertray damage*

17/ret	HUNGARIAN GP	Hungaroring	2	Scuderia Ferrari SpA SEFAC	3.5 Ferrari 641/2 V12	collision with Berger/6 laps behind
ret	BELGIAN GP	Spa	2	Scuderia Ferrari SpA SEFAC	3.5 Ferrari 641/2 V12	handling problems
4	ITALIAN GP	Monza	2	Scuderia Ferrari SpA SEFAC	3.5 Ferrari 641/2 V12	throttle problems
1	PORTUGUESE GP	Estoril	2	Scuderia Ferrari SpA SEFAC	3.5 Ferrari 641/2 V12	Pole
2	SPANISH GP	Jerez	2	Scuderia Ferrari SpA SEFAC	3.5 Ferrari 641/2 V12	
ret	JAPANESE GP	Suzuka	2	Scuderia Ferrari SpA SEFAC	3.5 Ferrari 641/2 V12	driveshaft
2	AUSTRALIAN GP	Adelaide	2	Scuderia Ferrari SpA SEFAC	3.5 Ferrari 641/2 V12	FL

1991

ret	US GP	Phoenix	5	Canon Williams Team	3.5 Williams FW14-Renault V10	gearbox
ret	BRAZILIAN GP	Interlagos	5	Canon Williams Team	3.5 Williams FW14-Renault V10	gearbox/FL
ret	SAN MARINO GP	Imola	5	Canon Williams Team	3.5 Williams FW14-Renault V10	collision with Brundle
2	MONACO GP	Monte Carlo	5	Canon Williams Team	3.5 Williams FW14-Renault V10	
6	CANADIAN GP	Montreal	5	Canon Williams Team	3.5 Williams FW14-Renault V10	leading-engine cut out last lap/FL
2	MEXICAN GP	Mexico City	5	Canon Williams Team	3.5 Williams FW14-Renault V10	FL
1	FRENCH GP	Magny Cours	5	Canon Williams Team	3.5 Williams FW14-Renault V10	FL
1	BRITISH GP	Silverstone	5	Canon Williams Team	3.5 Williams FW14-Renault V10	Pole/FL
1	GERMAN GP	Hockenheim	5	Canon Williams Team	3.5 Williams FW14-Renault V10	Pole
2	HUNGARIAN GP	Hungaroring	5	Canon Williams Team	3.5 Williams FW14-Renault V10	
ret	BELGIAN GP	Spa	5	Canon Williams Team	3.5 Williams FW14-Renault V10	voltage regulator
1	ITALIAN GP	Monza	5	Canon Williams Team	3.5 Williams FW14-Renault V10	
dsq	PORTUGUESE GP	Estoril	5	Canon Williams Team	3.5 Williams FW14-Renault V10	dsq-wheel change in pit lane/FL
1	SPANISH GP	Barcelona	5	Canon Williams Team	3.5 Williams FW14-Renault V10	
ret	JAPANESE GP	Suzuka	5	Canon Williams Team	3.5 Williams FW14-Renault V10	spun off
2*	AUSTRALIAN GP	Adelaide	5	Canon Williams Team	3.5 Williams FW14-Renault V10	race stopped 14 laps/*half points

1992 World Champion Driver

1	SOUTH AFRICAN GP	Kyalami	5	Canon Williams Team	3.5 Williams FW14B-Renault V10	Pole/FL
1	MEXICAN GP	Mexico City	5	Canon Williams Team	3.5 Williams FW14B-Renault V10	Pole
1	BRAZILIAN GP	Interlagos	5	Canon Williams Team	3.5 Williams FW14B-Renault V10	Pole
1	SPANISH GP	Barcelona	5	Canon Williams Team	3.5 Williams FW14B-Renault V10	Pole/FL
1	SAN MARINO GP	Imola	5	Canon Williams Team	3.5 Williams FW14B-Renault V10	Pole
2	MONACO GP	Monte Carlo	5	Canon Williams Team	3.5 Williams FW14B-Renault V10	stop for tyres when leadingPole/FL
ret	CANADIAN GP	Montreal	5	Canon Williams Team	3.5 Williams FW14B-Renault V10	spun off trying to pass Senna
1	FRENCH GP	Magny Cours	5	Canon Williams Team	3.5 Williams FW14B-Renault V10	aggregate of 2 parts/Pole/FL
1	BRITISH GP	Silverstone	5	Canon Williams Team	3.5 Williams FW14B-Renault V10	Pole/FL
1	GERMAN GP	Hockenheim	5	Canon Williams Team	3.5 Williams FW14B-Renault V10	Pole
2	HUNGARIAN GP	Hungaroring	5	Canon Williams Team	3.5 Williams FW14B-Renault V10	FL
2	BELGIAN GP	Spa	5	Canon Williams Team	3.5 Williams FW14B-Renault V10	Pole
ret	ITALIAN GP	Monza	5	Canon Williams Team	3.5 Williams FW14B-Renault V10	hydraulics/gearbox/Pole/FL
1	PORTUGUESE GP	Estoril	5	Canon Williams Team	3.5 Williams FW14B-Renault V10	Pole
ret	JAPANESE GP	Suzuka	5	Canon Williams Team	3.5 Williams FW14B-Renault V10	enginePole/FL
ret	AUSTRALIAN GP	Adelaide	5	Canon Williams Team	3.5 Williams FW14B-Renault V10	hit by Senna/Pole

GP Starts: 181   GP Wins: 30   Pole positions: 31   Fastest laps: 30   Points: 469

MANTOVANI, Sergio (I) b 22/5/1929

1953

	Race	Circuit	No	Entrant	Car/Engine	Comment
7*	ITALIAN GP	Monza	56	Officine Alfieri Maserati	2.0 Maserati A6GCM 6	* Musso took over/4 laps behind

1954

7	BELGIAN GP	Spa	30	Officine Alfieri Maserati	2.5 Maserati 250F 6	2 laps behind
5	GERMAN GP	Nürburgring	7	Officine Alfieri Maserati	2.5 Maserati 250F 6	
5	SWISS GP	Bremgarten	28	Officine Alfieri Maserati	2.5 Maserati 250F 6	2 laps behind
9	ITALIAN GP	Monza	18	Officine Alfieri Maserati	2.5 Maserati 250F 6	pit stop/6 laps behind
ret	SPANISH GP	Pedralbes	12	Officine Alfieri Maserati	2.5 Maserati 250F 6	brake problems-crashed

1955

ret	ARGENTINE GP	Buenos Aires	20	Officine Alfieri Maserati	2.5 Maserati 250F 6	fuel starvation/Musso/Behra c/drove
nc	"	" "	22	Officine Alfieri Maserati	2.5 Maserati 250F 6	Musso/Schell also drove/-13 laps

GP Starts: 7   GP Wins: 0   Pole positions: 0   Fastest laps: 0   Points: 4

SERGIO MANTOVANI

A young Italian businessman, Mantovani made a good impression in both sports and touring cars in 1952, finishing sixth in the Bari GP (second in class) in a Ferrari, and second in the GT Class of the Pescara 12 Hours in a Lancia Aurelia.

This led him to buy a Maserati, and he was soon assimilated into the works team, sharing a 2-litre sports car with Fangio to take third in the 1953 Targa Florio, and winning the Circuit of Caserta race. This led to a drive in that year's Italian GP, though he had to hand his car over to Musso in the race.

In 1954 he became a good, solid team member who could be relied upon to look after the car and bring it home, taking fifth places in the German and Swiss Grands Prix, and thirds in both the Syracuse and Rome non-championship events. Retained in the squad for 1955, Sergio was involved in a practice crash at the Valentino GP in Turin in which he sustained serious leg injuries which resulted in the amputation of one limb above the knee. His racing career was over, but he then became a member of the Italian Sporting Commission, thus retaining his links with the sport.

ROBERT MANZON

Manzon raced his own 1100 cc Cisitalia in 1947, taking wins at Angoulême and Comminges and chasing the Simca Gordinis sufficiently impressively in other events to persuade Amédée to sign him midway through the 1948 season. In his first race, at the Circuit des Ramparts in Angoulême (a circuit on which he always shone), he led the final and set fastest lap before retirement.

He was to become a mainstay of the team and in 1949 he was second to Trintignant at Angoulême, and runner-up to Sommer at Lausanne as well as winning the Bol d'Or at Montlhéry in a production Simca sports car with a special 1000 cc engine. The cars were gaining a reputation for unreliabilty because their engines were so highly stressed, but when they lasted good results often followed. In 1950 Manzon took fourth place in the World Championship French GP at Reims, while in the Formula 2 category he won the GP of Perigueux, the Circuit of Mettet in Belgium and was second at Roubaix and third in the Swiss GP at Bremgarten. The following season he triumphed only once, at Mettet again, but took second places at Les Sables d'Olonne, Rouen and Cadours.

Gordini introduced the new six-cylinder car for 1952, and this brought a much-needed boost in competitiveness. Robert put the extra performance to good use with some fine placings in the championship Grands Prix, including an excellent third at Spa behind the works Ferraris. His best non-title race finish was a second place shared with Bira at Marseilles, while in Gordini sports cars he won the Coupe du Salon at Montlhéry. One of his best-ever performances came at the beginning of 1953 in the Argentine GP when he lay second after a great drive before the car shed a wheel. He took fifth in the subsequent Libre race at Buenos Aires, but on his return to France he quit the team, racing a Lancia sports car for the remainder of the year before joining Louis Rosier's *équipe* in 1954. His best result was undoubtedly a third place behind two Mercedes-Benz making their stunning debut at Reims, although he did take a second at Bordeaux behind Gonzalez' works Ferrari.

In 1955 he was back in his spiritual home with *'Le Sorcier'*, but unhappily gained no real success, just a fifth place at Bordeaux. The following year saw heartbreak at Monaco, where he lay third until a gearbox failure just three laps from the finish. He did take a couple of wins – at the Naples GP, where he inherited the lead after the works Ferraris failed, and in the Pescara sports car race, where in the team's 2-litre sports car he defeated Taruffi's Ferrari after an outstanding drive. The much underrated Manzon decided to retire for both family and business reasons at the end of the season.

MANZON, Robert (F) b 12/4/1917

1950

	Race	Circuit	No	Entrant	Car/Engine	Comment
ret	MONACO GP	Monte Carlo	10	Equipe Simca Gordini	1.5 s/c Simca-Gordini Type 15 4	multiple accident
4	FRENCH GP	Reims	44	Equipe Simca Gordini	1.5 s/c Simca-Gordini Type 15 4	3 laps behind
ret	ITALIAN GP	Monza	44	Equipe Simca Gordini	1.5 s/c Simca-Gordini Type 15 4	transmission

1951

ret	FRENCH GP	Reims	30	Equipe Simca Gordini	1.5 s/c Simca-Gordini Type 15 4	engine
7	GERMAN GP	Nürburgring	82	Equipe Simca Gordini	1.5 s/c Simca-Gordini Type 15 4	1 lap behind
ret	ITALIAN GP	Monza	46	Equipe Simca Gordini	1.5 s/c Simca-Gordini Type 15 4	radiator
9	SPANISH GP	Pedralbes	14	Equipe Simca Gordini	1.5 s/c Simca-Gordini Type 15 4	

1952

ret	SWISS GP	Bremgarten	8	Equipe Gordini	2.0 Gordini Type 16 6	engine
3	BELGIAN GP	Spa	14	Equipe Gordini	2.0 Gordini Type 16 6	7 laps behind
4	FRENCH GP	Rouen	2	Equipe Gordini	2.0 Gordini Type 16 6	2 laps behind
ret	BRITISH GP	Silverstone	24	Equipe Gordini	2.0 Gordini Type 16 6	transmission
ret	GERMAN GP	Nürburgring	107	Equipe Gordini	2.0 Gordini Type 16 6	lost wheel
5	DUTCH GP	Zandvoort	10	Equipe Gordini	2.0 Gordini Type 16 6	3 laps behind
14	ITALIAN GP	Monza	2	Equipe Gordini	2.0 Gordini Type 16 6	9 laps behind

1953

ret	ARGENTINE GP	Buenos Aires	26	Equipe Gordini	2.0 Gordini Type 16 6	lost wheel

1954

3	FRENCH GP	Reims	34	Equipe Rosier	2.5 Ferrari 625 4	1 lap behind
ret	BRITISH GP	Silverstone	14	Equipe Rosier	2.5 Ferrari 625 4	cracked cylinder block
9	GERMAN GP	Nürburgring	24	Equipe Rosier	2.5 Ferrari 625 4	2 laps behind
dns	SWISS GP	Bremgarten	24	Scuderia Ferrari	2.5 Ferrari 553 4	practice accident
ret	ITALIAN GP	Monza	6	Equipe Rosier	2.5 Ferrari 625 4	engine
ret	SPANISH GP	Pedralbes	20	Equipe Rosier	2.5 Ferrari 625 4	engine

1955

ret	MONACO GP	Monte Carlo	8	Equipe Gordini	2.5 Gordini Type 16 6	gearbox
dns	"	"	8	Equipe Gordini	2.5 Gordini Type 32 8	practice only
ret	DUTCH GP	Zandvoort	20	Equipe Gordini	2.5 Gordini Type 16 6	transmission
ret	BRITISH GP	Aintree	22	Equipe Gordini	2.5 Gordini Type 16 6	transmission

1956

ret	MONACO GP	Monte Carlo	2	Equipe Gordini	2.5 Gordini Type 16 6	brakes crashed
dns	"	" "	2	Equipe Gordini	2.5 Gordini Type 32 8	practice only
9	FRENCH GP	Reims	30	Equipe Gordini	2.5 Gordini Type 32 8	5 laps behind
9	BRITISH GP	Silverstone	15	Equipe Gordini	2.5 Gordini Type 32 8	7 laps behind
ret	GERMAN GP	Nürburgring	10	Equipe Gordini	2.5 Gordini Type 32 8	suspension
ret	ITALIAN GP	Monza	10	Equipe Gordini	2.5 Gordini Type 32 8	gearbox

GP Starts: 28   GP Wins: 0   Pole positions: 0   Fastest laps: 0   Points: 16

MARIMÓN, Onofre (RA) b 19/12/1923 – d 31/7/1954

1951

	Race	Circuit	No	Entrant	Car/Engine	Comment
ret	FRENCH GP	Reims	50	Scuderia Milano	1.5 s/c Maserati 4CLT/Milano 4	engine

1953

	Race	Circuit	No	Entrant	Car/Engine	Comment
3	BELGIAN GP	Spa	28	Officine Alfieri Maserati	2.0 Maserati A6GCM 6	1 lap behind
9	FRENCH GP	Reims	22	Officine Alfieri Maserati	2.0 Maserati A6GCM 6	5 laps behind
ret	BRITISH GP	Silverstone	26	Officine Alfieri Maserati	2.0 Maserati A6GCM 6	engine
ret	GERMAN GP	Nürburgring	8	Officine Alfieri Maserati	2.0 Maserati A6GCM 6	suspension
ret	SWISS GP	Bremgarten	36	Officine Alfieri Maserati	2.0 Maserati A6GCM 6	oil pipe
ret	ITALIAN GP	Monza	54	Officine Alfieri Maserati	2.0 Maserati A6GCM 6	hit Ascari's spinning car

1954

	Race	Circuit	No	Entrant	Car/Engine	Comment
ret	ARGENTINE GP	Buenos Aires	4	Officine Alfieri Maserati	2.5 Maserati 250F 6	spun off
ret	BELGIAN GP	Spa	28	Officine Alfieri Maserati	2.5 Maserati 250F 6	engine
ret	FRENCH GP	Reims	12	Officine Alfieri Maserati	2.5 Maserati 250F 6	engine
3	BRITISH GP	Silverstone	33	Officine Alfieri Maserati	2.5 Maserati 250F 6	1 lap behind/FL (shared)
dns	GERMAN GP	Nürburgring	6	Officine Alfieri Maserati	2.5 Maserati 250F 6	fatal accident in practice

GP Starts: 11   GP Wins: 0   Pole positions: 0   Fastest laps: 1   Points: 8.14

MARKO, Helmut (A) b 27/4/1943

1971

	Race	Circuit	No	Entrant	Car/Engine	Comment
dns	GERMAN GP	Nürburgring	27	Ecurie Bonnier	3.0 McLaren M7C-Cosworth V8	practice only-only did 1 lap
11	AUSTRIAN GP	Österreichring	16	Yardley-BRM	3.0 BRM P153 V12	2 laps behind
ret	ITALIAN GP	Monza	21	Yardley-BRM	3.0 BRM P153 V12	engine
dns	"	"	20T	Yardley-BRM	3.0 BRM P160 V12	practice only
12	CANADIAN GP	Mosport Park	31	Yardley-BRM	3.0 BRM P153 V12	pit stop-fuel/4 laps behind
13	US GP	Watkins Glen	17	Yardley-BRM	3.0 BRM P160 V12	pit stop-fuel/2 laps behind

1972

	Race	Circuit	No	Entrant	Car/Engine	Comment
10	ARGENTINE GP	Buenos Aires	7	Austria-Marlboro BRM	3.0 BRM P153 V12	2 laps behind
14	SOUTH AFRICAN GP	Kyalami	24	Austria-Marlboro BRM	3.0 BRM P153 V12	3 laps behind
8	MONACO GP	Monte Carlo	26	Austria-Marlboro BRM	3.0 BRM P153B V12	3 laps behind
10	BELGIAN GP	Nivelles	27	Austria-Marlboro BRM	3.0 BRM P153B V12	2 laps behind
ret	FRENCH GP	Clermont Ferrand	25	Austria-Marlboro BRM	3.0 BRM P160B V12	stone pierced visor/eye injury

GP Starts: 9   GP Wins: 0   Pole positions: 0   Fastest laps: 0   Points: 0

ONOFRE MARIMÓN

A protégé of Fangio, who had frequently raced against his father, Domingo, in the long-distance South American road races, Onofre first made his mark in 1950 by winning the race at Mar del Plata in his 'Meccanica Nacional' special. The urge to race in Europe was overwhelming and Marimón came over briefly in 1951, racing for Scuderia Milano in the French GP and sharing a Talbot with Gonzalez at Le Mans.

He returned for a full season in 1953, making an immediate impression with third place in the Belgian GP, and second in the non-championship Modena GP. In 1954, with Fangio having been lured to Mercedes, and Gonzalez to Ferrari, Onofre found himself as effective Maserati team leader and he did well in the early-season races, winning the Rome GP at Castel Fusano and finishing third at Pau. In Grands Prix he tried hard to emulate his peers, but in practice for the German Grand Prix he failed to negotiate a corner, and his Maserati plunged through a hedge and somersaulted down a slope, killing its driver instantly.

HELMUT MARKO

Like many Austrian drivers, Marko, whose racing career had been delayed while he gained a doctorate in law, cut his teeth on Super Vee racers. In 1969 he drove the works McNamara in F3, but he had already tried his hand in sports cars, on which he concentrated the following year.

Driving Martini Racing's Porsche, Marko soon made his mark, finishing third at Le Mans in 1970 and then winning the classic race with Gijs van Lennep a year later. Luck generally deserted Helmut in other major events, but he handled a little Lola T212 sports car entered by Karl von Wendt to devastating effect in 1971, winning the Auvergne Trophy, the Cape 3 Hours and three rounds of the European 2-litre championship. By this time he had made a solid start to his Grand Prix career, his initial hire-drive agreement with BRM proving so satisfactory that he soon became a full team member.

For the 1972 season Marko had a BRM contract for Formula 1, and a seat in the Alfa Romeo sports car team, for whom he scored second places in both the Targa Florio and the Österreichring 1000 Km and thirds at Daytona and in the Nürburgring 1000 Km. His F1 season started well with fourth place in the non-championship Brazilian GP, but in the French GP at Clermont Ferrand a freak accident saw a stone thrown up by another car shatter his visor and embed itself in the unfortunate driver's eye. Happily Marko was able to bring the car safely to a halt, but the sight of the eye could not be saved, and a potentially fine Grand Prix career was lost.

Marko subsequently stayed within the sport working for Renault Austria, and more recently helped shape the career of his compatriot Karl Wendlinger.

MARR, Leslie (GB) b 14/8/1922

1954

	Race	Circuit	No	Entrant	Car/Engine	Comment
13	BRITISH GP	Silverstone	23	Leslie Marr	2.0 Connaught-Lea Francis A Type 4	8 laps behind

1955

	Race	Circuit	No	Entrant	Car/Engine	Comment
ret	BRITISH GP	Silverstone	38	Leslie Marr	2.5 Connaught-Alta B Type 4	brake pipe-spun off

GP Starts: 2   GP Wins: 0   Pole positions: 0   Fastest laps: 0   Points: 0

MARSH, Tony (GB) b 20/7/1931

1957

	Race	Circuit	No	Entrant	Car/Engine	Comment
15	GERMAN GP (F2)	Nürburgring	25	Ridgeway Managements	1.5 Cooper T43-Climax 4	4th in F2 class/5 laps behind

1958

	Race	Circuit	No	Entrant	Car/Engine	Comment
8	GERMAN GP (F2)	Nürburgring	30	Tony Marsh	1.5 Cooper T45-Climax 4	4th in F2 class

1961

	Race	Circuit	No	Entrant	Car/Engine	Comment
dns	BELGIAN GP	Spa	42	Tony Marsh	1.5 Lotus 18-Climax 4	car driven by Mairesse
ret	BRITISH GP	Aintree	48	Tony Marsh	1.5 Lotus 18-Climax 4	ignition
15	GERMAN GP	Nürburgring	37	Tony Marsh	1.5 Lotus 18-Climax 4	2 laps behind

GP Starts: 4   GP Wins: 0   Pole positions: 0   Fastest laps: 0   Points: 0

MARTIN, Eugène (F) b 24/5/1915

1950

	Race	Circuit	No	Entrant	Car/Engine	Comment
ret	BRITISH GP	Silverstone	17	Automobiles Talbot-Darracq SA	4.5 Lago-Talbot T26C-DA 6	engine-oil pressure
ret	SWISS GP	Bremgarten	8	Automobiles Talbot-Darracq SA	4.5 Lago-Talbot T26C-DA 6	crashed-injured

GP Starts: 2   GP Wins: 0   Pole positions: 0   Fastest laps: 0   Points: 0

LESLIE MARR

Marr was a professional artist who mainly raced his Connaught in national events during 1952-53, before trying his hand against tougher opposition in 1954, when he gained his greatest success in Libre events, placing third in the Glover Trophy, and third in the F2 class in the Aintree 200.

By 1955 Marr had taken delivery of a B-Type model, but after the British GP he raced it little until early 1956, when he drove splendidly to finish fourth in the New Zealand GP, after starting from the back of the grid without benefit of practice, and then took third place in the Lady Wigram Trophy at Christchurch.

TONY MARSH

Hill-climbs, trials, sprints, rallies – in fact almost every type of four-wheeled competition was sampled by Tony Marsh in the early fifties, when, at the wheel of the ex-Collins Cooper, he won his first three RAC hill-climb championships.

In 1957 he bought a Formula 2 Cooper, which he used to dominate Libre events at home and also raced on the Continent, making his debut in the German GP, where he took fourth in the F2 class. Over the next three seasons Marsh sensibly raced the Cooper in events where success was a realistic proposition, his best result being a win in the 1960 Lewis-Evans Trophy at Brands Hatch.

For 1961 Tony obtained a Lotus 18, which he drove in Grands Prix and even hill-climbs, winning five of the six events he entered, but despite a third on aggregate in the Brussels GP he soon set it aside in favour of a BRM. Then in 1962 a planned season with a works-tended BRM ended in legal action as Marsh felt the machine was unraceworthy. From then on he concentrated fully on the hill-climb scene, eventually replacing the BRM with a fearsome 4.3-litre Marsh-Oldsmobile special, with which he took another three titles to add to those won back in the fifties.

EUGÈNE MARTIN

Martin had a broad engineering background and when he began racing a BMW/Frazer-Nash in the late forties he soon modified it extensively, subsequently winning races at Angoulême and the GP of Lyons in 1947.

The latter victory put him in demand, and he briefly tried the CTA Arsenal before racing the Jicey during 1948-49. Invited to join Talbot for 1950, Martin crashed in only his second race for the team at Berne and was seriously injured, prompting his temporary retirement. He was to reappear occasionally, having acquired the Jicey, and drove a works Gordini at the 1954 Pau GP, which was to be his final race and unfortunately ended in a crash. He then concentrated on his new role as technical director of the Salmson company, whose machines were to bear a marked resemblance to the Martin cars Eugène had briefly marketed in 1952-53.

PIERLUIGI MARTINI

Little Martini had the resilience to shrug off a disastrous debut year in Grand Prix racing and sensibly return to shallower waters until he was truly ready to plunge back into the deep end. Since then he has become a well-respected part of the Grand Prix community, albeit with only a tantalising glimpse of ultimate success.

The nephew of Italian seventies racer Giancarlo Martini, Pierluigi spent a couple of years hidden in Italian F3 driving the ubiquitous Dallara before emerging as something of a surprise European F3 champion in 1983. At the wheel of a Pavesi Ralt, he put together a late-season run to snatch the title at the very last from under the nose of John Nielsen, but a second place on his Formula 2 debut in a Minardi that season may have given him ideas above his station. After he had tested a Brabham but failed to land a drive, 1984 saw a hapless attempt to qualify a works Toleman at Monza and his lack of experience was merely amplified during the 1985 season. The task of leading the singleton Minardi challenge was beyond him and he dropped back to F3000 for the 1986 season with the Pavesi team. It proved to be a good decision for, freed from the pressure of Formula 1, he soon found his feet to put in a determined bid for the championship, winning rounds at Imola, Mugello and Birmingham. Any hopes of a title win were dashed when he was disqualified in the final round at Jarama after some illegal tinkering with the car between the two parts of the interrupted race. The team lost their way the following year, constantly switching Ralt chassis, and Pierluigi was largely wasting his time. A move to the FIRST team in 1988 bounced him back to the front despite being hampered by a difficult March chassis, and a victory at Enna kept his interest in the series alive even though he had made a surprise return to Grand Prix racing with Minardi.

Scoring their first-ever championship point on his comeback in Detroit, the Italian soon found himself the spearhead of the little Faenza outfit's upward progress. In 1989 he hauled the team from the brink of the pre-qualification abyss to a brief but brilliant moment at Estoril when for one glorious lap a Minardi led a Grand Prix. At the last race of the year in Adelaide, he qualified third on the grid but had to settle for a distant sixth place on unsuitable Pirelli race tyres, and the following season was to prove relatively uneventful while Minardi waited with eager anticipation for the Ferrari power which they hoped would provide the leg-up required to place them among the front-runners. Sadly for Martini, the partnership was hardly a distinguished one, and at the end of the year he moved to Scuderia Italia along with the V12 engines. It was akin to being transferred from one First Division football team to another when the player was eyeing a move to the Premier League. Enduring a year of endless frustrations, Martini found himself without a drive when the team concluded a deal to race Lolas in 1993. He wasn't to know how lucky he was to miss out on that débâcle. He bided his time before keeping his Grand Prix career alive with a mid-season return to the homely confines of Minardi. After all this time, it is now hard to see him breaking out of the ranks of the also-ran teams – no matter how much he may deserve the chance.

MARTINI, Pierluigi (I) b 23/4/1961

1984

	Race	Circuit	No	Entrant	Car/Engine	Comment
dnq	ITALIAN GP	Monza	20	Toleman Group Motorsport	1.5 t/c Toleman TG184-Hart 4	

1985

	Race	Circuit	No	Entrant	Car/Engine	Comment
ret	BRAZILIAN GP	Rio	29	Minardi Team	3.0 Minardi M/185-Cosworth V8	engine
ret	PORTUGUESE GP	Estoril	29	Minardi Team	3.0 Minardi M/185-Cosworth V8	started from pit lane/spun off
ret	SAN MARINO GP	Imola	29	Minardi Team	1.5 t/c Minardi M/185-MM V6	turbo
dnq	MONACO GP	Monte Carlo	29	Minardi Team	1.5 t/c Minardi M/185-MM V6	no time set-knee injury in practice
ret	CANADIAN GP	Montreal	29	Minardi Team	1.5 t/c Minardi M/185-MM V6	accident
ret	US GP (DETROIT)	Detroit	29	Minardi Team	1.5 t/c Minardi M/185-MM V6	engine
ret	FRENCH GP	Paul Ricard	29	Minardi Team	1.5 t/c Minardi M/185-MM V6	accident with Berger
ret	BRITISH GP	Silverstone	29	Minardi Team	1.5 t/c Minardi M/185-MM V6	transmission1
11/ret	GERMAN GP	Nürburgring	29	Minardi Team	1.5 t/c Minardi M/185-MM V6	engine/5 laps behind
ret	AUSTRIAN GP	Österreichring	29	Minardi Team	1.5 t/c Minardi M/185-MM V6	suspension
ret	DUTCH GP	Zandvoort	29	Minardi Team	1.5 t/c Minardi M/185-MM V6	accident
ret	ITALIAN GP	Monza	29	Minardi Team	1.5 t/c Minardi M/185-MM V6	fuel pump
12	BELGIAN GP	Spa	29	Minardi Team	1.5 t/c Minardi M/185-MM V6	5 laps behind
ret	EUROPEAN GP	Brands Hatch	29	Minardi Team	1.5 t/c Minardi M/185-MM V6	accident
ret	SOUTH AFRICAN GP	Kyalami	29	Minardi Team	1.5 t/c Minardi M/185-MM V6	radiator
8	AUSTRALIAN GP	Adelaide	29	Minardi Team	1.5 t/c Minardi M/185-MM V6	4 laps behind

1988

	Race	Circuit	No	Entrant	Car/Engine	Comment
6	US GP (DETROIT)	Detroit	23	Lois Minardi Team	3.5 Minardi M188-Cosworth V8	1 lap behind
15	FRENCH GP	Paul Ricard	23	Lois Minardi Team	3.5 Minardi M188-Cosworth V8	3 laps behind
15	BRITISH GP	Silverstone	23	Lois Minardi Team	3.5 Minardi M188-Cosworth V8	2 laps behind
dnq	GERMAN GP	Hockenheim	23	Lois Minardi Team	3.5 Minardi M188-Cosworth V8	
ret	HUNGARIAN GP	Hungaroring	23	Lois Minardi Team	3.5 Minardi M188-Cosworth V8	collision with Piquet
dnq	BELGIAN GP	Spa	23	Lois Minardi Team	3.5 Minardi M188-Cosworth V8	
ret	ITALIAN GP	Monza	23	Lois Minardi Team	3.5 Minardi M188-Cosworth V8	engine

ret	PORTUGUESE GP	Estoril	23	Lois Minardi Team	3.5 Minardi M188-Cosworth V8	*engine*
ret	SPANISH GP	Jerez	23	Lois Minardi Team	3.5 Minardi M188-Cosworth V8	*gearbox*
13	JAPANESE GP	Suzuka	23	Lois Minardi Team	3.5 Minardi M188-Cosworth V8	*2 laps behind*
7	AUSTRALIAN GP	Adelaide	23	Lois Minardi Team	3.5 Minardi M188-Cosworth V8	*2 laps behind*

1989

ret	BRAZILIAN GP	Rio	23	Minardi Team SpA	3.5 Minardi M188B-Cosworth V8	*engine mounting*
ret	SAN MARINO GP	Imola	23	Minardi Team SpA	3.5 Minardi M188B-Cosworth V8	*gearbox*
ret	MONACO GP	Monte Carlo	23	Minardi Team SpA	3.5 Minardi M188B-Cosworth V8	*clutch*
ret	MEXICAN GP	Mexico City	23	Minardi Team SpA	3.5 Minardi M189-Cosworth V8	*engine*
ret	US GP (PHOENIX)	Phoenix	23	Minardi Team SpA	3.5 Minardi M189-Cosworth V8	*engine*
ret	CANADIAN GP	Montreal	23	Minardi Team SpA	3.5 Minardi M189-Cosworth V8	*collision with Modena*
ret	FRENCH GP	Paul Ricard	23	Minardi Team SpA	3.5 Minardi M189-Cosworth V8	*overheating*
5	BRITISH GP	Silverstone	23	Minardi Team SpA	3.5 Minardi M189-Cosworth V8	*pit stop-paper in radiator/-1 lap*
9	GERMAN GP	Hockenheim	23	Minardi Team SpA	3.5 Minardi M189-Cosworth V8	*chassis problems/1 lap behind*
ret	HUNGARIAN GP	Hungaroring	23	Minardi Team SpA	3.5 Minardi M189-Cosworth V8	*wheel bearing*
9	BELGIAN GP	Spa	23	Minardi Team SpA	3.5 Minardi M189-Cosworth V8	*pit stop-tyres/1 lap behind*
7	ITALIAN GP	Monza	23	Minardi Team SpA	3.5 Minardi M189-Cosworth V8	*1 lap behind*
5	PORTUGUESE GP	Estoril	23	Minardi Team SpA	3.5 Minardi M189-Cosworth V8	*led race for 1 lap/1 lap behind*
ret	SPANISH GP	Jerez	23	Minardi Team SpA	3.5 Minardi M189-Cosworth V8	*spun off*
6	AUSTRALIAN GP	Adelaide	23	Minardi Team SpA	3.5 Minardi M189-Cosworth V8	*3 laps behind*

1990

7	US GP (PHOENIX)	Phoenix	23	SCM Minardi Team	3.5 Minardi M189-Cosworth V8	*pit stop-tyres/1 lap behind*
9	BRAZILIAN GP	Interlagos	23	SCM Minardi Team	3.5 Minardi M189-Cosworth V8	*pit stop-tyres-brakes/2 laps behind*
dns	SAN MARINO GP	Imola	23	SCM Minardi Team	3.5 Minardi M190-Cosworth V8	*accident in practice*
ret	MONACO GP	Monte Carlo	23	SCM Minardi Team	3.5 Minardi M190-Cosworth V8	*electrics*
ret	CANADIAN GP	Montreal	23	SCM Minardi Team	3.5 Minardi M190-Cosworth V8	*hit by Suzuki*
12	MEXICAN GP	Mexico City	23	SCM Minardi Team	3.5 Minardi M190-Cosworth V8	*lack of power/1 lap behind*
ret	FRENCH GP	Paul Ricard	23	SCM Minardi Team	3.5 Minardi M190-Cosworth V8	*electrics*
ret	BRITISH GP	Silverstone	23	SCM Minardi Team	3.5 Minardi M190-Cosworth V8	*alternator*
ret	GERMAN GP	Hockenheim	23	SCM Minardi Team	3.5 Minardi M190-Cosworth V8	*engine*
ret	HUNGARIAN GP	Hungaroring	23	SCM Minardi Team	3.5 Minardi M190-Cosworth V8	*collision with Alesi*
15	BELGIAN GP	Spa	23	SCM Minardi Team	3.5 Minardi M190-Cosworth V8	*understeer/2 laps behind*
ret	ITALIAN GP	Monza	23	SCM Minardi Team	3.5 Minardi M190-Cosworth V8	*suspension*
11	PORTUGUESE GP	Estoril	23	SCM Minardi Team	3.5 Minardi M190-Cosworth V8	*2 laps behind*
ret	SPANISH GP	Jerez	23	SCM Minardi Team	3.5 Minardi M190-Cosworth V8	*loose wheel*
8	JAPANESE GP	Suzuka	23	SCM Minardi Team	3.5 Minardi M190-Cosworth V8	*1 lap behind*
9	AUSTRALIAN GP	Adelaide	23	SCM Minardi Team	3.5 Minardi M190-Cosworth V8	*2 laps behind*

1991

9/ret	US GP (PHOENIX)	Phoenix	23	SCM Minardi Team	3.5 Minardi M191-Ferrari V12	*engine*
ret	BRAZILIAN GP	Interlagos	23	SCM Minardi Team	3.5 Minardi M191-Ferrari V12	*spun off*
4	SAN MARINO GP	Imola	23	SCM Minardi Team	3.5 Minardi M191-Ferrari V12	*2 laps behind*
12	MONACO GP	Monte Carlo	23	SCM Minardi Team	3.5 Minardi M191-Ferrari V12	*stop & go penalty/6 laps behind*
7	CANADIAN GP	Montreal	23	SCM Minardi Team	3.5 Minardi M191-Ferrari V12	*1 lap behind*
ret	MEXICAN GP	Mexico City	23	SCM Minardi Team	3.5 Minardi M191-Ferrari V12	*spun off on Berger's oil*
9	FRENCH GP	Magny Cours	23	SCM Minardi Team	3.5 Minardi M191-Ferrari V12	*2 laps behind*
9	BRITISH GP	Silverstone	23	SCM Minardi Team	3.5 Minardi M191-Ferrari V12	*1 lap behind*
ret	GERMAN GP	Hockenheim	23	SCM Minardi Team	3.5 Minardi M191-Ferrari V12	*spun off on own oil*
ret	HUNGARIAN GP	Hungaroring	23	SCM Minardi Team	3.5 Minardi M191-Ferrari V12	*engine*
12	BELGIAN GP	Spa	23	SCM Minardi Team	3.5 Minardi M191-Ferrari V12	*2 laps behind*
ret	ITALIAN GP	Monza	23	SCM Minardi Team	3.5 Minardi M191-Ferrari V12	*spun off/brakes*
4	PORTUGUESE GP	Estoril	23	SCM Minardi Team	3.5 Minardi M191-Ferrari V12	
13	SPANISH GP	Barcelona	23	SCM Minardi Team	3.5 Minardi M191-Ferrari V12	*2 laps behind*
ret	JAPANESE GP	Suzuka	23	SCM Minardi Team	3.5 Minardi M191-Ferrari V12	*clutch*
ret	AUSTRALIAN GP	Adelaide	23	SCM Minardi Team	3.5 Minardi M191-Ferrari V12	*spun off in heavy rain*

1992

ret	SOUTH AFRICAN GP	Kyalami	22	Scuderia Italia SpA	3.5 BMS Dallara 192-Ferrari V12	*clutch*
ret	MEXICAN GP	Mexico City	22	Scuderia Italia SpA	3.5 BMS Dallara 192-Ferrari V12	*handling*
ret	BRAZILIAN GP	Interlagos	22	Scuderia Italia SpA	3.5 BMS Dallara 192-Ferrari V12	*clutch*
6	SPANISH GP	Barcelona	22	Scuderia Italia SpA	3.5 BMS Dallara 192-Ferrari V12	*2 laps behind*
6	SAN MARINO GP	Imola	22	Scuderia Italia SpA	3.5 BMS Dallara 192-Ferrari V12	*1 lap behind*
ret	MONACO GP	Monte Carlo	22	Scuderia Italia SpA	3.5 BMS Dallara 192-Ferrari V12	*accident lap 1*
8	CANADIAN GP	Montreal	22	Scuderia Italia SpA	3.5 BMS Dallara 192-Ferrari V12	*1 lap behind*
10	FRENCH GP	Magny Cours	22	Scuderia Italia SpA	3.5 BMS Dallara 192-Ferrari V12	*agg of two parts/2 laps behind*
15	BRITISH GP	Silverstone	22	Scuderia Italia SpA	3.5 BMS Dallara 192-Ferrari V12	*3 laps behind*
11	GERMAN GP	Hockenheim	22	Scuderia Italia SpA	3.5 BMS Dallara 192-Ferrari V12	*1 lap behind*
ret	HUNGARIAN GP	Hungaroring	22	Scuderia Italia SpA	3.5 BMS Dallara 192-Ferrari V12	*gearbox*
ret	BELGIAN GP	Spa	22	Scuderia Italia SpA	3.5 BMS Dallara 192-Ferrari V12	*spun off on lap 1*
8	ITALIAN GP	Monza	22	Scuderia Italia SpA	3.5 BMS Dallara 192-Ferrari V12	*1 lap behind*
ret	PORTUGUESE GP	Estoril	22	Scuderia Italia SpA	3.5 BMS Dallara 192-Ferrari V12	*damage from Patrese's debris*
10	JAPANESE GP	Suzuka	22	Scuderia Italia SpA	3.5 BMS Dallara 192-Ferrari V12	*1 lap behind*
ret	AUSTRALIAN GP	Adelaide	22	Scuderia Italia SpA	3.5 BMS Dallara 192-Ferrari V12	*collision with Grouillard-lap 1*

1993

ret	BRITISH GP	Silverstone	24	Minardi Team	3.5 Minardi M193-Ford HB V8	*cramp in arm*
14	GERMAN GP	Hockenheim	24	Minardi Team	3.5 Minardi M193-Ford HB V8	*1 lap behind*
ret	HUNGARIAN GP	Hungaroring	24	Minardi Team	3.5 Minardi M193-Ford HB V8	*spun off*
ret	BELGIAN GP	Spa	24	Minardi Team	3.5 Minardi M193-Ford HB V8	*spun off*
7	ITALIAN GP	Monza	24	Minardi Team	3.5 Minardi M193-Ford HB V8	*hit by Fittipaldi at finish/2 laps behind*
8	PORTUGUESE GP	Estoril	24	Minardi Team	3.5 Minardi M193-Ford HB V8	*2 laps behind*
10	JAPANESE GP	Suzuka	24	Minardi Team	3.5 Minardi M193-Ford HB V8	*2 laps behind*
ret	AUSTRALIAN GP	Phoenix	24	Minardi Team	3.5 Minardi M193-Ford HB V8	*gearbox*

GP Starts: 94   GP Wins: 0   Pole positions: 0   Fastest laps: 0   Points: 14

JOCHEN MASS

Maybe lacking the killer instinct which separates the winners from the rest, Jochen Mass was nevertheless a very talented racing driver who looked destined for the very top on the evidence of his early career, which began in 1970 with an Alfa saloon before he joined Ford Germany to race their Capri. He really shot to prominence in 1972 by winning the European touring car championship for drivers after major wins at Spa, Zandvoort, Silverstone and Jarama. In addition to a planned F3 programme, he also made his Formula 2 debut in the works March and scored a superb win in the Eifelrennen.

Retaining his Ford touring car links, Mass signed for the Surtees Formula 2 team in 1973, and won the rounds at Kinnekulle and Hockenheim. He finished a solid second in the championship standings and also earned his Grand Prix debut at Silverstone. Unfortunately his car was wiped out in the Jody Scheckter-instigated multiple shunt, but he was soon back in action, taking seventh place in the German GP. Promoted to the Surtees F1 team full-time in 1974, Jochen enjoyed a useful start to the year with a fourth place in the Medici GP in Brasilia and then second in the International Trophy race. Once the Grand Prix season proper got under way, however, things soon began to go wrong, with a succession of technical maladies afflicting the team. Things reached boiling point when a superb drive in the German GP was ended by engine failure, prompting him to follow Pace's example and quit in frustration. Picking up the vacant Yardley McLaren seat for the final two races of the season, Mass was offered a full works ride in place of the retired Denny Hulme for 1975 and emerged as an excellent number two to Fittipaldi, winning the shortened Spanish GP in Barcelona, and impressing mightily at both Paul Ricard and Watkins Glen.

The German's subordinate role in the team was to continue during the next two seasons as James Hunt breezed in to highlight the gulf that exists between champions and contenders. Jochen did have his moments, though, and was distinctly unlucky not to win the 1976 German GP, his gamble to run on slicks looking likely to pay off until Lauda's accident halted proceedings. He could, however, be relied upon to provide the team with plenty of top-six finishes and was happy to deliver. In 1977 a couple of Formula 2 races for March brought him victories at Hockenheim and the Nürburgring, and he began his long and tremendously successful sports car partnership with Jacky Ickx, winning three rounds of the World Championship of Makes in the Martini Racing Porsche.

Making the break from an increasingly down-trodden existence at McLaren, he joined the ATS team as number one driver in 1978, but the season was to be desperately disappointing and ended prematurely when Mass suffered a broken knee and thigh in a testing accident at Silverstone. It was to his credit that he made a strong comeback in 1979 with Arrows. Despite being in an outclassed car, he put in some spirited drives, none more stirring than at Monaco where he lay third until brake problems intervened. Continuing with the team for another season, he again proved a consistent performer. Ironically, his best placing was second in the Spanish GP, which was subsequently denied championship status, but he produced another excellent display at Monaco. Out of a drive for 1981, Jochen concentrated on sports car and G5 racing before an unhappy return to the Grand Prix arena with the RAM team in 1982.

Disillusioned after this final year of F1, Mass turned to sports car racing full-time. With Rothmans Porsche, he took eight wins between 1982 and 1985, before briefly switching to IMSA, and after racing a Brun Porsche in 1987 he joined Sauber, which eventually became the full works Mercedes-Benz team. He remained a very capable driver and his huge experience made him the ideal tutor to the German company's young lions, Schumacher, Wendlinger and Frentzen. Jochen scored three wins in 1988 and added five more in 1989, including a long-awaited and much deserved victory at Le Mans. In 1990 he won another two rounds but there were no successes the following year, when the programme was running down as Sauber looked towards Formula 1. In 1992 Mass moved into a team management role in the German touring car championship.

MASS, Jochen (D) b 30/9/1946

1973

	Race	Circuit	No	Entrant	Car/Engine	Comment
ret/dns	BRITISH GP	Silverstone	31	Team Surtees	3.0 Surtees TS14A-Cosworth V8	multiple accident/did not restart
7	GERMAN GP	Nürburgring	31	Team Surtees	3.0 Surtees TS14A-Cosworth V8	
ret	US GP	Watkins Glen	30	Team Surtees	3.0 Surtees TS14A-Cosworth V8	engine

1974

	Race	Circuit	No	Entrant	Car/Engine	Comment
ret	ARGENTINE GP	Buenos Aires	19	Team Surtees	3.0 Surtees TS16-Cosworth V8	engine
17	BRAZILIAN GP	Interlagos	19	Team Surtees	3.0 Surtees TS16-Cosworth V8	pit stop/2 laps behind
ret	SOUTH AFRICAN GP	Kyalami	19	Team Surtees	3.0 Surtees TS16-Cosworth V8	withdrawn after accident
ret	SPANISH GP	Jarama	19	Bang & Olufsen Team Surtees	3.0 Surtees TS16-Cosworth V8	gearbox
ret	BELGIAN GP	Nivelles	19	Bang & Olufsen Team Surtees	3.0 Surtees TS16-Cosworth V8	broken right rear upright
dns	MONACO GP	Monte Carlo	19	Bang & Olufsen Team Surtees	3.0 Surtees TS16-Cosworth V8	shortage of suspension parts
ret	SWEDISH GP	Anderstorp	19	Bang & Olufsen Team Surtees	3.0 Surtees TS16-Cosworth V8	suspension
ret	DUTCH GP	Zandvoort	19	Bang & Olufsen Team Surtees	3.0 Surtees TS16-Cosworth V8	c.v. joint
ret	FRENCH GP	Dijon	19	Bang & Olufsen Team Surtees	3.0 Surtees TS16-Cosworth V8	clutch
14	BRITISH GP	Brands Hatch	19	Bang & Olufsen Team Surtees	3.0 Surtees TS16-Cosworth V8	pit stop-puncture/7 laps behind
ret	GERMAN GP	Nürburgring	19	Bang & Olufsen Team Surtees	3.0 Surtees TS16-Cosworth V8	engine
16	CANADIAN GP	Mosport Park	33	Yardley Team McLaren	3.0 McLaren M23-Cosworth V8	spin/hit Peterson-pit stop/-8 laps
7	US GP	Watkins Glen	33	Yardley Team McLaren	3.0 McLaren M23-Cosworth V8	

1975

	Race	Circuit	No	Entrant	Car/Engine	Comment
14	ARGENTINE GP	Buenos Aires	2	Marlboro Team Texaco	3.0 McLaren M23-Cosworth V8	hit Scheckter-pit stop/3 laps behind
3	BRAZILIAN GP	Interlagos	2	Marlboro Team Texaco	3.0 McLaren M23-Cosworth V8	
6	SOUTH AFRICAN GP	Kyalami	2	Marlboro Team Texaco	3.0 McLaren M23-Cosworth V8	
1*	SPANISH GP	Montjuich Park	2	Marlboro Team Texaco	3.0 McLaren M23-Cosworth V8	accident-race stopped/*half points
6	MONACO GP	Monte Carlo	2	Marlboro Team Texaco	3.0 McLaren M23-Cosworth V8	
ret	BELGIAN GP	Zolder	2	Marlboro Team Texaco	3.0 McLaren M23-Cosworth V8	collision with Watson

Pos	Grand Prix	Circuit	No	Team	Car	Notes
ret	SWEDISH GP	Anderstorp	2	Marlboro Team Texaco	3.0 McLaren M23-Cosworth V8	water leak
ret	DUTCH GP	Zandvoort	2	Marlboro Team Texaco	3.0 McLaren M23-Cosworth V8	engine cut out-crashed
3	FRENCH GP	Paul Ricard	2	Marlboro Team Texaco	3.0 McLaren M23-Cosworth V8	FL
7/ret	BRITISH GP	Silverstone	2	Marlboro Team Texaco	3.0 McLaren M23-Cosworth V8	accident in rainstorm/1 lap behind
ret	GERMAN GP	Nürburgring	2	Marlboro Team Texaco	3.0 McLaren M23-Cosworth V8	tyre failure-crashed-lap 1
4	AUSTRIAN GP	Österreichring	2	Marlboro Team Texaco	3.0 McLaren M23-Cosworth V8	
ret	ITALIAN GP	Monza	2	Marlboro Team Texaco	3.0 McLaren M23-Cosworth V8	damaged suspension at chicane
3	US GP	Watkins Glen	2	Marlboro Team Texaco	3.0 McLaren M23-Cosworth V8	

1976

Pos	Grand Prix	Circuit	No	Team	Car	Notes
6	BRAZILIAN GP	Interlagos	12	Marlboro Team McLaren	3.0 McLaren M23-Cosworth V8	
3	SOUTH AFRICAN GP	Kyalami	12	Marlboro Team McLaren	3.0 McLaren M23-Cosworth V8	
5	US GP WEST	Long Beach	12	Marlboro Team McLaren	3.0 McLaren M23-Cosworth V8	
ret	SPANISH GP	Jarama	12	Marlboro Team McLaren	3.0 McLaren M23-Cosworth V8	engine/FL
6	BELGIAN GP	Zolder	12	Marlboro Team McLaren	3.0 McLaren M23-Cosworth V8	1 lap behind
5	MONACO GP	Monte Carlo	12	Marlboro Team McLaren	3.0 McLaren M23-Cosworth V8	1 lap behind
11	SWEDISH GP	Anderstorp	12	Marlboro Team McLaren	3.0 McLaren M23-Cosworth V8	1 lap behind
15	FRENCH GP	Paul Ricard	12	Marlboro Team McLaren	3.0 McLaren M23-Cosworth V8	hit by Reutemann-p stop/1 lap behind
ret	BRITISH GP	Brands Hatch	12	Marlboro Team McLaren	3.0 McLaren M23-Cosworth V8	clutch
3	GERMAN GP	Nürburgring	12	Marlboro Team McLaren	3.0 McLaren M23-Cosworth V8	
7	AUSTRIAN GP	Österreichring	12	Marlboro Team McLaren	3.0 McLaren M23-Cosworth V8	
9	DUTCH GP	Zandvoort	12	Marlboro Team McLaren	3.0 McLaren M26-Cosworth V8	1 lap behind
dns	"	"	12	Marlboro Team McLaren	3.0 McLaren M23-Cosworth V8	practice only
ret	ITALIAN GP	Monza	12	Marlboro Team McLaren	3.0 McLaren M23-Cosworth V8	ignition
dns	"	"	12	Marlboro Team McLaren	3.0 McLaren M26-Cosworth V8	practice only
5	CANADIAN GP	Mosport Park	12	Marlboro Team McLaren	3.0 McLaren M23-Cosworth V8	
4	US GP EAST	Watkins Glen	12	Marlboro Team McLaren	3.0 McLaren M23-Cosworth V8	
ret	JAPANESE GP	Mount Fuji	12	Marlboro Team McLaren	3.0 McLaren M23-Cosworth V8	slid off track

1977

Pos	Grand Prix	Circuit	No	Team	Car	Notes
ret	ARGENTINE GP	Buenos Aires	2	Marlboro Team McLaren	3.0 McLaren M23-Cosworth V8	engine cut out-spun off
ret	BRAZILIAN GP	Interlagos	2	Marlboro Team McLaren	3.0 McLaren M23-Cosworth V8	spun off
5	SOUTH AFRICAN GP	Kyalami	2	Marlboro Team McLaren	3.0 McLaren M23-Cosworth V8	
ret	US GP WEST	Long Beach	2	Marlboro Team McLaren	3.0 McLaren M23-Cosworth V8	rear end vibration
4	SPANISH GP	Jarama	2	Marlboro Team McLaren	3.0 McLaren M23-Cosworth V8	
4	MONACO GP	Monte Carlo	2	Marlboro Team McLaren	3.0 McLaren M23-Cosworth V8	
ret	BELGIAN GP	Zolder	2	Marlboro Team McLaren	3.0 McLaren M23-Cosworth V8	spun off
2	SWEDISH GP	Anderstorp	2	Marlboro Team McLaren	3.0 McLaren M23-Cosworth V8	
9	FRENCH GP	Dijon	2	Marlboro Team McLaren	3.0 McLaren M23-Cosworth V8	hit Reutemann-p stop/2 laps behind
4	BRITISH GP	Silverstone	2	Marlboro Team McLaren	3.0 McLaren M26-Cosworth V8	
dns	"	"	2	Marlboro Team McLaren	3.0 McLaren M23-Cosworth V8	practice only
ret	GERMAN GP	Hockenheim	2	Marlboro Team McLaren	3.0 McLaren M26-Cosworth V8	gearbox
dns	"	"	2	Marlboro Team McLaren	3.0 McLaren M23-Cosworth V8	practice only
6	AUSTRIAN GP	Österreichring	2	Marlboro Team McLaren	3.0 McLaren M23-Cosworth V8	pit stop/1 lap behind
ret	DUTCH GP	Zandvoort	2	Marlboro Team McLaren	3.0 McLaren M26-Cosworth V8	hit by Jones
4	ITALIAN GP	Monza	2	Marlboro Team McLaren	3.0 McLaren M26-Cosworth V8	
ret	US GP EAST	Watkins Glen	2	Marlboro Team McLaren	3.0 McLaren M26-Cosworth V8	fuel pump belt
3	CANADIAN GP	Mosport Park	2	Marlboro Team McLaren	3.0 McLaren M26-Cosworth V8	despite being hit by Hunt
ret	JAPANESE GP	Mount Fuji	2	Marlboro Team McLaren	3.0 McLaren M26-Cosworth V8	engine

1978

Pos	Grand Prix	Circuit	No	Team	Car	Notes
11	ARGENTINE GP	Buenos Aires	9	ATS Racing Team	3.0 ATS HS1-Cosworth V8	
7	BRAZILIAN GP	Rio	9	ATS Racing Team	3.0 ATS HS1-Cosworth V8	1 lap behind
ret	SOUTH AFRICAN GP	Kyalami	9	ATS Racing Team	3.0 ATS HS1-Cosworth V8	engine
ret	US GP WEST	Long Beach	9	ATS Racing Team	3.0 ATS HS1-Cosworth V8	brake master cylinder
dnq	MONACO GP	Monte Carlo	9	ATS Racing Team	3.0 ATS HS1-Cosworth V8	
11	BELGIAN GP	Zolder	9	ATS Racing Team	3.0 ATS HS1-Cosworth V8	pit stop-tyres/2 laps behind
9	SPANISH GP	Jarama	9	ATS Racing Team	3.0 ATS HS1-Cosworth V8	pit stop-tyres/1 lap behind
13	SWEDISH GP	Anderstorp	9	ATS Racing Team	3.0 ATS HS1-Cosworth V8	2 laps behind
13	FRENCH GP	Paul Ricard	9	ATS Racing Team	3.0 ATS HS1-Cosworth V8	1 lap behind
nc	BRITISH GP	Brands Hatch	9	ATS Racing Team	3.0 ATS HS1-Cosworth V8	pit stop/10 laps behind
ret	GERMAN GP	Hockenheim	9	ATS Racing Team	3.0 ATS HS1-Cosworth V8	suspension breakage-took Stuck off
dnq	AUSTRIAN GP	Österreichring	9	ATS Racing Team	3.0 ATS HS1-Cosworth V8	
dnq	DUTCH GP	Zandvoort	9	ATS Racing Team	3.0 ATS HS1-Cosworth V8	

1979

Pos	Grand Prix	Circuit	No	Team	Car	Notes
8	ARGENTINE GP	Buenos Aires	30	Warsteiner Arrows Racing Team	3.0 Arrows A1-Cosworth V8	2 laps behind
7	BRAZILIAN GP	Interlagos	30	Warsteiner Arrows Racing Team	3.0 Arrows A1-Cosworth V8	1 lap behind
12	SOUTH AFRICAN GP	Kyalami	30	Warsteiner Arrows Racing Team	3.0 Arrows A1-Cosworth V8	pit stop-tyre/4 laps behind
9	US GP WEST	Long Beach	30	Warsteiner Arrows Racing Team	3.0 Arrows A1-Cosworth V8	
8	SPANISH GP	Jarama	30	Warsteiner Arrows Racing Team	3.0 Arrows A1-Cosworth V8	
ret	BELGIAN GP	Zolder	30	Warsteiner Arrows Racing Team	3.0 Arrows A1-Cosworth V8	spun off-could not restart
6	MONACO GP	Monte Carlo	30	Warsteiner Arrows Racing Team	3.0 Arrows A1-Cosworth V8	pit stop-brake cooler/7 laps behind
15	FRENCH GP	Dijon	30	Warsteiner Arrows Racing Team	3.0 Arrows A2-Cosworth V8	handling/5 laps behind
ret	BRITISH GP	Silverstone	30	Warsteiner Arrows Racing Team	3.0 Arrows A2-Cosworth V8	gearbox
6	GERMAN GP	Hockenheim	30	Warsteiner Arrows Racing Team	3.0 Arrows A2-Cosworth V8	1 lap behind
ret	AUSTRIAN GP	Österreichring	30	Warsteiner Arrows Racing Team	3.0 Arrows A2-Cosworth V8	engine
6	DUTCH GP	Zandvoort	30	Warsteiner Arrows Racing Team	3.0 Arrows A2-Cosworth V8	2 laps behind
ret	ITALIAN GP	Monza	30	Warsteiner Arrows Racing Team	3.0 Arrows A2-Cosworth V8	suspension
dnq	CANADIAN GP	Montreal	30	Warsteiner Arrows Racing Team	3.0 Arrows A2-Cosworth V8	
dnq	US GP EAST	Watkins Glen	30	Warsteiner Arrows Racing Team	3.0 Arrows A2-Cosworth V8	

1980

Pos	Grand Prix	Circuit	No	Team	Car	Notes
ret	ARGENTINE GP	Buenos Aires	30	Warsteiner Arrows Racing Team	3.0 Arrows A3-Cosworth V8	gearbox
10	BRAZILIAN GP	Interlagos	30	Warsteiner Arrows Racing Team	3.0 Arrows A3-Cosworth V8	1 lap behind
6	SOUTH AFRICAN GP	Kyalami	30	Warsteiner Arrows Racing Team	3.0 Arrows A3-Cosworth V8	1 lap behind
7	US GP WEST	Long Beach	30	Warsteiner Arrows Racing Team	3.0 Arrows A3-Cosworth V8	pit stop-hit by Zunino/1 lap behind

	Race	Circuit	No	Entrant	Car/Engine	Comment
ret	BELGIAN GP	Zolder	30	Warsteiner Arrows Racing Team	3.0 Arrows A3-Cosworth V8	spun off
4	MONACO GP	Monte Carlo	30	Warsteiner Arrows Racing Team	3.0 Arrows A3-Cosworth V8	1 lap behind
10	FRENCH GP	Paul Ricard	30	Warsteiner Arrows Racing Team	3.0 Arrows A3-Cosworth V8	1 lap behind
13	BRITISH GP	Brands Hatch	30	Warsteiner Arrows Racing Team	3.0 Arrows A3-Cosworth V8	p stop-steering wheel/7 laps behind
8	GERMAN GP	Hockenheim	30	Warsteiner Arrows Racing Team	3.0 Arrows A3-Cosworth V8	
11	CANADIAN GP	Montreal	30	Warsteiner Arrows Racing Team	3.0 Arrows A3-Cosworth V8	3 laps behind
ret	US GP EAST	Watkins Glen	30	Warsteiner Arrows Racing Team	3.0 Arrows A3-Cosworth V8	driveshaft
	1982					
12	SOUTH AFRICAN GP	Kyalami	17	March Grand Prix Team	3.0 March 821-Cosworth V8	3 laps behind
10	BRAZILIAN GP	Rio	17	Rothmans March Grand Prix Team	3.0 March 821-Cosworth V8	pit stop/2 laps behind
8	US GP WEST	Long Beach	17	Rothmans March Grand Prix Team	3.0 March 821-Cosworth V8	3 laps behind
ret	BELGIAN GP	Zolder	17	Rothmans March Grand Prix Team	3.0 March 821-Cosworth V8	engine
dnq	MONACO GP	Monte Carlo	17	Rothmans March Grand Prix Team	3.0 March 821-Cosworth V8	
7	US GP (DETROIT)	Detroit	17	Rothmans March Grand Prix Team	3.0 March 821-Cosworth V8	1 lap behind
11	CANADIAN GP	Montreal	17	Rothmans March Grand Prix Team	3.0 March 821-Cosworth V8	pit stop/4 laps behind
ret	DUTCH GP	Zandvoort	17	Rothmans March Grand Prix Team	3.0 March 821-Cosworth V8	engine
10	BRITISH GP	Brands Hatch	17	Rothmans March Grand Prix Team	3.0 March 821-Cosworth V8	pit stop/3 laps behind
ret	FRENCH GP	Paul Ricard	17	Rothmans March Grand Prix Team	3.0 March 821-Cosworth V8	accident with Baldi

GP Starts: 104 (105)   GP Wins: 1   Pole positions: 0   Fastest laps: 2   Points: 71

MAX, Jean (F) b 27/7/1947

1971

	Race	Circuit	No	Entrant	Car/Engine	Comment
14	FRENCH GP	Paul Ricard	28	Frank Williams Racing Cars	3.0 March 701-Cosworth V8	pit stops/9 laps behind

GP Starts: 1   GP Wins: 0   Pole positions: 0   Fastest laps: 0   Points: 0

MAY, Michael (CH) b 18/8/1934

1961

	Race	Circuit	No	Entrant	Car/Engine	Comment
ret	MONACO GP	Monte Carlo	8	Scuderia Colonia	1.5 Lotus 18-Climax 4	oil pipe
11	FRENCH GP	Reims	46	Scuderia Colonia	1.5 Lotus 18-Climax 4	4 laps behind
dns	GERMAN GP	Nürburgring	25	Scuderia Colonia	1.5 Lotus 18-Climax 4	accident in practice

GP Starts: 1   GP Wins: 0   Pole positions: 0   Fastest laps: 0   Points: 0

MAYER, Tim (USA) b 22/2/1938 – d 28/2/1964

1962

	Race	Circuit	No	Entrant	Car/Engine	Comment
ret	US GP	Watkins Glen	23	Cooper Car Co	1.5 Cooper T53-Climax 4	ignition

GP Starts: 1   GP Wins: 0   Pole positions: 0   Fastest laps: 0   Points: 0

MAZET, François (F) b 25/2/1943

1971

	Race	Circuit	No	Entrant	Car/Engine	Comment
13	FRENCH GP	Paul Ricard	34	Jo Siffert Automobiles	3.0 March 701-Cosworth V8	5 laps behind

GP Starts: 1   GP Wins: 0   Pole positions: 0   Fastest laps: 0   Points: 0

JEAN MAX

Max spent much of his early career bound up in the Formula Ford and F3 GRAC projects, before switching to an F3 Tecno in 1970.

With Motul backing for 1971, he raced briefly in Formula 2 for Williams, handling the team's March 701 in that year's French GP. After a couple of unsuccessful outings for Rondel in Formula 2 the following year, Max returned to French F3 in 1973 with a Martini, again backed by the French oil giants.

TIM MAYER

An outstanding prospect, Tim soon graduated from racing an Austin Healey in 1959 to Formula Junior, winning the championship with a Cooper in 1962. After success in Penske's Cooper-Monaco, he was given a chance with an old works Cooper in the 1962 US GP and then joined Ken Tyrrell's FJ team for 1963. Mayer was set to race in Grands Prix for Cooper in 1964, but a hitherto successful Tasman series ended in disaster when the young American crashed fatally at Longford in Tasmania.

MICHAEL MAY

Principally an engineer, May nevertheless raced successfully in Formula Junior with a Stanguellini, winning the first Monaco race in 1959 and taking second places in the Eifelrennen and at Pau.

He showed great promise at the wheel of Seidel's Lotus in 1961, particularly at Monaco, but a practice crash at the Nürburgring persuaded him to pursue his original vocation, working on fuel injection development with both Porsche, for whom he was also a test driver, and then Ferrari in 1963.

FRANÇOIS MAZET

Mazet did well in two seasons of French F3 with Winfield Racing's Tecno and gained a seat as number two to Tim Schenken in the Sports Motor Formula 2 team for 1970. It was generally a disappointing year so, with Shell backing, he raced Siffert's Chevron in F2 when the Swiss star was committed elsewhere, a fourth place at Pau being his best result. He also raced a March under the team's banner at Paul Ricard, and did some ETC races for Ford Germany. Mazet was later involved with the Essex Petroleum sponsorship of Lotus in the early 1980s.

MENDITÉGUY, Carlos (RA) b 10/8/1915 – d 28/4/1973

	Race	Circuit	No	Entrant	Car/Engine	Comment
	1953					
ret	ARGENTINE GP	Buenos Aires	32	Equipe Gordini	2.0 Gordini Type 16 6	gearbox
	1954					
dns	ARGENTINE GP	Buenos Aires	36	Onofre Marimon	2.5 Maserati A6GCM/250F 6	engine in practice
	1955					
ret	ARGENTINE GP	Buenos Aires	24	Officine Alfieri Maserati	2.5 Maserati 250F 6	crashed
ret	"	" "	26	Officine Alfieri Maserati	2.5 Maserati 250F 6	fuel starvation/Bucci/Schell co-drove
5	ITALIAN GP	Monza	34	Officine Alfieri Maserati	2.5 Maserati 250F 6	1 lap behind
	1956					
ret	ARGENTINE GP	Buenos Aires	6	Officine Alfieri Maserati	2.5 Maserati 250F 6	half-shaft/led race
	1957					
3	ARGENTINE GP	Buenos Aires	8	Officine Alfieri Maserati	2.5 Maserati 250F 6	1 lap behind
ret	MONACO GP	Monte Carlo	36	Officine Alfieri Maserati	2.5 Maserati 250F 6	crashed at chicane-broken nose
ret	FRENCH GP	Rouen	8	Officine Alfieri Maserati	2.5 Maserati 250F 6	engine
ret	BRITISH GP	Aintree	8	Officine Alfieri Maserati	2.5 Maserati 250F 6	transmission
	1958					
7	ARGENTINE GP	Buenos Aires	6	Scuderia Sud Americana	2.5 Maserati 250F 6	4 laps behind
	1960					
4	ARGENTINE GP	Buenos Aires	6	Scuderia Centro Sud	2.5 Cooper T51-Maserati 4	

GP Starts: 10   GP Wins: 0   Pole positions: 0   Fastest laps: 0   Points: 9

CARLOS MENDITÉGUY

A fine all-round sportsman and top-ranked polo player, Menditéguy made his mark at the 1951 Peron Cup races of 1951 when his performances in an Alfa Romeo took the eye. From then on he was a regular local attraction when the Grand Prix teams visited for the Grands Prix and the Buenos Aires Libre races.

In 1956 Menditéguy led the Grand Prix until, missing a gear, he broke the car's half-shaft and slid the Maserati into a fence. Another fine drive in the Mendoza GP yielded only fourth place after low oil pressure had blunted his challenge, but he did share the winning Maserati sports car with Moss in the Buenos Aires 1000 Km.

Third place in the 1957 Grand Prix persuaded Maserati to give him an opportunity to race in Europe, but he had an unhappy sojourn, feeling his car was the least well prepared, while the team opined that he was too hard on the machinery. In mid-season he returned to Argentina in disgust. In 1958 he shared Godia's Maserati to take third place in the Buenos Aires City GP, and in 1960, in the last Argentine Grand Prix for more than a decade, showed his talent had not deserted him by taking a Centro Sud Cooper into fourth place.

ARTURO MERZARIO

'Little Art' made his name in the late sixties with works Fiat Abarths in both GT and European mountain-climb events. If one race advanced his career prospects, then it was the Mugello GP in 1969, which he won after a superb drive in the Abarth 2-litre, beating the likes of Vaccarella and de Adamich. This brought an invitation to join the Ferrari sports car team for 1970 and the start of a three-year association with the Scuderia.

His best season was probably 1972, Merzario making a sparkling Grand Prix debut at Brands Hatch, winning the Spa 1000 Km with Redman, the Targa Florio with Munari and the Rand 9 Hours with Regazzoni in the 312P. In addition, racing for Abarth, he was crowned European 2-litre champion. The following season saw Ferrari in something of a trough, but Merzario knuckled down to a hit-and-miss season of Formula 1 while team leader Ickx just gave up. His feisty spirit appealed to Frank Williams, who signed him for 1974. The season began with a third place in the Medici GP at Brasilia, but once the serious business began success was elusive. The pair ploughed on into the 1975 season but Merzario's fortunes in Formula 1 could hardly have been worse. By mid-season he had quit Williams to concentrate on his commitments with the Alfa sports car team, taking their T33 to wins at Dijon, Monza, Enna and the Nürburgring. After a brief liaison with Copersucar at Monza, Arturo lined up a works March drive for 1976, but the strain of running a four-car team showed and the Italian, unhappy with his lot, grabbed the chance to join Wolf-Williams in mid-season following the sudden departure of Ickx.

With no other options open to him, Merzario entered his own March in 1977 before the money ran out due to a lack of results. He had a good one-off drive for Shadow in Austria, but this was overlooked due to Alan Jones' splendid win in the sister car. While his Grand Prix career had been heading for the rocks for some time, Arturo managed to salvage his reputation somewhat by continuing his sports car success with Alfa Romeo, and in 1977 he won championship rounds at Dijon, Enna, Estoril and Paul Ricard in Autodelta's last fling. The following year Merzario took the brave and ultimately completely foolhardy step of fielding his own F1 chassis. Two versions of this appalling device were built during the next two seasons but the cars rarely looked capable of qualifying. Very much the poorer but seemingly no wiser, the little Italian persisted with his folly in 1980, making an equally fruitless attempt to mix it with the constructors in Formula 2 with his Merzario M1-BMW, which was just as embarrassing as his Grand Prix 'contender'.

MERZARIO, Arturo (I) b 11/3/1943

1972

	Race	Circuit	No	Entrant	Car/Engine	Comment
6	BRITISH GP	Brands Hatch	6	Scuderia Ferrari SpA SEFAC	3.0 Ferrari 312B2 F12	*pit stop-tyre/1 lap behind*
12	GERMAN GP	Nürburgring	19	Scuderia Ferrari SpA SEFAC	3.0 Ferrari 312B2 F12	*pit stop-oil pressure/1 lap behind*

1973

	Race	Circuit	No	Entrant	Car/Engine	Comment
9	ARGENTINE GP	Buenos Aires	20	Scuderia Ferrari SpA SEFAC	3.0 Ferrari 312B2 F12	*gearbox problems/4 laps behind*
4	BRAZILIAN GP	Interlagos	10	Scuderia Ferrari SpA SEFAC	3.0 Ferrari 312B2 F12	*1 lap behind*
4	SOUTH AFRICAN GP	Kyalami	9	Scuderia Ferrari SpA SEFAC	3.0 Ferrari 312B2 F12	*1 lap behind*
ret	MONACO GP	Monte Carlo	4	Scuderia Ferrari SpA SEFAC	3.0 Ferrari 312B3 F12	*oil pressure*
7	FRENCH GP	Paul Ricard	4	Scuderia Ferrari SpA SEFAC	3.0 Ferrari 312B3 F12	
7	AUSTRIAN GP	Österreichring	4	Scuderia Ferrari SpA SEFAC	3.0 Ferrari 312B3 F12	*1 lap behind*
ret	ITALIAN GP	Monza	4	Scuderia Ferrari SpA SEFAC	3.0 Ferrari 312B3 F12	*hit chicane-damaged suspension*
15	CANADIAN GP	Mosport Park	4	Scuderia Ferrari SpA SEFAC	3.0 Ferrari 312B3 F12	*pit stops-lost nose cone/-5 laps*
16	US GP	Watkins Glen	4	Scuderia Ferrari SpA SEFAC	3.0 Ferrari 312B3 F12	*pit stop-rear wing/4 laps behind*

1974

	Race	Circuit	No	Entrant	Car/Engine	Comment
ret	ARGENTINE GP	Buenos Aires	20	Frank Williams Racing Cars	3.0 Williams FW01-Cosworth V8	*engine*
ret	BRAZILIAN GP	Interlagos	20	Frank Williams Racing Cars	3.0 Williams FW01-Cosworth V8	*dirt in throttle slides*
6	SOUTH AFRICAN GP	Kyalami	20	Frank Williams Racing Cars	3.0 Williams FW02-Cosworth V8	
ret	SPANISH GP	Jarama	20	Frank Williams Racing Cars	3.0 Williams FW03-Cosworth V8	*hit and vaulted barrier*
ret	BELGIAN GP	Nivelles	20	Frank Williams Racing Cars	3.0 Williams FW03-Cosworth V8	*driveshaft*
ret	MONACO GP	Monte Carlo	20	Frank Williams Racing Cars	3.0 Williams FW03-Cosworth V8	*multiple accident*
dns	"	" "	20T	Frank Williams Racing Cars	3.0 Williams FW02-Cosworth V8	*practice only*
dns	SWEDISH GP	Anderstorp	20	Frank Williams Racing Cars	3.0 Williams FW02-Cosworth V8	*unwell*
ret	DUTCH GP	Zandvoort	20	Frank Williams Racing Cars	3.0 Williams FW02-Cosworth V8	*gearbox*
9	FRENCH GP	Dijon	20	Frank Williams Racing Cars	3.0 Williams FW02-Cosworth V8	*1 lap behind*
ret	BRITISH GP	Brands Hatch	20	Frank Williams Racing Cars	3.0 Williams FW03-Cosworth V8	*engine*
dns	"	" "	20	Frank Williams Racing Cars	3.0 Williams FW01-Cosworth V8	*practice only*
ret	GERMAN GP	Nürburgring	20	Frank Williams Racing Cars	3.0 Williams FW03-Cosworth V8	*throttle linkage*
ret	AUSTRIAN GP	Österreichring	20	Frank Williams Racing Cars	3.0 Williams FW03-Cosworth V8	*fuel pressure*
4	ITALIAN GP	Monza	20	Frank Williams Racing Cars	3.0 Williams FW03-Cosworth V8	
ret	CANADIAN GP	Mosport Park	20	Frank Williams Racing Cars	3.0 Williams FW03-Cosworth V8	*handling*
ret	US GP	Watkins Glen	20	Frank Williams Racing Cars	3.0 Williams FW03-Cosworth V8	*extinguisher caused electrical short*

1975

	Race	Circuit	No	Entrant	Car/Engine	Comment
nc	ARGENTINE GP	Buenos Aires	20	Frank Williams Racing Cars	3.0 Williams FW03-Cosworth V8	*2 p stops-fuel metering unit/-9 laps*
ret	BRAZILIAN GP	Interlagos	20	Frank Williams Racing Cars	3.0 Williams FW03-Cosworth V8	*fuel metering unit*
ret	SOUTH AFRICAN GP	Kyalami	20	Frank Williams Racing Cars	3.0 Williams FW03-Cosworth V8	*engine*
ret	SPANISH GP	Montjuich Park	20	Frank Williams Racing Cars	3.0 Williams FW04-Cosworth V8	*withdrew in protest over safety*
dnq	MONACO GP	Monte Carlo	20	Frank Williams Racing Cars	3.0 Williams FW03-Cosworth V8	
ret	BELGIAN GP	Zolder	20	Frank Williams Racing Cars	3.0 Williams FW03-Cosworth V8	*clutch*
11	ITALIAN GP	Monza	30	Copersucar-Fittipaldi	3.0 Fittipaldi FD03-Cosworth V8	*4 laps behind*

1976

	Race	Circuit	No	Entrant	Car/Engine	Comment
dnq	US GP WEST	Long Beach	35	Ovoro Team March	3.0 March 761-Cosworth V8	
ret	SPANISH GP	Jarama	35	Ovoro Team March	3.0 March 761-Cosworth V8	*gear linkage*
ret	BELGIAN GP	Zolder	35	Ovoro Team March	3.0 March 761-Cosworth V8	*engine*
dnq	MONACO GP	Monte Carlo	35	Ovoro Team March	3.0 March 761-Cosworth V8	*accident in practice*
14/ret	SWEDISH GP	Anderstorp	35	Ovoro Team March	3.0 March 761-Cosworth V8	*engine/2 laps behind*
9	FRENCH GP	Paul Ricard	35	Ovoro Team March	3.0 March 761-Cosworth V8	
ret	BRITISH GP	Brands Hatch	35	Ovoro Team March	3.0 March 761-Cosworth V8	*engine*
ret	GERMAN GP	Nürburgring	20	Walter Wolf Racing	3.0 Williams FW05-Cosworth V8	*brakes*
ret	AUSTRIAN GP	Österreichring	20	Walter Wolf Racing	3.0 Williams FW05-Cosworth V8	*spun off*
ret	DUTCH GP	Zandvoort	20	Walter Wolf Racing	3.0 Williams FW05-Cosworth V8	*spun off*
dns	ITALIAN GP	Monza	20	Walter Wolf Racing	3.0 Williams FW05-Cosworth V8	*withdrawn after practice*
ret	CANADIAN GP	Mosport Park	20	Walter Wolf Racing	3.0 Williams FW05-Cosworth V8	*spun off*
ret	US GP EAST	Watkins Glen	20	Walter Wolf Racing	3.0 Williams FW05-Cosworth V8	*spun, hit by Ertl*
ret	JAPANESE GP	Mount Fuji	20	Walter Wolf Racing	3.0 Williams FW05-Cosworth V8	*gearbox*

1977

	Race	Circuit	No	Entrant	Car/Engine	Comment
ret	SPANISH GP	Jarama	37	Team Merzario	3.0 March 761B-Cosworth V8	*suspension*
dnq	MONACO GP	Monte Carlo	37	Team Merzario	3.0 March 761B-Cosworth V8	
14	BELGIAN GP	Zolder	37	Team Merzario	3.0 March 761B-Cosworth V8	*pit stop-tyres-fuel pump/-5 laps*
ret	FRENCH GP	Dijon	37	Team Merzario	3.0 March 761B-Cosworth V8	*gearbox*
ret	BRITISH GP	Silverstone	37	Team Merzario	3.0 March 761B-Cosworth V8	*driveshaft*
dnq	GERMAN GP	Hockenheim	37	Team Merzario	3.0 March 761B-Cosworth V8	
ret	AUSTRIAN GP	Österreichring	16	Shadow Racing Team	3.0 Shadow DN8-Cosworth V8	*gear linkage*
dnq	DUTCH GP	Zandvoort	37	Team Merzario	3.0 March 761B-Cosworth V8	

1978

	Race	Circuit	No	Entrant	Car/Engine	Comment
ret	ARGENTINE GP	Buenos Aires	37	Team Merzario	3.0 Merzario A1-Cosworth V8	*differential*
dnq	BRAZILIAN GP	Rio	37	Team Merzario	3.0 Merzario A1-Cosworth V8	
ret	SOUTH AFRICAN GP	Kyalami	37	Team Merzario	3.0 Merzario A1-Cosworth V8	*radius rod mounting*
ret	US GP WEST	Long Beach	37	Team Merzario	3.0 Merzario A1-Cosworth V8	*gearbox*
dnpq	MONACO GP	Monte Carlo	37	Team Merzario	3.0 Merzario A1-Cosworth V8	
dnpq	BELGIAN GP	Zolder	37	Team Merzario	3.0 Merzario A1-Cosworth V8	
dnq	SPANISH GP	Jarama	37	Team Merzario	3.0 Merzario A1-Cosworth V8	
nc	SWEDISH GP	Anderstorp	37	Team Merzario	3.0 Merzario A1-Cosworth V8	*pit stop/8 laps behind*
dnq	FRENCH GP	Paul Ricard	37	Team Merzario	3.0 Merzario A1-Cosworth V8	
ret	BRITISH GP	Brands Hatch	37	Team Merzario	3.0 Merzario A1-Cosworth V8	*fuel pump*
dnq	GERMAN GP	Hockenheim	37	Team Merzario	3.0 Merzario A1-Cosworth V8	
dnq	AUSTRIAN GP	Österreichring	37	Team Merzario	3.0 Merzario A1-Cosworth V8	
ret	DUTCH GP	Zandvoort	37	Team Merzario	3.0 Merzario A1-Cosworth V8	*engine*
ret	ITALIAN GP	Monza	37	Team Merzario	3.0 Merzario A1-Cosworth V8	*engine*

ret	US GP EAST	Watkins Glen	37	Team Merzario	3.0 Merzario A1-Cosworth V8	*gearbox oil leak*
dnq	CANADIAN GP	Montreal	37	Team Merzario	3.0 Merzario A1-Cosworth V8	
	1979					
ret	ARGENTINE GP	Buenos Aires	24	Team Merzario	3.0 Merzario A1B-Cosworth V8	*accident in first start*
dnq	BRAZILIAN GP	Rio	24	Team Merzario	3.0 Merzario A1B-Cosworth V8	
dnq	SOUTH AFRICAN GP	Kyalami	24	Team Merzario	3.0 Merzario A1B-Cosworth V8	
ret	US GP WEST	Long Beach	24	Team Merzario	3.0 Merzario A1B-Cosworth V8	*engine*
dns	" "	" "	24	Team Merzario	3.0 Merzario A2-Cosworth V8	*practice only*
dnq	SPANISH GP	Jarama	24	Team Merzario	3.0 Merzario A2-Cosworth V8	
dnq	BELGIAN GP	Zolder	24	Team Merzario	3.0 Merzario A2-Cosworth V8	
dnq	FRENCH GP	Dijon	24	Team Merzario	3.0 Merzario A2-Cosworth V8	
dnq	BRITISH GP	Silverstone	24	Team Merzario	3.0 Merzario A2-Cosworth V8	
dnq	GERMAN GP	Hockenheim	24	Team Merzario	3.0 Merzario A2-Cosworth V8	
dnq	AUSTRIAN GP	Österreichring	24	Team Merzario	3.0 Merzario A2-Cosworth V8	
dnq	DUTCH GP	Zandvoort	24	Team Merzario	3.0 Merzario A2-Cosworth V8	
dnq	ITALIAN GP	Monza	24	Team Merzario	3.0 Merzario A2-Cosworth V8	
dnq	CANADIAN GP	Montreal	24	Team Merzario	3.0 Merzario A2-Cosworth V8	
dnq	US GP EAST	Watkins Glen	24	Team Merzario	3.0 Merzario A2-Cosworth V8	

GP Starts: 57   GP Wins: 0   Pole positions: 0   Fastest laps: 0   Points: 11

ROBERTO MIERES

Mieres was a natural athlete who excelled at rowing, yachting and rugby until a broken leg ended his interest in the oval-ball game. After reaching championship class at tennis, he turned to motor sport with an MG, which was soon replaced by a Mercedes SSK with which he won an important race at Rosario. Racing the ex-Varzi Bugatti, Mieres won the Argentine sports car championship, and as a result was invited to accompany Fangio and Gonzalez on a short trip to Europe, during which he took a Ferrari to fourth in the Geneva GP of 1950.

Returning home he waited for an opportunity to race abroad once more, which finally came in 1953, when Gordini invited him to replace the injured Behra. Little came his way in terms of results, but he drove brilliantly to finish fourth in the F1 Albi GP with the F2 car. In 1954 Roberto ordered a Maserati 250F, but he started the season with the interim A6GCM/250 and scored a superb second place in the Buenos Aires City GP. He was frustrated by the non-appearance of his new car for most of the year, but made the best of it, taking third at Pau and fourth in the International Trophy at Silverstone. When the 250F eventually arrived, Mieres immediately took fourth places in Swiss and Spanish GPs, so impressing the factory that he was taken on for 1955.

Ably supporting team leader Jean Behra, Mieres enjoyed a consistent season, doing particularly well in non-championship races, taking second in the Turin GP and third at both Pau and Bordeaux. Political upheaval at home prompted Mieres to retire from Grands Prix at the end of 1955 to tend his business intesests, and he returned to his earlier passion of yachting.

Roberto was tempted back behind the wheel, however. He finished fourth In the 1957 Buenos Aires 1000 Km in the Ecurie Ecosse Jaguar D-Type, while in 1958 he raced a Centro Sud Maserati 250 F in the Buenos Aires City GP, and shared a works Porsche with Barth and d'Orey in the 1000 Km, claiming a class win and fifth place overall, before quitting for good.

FRANÇOIS MIGAULT

A former Volant Shell winner, Migault seemed to have a promising future when he shone in Formula 3 during the 1970 and '71 seasons with a Tecno. His first Formula 2 races brought fourth place at Albi and fifth at Rouen, before he made his first attempt at Grands Prix with the enthusiastic but naïve Connew project in 1972. François marked time somewhat in 1973 with the F2 Pygmée, before joining compatriots Beltoise and Pescarolo in the Motul-backed BRM team for 1974. Despite making do with the worst of machinery, as befitted the third driver, Migault did well to qualify the car for most of the races, his best result being a fifth place in the International Trophy. Subsequently he scraped a handful of rides in 1975 with Hill and Williams, but nothing of note was achieved before an equally moribund year in Formula 2 with the works Osella in 1976.

Already experienced in sports cars, François had shared a Matra with Jabouille to take third place at Le Mans in 1974, and went one better in 1976, finishing second in the Mirage GR8. Since then he has become a perennial at his local Sarthe circuit, although outright success has so far eluded him (he was still trying in 1993), and he has recently been active in the USA, racing a Kudzu-Buick in IMSA.

JOHN MILES

The son of the late thespian Sir Bernard Miles, John chose not to pursue a life in the theatre, gaining numerous victories at club level in his Diva-Ford in 1964. Under the wing of Willment he continued his winning ways in 1965 and received a third-place Grovewood Award.

Scoring nine consecutive wins with the Willment Lotus Elan at the start of 1966, John soon became involved with the works team, racing the GT Europa and F3 Lotus 41 in 1967 and 1968 with tremendous success. A planned season with Lotus in Formula 2 in 1969 never took off, but he did finish third in the Rome GP and fifth at Hockhenheim from three starts before Colin Chapman entrusted him with the task of developing the Lotus 63 4WD car in five Grands Prix.

His reward was a place alongside Jochen Rindt in the Lotus team for the 1970 season, which started well with a fifth place in the Lotus 49C in South Africa, but gradually declined as Miles' apprehension over the fragility of the new Lotus 72 steadily grew. After Rindt's fatal crash at Monza, John was summarily replaced by Reine Wisell and his Grand Prix career was done. He found a ride in the DART sports car team the following season, but soon retired to concentrate on his new occupation as a motoring journalist, road-testing cars, before returning to Lotus in an engineering capacity.

MIERES, Roberto (RA) b 3/12/1924

1953

	Race	Circuit	No	Entrant	Car/Engine	Comment
ret	DUTCH GP	Zandvoort	22	Equipe Gordini	2.0 Gordini Type 16 6	transmission
ret	FRENCH GP	Reims	8	Equipe Gordini	2.0 Gordini Type 16 6	rear axle
6	ITALIAN GP	Monza	40	Equipe Gordini	2.0 Gordini Type 16 6	3 laps behind

1954

	Race	Circuit	No	Entrant	Car/Engine	Comment
ret	ARGENTINE GP	Buenos Aires	32	Roberto Mieres	2.5 Maserati A6GCM/250F 6	engine
ret	BELGIAN GP	Spa	24	Roberto Mieres	2.5 Maserati A6GCM/250F 6	fire
ret	FRENCH GP	Reims	16	Roberto Mieres	2.5 Maserati A6GCM/250F 6	engine
6	BRITISH GP	Silverstone	4	Roberto Mieres	2.5 Maserati A6GCM/250F 6	3 laps behind
ret	GERMAN GP	Nürburgring	8	Roberto Mieres	2.5 Maserati 250F 6	fuel leak
4	SWISS GP	Bremgarten	30	Officine Alfieri Maserati	2.5 Maserati 250F 6	2 laps behind
ret	ITALIAN GP	Monza	24	Officine Alfieri Maserati	2.5 Maserati 250F 6	suspension
4	SPANISH GP	Pedralbes	10	Officine Alfieri Maserati	2.5 Maserati 250F 6	1 lap behind

1955

	Race	Circuit	No	Entrant	Car/Engine	Comment
5	ARGENTINE GP	Buenos Aires	15	Officine Alfieri Maserati	2.5 Maserati 250F 6	5 laps behind
ret	MONACO GP	Monte Carlo	36	Officine Alfieri Maserati	2.5 Maserati 250F 6	rear axle
5*	BELGIAN GP	Spa	24	Officine Alfieri Maserati	2.5 Maserati 250F 6	* Behra took over/1 lap behind
4	DUTCH GP	Zandvoort	16	Officine Alfieri Maserati	2.5 Maserati 250F 6	FL/1 lap behind
ret	BRITISH GP	Aintree	6	Officine Alfieri Maserati	2.5 Maserati 250F 6	engine
7	ITALIAN GP	Monza	28	Officine Alfieri Maserati	2.5 Maserati 250F 6	2 laps behind

GP Starts: 17   GP Wins: 0   Pole positions: 0   Fastest laps: 1   Points: 13

MIGAULT, François (F) b 4/12/1944

1972

	Race	Circuit	No	Entrant	Car/Engine	Comment
dns	BRITISH GP	Brands Hatch	34	Darnvall Connew Racing Team	3.0 Connew PC1-Cosworth V8	suspension in practice
ret	AUSTRIAN GP	Österreichring	29	Darnvall Connew Racing Team	3.0 Connew PC1-Cosworth V8	rear wishbone mounting point

1974

	Race	Circuit	No	Entrant	Car/Engine	Comment
ret	ARGENTINE GP	Buenos Aires	37	Team BRM	3.0 BRM P160E V12	water leak
16	BRAZILIAN GP	Interlagos	37	Team BRM	3.0 BRM P160E V12	2 laps behind
15	SOUTH AFRICAN GP	Kyalami	37	Team BRM	3.0 BRM P160E V12	3 laps behind
ret	SPANISH GP	Jarama	37	Team BRM	3.0 BRM P160E V12	engine
16	BELGIAN GP	Nivelles	37	Team BRM	3.0 BRM P160E V12	3 laps behind
ret	MONACO GP	Monte Carlo	37	Team BRM	3.0 BRM P160E V12	brake failure-crashed
ret	DUTCH GP	Zandvoort	37	Team BRM	3.0 BRM P201 V12	gear linkage
dns	"	"	37	Team BRM	3.0 BRM P160E V12	practice only-Pescarolo in race
14	FRENCH GP	Dijon	37	Team BRM	3.0 BRM P160E V12	2 laps behind
nc	BRITISH GP	Brands Hatch	37	Team BRM	3.0 BRM P160E V12	2 pit stops-rear wing/-12 laps
dnq	GERMAN GP	Nürburgring	37	Team BRM	3.0 BRM P160E V12	
ret	ITALIAN GP	Monza	37	Team BRM	3.0 BRM P201 V12	gearbox

1975

	Race	Circuit	No	Entrant	Car/Engine	Comment
nc	SPANISH GP	Montjuich Park	23	Embassy Racing with Graham Hill	3.0 Hill GH1-Cosworth V8	hit Peterson-pit stop/-11 laps
ret	BELGIAN GP	Zolder	23	Embassy Racing with Graham Hill	3.0 Hill GH1-Cosworth V8	rear suspension sub-frame
dns	FRENCH GP	Paul Ricard	20	Frank Williams Racing Cars	3.0 Williams FW03-Cosworth V8	engine in practice

GP Starts: 13   GP Wins: 0   Pole positions: 0   Fastest laps: 0   Points: 0

MILES, John (GB) b 14/6/1943

1969

	Race	Circuit	No	Entrant	Car/Engine	Comment
ret	FRENCH GP	Clermont Ferrand	14	Gold Leaf Team Lotus	3.0 Lotus 63-Cosworth V8	fuel pump belt
10	BRITISH GP	Silverstone	9	Gold Leaf Team Lotus	3.0 Lotus 63-Cosworth V8	pit stop-gearbox/9 laps behind
ret	ITALIAN GP	Monza	6	Gold Leaf Team Lotus	3.0 Lotus 63-Cosworth V8	engine
ret	CANADIAN GP	Mosport Park	3	Gold Leaf Team Lotus	3.0 Lotus 63-Cosworth V8	gearbox
ret	MEXICAN GP	Mexico City	9	Gold Leaf Team Lotus	3.0 Lotus 63-Cosworth V8	fuel pump

1970

	Race	Circuit	No	Entrant	Car/Engine	Comment
5	SOUTH AFRICAN GP	Kyalami	10	Gold Leaf Team Lotus	3.0 Lotus 49C-Cosworth V8	1 lap behind
dnq	SPANISH GP	Jarama	19	Gold Leaf Team Lotus	3.0 Lotus 72-Cosworth V8	
dnq	MONACO GP	Monte Carlo	2T	Gold Leaf Team Lotus	3.0 Lotus 72-Cosworth V8	
dnq	"	"	2	Gold Leaf Team Lotus	3.0 Lotus 49C-Cosworth V8	
ret	BELGIAN GP	Spa	21	Gold Leaf Team Lotus	3.0 Lotus 72-Cosworth V8	fuel injection/tyres
dns	"	"	21	Gold Leaf Team Lotus	3.0 Lotus 49C-Cosworth V8	practice only-Rindt in race
7	DUTCH GP	Zandvoort	12	Gold Leaf Team Lotus	3.0 Lotus 72-Cosworth V8	2 laps behind
8	FRENCH GP	Clermont Ferrand	7	Gold Leaf Team Lotus	3.0 Lotus 72-Cosworth V8	
ret	BRITISH GP	Brands Hatch	6	Gold Leaf Team Lotus	3.0 Lotus 72-Cosworth V8	engine
ret	GERMAN GP	Hockenheim	16	Gold Leaf Team Lotus	3.0 Lotus 72-Cosworth V8	engine
ret	AUSTRIAN GP	Österreichring	7	Gold Leaf Team Lotus	3.0 Lotus 72C-Cosworth V8	front brake shaft
dns	ITALIAN GP	Monza	24	Gold Leaf Team Lotus	3.0 Lotus 72C-Cosworth V8	withdrawn after Rindt's fatal accident

GP Starts: 12   GP Wins: 0   Pole positions: 0   Fastest laps: 0   Points: 2

MILHOUX, André (B) 9/12/1928

1956

	Race	Circuit	No	Entrant	Car/Engine	Comment
ret	GERMAN GP	Nürburgring	11	Equipe Gordini	2.5 Gordini Type 32 8	misfire

GP Starts: 1   GP Wins: 0   Pole positions: 0   Fastest laps: 0   Points: 0

GERHARD MITTER

An outstanding driver, Mitter was an infrequent Grand Prix competitor who surely deserved more opportunities at the highest level, as he showed with his fourth place in de Beaufort's old Porsche in the 1963 German GP. As it was, he had to be content with just the annual outing at the Nürburgring, mainly in the Formula 2 class.

Gerhard was a top Formula Junior driver in the early sixties with his DKW-engined Lotus before joining Porsche in 1964. He was to become a mainstay of the German company's endurance racing programme, winning the Austrian GP in 1966 and the Targa Florio in 1969 and gaining many other fine placings, also becoming three-times European mountain-climb champion between 1966 and 1968.

In 1969 Mitter was also involved in the development of the Dornier-built BMW F2 contender, but he crashed fatally during practice for that year's German GP when, it was thought, a wheel may have come off the car.

STEFANO MODENA

Modena had served notice in karting that he was a man to watch, and when he finally got into Formula 3 he was soon a front-runner, taking fourth place in the Italian championship in 1986, impressing the F1 fraternity with a superb second place in the Monaco GP support race, and earning the title of 'European Champion' after victory in the one-off meeting at Imola.

Now with substantial backing, Modena moved straight into F3000 with the Onyx team and he took the championship at the first attempt, winning three races (at Vallelunga, Birmingham and Imola), but it was the way he went about the whole business that marked him as a special talent.

Much was expected of the tousle-haired Italian when he entered Grand Prix racing but after an end-of-season ride with Brabham he was forced to endure a discouraging learning year in 1988 with the uncompetitive EuroBrun before being given a chance to really show what he could do with Brabham in 1989. He finished in third place at Monaco, but the team lacked the financial recources to progress, and Stefano then marked time until 1991 when he moved to a Tyrrell team newly equipped with Honda power. Things started well with yet another superb display at Monaco, which ended with a broken engine when he lay second behind Senna, and then second place in the next race in Canada, but as the season wore on Modena seemed to lose heart too easily.

It was some surprise when he was signed to drive the Jordan-Yamaha in 1992, and it was to be a troubled season for the team which found the enigmatic Italian temperamentally unsuited to the situation. He scored a point in the last race of the year but was consigned to the wilderness for 1993, racing a BMW in the Italian touring car championship.

MITTER, Gerhard (D) b 30/8/1935 – d 1/8/1969

	Race	Circuit	No	Entrant	Car/Engine	Comment
1963						
ret	DUTCH GP	Zandvoort	34	Ecurie Maarsbergen	1.5 Porsche 718 F4	clutch
4	GERMAN GP	Nürburgring	26	Ecurie Maarsbergen	1.5 Porsche 718 F4	
1964						
9	GERMAN GP	Nürburgring	23	Team Lotus	1.5 Lotus 25-Climax V8	1 lap behind
1965						
ret	GERMAN GP	Nürburgring	3	Team Lotus	1.5 Lotus 25-Climax V8	water hose
1966						
dns	GERMAN GP	Nürburgring	30	Ron Harris Team Lotus	1.0 Lotus 44-Cosworth F2	withdrew-not fully fit after crash at Spa
1967						
ret	GERMAN GP (F2)	Nürburgring	20	Gerhard Mitter	1.6 Brabham BT23-Cosworth 4	engine
1969						
dns	GERMAN GP (F2)	Nürburgring	24	Bayerische Motoren Werke	BMW 269-4 F2	lost wheel-fatal accident

GP Starts: 5   GP Wins: 0   Pole positions: 0   Fastest laps: 0   Points: 3

MODENA, Stefano (I) b 12/5/1963

	Race	Circuit	No	Entrant	Car/Engine	Comment
1987						
ret	AUSTRALIAN GP	Adelaide	7	Motor Racing Developments	1.5 t/c Brabham BT56-BMW 4	driver exhaustion
1988						
ret	BRAZILIAN GP	Rio	33	EuroBrun Racing	3.5 EuroBrun ER188-Cosworth V8	engine cut out-fuel pump
nc	SAN MARINO GP	Imola	33	EuroBrun Racing	3.5 EuroBrun ER188-Cosworth V8	hit Palmer/gearbox trouble/-8 laps
dns	MONACO GP	Monte Carlo	33	EuroBrun Racing	3.5 EuroBrun ER188-Cosworth V8	excluded for missing weight check
dns	MEXICAN GP	Mexico City	33	EuroBrun Racing	3.5 EuroBrun ER188-Cosworth V8	excluded for rear wing infringement
12	CANADIAN GP	Montreal	33	EuroBrun Racing	3.5 EuroBrun ER188-Cosworth V8	3 laps behind

ret	US GP (DETROIT)	Detroit	33	EuroBrun Racing	3.5 EuroBrun ER188-Cosworth V8	*spun off*
14	FRENCH GP	Paul Ricard	33	EuroBrun Racing	3.5 EuroBrun ER188-Cosworth V8	*3 laps behind*
12	BRITISH GP	Silverstone	33	EuroBrun Racing	3.5 EuroBrun ER188-Cosworth V8	*1 lap behind*
ret	GERMAN GP	Hockenheim	33	EuroBrun Racing	3.5 EuroBrun ER188-Cosworth V8	*engine*
11	HUNGARIAN GP	Hungaroring	33	EuroBrun Racing	3.5 EuroBrun ER188-Cosworth V8	*4 laps behind*
dnq	BELGIAN GP	Spa	33	EuroBrun Racing	3.5 EuroBrun ER188-Cosworth V8	
dnq	ITALIAN GP	Monza	33	EuroBrun Racing	3.5 EuroBrun ER188-Cosworth V8	
dnq	PORTUGUESE GP	Estoril	33	EuroBrun Racing	3.5 EuroBrun ER188-Cosworth V8	
13	SPANISH GP	Jerez	33	EuroBrun Racing	3.5 EuroBrun ER188-Cosworth V8	*2 laps behind*
dnq	JAPANESE GP	Suzuka	33	EuroBrun Racing	3.5 EuroBrun ER188-Cosworth V8	
ret	AUSTRALIAN GP	Adelaide	33	EuroBrun Racing	3.5 EuroBrun ER188-Cosworth V8	*driveshaft*

1989

ret	BRAZILIAN GP	Rio	8	Motor Racing Developments	3.5 Brabham BT58-Judd V8	*driveshaft-c.v.joint*
ret	SAN MARINO GP	Imola	8	Motor Racing Developments	3.5 Brabham BT58-Judd V8	*spun into barrier*
3	MONACO GP	Monte Carlo	8	Motor Racing Developments	3.5 Brabham BT58-Judd V8	*1 lap behind*
10	MEXICAN GP	Mexico City	8	Motor Racing Developments	3.5 Brabham BT58-Judd V8	*1 lap behind*
ret	US GP (PHOENIX)	Phoenix	8	Motor Racing Developments	3.5 Brabham BT58-Judd V8	*brakes*
ret	CANADIAN GP	Montreal	8	Motor Racing Developments	3.5 Brabham BT58-Judd V8	*collision with Martini*
ret	FRENCH GP	Paul Ricard	8	Motor Racing Developments	3.5 Brabham BT58-Judd V8	*engine*
ret	BRITISH GP	Silverstone	8	Motor Racing Developments	3.5 Brabham BT58-Judd V8	*engine*
ret	GERMAN GP	Hockenheim	8	Motor Racing Developments	3.5 Brabham BT58-Judd V8	*engine*
11	HUNGARIAN GP	Hungaroring	8	Motor Racing Developments	3.5 Brabham BT58-Judd V8	*hit Sala-damaged nose cone/-1 lap*
ret	BELGIAN GP	Spa	8	Motor Racing Developments	3.5 Brabham BT58-Judd V8	*started from pit lane/handling*
dns	ITALIAN GP	Monza	8	Motor Racing Developments	3.5 Brabham BT58-Judd V8	*excluded-missed weight check*
14	PORTUGUESE GP	Estoril	8	Motor Racing Developments	3.5 Brabham BT58-Judd V8	*shock absorber/misfire/-2 laps*
ret	SPANISH GP	Jerez	8	Motor Racing Developments	3.5 Brabham BT58-Judd V8	*engine cut out-electrics*
ret	JAPANESE GP	Suzuka	8	Motor Racing Developments	3.5 Brabham BT58-Judd V8	*alternator*
8	AUSTRALIAN GP	Adelaide	8	Motor Racing Developments	3.5 Brabham BT58-Judd V8	*6 laps behind*

1990

5	US GP (PHOENIX)	Phoenix	8	Motor Racing Developments	3.5 Brabham BT58-Judd V8	*went up escape road*
ret	BRAZILIAN GP	Interlagos	8	Motor Racing Developments	3.5 Brabham BT58-Judd V8	*spun off*
ret	SAN MARINO GP	Imola	8	Motor Racing Developments	3.5 Brabham BT59-Judd V8	*brakes*
ret	MONACO GP	Monte Carlo	8	Motor Racing Developments	3.5 Brabham BT59-Judd V8	*transmission*
7	CANADIAN GP	Montreal	8	Motor Racing Developments	3.5 Brabham BT59-Judd V8	*2 laps behind*
11	MEXICAN GP	Mexico City	8	Motor Racing Developments	3.5 Brabham BT59-Judd V8	*1 lap behind*
13	FRENCH GP	Paul Ricard	8	Motor Racing Developments	3.5 Brabham BT59-Judd V8	*2 laps behind*
9	BRITISH GP	Silverstone	8	Motor Racing Developments	3.5 Brabham BT59-Judd V8	*spin-pit stop/2 laps behind*
ret	GERMAN GP	Hockenheim	8	Motor Racing Developments	3.5 Brabham BT59-Judd V8	*clutch on startline*
ret	HUNGARIAN GP	Hungaroring	8	Motor Racing Developments	3.5 Brabham BT59-Judd V8	*engine*
17/ret	BELGIAN GP	Spa	8	Motor Racing Developments	3.5 Brabham BT59-Judd V8	*engine*
ret	ITALIAN GP	Monza	8	Motor Racing Developments	3.5 Brabham BT59-Judd V8	*engine/5 laps behind*
ret	PORTUGUESE GP	Estoril	8	Motor Racing Developments	3.5 Brabham BT59-Judd V8	*gearbox*
ret	SPANISH GP	Jerez	8	Motor Racing Developments	3.5 Brabham BT59-Judd V8	*collision with Tarquini*
ret	JAPANESE GP	Suzuka	8	Motor Racing Developments	3.5 Brabham BT59-Judd V8	*spun off*
12	AUSTRALIAN GP	Adelaide	8	Motor Racing Developments	3.5 Brabham BT59-Judd V8	*pit stop-tyres/4 laps behind*

1991

4	US GP (PHOENIX)	Phoenix	4	Braun Tyrrell Honda	3.5 Tyrrell 020-Honda V10	
ret	BRAZILIAN GP	Interlagos	4	Braun Tyrrell Honda	3.5 Tyrrell 020-Honda V10	*gearshift*
ret	SAN MARINO GP	Imola	4	Braun Tyrrell Honda	3.5 Tyrrell 020-Honda V10	*engine*
ret	MONACO GP	Monte Carlo	4	Braun Tyrrell Honda	3.5 Tyrrell 020-Honda V10	*lay 2nd for 42 laps/engine*
2	CANADIAN GP	Montreal	4	Braun Tyrrell Honda	3.5 Tyrrell 020-Honda V10	
11	MEXICAN GP	Mexico City	4	Braun Tyrrell Honda	3.5 Tyrrell 020-Honda V10	*3 tyre stops/2 laps behind*
ret	FRENCH GP	Magny Cours	4	Braun Tyrrell Honda	3.5 Tyrrell 020-Honda V10	*gearbox*
7	BRITISH GP	Silverstone	4	Braun Tyrrell Honda	3.5 Tyrrell 020-Honda V10	*1 lap behind*
13	GERMAN GP	Hockenheim	4	Braun Tyrrell Honda	3.5 Tyrrell 020-Honda V10	*3 tyre stops/4 laps behind*
12	HUNGARIAN GP	Hungaroring	4	Braun Tyrrell Honda	3.5 Tyrrell 020-Honda V10	*2 laps behind*
ret	BELGIAN GP	Spa	4	Braun Tyrrell Honda	3.5 Tyrrell 020-Honda V10	*oil leak/fire*
ret	ITALIAN GP	Monza	4	Braun Tyrrell Honda	3.5 Tyrrell 020-Honda V10	*engine*
ret	PORTUGUESE GP	Estoril	4	Braun Tyrrell Honda	3.5 Tyrrell 020-Honda V10	*engine*
16	SPANISH GP	Jerez	4	Braun Tyrrell Honda	3.5 Tyrrell 020-Honda V10	*3 laps behind*
6	JAPANESE GP	Suzuka	4	Braun Tyrrell Honda	3.5 Tyrrell 020-Honda V10	*1 lap behind*
10	AUSTRALIAN GP	Adelaide	4	Braun Tyrrell Honda	3.5 Tyrrell 020-Honda V10	*heavy rain-race stopped at 14 laps*

1992

dnq	SOUTH AFRICAN GP	Kyalami	32	Sasol Jordan Yamaha	3.5 Jordan 192-Yamaha V12	
ret	MEXICAN GP	Mexico City	32	Sasol Jordan Yamaha	3.5 Jordan 192-Yamaha V12	*gearbox*
ret	BRAZILIAN GP	Interlagos	32	Sasol Jordan Yamaha	3.5 Jordan 192-Yamaha V12	*gearbox*
dnq	SPANISH GP	Barcelona	32	Sasol Jordan Yamaha	3.5 Jordan 192-Yamaha V12	
ret	SAN MARINO GP	Imola	32	Sasol Jordan Yamaha	3.5 Jordan 192-Yamaha V12	*gearbox*
ret	MONACO GP	Monte Carlo	32	Sasol Jordan Yamaha	3.5 Jordan 192-Yamaha V12	*crashed at Casino square*
ret	CANADIAN GP	Montreal	32	Sasol Jordan Yamaha	3.5 Jordan 192-Yamaha V12	*transmission*
ret	FRENCH GP	Magny Cours	32	Sasol Jordan Yamaha	3.5 Jordan 192-Yamaha V12	*engine*
ret	BRITISH GP	Silverstone	32	Sasol Jordan Yamaha	3.5 Jordan 192-Yamaha V12	*engine*
dnq	GERMAN GP	Hockenheim	32	Sasol Jordan Yamaha	3.5 Jordan 192-Yamaha V12	
ret	HUNGARIAN GP	Hungaroring	32	Sasol Jordan Yamaha	3.5 Jordan 192-Yamaha V12	*hit by Grouillard*
15	BELGIAN GP	Spa	32	Sasol Jordan Yamaha	3.5 Jordan 192-Yamaha V12	*2 laps behind*
dnq	ITALIAN GP	Monza	32	Sasol Jordan Yamaha	3.5 Jordan 192-Yamaha V12	
13	PORTUGUESE GP	Estoril	32	Sasol Jordan Yamaha	3.5 Jordan 192-Yamaha V12	*3 laps behind*
7	JAPANESE GP	Suzuka	32	Sasol Jordan Yamaha	3.5 Jordan 192-Yamaha V12	*1 lap behind*
6	AUSTRALIAN GP	Adelaide	32	Sasol Jordan Yamaha	3.5 Jordan 192-Yamaha V12	*1 lap behind*

GP Starts: 70   GP Wins: 0   Pole positions: 0   Fastest laps: 0   Points: 17

MONTGOMERIE-CHARRINGTON, Robin (GB) b 22/6/1915

1952

	Race	Circuit	No	Entrant	Car/Engine	Comment
ret	BELGIAN GP	Spa	40	Robin Montgomerie-Charrington	2.0 Aston Butterworth F4	misfire

GP Starts: 1   GP Wins: 0   Pole positions: 0   Fastest laps: 0   Points: 0

MORBIDELLI, Gianni (I) b 13/1/1968

1990

	Race	Circuit	No	Entrant	Car/Engine	Comment
dnq	US GP (PHOENIX)	Phoenix	21	Scuderia Italia	3.5 BMS Dallara F190-Cosworth V8	
14	BRAZILIAN GP	Interlagos	21	Scuderia Italia	3.5 BMS Dallara F190-Cosworth V8	pit stop-jammed throttle/-7 laps
ret	JAPANESE GP	Suzuka	24	SCM Minardi Team	3.5 Minardi M190-Cosworth V8	spun off
ret	AUSTRALIAN GP	Adelaide	24	SCM Minardi Team	3.5 Minardi M190-Cosworth V8	gearbox

1991

	Race	Circuit	No	Entrant	Car/Engine	Comment
ret	US GP (PHOENIX)	Phoenix	24	SCM Minardi Team	3.5 Minardi M191-Ferrari V12	gearbox
8	BRAZILIAN GP	Interlagos	24	SCM Minardi Team	3.5 Minardi M191-Ferrari V12	2 laps behind
ret	SAN MARINO GP	Imola	24	SCM Minardi Team	3.5 Minardi M191-Ferrari V12	gearbox
ret	MONACO GP	Monte Carlo	24	SCM Minardi Team	3.5 Minardi M191-Ferrari V12	gearbox
ret	CANADIAN GP	Montreal	24	SCM Minardi Team	3.5 Minardi M191-Ferrari V12	spun off
7	MEXICAN GP	Mexico City	24	SCM Minardi Team	3.5 Minardi M191-Ferrari V12	1 lap behind
ret	FRENCH GP	Magny Cours	24	SCM Minardi Team	3.5 Minardi M191-Ferrari V12	spun off
11	BRITISH GP	Silverstone	24	SCM Minardi Team	3.5 Minardi M191-Ferrari V12	2 laps behind
ret	GERMAN GP	Hockenheim	24	SCM Minardi Team	3.5 Minardi M191-Ferrari V12	engine
13	HUNGARIAN GP	Hungaroring	24	SCM Minardi Team	3.5 Minardi M191-Ferrari V12	2 laps behind
ret	BELGIAN GP	Spa	24	SCM Minardi Team	3.5 Minardi M191-Ferrari V12	engine
9	ITALIAN GP	Monza	24	SCM Minardi Team	3.5 Minardi M191-Ferrari V12	1 lap behind
9	PORTUGUESE GP	Estoril	24	SCM Minardi Team	3.5 Minardi M191-Ferrari V12	1 lap behind
14/ret	SPANISH GP	Barcelona	24	SCM Minardi Team	3.5 Minardi M191-Ferrari V12	spun off
ret	JAPANESE GP	Suzuka	24	SCM Minardi Team	3.5 Minardi M191-Ferrari V12	wheel bearing
6*	AUSTRALIAN GP	Adelaide	27	Scuderia Ferrari SpA	3.5 Fiat Ferrari 642 V12	shortened race/*half points awarded

1992

	Race	Circuit	No	Entrant	Car/Engine	Comment
ret	SOUTH AFRICAN GP	Kyalami	24	Minardi Team	3.5 Minardi M191B-Lamborghini V12	engine
ret	MEXICAN GP	Mexico City	24	Minardi Team	3.5 Minardi M191B-Lamborghini V12	spun off
7	BRAZILIAN GP	Interlagos	24	Minardi Team	3.5 Minardi M191B-Lamborghini V12	2 laps behind
ret	SPANISH GP	Barcelona	24	Minardi Team	3.5 Minardi M191B-Lamborghini V12	handling
ret	SAN MARINO GP	Imola	24	Minardi Team	3.5 Minardi M192-Lamborghini V12	transmission
ret	MONACO GP	Monte Carlo	24	Minardi Team	3.5 Minardi M192-Lamborghini V12	flat battery
11	CANADIAN GP	Montreal	24	Minardi Team	3.5 Minardi M192-Lamborghini V12	2 laps behind
8	FRENCH GP	Magny Cours	24	Minardi Team	3.5 Minardi M192-Lamborghini V12	agg of two parts/1 lap behind
17/ret	BRITISH GP	Silverstone	24	Minardi Teami	3.5 Minardi M192-Lamborghini V12	engine/6 laps behind
12	GERMAN GP	Hockenheim	24	Minardi Team	3.5 Minardi M192-Lamborghini V12	1 lap behind
dnq	HUNGARIAN GP	Hungaroring	24	Minardi Team	3.5 Minardi M192-Lamborghini V12	
16	BELGIAN GP	Spa	24	Minardi Team	3.5 Minardi M192-Lamborghini V12	2 laps behind
ret	ITALIAN GP	Monza	24	Minardi Team	3.5 Minardi M192-Lamborghini V12	engine
14	PORTUGUESE GP	Estoril	24	Minardi Team	3.5 Minardi M192-Lamborghini V12	3 laps behind
14	JAPANESE GP	Suzuka	24	Minardi Team	3.5 Minardi M192-Lamborghini V12	2 laps behind
10	AUSTRALIAN GP	Adelaide	24	Minardi Team	3.5 Minardi M192-Lamborghini V12	2 laps behind

GP Starts: 34   GP Wins: 0   Pole positions: 0   Fastest laps: 0   Points: 0.5

MORENO, Roberto (BR) b 11/2/1959

1982

	Race	Circuit	No	Entrant	Car/Engine	Comment
dnq	DUTCH GP	Zandvoort	12	John Player Team Lotus	3.0 Lotus 91-Cosworth V8	

1987

| ret | JAPANESE GP | Suzuka | 14 | Team El Charro AGS | 3.5 AGS JH22-Cosworth V8 | engine |
| 6 | AUSTRALIAN GP | Adelaide | 14 | Team El Charro AGS | 3.5 AGS JH22-Cosworth V8 | 3rd non-turbo/3 laps behind |

1989

dnq	BRAZILIAN GP	Rio	31	Coloni SpA	3.5 Coloni FC188B-Cosworth V8	
dnq	SAN MARINO GP	Imola	31	Coloni SpA	3.5 Coloni FC188B-Cosworth V8	
ret	MONACO GP	Monte Carlo	31	Coloni SpA	3.5 Coloni FC188B-Cosworth V8	gearbox
dnq	MEXICAN GP	Mexico City	31	Coloni SpA	3.5 Coloni FC188B-Cosworth V8	
dnq	US GP (PHOENIX)	Phoenix	31	Coloni SpA	3.5 Coloni FC188B-Cosworth V8	
ret	CANADIAN GP	Montreal	31	Coloni SpA	3.5 Coloni C3-Cosworth V8	transmission
dns	"	"	31	Coloni SpA	3.5 Coloni FC188B-Cosworth V8	practice only
dnq	FRENCH GP	Paul Ricard	31	Coloni SpA	3.5 Coloni C3-Cosworth V8	
ret	BRITISH GP	Silverstone	31	Coloni SpA	3.5 Coloni C3-Cosworth V8	gearbox
dnpq	GERMAN GP	Hockenheim	31	Coloni SpA	3.5 Coloni C3-Cosworth V8	
dnpq	HUNGARIAN GP	Hungaroring	31	Coloni SpA	3.5 Coloni C3-Cosworth V8	
dnpq	BELGIAN GP	Spa	31	Coloni SpA	3.5 Coloni C3-Cosworth V8	
dnpq	ITALIAN GP	Monza	31	Coloni SpA	3.5 Coloni C3-Cosworth V8	
ret	PORTUGUESE GP	Estoril	31	Coloni SpA	3.5 Coloni C3-Cosworth V8	electrics
dnpq	SPANISH GP	Jerez	31	Coloni SpA	3.5 Coloni C3-Cosworth V8	
dnpq	JAPANESE GP	Suzuka	31	Coloni SpA	3.5 Coloni C3-Cosworth V8	
dnpq	AUSTRALIAN GP	Adelaide	31	Coloni SpA	3.5 Coloni C3-Cosworth V8	

1990

| 13 | US GP (PHOENIX) | Phoenix | 33 | EuroBrun Racing | 3.5 EuroBrun ER189-Judd V8 | pit stop-flat battery/5 laps behind |
| dnpq | BRAZILIAN GP | Interlagos | 33 | EuroBrun Racing | 3.5 EuroBrun ER189-Judd V8 | |

ret	SAN MARINO GP	Imola	33	EuroBrun Racing	3.5 EuroBrun ER189-Judd V8	sticking throttle-lap 1
dnq	MONACO GP	Monte Carlo	33	EuroBrun Racing	3.5 EuroBrun EF189-Judd V8	
dnq	CANADIAN GP	Montreal	33	EuroBrun Racing	3.5 EuroBrun EF189-Judd V8	
excl	MEXICAN GP	Mexico City	33	EuroBrun Racing	3.5 EuroBrun EF189B-Judd V8	push start after spin in practice
dnpq	FRENCH GP	Paul Ricard	33	EuroBrun Racing	3.5 EuroBrun EF189B-Judd V8	
dnpq	BRITISH GP	Silverstone	33	EuroBrun Racing	3.5 EuroBrun EF189B-Judd V8	
dnpq	GERMAN GP	Hockenheim	33	EuroBrun Racing	3.5 EuroBrun EF189B-Judd V8	
dnpq	HUNGARIAN GP	Hungaroring	33	EuroBrun Racing	3.5 EuroBrun EF189B-Judd V8	
dnpq	BELGIAN GP	Spa	33	EuroBrun Racing	3.5 EuroBrun EF189B-Judd V8	
dnpq	ITALIAN GP	Monza	33	EuroBrun Racing	3.5 EuroBrun EF189B-Judd V8	
dnpq	PORTUGUESE GP	Estoril	33	EuroBrun Racing	3.5 EuroBrun EF189B-Judd V8	
dnpq	SPANISH GP	Jerez	33	EuroBrun Racing	3.5 EuroBrun EF189B-Judd V8	
2	JAPANESE GP	Suzuka	19	Benetton Formula	3.5 Benetton B190-Ford HB V8	
7	AUSTRALIAN GP	Adelaide	19	Benetton Formula	3.5 Benetton B190-Ford HB V8	pit stop-tyres/1 lap behind

1991

ret	US GP (PHOENIX)	Phoenix	19	Camel Benetton Ford	3.5 Benetton B190B-Ford HB V8	hit Patrese's spun car
7	BRAZILIAN GP	Interlagos	19	Camel Benetton Ford	3.5 Benetton B190B-Ford HB V8	1 lap behind
13/ret	SAN MARINO GP	Imola	19	Camel Benetton Ford	3.5 Benetton B190B-Ford HB V8	gearbox/engine/7 laps behind
4	MONACO GP	Monte Carlo	19	Camel Benetton Ford	3.5 Benetton B190B-Ford HB V8	1 lap behind
ret	CANADIAN GP	Montreal	19	Camel Benetton Ford	3.5 Benetton B190B-Ford HB V8	spun off-suspension damage
5	MEXICAN GP	Mexico City	19	Camel Benetton Ford	3.5 Benetton B190B-Ford HB V8	1 lap behind
ret	FRENCH GP	Magny Cours	19	Camel Benetton Ford	3.5 Benetton B190B-Ford HB V8	driver unwell
ret	BRITISH GP	Silverstone	19	Camel Benetton Ford	3.5 Benetton B190B-Ford HB V8	gearbox
8	GERMAN GP	Hockenheim	19	Camel Benetton Ford	3.5 Benetton B190B-Ford HB V8	1 lap behind
8	HUNGARIAN GP	Hungaroring	19	Camel Benetton Ford	3.5 Benetton B190B-Ford HB V8	1 lap behind
4	BELGIAN GP	Spa	19	Camel Benetton Ford	3.5 Benetton B190B-Ford HB V8	FL
ret	ITALIAN GP	Monza	32	Team 7UP Jordan	3.5 Jordan 191-Ford HB V8	spun off-brakes
10	PORTUGUESE GP	Estoril	32	Team 7UP Jordan	3.5 Jordan 191-Ford HB V8	1 lap behind
16	AUSTRALIAN GP	Adelaide	24	Minardi Team	3.5 Minardi M191-Ferrari V12	rain shortened race/1 lap behind

1992

dnpq	BRAZILIAN GP	Interlagos	34	Andrea Moda Formula	3.5 Moda S921-Judd V10	
dnpq	SPANISH GP	Barcelona	34	Andrea Moda Formula	3.5 Moda S921-Judd V10	
dnpq	SAN MARINO GP	Imola	34	Andrea Moda Formula	3.5 Moda S921-Judd V10	
ret	MONACO GP	Monte Carlo	34	Andrea Moda Formula	3.5 Moda S921-Judd V10	engine
dnpq	CANADIAN GP	Montreal	34	Andrea Moda Formula	3.5 Moda S921-Judd V10	
dnc	FRENCH GP	Magny Cours	34	Andrea Moda Formula	3.5 Moda S921-Judd V10	team failed to arrive for practice
dnpq	BRITISH GP	Silverstone	34	Andrea Moda Formula	3.5 Moda S921-Judd V10	
dnpq	GERMAN GP	Hockenheim	34	Andrea Moda Formula	3.5 Moda S921-Judd V10	
dnq	HUNGARIAN GP	Hungaroring	34	Andrea Moda Formula	3.5 Moda S921-Judd V10	
dnq	BELGIAN GP	Spa	34	Andrea Moda Formula	3.5 Moda S921-Judd V10	
dnp	ITALIAN GP	Monza	34	Andrea Moda Formula	3.5 Moda S921-Judd V10	team excluded from championship

GP Starts: 25   GP Wins: 0   Pole positions: 0   Fastest laps: 1   Points: 15

GIANNI MORBIDELLI

With a racing background (his family produced World Championship-winning motor cycles), Morbidelli raced karts from 1981 to 1986 before moving into Italian F3. Although he was certainly quick he was prone to accidents, which spoiled his 1988 season, but the following year he deservedly claimed the crown with his Forti Corse Dallara, earning a testing contract with Ferrari.

The 1990 season saw him make a brief unscheduled Grand Prix debut for Dallara in place of the indisposed Pirro, before he concentrated on his planned F3000 campaign with Forti, which got off to a slow start. Once he got to grips with the Lola he scored a fine win at Enna and, with Paolo Barilla out of favour at Minardi, Gianni finished the season back in Formula 1 with the luxury of a contract in his pocket for a full season with the Faenza team (and Ferrari power) in 1991. The campaign failed to live up to expectations, but Gianni impressed enough for Ferrari to draft him in to replace the departed Prost in Australia, where he finished sixth in the rain-shortened race to earn a priceless half-point.

He returned to Minardi in 1992, but the season was spent in the mire once more as they struggled to develop their Lamborghini-powered car. Without the necessary sponsorship to retain his place, Morbidelli then found himself dumped and was left to race in the Italian touring car championship, hoping for a return to the big league at some time in the future.

ROBERTO MORENO

A childhood friend and karting companion of Nelson Piquet, Roberto followed the future World Champion to Europe in 1979; he soon made a big impact in a Royale, and then in 1980 won 15 races and the British FF1600 championship in a van Diemen. A testing contract with Lotus gave Moreno the lifeline to sustain a Formula 3 career, while a victory in the Australian GP with a Ralt (beating Piquet and Jones) at the end of 1981 raised his profile greatly. He started 1982 winning in Formula Atlantic in the USA before having a disastrous outing for Lotus at Zandvoort, where he failed to qualify, which handicapped his career for a number of years. In 1984 he finished second to team-mate Thackwell in the Formula 2 championship, but a chance of a Formula 1 return with Toleman foundered when the team failed to tie up a tyre deal. This led Roberto to try his hand at IndyCar racing with Rick Galles, and while results were disappointing the little Brazilian impressed.

Returning to Europe in 1987, Moreno was back with Ralt in F3000, but his luck was out. Leading round after round, his car always seemed to hit trouble and he only managed to win one race, at Enna. Fortune did smile with a return to Grands Prix with the little AGS team which yielded a point in the Australian GP, but with no chance of racing with them in 1988 due to a lack of funds, Moreno was forced to stay in F3000, and showed his talent by clinching the championship with a virtually unsponsored Reynard, winning four rounds.

Buoyed by a testing contract with Ferrari, Roberto took up a drive with Coloni, then joined EuroBrun, only for the team to fold. Dramatically, after a run of non-qualifications, he was then given the Benetton seat in place of the injured Nannini, and a sensational debut in Japan saw him finish second to team-mate Piquet and gain a well-earned contract for 1991. His big season was something of an anti-climax, however, and Roberto found himself turfed out of the team, ironically after his best race of the year at Spa. After seeing out the season with Jordan and Minardi, Moreno was back at square one in 1992, with the hapless Andrea Moda outfit, though he did brilliantly to qualify the car at Monaco. When the team were finally thrown out of the championship Roberto was left with no option but to find a ride in Italian touring cars, but in 1993 he was enjoying his racing again with an Alfa in the French Supertourisme championship.

MORGAN, Dave (GB) b 7/8/1944

1975

	Race	Circuit	No	Entrant	Car/Engine	Comment
18/ret	BRITISH GP	Silverstone	19	National Organs-Team Surtees	3.0 Surtees TS16-Cosworth V8	crashed in rainstorm/6 laps behind

GP Starts: 1   GP Wins: 0   Pole positions: 0   Fastest laps: 1   Points: 0

MOSER, Silvio (CH) b 24/4/1941 – d 26/5/1974

1966

	Race	Circuit	No	Entrant	Car/Engine	Comment
dns	GERMAN GP (F2)	Nürburgring	35	Silvio Moser	1.0 Brabham BT16-Cosworth 4	engine in practice

1967

ret	BRITISH GP	Silverstone	22	Charles Vögele	2.7 Cooper T77-ATS V8	no oil pressure

1968

dnq	MONACO GP	Monte Carlo	21	Charles Vögele	3.0 Brabham BT20-Repco V8	
5	DUTCH GP	Zandvoort	22	Charles Vögele	3.0 Brabham BT20-Repco V8	3 laps behind
nc	BRITISH GP	Brands Hatch	19	Charles Vögele	3.0 Brabham BT20-Repco V8	pit stops-gearbox/28 laps behind
dnq	ITALIAN GP	Monza	12	Charles Vögele	3.0 Brabham BT20-Repco V8	

1969

ret	MONACO GP	Monte Carlo	17	Silvio Moser Racing Team	3.0 Brabham BT24-Cosworth V8	driveshaft
ret	DUTCH GP	Zandvoort	17	Silvio Moser Racing Team	3.0 Brabham BT24-Cosworth V8	steering/electrics
7	FRENCH GP	Clermont Ferrand	12	Silvio Moser Racing Team	3.0 Brabham BT24-Cosworth V8	2 laps behind
ret	ITALIAN GP	Monza	36	Silvio Moser Racing Team	3.0 Brabham BT24-Cosworth V8	fuel leak
ret	CANADIAN GP	Mosport Park	20	Silvio Moser Racing Team	3.0 Brabham BT24-Cosworth V8	put off road by Pease
6	US GP	Watkins Glen	19	Silvio Moser Racing Team	3.0 Brabham BT24-Cosworth V8	pit stop/10 laps behind
ret	MEXICAN GP	Mexico City	19	Silvio Moser Racing Team	3.0 Brabham BT24-Cosworth V8	fuel leak

1970

dnq	DUTCH GP	Zandvoort	29	Silvio Moser Racing Team	3.0 Bellasi-Cosworth V8	
dnq	FRENCH GP	Clermont Ferrand	24	Silvio Moser Racing Team	3.0 Bellasi-Cosworth V8	
dnq	GERMAN GP	Nürburgring	27	Silvio Moser Racing Team	3.0 Bellasi-Cosworth V8	
ret	AUSTRIAN GP	Österreichring	24	Silvio Moser Racing Team	3.0 Bellasi-Cosworth V8	radiator
dnq	ITALIAN GP	Monza	56	Silvio Moser Racing Team	3.0 Bellasi-Cosworth V8	

1971

ret	ITALIAN GP	Monza	27	Jolly Club Switzerland	3.0 Bellasi-Cosworth V8	shock absorber

GP Starts: 12   GP Wins: 0   Pole positions: 0   Fastest laps: 0   Points: 3

DAVE MORGAN

Having begun racing in 1965 with a Mini, Dave progressed to Formula 3 in 1970 with a March 703 and a highly competitive season ended in a controversial accident with James Hunt at Crystal Palace. Morgan was suspended for 12 months for 'dangerous driving', but happily he was subsequently allowed to continue his racing activities in Formula Atlantic in 1971.

The high point of his career came at the start of 1972 when his private Brabham took a surprise but well-earned win in the Formula 2 race at Mallory Park. Two seasons in the formula brought little more success, and Morgan returned to Formula Atlantic in 1974, but with the support of his sponsors Dave then organised his one Grand Prix drive with a Surtees in 1975. He then retired from the circuits, but returned in 1980-81, racing a Colt Lancer in the RAC Tricentrol series. More recently he has acted as Eric van de Poele's engineer in F3000 and Formula 1.

SILVIO MOSER

After racing Alfas in the early sixties this pleasant little Swiss driver switched to junior single-seaters in 1964 with huge success, both in European F3 and in the Temporada series, winning all four rounds in his Formula Junior Lotus.

Moser then moved into Formula 2 with his own team, but continued to race in F3 – where he was more competitive, winning races at Syracuse, La Chatre and Rosario. He then went into Formula 1 full-time , initially with an elderly Cooper-ATS, then with the ex-Ligier Brabham, scoring a fifth place at Zandvoort in 1968, and a sixth at Watkins Glen in 1969.

Silvio then embarked on a disastrous 1970 season with the hopeless Bellasi-Ford, which scuppered his immediate Grand Prix expectations. Returning to Formula 2, he drove a Brabham in 1971 and '72, taking second at the Monza Lottery GP, but had a thin time of it with a Surtees in 1973. Moser was planning to race a March in Formula 2 in 1974, as well as making a return to Grands Prix with a Bretscher Brabham, but he crashed a Lola sports car heavily in the Monza 1000 Km, sustaining serious internal and head injuries. Despite several operations, poor Moser died in hospital the following month without regaining consciousness.

STIRLING MOSS

The long career and many brilliant deeds of Stirling Moss far outstrip the space available to describe them here, and his successes are also far too numerous to list. Thus a broad brush must be used to give an impression of this patriotic and ultra-professional driver, who had a clear idea of his own worth. Without vanity, he quite soundly reasoned that the World Championship which the British public were so desperate for him to win was utterly meaningless as a measure of a driver's abilities. Painstaking and thorough in his approach, in his prime Stirling's mastery of the skills of his profession was absolute. Capable of driving just about any machine with equal excellence, Moss never gave less than 100 per cent and, no matter what the situation, he simply never gave up.

His career began in 1947 with a BMW 328, but he was soon scrapping it out in the rough and tumble of 500 cc racing with a Cooper-JAP. In 1950 he scored his first major success, winning the Tourist Trophy in a Jaguar XK120, and during the next three seasons he drove a variety of cars – HWM, Formula 3 Kieft, Frazer-Nash and Jaguar – sampling success in all of them. Only the ERA G-Type was a complete failure, and by 1953 Stirling's talents were coveted by Ferrari. Actually Moss had his eyes fixed on a seat with Mercedes-Benz, but Neubauer was not yet convinced that the youngster was ready. So for the 1954 season Moss bought a Maserati 250F and promptly took third place at Spa. Later in the year, he accepted the offer of a works car, and duly led the Mercedes of Fangio at Monza until the oil tank split. He was then signed by Mercedes for the 1955 season alongside the Maestro. In Grands Prix he watched and learned much from his august partner, scoring a famous victory in the British GP in the July sunshine at Aintree, and winning the Mille Miglia and the Targa Florio in the silver sports cars. Unfortunately the Le Mans disaster prompted Mercedes' withdrawal from the sport, and Stirling joined Maserati as number one driver in 1956. Despite wins at Monaco and Monza, retirements elsewhere cost him dear and the championship went to Fangio and Ferrari. It was a very productive year overall, however, with no fewer than 16 race wins in the 250F, the Maserati 300TS and the Vanwall among others.

His patriotism was at last rewarded when Vanwall offered him a machine worthy of his talents in 1957, and in the British GP Moss fulfilled a long-held ambition by giving a green car victory in a World Championship Grand Prix after taking over Brooks' sister entry. There were further wins at Pescara and Monza, and hopes were high for the championship in 1958. He started the season with a quite briliant win in Rob Walker's little Cooper before resuming the fight in Vandervell's machines. Once again the unreliability of the car torpedoed Moss's personal title chances but, with Brooks and Lewis-Evans backing him up, the team took the constructors' title before withdrawing from Grand Prix racing at the season's end.

By now Moss had ceased to worry unduly about the championship. Certainly Ferrari would have given anything to sign him, but he preferred the comfortable ambience of Walker's little team, with Rob himself offering discreet guidance and Alf Francis fettling the cars. Stirling possibly hindered his chances by switching about a bit too often, surmising that the BRP BRM would be better suited to Reims and Aintree, but he won in Portugal and Italy in the Walker Cooper. In 1960 Stirling had the choice of a Cooper and the new Lotus 18, which he used to win the Monaco GP, but in practice for the Belgian GP his Lotus shed a wheel, leaving him suffering from serious back injuries. Characteristically, he set himself impossible targets for his comeback and returned in time to take another win at the end of the year at Riverside.

In 1961 we saw the true genius of Moss at Monaco and particularly the Nürburgring, where he defeated the shark-nose Ferrari 156 V6 cars of Phil Hill and Taffy von Trips. These victories were inevitably just the tip of an iceberg of success that ran through the season, into the winter months at Nassau, and then across the world early in 1962 in Australia and New Zealand. On his return to Britain, Moss drove the pale-green UDT-entered Lotus to seventh in the Lombank Trophy before heading down to Goodwood for the Easter Monday meeting. Why he crashed is still not clear, but his car was wrecked and Stirling was hospitalised with serious head injuries. His recuperation was to be a slow one this time. Almost a year later he tried a car in a private test but his fears were realised. The sharp edge of his reflexes had gone, and wisely he decided he would not race again, thus leaving intact memories of a driver who always competed at the peak of his powers. Stirling then launched himself into myriad business ventures, many of which kept him in touch with the sport. In the late seventies he was tempted back to the track, mainly for fun, in historic cars and saloons.

MOSS, Stirling (GB) b 17/9/1929

1951

	Race	Circuit	No	Entrant	Car/Engine	Comment
8	SWISS GP	Bremgarten	14	HW Motors Ltd	2.0 HWM-Alta 4	2 laps behind

1952

	Race	Circuit	No	Entrant	Car/Engine	Comment
ret	SWISS GP	Bremgarten	46	HW Motors Ltd	2.0 HWM-Alta 4	withdrawn-hub failure of team-mate
ret	BELGIAN GP	Spa	32	ERA Ltd	2.0 ERA G Type-Bristol 6	engine
ret	BRITISH GP	Silverstone	12	ERA Ltd	2.0 ERA G Type-Bristol 6	engine
ret	DUTCH GP	Zandvoort	36	ERA Ltd	2.0 ERA G Type-Bristol 6	engine
ret	ITALIAN GP	Monza	32	Connaught Engineering	2.0 Connaught-Lea Francis A Type 4	engine

1953

	Race	Circuit	No	Entrant	Car/Engine	Comment
9	DUTCH GP	Zandvoort	34	Connaught Engineering	2.0 Connaught-Lea Francis A Type 4	7 laps behind
ret	FRENCH GP	Reims	36	Cooper Car Co	2.0 Cooper Alta Special-4	clutch
6	GERMAN GP	Nürburgring	19	Cooper Car Co	2.0 Cooper Alta Special Mk 11-4	1 lap behind
13	ITALIAN GP	Monza	28	Cooper Car Co	2.0 Cooper Alta Special Mk 11-4	p stop-fuel leak 10 laps behind

1954

	Race	Circuit	No	Entrant	Car/Engine	Comment
3	BELGIAN GP	Spa	22	Equipe Moss	2.5 Maserati 250F 6	1 lap behind
ret	BRITISH GP	Silverstone	7	A E Moss	2.5 Maserati 250F 6	gearbox/FL
ret	GERMAN GP	Nürburgring	16	A E Moss	2.5 Maserati 250F 6	engine

ret	SWISS GP	Bremgarten	32	Officine Alfieri Maserati	2.5 Maserati 250F 6	*oil pressure*
nc	ITALIAN GP	Monza	28	Officine Alfieri Maserati	2.5 Maserati 250F 6	*split oil tank/9 laps behind*
ret	SPANISH GP	Pedralbes	8	Officine Alfieri Maserati	2.5 Maserati 250F 6	*oil pump*

1955

ret	ARGENTINE GP	Buenos Aires	6	Daimler Benz AG	2.5 Mercedes-Benz W196 8	*fuel vapour lock*
4*	"	" "	8	Daimler Benz AG	2.5 Mercedes-Banz W196 8	**Herrmann/Kling also drove*
9/ret	MONACO GP	Monte Carlo	6	Daimler Benz AG	2.5 Mercedes-Benz W196 8	*engine/19 laps behind*
2	BELGIAN GP	Spa	14	Daimler Benz AG	2.5 Mercedes-Benz W196 8	
2	DUTCH GP	Zandvoort	10	Daimler Benz AG	2.5 Mercedes-Benz W196 8	
1	BRITISH GP	Aintree	12	Daimler Benz AG	2.5 Mercedes-Benz W196 8	*Pole/FL*
ret	ITALIAN GP	Monza	16	Daimler Benz AG	2.5 Mercedes-Benz W196 8	*engine/FL*

1956

ret	ARGENTINE GP	Buenos Aires	2	Officine Alfieri Maserati	2.5 Maserati 250F 6	*engine*
1	MONACO GP	Monte Carlo	28	Officine Alfieri Maserati	2.5 Maserati 250F 6	
ret	BELGIAN GP	Spa	30	Officine Alfieri Maserati	2.5 Maserati 250F 6	*lost wheel*
3*	"	"	34	Officine Alfieri Maserati	2.5 Maserati 250F 6	** took over Perdisa's car/FL*
ret	FRENCH GP	Reims	2	Officine Alfieri Maserati	2.5 Maserati 250F 6	*gear lever*
5*	"	"	6	Officine Alfieri Maserati	2.5 Maserati 250F 6	**took over Perdisa's car/-2 laps*
ret	BRITISH GP	Silverstone	7	Officine Alfieri Maserati	2.5 Maserati 250F 6	*gearbox/Pole/FL*
2	GERMAN GP	Nürburgring	7	Officine Alfieri Maserati	2.5 Maserati 250F 6	
1	ITALIAN GP	Monza	36	Officine Alfieri Maserati	2.5 Maserati 250F 6	*FL*

1957

8	ARGENTINE GP	Buenos Aires	4	Officine Alfieri Maserati	2.5 Maserati 250F 6	*p stop-throttle/-7 laps/Pole/FL*
ret	MONACO GP	Monte Carlo	18	Vandervell Products Ltd	2.5 Vanwall 4	*hit chicane*
ret	BRITISH GP	Aintree	18	Vandervell Products Ltd	2.5 Vanwall 4	*Brooks took over/engine/Pole*
1*	"	"	20	Vandervell Products Ltd	2.5 Vanwall 4	** took over from Brooks/FL*
5	GERMAN GP	Nürburgring	10	Vandervell Products Ltd	2.5 Vanwall 4	*suspension problems*
1	PESCARA GP	Pescara	26	Vandervell Products Ltd	2.5 Vanwall 4	*FL*
1	ITALIAN GP	Monza	18	Vandervell Products Ltd	2.5 Vanwall 4	

1958

1	ARGENTINE GP	Buenos Aires	14	R R C Walker Racing Team	1.9 Cooper T43-Climax 4	*tyres shot at finish*
ret	MONACO GP	Monte Carlo	28	Vandervell Products Ltd	2.5 Vanwall 4	*engine*
1	DUTCH GP	Zandvoort	1	Vandervell Products Ltd	2.5 Vanwall 4	*FL*
ret	BELGIAN GP	Spa	2	Vandervell Products Ltd	2.5 Vanwall 4	*dropped valve*
2	FRENCH GP	Reims	8	Vandervell Products Ltd	2.5 Vanwall 4	
ret	BRITISH GP	Silverstone	7	Vandervell Products Ltd	2.5 Vanwall 4	*engine/Pole*
ret	GERMAN GP	Nürburgring	7	Vandervell Products Ltd	2.5 Vanwall 4	*magneto/FL*
1	PORTUGUESE GP	Oporto	2	Vandervell Products Ltd	2.5 Vanwall 4	*Pole*
ret	ITALIAN GP	Monza	26	Vandervell Products Ltd	2.5 Vanwall 4	*gearbox/Pole*
1	MOROCCAN GP	Casablanca	8	Vandervell Products Ltd	2.5 Vanwall 4	*FL*

1959

ret	MONACO GP	Monte Carlo	30	R R C Walker Racing Team	2.5 Cooper T51-Climax 4	*transmission/Pole*
dns	MONACO GP	Monte Carlo	30	R R C Walker Racing Team	2.5 Cooper T51-BRM 4	*practice only*
ret	DUTCH GP	Zandvoort	11	R R C Walker Racing Team	2.5 Cooper T51-Climax 4	*gearbox/FL*
dns	"	"	15	Ecurie Maarsbergen	1.5 Porsche-RSK	*practice only*
dsq	FRENCH GP	Reims	2	British Racing Partnership	2.5 BRM P25 4	*outside assistance after spin/FL*
2	BRITISH GP	Aintree	6	British Racing Partnership	2.5 BRM P25 4	*FL (shared with McLaren)*
ret	GERMAN GP	AVUS	7	R R C Walker Racing Team	2.5 Cooper T51-Climax 4	*transmission-heat 1*
1	PORTUGUESE GP	Monsanto	4	R R C Walker Racing Team	2.5 Cooper T51-Climax 4	*Pole/FL*
1	ITALIAN GP	Monza	14	R R C Walker Racing Team	2.5 Cooper T51-Climax 4	*Pole*
ret	US GP	Sebring	7	R R C Walker Racing Team	2.5 Cooper T51-Climax 4	*transmission/Pole*

1960

ret	ARGENTINE GP	Buenos Aires	36	R R C Walker Racing Team	2.5 Cooper T51-Climax 4	*suspension/Pole/FL*
3*	"	" "	38	R R C Walker Racing Team	2.5 Cooper T51-Climax 4	** took over from Trintignant/no points*
dns	"	" "	36	R R C Walker Racing Team	2.5 Cooper T43-Climax 4	*practice only*
1	MONACO GP	Monte Carlo	28	R R C Walker Racing Team	2.5 Lotus 18-Climax 4	*Pole*
dns	"	" "	T	Reventlow Automobiles Inc	2.5 Scarab 4	*practice only*
4	DUTCH GP	Zandvoort	7	R R C Walker Racing Team	2.5 Lotus 18-Climax 4	*pit stop when 1st/Pole/FL*
dns	BELGIAN GP	Spa	12	R R C Walker Racing Team	2.5 Lotus 18-Cliamx 4	*practice accident/badly injured*
dsq	PORTUGUESE GP	Oporto	12	R R C Walker Racing Team	2.5 Lotus 18-Climax 4	*pushing car against traffic flow*
dns	"	"	12	R R C Walker Racing Team	2.5 Cooper T51-Climax 4	*practice only*
1	US GP	Riverside	5	R R C Walker Racing Team	2.5 Lotus 18-Climax 4	*Pole*

1961

1	MONACO GP	Monte Carlo	20	R R C Walker Racing Team	1.5 Lotus 18-Climax 4	*Pole/FL (shared with Ginther)*
dns	"	" "	20	R R C Walker Racing Team	1.5 Cooper T53-Climax 4	*practice only*
4	DUTCH GP	Zandvoort	14	R R C Walker Racing Team	1.5 Lotus 18-Climax 4	
dns	"	"	14	R R C Walker Racing Team	1.5 Cooper T53-Climax 4	*practice only*
8	BELGIAN GP	Spa	14	R R C Walker Racing Team	1.5 Lotus 18/21-Climax 4	
ret	FRENCH GP	Reims	26	R R C Walker Racing Team	1.5 Lotus 18/21-Climax 4	*brake pipe*
dns	"	"	26	UDT-Laystall Racing Team	1.5 Lotus 18-Climax 4	*practice only*
ret	BRITISH GP	Aintree	28	R R C Walker Racing Team	1.5 Lotus 18/21-Climax 4	*brake pipe*
dsq	"	"	26	R R C Walker Racing Team	1.5 Ferguson P99-Climax 4	*took over from Fairman/push start*
1	GERMAN GP	Nürburgring	7	R R C Walker Racing Team	1.5 Lotus 18/21-Climax 4	
ret	ITALIAN GP	Monza	28	R R C Walker Racing Team	1.5 Lotus 21-Climax 4	*wheel bearing/Ireland's works car*
dns	"	"	28	R R C Walker Racing Team	1.5 Lotus 18/21-Climax 4	*practice only*
dns	"	"	28	R R C Walker Racing Team	1.5 Lotus 18/21-Climax V8	*practice only*
ret	US GP	Watkins Glen	7	R R C Walker Racing Team	1.5 Lotus 18/21-Climax 4	*engine*
dns	"	" "	7	R R C Walker Racing Team	1.5 Lotus 18/21-Climax V8	*practice only*

GP Starts: 66   GP Wins: 16   Pole positions: 16   Fastest laps: 19   Points: 186.64

DAVID MURRAY

A chartered accountant by profession, Murray enthusiastically raced an ERA and then a 4CLT Maserati in British and Continental events, as well as taking in occasional rallies and hill-climbs.

He is perhaps best known, however, as the man who formed the famous Ecurie Ecosse team in 1952. After taking part in the British GP with the organisation's Cooper-Bristol, Murray then took on the chief management role in the team, masterminding their hugely successful sports car programme which culminated in the dark blue cars' wonderful triumphs at Le Mans in 1956 and 1957.

LUIGI MUSSO

The last of an ill-fated generation of Italian Grand Prix drivers, Musso followed one of his elder brothers into the sport with some less than earth-shattering performances, but he slowly gained experience and, armed with one of the latest Maserati sports cars for 1953, proved almost unbeatable as he sped to the Italian 2-litre championship.

So impressed were Maserati that he shared Mantovani's car at that year's Italian GP before racing works sports and Grand Prix machines the following season, when he was again sports car champion of Italy, winning the Circuit of Senigallia, and taking second in the Targa Florio and third in the Mille Miglia. In single-seaters he inherited a win in the Pescara GP, and took a fine second place in the Spanish GP at season's end. For 1955 Musso undertook another busy schedule of racing, scoring points only at Zandvoort, but taking second places in non-championship races at Syracuse, Bordeaux and Naples. Driving the Maserati T300S in sports car events, his only win came at the Monza Supercortemaggiore race with Behra.

In 1956 Luigi was invited to join the Scuderia Ferrari, and the association began on a high note when he shared the winning car with Fangio in the Argentine GP, following this with a second place in the Syracuse GP. Unfortunately a crash in the Nürburgring 1000 Km left him temporarily sidelined with a broken arm, though he made a contentious comeback at Monza, first refusing to hand his car to the waiting Fangio at a pit stop, then taking the lead of the Italian GP only for his steering to fail after a tyre threw a tread.

Something of a nearly-man, outright success seemed continually to elude the Italian in World Championship races in 1957. He was a runner-up in both France and Britain, as well as in the non-title Syracuse and Modena GPs, though he did at last take a victory at Reims in the GP de Marne. This sequence continued into 1958, when a succession of yet more second places (Argentine GP, Buenos Aires City GP, Buenos Aires 1000 Km and Monaco GP) was broken by victory in the Syracuse GP and the Targa Florio.

After crashing his Ferrari at Spa with tyre failure, Musso arrived at Reims for the French GP determined to make amends, but while he was chasing his team-mate Hawthorn he ran wide on the long Gueux curve at 150 mph. The car ran into a ditch and flipped, killing the driver instantly.

MUNARON, Gino (I) b 2/4/1928

1960

	Race	Circuit	No	Entrant	Car/Engine	Comment
13	ARGENTINE GP	Buenos Aires	14	Gino Munaron	2.5 Maserati 250F 6	8 laps behind
dnq	MONACO GP	Monte Carlo	30	Scuderia Eugenio Castellotti	2.5 Cooper T51-Ferrari 4	shared car with Scarlatti
ret	FRENCH GP	Reims	30	Scuderia Eugenio Castellotti	2.5 Cooper T51-Ferrari 4	transmission
15	BRITISH GP	Silverstone	21	Scuderia Eugenio Castellotti	2.5 Cooper T51-Ferrari 4	7 laps behind
ret	ITALIAN GP	Monza	4	Scuderia Eugenio Castellotti	2.5 Cooper T51-Ferrari 4	oil pipe

GP Starts: 4   GP Wins: 0   Pole positions: 0   Fastest laps: 0   Points: 0

MURRAY, David (GB) b 28/12/1909 – d 5/4/1973

1950

	Race	Circuit	No	Entrant	Car/Engine	Comment
ret	BRITISH GP	Silverstone	5	Scuderia Ambrosiana	1.5 s/c Maserati 4CLT/48 4	engine
ret	ITALIAN GP	Monza	50	Scuderia Ambrosiana	1.5 s/c Maserati 4CLT/48 4	gearbox/valves

1951

ret	BRITISH GP	Silverstone	15	Scuderia Ambrosiana	1.5 s/c Maserati 4CLT/48 4	valve springs
dns	GERMAN GP	Nürburgring	89	Scuderia Ambrosiana	1.5 s/c Maserati 4CLT/48 4	accident in practice

1952

ret	BRITISH GP	Silverstone	7	Ecurie Ecosse	2.0 Cooper T20-Bristol 6	engine/spark plugs

GP Starts: 4   GP Wins: 0   Pole positions: 0   Fastest laps: 0   Points: 0

MUSSO, Luigi (I) b 24/7/1924 – d 6/7/1958

1953

	Race	Circuit	No	Entrant	Car/Engine	Comment
7*	ITALIAN GP	Monza	56	Officine Alfieri Maserati	2.0 Maserati A6GCM 6	*took over from Mantovani/-4 laps

1954

dns	ARGENTINE GP	Buenos Aires	6	Officine Alfieri Maserati	2.5 Maserati A6GCM/250F 6	engine in practice
ret	ITALIAN GP	Monza	20	Officine Alfieri Maserati	2.5 Maserati 250F 6	transmission
2	SPANISH GP	Pedralbes	14	Officine Alfieri Maserati	2.5 Maserati 250F 6	

1955

	Race	Circuit	No	Entrant	Car/Engine	Comment
7	ARGENTINE GP	Buenos Aires	22	Officine Alfieri Maserati	2.5 Maserati 250F 6	*Mantovani/Schell co-drove/13 laps
ret	"	"	20	Officine Alfieri Maserati	2.5 Maserati 250F 6	fuel starvation/Behra/Mantovani
ret	MONACO GP	Monte Carlo	38	Officine Alfieri Maserati	2.5 Maserati 250F 6	transmission
7	BELGIAN GP	Spa	12	Officine Alfieri Maserati	2.5 Maserati 250F 6	2 laps behind
3	DUTCH GP	Zandvoort	18	Officine Alfieri Maserati	2.5 Maserati 250F 6	
5	BRITISH GP	Silverstone	4	Officine Alfieri Maserati	2.5 Maserati 250F 6	1 lap behind
ret	ITALIAN GP	Monza	30	Officine Alfieri Maserati	2.5 Maserati 250F 6	gearbox

1956

	Race	Circuit	No	Entrant	Car/Engine	Comment
1*	ARGENTINE GP	Buenos Aires	34	Scuderia Ferrari	2.5 Lancia-Ferrari D50 V8	* Fangio took over
ret	"	"	30	Scuderia Ferrari	2.5 Lancia-Ferrari D50 V8	switched to Fangio's car/fuel pump
ret	MONACO GP	Monte Carlo	24	Scuderia Ferrari	2.5 Lancia-Ferrari D50 V8	crashed avoiding Fangio
ret*	GERMAN GP	Nurburging	4	Scuderia Ferrari	2.5 Lancia-Ferrari D50 V8	* Castellotti took over and crashed
ret	ITALIAN GP	Monza	30	Scuderia Ferrari	2.5 Lancia-Ferrari D50 V8	steering arm-crashed

1957

	Race	Circuit	No	Entrant	Car/Engine	Comment
ret	ARGENTINE GP	Buenos Aires	12	Scuderia Ferrari	2.5 Lancia-Ferrari D50A V8	clutch
2	FRENCH GP	Rouen	10	Scuderia Ferrari	2.5 Lancia-Ferrari 801 V8	FL
2	BRITISH GP	Aintree	14	Scuderia Ferrari	2.5 Lancia-Ferrari 801 V8	
4	GERMAN GP	Nürburgring	6	Scuderia Ferrari	2.5 Lancia-Ferrari 801 V8	
ret	PESCARA GP	Pescara	34	Scuderia Ferrari	2.5 Lancia-Ferrari 801 V8	split oil tank-seized engine
8	ITALIAN GP	Monza	32	Scuderia Ferrari	2.5 Lancia-Ferrari 801 V8	5 laps behind

1958

	Race	Circuit	No	Entrant	Car/Engine	Comment
2	ARGENTINE GP	Buenos Aires	16	Scuderia Ferrari	2.4 Ferrari Dino 246 V6	
2	MONACO GP	Monte Carlo	34	Scuderia Ferrari	2.4 Ferrari Dino 246 V6	
7	DUTCH GP	Zandvoort	6	Scuderia Ferrari	2.4 Ferrari Dino 246 V6	pit stop/2 laps behind
ret	BELGIAN GP	Spa	18	Scuderia Ferrari	2.4 Ferrari Dino 246 V6	tyre-crashed at Stavelot
ret	FRENCH GP	Reims	2	Scuderia Ferrari	2.4 Ferrari Dino 246 V6	fatal accident

GP Starts: 24   GP Wins: 1   Pole positions: 0   Fastest laps: 1   Points: 44

NACKE, Bernhard (D) d 1980

1952

	Race	Circuit	No	Entrant	Car/Engine	Comment
ret	GERMAN GP	Nürburgring	30	Bernhard Nacke	2.0 BMW-Eigenbau 6	spark plugs

GP Starts: 1   GP Wins: 0   Pole positions: 0   Fastest laps: 0   Points: 0

SATORU NAKAJIMA

Nakajima was chosen by Honda to represent them on the Grand Prix stage after a glittering career in Japan which saw him win five Formula 2 titles, the last three consecutively between 1984 and '86.

Brought into the Lotus team alongside the brilliant Ayrton Senna, the Japanese driver inevitably appeared in an unfavourable light during his first season, and his number two status continued when Nelson Piquet took over as team leader in 1988-89, but Satoru quietly got on with the job as the fortunes of the Hethel outfit plummeted. His last race for the team was in the wet at Adelaide in 1989, and he astonished everyone as he made a mockery of the conditions to finish fourth and take fastest lap.

With help from long-time sponsors Honda and Epson, Satoru moved to Tyrrell in 1990, gaining the odd point with the nimble Cosworth car. He then endured a disappointing final year in F1, despite having V10 Honda power, and it was with some relief that he bowed out and retired from the sport, his head held high and no longer having to carry the burden of his fanatical countrymen's expectations.

NAKAJIMA, Satoru (J) b 23/2/1953

1987

	Race	Circuit	No	Entrant	Car/Engine	Comment
7	BRAZILIAN GP	Rio	11	Camel Team Lotus Honda	1.5 t/c Lotus 99T-Honda V6	pit stop-tyres/2 laps behind
6	SAN MARINO GP	Imola	11	Camel Team Lotus Honda	1.5 t/c Lotus 99T-Honda V6	pit stop-tyres/2 laps behind
5	BELGIAN GP	Spa	11	Camel Team Lotus Honda	1.5 t/c Lotus 99T-Honda V6	pit stop-tyres/1 lap behind

10	MONACO GP	Monte Carlo	11	Camel Team Lotus Honda	1.5 t/c Lotus 99T-Honda V6	*hit by Alliot/Capelli-pit stop/-3 laps*
ret	US GP (DETROIT)	Detroit	11	Camel Team Lotus Honda	1.5 t/c Lotus 99T-Honda V6	*accident with Campos*
nc	FRENCH GP	Paul Ricard	11	Camel Team Lotus Honda	1.5 t/c Lotus 99T-Honda V6	*p stops-tyre-wheel problems/-9 laps*
4	BRITISH GP	Silverstone	11	Camel Team Lotus Honda	1.5 t/c Lotus 99T-Honda V6	*pit stop-tyres/2 laps behind*
ret	GERMAN GP	Hockenheim	11	Camel Team Lotus Honda	1.5 t/c Lotus 99T-Honda V6	*turbo*
ret	HUNGARIAN GP	Hungaroring	11	Camel Team Lotus Honda	1.5 t/c Lotus 99T-Honda V6	*driveshaft*
13	AUSTRIAN GP	Österreichring	11	Camel Team Lotus Honda	1.5 t/c Lotus 99T-Honda V6	*pit stop-puncture/3 laps behind*
11	ITALIAN GP	Monza	11	Camel Team Lotus Honda	1.5 t/c Lotus 99T-Honda V6	*spin/pit stop-tyres/3 laps behind*
8	PORTUGUESE GP	Estoril	11	Camel Team Lotus Honda	1.5 t/c Lotus 99T-Honda V6	*pit stop-tyres/2 laps behind*
9	SPANISH GP	Jerez	11	Camel Team Lotus Honda	1.5 t/c Lotus 99T-Honda V6	*pit stop-tyres/2 laps behind*
ret	MEXICAN GP	Mexico City	11	Camel Team Lotus Honda	1.5 t/c Lotus 99T-Honda V6	*hit Warwick*
6	JAPANESE GP	Suzuka	11	Camel Team Lotus Honda	1.5 t/c Lotus 99T-Honda V6	
ret	AUSTRALIAN GP	Adelaide	11	Camel Team Lotus Honda	1.5 t/c Lotus 99T-Honda V6	*hydraulic leak*

1988

6	BRAZILIAN GP	Rio	2	Camel Team Lotus Honda	1.5 t/c Lotus 100T-Honda V6	*pit stop-tyres/1 lap behind*
8	SAN MARINO GP	Imola	2	Camel Team Lotus Honda	1.5 t/c Lotus 100T-Honda V6	*1 lap behind*
dnq	MONACO GP	Monte Carlo	2	Camel Team Lotus Honda	1.5 t/c Lotus 100T-Honda V6	
ret	MEXICAN GP	Mexico City	2	Camel Team Lotus Honda	1.5 t/c Lotus 100T-Honda V6	*turbo*
11	CANADIAN GP	Montreal	2	Camel Team Lotus Honda	1.5 t/c Lotus 100T-Honda V6	*pit stop-tyres/3 laps behind*
dnq	US GP (DETROIT)	Detroit	2	Camel Team Lotus Honda	1.5 t/c Lotus 100T-Honda V6	
7	FRENCH GP	Paul Ricard	2	Camel Team Lotus Honda	1.5 t/c Lotus 100T-Honda V6	*p stop-tyres/handling problem/-1 lap*
10	BRITISH GP	Silverstone	2	Camel Team Lotus Honda	1.5 t/c Lotus 100T-Honda V6	*lost 5th gear/1 lap behind*
9	GERMAN GP	Hockenheim	2	Camel Team Lotus Honda	1.5 t/c Lotus 100T-Honda V6	*1 lap behind*
7	HUNGARIAN GP	Hungaroring	2	Camel Team Lotus Honda	1.5 t/c Lotus 100T-Honda V6	*hit by Streiff/3 laps behind*
ret	BELGIAN GP	Spa	2	Camel Team Lotus Honda	1.5 t/c Lotus 100T-Honda V6	*engine*
ret	ITALIAN GP	Monza	2	Camel Team Lotus Honda	1.5 t/c Lotus 100T-Honda V6	*engine*
ret	PORTUGUESE GP	Estoril	2	Camel Team Lotus Honda	1.5 t/c Lotus 100T-Honda V6	*accident damage*
ret	SPANISH GP	Jerez	2	Camel Team Lotus Honda	1.5 t/c Lotus 100T-Honda V6	*spun off*
7	JAPANESE GP	Suzuka	2	Camel Team Lotus Honda	1.5 t/c Lotus 100T-Honda V6	*1 lap behind*
ret	AUSTRALIAN GP	Adelaide	2	Camel Team Lotus Honda	1.5 t/c Lotus 100T-Honda V6	*hit Gugelmin*

1989

8	BRAZILIAN GP	Rio	12	Camel Team Lotus	3.5 Lotus 101-Judd V8	*2 p stops-tyres/clutch/1 lap behind*
nc	SAN MARINO GP	Imola	12	Camel Team Lotus	3.5 Lotus 101-Judd V8	*pit stop-electrics/12 laps behind*
dnq	MONACO GP	Monte Carlo	12	Camel Team Lotus	3.5 Lotus 101-Judd V8	
ret	MEXICAN GP	Mexico City	12	Camel Team Lotus	3.5 Lotus 101-Judd V8	*gearbox-spun off*
ret	US GP (PHOENIX)	Phoenix	12	Camel Team Lotus	3.5 Lotus 101-Judd V8	*throttle cable bracket*
dnq	CANADIAN GP	Montreal	12	Camel Team Lotus	3.5 Lotus 101-Judd V8	
ret	FRENCH GP	Paul Ricard	12	Camel Team Lotus	3.5 Lotus 101-Judd V8	*electrics-engine cut out*
8	BRITISH GP	Silverstone	12	Camel Team Lotus	3.5 Lotus 101-Judd V8	*1 lap behind*
ret	GERMAN GP	Hockenheim	12	Camel Team Lotus	3.5 Lotus 101-Judd V8	*spun off*
ret	HUNGARIAN GP	Hungaroring	12	Camel Team Lotus	3.5 Lotus 101-Judd V8	*collision with Warwick*
dnq	BELGIAN GP	Spa	12	Camel Team Lotus	3.5 Lotus 101-Judd V8	
10	ITALIAN GP	Monza	12	Camel Team Lotus	3.5 Lotus 101-Judd V8	*2 pit stops-tyres/2 laps behind*
7	PORTUGUESE GP	Estoril	12	Camel Team Lotus	3.5 Lotus 101-Judd V8	*1 lap behind*
ret	SPANISH GP	Jerez	12	Camel Team Lotus	3.5 Lotus 101-Judd V8	*hit by Capelli-spun off*
ret	JAPANESE GP	Suzuka	12	Camel Team Lotus	3.5 Lotus 101-Judd V8	*engine*
4	AUSTRALIAN GP	Adelaide	12	Camel Team Lotus	3.5 Lotus 101-Judd V8	*FL in the rain*

1990

6	US GP (PHOENIX)	Phoenix	3	Tyrrell Racing Organisation	3.5 Tyrrell 018-Cosworth V8	*1 lap behind*
8	BRAZILIAN GP	Interlagos	3	Tyrrell Racing Organisation	3.5 Tyrrell 018-Cosworth V8	*collision with Senna/1 lap behind*
ret	SAN MARINO GP	Imola	3	Tyrrell Racing Organisation	3.5 Tyrrell 019-Cosworth V8	*hit Capelli-lap 1*
ret	MONACO GP	Monte Carlo	3	Tyrrell Racing Organisation	3.5 Tyrrell 019-Cosworth V8	*suspension*
11	CANADIAN GP	Montreal	3	Tyrrell Racing Organisation	3.5 Tyrrell 019-Cosworth V8	*3 laps behind*
ret	MEXICAN GP	Mexico City	3	Tyrrell Racing Organisation	3.5 Tyrrell 019-Cosworth V8	*collision with Suzuki*
ret	FRENCH GP	Paul Ricard	3	Tyrrell Racing Organisation	3.5 Tyrrell 019-Cosworth V8	*transmission*
ret	BRITISH GP	Silverstone	3	Tyrrell Racing Organisation	3.5 Tyrrell 019-Cosworth V8	*electrics*
ret	GERMAN GP	Hockenheim	3	Tyrrell Racing Organisation	3.5 Tyrrell 019-Cosworth V8	*engine*
ret	HUNGARIAN GP	Hungaroring	3	Tyrrell Racing Organisation	3.5 Tyrrell 019-Cosworth V8	*spun off*
ret	BELGIAN GP	Spa	3	Tyrrell Racing Organisation	3.5 Tyrrell 019-Cosworth V8	*misfire*
6	ITALIAN GP	Monza	3	Tyrrell Racing Organisation	3.5 Tyrrell 019-Cosworth V8	*1 lap behind*
dns	PORTUGUESE GP	Estoril	3	Tyrrell Racing Organisation	3.5 Tyrrell 019-Cosworth V8	*withdrawn-driver unwell*
ret	SPANISH GP	Jerez	3	Tyrrell Racing Organisation	3.5 Tyrrell 019-Cosworth V8	*spun off*
6	JAPANESE GP	Suzuka	3	Tyrrell Racing Organisation	3.5 Tyrrell 019-Cosworth V8	
ret	AUSTRALIAN GP	Adelaide	3	Tyrrell Racing Organisation	3.5 Tyrrell 019-Cosworth V8	*spun off*

1991

5	US GP (PHOENIX)	Phoenix	3	Braun Tyrrell Honda	3.5 Tyrrell 020-Honda V10	*1 lap behind*
ret	BRAZILIAN GP	Interlagos	3	Braun Tyrrell Honda	3.5 Tyrrell 020-Honda V10	*spun off*
ret	SAN MARINO GP	Imola	3	Braun Tyrrell Honda	3.5 Tyrrell 020-Honda V10	*transmission*
ret	MONACO GP	Monte Carlo	3	Braun Tyrrell Honda	3.5 Tyrrell 020-Honda V10	*spun and stalled*
10	CANADIAN GP	Montreal	3	Braun Tyrrell Honda	3.5 Tyrrell 020-Honda V10	*2 laps behind*
12	MEXICAN GP	Mexico City	3	Braun Tyrrell Honda	3.5 Tyrrell 020-Honda V10	*3 laps behind*
ret	FRENCH GP	Magny Cours	3	Braun Tyrrell Honda	3.5 Tyrrell 020-Honda V10	*spun off*
8	BRITISH GP	Silverstone	3	Braun Tyrrell Honda	3.5 Tyrrell 020-Honda V10	*1 lap behind*
ret	GERMAN GP	Hockenheim	3	Braun Tyrrell Honda	3.5 Tyrrell 020-Honda V10	*gearbox*
15	HUNGARIAN GP	Hungaroring	3	Braun Tyrrell Honda	3.5 Tyrrell 020-Honda V10	*3 laps behind*
ret	BELGIAN GP	Spa	3	Braun Tyrrell Honda	3.5 Tyrrell 020-Honda V10	*slid off at Les Combes*
ret	ITALIAN GP	Monza	3	Braun Tyrrell Honda	3.5 Tyrrell 020-Honda V10	*sticking throttle*
13	PORTUGUESE GP	Estoril	3	Braun Tyrrell Honda	3.5 Tyrrell 020-Honda V10	*3 laps behind*
17	SPANISH GP	Barcelona	3	Braun Tyrrell Honda	3.5 Tyrrell 020-Honda V10	*3 laps behind*
ret	JAPANESE GP	Suzuka	3	Braun Tyrrell Honda	3.5 Tyrrell 020-Honda V10	*suspension*
ret	AUSTRALIAN GP	Adelaide	3	Braun Tyrrell Honda	3.5 Tyrrell 020-Honda V10	*collision with Boutsen*

GP Starts: 74   GP Wins: 0   Pole positions: 0   Fastest laps: 1   Points: 16

NANNINI, Alessandro (I) b 7/7/1959

1986

	Race	Circuit	No	Entrant	Car/Engine	Comment
ret	BRAZILIAN GP	Rio	24	Minardi Team	1.5 t/c Minardi M185B-MM V6	clutch
dns	SPANISH GP	Jerez	24	Minardi Team	1.5 t/c Minardi M185B-MM V6	differential on parade lap
ret	SAN MARINO GP	Imola	24	Minardi Team	1.5 t/c Minardi M185B-MM V6	collision-suspension damage
dnq	MONACO GP	Monte Carlo	24	Minardi Team	1.5 t/c Minardi M185B-MM V6	
ret	BELGIAN GP	Spa	24	Minardi Team	1.5 t/c Minardi M185B-MM V6	gearbox
ret	CANADIAN GP	Montreal	24	Minardi Team	1.5 t/c Minardi M185B-MM V6	turbo
ret	US GP (DETROIT)	Detroit	24	Minardi Team	1.5 t/c Minardi M185B-MM V6	turbo
ret	FRENCH GP	Paul Ricard	24	Minardi Team	1.5 t/c Minardi M185B-MM V6	accident with Ghinzani
ret	BRITISH GP	Brands Hatch	24	Minardi Team	1.5 t/c Minardi M185B-MM V6	started from pit lane/driveshaft
ret	GERMAN GP	Hockenheim	24	Minardi Team	1.5 t/c Minardi M185B-MM V6	overheating
ret	HUNGARIAN GP	Hungaroring	24	Minardi Team	1.5 t/c Minardi M185B-MM V6	engine
ret	AUSTRIAN GP	Österreichring	24	Minardi Team	1.5 t/c Minardi M185B-MM V6	suspension-spun off
dns	"	"	24		1.5 t/c Minardi M186-MM V6	practice only
ret	ITALIAN GP	Monza	24	Minardi Team	1.5 t/c Minardi M185B-MM V6	electrics
nc	PORTUGUESE GP	Estoril	24	Minardi Team	1.5 t/c Minardi M185B-MM V6	pit stops/10 laps behind
14	MEXICAN GP	Mexico City	24	Minardi Team	1.5 t/c Minardi M185B-MM V6	pit stop-tyres/4 laps behind
ret	AUSTRALIAN GP	Adelaide	24	Minardi Team	1.5 t/c Minardi M185B-MM V6	crashed into barrier

1987

	Race	Circuit	No	Entrant	Car/Engine	Comment
ret	BRAZILIAN GP	Rio	24	Minardi Team	1.5 t/c Minardi M/187-MM V6	suspension
ret	SAN MARINO GP	Imola	24	Minardi Team	1.5 t/c Minardi M/187-MM V6	turbo
ret	BELGIAN GP	Spa	24	Minardi Team	1.5 t/c Minardi M/187-MM V6	turbo
ret	MONACO GP	Monte Carlo	24	Minardi Team	1.5 t/c Minardi M/187-MM V6	electrics
ret	US GP (DETROIT)	Detroit	24	Minardi Team	1.5 t/c Minardi M/187-MM V6	gearbox
ret	FRENCH GP	Paul Ricard	24	Minardi Team	1.5 t/c Minardi M/187-MM V6	turbo
ret	BRITISH GP	Silverstone	24	Minardi Team	1.5 t/c Minardi M/187-MM V6	engine
ret	GERMAN GP	Hockenheim	24	Minardi Team	1.5 t/c Minardi M/187-MM V6	engine
11	HUNGARIAN GP	Hungaroring	24	Minardi Team	1.5 t/c Minardi M/187-MM V6	3 laps behind
ret	AUSTRIAN GP	Österreichring	24	Minardi Team	1.5 t/c Minardi M/187-MM V6	engine/5 laps behind
16/ret	ITALIAN GP	Monza	24	Minardi Team	1.5 t/c Minardi M/187-MM V6	engine/4 laps behind
11/ret	PORTUGUESE GP	Estoril	24	Minardi Team	1.5 t/c Minardi M/187-MM V6	out of fuel
ret	SPANISH GP	Jerez	24	Minardi Team	1.5 t/c Minardi M/187-MM V6	turbo
ret	MEXICAN GP	Mexico City	24	Minardi Team	1.5 t/c Minardi M/187-MM V6	turbo
ret	JAPANESE GP	Suzuka	24	Minardi Team	1.5 t/c Minardi M/187-MM V6	engine
ret	AUSTRALIAN GP	Adelaide	24	Minardi Team	1.5 t/c Minardi M/187-MM V6	hit wall

1988

	Race	Circuit	No	Entrant	Car/Engine	Comment
ret	BRAZILIAN GP	Rio	19	Benetton Formula	3.5 Benetton B188-Cosworth V8	overheating
6	SAN MARINO GP	Imola	19	Benetton Formula	3.5 Benetton B188-Cosworth V8	1 lap behind
ret	MONACO GP	Monte Carlo	19	Benetton Formula	3.5 Benetton B188-Cosworth V8	gearbox
7	MEXICAN GP	Mexico City	19	Benetton Formula	3.5 Benetton B188-Cosworth V8	2 laps behind
ret	CANADIAN GP	Montreal	19	Benetton Formula	3.5 Benetton B188-Cosworth V8	ignition
ret	US GP (DETROIT)	Detroit	19	Benetton Formula	3.5 Benetton B188-Cosworth V8	front suspension damage
6	FRENCH GP	Paul Ricard	19	Benetton Formula	3.5 Benetton B188-Cosworth V8	1 lap behind
3	BRITISH GP	Silverstone	19	Benetton Formula	3.5 Benetton B188-Cosworth V8	two spins
18	GERMAN GP	Hockenheim	19	Benetton Formula	3.5 Benetton B188-Cosworth V8	p stop-throttle cable/4 laps behind/FL
ret	HUNGARIAN GP	Hungaroring	19	Benetton Formula	3.5 Benetton B188-Cosworth V8	water pipe leak
dsq	BELGIAN GP	Spa	19	Benetton Formula	3.5 Benetton B188-Cosworth V8	4th on road/illegal fuel
9	ITALIAN GP	Monza	19	Benetton Formula	3.5 Benetton B188-Cosworth V8	started Ifrom pit lane/1 lap behind
ret	PORTUGUESE GP	Estoril	19	Benetton Formula	3.5 Benetton B188-Cosworth V8	exhausted due to chassis vibration
3	SPANISH GP	Jerez	19	Benetton Formula	3.5 Benetton B188-Cosworth V8	
5	JAPANESE GP	Suzuka	19	Benetton Formula	3.5 Benetton B188-Cosworth V8	
ret	AUSTRALIAN GP	Adelaide	19	Benetton Formula	3.5 Benetton B188-Cosworth V8	spun off-could not restart

1989

	Race	Circuit	No	Entrant	Car/Engine	Comment
6	BRAZILIAN GP	Rio	19	Benetton Formula	3.5 Benetton B188-Cosworth V8	2 p stops-tyres/broken wing stay
4	SAN MARINO GP	Imola	19	Benetton Formula	3.5 Benetton B188-Cosworth V8	vibration in closing stages/-1 lap
8	MONACO GP	Monte Carlo	19	Benetton Formula	3.5 Benetton B188-Cosworth V8	brake fade-clipped barrier/-3 laps
4	MEXICAN GP	Mexico City	19	Benetton Formula	3.5 Benetton B188-Cosworth V8	
ret	US GP (PHOENIX)	Phoenix	19	Benetton Formula	3.5 Benetton B188-Cosworth V8	driver exhausted
dsq	CANADIAN GP	Montreal	19	Benetton Formula	3.5 Benetton B188-Cosworth V8	started from pit lane before green
ret	FRENCH GP	Paul Ricard	19	Benetton Formula	3.5 Benetton B189-Ford V8	suspension
3	BRITISH GP	Silverstone	19	Benetton Formula	3.5 Benetton B189-Ford V8	broken exhaust
ret	GERMAN GP	Hockenheim	19	Benetton Formula	3.5 Benetton B189-Ford V8	ignition
ret	HUNGARIAN GP	Hungaroring	19	Benetton Formula	3.5 Benetton B189-Ford V8	gearbox
5	BELGIAN GP	Spa	19	Benetton Formula	3.5 Benetton B189-Ford V8	
ret	ITALIAN GP	Monza	19	Benetton Formula	3.5 Benetton B189-Ford V8	brakes
4	PORTUGUESE GP	Estoril	19	Benetton Formula	3.5 Benetton B189-Ford V8	
ret	SPANISH GP	Jerez	19	Benetton Formula	3.5 Benetton B189-Ford V8	spun off
1*	JAPANESE GP	Suzuka	19	Benetton Formula	3.5 Benetton B189-Ford V8	*1st place car disqualified
2	AUSTRALIAN GP	Adelaide	19	Benetton Formula	3.5 Benetton B189-Ford V8	broken exhaust

1990

	Race	Circuit	No	Entrant	Car/Engine	Comment
11	US GP (PHOENIX)	Phoenix	19	Benetton Formula	3.5 Benetton B189B-Ford V8	2 p stops-accident damage/-2 laps
10	BRAZILIAN GP	Interlagos	19	Benetton Formula	3.5 Benetton B189B-Ford V8	collision with de Cesaris/-3 laps
3	SAN MARINO GP	Imola	19	Benetton Formula	3.5 Benetton B190-Ford V8	FL
ret	MONACO GP	Monte Carlo	19	Benetton Formula	3.5 Benetton B190-Ford V8	oil pressure
ret	CANADIAN GP	Montreal	19	Benetton Formula	3.5 Benetton B190-Ford V8	spun off
4	MEXICAN GP	Mexico City	19	Benetton Formula	3.5 Benetton B190-Ford V8	
16/ret	FRENCH GP	Paul Ricard	19	Benetton Formula	3.5 Benetton B190-Ford V8	15th place car dsq/engine/-5 laps
ret	BRITISH GP	Silverstone	19	Benetton Formula	3.5 Benetton B190-Ford V8	hit Patrese-spun and stalled
2	GERMAN GP	Hockenheim	19	Benetton Formula	3.5 Benetton B190-Ford V8	led race

ret	HUNGARIAN GP	Hungaroring	19	Benetton Formula	3.5 Benetton B190-Ford V8	collision with Senna
4	BELGIAN GP	Spa	19	Benetton Formula	3.5 Benetton B190-Ford V8	
8	ITALIAN GP	Monza	19	Benetton Formula	3.5 Benetton B190-Ford V8	long pit stop-tyres/1 lap behind
6	PORTUGUESE GP	Estoril	19	Benetton Formula	3.5 Benetton B190-Ford V8	
3	SPANISH GP	Jerez	19	Benetton Formula	3.5 Benetton B190-Ford V8	

GP Starts: 77   GP Wins: 1   Pole positions: 0   Fastest laps: 2   Points: 65

ALESSANDRO NANNINI

The beaming countenance and charming manner of Alessandro Nannini were among the more pleasing aspects of life in the Formula 1 paddock in the late eighties. Certainly it was Grand Prix racing's loss when his career was so devastatingly wrecked by a helicopter accident in which his right arm was severed. Surgeons were able to re-attach the limb but controlling an F1 car was now beyond him and the popular Italian's misfortune seemed all the more cruel since his Grand Prix prospects had been at their zenith.

Sandro began his racing activities off road with a Lancia Stratos, before turning to circuit racing in 1981 in Formula Italia. He then took a big jump into Formula 2 with Minardi in 1982, replacing the team's previous star, Michele Alboreto, who had moved into F1 with Tyrrell. Nannini soon proved himself a worthy successor and by the end of the season he had taken a second place at Misano. In 1983 Minardi produced a promising but initially unworkable new car, and Nannini had to resort to the old chassis to take another second place, this time at the Nürburgring. By 1984, still loyal to the team, Sandro's F2 career was really treading water, but everyone had seen the talent and Lancia signed him to drive for their sports car team between 1984 and 1986.

Having dispensed with the services of Pierluigi Martini, Minardi entered two cars in 1986, with Sandro very much the number two (in theory at least) to the experienced Andrea de Cesaris. He was to spend two seasons with the little team, which in truth had little hope of success. However, Sandro made his mark and, unlike a number of other Grand Prix talents, managed to escape to a front-line team before too many seasons at the back of the field could dull his edge. Chosen to partner Thierry Boutsen at Benetton, he proved more than a match for the Belgian, making the rostrum on two occasions. Nannini was thrust into the position of team leader in 1989 and took some time to adjust to the new situation, but once the new Ford engine arrived his season began to take off. He won the Japanese GP on a technical knock-out after Senna was excluded following his tête-à-tête with Prost, and then took a fine second to Boutsen's Williams in the rain-soaked Australian GP.

In 1990 Sandro was joined by the experienced and cunning Nelson Piquet, who immediately established a rapport with John Barnard in developing the B190. Having been somewhat overshadowed, Nannini suddenly found his form again at Hockenheim, where he led until finally giving best to Senna. The battle with the Brazilian was rejoined in Hungary, where Ayrton crassly elbowed the Benetton out of second place, ending his chances of a win. Certainly Sandro's star was in the ascendant, and there was reportedly a Ferrari contract being bandied about, if not for 1991, then certainly for some time in the future.

It was all to prove academic after the helicopter accident, but Nannini bravely fought back, to the admiration and great pleasure of the motor racing world. In 1992 he raced an Alfa Romeo successfully in the Italian touring car championship, before proving that he was not in the Alfa team on sentiment alone with some fine displays in the 1993 German series, backing his team-mate Larini superbly as they defeated the Mercedes on home territory.

EMANUELE NASPETTI

Driving for the top-notch Forti team, Naspetti won a titanic struggle to clinch the 1988 Italian F3 championship in only his second year of racing cars, having been in karting between 1980 and '86.

Drawing a blank in his first season of F3000, Naspetti then came under the wing of Eddie Jordan in 1990 but again disapppointed, scoring but a single point. It was a different story in 1991 when, with the advantage of a Heini Mader-tended Cosworth engine in his Forti Corse Reynard, the Italian came out of his shell to string together a run of four victories at Enna, Hockenheim, Brands Hatch and Spa. Still with Forti, he stayed in the formula for a fourth year in 1992, winning at Pau, but then jumped at the chance to join the Formula 1 March team, replacing Paul Belmondo in mid-season. Emanuele proved surprisingly quick to adapt, clinging tenaciously to his team-mate Wendlinger for most of his debut race at Spa.

Naspetti spent much of 1993 frustrated at the lack of a Formula 1 drive, but did make a one-off appearance for Jordan in Portugal as a reward for his efforts as a test driver.

NASPETTI, Emanuele (I) b 24/2/1968

1992

	Race	Circuit	No	Entrant	Car/Engine	Comment
12	BELGIAN GP	Spa	17	March F1	3.5 March CG911-Ilmor V10	1 lap behind
ret	ITALIAN GP	Monza	17	March F1	3.5 March CG911-Ilmor V10	collision with Wendlinger-spun off
11	PORTUGUESE GP	Estoril	17	March F1	3.5 March CG911-Ilmor V10	
13	JAPANESE GP	Suzuka	17	March F1	3.5 March CG911-Ilmor V10	2 laps behind
ret	AUSTRALIAN GP	Adelaide	17	March F1	3.5 March CG911-Ilmor V10	gearbox

1993

ret	PORTUGUESE GP	Estoril	15	Sasol Jordan	3.5 Jordan 193-Hart V10	engine fire

GP Starts: 6   GP Wins: 0   Pole positions: 0   Fastest laps: 0   Points: 0

MASSIMO NATILI

One of a number of promising Italian Formula Junior drivers tested by Scuderia Centro Sud, Massimo was given a handful of outings in 1961, none of which brought any success.

In 1962 he was lucky to survive a crash in a Monza FJ race, when an anonymous spectator pulled him from his blazing car with burns to face and legs. He reappeared for Centro Sud in 1963, and took a fourth place in the 1964 Rome GP with a Brabham-Giannini. He continued to race competitively in Italian F3 with a Brabham and was the 1965 1-litre national sports car champion with a Lotus 23.

BRIAN NAYLOR

A motor-dealer from Stockport and a former merchant navy radio officer who won awards for gallantry in the war, Naylor began racing in 1954 with a Cooper-MG but soon switched to a Lotus chassis, regularly clocking up victories the length and breadth of Britain. In 1957 he bought a Formula 2 Cooper, which he was to race in selected events, including Grands Prix, over the next three years.

Naylor was never content to drive standard fare, and experimented with a Maserati-engined Lotus before developing his own Cooper-based JBW-Maserati, which he ran with great success in Libre events but was outclassed in Formula 1 and Inter-Continental racing. Ill-health brought about his retirement at the end of the 1961 season.

TIFF NEEDELL

Tiff spent the formative years of his racing careeer in Formula Ford, winning the FF16000 championship in 1975 and finishing as runner-up in the FF2000 series the following year, when he won the premier Grovewood Award. After brief spells in Formula 3 and the Aurora F1/F2 championship, Needell's Grand Prix ambitions were thwarted in 1979, when he was refused a super-licence to drive the Ensign, although he was to get his opportunity in 1980.

By then, Tiff had extended his repertoire to encompass Japanese F2, touring cars, the Procar series and sports car racing, where he was to remain active throughout the eighties and beyond in tandem with his successful career as a journalist and broadcaster.

NATILI, Massimo (I) b 28/7/1935

1961

	Race	Circuit	No	Entrant	Car/Engine	Comment
ret	BRITISH GP	Aintree	62	Scuderia Centro Sud	1.5 Cooper T51-Maserati 4	gearbox
dnq	ITALIAN GP	Monza	60	Scuderia Centro Sud	1.5 Cooper T51-Maserati 4	practised-but entry taken by Lewis

GP Starts: 1 GP Wins: 0 Pole positions: 0 Fastest laps: 0 Points: 0

NAYLOR, Brian (GB) b 24/3/1959 – d 8/1989

1957

	Race	Circuit	No	Entrant	Car/Engine	Comment
13	GERMAN GP (F2)	Nürburgring	28	J B Naylor	1.5 Cooper T43-Climax 4	2nd in F2 class/2 laps behind

1958

ret	GERMAN GP (F2)	Nürburgring	29	J B Naylor	1.5 Cooper T45-Climax 4	fuel pump

1959

ret	BRITISH GP	Aintree	36	J B Naylor	2.5 JBW-Maserati 4	transmission

1960

dnq	MONACO GP	Monte Carlo	20	J B Naylor	2.5 JBW-Maserati 4	
13	BRITISH GP	Silverstone	25	J B Naylor	2.5 JBW-Maserati 4	pit stop/5 laps behind
ret	ITALIAN GP	Monza	6	J B Naylor	2.5 JBW-Maserati 4	gearbox
ret	US GP	Riverside	21	J B Naylor	2.5 JBW-Maserati 4	engine

1961

ret	ITALIAN GP	Monza	14	J B Naylor	1.5 JBW-Climax 4	engine

GP Starts: 7 GP Wins: 0 Pole positions: 0 Fastest laps: 0 Points: 0

NEEDELL, Tiff (GB) b 29/10/1951

1980

	Race	Circuit	No	Entrant	Car/Engine	Comment
ret	BELGIAN GP	Zolder	14	Unipart Racing Team	3.0 Ensign N180-Cosworth V8	engine
dnq	MONACO GP	Monte Carlo	14	Unipart Racing Team	3.0 Ensign N180-Cosworth V8	

GP Starts: 1 GP Wins: 0 Pole positions: 0 Fastest laps: 0 Points: 0

NEVE, Patrick (B) b 13/10/1949

1976

	Race	Circuit	No	Entrant	Car/Engine	Comment
ret	BELGIAN GP	Zolder	33	Tissot RAM Racing	3.0 Brabham BT44B-Cosworth V8	*driveshaft*
18	FRENCH GP	Paul Ricard	22	Team Ensign	3.0 Ensign N176-Cosworth V8	*1 lap behind*

1977

12	SPANISH GP	Jarama	27	Williams Grand Prix Engineering	3.0 March 761-Cosworth V8	*pit stop/4 laps behind*
10	BELGIAN GP	Zolder	27	Williams Grand Prix Engineering	3.0 March 761-Cosworth V8	*pit stop-tyres/2 laps behind*
15	SWEDISH GP	Anderstorp	27	Williams Grand Prix Engineering	3.0 March 761-Cosworth V8	*3 laps behind*
dnq	FRENCH GP	Dijon	27	Williams Grand Prix Engineering	3.0 March 761-Cosworth V8	
10	BRITISH GP	Silverstone	27	Williams Grand Prix Engineering	3.0 March 761-Cosworth V8	*2 laps behind*
dnq	GERMAN GP	Hockenheim	27	Williams Grand Prix Engineering	3.0 March 761-Cosworth V8	
9	AUSTRIAN GP	Österreichring	27	Williams Grand Prix Engineering	3.0 March 761-Cosworth V8	*1 lap behind*
dnq	DUTCH GP	Zandvoort	27	Williams Grand Prix Engineering	3.0 March 761-Cosworth V8	
7	ITALIAN GP	Monza	27	Williams Grand Prix Engineering	3.0 March 761-Cosworth V8	*2 laps behind*
18	US GP EAST	Watkins Glen	27	Williams Grand Prix Engineering	3.0 March 761-Cosworth V8	*4 laps behind*
ret	CANADIAN GP	Mosport Park	27	Williams Grand Prix Engineering	3.0 March 761-Cosworth V8	*oil pressure*

1978

dnpq	BELGIAN GP	Zolder	–	Patrick Neve	3.0 March 781S-Cosworth V8	*dnq for official practice sessions*

GP Starts: 10 GP Wins: 0 Pole positions: 0 Fastest laps: 0 Points: 0

NICHOLSON, John (NZ) b 6/10/1941

1974

	Race	Circuit	No	Entrant	Car/Engine	Comment
dnq	BRITISH GP	Brands Hatch	29	Pinch (Plant) Ltd	3.0 Lyncar 006-Cosworth V8	

1975

17/ret	BRITISH GP	Silverstone	32	Pinch (Plant) Ltd	3.0 Lyncar 009-Cosworth V8	*crashed in rainstorm/5 laps behind*

GP Starts: 1 GP Wins: 0 Pole positions: 0 Fastest laps: 0 Points: 0

PATRICK NEVE

A one-time pupil at the Jim Russell driving school, Neve later worked as an instructor to finance his own racing activities, but gained enough success in the school's Merlyn to set himself up for a successful year in 1974, winning the STP Formula Ford championship in a Lola T340.

Moving up to Formula 3 in 1975, Patrick drove well enough in the Safir to gain a test with Brabham and a drive with the RAM team in '76. After a couple of non-championship races, he was bundled out of the car by de Villota's banknotes in Spain, but raced in Belgium before departing for a one-off drive with Ensign.

The following year could have seen him make his breakthrough; he led a Formula 2 race at Silverstone until suspension problems dropped him to third place and then spent an unhappy Grand Prix season with the post-Wolf Frank Williams team running a March. The relationship ended in acrimony after the Canadian GP, and Neve's career never really recovered. After an abortive attempt to make the grid in Belgium in 1978, his planned season of Formula 2 with Kauhsen fell through when the German's sponsors pulled out, leaving the Belgian to race the unsuccessful Pilbeam. Thereafter he appeared only occasionally in BMW Procars and touring cars.

JOHN NICHOLSON

John had already tasted success in his native New Zealand with a Brabham BT18 when he made his way to England and walked straight into a job at McLaren working on their racing engines. When his urge to compete resurfaced, he quickly became a leading figure in Formula Atlantic, initially with a March and then with his own Lyncar-Nicholson, in which he won the 1973 and 1974 championships.

By 1973 he had established his own thriving engine business servicing and preparing Cosworths for McLaren and many others, which prevented him from undertaking a major racing programme abroad, but he did dip into Formula 1 with the Lyncar in British events, his best result being a sixth at the 1974 Race of Champions. Plans to purchase a McLaren M23 and have a real go fell through, much to Nicholson's dismay, but he did race subsequently in both Formula 2 and F5000 in 1976, and then took in the Peter Stuyvesant New Zealand series early in 1978, before concentrating on his business commitments and indulging his passion for speed with a new-found interest in powerboat racing.

NIEDERMAYR, Helmut (D) b 29/11/1915 – d 3/4/1985

1952

	Race	Circuit	No	Entrant	Car/Engine	Comment
nc	GERMAN GP	Nürburgring	124	Helmut Niedermayr	2.0 AFM 6-BMW 6	3 laps behind

GP Starts: 1　GP Wins: 0　Pole positions: 0　Fastest laps: 0　Points: 0

NIEMANN, Brausch (ZA) b 7/1/1939

1963

	Race	Circuit	No	Entrant	Car/Engine	Comment
14	SOUTH AFRICAN GP	East London	21	Ted Lanfear	1.5 Lotus 22-Ford 4	20 laps behind

1965

dnq	SOUTH AFRICAN GP	East London	27	Ted Lanfear	1.5 Lotus 22-Ford 4	

GP Starts: 1　GP Wins: 0　Pole positions: 0　Fastest laps: 0　Points: 0

GUNNAR NILSSON

This cheery and gregarious Swede was always his own man, and the courage and dignity he showed after the diagnosis of terminal cancer said as much for him as his all-too-brief motor racing career.

Having made a late start in the sport, Gunnar had his first full season of racing in Formula Super Vee in 1973, learning a great deal in a short time from the experienced Freddy Kottulinsky, who was instrumental in his early development. He also tried his hand at Formula 2 at Norisring and, given his novice status, did remarkably well to finish a lucky fourth on aggregate with a GRD. In 1974 he raced in the German Polifac F3 championship in a private March, and impressed sufficiently to bargain his way into the works team contesting the British series alongside Alex Ribeiro in 1975. Things could hardly have started better, as he won the first race at Thruxton to set up his year, which ended with him taking the BP championship. An end-of-season switch to Formula Atlantic merely underlined his talent as he won the last five rounds in succession in a Chevron B29.

Though tied to March and BMW for 1976, Nilsson got together with Ronnie Peterson to contrive a swap deal which saw Gunnar join the Lotus team at a time when it was at a low ebb. It was a gamble, but it soon paid off with Nilsson on the rostrum in his third race. The arrival of Mario Andretti only strengthened the team's hand as they sought to recapture past glories, and Gunnar benefited greatly from the American driver's guidance. Ken Tyrrell, no less, predicted that here was a future World Champion – praise indeed.

Happy to stay with Lotus for another year in 1977, Nilsson maintained his upward momentum during the first half of the season, culminating in his only Grand Prix win in the wet at Zolder when he memorably moved through the field before picking off the leader Niki Lauda with clinical precision. The second half of the year saw a sudden downturn in his fortunes as inconsistency set in. Of course no one knew it, but the cancer he had developed was already well advanced. With Peterson returning to the Lotus fold for 1978, Gunnar signed for the newly formed Arrows team, but in the event he was never well enough to drive the car. By the following autumn he was fighting to live just long enough to see his Gunnar Nilsson Cancer Treatment Campaign successfully launched, before passing away that October.

RODNEY NUCKEY

After showing a great deal of skill in his own F3 Cooper-Norton during the 1952 season, his record including wins at Falkenberg and Skarpnack in Sweden, Nuckey was sufficiently encouraged to purchase a Formula 2 Cooper-Bristol which he put to good use in 1953, taking a third place in the Syracuse GP, fourth in the London Trophy at Crystal Palace and fifth in the Eifelrennen. He continued to race the car in 1954, mainly in Formula Libre events, along with the Ecurie Richmond F3 Cooper.

NILSSON, Gunnar (S) b 20/11/1948 – d 20/10/1978

1976

	Race	Circuit	No	Entrant	Car/Engine	Comment
ret	SOUTH AFRICAN GP	Kyalami	6	John Player Team Lotus	3.0 Lotus 77-Cosworth V8	clutch
ret	US GP WEST	Long Beach	6	John Player Team Lotus	3.0 Lotus 77-Cosworth V8	suspension-crashed
3	SPANISH GP	Jarama	6	John Player Team Lotus	3.0 Lotus 77-Cosworth V8	
ret	BELGIAN GP	Zolder	6	John Player Team Lotus	3.0 Lotus 77-Cosworth V8	crashed
ret	MONACO GP	Monte Carlo	6	John Player Team Lotus	3.0 Lotus 77-Cosworth V8	engine
ret	SWEDISH GP	Anderstorp	6	John Player Team Lotus	3.0 Lotus 77-Cosworth V8	spun into barrier
ret	FRENCH GP	Paul Ricard	6	John Player Team Lotus	3.0 Lotus 77-Cosworth V8	transmission
ret	BRITISH GP	Brands Hatch	6	John Player Team Lotus	3.0 Lotus 77-Cosworth V8	engine
5	GERMAN GP	Nürburgring	6	John Player Team Lotus	3.0 Lotus 77-Cosworth V8	
3	AUSTRIAN GP	Österreichring	6	John Player Team Lotus	3.0 Lotus 77-Cosworth V8	
ret	DUTCH GP	Zandvoort	6	John Player Team Lotus	3.0 Lotus 77-Cosworth V8	crashed on oil
13	ITALIAN GP	Monza	6	John Player Team Lotus	3.0 Lotus 77-Cosworth V8	pit stop-broken nose/1 lap behind
12	CANADIAN GP	Mosport Park	6	John Player Team Lotus	3.0 Lotus 77-Cosworth V8	last away at start/1 lap behind
ret	US GP EAST	Watkins Glen	6	John Player Team Lotus	3.0 Lotus 77-Cosworth V8	engine
6	JAPANESE GP	Mount Fuji	6	John Player Team Lotus	3.0 Lotus 77-Cosworth V8	1 lap behind

1977

	Race	Circuit	No	Entrant	Car/Engine	Comment
dns	ARGENTINE GP	Buenos Aires	6	John Player Team Lotus	3.0 Lotus 78-Cosworth V8	Andretti drove car
5	BRAZILIAN GP	Interlagos	6	John Player Team Lotus	3.0 Lotus 78-Cosworth V8	2 pit stops-tyres/1 lap behind
12	SOUTH AFRICAN GP	Kyalami	6	John Player Team Lotus	3.0 Lotus 78-Cosworth V8	pit stop-tyres-new nose/-1 lap
8	US GP WEST	Long Beach	6	John Player Team Lotus	3.0 Lotus 78-Cosworth V8	1 lap behind
5	SPANISH GP	Jarama	6	John Player Team Lotus	3.0 Lotus 78-Cosworth V8	
ret	MONACO GP	Monte Carlo	6	John Player Team Lotus	3.0 Lotus 78-Cosworth V8	gearbox
1	BELGIAN GP	Zolder	6	John Player Team Lotus	3.0 Lotus 78-Cosworth V8	FL
19/ret	SWEDISH GP	Anderstorp	6	John Player Team Lotus	3.0 Lotus 78-Cosworth V8	wheel bearing/8 laps behind
4	FRENCH GP	Dijon	6	John Player Team Lotus	3.0 Lotus 78-Cosworth V8	
3	BRITISH GP	Silverstone	6	John Player Team Lotus	3.0 Lotus 78-Cosworth V8	
ret	GERMAN GP	Hockenheim	6	John Player Team Lotus	3.0 Lotus 78-Cosworth V8	engine
ret	AUSTRIAN GP	Österreichring	6	John Player Team Lotus	3.0 Lotus 78-Cosworth V8	engine
ret	DUTCH GP	Zandvoort	6	John Player Team Lotus	3.0 Lotus 78-Cosworth V8	hit Reutemann
ret	ITALIAN GP	Monza	6	John Player Team Lotus	3.0 Lotus 78-Cosworth V8	broken front upright
ret	US GP EAST	Watkins Glen	6	John Player Team Lotus	3.0 Lotus 78-Cosworth V8	hit by Peterson
ret	CANADIAN GP	Mosport Park	6	John Player Team Lotus	3.0 Lotus 78-Cosworth V8	throttle stuck-crashed
ret	JAPANESE GP	Mount Fuji	6	John Player Team Lotus	3.0 Lotus 78-Cosworth V8	gearbox

GP Starts: 31   GP Wins: 1   Pole positions: 0   Fastest laps: 1   Points: 31

NUCKEY, Rodney (GB) b 26/6/1929

1953

	Race	Circuit	No	Entrant	Car/Engine	Comment
11	GERMAN GP	Nürburgring	40	Rodney Nuckey	2.0 Cooper T23-Bristol 6	2 laps behind
	1954					
dns	BRITISH GP	Silverstone	30	Ecurie Richmond	2.0 Cooper T23-Bristol 6	Brandon drove car

GP Starts: 1   GP Wins: 0   Pole positions: 0   Fastest laps: 0   Points: 0

O'BRIEN, Robert (USA)

1952

	Race	Circuit	No	Entrant	Car/Engine	Comment
nc	BELGIAN GP	Spa	44	Robert O'Brien	1.5 Simca-Gordini Type 15 4	6 laps behind

GP Starts: 1   GP Wins: 0   Pole positions: 0   Fastest laps: 0   Points: 0

OLIVER, Jackie (GB) b 14/8/1942

1967

	Race	Circuit	No	Entrant	Car/Engine	Comment
5*	GERMAN GP (F2)	Nürburgring	24	Lotus Components Ltd	1.6 Lotus 48-Cosworth 4	* 1st in F2 class/no points scored

1968

ret	MONACO GP	Monte Carlo	10	Gold Leaf Team Lotus	3.0 Lotus 49-Cosworth V8	hit McLaren
5/ret	BELGIAN GP	Spa	2	Gold Leaf Team Lotus	3.0 Lotus 49B-Cosworth V8	driveshaft/2 laps behind
nc	DUTCH GP	Zandvoort	4	Gold Leaf Team Lotus	3.0 Lotus 49B-Cosworth V8	pit stops-water in electrics/-10 laps
dns	FRENCH GP	Rouen	14	Gold Leaf Team Lotus	3.0 Lotus 49B-Cosworth V8	accident in practice
ret	BRITISH GP	Brands Hatch	9	Gold Leaf Team Lotus	3.0 Lotus 49B-Cosworth V8	transmission
11	GERMAN GP	Nürburgring	21	Gold Leaf Team Lotus	3.0 Lotus 49B-Cosworth V8	1 lap behind
ret	ITALIAN GP	Monza	19	Gold Leaf Team Lotus	3.0 Lotus 49B-Cosworth V8	transmission/FL (disputed)
ret	CANADIAN GP	St Jovite	4	Gold Leaf Team Lotus	3.0 Lotus 49B-Cosworth V8	transmission
dns	US GP	Watkins Glen	11	Gold Leaf Team Lotus	3.0 Lotus 49B-Cosworth V8	accident in practice
3	MEXICAN GP	Mexico City	11	Gold Leaf Team Lotus	3.0 Lotus 49B-Cosworth V8	

1969

7	SOUTH AFRICAN GP	Kyalami	11	Owen Racing Organisation	3.0 BRM P133 V12	pit stop-3 laps behind
ret	SPANISH GP	Montjuich Park	11	Owen Racing Organisation	3.0 BRM P133 V12	burst oil pipe
ret	MONACO GP	Monte Carlo	11	Owen Racing Organisation	3.0 BRM P133 V12	hit Attwood-broke front wishbone
ret	DUTCH GP	Zandvoort	11	Owen Racing Organisation	3.0 BRM P133 V12	gearbox
ret	BRITISH GP	Silverstone	11	Owen Racing Organisation	3.0 BRM P133 V12	transmission
ret	GERMAN GP	Nürburgring	11	Owen Racing Organisation	3.0 BRM P138 V12	damaged sump
ret	ITALIAN GP	Monza	11	Owen Racing Organisation	3.0 BRM P139 V12	oil pressure
dns	"	"	11		3.0 BRM P138 V12	practice only
ret	CANADIAN GP	Mosport Park	11	Owen Racing Organisation	3.0 BRM P139 V12	engine
ret	US GP	Watkins Glen	11	Owen Racing Organisation	3.0 BRM P139 V12	engine
6	MEXICAN GP	Mexico City	11	Owen Racing Organisation	3.0 BRM P139 V12	2 laps behind

1970

ret	SOUTH AFRICAN GP	Kyalami	19	Owen Racing Organisation	3.0 BRM P153 V12	gear selection
ret	SPANISH GP	Jarama	15	Yardley Team BRM	3.0 BRM P153 V12	broken stub axle-hit Ickx-bad fire
ret	MONACO GP	Monte Carlo	16	Yardley Team BRM	3.0 BRM P153 V12	engine-throttle cable
ret	BELGIAN GP	Spa	2	Yardley Team BRM	3.0 BRM P153 V12	engine
ret	DUTCH GP	Zandvoort	2	Yardley Team BRM	3.0 BRM P153 V12	engine
ret	FRENCH GP	Clermont Ferrand	5	Yardley Team BRM	3.0 BRM P153 V12	engine
ret	BRITISH GP	Brands Hatch	23	Yardley Team BRM	3.0 BRM P153 V12	engine
ret	GERMAN GP	Hockenheim	18	Yardley Team BRM	3.0 BRM P153 V12	engine
5	AUSTRIAN GP	Österreichring	16	Yardley Team BRM	3.0 BRM P153 V12	1 lap behind
ret	ITALIAN GP	Monza	8	Yardley Team BRM	3.0 BRM P153 V12	engine
nc	CANADIAN GP	St Jovite	15	Yardley Team BRM	3.0 BRM P153 V12	pit stop-broken wishbone/-38 laps
ret	US GP	Watkins Glen	20	Yardley Team BRM	3.0 BRM P153 V12	engine

7	MEXICAN GP	Mexico City	20	Yardley Team BRM	3.0 BRM P153 V12	*1 lap behind*

1971

ret	BRITISH GP	Silverstone	11	Bruce McLaren Motor Racing	3.0 McLaren M14A-Cosworth V8	*hit Hill at start-broken radius rod*
9	AUSTRIAN GP	Österreichring	10	Bruce McLaren Motor Racing	3.0 McLaren M19A-Cosworth V8	*1 lap behind*
7	ITALIAN GP	Monza	14	Bruce McLaren Motor Racing	3.0 McLaren M14A-Cosworth V8	

1972

ret	BRITISH GP	Brands Hatch	14	Marlboro BRM	3.0 BRM P160B V12	*rear radius rod*

1973

ret	SOUTH AFRICAN GP	Kyalami	22	UOP Shadow Racing Team	3.0 Shadow DN1-Cosworth V8	*engine*
ret	SPANISH GP	Montjuich Park	19	UOP Shadow Racing Team	3.0 Shadow DN1-Cosworth V8	*oil leak*
ret	BELGIAN GP	Zolder	17	UOP Shadow Racing Team	3.0 Shadow DN1-Cosworth V8	*accident*
10	MONACO GP	Monte Carlo	17	UOP Shadow Racing Team	3.0 Shadow DN1-Cosworth V8	*6 laps behind*
ret	SWEDISH GP	Anderstorp	17	UOP Shadow Racing Team	3.0 Shadow DN1-Cosworth V8	*transmission*
ret	FRENCH GP	Paul Ricard	17	UOP Shadow Racing Team	3.0 Shadow DN1-Cosworth V8	*clutch*
ret	BRITISH GP	Silverstone	17	UOP Shadow Racing Team	3.0 Shadow DN1-Cosworth V8	*hit Lauda in first start*
ret	DUTCH GP	Zandvoort	17	UOP Shadow Racing Team	3.0 Shadow DN1-Cosworth V8	*stuck throttle-hit barrier*
8	GERMAN GP	Nürburgring	17	UOP Shadow Racing Team	3.0 Shadow DN1-Cosworth V8	
ret	AUSTRIAN GP	Österreichring	17	UOP Shadow Racing Team	3.0 Shadow DN1-Cosworth V8	*fuel leak*
11	ITALIAN GP	Monza	17	UOP Shadow Racing Team	3.0 Shadow DN1-Cosworth V8	*1 lap behind*
3	CANADIAN GP	Mosport Park	17	UOP Shadow Racing Team	3.0 Shadow DN1-Cosworth V8	
15	US GP	Watkins Glen	17	UOP Shadow Racing Team	3.0 Shadow DN1-Cosworth V8	*pit stop-loose wheels/4 laps behind*

1977

9	SWEDISH GP	Anderstorp	16	Shadow Racing Team	3.0 Shadow DN8-Cosworth V8	

GP Starts: 50   GP Wins: 0   Pole positions: 0   Fastest laps: 1   Points: 13

ONGAIS, Danny (USA) b 21/5/1942

1977

	Race	Circuit	No	Entrant	Car/Engine	Comment
ret	US GP EAST	Watkins Glen	14	Interscope Racing	3.0 Penske PC4-Cosworth V8	*spun off*
7	CANADIAN GP	Mosport Park	14	Interscope Racing	3.0 Penske PC4-Cosworth V8	*2 laps behind*

1978

ret	ARGENTINE GP	Buenos Aires	22	Team Tissot Ensign	3.0 Ensign N177-Cosworth V8	*rotor arm*
ret	BRAZILIAN GP	Rio	22	Team Tissot Ensign	3.0 Ensign N177-Cosworth V8	*brake disc mounting bolt*
dnpq	US GP WEST	Long Beach	39	Interscope Racing	3.0 Shadow DN9-Cosworth V8	
dnpq	DUTCH GP	Zandvoort	39	Interscope Racing	3.0 Shadow DN9-Cosworth V8	

GP Starts: 4   GP Wins: 0   Pole positions: 0   Fastest laps: 0   Points: 0

OPEL, Rikki von (FL) b 14/10/1947

1973

	Race	Circuit	No	Entrant	Car/Engine	Comment
15	FRENCH GP	Paul Ricard	29	Team Ensign	3.0 Ensign MN-Cosworth V8	*3 laps behind*
13	BRITISH GP	Silverstone	28	Team Ensign	3.0 Ensign MN-Cosworth V8	*pit stop-temperature gauge/-6 laps*
dns	DUTCH GP	Zandvoort	28	Team Ensign	3.0 Ensign MN-Cosworth V8	*suspension pick up in practice*
ret	AUSTRIAN GP	Österreichring	28	Team Ensign	3.0 Ensign MN-Cosworth V8	*fuel pressure*
ret	ITALIAN GP	Monza	28	Team Ensign	3.0 Ensign MN-Cosworth V8	*overheating*
nc	CANADIAN GP	Mosport Park	28	Team Ensign	3.0 Ensign MN-Cosworth V8	*2 pit stops-off road/12 laps behind*
ret	US GP	Watkins Glen	28	Team Ensign	3.0 Ensign MN-Cosworth V8	*stuck throttle*

1974

dns	ARGENTINE GP	Buenos Aires	22	Team Ensign	3.0 Ensign N174-Cosworth V8	*handling problems in practice*
ret	SPANISH GP	Jarama	8	Motor Racing Developments	3.0 Brabham BT44-Cosworth V8	*oil leak*
ret	BELGIAN GP	Nivelles	8	Motor Racing Developments	3.0 Brabham BT44-Cosworth V8	*oil pressure*
dnq	MONACO GP	Monte Carlo	8	Motor Racing Developments	3.0 Brabham BT44-Cosworth V8	
9	SWEDISH GP	Anderstorp	8	Motor Racing Developmants	3.0 Brabham BT44-Cosworth V8	*1 lap behind*
9	DUTCH GP	Zandvoort	8	Motor Racing Developments	3.0 Brabham BT44-Cosworth V8	*2 laps behind*
dnq	FRENCH GP	Dijon	8	Motor Racing Developments	3.0 Brabham BT44-Cosworth V8	

GP Starts: 10   GP Wins: 0   Pole positions: 0   Fastest laps: 0   Points: 0

---

d'OREY, Fritz (BR) b 25/3/1938

1959

	Race	Circuit	No	Entrant	Car/Engine	Comment
nc	FRENCH GP	Reims	38	Scuderia Centro Sud	2.5 Maserati 250F 6	*10 laps behind*
ret	BRITISH GP	Aintree	40	Scuderia Centro Sud	2.5 Maserati 250F 6	*out of brakes-crashed*
ret	US GP	Sebring	15	Camoradi USA	2.5 Tec Mec Maserati 250F 6	*oil leak*

GP Starts: 3   GP Wins: 0   Pole positions: 0   Fastest laps: 0   Points: 0

OWEN, Arthur (GB) b 23/3/1915

1960

	Race	Circuit	No	Entrant	Car/Engine	Comment
ret	ITALIAN GP	Monza	8	Arthur Owen	2.2 Cooper T45-Climax 4	*locked brakes-damaged suspension*

GP Starts: 1   GP Wins: 0   Pole positions: 0   Fastest laps: 0   Points: 0

JACK OLIVER

It's hard to believe the youthful-looking Oliver has been involved in motor sport for more than thirty years, having started racing with a Marcos way back in 1963. He really came to prominence, however, driving a Lotus Elan, with which he embarrassed many a more powerful GT car in 1965, before moving into single-seaters the following year, when he showed much promise but achieved little success in Formula 3.

Jack's breakthrough year was 1967 when he drove the Lotus Components F2 car, doing himself a power of good in the eyes of Colin Chapman by taking fifth overall and the F2 class win in the German GP. With the death of Jim Clark at Hockenheim, Oliver was promoted into the Lotus team as number two to Graham Hill, but had something of a torrid baptism, crashing in both the Monaco and French GPs before redeeming himself with a splendid performance at Brands Hatch, where he led the British GP until engine failure. Seen as nothing more than a stop-gap by Chapman, who had set his heart on having Jochen Rindt in the team, Oliver bowed out with a fine third place in Mexico to take up a two-year contract with BRM.

The following season was a miserable one for BRM, but Oliver salvaged his year by racing for John Wyer's Gulf team. Paired with Ickx, he won at Sebring and they then scored a famous victory at Le Mans, Jack's contribution to which is often overlooked. The second year of his BRM deal brought scarcely more joy than the first, even though he had the excellent P153 to drive. Apart from a fifth place in Austria and a third in the Gold Cup at Oulton Park, the catalogue of retirements made depressing reading. Jack's sharp, young, Essex personality didn't sit well with Louis Stanley, who preferred drivers cut from a different era, so a parting of the ways was probably inevitable. The season was not completely lost, for Oliver ventured into Can-Am with the Autocast project and took three second places. Meanwhile he returned to sports cars once more with Wyer, winning the Daytona 24 Hours and Monza 1000 Km, but was released after he preferred to take up an invitation to race Don Nichols' Shadow in Can-Am. Keen to keep his Formula 1 career afloat, Oliver arranged some drives in a third McLaren, and his versatility was proven when he stood in for Mark Donohue in Penske's Trans-Am Javelin to take third place at Riverside.

With the 1972 British GP being held at Brands Hatch (one of Jack's favourite circuits), he drove for BRM, but spent most of the season testing Shadow's latest Can-Am car. He got on well with Don Nichols, and when Shadow entered Grand Prix racing the following year Oliver had one of the drives. It was a perplexing season, with the DN1 chassis proving difficult to sort, but a wet race in Canada saw Jack take third place – although many insist that in fact he won, as the lap charts were thrown into confusion by the use of a pace car. Oliver concentrated on Can-Am alone in 1974 and it paid off handsomely with him winning the series at the fourth attempt in Nichols' machines. Although increasingly involved in the management side of things, Oliver contested the 1975 and 1976 US F5000 series, before a Formula 1 swansong as a driver in 1977. He took the Shadow DN8 into fifth place at the Race of Champions, and later in the year took part in his final Grand Prix in Sweden, finishing ninth.

Along with Alan Rees and Tony Southgate, Oliver quit Shadow at the end of the year and unveiled the 1978 Arrows Formula 1 car that was subsequently the centre of legal action from Nichols over design copyright. Since then Jack has kept his team on the Formula 1 grid, though a win still eludes him after 16 years. In 1990 he sold out to the Japanese Footwork concern, whose name the team now bears, but Oliver still remains at the helm as a director.

DANNY ONGAIS

This Hawaiian-born driver first found fame as a drag racer with the Vel's Parnelli team, before trying his hand in SCCA national racing in 1974. He then tackled US F5000 with Interscope Racing's Lola in 1975 and 1976, and although a win eluded him he was a regular contender. The following season Interscope ran him in USAC racing – where he shone, taking a win at Michigan – and in IMSA, where he won two rounds in a Porsche 935 turbo, and he made his Grand Prix debut at the end-of-year North American rounds in the team's Penske.

Danny's struggles in F1 in 1978 – he scraped onto the grid for the first two Grands Prix in the works Ensign, then floundered with the embarrassing Interscope Shadow – were in sharp contrast to his rapidly blossoming career in USAC, where he took five wins in the Parnelli VPJ6.

Although Danny enjoyed further success for Interscope in IMSA sports car events, winning the 1979 Daytona 24 Hours in a Porsche, and taking third place the following year, this was the high point of his IndyCar career, as he was to suffer appalling leg injuries in a crash at Indianapolis in 1981. Happily he recovered to make a return to the track but, although he raced until 1987, he was never quite the same force again.

RIKKI von OPEL

An heir to the Opel automobile fortune, von Opel began his racing career under the pseudonym 'Antonio Bronco', but soon reverted to his true name after a successful introduction to Formula Ford in 1970.

He jumped staight into F3 the following year with a Lotus and showed much promise, which was realised in 1972 when, driving the Iberia-sponsored works F3 Ensign, he took the Lombard North Central title and was so impressed with Mo Nunn's little team that he commissioned a Formula 1 car to go Grand Prix racing in 1973.

Inevitably with such an inexperienced pairing, success was thin on the ground and von Opel was damned as a playboy racer, which was unfair as he took the whole project very seriously indeed. When the opportunity arose to drive a pukka works Brabham at the beginning of the European season in 1974, Rikki grabbed it, reasoning that he could learn much in this established team.

After he was unable qualify the car at Dijon for the French GP, von Opel turned his back on the sport, having tried but failed to make the grade, to pursue other interests.

PACE, Carlos (BR) b 6/10/1944 – d 18/3/1977

1972

	Race	Circuit	No	Entrant	Car/Engine	Comment
17	SOUTH AFRICAN GP	Kyalami	22	Team Williams-Motul	3.0 March 711-Cosworth V8	lost 3 laps at start-fuel pump/-6 laps
6	SPANISH GP	Jarama	29	Team Williams-Motul	3.0 March 711-Cosworth V8	1 lap behind
17	MONACO GP	Monte Carlo	23	Team Williams-Motul	3.0 March 711-Cosworth V8	pit stop-electrics/8 laps behind
5	BELGIAN GP	Nivelles	16	Team Williams-Motul	3.0 March 711-Cosworth V8	1 lap behind
ret	FRENCH GP	Clermont Ferrand	17	Team Williams-Motul	3.0 March 711-Cosworth V8	engine
ret	BRITISH GP	Brands Hatch	25	Team Williams-Motul	3.0 March 711-Cosworth V8	collision-Reutemann/differential
nc	GERMAN GP	Nürburgring	21	Team Williams-Motul	3.0 March 711-Cosworth V8	long pit stop-handling/3 laps behind
nc	AUSTRIAN GP	Österreichring	23	Team Williams-Motul	3.0 March 711-Cosworth V8	pit stop-fuel leak/8 laps behind
ret	ITALIAN GP	Monza	26	Team Williams-Motul	3.0 March 711-Cosworth V8	hit by Regazzoni at chicane
9/ret	CANADIAN GP	Mosport Park	29	Team Williams-Motul	3.0 March 711-Cosworth V8	fuel pressure/2 laps behind
ret	US GP	Watkins Glen	27	Team Williams-Motul	3.0 March 711-Cosworth V8	fuel injection

1973

	Race	Circuit	No	Entrant	Car/Engine	Comment
ret	ARGENTINE GP	Buenos Aires	28	Brooke Bond Oxo-Team Surtees	3.0 Surtees TS14A-Cosworth V8	suspension
ret	BRAZILIAN GP	Interlagos	6	Brooke Bond Oxo-Team Surtees	3.0 Surtees TS14A-Cosworth V8	suspension
ret	SOUTH AFRICAN GP	Kyalami	11	Brooke Bond Oxo-Team Surtees	3.0 Surtees TS14A-Cosworth V8	burst tyre/crashed
ret	SPANISH GP	Montjuich Park	10	Brooke Bond Oxo-Team Surtees	3.0 Surtees TS14A-Cosworth V8	driveshaft
8	BELGIAN GP	Zolder	24	Brooke Bond Oxo-Team Surtees	3.0 Surtees TS14A-Cosworth V8	pit stop-rear wing4 laps behind
ret	MONACO GP	Monte Carlo	24	Brooke Bond Oxo-Team Surtees	3.0 Surtees TS14A-Cosworth V8	driveshaft
10	SWEDISH GP	Anderstorp	24	Brooke Bond Oxo-Team Surtees	3.0 Surtees TS14A-Cosworth V8	pit stop-tyres-vibration/-3 laps
13	FRENCH GP	Paul Ricard	24	Brooke Bond Oxo-Team Surtees	3.0 Surtees TS14A-Cosworth V8	pit stop-tyres/3 laps behind
ret/dns	BRITISH GP	Silverstone	24	Brooke Bond Oxo-Team Surtess	3.0 Surtees TS14A-Cosworth V8	multiple accident in first start
7	DUTCH GP	Zandvoort	24	Brooke Bond Oxo-Team Surtess	3.0 Surtees TS14A-Cosworth V8	p stop-tyres/engine problem/-3 laps
4	GERMAN GP	Nürburgring	24	Brooke Bond Oxo-Team Surtees	3.0 Surtees TS14A-Cosworth V8	FL
3	AUSTRIAN GP	Österreichring	24	Brooke Bond Oxo-Team Surtees	3.0 Surtees TS14A-Cosworth V8	FL
ret	ITALIAN GP	Monza	24	Brooke Bond Oxo-Team Surtees	3.0 Surtees TS14A-Cosworth V8	tyre failure
ret	CANADIAN GP	Mosport Park	24	Brooke Bond Oxo-Team Surtees	3.0 Surtees TS14A-Cosworth V8	broken wheel
ret	US GP	Watkins Glen	24	Brooke Bond Oxo-Team Surtees	3.0 Surtees TS14A-Cosworth V8	broken suspension

1974

	Race	Circuit	No	Entrant	Car/Engine	Comment
ret	ARGENTINE GP	Buenos Aires	18	Team Surtees	3.0 Surtees TS16-Cosworth V8	engine
4	BRAZILIAN GP	Interlagos	6	Team Surtees	3.0 Surtees TS16-Cosworth V8	1 lap behind
11	SOUTH AFRICAN GP	Kyalami	6	Bang & Olufsen Team Surtees	3.0 Surtees TS16-Cosworth V8	1 lap behind
13	SPANISH GP	Jarama	6	Bang & Olufsen Team Surtees	3.0 Surtees TS16-Cosworth V8	2 pit stops-tyres/6 laps behind
ret	BELGIAN GP	Nivelles	6	Bang & Olufsen Team Surtees	3.0 Surtees TS16-Cosworth V8	tyre vibration
ret	MONACO GP	Monte Carlo	6	Bang & Olufsen Team Surtees	3.0 Surtees TS16-Cosworth V8	multiple accident
ret	SWEDISH GP	Anderstorp	6	Bang & Olufsen Team Surtees	3.0 Surtees TS16-Cosworth V8	handling/withdrawn
dnq	FRENCH GP	Dijon	34	Hexagon Racing with John Goldie	3.0 Brabham BT42-Cosworth V8	
9	BRITISH GP	Brands Hatch	8	Motor Racing Developments	3.0 Brabham BT44-Cosworth V8	1 lap behind
12	GERMAN GP	Nürburgring	8	Motor Racing Developments	3.0 Brabham BT44-Cosworth V8	pit stop-handling
ret	AUSTRIAN GP	Österreichring	8	Motor Racing Developmants	3.0 Brabham BT44-Cosworth V8	fuel line
5	ITALIAN GP	Monza	8	Motor Racing Developments	3.0 Brabham BT44-Cosworth V8	pit stop-tyre/1 lap behind/FL
8	CANADIAN GP	Mosport Park	8	Motor Racing Developments	3.0 Brabham BT44-Cosworth V8	pit stop-tyre/1 lap behind
2	US GP	Watkins Glen	8	Motor Racing Developments	3.0 Brabham BT44-Cosworth V8	FL

1975

	Race	Circuit	No	Entrant	Car/Engine	Comment
ret	ARGENTINE GP	Buenos Aires	8	Martini Racing	3.0 Brabham BT44B-Cosworth V8	engine
1	BRAZILIAN GP	Interlagos	8	Martini Racing	3.0 Brabham BT44B-Cosworth V8	
4	SOUTH AFRICAN GP	Kyalami	8	Martini Racing	3.0 Brabham BT44B-Cosworth V8	Pole/FL
ret	SPANISH GP	Montjuich Park	8	Martini Racing	3.0 Brabham BT44B-Cosworth V8	accident avoiding Stommelen
3	MONACO GP	Monte Carlo	8	Martini Racing	3.0 Brabham BT44B-Cosworth V8	
8	BELGIAN GP	Zolder	8	Martini Racing	3.0 Brabham BT44B-Cosworth V8	1 lap behind
ret	SWEDISH GP	Anderstorp	8	Martini Racing	3.0 Brabham BT44B-Cosworth V8	spun off
5	DUTCH GP	Zandvoort	8	Martini Racing	3.0 Brabham BT44B-Cosworth V8	pit stop-tyres/1 lap behind
ret	FRENCH GP	Paul Ricard	8	Martini Racing	3.0 Brabham BT44B-Cosworth V8	driveshaft
2/ret	BRITISH GP	Silverstone	8	Martini Racing	3.0 Brabham BT44B-Cosworth V8	spun off in rainstorm/1 lap behind
ret	GERMAN GP	Nürburgring	8	Martini Racing	3.0 Brabham BT44B-Cosworth V8	rear upright
ret	AUSTRIAN GP	Österreichring	8	Martini Racing	3.0 Brabham BT44B-Cosworth V8	engine
ret	ITALIAN GP	Monza	8	Martini Racing	3.0 Brabham BT44B-Cosworth V8	throttle linkage
ret	US GP	Watkins Glen	8	Martini Racing	3.0 Brabham BT44B-Cosworth V8	collision with Depailler

1976

	Race	Circuit	No	Entrant	Car/Engine	Comment
10	BRAZILIAN GP	Interlagos	8	Martini Racing	3.0 Brabham BT45-Alfa Romeo F12	1 lap behind
ret	SOUTH AFRICAN GP	Kyalami	8	Martini Racing	3.0 Brabham BT45-Alfa Romeo F12	engine
9	US GP WEST	Long Beach	8	Martini Racing	3.0 Brabham BT45-Alfa Romeo F12	pit stop-handling/3 laps behind
6	SPANISH GP	Jarama	8	Martini Racing	3.0 Brabham BT45-Alfa Romeo F12	1 lap behind
ret	BELGIAN GP	Zolder	8	Martini Racing	3.0 Brabham BT45-Alfa Romeo F12	electrics
9	MONACO GP	Monte Carlo	8	Martini Racing	3.0 Brabham BT45-Alfa Romeo F12	2 laps behind
8	SWEDISH GP	Anderstorp	8	Martini Racing	3.0 Brabham BT45-Alfa Romeo F12	
4	FRENCH GP	Paul Ricard	8	Martini Racing	3.0 Brabham BT45-Alfa Romeo F12	
8	BRITISH GP	Brands Hatch	8	Martini Racing	3.0 Brabham BT45-Alfa Romeo F12	pit stops-tyres/3 laps behind
4	GERMAN GP	Nürburgring	8	Martini Racing	3.0 Brabham BT45-Alfa Romeo F12	
ret	AUSTRIAN GP	Österreichring	8	Martini Racing	3.0 Brabham BT45-Alfa Romeo F12	brake failure-hit barrier
ret	DUTCH GP	Zandvoort	8	Martini Racing	3.0 Brabham BT45-Alfa Romeo F12	oil leak
ret	ITALIAN GP	Monza	8	Martini Racing	3.0 Brabham BT45-Alfa Romeo F12	engine
7	CANADIAN GP	Mosport Park	8	Martini Racing	3.0 Brabham BT45-Alfa Romeo F12	
ret	US GP EAST	Watkins Glen	8	Martini Racing	3.0 Brabham BT45-Alfa Romeo F12	collision with Mass
ret	JAPANESE GP	Mount Fuji	8	Martini Racing	3.0 Brabham BT45-Alfa Romeo F12	withdrew due to conditions

1977

	Race	Circuit	No	Entrant	Car/Engine	Comment
2	ARGENTINE GP	Buenos Aires	8	Martini Racing	3.0 Brabham BT45-Alfa Romeo F12	
ret	BRAZILIAN GP	Interlagos	8	Martini Racing	3.0 Brabham BT45-Alfa Romeo F12	accident damage

| 13 | SOUTH AFRICAN GP | Kyalami | 8 | Martini Racing | 3.0 Brabham BT45B-Alfa Romeo F12 | pit stops-tyres/2 laps behind |
| dns | " | " | " | 8 | Martini Racing | 3.0 Brabham BT45-Alfa Romeo F12 | practice only |

GP Starts: 71 (72)   GP Wins: 1   Pole positions: 1   Fastest laps: 5   Points: 58

CARLOS PACE

A long-time friend and rival of the Fittipaldi brothers – fellow Paulistas – Pace raced for most of the sixties in Brazil, beginning in karts where his opponents included Wilson. Driving a variety of machines from Renault Gordinis to Formula Vee cars and a potent Alfa Romeo T33/2, Carlos took the Brazilian national championship three years in a row between 1967 and 1969.

Together with Wilson Fittipaldi, Carlos arrived in Europe in 1970 to contest a very competitive Formula 3 series with a Lotus 59 entered by Jim Russell. Despite his lack of knowledge of the British circuits, Pace was soon very much one of the front-runners and by the end of the year he had collected the Forward Trust championship. After spending his winter at home, where he endured a disappointing Torneio series, Carlos returned with a healthy dose of sponsorship which was eagerly accepted by Frank Williams, who provided a March for the Formula 2 season. Just as in F3 the previous year, Pace became one of the men to beat, and soon won a round at Imola, though the entry for this race wasn't one of the best.

Frank was keen to run Pace in his second F1 car in 1972, and the pair went 50/50 on a deal. While the unfortunate number one driver, Pescarolo, had a dreadful time, Carlos made good progress in the old March, taking valuable championship points in two of his first four races. Broadening his horizons, he briefly raced in Formula 2 with Pygmée, and then joined Ferrari's sports car team to take second place in the Österreichring 1000 Km, which brought an invitation from Gulf to race their Mirage at Watkins Glen, where he took third place. Late in the 1972 season, Pace dropped a bombshell on Williams by announcing his intention to join Surtees in 1973, and by the end-of-year Victory Race he was already installed in one of 'Big John's cars, taking second place in the TS9B. In 1973 he raced regularly for Surtees in Formula 1 and was a revelation. The highlights were his performances in Germany and Austria, but too many mechanical problems left him lowly placed in the final championship table. In tandem with F1, he drove for Ferrari in sports car events and, teamed with Merzario, took a string of placings, including second at Le Mans and the Nürburgring.

Despite the poor reliability of the Surtees, Carlos stayed with the team for 1974, but after a fourth place in his home GP, a succession of niggling problems blighted his prospects, and in mid-season he quit in frustration. It didn't take long for Bernie Ecclestone to bring him into the Brabham team alongside Carlos Reutemann and he soon proved to be every bit as competitive as his team-mate. A great drive in Austria was halted by a broken fuel line when victory seemed possible and he posted fastest race laps at Monza and Watkins Glen, where he served due notice of his intentions for the 1975 season. At Interlagos came the highlight of his career, his first Grand Prix win recorded in front of his ecstatic home fans, but luck rarely went his way throughout the year. His competitiveness was severely blunted in 1976 when Brabham ran Alfa Romeo engines, but he got stuck in and never gave up in his efforts to develop the car.

By the end of the year he was enthusiastic about his prospects for 1977. Second place in the Argentine Grand Prix vindicated his optimism, but prior to the start of the European season came the terrible news of his death in a light plane crash back in Brazil.

NELLO PAGANI

This aristocratic Italian was first and foremost a motor cycle racer, winning the inaugural 125 cc World Championship in 1949 on a Mondial and finishing second in the 500 cc class on the MV Agusta.

He was a talented car racer too, as witnessed by his wins at Pau in 1947 and 1948 in a Maserati, though his appearances on four wheels were necessarily limited.

In 1950 he drove a Maserati to seventh in his only Grand Prix appearance, at Bremgarten, and took a fourth at the Modena GP in a Simca-Gordini. Although he was to appear occasionally thereafter, taking second in class in the Mille Miglia with an OSCA in 1952, Pagani was more involved with the bike world, later managing the legendary MV Agusta team.

PAGANI, Nello (I)   b 11/10/1911

1950

	Race	Circuit	No	Entrant	Car/Engine	Comment
7	SWISS GP	Bremgarten	2	Scuderia Achille Varzi	1.5 s/c Maserati 4CLT/48 4	3 laps behind

GP Starts: 1   GP Wins: 0   Pole positions: 0   Fastest laps: 0   Points: 0

PALETTI, Riccardo (I) b 15/6/1958 – d 13/6/1982

1982

	Race	Circuit	No	Entrant	Car/Engine	Comment
dnq	SOUTH AFRICAN GP	Kyalami	32	Osella Squadra Corse	3.0 Osella FA1C-Cosworth V8	
dnpq	BRAZILIAN GP	Rio	32	Osella Squadra Corse	3.0 Osella FA1C-Cosworth V8	
dnq	US GP WEST	Long Beach	32	Osella Squadra Corse	3.0 Osella FA1C-Cosworth V8	
ret	SAN MARINO GP	Imola	32	Osella Squadra Corse	3.0 Osella FA1C-Cosworth V8	suspension
dnpq	BELGIAN GP	Zolder	32	Osella Sqaudra Corse	3.0 Osella FA1C-Cosworth V8	
dnpq	MONACO GP	Monte Carlo	32	Osella Squadra Corse	3.0 Osella FA1C-Cosworth V8	
dns	US GP (DETROIT)	Detroit	32	Osella Squadra Corse	3.0 Osella FA1C-Cosworth V8	crashed in a.m. warm-up
ret/dns	CANADIAN GP	Montreal	32	Osella Squadra Corse	3.0 Osella FA1C-Cosworth V8	fatal accident at first start

GP Starts: 1 (2)   GP Wins: 0   Pole positions: 0   Fastest laps: 0   Points: 0

PALM, Torsten (S) b 23/7/1947

1975

	Race	Circuit	No	Entrant	Car/Engine	Comment
dnq	MONACO GP	Monte Carlo	25	Polar Caravans	3.0 Hesketh 308-Cosworth V8	
10	SWEDISH GP	Anderstorp	32	Polar Caravans	3.0 Hesketh 308-Cosworth V8	2 laps behind

GP Starts: 1   GP Wins: 0   Pole positions: 0   Fastest laps: 0   Points: 0

RICCARDO PALETTI

Riccardo began racing at 19 in Italian SuperFord, but soon graduated to Formula 3 and then, after just 15 F3 races, made the big jump into Formula 2 – albeit briefly – at the end of 1979. Back for more at the end of 1980, Paletti drove sensibly within his limits and, with the benefit of winter testing, he joined the Onyx team full-time for 1981. The year started well with his March taking a second place at Silverstone and a third at Thruxton, but then his season tailed off disappointingly.

With the help of generous sponsorship, Paletti found himself a seat in the tiny Osella team for 1982, but the young Italian faced a steep learning curve. Sadly he never had the chance to progress, for in Montreal his Osella accelerated away from its place at the tail of the grid and hurtled into the back of the stalled Ferrari of Pironi at over 100 mph with devastating consequences. In a gruesome accident, Paletti suffered massive internal injuries and he died in hospital shortly afterwards.

TORSTEN PALM

After a little rallying in a Volvo, Torsten entered Scandinavian F3 with a Brabham in 1969, before teaming up with Picko Troberg for a programme that was successful at home but less so when they ventured abroad.

In 1973 Palm hired the second works Surtees for three Formula 2 races, taking a third place at Karlskoga, and he then had a handful of outings the following year, this time in a GRD, finishing sixth at the Salzburgring. Palm briefly surfaced in Grands Prix in 1975, hiring a Hesketh to contest two races before retiring to guide the career of the then promising Eje Elgh.

JONATHAN PALMER

A brilliant early career for Palmer failed to bring the truly competitive Grand Prix car his efforts had so obviously merited, and so another talent was never truly tested at the highest level.

Palmer's racing career took a back seat while he qualified as a doctor, but early races with a van Diemen in 1979 and 1980 brought him a drive with Dick Bennetts' crack Formula 3 team for 1981. In a superb year, Jonathan took seven pole positions and eight wins and set ten fastest laps to win the Marlboro F3 championship by a large margin from his rivals. A move into Formula 2 with the Ralt team brought him back down to earth with a jolt, as the team struggled to find a competitive set-up, but it was a different story in 1983 when, with the full attention of Honda, Jonathan and his team-mate Mike Thackwell dominated proceedings, Palmer winning six of the 12 rounds (five of them in a row at the end of the season) with a display of brilliant driving backed by much planning and hard work behind the scenes.

After a drive for Williams in the 1983 European GP, Palmer found himself first with the RAM team, then the ambitious but overstretched Zakspeed outfit, struggling even to gain sight of a top-six finish. Luckily he kept his competitive edge sharpened in sports cars; driving a Richard Lloyd Porsche, he won at Brands Hatch in 1984 with Jan Lammers and finished second at Le Mans in 1985, and in 1987 he won the Norisring race with Baldi in Brun's Porsche.

By now Palmer was at the start of a three-year association with Tyrrell. The first two years, spent struggling with a Cosworth against the turbo brigade, found him picking up the crumbs, but some excellent drives brought hard-earned points for the team and Jonathan won the Jim Clark Trophy for top non-turbo driver in 1987. A competitive new chassis allowed Palmer to take a splendid fifth at Imola in 1989, but his season sagged after the arrival of Jean Alesi, who stole the show. The season's finale saw a despondent Jonathan fail to qualify, and his Grand Prix career was over. In 1990 he acted as a test driver for McLaren-Honda and returned to competition in sports cars with a Porsche 962. More recently the personable and ever-talkative Palmer has moved into a commentary role for BBC TV.

PALMER, Jonathan (GB) b 7/11/1956

1983

	Race	Circuit	No	Entrant	Car/Engine	Comment
13	EUROPEAN GP	Brands Hatch	42	TAG Williams Team	3.0 Williams FW08C-Cosworth V8	pit stop-tyres/2 laps behind

1984

8*	BRAZILIAN GP	Rio	10	Skoal Bandit Formula 1 Team	1.5 t/c RAM 01-Hart 4	* 5th place car dsq/3 laps behind
ret	SOUTH AFRICAN GP	Kyalami	10	Skoal Bandit Formula 1 Team	1.5 t/c RAM 01-Hart 4	gearbox/electrics
10*	BELGIAN GP	Zolder	10	Skoal Bandit Formula 1 Team	1.5 t/c RAM 02-Hart 4	* 5th place car dsq/pit stop/-6 laps
9*	SAN MARINO GP	Imola	10	Skoal Bandit Formula 1 Team	1.5 t/c RAM 02-Hart 4	* 5th place car dsq/3 laps behind
13	FRENCH GP	Dijon	10	Skoal Bandit Formula 1 Team	1.5 t/c RAM 02-Hart 4	* 12th place car dsq/3 laps behind
dnq	MONACO GP	Monte Carlo	10	Skoal Bandit Formula 1 Team	1.5 t/c RAM 02-Hart 4	
ret	US GP (DETROIT)	Detroit	10	Skoal Bandit Formula 1 Team	1.5 t/c RAM 02-Hart 4	tyre failure-accident
ret	US GP (DALLAS)	Dallas	10	Skoal Bandit Formula 1 Team	1.5 t/c RAM 02-Hart 4	electrics
ret	BRITISH GP	Brands Hatch	10	Skoal Bandit Formula 1 Team	1.5 t/c RAM 02-Hart 4	steering failure-accident
ret	GERMAN GP	Hockenheim	10	Skoal Bandit Formula 1 Team	1.5 t/c RAM 02-Hart 4	turbo
9	AUSTRIAN GP	Österreichring	10	Skoal Bandit Formula 1 Team	1.5 t/c RAM 02-Hart 4	2 laps behind
9*	DUTCH GP	Zandvoort	10	Skoal Bandit Formula 1 Team	1.5 t/c RAM 02-Hart 4	* 8th & 9th place cars dsq/-4 laps
ret	ITALIAN GP	Monza	10	Skoal Bandit Formula 1 Team	1.5 t/c RAM 02-Hart 4	oil pressure
ret	EUROPEAN GP	Nürburgring	10	Skoal Bandit Formula 1 Team	1.5 t/c RAM 02-Hart 4	turbo
ret	PORTUGUESE GP	Estoril	10	Skoal Bandit Formula 1 Team	1.5 t/c RAM 02-Hart 4	gearbox

1985

ret	PORTUGUESE GP	Estoril	30	West Zakspeed Racing	1.5 t/c Zakspeed 841 4	suspension damage
dns	SAN MARINO GP	Imola	30	West Zakspeed Racing	1.5 t/c Zakspeed 841 4	engine misfire on warm-up
11	MONACO GP	Monte Carlo	30	West Zakspeed Racing	1.5 t/c Zakspeed 841 4	spin/4 laps behind
ret	FRENCH GP	Paul Ricard	30	West Zakspeed Racing	1.5 t/c Zakspeed 841 4	engine
ret	BRITISH GP	Silverstone	30	West Zakspeed Racing	1.5 t/c Zakspeed 841 4	engine
ret	GERMAN GP	Nürburgring	30	West Zakspeed Racing	1.5 t/c Zakspeed 841 4	alternator belt
ret	AUSTRIAN GP	Österreichring	30	West Zakspeed Racing	1.5 t/c Zakspeed 841 4	engine
ret	DUTCH GP	Zandvoort	30	West Zakspeed Racing	1.5 t/c Zakspeed 841 4	engine-oil pressure

1986

ret	BRAZILIAN GP	Rio	14	West Zakspeed Racing	1.5 t/c Zakspeed 861 4	cracked airbox
ret	SPANISH GP	Jerez	14	West Zakspeed Racing	1.5 t/c Zakspeed 861 4	accident with Jones
ret	SAN MARINO GP	Imola	14	West Zakspeed Racing	1.5 t/c Zakspeed 861 4	started from pit lane/brakes
12	MONACO GP	Monte Carlo	14	West Zakspeed Racing	1.5 t/c Zakspeed 861 4	pit stop/4 laps behind
13	BELGIAN GP	Spa	14	West Zakspeed Racing	1.5 t/c Zakspeed 861 4	pit stops-alternator belt/-5 laps
ret	CANADIAN GP	Montreal	14	West Zakspeed Racing	1.5 t/c Zakspeed 861 4	started from pit lane/engine
8	US GP (DETROIT)	Detroit	14	West Zakspeed Racing	1.5 t/c Zakspeed 861 4	2 laps behind
ret	FRENCH GP	Paul Ricard	14	West Zakspeed Racing	1.5 t/c Zakspeed 861 4	engine
9	BRITISH GP	Brands Hatch	14	West Zakspeed Racing	1.5 t/c Zakspeed 861 4	pit stop/6 laps behind
ret	GERMAN GP	Hockenheim	14	West Zakspeed Racing	1.5 t/c Zakspeed 861 4	engine
10	HUNGARIAN GP	Hungaroring	14	West Zakspeed Racing	1.5 t/c Zakspeed 861 4	pit stop-brakes/6 laps behind
ret	AUSTRIAN GP	Österreichring	14	West Zakspeed Racing	1.5 t/c Zakspeed 861 4	engine
ret	ITALIAN GP	Monza	14	West Zakspeed Racing	1.5 t/c Zakspeed 861 4	engine
12	PORTUGUESE GP	Estoril	14	West Zakspeed Racing	1.5 t/c Zakspeed 861 4	3 laps behind
10/ret	MEXICAN GP	Mexico City	14	West Zakspeed Racing	1.5 t/c Zakspeed 861 4	out of fuel/3 laps behind
9	AUSTRALIAN GP	Adelaide	14	West Zakspeed Racing	1.5 t/c Zakspeed 861 4	blk flagged-trailing bodywork/-5 laps

1987

10	BRAZILIAN GP	Rio	3	Data General Team Tyrrell	3.5 Tyrrell-016-Cosworth V8	1st non-turbo/3 laps behind
ret	SAN MARINO GP	Imola	3	Data General Team Tyrrell	3.5 Tyrrell-016-Cosworth V8	clutch
ret/dns	BELGIAN GP	Spa	3	Data General Team Tyrrell	3.5 Tyrrell-016-Cosworth V8	accident-Streiff/Streiff drove spare
5	MONACO GP	Monte Carlo	3	Data General Team Tyrrell	3.5 Tyrrell-016-Cosworth V8	1st non-turbo/2 laps behind
11	US GP (DETROIT)	Detroit	3	Data General Team Tyrrell	3.5 Tyrrell-016-Cosworth V8	1st non-turbo/3 laps behind
7	FRENCH GP	Paul Ricard	3	Data General Team Tyrrell	3.5 Tyrrell-016-Cosworth V8	2nd non-turbo/4 laps behind
8	BRITISH GP	Silverstone	3	Data General Team Tyrrell	3.5 Tyrrell-016-Cosworth V8	1st non-turbo/5 laps behind
5	GERMAN GP	Hockenheim	3	Data General Team Tyrrell	3.5 Tyrrell-016-Cosworth V8	2nd non-turbo/1 lap behind
7	HUNGARIAN GP	Hungroring	3	Data General Team Tyrrell	3.5 Tyrrell-016-Cosworth V8	1st non-turbo/2 laps behind
14	AUSTRIAN GP	Österreichring	3	Data General Team Tyrrell	3.5 Tyrrell-016-Cosworth V8	3rd non-turbo/5 laps behind
14	ITALIAN GP	Monza	3	Data General Team Tyrrell	3.5 Tyrrell-016-Cosworth V8	3rd non-turbo/3 laps behind
10	PORTUGUESE GP	Estoril	3	Data General Team Tyrrell	3.5 Tyrrell-016-Cosworth V8	std from pit lane/2nd non-turbo/-3 laps
ret	SPANISH GP	Jerez	3	Data General Team Tyrrell	3.5 Tyrrell-016-Cosworth V8	hit by Arnoux
7	MEXICAN GP	Mexico City	3	Data General Team Tyrrell	3.5 Tyrrell-016-Cosworth V8	2nd non-turbo/3 laps behind
8	JAPANESE GP	Suzuka	3	Data General Team Tyrrell	3.5 Tyrrell-016-Cosworth V8	1st non-turbo/1 lap behind
4	AUSTRALIAN GP	Adelaide	3	Data General Team Tyrrell	3.5 Tyrrell-016-Cosworth V8	1st non-turbo/2 laps behind

1988

ret	BRAZILIAN GP	Rio	3	Tyrrell Racing Organisation	3.5 Tyrrell 017-Cosworth V8	transmission
14	SAN MARINO GP	Imola	3	Tyrrell Racing Organisation	3.5 Tyrrell 017-Cosworth V8	engine problem/2 laps behind
5	MONACO GP	Monte Carlo	3	Tyrrrel Racing Organisation	3.5 Tyrrell 017-Cosworth V8	1 lap behind
dnq	MEXICAN GP	Mexico City	3	Tyrrell Racing Organisation	3.5 Tyrrell 017-Cosworth V8	
6	CANADIAN GP	Montreal	3	Tyrrell Racing Organisation	3.5 Tyrrell 017-Cosworth V8	cockpit problems/2 laps behind
5	US GP (DETROIT)	Detroit	3	Tyrrell Racing Organisation	3.5 Tyrrell 017-Cosworth V8	1 lap behind
ret	FRENCH GP	Paul Ricard	3	Tyrrell Racing Organisation	3.5 Tyrrell 017-Cosworth V8	engine
ret	BRITISH GP	Silverstone	3	Tyrrell Racing Organisation	3.5 Tyrrell 017-Cosworth V8	engine
11	GERMAN GP	Hockenheim	3	Tyrrell Racing Organisation	3.5 Tyrrell 017-Cosworth V8	1 lap behind
ret	HUNGARIAN GP	Hungaroring	3	Tyrrell Racing Organisation	3.5 Tyrrell 017-Cosworth V8	engine cut out
12*/ret	BELGIAN GP	Spa	3	Tyrrell Racing Organisation	3.5 Tyrrell 017-Cosworth V8	throttle/*3rd & 4th cars dsq/-4 laps
dnq	ITALIAN GP	Monza	3	Tyrrell Racing Organisation	3.5 Tyrrell 017-Cosworth V8	
ret	PORTUGUESE GP	Estoril	3	Tyrrell Racing Organisation	3.5 Tyrrell 017-Cosworth V8	overheating
ret	SPANISH GP	Jerez	3	Tyrrell Racing Organisation	3.5 Tyrrell 017-Cosworth V8	water radiator
12	JAPANESE GP	Suzuka	3	Tyrrell Racing Organisation	3.5 Tyrrell 017-Cosworth V8	1 lap behind
ret	AUSTRALIAN GP	Adelaide	3	Tyrrell Racing Organisation	3.5 Tyrrell 017-Cosworth V8	transmission

1989

7	BRAZILIAN GP	Rio	3	Tyrrell Racing Organisation	3.5 Tyrrell 017B-Cosworth V8	1 lap behind
5*	SAN MARINO GP	Imola	3	Tyrrell Racing Organisation	3.5 Tyrrell 018-Cosworth V8	* 4th car dsq/spin/1 lap behind
dns	"	"	3	Tyrrell Racing Organisation	3.5 Tyrrell 017B-Cosworth V8	practice only
9	MONACO GP	Monte Carlo	3	Tyrrell Racing Organisation	3.5 Tyrrell 018-Cosworth V8	3 laps behind
ret	MEXICAN GP	Mexico City	3	Tyrrell Racing Organisation	3.5 Tyrrell 018-Cosworth V8	throttle linkage
9/ret	US GP (PHOENIX)	Phoenix	3	Tyrrell Racing Organisation	3.5 Tyrrell 018-Cosworth V8	fuel shortage/6 laps behind
ret	CANADIAN GP	Montreal	3	Tyrrell Racing Organisation	3.5 Tyrrell 018-Cosworth V8	hit wall/FL
10	FRENCH GP	Paul Ricard	3	Tyrrell Racing Organisation	3.5 Tyrrell 018-Cosworth V8	5 pit stops-hit by Arnoux/-2 laps
ret	BRITISH GP	Silverstone	3	Tyrrell Racing Organisation	3.5 Tyrrell 018-Cosworth V8	spun off
ret	GERMAN GP	Hockenheim	3	Tyrrell Racing Organisation	3.5 Tyrrell 018-Cosworth V8	throttle cable
13	HUNGARIAN GP	Hungaroring	3	Tyrrell Racing Organisation	3.5 Tyrrell 018-Cosworth V8	pit stop-broken injector/-4 laps
14	BELGIAN GP	Spa	3	Tyrrell Racing Organisation	3.5 Tyrrell 018-Cosworth V8	misfire/2 laps behind
ret	ITALIAN GP	Monza	3	Tyrrell Racing Organisation	3.5 Tyrrell 018-Cosworth V8	engine
6	PORTUGUESE GP	Estoril	3	Tyrrell Racing Organisation	3.5 Tyrrell 018-Cosworth V8	1 lap behind
10	SPANISH GP	Jerez	3	Tyrrell Racing Organisation	3.5 Tyrrell 018-Cosworth V8	misfire/2 laps behind
ret	JAPANESE GP	Suzuka	3	Tyrrell Racing Organisation	3.5 Tyrrell 018-Cosworth V8	fuel leak
dnq	AUSTRALIAN GP	Adelaide	3	Tyrrell Racing Organisation	3.5 Tyrrell 018-Cosworth V8	

GP Starts: 81 (82)   GP Wins: 0   Pole positions: 0   Fastest laps: 0   Points: 15

PARKES, Mike (GB) b 24/9/1931 – d 28/8/1977

1959

	Race	Circuit	No	Entrant	Car/Engine	Comment
dnq	BRITISH GP (F2)	Aintree	60	David Fry	1.5 Fry-Climax 4 F2	

1966

2	FRENCH GP	Reims	22	Scuderia Ferrari SpA SEFAC	3.0 Ferrari 312/66-V12	
ret	DUTCH GP	Zandvoort	4	Scuderia Ferrari SpA SEFAC	3.0 Ferrari 312/66-V12	spun off
ret	GERMAN GP	Nürburgring	10	Scuderia Ferrari SpA SEFAC	3.0 Ferrari 312/66-V12	engine failure-crashed
2	ITALIAN GP	Monza	4	Scuderia Ferrari SpA SEFAC	3.0 Ferrari 312/66-V12	Pole

1967

5	DUTCH GP	Zandvoort	4	Scuderia Ferrari SpA SEFAC	3.0 Ferrari 312/66-V12	1 lap behind
ret	BELGIAN GP	Spa	3	Scuderia Ferrari SpA SEFAC	3.0 Ferrari 312/66-V12	went off on oil/broken legs

GP Starts: 6   GP Wins: 0   Pole positions: 1   Fastest laps: 0   Points: 14

MIKE PARKES

Born into a motoring family (his father was the chairman of Alvis cars), Mike first took to the circuits with an MG TD while working as an engineer with the Rootes group, and soon graduated to a Frazer Nash.

He started to race seriously in 1957 with a Lotus, bringing an invitation from Colin Chapman to act as reserve driver for the works team at Le Mans, and then became involved with David Fry's Formula 2 project, which was intended for Stuart Lewis-Evans. Apart from the occasional Libre success in minor events during 1958-59, the car was not really competitive and Mike failed to qualify it for the F2 class of the British GP at Aintree.

A few outings in Sir Gawaine Baillie's Lotus Elite during 1960 showed his potential but brought little by way of results, but his breakthrough came in 1961 when he raced for Tommy Sopwith's Equipe Endeavour in GT and Formula Junior events, and also handled Maranello Concessionaires' Ferrari GT, winning races regularly in all classes. The high point of his season was undoubtedly the Le Mans 24 Hours, in which he shared a Ferrari 3-litre Testa Rossa with Willy Mairesse to take a superb second place.

Although he began 1962 with a rare Formula 1 outing at Mallory Park, taking fourth place in the 1000 Guineas race in a Bowmaker Cooper, Parkes' immediate future remained in the sports and GT category. His superb form of the previous year was repeated with much the same machinery, his tally including a hat-trick of wins in one day at Brands Hatch. Another fine outing brought second place in the Nürburgring 1000 Km in the works Ferrari, and it was no surprise when he joined the Scuderia for the 1963 season as development engineer and reserve driver.

Over the next three seasons, Mike became one the world's leading sports car drivers, winning the Sebring 12 Hours and Spa 500 Km in 1964 – a season cut short by a testing accident – and the Monza 1000 Km in 1965. After John Surtees' sudden departure from the team, Mike was elevated to Grand Prix status and, with a special long chassis to accommodate his 6 ft 4in frame, he took second place on his debut in the French GP and repeated the feat at Monza. His success in sports cars continued, Parkes winning the Monza and Spa 1000 Km in 1966, and finishing second at Daytona, Monza and Le Mans in 1967, a season which started with much promise when he dead-heated with Scarfiotti to share a win at Syracuse and then demolished the opposition in the International Trophy at Silverstone. However, disaster struck in the Belgian GP when he crashed his Ferrari and suffered serious leg injuries.

Mike continued in a management role at Ferrari while he recovered from the accident, and made a tentative return in the Paris 1000 Km in 1969, returning to the track in 1970 and 1971 for NART and Scuderia Filipinetti. Though he could not repeat his previous triumphs, Parkes produced some useful performances, including a superb drive to fifth place in the 1972 Targa Florio with Peter Westbury in the little Lola T212. He was then involved in the Fiat 128 touring car programme before moving to Lancia to help develop the Stratos. Tragically, Parkes was killed in a road accident in 1977 when his car was involved in a collision with a lorry.

REG PARNELL

Something of a wayward performer in his youth, Reg Parnell matured to became one of Britain's most seasoned professionals and later a respected elder statesmen, guiding the fortunes of a new generation of Grand Prix talent.

He began racing in 1935 with an MG Magnette, and found success immediately before the war with a 4.7-litre Bugatti. The war years took away a large part of what should have been the prime of his career, but he did not idle his time away, purchasing a vast array of temporarily redundant racing machinery in readiness for peace.

Racing a Maserati and an ERA bought from Peter Whitehead, he was soon tackling Continental races with great gusto, but eventually the Maserati brought more success, particularly at Goodwood, where he seemed to be able to win at will. Such was the respect he commanded that Reg was invited to drive a works Alfa Romeo in the very first World Championship race at Silverstone in 1950, finishing an excellent third. In 1951 he drove Vandervell's 'Thinwall Special' Ferrari to points finishes in two Grands Prix, and won the International Trophy at Silverstone when the race was abandoned after a rainstorm. Less happy was his association with BRM and their problematic V16 car, which defeated even Reg's efforts. He found the ready-made Ferrari T500 – no longer a Grand Prix challenger due to the change in formula – just the ticket for national events, and chalked up many successes during the 1954 season. He later drove Rob Walker's Connaught on occasion as well as a Ferrari Super Squalo, which he used to win the 1957 New Zealand GP and the South Island race at Dunedin, before retiring to take up the full-time team manager's job at Aston Martin, having been a key member of the team since the early fifties.

When David Brown pulled out of racing, Reg was immediately in demand and spent 1961 and 1962 overseeing the Yeoman Credit and Bowmaker Lola teams, before setting up his own Reg Parnell Racing team which was still in its infancy when the sturdy Parnell died unexpectedly of peritonitis after a routine appendix operation in January 1964 at the age of 53.

TIM PARNELL

Big, bluff and affable, Tim never managed to match the success of his father Reg on the circuits, but he had an enjoyable career in minor Formula 1 and F2 races in the late fifties and early sixties.

Suitably encouraged by a sound Formula Junior season in 1960, Tim purchased a Lotus 18 in 1961, which he hauled to the far corners of the Continent in search of limited success, and also drove in two Grands Prix. Illness curtailed his 1962 campaign, but he returned in 1963, only for the sudden death of his father the following January to thrust him into the role of running the Parnell team.

He remained a team manager for the rest of the decade, latterly with the BRM works team. He also ran his own outfit, working with drivers such as Mike Spence (1966) and Pedro Rodriguez (1969).

PARNELL, Reg (GB) b 2/7/1911 – d 7/1/1964

	1950					
	Race	Circuit	No	Entrant	Car/Engine	Comment
3	BRITISH GP	Silverstone	4	Alfa Romeo SpA	1.5 s/c Alfa Romeo 158 8	guest driver
ret	FRENCH GP	Reims	32	Scuderia Ambrosiana	1.5 s/c Maserati 4CLT/48 4	engine
	1951					
4	FRENCH GP	Reims	26	G A Vandervell	4.5 Ferrari 375/Thinwall Spl V12	4 laps behind
5	BRITISH GP	Silverstone	6	BRM Ltd	1.5 s/c BRM P15 V16	5 laps behind
dns	ITALIAN GP	Monza	30	BRM Ltd	1.5 s/c BRM P15 V16	engine in practice
	1952					
7	BRITISH GP	Silverstone	8	A H M Bryde	2.0 Cooper T20-Bristol 6	3 laps behind
	1954					
ret	BRITISH GP	Silverstone	12	Scuderia Ambrosiana	2.5 Ferrari 500/625 4	water jacket

GP Starts: 6   GP Wins: 0   Pole positions: 0   Fastest laps: 0   Points: 9

PARNELL, Tim (GB) b 25/6/1932

	1959					
	Race	Circuit	No	Entrant	Car/Engine	Comment
dnq	BRITISH GP (F2)	Aintree	66	R H H Parnell	1.5 Cooper T45-Climax 4	
	1961					
ret	BRITISH GP	Aintree	38	Tim Parnell	1.5 Lotus 18-Climax 4	clutch
10	ITALIAN GP	Monza	16	Tim Parnell	1.5 Lotus 18-Climax 4	3 laps behind
	1963					
dnq	GERMAN GP	Nürburgring	30	Tim Parnell	1.5 Lotus 18/21-Climax 4	

GP Starts: 2   GP Wins: 0   Pole positions: 0   Fastest laps: 0   Points: 0

RICCARDO PATRESE

By the end of the 1993 season, the curtain finally seemed set to fall on the Formula 1 career of Riccardo Patrese, during which he had competed in a staggering total of 256 World Championship Grands Prix. During the 17 seasons that he had spent racing at the highest level, he had moved from a wild and cocksure *enfant terrible* to a contented and charming elder statesman, happy still to be part of the scene which had changed so much during his marathon innings.

A former karting whizz-kid who took the world title in 1974, Patrese moved into cars the following season in Formula Italia. He finished runner-up to Bruno Giacomelli and then embarked on a full season of Formula 3 in 1976. The ensuing fierce battle with Conny Andersson for the European championship went all the way to a bitter final round before the title fell to the Italian. Riccardo then enjoyed a successful year in Formula 2 with a Chevron but before long he had been propelled into the Shadow team to replace Zorzi. While his off-track demeanour ruffled a few feathers, there was certainly no doubting his talent behind the wheel. Patrese was part of the new breakaway Arrows team at the start of 1978 and he was sensationally quick, leading comfortably in South Africa until an engine failure robbed him of a deserved victory. Unfortunately his driving still had some rough edges, and in the emotional aftermath of Peterson's accident at Monza Riccardo was targeted for blame. The treatment he received would have broken a lesser man, but he simply got on with the job, although in retrospect staying loyal to Arrows could have been his biggest mistake. From 1979 through to 1981 he struggled to find sustained success with cars which showed occasional promise that remained unfulfilled, and secretly he must have regretted turning down the tempting opportunities he was offered in 1978.

A move to Brabham found him in a truly competitive environment, but a lucky win at Monaco was the highlight of an inconclusive year, disfigured by a rash of mistakes. It was a similar story in 1983, Riccardo tossing away victory at Imola early in the season yet signing off from the Brabham team with a perfect display at Kyalami to show what might have been. He certainly had time to ponder his wasted chances over the next few years as he became caught in a depressing downward spiral, struggling with the Benetton-sponsored Alfa for two seasons before returning to a Brabham team that was beginning its terminal decline. At least he had been able to savour the taste of success in his role as a works driver for Lancia Martini with wins at Silverstone and the Nürburgring in 1982, Kyalami in 1984 and Spa a year later.

When he was picked for the second Williams drive, most observers felt Patrese was extremely lucky to have been given such an opportunity, and he certainly failed to pull up any trees with the Judd-engined car in 1988. However, the following season, with Mansell off to Ferrari and Renault power at his disposal, a rejuvenated Riccardo appeared. Relaxed and confident, he forged an excellent working relationship with Patrick Head and was largely responsible for the development work which was to bring the Didcot team back to the top of the pile. Certainly he was unlucky not to win at least two races that year, but he put that to rights in 1990 with an emotional win at Imola, helping to erase his painful memories of 1983. Even the return of Mansell in 1991 – which Patrese took with great equanimity – failed to blunt his spirit, and he gave as good as he got, particularly in the first half of the season. Victories in Mexico and Portugal set the seal on what was probably his best-ever year. Statistically the following season, when he was runner-up to Mansell in the World Championship, was more successful, but his performances were less convincing, and he was very fortunate to escape unharmed after a horrifying coming-together with Berger at Estoril, but showed his steel by bouncing back with a win at Suzuka.

Accepting a lucrative contract with Benetton for 1993, Riccardo found it difficult to rediscover his recent sparkling form. A depressing early-season run was arrested by midsummer, but by then the Benetton management had already decided to dispense with the services of Grand Prix racing's most experienced campaigner.

PATRESE, Riccardo (I) b 17/4/1954

1977

	Race	Circuit	No	Entrant	Car/Engine	Comment
9	MONACO GP	Monte Carlo	16	Shadow Racing Team	3.0 Shadow DN8-Cosworth V8	*1 lap behind*
ret	BELGIAN GP	Zolder	16	Shadow Racing Team	3.0 Shadow DN8-Cosworth V8	*crashed*
ret	FRENCH GP	Dijon	16	Shadow Racing Team	3.0 Shadow DN8-Cosworth V8	*clutch/engine*
ret	BRITISH GP	Silverstone	16	Shadow Racing Team	3.0 Shadow DN8-Cosworth V8	*fuel pressure*
10/ret	GERMAN GP	Hockenheim	16	Shadow Racing Team	3.0 Shadow DN8-Cosworth V8	*lost wheel/5 laps behind*
13	DUTCH GP	Zandvoort	16	Shadow Racing Team	3.0 Shadow DN8-Cosworth V8	*pit stop/8 laps behind*
ret	ITALIAN GP	Monza	16	Shadow Racing Team	3.0 Shadow DN8-Cosworth V8	*spun off on oil*
10/ret	CANADIAN GP	Mosport Park	16	Shadow Racing Team	3.0 Shadow DN8-Cosworth V8	*spun off/4 laps behind*
6	JAPANESE GP	Mount Fuji	16	Shadow Racing Team	3.0 Shadow DN8-Cosworth V8	*1 lap behind*

1978

	Race	Circuit	No	Entrant	Car/Engine	Comment
10	BRAZILIAN GP	Rio	36	Arrows Racing Team	3.0 Arrows FA1-Cosworth V8	*2 pit stops-fuel/4 laps behind*
ret	SOUTH AFRICAN GP	Kyalami	35	Arrows Racing Team	3.0 Arrows FA1-Cosworth V8	*engine/led race*
6	US GP WEST	Long Beach	35	Arrows Racing Team	3.0 Arrows FA1-Cosworth V8	*pit stop-tyre/1 lap behind*
6	MONACO GP	Monte Carlo	35	Arrows Racing Team	3.0 Arrows FA1-Cosworth V8	
ret	BELGIUM GP	Zolder	35	Arrows Racing Team	3.0 Arrows FA1-Cosworth V8	*rear suspension*
ret	SPANISH GP	Jarama	35	Arrows Racing Team	3.0 Arrows FA1-Cosworth V8	*engine*
2	SWEDISH GP	Anderstorp	35	Arrows Racing Team	3.0 Arrows FA1-Cosworth V8	
8	FRENCH GP	Paul Ricard	35	Arrows Racing Team	3.0 Arrows FA1-Cosworth V8	
ret	BRITISH GP	Brands Hatch	35	Arrows Racing Team	3.0 Arrows FA1-Cosworth V8	*rear suspension after puncture*
9	GERMAN GP	Hockenheim	35	Arrows Racing Team	3.0 Arrows FA1-Cosworth V8	*1 lap behind*
ret	AUSTRIAN GP	Österreichring	35	Arrows Racing Team	3.0 Arrows A1-Cosworth V8	*collision with Ertl at restart*
ret	DUTCH GP	Zandvoort	35	Arrows Racing Team	3.0 Arrows A1-Cosworth V8	*collision with Pironi*
ret	ITALIAN GP	Monza	35	Arrows Racing Team	3.0 Arrows A1-Cosworth V8	*engine*
4	CANADIAN GP	Montreal	35	Arrows Racing Team	3.0 Arrows A1-Cosworth V8	

1979

	Race	Circuit	No	Entrant	Car/Engine	Comment
dns	ARGENTINE GP	Buenos Aires	29	Warsteiner Arrows Racing Team	3.0 Arrows A1-Cosworth V8	*accident in a.m. warm-up*

9	BRAZILIAN GP	Interlagos	29	Warsteiner Arrows Racing Team	3.0 Arrows A1-Cosworth V8	1 lap behind
11	SOUTH AFRICAN GP	Kyalami	29	Warsteiner Arrows Racing Team	3.0 Arrows A1-Cosworth V8	3 laps behind
ret	US GP WEST	Long Beach	29	Warsteiner Arrows Racing Team	3.0 Arrows A1-Cosworth V8	brakes
10	SPANISH GP	Jarama	29	Warsteiner Arrows Racing Team	3.0 Arrows A1-Cosworth V8	1 lap behind
5	BELGIUM GP	Zolder	29	Warsteiner Arrows Racing Team	3.0 Arrows A1-Cosworth V8	
ret	MONACO GP	Monte Carlo	29	Warsteiner Arrows Racing Team	3.0 Arrows A1-Cosworth V8	suspension
14	FRENCH GP	Dijon	29	Warsteiner Arrows Racing Team	3.0 Arrows A2-Cosworth V8	3 laps behind
ret	BRITISH GP	Silverstone	29	Warsteiner Arrows Racing Team	3.0 Arrows A2-Cosworth V8	gearbox
dns	"	"	29	Warsteiner Arrows Racing Team	3.0 Arrows A1-Cosworth V8	practice only
ret	GERMAN GP	Hockenheim	29	Warsteiner Arrows Racing Team	3.0 Arrows A1-Cosworth V8	puncture
ret	AUSTRIAN GP	Österreichring	29	Warsteiner Arrows Racing Team	3.0 Arrows A2-Cosworth V8	rear suspension
ret	DUTCH GP	Zandvoort	29	Warsteiner Arrows Racing Team	3.0 Arrows A2-Cosworth V8	brake failure-spun off
13	ITALIAN GP	Monza	29	Warsteiner Arrows Racing Team	3.0 Arrows A2-Cosworth V8	pit stop/3 laps behind
ret	CANADIAN GP	Montreal	29	Warsteiner Arrows Racing Team	3.0 Arrows A1-Cosworth V8	spun off-could not restart
dns	"	"	29	Warsteiner Arrows Racing Team	3.0 Arrows A1-Cosworth V8	practice only
ret	US GP EAST	Watkins Glen	29	Warsteiner Arrows Racing Team	3.0 Arrows A2-Cosworth V8	rear suspension

1980

ret	ARGENTINE GP	Buenos Aires	29	Warsteiner Arrows Racing Team	3.0 Arrows A3-Cosworth V8	engine
6	BRAZILIAN GP	Interlagos	29	Warsteiner Arrows Racing Team	3.0 Arrows A3-Cosworth V8	1 lap behind
ret	SOUTH AFRICAN GP	Kyalami	29	Warsteiner Arrows Racing Team	3.0 Arrows A3-Cosworth V8	locked brakes-accident
2	US GP WEST	Long Beach	29	Warsteiner Arrows Racing Team	3.0 Arrows A3-Cosworth V8	
ret	BELGIUM GP	Zolder	29	Warsteiner Arrows Racing Team	3.0 Arrows A3-Cosworth V8	spun off
8	MONACO GP	Monte Carlo	29	Warsteiner Arrows Racing Team	3.0 Arrows A3-Cosworth V8	hit by Arnoux-p stop/-3 laps/FL
9	FRENCH GP	Paul Ricard	29	Warsteiner Arrows Racing Team	3.0 Arrows A3-Cosworth V8	1 lap behind
9	BRITISH GP	Brands Hatch	29	Warsteiner Arrows Racing Team	3.0 Arrows A3-Cosworth V8	3 laps behind
9	GERMAN GP	Hockenheim	29	Warsteiner Arrows Racing Team	3.0 Arrows A3-Cosworth V8	1 lap behind
14	AUSTRIAN GP	Österreichring	29	Warsteiner Arrows Racing Team	3.0 Arrows A3-Cosworth V8	1 lap behind
ret	DUTCH GP	Zandvoort	29	Warsteiner Arrows Racing Team	3.0 Arrows A3-Cosworth V8	engine
ret	ITALIAN GP	Imola	29	Warsteiner Arrows Racing Team	3.0 Arrows A3-Cosworth V8	engine
ret	CANADIAN GP	Montreal	29	Warsteiner Arrows Racing Team	3.0 Arrows A3-Cosworth V8	collision with Prost
ret	US GP EAST	Watkins Glen	29	Warsteiner Arrows Racing Team	3.0 Arrows A3-Cosworth V8	spun off

1981

ret	US GP WEST	Long Beach	29	Arrows Racing Team	3.0 Arrows A3-Cosworth V8	fuel filter/Pole/led race
3	BRAZILIAN GP	Rio	29	Arrows Racing Team	3.0 Arrows A3-Cosworth V8	
7	ARGENTINE GP	Buenos Aires	29	Arrows Racing Team	3.0 Arrows A3-Cosworth V8	1 lap behind
2	SAN MARINO GP	Imola	29	Arrows Racing Team	3.0 Arrows A3-Cosworth V8	
ret/dns	BELGIUM GP	Zolder	29	Arrows Racing Team	3.0 Arrows A3-Cosworth V8	stalled-hit by Stohr at start/did not restart
ret	MONACO GP	Monte Carlo	29	Arrows Racing Team	3.0 Arrows A3-Cosworth V8	gearbox
ret	SPANISH GP	Jarama	29	Arrows Racing Team	3.0 Arrows A3-Cosworth V8	engine
14	FRENCH GP	Dijon	29	Arrows Racing Team	3.0 Arrows A3-Cosworth V8	3 laps behind
10/ret	BRITISH GP	Silverstone	29	Arrows Racing Team	3.0 Arrows A3-Cosworth V8	engine/4 laps behind
ret	GERMAN GP	Hockenheim	29	Arrows Racing Team	3.0 Arrows A3-Cosworth V8	engine
ret	AUSTRIAN GP	Österreichring	29	Arrows Racing Team	3.0 Arrows A3-Cosworth V8	engine
ret	DUTCH GP	Zandvoort	29	Arrows Racing Team	3.0 Arrows A3-Cosworth V8	suspension
ret	ITALIAN GP	Monza	29	Arrows Racing Team	3.0 Arrows A3-Cosworth V8	gearbox
ret	CANADIAN GP	Montreal	29	Arrows Racing Team	3.0 Arrows A3-Cosworth V8	spun off
11	CAESARS PALACE GP	Las Vegas	29	Arrows Racing Team	3.0 Arrows A3-Cosworth V8	2 pit stops/4 laps behind

1982

ret	SOUTH AFRICAN GP	Kyalami	2	Parmalat Racing Team	1.5 t/c Brabham BT50-BMW 4	turbo bearing
ret	BRAZILIAN GP	Rio	2	Parmalat Racing Team	3.0 Brabham BT49D-Cosworth V8	driver fatigue
3*	US GP WEST	Long Beach	2	Parmalat Racing Team	3.0 Brabham BT49C-Cosworth V8	* 3rd place car dsq
dns	"	"	2	Parmalat Racing Team	3.0 Brabham BT49D-Cosworth V8	practice only
ret	BELGIUM GP	Zolder	2	Parmalat Racing Team	1.5 t/c Brabham BT50-BMW 4	spun off
1	MONACO GP	Monte Carlo	2	Parmalat Racing Team	3.0 Brabham BT49D-Cosworth V8	FL
ret	US GP (DETROIT)	Detroit	2	Parmalat Racing Team	3.0 Brabham BT49D-Cosworth V8	hit barrier
2	CANADIAN GP	Montreal	2	Parmalat Racing Team	3.0 Brabham BT49D-Cosworth V8	
15	DUTCH GP	Zandvoort	2	Parmalat Racing Team	1.5 t/c Brabham BT50-BMW 4	pit stop-gear linkage/3 laps behind
ret	BRITISH GP	Brands Hatch	2	Parmalat Racing Team	1.5 t/c Brabham BT50-BMW 4	stalled at start-hit by Arnoux
ret	FRENCH GP	Paul Ricard	2	Parmalat Racing Team	1.5 t/c Brabham BT50-BMW 4	engine/FL
ret	GERMAN GP	Hockenheim	2	Parmalat Racing Team	1.5 t/c Brabham BT50-BMW 4	engine
ret	AUSTRIAN GP	Österreichring	2	Parmalat Racing Team	1.5 t/c Brabham BT50-BMW 4	engine
5	SWISS GP	Dijon	2	Parmalat Racing Team	1.5 t/c Brabham BT50-BMW 4	1 lap behind
ret	ITALIAN GP	Monza	2	Parmalat Racing Team	1.5 t/c Brabham BT50-BMW 4	clutch
ret	CAESARS PALACE GP	Las Vegas	2	Parmalat Racing Team	1.5 t/c Brabham BT50-BMW 4	clutch

1983

ret	BRAZILIAN GP	Rio	6	Fila Sport	1.5 t/c Brabham BT52-BMW 4	exhaust
10/ret	US GP WEST	Long Beach	6	Fila Sport	1.5 t/c Brabham BT52-BMW 4	distributor/3 laps behind
ret	FRENCH GP	Paul Ricard	6	Fila Sport	1.5 t/c Brabham BT52-BMW 4	overheating
ret	SAN MARINO GP	Imola	6	Fila Sport	1.5 t/c Brabham BT52-BMW 4	spun off when first/FL
ret	MONACO GP	Monte Carlo	6	Fila Sport	1.5 t/c Brabham BT52-BMW 4	electrics
ret	BELGIUM GP	Spa	6	Fila Sport	1.5 t/c Brabham BT52-BMW 4	engine
ret	US GP (DETROIT)	Detroit	6	Fila Sport	1.5 t/c Brabham BT52-BMW 4	brakes
ret	CANADIAN GP	Montreal	6	Fila Sport	1.5 t/c Brabham BT52-BMW 4	gearbox
ret	BRITISH GP	Silverstone	6	Fila Sport	1.5 t/c Brabham BT52B-BMW 4	turbo
3	GERMAN GP	Hockenheim	6	Fila Sport	1.5 t/c Brabham BT52B-BMW 4	
ret	AUSTRIAN GP	Österreichring	6	Fila Sport	1.5 t/c Brabham BT52B-BMW 4	overheating
9	DUTCH GP	Zandvoort	6	Fila Sport	1.5 t/c Brabham BT52B-BMW 4	pit stop-fuel/2 laps behind
ret	ITALIAN GP	Monza	6	Fila Sport	1.5 t/c Brabham BT52B-BMW 4	electrics/engine/Pole
7	EUROPEAN GP	Brands Hatch	6	Fila Sport	1.5 t/c Brabham BT52B-BMW 4	
1	SOUTH AFRICAN GP	Kyalami	6	Fila Sport	1.5 t/c Brabham BT52B-BMW 4	

1984

ret	BRAZILIAN GP	Rio	22	Benetton Team Alfa Romeo	1.5 t/c Alfa Romeo 184T V8	gearbox

4	SOUTH AFRICAN GP	Kyalami	22	Benetton Team Alfa Romeo	1.5 t/c Alfa Romeo 184T V8	*2 laps behind*
ret	BELGIUM GP	Zolder	22	Benetton Team Alfa Romeo	1.5 t/c Alfa Romeo 184T V8	*ignition*
ret	SAN MARINO GP	Imola	22	Benetton Team Alfa Romeo	1.5 t/c Alfa Romeo 184T V8	*electrics*
ret	FRENCH GP	Dijon	22	Benetton Team Alfa Romeo	1.5 t/c Alfa Romeo 184T V8	*engine*
ret	MONACO GP	Monte Carlo	22	Benetton Team Alfa Romeo	1.5 t/c Alfa Romeo 184T V8	*steering*
ret	CANADIAN GP	Montreal	22	Benetton Team Alfa Romeo	1.5 t/c Alfa Romeo 184T V8	*crashed*
ret	US GP (DETROIT)	Detroit	22	Benetton Team Alfa Romeo	1.5 t/c Alfa Romeo 184T V8	*spun off-suspension damage*
ret	US GP (DALLAS)	Dallas	22	Benetton Team Alfa Romeo	1.5 t/c Alfa Romeo 184T V8	*hit wall*
12*	BRITISH GP	Brands Hatch	22	Benetton Team Alfa Romeo	1.5 t/c Alfa Romeo 184T V8	*spin/*11th placed car dsq/-5 laps*
ret	GERMAN GP	Hockenheim	22	Benetton Team Alfa Romeo	1.5 t/c Alfa Romeo 184T V8	*fuel metering unit*
10/ret	AUSTRIAN GP	Österreichring	22	Benetton Team Alfa Romeo	1.5 t/c Alfa Romeo 184T V8	*out of fuel/3 laps behind*
ret	DUTCH GP	Zandvoort	22	Benetton Team Alfa Romeo	1.5 t/c Alfa Romeo 184T V8	*engine*
3	ITALIAN GP	Monza	22	Benetton Team Alfa Romeo	1.5 t/c Alfa Romeo 184T V8	*1 lap behind*
6	EUROPEAN GP	Nürburgring	22	Benetton Team Alfa Romeo	1.5 t/c Alfa Romeo 184T V8	*1 lap behind*
8	PORTUGUESE GP	Estoril	22	Benetton Team Alfa Romeo	1.5 t/c Alfa Romeo 184T V8	*1 lap behind*

1985

ret	BRAZILIAN GP	Rio	22	Benetton Team Alfa Romeo	1.5 t/c Alfa Romeo 185T V8	*puncture*
ret	PORTUGUESE GP	Estoril	22	Benetton Team Alfa Romeo	1.5 t/c Alfa Romeo 185T V8	*spun off*
ret	SAN MARINO GP	Imola	22	Benetton Team Alfa Romeo	1.5 t/c Alfa Romeo 185T V8	*engine*
ret	MONACO GP	Monte Carlo	22	Benetton Team Alfa Romeo	1.5 t/c Alfa Romeo 185T V8	*accident with Piquet*
10	CANADIAN GP	Montreal	22	Benetton Team Alfa Romeo	1.5 t/c Alfa Romeo 185T V8	*2 laps behind*
ret	US GP (DETROIT)	Detroit	22	Benetton Team Alfa Romeo	1.5 t/c Alfa Romeo 185T V8	*electrics*
11	FRENCH GP	Paul Ricard	22	Benetton Team Alfa Romeo	1.5 t/c Alfa Romeo 185T V8	*1 lap behind*
9	BRITISH GP	Silverstone	22	Benetton Team Alfa Romeo	1.5 t/c Alfa Romeo 185T V8	*3 laps behind*
ret	GERMAN GP	Nürburgring	22	Benetton Team Alfa Romeo	1.5 t/c Alfa Romeo 184T V8	*gearbox*
ret	AUSTRIAN GP	Österreichring	22	Benetton Team Alfa Romeo	1.5 t/c Alfa Romeo 184T V8	*engine*
ret	DUTCH GP	Zandvoort	22	Benetton Team Alfa Romeo	1.5 t/c Alfa Romeo 184T V8	*turbo*
ret	ITALIAN GP	Monza	22	Benetton Team Alfa Romeo	1.5 t/c Alfa Romeo 184T V8	*exhaust*
ret	BELGIUM GP	Spa	22	Benetton Team Alfa Romeo	1.5 t/c Alfa Romeo 184T V8	*engine*
9	EUROPEAN GP	Brands Hatch	22	Benetton Team Alfa Romeo	1.5 t/c Alfa Romeo 184T V8	*2 laps behind*
ret	SOUTH AFRICAN GP	Kyalami	22	Benetton Team Alfa Romeo	1.5 t/c Alfa Romeo 184T V8	*hit by Cheever-lap 1*
ret	AUSTRALIAN GP	Adelaide	22	Benetton Team Alfa Romeo	1.5 t/c Alfa Romeo 184T V8	*exhaust*

1986

ret	BRAZILIAN GP	Rio	7	Motor Racing Developments Ltd	1.5 t/c Brabham BT55-BMW 4	*split water pipe*
ret	SPANISH GP	Jerez	7	Motor Racing Developments Ltd	1.5 t/c Brabham BT55-BMW 4	*gearbox*
6/ret	SAN MARINO GP	Imola	7	Motor Racing Developments Ltd	1.5 t/c Brabham BT55-BMW 4	*out of fuel/2 laps behind*
ret	MONACO GP	Monte Carlo	7	Motor Racing Developments Ltd	1.5 t/c Brabham BT55-BMW 4	*fuel pump*
8	BELGIUM GP	Spa	7	Motor Racing Developments Ltd	1.5 t/c Brabham BT55-BMW 4	*started from pit lane/1 lap behind*
ret	CANADIAN GP	Montreal	7	Motor Racing Developments Ltd	1.5 t/c Brabham BT55-BMW 4	*turbo*
6	US GP (DETROIT)	Detroit	7	Motor Racing Developments Ltd	1.5 t/c Brabham BT55-BMW 4	*1 lap behind*
7	FRENCH GP	Paul Ricard	7	Motor Racing Developments Ltd	1.5 t/c Brabham BT55-BMW 4	*2 laps behind*
ret	BRITISH GP	Brands Hatch	7	Motor Racing Developments Ltd	1.5 t/c Brabham BT54-BMW 4	*engine*
ret	GERMAN GP	Hockenheim	7	Motor Racing Developments Ltd	1.5 t/c Brabham BT55-BMW 4	*turbo*
ret	HUNGARIAN GP	Hungaroring	7	Motor Racing Developments Ltd	1.5 t/c Brabham BT55-BMW 4	*spun off*
ret	AUSTRIAN GP	Österreichring	7	Motor Racing Developments Ltd	1.5 t/c Brabham BT55-BMW 4	*engine*
ret	ITALIAN GP	Monza	7	Motor Racing Developments Ltd	1.5 t/c Brabham BT55-BMW 4	*accident with Tambay*
ret	PORTUGUESE GP	Estoril	7	Motor Racing Developments Ltd	1.5 t/c Brabham BT55-BMW 4	*engine*
13/ret	MEXICAN GP	Mexico City	7	Motor Racing Developments Ltd	1.5 t/c Brabham BT55-BMW 4	*spun off/4 laps behind*
ret	AUSTRALIAN GP	Adelaide	7	Motor Racing Developments Ltd	1.5 t/c Brabham BT55-BMW 4	*engine-electrics*

1987

ret	BRAZILIAN GP	Rio	7	Motor Racing Developments Ltd	1.5 t/c Brabham BT56-BMW 4	*loose battery*
9	SAN MARINO GP	Imola	7	Motor Racing Developments Ltd	1.5 t/c Brabham BT56-BMW 4	*2 laps behind*
ret	BELGIUM GP	Spa	7	Motor Racing Developments Ltd	1.5 t/c Brabham BT56-BMW 4	*clutch*
ret	MONACO GP	Monte Carlo	7	Motor Racing Developments Ltd	1.5 t/c Brabham BT56-BMW 4	*electrics*
9	US GP (DETROIT)	Detroit	7	Motor Racing Developments Ltd	1.5 t/c Brabham BT56-BMW 4	*spun-hit Palmer/seat belt/-3 laps*
ret	FRENCH GP	Paul Ricard	7	Motor Racing Developments Ltd	1.5 t/c Brabham BT56-BMW 4	*transmission*
ret	BRITISH GP	Silverstone	7	Motor Racing Developments Ltd	1.5 t/c Brabham BT56-BMW 4	*engine*
ret	GERMAN GP	Hockenheim	7	Motor Racing Developments Ltd	1.5 t/c Brabham BT56-BMW 4	*turbo*
5	HUNGARIAN GP	Hungaroring	7	Motor Racing Developments Ltd	1.5 t/c Brabham BT56-BMW 4	*1 lap behind*
ret	AUSTRIAN GP	Österreichring	7	Motor Racing Developments Ltd	1.5 t/c Brabham BT56-BMW 4	*engine*
ret	ITALIAN GP	Monza	7	Motor Racing Developments Ltd	1.5 t/c Brabham BT56-BMW 4	*engine*
ret	PORTUGUESE GP	Estoril	7	Motor Racing Developments Ltd	1.5 t/c Brabham BT56-BMW 4	*engine*
13	SPANISH GP	Jerez	7	Motor Racing Developments Ltd	1.5 t/c Brabham BT56-BMW 4	*4 laps behind*
3	MEXICAN GP	Mexico City	7	Motor Racing Developments Ltd	1.5 t/c Brabham BT56-BMW 4	
11/ret	JAPANESE GP	Suzuka	7	Motor Racing Developments Ltd	1.5 t/c Brabham BT56-BMW 4	*engine/2 laps behind*
9/ret	AUSTRALIAN GP	Adelaide	5	Canon Williams Team	1.5 t/c Williams FW11B-Honda V6	*engine/6 laps behind*

1988

ret	BRAZILIAN GP	Rio	6	Canon Williams Team	3.5 Williams FW12-Judd V8	*overheating*
13	SAN MARINO GP	Imola	6	Canon Williams Team	3.5 Williams FW12-Judd V8	*pit stop-precautionary/handling/-2 laps*
6	MONACO GP	Monte Carlo	6	Canon Williams Team	3.5 Williams FW12-Judd V8	*1 lap behind*
ret	MEXICAN GP	Mexico City	6	Canon Williams Team	3.5 Williams FW12-Judd V8	*engine*
ret	CANADIAN GP	Montreal	6	Canon Williams Team	3.5 Williams FW12-Judd V8	*engine*
ret	US GP (DETROIT)	Detroit	6	Canon Williams Team	3.5 Williams FW12-Judd V8	*electrics*
ret	FRENCH GP	Paul Ricard	6	Canon Williams Team	3.5 Williams FW12-Judd V8	*brakes*
8	BRITISH GP	Silverstone	6	Canon Williams Team	3.5 Williams FW12-Judd V8	*1 lap behind*
ret	GERMAN GP	Hockenheim	6	Canon Williams Team	3.5 Williams FW12-Judd V8	*slid off*
6	HUNGARIAN GP	Hungaroring	6	Canon Williams Team	3.5 Williams FW12-Judd V8	*1 lap behind*
ret	BELGIUM GP	Spa	6	Canon Williams Team	3.5 Williams FW12-Judd V8	*engine*
7	ITALIAN GP	Monza	6	Canon Williams Team	3.5 Williams FW12-Judd V8	
ret	PORTUGUESE GP	Estoril	6	Canon Williams Team	3.5 Williams FW12-Judd V8	*radiator*
5	SPANISH GP	Jerez	6	Canon Williams Team	3.5 Williams FW12-Judd V8	*fined $10,000 for practice incident*
6	JAPANESE GP	Suzuka	6	Canon Williams Team	3.5 Williams FW12-Judd V8	
4	AUSTRALIAN GP	Adelaide	6	Canon Williams Team	3.5 Williams FW12-Judd V8	

1989

ret	BRAZILIAN GP	Rio	6	Canon Williams Team	3.5 Williams FW12C-Renault V10	engine/led race/FL
ret	SAN MARINO GP	Imola	6	Canon Williams Team	3.5 Williams FW12C-Renault V10	engine
15	MONACO GP	Monte Carlo	6	Canon Williams Team	3.5 Williams FW12C-Renault V10	pit stop-wing end/4 laps behind
2	MEXICAN GP	Mexico City	6	Canon Williams Team	3.5 Williams FW12C-Renault V10	
2	US GP (PHOENIX)	Phoenix	6	Canon Williams Team	3.5 Williams FW12C-Renault V10	
2	CANADIAN GP	Montreal	6	Canon Williams Team	3.5 Williams FW12C-Renault V10	pit stop-tyres/led race
3	FRENCH GP	Paul Ricard	6	Canon Williams Team	3.5 Williams FW12C-Renault V10	spin
ret	BRITISH GP	Silverstone	6	Canon Williams Team	3.5 Williams FW12C-Renault V10	stone burst radiator-crashed
4	GERMAN GP	Hockenheim	6	Canon Williams Team	3.5 Williams FW12C-Renault V10	p stop-tyres/vibration/gearbox/-1 lap
ret	HUNGARIAN GP	Hungaroring	6	Canon Williams Team	3.5 Williams FW12C-Renault V10	engine/Pole/led race
ret	BELGIAN GP	Spa	6	Canon Williams Team	3.5 Williams FW12C-Renault V10	collision with Alboreto
4	ITALIAN GP	Monza	6	Canon Williams Team	3.5 Williams FW12C-Renault V10	handling problems
ret	PORTUGUESE GP	Estoril	6	Canon Williams Team	3.5 Williams FW13-Renault V10	overheating
dns	"	"	6	Canon Williams Team	3.5 Williams FW12C-Renault V10	practice only
5	SPANISH GP	Jerez	6	Canon Williams Team	3.5 Williams FW12C-Renault V10	
dns	"	"	6	Canon Williams Team	3.5 Williams FW13-Renault V10	practice only
2*	JAPANESE GP	Suzuka	6	Canon Williams Team	3.5 Williams FW13-Renault V10	* 1st place car dsq
3	AUSTRALIAN GP	Adelaide	6	Canon Williams Team	3.5 Williams FW13-Renault V10	

1990

9	US GP (PHOENIX)	Phoenix	6	Canon Williams Renault	3.5 Williams FW13B-Renault V10	hit Grouillard-pit stop/1 lap behind
13/ret	BRAZILIAN GP	Interlagos	6	Canon Williams Renault	3.5 Williams FW13B-Renault V10	oil cooler/6 laps behind
1	SAN MARINO GP	Imola	6	Canon Williams Renault	3.5 Williams FW13B-Renault V10	
ret	MONACO GP	Monte Carlo	6	Canon Williams Renault	3.5 Williams FW13B-Renault V10	electrics-engine
ret	CANADIAN GP	Montreal	6	Canon Williams Renault	3.5 Williams FW13B-Renault V10	brakes
9	MEXICAN GP	Mexico City	6	Canon Williams Renault	3.5 Williams FW13B-Renault V10	spin-pit stop-tyres
6	FRENCH GP	Paul Ricard	6	Canon Williams Renault	3.5 Williams FW13B-Renault V10	pit stop-tyres/misfire
ret	BRITISH GP	Silverstone	6	Canon Williams Renault	3.5 Williams FW13B-Renault V10	hit by Nannini-damaged undertray
5	GERMAN GP	Hockenheim	6	Canon Williams Renault	3.5 Williams FW13B-Renault V10	pit stop-tyres
4	HUNGARIAN GP	Hungaroring	6	Canon Williams Renault	3.5 Williams FW13B-Renault V10	pit stop-tyres/FL
ret	BELGIAN GP	Spa	6	Canon Williams Renault	3.5 Williams FW13B-Renault V10	gearbox
5	ITALIAN GP	Monza	6	Canon Williams Renault	3.5 Williams FW13B-Renault V10	pit stop-tyres
7	PORTUGUESE GP	Estoril	6	Canon Williams Renault	3.5 Williams FW13B-Renault V10	long pit stop-tyres/1 lap behind
5	SPANISH GP	Jerez	6	Canon Williams Renault	3.5 Williams FW13B-Renault V10	2 pit stops-tyres
4	JAPANESE GP	Suzuka	6	Canon Williams Renault	3.5 Williams FW13B-Renault V10	pit stop-tyres/FL
6	AUSTRALIAN GP	Adelaide	6	Canon Williams Renault	3.5 Williams FW13B-Renault V10	spin-pit stop-tyres/1 lap behind

1991

ret	US GP (PHOENIX)	Phoenix	6	Canon Williams Team	3.5 Williams FW14-Renault V10	gearbox/spun
2	BRAZILIAN GP	Interlagos	6	Canon Williams Team	3.5 Williams FW14-Renault V10	
ret	SAN MARINO GP	Imola	6	Canon Williams Team	3.5 Williams FW14-Renault V10	elctrics/engine
ret	MONACO GP	Monte Carlo	6	Canon Williams Team	3.5 Williams FW14-Renault V10	hit Modena's oil-crashed
3	CANADIAN GP	Montreal	6	Canon Williams Team	3.5 Williams FW14-Renault V10	Pole
1	MEXICAN GP	Mexico City	6	Canon Williams Team	3.5 Williams FW14-Renault V10	Pole
5	FRENCH GP	Magny Cours	6	Canon Williams Team	3.5 Williams FW14-Renault V10	1 lap behind
ret	BRITISH GP	Silverstone	6	Canon Williams Team	3.5 Williams FW14-Renault V10	collision with Berger-lap 1
2	GERMAN GP	Hockenheim	6	Canon Williams Team	3.5 Williams FW14-Renault V10	FL
3	HUNGARIAN GP	Hungaroring	6	Canon Williams Team	3.5 Williams FW14-Renault V10	
5	BELGIAN GP	Spa	6	Canon Williams Team	3.5 Williams FW14-Renault V10	
ret	ITALIAN GP	Monza	6	Canon Williams Team	3.5 Williams FW14-Renault V10	clutch
1	PORTUGUESE GP	Estoril	6	Canon Williams Team	3.5 Williams FW14-Renault V10	Pole/*FL *(Mansell FL but dsq)
3	SPANISH GP	Barcelona	6	Canon Williams Team	3.5 Williams FW14-Renault V10	FL
3	JAPANESE GP	Suzuka	6	Canon Williams Team	3.5 Williams FW14-Renault V10	
5	AUSTRALIAN GP	Adelaide	6	Canon Williams Team	3.5 Williams FW14-Renault V10	race shortened-14 laps due to rain

1992

2	SOUTH AFRICAN GP	Kyalami	6	Canon Williams Team	3.5 Williams FW14B-Renault V10	
2	MEXICAN GP	Mexico City	6	Canon Williams Team	3.5 Williams FW14B-Renault V10	
2	BRAZILIAN GP	Interlagos	6	Canon Williams Team	3.5 Williams FW14B-Renault V10	FL
ret	SPANISH GP	Barcelona	6	Canon Williams Team	3.5 Williams FW14B-Renault V10	spun off
2	SAN MARINO GP	Imola	6	Canon Williams Team	3.5 Williams FW14B-Renault V10	FL
3	MONACO GP	Monte Carlo	6	Canon Williams Team	3.5 Williams FW14B-Renault V10	
ret	CANADIAN GP	Montreal	6	Canon Williams Team	3.5 Williams FW14B-Renault V10	gearbox
2*	FRENCH GP	Magny Cours	6	Canon Williams Team	3.5 Williams FW14B-Renault V10	*aggregate of two parts
2	BRITISH GP	Silverstone	6	Canon Williams Team	3.5 Williams FW14B-Renault V10	
8/ret	GERMAN GP	Hockenheim	6	Canon Williams Team	3.5 Williams FW14B-Renault V10	spun off-stalled/1 lap behind
ret	HUNGARIAN GP	Hungaroring	6	Canon Williams Team	3.5 Williams FW14B-Renault V10	engine/Pole
3	BELGIAN GP	Spa	6	Canon Williams Team	3.5 Williams FW14B-Renault V10	
5	ITALIAN GP	Monza	6	Canon Williams Team	3.5 Williams FW14B-Renault V10	led until car stuck in 4th gear
ret	PORTUGUESE GP	Estoril	6	Canon Williams Team	3.5 Williams FW14B-Renault V10	crashed after hitting Berger
1	JAPANESE GP	Suzuka	6	Canon Williams Team	3.5 Williams FW14B-Renault V10	
ret	AUSTRALIAN GP	Adelaide	6	Canon Williams Team	3.5 Williams FW14B-Renault V10	fuel pressure

1993

ret	SOUTH AFRICAN GP	Kyalami	6	Camel Benetton Ford	3.5 Benetton B192B-Ford HB V8	spun off
ret	BRAZILIAN GP	Interlagos	6	Camel Benetton Ford	3.5 Benetton B192B-Ford HB V8	active suspension
5	EUROPEAN GP	Donington	6	Camel Benetton Ford	3.5 Benetton B193-Ford HB V8	2 laps behind
ret	SAN MARINO GP	Imola	6	Camel Benetton Ford	3.5 Benetton B193B-Ford HB V8	spun off and stalled on lap 1
4	SPANISH GP	Barcelona	6	Camel Benetton Ford	3.5 Benetton B193B-Ford HB V8	1 lap behind
ret	MONACO GP	Monte Carlo	6	Camel Benetton Ford	3.5 Benetton B193B-Ford HB V8	engine
ret	CANADIAN GP	Montreal	6	Camel Benetton Ford	3.5 Benetton B193B-Ford HB V8	cramp
10	FRENCH GP	Magny Cours	6	Camel Benetton Ford	3.5 Benetton B193-Ford HB V8	p stop-colllision Fittipaldi/-2 laps
3	BRITISH GP	Silverstone	6	Camel Benetton Ford	3.5 Benetton B193-Ford HB V8	
5	GERMAN GP	Hockenheim	6	Camel Benetton Ford	3.5 Benetton B193-Ford HB V8	
2	HUNGARIAN GP	Hungaroring	6	Camel Benetton Ford	3.5 Benetton B193-Ford HB V8	

6	BELGIAN GP	Spa	6	Camel Benetton Ford	3.5 Benetton B193-Ford HB V8		1 lap behind
5	ITALIAN GP	Monza	6	Camel Benetton Ford	3.5 Benetton B193-Ford HB V8		active suspension/1 lap behind
16/ret	PORTUGUESE GP	Estoril	6	Camel Benetton Ford	3.5 Benetton B193-Ford HB V8		hit Warwick-spun off/-8 laps
ret	JAPANESE GP	Suzuka	6	Camel Benetton Ford	3.5 Benetton B193-Ford HB V8		split oil cooler-oil on tyres-crashed
8/ret	AUSTRALIAN GP	Adelaide	6	Camel Benetton Ford	3.5 Benetton B193-Ford HB V8		engine/2 laps behind

GP Starts: 255 (256)   GP Wins: 6   Pole positions: 8   Fastest laps: 13   Points: 281

PEASE, Al (CDN) b 15/10/1921

	Race	Circuit	No	Entrant	Car/Engine	Comment
	1967					
nc	CANADIAN GP	Mosport Park	11	Castrol Oils Ltd	2.7 Eagle TG101-Climax 4	43 laps behind
	1968					
dns	CANADIAN GP	St Jovite	25	Castrol Oils Ltd	2.7 Eagle TG101-Climax 4	engine in practice
	1969					
ret	CANADIAN GP	Mosport Park	69	John Maryon	2.7 Eagle TG101-Climax 4	black flagged/too slow

GP Starts: 1   GP Wins: 0   Pole positions: 0   Fastest laps: 0   Points: 0

PENSKE, Roger (USA) b 27/2/1937

	Race	Circuit	No	Entrant	Car/Engine	Comment
	1961					
8	US GP	Watkins Glen	6	John M Wyatt III	1.5 Cooper T53-Climax 4	4 laps behind
	1962					
9	US GP	Watkins Glen	14	Dupont Team Zerex	1.5 Lotus 24-Climax V8	4 laps behind

GP Starts: 2   GP Wins: 0   Pole positions: 0   Fastest laps: 0   Points: 0

PERDISA, Cesare (I) b 21/10/1932

	Race	Circuit	No	Entrant	Car/Engine	Comment
	1955					
ret*	MONACO GP	Monte Carlo	40	Officine Alfieri Maserati	2.5 Maserati 250F 6	* Behra took over and spun off
3*	"	"	34	Officine Alfieri Maserati	2.5 Maserati 250F 6	* took over Behra's car/1 lap behind
8	BELGIAN GP	Spa	26	Officine Alfieri Maserati	2.5 Maserati 250F 6	3 laps behind
	1956					
nc	MONACO GP	Monte Carlo	32	Officine Alfieri Maserati	2.5 Maserati 250F 6	pit stops/14 laps behind
3*	BELGIAN GP	Spa	24	Officine Alfieri Maserati	2.5 Maserati 250F 6	* Moss took over
5*	FRENCH GP	Reims	6	Officine Alfieri Maserati	2.5 Maserati 250F 6	* Moss took over/2 laps behind
7	BRITISH GP	Silverstone	9	Officine Alfieri Maserati	2.5 Maserati 250F 6	6 laps behind
dns	GERMAN GP	Nürburgring	8	Officine Alfieri Maserati	2.5 Maserati 250F 6	Maglioli drove car/Perdisa injured
	1957					
6*	ARGENTINE GP	Buenos Aires	18	Scuderia Ferrari	2.5 Lancia-Ferrari D50 V8	*Collins/von Trips co-drove/-2 laps

GP Starts: 8   GP Wins: 0   Pole positions: 0   Fastest laps: 0   Points: 5

PERKINS, Larry (AUS) b 18/3/1950

	Race	Circuit	No	Entrant	Car/Engine	Comment
	1974					
dnq	GERMAN GP	Nürburgring	30	Dalton-Amon International	3.0 Amon AF1-Cosworth V8	practice crash-hit barrier
	1976					
13	SPANISH GP	Jarama	37	HB Bewaking Alarm Systems	3.0 Boro Ensign N175-Cosworth V8	pit stop/3 laps behind
8	BELGIAN GP	Zolder	37	HB Bewaking Alarm Systems	3.0 Boro Ensign N175-Cosworth V8	1 lap behind
dnq	MONACO GP	Monte Carlo	37	HB Bewaking Alarm Systems	3.0 Boro Ensign N175-Cosworth V8	
ret	SWEDISH GP	Anderstorp	37	HB Bewaking Alarm Systems	3.0 Boro Ensign N175-Cosworth V8	engine
ret	DUTCH GP	Zandvoort	37	HB Bewaking Alarm Systems	3.0 Boro Ensign N175-Cosworth V8	spun off
ret	ITALIAN GP	Monza	40	HB Bewaking Alarm Systems	3.0 Boro Ensign N175-Cosworth V8	engine
17	CANADIAN GP	Mosport Park	8	Martini Racing	3.0 Brabham BT45-Alfa Romeo F12	spin/2 laps behind
ret	US GP EAST	Watkins Glen	8	Martini Racing	3.0 Brabham BT45-Alfa Romeo F12	front suspension
ret	JAPANESE GP	Mount Fuji	8	Martini Racing	3.0 Brabham BT45-Alfa Romeo F12	withdrawn due to conditions
	1977					
ret	BRAZILIAN GP	Interlagos	14	Rotary Watches Stanley BRM	3.0 BRM P207 V12	engine lost water
15	SOUTH AFRICAN GP	Kyalami	14	Rotary Watches Stanley BRM	3.0 BRM P201B/204 V12	engine on 10 cylinders/5 laps behind
12	BELGIAN GP	Zolder	7	Team Surtees	3.0 Surtees TS19-Cosworth V8	2 pit stops-tyres/3 laps behind
dnq	SWEDISH GP	Anderstorp	7	Team Surtees	3.0 Surtees TS19-Cosworth V8	
dnq	FRENCH GP	Dijon	7	Team Surtees	3.0 Surtees TS19-Cosworth V8	

GP Starts: 11   GP Wins: 0   Pole positions: 0   Fastest laps: 0   Points: 0

PERROT, Xavier (CH) b 1/2/1932

	Race	Circuit	No	Entrant	Car/Engine	Comment
	1969					
10	GERMAN GP (F2)	Nürburgring	30	Squadra Tartaruga	1.6 Brabham BT23C-Cosworth 4	6th in F2 class/1 lap behind

GP Starts: 1   GP Wins: 0   Pole positions: 0   Fastest laps: 0   Points: 0

AL PEASE

An amateur racer who had been on the Canadian racing scene from the early fifties with a Riley, Pease returned to the circuits in the early sixties with a Lotus 23 sports car, taking eighth place in the 1963 Canadian GP.

He had the backing to enble him to enter the original Eagle – hopelessly, as it turned out – in three successive Canadian GPs (1967-69). A sometime racer in Formula A, Pease handled a Lola T140-Chevrolet and a Brabham BT23B-Climax 4 with modest success during 1969 and 1970.

ROGER PENSKE

Roger Penske the racing driver has long since disappeared into the mists of time, to be replaced by the imposing figure who has built a business empire and progressively developed a small racing team, with Mark Donohue as driver, into the premier power in US single-seater racing, producing their own chassis for the IndyCar series.

However, Penske was a very good driver indeed. Racing a Porsche RSK, he won the SCCA 'F' category championship in 1960 before acquiring a Cooper-Monaco, which he modified and was later to rename the Zerex Special. Between 1961 and 1963 he gained many successes with this car and performed equally well in others, such as John Mecom's Ferrari GTO.

His drives in the US GPs of 1961 and 1962 offered him little but the chance to rub shoulders with the stars of the day, though he did bring his cars home to the finish. In 1964 he raced in future rival Jim Hall's Chaparral team, winning races at Monterey and Nassau and taking second place in the Riverside GP. At the end of the season Penske retired from driving to start his automobile business and the rest, as they say, is history.

CESARE PERDISA

From a wealthy publishing background, Perdisa first made his mark on the racing scene in 1954 with some excellent drives in his Maserati T200S sports car, finishing fourth at the Imola GP, fifth in the Portuguese GP and third at Syracuse. Proving this was no flash in the pan, the 1955 season saw wins at the Imola Shell GP and the Bari GP and second place at the Monza Supercortemaggiore in works machines, and his first Grand Prix, at Monaco, where Behra took over his car to share a third-place finish.

After missing the early-season Argentine races due to appendicitis, Perdisa was back in harness by Monaco, but again his points finishes were due in part to the efforts of another driver, this time Moss. Cesare was injured in a practice crash at the German Grand Prix and did not race for the Maserati team again. Lining up for rivals Ferrari in Argentina at the start of 1957, he took a shared sixth place in the Grand Prix, seventh in the Buenos Aires City GP, and won the 1000-km sports car race with co-drivers Gregory, Castellotti and Musso. However, on returning to Europe, perhaps due to pressure from his family, Cesare suddenly announced his retirement from racing.

LARRY PERKINS

Affectionately known as the 'Cowangie Kid' because he was from the tiny village of that name in Victoria, Larry came to Britain on the heels of Tim Schenken, with just as big a reputation, having left a winning trail through Formula Vee, Formula Ford and Australian F2 in three successive seasons between 1970 and 1972.

Once in Europe, Perkins finished fifth in the 1972 Formula Ford Festival before taking a shot at Formula 3 in 1973, his season improving after he switched to a Brabham. In 1974 Larry was involved in the ill-fated Amon F1 project and an unhappy attempt to qualify at the Nürburgring, before re-establishing his career back in F3 in 1975 with the works Ralt, winning the European championship.

Perkins landed a deal to drive the Boro (*née* Ensign) for the first part of 1976, and then came his big chance with Brabham, replacing the Ferrari-bound Reutemann for the final three races. To be frank, he blew it and found himself signing a contract to race the truly awful Stanley-BRM in 1977. After two races he gratefully jumped from the sinking ship, subsequently appearing briefly and unsuccessfully with Surtees.

Returning to Australia, Larry – now something of a big fish in a small pond – regained some pride winning the 1979 Australian F5000 series, before concentrating on a hugely successful and rewarding career in touring car racing, in which he was still a competitive force in 1993.

XAVIER PERROT

Perrot was a Swiss garage owner who had been competing since the early sixties in strictly national racing and hill-climbs with machines such as an Abarth-Simca and then a Lotus 23.

In 1968 he purchased an ex-Winklemann Racing Brabham to race in Formula 2, but found himself out of his depth. Not easily discouraged, Perrot was back for more in 1969, and by mid-season was looking more of a serious proposition, taking sixth in the F2 class in the German GP, and fourth in the Rhine Cup at Hockenheim. In 1970 he equipped himself with the latest March 702 and gained a somewhat lucky win in the Preis von Deutschland at the Nürburgring, which was the best result of the underrated Swiss driver's career. Perrot continued in Formula 2 in 1971 and into early 1972, gaining some useful results, and actually drove Siffert's March 701 in the Jochen Rindt Memorial Trophy F1 race at Hockenheim to finish 11th. Finding his F2 car ideally suited to hill-climbs, he successfully pursued this form of the sport thereafter.

PESCAROLO, Henri (F) b 25/9/1942

1968

	Race	Circuit	No	Entrant	Car/Engine	Comment
ret	CANADIAN GP	St Jovite	19	Matra Sports	3.0 Matra MS11 V12	oil pressure
dns	US GP	Watkins Glen	21T	Matra Sports	3.0 Matra MS11 V12	practice only
9	MEXICAN GP	Mexico City	9	Matra Sports	3.0 Matra MS11 V12	3 laps behind

1969

5	GERMAN GP (F2)	Nürburgring	26	Matra Sports	1.6 Matra MS7-Cosworth 4	1st in F2 class/no points scored

1970

7	SOUTH AFRICAN GP	Kyalami	4	Equipe Matra Elf	3.0 Matra-Simca MS120 V12	2 laps behind
ret	SPANISH GP	Jarama	22	Equipe Matra Elf	3.0 Matra-Simca MS120 V12	engine-con rod
3	MONACO GP	Monte Carlo	9	Equipe Matra Elf	3.0 Matra-Simca MS120 V12	
6/ret	BELGIAN GP	Spa	26	Equipe Matra Elf	3.0 Matra-Simca MS120 V12	out of fuel/1 lap behind
8	DUTCH GP	Zandvoort	24	Equipe Matra Elf	3.0 Matra-Simca MS120 V12	2 laps behind
5	FRENCH GP	Clermont Ferrand	20	Equipe Matra Elf	3.0 Matra-Simca MS120 V12	
ret	BRITISH GP	Brands Hatch	8	Equipe Matra Elf	3.0 Matra-Simca MS120 V12	spun off
6	GERMAN GP	Hockenheim	14	Equipe Matra Elf	3.0 Matra-Simca MS120 V12	pit stop-gearbox/1 lap behind
14	AUSTRIAN GP	Österreichring	20	Equipe Matra Elf	3.0 Matra-Simca MS120 V12	pit stop-wheel change/4 laps behind
ret	ITALIAN GP	Monza	42	Equipe Matra Elf	3.0 Matra-Simca MS120 V12	engine-valve spring
7	CANADIAN GP	St Jovite	24	Equipe Matra Elf	3.0 Matra-Simca MS120 V12	tyres shot/3 laps behind
8	US GP	Watkins Glen	7	Equipe Matra Elf	3.0 Matra-Simca MS120 V12	pit stops/3 laps behind
9	MEXICAN GP	Mexico City	7	Equipe Matra Elf	3.0 Matra-Simca MS120 V12	pit stop-gearbox/4 laps behind

1971

11	SOUTH AFRICAN GP	Kyalami	22	Frank Williams Racing Cars	3.0 March 701-Cosworth V8	2 laps behind
ret	SPANISH GP	Montjuich Park	27	Frank Williams Racing Cars	3.0 March 711-Cosworth V8	pit stop-rear wing-could not restart
8	MONACO GP	Monte Carlo	27	Frank Williams Racing Cars	3.0 March 711-Cosworth V8	pit stop-puncture/3 laps behind
13	DUTCH GP	Zandvoort	31	Frank Williams Racing Cars	3.0 March 711-Cosworth V8	spin-pit stop-nose cone/-8 laps
ret	FRENCH GP	Paul Ricard	27	Frank Williams Racing Cars	3.0 March 711-Cosworth V8	gearbox
4	BRITISH GP	Silverstone	26	Frank Williams Racing Cars	3.0 March 711-Cosworth V8	1 lap behind
ret	GERMAN GP	Nürburgring	14	Frank Williams Racing Cars	3.0 March 711-Cosworth V8	suspension
6	AUSTRIAN GP	Österreichring	25	Frank Williams Racing Cars	3.0 March 711-Cosworth V8	
ret	ITALIAN GP	Monza	16	Frank Williams Racing Cars	3.0 March 711-Cosworth V8	suspension/FL
dns	CANADIAN GP	Mosport Park	27	Frank Williams Racing Cars	3.0 March 711-Cosworth V8	went off in warm-up
ret	US GP	Watkins Glen	21	Frank Williams Racing Cars	3.0 March 711-Cosworth V8	engine

1972

8	ARGENTINE GP	Buenos Aires	23	Team Williams-Motul	3.0 March 721-Cosworth V8	engine
11	SOUTH AFRICAN GP	Kyalami	21	Team Williams-Motul	3.0 March 721-Cosworth V8	1 lap behind
11	SPANISH GP	Jarama	14	Team Williams-Motul	3.0 March 721-Cosworth V8	4 laps behind
ret	MONACO GP	Monte Carlo	22	Team Williams-Motul	3.0 March 721-Cosworth V8	aquaplaned-hit barrier
nc	BELGIAN GP	Nivelles	15	Team Williams-Motul	3.0 March 721-Cosworth V8	pit stop-throttle problems/-26 laps
dns	FRENCH GP	Clermont Ferrand	16	Team Williams-Motul	3.0 March 721-Cosworth V8	crashed in practice
ret	BRITISH GP	Brands Hatch	24	Team Williams-Motul	3.0 Politoys FX3-Cosworth V8	steering failure-accident
ret	GERMAN GP	Nürburgring	20	Team Williams-Motul	3.0 March 721-Cosworth V8	crashed while 6th
dns	AUSTRIAN GP	Österreichring	22	Team Williams-Motul	3.0 March 721-Cosworth V8	accident in practice
dnq	ITALIAN GP	Monza	25	Team Williams-Motul	3.0 March 721-Cosworth V8	accident in practice
13	CANADIAN GP	Mosport Park	28	Team Williams-Motul	3.0 March 721-Cosworth V8	pit stop-handling/7 laps behind
14	US GP	Watkins Glen	26	Team Williams-Motul	3.0 March 721-Cosworth V8	2 laps behind

1973

8	SPANISH GP	Montjuich Park	11	STP March Racing Team	3.0 March 721G/731-Cosworth V8	2 laps behind
ret	FRENCH GP	Paul Ricard	26	Frank Williams Racing Cars	3.0 Iso Williams 1R-Cosworth V8	overheating
10	GERMAN GP	Nürburgring	26	Frank Williams Racing Cars	3.0 Iso Williams 1R-Cosworth V8	

1974

9	ARGENTINE GP	Buenos Aires	15	Motul Team BRM	3.0 BRM P160E V12	1 lap behind
14	BRAZILIAN GP	Interlagos	15	Motul Team BRM	3.0 BRM P160E V12	2 laps behind
18	SOUTH AFRICAN GP	Kyalami	15	Motul Team BRM	3.0 BRM P160E V12	hit Mass-nose cone-2 p stops/-6 laps
12	SPANISH GP	Jarama	15	Motul Team BRM	3.0 BRM P160E V12	pit stop/4 laps behind
ret	BELGIAN GP	Nivelles	15	Motul Team BRM	3.0 BRM P106E V12	spun off
ret	MONACO GP	Monte Carlo	15	Motul Team BRM	3.0 BRM P160E V12	gearbox
ret	SWEDISH GP	Anderstorp	15	Motul Team BRM	3.0 BRM P201 V12	fire on lap 1
ret	DUTCH GP	Zandvoort	15	Motul Team BRM	3.0 BRM P160E V12	handling
dns	"	"	15	Motul Team BRM	3.0 BRM P201 V12	practice only
ret	FRENCH GP	Dijon	15	Motul Team BRM	3.0 BRM P201 V12	clutch on startline
ret	BRITISH GP	Brands Hatch	15	Motul Team BRM	3.0 BRM P201 V12	engine
10	GERMAN GP	Nürburgring	15	Motul Team BRM	3.0 BRM P201 V12	
ret	ITALIAN GP	Monza	15	Motul Team BRM	3.0 BRM P201 V12	engine

1976

dnq	MONACO GP	Monte Carlo	38	Team Norev Racing/BS Fabrications	3.0 Surtees TS19-Cosworth V8	
ret	FRENCH GP	Paul Ricard	38	Team Norev Racing/BS Fabrications	3.0 Surtees TS19-Cosworth V8	rear hub
ret	BRITISH GP	Brands Hatch	38	Team Norev Racing/BS Fabrications	3.0 Surtees TS19-Cosworth V8	fuel pressure
dnq	GERMAN GP	Nürburgring	38	Team Norev Racing/BS Fabrications	3.0 Surtees TS19-Cosworth V8	fuel system problems
9	AUSTRIAN GP	Österreichring	38	Team Norev Racing/BS Fabrications	3.0 Surtees TS19-Cosworth V8	2 laps behind
11	DUTCH GP	Zandvoort	38	Team Norev Racing/BS Fabrications	3.0 Surtees TS19-Cosworth V8	1 lap behind
17	ITALIAN GP	Monza	38	Team Norev Racing/BS Fabrications	3.0 Surtees TS19-Cosworth V8	pit stop/3 laps behind
19	CANADIAN GP	Mosport Park	38	Team Norev Racing/BS Fabrications	3.0 Surtees TS19-Cosworth V8	3 laps behind
nc	US GP EAST	Watkins Glen	38	Team Norev Racing/BS Fabrications	3.0 Surtees TS19-Cosworth V8	hit chicane-pit stop/11 laps behind

GP Starts: 57   GP Wins: 0   Pole positions: 0   Fastest laps: 1   Points: 12

HENRI PESCAROLO

Pescarolo started his competition career in a minor way during 1965 with a Lotus Seven, and was soon offered the third place in the Matra F3 team for the following year. It proved to be something of a false start to his Formula 3 career, as his car was not ready until mid-season. It was a different story in 1967, however, when he became the man to beat, winning the European championship. His wins that year included the important events at Barcelona, Monaco, Rouen and Zandvoort, so his promotion to the Formula 2 team in 1968 was a formality. Supporting Beltoise, Henri put in some excellent drives, taking second places at Barcelona, Hockenheim, Zandvoort and Hockenheim again before finishing the year with his first win at Albi. Highly regarded by Matra, he was given a run in the second V12 car in the end-of-season Grands Prix.

Pescarolo's career then received a big setback when, while testing the Matra sports car at Le Mans, he crashed on the Mulsanne Straight and suffered serious burns which laid him low until mid-season. Henri did well to return at the German GP, where he took the F2 Matra into fifth place overall and won the small-capacity class, and the season ended on a bright note when he shared the MS630 sports car with Beltoise to win the Paris 1000 Km at Montlhéry. With Matra now committed to their own Grand Prix project once more, Beltoise returned from his year with Tyrrell and Pescarolo joined him in the Matra V12s. Henri put in some solid performances that year, with a third place at Monaco his best finish. He was also a member of the sports car squad, taking victory in the Buenos Aires 1000 Km with Beltoise.

Pescarolo was surplus to requirements at Matra in 1971 and took some backing from Motul to Frank Williams, which enabled the team to go racing in both F1 and F2. Henri started the season with the old March 701 and picked up a second place on aggregate in the non-title Argentine GP, but Frank Williams was soon over-extended both financially and logistically, which showed in the team's preparation and lack of competitiveness as the year wore on. Meanwhile Pescarolo pursued a parallel programme in sports cars with Alfa Romeo, winning the BOAC 1000 Km with de Adamich. Despite all the problems, Henri was back in the Williams fold in 1972. It turned out to be a miserable season for all concerned as his March 721 was involved in a succession of crashes which required extensive and expensive rebuilds and, to cap it all, the prototype Politoys was written off in the midst of all this on its Brands Hatch debut. Fortunately Pescarolo escaped the carnage largely unhurt, and was buoyed up by his Le Mans win with Graham Hill in the Matra. Racing for the smart Rondel squad in Formula 2, Henri also won at Enna that year, and took another victory at Thruxton in 1973 after bringing Motul sponsorship to the team. With only the occasional Grand Prix ride that season, Pescarolo returned to Matra for a hugely successful programme of sports car racing, winning at Vallelunga, Dijon, Le Mans (for the second time), the Österreichring and Watkins Glen.

With Motul backing once more, Pescarolo made a full-time return to Grand Prix racing with BRM in 1974, but the team had lost their way, and his only decent finish came in the International Trophy where he was fourth. His partnership with Larrousse at Matra was still a potent one, however, and Henri completed a hat-trick of Le Mans victories and scored other wins at Monza and the Österreichring. By now, of course, he was widely recognised as one of sports car racing's best talents and in 1975 he returned to Alfa Romeo, winning rounds at Spa, the Österreichring and Watkins Glen, all with Derek Bell.

Henri made a last attempt to find success in Formula 1 with a privately entered Surtees in 1976, but neither he nor the car was remotely competitive. From then on Pescarolo concentrated on his sports car career, taking a fourth win at Le Mans in 1984, and raising his tally of World Championship victories to 21 by the end of 1986. In 1991 he shared the winning Porsche at the Daytona 24-hour race, subsequently continuing his career in IMSA, and in 1993 he took part in his 27th Le Mans 24 Hours, finishing ninth.

ALESSANDRO PESENTI-ROSSI

Pesenti-Rossi was regarded as an Italian national F3 racer of little pedigree until 1974, when he did well in his GRD at home and undertook a couple of Formula 2 races with a Beta-backed March. In 1975 Alessandro again achieved some success, including a second place on aggregate at Mugello.

Somewhat ambitiously he made a short-lived attempt to break into Grand Prix racing in mid-1976 with a privately entered Tyrrell. He and his backers sensibly decided to invest their money more wisely the following year when he returned to Formula 2 with a March 772, though three fourth places on home soil (at Vallelunga, Mugello and Misano) were the best he could muster. After he failed to qualify for the Preis von Württemberg at Hockenheim in a Chevron at the start of 1978, no more was seen of the wiry Italian at this level.

PESENTI-ROSSI, Alessandro (I) b 31/8/1942

1976

	Race	Circuit	No	Entrant	Car/Engine	Comment
14	GERMAN GP	Nürburgring	40	Scuderia Gulf Rondini	3.0 Tyrrell 007-Cosworth V8	1 lap behind
11	AUSTRIAN GP	Österreichring	39	Scuderia Gulf Rondini	3.0 Tyrrell 007-Cosworth V8	3 laps behind
dnq	DUTCH GP	Zandvoort	40	Scuderia Gulf Rondini	3.0 Tyrrell 007-Cosworth V8	
18	ITALIAN GP	Monza	37	Scuderia Gulf Rondini	3.0 Tyrrell 007-Cosworth V8	3 laps behind

GP Starts: 3   GP Wins: 0   Pole positions: 0   Fastest laps: 0   Points: 0

PETERS, Josef (D) b 16/9/1914

1952

	Race	Circuit	No	Entrant	Car/Engine	Comment
ret	GERMAN GP	Nürburgring	129	Josef Peters	2.0 Veritas RS 6-BMW 6 (sports car)	

GP Starts: 1   GP Wins: 0   Pole positions: 0   Fastest laps: 0   Points: 0

RONNIE PETERSON

Everybody loved Ronnie. Whatever your allegiances, the big blond Swede was *the* entertainer of the early seventies, thrilling everyone with his astonishing car control. Just watching him drift a Lotus 72 through the old Woodcote Corner was worth the price of admission alone. With all that natural talent, he should surely have been a World Champion, but sadly luck decreed otherwise.

Ronnie was Swedish karting champion between 1963 and 1966 and then switched to Formula 3, at first in a home-brewed special before acquiring a Tecno for 1968. This proved to be a wise move as he took his national championship, and gained a place in the works F3 team for the following year. At this time his big rival was compatriot Reine Wisell, and he and Ronnie were to have many duels in the 1-litre F3 formula. Peterson won the prestigious Monaco race during a successful 1969 season which brought the offer of a three-year contract with March from 1970. He gained some valuable experience in his first year with the Colin Crabbe-entered F1 car and ran a full season of Formula 2 guided by Malcolm Guthrie.

Promoted to the full works teams the following season, he quickly established himself as one of the world's leading talents, scoring four second places in Grands Prix to finish as runner-up in the World Championship, while in Formula 2 he displayed Rindt-like qualities to take the European championship with five wins. Locked into the final year of his March deal, Peterson was lumbered with the hopeless 721X in 1972 and things improved only marginally when the hastily cobbled-together 721G was pressed into service. His racing in F2 was limited by a successful sports car programme for Ferrari; teamed with Schenken, he won at Buenos Aires and the Nürburgring and took four second places.

Ronnie joined Lotus for 1973 but his slow start to the season eventually counted against him when a late burst of four wins took him into third place in the championship. So dominant was his form that team-mate Emerson Fittipaldi opted for McLaren for 1974, allowing Jacky Ickx to partner Peterson. The season was desperately disappointing because of the difficulties experienced with the new Lotus 76, but the compensation for the Swede's army of admirers was the opportunity to savour his sublime driving talent a little longer at the wheel of the now aged Lotus 72E. Wins at Monaco, Dijon and Monza were the stuff of true genius. Peterson was forced to soldier on in the old faithful during 1975 while a new car was prepared, and he could no longer compensate for its deficiencies. Unfortunately, when the Type 77 was introduced at the opening race of 1976 it appeared to be another lemon, and then Ronnie contrived to collide with new team-mate Mario Andretti. This was the final straw for Peterson, who engineered a move back to March for the rest of the season. In the underfinanced little team's car he managed to score a brilliant win at Monza, before being tempted to Tyrrell for 1977. However, the six-wheeler was just not suited to Ronnie's style, and he was regularly outpaced by team-mate Depailler. By the end of the year his reputation had been seriously dented, but salvation was nigh. Colin Chapman took him back, albeit strictly as number two to Andretti, to race the superb Lotus 79.

Keeping his word, Peterson was content to play the support role in the team. Mario headed for his deserved championship win and Ronnie picked up the crumbs, in the shape of wins in South Africa and Austria. However, tragedy lay around the corner. At Monza he became embroiled in a first-lap multiple crash, which left him suffering from severe leg injuries. Worse was to come, for once in hospital complications set in. He slipped into a coma and within hours he was gone. The sense of disbelief was matched only by the grief felt throughout motor racing. For Lotus, what should have been a time of great joy became instead a period of hollow celebration.

PETERSON, Ronnie (S) b 14/2/1944 – d 11/9/1978

1970

	Race	Circuit	No	Entrant	Car/Engine	Comment
7	MONACO GP	Monte Carlo	23	Antique Automobiles Racing Team	3.0 March 701-Cosworth V8	2 laps behind
nc	BELGIAN GP	Spa	14	Antique Automobiles Racing Team	3.0 March 701-Cosworth V8	spin-pit stop/8 laps behind
9	DUTCH GP	Zandvoort	22	Colin Crabbe Racing	3.0 March 701-Cosworth V8	2 laps behind
ret	FRENCH GP	Clermont Ferrand	18	Colin Crabbe Racing	3.0 March 701-Cosworth V8	transmission
9	BRITISH GP	Brands Hatch	27	Colin Crabbe Racing	3.0 March 701-Cosworth V8	pit stop-clutch/8 laps behind
ret	GERMAN GP	Hockenheim	22	Colin Crabbe Racing	3.0 March 701-Cosworth V8	engine
ret	ITALIAN GP	Monza	52	Colin Crabbe Racing	3.0 March 701-Cosworth V8	engine
nc	CANADIAN GP	St Jovite	26	Colin Crabbe Racing	3.0 March 701-Cosworth V8	pit stops-fuel leak/25 laps behind
11	US GP	Watkins Glen	29	Colin Crabbe Racing	3.0 March 701-Cosworth V8	2 pit stops-tyres/4 laps behind

1971

	Race	Circuit	No	Entrant	Car/Engine	Comment
10	SOUTH AFRICAN GP	Kyalami	7	STP March Racing Team	3.0 March 711-Cosworth V8	pit stop-plug lead/2 laps behind
ret	SPANISH GP	Montjuich Park	18	STP March Racing Team	3.0 March 711-Cosworth V8	ignition
2	MONACO GP	Monte Carlo	17	STP March Racing Team	3.0 March 711-Cosworth V8	
4	DUTCH GP	Zandvoort	16	STP March Racing Team	3.0 March 711-Cosworth V8	2 laps behind
dns	"	"	16T	STP March Racing Team	3.0 March 711-Alfa Romeo V8	practice only/qualified in this car
ret	FRENCH GP	Paul Ricard	17	STP March Racing Team	3.0 March 711-Alfa Romeo V8	engine
2	BRITISH GP	Silverstone	18	STP March Racing Team	3.0 March 711-Cosworth V8	
5	GERMAN GP	Nürburgring	15	STP March Racing Team	3.0 March 711-Cosworth V8	pit stop-radiator cover
8	AUSTRIAN GP	Österreichring	17	STP March Racing Team	3.0 March 711-Cosworth V8	handling problems/1 lap behind
2	ITALIAN GP	Monza	25	STP March Racing Team	3.0 March 711-Cosworth V8	
2	CANADIAN GP	Mosport Park	17	STP March Racing Team	3.0 March 711-Cosworth V8	
3	US GP	Watkins Glen	25	STP March Racing Team	3.0 March 711-Cosworth V8	

1972

	Race	Circuit	No	Entrant	Car/Engine	Comment
6	ARGENTINE GP	Buenos Aires	14	STP March Racing Team	3.0 March 721-Cosworth V8	spin/1 lap behind
5	SOUTH AFRICAN GP	Kyalami	3	STP March Racing Team	3.0 March 721-Cosworth V8	handling problems
ret	SPANISH GP	Jarama	2	STP March Racing Team	3.0 March 721X-Cosworth V8	fuel leak/suspension/body damage
11	MONACO GP	Monte Carlo	3	STP March Racing Team	3.0 March 721X-Cosworth V8	hit Ickx-pit stop/4 laps behind
dns	"	"	3T	STP March Racing Team	3.0 March 721-Cosworth V8	practice only
9	BELGIAN GP	Nivelles	11	STP March Racing Team	3.0 March 721X-Cosworth V8	2 laps behind
5	FRENCH GP	Clermont Ferrand	12	STP March Racing Team	3.0 March 721G-Cosworth V8	broken roll bar
7/ret	BRITISH GP	Brands Hatch	3	STP March Racing Team	3.0 March 721G-Cosworth V8	out of fuel-spun off/2 laps behind

3	GERMAN GP	Nürburgring	10	STP March Racing Team	3.0 March 721G-Cosworth V8	spin
12	AUSTRIAN GP	Österreichring	5	STP March Racing Team	3.0 March 721G-Cosworth V8	pit stop-fuel/2 laps behind
9	ITALIAN GP	Monza	19	STP March Racing Team	3.0 March 721G-Cosworth V8	pit stop-handling/1 lap behind
dsq	CANADIAN GP	Mosport Park	25	STP March Racing Team	3.0 March 721G-Cosworth V8	push start after collision
4	US GP	Watkins Glen	4	STP March Racing Team	3.0 March 721G-Cosworth V8	accident in practice

1973

ret	ARGENTINE GP	Buenos Aires	4	John Player Team Lotus	3.0 Lotus 72D-Cosworth V8	oil pressure
ret	BRAZILIAN GP	Interlagos	2	John Player Team Lotus	3.0 Lotus 72D-Cosworth V8	rear wheel/Pole
11	SOUTH AFRICAN GP	Kyalami	2	John Player Team Lotus	3.0 Lotus 72D-Cosworth V8	pit stop-throttle linkage/6 laps behind
ret	SPANISH GP	Montjuich Park	2	John Player Team Lotus	3.0 Lotus 72E-Cosworth V8	gearbox/Pole/FL
ret	BELGIAN GP	Zolder	2	John Player Team Lotus	3.0 Lotus 72E-Cosworth V8	spun off/Pole
3	MONACO GP	Monte Carlo	2	John Player Team Lotus	3.0 Lotus 72E-Cosworth V8	engine problems/1 lap behind
2	SWEDISH GP	Anderstorp	2	John Player Team Lotus	3.0 Lotus 72E-Cosworth V8	puncture last lap when 1st/Pole
1	FRENCH GP	Paul Ricard	2	John Player Team Lotus	3.0 Lotus 72E-Cosworth V8	
2	BRITISH GP	Silverstone	2	John Player Team Lotus	3.0 Lotus 72E-Cosworth V8	Pole
11/ret	DUTCH GP	Zandvoort	2	John Player Team Lotus	3.0 Lotus 72E-Cosworth V8	engine/gearbox/Pole/FL/6 laps behind
ret	GERMAN GP	Nürburgring	2	John Player Team Lotus	3.0 Lotus 72E-Cosworth V8	distributor
1	AUSTRIAN GP	Österreichring	2	John Player Team Lotus	3.0 Lotus 72E-Cosworth V8	
1	ITALIAN GP	Monza	2	John Player Team Lotus	3.0 Lotus 72E-Cosworth V8	Pole
ret	CANADIAN GP	Mosport Park	2	John Player Team Lotus	3.0 Lotus 72E-Cosworth V8	puncture-spun off/Pole
1	US GP	Watkins Glen	2	John Player Team Lotus	3.0 Lotus 72E-Cosworth V8	Pole

1974

13	ARGENTINE GP	Buenos Aires	1	John Player Team Lotus	3.0 Lotus 72E-Cosworth V8	pit stop-battery-tyres/Pole/-5 laps
6	BRAZILIAN GP	Interlagos	1	John Player Team Lotus	3.0 Lotus 72E-Cosworth V8	pit stop-tyre/1 lap behind
ret	SOUTH AFRICAN GP	Kyalami	1	John Player Team Lotus	3.0 Lotus 76-Cosworth V8	hit Ickx
dns	"	"	1	John Player Team Lotus	3.0 Lotus 76-Cosworth V8	practice only
ret	SPANISH GP	Jarama	1	John Player Team Lotus	3.0 Lotus 76-Cosworth V8	engine
ret	BELGIAN GP	Nivelles	1	John Player Team Lotus	3.0 Lotus 76-Cosworth V8	fuel leak
dns	"	"	1T	John Player Team Lotus	3.0 Lotus 72E-Cosworth V8	practice only
1	MONACO GP	Monte Carlo	1	John Player Team Lotus	3.0 Lotus 72E-Cosworth V8	FL
ret	SWEDISH GP	Anderstorp	1	John Player Team Lotus	3.0 Lotus 72E-Cosworth V8	driveshaft
dns	"	"	1T	John Player Team Lotus	3.0 Lotus 76-Cosworth V8	practice only
8	DUTCH GP	Zandvoort	1	John Player Team Lotus	3.0 Lotus 72E-Cosworth V8	pit stop-tyres/FL/2 laps behind
1	FRENCH GP	Dijon	1	John Player Team Lotus	3.0 Lotus 72E-Cosworth V8	
dns	"	"	1T	John Player Team Lotus	3.0 Lotus 76-Cosworth V8	practice only
10	BRITISH GP	Brands Hatch	1	John Player Team Lotus	3.0 Lotus 72E-Cosworth V8	pit stops-tyres/2 laps behind
4	GERMAN GP	Nürburgring	1	John Player Team Lotus	3.0 Lotus 76-Cosworth V8	
dns	"	"	1	John Player Team Lotus	3.0 Lotus 72E-Cosworth V8	practice only
ret	AUSTRIAN GP	Österreichring	1	John Player Team Lotus	3.0 Lotus 72E-Cosworth V8	driveshaft
dns	"	"	1T	John Player Team Lotus	3.0 Lotus 76-Cosworth V8	practice only
1	ITALIAN GP	Monza	1	John Player Team Lotus	3.0 Lotus 72E-Cosworth V8	
dns	"	"	1	John Player Team Lotus	3.0 Lotus 76-Cosworth V8	practice only
3	CANADIAN GP	Mosport Park	1	John Player Team Lotus	3.0 Lotus 72E-Cosworth V8	
ret	US GP	Watkins Glen	1	John Player Team Lotus	3.0 Lotus 72E-Cosworth V8	fuel line

1975

ret	ARGENTINE GP	Buenos Aires	5	John Player Team Lotus	3.0 Lotus 72E-Cosworth V8	brakes/gearbox
15	BRAZILIAN GP	Interlagos	5	John Player Team Lotus	3.0 Lotus 72E-Cosworth V8	stalled on grid-last away/-2 laps
10	SOUTH AFRICAN GP	Kyalami	5	John Player Team Lotus	3.0 Lotus 72E-Cosworth V8	pit stop-tyres/1 lap behind
ret	SPANISH GP	Montjuich Park	5	John Player Team Lotus	3.0 Lotus 72E-Cosworth V8	collision with Migault
4	MONACO GP	Monte Carlo	5	John Player Team Lotus	3.0 Lotus 72E-Cosworth V8	
ret	BELGIAN GP	Zolder	5	John Player Team Lotus	3.0 Lotus 72E-Cosworth V8	brake failure-went off
9	SWEDISH GP	Anderstorp	5	John Player Team Lotus	3.0 Lotus 72E-Cosworth V8	1 lap behind
15/ret	DUTCH GP	Zandvoort	5	John Player Team Lotus	3.0 Lotus 72E-Cosworth V8	out of fuel/6 laps behind
10	FRENCH GP	Paul Ricard	5	John Player Team Lotus	3.0 Lotus 72E-Cosworth V8	
ret	BRITISH GP	Silverstone	5	John Player Team Lotus	3.0 Lotus 72E-Cosworth V8	engine
ret	GERMAN GP	Nürburgring	5	John Player Team Lotus	3.0 Lotus 72E-Cosworth V8	clutch
5	AUSTRIAN GP	Österreichring	5	John Player Team Lotus	3.0 Lotus 72E-Cosworth V8	
ret	ITALIAN GP	Monza	5	John Player Team Lotus	3.0 Lotus 72E-Cosworth V8	engine
5	US GP	Watkins Glen	5	John Player Team Lotus	3.0 Lotus 72E-Cosworth V8	

1976

ret	BRAZILIAN GP	Interlagos	5	John Player Team Lotus	3.0 Lotus 77-Cosworth V8	collision with Andretti
ret	SOUTH AFRICAN GP	Kyalami	10	March Engineering	3.0 March 761-Cosworth V8	accident with Depailler
10	US GP WEST	Long Beach	10	Theodore Racing	3.0 March 761-Cosworth V8	pit stop-boiling brake fluid/-3 laps
ret	SPANISH GP	Jarama	10	March Engineering	3.0 March 761-Cosworth V8	transmission
ret	BELGIAN GP	Zolder	10	March Engineering	3.0 March 761-Cosworth V8	spun avoiding Reutemann
ret	MONACO GP	Monte Carlo	10	March Engineering	3.0 March 761-Cosworth V8	spun off
7	SWEDISH GP	Anderstorp	10	March Engineering	3.0 March 761-Cosworth V8	
19/ret	FRENCH GP	Paul Ricard	10	March Engineering	3.0 March 761-Cosworth V8	fuel metering unit/3 laps behind
ret	BRITISH GP	Brands Hatch	10	March Engineering	3.0 March 761-Cosworth V8	fuel pressure
ret	GERMAN GP	Nürburgring	10	March Engineering	3.0 March 761-Cosworth V8	went off at Flugplatz
6	AUSTRIAN GP	Österreichring	10	March Engineering	3.0 March 761-Cosworth V8	
ret	DUTCH GP	Zandvoort	10	March Engineering	3.0 March 761-Cosworth V8	oil pressure/Pole
1	ITALIAN GP	Monza	10	March Engineering	3.0 March 761-Cosworth V8	FL
9	CANADIAN GP	Mosport Park	10	March Engineering	3.0 March 761-Cosworth V8	1 lap behind
ret	US GP EAST	Watkins Glen	10	March Engineering	3.0 March 761-Cosworth V8	front suspension bulkhead
ret	JAPANESE GP	Mount Fuji	10	March Engineering	3.0 March 761-Cosworth V8	engine cut out

1977

ret	ARGENTINE GP	Buenos Aires	3	Elf Team Tyrrell	3.0 Tyrrell P34-Cosworth V8	spun off
ret	BRAZILIAN GP	Interlagos	3	Elf Team Tyrrell	3.0 Tyrrell P34-Cosworth V8	accident avoiding Mass-Regazzoni
ret	SOUTH AFRICAN GP	Kyalami	3	Elf Team Tyrrell	3.0 Tyrrell P34-Cosworth V8	fuel pressure
ret	US GP WEST	Long Beach	3	Elf Team Tyrrell	3.0 Tyrrell P34-Cosworth V8	fuel line
8	SPANISH GP	Jarama	3	Elf Team Tyrrell	3.0 Tyrrell P34-Cosworth V8	1 lap behind

	Race	Circuit	No	Entrant	Car/Engine	Comment
ret	MONACO GP	Monte Carlo	3	Elf Team Tyrrell	3.0 Tyrrell P34-Cosworth V8	brakes
3	BELGIAN GP	Zolder	3	Elf Team Tyrrell	3.0 Tyrrell P34-Cosworth V8	
ret	SWEDISH GP	Anderstorp	3	Elf Team Tyrrell	3.0 Tyrrell P34-Cosworth V8	ignition
12	FRENCH GP	Dijon	3	Elf Team Tyrrell	3.0 Tyrrell P34-Cosworth V8	pit stop-tyres/3 laps behind
ret	BRITISH GP	Silverstone	3	Elf Team Tyrrell	3.0 Tyrrell P34-Cosworth V8	engine
9/ret	GERMAN GP	Hockenheim	3	Elf Team Tyrrell	3.0 Tyrrell P34-Cosworth V8	engine/5 laps behind
5	AUSTRIAN GP	Österreichring	3	Elf Team Tyrrell	3.0 Tyrrell P34-Cosworth V8	
ret	DUTCH GP	Zandvoort	3	Elf Team Tyrrell	3.0 Tyrrell P34-Cosworth V8	ignition
6	ITALIAN GP	Monza	3	Elf Team Tyrrell	3.0 Tyrrell P34-Cosworth V8	
16	US GP EAST	Watkins Glen	3	Elf Team Tyrrell	3.0 Tyrrell P34-Cosworth V8	pit stops-tyres/FL/3 laps behind
ret	CANADIAN GP	Mosport Park	3	Elf Team Tyrrell	3.0 Tyrrell P34-Cosworth V8	fuel leak
ret	JAPANESE GP	Mount Fuji	3	Elf Team Tyrrell	3.0 Tyrrell P34-Cosworth V8	hit by Villeneuve

1978

	Race	Circuit	No	Entrant	Car/Engine	Comment
5	ARGENTINE GP	Buenos Aires	6	John Player Team Lotus	3.0 Lotus 78-Cosworth V8	
ret	BRAZILIAN GP	Rio	6	John Player Team Lotus	3.0 Lotus 78-Cosworth V8	collision with Villeneuve/Pole
1	SOUTH AFRICAN GP	Kyalami	6	John Player Team Lotus	3.0 Lotus 78-Cosworth V8	took lead on last lap
4	US GP WEST	Long Beach	6	John Player Team Lotus	3.0 Lotus 78-Cosworth V8	pit stop-tyres
ret	MONACO GP	Monte Carlo	6	John Player Team Lotus	3.0 Lotus 78-Cosworth V8	gearbox
2	BELGIAN GP	Zolder	6	John Player Team Lotus	3.0 Lotus 78-Cosworth V8	pit stop-tyre/FL
2	SPANISH GP	Jarama	6	John Player Team Lotus	3.0 Lotus 79-Cosworth V8	
3	SWEDISH GP	Anderstorp	6	John Player Team Lotus	3.0 Lotus 79-Cosworth V8	held up by Patrese
2	FRENCH GP	Paul Ricard	6	John Player Team Lotus	3.0 Lotus 79-Cosworth V8	
ret	BRITISH GP	Brands Hatch	6	John Player Team Lotus	3.0 Lotus 79-Cosworth V8	fuel pump/Pole
ret	GERMAN GP	Hockenheim	6	John Player Team Lotus	3.0 Lotus 79-Cosworth V8	gearbox/FL
1	AUSTRIAN GP	Österreichring	6	John Player Team Lotus	3.0 Lotus 79-Cosworth V8	Pole/FL
2	DUTCH GP	Zandvoort	6	John Player Team Lotus	3.0 Lotus 79-Cosworth V8	
ret/dns	ITALIAN GP	Monza	6	John Player Team Lotus	3.0 Lotus 78-Cosworth V8	fatal accident at 1st start
dns	"	"	6	John Player Team Lotus	3.0 Lotus 79-Cosworth V8	practice accident-car damaged

GP Starts: 123 (124)   GP Wins: 10   Pole positions: 14   Fastest laps: 9   Points: 206

PICARD, François (F) b 26/4/1921

1958

	Race	Circuit	No	Entrant	Car/Engine	Comment
ret	MOROCCAN GP (F2)	Casablanca	54	R R C Walker Racing Team	1.5 Cooper T43-Climax 4	hit Gendebien's spinning car/injured

GP Starts: 1   GP Wins: 0   Pole positions: 0   Fastest laps: 0   Points: 0

PIETERSE, Ernest (ZA) b 4/7/1938

1962

	Race	Circuit	No	Entrant	Car/Engine	Comment
10	SOUTH AFRICAN GP	East London	14	Ernest Pieterse	1.5 Lotus 21-Climax 4	11 laps behind

1963

ret	SOUTH AFRICAN GP	East London	7	Lawson Organisation	1.5 Lotus 21-Climax 4	engine

1965

dnq	SOUTH AFRICAN GP	East London	22	Lawson Organisation	1.5 Lotus 21-Climax 4	

GP Starts: 2   GP Wins: 0   Pole positions: 0   Fastest laps: 0   Points: 0

PIETSCH, Paul (D) b 20/6/1911

1950

	Race	Circuit	No	Entrant	Car/Engine	Comment
ret	ITALIAN GP	Monza	28	Paul Pietsch	1.5 s/c Maserati 4CLT/48	engine at start

1951

ret	GERMAN GP	Nürburgring	78	Alfa Romeo SpA	1.5 s/c Alfa Romeo 159 8	spun off

1952

ret	GERMAN GP	Nürburgring	127	Motor-Presse-Verlag	2.0 Veritas Meteor 6	gearbox

GP Starts: 3   GP Wins: 0   Pole positions: 0   Fastest laps: 0   Points: 0

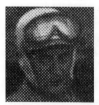

FRANÇOIS PICARD

Picard began racing in 1949, initially with a Renault 4CV, before switching to a Porsche, with which he won the 1952 Circuit of Agadir. From 1953 on he became a well-known Ferrari privateer, racing mainly in France and North Africa. He gained some good results partnering Charles Pozzi, the pair winning their class at both the Reims and Hyères 12-hour races in 1954. Over the next two seasons, Picard ran a Ferrari 500 Monza, taking numerous placings including second at the 1955 Coupe de Paris, and third in the Agadir GP and Paris 1000 Km in 1956. He continued in sports cars until the Moroccan GP of 1958, when he drove in his first, and only, single-seater race in Rob Walker's Cooper. The unlucky Picard crashed into Gendebien's spinning car, sustaining serious injuries which left him incapacitated for six months. Happily he recovered, but he never raced again.

PAUL PIETSCH

Pietsch was a notable pre-war driver who, after success aplenty in hill-climbs from the early thirties with an Alfa Romeo 'Monza', was invited to join the Auto Union team in 1935. He did not get many opportunities to race, but shared the third-place car in the 1935 Italian GP with Rosemeyer, before branching out on his own with a Maserati, with which he led the 1939 German GP until plug trouble dropped him to third.

After the war Pietsch concentrated on building up his thriving publishing business, but he found time to race a Maserati and a Veritas, winning the Eifelrennen in the latter in 1951. He was given a works Alfa Romeo for that year's German GP, but crashed heavily in the race when lying fifth, escaping injury, and after another serious accident at AVUS the following year Pietsch decided to quit for good.

ANDRÉ PILETTE

André's father, who had raced at Indianapolis in 1912, finishing fifth, and taken third place in the French GP the same year, died when he was only three. Nevertheless tales of his exploits were to set the youngster on course for a career in motor sport.

After gaining some experience in the late forties with his own machines, Pilette joined the Ecurie Belgique, finally taking their Talbot to sixth place in the 1951 Belgian GP. Then, at the Dutch GP, he had the first of two huge accidents in which he was seriously injured (the second at Albi in 1952 wrote off the Talbot). He reappeared in Claes' Connaught at the Grand Prix at Spa in 1953, and then aligned himself with Gordini for 1954. He competed in only three Grands Prix, but raced in a good number of non-title races, his best results being second places at Chimay and Cadours. Back with his countrymen to form Ecurie Nationale Belge in 1955, Pilette ironically only found success in the Coupe de Paris in a Gordini.

The 1956 season started well, but then he had another bad accident in practice for the German GP, which sidelined him for nearly two years. He finished fourth at Le Mans in 1959, and then second in 1960 with Ricardo Rodriguez in a NART Ferrari.

In 1961 André reappeared in single-seaters, with the ENB Emeryson-Climax, which proved a total flop, but, being a glutton for punishment, he was back in 1963 with an old Lotus 18/21 four-cylinder, before a final fling in the ex-Powell Scirocco in 1964. Subsequently he opened a racing school at Zolder which he ran until the late eighties.

TEDDY PILETTE

Teddy followed his father André into the sport but cleared his own path, setting out in Formula Junior in 1962, then having a spell with the Fiat-Abarth GT team.

In 1965 he used a Fiat-Abarth saloon to win his class in the Belgian championship, and he then became involved in what was to be a long-term association with Count van der Straten's VDS team, first driving an Alfa Romeo T33 and then a Lola T70.

In 1971, Pilette began racing in F5000 which is where he found his greatest success, winnng the European championship with a Chevron B28 in 1973 and repeating the feat with a Lola T400 in 1975, before heading for a season in the United States.

Pilette finally emulated his father's achievement by starting a Grand Prix in 1974, in a rented Brabham, and later became another of the masochists who tried to qualify the lumbering Stanley-BRM in 1977, even campaigning the dreadful car in the British Aurora AFX series the following year.

PILETTE, André (B) b 6/10/1918

	Race	Circuit	No	Entrant	Car/Engine	Comment
	1951					
6	BELGIAN GP	Spa	24	Ecurie Belgique	4.5 Lago-Talbot T26C 6	*3 laps behind*
	1953					
nc	BELGIAN GP	Spa	40	Ecurie Belge	2.0 Connaught A Type-Lea Francis 4	*7 laps behind*
	1954					
5	BELGIAN GP	Spa	18	Equipe Gordini	2.5 Gordini Type 16 6	*1 lap behind*
9	BRITISH GP	Silverstone	19	Equipe Gordini	2.5 Gordini Type 16 6	*4 laps behind*
ret	GERMAN GP	Nürburgring	12	Equipe Gordini	2.5 Gordini Type 16 6	*gearbox*
	1956					
6*	MONACO GP	Monte Carlo	4	Equipe Gordini	2.5 Gordini Type 32 8	** took over from Bayol/-12 laps*
6	BELGIAN GP	Spa	20	Scuderia Ferrari	2.5 Lancia-Ferrari D50 V8	*3 laps behind*
11	FRENCH GP	Reims	34	Equipe Gordini	2.5 Gordini Type 16 6	*6 laps behind*
dns	GERMAN GP	Nürburgring	11	Equipe Gordini	2.5 Gordini Type 32 8	*practice accident*
	1961					
dnq	ITALIAN GP	Monza	68	André Pilette	1.5 Emeryson P-Climax 4	
	1963					
dnq	GERMAN GP	Nürburgring	29	Tim Parnell	1.5 Lotus 18/21-Climax 4	
dnq	ITALIAN GP	Monza	46	André Pilette	1.5 Lotus 18/21-Climax 4	
	1964					
ret	BELGIAN GP	Spa	28	Equipe Scirocco Belge	1.5 Scirocco 02-Climax V8	*engine*
dnq	GERMAN GP	Nürburgring	28	Equipe Scirocco Belge	1.5 Scirocco 02-Climax V8	

GP Starts: 9 GP Wins: 0 Pole positions: 0 Fastest laps: 0 Points: 0

PILETTE, Teddy (B) b 26/7/1942

	Race	Circuit	No	Entrant	Car/Engine	Comment
	1974					
17	BELGIAN GP	Nivelles	34	Motor Racing Developments	3.0 Brabham BT42-Cosworth V8	*pit stop-tyres/4 laps behind*
	1977					
dnq	GERMAN GP	Hockenheim	40	Stanley BRM	3.0 BRM P207 V12	
dnq	DUTCH GP	Zandvoort	29	Stanley BRM	3.0 BRM P207 V12	
dnq	ITALIAN GP	Monza	29	Stanley BRM	3.0 BRM P207 V12	

GP Starts: 1 GP Wins: 0 Pole positions: 0 Fastest laps: 0 Points: 0

PIOTTI, Luigi (I)

	Race	Circuit	No	Entrant	Car/Engine	Comment
	1955					
dns	ITALIAN GP	Monza	46	Scuderia Volpini/Luigi Piotti	2.5 Arzani-Volpini 4	*mechanical problems in practice*
	1956					
ret	ARGENTINE GP	Buenos Aires	8	Officine Alfieri Maserati	2.5 Maserati 250F 6	*collision with Collins*
ret	GERMAN GP	Nürburgring	18	Luigi Piotti	2.5 Maserati 250F 6	*engine*
6	ITALIAN GP	Monza	40	Luigi Piotti	2.5 Maserati 250F 6	*3 laps behind*

1957

10	ARGENTINE GP	Buenos Aires	28	Luigi Piotti	2.5 Maserati 250F 6	10 laps behind
dnq	MONACO GP	Monte Carlo	42	Luigi Piotti	2.5 Maserati 250F 6	
ret	PESCARA GP	Pescara	12	Luigi Piotti	2.5 Maserati 250F 6	*transmission*
ret	ITALIAN GP	Monza	12	Luigi Piotti	2.5 Maserati 250F 6	*engine*

1958

dnq	MONACO GP	Monte Carlos	54	Automobili OSCA	1.5 OSCA 4 sports car	

GP Starts: 6   GP Wins: 0   Pole positions: 0   Fastest laps: 0   Points: 0

LUIGI PIOTTI

A businessman and part-time racer, Piotti achieved minor success in sports cars, including a class win in the 1952 Tour of Sicily in an OSCA, third place in a rather weak Targa Florio with a Lancia in 1954 and a win in the Hyères 12 Hours the same year in a Ferrari with Trintignant.

He made his Formula 1 debut in 1955, taking seventh place in the Syracuse GP in a works Maserati 250F, before purchasing a car for the 1956 season, in which he proved hopelessly slow, especially in the Argentine GP where he continually balked faster cars, eventually colliding with Collins' Ferrari. Later he caused a furore at the Italian GP by using his car to push Moss's fuel-starved machine into the pits and thus give the Englishman a chance to win the race. Piotti plodded through the 1957 season with the Maserati, and after finding little success in an OSCA in 1958 wisely returned to a more sedate occupation.

DAVID PIPER

From farming stock, Piper began his career by competing in sprints and hill-climbs, but soon hit the circuits in a little Lotus XI before buying a Lotus 16 with which, by swapping engines, he raced in both F1 and F2 in 1959-60, perhaps his best result in the car being a second place in the 1960 Lady Wigram Trophy in New Zealand.

In 1961 he joined Jo Siffert on the Continent for a season of Formula Junior racing, before returning home to drive the F1 Gilby in the Gold Cup. Although he did a handful of national F1 races in 1962, he had become disillusioned with single-seaters and bought a Ferrari GTO, which gave his career a new lease of life.

Between 1962 and 1970, Piper raced all over the world in his own Ferraris and later Porsches, occasionally winning races in places as far afield as South Africa, Angola, Sweden and Japan, but always proving a reliable driver and a consistent finisher. In 1970 Piper crashed his Porsche 917 while working on the Steve McQueen film *Le Mans*, and had the lower part of a leg amputated. Later on, he returned to race in historic events.

NELSON PIQUET

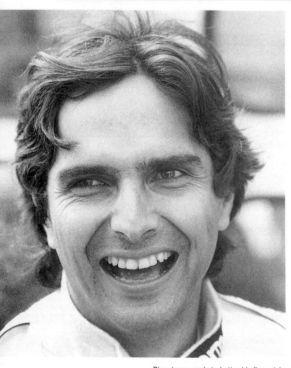

Three world titles testify to the standing of Nelson Piquet, yet many begrudge him his successes, feeling they were not earned in the manner of a true champion. Of course the Brazilian couldn't have cared less. Racing above all to please himself, he went about things in his own way and that approach generally paid dividends. Never happier than when he had some technical advantage to exploit, Nelson felt no embarrassment at using that edge to beat his hapless rivals.

Having raced karts and Super Vee cars in Brazil, Nelson came to Europe in 1977 to tackle the European F3 series, winning two rounds after switching to a Ralt chassis. The following year he concentrated on F3 once more, this time in Britain. His initial object was to beat his Brazilian rival Chico Serra, who was getting a good press back at home, but eventually it was Derek Warwick who was to be his sternest challenger for the two championships on offer that year. They ended up taking one apiece, but by now Nelson was interesting Formula 1 teams. Mo Nunn gave him a debut in his forgiving Ensign, before the heavy steering of the BS Fabrications McLaren posed more searching questions. However, his practice performance in the third Brabham-Alfa at Montreal prompted Bernie Ecclestone to offer him a contract for 1979.

A superb drive in the Race of Champions took him into second place, and though the Grand Prix season yielded little by way of hard results Nelson was clearly a driver destined for the very top. When Lauda quit towards the end of the season Brabham did not have far to look for a new team leader to handle the Cosworth-powered BT49 in 1980. Nelson took three Grand Prix wins and finished runner-up to Alan Jones that year, and was to go all the way in 1981. After a tense and closely fought season, Piquet typically did just enough to edge out Carlos Reutemann in the final race at Caesars Palace. Realising that turbo power was now a necessity, Brabham spent the 1982 season bringing their new BMW-engined car to a competitive state – something achieved when Nelson won in Montreal – and then trying to make it reliable. The knowledge gained was then incorporated into the design of Gordon Murray's flat-bottomed 1983 contender which was tailored to the mid-race refuelling tactics the team had pioneered the previous year. At the wheel of the splendid little BT52, Piquet battled with Prost for the title, whittling away the Frenchman's lead before taking the crown at the last gasp at Kyalami. In 1984 the Brabham was no match for the McLarens and even Nelson was left in their wake but, digging deep, he conjured up back-to-back wins in Montreal and Detroit to salvage something from a disappointing year. The end of the superb Piquet-Brabham relationship came in 1985, with Nelson hamstrung by running uncompetitive Pirellis, but there was one last win, at Paul Ricard, when the hard-compound Italian tyres held sway.

Piquet was ready to better his financial position and signed for Williams for 1986. The season should have been a walk-over for the Didcot team, but the atmosphere soon became strained as Nigel Mansell refused to play second fiddle and set about launching his own title bid. The upshot was that Alain Prost stole the championship at the death, leaving Nelson fuming over Williams' indecisive handling of team tactics. Honda were not pleased either, and would switch to McLaren at the end of the following season. Piquet knew the score in 1987, and set about winning the title despite Mansell. With a good deal of fortune and some help from his luckless team-mate, Nelson did just that. His third title may have been achieved more by stealth than by absolute speed, but the results justified the means in Piquet's book. A two-year spell at Lotus was a complete disaster for all concerned. The massive retainer Nelson picked up from Camel was out of all proportion to his on-track return, and while his bank balance may never have been higher than it was at the end of 1989, never was his stock so low. His subsequent inclusion in the Benetton team for 1990 was greeted with huge surprise, but as the season wore on the wisdom of the move became apparent. Nelson struck up a good working relationship with John Barnard and the pair brought the Benetton B190 to a very competitive pitch, Nelson exploiting others' misfortune to win both the Japanese and Australian GPs. Even his sternest critics were forced to admit that his drive in Adelaide was right out of the top drawer. He was to take one more very fortuitous (but highly satisfying) win at Mansell's expense in Canada the following year before being swept away amid the personnel changes that engulfed the team that season.

With no suitable F1 offers available, Piquet decided to try his hand at the Indianapolis 500 in 1992. Unfortunately a huge crash in practice left him with very badly crushed feet and legs, easily the most severe injuries he had suffered in his long career, and his rehabilitation was long and painful. Nelson vowed never to return to the cockpit but, once fit, he was back at the Brickyard in 1993, and by qualifying for the race he finished the job left uncompleted 12 months earlier.

PIPER, David (GB) b 2/12/1930

1959

	Race	Circuit	No	Entrant	Car/Engine	Comment
ret	BRITISH GP	Aintree	64	Dorchester Service Station	1.5 Lotus 16-Climax 4 F2	engine-head gasket

1960

dns	FRENCH GP	Reims	34	Robert Bodle Ltd	2.5 Lotus 16-Climax 4	engine in practice
12	BRITISH GP	Silverstone	26	Robert Bodle Ltd	2.5 Lotus 16-Climax 4	5 laps behind

GP Starts: 2 GP Wins: 0 Pole positions: 0 Fastest laps: 0 Points:

PIQUET, Nelson (BR) b 17/8/1952

1978

	Race	Circuit	No	Entrant	Car/Engine	Comment
ret	GERMAN GP	Hockenheim	22	Team Tissot Ensign	3.0 Ensign N177-Cosworth V8	engine
ret/dns	AUSTRIAN GP	Österreichring	29	BS Fabrications	3.0 McLaren M23-Cosworth V8	slid off-first start/did not restart
ret	DUTCH GP	Zandvoort	29	BS Fabrications	3.0 McLaren M23-Cosworth V8	driveshaft
9	ITALIAN GP	Monza	29	BS Fabrications	3.0 McLaren M23-Cosworth V8	
11	CANADIAN GP	Montreal	66	Parmalat Racing Team	3.0 Brabham BT46-Alfa Romeo F12	1 lap behind

1979

ret/dns	ARGENTINE GP	Buenos Aires	6	Parmalat Racing Team	3.0 Brabham BT46-Alfa Romeo F12	accident in first start-hurt foot
ret	BRAZILIAN GP	Interlagos	6	Parmalat Racing Team	3.0 Brabham BT48-Alfa Romeo V12	hit Reutemann
7	SOUTH AFRICAN GP	Kyalami	6	Parmalat Racing Team	3.0 Brabham BT48-Alfa Romeo V12	1 lap behind
8	US GP WEST	Long Beach	6	Parmalat Racing Team	3.0 Brabham BT48-Alfa Romeo V12	pit stop-tyres/2 laps behind
ret	SPANISH GP	Jarama	6	Parmalat Racing Team	3.0 Brabham BT48-Alfa Romeo V12	fuel metering unit
ret	BELGIAN GP	Zolder	6	Parmalat Racing Team	3.0 Brabham BT48-Alfa Romeo V12	engine
ret	MONACO GP	Monte Carlo	6	Parmalat Racing Team	3.0 Brabham BT48-Alfa Romeo V12	driveshaft
ret	FRENCH GP	Dijon	6	Parmalat Racing Team	3.0 Brabham BT48-Alfa Romeo V12	spun off
ret	BRITISH GP	Silverstone	6	Parmalat Racing Team	3.0 Brabham BT48-Alfa Romeo V12	spun off-could not restart
12/ret	GERMAN GP	Hockenheim	6	Parmalat Racing Team	3.0 Brabham BT48-Alfa Romeo V12	engine/3 laps behind
ret	AUSTRIAN GP	Österreichring	6	Parmalat Racing Team	3.0 Brabham BT48-Alfa Romeo V12	engine
4	DUTCH GP	Zandvoort	6	Parmalat Racing Team	3.0 Brabham BT48-Alfa Romeo V12	1 lap behind
ret	ITALIAN GP	Monza	6	Parmalat Racing Team	3.0 Brabham BT48-Alfa Romeo V12	collision with Regazzoni
ret	CANADIAN GP	Montreal	6	Parmalat Racing Team	3.0 Brabham BT49-Cosworth V8	gearbox
ret	US GP EAST	Watkins Glen	6	Parmalat Racing Team	3.0 Brabham BT49-Cosworth V8	driveshaft

1980

2	ARGENTINE GP	Buenos Aires	5	Parmalat Racing Team	3.0 Brabham BT49-Cosworth V8	
ret	BRAZILIAN GP	Interlagos	5	Parmalat Racing Team	3.0 Brabham BT49-Cosworth V8	suspension failure-accident
4	SOUTH AFRICAN GP	Kyalami	5	Parmalat Racing Team	3.0 Brabham BT49-Cosworth V8	
1	US GP WEST	Long Beach	5	Parmalat Racing Team	3.0 Brabham BT49-Cosworth V8	Pole/FL
ret	BELGIAN GP	Zolder	5	Parmalat Racing Team	3.0 Brabham BT49-Cosworth V8	crashed into catch fence
3	MONACO GP	Monte Carlo	5	Parmalat Racing Team	3.0 Brabham BT49-Cosworth V8	
4	FRENCH GP	Paul Ricard	5	Parmalat Racing Team	3.0 Brabham BT49-Cosworth V8	
2	BRITISH GP	Brands Hatch	5	Parmalat Racing Team	3.0 Brabham BT49-Cosworth V8	
4	GERMAN GP	Hockenheim	5	Parmalat Racing Team	3.0 Brabham BT49-Cosworth V8	
5	AUSTRIAN GP	Österreichring	5	Parmalat Racing Team	3.0 Brabham BT49-Cosworth V8	
1	DUTCH GP	Zandvoort	5	Parmalat Racing Team	3.0 Brabham BT49-Cosworth V8	
1	ITALIAN GP	Imola	5	Parmalat Racing Team	3.0 Brabham BT49-Cosworth V8	
ret	CANADIAN GP	Montreal	5	Parmalat Racing Team	3.0 Brabham BT49-Cosworth V8	engine/Pole
ret	US GP EAST	Watkins Glen	5	Parmalat Racing Team	3.0 Brabham BT49-Cosworth V8	spun off-push started

1981 World Champion Driver

3	US GP WEST	Long Beach	5	Parmalat Racing Team	3.0 Brabham BT49C-Cosworth V8	
12	BRAZILIAN GP	Rio	5	Parmalat Racing Team	3.0 Brabham BT49C-Cosworth V8	pit stop-tyres/Pole/2 laps behind
1	ARGENTINE GP	Buenos Aires	5	Parmalat Racing Team	3.0 Brabham BT49C-Cosworth V8	Pole/FL
1	SAN MARINO GP	Imola	5	Parmalat Racing Team	3.0 Brabham BT49C-Cosworth V8	
ret	BELGIAN GP	Zolder	5	Parmalat Racing Team	3.0 Brabham BT49C-Cosworth V8	collision with Jones
ret	MONACO GP	Monte Carlo	5	Parmalat Racing Team	3.0 Brabham BT49C-Cosworth V8	spun off/Pole
ret	SPANISH GP	Jarama	5	Parmalat Racing Team	3.0 Brabham BT49C-Cosworth V8	collision with Andretti
3	FRENCH GP	Dijon	5	Parmalat Racing Team	3.0 Brabham BT49C-Cosworth V8	
ret	BRITISH GP	Silverstone	5	Parmalat Racing Team	3.0 Brabham BT49C-Cosworth V8	tyre failure-accident
dns	"	"	5	Parmalat Racing Team	1.5 t/c Brabham BT50-BMW 4	practice only
1	GERMAN GP	Hockenheim	5	Parmalat Racing Team	3.0 Brabham BT49C-Cosworth V8	
3	AUSTRIAN GP	Österreichring	5	Parmalat Racing Team	3.0 Brabham BT49C-Cosworth V8	
2	DUTCH GP	Zandvoort	5	Parmalat Racing Team	3.0 Brabham BT49C-Cosworth V8	
6/ret	ITALIAN GP	Monza	5	Parmalat Racing Team	3.0 Brabham BT49C-Cosworth V8	engine on last lap when 3rd/-1 lap
5	CANADIAN GP	Montreal	5	Parmalat Racing Team	3.0 Brabham BT49C-Cosworth V8	Pole/1 lap behind
5	CAESARS PALACE GP	Las Vegas	5	Parmalat Racing Team	3.0 Brabham BT49C-Cosworth V8	

1982

ret	SOUTH AFRICAN GP	Kyalami	1	Parmalat Racing Team	1.5 t/c Brabham BT50-BMW 4	spun off
dsq*	BRAZILIAN GP	Rio	1	Parmalat Racing Team	3.0 Brabham BT49D-Cosworth V8	* due water cooled brakes/1st/FL
ret	US GP WEST	Long Beach	1	Parmalat Racing Team	3.0 Brabham BT49D-Cosworth V8	hit wall
5*	BELGIAN GP	Zolder	1	Parmalat Racing Team	1.5 t/c Brabham BT50-BMW 4	* 3rd place car dsq/pit stop/-3 laps
ret	MONACO GP	Monte Carlo	1	Parmalat Racing Team	1.5 t/c Brabham BT50-BMW 4	gearbox
dnq	US GP (DETROIT)	Detroit	1	Parmalat Racing Team	1.5 t/c Brabham BT50-BMW 4	
1	CANADIAN GP	Montreal	1	Parmalat Racing Team	1.5 t/c Brabham BT50-BMW 4	
2	DUTCH GP	Zandvoort	1	Parmalat Racing Team	1.5 t/c Brabham BT50-BMW 4	
ret	BRITISH GP	Brands Hatch	1	Parmalat Racing Team	1.5 t/c Brabham BT50-BMW 4	fuel metering unit
ret	FRENCH GP	Paul Ricard	1	Parmalat Racing Team	1.5 t/c Brabham BT50-BMW 4	engine
ret	GERMAN GP	Hockenheim	1	Parmalat Racing Team	1.5 t/c Brabham BT50-BMW 4	accident with Salazar/FL
ret	AUSTRIAN GP	Österreichring	1	Parmalat Racing Team	1.5 t/c Brabham BT50-BMW 4	engine/Pole/FL

4	SWISS GP	Dijon	1	Parmalat Racing Team	1.5 t/c Brabham BT50-BMW 4	*pit stop-tyres/fuel/1 lap behind*
ret	ITALIAN GP	Monza	1	Parmalat Racing Team	1.5 t/c Brabham BT50-BMW 4	*clutch*
ret	CAESARS PALACE GP	Las Vegas	1	Parmalat Racing Team	1.5 t/c Brabham BT50-BMW 4	*spark plug electrode*

1983 World Champion Driver

1	BRAZILIAN GP	Rio	5	Fila Sport	1.5 t/c Brabham BT52-BMW 4	*FL*
ret	US GP WEST	Long Beach	5	Fila Sport	1.5 t/c Brabham BT52-BMW 4	*throttle linkage*
2	FRENCH GP	Paul Ricard	5	Fila Sport	1.5 t/c Brabham BT52-BMW 4	*pit stop-fuel*
ret	SAN MARINO GP	Imola	5	Fila Sport	1.5 t/c Brabham BT52-BMW 4	*engine*
2	MONACO GP	Monte Carlo	5	Fila Sport	1.5 t/c Brabham BT52-BMW 4	*FL*
4	BELGIAN GP	Spa	5	Fila Sport	1.5 t/c Brabham BT52-BMW 4	
4	US GP (DETROIT)	Detroit	5	Fila Sport	1.5 t/c Brabham BT52-BMW 4	
ret	CANADIAN GP	Montreal	5	Fila Sport	1.5 t/c Brabham BT52-BMW 4	*throttle cable*
2	BRITISH GP	Silverstone	5	Fila Sport	1.5 t/c Brabham BT52B-BMW 4	
13/ret	GERMAN GP	Hockenheim	5	Fila Sport	1.5 t/c Brabham BT52B-BMW 4	*fire-leaking fuel/3 laps behind*
3	AUSTRIAN GP	Österreichring	5	Fila Sport	1.5 t/c Brabham BT52B-BMW 4	
ret	DUTCH GP	Zandvoort	5	Fila Sport	1.5 t/c Brabham BT52B-BMW 4	*accident with Prost/Pole*
1	ITALIAN GP	Monza	5	Fila Sport	1.5 t/c Brabham BT52B-BMW 4	*FL*
1	EUROPEAN GP	Brands Hatch	5	Fila Sport	1.5 t/c Brabham BT52B-BMW 4	
3	SOUTH AFRICAN GP	Kyalami	5	Fila Sport	1.5 t/c Brabham BT52B-BMW 4	*FL*

1984

ret	BRAZILIAN GP	Rio	1	MRD International	1.5 t/c Brabham BT53-BMW 4	*engine*
ret	SOUTH AFRICAN GP	Kyalami	1	MRD International	1.5 t/c Brabham BT53-BMW 4	*turbo/Pole*
9*/ret	BELGIAN GP	Zolder	1	MRD International	1.5 t/c Brabham BT53-BMW 4	*engine/*6th place car dsq/-4 laps*
ret	SAN MARINO GP	Imola	1	MRD International	1.5 t/c Brabham BT53-BMW 4	*turbo/Pole/FL*
ret	FRENCH GP	Dijon	1	MRD International	1.5 t/c Brabham BT53-BMW 4	*turbo*
ret	MONACO GP	Monte Carlo	1	MRD International	1.5 t/c Brabham BT53-BMW 4	*wet electrics*
1	CANADIAN GP	Montreal	1	MRD International	1.5 t/c Brabham BT53-BMW 4	*Pole/FL*
1	US GP (DETROIT)	Detroit	1	MRD International	1.5 t/c Brabham BT53-BMW 4	*Pole*
ret	US GP (DALLAS)	Dallas	1	MRD International	1.5 t/c Brabham BT53-BMW 4	*jammed throttle hit wall*
7	BRITISH GP	Brands Hatch	1	MRD International	1.5 t/c Brabham BT53-BMW 4	*lost turbo boost/1 lap behind/Pole*
ret	GERMAN GP	Hockenheim	1	MRD International	1.5 t/c Brabham BT53-BMW 4	*gearbox*
2	AUSTRIAN GP	Österreichring	1	MRD International	1.5 t/c Brabham BT53-BMW 4	*Pole*
ret	DUTCH GP	Zandvoort	1	MRD International	1.5 t/c Brabham BT53-BMW 4	*oil pressure-loose oil union*
ret	ITALIAN GP	Monza	1	MRD International	1.5 t/c Brabham BT53-BMW 4	*engine/Pole*
3	EUROPEAN GP	Nürburgring	1	MRD International	1.5 t/c Brabham BT53-BMW 4	*Pole/FL (shared with Alboreto)*
6	PORTUGUESE GP	Estoril	1	MRD International	1.5 t/c Brabham BT53-BMW 4	*spin/1 lap behind/Pole*

1985

ret	BRAZILIAN GP	Rio	7	Motor Racing Developments Ltd	1.5 t/c Brabham BT54-BMW 4	*transmission*
ret	PORTUGUESE GP	Estoril	7	Motor Racing Developments Ltd	1.5 t/c Brabham BT54-BMW 4	*tyres/handling*
8	SAN MARINO GP	Imola	7	Motor Racing Developments Ltd	1.5 t/c Brabham BT54-BMW 4	*pit stop-tyres/3 laps behind*
ret	MONACO GP	Monte Carlo	7	Motor Racing Developments Ltd	1.5 t/c Brabham BT54-BMW 4	*accident with Patrese*
ret	CANADIAN GP	Montreal	7	Motor Racing Developments Ltd	1.5 t/c Brabham BT54-BMW 4	*transmission*
6	US GP (DETROIT)	Detroit	7	Motor Racing Developments Ltd	1.5 t/c Brabham BT54-BMW 4	*1 lap behind*
1	FRENCH GP	Paul Ricard	7	Motor Racing Developments Ltd	1.5 t/c Brabham BT54-BMW 4	
4	BRITISH GP	Silverstone	7	Motor Racing Developmants Ltd	1.5 t/c Brabham BT54-BMW 4	*1 lap behind*
ret	GERMAN GP	Nürburgring	7	Motor Racing Developments Ltd	1.5 t/c Brabham BT54-BMW 4	*turbo*
ret	AUSTRIAN GP	Österreichring	7	Motor Racing Developments Ltd	1.5 t/c Brabham BT54-BMW 4	*exhaust*
8	DUTCH GP	Zandvoort	7	Motor Racing Developments Ltd	1.5 t/c Brabham BT54-BMW 4	*stalled on grid/1 lap behind/Pole*
2	ITALIAN GP	Monza	7	Motor Racing Developments Ltd	1.5 t/c Brabham BT54-BMW 4	
5	BELGIAN GP	Spa	7	Motor Racing Developments Ltd	1.5 t/c Brabham BT54-BMW 4	*1 lap behind*
ret	EUROPEAN GP	Brands Hatch	7	Motor Racing Developments Ltd	1.5 t/c Brabham BT54-BMW 4	*hit Rosberg's spinning car*
ret	SOUTH AFRICAN GP	Kyalami	7	Motor Racing Developments Ltd	1.5 t/c Brabham BT54-BMW 4	*engine*
ret	AUSTRALIAN GP	Adelaide	7	Motor Racing Developments Ltd	1.5 t/c Brabham BT54-BMW 4	*electrical fire*

1986

1	BRAZILIAN GP	Rio	6	Canon Williams Team	1.5 t/c Williams FW11-Honda V6	*FL*
ret	SPANISH GP	Jerez	6	Canon Williams Team	1.5 t/c Williams FW11-Honda V6	*overheating*
2	SAN MARINO GP	Imola	6	Canon Williams Team	1.5 t/c Williams FW11-Honda V6	*FL*
7	MONACO GP	Monte Carlo	6	Canon Williams Team	1.5 t/c Williams FW11-Honda V6	*1 lap behind*
ret	BELGIAN GP	Spa	6	Canon Williams Team	1.5 t/c Williams FW11-Honda V6	*turbo boost control/Pole*
3	CANADIAN GP	Montreal	6	Canon Williams Team	1.5 t/c Williams FW11-Honda V6	*FL*
ret	US GP (DETROIT)	Detroit	6	Canon Williams Team	1.5 t/c Williams FW11-Honda V6	*hit wall/FL*
3	FRENCH GP	Paul Ricard	6	Canon Williams Team	1.5 t/c Williams FW11-Honda V6	
2	BRITISH GP	Brands Hatch	6	Canon Williams Team	1.5 t/c Williams FW11-Honda V6	*Pole*
1	GERMAN GP	Hockenheim	6	Canon Williams Team	1.5 t/c Williams FW11-Honda V6	
1	HUNGARIAN GP	Hungaroring	6	Canon Williams Team	1.5 t/c Williams FW11-Honda V6	*FL*
ret	AUSTRIAN GP	Österreichring	6	Canon Williams Team	1.5 t/c Williams FW11-Honda V6	*engine*
1	ITALIAN GP	Monza	6	Canon Williams Team	1.5 t/c Williams FW11-Honda V6	
3	PORTUGUESE GP	Estoril	6	Canon Williams Team	1.5 t/c Williams FW11-Honda V6	
4	MEXICAN GP	Mexico City	6	Canon Williams Team	1.5 t/c Williams FW11-Honda V6	*1 lap behind/FL*
2	AUSTRALIAN GP	Adelaide	6	Canon Williams Team	1.5 t/c Williams FW11-Honda V6	*precautionary tyre stop/FL*

1987 World Champion Driver

2	BRAZILIAN GP	Rio	6	Canon Williams Team	1.5 t/c Williams FW11B-Honda V6	*FL*
dns	SAN MARINO GP	Imola	6	Canon Williams Team	1.5 t/c Williams FW11B-Honda V6	*practice accident/not allowed to start*
ret	BELGIAN GP	Spa	6	Canon Williams Team	1.5 t/c Williams FW11B-Honda V6	*turbo sensor*
2	MONACO GP	Monte Carlo	6	Canon Williams Team	1.5 t/c Williams FW11B-Honda V6	
2	US GP (DETROIT)	Detroit	6	Canon Williams Team	1.5 t/c Williams FW11B-Honda V6	
2	FRENCH GP	Paul Ricard	6	Canon Williams Team	1.5 t/c Williams FW11B-Honda V6	*FL*
2	BRITISH GP	Silverstone	6	Canon Williams Team	1.5 t/c Williams FW11B-Honda V6	*Pole*
1	GERMAN GP	Hockenheim	6	Canon Williams Team	1.5 t/c Williams FW11B-Honda V6	
1	HUNGARIAN GP	Hungaroring	6	Canon Williams Team	1.5 t/c Williams FW11B-Honda V6	*FL*
2	AUSTRIAN GP	Österreichring	6	Canon Williams Team	1.5 t/c Williams FW11B-Honda V6	*Pole*
1	ITALIAN GP	Monza	6	Canon Williams Team	1.5 t/c Williams FW11B-Honda V6	*Pole*

3	PORTUGUESE GP	Estoril	6	Canon Williams Team	1.5 t/c Williams FW11B-Honda V6	
4	SPANISH GP	Jerez	6	Canon Williams Team	1.5 t/c Williams FW11B-Honda V6	*Pole*
2	MEXICAN GP	Mexico City	6	Canon Williams Team	1.5 t/c Williams FW11B-Honda V6	*FL*
15/ret	JAPANESE GP	Suzuka	6	Canon Williams Team	1.5 t/c Williams FW11B-Honda V6	*engine/6 laps behind*
ret	AUSTRALIAN GP	Adelaide	6	Canon Williams Team	1.5 t/c Williams FW11B-Honda V6	*brakes/gear linkage*

1988

3	BRAZILIAN GP	Rio	1	Camel Team Lotus Honda	1.5 t/c Lotus 100T-Honda V6	
3	SAN MARINO GP	Imola	1	Camel Team Lotus Honda	1.5 t/c Lotus 100T-Honda V6	*1 lap behind*
ret	MONACO GP	Monte Carlo	1	Camel Team Lotus Honda	1.5 t/c Lotus 100T-Honda V6	*accident damage*
ret	MEXICAN GP	Mexico City	1	Camel Team Lotus Honda	1.5 t/c Lotus 100T-Honda V6	*engine*
4	CANADIAN GP	Montreal	1	Camel Team Lotus Honda	1.5 t/c Lotus 100T-Honda V6	*1 lap behind*
ret	US GP (DETROIT)	Detroit	1	Camel Team Lotus Honda	1.5 t/c Lotus 100T-Honda V6	*spun off*
5	FRENCH GP	Paul Ricard	1	Camel Team Lotus Honda	1.5 t/c Lotus 100T-Honda V6	*1 lap behind*
5	BRITISH GP	Silverstone	1	Camel Team Lotus Honda	1.5 t/c Lotus 100T-Honda V6	
ret	GERMAN GP	Hockenheim	1	Camel Team Lotus Honda	1.5 t/c Lotus 100T-Honda V6	*dry tyres-wet race-spun off*
8	HUNGARIAN GP	Hungaroring	1	Camel Team Lotus Honda	1.5 t/c Lotus 100T-Honda V6	*hit Martini-pit stop/3 laps behind*
4*	BELGIAN GP	Spa	1	Camel Team Lotus Honda	1.5 t/c Lotus 100T-Honda V6	** 3rd & 4th place cars dsq*
ret	ITALIAN GP	Monza	1	Camel Team Lotus Honda	1.5 t/c Lotus 100T-Honda V6	*clutch/spun off*
ret	PORTUGUESE GP	Estoril	1	Camel Team Lotus Honda	1.5 t/c Lotus 100T-Honda V6	*clutch*
8	SPANISH GP	Jerez	1	Camel Team Lotus Honda	1.5 t/c Lotus 100T-Honda V6	
ret	JAPANESE GP	Suzuka	1	Camel Team Lotus Honda	1.5 t/c Lotus 100T-Honda V6	*driver unwell*
3	AUSTRALIAN GP	Adelaide	1	Camel Team Lotus Honda	1.5 t/c Lotus 100T-Honda V6	

1989

ret	BRAZILIAN GP	Rio	11	Camel Team Lotus	3.5 Lotus 101-Judd V8	*fuel pump*
ret	SAN MARINO GP	Imola	11	Camel Team Lotus	3.5 Lotus 101-Judd V8	*engine*
ret	MONACO GP	Monte Carlo	11	Camel Team Lotus	3.5 Lotus 101-Judd V8	*collision with de Cesaris*
11	MEXICAN GP	Mexico City	11	Camel Team Lotus	3.5 Lotus 101-Judd V8	*understeer/1 lap behind*
ret	US GP (PHOENIX)	Phoenix	11	Camel Team Lotus	3.5 Lotus 101-Judd V8	*hit wall*
4	CANADIAN GP	Montreal	11	Camel Team Lotus	3.5 Lotus 101-Judd V8	*2 pit stops-tyres/low oil pressure*
8	FRENCH GP	Paul Ricard	11	Camel Team Lotus	3.5 Lotus 101-Judd V8	*2 pit stops-tyres/2 laps behind*
4	BRITISH GP	Silverstone	11	Camel Team Lotus	3.5 Lotus 101-Judd V8	
5	GERMAN GP	Hockenheim	11	Camel Team Lotus	3.5 Lotus 101-Judd V8	*pit stop-tyres/1 lap behind*
6	HUNGARIAN GP	Hungaroring	11	Camel Team Lotus	3.5 Lotus 101-Judd V8	*pit stop-tyres*
dnq	BELGIAN GP	Spa	11	Camel Team Lotus	3.5 Lotus 101-Judd V8	
ret	ITALIAN GP	Monza	11	Camel Team Lotus	3.5 Lotus 101-Judd V8	*spun avoiding Gachot*
ret	PORTUGUESE GP	Estoril	11	Camel Team Lotus	3.5 Lotus 101-Judd V8	*collision with Caffi*
8	SPANISH GP	Jerez	11	Camel Team Lotus	3.5 Lotus 101-Judd V8	*2 pit stops-tyres-puncture/-2 laps*
4	JAPANESE GP	Suzuka	11	Camel Team Lotus	3.5 Lotus 101-Judd V8	*1st place car dsq*
ret	AUSTRALIAN GP	Adelaide	11	Camel Team Lotus	3.5 Lotus 101-Judd V8	*hit Ghinzani in rain*

1990

4	US GP (PHOENIX)	Phoenix	20	Benetton Formula	3.5 Benetton B189B-Ford HB V8	*pit stop-tyres*
6	BRAZILIAN GP	Interlagos	20	Benetton Formula	3.5 Benetton B189B-Ford HB V8	*1 lap behind*
5	SAN MARINO GP	Imola	20	Benetton Formula	3.5 Benetton B190-Ford HB V8	*collision with Alesi/pit stop-tyres*
dsq	MONACO GP	Monte Carlo	20	Benetton Formula	3.5 Benetton B190-Ford HB V8	*spin-push start-black flagged*
2	CANADIAN GP	Montreal	20	Benetton Formula	3.5 Benetton B190-Ford HB V8	
6	MEXICAN GP	Mexico City	20	Benetton Formula	3.5 Benetton B190-Ford HB V8	*pit stop-tyres*
4	FRENCH GP	Paul Ricard	20	Benetton Formula	3.5 Benetton B190-Ford HB V8	*pit stop-tyres*
5	BRITISH GP	Silverstone	20	Benetton Formula	3.5 Benetton B190-Ford HB V8	*started from back/lost rear bodywork*
ret	GERMAN GP	Hockenheim	20	Benetton Formula	3.5 Benetton B190-Ford HB V8	*engine*
3	HUNGARIAN GP	Hungaroring	20	Benetton Formula	3.5 Benetton B190-Ford HB V8	*electrical problems*
5	BELGIAN GP	Spa	20	Benetton Formula	3.5 Benetton B190-Ford HB V8	*raced spare/understeer/no clutch*
7	ITALIAN GP	Monza	20	Benetton Formula	3.5 Benetton B190-Ford HB V8	*pit stop-puncture/1 lap behind*
5	PORTUGUESE GP	Estoril	20	Benetton Formula	3.5 Benetton B190-Ford HB V8	*pit stop-tyres*
ret	SPANISH GP	Jerez	20	Benetton Formula	3.5 Benetton B190-Ford HB V8	*electrics*
1	JAPANESE GP	Suzuka	20	Benetton Formula	3.5 Benetton B190-Ford HB V8	
1	AUSTRALIAN GP	Adelaide	20	Benetton Formula	3.5 Benetton B190-Ford HB V8	

1991

ret	US GP (PHOENIX)	Phoenix	20	Camel Benetton Ford	3.5 Benetton B190B-Ford HB V8	
5	BRAZILIAN GP	Interlagos	20	Camel Benetton Ford	3.5 Benetton B190B-Ford HB V8	
ret	SAN MARINO GP	Imola	20	Camel Benetton Ford	3.5 Benetton B191-Ford HB V8	*spun off lap 1*
ret	MONACO GP	Monte Carlo	20	Camel Benetton Ford	3.5 Benetton B191-Ford HB V8	*hit by Berger-suspension damage*
1	CANADIAN GP	Montreal	20	Camel Benetton Ford	3.5 Benetton B191-Ford HB V8	
ret	MEXICAN GP	Mexico City	20	Camel Benetton Ford	3.5 Benetton B191-Ford HB V8	*wheel bearing*
8	FRENCH GP	Magny Cours	20	Camel Benetton Ford	3.5 Benetton B191-Ford HB V8	*2 laps behind*
5	BRITISH GP	Silverstone	20	Camel Benetton Ford	3.5 Benetton B191-Ford HB V8	
ret	GERMAN GP	Hockenheim	20	Camel Benetton Ford	3.5 Benetton B191-Ford HB V8	*engine*
ret	HUNGARIAN GP	Hungaroring	20	Camel Benetton Ford	3.5 Benetton B191-Ford HB V8	*gearbox*
3	BELGIAN GP	Spa	20	Camel Benetton Ford	3.5 Benetton B191-Ford HB V8	
6	ITALIAN GP	Monza	20	Camel Benetton Ford	3.5 Benetton B191-Ford HB V8	
5	PORTUGUESE GP	Estoril	20	Camel Benetton Ford	3.5 Benetton B191-Ford HB V8	
11	SPANISH GP	Barcelona	20	Camel Benetton Ford	3.5 Benetton B191-Ford HB V8	*electrical problem/wet set up/-2 laps*
7	JAPANESE GP	Suzuka	20	Camel Benetton Ford	3.5 Benetton B191-Ford HB V8	*1lap behind*
4	AUSTRALIAN GP	Adelaide	20	Camel Benetton Ford	3.5 Benetton B191-Ford HB V8	*race shortened-14 laps due to rain*

GP Starts: 202 (204)   GP Wins: 23   Pole positions: 24   Fastest laps: 23   Points: 485.5

PIROCCHI, Renato (I) b 26/3/1933

1961

	Race	Circuit	No	Entrant	Car/Engine	Comment
12	ITALIAN GP	Monza	58	Pescara Racing Club	1.5 Cooper T51-Maserati 4	*5 laps behind*

GP Starts: 1   GP Wins: 0   Pole positions: 0   Fastest laps: 0   Points: 0

PIRONI, Didier (F) b 26/3/1952 – d 23/8/1987

1978

	Race	Circuit	No	Entrant	Car/Engine	Comment
14	ARGENTINE GP	Buenos Aires	3	Elf Team Tyrrell	3.0 Tyrrell 008-Cosworth V8	1 lap behind
6	BRAZILIAN GP	Rio	3	Elf Team Tyrrell	3.0 Tyrrell 008-Cosworth V8	1 lap behind
6	SOUTH AFRICAN GP	Kyalami	3	Elf Team Tyrrell	3.0 Tyrrell 008-Cosworth V8	1 lap behind
ret	US GP WEST	Long Beach	3	Elf Team Tyrrell	3.0 Tyrrell 008-Cosworth V8	gearbox
5	MONACO GP	Monte Carlo	3	Elf Team Tyrrell	3.0 Tyrrell 008-Cosworth V8	
6	BELGIAN GP	Zolder	3	Elf Team Tyrrell	3.0 Tyrrell 008-Cosworth V8	1 lap behind
12	SPANISH GP	Jarama	3	Elf Team Tyrrell	3.0 Tyrrell 008-Cosworth V8	pit stop/distributor/4 laps behind
ret	SWEDISH GP	Anderstorp	3	Elf Team Tyrrell	3.0 Tyrrell 008-Cosworth V8	collision with Brambilla
10	FRENCH GP	Paul Ricard	3	Elf Team Tyrrell	3.0 Tyrrell 008-Cosworth V8	
ret	BRITISH GP	Brands Hatch	3	Elf Team Tyrrell	3.0 Tyrrell 008-Cosworth V8	gearbox mounting bolts
5	GERMAN GP	Hockenheim	3	Elf Team Tyrrell	3.0 Tyrrell 008-Cosworth V8	
ret	AUSTRIAN GP	Österreichring	3	Elf Team Tyrrell	3.0 Tyrrell 008-Cosworth V8	crashed
ret	DUTCH GP	Zandvoort	3	Elf Team Tyrrell	3.0 Tyrrell 008-Cosworth V8	accident with Patrese
ret/dns	ITALIAN GP	Monza	3	Elf Team Tyrrell	3.0 Tyrrell 008-Cosworth V8	accident-first start/did not restart
10	US GP EAST	Watkins Glen	3	Elf Team Tyrrell	3.0 Tyrrell 008-Cosworth V8	1 lap behind
7	CANADIAN GP	Montreal	3	Elf Team Tyrrell	3.0 Tyrrell 008-Cosworth V8	

1979

	Race	Circuit	No	Entrant	Car/Engine	Comment
ret/dns	ARGENTINE GP	Buenos Aires	3	Team Tyrrell	3.0 Tyrrell 009-Cosworth V8	accident-first start/did not restart
4	BRAZILIAN GP	Interlagos	3	Team Tyrrell	3.0 Tyrrell 009-Cosworth V8	
ret	SOUTH AFRICAN GP	Kyalami	3	Team Tyrrell	3.0 Tyrrell 009-Cosworth V8	throttle linkage
dsq	US GP WEST	Long Beach	3	Team Tyrrell	3.0 Tyrrell 009-Cosworth V8	push start
6	SPANISH GP	Jarama	3	Team Tyrrell	3.0 Tyrrell 009-Cosworth V8	
3	BELGIAN GP	Zolder	3	Candy Tyrrell Team	3.0 Tyrrell 009-Cosworth V8	
ret	MONACO GP	Monte Carlo	3	Candy Tyrrell Team	3.0 Tyrrell 009-Cosworth V8	accident with Lauda
ret	FRENCH GP	Dijon	3	Candy Tyrrell Team	3.0 Tyrrell 009-Cosworth V8	suspension
10	BRITISH GP	Silverstone	3	Candy Tyrrell Team	3.0 Tyrrell 009-Cosworth V8	pit stop/2 laps behind
9	GERMAN GP	Hockenheim	3	Candy Tyrrell Team	3.0 Tyrrell 009-Cosworth V8	pit stop/1 lap behind
7	AUSTRIAN GP	Österreichring	3	Candy Tyrrell Team	3.0 Tyrrell 009-Cosworth V8	1 lap behind
ret	DUTCH GP	Zandvoort	3	Candy Tyrrell Team	3.0 Tyrrell 009-Cosworth V8	rear suspension
10	ITALIAN GP	Monza	3	Candy Tyrrell Team	3.0 Tyrrell 009-Cosworth V8	p stop-hit by Watson/1 lap behind
5	CANADIAN GP	Montreal	3	Candy Tyrrell Team	3.0 Tyrrell 009-Cosworth V8	1 lap behind
3	US GP EAST	Watkins Glen	3	Candy Tyrrell Team	3.0 Tyrrell 009-Cosworth V8	

1980

	Race	Circuit	No	Entrant	Car/Engine	Comment
ret	ARGENTINE GP	Buenos Aires	25	Equipe Ligier Gitanes	3.0 Ligier JS11/15-Cosworth V8	engine
4	BRAZILIAN GP	Interlagos	25	Equipe Ligier Gitanes	3.0 Ligier JS11/15-Cosworth V8	
3	SOUTH AFRICAN GP	Kyalami	25	Equipe Ligier Gitanes	3.0 Ligier JS11/15-Cosworth V8	
6	US GP WEST	Long Beach	25	Equipe Ligier Gitanes	3.0 Ligier JS11/15-Cosworth V8	1 lap behind
1	BELGIAN GP	Zolder	25	Equipe Ligier Gitanes	3.0 Ligier JS11/15-Cosworth V8	
ret	MONACO GP	Monte Carlo	25	Equipe Ligier Gitanes	3.0 Ligier JS11/15-Cosworth V8	gearbox/hit barrier when 1st/Pole
2	FRENCH GP	Paul Ricard	25	Equipe Ligier Gitanes	3.0 Ligier JS11/15-Cosworth V8	
ret	BRITISH GP	Brands Hatch	25	Equipe Ligier Gitanes	3.0 Ligier JS11/15-Cosworth V8	rim/tyre failure/crashed/Pole/FL
ret	GERMAN GP	Hockenheim	25	Equipe Ligier Gitanes	3.0 Ligier JS11/15-Cosworth V8	driveshaft
ret	AUSTRIAN GP	Österreichring	25	Equipe Ligier Gitanes	3.0 Ligier JS11/15-Cosworth V8	handling
ret	DUTCH GP	Zandvoort	25	Equipe Ligier Gitanes	3.0 Ligier JS11/15-Cosworth V8	accident with de Angelis
6	ITALIAN GP	Imola	25	Equipe Ligier Gitanes	3.0 Ligier JS11/15-Cosworth V8	1 lap behind
3*	CANADIAN GP	Montreal	25	Equipe Ligier Gitanes	3.0 Ligier JS11/15-Cosworth V8	* 1st on road but 1 min penalty/FL
3	US GP EAST	Watkins Glen	25	Equipe Ligier Gitanes	3.0 Ligier JS11/15-Cosworth V8	

1981

	Race	Circuit	No	Entrant	Car/Engine	Comment
ret	US GP WEST	Long Beach	28	Scuderia Ferrari SpA SEFAC	1.5 t/c Ferrari 126CK V6	engine
ret	BRAZILIAN GP	Rio	28	Scuderia Ferrari SpA SEFAC	1.5 t/c Ferrari 126CK V6	collision with Prost
ret	ARGENTINE GP	Buenos Aires	28	Scuderia Ferrari SpA SEFAC	1.5 t/c Ferrari 126CK V6	engine
5	SAN MARINO GP	Imola	28	Scuderia Ferrari SpA SEFAC	1.5 t/c Ferrari 126CK V6	
8	BELGIAN GP	Zolder	28	Scuderia Ferrari SpA SEFAC	1.5 t/c Ferrari 126CK V6	led race until brake problems
4	MONACO GP	Monte Carlo	28	Scuderia Ferrari SpA SEFAC	1.5 t/c Ferrari 126CK V6	1 lap behind
15	SPANISH GP	Jarama	28	Scuderia Ferrari SpA SEFAC	1.5 t/c Ferrari 126CK V6	pit stop/new nose/tyres/-4 laps
5	FRENCH GP	Dijon	28	Scuderia Ferrari SpA SEFAC	1.5 t/c Ferrari 126CK V6	1 lap behind
ret	BRITISH GP	Silverstone	28	Scuderia Ferrari SpA SEFAC	1.5 t/c Ferrari 126CK V6	engine
ret	GERMAN GP	Hockenheim	28	Scuderia Ferrari SpA SEFAC	1.5 t/c Ferrari 126CK V6	engine
9	AUSTRIAN GP	Österreichring	28	Scuderia Ferrari SpA SEFAC	1.5 t/c Ferrari 126CK V6	1 lap behind
ret	DUTCH GP	Zandvoort	28	Scuderia Ferrari SpA SEFAC	1.5 t/c Ferrari 126CK V6	accident with Tambay
5	ITALIAN GP	Monza	28	Scuderia Ferrari SpA SEFAC	1.5 t/c Ferrari 126CK V6	
ret	CANADIAN GP	Montreal	28	Scuderia Ferrari SpA SEFAC	1.5 t/c Ferrari 126CK V6	engine
9	CAESARS PALACE GP	Las Vegas	28	Scuderia Ferrari SpA SEFAC	1.5 t/c Ferrari 126CK V6	p stops/tyres/damage check/FL/-2 laps

1982

	Race	Circuit	No	Entrant	Car/Engine	Comment
18	SOUTH AFRICAN GP	Kyalami	28	Scuderia Ferrari SpA SEFAC	1.5 t/c Ferrari 126C2 V6	pit stops/tyres/6 laps behind
6*	BRAZILIAN GP	Rio	28	Scuderia Ferrari SpA SEFAC	1.5 t/c Ferrari 126C2 V6	pit stop/tyres/*1st & 2nd cars dsq
ret	US GP WEST	Long Beach	28	Scuderia Ferrari SpA SEFAC	1.5 t/c Ferrari 126C2 V6	hit wall
1	SAN MARINO GP	Imola	28	Scuderia Ferrari SpA SEFAC	1.5 t/c Ferrari 126C2 V6	overtook Villeneuve on last lap/FL
dns	BELGIAN GP	Zolder	28	Scuderia Ferrari SpA SEFAC	1.5 t/c Ferrari 126C2 V6	withdrawn after Villeneuve's accident
2/ret	MONACO GP	Monte Carlo	28	Scuderia Ferrari SpA SEFAC	1.5 t/c Ferrari 126C2 V6	electrics/1 lap behind
3	US GP (DETROIT)	Detroit	28	Scuderia Ferrari SpA SEFAC	1.5 t/c Ferrari 126C2 V6	
9	CANADIAN GP	Montreal	28	Scuderia Ferrari SpA SEFAC	1.5 t/c Ferrari 126C2 V6	p stop/mechanical/Pole/FL/-3 laps
1	DUTCH GP	Zandvoort	28	Scuderia Ferrari SpA SEFAC	1.5 t/c Ferrari 126C2 V6	
2	BRITISH GP	Brands Hatch	28	Scuderia Ferrari SpA SEFAC	1.5 t/c Ferrari 126C2 V6	
3	FRENCH GP	Paul Ricard	28	Scuderia Ferrari SpA SEFAC	1.5 t/c Ferrari 126C2 V6	
dns	GERMAN GP	Hockenheim	28	Scuderia Ferrari SpA SEFAC	1.5 t/c Ferrari 126C2 V6	practice accident/seriously injured/Pole

GP Starts: 68 (70)   GP Wins: 3   Pole positions: 4   Fastest laps: 5   Points: 101

DIDIER PIRONI

Pironi's ambition to become France's first-ever World Champion driver was never realised. The crash at Hockenheim in 1982 which destroyed his career and almost cost him his legs would see to that, leaving the cool and unemotional Frenchman to fight the greater battle of learning to walk again, while Alain Prost was enjoying his nation's plaudits in 1985.

Didier's interest in motor racing was awakened by a visit to a meeting with his cousin José Dolhem, and as soon as he was old enough he attended the Winfield racing school, winning the prize of an Elf-sponsored Martini for 1973. It was a hard learning year for the young Pironi, who, rather than whingeing, clinically analysed all the ingredients that were lacking in his first season and set about putting them into place for his return in 1974. His attention to detail obviously paid dividends for Pironi became French Formule Renault champion at the wheel of a Martini MK14.

Moving into Formule Super Renault in 1975 as number two to René Arnoux, Didier dutifully supported his team-mate before taking over the number one seat a year later. His dominance was almost total and he ran away with the championship, gaining promotion to the Elf Martini Formula 2 squad in 1977, again as number two to Arnoux. While he was finding his feet in this category, Pironi gambled on dropping into Formula 3 for just one event, the Monaco Formula 3 race. His reasoning was sound, for a win here would be a valuable calling card in his future dealings. Naturally mission was accomplished and he resumed his Formula 2 racing with the air of a man who knew his destiny. Raising his game, by the end of the year he had taken his first win at Estoril, and earned a Grand Prix contract with Tyrrell for the 1978 season.

As one now expected of this coolest of customers, his first tilt at the big time was accomplished with all the aplomb of a seasoned veteran. Finishing four of his first six races in the points maybe raised expectations a little too high, as he ended the year with a few shunts. However, there was also the considerable kudos of a win at Le Mans in the Elf-backed Alpine-Renault to reinforce his burgeoning reputation. In fact Didier was top of the turbo team's shopping list for 1979, but Tyrrell kept him to his contract, and thus he spent the year looking for an escape route, which he found in the shape of a move to Ligier for 1980.

Overshadowing the incumbent, Jacques Laffite, with some stunning drives, Pironi took his first Grand Prix win at Zolder, and was unlucky not to win the British GP at Brands Hatch after a brilliant drive through the field. With Jody Scheckter heading for retirement, another door opened for Didier, who joined Villeneuve at Maranello for 1981. The new turbo cars were unrefined, but Gilles was at his brilliant best, leaving Pironi groping somewhat for the first time. Clearly a single fourth place was unacceptable to Ferrari, but it was doubly so to Pironi, who resolved not to be found wanting in 1982.

Four races into what was to prove a bitter and tragic season came a flashpoint at Imola when Pironi stole the win from Villeneuve on the last lap against team orders. All lines of communication between the two drivers were cut. Two weeks later at Zolder came Villeneuve's horrendous fatal accident, and previous feudings were now irrelevant. Didier, now centre stage at Ferrari, unleashed a superb run of impressive performances which came to an end when, unsighted in pouring rain, he ran into Prost's Renault in practice for the German GP. Pironi's season was over and his total of 39 points left him tantalisingly within touching distance of the title before Keke Rosberg edged him out by a mere five points.

Although, almost miraculously, Pironi's feet and ankles were saved, he would never regain the feel and movement necessary to allow him to return to the cockpit. For thrills he turned to the dangerous sport of powerboat racing, which became a lethal pastime when he crashed off the Isle of Wight in August 1987.

PIRRO Emanuele (I) b 12/1/1962

1989

	Race	Circuit	No	Entrant	Car/Engine	Comment
9	FRENCH GP	Paul Ricard	20	Benetton Formula Ltd	3.5 Benetton B188-Cosworth V8	2 laps behind
11	BRITISH GP	Silverstone	20	Benetton Formula Ltd	3.5 Benetton B189-Cosworth V8	2 laps behind
ret	GERMAN GP	Hockenheim	20	Benetton Formula Ltd	3.5 Benetton B189-Cosworth V8	accident
8	HUNGARIAN GP	Hungaroring	20	Benetton Formula Ltd	3.5 Benetton B189-Cosworth V8	1 lap behind
10	BELGIAN GP	Spa	20	Benetton Formula Ltd	3.5 Benetton B189-Cosworth V8	1 lap behind
ret	ITALIAN GP	Monza	20	Benetton Formula Ltd	3.5 Benetton B189-Cosworth V8	clutch on lap 1
ret	PORTUGUESE GP	Estoril	20	Benetton Formula Ltd	3.5 Benetton B189-Cosworth V8	shock absorber
ret	SPANISH GP	Jerez	20	Benetton Formula Ltd	3.5 Benetton B189-Cosworth V8	leg cramp-spun off when 4th
ret	JAPANESE GP	Suzuka	20	Benetton Formula Ltd	3.5 Benetton B189-Cosworth V8	accident with de Cesaris
5	AUSTRALIAN GP	Adelaide	20	Benetton Formula Ltd	3.5 Benetton B189-Cosworth V8	2 laps behind

1990

	Race	Circuit	No	Entrant	Car/Engine	Comment
ret	SAN MARINO GP	Imola	21	Scuderia Italia SpA	3.5 BMS Dallara 190-Cosworth V8	engine
ret/dns	MONACO GP	Monte Carlo	21	Scuderia Italia SpA	3.5 BMS Dallara 190-Cosworth V8	stalled on dummy grid/did not start
ret	CANADIAN GP	Montreal	21	Scuderia Italia SpA	3.5 BMS Dallara 190-Cosworth V8	collided with Alboreto
ret	MEXICAN GP	Mexico City	21	Scuderia Italia SpA	3.5 BMS Dallara 190-Cosworth V8	engine
ret	FRENCH GP	Paul Ricard	21	Scuderia Italia SpA	3.5 BMS Dallara 190-Cosworth V8	brakes-spun off
11	BRITISH GP	Silverstone	21	Scuderia Italia SpA	3.5 BMS Dallara 190-Cosworth V8	2 laps behind
ret	GERMAN GP	Hockenheim	21	Scuderia Italia SpA	3.5 BMS Dallara 190-Cosworth V8	startline collision with Brabham
10	HUNGARIAN GP	Hungaroring	21	Scuderia Italia SpA	3.5 BMS Dallara 190-Cosworth V8	1 lap behind
ret	BELGIAN GP	Spa	21	Scuderia Italia SpA	3.5 BMS Dallara 190-Cosworth V8	cracked water pipe
ret	ITALIAN GP	Monza	21	Scuderia Italia SpA	3.5 BMS Dallara 190-Cosworth V8	gearbox-spun off
15	PORTUGUESE GP	Estoril	21	Scuderia Italia SpA	3.5 BMS Dallara 190-Cosworth V8	3 laps behind
ret	SPANISH GP	Jerez	21	Scuderia Italia SpA	3.5 BMS Dallara 190-Cosworth V8	spun off
ret	JAPANESE GP	Suzuka	21	Scuderia Italia SpA	3.5 BMS Dallara 190-Cosworth V8	engine
ret	AUSTRALIAN GP	Adelaide	21	Scuderia Italia SpA	3.5 BMS Dallara 190-Cosworth V8	engine

1991

	Race	Circuit	No	Entrant	Car/Engine	Comment
ret	US GP (PHOENIX)	Phoenix	21	Scuderia Italia SpA	3.5 BMS Dallara 191-Judd V10	clutch
11	BRAZILIAN GP	Rio	21	Scuderia Italia SpA	3.5 BMS Dallara 191-Judd V10	3 laps behind
dnpq	SAN MARINO GP	Imola	21	Scuderia Italia SpA	3.5 BMS Dallara 191-Judd V10	
6	MONACO GP	Monte Carlo	21	Scuderia Italia SpA	3.5 BMS Dallara 191-Judd V10	1 lap behind

9	CANADIAN GP	Montreal	21	Scuderia Italia SpA	3.5 BMS Dallara 191-Judd V10	1 lap behind
dnpq	MEXICAN GP	Mexico City	21	Scuderia Italia SpA	3.5 BMS Dallara 191-Judd V10	
dnpq	FRENCH GP	Magny Cours	21	Scuderia Italia SpA	3.5 BMS Dallara 191-Judd V10	
10	BRITISH GP	Silverstone	21	Scuderia Italia SpA	3.5 BMS Dallara 191-Judd V10	2 laps behind
10	GERMAN GP	Hockenheim	21	Scuderia Italia SpA	3.5 BMS Dallara 191-Judd V10	1 lap behind
ret	HUNGARIAN GP	Hungaroring	21	Scuderia Italia SpA	3.5 BMS Dallara 191-Judd V10	engine-oil pressure
8	BELGIAN GP	Spa	21	Scuderia Italia SpA	3.5 BMS Dallara 191-Judd V10	1 lap behind
10	ITALIAN GP	Monza	21	Scuderia Italia SpA	3.5 BMS Dallara 191-Judd V10	1 lap behind
ret	PORTUGUESE GP	Estoril	21	Scuderia Italia SpA	3.5 BMS Dallara 191-Judd V10	engine
15	SPANISH GP	Barcelona	21	Scuderia Italia SpA	3.5 BMS Dallara 191-Judd V10	3 laps behind
ret	JAPANESE GP	Suzuka	21	Scuderia Italia SpA	3.5 BMS Dallara 191-Judd V10	spun off avoiding de Cesaris
7	AUSTRALIAN GP	Adelaide	21	Scuderia Italia SpA	3.5 BMS Dallara 191-Judd V10	race stopped after 14 laps-rain

GP Starts: 36 (37)   GP Wins: 0   Pole positions: 0   Fastest laps: 0   Points: 3

EMANUELE PIRRO

Something of a nearly-man, Pirro's career is a tale of ups and downs, as the unlucky Italian has always seemed to fall short of ultimate success in most of the categories he has raced in.

Moving from karts to Formula Fiat, he won the championship in 1980 before graduating to the European Formula 3 series, taking the runner-up slot behind Euroracing team-mate Larrauri in 1982. When the teamwent to F1 in 1983, Pirro had to find a ride elsewhere and after a bright start faded to third in the championship. Stepping up to Formula 2 for 1984 with Onyx, he established a good rapport with the team, and stayed with them for F3000 in 1985, victories at Thruxton and Vallelunga earning him a Brabham F1 test which came to nought. So it was back to F3000 in 1986, and second place in the championship behind Capelli, a mid-season slump costing Pirro his title chance.

Still seeking an F1 ride, Emanuele busied himself with some superb performances in BMW touring cars, and took on the role of test driver for McLaren before replacing Herbert at Benetton midway through 1989. His half-season was not productive enough, and he was dropped for 1990, finding a place in the Dallara squad for the next two seasons. With no worthwhile results to speak of, Pirro found himself passed over in favour of fresher talent in 1992, switching to the Italian touring car championship with a Bigazzi BMW.

ERIC van de POELE

This popular Belgian began his career in French Formula 3 in 1984, before a season in Belgian Group N and the Benelux Formula Ford championships. Eric then briefly tasted the German F3 series but really made a name for himself in the Zakspeed BMW Junior team, winning the German championship, with the added highlight of a victory in the Spa 24 Hours with Theys and Martin.

After another season of touring cars with Schnitzer BMW, Eric made the break into single-seaters at last with an F3000 drive with GA Motorsports in 1989. He was to enjoy two happy years with the team, taking second place in the 1990 championship after three wins (Pau, Birmingham and Nogaro).

With long-time sponsors Lease Plan behind him, Eric joined the newly formed Lambo team for a crack at Grands Prix in 1991. The car was never a competitive proposition, but mysteriously it ran very well at Imola, van de Poele holding a secure fifth place until a fuel pump failure on the last lap. For 1992 Eric threw in his lot with the by now distinctly shaky Brabham team for another frustrating string of non-qualifications, before jumping out of the frying pan and into the fire with a Fondmetal team also facing imminent extinction. He was on the sidelines for much of 1993 and his future appears to lie in a return to touring cars.

POELE van de, Eric (B) b 30/9/1961

	Race	Circuit	No	Entrant	Car/Engine	Comment
	1991					
dnpq	US GP (PHOENIX)	Phoenix	35	Modena Team SpA	3.5 Lambo 291-Lamborghini V12	
dnpq	BRAZILIAN GP	Interlagos	35	Modena Team SpA	3.5 Lambo 291-Lamborghini V12	
9/ret	SAN MARINO GP	Imola	35	Modena Team SpA	3.5 Lambo 291-Lamborghini V12	fuel pump/4 laps behind
dnpq	MONACO GP	Monte Carlo	35	Modena Team SpA	3.5 Lambo 291-Lamborghini V12	
dnpq	CANADIAN GP	Montreal	35	Modena Team SpA	3.5 Lambo 291-Lamborghini V12	
dnpq	MEXICAN GP	Mexico City	35	Modena Team SpA	3.5 Lambo 291-Lamborghini V12	
dnpq	FRENCH GP	Magny Cours	35	Modena Team SpA	3.5 Lambo 291-Lamborghini V12	
dnpq	BRITISH GP	Silverstone	35	Modena Team SpA	3.5 Lambo 291-Lamborghini V12	
dnq	GERMAN GP	Hockenheim	35	Modena Team SpA	3.5 Lambo 291-Lamborghini V12	
dnq	HUNGARIAN GP	Hungaroring	35	Modena Team SpA	3.5 Lambo 291-Lamborghini V12	
dnq	BELGIAN GP	Spa	35	Modena Team SpA	3.5 Lambo 291-Lamborghini V12	
dnq	ITALIAN GP	Monza	35	Modena Team SpA	3.5 Lambo 291-Lamborghini V12	
dnq	PORTUGUESE GP	Estoril	35	Modena Team SpA	3.5 Lambo 291-Lamborghini V12	
dnq	SPANISH GP	Barcelona	35	Modena Team SpA	3.5 Lambo 291-Lamborghini V12	
dnq	JAPANESE GP	Suzuka	35	Modena Team SpA	3.5 Lambo 291-Lamborghini V12	
dnq	AUSTRALIAN GP	Adelaide	35	Modena Team SpA	3.5 Lambo 291-Lamborghini V12	
	1992					
13	SOUTH AFRICAN GP	Kyalami	7	Motor Racing Developments Ltd	3.5 Brabham BT60B-Judd V10	4 laps behind
dnq	MEXICAN GP	Mexico City	7	Motor Racing Developments Ltd	3.5 Brabham BT60B-Judd V10	
dnq	BRAZILIAN GP	Interlagos	7	Motor Racing Developments Ltd	3.5 Brabham BT60B-Judd V10	
dnq	SPANISH GP	Barcelona	7	Motor Racing Developments Ltd	3.5 Brabham BT60B-Judd V10	
dnq	SAN MARINO GP	Imola	7	Motor Racing Developments Ltd	3.5 Brabham BT60B-Judd V10	
dnq	MONACO GP	Monte Carlo	7	Motor Racing Developments Ltd	3.5 Brabham BT60B-Judd V10	
dnq	CANADIAN GP	Montreal	7	Motor Racing Developments Ltd	3.5 Brabham BT60B-Judd V10	
dnq	FRENCH GP	Magny Cours	7	Motor Racing Developments Ltd	3.5 Brabham BT60B-Judd V10	
dpq	BRITISH GP	Silverstone	7	Motor Racing Developments Ltd	3.5 Brabham BT60B-Judd V10	
dnq	GERMAN GP	Hockenheim	7	Motor Racing Developments Ltd	3.5 Brabham BT60B-Judd V10	
ret	HUNGARIAN GP	Hungaroring	14	Fondmetal	3.5 Fondmetal GR02-Ford HB V8	multiple collision-spun off-lap 1
10	BELGIAN GP	Spa	14	Fondmetal	3.5 Fondmetal GR02-Ford HB V8	1 lap behind
ret	ITALIAN GP	Monza	14	Fondmetal	3.5 Fondmetal GR02-Ford HB V8	clutch

GP Starts: 5   GP Wins: 0   Pole positions: 0   Fastest laps: 0   Points: 0

DENNIS POORE

A British hill-climb champion in 1950 with his Alfa Romeo 3.8S, Poore, a wealthy industrialist, briefly became a member of the Connaught Racing Syndicate in 1952, scoring a fine fourth place in the British GP. He then severed his connections with the Send concern and linked up with the Aston Martin sports car team, winning the 1955 Goodwood International 9 Hours in a DB3S with Peter Walker.

He continued to race his old Alfa Romeo in numerous events during this period, winning the Dick Seaman Trophy race three times in a row between 1951 and 1953.

ALFONSO de PORTAGO

One of the most colourful characters ever to have been seen in motor racing, 'Fon' was a fantastic all-round sportsman. A Spanish nobleman, he was three times French amateur champion jockey, and appeared twice at Aintree – where he never raced cars – in the Grand National steeplechase; he was an international-class swimmer; and in addition he created the Spanish bobsleigh team to take part in the 1956 Winter Olympics.

He took up motor racing in 1954, briefly sharing Schell's big 4.5-litre Ferrari on its way to second place in the Buenos Aires 1000 Km, but usually handled less potent machinery to begin with, his Maserati 2-litre winning a race at Metz.

In 1955 de Portago joined the Scuderia Ferrari and while his F1 outings were restricted to non-championship races his sports car programme saw him take second in the Venezuelan GP and win the Governor's Cup at Nassau. He was included in Ferrari's large Grand Prix squad during 1956, sharing the second-place car in the British GP with Collins, while in sports cars the highlight of his season was a win in the Tour de France in his Ferrari GT.

The 1957 season started well with a shared fifth place in the Argentine GP and success in sports car events, de Portago taking a win at Montlhéry and third places in both the Buenos Aires 1000 Km and the Cuban GP, the latter after a brilliant drive when time was lost at a long pit stop. He was unhappy at taking part in the Mille Miglia, which he considered unnecessarily dangerous, but he competed nevertheless, only for disaster to strike less than 120 km before the finish. It is thought that a tyre burst, hurling the Ferrari of de Portago and his long-time friend and co-driver Ed Nelson into the crowd. Ten unfortunate spectators were killed, along with the car's occupants, and the famous road race was banned forthwith by the Italian government.

POLLET, Jacques (F) b 2/7/1932

	1954					
	Race	Circuit	No	Entrant	Car/Engine	Comment
ret	FRENCH GP	Reims	26	Equipe Gordini	2.5 Gordini Type 16 6	
ret	SPANISH GP	Pedralbes	48	Equipe Gordini	2.5 Gordini Type 16 6	mechanical
	1955					
7	MONACO GP	Monte Carlo	10	Equipe Gordini	2.5 Gordini Type 16 6	
10	DUTCH GP	Zandvoort	24	Equipe Gordini	2.5 Gordini Type 16 6	10 laps behind
ret	ITALIAN GP	Monza	26	Equipe Gordini	2.5 Gordini Type 16 6	mechanical

GP Starts: 5   GP Wins: 0   Pole positions: 0   Fastest laps: 0   Points: 0

PON, Ben (NL) b 9/12/1936

	1962					
	Race	Circuit	No	Entrant	Car/Engine	Comment
ret	DUTCH GP	Zandvoort	15	Ecurie Maarsbergen	1.5 Porsche 787 F4	spun off

GP Starts: 1   GP Wins: 0   Pole positions: 0   Fastest laps: 0   Points: 0

POORE, Dennis (GB) b 19/8/1916 – d 12/2/1987

	1952					
	Race	Circuit	No	Entrant	Car/Engine	Comment
4	BRITISH GP	Silverstone	6	Connaught Engineering	2.0 Connaught A Type 4	
12	ITALIAN GP	Monza	30	Connaught Racing Syndicate	2.0 Connaught A Type 4	

GP Starts: 3   GP Wins: 0   Pole positions: 0   Fastest laps: 0   Points: 3

PORTAGO, Alfonso de (E) b 11/10/1928 – d 12/5/1957

	1956					
	Race	Circuit	No	Entrant	Car/Engine	Comment
ret	FRENCH GP	Reims	16	Scuderia Ferrari	2.5 Lancia-Ferrari D50 V8	gearbox
2*	BRITISH GP	Silverstone	4	Scuderia Ferrari	2.5 Lancia-Ferrari D50 V8	* Collins took over car
10*	"	"	3	Scuderia Ferrari	2.5 Lancia-Ferrari D50 V8	* took over Castellotti's car
ret*	GERMAN GP	Nürburgring	5	Scuderia Ferrari	2.5 Lancia-Ferrari D50 V8	* Collins took over/crashed
ret	ITALIAN GP	Monza	20	Scuderia Ferrari	2.5 Lancia-Ferrari D50 V8	puncture
	1957					
5*	ARGENTINE GP	Buenos Aires	20	Scuderia Ferrari	2.5 Lancia-Ferrari D50 V8	* took over Gonzalez's car

GP Starts: 5   GP Wins: 0   Pole positions: 0   Fastest laps: 0   Points: 4

POSEY, Sam (USA) b 26/5/1944

	Race	Circuit	No	Entrant	Car/Engine	Comment
	1971					
ret	US GP	Watkins Glen	19	Team Surtees	3.0 Surtees TS9-Cosworth V8	engine
	1972					
12	US GP	Watkins Glen	34	Champcarr Inc	3.0 Surtees TS9B-Cosworth V8	2 laps behind

GP Starts: 2   GP Wins: 0   Pole positions: 0   Fastest laps: 0   Points: 0

POZZI, Charles (F) b 27/85/1909

	Race	Circuit	No	Entrant	Car/Engine	Comment
	1950					
6*	FRENCH GP	Reims	26	Charles Pozzi	4.5 Lago-Talbot T26C 6	* Rosier took over

GP Starts: 1   GP Wins: 0   Pole positions: 0   Fastest laps: 0   Points: 0

PRETORIOUS, Jackie (ZA) b 22/11/1934

	Race	Circuit	No	Entrant	Car/Engine	Comment
	1965					
dnpq	SOUTH AFRICAN GP	East London	29	Jackie Pretorious	1.5 LDS 03-Alfa Romeo 4	did not qualify for official practice
	1968					
nc	SOUTH AFRICAN GP	Kyalami	23	Team Pretoria	2.7 Brabham BT7-Climax 4	10 laps behind
	1971					
ret	SOUTH AFRICAN GP	Kyalami	25	Team Gunston	3.0 Brabham BT26A-Cosworth V8	engine
	1973					
ret	SOUTH AFRICAN GP	Kyalami	20	Frank Williams Racing Cars	3.0 Iso Williams FX3B-Cosworth V8	overheating

GP Starts: 3   GP Wins: 0   Pole positions: 0   Fastest laps: 0   Points: 0

PROPHET, David (GB) b 9/10/1937 – d 29/3/1981

	Race	Circuit	No	Entrant	Car/Engine	Comment
	1963					
ret	SOUTH AFRICAN GP	East London	22	David Prophet	1.5 Brabham BT6-Ford 4	oil pressure
	1965					
14	SOUTH AFRICAN GP	East London	19	David Prophet Racing	1.5 Brabham BT10-Ford 4	14 laps behind

GP Starts: 2   GP Wins: 0   Pole positions: 0   Fastest laps: 0   Points: 0

SAM POSEY

Posey was a versatile American driver who loved the ambience of Formula 1 and wanted to make a real impact on the Grand Prix scene, but never had the chance to do so.

In the late sixties, he made an impression in Can-Am and sports cars, and he finished fourth at Daytona and Le Mans in 1970, but his real success came in Formula A, Sam challenging Hobbs and McRae for the championships of 1971 and 1972.

After a brief tilt at USAC, finishing fifth at both Indianapolis and Pocono in 1972, and sixth at Ontario in 1973, Sam focused his attentions on IMSA and sports car racing and was a Le Mans regular for many years.

JACKIE PRETORIOUS

A leading light on the thriving South African racing scene in the 1960s, Jackie handled the local Serrurier-built LDS-Climax in national events, but used a Lotus to finish ninth in the non-championship 1966 Grand Prix. Between 1968 and 1970 he was successful in Lola single-seaters and sports cars entered by Serrurier, but his best season was predictably when handling the Team Gunston Brabham BT26A in 1971, Pretorious winning championship races at Killarney and the Natal Roy Hesketh circuit.

At the 1973 South African Grand Prix, Jackie was called in by Williams to replace Nanni Galli, injured in an earlier testing accident, before returning to business in the local series with his ex-Motul Brabham BT38.

CHARLES POZZI

A shrewd motor dealer who traded in luxury cars after the war, Pozzi was briefly associated with Paul Vallée's Ecurie France before leaving together with Eugène Chaboud. The pair formed their own team, Ecurie Leutitia, usually fielding Delahayes, with one of which Pozzi won the 1949 Comminges GP at St Gaudens. In 1950 he shared Rosier's Talbot in the French GP, but for the most part he confined himself to sports cars, winning

the Casablanca 12 Hours in a Talbot in 1952. During 1953-54 he raced François Picard's Ferrari, before pressure of business forced his retirement, as he was by now the importer for both Chrysler and Rolls-Royce in France. He maintained his interest in the sport for many years and, having become the Ferrari importer, he entered Daytonas and 512Bs at Le Mans throughout the seventies.

DAVID PROPHET

Never a driver likely to make an impression above national level, Prophet, a Midlands motor trader, raced enthusiastically in some serious machinery for more than a decade. While competing in Formula Junior, he took his Brabham to South Africa late in the 1963 season and raced in the national Grand Prix, also taking sixth place on aggregate in the Rand GP.

David raced in European F2 from 1964 to 1967 with little success, but found more joy in sports cars, particularly with the Lotus 30. In 1968-69, he raced his Ford GT40 and then a Lola T70, before becoming a regular competitor in Formula 5000 in 1970 with a McLaren 10B which he then took to the non-championship 1971 Argentine GP to claim a lucrative fourth place on aggregate after more fancied runners had fallen by the wayside. He was killed in 1981 when the helicopter in which he was leaving the Silverstone circuit crashed just after take-off.

ALAIN PROST

Try comparing some great racing drivers with the work of famous artists: for Senna read Dali, Stewart – Warhol, Lauda – Mondrian; and Prost? Well, perhaps Monet. His work seems easy, but what nuance and depth when you look closely. Only a bit of fun, but drivers, just like painters, have their own personalities which are reflected on the canvas of the Grand Prix track.

At the time of writing Prost has just retired, having won four World Championships and 51 Grands Prix and amassed nearly 800 points from 199 starts. Simple mathematics tell the story: an average of four points from every Grand Prix. Yet despite these staggering statistics, there are plenty of fans who wouldn't give the Frenchman the time of day. Perhaps only Stewart can divide opinion so sharply, and the issues were much clearer in his case, being centred on safety.

Prost's car racing career has been set on a stellar path from the start. After racing karts in the company of Cheever and Patrese he turned to cars in 1975, enrolling at the Winfield school. He won the traditional Pilote Elf prize of a car for the following season's Formule Renault series and certainly put it to good use, winning 12 of 13 races. Promotion to Formule Super Renault duly followed, and eight wins later that trophy went on the Prost mantelpiece as well. Moving into Formula 3 in 1978, the Martini MK21B-Renault was not truly competitive until a close-season revamp saw the car emerge as the MK27. Alain proved virtually unbeatable with it, taking the European and French titles and the all-important Monaco F3 race. He was ready for Formula 1, and McLaren were the first takers.

In 1980 the team were not in great shape and on the point of total transition, but Prost was unfazed and scored points in his first two Grands Prix. Even in that first season the traits that have since served him so well were there: the smooth driving style, the willingness to speak his mind honestly and a genuine concern about the sport and its image. The chance to join Renault for 1991 was too good to turn down and Prost moved in to completely flummox partner Arnoux. Alain scored three wins that year and two more were added in 1982, but there could have been many others if the Renault had not let him down so often. It was largely thanks to Prost that the RE30B had reached such a competitive position, and he was just as formidable a force in 1983 with its successor. Apart from an error at Zandvoort he hardly put a foot wrong, yet still the championship slipped through his fingers at the very last. Renault and the French press pointed the finger of blame at a bemused Prost, who took the only course of action possible and high-tailed it to McLaren, who knew better than to look a gift horse in the mouth. While the Renault F1 effort slid into oblivion over the next two seasons, Alain was busy winning the small matter of 12 Grands Prix. In 1984 he lost out to Niki Lauda by just half a point, but finally cracked it to become the first French World Champion in 1985.

With Williams-Honda dominant in 1986, few gave Alain any hope of retaining his crown, but he hung in, picking up every point possible and coaxing four wins from the McLaren-TAG to steal the title in Adelaide. The following year even Prost's

powers were unable to halt the Williams steamroller, but he did overtake Jackie Stewart's long-standing total of Grand Prix wins in Portugal. Then in 1988 Prost too had Honda power, but with the Japanese V6 came Ayrton Senna. That first season saw a McLaren carve-up, with the pair winning all but one of the 16 races. Senna had the edge and Prost, at times non-plussed, had to settle for second-best for once. It was a different story in 1989; Alain raised his game and the battle was on, especially after a steady deterioration in the drivers' relationship. The title was settled in the Frenchman's favour when he subtly chopped the Brazilian at Suzuka. It was truly an awful way to decide a championship, and yet history repeated itself in 1990, except that Alain was now on the receiving end as Senna drove into the back of his Ferrari at the start. This wiped out a season's truly brilliant endeavour by Prost, who had moved into his new environment and immediately given the Italian team a real sense of purpose. Unfortunately this was not to be maintained in 1991, when Maranello politics and intrigue reached new heights, with Prost locked in bitter off-track arguments. When it finally arrived, the new 643 was disappointing and by the season's end the Frenchman had been fired for his outspoken views.

Disillusioned, he took a year's sabbatical from the cockpit, despite massive pressure to try and persuade him to join Ligier. This move left him plenty of time to weigh up his options and by mid-1992 he had tied up a deal to join Williams in 1993, expecting to partner Nigel Mansell. Of course it is now history that Nigel chose to vacate his seat, leaving Prost in a very strong position to take his fourth World Championship. In a no-win situation, Alain got the job done in his usual undramatic style, his season yielding another seven wins. With the prospect of Ayrton Senna joining the team in 1994, Prost concluded that he just didn't need the aggravation, and announced his impending retirement at Estoril – though overtures from McLaren's Ron Dennis could yet tempt the mercurial little Frenchman to change his mind.

PROST, Alain (F) b 24/2/1955

1980

	Race	Circuit	No	Entrant	Car/Engine	Comment
6	ARGENTINE GP	Buenos Aires	8	Marlboro Team McLaren	3.0 McLaren M29-Cosworth V8	1 lap behind
5	BRAZILIAN GP	Interlagos	8	Marlboro Team McLaren	3.0 McLaren M29-Cosworth V8	
dns	SOUTH AFRICAN GP	Kyalami	8	Marlboro Team McLaren	3.0 McLaren M29-Cosworth V8	practice accident/hurt wrist
ret	BELGIAN GP	Zolder	8	Marlboro Team McLaren	3.0 McLaren M29-Cosworth V8	transmission
ret	MONACO GP	Monte Carlo	8	Marlboro Team McLaren	3.0 McLaren M29-Cosworth V8	multiple accident on first lap
ret	FRENCH GP	Paul Ricard	8	Marlboro Team McLaren	3.0 McLaren M29-Cosworth V8	transmission
6	BRITISH GP	Brands Hatch	8	Marlboro Team McLaren	3.0 McLaren M29-Cosworth V8	1 lap behind
11	GERMAN GP	Hockenheim	8	Marlboro Team McLaren	3.0 McLaren M29-Cosworth V8	pit stops/tyre/skirt problems
7	AUSTRIAN GP	Österreichring	8	Marlboro Team McLaren	3.0 McLaren M29-Cosworth V8	
6	DUTCH GP	Zandvoort	8	Marlboro Team McLaren	3.0 McLaren M30-Cosworth V8	
7	ITALIAN GP	Imola	8	Marlboro Team McLaren	3.0 McLaren M30-Cosworth V8	1 lap behind
ret	CANADIAN GP	Montreal	8	Marlboro Team McLaren	3.0 McLaren M30-Cosworth V8	suspension failure/accident
dns	US GP EAST	Watkins Glen	8	Marlboro Team McLaren	3.0 McLaren M30-Cosworth V8	practice accident

1981

	Race	Circuit	No	Entrant	Car/Engine	Comment
ret	US GP WEST	Long Beach	15	Equipe Renault Elf	1.5 t/c Renault RE22B V6	hit by de Cesaris
ret	BRAZILIAN GP	Rio	15	Equipe Renault Elf	1.5 t/c Renault RE22B V6	hit by Pironi

3	ARGENTINE GP	Buenos Aires	15	Equipe Renault Elf	1.5 t/c Renault RE22B V6	
ret	SAN MARINO GP	Imola	15	Equipe Renault Elf	1.5 t/c Renault RE22B V6	gearbox
ret	BELGIAN GP	Zolder	15	Equipe Renault Elf	1.5 t/c Renault RE30 V6	clutch
ret	MONACO GP	Monte Carlo	15	Equipe Renault Elf	1.5 t/c Renault RE30 V6	engine
ret	SPANISH GP	Jarama	15	Equipe Renault Elf	1.5 t/c Renault RE30 V6	spun off
1*	FRENCH GP	Dijon	15	Equipe Renault Elf	1.5 t/c Renault RE30 V6	* 2nd first race/1st second race/FL
ret	BRITISH GP	Silverstone	15	Equipe Renault Elf	1.5 t/c Renault RE30 V6	engine
2	GERMAN GP	Hockenheim	15	Equipe Renault Elf	1.5 t/c Renault RE30 V6	Pole
ret	AUSTRIAN GP	Österreichring	15	Equipe Renault Elf	1.5 t/c Renault RE30 V6	front suspension
1	DUTCH GP	Zandvoort	15	Equipe Renault Elf	1.5 t/c Renault RE30 V6	Pole
1	ITALIAN GP	Monza	15	Equipe Renault Elf	1.5 t/c Renault RE30 V6	
ret	CANADIAN GP	Montreal	15	Equipe Renault Elf	1.5 t/c Renault RE30 V6	accident with Mansell
2	CAESARS PALACE GP	Las Vegas	15	Equipe Renault Elf	1.5 t/c Renault RE30 V6	

1982

1	SOUTH AFRICAN GP	Kyalami	15	Equipe Renault Elf	1.5 t/c Renault RE30B V6	FL
1*	BRAZILIAN GP	Rio	15	Equipe Renault Elf	1.5 t/c Renault RE30B V6	* 1st & 2nd place cars dsq/Pole
ret	US GP WEST	Long Beach	15	Equipe Renault Elf	1.5 t/c Renault RE30B V6	brake problems/hit wall
ret	SAN MARINO GP	Imola	15	Equipe Renault Elf	1.5 t/c Renault RE30B V6	engine
ret	BELGIAN GP	Zolder	15	Equipe Renault Elf	1.5 t/c Renault RE30B V6	spun off/Pole
7/ret	MONACO GP	Monte Carlo	15	Equipe Renault Elf	1.5 t/c Renault RE30B V6	spun off/3 laps behind
nc	US GP (DETROIT)	Detroit	15	Equipe Renault Elf	1.5 t/c Renault RE30B V6	p stop/fuel pump/Pole/FL/-8 laps
ret	CANADIAN GP	Montreal	15	Equipe Renault Elf	1.5 t/c Renault RE30B V6	engine
ret	DUTCH GP	Zandvoort	15	Equipe Renault Elf	1.5 t/c Renault RE30B V6	engine
6	BRITISH GP	Brands Hatch	15	Equipe Renault Elf	1.5 t/c Renault RE30B V6	
2	FRENCH GP	Paul Ricard	15	Equipe Renault Elf	1.5 t/c Renault RE30B V6	Arnoux won against team orders
ret	GERMAN GP	Hockenheim	15	Equipe Renault Elf	1.5 t/c Renault RE30B V6	fuel injection
8/ret	AUSTRIAN GP	Österreichring	15	Equipe Renault Elf	1.5 t/c Renault RE30B V6	fuel injection/5 laps behind
2	SWISS GP	Dijon	15	Equipe Renault Elf	1.5 t/c Renault RE30B V6	Pole/FL
ret	ITALIAN GP	Monza	15	Equipe Renault Elf	1.5 t/c Renault RE30B V6	fuel injection
4	CAESARS PALACE GP	Las Vegas	15	Equipe Renault Elf	1.5 t/c Renault RE30B V6	Pole

1983

7	BRAZILIAN GP	Rio	15	Equipe Renault Elf	1.5 t/c Renault RE30C V6	1 lap behind
11	US GP WEST	Long Beach	15	Equipe Renault Elf	1.5 t/c Renault RE40 V6	pit stip/misfire/3laps behind
1	FRENCH GP	Paul Ricard	15	Equipe Renault Elf	1.5 t/c Renault RE40 V6	Pole/FL
2	SAN MARINO GP	Imola	15	Equipe Renault Elf	1.5 t/c Renault RE40 V6	
3	MONACO GP	Monte Carlo	15	Equipe Renault Elf	1.5 t/c Renault RE40 V6	
1	BELGIAN GP	Spa	15	Equipe Renault Elf	1.5 t/c Renault RE40 V6	Pole
8	US GP (DETROIT)	Detroit	15	Equipe Renault Elf	1.5 t/c Renault RE40 V6	pit stop/fuel/1 lap behind
5	CANADIAN GP	Montreal	15	Equipe Renault Elf	1.5 t/c Renault RE40 V6	1 lap behind
1	BRITISH GP	Silverstone	15	Equipe Renault Elf	1.5 t/c Renault RE40 V6	FL
4	GERMAN GP	Hockenheim	15	Equipe Renault Elf	1.5 t/c Renault RE40 V6	
1	AUSTRIAN GP	Österreichring	15	Equipe Renault Elf	1.5 t/c Renault RE40 V6	FL
ret	DUTCH GP	Zandvoort	15	Equipe Renault Elf	1.5 t/c Renault RE40 V6	collision with Piquet
ret	ITALIAN GP	Monza	15	Equipe Renault Elf	1.5 t/c Renault RE40 V6	turbo
2	EUROPEAN GP	Brands Hatch	15	Equipe Renault Elf	1.5 t/c Renault RE40 V6	
ret	SOUTH AFRICAN GP	Kyalami	15	Equipe Renault Elf	1.5 t/c Renault RE40 V6	turbo

1984

1	BRAZILIAN GP	Rio	7	Marlboro McLaren International	1.5 t/c McLaren MP4/2-TAG V6	FL
2	SOUTH AFRICAN GP	Kyalami	7	Marlboro McLaren International	1.5 t/c McLaren MP4/2-TAG V6	started from pit lane
ret	BELGIAN GP	Zolder	7	Marlboro McLaren International	1.5 t/c McLaren MP4/2-TAG V6	distributor
1	SAN MARINO GP	Imola	7	Marlboro McLaren International	1.5 t/c McLaren MP4/2-TAG V6	
7	FRENCH GP	Dijon	7	Marlboro McLaren International	1.5 t/c McLaren MP4/2-TAG V6	2 pit stops/loose wheel/FL
1	MONACO GP	Monte Carlo	7	Marlboro McLaren International	1.5 t/c McLaren MP4/2-TAG V6	rain shortened race/half points/Pole
3	CANADIAN GP	Montreal	7	Marlboro McLaren International	1.5 t/c McLaren MP4/2-TAG V6	
4*	US GP (DETROIT)	Detroit	7	Marlboro McLaren International	1.5 t/c McLaren MP4/2-TAG V6	* 2nd place car disqualified
ret	US GP (DALLAS)	Dallas	7	Marlboro McLaren International	1.5 t/c McLaren MP4/2-TAG V6	hit wall
ret	BRITISH GP	Brands Hatch	7	Marlboro McLaren International	1.5 t/c McLaren MP4/2-TAG V6	gearbox
1	GERMAN GP	Hockenheim	7	Marlboro McLaren International	1.5 t/c McLaren MP4/2-TAG V6	Pole/FL
ret	AUSTRIAN GP	Österreichring	7	Marlboro McLaren International	1.5 t/c McLaren MP4/2-TAG V6	spun off
1	DUTCH GP	Zandvoort	7	Marlboro McLaren International	1.5 t/c McLaren MP4/2-TAG V6	Pole
ret	ITALIAN GP	Monza	7	Marlboro McLaren International	1.5 t/c McLaren MP4/2-TAG V6	engine
1	EUROPEAN GP	Nürburgring	7	Marlboro McLaren International	1.5 t/c McLaren MP4/2-TAG V6	
1	PORTUGUESE GP	Estoril	7	Marlboro McLaren International	1.5 t/c McLaren MP4/2-TAG V6	

1985 World Champion Driver

1	BRAZILIAN GP	Rio	2	Marlboro McLaren International	1.5 t/c McLaren MP4/2B-TAG V6	FL
ret	PORTUGUESE GP	Estoril	2	Marlboro McLaren International	1.5 t/c McLaren MP4/2B-TAG V6	spun off
dsq	SAN MARINO GP	Imola	2	Marlboro McLaren International	1.5 t/c McLaren MP4/2B-TAG V6	underweight/1st on the road/FL
1	MONACO GP	Monte Carlo	2	Marlboro McLaren International	1.5 t/c McLaren MP4/2B-TAG V6	
3	CANADIAN GP	Montreal	2	Marlboro McLaren International	1.5 t/c McLaren MP4/2B-TAG V6	
ret	US GP (DETROIT)	Detroit	2	Marlboro McLaren International	1.5 t/c McLaren MP4/2B-TAG V6	brake failure/accident
3	FRENCH GP	Paul Ricard	2	Marlboro McLaren International	1.5 t/c McLaren MP4/2B-TAG V6	
1	BRITISH GP	Silverstone	2	Marlboro McLaren International	1.5 t/c McLaren MP4/2B-TAG V6	FL
2	GERMAN GP	Nürburgring	2	Marlboro McLaren International	1.5 t/c McLaren MP4/2B-TAG V6	
1	AUSTRIAN GP	Österreichring	2	Marlboro McLaren International	1.5 t/c McLaren MP4/2B-TAG V6	Pole/FL
2	DUTCH GP	Zandvoort	2	Marlboro McLaren International	1.5 t/c McLaren MP4/2B-TAG V6	FL
1	ITALIAN GP	Monza	2	Marlboro McLaren International	1.5 t/c McLaren MP4/2B-TAG V6	
3	BELGIAN GP	Spa	2	Marlboro McLaren International	1.5 t/c McLaren MP4/2B-TAG V6	Pole/FL
4	EUROPEAN GP	Brands Hatch	2	Marlboro McLaren International	1.5 t/c McLaren MP4/2B-TAG V6	
3	SOUTH AFRICAN GP	Kyalami	2	Marlboro McLaren International	1.5 t/c McLaren MP4/2B-TAG V6	
ret	AUSTRALIAN GP	Adelaide	2	Marlboro McLaren International	1.5 t/c McLaren MP4/2B-TAG V6	engine

1986 World Champion Driver

ret	BRAZILIAN GP	Rio	1	Marlboro McLaren International	1.5 t/c McLaren MP4/2C-TAG V6	engine

3	SPANISH GP	Jerez	1	Marlboro McLaren International	1.5 t/c McLaren MP4/2C-TAG V6	
1	SAN MARINO GP	Imola	1	Marlboro McLaren International	1.5 t/c McLaren MP4/2C-TAG V6	
1	MONACO GP	Monte Carlo	1	Marlboro McLaren International	1.5 t/c McLaren MP4/2C-TAG V6	Pole/FL
6	BELGIAN GP	Spa	1	Marlboro McLaren International	1.5 t/c McLaren MP4/2C-TAG V6	first lap collision and spin/FL
2	CANADIAN GP	Montreal	1	Marlboro McLaren International	1.5 t/c McLaren MP4/2C-TAG V6	
3	US GP (DETROIT)	Detroit	1	Marlboro McLaren International	1.5 t/c McLaren MP4/2C-TAG V6	
2	FRENCH GP	Paul Ricard	1	Marlboro McLaren International	1.5 t/c McLaren MP4/2C-TAG V6	
3	BRITISH GP	Brands Hatch	1	Marlboro McLaren International	1.5 t/c McLaren MP4/2C-TAG V6	
6/ret	GERMAN GP	Hockenheim	1	Marlboro McLaren International	1.5 t/c McLaren MP4/2C-TAG V6	out of fuel
ret	HUNGARIAN GP	Hungaroring	1	Marlboro McLaren International	1.5 t/c McLaren MP4/2C-TAG V6	accident with Arnoux
1	AUSTRIAN GP	Österreichring	1	Marlboro McLaren International	1.5 t/c McLaren MP4/2C-TAG V6	
dsq	ITALIAN GP	Monza	1	Marlboro McLaren International	1.5 t/c McLaren MP4/2C-TAG V6	late car change after green flag
2	PORTUGUESE GP	Estoril	1	Marlboro McLaren International	1.5 t/c McLaren MP4/2C-TAG V6	
2	MEXICAN GP	Mexico City	1	Marlboro McLaren International	1.5 t/c McLaren MP4/2C-TAG V6	
1	AUSTRALIAN GP	Adelaide	1	Marlboro McLaren International	1.5 t/c McLaren MP4/2C-TAG V6	

1987

1	BRAZILIAN GP	Rio	1	Marlboro McLaren International	1.5 t/c McLaren MP4/3-TAG V6	
ret	SAN MARINO GP	Imola	1	Marlboro McLaren International	1.5 t/c McLaren MP4/3-TAG V6	alternator
1	BELGIAN GP	Spa	1	Marlboro McLaren International	1.5 t/c McLaren MP4/3-TAG V6	FL
9/ret	MONACO GP	Monte Carlo	1	Marlboro McLaren International	1.5 t/c McLaren MP4/3-TAG V6	engine/3 laps behind
3	US GP (DETROIT)	Detroit	1	Marlboro McLaren International	1.5 t/c McLaren MP4/3-TAG V6	
3	FRENCH GP	Paul Ricard	1	Marlboro McLaren International	1.5 t/c McLaren MP4/3-TAG V6	
ret	BRITISH GP	Silverstone	1	Marlboro McLaren International	1.5 t/c McLaren MP4/3-TAG V6	clutch bearings/electrics
7/ret	GERMAN GP	Hockenheim	1	Marlboro McLaren International	1.5 t/c McLaren MP4/3-TAG V6	alternator belt/5 laps behind
3	HUNGARIAN GP	Hungaroring	1	Marlboro McLaren International	1.5 t/c McLaren MP4/3-TAG V6	
6	AUSTRIAN GP	Österreichring	1	Marlboro McLaren International	1.5 t/c McLaren MP4/3-TAG V6	started from pit lane/2 laps behind
15	ITALIAN GP	Monza	1	Marlboro McLaren International	1.5 t/c McLaren MP4/3-TAG V6	pit stop/misfire/4 laps behind
1	PORTUGUESE GP	Estoril	1	Marlboro McLaren International	1.5 t/c McLaren MP4/3-TAG V6	
2	SPANISH GP	Jerez	1	Marlboro McLaren International	1.5 t/c McLaren MP4/3-TAG V6	
ret	MEXICAN GP	Mexico City	1	Marlboro McLaren International	1.5 t/c McLaren MP4/3-TAG V6	accident with Piquet
7	JAPANESE GP	Suzuka	1	Marlboro McLaren International	1.5 t/c McLaren MP4/3-TAG V6	pit stop/puncture/FL/1 lap behind
ret	AUSTRALIAN GP	Adelaide	1	Marlboro McLaren International	1.5 t/c McLaren MP4/3-TAG V6	brake problem/accident

1988

1	BRAZILIAN GP	Rio	11	Honda Marlboro McLaren	1.5 t/c McLaren MP4/4-Honda V6	
2	SAN MARINO GP	Imola	11	Honda Marlboro McLaren	1.5 t/c McLaren MP4/4-Honda V6	FL
1	MONACO GP	Monte Carlo	11	Honda Marlboro McLaren	1.5 t/c McLaren MP4/4-Honda V6	
1	MEXICAN GP	Mexico City	11	Honda Marlboro McLaren	1.5 t/c McLaren MP4/4-Honda V6	FL
2	CANADIAN GP	Montreal	11	Honda Marlboro McLaren	1.5 t/c McLaren MP4/4-Honda V6	
2	US GP (DETROIT)	Detroit	11	Honda Marlboro McLaren	1.5 t/c McLaren MP4/4-Honda V6	FL
1	FRENCH GP	Paul Ricard	11	Honda Marlboro McLaren	1.5 t/c McLaren MP4/4-Honda V6	Pole/FL
ret	BRITISH GP	Silverstone	11	Honda Marlboro McLaren	1.5 t/c McLaren MP4/4-Honda V6	handling in wet conditions
2	GERMAN GP	Hockenheim	11	Honda Marlboro McLaren	1.5 t/c McLaren MP4/4-Honda V6	
2	HUNGARIAN GP	Hungaroring	11	Honda Marlboro McLaren	1.5 t/c McLaren MP4/4-Honda V6	FL
2	BELGIAN GP	Spa	11	Honda Marlboro McLaren	1.5 t/c McLaren MP4/4-Honda V6	
ret	ITALIAN GP	Monza	11	Honda Marlboro McLaren	1.5 t/c McLaren MP4/4-Honda V6	engine
1	PORTUGUESE GP	Estoril	11	Honda Marlboro McLaren	1.5 t/c McLaren MP4/4-Honda V6	Pole
1	SPANISH GP	Jerez	11	Honda Marlboro McLaren	1.5 t/c McLaren MP4/4-Honda V6	FL
2	JAPANESE GP	Suzuka	11	Honda Marlboro McLaren	1.5 t/c McLaren MP4/4-Honda V6	
1	AUSTRALIAN GP	Adelaide	11	Honda Marlboro McLaren	1.5 t/c McLaren MP4/4-Honda V6	FL

1989 World Champion Driver

2	BRAZILIAN GP	Rio	2	Honda Marlboro McLaren	3.5 McLaren MP4/5-Honda V10	
2	SAN MARINO GP	Imola	2	Honda Marlboro McLaren	3.5 McLaren MP4/5-Honda V10	Aggregate of two parts/FL
2	MONACO GP	Monte Carlo	2	Honda Marlboro McLaren	3.5 McLaren MP4/5-Honda V10	FL
5	MEXICAN GP	Mexico City	2	Honda Marlboro McLaren	3.5 McLaren MP4/5-Honda V10	wrong choice of tyre type
1	US GP (PHOENIX)	Phoenix	2	Honda Marlboro McLaren	3.5 McLaren MP4/5-Honda V10	
ret	CANADIAN GP	Montreal	2	Honda Marlboro McLaren	3.5 McLaren MP4/5-Honda V10	suspension failure
1	FRENCH GP	Paul Ricard	2	Honda Marlboro McLaren	3.5 McLaren MP4/5-Honda V10	Pole
1	BRITISH GP	Silverstone	2	Honda Marlboro McLaren	3.5 McLaren MP4/5-Honda V10	
2	GERMAN GP	Hockenheim	2	Honda Marlboro McLaren	3.5 McLaren MP4/5-Honda V10	
4	HUNGARIAN GP	Hungaroring	2	Honda Marlboro McLaren	3.5 McLaren MP4/5-Honda V10	late tyre stop
2	BELGIAN GP	Spa	2	Honda Marlboro McLaren	3.5 McLaren MP4/5-Honda V10	FL
1	ITALIAN GP	Monza	2	Honda Marlboro McLaren	3.5 McLaren MP4/5-Honda V10	FL
2	PORTUGUESE GP	Estoril	2	Honda Marlboro McLaren	3.5 McLaren MP4/5-Honda V10	
3	SPANISH GP	Jerez	2	Honda Marlboro McLaren	3.5 McLaren MP4/5-Honda V10	
ret	JAPANESE GP	Suzuka	2	Honda Marlboro McLaren	3.5 McLaren MP4/5-Honda V10	accident with Senna/FL
dns	AUSTRALIAN GP	Adelaide	2	Honda Marlboro McLaren	3.5 McLaren MP4/5-Honda V10	refused to start due to conditions

1990

ret	US GP (PHOENIX)	Phoenix	1	Scuderia Ferrari SpA	3.5 Fiat Ferrari 641 V12	engine oil leak
1	BRAZILIAN GP	Rio	1	Scuderia Ferrari SpA	3.5 Fiat Ferrari 641 V12	
4	SAN MARINO GP	Imola	1	Scuderia Ferrari SpA	3.5 Fiat Ferrari 641 V12	
ret	MONACO GP	Monte Carlo	1	Scuderia Ferrari SpA	3.5 Fiat Ferrari 641 V12	electrics
5	CANADIAN GP	Montreal	1	Scuderia Ferrari SpA	3.5 Fiat Ferrari 641 V12	worn brakes
1	MEXICAN GP	Mexico City	1	Scuderia Ferrari SpA	3.5 Fiat Ferrari 641 V12	FL
1	FRENCH GP	Paul Ricard	1	Scuderia Ferrari SpA	3.5 Fiat Ferrari 641 V12	
1	BRITISH GP	Silverstone	1	Scuderia Ferrari SpA	3.5 Fiat Ferrari 641 V12	
4	GERMAN GP	Hockenheim	1	Scuderia Ferrari SpA	3.5 Fiat Ferrari 641 V12	
ret	HUNGARIAN GP	Hungaroring	1	Scuderia Ferrari SpA	3.5 Fiat Ferrari 641 V12	clutch seized-spun off
2	BELGIAN GP	Spa	1	Scuderia Ferrari SpA	3.5 Fiat Ferrari 641 V12	FL
2	ITALIAN GP	Monza	1	Scuderia Ferrari SpA	3.5 Fiat Ferrari 641 V12	
3	PORTUGUESE GP	Estoril	1	Scuderia Ferrari SpA	3.5 Fiat Ferrari 641 V12	
1	SPANISH GP	Jerez	1	Scuderia Ferrari SpA	3.5 Fiat Ferrari 641 V12	
ret	JAPANESE GP	Suzuka	1	Scuderia Ferrari SpA	3.5 Fiat Ferrari 641 V12	first corner accident with Senna
3	AUSTRALIAN GP	Adelaide	1	Scuderia Ferrari SpA	3.5 Fiat Ferrari 641 V12	

1991

	Race	Circuit	No	Entrant	Car/Engine	Comment
2	US GP (PHOENIX)	Phoenix	27	Scuderia Ferrari SpA	3.5 Fiat Ferrari 642 V12	
4	BRAZILIAN GP	Interlagos	27	Scuderia Ferrari SpA	3.5 Fiat Ferrari 642 V12	
dns	SAN MARINO GP	Imola	27	Scuderia Ferrari SpA	3.5 Fiat Ferrari 642 V12	spun off on parade lap
5	MONACO GP	Monte Carlo	27	Scuderia Ferrari SpA	3.5 Fiat Ferrari 642 V12	late pit stop-tyres/FL/1 lap behind
ret	CANADIAN GP	Montreal	27	Scuderia Ferrari SpA	3.5 Fiat Ferrari 642 V12	gearbox
ret	MEXICAN GP	Mexico City	27	Scuderia Ferrari SpA	3.5 Fiat Ferrari 642 V12	alternator
2	FRENCH GP	Magny Cours	27	Scuderia Ferrari SpA	3.5 Fiat Ferrari 643 V12	
3	BRITISH GP	Silverstone	27	Scuderia Ferrari SpA	3.5 Fiat Ferrari 643 V12	
ret	GERMAN GP	Hockenheim	27	Scuderia Ferrari SpA	3.5 Fiat Ferrari 643 V12	spun off unable to restart
ret	HUNGARIAN GP	Hungaroring	27	Scuderia Ferrari SpA	3.5 Fiat Ferrari 643 V12	engine
ret	BELGIAN GP	Spa	27	Scuderia Ferrari SpA	3.5 Fiat Ferrari 643 V12	engine
3	ITALIAN GP	Monza	27	Scuderia Ferrari SpA	3.5 Fiat Ferrari 643 V12	
ret	PORTUGUESE GP	Estoril	27	Scuderia Ferrari SpA	3.5 Fiat Ferrari 643 V12	engine
2	SPANISH GP	Barcelona	27	Scuderia Ferrari SpA	3.5 Fiat Ferrari 643 V12	
4	JAPANESE GP	Suzuka	27	Scuderia Ferrari SpA	3.5 Fiat Ferrari 643 V12	

1993 World Champion Driver

	Race	Circuit	No	Entrant	Car/Engine	Comment
1	SOUTH AFRICAN GP	Kyalami	2	Canon Williams Team	3.5 Williams FW15B-Renault V10	Pole/FL
ret	BRAZILIAN GP	Interlagos	2	Canon Williams Team	3.5 Williams FW15B-Renault V10	Spun off in rainstorm/Pole
3	EUROPEAN GP	Donington	2	Canon Williams Team	3.5 Williams FW15B-Renault V10	Pole
1	SAN MARINO GP	Imola	2	Canon Williams Team	3.5 Williams FW15B-Renault V10	Pole/FL
1	SPANISH GP	Barcelona	2	Canon Williams Team	3.5 Williams FW15B-Renault V10	Pole
4	MONACO GP	Monte Carlo	2	Canon Williams Team	3.5 Williams FW15B-Renault V10	Jump start-stop & go pen/Pole/FL
1	CANADIAN GP	Montreal	2	Canon Williams Team	3.5 Williams FW15B-Renault V10	Pole
1	FRENCH GP	Magny Cours	2	Canon Williams Team	3.5 Williams FW15B-Renault V10	
1	BRITISH GP	Silverstone	2	Canon Williams Team	3.5 Williams FW15B-Renault V10	50th Grand Prix win/Pole
1	GERMAN GP	Hockenheim	2	Canon Williams Team	3.5 Williams FW15B-Renault V10	stop & go penalty/Pole
12	HUNGARIAN GP	Hungaroring	2	Canon Williams Team	3.5 Williams FW15B-Renault V10	started at back/stop-wing/Pole/FL/-7 laps
3	BELGIAN GP	Spa	2	Canon Williams Team	3.5 Williams FW15B-Renault V10	Pole/FL
12	ITALIAN GP	Monza	2	Canon Williams Team	3.5 Williams FW15B-Renault V10	engine/5 laps behind/Pole
2	PORTUGUESE GP	Estoril	2	Canon Williams Team	3.5 Williams FW15B-Renault V10	
2	JAPANESE GP	Suzuka	2	Canon Williams Team	3.5 Williams FW15B-Renault V10	Pole/FL
2	AUSTRALIAN GP	Adelaide	2	Canon Williams Team	3.5 Williams FW15B-Renault V10	

GP Starts: 199 (200)   GP Wins: 51   Pole positions: 32   Fastest laps: 37   Points: 798.5

PRYCE, Tom (GB) b 11/6/1949 – d 5/3/1977

1974

	Race	Circuit	No	Entrant	Car/Engine	Comment
ret	BELGIAN GP	Nivelles	42	Token Racing	3.0 Token RJ02-Cosworth V8	collision with Scheckter
ret	DUTCH GP	Zandvoort	16	UOP Shadow Racing Team	3.0 Shadow DN3-Cosworth V8	collision with Hunt
ret	FRENCH GP	Dijon	16	UOP Shadow Racing Team	3.0 Shadow DN3-Cosworth V8	collision with Hunt
8	BRITISH GP	Brands Hatch	16	UOP Shadow Racing Team	3.0 Shadow DN3-Cosworth V8	1 lap behind
6	GERMAN GP	Nürburgring	16	UOP Shadow Racing Team	3.0 Shadow DN3-Cosworth V8	
ret	AUSTRIAN GP	Österreichring	16	UOP Shadow Racing Team	3.0 Shadow DN3-Cosworth V8	spun off-could not restart
10	ITALIAN GP	Monza	16	UOP Shadow Racing Team	3.0 Shadow DN3-Cosworth V8	2 laps behind
ret	CANADIAN GP	Mosport Park	16	UOP Shadow Racing Team	3.0 Shadow DN3-Cosworth V8	engine
nc	US GP	Watkins Glen	16	UOP Shadow Racing Team	3.0 Shadow DN3-Cosworth V8	2 p stops/nose cone/misfire/-12 laps

1975

	Race	Circuit	No	Entrant	Car/Engine	Comment
12/ret	ARGENTINE GP	Buenos Aires	16	UOP Shadow Racing Team	3.0 Shadow DN3B-Cosworth V8	transmission/2 laps behind
ret	BRAZILIAN GP	Interlagos	16	UOP Shadow Racing Team	3.0 Shadow DN3B-Cosworth V8	spun off
9	SOUTH AFRICAN GP	Kyalami	16	UOP Shadow Racing Team	3.0 Shadow DN5-Cosworth V8	1 lap behind
ret	SPANISH GP	Montjuich Park	16	UOP Shadow Racing Team	3.0 Shadow DN5-Cosworth V8	collision with Brise
ret	MONACO GP	Monte Carlo	16	UOP Shadow Racing Team	3.0 Shadow DN5-Cosworth V8	hit barrier-damaged rear wing
6	BELGIAN GP	Zolder	16	UOP Shadow Racing Team	3.0 Shadow DN5-Cosworth V8	
ret	SWEDISH GP	Anderstorp	16	UOP Shadow Racing Team	3.0 Shadow DN5-Cosworth V8	spun off-could not restart
6	DUTCH GP	Zandvoort	16	UOP Shadow Racing Team	3.0 Shadow DN5-Cosworth V8	1 lap behind
ret	FRENCH GP	Paul Ricard	16	UOP Shadow Racing Team	3.0 Shadow DN5-Cosworth V8	transmission
ret	BRITISH GP	Silverstone	16	UOP Shadow Racing Team	3.0 Shadow DN5-Cosworth V8	spun off/Pole
4	GERMAN GP	Nürburgring	16	UOP Shadow Racing Team	3.0 Shadow DN5-Cosworth V8	
3	AUSTRIAN GP	Österreichring	16	UOP Shadow Racing Team	3.0 Shadow DN5-Cosworth V8	
6	ITALIAN GP	Monza	16	UOP Shadow Racing Team	3.0 Shadow DN5-Cosworth V8	
nc	US GP	Watkins Glen	16	UOP Shadow Racing Team	3.0 Shadow DN5-Cosworth V8	pit stops/misfire/7 laps behind

1976

	Race	Circuit	No	Entrant	Car/Engine	Comment
3	BRAZILIAN GP	Interlagos	16	Shadow Racing Team	3.0 Shadow DN5-Cosworth V8	
7	SOUTH AFRICAN GP	Kyalami	16	Shadow Racing Team	3.0 Shadow DN5-Cosworth V8	1 lap behind
ret	US GP WEST	Long Beach	16	Shadow Racing Team	3.0 Shadow DN5-Cosworth V8	driveshaft
8	SPANISH GP	Jarama	16	Shadow Racing Team	3.0 Shadow DN5-Cosworth V8	1 lap behind
10	BELGIAN GP	Zolder	16	Shadow Racing Team	3.0 Shadow DN5-Cosworth V8	2 laps behind
7	MONACO GP	Monte Carlo	16	Shadow Racing Team	3.0 Shadow DN5-Cosworth V8	1 lap behind
9	SWEDISH GP	Anderstorp	16	Shadow Racing Team	3.0 Shadow DN5-Cosworth V8	1 lap behind
8	FRENCH GP	Paul Ricard	16	Shadow Racing Team	3.0 Shadow DN5-Cosworth V8	
4	BRITISH GP	Brands Hatch	16	Shadow Racing Team	3.0 Shadow DN5-Cosworth V8	1 lap behind
8	GERMAN GP	Nürburgring	16	Shadow Racing with Tabatip	3.0 Shadow DN5-Cosworth V8	
ret	AUSTRIAN GP	Österreichring	16	Shadow Racing with Tabatip	3.0 Shadow DN5-Cosworth V8	brakes
4	DUTCH GP	Zandvoort	16	Shadow Racing Team	3.0 Shadow DN5-Cosworth V8	
8	ITALIAN GP	Monza	16	Shadow Racing Team	3.0 Shadow DN8-Cosworth V8	
11	CANADIAN GP	Mosport Park	16	Shadow Racing Team	3.0 Shadow DN8-Cosworth V8	1 lap behind
ret	US GP EAST	Watkins Glen	16	Shadow Racing Team	3.0 Shadow DN8-Cosworth V8	engine
ret	JAPANESE GP	Mount Fuji	16	Shadow Racing Team	3.0 Shadow DN8-Cosworth V8	engine-seized

1977

nc	ARGENTINE GP	Buenos Aires	16	Shadow Racing Team	3.0 Shadow DN8-Cosworth V8	pit stop/gear selection/8 laps behind
ret	BRAZILIAN GP	Interlagos	16	Shadow Racing Team	3.0 Shadow DN8-Cosworth V8	engine
ret	SOUTH AFRICAN GP	Kyalami	16	Shadow Racing Team	3.0 Shadow DN8-Cosworth V8	fatal accident

GP Starts: 42   GP Wins: 0   Pole positions: 1   Fastest laps: 0   Points: 19

PURLEY, David (GB)   b 26/1/1945 – d 2/7/1985

1973

	Race	Circuit	No	Entrant	Car/Engine	Comment
ret	MONACO GP	Monte Carlo	18	LEC Refrigeration Racing	3.0 March 731-Cosworth V8	oil tank
dns	BRITISH GP	Silverstone	18	LEC Refrigeration Racing	3.0 March 731-Cosworth V8	practice accident
ret	DUTCH GP	Zandvoort	18	LEC Refrigeration Racing	3.0 March 731-Cosworth V8	stopped-tried help Roger Williamson
15	GERMAN GP	Nürburgring	18	LEC Refrigeration Racing	3.0 March 731-Cosworth V8	1 lap behind
9	ITALIAN GP	Monza	29	LEC Refrigeration Racing	3.0 March 731-Cosworth V8	1 lap behind

1974

dnq	BRITISH GP	Brands Hatch	42	Team Harper-Token Racing	3.0 Token RJ02-Cosworth V8	

1977

dnq	SPANISH GP	Jarama	31	LEC Refrigeration Racing	3.0 LEC CRP1-Cosworth V8	
13	BELGIAN GP	Zolder	31	LEC Refrigeration Racing	3.0 LEC CRP1-Cosworth V8	3 laps behind
14	SWEDISH GP	Anderstorp	31	LEC Refrigeration Racing	3.0 LEC CRP1-Cosworth V8	2 laps behind
ret	FRENCH GP	Dijon	31	LEC Refrigeration Racing	3.0 LEC CRP1-Cosworth V8	brake failure/accident
dnpq	BRITISH GP	Silverstone	31	LEC Refrigeration Racing	3.0 LEC CRP1-Cosworth V8	accident in practice/badly injured

GP Starts: 7   GP Wins: 0   Pole positions: 0   Fastest laps: 0   Points: 0

TOM PRYCE

Tom Pryce's death at Kyalami in 1977 robbed Britain of one of its great natural talents of the era who, had he survived, would surely have gone on to achieve much greater things. The quiet and reserved Welshman had got into motor racing in 1970 via a competition in the *Daily Express* in which he won a Lola T200 Formula Ford. He made a good start in the car before switching to the Formula 100 series in 1971, where he dominated in his TAS Racing Royale. This success took him to the works Royale team to race in Formula Super Vee before embarking on a Formula 3 season with the team in 1972. Unfortunately this effort was hampered by a lack of finance, and Tom's season was interrupted by a broken leg sustained in a heat of the Monaco F3 race.

Royale ran Tom in Formula Atlantic in 1973 and he was enjoying a successful season when he was given an opportunity to drive the Motul Rondel F2 car in selected races. A second place at Norisring signified better things ahead, and sure enough in 1974 Tom joined the little Token team for the International Trophy and Belgian GP. When the team's entry for Monaco was refused due to the Welshman's lack of experience, he contested the F3 support race instead and, in an astonishing display of dominance, simply drove into the distance to win by the proverbial country mile.

With Shadow still looking for a suitable replacement for the late Peter Revson, Pryce was drafted into the team after Brian Redman had decided not to stay. In only his second race at Dijon he put the car onto the second row of the grid and that was enough for Don Nichols to decide he had found his man. The 1975 season started well with a win in the Race of Champions, but it was an up-and-down year, pole position for the British GP and superb drives in both Germany and Austria being the highlights. The team received a major setback when UOP, their main sponsor, pulled out at the end of the year and the subsequent cash shortage certainly hindered both the team's and Tom's progress in 1976, the Welshman loyally staying on when plenty of others would have been seeking to better their lot elsewhere. The 1977 season began with new sponsors and a fresh enthusiasm, but a bizarre and horrendous accident at Kyalami cruelly cut him down. Thankfully he was probably already dead as his car hurtled towards oblivion, having hit an errant marshal as he crossed the track carrying a fire extinguisher.

DAVID PURLEY

Some drivers leave behind memories far greater than the sum of their deeds, and David Purley was undoubtedly such a man: a model of personal courage, a great sportsman, and a fine racing driver as well. He began racing with a big Cobra in 1968, then moved on to a Chevron GT, before taking a shot at Formula 3 in 1970 in his family-backed Lec Refrigeration Brabham. At this stage he was a little wild and wayward, and he certainly relished the dangerous challenge presented by events such as the GP of Chimay, taking a hat-trick of wins on this road circuit between 1970 and '72.

By 1972 Purley had progressed to Formula 2, taking a splendid third place at Pau, but in 1973 he dropped down for a season of Formula Atlantic, during the course of which he hired a March to go Grand Prix racing for the first time. Although his results were forgettable, his actions at the Dutch GP when he single-handedly tried in vain to save poor Roger Williamson were certainly not. David's bravery won him the George Medal, and the admiration of the Grand Prix world.

In 1974 Purley teamed up with Peter Harper to race in Formula 2 once more and enjoyed a successful season, taking second places at the Salzburgring, Rouen and Enna, and in the end-of-year Macau GP. Back under his own Lec banner, Purley then contested two seasons of F5000 with a Chevron, taking the Shellsport championship in 1976 with six victories.

Seeing Formula 1 as unfinished business, David commissioned his own Lec chassis to race in 1977, taking a sixth place in the Race of Champions, and then briefly leading the wet Belgian GP during a round of pit stops. Disaster struck in practice for the British GP when he crashed his car, sustaining horrendous multiple injuries that would have killed a man of lesser fortitude. Displaying incredible will to survive and then recover, Purley endured months of rehabilitation, racing his Porsche in club events in preparation for a serious return to the track in the Aurora series towards the end of 1979. He may have competed in only four rounds, but a fourth place at Snetterton was an amazing achievement.

Purley then restricted his racing to occasional club events, but his love for speed and danger remained unquenchable. He took up aerobatics with a Pitts Special biplane, until fate at last caught up with him in July 1985, when his plane crashed into the sea off Bognor Regis. One of Britain's greatest characters had finally run out of luck.

DIETER QUESTER

Since coming into motor racing in 1965, after many years competing in speedboats and motor cycling, Quester has been identified with the BMW marque for the bulk of his long career. He really came to prominence driving touring cars in 1968, and was then part of BMW's largely unsuccessful Formula 2 programme, managing a victory at Hockenheim at the end of 1970. Quester switched to a March for 1971, and performed well, winning the Lottery GP and scoring five second places. It was around this period that, frustrated at being unable to get a Formula 1 ride, he more than once seriously considered retirement, but he carried on and eventually drove a rented Surtees in the 1974 Austrian GP. Subsequently concentrating on sports cars and saloons, he was European G2 champion in 1977 and a regular in the BMW Procar series of 1979-80, while over the last decade he has been a permanent fixture in BMW touring cars in the European, German and Austrian championships.

IAN RABY

A car dealer from Brighton, Raby began racing in the early fifties in Formula 3 with specials which he christened 'Puddle Jumper', but he wasn't really competitive until he raced a Cooper in 1956. After two years with Cooper and Elva sports cars, Raby returned to single-seaters in 1959-60 with both a Cooper and a Hume-Climax, gaining success only in modest Formula Libre races.

In 1961-62 he raced mainly in Formula Junior, before buying the Gilby-BRM from Syd Greene to race in Formula 1 in 1963. Ian gained a third place at Vallelunga in the Rome GP, but precious little else, and in 1964-65 he relied on a Brabham BT3, still no more than making up the numbers.

With the new 3-litre formula in operation for 1966, Raby stepped down into F2 with a Brabham BT14-Cosworth. He scored a good fourth place at the Eifelrennen, before a crash at Brands Hatch curtailed his season. Despite his relatively old age, Ian undertook a full season of Formula 2 in 1967, gaining the occasional top-six finish, before a serious crash at Zandvoort left him hospitalised with multiple injuries to which he succumed some weeks later.

BOBBY RAHAL

From the start, Rahal was refreshingly different from most American drivers in that he wanted to go road racing, and was prepared to come to Europe and measure himself against the best talent around. After three years (1975-77) in Canadian Formula Atlantic, where he was somewhat overshadowed by the exploits of Gilles Villeneuve, Bobby crossed the Atlantic for a selection of Formula 3 races with Walter Wolf Racing. He did well enough to be offered a drive with the team in the end-of-season US and Canadian GPs, the latter in the old WR1 chassis, which had been dragged from a museum after he had pranged his WR5 in practice. Determined to make the grade, he came back to Europe in 1979 for a full Formula 2 season with a works Chevron, scoring some good finishes in a car which was not the most competitive around. That was the end of Rahal's dreams of Formula 1, however, for in 1980 he went Can-Am racing, which was to be followed by a successful year in endurance events, Bobby winning the Daytona 24 Hours and taking second place at Brands Hatch in a Porsche 935 turbo.

In 1982 he moved into IndyCar racing, winning the Cleveland race and finishing second in the PPG Cup, and in 1986, racing for Truesports, Rahal won the championship and the Indy 500. He won the title again in 1992, having set up his own team in partnership with Carl Hogan, and by the end of 1993 he had taken 24 wins and amassed more than $12 million in prize money. With a Honda engine deal for 1994, more success seems imminent.

NANO da SILVA RAMOS

Holding dual French-Brazilian nationality, Ramos took part in his first races in Rio with an MG but wasn't really interested in the sport until he returned to France and purchased an Aston Martin DB2, with which he won the Rallye de Sable in 1953. After more success in the car the following year, Ramos joined the Gordini team for 1955 and 1956, racing their Grand Prix and sports cars, and suffering the usual mixture of speed and unreliability associated with that marque. In single-seaters he finished fifth in the 1956 International Trophy and did well to claim points at Monaco, but achieved little else, while in sports car racing he scored a win for the team at Montlhéry against very poor opposition. Equipe Gordini were on their last legs early in 1957, but Ramos took sixth place at Pau in the streamliner before their demise, and returned in an Alan Brown Cooper the following year to finish second. In 1959 he raced briefly for Scuderia Centro Sud, claiming a very distant fourth in their outdated Maserati 250F in the Aintree 200.

PIERRE-HENRI RAPHANEL

After finishing third in the 1984 series, Raphanel was French Formula 3 champion in 1985, successfully defending his early-season lead from ORECA team-mate Yannick Dalmas as the season wore on.

Promoted into the ORECA F3000 team for 1986, Raphanel soon found his feet and ended the season looking a good bet for honours in 1987, but somehow he failed to spark thereafter, enduring two lacklustre seasons. At the end of 1988 he stood in for his former team-mate Dalmas at Larrousse, but gearbox problems stymied his chances of qualifying. Signing to race for Coloni in 1989, he found himself among the early-risers attempting to pre-qualify, and did extremely well to get on the grid at Monaco. A mid-season move to Rial merely meant that he could turn up a little later for practice, but he was still to find his Sundays free.

Since 1990 Raphanel has been driving in Japanese Group C and touring cars, and has figured in Toyota's Le Mans challenge, finishing second in 1992.

QUESTER, Dieter (A) b 30/5/1939

1969

	Race	Circuit	No	Entrant	Car/Engine	Comment
dns	GERMAN GP	Nürburgring	25	Bayerische Moteren Werke	1.6 BMW 269 4 F2	*withdrawn after Mitter's accident*

1974

9	AUSTRIAN GP	Österreichring	28	Memphis International-Team Surtees	3.0 Surtees TS16-Cosworth V8	*3 laps behind*

GP Starts: 1   GP Wins: 0   Pole positions: 0   Fastest laps: 0   Points: 0

RABY, Ian (GB) b 22/9/1921 – 7/11/1967

1963

	Race	Circuit	No	Entrant	Car/Engine	Comment
ret	BRITISH GP	Silverstone	26	Ian Raby (Racing)	1.5 Gilby-BRM V8	*gearbox*
dnq	GERMAN GP	Nürburgring	25	Ian Raby (Racing)	1.5 Gilby-BRM V8	
dnq	ITALIAN GP	Monza	50	Ian Raby (Racing)	1.5 Gilby-BRM V8	

1964

ret	BRITISH GP	Brands Hatch	23	Ian Raby (Racing)	1.5 Brabham BT3-BRM V8	*accident*
dnq	ITALIAN GP	Monza	23	Ian Raby (Racing)	1.5 Brabham BT3-BRM V8	

1965

11	BRITISH GP	Silverstone	24	Ian Raby (Racing)	1.5 Brabham BT3-BRM V8	*7 laps behind*
dnq	GERMAN GP	Nürburgring	23	Ian Raby (Racing)	1.5 Brabham BT3-BRM V8	

GP Starts: 3   GP Wins: 0   Pole positions: 0   Fastest laps: 0   Points: 0

RAHAL, Bobby (USA) b 10/1/1953

1978

	Race	Circuit	No	Entrant	Car/Engine	Comment
12	US GP EAST	Watkins Glen	21	Walter Wolf Racing	3.0 Wolf WR5-Cosworth V8	*1 lap behind*
ret	CANADIAN GP	Montreal	21	Walter Wolf Racing	3.0 Wolf WR1-Cosworth V8	*fuel system*
dns	"	"	21	Walter Wolf Racing	3.0 Wolf WR5-Cosworth V8	*practice accident*

GP Starts: 2   GP Wins: 0   Pole positions: 0   Fastest laps: 0   Points: 0

RAMOS, Nano da Silva (F/BR) b 7/12/1925

1955

	Race	Circuit	No	Entrant	Car/engine	Comment
8	DUTCH GP	Zandvoort	22	Equipe Gordini	2.5 Gordini Type 16 6	*8 laps behind*
ret	BRITISH GP	Aintree	24	Equipe Gordini	2.5 Gordini Type 16 6	*engine*
ret	ITALIAN GP	Monza	22	Equipe Gordini	2.5 Gordini Type 16 6	*mechanical*
dns	"	"	22	Equipe Gordini	2.5 Gordini Type 32 8	*practice only*

1956

5	MONACO GP	Monte Carlo	6	Equipe Gordini	2.5 Gordini Type 16 6	*7 laps behind*
8	FRENCH GP	Reims	32	Equipe Gordini	2.5 Gordini Type 32 8	*4 laps behind*
ret	BRITISH GP	Silverstone	14	Equipe Gordini	2.5 Gordini Type 32 8	*rear axle*
ret	ITALIAN GP	Monza	8	Equipe Gordini	2.5 Gordini Type 32 8	*engine*

GP Starts: 7   GP Wins: 0   Pole positions: 0   Fastest laps: 0   Points: 2

RAPHANEL, Pierre-Henri (F) b 27/5/1961

1988

	Race	Circuit	No	Entrant	Car/engine	Comment
dnq	AUSTRALIAN GP	Adelaide	29	Larrousse Calmels	3.5 Lola LC88-Cosworth V8	

1989

dnpq	BRAZILIAN GP	Rio	32	Coloni SpA	3.5 Coloni FC88-Cosworth V8	
dnpq	SAN MARINO GP	Imola	32	Coloni SpA	3.5 Coloni FC88-Cosworth V8	
ret	MONACO GP	Monte Carlo	32	Coloni SpA	3.5 Coloni FC88-Cosworth V8	*gearbox*
dnpq	MEXICAN GP	Mexico City	32	Coloni SpA	3.5 Coloni FC88-Cosworth V8	
dnpq	US GP (PHOENIX)	Phoenix	32	Coloni SpA	3.5 Coloni FC88-Cosworth V8	
dnpq	CANADIAN GP	Montreal	32	Coloni SpA	3.5 Coloni C3-Cosworth V8	
dnpq	FRENCH GP	Paul Ricard	32	Coloni SpA	3.5 Coloni C3-Cosworth V8	
dnpq	BRITISH GP	Silverstone	32	Coloni SpA	3.5 Coloni FC3-Cosworth V8	
dnpq	GERMAN GP	Hockenheim	32	Coloni SpA	3.5 Coloni FC3-Cosworth V8	
dnpq	HUNGARIAN GP	Hungaroring	32	Coloni SpA	3.5 Coloni FC88-Cosworth V8	
dnq	BELGIAN GP	Spa	39	Rial Racing	3.5 Rial ARC2-Cosworth V8	
dnq	ITALIAN GP	Monza	39	Rial Racing	3.5 Rial ARC2-Cosworth V8	
dnq	PORTUGUESE GP	Estoril	39	Rial Racing	3.5 Rial ARC2-Cosworth V8	
dnq	SPANISH GP	Jerez	39	Rial Racing	3.5 Rial ARC2-Cosworth V8	
dnq	JAPANESE GP	Suzuka	39	Rial Racing	3.5 Rial ARC2-Cosworth V8	
dnq	AUSTRALIAN GP	Adelaide	39	Rial Racing	3.5 Rial ARC2-Cosworth V8	

GP Starts: 1   GP Wins: 0   Pole positions: 0   Fastest laps: 0   Points: 0

HECTOR REBAQUE

An ambitious young Mexican hot-shot, Rebaque came to England in 1974 as a raw 18-year-old to try his hand at Formula Atlantic as a protégé of Fred Opert in a Chevron. The following year, he moved into Formula 2 in Opert's Chevron, before returning across the pond to contest the Canadian Formula Atlantic series in 1975 and 1976.

Itching to get into Grand Prix racing, Hector joined the Hesketh team for a few outings in 1977, qualifying just once. Determined to succeed, he set up his own team the following season, fielding ex-works Lotus 78s, but managed only one top-six finish, in Germany. For 1979 he had Lotus 79s at his disposal but results remained discouraging, so he took the brave – if foolhardy – step of commissioning his own chassis, which only appeared for the last three Grands Prix of the year before the team folded.

In 1980 Hector kicked his heels until the opportunity arose to join Brabham in place of Zunino. Now in a top-notch car, it was up to the driver to prove himself, and on occasion he showed a good turn of speed. In Argentina in 1981, for example, he had the BT49C in a comfortable second place until a rotor arm broke.

Rebaque briefly tried his hand at IndyCar racing in 1982, luckily winning a race at Elkhart Lake when many of the leaders ran out of fuel, but after a mid-season crash at Michigan he developed a distinct aversion to ovals, and retired at season's end at the age of 29.

BRIAN REDMAN

A racing driver for well over 30 years, Brian Redman had the talent to have become a Grand Prix winner, but his distaste for the high-pressure Formula 1 environment prompted him to turn his back on the GP paddock to enjoy an enormously successful and rewarding career in other forms of racing which has lasted into his fifties.

After early outings with a Mini, Redman made a name for himself in 1965 with a Jaguar E-Type before campaigning a Lola T70 in 1966. His career gradually gained momentum during 1967 in Formula 2 – with David Bridges' Lola – and sports car events, Brian winning the Rand 9 Hours in a Mirage with Ickx. In 1968 he had his first taste of Grand Prix racing with Cooper, which ended with a broken arm after a crash at Spa when his car's suspension failed. This came after a run of impressive performances, most notably victories in the BOAC 500 and Spa 1000 Km with Ickx in the GT40 and a brilliant drive in the F2 Eifelrennen with the Ferrari Dino that brought an offer of a works drive, which he declined.

Redman then began a long period in sports car racing (1969-73) with Porsche and Ferrari, winning virtually all the major classics with the striking exception of Le Mans, which has strangely eluded him. He made occasional returns to Grand Prix racing, usually as a replacement driver, but often without the benefit of testing and preparation. However, by this time Brian had established himself as the man to beat in US F5000, winning three successive titles between 1974 and 1976 in the Haas/Hall Lola.

Overcoming serious injuries received at the start of 1977 when his Can-Am Lola flipped, Brian was soon back, winning at Sebring in 1978 and taking the IMSA title in 1981. Based in Florida, Redman has since graced a wide variety of classes, racing as competitively as ever and revelling in the less-pressured atmosphere of motor sport in North America.

ALAN REES

A very useful driver in Formula Junior, Rees drove for the works Lotus team in 1962, taking three wins before a crash in a Lotus 23 at the Nürburgring 1000 Km sports car race curtailed his season.

For 1963, he joined the Roy Winkelmann team and would become its mainstay as both driver and, later, team manager. Concentrating on Formula 2 between 1964 and 1968, Rees drove countless races in the team's Brabhams, often beating the stars of the day, such as Rindt, Stewart and Clark. However, his Grand Prix opportunities were limited to a couple of races in the Winkelmann F2 car and a single outing in a rather tired works Cooper at the 1967 British GP.

By the end of 1968, Rees had decided that he was not going to progress any further as a driver and he retired to the team manager's role, before becoming a founder member of March, later acting as team manager of Shadow and Arrows.

REBAQUE, Hector (MEX) b 5/2/1956

1977

	Race	Circuit	No	Entrant	Car/Engine	Comment
dnq	BELGIAN GP	Zolder	39	Hesketh Racing	3.0 Hesketh 308E-Cosworth V8	
dnq	SWEDISH GP	Anderstorp	39	Hesketh Racing	3.0 Hesketh 308E-Cosworth V8	
dnq	FRENCH GP	Dijon	39	Hesketh Racing	3.0 Hesketh 308E-Cosworth V8	
ret	GERMAN GP	Hockenheim	25	Hesketh Racing	3.0 Hesketh 308E-Cosworth V8	*battery*
dnq	AUSTRIAN GP	Österreichring	25	Hesketh Racing	3.0 Hesketh 308E-Cosworth V8	
dnq	DUTCH GP	Zandvoort	25	Hesketh Racing	3.0 Hesketh 308E-Cosworth V8	

1978

	Race	Circuit	No	Entrant	Car/Engine	Comment
dnq	ARGENTINE GP	Buenos Aires	25	Team Rebaque	3.0 Lotus 78-Cosworth V8	
ret	BRAZILIAN GP	Rio	25	Team Rebaque	3.0 Lotus 78-Cosworth V8	*driver fatigue*
10	SOUTH AFRICAN GP	Kyalami	25	Team Rebaque	3.0 Lotus 78-Cosworth V8	*1 lap behind*
dnpq	US GP WEST	Long Beach	25	Team Rebaque	3.0 Lotus 78-Cosworth V8	
dnpq	MONACO GP	Monte Carlo	25	Team Rebaque	3.0 Lotus 78-Cosworth V8	
dnpq	BELGIAN GP	Zolder	25	Team Rebaque	3.0 Lotus 78-Cosworth V8	
ret	SPANISH GP	Jarama	25	Team Rebaque	3.0 Lotus 78-Cosworth V8	*exhaust system*
12	SWEDISH GP	Anderstorp	25	Team Rebaque	3.0 Lotus 78-Cosworth V8	*2 laps behind*
dnq	FRENCH GP	Paul Ricard	25	Team Rebaque	3.0 Lotus 78-Cosworth V8	
ret	BRITISH GP	Brands Hatch	25	Team Rebaque	3.0 Lotus 78-Cosworth V8	*gearbox*
6	GERMAN GP	Hockenheim	25	Team Rebaque	3.0 Lotus 78-Cosworth V8	
ret	AUSTRIAN GP	Österreichring	25	Team Rebaque	3.0 Lotus 78-Cosworth V8	*clutch*
11	DUTCH GP	Zandvoort	25	Team Rebaque	3.0 Lotus 78-Cosworth V8	*1 lap behind*
dnq	ITALIAN GP	Monza	25	Team Rebaque	3.0 Lotus 78-Cosworth V8	
ret	US GP EAST	Watkins Glen	25	Team Rebaque	3.0 Lotus 78-Cosworth V8	*clutch*
dnq	CANADIAN GP	Montreal	25	Team Rebaque	3.0 Lotus 78-Cosworth V8	

1979

ret	ARGENTINE GP	Buenos Aires	31	Team Rebaque	3.0 Lotus 79-Cosworth V8	suspension
dnq	BRAZILIAN GP	Interlagos	31	Team Rebaque	3.0 Lotus 79-Cosworth V8	
ret	SOUTH AFRICAN GP	Kyalami	31	Team Rebaque	3.0 Lotus 79-Cosworth V8	engine
ret	US GP WEST	Long Beach	31	Team Rebaque	3.0 Lotus 79-Cosworth V8	accident with Daly
ret	SPANISH GP	Jarama	31	Team Rebaque	3.0 Lotus 79-Cosworth V8	engine
ret	BELGIAN GP	Zolder	31	Team Rebaque	3.0 Lotus 79-Cosworth V8	driveshaft
12	FRENCH GP	Dijon	31	Team Rebaque	3.0 Lotus 79-Cosworth V8	2 laps behind
9	BRITISH GP	Silverstone	31	Team Rebaque	3.0 Lotus 79-Cosworth V8	2 laps behind
ret	GERMAN GP	Hockenheim	31	Team Rebaque	3.0 Lotus 79-Cosworth V8	handling
dnq	AUSTRIAN GP	Österreichring	31	Team Rebaque	3.0 Lotus 79-Cosworth V8	
7	DUTCH GP	Zandvoort	31	Team Rebaque	3.0 Lotus 79-Cosworth V8	2 laps behind
dnq	ITALIAN GP	Monza	31	Team Rebaque	3.0 Rebaque HR100-Cosworth V8	
ret	CANADIAN GP	Montreal	31	Team Rebaque	3.0 Rebaque HR100-Cosworth V8	engine mounting
dnq	US GP EAST	Watkins Glen	31	Team Rebaque	3.0 Rebaque HR100-Cosworth V8	

1980

7	BRITISH GP	Brands Hatch	6	Parmalat Racing Team	3.0 Brabham BT49-Cosworth V8	2 laps behind
ret	GERMAN GP	Hockenheim	6	Parmalat Racing Team	3.0 Brabham BT49-Cosworth V8	gearbox
10	AUSTRIAN GP	Österreichring	6	Parmalat Racing Team	3.0 Brabham BT49-Cosworth V8	1 lap behind
ret	DUTCH GP	Zandvoort	6	Parmalat Racing Team	3.0 Brabham BT49-Cosworth V8	gearbox
ret	ITALIAN GP	Imola	6	Parmalat Racing Team	3.0 Brabham BT49-Cosworth V8	broken rear suspension
6	CANADIAN GP	Montreal	6	Parmalat Racing Team	3.0 Brabham BT49-Cosworth V8	1 lap behind
ret	US GP EAST	Watkins Glen	6	Parmalat Racing Team	3.0 Brabham BT49-Cosworth V8	engine

1981

ret	US GP WEST	Long Beach	6	Parmalat Racing Team	3.0 Brabham BT49C-Cosworth V8	accident
ret	BRAZILIAN GP	Rio	6	Parmalat Racing Team	3.0 Brabham BT49C-Cosworth V8	rear suspension damage
ret	ARGENTINE GP	Buenos Aires	6	Parmalat Racing Team	3.0 Brabham BT49C-Cosworth V8	distibutor rotor arm
4	SAN MARINO GP	Imola	6	Parmalat Racing Team	3.0 Brabham BT49C-Cosworth V8	
ret	BELGIAN GP	Zolder	6	Parmalat Racing Team	3.0 Brabham BT49C-Cosworth V8	accident
dnq	MONACO GP	Monte Carlo	6	Parmalat Racing Team	3.0 Brabham BT49C-Cosworth V8	
ret	SPANISH GP	Jarama	6	Parmalat Racing Team	3.0 Brabham BT49C-Cosworth V8	gearbox
9	FRENCH GP	Dijon	6	Parmalat Racing Team	3.0 Brabham BT49C-Cosworth V8	2 laps behind
5	BRITISH GP	Silverstone	6	Parmalat Racing Team	3.0 Brabham BT49C-Cosworth V8	1 lap behind
4	GERMAN GP	Hockenheim	6	Parmalat Racing Team	3.0 Brabham BT49C-Cosworth V8	
ret	AUSTRIAN GP	Österreichring	6	Parmalat Racing Team	3.0 Brabham BT49C-Cosworth V8	clutch
4	DUTCH GP	Zandvoort	6	Parmalat Racing Team	3.0 Brabham BT49C-Cosworth V8	1 lap behind
ret	ITALIAN GP	Monza	6	Parmalat Racing Team	3.0 Brabham BT49C-Cosworth V8	electrics
ret	CANADIAN GP	Montreal	6	Parmalat Racing Team	3.0 Brabham BT49C-Cosworth V8	spun off
ret	CAESARS PALACE GP	Las Vegas	6	Parmalat Racing Team	3.0 Brabham BT49C-Cosworth V8	spun off

GP Starts: 41   GP Wins: 0   Pole positions: 0   Fastest laps: 0   Points: 13

REDMAN, Brian (GB) b 9/3/1937

1968

	Race	Circuit	No	Entrant	Car/Engine	Comment
ret	SOUTH AFRICAN GP	Kyalami	14	Cooper Car Co	3.0 Cooper T81B-Maserati V12	overheating/oil leak
3	SPANISH GP	Jarama	14	Cooper Car Co	3.0 Cooper T86B-BRM V12	
ret	BELGIAN GP	Spa	16	Cooper Car Co	3.0 Cooper T86B-BRM V12	accident/broken suspension

1970

dnp	SOUTH AFRICAN GP	Kyalami	11	Rob Walker Racing Team	3.0 Lotus 49C-Cosworth V8	did not practice, stand-by for Hill
dns	BRITISH GP	Brands Hatch	25	Frank Williams Racing Cars	3.0 de Tomaso 505-Cosworth V8	hub failure in practice
dnq	GERMAN GP	Hockenheim	25	Frank Williams Racing Cars	3.0 de Tomaso 505-Cosworth V8	

1971

7	SOUTH AFRICAN GP	Kyalami	28	Team Surtees	3.0 Surtees TS7-Cosworth V8	1 lap behind

1972

5	MONACO GP	Monte Carlo	15	Yardley Team McLaren	3.0 McLaren M19A-Cosworth V8	pit stop/puncture
9	FRENCH GP	Clermont Ferrand	11	Yardley Team McLaren	3.0 McLaren M19A-Cosworth V8	
5	GERMAN GP	Nürburgring	15	Yardley Team McLaren	3.0 McLaren M19A-Cosworth V8	
ret	US GP	Watkins Glen	15	Marlboro BRM	3.0 BRM P180 V12	engine

1973

dsq	US GP	Watkins Glen	31	Shadow Racing Team	3.0 Shadow DN1-Cosworth V8	outside assistance

1974

7	SPANISH GP	Jarama	16	UOP Shadow Racing Team	3.0 Shadow DN3-Cosworth V8	3 laps behind
18/ret	BELGIAN GP	Nivelles	16	UOP Shadow Racing Team	3.0 Shadow DN3-Cosworth V8	engine/5 laps behind
ret	MONACO GP	Monte Carlo	16	UOP Shadow Racing Team	3.0 Shadow DN3-Cosworth V8	multiple accident

GP Starts: 12   GP Wins: 0   Pole positions: 0   Fastest laps: 0   Points: 8

REES, Alan (GB) b 12/1/1938

1966

	Race	Circuit	No	Entrant	Car/Engine	Comment
ret	GERMAN GP (F2)	Nürburgring	29	Roy Winkelmann Racing	1.0 Brabham BT18-Cosworth 4 F2	gearbox/engine

1967

9	BRITISH GP	Silverstone	14	Cooper Car Co	3.0 Cooper T81-Maserati V12	4 laps behind
7*	GERMAN GP (F2)	Nürburgring	22	Roy Winkelmann Racing	1.6 Brabham BT23-Cosworth 4 F2	* 2nd in F2 class

GP Starts: 3   GP Wins: 0   Pole positions: 0   Fastest laps: 0   Points: 0

CLAY REGAZZONI

A driver right out of the old school, Regazzoni took no prisoners with his rough-and-ready approach to racing during his early days of Formula 3. And while he may have tempered his approach in the ensuing years, he was always liable to revert to type, leaving his competitors a little wary as they locked horns with the hard-racing Swiss.

After competing with a Healey Sprite, Clay joined forces with fellow countryman Silvio Moser to race F2 and F3 Brabhams in 1965-66 before switching to Tecnos. Regazzoni joined the works team in 1968 to compete in the European Formula 2 championship, where some of his driving tactics became a cause for concern. Things reached a low ebb in mid-season, when he was disqualified for overtaking at the site of an accident at Monza and then, in the next race at Zandvoort, was involved in Chris Lambert's fatal accident. The fall-out from this incident was to last for some considerable time, and though Regazzoni was absolved from blame some mud would always stick. The 1969 season brought an invitation from Ferrari to race their 166 Dino, but little of note was achieved, and he soon returned to the Tecno ranks. This proved a wise decision, for the team's F2 car really came good in 1970. Up to this point Clay had been regarded as something of a neanderthal, but wins at Hockenheim, Paul Ricard, Enna and Imola helped dispel this image and he jumped into the Ferrari F1 team with no qualms at all. Fourth place on his debut was a great effort, but better was to come when, after a splendid second at the Österreichring, he took the ultimate prize for a Ferrari driver, winning the Italian GP at Monza. His place was now secure, but over the next two seasons, apart from the Race of Champions in 1971, there were to be no more wins – some good performances to be sure, but too many incidents for the Scuderia's liking. Thus at the end of 1972 he was released, but soon found a seat with the Marlboro BRM squad.

Regazzoni took his change of circumstances with equanimity and started the season with a great drive in the Argentine GP, taking pole and leading the race for 30 laps before troubles dropped him back. His year was largely spent in midfield anonymity, however, before a surprise recall to Ferrari, who were restructuring after a terrible year. The 1974 season was probably the Swiss driver's finest. There were off-track excursions but he was a remarkably consistent finisher and took a superb win at the Nürburgring to get within touching distance of the World Championship. His value to Ferrari at this period was immense, Clay proving the ideal foil for Niki Lauda, quite capable of picking up the pieces if necessary, as in the non-title Swiss GP and then the Italian GP at Monza the following season. Unfortunately there was still the occasional brainstorm, and his tactics at Watkins Glen, where he blatantly blocked Fittipaldi, were a disgrace. In 1976 we saw the same cocktail – a brilliant win at Long Beach, and a crass first-corner manoeuvre at Paddock Bend in the infamous British GP. Certainly his form began to tail off towards the end of that year, and his services were no longer required.

Joining the little Ensign squad for 1977 was akin to leaving the Ritz to dine at Wimpy, but Regazzoni was happy just to be part of the scene. There were, of course, the inevitable crashes, but a couple of fifth places near the end of the season kept Mo Nunn happy enough. Clay was tempted by the lure of Indianapolis that year, and qualified in a Theodore McLaren, but retired the car in the race with a water leak. His Swiss connections helped him into the Shadow team for 1978, but apart from Anderstorp it was a pretty dismal year. It was difficult to see much future for Regazzoni by this stage, but Frank Williams was to take Clay on board. He reasoned that in a good car he had been almost as quick as Lauda, and his experience would be an asset in the team's expanded two-car operation. Frank's hunch was to prove correct, as Clay won at Silverstone to score the Williams team's first-ever Grand Prix win, and a special place in their history. Sentiment didn't cloud Williams' judgement when it came to his 1980 line-up, however, and when Carlos Reutemann became available Regazzoni was out.

Unperturbed, Clay counted his blessings and headed back to Ensign. The team now had a healthier budget and a new car, but the season was only four races old when disaster struck. In the Grand Prix at Long Beach, the brake pedal snapped, leaving his red, white and blue machine hurtling down the escape road into a parked Brabham. Poor Regazzoni sustained serious spinal damage, which has since confined him to a wheelchair, but despite this crippling injury, Clay has lost none of his enthusiasm for the sport, working regularly as a commentator for Swiss TV.

REGAZZONI, Clay (Gianclaudio) (CH) b 5/12/1939

1970

	Race	Circuit	No	Entrant	Car/Engine	Comment
4	DUTCH GP	Zandvoort	26	Scuderia Ferrari SpA SEFAC	3.0 Ferrari 312B F12	1 lap behind
4	BRITISH GP	Brands Hatch	4	Scuderia Ferrari SpA SEFAC	3.0 Ferrari 312B F12	
ret	GERMAN GP	Hockenheim	15	Scuderia Ferrari SpA SEFAC	3.0 Ferrari 312B F12	gearbox problems/spun off
2	AUSTRIAN GP	Österreichring	2	Scuderia Ferrari SpA SEFAC	3.0 Ferrari 312B F12	FL
1	ITALIAN GP	Monza	4	Scuderia Ferrari SpA SEFAC	3.0 Ferrari 312B F12	FL
2	CANADIAN GP	St Jovite	19	Scuderia Ferrari SpA SEFAC	3.0 Ferrari 312B F12	FL
13	US GP	Watkins Glen	4	Scuderia Ferrari SpA SEFAC	3.0 Ferrari 312B F12	pit stop/fuel pipe/7 laps behind
2	MEXICAN GP	Mexico City	4	Scuderia Ferrari SpA SEFAC	3.0 Ferrari 312B F12	Pole

1971

	Race	Circuit	No	Entrant	Car/Engine	Comment
3	SOUTH AFRICAN GP	Kyalami	5	Scuderia Ferrari SpA SEFAC	3.0 Ferrari 312B F12	
ret	SPANISH GP	Montjuich Park	5	Scuderia Ferrari SpA SEFAC	3.0 Ferrari 312B F12	engine
dns	"	"	5T	Scuderia Ferrari SpA SEFAC	3.0 Ferrari 312B2 F12	practice only
ret	MONACO GP	Monte Carlo	3	Scuderia Ferrari SpA SEFAC	3.0 Ferrari 312B2 F12	hit chicane-suspension
3	DUTCH GP	Zandvoort	3	Scuderia Ferrari SpA SEFAC	3.0 Ferrari 312B2 F12	late spin/1 lap behind
dns	"	"	3T	Scuderia Ferrari SpA SEFAC	3.0 Ferrari 312B F12	practice only
ret	FRENCH GP	Paul Ricard	5	Scuderia Ferrari SpA SEFAC	3.0 Ferrari 312B2 F12	spun off-damaged wheel
ret	BRITISH GP	Silverstone	5	Scuderia Ferrari SpA SEFAC	3.0 Ferrari 312B2 F12	engine/Pole
3	GERMAN GP	Nürburgring	6	Scuderia Ferrari SpA SEFAC	3.0 Ferrari 312B2 F12	
dns	"	"	31	Scuderia Ferrari SpA SEFAC	3.0 Ferrari 312B F12	practice only
ret	AUSTRIAN GP	Österreichring	5	Scuderia Ferrari SpA SEFAC	3.0 Ferrari 312B2 F12	engine
ret	ITALIAN GP	Monza	4	Scuderia Ferrari SpA SEFAC	3.0 Ferrari 312B2 F12	engine damper
ret	CANADIAN GP	Mosport Park	5	Scuderia Ferrari SpA SEFAC	3.0 Ferrari 312B2 F12	electrical fire/accident
dns	"	" "	25T	Scuderia Ferrari SpA SEFAC	3.0 Ferrari 312B2 F12	practice only
6	US GP	Watkins Glen	5	Scuderia Ferrari SpA SEFAC	3.0 Ferrari 312B2 F12	spin

1972

	Race	Circuit	No	Entrant	Car/Engine	Comment
4	ARGENTINE GP	Buenos Aires	9	Scuderia Ferrari SpA SEFAC	3.0 Ferrari 312B2 F12	
12	SOUTH AFRICAN GP	Kyalami	6	Scuderia Ferrari SpA SEFAC	3.0 Ferrari 312B2 F12	pit stop/tyres/2 laps behind
3	SPANISH GP	Jarama	6	Scuderia Ferrari SpA SEFAC	3.0 Ferrari 312B2 F12	1 lap behind
ret	MONACO GP	Monte Carlo	7	Scuderia Ferrari SpA SEFAC	3.0 Ferrari 312B2 F12	hit barrier
ret	BELGIAN GP	Nivelles	30	Scuderia Ferrari SpA SEFAC	3.0 Ferrari 312B2 F12	hit Galli's spinning car
2	GERMAN GP	Nürburgring	9	Scuderia Ferrari SpA SEFAC	3.0 Ferrari 312B2 F12	hit Stewart on last lap
ret	AUSTRIAN GP	Österreichring	19	Scuderia Ferrari SpA SEFAC	3.0 Ferrari 312B2 F12	fuel pressure
ret	ITALIAN GP	Monza	5	Scuderia Ferrari SpA SEFAC	3.0 Ferrari 312B2 F12	hit Pace at chicane
5	CANADIAN GP	Mosport Park	11	Scuderia Ferrari SpA SEFAC	3.0 Ferrari 312B2 F12	handling problems
8	US GP	Watkins Glen	8	Scuderia Ferrari SpA SEFAC	3.0 Ferrari 312B2 F12	exhaust fell off/1 lap behind

1973

	Race	Circuit	No	Entrant	Car/Engine	Comment
7	ARGENTINE GP	Buenos Aires	32	Marlboro BRM	3.0 BRM P160D V12	Pole/3 laps behind
6	BRAZILIAN GP	Interlagos	14	Marlboro BRM	3.0 BRM P160D V12	1 lap behind
ret	SOUTH AFRICAN GP	Kyalami	14	Marlboro BRM	3.0 BRM P160D V12	multiple accident/rescued by Hailwood
9	SPANISH GP	Montjuich Park	14	Marlboro BRM	3.0 BRM P160E V12	pit stops/tyres/6 laps behind
10/ret	BELGIAN GP	Zolder	19	Marlboro BRM	3.0 BRM P160E V12	spun off
ret	MONACO GP	Monte Carlo	14	Marlboro BRM	3.0 BRM P160E V12	boiling brake fluid
9	SWEDISH GP	Anderstorp	14	Marlboro BRM	3.0 BRM P160E V12	3 laps behind
12	FRENCH GP	Paul Ricard	14	Marlboro BRM	3.0 BRM P160E V12	1 lap behind
7	BRITISH GP	Silverstone	14	Marlboro BRM	3.0 BRM P160E V12	
8	DUTCH GP	Zandvoort	14	Marlboro BRM	3.0 BRM P160E V12	2 pit stops/tyre/fuel/4 laps behind
ret	GERMAN GP	Nürburgring	14	Marlboro BRM	3.0 BRM P160E V12	engine
6	AUSTRIAN GP	Österreichring	14	Marlboro BRM	3.0 BRM P160E V12	
ret	ITALIAN GP	Monza	14	Marlboro BRM	3.0 BRM P160E V12	coil
8	US GP	Watkins Glen	14	Marlboro BRM	3.0 BRM P160E V12	1 lap behind

1974

	Race	Circuit	No	Entrant	Car/Engine	Comment
3	ARGENTINE GP	Buenos Aires	11	Scuderia Ferrari SpA SEFAC	3.0 Ferrari 312B3 F12	FL
2	BRAZILIAN GP	Interlagos	11	Scuderia Ferrari SpA SEFAC	3.0 Ferrari 312B3 F12	FL
ret	SOUTH AFRICAN GP	Kyalami	11	Scuderia Ferrari SpA SEFAC	3.0 Ferrari 312B3 F12	oil pressure
2	SPANISH GP	Jarama	11	Scuderia Ferrari SpA SEFAC	3.0 Ferrari 312B3 F12	
4	BELGIAN GP	Nivelles	11	Scuderia Ferrari SpA SEFAC	3.0 Ferrari 312B3 F12	Pole
4	MONACO GP	Monte Carlo	11	Scuderia Ferrari SpA SEFAC	3.0 Ferrari 312B3 F12	
ret	SWEDISH GP	Anderstorp	11	Scuderia Ferrari SpA SEFAC	3.0 Ferrari 312B3 F12	transmission
2	DUTCH GP	Zandvoort	11	Scuderia Ferrari SpA SEFAC	3.0 Ferrari 312B3 F12	
3	FRENCH GP	Dijon	11	Scuderia Ferrari SpA SEFAC	3.0 Ferrari 312B3 F12	
4	BRITISH GP	Brands Hatch	11	Scuderia Ferrari SpA SEFAC	3.0 Ferrari 312B3 F12	
1	GERMAN GP	Nürburgring	11	Scuderia Ferrari SpA SEFAC	3.0 Ferrari 312B3 F12	
5	AUSTRIAN GP	Österreichring	11	Scuderia Ferrari SpA SEFAC	3.0 Ferrari 312B3 F12	pit stop/tyre/FL
ret	ITALIAN GP	Monza	11	Scuderia Ferrari SpA SEFAC	3.0 Ferrari 312B3 F12	engine oil seal
2	CANADIAN GP	Mosport Park	11	Scuderia Ferrari SpA SEFAC	3.0 Ferrari 312B3 F12	
11	US GP	Watkins Glen	11	Scuderia Ferrari SpA SEFAC	3.0 Ferrari 312B3 F12	3 pit stops/handling/4 laps behind

1975

	Race	Circuit	No	Entrant	Car/Engine	Comment
4	ARGENTINE GP	Buenos Aires	12	Scuderia Ferrari SpA SEFAC	3.0 Ferrari 312B3 F12	
4	BRAZILIAN GP	Interlagos	12	Scuderia Ferrari SpA SEFAC	3.0 Ferrari 312B3 F12	
16/ret	SOUTH AFRICAN GP	Kyalami	12	Scuderia Ferrari SpA SEFAC	3.0 Ferrari 312T F12	throttle linkage/7 laps behind
nc	SPANISH GP	Montjuich Park	12	Scuderia Ferrari SpA SEFAC	3.0 Ferrari 312T F12	pit stop-collision/4 laps behind
ret	MONACO GP	Monte Carlo	12	Scuderia Ferrari SpA SEFAC	3.0 Ferrari 312T F12	spun off-damaged suspension
5	BELGIAN GP	Zolder	12	Scuderia Ferrari SpA SEFAC	3.0 Ferrari 312T F12	pit stop/tyre/FL
3	SWEDISH GP	Anderstorp	12	Scuderia Ferrari SpA SEFAC	3.0 Ferrari 312T F12	
3	DUTCH GP	Zandvoort	12	Scuderia Ferrari SpA SEFAC	3.0 Ferrari 312T F12	
ret	FRENCH GP	Paul Ricard	12	Scuderia Ferrari SpA SEFAC	3.0 Ferrari 312T F12	engine
13	BRITISH GP	Silverstone	12	Scuderia Ferrari SpA SEFAC	3.0 Ferrari 312T F12	pit stops/tyres/FL/2 laps behind
ret	GERMAN GP	Nürburgring	12	Scuderia Ferrari SpA SEFAC	3.0 Ferrari 312T F12	engine/FL

Pos	Grand Prix	Circuit	No	Entrant	Car	Notes
7	AUSTRIAN GP	Österreichring	12	Scuderia Ferrari SpA SEFAC	3.0 Ferrari 312T F12	
1	ITALIAN GP	Monza	12	Scuderia Ferrari SpA SEFAC	3.0 Ferrari 312T F12	*FL*
ret	US GP	Watkins Glen	12	Scuderia Ferrari SpA SEFAC	3.0 Ferrari 312T F12	*withdrawn in protest over reprimand*

1976

Pos	Grand Prix	Circuit	No	Entrant	Car	Notes
7	BRAZILIAN GP	Interlagos	2	Scuderia Ferrari SpA SEFAC	3.0 Ferrari 312T F12	*pit stop/tyre*
ret	SOUTH AFRICAN GP	Kyalami	2	Scuderia Ferrari SpA SEFAC	3.0 Ferrari 312T F12	*engine*
1	US GP WEST	Long Beach	2	Scuderia Ferrari SpA SEFAC	3.0 Ferrari 312T F12	*Pole/FL*
11	SPANISH GP	Jarama	2	Scuderia Ferrari SpA SEFAC	3.0 Ferrari 312T2 F12	*pit stop/gear selection/3 laps behind*
2	BELGIAN GP	Zolder	2	Scuderia Ferrari SpA SEFAC	3.0 Ferrari 312T2 F12	
14/ret	MONACO GP	Monte Carlo	2	Scuderia Ferrari SpA SEFAC	3.0 Ferrari 312T2 F12	*spun off/FL/5 laps behind*
6	SWEDISH GP	Anderstorp	2	Scuderia Ferrari SpA SEFAC	3.0 Ferrari 312T2 F12	
ret	FRENCH GP	Paul Ricard	2	Scuderia Ferrari SpA SEFAC	3.0 Ferrari 312T2 F12	*engine-spun off*
ret/dsq	BRITISH GP	Brands Hatch	2	Scuderia Ferrari SpA SEFAC	3.0 Ferrari 312T2 F12	*accident/used training car in restart*
9	GERMAN GP	Nürburgring	2	Scuderia Ferrari SpA SEFAC	3.0 Ferrari 312T2 F12	*pit stop/nose cone*
2	DUTCH GP	Zandvoort	2	Scuderia Ferrari SpA SEFAC	3.0 Ferrari 312T2 F12	*FL*
2	ITALIAN GP	Monza	2	Scuderia Ferrari SpA SEFAC	3.0 Ferrari 312T2 F12	
6	CANADIAN GP	Mosport Park	2	Scuderia Ferrari SpA SEFAC	3.0 Ferrari 312T2 F12	*1 lap behind*
7	US GP EAST	Watkins Glen	2	Scuderia Ferrari SpA SEFAC	3.0 Ferrari 312T2 F12	*1 lap behind*
5	JAPANESE GP	Mount Fuji	2	Scuderia Ferrari SpA SEFAC	3.0 Ferrari 312T2 F12	*pit stop/tyre*

1977

Pos	Grand Prix	Circuit	No	Entrant	Car	Notes
6	ARGENTINE GP	Buenos Aires	22	Team Tissot Ensign with Castrol	3.0 Ensign N177-Cosworth V8	*2 laps behind*
ret	BRAZILIAN GP	Interlagos	22	Team Tissot Ensign with Castrol	3.0 Ensign N177-Cosworth V8	*hit catch-fencing spun onto track*
9	SOUTH AFRICAN GP	Kyalami	22	Team Tissot Ensign with Castrol	3.0 Ensign N177-Cosworth V8	
ret	US GP WEST	Long Beach	22	Team Tissot Ensign with Castrol	3.0 Ensign N177-Cosworth V8	*gearbox*
ret	SPANISH GP	Jarama	22	Team Tissot Ensign with Castrol	3.0 Ensign N177-Cosworth V8	*collision with Brambilla*
dnq	MONACO GP	Monte Carlo	22	Team Tissot Ensign with Castrol	3.0 Ensign N177-Cosworth V8	
ret	BELGIAN GP	Zolder	22	Team Tissot Ensign with Castrol	3.0 Ensign N177-Cosworth V8	*engine*
7	SWEDISH GP	Anderstorp	22	Team Tissot Ensign with Castrol	3.0 Ensign N177-Cosworth V8	
7	FRENCH GP	Dijon	22	Team Tissot Ensign with Castrol	3.0 Ensign N177-Cosworth V8	*1 lap behind*
dnq	BRITISH GP	Silverstone	22	Team Tissot Ensign with Castrol	3.0 Ensign N177-Cosworth V8	
ret	GERMAN GP	Hockenheim	22	Team Tissot Ensign with Castrol	3.0 Ensign N177-Cosworth V8	*startline accident*
ret	AUSTRIAN GP	Österreichring	22	Team Tissot Ensign with Castrol	3.0 Ensign N177-Cosworth V8	*spun off*
ret	DUTCH GP	Zandvoort	22	Team Tissot Ensign with Castrol	3.0 Ensign N177-Cosworth V8	*throttle cable*
5	ITALIAN GP	Monza	22	Team Tissot Ensign with Castrol	3.0 Ensign N177-Cosworth V8	
5	US GP EAST	Watkins Glen	22	Team Tissot Ensign with Castrol	3.0 Ensign N177-Cosworth V8	
ret	CANADIAN GP	Mosport Park	22	Team Tissot Ensign with Castrol	3.0 Ensign N177-Cosworth V8	*crashed on lap 1*
ret	JAPANESE GP	Mount Fuji	22	Team Tissot Ensign with Castrol	3.0 Ensign N177-Cosworth V8	*engine*

1978

Pos	Grand Prix	Circuit	No	Entrant	Car	Notes
15	ARGENTINE GP	Buenos Aires	17	Shadow Racing Team	3.0 Shadow DN8-Cosworth V8	*pit stop/tyre/1 lap behind*
5	BRAZILIAN GP	Rio	17	Shadow Racing Team	3.0 Shadow DN8-Cosworth V8	*1 lap behind*
dnq	SOUTH AFRICAN GP	Kyalami	17	Shadow Racing Team	3.0 Shadow DN8-Cosworth V8	
10	US GP WEST	Long Beach	17	Shadow Racing Team	3.0 Shadow DN8-Cosworth V8	*1 lap behind*
dnq	MONACO GP	Monte Carlo	17	Shadow Racing Team	3.0 Shadow DN9-Cosworth V8	
ret	BELGIAN GP	Zolder	17	Shadow Racing Team	3.0 Shadow DN9-Cosworth V8	*differential*
15/ret	SPANISH GP	Jarama	17	Shadow Racing Team	3.0 Shadow DN9-Cosworth V8	*fuel union/8 laps behind*
5	SWEDISH GP	Anderstorp	17	Shadow Racing Team	3.0 Shadow DN9-Cosworth V8	*1 lap behind*
ret	FRENCH GP	Paul Ricard	17	Shadow Racing Team	3.0 Shadow DN9-Cosworth V8	*electrics*
ret	BRITISH GP	Brands Hatch	17	Shadow Racing Team	3.0 Shadow DN9-Cosworth V8	*gearbox*
dnq	GERMAN GP	Hockenheim	17	Shadow Racing Team	3.0 Shadow DN9-Cosworth V8	
nc	AUSTRIAN GP	Österreichring	17	Shadow Racing Team	3.0 Shadow DN9-Cosworth V8	*pit stop/tyres/7 laps behind*
dnq	DUTCH GP	Zandvoort	17	Shadow Racing Team	3.0 Shadow DN9-Cosworth V8	
nc	ITALIAN GP	Monza	17	Shadow Racing Team	3.0 Shadow DN9-Cosworth V8	*pit stops/7 laps behind*
14	US GP EAST	Watkins Glen	17	Shadow Racing Team	3.0 Shadow DN9-Cosworth V8	*pit stop/tyres/3 laps behind*
dnq	CANADIAN GP	Montreal	17	Shadow Racing Team	3.0 Shadow DN9-Cosworth V8	

1979

Pos	Grand Prix	Circuit	No	Entrant	Car	Notes
10	ARGENTINE GP	Buenos Aires	28	Albilad-Saudia Racing Team	3.0 Williams FW06-Cosworth V8	*pit stop/tyres/2 laps behind*
15	BRAZILIAN GP	Interlagos	28	Albilad-Saudia Racing Team	3.0 Williams FW06-Cosworth V8	*pit stop/damage check/-2 laps*
9	SOUTH AFRICAN GP	Kyalami	28	Albilad-Saudia Racing Team	3.0 Williams FW06-Cosworth V8	*2 laps behind*
ret	US GP WEST	Long Beach	28	Albilad-Saudia Racing Team	3.0 Williams FW06-Cosworth V8	*engine*
ret	SPANISH GP	Jarama	28	Albilad-Saudia Racing Team	3.0 Williams FW07-Cosworth V8	*engine*
ret	BELGIAN GP	Zolder	28	Albilad-Saudia Racing Team	3.0 Williams FW07-Cosworth V8	*accident-Scheckter & Villeneuve*
2	MONACO GP	Monte Carlo	28	Albilad-Saudia Racing Team	3.0 Williams FW07-Cosworth V8	
6	FRENCH GP	Dijon	28	Albilad-Saudia Racing Team	3.0 Williams FW07-Cosworth V8	
1	BRITISH GP	Silverstone	28	Albilad-Saudia Racing Team	3.0 Williams FW07-Cosworth V8	*FL*
2	GERMAN GP	Hockenheim	28	Albilad-Saudia Racing Team	3.0 Williams FW07-Cosworth V8	
5	AUSTRIAN GP	Österreichring	28	Albilad-Saudia Racing Team	3.0 Williams FW07-Cosworth V8	
ret	DUTCH GP	Zandvoort	28	Albilad-Saudia Racing Team	3.0 Williams FW07-Cosworth V8	*accident with Arnoux at the start*
3	ITALIAN GP	Monza	28	Albilad-Saudia Racing Team	3.0 Williams FW07-Cosworth V8	*FL*
3	CANADIAN GP	Montreal	28	Albilad-Saudia Racing Team	3.0 Williams FW07-Cosworth V8	
ret	US GP EAST	Watkins Glen	28	Albilad-Saudia Racing Team	3.0 Williams FW07-Cosworth V8	*collision with Piquet*

1980

Pos	Grand Prix	Circuit	No	Entrant	Car	Notes
nc	ARGENTINE GP	Buenos Aires	14	Unipart Racing Team	3.0 Ensign N180-Cosworth V8	*3 pit stops/throttle/9 laps behind*
ret	BRAZILIAN GP	Interlagos	14	Unipart Racing Team	3.0 Ensign N180-Cosworth V8	*handling*
9	SOUTH AFRICAN GP	Kyalami	14	Unipart Racing Team	3.0 Ensign N180-Cosworth V8	*1 lap behind*
ret	US GP WEST	Long Beach	14	Unipart Racing Team	3.0 Ensign N180-Cosworth V8	*brake failure/accident/paralysed*

GP Starts: 132   GP Wins: 5   Pole positions: 5   Fastest laps: 15   Points: 212

REUTEMANN, Carlos (R) b 12/4/1942

1972

	Race	Circuit	No	Entrant	Car/Engine	Comment
7	ARGENTINE GP	Buenos Aires	2	Motor Racing Developments	3.0 Brabham BT34-Cosworth V8	pit stop/loose air box/Pole/-2 laps
ret	SOUTH AFRICAN GP	Kyalami	20	Motor Racing Developments	3.0 Brabham BT34-Cosworth V8	fuel line
13	BELGIAN GP	Nivelles	19	Motor Racing Developments	3.0 Brabham BT37-Cosworth V8	pit stops/clutch/gear lever/-4 laps
12	FRENCH GP	Clermont Ferrand	20	Motor Racing Developments	3.0 Brabham BT37-Cosworth V8	1 lap behind
8	BRITISH GP	Brands Hatch	27	Motor Racing Developments	3.0 Brabham BT37-Cosworth V8	pit stop/wheels/3 laps behind
ret	GERMAN GP	Nürburgring	12	Motor Racing Developments	3.0 Brabham BT37-Cosworth V8	gearbox
ret	AUSTRIAN GP	Österreichring	17	Motor Racing Developments	3.0 Brabham BT37-Cosworth V8	fuel metering unit
ret	ITALIAN GP	Monza	30	Motor Racing Developments	3.0 Brabham BT37-Cosworth V8	hit chicane-suspension damage
4	CANADIAN GP	Mosport Park	8	Motor Racing Developments	3.0 Brabham BT37-Cosworth V8	
ret	US GP	Watkins Glen	29	Motor Racing Developments	3.0 Brabham BT37-Cosworth V8	engine

1973

	Race	Circuit	No	Entrant	Car/Engine	Comment
ret	ARGENTINE GP	Buenos Aires	10	Motor Racing Developments	3.0 Brabham BT37-Cosworth V8	gearbox
11	BRAZILIAN GP	Interlagos	17	Motor Racing Developments	3.0 Brabham BT37-Cosworth V8	pit stop/fuel metering unit/-2 laps
7	SOUTH AFRICAN GP	Kyalami	18	Motor Racing Developments	3.0 Brabham BT37-Cosworth V8	pit stop/tyre/2 laps behind
ret	SPANISH GP	Montjuich Park	18	Motor Racing Developments	3.0 Brabham BT42-Cosworth V8	driveshaft
ret	BELGIAN GP	Zolder	10	Motor Racing Developments	3.0 Brabham BT42-Cosworth V8	oil leak
ret	MONACO GP	Monte Carlo	10	Motor Racing Developments	3.0 Brabham BT42-Cosworth V8	gearbox
4	SWEDISH GP	Anderstorp	10	Motor Racing Developments	3.0 Brabham BT42-Cosworth V8	
3	FRENCH GP	Paul Ricard	10	Motor Racing Developments	3.0 Brabham BT42-Cosworth V8	
6	BRITISH GP	Silverstone	10	Motor Racing Developments	3.0 Brabham BT42-Cosworth V8	
ret	DUTCH GP	Zandvoort	10	Motor Racing Developments	3.0 Brabham BT42-Cosworth V8	burst tyre
ret	GERMAN GP	Nürburgring	10	Motor Racing Developments	3.0 Brabham BT42-Cosworth V8	engine
4	AUSTRIAN GP	Österreichring	10	Motor Racing Developments	3.0 Brabham BT42-Cosworth V8	
6	ITALIAN GP	Monza	10	Motor Racing Developments	3.0 Brabham BT42-Cosworth V8	
8	CANADIAN GP	Mosport Park	10	Motor Racing Developments	3.0 Brabham BT42-Cosworth V8	pit stop/tyres/2 laps behind
3	US GP	Watkins Glen	10	Motor Racing Developments	3.0 Brabham BT42-Cosworth V8	

1974

	Race	Circuit	No	Entrant	Car/Engine	Comment
7	ARGENTINE GP	Buenos Aires	7	Motor Racing Developments	3.0 Brabham BT44-Cosworth V8	led race/out of fuel/1 lap behind
7	BRAZILIAN GP	Interlagos	7	Motor Racing Developments	3.0 Brabham BT44-Cosworth V8	led race/tyre problems/-1 lap
1	SOUTH AFRICAN GP	Kyalami	7	Motor Racing Developments	3.0 Brabham BT44-Cosworth V8	FL
ret	SPANISH GP	Jarama	7	Motor Racing Developments	3.0 Brabham BT44-Cosworth V8	spun off
ret	BELGIAN GP	Nivelles	7	Motor Racing Developments	3.0 Brabham BT44-Cosworth V8	broken fuel line
ret	MONACO GP	Monte Carlo	7	Motor Racing Developments	3.0 Brabham BT44-Cosworth V8	hit Peterson
ret	SWEDISH GP	Anderstorp	7	Motor Racing Developments	3.0 Brabham BT44-Cosworth V8	oil leak
12	DUTCH GP	Zandvoort	7	Motor Racing Developments	3.0 Brabham BT44-Cosworth V8	pit stop/tyres/4 laps behind
ret	FRENCH GP	Dijon	7	Motor Racing Developments	3.0 Brabham BT44-Cosworth V8	handling
6	BRITISH GP	Brands Hatch	7	Motor Racing Developments	3.0 Brabham BT44-Cosworth V8	spin/1 lap behind
3	GERMAN GP	Nürburgring	7	Motor Racing Developments	3.0 Brabham BT44-Cosworth V8	
1	AUSTRIAN GP	Österreichring	7	Motor Racing Developments	3.0 Brabham BT44-Cosworth V8	
ret	ITALIAN GP	Monza	7	Motor Racing Developments	3.0 Brabham BT44-Cosworth V8	gearbox
9	CANADIAN GP	Mosport Park	7	Motor Racing Developments	3.0 Brabham BT44-Cosworth V8	pit stop/tyres/1 lap behind
1	US GP	Watkins Glen	7	Motor Racing Developments	3.0 Brabham BT44-Cosworth V8	Pole

1975

	Race	Circuit	No	Entrant	Car/Engine	Comment
3	ARGENTINE GP	Buenos Aires	7	Martini Racing	3.0 Brabham BT44B-Cosworth V8	led race
8	BRAZILIAN GP	Interlagos	7	Martini Racing	3.0 Brabham BT44B-Cosworth V8	pit stop/tyre/led race
2	SOUTH AFRICAN GP	Kyalami	7	Martini Racing	3.0 Brabham BT44B-Cosworth V8	
3*	SPANISH GP	Montjuich Park	7	Martini Racing	3.0 Brabham BT44B-Cosworth V8	race stopped/*half points/-1 lap
9	MONACO GP	Monte Carlo	7	Martini Racing	3.0 Brabham BT44B-Cosworth V8	wrong tyre choice/2 laps behind
3	BELGIAN GP	Zolder	7	Martini Racing	3.0 Brabham BT44B-Cosworth V8	
2	SWEDISH GP	Anderstorp	7	Martini Racing	3.0 Brabham BT44B-Cosworth V8	led race
4	DUTCH GP	Zandvoort	7	Martini Racing	3.0 Brabham BT44B-Cosworth V8	pit stop//tyres/1 lap behind
14	FRENCH GP	Paul Ricard	7	Martini Racing	3.0 Brabham BT44B-Cosworth V8	pit stop/tyres/1 lap behind
ret	BRITISH GP	Silverstone	7	Martini Racing	3.0 Brabham BT44B-Cosworth V8	engine
1	GERMAN GP	Nürburgring	7	Martini Racing	3.0 Brabham BT44B-Cosworth V8	
14	AUSTRIAN GP	Österreichring	7	Martini Racing	3.0 Brabham BT44B-Cosworth V8	1 lap behind
4	ITALIAN GP	Monza	7	Martini Racing	3.0 Brabham BT44B-Cosworth V8	
ret	US GP	Watkins Glen	7	Martini Racing	3.0 Brabham BT44B-Cosworth V8	engine

1976

	Race	Circuit	No	Entrant	Car/Engine	Comment
12/ret	BRAZILIAN GP	Interlagos	7	Martini Racing	3.0 Brabham BT45-Alfa Romeo F12	out of fuel/3 laps behind
ret	SOUTH AFRICAN GP	Kyalami	7	Martini Racing	3.0 Brabham BT45-Alfa Romeo F12	engine
ret	US GP WEST	Long Beach	7	Martini Racing	3.0 Brabham BT45-Alfa Romeo F12	collision with Brambilla
4	SPANISH GP	Jarama	7	Martini Racing	3.0 Brabham BT45-Alfa Romeo F12	
ret	BELGIAN GP	Zolder	7	Martini Racing	3.0 Brabham BT45-Alfa Romeo F12	engine
ret	MONACO GP	Monte Carlo	7	Martini Racing	3.0 Brabham BT45-Alfa Romeo F12	collision with Jones
ret	SWEDISH GP	Anderstorp	7	Martini Racing	3.0 Brabham BT45-Alfa Romeo F12	engine
11	FRENCH GP	Paul Ricard	7	Martini Racing	3.0 Brabham BT45-Alfa Romeo F12	
ret	BRITISH GP	Brands Hatch	7	Martini Racing	3.0 Brabham BT45-Alfa Romeo F12	oil pressure
ret	GERMAN GP	Nürburgring	7	Martini Racing	3.0 Brabham BT45-Alfa Romeo F12	engine
ret	AUSTRIAN GP	Österreichring	7	Martini Racing	3.0 Brabham BT45-Alfa Romeo F12	clutch
ret	DUTCH GP	Zandvoort	7	Martini Racing	3.0 Brabham BT45-Alfa Romeo F12	clutch
9	ITALIAN GP	Monza	35	Scuderia Ferrari SpA SEFAC	3.0 Ferrari 312T2 F12	

1977

	Race	Circuit	No	Entrant	Car/Engine	Comment
3	ARGENTINE GP	Buenos Aires	12	Scuderia Ferrari SpA SEFAC	3.0 Ferrari 312T2 F12	
1	BRAZILIAN GP	Interlagos	12	Scuderia Ferrari SpA SEFAC	3.0 Ferrari 312T2 F12	
8	SOUTH AFRICAN GP	Kyalami	12	Scuderia Ferrari SpA SEFAC	3.0 Ferrari 312T2 F12	
ret	US GP WEST	Long Beach	12	Scuderia Ferrari SpA SEFAC	3.0 Ferrari 312T2 F12	collision with Lunger
2	SPANISH GP	Jarama	12	Scuderia Ferrari SpA SEFAC	3.0 Ferrari 312T2 F12	
3	MONACO GP	Monte Carlo	12	Scuderia Ferrari SpA SEFAC	3.0 Ferrari 312T2 F12	

ret	BELGIAN GP	Zolder	12	Scuderia Ferrari SpA SEFAC	3.0 Ferrari 312T2 F12	*spun off*
3	SWEDISH GP	Anderstorp	12	Scuderia Ferrari SpA SEFAC	3.0 Ferrari 312T2 F12	
6	FRENCH GP	Dijon	12	Scuderia Ferrari SpA SEFAC	3.0 Ferrari 312T2 F12	*1 lap behind*
15	BRITISH GP	Silverstone	12	Scuderia Ferrari SpA SEFAC	3.0 Ferrari 312T2 F12	*pit stop/brake problem/-6 laps*
4	GERMAN GP	Hockenheim	12	Scuderia Ferrari SpA SEFAC	3.0 Ferrari 312T2 F12	
4	AUSTRIAN GP	Österreichring	12	Scuderia Ferrari SpA SEFAC	3.0 Ferrari 312T2 F12	
6	DUTCH GP	Zandvoort	12	Scuderia Ferrari SpA SEFAC	3.0 Ferrari 312T2 F12	*pit stop/wing damage/-2 laps*
ret	ITALIAN GP	Monza	12	Scuderia Ferrari SpA SEFAC	3.0 Ferrari 312T2 F12	*spun off on oil*
6	US GP EAST	Watkins Glen	12	Scuderia Ferrari SpA SEFAC	3.0 Ferrari 312T2 F12	*1 lap behind*
ret	CANADIAN GP	Mosport Park	12	Scuderia Ferrari SpA SEFAC	3.0 Ferrari 312T2 F12	*fuel pressure*
2	JAPANESE GP	Mount Fuji	12	Scuderia Ferrari SpA SEFAC	3.0 Ferrari 312T2 F12	

1978

7	ARGENTINE GP	Buenos Aires	11	Scuderia Ferrari SpA SEFAC	3.0 Ferrari 312T2 F12	*pit stop/tyres*
1	BRAZILIAN GP	Rio	11	Scuderia Ferrari SpA SEFAC	3.0 Ferrari 312T2 F12	*FL*
ret	SOUTH AFRICAN GP	Kyalami	11	Scuderia Ferrari SpA SEFAC	3.0 Ferrari 312T3 F12	*spun off on oil*
1	US GP WEST	Long Beach	11	Scuderia Ferrari SpA SEFAC	3.0 Ferrari 312T3 F12	*Pole*
8	MONACO GP	Monte Carlo	11	Scuderia Ferrari SpA SEFAC	3.0 Ferrari 312T3 F12	*p stop/hit kerb/damaged tyres/Pole*
3	BELGIAN GP	Zolder	11	Scuderia Ferrari SpA SEFAC	3.0 Ferrari 312T3 F12	
ret	SPANISH GP	Jarama	11	Scuderia Ferrari SpA SEFAC	3.0 Ferrari 312T3 F12	*driveshaft/accident*
10	SWEDISH GP	Anderstorp	11	Scuderia Ferrari SpA SEFAC	3.0 Ferrari 312T3 F12	*pit stops/tyres/1 lap behind*
18	FRENCH GP	Paul Ricard	11	Scuderia Ferrari SpA SEFAC	3.0 Ferrari 312T3 F12	*pit stops/tyres/1 lap behind*
1	BRITISH GP	Brands Hatch	11	Scuderia Ferrari SpA SEFAC	3.0 Ferrari 312T3 F12	*pit stops/tyres/FL/5 laps behind*
ret	GERMAN GP	Hockenheim	11	Scuderia Ferrari SpA SEFAC	3.0 Ferrari 312T3 F12	*fuel vaporisation*
dsq	AUSTRIAN GP	Österreichring	11	Scuderia Ferrari SpA SEFAC	3.0 Ferrari 312T3 F12	*outside assistance following spin*
7	DUTCH GP	Zandvoort	11	Scuderia Ferrari SpA SEFAC	3.0 Ferrari 312T3 F12	
3	ITALIAN GP	Monza	11	Scuderia Ferrari SpA SEFAC	3.0 Ferrari 312T3 F12	
1	US GP EAST	Watkins Glen	11	Scuderia Ferrari SpA SEFAC	3.0 Ferrari 312T3 F12	
3	CANADIAN GP	Montreal	11	Scuderia Ferrari SpA SEFAC	3.0 Ferrari 312T3 F12	

1979

2	ARGENTINE GP	Buenos Aires	2	Martini Racing Team Lotus	3.0 Lotus 79-Cosworth V8	
3	BRAZILIAN GP	Interlagos	2	Martini Racing Team Lotus	3.0 Lotus 79-Cosworth V8	
5	SOUTH AFRICAN GP	Kyalami	2	Martini Racing Team Lotus	3.0 Lotus 79-Cosworth V8	
ret	US GP WEST	Long Beach	2	Martini Racing Team Lotus	3.0 Lotus 79-Cosworth V8	*broken driveshaft*
2	SPANISH GP	Jarama	2	Martini Racing Team Lotus	3.0 Lotus 79-Cosworth V8	
4	BELGIAN GP	Zolder	2	Martini Racing Team Lotus	3.0 Lotus 79-Cosworth V8	
3	MONACO GP	Monte Carlo	2	Martini Racing Team Lotus	3.0 Lotus 79-Cosworth V8	
13/ret	FRENCH GP	Dijon	2	Martini Racing Team Lotus	3.0 Lotus 79-Cosworth V8	*accident with Rosberg/3 laps behind*
8	BRITISH GP	Silverstone	2	Martini Racing Team Lotus	3.0 Lotus 79-Cosworth V8	*pit stop/tyre/2 laps behind*
ret	GERMAN GP	Hockenheim	2	Martini Racing Team Lotus	3.0 Lotus 79-Cosworth V8	*collision with Mass/spun off*
ret	AUSTRIAN GP	Österreichring	2	Martini Racing Team Lotus	3.0 Lotus 79-Cosworth V8	*handling*
ret	DUTCH GP	Zandvoort	2	Martini Racing Team Lotus	3.0 Lotus 79-Cosworth V8	*collision with Jarier*
7	ITALIAN GP	Monza	2	Martini Racing Team Lotus	3.0 Lotus 79-Cosworth V8	
ret	CANADIAN GP	Montreal	2	Martini Racing Team Lotus	3.0 Lotus 79-Cosworth V8	*rear suspension*
ret	US GP EAST	Watkins Glen	2	Martini Racing Team Lotus	3.0 Lotus 79-Cosworth V8	*spun off*

1980

ret	ARGENTINE GP	Buenos Aires	28	Albilad-Williams Racing Team	3.0 Williams FW07B-Cosworth V8	*engine*
ret	BRAZILIAN GP	Interlagos	28	Albilad-Williams Racing Team	3.0 Williams FW07B-Cosworth V8	*driveshaft*
5	SOUTH AFRICAN GP	Kyalami	28	Albilad-Williams Racing Team	3.0 Williams FW07B-Cosworth V8	*1 lap behind*
ret	US GP WEST	Long Beach	28	Albilad-Williams Racing Team	3.0 Williams FW07B-Cosworth V8	*driveshaft*
3	BELGIAN GP	Zolder	28	Albilad-Williams Racing Team	3.0 Williams FW07B-Cosworth V8	
1	MONACO GP	Monte Carlo	28	Albilad-Williams Racing Team	3.0 Williams FW07B-Cosworth V8	
6	FRENCH GP	Paul Ricard	28	Albilad-Williams Racing Team	3.0 Williams FW07B-Cosworth V8	
3	BRITISH GP	Brands Hatch	28	Albilad-Williams Racing Team	3.0 Williams FW07B-Cosworth V8	
2	GERMAN GP	Hockenheim	28	Albilad-Williams Racing Team	3.0 Williams FW07B-Cosworth V8	
3	AUSTRIAN GP	Österreichring	28	Albilad-Williams Racing Team	3.0 Williams FW07B-Cosworth V8	
4	DUTCH GP	Zandvoort	28	Albilad-Williams Racing Team	3.0 Williams FW07B-Cosworth V8	
3	ITALIAN GP	Imola	28	Albilad-Williams Racing Team	3.0 Williams FW07B-Cosworth V8	
2	CANADIAN GP	Montreal	28	Albilad-Williams Racing Team	3.0 Williams FW07B-Cosworth V8	
2	US GP EAST	Watkins Glen	28	Albilad-Williams Racing Team	3.0 Williams FW07B-Cosworth V8	

1981

2	US GP WEST	Long Beach	2	Albilad-Williams Racing Team	3.0 Williams FW07C-Cosworth V8	
1	BRAZILIAN GP	Rio	2	Albilad-Williams Racing Team	3.0 Williams FW07C-Cosworth V8	
2	ARGENTINE GP	Buenos Aires	2	Albilad-Williams Racing Team	3.0 Williams FW07C-Cosworth V8	
3	SAN MARINO GP	Imola	2	Albilad-Williams Racing Team	3.0 Williams FW07C-Cosworth V8	
1	BELGIAN GP	Zolder	2	Albilad-Williams Racing Team	3.0 Williams FW07C-Cosworth V8	*Pole/FL*
ret	MONACO GP	Monte Carlo	2	Albilad-Williams Racing Team	3.0 Williams FW07C-Cosworth V8	*gearbox*
4	SPANISH GP	Jarama	2	TAG Williams Team	3.0 Williams FW07C-Cosworth V8	
10	FRENCH GP	Dijon	2	TAG Williams Team	3.0 Williams FW07C-Cosworth V8	*misfire/2 laps behind*
2	BRITISH GP	Silverstone	2	TAG Williams Team	3.0 Williams FW07C-Cosworth V8	
ret	GERMAN GP	Hockenheim	2	TAG Williams Team	3.0 Williams FW07C-Cosworth V8	*engine*
5	AUSTRIAN GP	Österreichring	2	TAG Williams Team	3.0 Williams FW07C-Cosworth V8	
ret	DUTCH GP	Zandvoort	2	TAG Williams Team	3.0 Williams FW07C-Cosworth V8	*accident with Laffite*
3	ITALIAN GP	Monza	2	TAG Williams Team	3.0 Williams FW07C-Cosworth V8	*FL*
10	CANADIAN GP	Montreal	2	TAG Williams Team	3.0 Williams FW07C-Cosworth V8	*wrong tyre choice in rain/-3 laps*
8	CAESARS PALACE GP	Las Vegas	2	TAG Williams Team	3.0 Williams FW07C-Cosworth V8	*handling problems/Pole/-1 lap*

1982

2	SOUTH AFRICAN GP	Kyalami	5	TAG Williams Team	3.0 Williams FW07C-Cosworth V8	
ret	BRAZILIAN GP	Rio	5	TAG Williams Team	3.0 Williams FW07C-Cosworth V8	*accident with Arnoux*

GP Starts: 146   GP Wins: 12   Pole positions: 6   Fastest laps: 6   Points: 310

CARLOS REUTEMANN

Carlos Reutemann was certainly the enigma of his times. Picturing some of his majestic Grand Prix wins, it seems impossible to believe that here was anything other than a World Champion. Yet there were days when his performance was so lacklustre that you would cringe with embarrassment at his feeble showing. That was the contradiction of this deep-thinking perfectionist, who was ultimately unable to summon from within himself the consistency which must underpin any championship success.

Carlos was a cattle-rancher's son from Santa Fe, Argentina, who began racing in 1965. Competing mainly in saloons such as Ford Torinos, he soon became one of the country's top talents, gaining some valuable single-seater experience in the 1968 Temporada Formula 2 series. In 1970 he was chosen by the Automovil Club Argentino for a sponsored season in Europe racing a Brabham BT30. The year passed relatively uneventfully, with Carlos learning a great deal and taking the occasional top-six finish. Returning home, he served notice of his talent by taking an aggregate third place in the non-championship Argentine GP in an elderly McLaren M7C. Back in Europe for another season of Formula 2, Reutemann really came good in the latter stages of the year. Although he won only at Hockenheim, there were plenty of brilliant performances and he finished runner-up to Ronnie Peterson in the final standings.

Having newly acquired the Brabham team, Bernie Ecclestone signed Carlos for 1972 and the Argentinian was to make a sensational GP debut at Buenos Aires, putting the hitherto unloved Brabham BT34 on pole position before finishing seventh. Reutemann then won the non-title Brazilian GP at Interlagos to underline his vast promise, but his momentum was broken soon after his return to Europe when a nasty crash at Thruxton in the F2 Rondel Brabham left him with a crushed ankle. This injury proved troublesome and slow to mend, which knocked his confidence for the rest of that year.

The 1973 season saw him back in the groove, particularly once the new BT42 was introduced. There were flashes of brilliance and he soon became a regular top-six finisher. With the superb BT44 at his disposal at the start of 1974, Reutemann launched a ferocious opening onslaught, leading the first two Grands Prix before encountering problems, and then winning the third, at Kyalami. But, just as suddenly, his form then vanished before mysteriously reappearing when he won the Austrian GP with a stunning performance. There was another victory at Watkins Glen which prompted thoughts that a World Championship bid was on the cards for the following season, but once again he flattered to deceive. Winning the German GP was the high-point, but he seemed unsettled by the competitive presence of new team-mate Carlos Pace. Things took a turn for the worse in 1976, when Brabham became involved in the Alfa engine project. The powerplant was woefully unreliable, and Reutemann soon became fed up with the situation. He engineered his way out of his contract to join Ferrari, who were anxious to find a replacement for the recently injured Niki Lauda, but in the event Carlos raced only at Monza due to the Austrian's amazing recovery. Despite a win in the Brazilian GP at the beginning of 1977, Reutemann was completely overshadowed by Lauda, who with total disdain took great delight in heaping any little humiliation he could upon the Argentinian.

With the Rat's two-fingered departure at the end of the year, Carlos was promoted to lead the Ferrari challenge in 1978, and his form certainly improved, Reutemann taking four wins including a brilliantly judged performance to outwit Lauda at Brands Hatch. Despite this success, he found himself unwanted by Ferrari and joined Lotus in 1979, which was in hindsight the worst possible move. The new Lotus 80 was a technical nightmare and Reutemann stuck resolutely with the 79, with which, to be fair, he put in some brilliant performances which went largely unregarded. Frank Williams still had faith in him and for 1980 Carlos was included in the team alongside Alan Jones. It was a mystery that a driver of such experience should take such a long time to come to terms with his situation; a win at Monaco was achieved by caution and he seemed content to let Jones force the pace as the Australian charged towards his well-deserved championship. The following season saw a far more aggressive Reutemann. He took the FOCA-only South African GP and then embarked on an early-season run of brilliant performances to put himself in a seemingly impregnable position. Then, almost inevitably, came the slump. The title went down to the line at Las Vegas, and Carlos set himself for glory with an utterly brilliant lap to gain pole positon. But once the lights went green Reutemann, his confidence sapped by a mysterious handling problem encountered in the warm-up, just seemed to fade away. A season's work appeared to be tossed away without so much as a whimper as Nelson Piquet snatched the title by a point.

Reutemann was back in 1982, but perhaps the roll of the dice at Caesars Palace still weighed heavily on the mind of this introspective and complex man. Just two races into the season, he suddenly retired for reasons that have never really been explained. An enigma to the end.

LANCE REVENTLOW

The multi-millionaire son of Woolworth heiress Barbara Hutton, Reventlow began competing in the mid-fifties with a Mercedes before getting his hands on an 1100 cc Cooper to race in the US in 1956. The following year he came to Europe to buy a Maserati sports car, which he crashed badly at Snetterton, escaping unharmed. He also raced an F2 Cooper briefly, before returning home.

Reventlow then decided to build his own sports car, the Scarab, for 1958. It was a success and, with Chuck Daigh, Lance ambitiously planned a front-engined Grand Prix car which the pair would drive, but when it finally appeared in 1960 the outdated design was hopelessly outclassed. So frustrated were the drivers that, by the British GP, the car had been temporarily abandoned in favour of a third works Cooper. Both Lance and Daigh practised in it, but Chuck, being the faster, drove it in the race. The Scarab project struggled on in the hope of some success in the 1961 Inter-Continental Formula, but when that folded, so did the team.

Reventlow returned to the States to race a new Scarab rear-engined sports car briefly before losing interest in the sport completely. He was killed in 1972, when he was a passenger in a light aeroplane which crashed in bad weather over the Rocky Mountains.

REVENTLOW, Lance (USA) b 24/2/1936 – 24/7/1972

	1960					
	Race	Circuit	No	Entrant	Car/Engine	Comment
dnq	MONACO GP	Monte Carlo	48	Reventlow Automobiles Inc	2.4 Scarab 4	
dns	DUTCH GP	Zandvoort	21	Reventlow Automobiles Inc	2.4 Scarab 4	dispute over starting money
ret	BELGIAN GP	Spa	28	Reventlow Automobiles Inc	2.4 Scarab 4	engine
dns	BRITISH GP	Silverstone	3	Cooper Car Co	2.5 Cooper T51-Climax 4	practised but car driven by Daigh

GP Starts: 1   GP Wins: 0   Pole positions: 0   Fastest laps: 0   Points: 0

PETER REVSON

Despite his family being a part of the Revlon cosmetics empire, Peter Revson made his way in motor racing very much under his own steam. He was initially regarded rather unfairly as just another American rich-kid playboy after his first unsuccessful attempts at Grand Prix racing, but eventually returned to fulfil his long-held ambition of winning a Grand Prix and, almost as importantly, win the respect and admiration of his peers.

Peter's career started in Hawaii with a Morgan which he shipped back to the States and raced there before trying his hand in a Formula Junior Taraschi. However, the lure of European racing, not to mention European culture, exerted a great pull on the young Revson, who cashed in everything he could to finance his expedition in 1963. Leading the nomadic existence that was so typical of the time, which often meant living out of the transporter, he raced a Formula Junior Cooper on the Continent and won the Copenhagen GP, but soon laid plans for a Formula 1 assault. Reg Parnell's team had lost their sponsor and took Peter under their wing by way of a semi-works deal. His first tilt at Formula 1 in 1964 brought little cheer except a fourth place at Solitude, and he changed tack in 1965, joining the works Lotus F2 team run for the factory by Ron Harris. A win in the Eifelrennen was lost when he went off on the last lap but he finished second and, dropping into F3, also took the Monaco support race. Despite the season's progress, the gloss was wearing off Revson's European idyll and he headed back to the States to race a little Brabham BT8 sports car, winning his class at Seattle and Las Vegas.

For the 1966 season Revson joined Skip Scott in a Ford GT40 and over the next three seasons he began to build his career in big sports cars in Can-Am and Trans-Am before stepping back into single-seaters with a fine drive to fifth at Indianapolis in 1969. The following season he took second at Sebring with actor Steve McQueen in a Porsche 908 and then raced Carl Haas's Lola in Can-Am. In 1971 he joined the McLaren team to contest the money-spinning series, winning five rounds in the McLaren M8F, and his performance when taking second place in the Indy 500 for McLaren raised his profile greatly. He was invited to drive for Tyrrell at Watkins Glen in a one-off Grand Prix return before arranging a full season of both Formula 1 and Can-Am with McLaren in 1972. The team's F1 M19 wasn't quite a winner, but Peter did a superb job with plenty of placings and few mistakes despite having to miss some races due to clashing USAC commitments. Revson stayed with the team in 1973 and once behind the wheel of the M23 proved a winner at last. His performance in the British GP was exemplary. On a damp track he first grabbed the initiative and then controlled the later stages to score a beautifully judged victory. There was one more win to follow in the rain-soaked confusion of Mosport, but by now internal pressures were afflicting the team, and Peter in particular. Emerson Fittipaldi was moving in for 1974 with massive support from Marlboro and Texaco and Teddy Mayer was willing to run Revson only as a third entry in Yardley colours. Not surprisingly Revson decided to seek better treatment elsewhere, joining the Shadow team. The season started with great promise as the new DN3 showed a fair turn of speed, but in testing for the South African GP at Kyalami tragedy struck when a suspension failure is thought to have caused the car to crash into a guard rail. The car was totally destroyed in the massive impact and Revson had no chance of survival.

JOHN RHODES

A Formula Junior regular in the early sixties, Rhodes raced the Midland Racing Partnership Cooper in 1961, with victory in the minor Irish FJ championship providing the highlight of his season.

In 1962 he raced for Bob Gerard, taking 13th in the International Trophy in a Cooper and driving an Ausper-Ford in Formula Junior events. He signed to race for Ken Tyrrell in the formula the following year, but also began to drive the works Mini-Coopers with which he was to become synonymous throughout the sixties.

John's single-seater outings were then confined to a few races with Bob Gerard's faithful old Cooper in 1965, the car proving to be very slow in his only Grand Prix appearance at Silverstone.

ALEX RIBEIRO

The 1973 Brazilian Formula Ford champion with five wins from seven starts, Alex then headed for Europe and an excellent first season in F3 with the works GRD, winning three rounds. His career continued its upward trend with the works F3 March in 1975, which led to a full season for the team in Formula 2 in 1976. Although a win eluded him, he was, with Arnoux, usually the fastest man around. Hiring a Hesketh, Alex made a steady F1 debut in the US GP, before taking on his only full Grand Prix season with the works-supported March in 1977. It was to be a disastrous campaign, with drivers and management blaming each other for the cars' disappointing performances.

Back in Formula 2 in 1978 with his own 'Jesus Saves Racing' March 782, Alex initially showed he had lost none of his talent with a brilliant win at the Nürburgring, but gradually his season tailed off and the little team lost heart.

In 1979, Ribeiro reappeared with Fittipaldi at the non-championship Dino Ferrari GP, but retired early on. He was later invited to drive for the team in the end-of-season North American races, but failed to qualify the cars on both occasions.

REVSON, Peter (USA) b 27/2/1939 – d 22/3/1974

1964

	Race	Circuit	No	Entrant	Car/Engine	Comment
dnq	MONACO GP	Monte Carlo	2	Revson Racing (America)	1.5 Lotus 24-BRM V8	
dsq	BELGIAN GP	Spa	29	Reg Parnell (Racing)	1.5 Lotus 24-BRM V8	push start
dns	FRENCH GP	Rouen	36	Reg Parnell (Racing)	1.5 Lotus 25-BRM V8	car driven by Hailwood
ret	BRITISH GP	Brands Hatch	24	Revson Racing (America)	1.5 Lotus 24-BRM V8	gear selectors
14/ret	GERMAN GP	Nürburgring	27	Revson Racing (America)	1.5 Lotus 24-BRM V8	accident
13	ITALIAN GP	Monza	38	Revson Racing (America)	1.5 Lotus 24-BRM V8	

1971

	Race	Circuit	No	Entrant	Car/Engine	Comment
ret	US GP	Watkins Glen	10	Elf Team Tyrrell	3.0 Tyrrell 001-Cosworth V8	clutch

1972

	Race	Circuit	No	Entrant	Car/Engine	Comment
ret	ARGENTINE GP	Buenos Aires	18	Team Yardley McLaren	3.0 McLaren M19A-Cosworth V8	engine
3	SOUTH AFRICAN GP	Kyalami	14	Team Yardley McLaren	3.0 McLaren M19A-Cosworth V8	
5	SPANISH GP	Jarama	20	Team Yardley McLaren	3.0 McLaren M19A-Cosworth V8	1 lap behind
7	BELGIAN GP	Nivelles	10	Team Yardley McLaren	3.0 McLaren M19A-Cosworth V8	2 laps behind
3	BRITISH GP	Brands Hatch	19	Team Yardley McLaren	3.0 McLaren M19A-Cosworth V8	
3	AUSTRIAN GP	Österreichring	14	Team Yardley McLaren	3.0 McLaren M19C-Cosworth V8	
dns	"	"	14T	Team Yardley McLaren	3.0 McLaren M19A-Cosworth V8	practice only
4	ITALIAN GP	Monza	15	Team Yardley McLaren	3.0 McLaren M19C-Cosworth V8	
dns	"	"	14T	Team Yardley McLaren	3.0 McLaren M19A-Cosworth V8	practice only
2	CANADIAN GP	Mosport Park	19	Team Yardley McLaren	3.0 McLaren M19C-Cosworth V8	Pole
dns	"	"	19T	Team Yardley McLaren	3.0 McLaren M19A-Cosworth V8	practice only
18/ret	US GP	Watkins Glen	20	Team Yardley McLaren	3.0 McLaren M19C-Cosworth V8	ignition/5 laps behind

1973

	Race	Circuit	No	Entrant	Car/Engine	Comment
8	ARGENTINE GP	Buenos Aires	16	Yardley Team McLaren	3.0 McLaren M19C-Cosworth V8	tyre problems/4 laps behind
ret	BRAZILIAN GP	Interlagos	8	Yardley Team McLaren	3.0 McLaren M19C-Cosworth V8	gearbox
2	SOUTH AFRICAN GP	Kyalami	6	Yardley Team McLaren	3.0 McLaren M19C-Cosworth V8	
4	SPANISH GP	Montjuich Park	6	Yardley Team McLaren	3.0 McLaren M23-Cosworth V8	1 lap behind
ret	BELGIAN GP	Zolder	8	Yardley Team McLaren	3.0 McLaren M23-Cosworth V8	spun off
5	MONACO GP	Monte Carlo	8	Yardley Team McLaren	3.0 McLaren M23-Cosworth V8	2 laps behind
7	SWEDISH GP	Anderstorp	8	Yardley Team McLaren	3.0 McLaren M23-Cosworth V8	1 lap behind
1	BRITISH GP	Silverstone	8	Yardley Team McLaren	3.0 McLaren M23-Cosworth V8	
4	DUTCH GP	Zandvoort	8	Yardley Team McLaren	3.0 McLaren M23-Cosworth V8	
9	GERMAN GP	Nürburgring	8	Yardley Team McLaren	3.0 McLaren M23-Cosworth V8	
ret	AUSTRIAN GP	Österreichring	8	Yardley Team McLaren	3.0 McLaren M23-Cosworth V8	clutch
3	ITALIAN GP	Monza	8	Yardley Team McLaren	3.0 McLaren M23-Cosworth V8	
1	CANADIAN GP	Mosport Park	8	Yardley Team McLaren	3.0 McLaren M23-Cosworth V8	
5	US GP	Watkins Glen	8	Yardley Team McLaren	3.0 McLaren M23-Cosworth V8	

1974

	Race	Circuit	No	Entrant	Car/Engine	Comment
ret	ARGENTINE GP	Buenos Aires	16	UOP Shadow Racing Team	3.0 Shadow DN3-Cosworth V8	collision-Hailwood and Regazzoni
ret	BRAZILIAN GP	Interlagos	16	UOP Shadow Racing Team	3.0 Shadow DN3-Cosworth V8	overheating
dns	SOUTH AFRICAN GP	Kyalami	16	UOP Shadow Racing Team	3.0 Shadow DN3-Cosworth V8	fatal accident in pre-race practice

GP Starts: 30   GP Wins: 2   Pole positions: 1   Fastest laps: 0   Points: 61

RHODES, John (GB) b 18/8/1927

1965

	Race	Circuit	No	Entrant	Car/Engine	Comment
ret	BRITISH GP	Silverstone	20	Gerard Racing	1.5 Cooper T60-Climax V8	ignition

GP Starts: 1   GP Wins: 0   Pole positions: 0   Fastest laps: 0   Points: 0

RIBEIRO, Alex (BR) b 7/11/1948

1976

	Race	Circuit	No	Entrant	Car/Engine	Comment
12	US GP EAST	Watkins Glen	25	Hesketh Racing with Rizla/Penthouse	3.0 Hesketh 308D-Cosworth V8	2 laps behind

1977

	Race	Circuit	No	Entrant	Car/Engine	Comment
ret	ARGENTINE GP	Buenos Aires	9	Hollywood March Racing	3.0 March 761B-Cosworth V8	broken gear lever
ret	BRAZILIAN GP	Interlgos	9	Hollywood March Racing	3.0 March 761B-Cosworth V8	engine
ret	SOUTH AFRICAN GP	Kyalami	9	Hollywood March Racing	3.0 March 761B-Cosworth V8	engine
ret	US GP WEST	Long Beach	9	Hollywood March Racing	3.0 March 761B-Cosworth V8	gearbox oil leak
dnq	SPANISH GP	Jarama	9	Hollywood March Racing	3.0 March 761B-Cosworth V8	
dnq	MONACO GP	Monte Carlo	9	Hollywood March Racing	3.0 March 761B-Cosworth V8	accident in practice
dnq	BELGIAN GP	Zolder	9	Hollywood March Racing	3.0 March 761B-Cosworth V8	
dnq	SWEDISH GP	Anderstorp	9	Hollywood March Racing	3.0 March 761B-Cosworth V8	
dnq	FRENCH GP	Dijon	9	Hollywood March Racing	3.0 March 761B-Cosworth V8	
dnq	BRITISH GP	Silverstone	9	Hollywood March Racing	3.0 March 761B-Cosworth V8	
8	GERMAN GP	Hockenheim	9	Hollywood March Racing	3.0 March 761B-Cosworth V8	1 lap behind
dnq	AUSTRIAN GP	Österreichring	9	Hollywood March Racing	3.0 March 761B-Cosworth V8	accident in practice
11	DUTCH GP	Zandvoort	9	Hollywood March Racing	3.0 March 761B-Cosworth V8	3 laps behind
dnq	ITALIAN GP	Monza	9	Hollywood March Racing	3.0 March 761B-Cosworth V8	3 laps behind
15	US GP EAST	Watkins Glen	9	Hollywood March Racing	3.0 March 761B-Cosworth V8	
8	CANADIAN GP	Mosport Park	9	Hollywood March Racing	3.0 March 761B-Cosworth V8	2 laps behind
12	JAPANESE GP	Mount Fuji	9	Hollywood March Racing	3.0 March 761B-Cosworth V8	4 laps behind

1979

	Race	Circuit	No	Entrant	Car/Engine	Comment
dnq	CANADIAN GP	Montreal	19	Fittipaldi Automotive	3.0 Fittipaldi F6A-Cosworth V8	
dnq	US GP EAST	Watkins Glen	19	Fittipaldi Automotive	3.0 Fittipaldi F6A-Cosworth V8	

GP Starts: 10   GP Wins: 0   Pole positions: 0   Fastest laps: 0   Points: 0

RIESS, Fritz (D) b 11/7/1922

1952

Race	Circuit	No	Entrant	Car/Engine	Comment
7 GERMAN GP	Nürburgring	121	Fritz Riess	2.0 Veritas RS 6 sports car	2 laps behind

GP Starts: 1   GP Wins: 0   Pole positions: 0   Fastest laps: 0   Points: 0

FRITZ RIESS

Having shown much promise in Hermann Holbein's beautifully constructed HH single-seater in 1948, Riess then switched to AFM and in 1950 he enjoyed some fine tussles with Ulmen's Veritas-Meteor, winning the Eifelrennen and finishing second to Ulmen at Sachsenring. He continued with the team the following year, winning at the Riem airfield circuit and then taking second place behind Pietsch in the Eifelrennen, before successfully joining the ranks of the Veritas runners in 1952 with his two-seater sports model.

Invited by Mercedes to join their team for Le Mans, Riess shared the winning 300SL with Lang and then finished third in the Prix de Berne at Bremgarten. He raced infrequently from 1953 onwards but was still active in 1957, when he took a class win in the Nürburgring 1000 Km, again in a Mercedes-Benz 300SL.

JOCHEN RINDT

You really needed to see Rindt in action to appreciate his genius. The little skittering Formula 2 cars were thrown to the limits of their adhesion as he almost danced them to win after win. Then his phenomenal skill took the huge overweight Cooper-Maserati into undreamed-of angles as the unwieldy beast was driven with such ferocity that, inevitably perhaps, finishes were few and far between.

Although Rindt had been around in Formula Junior and taken part in the non-championship 1963 Austrian GP, his potential remained hidden until he burst upon an unsuspecting British public at a big Formula 2 race at Crystal Palace in 1964. Sensationally he defeated the established aces of the day in the formula that was to become largely his personal domain in future years. With the Zeltweg race part of the championship calendar that year, Rindt hired Rob Walker's Brabham. Though he retired in the race, Jochen was keen to drive for Walker's *équipe* in 1965, but while Rob greatly admired the Austrian's talents he felt he would be better off at Cooper.

His first season with the team was spent learning the ropes under the tutelage of Bruce McLaren, and success was found more regularly in Formula 2, although his big win that year was at Le Mans where he took a NART-entered Ferrari 250LM to an unlikely victory with Masten Gregory. Cooper's competitiveness was restored in 1966 when Jochen emerged as a true front-runner, although he was pushed aside somewhat by the mid-season arrival of John Surtees. Signing a three-year deal with Cooper proved to have been a big mistake when Rindt was trapped in a poor car in 1967, but he spent his energies making up for it in Formula 2, taking Roy Winkelmann's Brabham to nine victories and four second places from 15 starts.

Joining a Brabham team fresh from two World Championships should have been the passport to well-deserved Grand Prix success for Rindt but, alas, it was not to be. The latest Repco engine proved to be hopelessly unreliable and Jochen was left with just a couple of third places at the end of the year. He also had a shot at Indianapolis in the team's BT25-Repco, but his race ended in retirement. Rindt's Formula 2 success continued unabated, but the lack of Grand Prix success led him to accept a drive at Lotus alongside Graham Hill for the 1969 season. Although he had equal status with the new World Champion, it soon became clear during the Tasman series that he had the edge, Jochen winning races at Christchurch and Warwick Farm.

The European season started badly for Rindt when he crashed in the Spanish GP after the massive rear aerofoil collapsed, putting him into hospital. He was back to his best by the British GP, where he fought a glorious duel with Stewart's Matra before minor problems dropped him from contention. He could not be denied much longer, however, taking his long-awaited maiden Grand Prix victory at Watkins Glen. Although Colin Chapman had supplied Rindt with a car worthy of his talents, theirs was an uneasy alliance. Jochen would dearly have liked to have returned to Brabham – now a competitive force again – but in the end lashings of money, the promise of total number-one status and a ground-breaking new car for 1970 held sway.

After starting the year in the old Lotus 49, taking second in the Race of Champions, Rindt gave the sensational-looking Lotus 72 its debut in Spain. However, it still needed some development and for Monaco Jochen was back in the old car. It was here he took perhaps his most famous victory, his incredible late-race charge forcing Jack Brabham into a final-corner error. The new 72 was finally considered fully raceworthy at Zandvoort and Jochen scored the first of four successive wins which put him within touching distance of the title. At Brands Hatch he was very lucky, as Brabham ran out of fuel on the last lap, but at Hockenheim he and Jacky Ickx gave a wonderful display of high-speed artistry. Having previously agreed places on the circuit where overtaking manoeuvres were acceptable, both drivers fought a great battle within those parameters. At the finish Chapman, who by now had grown much closer to Rindt than had seemed possible a year before, offered his congratulations. 'A monkey could have won in your car today,' was Jochen's retort. Then came Monza. There were rumours of retirement, for Jochen had lost close friends Bruce McLaren and Piers Courage in accidents in the preceding months. However, during practice 'something broke' on the car, which veered at enormous speed into the barrier. The front of the Lotus was totally destroyed and poor Rindt was pronounced dead on arrival at hospital in Milan. A month later at Watkins Glen, the inexperienced Emerson Fittipaldi took the Lotus 72 to a surprise victory, thus ensuring that Rindt became the sport's first, and thankfully only, posthumous World Champion.

RINDT, Jochen (A) b 18/4/1942 – d 5/9/1970

1964

	Race	Circuit	No	Entrant	Car/Engine	Comment
ret	AUSTRIAN GP	Zeltweg	12	Rob Walker Racing Team	1.5 Brabham BT11-BRM V8	steering

1965

	Race	Circuit	No	Entrant	Car/Engine	Comment
ret	SOUTH AFRICAN GP	East London	10	Cooper Car Co	1.5 Cooper T73-Climax V8	electrics
dnq	MONACO GP	Monte Carlo	8	Cooper Car Co	1.5 Cooper T77-Climax V8	
11	BELGIAN GP	Spa	5	Cooper Car Co	1.5 Cooper T77-Climax V8	3 laps behind
ret	FRENCH GP	Clermont Ferrand	20	Cooper Car Co	1.5 Cooper T77-Climax V8	collision with Amon
14/ret	BRITISH GP	Silverstone	10	Cooper Car Co	1.5 Cooper T77-Climax V8	engine
ret	DUTCH GP	Zandvoort	20	Cooper Car Co	1.5 Cooper T77-Climax V8	no oil pressure
4	GERMAN GP	Nürburgring	11	Cooper Car Co	1.5 Cooper T77-Climax V8	
8	ITALIAN GP	Monza	18	Cooper Car Co	1.5 Cooper T77-Climax V8	2 laps behind
6	US GP	Watkins Glen	10	Cooper Car Co	1.5 Cooper T77-Climax V8	2 laps behind
ret	MEXICAN GP	Mexico City	10	Cooper Car Co	1.5 Cooper T77-Climax V8	ignition

1966

	Race	Circuit	No	Entrant	Car/Engine	Comment
ret	MONACO GP	Monte Carlo	10	Cooper Car Co	3.0 Cooper T81-Maserati V12	engine
2	BELGIAN GP	Spa	19	Cooper Car Co	3.0 Cooper T81-Maserati V12	
4	FRENCH GP	Reims	6	Cooper Car Co	3.0 Cooper T81-Maserati V12	2 laps behind
5	BRITISH GP	Brands Hatch	11	Cooper Car Co	3.0 Cooper T81-Maserati V12	1 lap behind
ret	DUTCH GP	Zandvoort	26	Cooper Car Co	3.0 Cooper T81-Maserati V12	crashed
3	GERMAN GP	Nürburgring	8	Cooper Car Co	3.0 Cooper T81-Maserati V12	
4	ITALIAN GP	Monza	16	Cooper Car Co	3.0 Cooper T81-Maserati V12	flat tyre last lap/1 lap behind
2	US GP	Watkins Glen	8	Cooper Car Co	3.0 Cooper T81-Maserati V12	1 lap behind
ret	MEXICAN GP	Mexico City	8	Cooper Car Co	3.0 Cooper T81-Maserati V12	lost wheel-suspension bolt

1967

	Race	Circuit	No	Entrant	Car/Engine	Comment
ret	SOUTH AFRICAN GP	Kyalami	3	Cooper Car Co	3.0 Cooper T81-Maserati V12	engine
ret	MONACO GP	Monte Carlo	10	Cooper Car Co	3.0 Cooper T81-Maserati V12	gearbox
ret	DUTCH GP	Zandvoort	12	Cooper Car Co	3.0 Cooper T81B-Maserati V12	suspension
4	BELGIAN GP	Spa	29	Cooper Car Co	3.0 Cooper T81B-Maserati V12	
ret	FRENCH GP	Le Mans	12	Cooper Car Co	3.0 Cooper T81B-Maserati V12	engine
ret	BRITISH GP	Silverstone	11	Cooper Car Co	3.0 Cooper T86-Maserati V12	engine
dns	"	"	11		3.0 Cooper T81B-Maserati V12	practice only
ret	GERMAN GP	Nürburgring	5	Cooper Car Co	3.0 Cooper T86-Maserati V12	engine-overheating
dns	"	"	5		3.0 Cooper T81B-Maserati V12	practice only
ret	CANADIAN GP	Mosport Park	71	Cooper Car Co	3.0 Cooper T81-Maserati V12	ignition
4	ITALIAN GP	Monza	30	Cooper Car Co	3.0 Cooper T86-Maserati V12	
ret	US GP	Watkins Glen	4	Cooper Car Co	3.0 Cooper T81B-Maserati V12	engine
dns	"	" "	21		3.0 Cooper T86-Maserati V12	Ickx drove car in race

1968

	Race	Circuit	No	Entrant	Car/Engine	Comment
3	SOUTH AFRICAN GP	Kyalami	3	Brabham Racing Organisation	3.0 Brabham BT24-Repco V8	
ret	SPANISH GP	Jarama	4	Brabham Racing Organisation	3.0 Brabham BT24-Repco V8	low oil pressure
ret	MONACO GP	Monte Carlo	3	Brabham Racing Organisation	3.0 Brabham BT24-Repco V8	spun off
ret	BELGIAN GP	Spa	19	Brabham Racing Organisation	3.0 Brabham BT26-Repco V8	engine
ret	DUTCH GP	Zandvoort	6	Brabham Racing Organisation	3.0 Brabham BT26-Repco V8	damp ignition
ret	FRENCH GP	Rouen	2	Brabham Racing Organisation	3.0 Brabham BT26-Repco V8	fuel leak/Pole
ret	BRITISH GP	Brands Hatch	4	Brabham Racing Organisation	3.0 Brabham BT26-Repco V8	fuel system
dns	"	"	4	Brabham Racing Organisation	3.0 Brabham BT24-Repco V8	practice only
3	GERMAN GP	Nürburgring	5	Brabham Racing Organisation	3.0 Brabham BT26-Repco V8	
ret	ITALIAN GP	Monza	11	Brabham Racing Organisation	3.0 Brabham BT26-Repco V8	engine
ret	CANADIAN GP	St Jovite	6	Brabham Racing Organisation	3.0 Brabham BT26-Repco V8	engine/Pole
ret	US GP	Watkins Glen	4	Brabham Racing Organisation	3.0 Brabham BT26-Repco V8	engine
ret	MEXICAN GP	Mexico City	4	Brabham Racing Organisation	3.0 Brabham BT26-Repco V8	ignition

1969

	Race	Circuit	No	Entrant	Car/Engine	Comment
ret	SOUTH AFRICAN GP	Kyalami	2	Gold Leaf Team Lotus	3.0 Lotus 49B-Cosworth V8	fuel pump
ret	SPANISH GP	Montjuich Park	2	Gold Leaf Team Lotus	3.0 Lotus 49B-Cosworth V8	broken rear wing/accident/Pole/FL
ret	DUTCH GP	Zandvoort	2	Gold Leaf Team Lotus	3.0 Lotus 49B-Cosworth V8	driveshaft/Pole
ret	FRENCH GP	Clermont Ferrand	15	Gold Leaf Team Lotus	3.0 Lotus 49B-Cosworth V8	driver unwell-double vision
4	BRITISH GP	Silverstone	2	Gold Leaf Team Lotus	3.0 Lotus 49B-Cosworth V8	pit stops/rear wing/fuel/Pole
ret	GERMAN GP	Nürburgring	2	Gold Leaf Team Lotus	3.0 Lotus 49B-Cosworth V8	ignition
2	ITALIAN GP	Monza	4	Gold Leaf Team Lotus	3.0 Lotus 49B-Cosworth V8	Pole
3	CANADIAN GP	Mosport Park	2	Gold Leaf Team Lotus	3.0 Lotus 49B-Cosworth V8	
dns	"	" "	T	Gold Leaf Team Lotus	3.0 Lotus 63-Cosworth V8 4WD	practice only
1	US GP	Watkins Glen	2	Gold Leaf Team Lotus	3.0 Lotus 49B-Cosworth V8	Pole/FL
ret	MEXICAN GP	Mexico City	2	Gold Leaf Team Lotus	3.0 Lotus 49B-Cosworth V8	broken front suspension

1970 World Champion Driver

	Race	Circuit	No	Entrant	Car/Engine	Comment
13/ret	SOUTH AFRICAN GP	Kyalami	9	Gold Leaf Team Lotus	3.0 Lotus 49C-Cosworth V8	engine
ret	SPANISH GP	Jarama	3	Gold Leaf Team Lotus	3.0 Lotus 49C-Cosworth V8	ignition
1	MONACO GP	Monte Carlo	3	Gold Leaf Team Lotus	3.0 Lotus 49C-Cosworth V8	FL
ret	BELGIAN GP	Spa	20	Gold Leaf Team Lotus	3.0 Lotus 49C-Cosworth V8	engine
dns	"	"	20	Gold Leaf Team Lotus	3.0 Lotus 72-Cosworth V8	practice only
1	DUTCH GP	Zandvoort	10	Gold Leaf Team Lotus	3.0 Lotus 72-Cosworth V8	Pole
1	FRENCH GP	Clermont Ferrand	6	Gold Leaf Team Lotus	3.0 Lotus 72-Cosworth V8	
1	BRITISH GP	Brands Hatch	5	Gold Leaf Team Lotus	3.0 Lotus 72-Cosworth V8	Pole
1	GERMAN GP	Hockenheim	2	Gold Leaf Team Lotus	3.0 Lotus 72-Cosworth V8	
ret	AUSTRIAN GP	Österreichring	6	Gold Leaf Team Lotus	3.0 Lotus 72-Cosworth V8	engine/Pole
dns	ITALIAN GP	Monza	22	Gold Leaf Team Lotus	3.0 Lotus 72-Cosworth V8	fatal accident in practice

GP Starts: 60   GP Wins: 6   Pole positions: 10   Fastest laps: 3   Points: 109

RICHARD ROBARTS

A Formula Ford club racer from 1969 to 1972, Robarts drove an F3 GRD in 1973, sharing the Lombard North Central championship with Tony Brise.

Richard bought the second seat in the Brabham team for 1974, but when his backing fell through, he lost his place to the well-funded Rikki von Opel. A hoped-for second chance with Williams in Sweden later that year failed to materialise when Tom Belso took over the car at the last minute, which left Robarts pretty much in the wilderness until he found the necessary sponsorship to go racing in Formula 2 in 1976 with a year-old March. He found the level of competition a bit too hot, but enjoyed some success with occasional outings in the Shellsport G8 series.

PEDRO RODRIGUEZ

Pedro Rodriguez looked just great in a late-sixties Grand Prix car. His head seemed perpetually laid right back, and you could clearly see his eyes staring through the big aviator goggles as he went about his work. Aesthetics aside, that his talent went largely unregarded in Formula 1 is something of a mystery, and it was only right at the end of his life that his legend was forged.

Two years older than his brother Ricardo, Pedro was racing bikes by the age of 12 and a Jaguar XK120 by the time he was 15. He was soon joined by his sibling and the pair became notorious for their daring exploits in the late fifties. Attracting the attention of Luigi Chinetti, Pedro began racing his NART Ferraris, taking second place in the 1958 Nassau Trophy. The brothers eventually came to Europe and set about building a brilliant reputation in Chinetti's Ferraris, winning both the Nürburgring and Paris 1000 Km in 1961.

The death of Ricardo in Mexico at the end of 1962 was a devasting blow for Pedro, who nevertheless carried on racing, but was largely restricted to North America during 1963 and 1964. There were wins at Daytona in the GT class in 1963, and outright in 1964, sharing a GTO with Phil Hill. There were also end-of-year F1 drives for Lotus and Ferrari, but no offers of permanent Grand Prix employment came his way, so the little Mexican stuck it out in sports car racing, taking the occasional single-seater opportunities he was given. For the 1967 South African GP, Pedro was offered a works Cooper drive, but no deal beyond that. In a race of high attrition, he drove steadily to score a surprise win, a feat which eluded even Rindt during his spell with the team. Rodriguez was naturally then taken on for the rest of the year, but the car was rapidly becoming uncompetitive, and he did well just to scrape the odd point thereafter. His season was also interrupted by injury when an accident at Enna in the F2 Protos left him with a broken foot.

Pedro joined BRM in 1968 and, after an unsuccessful Tasman series, started the season in fine form, taking a memorable second place in the Race of Champions when he sliced through the field after being left at the start. After a rather lucky second place at Spa, the season slid into mediocrity as the team lost their way, and it was Pedro who paid the price, making way for John Surtees in 1969. As luck would have it, that was to be a terrible year at Bourne, and Pedro was fortunate to be out of the firing line, racing Tim Parnell's semi-works machine until he accepted an offer to drive the equally disappointing Ferrari.

Rodriguez had become much in demand as a sports car driver following his 1968 Le Mans victory with Bianchi in John Wyer's Ford GT40. He drove for both Ferrari and Matra the following year, before returning to Wyer in 1970. He was also back at BRM, and this time they had come up with a really good car in the P153. There were two races that year which Pedro would leave as a legacy to the portfolio of great motor racing performances. At Brands Hatch, driving the fearsome Gulf Porsche 917, he produced an unforgettable display in the rain to win the 1000 Km by a five-lap margin, and then in the Belgian GP at Spa he drove a masterful race, almost to the point of perfection, to beat Amon's March. He would score no more Grand Prix victories, only a win in the 1971 Rothmans Trophy at Oulton Park, but he continued to drive the Porsche with a fearlessness that was frightening. In 1971 Rodriguez won the Daytona 24 Hours, Monza 1000 Km and Spa 1000 Km with Jack Oliver, and the Österreichring 1000 Km with Richard Attwood to confirm his position as sports car racing's leading exponent.

Pedro lived for racing, and could not refuse the offer of a drive in an Interserie round at Norisring. Driving Herbert Müller's Ferrari 512M, Rodriguez crashed heavily when a tyre was thought to have deflated. The car burst into flames and when the driver was finally released he was found to have succumbed to multiple injuries.

RISELEY-PRITCHARD, John (GB) b 17/1/1924

1954

	Race	Circuit	No	Entrant	Car/Engine	Comment
ret	BRITISH GP	Silverstone	24	R R C Walker Racing Team	2.0 Connaught A Type 4	spun off

GP Starts: 1   GP Wins: 0   Pole positions: 0   Fastest laps: 0   Points: 0

ROBARTS, Richard (GB) b 22/9/1944

1974

	Race	Circuit	No	Entrant	Car/Engine	Comment
ret	ARGENTINE GP	Buenos Aires	38	Motor Racing Developments	3.0 Brabham BT44-Cosworth V8	gearbox
15	BRAZILIAN GP	Interlagos	38	Motor Racing Developments	3.0 Brabham BT44-Cosworth V8	2 laps behind
17	SOUTH AFRICAN GP	Kyalami	38	Motor Racing Developments	3.0 Brabham BT44-Cosworth V8	4 laps behind
dns	SWEDISH GP	Anderstorp	20	Frank Williams Racing Cars	3.0 Iso Williams FW02-Cosworth V8	car driven by Belso

GP Starts: 3   GP Wins: 0   Pole positions: 0   Fastest laps: 0   Points: 0

RODRIGUEZ LARRETA, Alberto (RA) b 14/1/1934

1960

	Race	Circuit	No	Entrant	Car/Engine	Comment
9	ARGENTINE GP	Buenos Aires	46	Team Lotus	2.5 Lotus 16-Climax 4	3rd works car/3 laps behind

GP Starts: 1   GP Wins: 0   Pole positions: 0   Fastest laps: 0   Points: 0

RODRIGUEZ, Pedro (MEX) b 18/1/1940 – d 11/7/1971

1963

	Race	Circuit	No	Entrant	Car/Engine	Comment
ret	US GP	Watkins Glen	10	Team Lotus	1.5 Lotus 25-Climax V8	engine
ret	MEXICAN GP	Mexico City	10	Team Lotus	1.5 Lotus 25-Climax V8	rear suspension

1964

6	MEXICAN GP	Mexico City	18	North American Racing Team	1.5 Ferrari 156 V6	

1965

5	US GP	Watkins Glen	14	North American Racing Team	1.5 Ferrari 1512 F12	2 laps behind
7	MEXICAN GP	Mexico City	14	North American Racing Team	1.5 Ferrari 1512 F12	3 laps behind

1966

10/ret	FRENCH GP	Reims	2	Team Lotus	2.0 Lotus 33-Climax V8	engine-broken oil pipe
ret	GERMAN GP (F2)	Nürburgring	31	Ron Harris-Team Lotus	1.0 Lotus 44-Cosworth 4 F2	engine
ret	US GP	Watkins Glen	11	Team Lotus	2.0 Lotus 33-BRM V8	starter motor after pit stop
ret	MEXICAN GP	Mexico City	11	Team Lotus	2.0 Lotus 33-Climax V8	gearbox

1967

1	SOUTH AFRICAN GP	Kyalami	4	Cooper Car Co	3.0 Cooper T81-Maserati V12	
5	MONACO GP	Monte Carlo	11	Cooper Car Co	3.0 Cooper T81-Maserati V12	4 laps behind
ret	DUTCH GP	Zandvoort	14	Cooper Car Co	3.0 Cooper T81-Maserati V12	gearbox
ret	BELGIAN GP	Spa	30	Cooper Car Co	3.0 Cooper T81-Maserati V12	engine/3 laps behind
6	FRENCH GP	Le Mans	14	Cooper Car Co	3.0 Cooper T81-Maserati V12	4 laps behind
5	BRITISH GP	Silverstone	12	Cooper Car Co	3.0 Cooper T81-Maserati V12	1 lap behind
8	GERMAN GP	Nürburgring	6	Cooper Car Co	3.0 Cooper T81-Maserati V12	2 laps behind
dns	"	"	6	Cooper Car Co	3.0 Cooper T86-Maserati V12	practice only
6	MEXICAN GP	Mexico City	21	Cooper Car Co	3.0 Cooper T81B-Maserati V12	

1968

ret	SOUTH AFRICAN GP	Kyalami	11	Owen Racing Organisation	3.0 BRM P126 V12	ignition/boiling fuel
ret	SPANISH GP	Jarama	9	Owen Racing Organisation	3.0 BRM P133 V12	crashed
ret	MONACO GP	Monte Carlo	4	Owen Racing Organisation	3.0 BRM P133 V12	hit barrier
2	BELGIAN GP	Spa	11	Owen Racing Organisation	3.0 BRM P133 V12	
3	DUTCH GP	Zandvoort	15	Owen Racing Organisation	3.0 BRM P133 V12	1 lap behind
12	FRENCH GP	Rouen	20	Owen Racing Organisation	3.0 BRM P133 V12	pit stops/gearbox/led race/FL/-7 laps
ret	BRITISH GP	Brands Hatch	10	Owen Racing Organisation	3.0 BRM P133 V12	timing chain
dns	"	"	10	Owen Racing Organisation	3.0 BRM P126 V12	practice only
6	GERMAN GP	Nürburgring	10	Owen Racing Organisation	3.0 BRM P133 V12	
ret	ITALIAN GP	Monza	26	Owen Racing Organisation	3.0 BRM P138 V12	engine
3	CANADIAN GP	St Jovite	16	Owen Racing Organisation	3.0 BRM P133 V12	
ret	US GP	Watkins Glen	8	Owen Racing Organisation	3.0 BRM P133 V12	broken rear suspension
dns	"	"	8	Owen Racing Organisation	3.0 BRM P138 V12	practice only
4	MEXICAN GP	Mexico City	8	Owen Racing Organisation	3.0 BRM P133 V12	2 laps behind

1969

ret	SOUTH AFRICAN GP	Kyalami	12	Reg Parnell (Racing) Ltd	3.0 BRM P126 V12	engine
ret	SPANISH GP	Montjuich Park	9	Reg Parnell (Racing) Ltd	3.0 BRM P126 V12	engine
ret	MONACO GP	Monte Carlo	10	Reg Parnell (Racing) Ltd	3.0 BRM P126 V12	engine
ret	BRITISH GP	Silverstone	12	Scuderia Ferrari SpA SEFAC	3.0 Ferrari 312/68/69 V12	engine
6	ITALIAN GP	Monza	10	Scuderia Ferrari SpA SEFAC	3.0 Ferrari 312/68/69 V12	2 laps behind
ret	CANADIAN GP	Mosport Park	6	North American Racing Team	3.0 Ferrari 312/68/69 V12	oil pressure
5	US GP	Watkins Glen	12	North American Racing Team	3.0 Ferrari 312/68/69 V12	7 laps behind
7	MEXICAN GP	Mexico City	12	North American Racing Team	3.0 Ferrari 312/68/69 V12	2 laps behind

1970

9	SOUTH AFRICAN GP	Kyalami	20	Owen Racing Organisation	3.0 BRM P153 V12	pit stop/misfire/4 laps behind
ret	SPANISH GP	Jarama	10	Yardley Team BRM	3.0 BRM P153 V12	withdrawn after Oliver's accident
6	MONACO GP	Monte Carlo	17	Yardley Team BRM	3.0 BRM P153 V12	pit stop/sticking throttle
1	BELGIAN GP	Spa	1	Yardley Team BRM	3.0 BRM P153 V12	

10	DUTCH GP	Zandvoort	1	Yardley Team BRM	3.0 BRM P153 V12		2 pit stops/loose nose cone
ret	FRENCH GP	Clermont Ferrand	3	Yardley Team BRM	3.0 BRM P153 V12		gearbox
ret	BRITISH GP	Brands Hatch	22	Yardley Team BRM	3.0 BRM P153 V12		spun off
ret	GERMAN GP	Hockenheim	6	Yardley Team BRM	3.0 BRM P153 V12		ignition
4	AUSTRIAN GP	Österreichring	17	Yardley Team BRM	3.0 BRM P153 V12		
ret	ITALIAN GP	Monza	10	Yardley Team BRM	3.0 BRM P153 V12		engine
4	CANADIAN GP	St Jovite	14	Yardley Team BRM	3.0 BRM P153 V12		pit stop/fuel
2	US GP	Watkins Glen	19	Yardley Team BRM	3.0 BRM P153 V12		pit stop when 1st/fuel
6	MEXICAN GP	Mexico City	19	Yardley Team BRM	3.0 BRM P153 V12		

1971

ret	SOUTH AFRICAN GP	Kyalami	16	Yardley-BRM	3.0 BRM P160 V12	overheating
dns	"	"	16T	Yardley-BRM	3.0 BRM P153 V12	practice only
4	SPANISH GP	Montjuich Park	14	Yardley-BRM	3.0 BRM P160 V12	
9	MONACO GP	Monte Carlo	15	Yardley-BRM	3.0 BRM P160 V12	pit stop/wheel change/-4 laps
dns	"	"	15T	Yardley-BRM	3.0 BRM P153 V12	practice only
2	DUTCH GP	Zandvoort	8	Yardley-BRM	3.0 BRM P160 V12	led race
ret	FRENCH GP	Paul Ricard	15	Yardley-BRM	3.0 BRM P160 V12	coil

GP Starts: 55   GP Wins: 2   Pole positions: 10   Fastest laps: 1   Points: 71

RODRIGUEZ, Ricardo (MEX) b 14/2/1942 – d 1/11/1962

1961

	Race	Circuit	No	Entrant	Car/Engine	Comment
ret	ITALIAN GP	Monza	8	Scuderia Ferrari SpA SEFAC	1.5 Ferrari 156 V6	fuel pump

1962

ret	DUTCH GP	Zandvoort	3	Scuderia Ferrari SpA SEFAC	1.5 Ferrari 156 V6	crashed
dns	MONACO GP	Monte Carlo	40T	Scuderia Ferrari SpA SEFAC	1.5 Ferrari 156 V6	practised in Mairesse car
4	BELGIAN GP	Spa	12	Scuderia Ferrari SpA SEFAC	1.5 Ferrari 156 V6	
6	GERMAN GP	Nürburgring	3	Scuderia Ferrari SpA SEFAC	1.5 Ferrari 156 V6	
14	ITALIAN GP	Monza	4	Scuderia Ferrari SpA SEFAC	1.5 Ferrari 156 V6	pit stops/ignition/23 laps behind

GP Starts: 5   GP Wins: 0   Pole positions: 0   Fastest laps: 0   Points: 4

ROL, Franco (I) b 1908 – d 5/6/1977

1950

	Race	Circuit	NO	Entrant	Car/Engine	Comment
ret	MONACO GP	Monte Carlo	44	Officine Alfieri Maserati	1.5 s/c Maserati 4CLT/48 4	multiple accident
ret	FRENCH GP	Reims	28	Officine Alfieri Maserati	1.5 s/c Maserati 4CLT/48 4	engine
ret	ITALIAN GP	Monza	4	Officine Alfieri Maserati	1.5 s/c Maserati 4CLT/48 4	

1951

9	ITALIAN GP	Monza	44	OSCA Automobili	4.5 OSCA 4500G V12	13 laps behind

1952

ret	ITALIAN GP	Monza	24	Officine Alfieri Maserati	2.0 Maserati A6GCM 6	engine

GP Starts: 5   GP Wins: 0   Pole positions: 0   Fastest laps: 0   Points: 0

ROLT, Tony (GB) b 16/10/1918

1950

	Race	Circuit	No	Entrant	Car/Engine	Comment
ret	BRITISH GP	Silverstone	9	Peter Walker	1.5 s/c ERA E Type 6	car shared with Walker/gearbox

1953

ret	BRITISH GP	Silverstone	14	R R C Walker Racing Team	2.0 Connaught A Type 4	driveshaft

1955

ret*	BRITISH GP	Aintree	36	R R C Walker Racing Team	2.5 Connaught B Type 4	*taken over by Walker/throttle

GP Starts: 3   GP Wins: 0   Pole positions: 0   Fastest laps: 0   Points: 0

ROOS, Bertil (S) b 12/10/1943

1974

	Race	Circuit	No	Entrant	Car/Engine	Comment
ret	SWEDISH GP	Anderstorp	16	UOP Shadow Racing Team	3.0 Shadow DN3-Cosworth V8	transmission

GP Starts: 1   GP Wins: 0   Pole positions: 0   Fastest laps: 0   Points: 0

ROOYEN, Basil van (ZA) b 19/4/1938

1968

	Race	Circuit	No	Entrant	Car/Engine	Comment
ret	SOUTH AFRICAN GP	Kyalami	25	John Love	2.7 Cooper T75-Climax 4	head gasket

1969

ret	SOUTH AFRICAN GP	Kyalami	18	Team Lawson	3.0 McLaren M7A-Cosworth V8	brakes

GP Starts: 2   GP Wins: 0   Pole positions: 0   Fastest laps: 0   Points: 0

RICARDO RODRIGUEZ

The younger of the two racing Rodriguez brothers, Ricardo gave up bike racing at the age of 14, having won the Mexican championship, to race an Opel sedan. By 1957 he was already competing abroad, taking a class win in the Nassau Tourist Trophy with a Porsche Spyder.

The brothers Rodriguez came to Europe in 1960 with a NART Ferrari, though it was with André Pilette that Ricardo gained his best result, a second at Le Mans in a 250GT. Teamed with Pedro, he took third in the Sebring 12 Hours and second in the Nürburgring 1000 Km.

Invited by the Scuderia to join their Grand Prix line-up for the Italian GP, he sensationally put the car on the front row of the grid alongside the ill-fated championship favourite, von Trips. Not surprisingly he was signed by the team for a full season in 1962, but the car was far from the dominant machine of just a year earlier and young Ricardo, still a little wild and fearless, was used selectively. In a bright start, the Mexican took second place at the Pau GP, before confirming his outstanding potential in a number of World Championship rounds. In sports car racing he was out of luck, except for a win in the Targa Florio sharing a Ferrari 246 V6 with Gendebien and Mairesse.

When Ferrari decided not to enter their cars for the non-championship Mexican GP, Ricardo arranged to race one of Rob Walker's Lotus-Climax V8s. Striving for pole position, the young charger came unstuck, crashing on the banking and dying from multiple injuries.

TONY ROLT

Perhaps the brightest young talent of a generation of pre-war amateur drivers, Rolt, an Army officer who would become a celebrated resident of Colditz Castle, won the British Empire Trophy at Donington in an ERA as a 19-year-old before the outbreak of hostilities. When peace returned he was soon back in action with an Alfa Romeo, a Delage and a Nash-Healey. Although he shared Peter Walker's ERA at the 1950 British GP, in the main Rolt restricted himself to national racing, enjoying himself with Rob Walker's Delage in 1951 and, in his only HWM drive, taking second place in the 1952 International Trophy behind team-mate Lance Macklin.

Between 1953 and 1955, Rolt raced Walker's dark-blue Connaught with great succes in national events, winning numerous Formula 2, Libre and handicap races, and also drove for the works Jaguar sports car team, paired with the extrovert Duncan Hamilton. This larger-than-life duo won the Le Mans 24-hour race in 1953, and took second place the following year both at Le Mans and in the Reims 12 Hours.

BERTIL ROOS

A graduate of the Opert driving school, where he was later an instructor, the self-confident Roos looked to have a bright future after winning the 1973 US Super Vee title and doing well in both European Formula 2 and Canadian Formula Atlantic. His big opportunity came when Shadow invited him to drive their car in the 1974 Swedish GP, but it was an unhappy and brief alliance, the Swede failing to impress the team and subsequently being passed over in favour of Tom Pryce.

Thereafter, Roos returned to Atlantic racing in the USA and Canada.

BASIL van ROOYEN

Having shown his talent as early as 1963, when he beat Lotus Cortina ace John Whitmore in an identical machine, Basil was a dominant force in saloons in South Africa for many years, handling a variety of cars including Ford Mustangs and Alfa Romeo GTs. With backing from STP he also moved into national single-seaters in 1968 with a Brabham BT24, although he had to make do with John Love's old Cooper for the Grand Prix.

In 1969, van Rooyen had a McLaren M7A at his disposal, but afer a couple of wins in the car he wrote it off in a big way at Kyalami, returning to the more comfortable environment of saloon cars until 1973, when he virtually retired from racing. However, when Formula Atlantic was introduced in 1975, Basil was tempted back into single-seaters with a Chevron for a couple of seasons.

KEKE ROSBERG

The buccaneering Finn became a firm favourite in the mid-eighties after he had taken a surprise World Championship win in a season clouded by tragedy. His subsequent exuberant performances, stabbing the turbo-powered Williams around the world's circuits with frightening commitment, did much to supply the entertainment factor which was often missing from the sport.

Born in Sweden of Finnish parentage, Keijo Rosberg was three times his country's karting champion before moving with equal success into the rough-and-tumble world of Formula Vee and Super Vee, taking the Castrol GTX title in the latter category in 1975. He found a seat in the Toj Formula 2 team in 1976, but apart from a fourth place at Rouen this was not a successful alliance. By the end of the year Keke had linked up with Fred Opert, who satisfied the Finn's insatiable appetite for racing in 1977 by running him first in New Zealand, where he took the Stuyvesant title, and then in the European Formula 2 championship and the Labatt's Atlantic series in North America.

There was no let-up the following year when Rosberg undertook a mind-numbing schedule which totalled some forty races. In addition to repeating the previous season's marathon stint for Opert, Keke moved into Formula 1 and scored a shock win in a rain-drenched International Trophy race for the new Theodore team. Although this result was something of a fluke, there was no doubting the Finn's stunning car control, and his name was noted down as one to watch by Formula 1 team managers. In World Championship races, of course, it was a different story, as he struggled to make an impression in three different makes of car.

Resigned to a season of Can-Am in 1979, Rosberg was often quicker but, tellingly, also more erratic than champion Jacky Ickx, but a route back into Grand Prix racing was to re-open after James Hunt's sudden retirement. His half-season in a difficult car failed to provide any satisfactory results, but he was back in the frame to stay. When Wolf amalgamated with Fittipaldi for 1980 Keke was part of the package, and on his maiden outing at Buenos Aires he scored his first championship points. However, the team lacked the technical and financial resources to make a real impact and Rosberg was forced to make up the numbers until the end of 1981 when it closed its doors.

The cards suddenly began to fall for the Finn when he took over the Williams seat vacated by Alan Jones at the start of 1982. Within two races the team's other star driver, Carlos Reutemann, had also walked away from Grand Prix racing and suddenly Keke was leading the team. Showing incredible maturity for one not familiar with racing at the sharp end of the grid, Rosberg made the odd mistake but maximised every potential points-scoring opportunity and took a splendidly thought-out win in the Swiss GP at Dijon. By the end of the year he had overhauled the unfortunate Didier Pironi's points total and claimed a fairytale World Championship triumph. The following year saw Keke hampered by a lack of turbo power, but this didn't prevent him taking a classic win, driving on slicks throughout, on a damp track at Monaco. He took the Cosworth car into battle with great ferocity elsewhere, never admitting defeat when many others would have been content merely to cruise round. When he finally got a turbo engine himself, Keke was to be frustrated by the poor handling of the Williams chassis, but nevertheless he scored perhaps the best win of his career in searing heat in Dallas in 1984 when most of his rivals failed to avoid a meeting with the concrete walls. Rosberg's relationship with Williams was never completely harmonious and he wanted away at the end of the season but, forced to see out his contract, he got on with the job without further complaint. Initially at least, he was unhappy with the arrival of Nigel Mansell for 1985 but soon established a rapport with his new team-mate. Having agreed a lucrative deal with McLaren, Rosberg signed off from Williams with a sparkling win in Adelaide to start the final short chapter of his Grand Prix career, but the partnership was to be something of disappointment for both sides, with Keke rather taken aback by his inability to come to terms with Alain Prost.

Rosberg quit without regrets, but stayed closely involved with the sport, making a return to the wheel in the World Sports Car Championship with Peugeot in 1991. With Dalmas, he took wins at both Magny Cours and Mexico, before switching to the German touring car championship the following year to race a Mercedes. Perhaps more important has become his role in guiding young Finnish talent, the careers of both Mika Häkkinen and J J Lehto prospering under his shrewd managership.

ROSBERG, Keke (Keijo) (SF) b 6/12/1948

1978

	Race	Circuit	No	Entrant	Car/Engine	Comment
ret	SOUTH AFRICAN GP	Kyalami	32	Theodore Racing Hong Kong	3.0 Theodore TR1-Cosworth V8	clutch/engine/fuel leak
dnpq	US GP WEST	Long Beach	32	Theodore Racing Hong Kong	3.0 Theodore TR1-Cosworth V8	
dnpq	MONACO GP	Monte Carlo	32	Theodore Racing Hong Kong	3.0 Theodore TR1-Cosworth V8	
dnq	BELGIAN GP	Zolder	32	Theodore Racing Hong Kong	3.0 Theodore TR1-Cosworth V8	
dnpq	SPANISH GP	Jarama	32	Theodore Racing Hong Kong	3.0 Theodore TR1-Cosworth V8	
15	SWEDISH GP	Anderstorp	10	ATS Racing Team	3.0 ATS HS1-Cosworth V8	pit stops/ignition/clutch/-7 laps
16	FRENCH GP	Paul Ricard	10	ATS Racing Team	3.0 ATS HS1-Cosworth V8	2 laps behind
ret	BRITISH GP	Brands Hatch	10	ATS Racing Team	3.0 ATS HS1-Cosworth V8	front suspension
10	GERMAN GP	Hockenheim	32	Theodore Racing Hong Kong	3.0 Wolf WR3-Cosworth V8	pit stop/nose cone/3 laps behind
nc	AUSTRIAN GP	Österreichring	32	Theodore Racing Hong Kong	3.0 Wolf WR3-Cosworth V8	pit stop/tyres/7 laps behind
ret	DUTCH GP	Zandvoort	32	Theodore Racing Hong Kong	3.0 Wolf WR4-Cosworth V8	stuck throttle/accident
dns	"	"	32	Theodore Racing Hong Kong	3.0 Wolf WR3-Cosworth V8	practice only

dnpq	ITALIAN GP	Monza	32	Theodore Racing Hong Kong	3.0 Wolf WR4-Cosworth V8	
ret	US GP EAST	Watkins Glen	32	ATS Racing Team	3.0 ATS D1-Cosworth V8	gear linkage
nc	CANADIAN GP	Montreal	32	ATS Racing Team	3.0 ATS D1-Cosworth V8	pit stops/misfire/12 laps behind

1979

9	FRENCH GP	Dijon	20	Olympus Cameras Wolf Racing	3.0 Wolf WR8-Cosworth V8	gearbox problems/1 lap behind
ret	BRITISH GP	Silverstone	20	Olympus Cameras Wolf Racing	3.0 Wolf WR7-Cosworth V8	fuel system
dns	"	"	20	Olympus Cameras Wolf Racing	3.0 Wolf WR9-Cosworth V8	practice only
ret	GERMAN GP	Hockenheim	20	Olympus Cameras Wolf Racing	3.0 Wolf WR8-Cosworth V8	engine
dns	"	"	20	Olympus Cameras Wolf Racing	3.0 Wolf WR9-Cosworth V8	practice only
ret	AUSTRIAN GP	Österreichring	20	Olympus Cameras Wolf Racing	3.0 Wolf WR9-Cosworth V8	electrics
dns	"	"	20	Olympus Cameras Wolf Racing	3.0 Wolf WR9-Cosworth V8	practice only
ret	DUTCH GP	Zandvoort	20	Olympus Cameras Wolf Racing	3.0 Wolf WR9-Cosworth V8	engine
ret	ITALIAN GP	Monza	20	Olympus Cameras Wolf Racing	3.0 Wolf WR8-Cosworth V8	engine
dns	"	"	20	Olympus Cameras Wolf Racing	3.0 Wolf WR9-Cosworth V8	practice only
dnq	CANADIAN GP	Montreal	20	Olympus Cameras Wolf Racing	3.0 Wolf WR9-Cosworth V8	
ret	US GP EAST	Watkins Glen	20	Olympus Cameras Wolf Racing	3.0 Wolf WR8/9-Cosworth V8	collision with Pironi

1980

3	ARGENTINE GP	Buenos Aires	21	Skol Fittipaldi Team	3.0 Fittipaldi F7-Cosworth V8	
9	BRAZILIAN GP	Interlagos	21	Skol Fittipaldi Team	3.0 Fittipaldi F7-Cosworth V8	1 lap behind
ret	SOUTH AFRICAN GP	Kyalami	21	Skol Fittipaldi Team	3.0 Fittipaldi F7-Cosworth V8	brake failure/crashed
ret	US GP WEST	Long Beach	21	Skol Fittipaldi Team	3.0 Fittipaldi F7-Cosworth V8	overheating
7	BELGIAN GP	Zolder	21	Skol Fittipaldi Team	3.0 Fittipaldi F7-Cosworth V8	1 lap behind
dnq	MONACO GP	Monte Carlo	21	Skol Fittipaldi Team	3.0 Fittipaldi F7-Cosworth V8	
ret	FRENCH GP	Paul Ricard	21	Skol Fittipaldi Team	3.0 Fittipaldi F7-Cosworth V8	crashed
dnq	BRITISH GP	Brands Hatch	21	Skol Fittipaldi Team	3.0 Fittipaldi F7-Cosworth V8	
ret	GERMAN GP	Hockenheim	21	Skol Fittipaldi Team	3.0 Fittipaldi F8-Cosworth V8	wheel bearing
16	AUSTRIAN GP	Österreichring	21	Skol Fittipaldi Team	3.0 Fittipaldi F8-Cosworth V8	pit stop/2 laps behind
dnq	DUTCH GP	Zandvoort	21	Skol Fittipaldi Team	3.0 Fittipaldi F8-Cosworth V8	
5	ITALIAN GP	Imola	21	Skol Fittipaldi Team	3.0 Fittipaldi F8-Cosworth V8	1 lap behind
9	CANADIAN GP	Montreal	21	Skol Fittipaldi Team	3.0 Fittipaldi F8-Cosworth V8	2 laps behind
10	US GP EAST	Watkins Glen	21	Skol Fittipaldi Team	3.0 Fittipaldi F8-Cosworth V8	2 laps behind

1981

ret	US GP WEST	Long Beach	20	Fittipaldi Automotive	3.0 Fittipaldi F8C-Cosworth V8	rotor arm
9	BRAZILIAN GP	Rio	20	Fittipaldi Automotive	3.0 Fittipaldi F8C-Cosworth V8	1 lap behind
ret	ARGENTINE GP	Buenos Aires	20	Fittipaldi Automotive	3.0 Fittipaldi F8C-Cosworth V8	fuel pump belt
ret	SAN MARINO GP	Imola	20	Fittipaldi Automotive	3.0 Fittipaldi F8C-Cosworth V8	engine
ret	BELGIAN GP	Zolder	20	Fittipaldi Automotive	3.0 Fittipaldi F8C-Cosworth V8	broken gear lever
dnq	MONACO GP	Monte Carlo	20	Fittipaldi Automotive	3.0 Fittipaldi F8C-Cosworth V8	
12	SPANISH GP	Jarama	20	Fittipaldi Automotive	3.0 Fittipaldi F8C-Cosworth V8	2 laps behind
ret	FRENCH GP	Dijon	20	Fittipaldi Automotive	3.0 Fittipaldi F8C-Cosworth V8	broken rear cross beam
ret	BRITISH GP	Silverstone	20	Fittipaldi Automotive	3.0 Fittipaldi F8C-Cosworth V8	rear suspension
dnq	GERMAN GP	Hockenheim	20	Fittipaldi Automotive	3.0 Fittipaldi F8C-Cosworth V8	
dnq	DUTCH GP	Zandvoort	20	Fittipaldi Automotive	3.0 Fittipaldi F8C-Cosworth V8	
dnq	ITALIAN GP	Monza	20	Fittipaldi Automotive	3.0 Fittipaldi F8C-Cosworth V8	
dnq	CANADIAN GP	Montreal	20	Fittipaldi Automotive	3.0 Fittipaldi F8C-Cosworth V8	
10	CAESARS PALACE GP	Las Vegas	20	Fittipaldi Automotive	3.0 Fittipaldi F8C-Cosworth V8	3 laps behind

1982 World Champion Driver

5	SOUTH AFRICAN GP	Kyalami	6	TAG Williams Team	3.0 Williams FW07C-Cosworth V8	
dsq	BRAZILIAN GP	Rio	6	TAG Williams Team	3.0 Williams FW07C-Cosworth V8	illegal brakes/2nd on road
2	US GP WEST	Long Beach	6	TAG Williams Team	3.0 Williams FW07C-Cosworth V8	
2	BELGIAN GP	Zolder	6	TAG Williams Team	3.0 Williams FW08-Cosworth V8	
ret	MONACO GP	Monte Carlo	6	TAG Williams Team	3.0 Williams FW08-Cosworth V8	front suspension
4	US GP (DETROIT)	Detroit	6	TAG Williams Team	3.0 Williams FW08-Cosworth V8	
ret	CANADIAN GP	Montreal	6	TAG Williams Team	3.0 Williams FW08-Cosworth V8	gearbox
3	DUTCH GP	Zandvoort	6	TAG Williams Team	3.0 Williams FW08-Cosworth V8	
ret	BRITISH GP	Brands Hatch	6	TAG Williams Team	3.0 Williams FW08-Cosworth V8	fuel pressure/Pole
5	FRENCH GP	Paul Ricard	6	TAG Williams Team	3.0 Williams FW08-Cosworth V8	
3	GERMAN GP	Hockenheim	6	TAG Williams Team	3.0 Williams FW08-Cosworth V8	1 lap behind
2	AUSTRIAN GP	Österreichring	6	TAG Williams Team	3.0 Williams FW08-Cosworth V8	
1	SWISS GP	Dijon	6	TAG Williams Team	3.0 Williams FW08-Cosworth V8	
8	ITALIAN GP	Monza	6	TAG Williams Team	3.0 Williams FW08-Cosworth V8	pit stop/lost rear wing/-2 laps
5	CAESARS PALACE GP	Las Vegas	6	TAG Williams Team	3.0 Williams FW08-Cosworth V8	

1983

dsq	BRAZILIAN GP	Rio	1	TAG Williams Team	3.0 Williams FW08C-Cosworth V8	push start at p stop/Pole/2nd on road
ret	US GP WEST	Long Beach	1	TAG Williams Team	3.0 Williams FW08C-Cosworth V8	accident with Jarier
5	FRENCH GP	Paul Ricard	1	TAG Williams Team	3.0 Williams FW08C-Cosworth V8	1 lap behind
4	SAN MARINO GP	Imola	1	TAG Williams Team	3.0 Williams FW08C-Cosworth V8	1 lap behind
1	MONACO GP	Monte Carlo	1	TAG Williams Team	3.0 Williams FW08C-Cosworth V8	
5	BELGIAN GP	Spa	1	TAG Williams Team	3.0 Williams FW08C-Cosworth V8	
2	US GP (DETROIT)	Detroit	1	TAG Williams Team	3.0 Williams FW08C-Cosworth V8	
4	CANADIAN GP	Montreal	1	TAG Williams Team	3.0 Williams FW08C-Cosworth V8	
11	BRITISH GP	Silverstone	1	TAG Williams Team	3.0 Williams FW08C-Cosworth V8	pit stop/tyres/2 laps behind
10	GERMAN GP	Hockenheim	1	TAG Williams Team	3.0 Williams FW08C-Cosworth V8	pit stop/tyres/1 lap behind
8	AUSTRIAN GP	Österreichring	1	TAG Williams Team	3.0 Williams FW08C-Cosworth V8	pit stop/tyres/2 laps behind
ret	DUTCH GP	Zandvoort	1	TAG Williams Team	3.0 Williams FW08C-Cosworth V8	misfire
11*	ITALIAN GP	Monza	1	TAG Williams Team	3.0 Williams FW08C-Cosworth V8	* 9th on road/1 min pen/-1 lap
ret	EUROPEAN GP	Brands Hatch	1	TAG Williams Team	3.0 Williams FW08C-Cosworth V8	engine
5	SOUTH AFRICAN GP	Kyalami	1	TAG Williams Team	1.5 t/c Williams FW09-Honda V6	pit stop/tyres/1 lap behind

1984

2	BRAZILIAN GP	Rio	6	Williams Grand Prix Engineering	1.5 t/c Williams FW09-Honda V6	
ret	SOUTH AFRICAN GP	Kyalami	6	Williams Grand Prix Engineering	1.5 t/c Williams FW09-Honda V6	loose wheel nut-lost wheel

4/ret	BELGIAN GP	Zolder	6	Williams Grand Prix Engineering	1.5 t/c Williams FW09-Honda V6	*out of fuel/1 lap behind*
ret	SAN MARINO GP	Imola	6	Williams Grand Prix Engineering	1.5 t/c Williams FW09-Honda V6	*electrics*
6	FRENCH GP	Dijon	6	Williams Grand Prix Engineering	1.5 t/c Williams FW09-Honda V6	*1 lap behind*
4	MONACO GP	Monte Carlo	6	Williams Grand Prix Engineering	1.5 t/c Williams FW09-Honda V6	*3rd car dsq/race stopped-half pts only*
ret	CANADIAN GP	Montreal	6	Williams Grand Prix Engineering	1.5 t/c Williams FW09-Honda V6	*fuel system*
ret	US GP (DETROIT)	Detroit	6	Williams Grand Prix Engineering	1.5 t/c Williams FW09-Honda V6	*exhaust/turbo*
1	US GP (DALLAS)	Dallas	6	Williams Grand Prix Engineering	1.5 t/c Williams FW09-Honda V6	
ret	BRITISH GP	Brands Hatch	6	Williams Grand Prix Engineering	1.5 t/c Williams FW09B-Honda V6	*intercooler hose/engine*
ret	GERMAN GP	Hockenheim	6	Williams Grand Prix Engineering	1.5 t/c Williams FW09B-Honda V6	*electrics*
ret	AUSTRIAN GP	Österreichring	6	Williams Grand Prix Engineering	1.5 t/c Williams FW09B-Honda V6	*handling*
8/ret	DUTCH GP	Zandvoort	6	Williams Grand Prix Engineering	1.5 t/c Williams FW09B-Honda V6	*8th & 9th cars dsq/out of fuel*
ret	ITALIAN GP	Monza	6	Williams Grand Prix Engineering	1.5 t/c Williams FW09B-Honda V6	*engine*
ret	EUROPEAN GP	Nürburgring	6	Williams Grand Prix Engineering	1.5 t/c Williams FW09B-Honda V6	*hit by Senna*
ret	PORTUGUESE GP	Estoril	6	Williams Grand Prix Engineering	1.5 t/c Williams FW09B-Honda V6	*engine*

1985

ret	BRAZILIAN GP	Rio	6	Canon Williams Team	1.5 t/c Williams FW10-Honda V6	*turbo*
ret	PORTUGUESE GP	Estoril	6	Canon Williams Team	1.5 t/c Williams FW10-Honda V6	*spun off*
ret	SAN MARINO GP	Imola	6	Canon Williams Team	1.5 t/c Williams FW10-Honda V6	*throttle linkage/brakes*
8	MONACO GP	Monte Carlo	6	Canon Williams Team	1.5 t/c Williams FW10-Honda V6	*2 laps behind*
4	CANADIAN GP	Montreal	6	Canon Williams Team	1.5 t/c Williams FW10-Honda V6	
1	US GP (DETROIT)	Detroit	6	Canon Williams Team	1.5 t/c Williams FW10-Honda V6	
2	FRENCH GP	Paul Ricard	6	Canon Williams Team	1.5 t/c Williams FW10-Honda V6	*Pole/FL*
ret	BRITISH GP	Silverstone	6	Canon Williams Team	1.5 t/c Williams FW10-Honda V6	*exhaust/Pole*
12/ret	GERMAN GP	Nürburgring	6	Canon Williams Team	1.5 t/c Williams FW10-Honda V6	*brake caliper/5 laps behind*
ret	AUSTRIAN GP	Österreichring	6	Canon Williams Team	1.5 t/c Williams FW10-Honda V6	*engine*
ret	DUTCH GP	Zandvoort	6	Canon Williams Team	1.5 t/c Williams FW10-Honda V6	*engine*
ret	ITALIAN GP	Monza	6	Canon Williams Team	1.5 t/c Williams FW10-Honda V6	*engine*
4	BELGIAN GP	Spa	6	Canon Williams Team	1.5 t/c Williams FW10-Honda V6	
3	EUROPEAN GP	Brands Hatch	6	Canon Williams Team	1.5 t/c Williams FW10-Honda V6	
2	SOUTH AFRICAN GP	Kyalami	6	Canon Williams Team	1.5 t/c Williams FW10-Honda V6	*FL*
1	AUSTRALIAN GP	Adelaide	6	Canon Williams Team	1.5 t/c Williams FW10-Honda V6	*FL*

1986

ret	BRAZILIAN GP	Rio	2	Marlboro McLaren International	1.5 t/c McLaren MP4/2C-TAG V6	*engine*
4	SPANISH GP	Jerez	2	Marlboro McLaren International	1.5 t/c McLaren MP4/2C-TAG V6	
5/ret	SAN MARINO GP	Imola	2	Marlboro McLaren International	1.5 t/c McLaren MP4/2C-TAG V6	*out of fuel/2 laps behind*
2	MONACO GP	Monte Carlo	2	Marlboro McLaren International	1.5 t/c McLaren MP4/2C-TAG V6	
ret	BELGIAN GP	Spa	2	Marlboro McLaren International	1.5 t/c McLaren MP4/2C-TAG V6	*engine*
4	CANADIAN GP	Montreal	2	Marlboro McLaren International	1.5 t/c McLaren MP4/2C-TAG V6	
ret	US GP (DETROIT)	Detroit	2	Marlboro McLaren International	1.5 t/c McLaren MP4/2C-TAG V6	*transmission*
4	FRENCH GP	Paul Ricard	2	Marlboro McLaren International	1.5 t/c McLaren MP4/2C-TAG V6	
ret	BRITISH GP	Brands Hatch	2	Marlboro McLaren International	1.5 t/c McLaren MP4/2C-TAG V6	*gearbox*
5/ret	GERMAN GP	Hockenheim	2	Marlboro McLaren International	1.5 t/c McLaren MP4/2C-TAG V6	*out of fuel/1 lap behind/Pole*
ret	HUNGARIAN GP	Hungaroring	2	Marlboro McLaren International	1.5 t/c McLaren MP4/2C-TAG V6	*rear suspension*
9/ret	AUSTRIAN GP	Österreichring	2	Marlboro McLaren International	1.5 t/c McLaren MP4/2C-TAG V6	*electrics/5 laps behind*
4	ITALIAN GP	Monza	2	Marlboro McLaren International	1.5 t/c McLaren MP4/2C-TAG V6	
ret	PORTUGUESE GP	Estoril	2	Marlboro McLaren International	1.5 t/c McLaren MP4/2C-TAG V6	*engine*
ret	MEXICAN GP	Mexico City	2	Marlboro McLaren International	1.5 t/c McLaren MP4/2C-TAG V6	*puncture*
ret	AUSTRALIAN GP	Adelaide	2	Marlboro McLaren International	1.5 t/c McLaren MP4/2C-TAG V6	*tyre failure when leading*

GP Starts: 114   GP Wins: 5   Pole positions: 5   Fastest laps: 3   Points: 159.5

ROSIER, Louis (F) b 5/11/1905 – d 29/10/1956

1950

	Race	Circuit	No	Entrant	Car/Engine	Comment
5	BRITISH GP	Silverstone	15	Ecurie Rosier	4.5 Lago-Talbot T26C 6	*2 laps behind*
ret	MONACO GP	Monte Carlo	16	Ecurie Rosier	4.5 Lago-Talbot T26C 6	*multiple accident*
3	SWISS GP	Bremgarten	10	Automobiles Talbot-Darracq SA	4.5 Lago-Talbot T26C-DA 6	*1 lap behind*
3	BELGIAN GP	Spa	14	Automobiles Talbot-Darracq SA	4.5 Lago-Talbot T26C-DA 6	
ret	FRENCH GP	Reims	20	Automobiles Talbot-Darracq SA	4.5 Lago-Talbot T26C-DA 6	*overheating*
6*	"	"	26	Charles Pozzi	4.5 Lago-Talbot T26C 6	** took Pozzi's car/8 laps behind*
4	ITALIAN GP	Monza	58	Ecurie Rosier	4.5 Lago-Talbot T26C 6	*5 laps behind*

1951

9	SWISS GP	Bremgarten	8	Ecurie Rosier	4.5 Lago-Talbot T26C-DA 6	*3 laps behind*
4	BELGIAN GP	Spa	14	Ecurie Rosier	4.5 Lago-Talbot T26C-DA 6	*2 laps behind*
ret	FRENCH GP	Reims	40	Ecurie Rosier	4.5 Lago-Talbot T26C-DA 6	*transmisssion-rear axle*
10	BRITISH GP	Silverstone	22	Ecurie Rosier	4.5 Lago-Talbot T26C-DA 6	*7 laps behind*
8	GERMAN GP	Nürburgring	84	Ecurie Rosier	4.5 Lago-Talbot T26C-DA 6	*1 lap behind*
7	ITALIAN GP	Monza	18	Ecurie Rosier	4.5 Lago-Talbot T26C-DA 6	*7 laps behind*
7	SPANISH GP	Pedrlbes	28	Ecurie Rosier	4.5 Lago-Talbot T26C-DA 6	*6 laps behind*

1952

ret	SWISS GP	Bremgarten	12	Ecurie Rosier	2.0 Ferrari 500 4	*crashed*
ret	BELGIAN GP	Spa	22	Ecurie Rosier	2.0 Ferrari 500 4	*transmission*
ret	FRENCH GP	Rouen	14	Ecurie Rosier	2.0 Ferrari 500 4	*engine*
10	ITALIAN GP	Monza	62	Ecurie Rosier	2.0 Ferrari 500 4	*5 laps behind*

1953

7	DUTCH GP	Zandvoort	10	Ecurie Rosier	2.0 Ferrari 500 4	*4 laps behind*
8	BELGIAN GP	Spa	32	Ecurie Rosier	2.0 Ferrari 500 4	*3 laps behind*
8	FRENCH GP	Reims	44	Ecurie Rosier	2.0 Ferrari 500 4	*4 laps behind*
10	BRITISH GP	Silverstone	9	Ecurie Rosier	2.0 Ferrari 500 4	*12 laps behind*
10	GERMAN GP	Nürburgring	20	Ecurie Rosier	2.0 Ferrari 500 4	*1 lap behind*

ret	SWISS GP	Bremgarten	10	Ecurie Rosier	2.0 Ferrari 500 4	*spun off*
nc	ITALIAN GP	Monza	64	Ecurie Rosier	2.0 Ferrari 500 4	*15 laps behind*
1954						
ret	ARGENTINE GP	Buenos Aires	24	Ecurie Rosier	2.5 Ferrari 500/625 4	*spun off*
ret	FRENCH GP	Reims	36	Ecurie Rosier	2.5 Ferrari 500/625 4	*engine*
ret	BRITISH GP	Silverstone	15	Ecurie Rosier	2.5 Ferrari 500/625 4	*engine*
8	GERMAN GP	Nürburgring	25	Ecurie Rosier	2.5 Ferrari 500/625 4	*1 lap behind*
8	ITALIAN GP	Monza	26	Officine Alfieri Maserati	2.5 Maserati 250F 6	*6 laps behind*
7	SPANISH GP	Pedralbes	26	Ecurie Rosier	2.5 Maserati 250F 6	*6 laps behind*
1955						
ret	MONACO GP	Monte Carlo	14	Ecurie Rosier	2.5 Maserati 250F 6	*split oil tank*
9	BELGIAN GP	Spa	28	Ecurie Rosier	2.5 Maserati 250F 6	*3 laps behind*
9	DUTCH GP	Zandvoort	28	Ecurie Rosier	2.5 Maserati 250F 6	*8 laps behind*
1956						
ret	MONACO GP	Monte Carlo	8	Ecurie Rosier	2.5 Maserati 250F 6	*engine*
8	BELGIAN GP	Spa	24	Ecurie Rosier	2.5 Maserati 250F 6	*3 laps behind*
6	FRENCH GP	Reims	36	Ecurie Rosier	2.5 Maserati 250F 6	*3 laps behind*
ret	BRITISH GP	Silverstone	27	Ecurie Rosier	2.5 Maserati 250F 6	*carburettor union*
5	GERMAN GP	Nürburgring	15	Ecurie Rosier	2.5 Maserati 250F 6	*3 laps behind*

GP Starts: 38   GP Wins: 0   Pole positions: 0   Fastest laps: 0   Points: 18

LOUIS ROSIER

A former motor cycle racer and hill-climb specialist, Rosier had just started to develop his racing career when the war intervened, and it was 1947 before this garage owner from Clermont Ferrand could compete on a wider stage.

Equipped with his self-prepared Talbot, Rosier won the 1947 Albi GP after more speedy opponents had dropped out and this win obviously set the tone for the rest of his career, for he usually raced well within his limits and placed great store by strategy and reliability as a route to success. In 1948, as a member of the Ecurie France team, he took delivery of a single-seater Lago-Talbot, winning the Grand Prix du Salon and finishing fourth at the Comminges, Pau and British GPs. The following season, with the Talbot probably at its peak relative to the opposition, Rosier won the Belgian GP and, with a succession of steady finishes, was crowned champion of France, a title he was to hold for four years.

Alfa Romeo ruled the roost in 1950, the year of the inaugural World Championship, but the crafty Rosier was always well placed to pick up the pieces, and he took some good points-scoring finishes in championship Grands Prix, as well as winning the Albi and Dutch GPs. Adapting his Talbot to sports car specification, he also won that season's Le Mans 24-hour race with his son Jean-Louis, though it was the father who was the pillar of the achievement, driving for some 20 hours. By 1951 the Talbot was no longer a competitive proposition, but Louis still managed to coax the elderly car to the finish with astonishing consistency, winning the non-championship Dutch and Bordeaux GPs.

The 1952 season brought a change of regulations, and Rosier lost no time in getting his hands on a Ferrari T375 and a state-of-the-art Ferrari T500 F2 car. The Italian machines were naturally painted French blue, and Rosier quickly put one of them to good use, winning the Albi GP in the big-engined model. For 1953 he continued with the same equipment, taking yet another win in the Albi GP and a victory in the Sables d'Olonne GP with the T500, while his old Talbot was brought out for the Reims 12 Hours, in which he took second place with Giraud-Cabantous.

By now Rosier was well past his best as a driver, but he pushed ahead undaunted the following season, and after racing a Ferrari 625 he bought a Maserati 250F which he continued to campaign in Grands Prix and non-championship events in a steady and reliable fashion, as well as handling his own Ferrari 3-litre sports car. Ironically, Rosier shared a Maserati T300S with Behra to win the 1956 Paris 1000 Km, his last win, before returning to the Montlhéry circuit he knew so well in this Ferrari for the Coupe du Salon. In pouring rain, Rosier overturned his car and suffered severe head injuries from which he died three weeks later. He was posthumously awarded the French Order of the Nation.

HUUB ROTHENGATTER

A tall, genial Dutchman, Rothengatter successfully financed a Grand Prix career after a fairly unspectacular climb through the ranks. Graduating to Formula 2 in 1979 with a Chevron, he looked a little rough round the edges, but the following season, equipped with a Toleman, he improved immensely and scored an excellent win at Zolder.

At this point Rothengatter harboured hopes of a Formula 1 ride, but in the event he missed the first half of 1981 completely before making a brief return to F2, and it was not until 1984 that he finally realised his ambition with the Spirit team, now shorn of Honda power. Halfway through the following season he joined Osella in place of Ghinzani, who had moved to Toleman, and he then had a year with Zakspeed. Huub had basically just been making up the numbers, but he remained remarkably cheerful nevertheless, clearly enjoying his bit part on the Grand Prix stage.

LLOYD RUBY

This Indianapolis 500 perennial began racing midgets after the war, but it was more than a decade before he joined the USAC trail, soon developing a reputation as a shrewd tactician who looked after his cars. However, he never succeded in winning the '500' – third place in 1964 was his best finish – though he came heart-breakingly close on a number of occasions, notably in 1969, when a routine pit stop went disastrously wrong.

In the early sixties Ruby also went sports car racing with a Lotus Monte Carlo, and became a local attraction at the 1961 US GP in a guest appearance in a Lotus 18. His mechanical sympathy prompted Ford to take him into their sports car team to develop their prototype and he won the Daytona 24 Hours in 1965 and 1966 with Ken Miles. This experienced pairing also took a win at Sebring in 1966, but injury caused Lloyd to miss Le Mans and a chance of victory.

TROY RUTTMAN

While Lloyd Ruby tried in vain to win the Indy 500 for more than two decades, Troy Ruttman was only 22 when he triumphed at the Brickyard at only his fourth attempt in 1952, becoming the youngest driver to win the classic event. However, it could easily have been his last year in racing for he was later seriously injured in a sprint car race at Cedar Rapids, Iowa, and didn't return to action until 1954.

Thereafter he raced fairly infrequently, though he was invited to compete in the 1957 'Two Worlds Trophy' race at Monza, finishing second. He returned for the race in 1958, and stayed on in Europe to try his hand at Grand Prix racing with Scuderia Centro Sud. In conflict with the American racing authorities, allegedly over his love for gambling, Troy returned to Indianapolis in 1960, leading briefly. Then, in addition to his annual trips to the Speedway, Troy successfully took up stock-car racing with Mercury, before suddenly announcing his retirement from the sport immediately after completing his final Indy 500 in 1964.

PETER RYAN

This Canadian youngster built a fine reputation during his tragically short career, initially at the wheel of a Porsche with which he won a thrilling Sundown GP at Harewood in 1961. That triumph was followed by victory in the Canadian GP at Mosport in a Lotus 23, Ryan beating a similar car handled by no less a driver than Stirling Moss.

In 1962, Peter came to Europe for a planned season of Formula Junior in a works Lotus, but in the event he was loaned to the Ian Walker stable. Ryan immediately confirmed his promise by beating Peter Arundell in the works car at Mallory Park, but sadly, during a heat of the Coupe de Vitesse des Juniors at Reims, Peter's Lotus was involved in a collision with the Gemini of Bill Moss. The young Canadian was thrown from his machine and died from internal injuries.

'BOB' SAID

Born in New York of Syrian-Russian parents, Said holds the distinction of being the first American to win a post-war European race – at Rouen with an OSCA in 1953 – having already made his mark at home in a Jaguar and his Cisitalia sports car, with which he won the Seneca Cup at Watkins Glen. His two seasons in Europe went pretty well; he won the Anerley Trophy in 1953 with the OSCA, then switched to a Ferrari for 1954, taking second place in the Bari GP and the Trullo d'Oro at Castellana.

Briefly dropping out of racing to lose a bundle in real-estate, Said returned to the tracks late in 1957, winning his class at Nassau with a Ferrari. He drove Paul Emery's ancient Connaught at Sebring in 1959 and continued to race in minor events until 1962, when, 'dead broke', he borrowed $2,600 to venture into property speculation once more. This time his gamble paid off and within two years he had made a million dollars.

ROTHENGATTER, Huub (NL) b 8/10/1954

1984

	Race	Circuit	No	Entrant	Car/Engine	Comment
nc	CANADIAN GP	Montreal	21	Spirit Racing	1.5 t/c Spirit 101-Hart 4	engine problems/14 laps behind
dnq	US GP (DETROIT)	Detroit	21	Spirit Racing	1.5 t/c Spirit 101-Cosworth V8	
ret	US GP (DALLAS)	Dallas	21	Spirit Racing	1.5 t/c Spirit 101-Hart 4	fuel leak in cockpit
nc	BRITISH GP	Brands Hatch	21	Spirit Racing	1.5 t/c Spirit 101-Hart 4	pit stop/nose cone/9 laps behind
9*	GERMAN GP	Hockenheim	21	Spirit Racing	1.5 t/c Spirit 101-Hart 4	* 9th place car dsq/4 laps behind
nc	AUSTRIAN GP	Österreichring	21	Spirit Racing	1.5 t/c Spirit 101-Hart 4	pit stop/exhaust/28laps behind
dnq/ret	DUTCH GP	Zandvoort	21	Spirit Racing	1.5 t/c Spirit 101-Hart 4	allowed to start/throttle cable
8	ITALIAN GP	Monza	21	Spirit Racing	1.5 t/c Spirit 101-Hart 4	3 laps behind

1985

	Race	Circuit	No	Entrant	Car/Engine	Comment
ret	GERMAN GP	Nürburgring	24	Osella Squadra Corse	1.5 t/c Osella FA1G-Alfa Romeo V8	gearbox
9	AUSTRIAN GP	Österreichring	24	Osella Squadra Corse	1.5 t/c Osella FA1G-Alfa Romeo V8	4 laps behind
nc	DUTCH GP	Zandvoort	24	Osella Squadra Corse	1.5 t/c Osella FA1G-Alfa Romeo V8	24 laps behind
ret	ITALIAN GP	Monza	24	Osella Squadra Corse	1.5 t/c Osella FA1G-Alfa Romeo V8	engine
nc	BELGIAN GP	Spa	24	Osella Squadra Corse	1.5 t/c Osella FA1G-Alfa Romeo V8	6 laps behind
dnq	EUROPEAN GP	Brands Hatch	24	Osella Squadra Corse	1.5 t/c Osella FA1G-Alfa Romeo V8	
ret	SOUTH AFRICAN GP	Kyalami	24	Osella Squadra Corse	1.5 t/c Osella FA1G-Alfa Romeo V8	electrics
7	AUSTRALIAN GP	Adelaide	24	Osella Squadra Corse	1.5 t/c Osella FA1G-Alfa Romeo V8	4 laps behind

1986

	Race	Circuit	No	Entrant	Car/Engine	Comment
ret	SAN MARINO GP	Imola	29	West Zakspeed Racing	1.5 t/c Zakspeed 861 4	turbo
dnq	MONACO GP	Monte Carlo	29	West Zakspeed Racing	1.5 t/c Zakspeed 861 4	
ret	BELGIAN GP	Spa	29	West Zakspeed Racing	1.5 t/c Zakspeed 861 4	alternator/battery
12	CANADIAN GP	Montreal	29	West Zakspeed Racing	1.5 t/c Zakspeed 861 4	6 laps behind
dns	US GP (DETROIT)	Detroit	29	West Zakspeed Racing	1.5 t/c Zakspeed 861 4	electrical problems-warm-up lap
ret	FRENCH GP	Paul Ricard	29	West Zakspeed Racing	1.5 t/c Zakspeed 861 4	hit Dumfries
ret	BRITISH GP	Brands Hatch	29	West Zakspeed Racing	1.5 t/c Zakspeed 861 4	engine
ret	GERMAN GP	Hockenheim	29	West Zakspeed Racing	1.5 t/c Zakspeed 861 4	gearbox
ret	HUNGARIAN GP	Hungaroring	29	West Zakspeed Racing	1.5 t/c Zakspeed 861 4	oil radiator
8	AUSTRIAN GP	Österreichring	29	West Zakspeed Racing	1.5 t/c Zakspeed 861 4	4 laps behind
ret	ITALIAN GP	Monza	29	West Zakspeed Racing	1.5 t/c Zakspeed 861 4	engine
ret	PORTUGUESE GP	Estoril	29	West Zakspeed Racing	1.5 t/c Zakspeed 861 4	transmission
dns	MEXICAN GP	Mexico City	29	West Zakspeed Racing	1.5 t/c Zakspeed 861 4	practice accident/no spare car
ret	AUSTRALIAN GP	Adelaide	29	West Zakspeed Racing	1.5 t/c Zakspeed 861 4	rear suspension

GP Starts: 26   GP Wins: 0   Pole positions: 0   Fastest laps: 0   Points: 0

RUBY, Lloyd (USA) b 12/1/1928

1961

	Race	Circuit	No	Entrant	Car/Engine	Comment
ret	US GP	Watkins Glen	26	J Frank Harrison	1.5 Lotus 18-Climax 4	magneto

GP Starts: 1   GP Wins: 0   Pole positions: 0   Fastest laps: 0   Points: 0

RUSSO, Giacomo see 'Geki'

RUTTMAN, Troy (USA) b 11/3/1930

1958

	Race	Circuit	No	Entrant	Car/Engine	Comment
10	FRENCH GP	Reims	30	Scuderia Centro Sud	2.5 Maserati 250F 6	5 laps behind
dns	GERMAN GP	Nürburgring	14	Scuderia Centro Sud	2.5 Maserati 250F 6	engine in practice

GP Starts: 1   GP Wins: 0   Pole positions: 0   Fastest laps: 0   Points: 0

RYAN, Peter (CDN) b 10/6/1942 – d 2/7/1962

1961

	Race	Circuit	No	Entrant	Car/Engine	Comment
9	US GP	Watkins Glen	16	J Wheeler Autosport	1.5 Lotus 18/21-Climax 4	4 laps behind

GP Starts: 1   GP Wins: 0   Pole positions: 0   Fastest laps: 0   Points: 0

SAID, 'Bob' (Boris) (USA) b 5/5/1932

1959

	Race	Circuit	No	Entrant	Car/Engine	Comment
ret	US GP	Sebring	18	Connaught Cars-Paul Emery	2.5 Connaught D Type Alta 4	spun off on lap 1

GP Starts: 1   GP Wins: 0   Pole positions: 0   Fastest laps: 0   Points: 0

LUIS PEREZ SALA

This Spanish driver contested the 1985 Italian F3 championship with the Pavesi team's Ralt-Alfa, winning a round of the series, but didn't pull up any trees. However, he was a different proposition when he moved up to Formula 3000 with Pavesi the following season. Luis was well served by his team and, in his own quiet way, soon got to grips with the formula , winning two rounds (at Enna and Birmingham). Backing these victories up with a consistent finishing record, he took fifth place in the points table.

This excellent first season booked him a place in the works Lola team for 1987, and he again won two races (at Donington and Le Mans) but was unable to stop Stefano Modena's title charge, having to settle for the runner-up slot.

With Spanish backing, Sala joined his former rival Adrian Campos at Minardi for 1988 and looked quite promising in the early races, but once his countryman had been replaced by Pierluigi Martini the picture changed. Suddenly Luis was very much second-best within the team, particularly the following season when Minardi were quite capable of scoring points. At the end of the year he was out, and today he can be found contesting the Spanish touring car championship, along with his former team-mate Campos.

ELISEO SALAZAR

A virtual unknown when he came to Britain in 1979 to contest the Vandervell F3 championship, Salazar made a good impression with some gritty performances, despite being saddled with the initially temperamental 'ground-effect' Ralt RT3 while his rivals ran more proven machinery. For 1980 the Chilean switched to the Aurora British F1 series with the RAM Racing Williams FW07 and won three races (including the once prestigious International Trophy), but finished second to his team-mate, Emilio de Villota, in the championship.

With much-needed financial backing available, Salazar joined the revamped March team the following season but soon became disillusioned and took his cash to Ensign, where he put in some excellent performances, finishing in sixth place at Zandvoort. For 1982, Eliseo joined the autocratic Gunther Schmid's ATS team but, apart from a fifth place at Imola, he was largely in the shadow of Manfred Winkelhock. However, he was involved in a much publicised incident at Hockenheim after being involved in a collision with Nelson Piquet, when he was assaulted by the irate Brazilian.

His options now limited if he wished to stay in Formula 1, Salazar went back to RAM for 1983 but, perhaps predictably, things rapidly disintegrated, and after a string of non-qualifications he found himself out of a drive.

SALA, Luis Perez (E) b 5/5/1959

1988

	Race	Circuit	No	Entrant	Car/Engine	Comment
ret	BRAZILIAN GP	Rio	24	Lois Minardi Team	3.5 Minardi M188-Cosworth V8	*rear wing mounting*
11	SAN MARINO GP	Imola	24	Lois Minardi Team	3.5 Minardi M188-Cosworth V8	*2 laps behind*

	Race	Circuit	No	Entrant	Car/Engine	Comment
ret	MONACO GP	Monte Carlo	24	Lois Minardi Team	3.5 Minardi M188-Cosworth V8	suspension
11	MEXICAN GP	Mexico City	24	Lois Minardi Team	3.5 Minardi M188-Cosworth V8	4 laps behind
13	CANADIAN GP	Montreal	24	Lois Minardi Team	3.5 Minardi M188-Cosworth V8	5 laps behind
ret	US GP (DETROIT)	Detroit	24	Lois Minardi Team	3.5 Minardi M188-Cosworth V8	gearbox
nc	FRENCH GP	Paul Ricard	24	Lois Minardi Team	3.5 Minardi M188-Cosworth V8	4 pit stops-electrics/10 laps behind
ret	BRITISH GP	Silverstone	24	Lois Minardi Team	3.5 Minardi M188-Cosworth V8	ran into back of Streiff on lap 1
dnq	GERMAN GP	Hockenheim	24	Lois Minardi Team	3.5 Minardi M188-Cosworth V8	
10	HUNGARIAN GP	Hungaroring	24	Lois Minardi Team	3.5 Minardi M188-Cosworth V8	4 laps behind
dnq	BELGIAN GP	Spa	24	Lois Minardi Team	3.5 Minardi M188-Cosworth V8	
ret	ITALIAN GP	Monza	24	Lois Minardi Team	3.5 Minardi M188-Cosworth V8	gearbox
8	PORTUGUESE GP	Estoril	24	Lois Minardi Team	3.5 Minardi M188-Cosworth V8	2 laps behind
12	SPANISH GP	Jerez	24	Lois Minardi Team	3.5 Minardi M188-Cosworth V8	2 laps behind
15	JAPANESE GP	Suzuka	24	Lois Minardi Team	3.5 Minardi M188-Cosworth V8	2 laps behind
ret	AUSTRALIAN GP	Adelaide	24	Lois Minardi Team	3.5 Minardi M188-Cosworth V8	engine

1989

	Race	Circuit	No	Entrant	Car/Engine	Comment
ret	BRAZILIAN GP	Rio	24	Lois Minardi Team	3.5 Minardi M188B-Cosworth V8	collision-Grouillard on first lap
ret	SAN MARINO GP	Imola	24	Lois Minardi Team	3.5 Minardi M188B-Cosworth V8	spun off
ret	MONACO GP	Monte Carlo	24	Lois Minardi Team	3.5 Minardi M188B-Cosworth V8	cockpit fire
dnq	MEXICAN GP	Mexico City	24	Lois Minardi Team	3.5 Minardi M189-Cosworth V8	
ret	US GP (PHOENIX)	Phoenix	24	Lois Minardi Team	3.5 Minardi M189-Cosworth V8	overheating
ret	CANADIAN GP	Montreal	24	Lois Minardi Team	3.5 Minardi M189-Cosworth V8	started from pit lane/crashed
dnq	FRENCH GP	Paul Ricard	24	Lois Minardi Team	3.5 Minardi M189-Cosworth V8	
6	BRITISH GP	Silverstone	24	Lois Minardi Team	3.5 Minardi M189-Cosworth V8	1 lap behind
dnq	GERMAN GP	Hockenheim	24	Lois Minardi Team	3.5 Minardi M189-Cosworth V8	
ret	HUNGARIAN GP	Hungaroring	24	Lois Minardi Team	3.5 Minardi M189-Cosworth V8	accident with Modena
15	BELGIAN GP	Spa	24	Lois Minardi Team	3.5 Minardi M189-Cosworth V8	3 laps behind
8	ITALIAN GP	Monza	24	Lois Minardi Team	3.5 Minardi M189-Cosworth V8	2 laps behind
12	PORTUGUESE GP	Estoril	24	Lois Minardi Team	3.5 Minardi M189-Cosworth V8	2 laps behind
ret	SPANISH GP	Jerez	24	Lois Minardi Team	3.5 Minardi M189-Cosworth V8	collision with Gugelmin
ret	JAPANESE GP	Suzuka	24	Lois Minardi Team	3.5 Minardi M189-Cosworth V8	forced off by Nakajima on lap 1
dnq	AUSTRALIAN GP	Adelaide	24	Lois Minardi Team	3.5 Minardi M189-Cosworth V8	

GP Starts: 26   GP Wins: 0   Pole positions: 0   Fastest laps: 0   Points: 1

SALAZAR, Eliseo (RCH) b 14/11/1954

1981

	Race	Circuit	No	Entrant	Car/Engine	Comment
dnq	US GP WEST	Long Beach	18	March Grand Prix Team	3.0 March 811-Cosworth V8	
dnq	BRAZILIAN GP	Rio	18	March Grand Prix Team	3.0 March 811-Cosworth V8	
dnq	ARGENTINE GP	Buenos Aires	18	March Grand Prix Team	3.0 March 811-Cosworth V8	
ret	SAN MARINO GP	Imola	17	March Grand Prix Team	3.0 March 811-Cosworth V8	oil pressure
dnq	BELGIAN GP	Zolder	17	March Grand Prix Team	3.0 March 811-Cosworth V8	
dnpq	MONACO GP	Monte Carlo	17	March Grand Prix Team	3.0 March 811-Cosworth V8	
14	SPANISH GP	Jarama	14	Ensign Racing	3.0 Ensign 180B-Cosworth V8	3 laps behind
ret	FRENCH GP	Dijon	14	Ensign Racing	3.0 Ensign 180B-Cosworth V8	rear suspension
dnq	BRITISH GP	Silverstone	14	Ensign Racing	3.0 Ensign 180B-Cosworth V8	
nc	GERMAN GP	Hockenheim	14	Ensign Racing	3.0 Ensign 180B-Cosworth V8	pit stop/brake problems/-6 laps
ret	AUSTRIAN GP	Österreichring	14	Ensign Racing	3.0 Ensign 180B-Cosworth V8	engine
6	DUTCH GP	Zandvoort	14	Ensign Racing	3.0 Ensign 180B-Cosworth V8	2 laps behind
ret	ITALIAN GP	Monza	14	Ensign Racing	3.0 Ensign 180B-Cosworth V8	tyre failure
ret	CANADIAN GP	Montreal	14	Ensign Racing	3.0 Ensign 180B-Cosworth V8	spun off
nc	CAESARS PALACE GP	Las Vegas	14	Ensign Racing	3.0 Ensign 180B-Cosworth V8	pit stop/brake problems/-14 laps

1982

	Race	Circuit	No	Entrant	Car/Engine	Comment
9	SOUTH AFRICAN GP	Kyalami	10	Team ATS	3.0 ATS D5-Cosworth V8	2 laps behind
ret	BRAZILIAN GP	Rio	10	Team ATS	3.0 ATS D5-Cosworth V8	engine
ret	US GP WEST	Long Beach	10	Team ATS	3.0 ATS D5-Cosworth V8	hit wall
5	SAN MARINO GP	Imola	10	Team ATS	3.0 ATS D5-Cosworth V8	3 laps behind
ret	BELGIAN GP	Zolder	10	Team ATS	3.0 ATS D5-Cosworth V8	startline accident
ret	MONACO GP	Monte Carlo	10	Team ATS	3.0 ATS D5-Cosworth V8	fire extinguisher went off
ret	US GP (DETROIT)	Detroit	10	Team ATS	3.0 ATS D5-Cosworth V8	crashed
ret	CANADIAN GP	Montreal	10	Team ATS	3.0 ATS D5-Cosworth V8	transmission
13	DUTCH GP	Zandvoort	10	Team ATS	3.0 ATS D5-Cosworth V8	2 laps behind
dnq	BRITISH GP	Brands Hatch	10	Team ATS	3.0 ATS D5-Cosworth V8	
ret	FRENCH GP	Paul Ricard	10	Team ATS	3.0 ATS D5-Cosworth V8	crashed
ret	GERMAN GP	Hockenheim	10	Team ATS	3.0 ATS D5-Cosworth V8	accident with Piquet
dnq	AUSTRIAN GP	Österreichring	10	Team ATS	3.0 ATS D5-Cosworth V8	
14	SWISS GP	Dijon	10	Team ATS	3.0 ATS D5-Cosworth V8	3 laps behind
9	ITALIAN GP	Monza	10	Team ATS	3.0 ATS D5-Cosworth V8	2 laps behind
dnq	CAESARS PALACE GP	Las Vegas	10	Team ATS	3.0 ATS D5-Cosworth V8	

1983

	Race	Circuit	No	Entrant	Car/Engine	Comment
15	BRAZILIAN GP	Rio	17	RAM Automotive Team March	3.0 March RAM 01-Cosworth V8	4 laps behind
ret	US GP WEST	Long Beach	17	RAM Automotive Team March	3.0 March RAM 01-Cosworth V8	gear linkage
dnq	FRENCH GP	Paul Ricard	17	RAM Automotive Team March	3.0 March RAM 01-Cosworth V8	
dnq	SAN MARINO GP	Imola	17	RAM Automotive Team March	3.0 March RAM 01-Cosworth V8	
dnq	MONACO GP	Monte Carlo	17	RAM Automotive Team March	3.0 March RAM 01-Cosworth V8	
dnq	BELGIAN GP	Spa	17	RAM Automotive Team March	3.0 March RAM 01-Cosworth V8	

GP Starts: 24   GP Wins: 0   Pole positions: 0   Fastest laps: 0   Points: 3

ROY SALVADORI

While not possessing the talent of his contemporaries Moss, Hawthorn, Collins and Brooks, Salvadori was a fine all-round driver, particularly in sports cars, who became a household name in Britain thanks to his many victories in races on home soil. Though born of Italian parentage, Salvadori was very much a Londoner at heart, and began racing for fun in 1946 before entering selected events the following year in an Alfa Romeo. Deciding to pursue a professional career, Roy sampled a variety of machines including a Healey, a Jaguar and a Frazer Nash on his way up the ladder.

In 1952 he campaigned a four-cylinder Ferrari in the British GP and a few other minor races in addition to racing Tony Crook's Frazer Nash, but his sights were by now set on Grand Prix racing and he joined Connaught for the 1953 season. While he drew a blank in the World Championship races, there were plenty of successful outings in national events. He was happy to compete in almost any type of machine and often took part in three or more races during a single race meeting.

Joining Syd Greene to race his potent Maserati 250F, Salvadori again concentrated on events at home during 1954-56, but by this time he was already a regular member of the Aston Martin sports car team, a role he was to fulfil right to the end of their programme, which finished on such a high note in 1959 when Roy shared the winning DBR1 at Le Mans with Carroll Shelby.

For 1957 Roy aligned himself with Cooper as they developed their rear-engined Formula 2 car in preparation for a full season of Grands Prix the following year. Fifth place in the British GP at Aintree put him among the championship points scorers for the first time, and in non-title races he took a second at Caen and a fourth at Reims. The 1958 season saw the Surbiton team's first sustained effort at the top level, and Brabham and Salvadori both scored some excellent results. Roy's second place to Brooks in the German GP may have been distant but it was a portent of even greater things to follow, but Roy was sadly not to be part of the great works Cooper triumph.

In 1959 Salvadori continued to drive Coopers in Formula 2, but for Tommy Atkins, his best result being a win in the London Trophy at Crystal Palace. Meanwhile Aston Martin had ambitiously decided to embark on a Grand Prix programme of their own and Roy was to be one of the drivers, but crucially they had opted to adopt the traditional front-engined layout which, of course, was soon doomed to oblivion. Their cars were superbly crafted and beautifully turned out, but after Salvadori had scored a totally misleading second place in the International Trophy early in 1959, they proved to be a major disappointment. The engine just didn't possess enough power and, depite major reworkings, the project was a hopeless failure which drifted on into 1960, by which time the writing was well and truly on the wall.

The following season Roy joined John Surtees in Reg Parnell's well-funded Yeoman Credit-backed team racing Coopers. However,the Surbiton-built cars had had their day, as Colin Chapman had devoured every lesson they had to offer and combined them with his own thinking to push his Lotus 18 and 21 models to the fore. Salvadori was as close as he ever would be to winning a Grand Prix at Watkins Glen that year when he was closing in on Innes Ireland's leading Lotus before the engine failed. The team had high hopes for 1962 with the new Lola chassis, but it was to be a desperately disappointing season for Salvadori, who was totally overshadowed by Surtees, almost being reduced to the role of hack driver. Wisely perhaps, he decided that Grand Prix success was now beyond his reach, and he returned to sports and touring car racing with Tommy Atkins' Cooper Monaco, Shelby Cobra and Jaguar E-Type cars. Although his front-line career was behind him, there was no easing up in his driving style, for Roy had never taken any prisoners and he wasn't going to change his approach in the twilight of his career!

By the time he retired early in 1965 Salvadori had driven on most of the world's circuits. He knew the risks attendant on them, for he had seen many of his peers perish over his long career, and indeed had come perilously close to joining them on more than one occasion. He also knew his own worth and the thought of racing without starting money was anathema to him. After his driving days were over, he became the team manager at Cooper in 1966-67, before retiring to Monaco in the late sixties, where he resides to this day. His apartment overlooking the Monte Carlo circuit still attracts many old friends from his racing days for a wonderful view of the Grand Prix each May.

CONSALVO SANESI

Sanesi's main role at Alfa Romeo was as a test driver, but he was also given numerous opportunities to drive the superb Tipo 158/159 series cars in races. In 1946, he won his heat and finished third in the Milan GP, while in 1947 he was second to Varzi at Bari and third in the Italian GP held at Sempione Park after claiming pole position.

The following year saw Consalvo take second place in the French GP and third with fastest lap at the Monza Autodrome GP. In 1949 Alfa Corse did not compete in Formula 1, though Sanesi finished second in the touring car class in the Mille Miglia with an Alfa, and when the team returned in 1950 he drove in only one Grand Prix but won the Coppa Inter Europa sports car race at Monza.

Consalvo had his most active Grand Prix season in 1951, scoring points in two of his four starts, but after Alfa's withdrawal from Grand Prix racing at the end of the year, he concentrated fully on sports cars, winning his class in the 1954 Carrera Panamericana. A testing accident later that year with the Disco Volante left him with serious injuries, but he returned to competition in 1955, taking second place in the Verminico hill-climb with a 1.9 Alfa.

SALVADORI, Roy (GB) b 12/5/1922

1952

	Race	Circuit	No	Entrant	Car/Engine	Comment
8	BRITISH GP	Silverstone	14	G Caprara	2.0 Ferrari 500 4	3 laps behind

1953

	Race	Circuit	No	Entrant	Car/Engine	Comment
ret	DUTCH GP	Zandvoort	26	Connaught Engineering	2.0 Connaught A Type 4	engine
ret	FRENCH GP	Reims	50	Connaught Engineering	2.0 Connaught A Type 4	ignition
ret	BRITISH GP	Silverstone	12	Connaught Engineering	2.0 Connaught A Type 4	radius rod
ret	GERMAN GP	Nürburgring	15	Connaught Engineering	2.0 Connaught A Type 4	engine
ret	ITALIAN GP	Monza	22	Connaught Engineering	2.0 Connaught A Type 4	throttle cable

1954

	Race	Circuit	No	Entrant	Car/Engine	Comment
ret	FRENCH GP	Reims	44	Gilby Engineering Ltd	2.5 Maserati 250F 6	driveshaft
ret	BRITISH GP	Silverstone	5	Gilby Engineering Ltd	2.5 Maserati 250F 6	oil pipe
dns	SWISS GP	Bremgarten	28	Officine Alfieri Maserati	2.5 Maserati 250F 6	Mantovani drove car

1955

	Race	Circuit	No	Entrant	Car/Engine	Comment
ret	BRITISH GP	Aintree	44	Gilby Engineering Ltd	2.5 Maserati 250F 6	gearbox

1956

	Race	Circuit	No	Entrant	Car/Engine	Comment
ret	BRITISH GP	Silverstone	28	Gilby Engineering Ltd	2.5 Maserati 250F 6	fuel starvation
ret	GERMAN GP	Nürburgring	16	Gilby Engineering Ltd	2.5 Maserati 250F 6	rear suspension
nc	ITALIAN GP	Monza	44	Gilby Engineering Ltd	2.5 Maserati 250F 6	9 laps behind

1957

	Race	Circuit	No	Entrant	Car/Engine	Comment
dnq	MONACO GP	Monte Carlo	8	Owen Racing Organisation	2.5 BRM P25 4	
ret	FRENCH GP	Rouen	20	Vandervell Products Ltd	2.5 Vanwall 4	engine
5	BRITISH GP	Aintree	36	Cooper Car Co	2.0 Cooper T43-Climax 4	5 laps behind
ret	GERMAN GP (F2)	Nürburgring	23	Cooper Car Co	1.5 Cooper T43-Climax 4	transmission
ret	PESCARA GP	Pescara	22	Cooper Car Co	1.5 Cooper T43-Climax 4	suspension

1958

	Race	Circuit	No	Entrant	Car/Engine	Comment
ret	MONACO GP	Monte Carlo	18	Cooper Car Co	2.0 Cooper T45-Climax 4	gearbox
4	DUTCH GP	Zandvoort	7	Cooper Car Co	2.2 Cooper T45-Climax 4	1 lap behind
8	BELGIAN GP	Spa	24	Cooper Car Co	2.0 Cooper T45-Climax 4	1 lap behind
nc	FRENCH GP	Reims	20	Cooper Car Co	2.0 Cooper T45-Climax 4	clutch slip/13 laps behind
3	BRITISH GP	Silverstone	10	Cooper Car Co	2.2 Cooper T45-Climax 4	
2	GERMAN GP	Nürburgring	10	Cooper Car Co	2.2 Cooper T45-Climax 4	
9	PORTUGUESE GP	Oporto	16	Cooper Car Co	2.0 Cooper T45-Climax 4	4 laps behind
nc*	ITALIAN GP	Monza	6	Cooper Car Co	2.2 Cooper T45-Climax 4	* 4th on road but 8 laps behind
7	MOROCCAN GP	Casablanca	28	Cooper Car Co	2.2 Cooper T45-Climax 4	2 laps behind

1959

	Race	Circuit	No	Entrant	Car/Engine	Comment
ret	MONACO GP	Monte Carlo	38	High Efficiency Motors	2.5 Cooper T45-Maserati 4	transmisssion
ret	DUTCH GP	Zandvoort	4	David Brown Corporation	2.5 Aston Martin DBR4/250 6	overheating
ret	FRENCH GP	Reims	16	High Efficiency Motors	2.5 Cooper T45-Maserati 4	engine
6	BRITISH GP	Aintree	2	David Brown Corporation	2.5 Aston Martin DBR4/250 6	1 lap behind
6	PORTUGUESE GP	Monsanto	10	David Brown Corporation	2.5 Aston Martin DBR4/250 6	3 laps behind
ret	ITALIAN GP	Monza	24	David Brown Corporation	2.5 Aston Martin DBR4/250 6	engine
ret	US GP	Sebring	12	High Efficiency Motors	2.5 Cooper T45-Maserati 4	transmission

1960

	Race	Circuit	No	Entrant	Car/Engine	Comment
ret	MONACO GP	Monte Carlo	14	High Efficiency Motors	2.5 Cooper T51-Climax 4	overheating
dns	DUTCH GP	Zandvoort	17	David Brown Corporation	2.5 Aston Martin DBR4/250 6	withdrawn-starting money dispute
ret	BRITISH GP	Silverstone	18	David Brown Corporation	2.5 Aston Martin DBR4/250 6	steering
8	US GP	Riverside	14	High Efficiency Motors	2.5 Cooper T51-Climax 4	2 laps behind

1961

	Race	Circuit	No	Entrant	Car/Engine	Comment
8	FRENCH GP	Reims	42	Yeoman Credit Racing Team	1.5 Cooper T53-Climax 4	1 lap behind
6	BRITISH GP	Aintree	36	Yeoman Credit Racing Team	1.5 Cooper T53-Climax 4	
10	GERMAN GP	Nürburgring	19	Yeoman Credit Racing Team	1.5 Cooper T53-Climax 4	
6	ITALIAN GP	Monza	40	Yeoman Credit Racing Team	1.5 Cooper T53-Climax 4	1 lap behind
ret	US GP	Watkins Glen	19	Yeoman Credit Racing Team	1.5 Cooper T53-Climax 4	engine when 2nd

1962

	Race	Circuit	No	Entrant	Car/Engine	Comment
ret	DUTCH GP	Zandvoort	20	Bowmaker Racing Team	1.5 Lola 4-Climax V8	withdrawn after Surtees' accident
ret	MONACO GP	Monte Carlo	26	Bowmaker Racing Team	1.5 Lola 4-Climax V8	suspension
ret	FRENCH GP	Rouen	20	Bowmaker Racing Team	1.5 Lola 4-Climax V8	oil pressure
ret	BRITISH GP	Aintree	26	Bowmaker Racing Team	1.5 Lola 4-Climax V8	battery
ret	GERMAN GP	Nürburgring	15	Bowmaker Racing Team	1.5 Lola 4-Climax V8	gearbox
ret	ITALIAN GP	Monza	44	Bowmaker Racing Team	1.5 Lola 4-Climax V8	engine
dns	US GP	Watkins Glen	19	Bowmaker Racing Team	1.5 Lola 4-Climax V8	Surtees drove car
ret	SOUTH AFRICAN GP	Kyalami	7	Bowmaker Racing Team	1.5 Lola 4-Climax V8	fuel leak-split tank

GP Starts: 47   GP Wins: 0   Pole positions: 0   Fastest laps: 0   Points: 19

SANESI, Consalvo (I) b 28/3/1911

1950

	Race	Circuit	No	Entrant	Car/Engine	Comment
ret	ITALIAN GP	Monza	46	Scuderia Alfa Romeo SpA	1.5 s/c Alfa Romeo 158 8	engine

1951

	Race	Circuit	No	Entrant	Car/Engine	Comment
4	SWISS GP	Bremgarten	28	Scuderia Alfa Romeo SpA	1.5 s/c Alfa Romeo 159 8	1 lap behind
ret	BELGIAN GP	Spa	6	Scuderia Alfa Romeo SpA	1.5 s/c Alfa Romeo 159 8	radiator
10	FRENCH GP	Reims	6	Scuderia Alfa Romeo SpA	1.5 s/c Alfa Romeo 159 8	pushed car to finish
6	BRITISH GP	Silverstone	3	Scuderia Alfa Romeo SpA	1.5 s/c Alfa Romeo 159 8	

GP Starts: 5   GP Wins: 0   Pole positions: 0   Fastest laps: 0   Points: 3

SCARFIOTTI, Ludovico (I) b 18/10/1933 – d 8/6/1968

1963

	Race	Circuit	No	Entrant	Car/Engine	Comment
6	DUTCH GP	Zandvoort	4	Scuderia Ferrari SpA SEFAC	1.5 Ferrari 156 V6	2 laps behind
dns	FRENCH GP	Reims	4	Scuderia Ferrari SpA SEFAC	1.5 Ferrari 156 V6	practice accident

1964

	Race	Circuit	No	Entrant	Car/Engine	Comment
9	ITALIAN GP	Monza	6	Scuderia Ferrari SpA SEFAC	1.5 Ferrari 156 V6	1 lap behind

1965

	Race	Circuit	No	Entrant	Car/Engine	Comment
dns	MEXICAN GP	Mexico City	24	Scuderia Ferrari SpA SEFAC	1.5 Ferrari 1512 F12	car driven by Rodriguez

1966

	Race	Circuit	No	Entrant	Car/Engine	Comment
ret	GERMAN GP	Nürburgring	11	Scuderia Ferrari SpA SEFAC	2.4 Ferrari Dino 246 V6	electrics
1	ITALIAN GP	Monza	6	Scuderia Ferrari SpA SEFAC	3.0 Ferrari 312/66 V12	FL

1967

	Race	Circuit	No	Entrant	Car/Engine	Comment
6	DUTCH GP	Zandvoort	22	Scuderia Ferrari SpA SEFAC	3.0 Ferrari 312/67 V12	1 lap behind
nc	BELGIAN GP	Spa	2	Scuderia Ferrari SpA SEFAC	3.0 Ferrari 312/67 V12	pit stop-hydraulic pipe/-4 laps
ret	ITALIAN GP	Monza	10	Anglo American Racers	3.0 Eagle T1G-Weslake V12	engine

1968

	Race	Circuit	No	Entrant	Car/Engine	Comment
ret	SOUTH AFRICAN GP	Kyalami	15	Cooper Car Co	3.0 Cooper T86-Maserati V12	broken brake line/accident/slight burns
4	SPANISH GP	Jarama	15	Cooper Car Co	3.0 Cooper T86B-BRM V12	1 lap behind
4	MONACO GP	Monte Carlo	6	Cooper Car Co	3.0 Cooper T86B-BRM V12	pit stop/wheel change/-4 laps

GP Starts: 10   GP Wins: 1   Pole positions: 0   Fastest laps: 1   Points: 17

SCARLATTI, Giorgio (I) b 2/10/1921

1956

	Race	Circuit	No	Entrant	Car/Engine	Comment
dnq	MONACO GP	Monte Carlo	36	Giorgio Scarlatti	2.0 Ferrari 500 4	
ret	GERMAN GP	Nürburgring	14	Scuderia Centro Sud	2.0 Ferrari 500 4	mechnical

1957

	Race	Circuit	No	Entrant	Car/Engine	Comment
ret*	MONACO GP	Monte Carlo	34	Officine Alfieri Maserati	2.5 Maserati 250F 6	*Schell took over/oil pressure
10	GERMAN GP	Nürburgring	4	Officine Alfieri Maserati	2.5 Maserati 250F 6	1 lap behind
6	PESCARA GP	Pescara	8	Officine Alfieri Maserati	2.5 Maserati 250F 6	1 lap behind
5*	ITALIAN GP	Monza	8	Officine Alfieri Maserati	2.5 Maserati 250F 6	* Schell took over

1958

	Race	Circuit	No	Entrant	Car/Engine	Comment
ret	MONACO GP	Monte Carlo	46	Giorgio Scarlatti	2.5 Maserati 250F 6	engine
ret	DUTCH GP	Zandvoort	10	Giorgio Scarlatti	2.5 Maserati 250F 6	rear axle

1959

	Race	Circuit	No	Entrant	Car/Engine	Comment
dnq	MONACO GP	Monte Carlo	54	Scuderia Ugolini	2.5 Maserati 250F 6	
nc	FRENCH GP	Reims	40	Scuderia Ugolini	2.5 Maserati 250F 6	9 laps behind
12	ITALIAN GP	Monza	10	Cooper Car Co	2.5 Cooper T51-Climax 4	4 laps behind

1960

	Race	Circuit	No	Entrant	Car/Engine	Comment
ret	ARGENTINE GP	Buenos Aires	8	Giorgio Scarlatti	2.5 Maserati 250F 6	overheating
dnq	MONACO GP	Monte Carlo	30	Scuderia Castellotti	2.5 Cooper T51-Ferrari 4	
ret	ITALIAN GP	Monza	36	Scuderia Castellotti	2.5 Cooper T51-Maserati 4	throttle cable

1961

	Race	Circuit	No	Entrant	Car/Engine	Comment
ret	FRENCH GP	Reims	34	Scuderia Serenissima	1.5 de Tomaso F1 001-OSCA 4	engine
dns	"	"	32	Scuderia Serenissima	1.5 Cooper T51-Maserati 4	car driven by Trintignant in race

GP Starts: 12   GP Wins: 0   Pole positions: 0   Fastest laps: 0   Points: 1

SCHECKTER, Ian (ZA) b 22/8/1947

1974

	Race	Circuit	No	Entrant	Car/Engine	Comment
13	SOUTH AFRICAN GP	Kyalami	29	Team Gunston	3.0 Lotus 72-Cosworth V8	2 laps behind
dnq	AUSTRIAN GP	Österreichring	31	Hesketh Racing	3.0 Hesketh 308-Cosworth V8	

1975

	Race	Circuit	No	Entrant	Car/Engine	Comment
ret	SOUTH AFRICAN GP	Kyalami	32	Lexington Racing	3.0 Tyrrell 007-Cosworth V8	spun off
ret	SWEDISH GP	Anderstorp	21	Frank Williams Racing Cars	3.0 Williams FW04-Cosworth V8	burst tyre/spun off
12	DUTCH GP	Zandvoort	21	Frank Williams Racing Cars	3.0 Williams FW03-Cosworth V8	5 laps behind

1976

	Race	Circuit	No	Entrant	Car/Engine	Comment
ret	SOUTH AFRICAN GP	Kyalami	15	Lexington Racing	3.0 Tyrrell 007-Cosworth V8	collision with Leclère

1977

	Race	Circuit	No	Entrant	Car/Engine	Comment
ret	ARGENTINE GP	Buenos Aires	10	Team Rothmans International	3.0 March 761B-Cosworth V8	battery terminal
ret	BRAZILIAN GP	Interlagos	10	Team Rothmans International	3.0 March 761B-Cosworth V8	transmission
11	SPANISH GP	Jarama	10	Team Rothmans International	3.0 March 761B-Cosworth V8	3 laps behind
dnq	MONACO GP	Monte Carlo	10	Team Rothmans International	3.0 March 761B-Cosworth V8	driver injured
ret	BELGIAN GP	Zolder	10	Team Rothmans International	3.0 March 761B-Cosworth V8	spun off
dns	"	"	10	Team Rothmans International	3.0 March 771-Cosworth V8	practice only
ret	SWEDISH GP	Anderstorp	10	Team Rothmans International	3.0 March 761B-Cosworth V8	driveshaft
nc	FRENCH GP	Dijon	10	Team Rothmans International	3.0 March 761B-Cosworth V8	11 laps behind
ret	BRITISH GP	Silverstone	10	Team Rothmans International	3.0 March 761B-Cosworth V8	spun off
ret	GERMAN GP	Hockenheim	10	Team Rothmans International	3.0 March 761B-Cosworth V8	clutch
ret	AUSTRIAN GP	Österreichring	10	Team Rothmans International	3.0 March 761B-Cosworth V8	spun off
10	DUTCH GP	Zandvoort	10	Team Rothmans International	3.0 March 771-Cosworth V8	2 laps behind
ret	ITALIAN GP	Monza	10	Team Rothmans International	3.0 March 771-Cosworth V8	transmission
ret	US GP EAST	Watkins Glen	10	Team Rothmans International	3.0 March 771-Cosworth V8	crashed at chicane
ret	CANADIAN GP	Mosport Park	10	Team Rothmans International	3.0 March 771-Cosworth V8	engine

GP Starts: 18   GP Wins: 0   Pole positions: 0   Fastest laps: 0   Points: 0

LUDOVICO SCARFIOTTI

A great all-rounder who wasn't out of the top drawer, Scarfiotti nevertheless had his moment of glory in 1966, taking the 3-litre Ferrari to a momentous victory in front of the rapturous *'tifosi'* at Monza on a glorious September afternoon. It was the zenith of a career that had started a decade earlier in a far more modest Fiat 1100 saloon. Winning his class in the Mille Miglia in 1956 and 1957, Scarfiotti originally raced just for fun – as he could afford to, being related to the wealthy Agnelli family who, of course, controlled the FIAT empire. He tested a works Ferrari sports car as early as 1958, but had to be content with campaigning a little 2-litre OSCA, taking second place in the Naples GP at Posillipo.

Ludovico finally joined the Scuderia's sports car team in 1960, sharing the fourth-place car with Cabianca and Mairesse in the Targa Florio. His first real success came in 1962 when he took the European mountain-climb championship in Ferrari's 2-litre V6 car, and this confirmed his place in the works team for 1963 alongside Surtees and Mairesse, when the rest of the Scuderia's drivers were being shown the door. His early-season sports car outings were encouraging. Sharing the 250P with Surtees, he won at Sebring and he later won at Le Mans, this time with Bandini. Impressed with his efforts, Ferrari rewarded him with his Grand Prix debut at Zandvoort and after a steady drive he took sixth place, enough to earn another opportunity at Reims. Unfortunately a practice crash in which he hit a telegraph pole left him with leg injuries serious enough not only to keep him out for some while but also to prompt him to announce his retirement from F1.

Scarfiotti was back in action in 1964, winning the Nürburgring 1000 Km with Vaccarella in the works Ferrari 275P and finishing second at Mosport in the 330P. Contrary to his earlier intentions, he was back in a Ferrari single-seater at Monza, but was mostly used by the Scuderia in sports cars the following year. Driving the lovely 1.6-litre Ferrari Dino, Ludovico took his second mountain-climb championship, and he was also second in the Monza 1000 Km.

The 1966 season was his best, but only courtesy of his famous Italian GP victory, as little else was achieved bar a second place in the Nürburgring 1000 Km. Scarfiotti was one of four drivers (Bandini, Parkes and newcomer Amon were the others) representing Ferrari in 1967, and the season started well with second places with the Ferrari P4 sports car at Daytona and in the Monza 1000 Km. Then came a fifth place in the Race of Champions and a staged dead-heat with Parkes to win the Syracuse GP before the first disaster. Bandini was killed at Monaco and soon Parkes – with whom Scarfiotti had just taken a second place at Le Mans – was badly injured at Spa. 'Lulu' seemed to lose heart and after a dispute with the management took his leave, appearing in Dan Gurney's Eagle at Monza.

For 1968 Scarfiotti found himself a berth at Cooper. The cars were slow but reliable, and he managed to pick up a couple of fourth-place finishes. Although he had forsaken Ferrari, his sports car talents were not about to be allowed to go to waste, and he signed for Porsche to race their prototypes. A second place in the BOAC 500 at Brands was to be his best placing for the Stuttgart firm, for while practising for the Rossfeld hill-climb in June 1968 he inexplicably ran straight on at a corner and crashed into a clump of trees with fatal consequences.

GIORGIO SCARLATTI

A solid and dependable but not too quick Italian sports car driver, Scarlatti raced a Maserati T200S in 1954-55, his best finishes being a second in class in the Tour of Sicily, and third places at Bari and Caserta. At this time he bought a Ferrari 500 to race in Formula 1, but after a fourth place in the 1956 Naples GP he proved to be hopelessly slow in his efforts to qualify at Monaco.

For 1957, Giorgio aligned himself with the works Maserati team and shared a point with Schell for their fifth place in the Italian GP, taking another fifth at the Modena GP and sixth at the Pescara GP, although he was ten minutes behind the winner.

After the works team had closed their doors, Scarlatti soldiered on with the 250F, sharing fourth place in the Buenos Aires City GP after Behra took over the car, and earned third place (and a class win) in the Targa Florio when he partnered Behra in the Frenchman's Porsche. In 1959, Giorgio again raced the outdated Maserati, but disappointed when entrusted with the third works Cooper at Monza in place of the injured Gregory.

He continued to race various ill-prepared single-seaters without success until 1961, though he did a little better in sports cars, winning that year's Pescara 4 Hours with a young Lorenzo Bandini in a Ferrari 246 V6.

IAN SCHECKTER

Ian, the elder brother of World Champion Jody, followed his brother to Europe in mid-1972 after winning the domestic Formula Ford series with a Merlyn. After a brief stay, during which he proved his competitiveness, Scheckter returned to South Africa to contest the national championship in a Team Gunston Chevron and attempt to break Dave Charlton's stranglehold on the title.

Ian made his Grand Prix debut at Kyalami in 1974 and had a handful of Formula 1 outings over the next couple of years, but it was only after he had finally clinched the South African championship (by now for Formula Atlantic cars) in 1976 that he took up the offer of a full-time Grand Prix drive with March in 1977. The season was an utter shambles for the bewildered Scheckter, who managed just two finishes from 13 starts, and his Formula 1 career was buried. He returned home to renew his successful association with Lexington Racing, winning the Atlantic tiles in 1977-78 and 1978-79, before switching to saloon car racing with BMW South Africa's 535i.

JODY SCHECKTER

Jody was a prodigy who burst upon the motor racing scene in much the same manner as Ricardo Rodriguez had done a decade earlier. Immensely talented, brave almost to the point of being foolhardy and blindingly quick in any car he chose to drive, Jody somehow managed to avoid the 'Grim Reaper' in those wild early days to become a dry-humoured, somewhat world-weary elder statesman who had got the risks under control and knew his destiny.

Jody started his racing early, running a go-kart at 12 before moving on to motor cycles and then saloons by the age of 18. His home-built Renault proved to be tremendously successful in the youngster's hands, and he scored numerous victories before his racing took a back seat to a spell of National Service. Towards the end of 1970, Team Lawson entrusted their Mazda to the youngster in the Springbok series, and he finished fifth in the Bulawayo 3 Hours and won his class in the Goldfields 9 Hours. His immediate ambition, though, was to do well in the Formula Ford Sunshine series and thus win the 'Driver to Europe' prize that went with it. Sure enough, young Jody in his Lola T200 Formula Ford did exactly that and was on his way to England early in 1971.

The headstrong Scheckter got himself into a Merlyn at Brands, and sensationally led the race until he spun. This set the pattern for his short Formula Ford career. Spin or win seemed to be the order of the day until, after a few races, he felt he needed the tougher challenge of Formula 3, jumping into the deep end with an EMC and then a works Merlyn. By the end of the year he was winning at this level, in addition to hustling a Ford Escort Mexico indecently quickly. McLaren were first in with their pen, and Jody was signed to race for their Formula 2 team in 1972.

Generally his luck was out with the McLaren M21, but he did manage one win in the Greater London Trophy at Crystal Palace. As a bonus the team gave him his Grand Prix debut at Watkins Glen, where he kept the lid on things and finished a creditable ninth. McLaren kept him on for the 1973 season, though with Revson and Hulme on board they didn't really have room to accommodate him. Perhaps they wished they hadn't when his 1973 Grand Prix season turned into a succession of accidents, the most serious incident being his infamous spin at the beginning of the British GP which not only halted the race but wiped out a good proportion of the field. Ever the paradox at this stage of his career, Jody also raced for Sid Taylor in America, winning the L & M F5000 series in a Trojan, and competed in Can-Am with a Porsche 917 – completely without mishap.

With McLaren unable to offer Jody a firm deal for 1974, Ken Tyrrell stepped in and signed the South African to head his team, newly shorn of the retired Jackie Stewart and deceased François Cevert. It was to prove an inspired choice as the still relatively inexperienced charger took two Grand Prix wins and finished third in the championship table. Jody found it hard to maintain his scintillating form the following season, but he did have the wonderful bonus of winning the South African GP. In 1976 Tyrrell launched the bizarre but effective six-wheel P34 car. In Scheckter's hands this became a serious machine, Jody taking it to a historic victory in Sweden and racking up the points regularly elsewhere to finish a creditable third in the World Championship behind Hunt and Lauda. It was also a year when Scheckter achieved another ambition by winning the Wynn's 1000 Km at Kyalami in a BMW with Nilsson and Grohs.

Out of sync with the Tyrrell philosophy, Jody took a big gamble in joining Wolf for 1977, but it paid off immediately when he gave the restructured team a winning debut in the Argentine GP. The car wasn't consistently good at every circuit, but Jody never let that become a problem. Two more wins were to follow and second place to Lauda in the championship was his reward. His 1978 season was not so productive, the new Wolf chassis being far more troublesome than the relatively straightforward machine of the previous year. An offer from Ferrari for 1979 was too good to refuse, and the wild man of the early days was now but a distant memory. Indeed, incredible though it may seem, he was now driving almost conservatively. Certainly he had everything weighed up and his performances were the model of economy, Scheckter doing just enough and no more, but he was able to clinch the World Championship in style, with a win at Monza.

His ambition realised, Jody planned just one more year. As it happened it was easily the worst of his career, leaving the South African frustrated and a little bemused. The ultimate humiliation came at Montreal where he failed to qualify; he knew it was just one of those things, that circumstances had conspired against him, but it hurt his pride none the less. Scheckter came in with a bang but went out with a whimper, but he walked away unhurt and there were a few people who didn't believe that possible in 1973.

Ever his own man, since retiring Jody has settled in the United States, beginning a new life without even mentioning his deeds. Most of his new acquaintances know nothing of Jody the Formula 1 World Champion, and that's exactly the way he wants it. The past is the past, and it's the future that counts.

SCHECKTER, Jody (ZA) b 29/1/1950

1972

	Race	Circuit	No	Entrant	Car/Engine	Comment
9	US GP	Watkins Glen	21	Yardley Team McLaren	3.0 McLaren M19A-Cosworth V8	1 lap behind

1973

	Race	Circuit	No	Entrant	Car/Engine	Comment
9/ret	SOUTH AFRICAN GP	Kyalami	7	Yardley Team McLaren	3.0 McLaren M19C-Cosworth V8	engine/4 laps behind
ret	FRENCH GP	Paul Ricard	8	Yardley Team McLaren	3.0 McLaren M23-Cosworth V8	collision-Fittipaldi/suspension
ret/dns	BRITISH GP	Silverstone	30	Yardley Team McLaren	3.0 McLaren M23-Cosworth V8	spun, caused multiple accident 1st start
ret	CANADIAN GP	Mosport Park	0	Yardley Team McLaren	3.0 McLaren M23-Cosworth V8	accident with Cevert
ret	US GP	Watkins Glen	0	Yardley Team McLaren	3.0 McLaren M23-Cosworth V8	suspension

1974

	Race	Circuit	No	Entrant	Car/Engine	Comment
ret	ARGENTINE GP	Buenos Aires	3	Elf Team Tyrrell	3.0 Tyrrell 006-Cosworth V8	cylinder head gasket
13	BRAZILIAN GP	Interlagos	3	Elf Team Tyrrell	3.0 Tyrrell 006-Cosworth V8	1 lap behind
8	SOUTH AFRICAN GP	Kyalami	3	Elf Team Tyrrell	3.0 Tyrrell 006-Cosworth V8	

5	SPANISH GP	Jarama	3	Elf Team Tyrrell	3.0 Tyrrell 007-Cosworth V8	2 laps behind
dns	"		3	Elf Team Tyrrell	3.0 Tyrrell 006-Cosworth V8	practice only
3	BELGIAN GP	Nivelles	3	Elf Team Tyrrell	3.0 Tyrrell 007-Cosworth V8	
2	MONACO GP	Monte Carlo	3	Elf Team Tyrrell	3.0 Tyrrell 007-Cosworth V8	
1	SWEDISH GP	Anderstorp	3	Elf Team Tyrrell	3.0 Tyrrell 007-Cosworth V8	
5	DUTCH GP	Zandvoort	3	Elf Team Tyrrell	3.0 Tyrrell 007-Cosworth V8	
4	FRENCH GP	Dijon	3	Elf Team Tyrrell	3.0 Tyrrell 007-Cosworth V8	FL
1	BRITISH GP	Brands Hatch	3	Elf Team Tyrrell	3.0 Tyrrell 007-Cosworth V8	
2	GERMAN GP	Nürburgring	3	Elf Team Tyrrell	3.0 Tyrrell 007-Cosworth V8	FL
ret	AUSTRIAN GP	Österreichring	3	Elf Team Tyrrell	3.0 Tyrrell 007-Cosworth V8	engine
3	ITALIAN GP	Monza	3	Elf Team Tyrrell	3.0 Tyrrell 007-Cosworth V8	
ret	CANADIAN GP	Mosport Park	3	Elf Team Tyrrell	3.0 Tyrrell 007-Cosworth V8	brake failure/accident
ret	US GP	Watkins Glen	3	Elf Team Tyrrel	3.0 Tyrrell 007-Cosworth V8	fuel pipe

1975

11	ARGENTINE GP	Buenos Aires	3	Elf Team Tyrrell	3.0 Tyrrell 007-Cosworth V8	1 lap behind
ret	BRAZILIAN GP	Interlagos	3	Elf Team Tyrrel	3.0 Tyrrell 007-Cosworth V8	oil tank
1	SOUTH AFRICAN GP	Kyalami	3	Elf Team Tyrrell	3.0 Tyrrell 007-Cosworth V8	
ret	SPANISH GP	Montjuich Park	3	Elf Team Tyrrell	3.0 Tyrrell 007-Cosworth V8	engine
7	MONACO GP	Monte Carlo	3	Elf Team Tyrrell	3.0 Tyrrell 007-Cosworth V8	1 lap behind
2	BELGIAN GP	Zolder	3	Elf Team Tyrrell	3.0 Tyrrell 007-Cosworth V8	
7	SWEDISH GP	Anderstorp	3	Elf Team Tyrrell	3.0 Tyrrell 007-Cosworth V8	1 lap behind
16/ret	DUTCH GP	Zandvoort	3	Elf Team Tyrrell	3.0 Tyrrell 007-Cosworth V8	engine/8 laps behind
9	FRENCH GP	Paul Ricard	3	Elf Team Tyrrell	3.0 Tyrrell 007-Cosworth V8	
3/ret	BRITISH GP	Silverstone	3	Elf Team Tyrrell	3.0 Tyrrell 007-Cosworth V8	spun off in rainstorm/1 lap behind
ret	GERMAN GP	Nürburgring	3	Elf Team Tyrrell	3.0 Tyrrell 007-Cosworth V8	tyre failure/accident
8	AUSTRIAN GP	Österreichring	3	Elf Team Tyrrell	3.0 Tyrrell 007-Cosworth V8	1 lap behind
8	ITALIAN GP	Monza	3	Elf Team Tyrrell	3.0 Tyrrell 007-Cosworth V8	1 lap behind
6	US GP	Watkins Glen	3	Elf Team Tyrrell	3.0 Tyrrell 007-Cosworth V8	

1976

5	BRAZILIAN GP	Interlgos	3	Elf Team Tyrrell	3.0 Tyrrell 007-Cosworth V8	
4	SOUTH AFRICAN GP	Kyalami	3	Elf Team Tyrrell	3.0 Tyrrell 007-Cosworth V8	
ret	US GP WEST	Long Beach	3	Elf Team Tyrrell	3.0 Tyrrell 007-Cosworth V8	suspension
ret	SPANISH GP	Jarama	3	Elf Team Tyrrell	3.0 Tyrrell 007-Cosworth V8	oil pump belt
4	BELGIAN GP	Zolder	3	Elf Team Tyrrell	3.0 Tyrrell P34-Cosworth V8	
2	MONACO GP	Monte Carlo	3	Elf Team Tyrrell	3.0 Tyrrell P34-Cosworth V8	
1	SWEDISH GP	Anderstorp	3	Elf Team Tyrrell	3.0 Tyrrell P34-Cosworth V8	Pole
6	FRENCH GP	Paul Ricard	3	Elf Team Tyrrell	3.0 Tyrrell P34-Cosworth V8	
2*	BRITISH GP	Brands Hatch	3	Elf Team Tyrrell	3.0 Tyrrell P34-Cosworth V8	* 1st place car disqualified
dns	"	"	3	Elf Team Tyrrell	3.0 Tyrrell 007-Cosworth V8	practice only
2	GERMAN GP	Nürburgring	3	Elf Team Tyrrell	3.0 Tyrrell P34-Cosworth V8	FL
ret	AUSTRIAN GP	Österreichring	3	Elf Team Tyrrell	3.0 Tyrrell P34-Cosworth V8	suspension/accident
5	DUTCH GP	Zandvoort	3	Elf Team Tyrrell	3.0 Tyrrell P34-Cosworth V8	
5	ITALIAN GP	Monza	3	Elf Team Tyrrell	3.0 Tyrrell P34-Cosworth V8	
4	CANADIAN GP	Mosport Park	3	Elf Team Tyrrell	3.0 Tyrrell P34-Cosworth V8	
2	US GP EAST	Watkins Glen	3	Elf Team Tyrrell	3.0 Tyrrell P34-Cosworth V8	
ret	JAPANESE GP	Mount Fuji	3	Elf Team Tyrrell	3.0 Tyrrell P34-Cosworth V8	overheating

1977

1	ARGENTINE GP	Buenos Aires	20	Walter Wolf Racing	3.0 Wolf WR1-Cosworth V8	
ret	BRAZILIAN GP	Interlagos	20	Walter Wolf Racing	3.0 Wolf WR1-Cosworth V8	engine
2	SOUTH AFRICAN GP	Kyalami	20	Walter Wolf Racing	3.0 Wolf WR1-Cosworth V8	
dns	"	"	20	Walter Wolf Racing	3.0 Wolf WR2-Cosworth V8	practice only
3	US GP WEST	Long Beach	20	Walter Wolf Racing	3.0 Wolf WR1-Cosworth V8	puncture when 1st
3	SPANISH GP	Jarama	20	Walter Wolf Racing	3.0 Wolf WR2-Cosworth V8	
1	MONACO GP	Monte Carlo	20	Walter Wolf Racing	3.0 Wolf WR1-Cosworth V8	FL
dns	"	"	20	Walter Wolf Racing	3.0 Wolf WR3-Cosworth V8	practice only
ret	BELGIAN GP	Zolder	20	Walter Wolf Racing	3.0 Wolf WR3-Cosworth V8	engine
dns	"	"	20	Walter Wolf Racing	3.0 Wolf WR2-Cosworth V8	practice only
ret	SWEDISH GP	Anderstorp	20	Walter Wolf Racing	3.0 Wolf WR1-Cosworth V8	hit Watson
dns	"	"	20	Walter Wolf Racing	3.0 Wolf WR2-Cosworth V8	practice only
ret	FRENCH GP	Dijon	20	Walter Wolf Racing	3.0 Wolf WR3-Cosworth V8	hit by Regazzoni
ret	BRITISH GP	Silverstone	20	Walter Wolf Racing	3.0 Wolf WR1-Cosworth V8	engine
2	GERMAN GP	Hockenheim	20	Walter Wolf Racing	3.0 Wolf WR2-Cosworth V8	Pole
ret	AUSTRIAN GP	Österreichring	20	Walter Wolf Racing	3.0 Wolf WR3-Cosworth V8	spun off
dns	"	"	20	Walter Wolf Racing	3.0 Wolf WR1-Cosworth V8	practice only
3	DUTCH GP	Zandvoort	20	Walter Wolf Racing	3.0 Wolf WR2-Cosworth V8	1 lap behind
ret	ITALIAN GP	Monza	20	Walter Wolf Racing	3.0 Wolf WR1-Cosworth V8	engine
3	US GP EAST	Watkins Glen	20	Walter Wolf Racing	3.0 Wolf WR1-Cosworth V8	
1	CANADIAN GP	Mosport Park	20	Walter Wolf Racing	3.0 Wolf WR1-Cosworth V8	
10	JAPANESE GP	Mount Fuji	20	Walter Wolf Racing	3.0 Wolf WR3-Cosworth V8	pit stop/tyres/FL

1978

10	ARGENTINE GP	Buenos Aires	20	Walter Wolf Racing	3.0 Wolf WR4-Cosworth V8	
dns	"	"	20	Walter Wolf Racing	3.0 Wolf WR1-Cosworth V8	practice only
ret	BRAZILIAN GP	Rio	20	Walter Wolf Racing	3.0 Wolf WR1-Cosworth V8	collision-Tambay/suspension
ret	SOUTH AFRICAN GP	Kyalami	20	Walter Wolf Racing	3.0 Wolf WR1-Cosworth V8	engine cut out/accident
dns	"	"	20	Walter Wolf Racing	3.0 Wolf WR3-Cosworth V8	practice only
ret	US GP WEST	Long Beach	20	Walter Wolf Racing	3.0 Wolf WR3-Cosworth V8	hit by Tambay
dns	"	"	20	Walter Wolf Racing	3.0 Wolf WR1-Cosworth V8	practice only
3	MONACO GP	Monte Carlo	20	Walter Wolf Racing	3.0 Wolf WR1-Cosworth V8	
dns	"	"	20	Walter Wolf Racing	3.0 Wolf WR5-Cosworth V8	practice only
ret	BELGIAN GP	Zolder	20	Walter Wolf Racing	3.0 Wolf WR1-Cosworth V8	spun off
4	SPANISH GP	Jarama	20	Walter Wolf Racing	3.0 Wolf WR1-Cosworth V8	
ret	SWEDISH GP	Anderstorp	20	Walter Wolf Racing	3.0 Wolf WR5-Cosworth V8	overheating
6	FRENCH GP	Paul Ricard	20	Walter Wolf Racing	3.0 Wolf WR5-Cosworth V8	

ret	BRITISH GP	Brands Hatch	20	Walter Wolf Racing	3.0 Wolf WR5-Cosworth V8	*gearbox*
dns	"	"	20	Walter Wolf Racing	3.0 Wolf WR6-Cosworth V8	*practice only*
2	GERMAN GP	Hockenheim	20	Walter Wolf Racing	3.0 Wolf WR5-Cosworth V8	
ret/dns	AUSTRIAN GP	Österreichring	20	Walter Wolf Racing	3.0 Wolf WR5-Cosworth V8	*spun off in first race/did not restart*
12	DUTCH GP	Zandvoort	20	Walter Wolf Racing	3.0 Wolf WR5-Cosworth V8	*handling problems/2 laps behind*
dns	"	"	20	Walter Wolf Racing	3.0 Wolf WR6-Cosworth V8	*practice only*
12	ITALIAN GP	Monza	20	Walter Wolf Racing	3.0 Wolf WR5-Cosworth V8	*did not practice this car/-1 lap*
dns	"	"	20	Walter Wolf Racing	3.0 Wolf WR6-Cosworth V8	*practice accident*
3	US GP EAST	Watkins Glen	20	Walter Wolf Racing	3.0 Wolf WR6-Cosworth V8	
2	CANADIAN GP	Montreal	20	Walter Wolf Racing	3.0 Wolf WR6-Cosworth V8	

1979 World Champion Driver

ret/dns	ARGENTINE GP	Buenos Aires	11	Scuderia Ferrari SpA SEFAC	3.0 Ferrari 312T3 F12	*hurt wrist in first start/did not restart*
6	BRAZILIAN GP	Interlagos	11	Scuderia Ferrari SpA SEFAC	3.0 Ferrari 312T3 F12	*1 lap behind*
2	SOUTH AFRICAN GP	Kyalami	11	Scuderia Ferrari SpA SEFAC	3.0 Ferrari 312T4 F12	*pit stop/tyres when 1st*
2	US GP WEST	Long Beach	11	Scuderia Ferrari SpA SEFAC	3.0 Ferrari 312T4 F12	
4	SPANISH GP	Jarama	11	Scuderia Ferrari SpA SEFAC	3.0 Ferrari 312T4 F12	
1	BELGIAN GP	Zolder	11	Scuderia Ferrari SpA SEFAC	3.0 Ferrari 312T4 F12	
1	MONACO GP	Monte Carlo	11	Scuderia Ferrari SpA SEFAC	3.0 Ferrari 312T4 F12	*Pole*
7	FRENCH GP	Dijon	11	Scuderia Ferrari SpA SEFAC	3.0 Ferrari 312T4 F12	*pit stop/tyres/1 lap behind*
5	BRITISH GP	Silverstone	11	Scuderia Ferrari SpA SEFAC	3.0 Ferrari 312T4 F12	*1 lap behind*
4	GERMAN GP	Hockenheim	11	Scuderia Ferrari SpA SEFAC	3.0 Ferrari 312T4 F12	
4	AUSTRIAN GP	Österreichring	11	Scuderia Ferrari SpA SEFAC	3.0 Ferrari 312T4 F12	
2	DUTCH GP	Zandvoort	11	Scuderia Ferrari SpA SEFAC	3.0 Ferrari 312T4 F12	
1	ITALIAN GP	Monza	11	Scuderia Ferrari SpA SEFAC	3.0 Ferrari 312T4 F12	
4	CANADIAN GP	Montreal	11	Scuderia Ferrari SpA SEFAC	3.0 Ferrari 312T4 F12	*pit stop/tyres/1 lap behind*
ret	US GP EAST	Watkins Glen	11	Scuderia Ferrari SpA SEFAC	3.0 Ferrari 312T4 F12	*tyre failure*

1980

ret	ARGENTINE GP	Buenos Aires	1	Scuderia Ferrari SpA SEFAC	3.0 Ferrari 312T5 F12	*engine*
ret	BRAZILIAN GP	Interlagos	1	Scuderia Ferrari SpA SEFAC	3.0 Ferrari 312T5 F12	*engine*
ret	SOUTH AFRICAN GP	Kyalami	1	Scuderia Ferrari SpA SEFAC	3.0 Ferrari 312T5 F12	*engine/electrics*
5	US GP WEST	Long Beach	1	Scuderia Ferrari SpA SEFAC	3.0 Ferrari 312T5 F12	*pit stop/tyres/1 lap behind*
8	BELGIAN GP	Zolder	1	Scuderia Ferrari SpA SEFAC	3.0 Ferrari 312T5 F12	*2 laps behind*
ret	MONACO GP	Monte Carlo	1	Scuderia Ferrari SpA SEFAC	3.0 Ferrari 312T5 F12	*handling*
12	FRENCH GP	Paul Ricard	1	Scuderia Ferrari SpA SEFAC	3.0 Ferrari 312T5 F12	*2 pit stops/tyres*
10	BRITISH GP	Brands Hatch	1	Scuderia Ferrari SpA SEFAC	3.0 Ferrari 312T5 F12	*pit stop/nose cone/3 laps behind*
13	GERMAN GP	Hockenheim	1	Scuderia Ferrari SpA SEFAC	3.0 Ferrari 312T5 F12	*pit stop/tyres/1 lap behind*
13	AUSTRIAN GP	Österreichring	1	Scuderia Ferrari SpA SEFAC	3.0 Ferrari 312T5 F12	*pit stop/tyres/1 lap behind*
9	DUTCH GP	Zandvoort	1	Scuderia Ferrari SpA SEFAC	3.0 Ferrari 312T5 F12	*2 pit stops/tyres/2 laps behind*
8	ITALIAN GP	Imola	1	Scuderia Ferrari SpA SEFAC	3.0 Ferrari 312T5 F12	*1 lap behind*
dnq	CANADIAN GP	Montreal	1	Scuderia Ferrari SpA SEFAC	3.0 Ferrari 312T5 F12	
11	US GP EAST	Watkins Glen	1	Scuderia Ferrari SpA SEFAC	3.0 Ferrari 312T5 F12	*1 lap behind*

GP Starts: 109 (112)   GP Wins: 10   Pole positions: 3   Fastest laps: 5   Points: 255

HARRY SCHELL

Born in Paris but of American parents, Harry O'Reilly Schell was a fun-loving extrovert who was one of the great characters of the fifties motor racing scene. His childhood during the thirties was filled by racing, for his father Laury was the patron of Ecurie Bleue, a team which raced Delahayes and Talbots. His mother Lucy took over the running of the team following the death of her husband in a road accident and ran René Dreyfus at Indianapolis just before the war. Young Harry was on that trip, and resolved to race himself once old enough.

The war saw him serving in the US military in Finland, and by the late forties he was taking his first steps in racing. In 1949 he managed a second place with a Talbot in the Coupe du Salon at Montlhéry but it was the following year, when he raced a Cooper-JAP, that brought him success. Schell handled the little car with great verve, frequently embarrassing Formula 2 opposition. At the Circuit du Lac, in Aix-les-Bains, he succeeded in beating the works Ferrari in his heat and comfortably led the final before being forced into retirement. He managed to gain an entry for the Monaco GP that year but was eliminated in the first-lap multiple crash, but at Bremgarten he enjoyed his first taste of a real Grand Prix machine, taking a Talbot into eighth place.

Schell mainly raced Maseratis entered by Ecurie Platé in 1951 and 1952, but started to gain solid results only when he joined forces with Simca Gordini. A second place in the Cadours GP of 1952 encouraged both parties to continue together the following year, when Harry was out of luck in the championship Grands Prix, but took a string of good finishes in the French championship rounds. Schell ran his own Maserati A6GCM in 1954, taking second place at Castelfusano and thirds at Pescara and Aintree, but by the end-of-season Spanish GP he had his own Maserati 250F and caused something of a stir as he drove off into the distance at the start, only losing the lead to Fangio after a spin and eventually retiring with transmission failure. There was talk of the American running on half-tanks to break up the opposition, but he had certainly made his mark, for both Vanwall and Ferrari used his services in 1955, and he won some minor events for Tony Vandervell. Schell showed the green machines' startling potential in 1956 when he put on a marvellous show at Reims, snapping at the heels of the works Ferraris, and scored a win in the Caen GP before taking his leave to join the works Maserati team in 1957.

Harry fulfilled a useful subordinate role to Fangio, recording a number of good results, including a fine if distant third place at Pescara. He also took second place at Pau and third at Modena before arranging to join BRM for the 1958 and 1959 seasons. Harry proved an excellent acquisition for the Bourne team, his second place at Zandvoort being the closest the American would ever get to that elusive Grand Prix win. At the end of the 1959 season he purchased a Cooper-Climax which he raced under the Ecurie Bleue banner as a privateer. He also raced the car at the beginning of 1960 before joining the Yeoman Credit team. It was while practising one of their cars for the International Trophy in the wet at Silverstone that he was to lose his life, crashing after the Cooper got away from him on one of the circuit's fast bends. Harry was an immensely popular character, and his death was a great loss to the racing scene as it moved into a new era.

SCHELL, Harry (F/USA) b 29/6/1921 – d 13/5/1960

1950

	Race	Circuit	No	Entrant	Car/Engine	Comment
ret	MONACO GP	Monte Carlo	8	Horschell Racing Corp	1.1 Cooper T12-JAP V2	multiple accident
8	SWISS GP	Bremgarten	44	Ecurie Bleue	4.5 Lago-Talbot T26C 6	3 laps behind

1951

12	SWISS GP	Bremgarten	32	Enrico Platé	1.5 s/c Maserati 4CLT/48 4	4 laps behind
ret	FRENCH GP	Reims	20	Enrico Platé	1.5 s/c Maserati 4CLT/48 4	steering

1952

ret	SWISS GP	Bremgarten	40	Enrico Platé	2.0 Maserati 4CLT/Platé 4	engine
ret	FRENCH GP	Rouen	18	Enrico Platé	2.0 Maserati 4CLT/Platé 4	gearbox
ret	"	"	16	Enrico Platé	2.0 Maserati 4CLT/Platé 4	took over from de Graffenried/brakes
17	BRITISH GP	Silverstone	33	Enrico Platé	2.0 Maserati 4CLT/Platé 4	7 laps behind

1953

7*	ARGENTINE GP	Buenos Aires	28	Equipe Gordini	2.0 Gordini Type 16 6	* took over from Trintignant/-6 laps
ret	DUTCH GP	Zandvoort	20	Equipe Gordini	2.0 Gordini Type 16 6	transmission
7	BELGIAN GP	Spa	20	Equipe Gordini	2.0 Gordini Type 16 6	3 laps behind
ret	FRENCH GP	Reims	6	Equipe Gordini	2.0 Gordini Type 16 6	engine
ret	BRITISH GP	Silverstone	28	Equipe Gordini	2.0 Gordini Type 16 6	magneto
ret	GERMAN GP	Nürburgring	11	Equipe Gordini	2.0 Gordini Type 16 6	head gasket
9	ITALIAN GP	Monza	38	Equipe Gordini	2.0 Gordini Type 16 6	5 laps behind

1954

6	ARGENTINE GP	Buenos Aires	28	Harry Schell	2.5 Maserati A6GCM/250F 6	3 laps behind
ret	FRENCH GP	Reims	48	Harry Schell	2.5 Maserati A6GCM/250F 6	engine
12	BRITISH GP	Silverstone	3	Harry Schell	2.5 Maserati A6GCM/250F 6	7 laps behind
7	GERMAN GP	Nürburgring	15	Harry Schell	2.5 Maserati A6GCM/250F 6	
ret	SWISS GP	Bremgarten	34	Officine Alfieri Maserati	2.5 Maserati 250F 6	oil pump
ret	SPANISH GP	Pedralbes	24	Harry Schell	2.5 Maserati 250F 6	transmission-rear axle

1955

6*	ARGENTINE GP	Buenos Aires	28	Officine Alfieri Maserati	2.5 Maserati 250F 6	* Behra took over
nc*	"	"	22	Officine Alfieri Maserati	2.5 Maserati 250F 6	* Mantovani/Musso also drove
ret*	"	"	26	Officine Alfieri Maserati	2.5 Maserati 250F 6	* fuel starvation/Bucci/Menditéguy drove
ret	MONACO GP	Monte Carlo	46	Scuderia Ferrari	2.5 Ferrari 555 4	engine
dns	BELGIAN GP	Spa	4	Scuderia Ferrari	2.5 Ferrari 555 4	Trintignant drove car
ret	BRITISH GP	Aintree	30	Vandervell Products Ltd	2.5 Vanwall 4	accelerator
nc*	"	"	28	Vandervell Products Ltd	2.5 Vanwall 4	took over Wharton's car/-18 laps
ret	ITALIAN GP	Monza	42	Vandervell Products Ltd	2.5 Vanwall 4	suspension

1956

ret	MONACO GP	Monte Carlo	16	Vandervell Products Ltd	2.5 Vanwall 4	spun off avoiding Fangio
4	BELGIAN GP	Spa	10	Vandervell Products Ltd	2.5 Vanwall 4	2 laps behind
ret	FRENCH GP	Reims	22	Vandervell Products Ltd	2.5 Vanwall 4	engine
10*	"	"	24	Vandervell Products Ltd	2.5 Vanwall 4	* took over Hawthorn's car
ret	BRITISH GP	Silverstone	16	Vandervell Products Ltd	2.5 Vanwall 4	fuel pipe
ret	GERMAN GP	Nürburgring	12	Scuderia Centro Sud	2.5 Maserati 250F 6	overheating
ret	ITALIAN GP	Monza	18	Vandervell Products Ltd	2.5 Vanwall 4	transmission

1957

4	ARGENTINE GP	Buenos Aires	22	Scuderia Centro Sud	2.5 Maserati 250F 6	
ret*	MONACO GP	Monte Carlo	38	Officine Alfieri Maserati	2.5 Maserati 250F 6	king pins
ret	"	"	34	Officine Alfieri Maserati	2.5 Maserati 250F 6	* took Scarlatti's car/mechanical
5	FRENCH GP	Rouen	6	Officine Alfieri Maserati	2.5 Maserati 250F 6	7 laps behind
ret	BRITISH GP	Aintree	6	Officine Alfieri Maserati	2.5 Maserati 250F 6	water pump
7	GERMAN GP	Nürburgring	3	Officine Alfieri Maserati	2.5 Maserati 250F 6	
3	PESCARA GP	Pescara	6	Officine Alfieri Maserati	2.5 Maserati 250F 6	
ret	ITALIAN GP	Monza	4	Officine Alfieri Maserati	2.5 Maserati 250F 6	water pump
5*	"	"	8	Officine Alfieri Maserati	2.5 Maserati 250F 6	* took over Scarlatti's car/-3 laps

1958

6	ARGENTINE GP	Buenos Aires	8	Joakim Bonnier	2.5 Maserati 250F 6	2 laps behind
5	MONACO GP	Monte Carlo	8	Owen Racing Organisation	2.5 BRM P25 4	9 laps behind
2	DUTCH GP	Zandvoort	15	Owen Racing Organisation	2.5 BRM P25 4	
5	BELGIAN GP	Spa	10	Owen Racing Organisation	2.5 BRM P25 4	1 lap behind
ret	FRENCH GP	Reims	16	Owen Racing Organisation	2.5 BRM P25 4	overheating
5	BRITISH GP	Silverstone	20	Owen Racing Organisation	2.5 BRM P25 4	
ret	GERMAN GP	Nürburgring	6	Owen Racing Organisation	2.5 BRM P25 4	brakes
6	PORTUGUESE GP	Oporto	10	Owen Racing Organisation	2.5 BRM P25 4	1 lap behind
ret	ITALIAN GP	Monza	10	Owen Racing Organisation	2.5 BRM P25 4	collision with Von Trips on grid
5	MOROCCAN GP	Casablanca	16	Owen Racing Organisation	2.5 BRM P25 4	

1959

ret	MONACO GP	Monte Carlo	16	Owen Racing Organisation	2.5 BRM P25 4	engine
ret	DUTCH GP	Zandvoort	6	Owen Racing Organisation	2.5 BRM P25 4	engine
7	FRENCH GP	Reims	6	Owen Racing Organisation	2.5 BRM P25 4	3 laps behind
4	BRITISH GP	Aintree	8	Owen Racing Organisation	2.5 BRM P25 4	1 lap behind
nc	GERMAN GP	AVUS	10	Owen Racing Organisation	2.5 BRM P25 4	5th heat 1/nc heat 2/-11 laps
5	PORTUGUESE GP	Monsanto	6	Owen Racing Organisation	2.5 BRM P25 4	3 laps behind
7	ITALIAN GP	Monza	2	Owen Racing Organisation	2.5 BRM P25 4	2 laps behind
ret	US GP	Sebring	19	Ecurie Bleue	2.2 Cooper T51-Climax 4	clutch

1960

ret	ARGENTINE GP	Buenos Aires	34	Ecurie Bleue	2.2 Cooper T51-Climax 4	fuel pump

GP Starts: 56   GP Wins: 0   Pole positions: 0   Fastest laps: 0   Points: 30

SCHENKEN, Tim (AUS) b 26/9/1943

1970

ret	AUSTRIAN GP	Österreichring	26	Frank Williams Racing Cars	3.0 de Tomaso 505-Cosworth V8	*engine*
ret	ITALIAN GP	Monza	54	Frank Williams Racing Cars	3.0 de Tomaso 505-Cosworth V8	*engine*
nc	CANADIAN GP	St Jovite	10	Frank Williams Racing Cars	3.0 de Tomaso 505-Cosworth V8	*pit stop/shock absorber-11 laps*
ret	US GP	Watkins Glen	30	Frank Williams Racing Cars	3.0 de Tomaso 505-Cosworth V8	*rear suspension*

1971

9	SPANISH GP	Montjuich Park	8	Motor Racing Developments	3.0 Brabham BT33-Cosworth V8	*3 laps behind*
10	MONACO GP	Monte Carlo	8	Motor Racing Developments	3.0 Brabham BT33-Cosworth V8	*pit stop-wheel change/-4 laps*
ret	DUTCH GP	Zandvoort	25	Motor Racing Developments	3.0 Brabham BT33-Cosworth V8	*collision with Pescarolo*
12/ret	FRENCH GP	Paul Ricard	8	Motor Racing Developments	3.0 Brabham BT33-Cosworth V8	*engine-oil pressure/-5 laps*
12/ret	BRITISH GP	Silverstone	8	Motor Racing Developments	3.0 Brabham BT33-Cosworth V8	*gearbox/5 laps behind*
6	GERMAN GP	Nürburgring	25	Motor Racing Developments	3.0 Brabham BT33-Cosworth V8	
3	AUSTRIAN GP	Österreichring	8	Motor Racing Developments	3.0 Brabham BT33-Cosworth V8	
ret	ITALIAN GP	Monza	11	Motor Racing Developments	3.0 Brabham BT33-Cosworth V8	*rear subframe*
ret	CANADIAN GP	Mosport Park	8	Motor Racing Developments	3.0 Brabham BT33-Cosworth V8	*transistor box*
ret	US GP	Watkins Glen	23	Motor Racing Developments	3.0 Brabham BT33-Cosworth V8	*valve*

1972

5	ARGENTINE GP	Buenos Aires	19	Brooke Bond Oxo/Rob Walker/Team Surtees	3.0 Surtees TS9A-Cosworth V8	
ret	SOUTH AFRICAN GP	Kyalami	16	Brooke Bond Oxo/Rob Walker/Team Surtees	3.0 Surtees TS9A-Cosworth V8	*engine*
8	SPANISH GP	Jarama	12	Brooke Bond Oxo/Rob Walker/Team Surtees	3.0 Surtees TS9B-Cosworth V8	*2 laps behind*
ret	MONACO GP	Monte Carlo	10	Team Surtees	3.0 Surtees TS9B-Cosworth V8	*hit barrier*
ret	BELGIAN GP	Nivelles	35	Team Surtees	3.0 Surtees TS9B-Cosworth V8	*engine*
17	FRENCH GP	Clermont Ferrand	27	Flame Out-Team Surtees	3.0 Surtees TS9B-Cosworth V8	*pit stop/fuel pressure/-2 laps*
ret	BRITISH GP	Brands Hatch	22	Flame Out-Team Surtees	3.0 Surtees TS9B-Cosworth V8	*broken rear suspension mounting*
14	GERMAN GP	Nürburgring	15	Team Surtees	3.0 Surtees TS9B-Cosworth V8	*pit stops/tyre/electrical/1 lap behind*
11	AUSTRIAN GP	Österreichring	24	Team Surtees	3.0 Surtees TS9B-Cosworth V8	*pit stop/tyres/2 laps behind*
ret	ITALIAN GP	Monza	8	Team Surtees	3.0 Surtees TS9B-Cosworth V8	*hit chicane*
7	CANADIAN GP	Mosport Park	22	Team Surtees	3.0 Surtees TS9B-Cosworth V8	*1 laps behind*
ret	US GP	Watkins Glen	22	Team Surtees	3.0 Surtees TS14-Cosworth V8	*oil leak*

1973

14	CANADIAN GP	Mosport Park	26	Frank Williams Racing Cars	3.0 Iso Williams 1R-Cosworth V8	*pit stop/tyres/5 laps behind*

1974

14/ret	SPANISH GP	Jarama	23	Trojan-Tauranac Racing	3.0 Trojan T103-Cosworth V8	*spun off*
10	BELGIAN GP	Nivelles	41	Trojan-Tauranac Racing	3.0 Trojan T103-Cosworth V8	*2 laps behind*
ret	MONACO GP	Monte Carlo	23	Trojan-Tauranac Racing	3.0 Trojan T103-Cosworth V8	*multiple accident*
dnq	DUTCH GP	Zandvoort	23	Trojan-Tauranac Racing	3.0 Trojan T103-Cosworth V8	
ret	BRITISH GP	Brands Hatch	23	Trojan-Tauranac Racing	3.0 Trojan T103-Cosworth V8	*suspension*
dnq	GERMAN GP	Nürburgring	23	Trojan-Tauranac Racing	3.0 Trojan T103-Cosworth V8	
10	AUSTRIAN GP	Österreichring	23	Trojan-Tauranac Racing	3.0 Trojan T103-Cosworth V8	*4 laps behind*
ret	ITALIAN GP	Monza	29	Trojan-Tauranac Racing	3.0 Trojan T103-Cosworth V8	*gear selection*
dsq	US GP	Watkins Glen	31	John Player Team Lotus	3.0 Lotus 76-Cosworth V8	*started unofficially-2nd reserve*

GP Starts: 34 GP Wins: 0 Pole positions: 0 Fastest laps: 0 Points: 7

SCHERRER, Albert (CH) b 28/2/1908 – d 5/7/1986

1953

	Race	Circuit	No	Entrant	Car/Engine	Comment
nc	SWISS GP	Bremgarten	18	HW Motors	2.0 HWM-Alta 4	*still runnng-not classified*

GP Starts: 1 GP Wins: 0 Pole positions: 0 Fastest laps: 0 Points: 0

SCHILLER, Heinz (CH) b 25/1/1930

1962

	Race	Circuit	No	Entrant	Car/Engine	Entrant
ret	GERMAN GP	Nürburgring	28	Ecurie Filipinetti	1.5 Lotus 24-BRM V8	*oil pressure*

GP Starts: 1 GP Wins: 0 Pole positions: 0 Fastest laps: 0 Points: 0

SCHLESSER, Jean-Louis (F) b 12/9/1952

1983

	Race	Circuit	No	Entrant	Car/Engine	Comment
dnq	FRENCH GP	Paul Ricard	18	RAM Automotive Team March	3.0 March-RAM 01-Cosworth V8	

1988

11	ITALIAN GP	Monza	5	Canon Williams Team	3.5 Williams FW12-Judd V8	*collided with Senna/2 laps behind*

GP Starts: 1 GP Wins: 0 Pole positions: 0 Fastest laps: 0 Points: 0

SCHLESSER, Jo (F) b 18/5/1928 – d 7/7/1968

1966

	Race	Circuit	No	Entrant	Car/Engine	Comment
10	GERMAN GP (F2)	Nürburgring	33	Matra Sports	1.0 Matra MS5-BRM 4 F2	*3rd in F2 class/1 lap behind*

1967

ret	GERMAN GP (F2)	Nürburgring	23	Ecurie Ford-France	1.6 Matra MS5-Cosworth 4 F2	*clutch*

1968

ret	FRENCH GP	Rouen	18	Honda Racing (France)	3.0 Honda RA302 V8	*fatal accident*

GP Starts: 3 GP Wins: 0 Pole positions: 0 Fastest laps: 0 Points: 0

TIM SCHENKEN

With 42 wins in Formula Ford and a Grovewood Award in 1968, Tim Schenken was obviously a man to watch, and in 1969 he continued the good work in Rodney Bloor's Sports Motors Formula 3 Brabham at home and abroad, winning the French Craven A title.

For 1970 Tim and the Sports Motors team took the step up to Formula 2 and had an up-and-down season, the best results being second at Paul Ricard, and third at Pau and Mantorp Park. Schenken also made his Grand Prix debut, coming into a Williams team still reeling from the loss of Piers Courage, but he could do nothing with the de Tomaso.

The following season he appeared to have made the big breakthrough. Signed as number two to Graham Hill in the Brabham team, Tim was restricted to the old BT33, (possibly an advantage) but overshadowed the former World Champion for much of the year. Schenken's two points finishes were not really just reward for his efforts, though in non-title races he took third place in the International Trophy and fourth in the Race of Champions.

In 1972 he made what turned out to be the biggest mistake of his career, joining Team Surtees for a season which effectively sabotaged his long-term Grand Prix ambitions. There was some solace, for he had been leading the Rondel Formula 2 outfit with distinction and was invited to join the Ferrari sports car team, for whom he scored a win in the Buenos Aires 1000 Km and the Nürburgring 1000 Km in addition to four second places, all paired with Peterson.

After ambitious plans to race a Formula 1 Rondel failed to materialise in 1973 and the Trojan project with his old Brabham boss Ron Tauranac turned into an embarrassing failure in 1974, poor Tim must have thought things couldn't get worse, but they did when he was invited to handle a Lotus 76 in the 1974 US GP and found the car almost undriveable, his one race for the Hethel team ending in non-qualification.

Schenken then embarked on a programme of sports car and GT racing for George Loos, racing his stable of Porsches during 1975-77 and winning the Nürburgring 1000 Km with Hezemans and Stommelen in 1977. Tim also shared the Jaguar XJ12C with John Fitzpatrick in the 1977 European GT championship, before retiring to concentrate on his Tiga racing car business with partner Howden Ganley.

JEAN-LOUIS SCHLESSER

A nephew of the late Jo Schlesser, Jean-Louis is a driver who missed the Formula 1 boat, and unfortunately the immensely popular Frenchman will be best remembered for inadvertently tangling with Ayrton Senna near the end of the 1988 Italian GP as the Brazilian was about to lap his Williams.

A graduate of Formule Renault, Schlesser got bogged down in French Formula 3 and production racing before turning to the European F3 championship in 1981. However, his Martini was saddled with the wrong brand of tyres and the undoubted high spot of the year was a terrific second place at Le Mans, sharing a Rondeau with Jacky Haran and Philippe Streiff. Still determined to succeed in single-seaters, Jean-Louis joined the Maurer team alongside Bellof in 1982, but it was another season of frustration, as he did not enjoy the best of equipment.

In 1983 Schlesser began work as a test driver for Williams, and attempted to qualify the RAM for the French GP. He then returned to production cars, winning the French championship in 1985, before Tom Walkinshaw signed him for the TWR Jaguar sports car team in 1986. Disappointingly, finishes were thin on the ground and he was released, ultimately joining the Kouros Sauber team, which, in 1988, became the official representative of the Mercedes factory. Schlesser scored two wins and finished second to Martin Brundle in the points standings and the following season he made no mistake, winning five rounds (Suzuka, Jarama, the Nürburgring, Donington and Mexico City) to claim the World Sports Car Championship, a feat he repeated in 1990, when he shared the title with Mauro Baldi.

JO SCHLESSER

A true all-rounder and as brave as they come, Schlesser loved every form of motor sport and competed in as many of them as he possibly could during a career that started in 1952, when he rallied a Panhard. He tried the current French vogue of monomill racing in 1954, but his serious competition activities were then put on hold for three years while he was working in Mozambique. Back in Europe in 1957, he finished second in the Liège-Rome-Liège Rally with a Mercedes, which he soon replaced with a Ferrari 250 GT, but success did not really come until 1960 when he took second in class at the Nürburgring 1000 Km, and second overall in the Rouen GP. This was in contrast to his rather disappointing year in a Formula 2 Cooper, a sixth place at Syracuse his only result worth mentioning. His 1961 season was curtailed by a very big accident at Le Mans which left him with a badly broken arm and leg, but he was back in action the following year with a Formula Junior Brabham, putting in some superb drives to become one of the formula's leading protagonists.

The advent of the 1-litre Formula 2 in 1964 gave Jo the chance to pit himself against some of racing's top names, and he became a respected member of the Continental F2 fraternity, joining the Matra works team in 1966 and running the same car under the Ford France banner the following year before setting up a team with his great friend Guy Ligier to race McLarens in 1968. Since 1965 Schlesser had also made something of name for himself at the wheel of powerful sports cars including a Shelby Cobra and then the Ford France GT40, winning the Reims 12-hour race in 1967, paired with Ligier.

However, his Grand Prix experience was limited to just two outings in the Formula 2 class of the German GP when he was invited to race the totally unproven air-cooled Honda in the 1968 French GP – it must be said, much against the wishes of John Surtees. In the opening laps of the race, Schlesser lost control of the car in pouring rain, crashing it into an earth bank, whereupon it burst into flames, swiftly claiming the life of its 41-year-old driver.

BERND SCHNEIDER

A graduate of Formula Ford 1600 and FF2000, Schneider finished equal third in his first year of German F3 in 1986, but when he came back to slaughter the opposition in 1988, winning seven of the eight rounds he contested, many watchers were convinced that here at last was a German with a big future. Little did they realise that it would be at the wheel of Mercedes touring cars that he would taste success rather than in Grand Prix racing, where two miserable seasons with Zakspeed and a couple of drives with Arrows left him washed up at the age of 26.

Bernd drove a Kremer Porsche in Interserie racing in 1990 and then raced in IMSA for the Joest team, before reviving his career in a Zakspeed Mercedes. He switched to an AMG works car for 1992-93 and is now considered the fastest driver in the Mercedes squad, but the scintillating form of Larini and the Alfas in 1993 means he is still hunting for the championship title.

SCHNEIDER, Bernd (D) b 20/7/1964

1988

	Race	Circuit	No	Entrant	Car/Engine	Comment
dnq	BRAZILIAN GP	Rio	10	West Zakspeed Racing	1.5 t/c Zakspeed 881 4	
dnq	SAN MARINO GP	Imola	10	West Zakspeed Racing	1.5 t/c Zakspeed 881 4	
dnq	MONACO GP	Monte Carlo	10	West Zakspeed Racing	1.5 t/c Zakspeed 881 4	
ret	MEXICAN GP	Mexico City	10	West Zakspeed Racing	1.5 t/c Zakspeed 881 4	engine
dnq	CANADIAN GP	Montreal	10	West Zakspeed Racing	1.5 t/c Zakspeed 881 4	
dnq	US GP (DETROIT)	Detroit	10	West Zakspeed Racing	1.5 t/c Zakspeed 881 4	
ret	FRENCH GP	Paul Ricard	10	West Zakspeed Racing	1.5 t/c Zakspeed 881 4	gearbox
dnq	BRITISH GP	Silverstone	10	West Zakspeed Racing	1.5 t/c Zakspeed 881 4	
12	GERMAN GP	Hockenheim	10	West Zakspeed Racing	1.5 t/c Zakspeed 881 4	1 lap behind
dnq	HUNGARIAN GP	Hungaroring	10	West Zakspeed Racing	1.5 t/c Zakspeed 881 4	
15/ret	BELGIAN GP	Spa	10	West Zakspeed Racing	1.5 t/c Zakspeed 881 4	gearbox/5 laps behind
ret	ITALIAN GP	Monza	10	West Zakspeed Racing	1.5 t/c Zakspeed 881 4	engine
dnq	PORTUGUESE GP	Estoril	10	West Zakspeed Racing	1.5 t/c Zakspeed 881 4	
dnq	SPANISH GP	Jerez	10	West Zakspeed Racing	1.5 t/c Zakspeed 881 4	
ret	JAPANESE GP	Suzuka	10	West Zakspeed Racing	1.5 t/c Zakspeed 881 4	feeling effects of practice accident
dnq	AUSTRALIAN GP	Adelaide	10	West Zakspeed Racing	1.5 t/c Zakspeed 881 4	

1989

	Race	Circuit	No	Entrant	Car/Engine	Comment
ret	BRAZILIAN GP	Rio	34	West Zakspeed Racing	3.5 Zakspeed 891-Yamaha V8	collision with Cheever
dnpq	SAN MARINO GP	Imola	34	West Zakspeed Racing	3.5 Zakspeed 891-Yamaha V8	
dnpq	MONACO GP	Monte Carlo	34	West Zakspeed Racing	3.5 Zakspeed 891-Yamaha V8	
dnpq	MEXICAN GP	Mexico City	34	West Zakspeed Racing	3.5 Zakspeed 891-Yamaha V8	
dnpq	US GP (PHOENIX)	Phoenix	34	West Zakspeed Racing	3.5 Zakspeed 891-Yamaha V8	
dnpq	CANADIAN GP	Montreal	34	West Zakspeed Racing	3.5 Zakspeed 891-Yamaha V8	
dnpq	FRENCH GP	Paul Ricard	34	West Zakspeed Racing	3.5 Zakspeed 891-Yamaha V8	
dnpq	BRITISH GP	Silverstone	34	West Zakspeed Racing	3.5 Zakspeed 891-Yamaha V8	
dnpq	GERMAN GP	Hockenheim	34	West Zakspeed Racing	3.5 Zakspeed 891-Yamaha V8	
dnpq	HUNGARIAN GP	Hungaroring	34	West Zakspeed Racing	3.5 Zakspeed 891-Yamaha V8	
dnpq	BELGIAN GP	Spa	34	West Zakspeed Racing	3.5 Zakspeed 891-Yamaha V8	
dnpq	ITALIAN GP	Monza	34	West Zakspeed Racing	3.5 Zakspeed 891-Yamaha V8	
dnpq	PORTUGUESE GP	Estoril	34	West Zakspeed Racing	3.5 Zakspeed 891-Yamaha V8	
dnpq	SPANISH GP	Jerez	34	West Zakspeed Racing	3.5 Zakspeed 891-Yamaha V8	
ret	JAPANESE GP	Suzuka	34	West Zakspeed Racing	3.5 Zakspeed 891-Yamaha V8	engine on lap 1
dnpq	AUSTRALIAN GP	Adelaide	34	West Zakspeed Racing	3.5 Zakspeed 891-Yamaha V8	

1989

	Race	Circuit	No	Entrant	Car/Engine	Comment
12	US GP (PHOENIX)	Phoenix	10	Footwork Arrows Racing	3.5 Arrows A11-Cosworth V8	2 laps behind
dnq	SPANISH GP	Jerez	10	Footwork Arrows Racing	3.5 Arrows A11-Cosworth V8	

GP Starts: 9   GP Wins: 0   Pole positions: 0   Fastest laps: 0   Points: 0

SCHOELLER, Rudolf (CH) d 1980

1952

	Race	Circuit	No	Entrant	Car/Engine	Comment
ret	GERMAN GP	Nürburgring	118	Ecurie Espadon	2.0 Ferrari 212 V12	shock absober

GP Starts: 1   GP Wins: 0   Pole positions: 0   Fastest laps: 0   Points: 0

SCHROEDER, Bob (USA) b 11/5/1926

1962

	Race	Circuit	No	Entrant	Car/Engine	Comment
10	US GP	Watkins Glen	26	John Mecom	1.5 Lotus 24-Climax V8	hired Rob Walker's car/-7 laps

GP Starts: 1   GP Wins: 0   Pole positions: 0   Fastest laps: 0   Points: 0

MICHAEL SCHUMACHER

When Michael Schumacher burst upon the Grand Prix stage with a sensational debut for Jordan at Spa, the Grand Prix hype-machine went into overdrive, billing this young 'unknown' as the next Senna. In truth Michael's racing career had been very carefully groomed before he ever stepped into a Formula 1 car, and he had the comforting prospect of major manufacturer and commercial backing with which to develop his top-level career.

A former karting star with but a single season of Formula Ford 1600 and Formula König in 1988 behind him, Schumacher was signed by leading German F3 team OTS to support Heinz-Harald Frentzen in 1989. It was a closely contested season, with the pair both finishing just one point behind series winner Karl Wendlinger. It was then that Mercedes sporting director Jochen Neerpasch stepped in with his junior driver scheme which placed all three drivers in the Sauber-Mercedes Group C programme for 1990. Under the wise tutelage of Jochen Mass, the trio were schooled in the art of handling big, powerful cars in a very disciplined and professional framework. Schumacher finished in second place in the three races he started at Dijon, the Nürburgring and Mexico City, this last result becoming a win when the sister car was disqualified. In parallel to his sports car drives, Michael was back in German F3, and this time won the series comfortably. He also took in two end-of-season races at Fuji and Macau, and confirmed his talent by winning them both.

Most drivers would be wanting to try their hand at F3000 by this time, but Michael was happy to stay within the confines of the Mercedes team. This second season saw a change of emphasis with the young lions Schumacher and Wendlinger paired together and allowed their heads. Both did an excellent job, but the consensus was that Michael had the edge, the pair's reward after a trouble-strewn year being victory in the round at Autopolis. With a Formula 1 drive inevitable sooner (as it would turn out) or later, nothing was left to chance and Neerpasch arranged for Schumacher to race a Formula 3000 car at Sugo, well away from the glare of publicity. He finished second and enjoyed the different experience of racing a powerful single-seater.

A month later came the Jordan drive at Spa which, after his stirring deeds in practice, ended disappointingly when Michael's clutch failed at the start. Suddenly Schumacher was a hot property and after much legal wrangling the somewhat bemused driver was whisked off to join the Benetton team in time for the next race at Monza. Three points-scoring finishes in the first three races were more than enough evidence for Flavio Briatore to plan the team's future around the German star and he was not to disappoint. In his first full Grand Prix season Michael proved to be not only very quick but also remarkably consistent, rarely making costly mistakes and putting in some scintillating performances such as his second place to Mansell in the rain at Barcelona and his climb through the field to third at Monza after being left at the start. Of course, the supreme moment was his fully deserved, if slightly fortunate, win at Spa where he made his own luck – and reaped the rewards.

The 1993 season provided more evidence of Schumacher's increasing maturity. Only the Williams team's dominance stood between him and the winner's step on the podium on numerous occasions and he took a superbly thought-out win at Estoril. Committed to Benetton for the foreseeable future, Michael will be hoping that the team can provide him with the equipment he needs in his quest to become the first German driver to win the World Championship.

SCHUMACHER Michael (D) b 3/1/1969

	Race	Circuit	No	Entrant	Car/Engine	Comment
	1991					
ret	BELGIAN GP	Spa	32	Team 7UP Jordan	3.5 Jordan 191-Ford HB V8	clutch at start
5	ITALIAN GP	Monza	19	Camel Benetton Ford	3.5 Benetton B191-Ford HB V8	
6	PORTUGUESE GP	Estoril	19	Camel Benetton Ford	3.5 Benetton B191-Ford HB V8	
6	SPANISH GP	Barcelona	19	Camel Benetton Ford	3.5 Benetton B191-Ford HB V8	
ret	JAPANESE GP	Suzuka	19	Camel Benetton Ford	3.5 Benetton B191-Ford HB V8	engine
ret	AUSTRALIAN GP	Adelaide	19	Camel Benetton Ford	3.5 Benetton B191-Ford HB V8	collision with Alesi
	1992					
4	SOUTH AFRICAN GP	Kyalami	19	Camel Benetton Ford	3.5 Benetton B191B-Ford HB V8	
3	MEXICAN GP	Mexico City	19	Camel Benetton Ford	3.5 Benetton B191B-Ford HB V8	
3	BRAZILIAN GP	Interlagos	19	Camel Benetton Ford	3.5 Benetton B191B-Ford HB V8	
2	SPANISH GP	Barcelona	19	Camel Benetton Ford	3.5 Benetton B192-Ford HB V8	
ret	SAN MARINO GP	Imola	19	Camel Benetton Ford	3.5 Benetton B192-Ford HB V8	spun-suspension damage
4	MONACO GP	Monte Carlo	19	Camel Benetton Ford	3.5 Benetton B192-Ford HB V8	
2	CANADIAN GP	Montreal	19	Camel Benetton Ford	3.5 Benetton B192-Ford HB V8	
ret	FRENCH GP	Magny Cours	19	Camel Benetton Ford	3.5 Benetton B192-Ford HB V8	accident-collision Senna
4	BRITISH GP	Silverstone	19	Camel Benetton Ford	3.5 Benetton B192-Ford HB V8	
3	GERMAN GP	Hockenheim	19	Camel Benetton Ford	3.5 Benetton B192-Ford HB V8	
ret	HUNGARIAN GP	Hungaroring	19	Camel Benetton Ford	3.5 Benetton B192-Ford HB V8	collision-lost rear wing/spun off
1	BELGIAN GP	Spa	19	Camel Benetton Ford	3.5 Benetton B192-Ford HB V8	FL
3	ITALIAN GP	Monza	19	Camel Benetton Ford	3.5 Benetton B192-Ford HB V8	clutch
7	PORTUGUESE GP	Estoril	19	Camel Benetton Ford	3.5 Benetton B192-Ford HB V8	started from back/puncture/-2 laps
ret	JAPANESE GP	Suzuka	19	Camel Benetton Ford	3.5 Benetton B192-Ford HB V8	gearbox
2	AUSTRALIAN GP	Adelaide	19	Camel Benetton Ford	3.5 Benetton B192-Ford HB V8	FL
	1993					
ret	SOUTH AFRICAN GP	Kyalami	5	Camel Benetton Ford	3.5 Benetton B192B-Ford HB V8	collision with Senna
3	BRAZILIAN GP	Interlagos	5	Camel Benetton Ford	3.5 Benetton B192B-Ford HB V8	FL

	Race	Circuit	No	Entrant	Car/Engine	Comment
ret	EUROPEAN GP	Donington	5	Camel Benetton Ford	3.5 Benetton B193B-Ford HB V8	
2	SAN MARINO GP	Imola	5	Camel Benetton Ford	3.5 Benetton B193B-Ford HB V8	
3	SPANISH GP	Barcelona	5	Camel Benetton Ford	3.5 Benetton B193B-Ford HB V8	FL
ret	MONACO GP	Monte Carlo	5	Camel Benetton Ford	3.5 Benetton B193B-Ford HB V8	active hydraulics/fire
2	CANADIAN GP	Montreal	5	Camel Benetton Ford	3.5 Benetton B193B-Ford HB V8	FL
3	FRENCH GP	Magny Cours	5	Camel Benetton Ford	3.5 Benetton B193B-Ford HB V8	FL
2	BRITISH GP	Silverstone	5	Camel Benetton Ford	3.5 Benetton B193B-Ford HB V8	
2	GERMAN GP	Hockenheim	5	Camel Benetton Ford	3.5 Benetton B193B-Ford HB V8	FL
ret	HUNGARIAN GP	Hungaroring	5	Camel Benetton Ford	3.5 Benetton B193B-Ford HB V8	engine
2	BELGIAN GP	Spa	5	Camel Benetton Ford	3.5 Benetton B193B-Ford HB V8	
ret	ITALIAN GP	Monza	5	Camel Benetton Ford	3.5 Benetton B193B-Ford HB V8	engine
1	PORTUGUESE GP	Estoril	5	Camel Benetton Ford	3.5 Benetton B193B-Ford HB V8	
ret	JAPANESE GP	Suzuka	5	Camel Benetton Ford	3.5 Benetton B193B-Ford HB V8	collision Hill/suspension damage
ret	AUSTRALIAN GP	Adelaide	5	Camel Benetton Ford	3.5 Benetton B193B-Ford HB V8	engine

GP Starts: 38   GP Wins: 2   Pole positions: 0   Fastest laps: 7   Points: 109

SCHUPPAN, Vern (AUS) b 19/3/1943

1972

	Race	Circuit	No	Entrant	Car/Engine	Comment
dns	BELGIAN GP	Nivelles	26	Marlboro BRM	3.0 BRM P153B V12	Marko raced car

1974

15	BELGIAN GP	Nivelles	22	Team Ensign	3.0 Ensign N174-Cosworth V8	pit stop/fuel feed/3 laps behind
ret	MONACO GP	Monte Carlo	22	Team Ensign	3.0 Ensign N174-Cosworth V8	spun off
dsq	SWEDISH GP	Anderstorp	22	Team Ensign	3.0 Ensign N174-Cosworth V8	started unofficially
ret/dsq*	DUTCH GP	Zandvoort	22	Team Ensign	3.0 Ensign N174-Cosworth V8	fuel line/*tyre change outside pits
dnq	FRENCH GP	Dijon	22	Team Ensign	3.0 Ensign N174-Cosworth V8	
dnq	BRITISH GP	Brands Hatch	22	Team Ensign	3.0 Ensign N174-Cosworth V8	
ret	GERMAN GP	Nürburgring	22	Team Ensign	3.0 Ensign N174-Cosworth V8	transmission

1975

ret	SWEDISH GP	Anderstorp	22	Embassy Racing with Graham Hill	3.0 Hill GH1-Cosworth V8	driveshaft
ret	"	"	22T	Embassy Racing with Graham Hill	3.0 Lola T370-Cosworth V8	practice only

1977

12	BRITISH GP	Silverstone	18	Team Surtees	3.0 Surtees TS19-Cosworth V8	
7	GERMAN GP	Hockenheim	18	Team Surtees	3.0 Surtees TS19-Cosworth V8	1 lap behind
16	AUSTRIAN GP	Österreichring	18	Team Surtees	3.0 Surtees TS19-Cosworth V8	pit stop/tyres/2 laps behind
dnq	DUTCH GP	Zandvoort	18	Team Surtees	3.0 Surtees TS19-Cosworth V8	

GP Starts: 9   GP Wins: 0   Pole positions: 0   Fastest laps: 0   Points: 0

SCHWELM, Adolfo J Cruz (RA) b 28/6/1923

1953

	Race	Circuit	No	Entrant	Car/Engine	Comment
ret	ARGENTINE GP	Buenos Aires	24	Cooper Car Co	2.0 Cooper T20-Bristol 6	broken stub axle-lost wheel

GP Starts: 1   GP Wins: 0   Pole positions: 0   Fastest laps: 0   Points: 0

SCOTT-BROWN, Archie (GB) b 13/5/1937 – d 19/5/1958

1956

	Race	Circuit	No	Entrant	Car/Engine	Comment
ret	BRITISH GP	Silverstone	19	Connaught Engineering	2.5 Connaught-Alta B Type 4	lost wheel

GP Starts: 1   GP Wins: 0   Pole positions: 0   Fastest laps: 0   Points: 0

SCOTTI, Piero (I) b 11/11/1909

1956

	Race	Circuit	No	Entrant	Car/Engine	Comment
ret	BELGIAN GP	Spa	28	Piero Scotti	2.5 Connaught-Alta B Type 4	oil pressure

GP Starts: 1   GP Wins: 0   Pole positions: 0   Fastest laps: 0   Points: 0

SEIDEL, Wolfgang (D) b 4/7/1926 – d 1/3/1987

1953

	Race	Circuit	No	Entrant	Car/Engine	Comment
16	GERMAN GP	Nürburgring	22	Wolfgang Seidel	2.0 Veritas RS 6	4 laps behind

1958

ret	BELGIAN GP	Spa	32	Scuderia Centro Sud	2.5 Maserati 250F 6	engine
ret	GERMAN GP (F2)	Nürburgring	22	R R C Walker Racing Team	1.5 Cooper T43-Climax 4	suspension
ret	MOROCCAN GP	Casablanca	24	Scuderia Centro Sud	2.5 Maserati 250F 6	accident

1960

9	ITALIAN GP	Monza	10	Wolfgang Seidel	1.5 Cooper T45-Climax 4	

1961

dns	BELGIAN GP	Spa	48	Scuderia Colonia	1.5 Lotus 18-Climax 4	car raced by Bianchi
17	BRITISH GP	Aintree	52	Scuderia Colonia	1.5 Lotus 18-Climax 4	17 laps behind

ret	GERMAN GP	Nürburgring	26	Scuderia Colonia	1.5 Lotus 18-Climax 4	*steering*
ret	ITALIAN GP	Monza	56	Scuderia Colonia	1.5 Lotus 18-Climax 4	*engine*
1962						
10	DUTCH GP	Zandvoort	16	Ecurie Maarsbergen	1.5 Emeryson 1006-Climax 4	*28 laps behind*
ret	BRITISH GP	Aintree	44	Autosport Team Wolfgang Seidel	1.5 Lotus 24-BRM V8	*brakes/overheating*
dnq	GERMAN GP	Nürburgring	34	Autosport Team Wolfgang Seidel	1.5 Lotus 24-BRM V8	

GP Starts: 10   GP Wins: 0   Pole positions: 0   Fastest laps: 0   Points: 0

VERN SCHUPPAN

After a few successful years in karting, this tall, blond Australian came to Britain in 1969 to race in Formula Ford, but it was when he moved into Formula Atlantic with a works Palliser in 1971 that he made the breakthrough, winning the Yellow Pages championship. After a Tyrrell test, Vern was contracted as a junior driver for BRM, but his opportunities were restricted to a couple of non-title events – in which he did well, taking fifth place in the Gold Cup and fourth in the John Player Challenge at Brands Hatch. It was much the same the following year, with Vern kicking his heels in F1, so he accepted an offer to join the Gulf/Wyer team to replace the injured Watson, taking second place in the Spa 1000 Km with Ganley.

For 1974, Schuppan settled into an F5000 programme with Theodore Racing, and although a Grand Prix chance came with Ensign he dropped out after a few races. His later F1 outings with Hill and Surtees were equally unproductive, but he was already concentrating on building a career in sports cars and F5000, joining Dan Gurney's Eagle team in 1975.

In 1976, Vern hit the USAC trail, earning the 'Rookie of the Year' award at Indianapolis that year, but his best finish was to be third at Indy in 1981. In the early eighties Schuppan became heavily involved in endurance racing, winning the Le Mans 24 Hours in 1983 for the powerful Rothmans Porsche factory team with Holbert and Haywood. Thereafter Vern became a successful Porsche entrant in the FIA and Japanese sports car series, developing the basic design on behalf of customers around the world.

ARCHIE SCOTT-BROWN

A tiny Scot who made light of the disability of having a partly formed right arm, Archie drew admiration from everyone for the amazing way he handled any type of machinery – Fangio for one thought his car control was phenomenal.

He began racing in 1950 in a minor way in an MG TD, but it was 1954 before he began to make his mark, forming a great partnership with Brian Lister to race his Lister-Bristol. Soon Archie was winning club and national events all over the country with the car, and he earned himself a chance in the Connaught F1 team for 1956, taking part in the British Grand Prix and finishing second in the International Trophy race.

However, he continued to race in sports cars and was back with Lister for 1957, handling his ferocious Lister-Jaguar. By this time Scott-Brown was greatly frustrated by his inability to gain an international licence, which stopped him competing abroad. He did obtain permission to race in New Zealand early in 1958, winning the Lady Wigram Trophy, but the following May, when competing in a big sports car race at Spa, he lost control of his Lister on a piece of damp track while dicing with Masten Gregory. He crashed into a field and the car burst into flames, the luckless Scot dying from his injuries the following day.

PIERO SCOTTI

Scotti was an Italian businessman who raced Ferrari sports cars in the early fifties, taking third place in the 1951 Mille Miglia, and sharing a works car with Farina to win the Casablanca 12 Hours. He continued to find success in minor events before trying his hand at Formula 1 in 1956.

He bought an F1 Connaught on hire-purchase and took seventh in the International Trophy, but after the Belgian Grand Prix at Spa he returned the car to the factory and gave up racing.

WOLFGANG SEIDEL

An enthusiastic German, Seidel raced intermittently in Grands Pix for a decade without any success, despite campaigning some quite decent machinery on occasion.

He competed regularly in sports car events as a privateer, but sometimes drove for the works Ferrari and Porsche teams. Seidel's best result was a victory in the 1959 Targa Florio, sharing with Barth, but he was placed on numerous occasions, including second in the 1957 Reims 12 Hours with Phil Hill and third at Sebring in 1958 with Behra.

AYRTON SENNA

The wonder of the age, Senna's colossal talent has bestrode Grand Prix racing for a decade. He has virtually made it his own personal fiefdom (in the widest sense) with a frightening intensity and commitment that can be viewed as bordering on arrogance . Yet Senna's creed is simplicity itself; his talent, just like that of a great musician, must be continually developed day by day, year after year. To achieve this goal everything else must match his expectations: the machine and organisation at his disposal must perform to his exacting standards or they serve no useful purpose. Toleman, Lotus, and now even McLaren have been blessed by his gifts, but have been immediately discarded when no longer of use. He finds the mundane trivialities that surround racing a tiresome chore. The media, at best barely tolerated, must now scuffle round in huge posses as if attending royalty, hanging onto every considered utterance, delivered precisely and without emotion in any one of a number

of languages. The gauche youngster who stepped into a Toleman at the beginning of 1984 now inhabits a place in the stratosphere, where the real world hardly seems to intrude. Lear jets, helicopters descending onto skyscraper corporate offices – the Senna industry worldwide mushrooms in a way which calls to mind Joseph Heller's gloriously improbable Milo Minderbinder.

From a well-to-do Brazilian family, Ayrton was racing karts from a very early age and in fact had amassed eight seasons' experience before coming to Britain to make his Formula Ford debut in 1981. Twelve wins ensured the FF1600 title was won, and the Brazilian returned the following year to continue his climb to fame and fortune in the FF2000 series. A tally of 21 wins from 27 starts tells its own story. In 1983 Ayrton joined the West Surrey Racing F3 team and became embroiled in a fabulous tussle for the Marlboro championship with Martin Brundle. In the end Senna's early-season run of wins kept him in front when the title was decided, and after testing for both Williams and McLaren he agreed to drive for Toleman in Formula 1 in 1984.

The phenomenal talent was soon in evidence, with his drive in the wet at Monaco outstanding. Senna was poised to challenge Prost for the lead when the race was controversially stopped, but he had made his mark on an event he was to win for a staggering sixth time in 1993. When it became clear that Toleman were not able to provide Ayrton with the means to win, the Brazilian engineered his way out of his contract and joined Lotus. Almost immediately his first Grand Prix victory arrived, his skills in the wet at Estoril provoking memories of the great Jacky Ickx. Over the next three seasons Senna proved to be the fastest man around, certainly in qualifying, as he amassed 16 pole positions, but only six wins, due in part to the fragility of the Lotus. It was crystal clear to Senna that to win the championship he needed a Honda engine, but definitely not a Lotus, and for 1988 he joined the McLaren team to partner Alain Prost. Senna was supremely confident of his ability to outdrive the Frenchman, and was as good as his word. In a season which saw McLaren take victory in all bar one of the 16 races, Ayrton emerged triumphant in a manner more convincing than the eight-wins-to-seven margin suggests. Relationships between the two superstars were never more than cordial at best, and they broke down completely in 1989 as both drivers waged war within the confines of the team. This time the championship battle ended in Prost's favour after the Brazilian was deftly taken out by the Frenchman at the Suzuka chicane. By this time, of course, Prost had nothing to lose, having already decided to take his leave of McLaren, though he and Senna were to be embroiled in further controversy the following season. With Prost needing points at Suzuka to maintain Ferrari's challenge , Ayrton seemed to take his revenge, driving into the back of Prost's car at the first corner. It was an unworthy way for the title to be decided, wiping away the memory of some great performances earlier in the season.

In many ways 1991 was Senna's finest championship triumph to date. The new V12 Honda was not initially markedly superior to its lighter predecessor, despite the impression given by Ayrton's four straight wins from the start of the season. In fact these had been extremely hard-won triumphs that had demanded every ounce of the Brazilian's skill and guile. The following season found Senna in the unusual position of underdog, Williams and Renault finally having found the edge and the ability to sustain it. Ayrton predictably gave his all, winning at Monaco, Hungary and Monza, but perceived shortcomings at McLaren were already irking him and his frustration was probably not helped by his inability to muscle into a Williams drive alongside Prost in 1993. During the winter months McLaren were having to come to terms with the loss of Honda power and hoping that the replacement Ford engine would be sufficiently promising to tempt the unhappy Brazilian to continue. In the event Senna deigned to drive – initially on a race-by-race basis for a reported fee of $1 million per race. Luckily for us mortals, he served up a number of superlative performances which can seldom have been bettered at any time in the history of motor racing. Brazil, Donington and Adelaide showed us all why he truly is a driver on a par with the sport's all-time greats.

Senna's goal must now be to win more races and more championships than anyone else. What Ayrton wants, Ayrton gets. For 1994 he has his coveted Williams-Renault and, all things being equal, it would be a brave man who bets against him re-writing the history books in the future.

SENNA, Ayrton (BR) b 21/3/1960

1984

	Race	Circuit	No	Entrant	Car/Engine	Comment
ret	BRAZILIAN GP	Rio	19	Toleman Group Motorsport	1.5 t/c Toleman TG183B-Hart 4	turbo boost pressure
6	SOUTH AFRICAN GP	Kyalami	19	Toleman Group Motorsport	1.5 t/c Toleman TG183B-Hart 4	3 laps behind
6*	BELGIAN GP	Spa	19	Toleman Group Motorsport	1.5 t/c Toleman TG183B-Hart 4	*6th place car dsq/2 laps behind
dnq	SAN MARINO GP	Imola	19	Toleman Group Motorsport	1.5 t/c Toleman TG183B-Hart 4	tyre problems
ret	FRENCH GP	Dijon	19	Toleman Group Motorsport	1.5 t/c Toleman TG184-Hart 4	turbo
2	MONACO GP	Monte Carlo	19	Toleman Group Motorsport	1.5 t/c Toleman TG184-Hart 4	race stopped/rain/FL/half points
7	CANADIAN GP	Montreal	19	Toleman Group Motorsport	1.5 t/c Toleman TG184-Hart 4	2 laps behind
ret	US GP (DETROIT)	Detroit	19	Toleman Group Motorsport	1.5 t/c Toleman TG184-Hart 4	broken wishbone/crashed

ret	US GP (DALLAS)	Dallas	19	Toleman Group Motorsport	1.5 t/c Toleman TG184-Hart 4	*driveshaft*
3	BRITISH GP	Brands Hatch	19	Toleman Group Motorsport	1.5 t/c Toleman TG184-Hart 4	
ret	GERMAN GP	Hockenheim	19	Toleman Group Motorsport	1.5 t/c Toleman TG184-Hart 4	*rear wing failure/accident*
ret	AUSTRIAN GP	Österreichring	19	Toleman Group Motorsport	1.5 t/c Toleman TG184-Hart 4	*oil pressure*
ret	DUTCH GP	Zandvoort	19	Toleman Group Motorsport	1.5 t/c Toleman TG184-Hart 4	*engine*
ret	EUROPEAN GP	Nürburgring	19	Toleman Group Motorsport	1.5 t/c Toleman TG184-Hart 4	*hit Rosberg*
3	PORTUGUESE GP	Estoril	19	Toleman Group Motorsport	1.5 t/c Toleman TG184-Hart 4	

1985

ret	BRAZILIAN GP	Rio	12	John Player Special Team Lotus	1.5 t/c Lotus 97T-Renault V6	*electrics*
1	PORTUGUESE GP	Estoril	12	John Player Special Team Lotus	1.5 t/c Lotus 97T-Renault V6	*Pole/FL*
7/ret	SAN MARINO	Imola	12	John Player Special Team Lotus	1.5 t/c Lotus 97T-Renault V6	*out of fuel/Pole*
ret	MONACO GP	Monte Carlo	12	John Player Special Team Lotus	1.5 t/c Lotus 97T-Renault V6	*engine/Pole*
16	CANADIAN GP	Montreal	12	John Player Special Team Lotus	1.5 t/c Lotus 97T-Renault V6	*pit stop/turbo pipe loose/FL/-5 laps*
ret	US GP (DETROIT)	Detroit	12	John Player Special Team Lotus	1.5 t/c Lotus 97T-Renault V6	*hit wall/Pole/FL*
ret	FRENCH GP	Paul Ricard	12	John Player Special Team Lotus	1.5 t/c Lotus 97T-Renault V6	*engine/accident*
10	BRITISH GP	Silverstone	12	John Player Special Team Lotus	1.5 t/c Lotus 97T-Renault V6	*fuel injection problems/-5 laps*
ret	GERMAN GP	Nürburgring	12	John Player Special Team Lotus	1.5 t/c Lotus 97T-Renault V6	*driveshaft*
2	AUSTRIAN GP	Österreichring	12	John Player Special Team Lotus	1.5 t/c Lotus 97T-Renault V6	
3	DUTCH GP	Zandvoort	12	John Player Special Team Lotus	1.5 t/c Lotus 97T-Renault V6	
3	ITALIAN GP	Monza	12	John Player Special Team Lotus	1.5 t/c Lotus 97T-Renault V6	*Pole*
1	BELGIAN GP	Spa	12	John Player Special Team Lotus	1.5 t/c Lotus 97T-Renault V6	
2	EUROPEAN GP	Brands Hatch	12	John Player Special Team Lotus	1.5 t/c Lotus 97T-Renault V6	*Pole*
ret	SOUTH AFRICAN GP	Kyalami	12	John Player Special Team Lotus	1.5 t/c Lotus 97T-Renault V6	*engine*
ret	AUSTRALIAN GP	Adelaide	12	John Player Special Team Lotus	1.5 t/c Lotus 97T-Renault V6	*engine/Pole*

1986

2	BRAZILIAN GP	Rio	12	John Player Special Team Lotus	1.5 t/c Lotus 98T-Renault V6	*incident with Mansell/Pole*
1	SPANISH GP	Jerez	12	John Player Special Team Lotus	1.5 t/c Lotus 98T-Renault V6	*Pole*
ret	SAN MARINO GP	Imola	12	John Player Special Team Lotus	1.5 t/c Lotus 98T-Renault V6	*wheel bearing/Pole*
3	MONACO GP	Monte Carlo	12	John Player Special Team Lotus	1.5 t/c Lotus 98T-Renault V6	
2	BELGIAN GP	Spa	12	John Player Special Team Lotus	1.5 t/c Lotus 98T-Renault V6	
5	CANADIAN GP	Montreal	12	John Player Special Team Lotus	1.5 t/c Lotus 98T-Renault V6	*1 lap behind*
1	US GP (DETROIT)	Detroit	12	John Player Special Team Lotus	1.5 t/c Lotus 98T-Renault V6	*Pole*
ret	FRENCH GP	Paul Ricard	12	John Player Special Team Lotus	1.5 t/c Lotus 98T-Renault V6	*spun off on oil/Pole*
ret	BRITISH GP	Brands Hatch	12	John Player Special Team Lotus	1.5 t/c Lotus 98T-Renault V6	*gearbox*
2	GERMAN GP	Hockenheim	12	John Player Special Team Lotus	1.5 t/c Lotus 98T-Renault V6	
2	HUNGARIAN GP	Hungaroring	12	John Player Special Team Lotus	1.5 t/c Lotus 98T-Renault V6	*Pole*
ret	AUSTRIAN GP	Österreichring	12	John Player Special Team Lotus	1.5 t/c Lotus 98T-Renault V6	*engine*
ret	ITALIAN GP	Monza	12	John Player Special Team Lotus	1.5 t/c Lotus 98T-Renault V6	*transmission*
4	PORTUGUESE GP	Estoril	12	John Player Special Team Lotus	1.5 t/c Lotus 98T-Renault V6	*1 lap behind/Pole*
3	MEXICAN GP	Mexico City	12	John Player Special Team Lotus	1.5 t/c Lotus 98T-Renault V6	*Pole*
ret	AUSTRALIAN GP	Adelaide	12	John Player Special Team Lotus	1.5 t/c Lotus 98T-Renault V6	*engine*

1987

ret	BRAZILIAN GP	Rio	12	Camel Team Lotus Honda	1.5 t/c Lotus 99T-Honda V6	*engine*
2	SAN MARINO GP	Imola	12	Camel Team Lotus Honda	1.5 t/c Lotus 99T-Honda V6	*Pole*
ret	BELGIAN GP	Spa	12	Camel Team Lotus Honda	1.5 t/c Lotus 99T-Honda V6	*accident with Mansell*
1	MONACO GP	Monte Carlo	12	Camel Team Lotus Honda	1.5 t/c Lotus 99T-Honda V6	*FL*
1	US GP (DETROIT)	Detroit	12	Camel Team Lotus Honda	1.5 t/c Lotus 99T-Honda V6	*FL*
4	FRENCH GP	Paul Ricard	12	Camel Team Lotus Honda	1.5 t/c Lotus 99T-Honda V6	*1 lap behind*
3	BRITISH GP	Silverstone	12	Camel Team Lotus Honda	1.5 t/c Lotus 99T-Honda V6	*1 lap behind*
3	GERMAN GP	Hockenheim	12	Camel Team Lotus Honda	1.5 t/c Lotus 99T-Honda V6	*1 lap behind*
2	HUNGARIAN GP	Hungaroring	12	Camel Team Lotus Honda	1.5 t/c Lotus 99T-Honda V6	
5	AUSTRIAN GP	Österreichring	12	Camel Team Lotus Honda	1.5 t/c Lotus 99T-Honda V6	*2 laps behind*
2	ITALIAN GP	Monza	12	Camel Team Lotus Honda	1.5 t/c Lotus 99T-Honda V6	*FL*
7	PORTUGUESE GP	Estoril	12	Camel Team Lotus Honda	1.5 t/c Lotus 99T-Honda V6	*pit stop/throttle problems/-2 laps*
5	SPANISH GP	Jerez	12	Camel Team Lotus Honda	1.5 t/c Lotus 99T-Honda V6	*tyre problems*
ret	MEXICAN GP	Mexico City	12	Camel Team Lotus Honda	1.5 t/c Lotus 99T-Honda V6	*clutch-spun off*
2	JAPANESE GP	Suzuka	12	Camel Team Lotus Honda	1.5 t/c Lotus 99T-Honda V6	
dsq*	AUSTRALIAN GP	Adelaide	12	Camel Team Lotus Honda	1.5 t/c Lotus 99T-Honda V6	*2nd on road/* oversize brake ducts*

1988 World Champion Driver

dsq	BRAZILIAN GP	Rio	12	Honda Marlboro McLaren	1.5 t/c McLaren MP4/4-Honda V6	*changed cars illegally/Pole*
1	SAN MARINO GP	Imola	12	Honda Marlboro McLaren	1.5 t/c McLaren MP4/4-Honda V6	*Pole*
ret	MONACO GP	Monte Carlo	12	Honda Marlboro McLaren	1.5 t/c McLaren MP4/4-Honda V6	*hit barrier when 1st/Pole/FL*
2	MEXICAN GP	Mexico City	12	Honda Marlboro McLaren	1.5 t/c McLaren MP4/4-Honda V6	*Pole*
1	CANADIAN GP	Montreal	12	Honda Marlboro McLaren	1.5 t/c McLaren MP4/4-Honda V6	*Pole/FL*
1	US GP (DETROIT)	Detroit	12	Honda Marlboro McLaren	1.5 t/c McLaren MP4/4-Honda V6	*Pole*
2	FRENCH GP	Paul Ricard	12	Honda Marlboro McLaren	1.5 t/c McLaren MP4/4-Honda V6	
1	BRITISH GP	Silverstone	12	Honda Marlboro McLaren	1.5 t/c McLaren MP4/4-Honda V6	
1	GERMAN GP	Hockenheim	12	Honda Marlboro McLaren	1.5 t/c McLaren MP4/4-Honda V6	*Pole*
1	HUNGARIAN GP	Hungaroring	12	Honda Marlboro McLaren	1.5 t/c McLaren MP4/4-Honda V6	*Pole*
1	BELGIAN GP	Spa	12	Honda Marlboro McLaren	1.5 t/c McLaren MP4/4-Honda V6	*Pole*
10/ret	ITALIAN GP	Monza	12	Honda Marlboro McLaren	1.5 t/c McLaren MP4/4-Honda V6	*collision-Schlesser/Pole/-2 laps*
6	PORTUGUESE GP	Estoril	12	Honda Marlboro McLaren	1.5 t/c McLaren MP4/4-Honda V6	*hit by Mansell/p stop damage check*
4	SPANISH GP	Jerez	12	Honda Marlboro McLaren	1.5 t/c McLaren MP4/4-Honda V6	*pit stop/tyres/Pole*
1	JAPANESE GP	Suzuka	12	Honda Marlboro McLaren	1.5 t/c McLaren MP4/4-Honda V6	*Pole/FL/then record 8th win of year*
2	AUSTRALIAN GP	Adelaide	12	Honda Marlboro McLaren	1.5 t/c McLaren MP4/4-Honda V6	*Pole*

1989

11	BRAZILIAN GP	Rio	1	Honda Marlboro McLaren	3.5 McLaren MP4/5-Honda V10	*lap 1 collision/4 p stops/Pole/-2 laps*
1	SAN MARINO GP	Imola	1	Honda Marlboro McLaren	3.5 McLaren MP4/5-Honda V10	*aggregate of two parts/Pole*
1	MONACO GP	Monte Carlo	1	Honda Marlboro McLaren	3.5 McLaren MP4/5-Honda V10	*Pole*
1	MEXICAN GP	Mexico City	1	Honda Marlboro McLaren	3.5 McLaren MP4/5-Honda V10	*Pole*
ret	US GP (PHOENIX)	Phoenix	1	Honda Marlboro McLaren	3.5 McLaren MP4/5-Honda V10	*electrics/Pole/FL*
7/ret	CANADIAN GP	Montreal	1	Honda Marlboro McLaren	3.5 McLaren MP4/5-Honda V10	*engine/3 laps behind*

ret	FRENCH GP	Paul Ricard	1	Honda Marlboro McLaren	3.5 McLaren MP4/5-Honda V10	*transmission at start*
ret	BRITISH GP	Silverstone	1	Honda Marlboro McLaren	3.5 McLaren MP4/5-Honda V10	*gearbox-spun off/Pole*
1	GERMAN GP	Hockenheim	1	Honda Marlboro McLaren	3.5 McLaren MP4/5-Honda V10	*Pole/FL*
2	HUNGARIAN GP	Hungaroring	1	Honda Marlboro McLaren	3.5 McLaren MP4/5-Honda V10	
1	BELGIAN GP	Spa	1	Honda Marlboro McLaren	3.5 McLaren MP4/5-Honda V10	*Pole*
ret	ITALIAN GP	Monza	1	Honda Marlboro McLaren	3.5 McLaren MP4/5-Honda V10	*engine/Pole*
ret	PORTUGUESE GP	Estoril	1	Honda Marlboro McLaren	3.5 McLaren MP4/5-Honda V10	*collision with Mansell/Pole*
1	SPANISH GP	Jerez	1	Honda Marlboro McLaren	3.5 McLaren MP4/5-Honda V10	*Pole/FL*
dsq	JAPANESE GP	Suzuka	1	Honda Marlboro McLaren	3.5 McLaren MP4/5-Honda V10	*1st/collision-rejoined illegally/Pole*
ret	AUSTRALIAN GP	Adelaide	1	Honda Marlboro McLaren	3.5 McLaren MP4/5-Honda V10	*collision with Brundle/Pole*

1990 World Champion Driver

1	US GP (PHOENIX)	Phoenix	27	Honda Marlboro McLaren	3.5 McLaren MP4/5B-Honda V10	
3	BRAZILIAN GP	Interlagos	27	Honda Marlboro McLaren	3.5 McLaren MP4/5B-Honda V10	*p stop/collision with Nakajima/Pole*
ret	SAN MARINO GP	Imola	27	Honda Marlboro McLaren	3.5 McLaren MP4/5B-Honda V10	*wheel rim damage spun off/Pole*
1	MONACO GP	Monza	27	Honda Marlboro McLaren	3.5 McLaren MP4/5B-Honda V10	*Pole/FL*
1	CANADIAN GP	Montreal	27	Honda Marlboro McLaren	3.5 McLaren MP4/5B-Honda V10	*Pole*
20/ret	MEXICAN GP	Mexico City	27	Honda Marlboro McLaren	3.5 McLaren MP4/5B-Honda V10	*puncture/6 laps behind*
3	FRENCH GP	Paul Ricard	27	Honda Marlboro McLaren	3.5 McLaren MP4/5B-Honda V10	
3	BRITISH GP	Silverstone	27	Honda Marlboro McLaren	3.5 McLaren MP4/5B-Honda V10	*spun at Copse*
1	GERMAN GP	Hockenheim	27	Honda Marlboro McLaren	3.5 McLaren MP4/5B-Honda V10	*Pole*
2	HUNGARIAN GP	Hungaroring	27	Honda Marlboro McLaren	3.5 McLaren MP4/5B-Honda V10	*puncture-p stop/collision with Nannini*
1	BELGIAN GP	Spa	27	Honda Marlboro McLaren	3.5 McLaren MP4/5B-Honda V10	*Pole*
1	ITALIAN GP	Monza	27	Honda Marlboro McLaren	3.5 McLaren MP4/5B-Honda V10	*Pole/FL*
2	PORTUGUESE GP	Estoril	27	Honda Marlboro McLaren	3.5 McLaren MP4/5B-Honda V10	*pit stop-tyres*
ret	SPANISH GP	Jerez	27	Honda Marlboro McLaren	3.5 McLaren MP4/5B-Honda V10	*punctured radiator/engine/Pole*
ret	JAPANESE GP	Suzuka	27	Honda Marlboro McLaren	3.5 McLaren MP4/5B-Honda V10	*collision with Prost/Pole*
ret	AUSTRALIAN GP	Adelaide	27	Honda Marlboro McLaren	3.5 McLaren MP4/5B-Honda V10	*missed 2nd gear-crashed/Pole*

1991 World Champion Driver

1	US GP (PHOENIX)	Phoenix	1	Honda Marlboro McLaren	3.5 McLaren MP4/6-Honda V12	*Pole*
1	BRAZILIAN GP	Interlagos	1	Honda Marlboro McLaren	3.5 McLaren MP4/6-Honda V12	*lost 3rd-5th gears/Pole*
1	SAN MARINO GP	Imola	1	Honda Marlboro McLaren	3.5 McLaren MP4/6-Honda V12	*Pole*
1	MONACO GP	Monte Carlo	1	Honda Marlboro McLaren	3.5 McLaren MP4/6-Honda V12	*Pole*
ret	CANADIAN GP	Montreal	1	Honda Marlboro McLaren	3.5 McLaren MP4/6-Honda V12	*electrics/alternator*
3	MEXICAN GP	Mexico City	1	Honda Marlboro McLaren	3.5 McLaren MP4/6-Honda V12	
3	FRENCH GP	Magny Cours	1	Honda Marlboro McLaren	3.5 McLaren MP4/6-Honda V12	
4	BRITISH GP	Silverstone	1	Honda Marlboro McLaren	3.5 McLaren MP4/6-Honda V12	*out of fuel/1 lap behind*
7	GERMAN GP	Hockenheim	1	Honda Marlboro McLaren	3.5 McLaren MP4/6-Honda V12	*out of fuel/1 lap behind*
1	HUNGARIAN GP	Hungaroring	1	Honda Marlboro McLaren	3.5 McLaren MP4/6-Honda V12	*Pole*
1	BELGIAN GP	Spa	1	Honda Marlboro McLaren	3.5 McLaren MP4/6-Honda V12	*Pole*
2	ITALIAN GP	Monza	1	Honda Marlboro McLaren	3.5 McLaren MP4/6-Honda V12	*Pole/FL*
2	PORTUGUESE GP	Estoril	1	Honda Marlboro McLaren	3.5 McLaren MP4/6-Honda V12	
5	SPANISH GP	Barcelona	1	Honda Marlboro McLaren	3.5 McLaren MP4/6-Honda V12	*spin*
2	JAPANESE GP	Suzuka	1	Honda Marlboro McLaren	3.5 McLaren MP4/6-Honda V12	*allowed Berger to win/FL*
1	AUSTRALIAN GP	Adelaide	1	Honda Marlboro McLaren	3.5 McLaren MP4/6-Honda V12	*rain shortened race-half points/Pole*

1992

3	SOUTH AFRICAN GP	Kyalami	1	Honda Marlboro McLaren	3.5 McLaren MP4/6B-Honda V12	
ret	MEXICAN GP	Mexico City	1	Honda Marlboro McLaren	3.5 McLaren MP4/6B-Honda V12	*transmission*
ret	BRAZILIAN GP	Interlagos	1	Honda Marlboro McLaren	3.5 McLaren MP4/7A-Honda V12	*electrics*
	"	"	1	Honda Marlboro McLaren	3.5 McLaren MP4/6B-Honda V12	*practice only*
9/ret	SPANISH GP	Barcelona	1	Honda Marlboro McLaren	3.5 McLaren MP4/7A-Honda V12	*spun off/3 laps behind*
3	SAN MARINO GP	Imola	1	Honda Marlboro McLaren	3.5 McLaren MP4/7A-Honda V12	
1	MONACO GP	Monte Carlo	1	Honda Marlboro McLaren	3.5 McLaren MP4/7A-Honda V12	
ret	CANADIAN GP	Montreal	1	Honda Marlboro McLaren	3.5 McLaren MP4/7A-Honda V12	*electrics/Pole*
ret	FRENCH GP	Magny Cours	1	Honda Marlboro McLaren	3.5 McLaren MP4/7A-Honda V12	*collision damage lap 1*
ret	BRITISH GP	Silverstone	1	Honda Marlboro McLaren	3.5 McLaren MP4/7A-Honda V12	*transmission*
2	GERMAN GP	Hockenheim	1	Honda Marlboro McLaren	3.5 McLaren MP4/7A-Honda V12	
1	HUNGARIAN GP	Hungaroring	1	Honda Marlboro McLaren	3.5 McLaren MP4/7A-Honda V12	
5	BELGIAN GP	Spa	1	Honda Marlboro McLaren	3.5 McLaren MP4/7A-Honda V12	*gambled to stay on slicks*
1	ITALIAN GP	Monza	1	Honda Marlboro McLaren	3.5 McLaren MP4/7A-Honda V12	
3	PORTUGUESE GP	Estoril	1	Honda Marlboro McLaren	3.5 McLaren MP4/7A-Honda V12	*pit stops-handling/1 lap behind/FL*
ret	JAPANESE GP	Suzuka	1	Honda Marlboro McLaren	3.5 McLaren MP4/7A-Honda V12	*engine*
ret	AUSTRALIAN GP	Adelaide	1	Honda Marlboro McLaren	3.5 McLaren MP4/7A-Honda V12	*ran into back of Mansell*

1993

2	SOUTH AFRICAN GP	Kyalami	8	Marlboro McLaren	3.5 McLaren MP4/8-Ford HB V8	
1	BRAZILIAN GP	Interlagos	8	Marlboro McLaren	3.5 McLaren MP4/8-Ford HB V8	
1	EUROPEAN GP	Donington	8	Marlboro McLaren	3.5 McLaren MP4/8-Ford HB V8	*FL*(set via pit lane without stopping)*
ret	SAN MARINO GP	Imola	8	Marlboro McLaren	3.5 McLaren MP4/8-Ford HB V8	*hydraulic failure*
2	SPANISH GP	Barcelona	8	Marlboro McLaren	3.5 McLaren MP4/8-Ford HB V8	
1	MONACO GP	Monte Carlo	8	Marlboro McLaren	3.5 McLaren MP4/8-Ford HB V8	*6th Monaco win-new record*
18/ret	CANADIAN GP	Montreal	8	Marlboro McLaren	3.5 McLaren MP4/8-Ford HB V8	*electrics/7 laps behind*
4	FRENCH GP	Magny Cours	8	Marlboro McLaren	3.5 McLaren MP4/8-Ford HB V8	
5/ret	BRITISH GP	Silverstone	8	Marlboro McLaren	3.5 McLaren MP4/8-Ford HB V8	*out of fuel-last lap/1 lap behind*
4	GERMAN GP	Hockenheim	8	Marlboro McLaren	3.5 McLaren MP4/8-Ford HB V8	*collision-spin lap 1*
ret	HUNGARIAN GP	Hungaroring	8	Marlboro McLaren	3.5 McLaren MP4/8-Ford HB V8	*throttle*
4	BELGIAN GP	Spa	8	Marlboro McLaren	3.5 McLaren MP4/8-Ford HB V8	
ret	ITALIAN GP	Monza	8	Marlboro McLaren	3.5 McLaren MP4/8-Ford HB V8	*ran into back of Brundle*
ret	PORTUGUESE GP	Estoril	8	Marlboro McLaren	3.5 McLaren MP4/8-Ford HB V8	*engine*
1	JAPANESE GP	Suzuka	8	Marlboro McLaren	3.5 McLaren MP4/8-Ford HB V8	
1	AUSTRALIAN GP	Adelaide	8	Marlboro McLaren	3.5 McLaren MP4/8-Ford HB V8	*Pole*

GP Starts: 158   GP Wins: 41   Pole positions: 62   Fastest laps: 19   Points: 614

DORINO SERAFINI

This ex-Gilera motor cycle racer's career prospects on four wheels were spoilt by a very serious accident in the 1947 Comminges GP when the steering column failed on his Maserati. It put him out of action for some time, and he was never quite the same prospect subsequently. Joining Ferrari for 1950, Serafini shared the second-place Ferrari with Ascari in his only Grand Prix start, and took a number of other second places – notably at Pedralbes, in the F1 car, and in the Eva Peron Cup race at Buenos Aires and the Circuit of Garda with the F2 T166.

It was much the same story in 1951 with second places again in both the Syracuse and San Remo GPs, before another big accident – this time in the Mille Miglia – left him with a broken arm and leg. Thereafter Dorino raced less frequently but he returned to contest the 1954 Brescia-Rome-Brescia classic, taking seventh place overall and first in the GT class with his Lancia.

CHICO SERRA

A contemporary and bitter rival of fellow countryman Nelson Piquet, Serra enjoyed an outstanding Formula Ford season in 1977, winning the Townsend Thoresen FF1600 championship, before stepping into Formula 3 with the Ron Dennis-run Project Four March. It was a strong year, with Piquet and Warwick among the opposition, but Chico was unflustered, escaping a huge accident at Mallory Park to finish third in the Vandervell series and joint-second with Warwick in the BP championship.

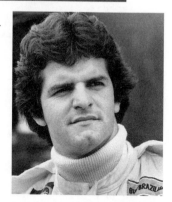

Back in Formula 3 in 1979, Serra made no mistake, winning the 20-round Vandervell championship, taking five victories and seven second places, and putting his Project Four March on the front row no fewer than 16 times. Moving into Formula 2 along with the team, Chico found the going tough, being very much the number two driver to Andrea de Cesaris.

Joining Emerson Fittipaldi to race his fading team's cars in Grands Prix, Serra struggled, but when he managed to get the car onto the grid more often than not brought it home to the finish, gaining his only championship point at Zolder in 1982. After the team closed its doors, Serra briefly raced the Arrows while Alan Jones prevaricated over the prospect of a GP comeback with the team, before losing out to Thierry Boutsen. A dispirited Serra returned to his homeland, no doubt ruefully watching Piquet's continued success. He didn't turn his back on the sport, however, and continues to race saloons in his native Brazil.

SERAFINI, Dorino (I) b 22/7/1909

1950

	Race	Circuit	No	Entrant	Car/Engine	Comment
2*	ITALIAN GP	Monza	48	Scuderia Ferrari	4.5 Ferrari 375F1 V12	* car taken over by Ascari

GP Starts: 1   GP Wins: 0   Pole positions: 0   Fastest laps: 0   Points: 3

SERRA, Chico (Francisco) (BR) b 3/2/1957

1981

	Race	Circuit	No	Entrant	Car/Engine	Comment
7	US GP WEST	Long Beach	21	Fittipaldi Automotive	3.0 Fittipaldi F8C-Cosworth V8	2 laps behind
ret	BRAZILIAN GP	Rio	21	Fittipaldi Automotive	3.0 Fittipaldi F8C-Cosworth V8	startline collision
ret	ARGENTINE GP	Buenos Aires	21	Fittipaldi Automotive	3.0 Fittipaldi F8C-Cosworth V8	gearbox
dnq	SAN MARINO GP	Imola	21	Fittipaldi Automotive	3.0 Fittipaldi F8C-Cosworth V8	
ret	BELGIAN GP	Zolder	211	Fittipaldi Automotive	3.0 Fittipaldi F8C-Cosworth V8	engine
dnq	MONACO GP	Monte Carlo	21	Fittipaldi Automotive	3.0 Fittipaldi F8C-Cosworth V8	
11	SPANISH GP	Jarama	21	Fittipaldi Automotive	3.0 Fittipaldi F8C-Cosworth V8	1 lap behind
dns	FRENCH GP	Dijon	21	Fittipaldi Automotive	3.0 Fittipaldi F8C-Cosworth V8	accident in warm-up
dnq	BRITISH GP	Silverstone	21	Fittipaldi Automotive	3.0 Fittipaldi F8C-Cosworth V8	
dnq	GERMAN GP	Hockenheim	21	Fittipaldi Automotive	3.0 Fittipaldi F8C-Cosworth V8	
dnq	DUTCH GP	Zandvoort	21	Fittipaldi Automotive	3.0 Fittipaldi F8C-Cosworth V8	
dnq	ITALIAN GP	Monza	21	Fittipaldi Automotive	3.0 Fittipaldi F8C-Cosworth V8	
dnq	CANADIAN GP	Montreal	21	Fittipaldi Automotive	3.0 Fittipaldi F8C-Cosworth V8	
dnq	CAESARS PALACE GP	Las Vegas	21	Fittipaldi Automotive	3.0 Fittipaldi F8C-Cosworth V8	

1982

	Race	Circuit	No	Entrant	Car/Engine	Comment
17	SOUTH AFRICAN GP	Kyalami	20	Fittipaldi Automotive	3.0 Fittipaldi F8D-Cosworth V8	5 laps behind
ret	BRAZILIAN GP	Rio	20	Fittipaldi Automotive	3.0 Fittipaldi F8D-Cosworth V8	spun off
dnq	US GP WEST	Long Beach	20	Fittipaldi Automotive	3.0 Fittipaldi F8D-Cosworth V8	
6	BELGIAN GP	Zolder	20	Fittipaldi Automotive	3.0 Fittipaldi F8D-Cosworth V8	3 laps behind
dnq	MONACO GP	Monte Carlo	20	Fittipaldi Automotive	3.0 Fittipaldi F8D-Cosworth V8	
11	US GP (DETROIT)	Detroit	20	Fittipaldi Automotive	3.0 Fittipaldi F8D-Cosworth V8	3 laps behind
dnq	CANADIAN GP	Montreal	20	Fittipaldi Automotive	3.0 Fittipaldi F8D-Cosworth V8	
ret	DUTCH GP	Zandvoort	20	Fittipaldi Automotive	3.0 Fittipaldi F8D-Cosworth V8	fuel pump
ret	BRITISH GP	Brands Hatch	20	Fittipaldi Automotive	3.0 Fittipaldi F8D-Cosworth V8	accident with Jarier
dnq	FRENCH GP	Paul Ricard	20	Fittipaldi Automotive	3.0 Fittipaldi F9-Cosworth V8	
11	GERMAN GP	Hockenheim	20	Fittipaldi Automotive	3.0 Fittipaldi F9-Cosworth V8	2 laps behind
7	AUSTRIAN GP	Österreichring	20	Fittipaldi Automotive	3.0 Fittipaldi F9-Cosworth V8	3 laps behind
dnq	SWISS GP	Dijon	20	Fittipaldi Automotive	3.0 Fittipaldi F9-Cosworth V8	
11	ITALIAN GP	Monza	20	Fittipaldi Automotive	3.0 Fittipaldi F9-Cosworth V8	3 laps behind
dnq	CAESARS PALACE GP	Las Vegas	20	Fittipaldi Automotive	3.0 Fittipaldi F9-Cosworth V8	

1983

	Race	Circuit	No	Entrant	Car/Engine	Comment
9	BRAZILIAN GP	Rio	30	Arrows Racing Team	3.0 Arrows A6-Cosworth V8	1 lap behind
ret	FRENCH GP	Paul Ricard	30	Arrows Racing Team	3.0 Arrows A6-Cosworth V8	gearbox
8	SAN MARINO GP	Imola	30	Arrows Racing Team	3.0 Arrows A6-Cosworth V8	2 laps behind
7	MONACO GP	Monte Carlo	30	Arrows Racing Team	3.0 Arrows A6-Cosworth V8	2 laps behind

GP Starts: 18   GP Wins: 0   Pole positions: 0   Fastest laps: 0   Points: 1

SERRURIER, Doug (ZA) b 9/12/1920

1962

	Race	Circuit	No	Entrant	Car/Engine	Comment
ret	SOUTH AFRICAN GP	East London	21	Otelle Nucci	1.5 LDS 06-Alfa Romeo 4	radiator leak
	1963					
11	SOUTH AFRICAN GP	East London	16	Otelle Nucci	1.5 LDS 06-Alfa Romeo 4	7 laps behind
	1965					
dnq	SOUTH AFRICAN GP	East London	21	Otelle Nucci	1.5 LDS 07-Climax 4	

GP Starts: 2   GP Wins: 0   Pole positions: 0   Fastest laps: 0   Points: 0

SERVOZ-GAVIN, Johnny (Georges) (F) b 18/1/1942

1967

	Race	Circuit	No	Entrant	Car/Engine	Comment
ret	MONACO GP	Monte Carlo	2	Matra Sports	1.6 Matra MS7-Cosworth 4 F2	fuel injection unit drive
	1968					
ret	MONACO GP	Monte Carlo	11	Matra International	3.0 Matra MS10-Cosworth V8	hit chicane-broken driveshaft
ret	FRENCH GP	Rouen	32	Cooper Car Co	3.0 Cooper T86B-BRM V12	spun off-hit tree
2	ITALIAN GP	Monza	5	Matra International	3.0 Matra MS10-Cosworth V8	
ret	CANADIAN GP	St Jovite	15	Matra International	3.0 Matra MS10-Cosworth V8	spun off
ret	MEXICAN GP	Mexico City	23	Matra International	3.0 Matra MS10-Cosworth V8	engine/8 laps behind
	1969					
ret	GERMAN GP (F2)	Nürburgring	27	Matra International	1.6 Matra MS7-Cosworth 4	engine/FL-F2 class
6	CANADIAN GP	Mosport Park	19	Matra International	3.0 Matra MS84-Cosworth V8	6 laps behind
7	US GP	Watkins Glen	16	Matra International	3.0 Matra MS84-Cosworth V8	2 p stops-rear wheel bearing/-16 laps
8	MEXICAN GP	Mexico City	16	Matra International	3.0 Matra MS84-Cosworth V8	2 laps behind
	1970					
ret	SOUTH AFRICAN GP	Kyalami	2	Tyrrell Racing Organisation	3.0 March 701-Cosworth V8	engine
5	SPANISH GP	Jarama	16	Tyrrell Racing Organisation	3.0 March 701-Cosworth V8	
dnq	MONACO GP	Monte Carlo	20	Tyrrell Racing Organisation	3.0 March 701-Cosworth V8	

GP Starts: 12   GP Wins: 0   Pole positions: 0   Fastest laps: 0   Points: 9

SETTEMBER, Tony (USA) b 1930

1962

	Race	Circuit	No	Entrant	Car/Engine	Comment
11	BRITISH GP	Aintree	40	Emeryson Cars	1.5 Emeryson 1004-Climax 4	4 laps behind
ret	ITALIAN GP	Monza	48	Emeryson Cars	1.5 Emeryson 1004-Climax 4	cylinder head gasket
	1963					
8/ret	BELGIAN GP	Spa	24	Scirocco Powell (Racing Cars)	1.5 Scirocco 01-BRM V8	accident/5 laps behind
ret	FRENCH GP	Reims	38	Scirocco Powell (Racing Cars)	1.5 Scirocco 01-BRM V8	rear hub bearing
ret	BRITISH GP	Silverstone	15	Scirocco Powell (Racing Cars)	1.5 Scirocco 01-BRM V8	ignition
ret	GERMAN GP	Nürburgring	23	Scirocco Powell (Racing Cars)	1.5 Scirocco 01-BRM V8	accident
dnq	ITALIAN GP	Monza	34	Scirocco Powell (Racing Cars)	1.5 Scirocco 01-BRM V8	

GP Starts: 6   GP Wins: 0   Pole positions: 0   Fastest laps: 0   Points: 0

SHARP, 'Hap' (James R) (USA) b 1/1/1928 – d 5/1993

1961

	Race	Circuit	No	Entrant	Car/Engine	Comment
10	US GP	Watkins Glen	3	'Hap' Sharp	1.5 Cooper T53-Climax 4	3rd works car/7 laps behind
	1962					
11	US GP	Watkins Glen	24	'Hap' Sharp	1.5 Cooper T53-Climax 4	9 laps behind
	1963					
ret	US GP	Watkins Glen	22	Reg Parnell (Racing)	1.5 Lotus 24-BRM V8	engine
7	MEXICAN GP	Mexico City	22	Reg Parnell (Racing)	1.5 Lotus 24-BRM V8	4 laps behind
	1964					
nc	US GP	Watkins Glen	23	Rob Walker Racing Team	1.5 Brabham BT11-BRM V8	long stop engine/45 laps behind
13	MEXICAN GP	Mexico City	23	Rob Walker Racing Team	1.5 Brabham BT11-BRM V8	5 laps behind

GP Starts: 6   GP Wins: 0   Pole positions: 0   Fastest laps: 0   Points: 0

SHAWE-TAYLOR, Brian (GB) b 29/1/1913

1950

	Race	Circuit	No	Entrant	Car/Engine	Comment
10*	BRITISH GP	Silverstone	10	Joe Fry	1.5 s/c Maserati 4CL 4	* Fry also drove/6 laps behind
	1951					
dns	FRENCH GP	Reims	26	G A Vandervell	4.5 Ferrari 375F1	Parnell drove car
8	BRITISH GP	Silverstone	9	Brian Shawe-Taylor	1.5 s/c ERA B Type 6	6 laps behind

GP Starts: 2   GP Wins: 0   Pole positions: 0   Fastest laps: 0   Points: 0

DOUG SERRURIER

A mainstay of the South African motor racing scene as driver, constructor and later entrant, Doug – a former speedway rider – initially raced a Triumph TR2 in the mid-fifties, before starting work on the first of his LDS specials. This led to his Cooper-based LDS-Alfa of 1961, and a series of these gradually evolving cars, later based upon Brabham designs, were then developed during the early sixties, to be driven, for the main part, by Serrurier himself and another veteran, Sam Tingle.

By 1966 it was becoming increasingly impractical to compete with the major constructors, so, after sharing Roy Pierpoint's Lola T70 to take second place in the Cape Town 3 Hours, Serrurier decided to buy one of these cars, which he then shared with Jackie Pretorious, winning the Roy Hesketh 3 Hours in 1967. After retiring from racing at the end of 1969, Serrurier entered Pretorious in the South African series with a Surtees.

JOHNNY SERVOZ-GAVIN

Georges 'Johnny' Servoz-Gavin was the handsome blond playboy racer who loved the good life, but significantly he also possessed a great deal of talent.

After being thrown out of the Winfield driving school in 1963, 'Johnny' did a little rallying in 1964, before spending all his money on a Brabham for 1965. He was wild but fast, taking fourth place in the French F3 series to earn a drive with Matra in 1966. Promoted to the Matra Formula 2 team for 1967, his results were moderate, and only a splendid fourth in the F1/F2 non-title Spanish GP kept him on board.

An accident to Jackie Stewart early in 1968 brought the Frenchman a glorious opportunity to show his ability. In Ken Tyrrell's Matra he sensationally led the Monaco GP, but clipped a barrier which broke a driveshaft. Later in the season he redeemed himself with a superb second place in the Italian GP, but he still lacked a full-time Grand Prix ride. For 1969 he concentrated on the European F2 championship, and with victory in the Rome GP took the title of top non-graded driver. In Grands Prix, he was mainly entrusted with the Matra MS84, and succeeded in gaining a point with it at Mosport, the only time any 4WD car achieved this feat.

For 1970, 'Johnny' was paired with Jackie Stewart in the Tyrrell team, running the difficult March 701. He finished fifth in the Spanish GP, but failed to qualify at Monaco, which caused him suddenly to announce his retirement. Ultimately he had decided that the risks inherent in racing at the time were not worthwhile, but there was also, apparently, a problem with his vision, which may have been the deciding factor.

TONY SETTEMBER

A Calfornian of Italian descent, Tony raced Corvettes and a Mercedes 300SL in the States before coming to Europe, initially driving a WRE-Maserati sports car, and taking a win in the Naples GP at Posillipo but little else before returning home. After persuading his wealthy friend Hugh Powell to provide suitable funding, Settember commissioned Emeryson to build a chassis for the 1962 season, but the driver did not fit the car properly and relationships in the team became strained when no success was achieved.

In the event Paul Emery departed before the season was out, and the two Americans formed the Scirocco-Powell team for 1963, using BRM power. The car was attractive but slow, Settember being flattered by an inherited second-place finish in the non-championship Austrian GP, some five laps down. When Powell finally called a halt to proceedings, Settember continued his racing activities in the US with Lotus 23 and 30 sports cars, and then an AC Cobra, before trying his hand at Can-Am in the late sixties with a Lola T70. He reappeared in the early seventies in the L & M F5000 series between 1972 and 1974, but never seriously threatened the front-runners.

'HAP' SHARP

A Texan involved in the oil-drilling business, Sharp was a long-time associate of Jim Hall who became closely involved in the Chaparral project, mainly racing in the USRRC series. In 1964, 'Hap' was fifth overall in the championship and also won the Nassau Trophy teamed with Roger Penske. Improving on this the following year, he took third overall in the series and won the Sebring 12 Hours with Hall, recording six other big wins including another Nassau victory.

A great Formula 1 enthusiast, Sharp had the wherewithal to arrange a succession of Grand Prix drives on the North American continent in the early sixties, coming close to scoring a point in Mexico City in 1963 in Reg Parnell's Lotus-BRM. After retiring from the sport, Sharp suffered from personal problems which resulted in his suicide in May 1993.

BRIAN SHAWE-TAYLOR

A garage proprietor from Gloucestershire, Shawe-Taylor had gained success before the war, winning the 1939 Nuffield Trophy, and after the hostilities he reappeared with a B-Type ERA. When his entry for the 1950 British GP was refused on the grounds that his car was too old, he shared Joe Fry's Maserati instead. He was developing a reputation as a very quick driver, and in 1951 he practised Tony Vandervell's Ferrari at Reims, but in the event Parnell raced the car.

Having scored some good placings with the ERA at Goodwood (second in both the Richmond Trophy and the Chichester Cup), Brian was granted an entry for the British GP, and succeeded in finishing eighth, the first privateer home. He shared a works Aston Martin with Abecassis at Le Mans and finished fifth, before an accident in the Daily Graphic Trophy at Goodwood, when he spun the ERA and was hit by Branca's car. Seriously injured, this promising driver recovered, but never raced again.

SHELBY, Carroll (USA) b 11/1/1923

1958

	Race	Circuit	No	Entrant	Car/Engine	Comment
ret	FRENCH GP	Reims	28	Scuderia Centro Sud	2.5 Maserati 250F 6	engine
9	BRITISH GP	Silverstone	5	Scuderia Centro Sud	2.5 Maserati 250F 6	
9/ret	PORTUGUESE GP	Oporto	28	Temple Buell	2.5 Maserati 250F 6	crashed-brakes
ret	ITALIAN GP	Monza	34	Temple Buell	2.5 Maserati 250F 6	mechanical
4*	"	"	32	Scuderia Centro Sud	2.5 Maserati 250F 6	Gregory's car-*no pts-not nominated

1959

	Race	Circuit	No	Entrant	Car/Engine	Comment
ret	DUTCH GP	Zandvoort	5	David Brown Corporation	2.5 Aston-Martin DBR4/250 6	engine
11/ret	BRITISH GP	Aintree	4	David Brown Corporation	2.5 Aston-Martin DBR4/250 6	magneto
8	PORTUGUESE GP	Monsanto	9	David Brown Corporation	2.5 Aston-Martin DBR4/250 6	4 laps behind
10	ITALIAN GP	Monza	26	David Brown Corporation	2.5 Aston-Martin DBR4/250 6	2 laps behind

GP Starts: 2   GP Wins: 0   Pole positions: 0   Fastest laps: 0   Points: 0

SHELLY, Tony (NZ) b 2/2/1937

1962

	Race	Circuit	No	Entrant	Car/Engine	Comment
ret	BRITISH GP	Aintree	48	John Dalton	1.5 Lotus 18/21-Climax 4	cylinder head gasket
dnq	GERMAN GP	Nürburgring	29	John Dalton	1.5 Lotus 18/21-Climax 4	
dnq	ITALIAN GP	Monza	60	Autosport Team Wolfgang Seidel	1.5 Lotus 24-BRM V8	

GP Starts: 1   GP Wins: 0   Pole positions: 0   Fastest laps: 0   Points: 0

CARROLL SHELBY

This hard-bitten Texan began racing in 1952 with an MG TC, winning his first event. He soon progressed to more potent machinery with an Allard-Cadillac and a Ferrari in 1953, and the following season he competed abroad for the first time, racing in Argentina before coming over to Europe to drive David Brown's Aston Martin DB3S.

In 1955 Shelby continued to race in sports car events, sharing a Ferrari with Phil Hill to take second place in the Sebring 12 Hours, and also made his F1 debut for Maserati with a sixth place in the Syracuse GP. Staying in the US for 1956, Carroll virtually swept the board in SCCA circles, winning 27 races – 19 of them consecutively – in his Ferrari. Driving a Ferrari for John Edgar in 1957, Shelby finished second to Fangio in the Cuban GP, and he continued his winning ways in SCCA, overcoming a nasty crash at Riverside in which he sustained facial injuries.

Tempted back to Europe in 1958, Shelby raced the outdated Maserati 250F, and was unfortunate to be stripped of his points at Monza after taking over Gregory's car to earn a fourth-place finish. He also renewed his association with Aston Martin, finishing third with Lewis-Evans in the Tourist Trophy at Goodwood to set up a full season in both Formula 1 and sports cars in 1959.

The Grand Prix project was a huge disappointment. Although the front-engined cars were beautifully made, their reliability was suspect and they were unable to compete with the fleet little Coopers. In direct contrast, the sports car programme went well and the Feltham team eventually took the World Sports Car Championship, Carroll playing his part by winning the Le Mans 24 Hours with Salvadori, and the Tourist Trophy at Goodwood with Moss and Fairman.

In 1960 Shelby competed in SCCA events once more, but by this time he was suffering from heart trouble, and retired at season's end. It was the beginning of a new chapter, though, as Shelby was to gain even greater fame, first developing the AC Cobra, and then overseeing Ford's massive and ultimately successful assault on the Le Mans 24-hour race.

TONY SHELLY

A popular New Zealander who made a promising start to his career by winning the first big race he contested at Teretonga with a Cooper in 1958, Shelly became a leading driver down-under before coming to Europe in 1962 to race, mainly in non-championship events, for John Dalton. Considering his unfamiliarity with the tracks, Tony acquitted himself very well, taking his four-cylinder Lotus 18 into fifth place in the Lombank Trophy, and following that with a third in the Lavant Cup. He went back to New Zealand at the end of the season and never returned, racing down-under in 1963-64 before retiring, though he did have occasional outings in later years.

JO SIFFERT

Siffert could be a wild and hairy driver, but how the fans loved him, perhaps because he was a man who chanced his arm a little more than most. Chiefly remembered for the 1968 British Grand Prix when, in Rob Walker's dark-blue Lotus 49, he withstood all Chris Amon's attempts to pass in the Ferrari to take a fairy-tale victory, 'Seppi' was a very underrated Grand Prix driver, having spent the bulk of his career uncomplainingly in second-rank equipment. He had the heart of a lion and, despite his frail appearance, was an immensely tough and doughty competitor – no doubt born of his motor cycling career, during which he won the 350 cc Swiss championship on a Gilera and passengered Edgar Strub in the 1959 sidecar World Championship.

Siffert's first competition on four wheels came in 1960 when he raced in Formula Junior, but he really came to prominence the following year when, driving a Lotus 21, he won the Eifelrennen race among others to emerge as joint European Formula Junior champion with Tony Maggs. For 1962, Siffert decided to step up to Formula 1 with Ecurie Filipinetti. No results of note were achieved but he plugged away into 1963, buying the Filipinetti Lotus 24-BRM to run as an independent. He finally took a championship point at Reims and also won a poorly supported Syracuse GP and took second in the Imola GP.

Purchasing a Brabham for 1964 increased his Grand Prix competitiveness and he scored a superb win in the Mediterranean GP, in which even the great Jim Clark had to take second best, the final margin being a tenth of a second. Amazingly 'Seppi' was to repeat the victory in 1965 when he again saw off the great Scot, this time by the huge margin of three-tenths of a second! Jo had joined the Walker team at the beginning of the year and was to strike up a wonderful relationship with Rob which saw them through the many tough times that were to follow.

The 1966-67 seasons were a period of struggle when Siffert scraped the occasional point but top-three finishes were achieved only in non-title races. Hopes were high for 1968 when Walker persuaded Colin Chapman to provide him with a Lotus 49, and after the team's wonderful day at Brands Hatch 'Seppi' was a front-runner for the rest of the year and sometimes quicker than the works car of Graham Hill. He was to stay with Rob for one more season which, after a bright start, faded disappointingly. By this time Siffert had established himself as a star of the Porsche sports car team, having won five major races in the 1969 season alone. A tempting offer from Ferrari was dangled in front of him but Porsche, desperate not to lose his services, paid for him to join the STP March team for 1970. It was an absolutely disastrous Grand Prix year for 'Seppi', only partly salvaged by success in Formula 2 with the works BMW and in sports car racing with the Gulf Porsche team, for whom he won the Targa Florio, the Spa 1000 Km and the Österreichring 1000 Km, all with Brian Redman.

Siffert set out on a hectic racing programme in 1971. He joined the BRM Formula 1 team, purchased a Chevron to race in F2 and a Porsche 917 for Can-Am and continued to race the works Porsche with Gulf/John Wyer. The season was a very successful one for 'Seppi'. Apart from his dominant BRM triumph in the Austrian GP, he took plenty of top-three finishes in the other formulae and the popular Swiss had much to look forward to in 1972 when he arrived at Brands Hatch for the season's finale, the Rothmans Victory Race. However, during the race a suspension failure sent the BRM P160 hurtling into a bank, the car bursting into flames. Poor Siffert was trapped in the wreckage and when he was finally extricated was found to have died of asphyxia, having survived the initial impact with a broken leg. Coming so soon after the loss of Pedro Rodriguez, the death of another of the sport's great 'tigers' was hard to bear.

SIFFERT, Jo (CH) b 7/7/1936 – d 24/10/1971

1962

	Race	Circuit	No	Entrant	Car/Engine	Comment
dnq	MONACO GP	Monte Carlo	46	Ecurie Nationale Suisse	1.5 Lotus 21-Climax 4	
10	BELGIAN GP	Spa	22	Ecurie Filipinetti	1.5 Lotus 21-Climax 4	3 laps behind
ret	FRENCH GP	Rouen	40	Ecurie Filipinetti	1.5 Lotus 24-BRM V8	clutch
dns	"	"	40	Ecurie Filipinetti	1.5 Lotus 21-Climax 4	practice only
12	GERMAN GP	Nürburgring	19	Ecurie Filipinetti	1.5 Lotus 21-Climax 4	
dnq	ITALIAN GP	Monza	42	Ecurie Filipinetti	1.5 Lotus 24-BRM V8	

1963

	Race	Circuit	No	Entrant	Car/Engine	Comment
ret	MONACO GP	Monte Carlo	25	Siffert Racing Team	1.5 Lotus 24-BRM V8	engine
ret	BELGIAN GP	Spa	28	Siffert Racing Team	1.5 Lotus 24-BRM V8	crashed in rain storm
7	DUTCH GP	Zandvoort	36	Siffert Racing Team	1.5 Lotus 24-BRM V8	3 laps behind
6	FRENCH GP	Reims	36	Siffert Racing Team	1.5 Lotus 24-BRM V8	1 lap behind
ret	BRITISH GP	Silverstone	25	Siffert Racing Team	1.5 Lotus 24-BRM V8	gearbox
9/ret	GERMAN GP	Nürburgring	18	Siffert Racing Team	1.5 Lotus 24-BRM V8	differential/5 laps behind
ret	ITALIAN GP	Monza	54	Siffert Racing Team	1.5 Lotus 24-BRM V8	oil pressure
ret	US GP	Watkins Glen	14	Siffert Racing Team	1.5 Lotus 24-BRM V8	gearbox
9	MEXICAN GP	Mexico City	14	Siffert Racing Team	1.5 Lotus 24-BRM V8	6 laps behind

1964

	Race	Circuit	No	Entrant	Car/Engine	Comment
nc	MONACO GP	Monte Carlo	24	Siffert Racing Team	1.5 Lotus 24-BRM V8	p stops-misfire etc/22 laps behind
nc	DUTCH GP	Zandvoort	36	Siffert Racing Team	1.5 Brabham BT11-BRM V8	p stops-misfire/25 laps behind
ret	BELGIAN GP	Spa	17	Siffert Racing Team	1.5 Brabham BT11-BRM V8	engine
ret	FRENCH GP	Rouen	30	Siffert Racing Team	1.5 Brabham BT11-BRM V8	clutch
11	BRITISH GP	Brands Hatch	20	Siffert Racing Team	1.5 Brabham BT11-BRM V8	4 laps behind
4	GERMAN GP	Nürburgring	19	Siffert Racing Team	1.5 Brabham BT11-BRM V8	
ret	AUSTRIAN GP	Zeltweg	20	Siffert Racing Team	1.5 Brabham BT11-BRM V8	accident
7	ITALIAN GP	Monza	12	Siffert Racing Team	1.5 Brabham BT11-BRM V8	1 lap behind
3	US GP	Watkins Glen	22	Rob Walker Racing Team	1.5 Brabham BT11-BRM V8	1 lap behind
ret	MEXICAN GP	Mexico City	22	Rob Walker Racing Team	1.5 Brabham BT11-BRM V8	fuel pump

1965

	Race	Circuit	No	Entrant	Car/Engine	Comment
7	SOUTH AFRICAN GP	East London	12	Rob Walker Racing Team	1.5 Brabham BT11-BRM V8	2 laps behind
6	MONACO GP	Monte Carlo	14	Rob Walker Racing Team	1.5 Brabham BT11-BRM V8	2 laps behind

8	BELGIAN GP	Spa	21	Rob Walker Racing Team	1.5 Brabham BT11-BRM V8	*1 lap behind*
6	FRENCH GP	Clermont Ferrand	36	Rob Walker Racing Team	1.5 Brabham BT11-BRM V8	*1 lap behind*
9	BRITISH GP	Silverstone	16	Rob Walker Racing Team	1.5 Brabham BT11-BRM V8	*2 laps behind*
13	DUTCH GP	Zandvoort	28	Rob Walker Racing Team	1.5 Brabham BT11-BRM V8	*long stop-fuel starvation/-25 laps*
ret	GERMAN GP	Nürburgring	17	Rob Walker Racing Team	1.5 Brabham BT11-BRM V8	*engine*
ret	ITALIAN GP	Monza	44	Rob Walker Racing Team	1.5 Brabham BT11-BRM V8	*gearbox*
11	US GP	Watkins Glen	16	Rob Walker Racing Team	1.5 Brabham BT11-BRM V8	*p stop clutch slip/11 laps behind*
4	MEXICAN GP	Mexico City	16	Rob Walker Racing Team	1.5 Brabham BT11-BRM V8	

1966

ret	MONACO GP	Monte Carlo	14	Rob Walker Racing Team	2.0 Brabham BT11-BRM V8	*clutch*
ret	BELGIAN GP	Spa	21	Rob Walker Racing Team	3.0 Cooper T81-Maserati V12	*engine*
ret	FRENCH GP	Reims	38	Rob Walker Racing Team	3.0 Cooper T81-Maserati V12	*overheating*
12	BRITISH GP	Brands Hatch	20	Rob Walker Racing Team	3.0 Cooper T81-Maserati V12	*pit stop-overheating/10 laps behind*
ret	DUTCH GP	Zandvoort	28	Rob Walker Racing Team	3.0 Cooper T81-Maserati V12	*engine*
ret	ITALIAN GP	Monza	36	Rob Walker Racing Team	3.0 Cooper T81-Maserati V12	*engine*
4	US GP	Watkins Glen	19	Rob Walker Racing Team	3.0 Cooper T81-Maserati V12	*3 laps behind*
ret	MEXICAN GP	Mexico City	19	Rob Walker Racing Team	3.0 Cooper T81-Maserati V12	*suspension bolt*

1967

ret	SOUTH AFRICAN GP	Kyalami	12	Rob Walker/Jack Durlacher Racing	3.0 Cooper T81-Maserati V12	*engine*
ret	MONACO GP	Monte Carlo	12	Rob Walker/Jack Durlacher Racing	3.0 Cooper T81-Maserati V12	*engine*
10	DUTCH GP	Zandvoort	12	Rob Walker/Jack Durlacher Racing	3.0 Cooper T81-Maserati V12	*pit stop-overheating/7 laps behind*
7	BELGIAN GP	Spa	12	Rob Walker/Jack Durlacher Racing	3.0 Cooper T81-Maserati V12	*1 lap behind*
4	FRENCH GP	Le Mans	12	Rob Walker/Jack Durlacher Racing	3.0 Cooper T81-Maserati V12	*3 laps behind*
ret	BRITISH GP	Silverstone	12	Rob Walker/Jack Durlacher Racing	3.0 Cooper T81-Maserati V12	*engine*
9/ret	GERMAN GP	Nürburgring	12	Rob Walker/Jack Durlacher Racing	3.0 Cooper T81-Maserati V12	*fuel pump/3 laps behind*
dns	CANADIAN GP	Mosport Park	12	Rob Walker/Jack Durlacher Racing	3.0 Cooper T81-Maserati V12	*starter ring on way to grid*
ret	ITALIAN GP	Monza	12	Rob Walker/Jack Durlacher Racing	3.0 Cooper T81-Maserati V12	*crashed-puncture*
4	US GP	Watkins Glen	12	Rob Walker/Jack Durlacher Racing	3.0 Cooper T81-Maserati V12	*2 laps behind*
12/ret	MEXICAN GP	Mexico City	12	Rob Walker/Jack Durlacher Racing	3.0 Cooper T81-Maserati V12	*engine-no water/6 laps behind*

1968

7	SOUTH AFRICAN GP	Kyalami	19	Rob Walker/Jack Durlacher Racing	3.0 Cooper T81-Maserati V12	*3 laps behind*
ret	SPANISH GP	Jarama	16	Rob Walker/Jack Durlacher Racing	3.0 Lotus 49-Cosworth V8	*transmission vibration*
ret	MONACO GP	Monte Carlo	17	Rob Walker/Jack Durlacher Racing	3.0 Lotus 49-Cosworth V8	*transmission*
ret	BELGIAN GP	Spa	3	Rob Walker/Jack Durlacher Racing	3.0 Lotus 49-Cosworth V8	*oil pressure/3 laps behind*
ret	DUTCH GP	Zandvoort	21	Rob Walker/Jack Durlacher Racing	3.0 Lotus 49-Cosworth V8	*gear selectors*
11	FRENCH GP	Rouen	34	Rob Walker/Jack Durlacher Racing	3.0 Lotus 49-Cosworth V8	*6 laps behind*
1	BRITISH GP	Brands Hatch	22	Rob Walker/Jack Durlacher Racing	3.0 Lotus 49B-Cosworth V8	*FL*
ret	GERMAN GP	Nürburgring	16	Rob Walker/Jack Durlacher Racing	3.0 Lotus 49B-Cosworth V8	*wet ignition*
ret	ITALIAN GP	Monza	20	Rob Walker/Jack Durlacher Racing	3.0 Lotus 49B-Cosworth V8	*shock absorber mounting*
ret	CANADIAN GP	St Jovite	12	Rob Walker/Jack Durlacher Racing	3.0 Lotus 49B-Cosworth V8	*oil leak/FL*
5	US GP	Watkins Glen	16	Rob Walker/Jack Durlacher Racing	3.0 Lotus 49B-Cosworth V8	*pit stop-fuel/3 laps behind*
6	MEXICAN GP	Mexico City	16	Rob Walker/Jack Durlacher Racing	3.0 Lotus 49B-Cosworth V8	*pit stop-throttle/Pole/Fastest lap*

1969

4	SOUTH AFRICAN GP	Kyalami	4	Rob Walker/Jack Durlacher Racing	3.0 Lotus 49B-Cosworth V8	
ret	SPANISH GP	Montjuich Park	10	Rob Walker/Jack Durlacher Racing	3.0 Lotus 49B-Cosworth V8	*engine*
3	MONACO GP	Monte Carlo	9	Rob Walker/Jack Durlacher Racing	3.0 Lotus 49B-Cosworth V8	
2	DUTCH GP	Zandvoort	10	Rob Walker/Jack Durlacher Racing	3.0 Lotus 49B-Cosworth V8	
9	FRENCH GP	Clermont Ferrand	3	Rob Walker/Jack Durlacher Racing	3.0 Lotus 49B-Cosworth V8	*pit stop-damaged nose/-4 laps*
8	BRITISH GP	Silverstone	10	Rob Walker/Jack Durlacher Racing	3.0 Lotus 49B-Cosworth V8	*pit stop-fuel/3 laps behind*
5*/ret	GERMAN GP	Nürburgring	11	Rob Walker/Jack Durlacher Racing	3.0 Lotus 49B-Cosworth V8	*accident/*11th behind F2 cars/-2 laps*
8/ret	ITALIAN GP	Monza	30	Rob Walker/Jack Durlacher Racing	3.0 Lotus 49B-Cosworth V8	*engine/4 laps behind*
ret	CANADIAN GP	Mosport Park	9	Rob Walker/Jack Durlacher Racing	3.0 Lotus 49B-Cosworth V8	*driveshaft*
ret	US GP	Watkins Glen	10	Rob Walker/Jack Durlacher Racing	3.0 Lotus 49B-Cosworth V8	*fuel metering unit drive belt*
ret	MEXICAN GP	Mexico City	10	Rob Walker/Jack Durlacher Racing	3.0 Lotus 49B-Cosworth V8	*collision with Courage*

1970

10	SOUTH AFRICAN GP	Kyalami	16	March Engineering	3.0 March 701-Cosworth V8	*pit stop-broken exhaust/-5 laps*
dnq	SPANISH GP	Jarama	14	March Engineering	3.0 March 701-Cosworth V8	
8	MONACO GP	Monte Carlo	19	March Engineering	3.0 March 701-Cosworth V8	*engine misfire/4 laps behind*
7	BELGIAN GP	Spa	9	March Engineering	3.0 March 701-Cosworth V8	*engine fuel feed/2 laps behind*
ret	DUTCH GP	Zandvoort	9	March Engineering	3.0 March 701-Cosworth V8	*engine*
ret	FRENCH GP	Clermont Ferrand	12	March Engineering	3.0 March 701-Cosworth V8	*accident-locked brakes*
ret	BRITISH GP	Brands Hatch	15	March Engineering	3.0 March 701-Cosworth V8	*rear suspension bracket*
8/ret	GERMAN GP	Hockenheim	12	March Engineering	3.0 March 701-Cosworth V8	*engine/3 laps behind*
9	AUSTRIAN GP	Österreichring	3	March Engineering	3.0 March 701-Cosworth V8	*1 lap behind*
ret	ITALIAN GP	Monza	50	March Engineering	3.0 March 701-Cosworth V8	*engine*
ret	CANADIAN GP	St Jovite	21	March Engineering	3.0 March 701-Cosworth V8	*engine*
9	US GP	Watkins Glen	11	March Engineering	3.0 March 701-Cosworth V8	*pit stop-tyre/3 laps behind*
ret	MEXICAN GP	Mexico City	11	March Engineering	3.0 March 701-Cosworth V8	*engine*

1971

ret	SOUTH AFRICAN GP	Kyalami	17	Yardley-BRM	3.0 BRM P153 V12	*overheating*
ret	SPANISH GP	Montjuich Park	15	Yardley-BRM	3.0 BRM P160 V12	*gear linkage*
ret	MONACO GP	Monte Carlo	14	Yardley-BRM	3.0 BRM P160 V12	*engine*
6	DUTCH GP	Zandvoort	9	Yardley-BRM	3.0 BRM P160 V12	*2 laps behind*
4	FRENCH GP	Paul Ricard	14	Yardley-BRM	3.0 BRM P160 V12	
9	BRITISH GP	Silverstone	16	Yardley-BRM	3.0 BRM P160 V12	*2 p stops-loose condenser/-2 laps*
ret	GERMAN GP	Nürburgring	21	Yardley-BRM	3.0 BRM P160 V12	*suspension*
1	AUSTRIAN GP	Österreichring	14	Yardley-BRM	3.0 BRM P160 V12	*Pole/FL*
9	ITALIAN GP	Monza	20	Yardley-BRM	3.0 BRM P160 V12	*stuck in gear for final laps/-2 laps*
9	CANADIAN GP	Mosport Park	14	Yardley-BRM	3.0 BRM P160 V12	*p stop dirt in nose of car/-3 laps*
2	US GP	Watkins Glen	14	Yardley-BRM	3.0 BRM P160 V12	

GP Starts: 96   GP Wins: 2   Pole positions: 2   Fastest laps: 4   Points: 68

ANDRÉ SIMON

Now a somewhat forgotten figure, Simon was a key member of the Simca-Gordini team in 1950, taking a string of second-place finishes (German GP, Aix-les-Bains, Angoulême, Reims, Geneva and Périgueux) that year. He contnued to race the light-blue cars in both Grands Prix and Formula 2 the following season, winning at Les Sables d'Olonne. For 1952 Simon joined Ferrari but raced in only a few events, although he did share the winning T500 with Ascari at Comminges, and took second place in the Paris GP and the Autodrome GP at Monza, and fourth in the Monaco sports car race.

From 1953 on, André raced intermittently as an independent in both Grands Prix and sports car events, taking a third for Gordini in the 1954 International Trophy. In 1955 he replaced the injured Herrmann in the Mercedes at short notice at Monaco and also raced the German team's sports cars, taking third in the Tourist Trophy. Driving a Maserati 250F, Simon won the Albi GP in 1955, but it was by then a much less important event than in previous years. He raced in a few more Grands Prix without success, his last decent placing being second in the rain-soaked 1956 Caen GP in a Gordini.

Turning to sports car and GT racing, Simon was third in the Paris 1000 Km at Montlhéry in Schlesser's Ferrari, and third in the Auvergne Trophy and Coupe de la Marne Debouteville at Rouen in 1961, also in a Ferrari. In 1962 he won the Tour de France with co-driver Dupeyren – his last major win, though he continued racing through until 1965 when he finished 12th in the Nürburgring 1000 Km in a Ford France AC Cobra with his old friend Jo Schlesser.

MOISES SOLANA

Solana was first and foremost an expert exponent of the sport of jai-alai, and so good was he at this that it provided him with the means to go motor racing, though he rarely competed outside Mexico. In 1962 he arranged to drive a Bowmaker Lola in the non-championship F1 race there, but he rejected the car in practice, claiming it was not satisfactory. From then on he found the cars he drove acceptable, but was unable to score any worthwhile results, despite some excellent qualifying performances, which included seventh fastest for the 1967 US GP.

Most of his sorties outside Mexico were across the border in USRRC races, but he did come to Europe once to race a Lotus 48 F2 car at the Madrid GP in 1967, when he finished 11th. Solana was killed in 1969 while competing in the Valle de Bravo hill-climb when he lost control of his McLaren M6B, which crashed into a bridge and caught fire.

SIMON, André (F) b 5/1/1920

1951

	Race	Circuit	No	Entrant	Car/Engine	Comment
ret	FRENCH GP	Reims	34	Equipe Gordini	1.5 s/c Simca-Gordini Type 15 4	engine
ret	GERMAN GP	Nürburgring	83	Equipe Gordini	1.5 s/c Simca-Gordini Type 15 4	engine
6	ITALIAN GP	Monza	48	Equipe Gordini	1.5 s/c Simca-Gordini Type 15 4	6 laps behind
ret	SPANISH GP	Pedralbes	16	Equipe Gordini	1.5 s/c Simca-Gordini Type 15 4	engine

1952

ret*	SWISS GP	Bremgarten	32	Scuderia Ferrari	2.0 Ferrari 500 4	* Farina took over/magneto
6	ITALIAN GP	Monza	8	Scuderia Ferrari	2.0 Ferrari 500 4	1 lap behind

1955

ret	MONACO GP	Monte Carlo	4	Daimler Benz AG	2.5 Mercedes-Benz W196 8	drove Herrmann's car/oil pipe
dns	" "	16	Ecurie Rosier	2.5 Maserati 250F 6	practice only-drove Mercedes
ret	BRITISH GP	Aintree	8	Officine Alfieri Maserati	2.5 Maserati 250F 6	gearbox

1956

ret	FRENCH GP	Reims	42	André Simon	2.5 Maserati 250F 6	mechanical
9	ITALIAN GP	Monza	12	Equipe Gordini	2.5 Gordini Type 16 8	5 laps behind

1957

dnq	MONACO GP	Monte Carlo	4	Scuderia Centro Sud	2.5 Maserati 250F 6	
nc*	ITALIAN GP	Monza	28	Ottorino Volonterio	2.5 Maserati 250F 6	* Volonterio took over/-15 laps

GP Starts: 11   GP Wins: 0   Pole positions: 0   Fastest laps: 0   Points: 0

SOLANA, Moises (MEX) b 1936 – d 27/7/1969

1963

	Race	Circuit	No	Entrant	Car/Engine	Comment
11/ret	MEXICAN GP	Mexico City	13	Scuderia Centro Sud	1.5 BRM P57 V8	cam follower/8 laps behind
	1964					
10	MEXICAN GP	Mexico City	17	Team Lotus	1.5 Lotus 33-Climax V8	2 laps behind
	1965					
12	US GP	Watkins Glen	18	Team Lotus	1.5 Lotus 25-Climax V8	15 laps behind
ret	MEXICAN GP	Mexico City	18	Team Lotus	1.5 Lotus 25-Climax V8	ignition
	1966					
ret	MEXICAN GP	Mexico City	9	Cooper Car Co	3.0 Cooper T81-Maserati V12	overheating
	1967					
ret	US GP	Watkins Glen	18	Team Lotus	3.0 Lotus 49-Cosworth V8	electrics-ignition
ret	MEXICAN GP	Mexico City	18	Team Lotus	3.0 Lotus 49-Cosworth V8	front suspension
	1968					
ret	MEXICAN GP	Mexico City	12	Gold Leaf Team Lotus	3.0 Lotus 49B-Cosworth V8	collapsed wing

GP Starts: 8   GP Wins: 0   Pole positions: 0   Fastest laps: 0   Points: 0

ALEX SOLER-ROIG

From a wealthy background, this sophisticated Spaniard had the means to try his hand at Formula 1 over a three-year period but it was obvious that he lacked the hunger or speed to be truly competitive.

He won his first event, a hill-climb, in 1960, and continued to race in his own country, usually with a Porsche, until he joined the European Formula 2 circus in 1967 for his first sustained attempt at professional racing. His season with the Lola was not too successful, so in 1968 he switched to sports car and GT racing, winning the Jarama 6 Hours with Rindt, and finishing fourth in the Sebring 12 Hours with Lins, both in Porsches. Alex finished second in the Buenos Aires 1000 Km in 1970 with his Porsche 908, again teamed with Rindt, and cleaned up in Spanish G5/6 races with his Porsche 917. After failing to qualify for a Grand Prix in three attempts with Lotus, Soler-Roig joined March for the 1971 season, but although he made the grids he felt dissatisfied with the engines he was given and quit in mid-season, preferring to concentrate on his drive in the European touring car championship with Ford Germany, which yielded two victories in the Capri, co-driving with Glemser. His short spell in the Marlboro BRM team at the beginning of 1972 was a disaster, but a return to touring cars brought further wins at Zandvoort and Jarama with the help of such talents asGlemser, Mass and Larrousse before Alex called it a day at the end of the season.

RAYMOND SOMMER

Given the format of this book, Raymond Sommer's entry is brief, and unfortunately lack of space prevents me from writing more fully about this truly exceptional individual, who surely epitomised all that is good about motor racing – courage, tenacity, enthusiasm, persistence and sportsmanship.

He first came to fame by defeating the works Alfas in his private machine at Le Mans in 1932, driving for all but three of the 24 hours. The following year he won again, this time with the legendary Nuvolari. Raymond was soon racing in Grands Prix, usually as an independent, for he could not bear the constraints teams might impose. Thus he had to make do with whatever machinery was available, and always drove it to its limits, taking great delight when he managed to beat a car from the mighty Scuderia Ferrari or Mercedes teams. In this context, his record of successes was remarkable, even if he failed to win a monoposto Grand Prix outright before the war, though he did win the French sports car GP with Wimille in 1936.

After the war, Sommer was soon back in action, and in 1946 he enjoyed his best season, which included a famous victory in the GP of St Cloud, when the works Alfa 158s failed. In 1947 he was out of action after inadvertently swallowing some methanol at the Pau GP, but he returned with a semi-works Ferrari the following year, winning the Reims F2 race. Equipping himself with a big Talbot, Sommer was like a cat among the pigeons in 1949, hammering the car for all it was worth and frequently mixing it with the Italians, who viewed his on-the-edge, no-quarter-asked-or-given style with some concern.

He was driving as well as ever in 1950, scoring a fourth place at Monaco in his nimble Formula 2 Ferrari (with which he also took F2 wins at Roubaix, Aix-les-Bains and Bremgarten). He reverted to his Talbot for the later championship Grands Prix, where power was all, but no points were gained. It came as a huge shock when the motor racing world learned of his death while competing in a minor end-of-season 500 cc race at Cadours when, it is thought, a wheel bearing seized on his Cooper.

'MIKE SPARKEN'

This Frenchman was a great amateur enthusiast who raced sports cars under a pseudonym. In 1952 ran an Aston Martin DB2 and won his class at Montlhéry, but much of his success came in North African events. He won the 1955 sports car race at Agadir in his 3-litre Ferrari T750S, which he brought to England and drove impressively in the British Empire Trophy before the clutch failed, and at Goodwood, where he placed second. His only single-seater drive of any note was at the wheel of the works Gordini at the British GP that year.

MIKE SPENCE

Spence overcame polio as a child with no ill effects, and from a young age he harboured dreams of becoming a racing driver. After his Army service was finished he took up club racing in 1958 with a Turner, before going into Formula Junior in 1960 with a Cooper-Austin. He made his Formula 1 debut the following year with an Emeryson-Climax at Solitude, and won the minor Commander York Trophy at Silverstone in the same car. For 1962, Spence entered his own Formula Junior Lotus under the wing of Ian Walker's team, with Mike preparing the car himself in the evenings after his day job was done. He had only one big win – at Reims – but scored many placings and was taken on by Lotus on a three-year contract in 1963.

The fair-haired Englishman drove in the Formula Junior team, but the car proved difficult to handle and Mike's confidence dropped. However, things gradually came round when the car was made more competitive, and he enjoyed a late-season boost when he stood in for the injured Trevor Taylor at Monza. In 1964 Mike was planning a season of Formula 2 and the occasional Grand Prix when he found himself thrust into the F1 team after Arundell's accident. For one so inexperienced he coped well, especially as Peter had made such a big impression in his few starts. Colin Chapman had no hesitation in keeping Spence in the team with Jim Clark for 1965, and he soon repaid that faith by winning the Race of Champions and performing well on other occasions. With Arundell fit to return for 1966, Mike was out of a drive, but he bade farewell by winning the non-championship South African GP on New Year's Day, before spending the rest of the year marking time with Tim Parnell's team. Joining the works BRM line-up for 1967 was a step back up, but he was given the task of sorting the troublesome BRM H16 car and did superbly to bring it to five points finishes. He also raced the fabulous winged Chaparral with Phil Hill, which was quick but fragile, suffering repeated transmission failures, but at Brands Hatch in the BOAC 500 the car had its great day, crushing the Ferraris.

In 1968, Mike Spence had been racing for ten years; it had been a long haul to the top, but suddenly his talent had begun to flower, and he was about to take his rightful place among the very top echelon of his profession. Yet fate would decree otherwise. The shadow of Jim Clark, which had, perhaps inevitably, held him back throughout his years at Lotus, passed over him once more as he took over the late Scotsman's Lotus for the forthcoming Indianapolis 500. In qualifying everything had gone well, but when Spence took a team-mate's car out for a few shakedown laps, he lost control and crashed into the wall. The right-front wheel flew back and struck the driver's head, and poor Spence died in hospital a few hours later.

SOLER-ROIG, Alex (E) b 29/10/1932

1970

	Race	Circuit	No	Entrant	Car/Engine	Comment
dnq	SPANISH GP	Jarama	23	Garvey Team Lotus	3.0 Lotus 49C-Cosworth V8	
dnq	BELGIAN GP	Spa	22	World Wide Racing	3.0 Lotus 72-Cosworth V8	
dnq	FRENCH GP	Clermont Ferrand	9	World Wide Racing	3.0 Lotus 49C-Cosworth V8	

1971

	Race	Circuit	No	Entrant	Car/Engine	Comment
ret	SOUTH AFRICAN GP	Kyalami	26	STP March	3.0 March 711-Cosworth V8	engine
ret	SPANISH GP	Montjuich Park	19	STP March	3.0 March 711-Cosworth V8	fuel line
dnq	MONACO GP	Monte Carlo	18	STP March	3.0 March 711-Cosworth V8	
ret	DUTCH GP	Zandvoort	19	STP March	3.0 March 711-Cosworth V8	engine
ret	FRENCH GP	Paul Ricard	18	STP March	3.0 March 711-Cosworth V8	fuel pump

1972

	Race	Circuit	No	Entrant	Car/Engine	Comment
ret	ARGENTINE GP	Buenos Aires	6	España Marlboro BRM	3.0 BRM P160B V12	accident-stuck throttle
ret	SPANISH GP	Jarama	28	España Marlboro BRM	3.0 BRM P160B V12	accident-no gears

GP Starts: 6 GP Wins: 0 Pole positions: 0 Fastest laps: 0 Points: 0

SOMMER, Raymond (F) b 31/8/1906 – d 10/9/1950

1950

	Race	Circuit	No	Entrant	Car/Engine	Comment
4	MONACO GP	Monte Carlo	42	Scuderia Ferrari	1.5 s/c Ferrari 125/F1	
ret	SWISS GP	Bremgarten	20	Scuderia Ferrari	2.0 Ferrari 166/F2	suspension
ret	BELGIAN GP	Spa	6	Raymond Sommer	4.5 Lago-Talbot T26C 6	engine
ret	FRENCH GP	Reims	12	Automobiles Talbot-Darracq	4.5 Lago-Talbot T26C-GS 6	engine
ret	ITALIAN GP	Monza	12	Raymond Sommer	4.5 Lago-Talbot T26C 6	gearbox

GP Starts: 5 GP Wins: 0 Pole positions: 0 Fastest laps: 0 Points: 3

'SPARKEN, Mike' (Michel Poberejsky) (F) b 16/6/1930

1955

	Race	Circuit	No	Entrant	Car/Engine	Comment
7	BRITISH GP	Aintree	26	Equipe Gordini	2.5 Gordini Type 16 6	9 laps behind

GP Starts: 1 GP Wins: 0 Pole positions: 0 Fastest laps: 0 Points: 0

SPENCE, Mike (GB) b 30/12/1936 – d 7/5/1968

1963

	Race	Circuit	No	Entrant	Car/Engine	Comment
13/ret	ITALIAN GP	Monza	6	Team Lotus	1.5 Lotus 25-Climax V8	oil pressure/13 laps behind

1964

	Race	Circuit	No	Entrant	Car/Engine	Comment
9	BRITISH GP	Brands Hatch	2	Team Lotus	1.5 Lotus 25-Climax V8	3 laps behind
8	GERMAN GP	Nürburgring	2	Team Lotus	1.5 Lotus 33-Climax V8	1 lap behind
dns	"	"	23	Team Lotus	1.5 Lotus 33-Climax V8	practice only-Mitter's car
ret	AUSTRIAN GP	Zeltweg	2	Team Lotus	1.5 Lotus 33-Climax V8	driveshaft
6	ITALIAN GP	Monza	10	Team Lotus	1.5 Lotus 33-Climax V8	1 lap behind
7	US GP	Watkins Glen	2	Team Lotus	1.5 Lotus 33-Climax V8	fuel starvation/Clark took car/-8 laps
ret	"	"	1	Team Lotus	1.5 Lotus 33-Climax V8	fuel injection/given Clark's car
4	MEXICAN GP	Mexico City	2	Team Lotus	1.5 Lotus 25-Climax V8	
dns	"	" "	1	Team Lotus	1.5 Lotus 33-Climax V8	practice only

1965

	Race	Circuit	No	Entrant	Car/Engine	Comment
4	SOUTH AFRICAN GP	East London	6	Team Lotus	1.5 Lotus 33-Climax V8	
7	BELGIAN GP	Spa	18	Team Lotus	1.5 Lotus 33-Climax V8	1 lap behind
7	FRENCH GP	Clermont Ferrand	8	Team Lotus	1.5 Lotus 33-Climax V8	1 lap behind
4	BRITISH GP	Silverstone	6	Team Lotus	1.5 Lotus 33-Climax V8	
dns	"		77	Team Lotus	1.5 Lotus 25-Climax V8	practice only
8	DUTCH GP	Zandvoort	8	Team Lotus	1.5 Lotus 25-Climax V8	1 lap behind
ret	GERMAN GP	Nürburgring	2	Team Lotus	1.5 Lotus 33-Climax V8	driveshaft
11/ret	ITALIAN GP	Monza	26	Team Lotus	1.5 Lotus 33-Climax V8	alternator/13 laps behind
dns	"	"	28	Team Lotus	1.5 Lotus 25-Climax V8	practice only
ret	US GP	Watkins Glen	6	Team Lotus	1.5 Lotus 33-Climax V8	engine
dns	"	" "	18	Team Lotus	1.5 Lotus 25-Climax V8	practice only
3	MEXICAN GP	Mexico City	6	Team Lotus	1.5 Lotus 33-Climax V8	

1966

	Race	Circuit	No	Entrant	Car/Engine	Comment
ret	MONACO GP	Monte Carlo	6	Reg Parnell Racing Ltd	2.0 Lotus 25-BRM V8	rear suspension
ret	BELGIAN GP	Spa	16	Reg Parnell Racing Ltd	2.0 Lotus 25-BRM V8	accident in rain storm
ret	FRENCH GP	Reims	32	Reg Parnell Racing Ltd	2.0 Lotus 25-BRM V8	clutch
ret	BRITISH GP	Brands Hatch	17	Reg Parnell Racing Ltd	2.0 Lotus 25-BRM V8	oil leak
5	DUTCH GP	Zandvoort	32	Reg Parnell Racing Ltd	2.0 Lotus 25-BRM V8	3 laps behind
ret	GERMAN GP	Nürburgring	15	Reg Parnell Racing Ltd	2.0 Lotus 25-BRM V8	electrics
5	ITALIAN GP	Monza	42	Reg Parnell Racing Ltd	2.0 Lotus 25-BRM V8	1 lap behind
ret	US GP	Watkins Glen	18	Reg Parnell Racing Ltd	2.0 Lotus 25-BRM V8	electrics
dns	MEXICAN GP	Mexico City	18	Reg Parnell Racing Ltd	2.0 Lotus 25-BRM V8	accident in practice

1967

	Race	Circuit	No	Entrant	Car/Engine	Comment
ret	SOUTH AFRICAN GP	Kyalami	6	Owen Racing Organisation	3.0 BRM P83 H16	oil pipe
6	MONACO GP	Monte Carlo	5	Owen Racing Organisation	3.0 BRM P83 H16	4 laps behind

8	DUTCH GP	Zandvoort	10	Owen Racing Organisation	3.0 BRM P83 H16	*gearbox problems/3 laps behind*
5	BELGIAN GP	Spa	12	Owen Racing Organisation	3.0 BRM P83 H16	*1 lap behind*
dns	"	"	14	Owen Racing Organisation	2.1 BRM P261 V8	*practice only*
ret	FRENCH GP	Le Mans	11	Owen Racing Organisation	3.0 BRM P83 H16	*driveshaft*
ret	BRITISH GP	Silverstone	4	Owen Racing Organisation	3.0 BRM P83 H16	*ignition*
ret	GERMAN GP	Nürburgring	12	Owen Racing Organisation	3.0 BRM P83 H16	*transmission*
5	CANADIAN GP	Mosport Park	16	Owen Racing Organisation	3.0 BRM P83 H16	*3 laps behind*
5	ITALIAN GP	Monza	36	Owen Racing Organisation	3.0 BRM P83 H16	*1 lap behind*
ret	US GP	Watkins Glen	8	Owen Racing Organisation	3.0 BRM P83 H16	*engine*
5	MEXICAN GP	Mexico City	8	Owen Racing Organisation	3.0 BRM P83 H16	*2 laps behind*
	1968					
ret	SOUTH AFRICAN GP	Kyalami	12	Owen Racing Organisation	3.0 BRM P115 H16	*boiling fuel*
dns	" "	"	11	Owen Racing Organisation	3.0 BRM P126 V12	*practice only-Rodriguez raced car*

GP Starts: 36   GP Wins: 0   Pole positions: 0   Fastest laps: 0   Points: 27

STACEY, Alan (GB) b 29/8/1933 – d 19/6/1960

	1958					
	Race	*Circuit*	*No*	*Entrant*	*Car/Engine*	*Comment*
ret	BRITISH GP	Silverstone	18	Team Lotus	2.0 Lotus 16-Climax 4	*overheating*
	1959					
8	BRITISH GP	Aintree	30	Team Lotus	2.5 Lotus 16-Climax 4	*4 laps behind*
ret	US GP	Sebring	11	Team Lotus	2.5 Lotus 16-Climax 4	*clutch*
	1960					
ret	ARGENTINE GP	Buenos Aires	22	Team Lotus	2.5 Lotus 16-Climax 4	*electrics*
ret	MONACO GP	Monte Carlo	24	Team Lotus	2.5 Lotus 18-Climax 4	*engine mountings*
ret	DUTCH GP	Zandvoort	5	Team Lotus	2.5 Lotus 18-Climax 4	*transmission*
ret	BELGIAN GP	Spa	16	Team Lotus	2.5 Lotus 18-Climax 4	*fatal accident-bird flew in face*

GP Starts: 7   GP Wins: 0   Pole positions: 0   Fastest laps: 0   Points: 0

STARRABBA, Prince Gaetano (I) b 3/12/1932

	1961					
	Race	*Circuit*	*No*	*Entrant*	*Car/Engine*	*Comment*
ret	ITALIAN GP	Monza	72	Prince Gaetano Starrabba	1.5 Lotus 18-Maserati 4	*engine*

GP Starts: 1   GP Wins: 0   Pole positions: 0   Fastest laps: 0   Points: 0

STEWART, Ian (GB) b 15/7/1929

	1953					
	Race	*Circuit*	*No*	*Entrant*	*Car/Engine*	*Comment*
ret	BRITISH GP	Silverstone	15	Ecurie Ecosse	2.0 Connaught A Type-Lea Francis 4	*engine*

GP Starts: 1   GP Wins: 0   Pole positions: 0   Fastest laps: 0   Points: 0

ALAN STACEY

Stacey made his competition debut in 1955 and spent three years in club racing – almost exclusively at the wheel of Lotus XI sports cars. He won seven races with his own car in 1956, before gaining an invitation to drive for the works during the following season.

Alan had the handicap of an artificial lower right leg, but this proved no obstacle to his racing, nor did it seem to limit his competitiveness, otherwise Colin Chapman would certainly not have signed him to race his sports cars full-time for 1958. He won the Farningham Trophy at Brands Hatch, and scored another victory at Crystal Palace, also taking third place in the Rouen GP. Stacey made his Grand Prix debut at Silverstone that year but, in common with his team-mates Innes Ireland and Graham Hill, he was to suffer a frustrating 1959 season as a lack of reliability undermined the Lotus team's efforts in F1, F2 and sports car racing.

With Hill departing for BRM, Alan was promoted to the position of Ireland's number two in 1960, and once the European season started he had one of Chapman's stunning rear-engined Lotus 18s to drive. He finished fourth in the International Trophy race, but retired at both Monaco and Zandvoort, where he lay in third place before transmission trouble. However, during practice for the Belgian GP at Spa the luckless Stacey was hit full in the face by a bird, losing consciousness and crashing to his death.

IAN STEWART

Not related to the brothers Jackie and Jimmy, this young Scot mainly raced his Jaguar XK120 north of the border in 1951, before coming to prominence as a founder member of the Ecurie Ecosse team in 1952, winning the Jersey Road Race, the Wakefield Trophy and other sports car events in their Jaguar C-Type. For 1953, the team laid more ambitious plans, running a Formula 2 Connaught, which Ian handled in the British GP and Libre events, and contesting Continental sports car races, Stewart finishing second in the Nürburgring 1000 Km, with Salvadori, and fourth at Le Mans, with Peter Whitehead.

The following season began with an accident in the Buenos Aires 1000 Km in the team's D-Type from which he escaped with minor injuries, and when he got married shortly afterwards Ian decided to retire from the sport and concentrate on his business interests.

JACKIE STEWART

Jackie Stewart was the driving force behind the transformation of motor racing from a sport where death was almost routine. When Stewart began racing, the risks were blithely accepted with a shrug of the shoulders as an occupational hazard. But the determined little Scot, who was to see many of his friends and colleagues perish, pursued his campaign with remarkable fervour long after his own retirement and he more than any other individual is responsible for the emergence of the highly organised and remarkably safe sport we know today. As if this weren't enough, Stewart was also a truly great racing driver, a triple World Champion who was a more than worthy successor to his great idol Jim Clark.

Motor racing was part of the family as the young Jackie was growing up, for his brother Jimmy – eight years his senior – was a driver for Ecurie Ecosse. Unfortunately a serious crash ended the elder Stewart's career in 1955. However, young Jackie was more interested in clay pigeon shooting. He was an excellent shot, winning many tournaments at home and abroad, and was hoping to take part in the 1960 Rome Olympics, but missed the team when he had an 'off day' at the final trials. It was to be the biggest disappointment of his sporting life, worse than anything that he ever suffered during his racing days.

Jackie's circuit career began in a casual way, at the wheel of a Healey Sprite and a Marcos, before he joined Ecurie Ecosse in 1963. Driving the team's GT and touring cars, Stewart virtually swept the board. While still racing for Ecosse, Jackie came under the guidance of Ken Tyrrell to race a Cooper-BMC in Formula 3, where he set about thrashing the opposition. Colin Chapman tried him in his Ron Harris Formula 2 team and liked what he saw, putting the Scot into a Formula 1 Lotus for the Rand GP at Kyalami, where he retired in the first heat but won the second.

Offered a seat alongside Jim Clark for 1965, Stewart wisely declined, preferring to join BRM, where he could learn his trade with Graham Hill and not face the pressure of being compared directly with his fellow Scot. A second place in the Race of Champions and a win in the International Trophy gave fair notice that here was a special talent, and his Grand Prix performances went from strength to strength, culminating in his first World Championship win at Monza. In the 1966 Tasman series Stewart took the BRM to four victories, and he then won the opening Grand Prix of the year at Monaco in the 2-litre car. Then his luck changed. Victory seemed certain at the Indianapolis 500 until an engine failure close to the finish, and on his return to Europe he crashed the BRM in a rainstorm at Spa. Lying trapped in the car for some time soaked in petrol with a cracked collar-bone was an experience that the Scot would never forget, and no doubt acted as a catalyst for his subsequent safety crusade.

Jackie stayed with BRM for a third season in 1967, but it was a disappointing year with the H16 car proving woefully unreliable. His second place with it in Belgium was a remarkable achievement, especially as he was obliged to hold it in gear for much of the race. The only compensation was a drive for Ferrari in the BOAC 500 at Brands Hatch, where he shared a P4 with Chris Amon, the pair taking second place and clinching the championship for Maranello. Of more importance, however, was his developing working partnership with Ken Tyrrell and Matra, Jackie taking the French Formula 2 car to victory in four of the last five races of the season as a prelude to a Formula 1 effort in 1968.

At last Stewart was in a competitive car, and following the death of Jim Clark he looked the favourite to take the title. Unfortunately his season was interrupted by a crash in a Formula 2 race which sidelined him with a wrist injury. Though he missed only two Grands Prix, it was enough to crucially blunt his title challenge. A feature of the year was his brilliant win in the German GP in the most appalling conditions, truly one of his greatest drives, and there was no stopping him in 1969 as he swept to his first championship with six Grand Prix wins in the Matra MS80, a car he loved to drive.

For the 1970 season Tyrrell was forced to resort to a March chassis, for Matra were running their own operation once more. However, despite a promising start with wins in the Race of Champions and the Spanish GP and a second place in the International Trophy, all was not well. The car was not up to the expectations of a World Champion, and therefore not of the required standard, and Tyrrell secretly set Derek Gardner to work building his own Grand Prix challenger at the greatest possible speed. The new car was unveiled at the Canadian GP where Stewart took pole position. The future was now clear and Tyrrell was henceforth to build his own cars. The 1971 season saw Jackie back at his brilliant best, using the new Tyrrell to devastating effect, winning six Grands Prix and easily taking his second World Championship. He was much in demand that year and undertook the ten-round Can-Am series for Carl Haas. Stewart won two rounds in the Lola, but the strain of trans-Atlantic travel was already taking its toll.

Jackie's health was to suffer in 1972 due to an ulcer which caused him to miss six weeks of the season, enough to see his title chances disappear as an ebullient Emerson Fittipaldi made the most of his opportunities with his Lotus 72. Not that Stewart was about to let his title slip away without a fight. He won the French GP on his return and finished the year on a winning note with back-to-back wins at Mosport and Watkins Glen to sound a warning that he would not be so easy to beat in 1973. And so it was to prove. By this time Stewart was the complete driver, mentally and physically prepared to cope with every eventuality. He won as he pleased at Kyalami, Monte Carlo, Zandvoort and the Nürburgring, thus passing the late Jim Clark's number of wins to set a new record total of 27. His last race in Europe was one of his greatest. As he climbed through the field after a puncture at Monza to take fourth place, it was a stirring sight to see him forced to drive at the limit lap after lap, picking off one car after another.

Jackie had decided to retire after the US GP at Watkins Glen in what would have been his 100th Grand Prix start, but the weekend was to be clouded by tragedy as his team-mate François Cevert was killed in practice. The Tyrrell team withdrew their cars, and the wonderful career of John Young Stewart was over. Since then, of course, Jackie has worked harder than ever. He has been seen regularly at the circuits, imparting his wisdom to a new generation of racers. His son Paul, much against his parents' wishes, has raced with some success, but now runs his own team with a degree of professionalism reflecting the high standards established by his father.

STEWART, Jackie (John Young) (GB) b 11/6/1939

1965

	Race	Circuit	No	Entrant	Car/Engine	Comment
6	SOUTH AFRICAN GP	East London	4	Owen Racing Organisation	1.5 BRM P261 V8	*2 laps behind*
3	MONACO GP	Monte Carlo	4	Owen Racing Organisation	1.5 BRM P261 V8	
2	BELGIAN GP	Spa	8	Owen Racing Organisation	1.5 BRM P261 V8	
2	FRENCH GP	Clermont Ferrand	12	Owen Racing Organisation	1.5 BRM P261 V8	
5	BRITISH GP	Silverstone	4	Owen Racing Organisation	1.5 BRM P261 V8	
2	DUTCH GP	Zandvoort	12	Owen Racing Organisation	1.5 BRM P261 V8	
ret	GERMAN GP	Nürburgring	10	Owen Racing Organisation	1.5 BRM P261 V8	*suspension*
1	ITALIAN GP	Monza	32	Owen Racing Organisation	1.5 BRM P261 V8	
ret	US GP	Watkins Glen	4	Owen Racing Organisation	1.5 BRM P261 V8	*suspension*
ret	MEXICAN GP	Mexico city	4	Owen Racing Organisation	1.5 BRM P261 V8	*clutch*

1966

	Race	Circuit	No	Entrant	Car/Engine	Comment
1	MONACO GP	Monte Carlo	12	Owen Racing Organisation	2.0 BRM P261 V8	
ret	BELGIAN GP	Spa	15	Owen Racing Organisation	2.0 BRM P261 V8	*spun off in rainstorm-injured*
dns	"	"	15	Owen Racing Organisation	3.0 BRM P83 H16	*practice only*
ret	BRITISH GP	Brands Hatch	4	Owen Racing Organisation	2.0 BRM P261 V8	*engine*
4	DUTCH GP	Zandvoort	14	Owen Racing Organisation	2.0 BRM P261 V8	*2 laps behind*
5	GERMAN GP	Nürburgring	6	Owen Racing Organisation	2.0 BRM P261 V8	
ret	ITALIAN GP	Monza	28	Owen Racing Organisation	3.0 BRM P83 H16	*fuel leak*
ret	US GP	Watkins glen	4	Owen Racing Organisation	3.0 BRM P83 H16	*engine*
ret	MEXICAN GP	Mexico City	4	Owen Racing Organisation	3.0 BRM P83 H16	*oil leak*

1967

	Race	Circuit	No	Entrant	Car/Engine	Comment
ret	SOUTH AFRICAN GP	Kyalami	5	Owen Racing Organisation	3.0 BRM P83 H16	*engine*
ret	MONACO GP	Monte Carlo	4	Owen Racing Organisation	2.1 BRM P261 V8	*transmission*
dns	"	"	4T	Owen Racing Organisation	3.0 BRM P83 H16	*practice only*
ret	DUTCH GP	Zandvoort	9	Owen Racing Organisation	3.0 BRM P83 H16	*brakes*
2	BELGIAN GP	Spa	14	Owen Racing Organisation	3.0 BRM P83 H16	
dns	"	"	12	Owen Racing Organisation	2.1 BRM P261 V8	*practice only*
3	FRENCH GP	Le Mans	10	Owen Racing Organisation	2.1 BRM P261 V8	*1 lap behind*
dns	"	"	10	Owen Racing Organisation	3.0 BRM P83 H16	*practice only*
ret	BRITISH GP	Silverstone	3	Owen Racing Organisation	3.0 BRM P83 H16	*transmission*
ret	GERMAN GP	Nürburgring	11	Owen Racing Organisation	3.0 BRM P115 H16	*transmission*
dns	"	"	11	Owen Racing Organisation	3.0 BRM P83 H16	*practice only*
ret	CANADIAN GP	Mosport Park	15	Owen Racing Organisation	3.0 BRM P115 H16	*spun off*
ret	ITALIAN GP	Monza	34	Owen Racing Organisation	3.0 BRM P115 H16	*engine*
ret	US GP	Watkins Glen	7	Owen Racing Organisation	3.0 BRM P115 H16	*fuel metering unit belt*
ret	MEXICAN GP	Mexico City	7	Owen Racing Organisation	3.0 BRM P115 H16	*engine vibration*

1968

	Race	Circuit	No	Entrant	Car/Engine	Comment
ret	SOUTH AFRICAN GP	Kyalami	16	Matra International	3.0 Matra MS9-Cosworth V8	*engine*
dns	"	"	26	Matra International	1.6 Matra MS7-Cosworth 4	*practice only*
4	BELGIAN GP	Spa	7	Matra International	3.0 Matra MS10-Cosworth V8	*pit stop-fuel/1 lap behind*
1	DUTCH GP	Zandvoort	8	Matra International	3.0 Matra MS10-Cosworth V8	
3	FRENCH GP	Rouen	28	Matra International	3.0 Matra MS10-Cosworth V8	*pit stop-tyres/1 lap behind*
6	BRITISH GP	Brands Hatch	14	Matra International	3.0 Matra MS10-Cosworth V8	*2 laps behind*
1	GERMAN GP	Nürburgring	6	Matra International	3.0 Matra MS10-Cosworth V8	*FL*
ret	ITALIAN GP	Monza	4	Matra International	3.0 Matra MS10-Cosworth V8	*engine*
6	CANADIAN GP	St Jovite	14	Matra International	3.0 Matra MS10-Cosworth V8	*p stop-suspension problems/-7 laps*
1	US GP	Watkins Glen	15	Matra International	3.0 Matra MS10-Cosworth V8	*FL*
7	MEXICAN GP	Mexico City	15	Matra International	3.0 Matra MS10-Cosworth V8	*fuel feed problems/1 lap behind*

1969 World Champion Driver

	Race	Circuit	No	Entrant	Car/Engine	Comment
1	SOUTH AFRICAN GP	Kyalami	7	Matra International	3.0 Matra MS10-Cosworth V8	*FL*
dns	"	"	20	Matra International	3.0 Matra MS80-Cosworth V8	*practice only*
1	SPANISH GP	Montjuich Park	7	Matra International	3.0 Matra MS80-Cosworth V8	
ret	MONACO GP	Monte Carlo	7	Matra International	3.0 Matra MS80-Cosworth V8	*driveshaft/Pole/FL*
1	DUTCH GP	Zandvoort	4	Matra International	3.0 Matra MS80-Cosworth V8	*FL*
dns	"	"	4T	Matra International	3.0 Matra MS84-Cosworth V8 4WD	*practice only*
1	FRENCH GP	Clermont Ferrand	2	Matra International	3.0 Matra MS80-Cosworth V8	*Pole/FL*
dns	"	"	2T	Matra International	3.0 Matra MS84-Cosworth V8 4WD	*practice only*
1	BRITISH GP	Silverstone	3	Matra International	3.0 Matra MS80-Cosworth V8	*FL*
dns	"	"	30	Matra International	3.0 Matra MS84-Cosworth V8 4WD	*practice only*
2	GERMAN GP	Nürburgring	7	Matra International	3.0 Matra MS80-Cosworth V8	
dns	"	"	7T	Matra International	3.0 Matra MS84-Cosworth V8 4WD	*practice only*
1	ITALIAN GP	Monza	20	Matra International	3.0 Matra MS80-Cosworth V8	
dns	"	"	24	Matra International	3.0 Matra MS84-Cosworth V8 4WD	*practice only*
ret	CANADIAN GP	Mosport Park	17	Matra International	3.0 Matra MS80-Cosworth V8	*hit by Ickx*
ret	US GP	Watkins Glen	3	Matra International	3.0 Matra MS80-Cosworth V8	*engine*
dns	"	"	3	Matra International	3.0 Matra MS84-Cosworth V8 4WD	*practice only*
4	MEXICAN GP	Mexico City	3	Matra International	3.0 Matra MS80-Cosworth V8	

1970

	Race	Circuit	No	Entrant	Car/Engine	Comment
3	SOUTH AFRICAN GP	Kyalami	1	Tyrrell Racing Organisation	3.0 March 701-Cosworth V8	*Pole*
1	SPANISH GP	Jarama	1	Tyrrell Racing Organisation	3.0 March 701-Cosworth V8	
ret	MONACO GP	Monte Carlo	21	Tyrrell Racing Organisation	3.0 March 701-Cosworth V8	*engine/Pole*
ret	BELGIAN GP	Spa	11	Tyrrell Racing Organisation	3.0 March 701-Cosworth V8	*engine/Pole*
2	DUTCH GP	Zandvoort	5	Tyrrell Racing Organisation	3.0 March 701-Cosworth V8	
9	FRENCH GP	Clermont Ferrand	9	Tyrrell Racing Organisation	3.0 March 701-Cosworth V8	*pit stop-ignition*
ret	BRITISH GP	Brands Hatch	1	Tyrrell Racing Organisation	3.0 March 701-Cosworth V8	*melted clutch line-fire*
ret	GERMAN GP	Hockenheim	1	Tyrrell Racing Organisation	3.0 March 701-Cosworth V8	*engine*
ret	AUSTRIAN GP	Österreichring	1	Tyrrell Racing Organisation	3.0 March 701-Cosworth V8	*split fuel line*
2	ITALIAN GP	Monza	18	Tyrrell Racing Organisation	3.0 March 701-Cosworth V8	

	Race	Circuit	No	Entrant	Car/Engine	Comment
dns	"	"	18	Tyrrell Racing Organisation	3.0 Tyrrell 001-Cosworth V8	*practice only*
ret	CANADIAN GP	St Jovite	3	Tyrrell Racing Organisation	3.0 Tyrrell 001-Cosworth V8	*broken stub axle/Pole*
dns	" "	" "	1	Tyrrell Racing Organisation	3.0 March 701-Cosworth V8	*practice only*
ret	US GP	Watkins Glen	1	Tyrrell Racing Organisation	3.0 Tyrrell 001-Cosworth V8	*engine*
dns	"	"	33	Tyrrell Racing Organisation	3.0 March 701-Cosworth V8	*practice only*
ret	MEXICAN GP	Mexico City	1	Tyrrell Racing Organisation	3.0 Tyrrell 001-Cosworth V8	*steering-hit dog*

1971 World Champion Driver

	Race	Circuit	No	Entrant	Car/Engine	Comment
2	SOUTH AFRICAN GP	Kyalami	9	Elf Team Tyrrell	3.0 Tyrrell 001-Cosworth V8	*Pole*
dns	"	"	10	Elf Team Tyrrell	3.0 Tyrrell 002-Cosworth V8	*practice only*
1	SPANISH GP	Montjuich Park	11	Elf Team Tyrrell	3.0 Tyrrell 003-Cosworth V8	
dns	"	"	11T	Elf Team Tyrrell	3.0 Tyrrell 001-Cosworth V8	*practice only*
1	MONACO GP	Monte Carlo	11	Elf Team Tyrrell	3.0 Tyrrell 003-Cosworth V8	*Pole/FL*
dns	"	" "	11T	Elf Team Tyrrell	3.0 Tyrrell 001-Cosworth V8	*practice only*
11	DUTCH GP	Zandvoort	5	Elf Team Tyrrell	3.0 Tyrrell 003-Cosworth V8	*spin in rain/5 laps behind*
dns	"	"	5T	Elf Team Tyrrell	3.0 Tyrrell 001-Cosworth V8	*practice only*
1	FRENCH GP	Paul Ricard	11	Elf Team Tyrrell	3.0 Tyrrell 003-Cosworth V8	*Pole/FL*
dns	"	" "	11T	Elf Team Tyrrell	3.0 Tyrrell 001-Cosworth V8	*practice only*
1	BRITISH GP	Silverstone	12	Elf Team Tyrrell	3.0 Tyrrell 003-Cosworth V8	*FL*
1	GERMAN GP	Nürburgring	2	Elf Team Tyrrell	3.0 Tyrrell 003-Cosworth V8	*Pole*
dns	"	"	2T	Elf Team Tyrrell	3.0 Tyrrell 001-Cosworth V8	*practice only*
ret	AUSTRIAN GP	Österreichring	11	Elf Team Tyrrell	3.0 Tyrrell 003-Cosworth V8	*lost wheel*
dns	"	"	11T	Elf Team Tyrrell	3.0 Tyrrell 001-Cosworth V8	*practice only*
ret	ITALIAN GP	Monza	30	Elf Team Tyrrell	3.0 Tyrrell 003-Cosworth V8	*engine*
1	CANADIAN GP	Mosport Park	11	Elf Team Tyrrell	3.0 Tyrrell 003-Cosworth V8	*Pole*
dns	"	" "	11T	Elf Team Tyrrell	3.0 Tyrrell 001-Cosworth V8	*practice only*
5	US GP	Watkins Glen	8	Elf Team Tyrrell	3.0 Tyrrell 003-Cosworth V8	*chunking tyres/Pole*

1972

	Race	Circuit	No	Entrant	Car/Engine	Comment
1	ARGENTINE GP	Buenos Aires	21	Elf Team Tyrrell	3.0 Tyrrell 003-Cosworth V8	*FL*
ret	SOUTH AFRICAN GP	Kyalami	1	Elf Team Tyrrell	3.0 Tyrrell 003-Cosworth V8	*gearbox/Pole*
dns	" "	"	1T	Elf Team Tyrrell	3.0 Tyrrell 004-Cosworth V8	*practice only*
ret	SPANISH GP	Jarama	1	Elf Team Tyrrell	3.0 Tyrrell 003-Cosworth V8	*spun-holed radiator*
dns	"	"	1T	Elf Team Tyrrell	3.0 Tyrrell 004-Cosworth V8	*practice only*
4	MONACO GP	Monte Carlo	1	Elf Team Tyrrell	3.0 Tyrrell 004-Cosworth V8	*2 spins/misfire/2 laps behind*
dns	"	" "	1T	Elf Team Tyrrell	3.0 Tyrrell 003-Cosworth V8	*practice only*
1	FRENCH GP	Clermont Ferrand	4	Elf Team Tyrrell	3.0 Tyrrell 003-Cosworth V8	
2	BRITISH GP	Brands Hatch	1	Elf Team Tyrrell	3.0 Tyrrell 005-Cosworth V8	*FL*
dns	"	" "	1	Elf Team Tyrrell	3.0 Tyrrell 003-Cosworth V8	*accident in practice*
11/ret	GERMAN GP	Nürburgring	1	Elf Team Tyrrell	3.0 Tyrrell 003-Cosworth V8	*collision with Regazzoni/-1 lap*
7	AUSTRIAN GP	Österreichring	1	Elf Team Tyrrell	3.0 Tyrrell 005-Cosworth V8	*handling problems*
ret	ITALIAN GP	Monza	1	Elf Team Tyrrell	3.0 Tyrrell 004-Cosworth V8	*transmission*
dns	"	"	1T	Elf Team Tyrrell	3.0 Tyrrell 003-Cosworth V8	*practice only*
1	CANADIAN GP	Mosport Park	1	Elf Team Tyrrell	3.0 Tyrrell 005-Cosworth V8	*FL*
dns	"	" "	1T	Elf Team Tyrrell	3.0 Tyrrell 004-Cosworth V8	*practice only*
dns	"	" "	2T	Elf Team Tyrrell	3.0 Tyrrell 006-Cosworth V8	*practice only*
1	US GP	Watkins Glen	1	Elf Team Tyrrell	3.0 Tyrrell 005-Cosworth V8	*Pole/FL*

1973 World Champion Driver

	Race	Circuit	No	Entrant	Car/Engine	Comment
3	ARGENTINE GP	Buenos Aires	6	Elf Team Tyrrell	3.0 Tyrrell 005-Cosworth V8	*slow puncture*
2	BRAZILIAN GP	Rio	3	Elf Team Tyrrell	3.0 Tyrrell 005-Cosworth V8	
1	SOUTH AFRICAN GP	Kyalami	3	Elf Team Tyrrell	3.0 Tyrrell 006-Cosworth V8	
dns	"	"	3	Elf Team Tyrrell	3.0 Tyrrell 006-Cosworth V8	*accident in practice-brake failure*
ret	SPANISH GP	Montjuich Park	3	Elf Team Tyrrell	3.0 Tyrrell 006-Cosworth V8	*disc brake mounting*
dns	"	"	3T	Elf Team Tyrrell	3.0 Tyrrell 005-Cosworth V8	*practice only*
1	BELGIAN GP	Zolder	5	Elf Team Tyrrell	3.0 Tyrrell 006-Cosworth V8	
1	MONACO GP	Monte Carlo	5	Elf Team Tyrrell	3.0 Tyrrell 006-Cosworth V8	*Pole*
dns	"	"	5T	Elf Team Tyrrell	3.0 Tyrrell 006-Cosworth V8	*practice only*
5	SWEDISH GP	Anderstorp	5	Elf Team Tyrrell	3.0 Tyrrell 006-Cosworth V8	*brake problems*
dns	"	"	5T	Elf Team Tyrrell	3.0 Tyrrell 005-Cosworth V8	*practice only*
4	FRENCH GP	Paul Ricard	5	Elf Team Tyrrell	3.0 Tyrrell 006-Cosworth V8	*Pole*
dns	"	" "	5T	Elf Team Tyrrell	3.0 Tyrrell 005-Cosworth V8	*practice only*
10	BRITISH GP	Silverstone	5	Elf Team Tyrrell	3.0 Tyrrell 006-Cosworth V8	*spin-p stop to remove debris/-1 lap*
dns	"	"	42	Elf Team Tyrrell	3.0 Tyrrell 005-Cosworth V8	*practice only*
1	DUTCH GP	Zandvoort	5	Elf Team Tyrrell	3.0 Tyrrell 006-Cosworth V8	
dns	"	"	5T	Elf Team Tyrrell	3.0 Tyrrell 005-Cosworth V8	*practice only*
1	GERMAN GP	Nürburgring	5	Elf Team Tyrrell	3.0 Tyrrell 006-Cosworth V8	*Pole*
dns	"	"	5T	Elf Team Tyrrell	3.0 Tyrrell 005-Cosworth V8	*practice only*
2	AUSTRIAN GP	Österreichring	5	Elf Team Tyrrell	3.0 Tyrrell 005-Cosworth V8	
4	ITALIAN GP	Monza	5	Elf Team Tyrrell	3.0 Tyrrell 006-Cosworth V8	*pit stop-tyres/FL*
5	CANADIAN GP	Mosport Park	5	Elf Team Tyrrell	3.0 Tyrrell 006-Cosworth V8	*1 lap behind*
dns	US GP	Watkins Glen	5	Elf Team Tyrrell	3.0 Tyrrell 006-Cosworth V8	*withdrawn following Cevert's death*

GP Starts: 99　GP Wins: 27　Pole positions: 17　Fastest laps: 15　Points: 360

STEWART, Jimmy (GB) b 6/3/1931

1953

	Race	Circuit	No	Entrant	Car/Engine	Comment
ret	BRITISH GP	Silverstone	18	Ecurie Ecosse	2.0 Cooper T20-Bristol 6	*spun off*

GP Starts: 1　GP Wins: 0　Pole positions: 0　Fastest laps: 0　Points: 0

SIEGFRIED STOHR

Born in Rimini of an Italian mother and a German father, Stohr won the 1978 Italian F3 championship with a Chevron, a title which at that time was very much secondary to the European crown. Nevertheless the former karting ace moved into Formula 2 for 1979, taking second places at Vallelunga and Pau with a Chevron before switching less successfully to a March. Securing sponsorship from Beta, Stohr joined the Alan Docking team to race a Toleman in 1980 and did a sound job, scoring a win at Enna and earning fourth place in the championship.

Taking his sponsorship along to Arrows the following season, Stohr never really got to grips with things in his one shot at Grand Prix racing, being very much the number two to Riccardo Patrese.

ROLF STOMMELEN

While both Ahrens and Mitter promised much but failed to make a permanent mark on Grand Prix racing, Rolf Stommelen became the first German driver since von Trips to appear regularly on the F1 starting grids.

After campaigning his private Porsche 904 GTS in 1964-65, Rolf was invited to join the works team for endurance racing. He soon became a key member of the team, winning the 1967 Targa Florio with Paul Hawkins, and the Daytona 24 Hours and Paris 1000 Km in 1968, as well as taking many placings. He was also successfully involved in Porsche's European mountain-climb programme with the 2-litre Bergspyder.

After dipping his toe into the water by competing in the 1969 German GP with a hired F2 Lotus, Stommelen gained sponsorship for a full F1 season in 1970 with a works Brabham and showed distinct promise, highlighted by a brilliant drive in Austria when he drove from 18th to finish third. He was also busy making his mark in Formula 2 with the Eifelland Caravans Brabham, and was a works driver for the Alfa Romeo sports car team, for whom he drove until 1974.

For 1971, Stommelen took his sponsorship to Surtees, but the partnership produced little and relationships were strained, so it was no surprise when he branched out on his own for 1972 with the curious-looking March-based Eifelland-Ford, which performed even more lamely than its appearance promised. Temporarily on the Formula 1 sidelines after this fiasco, Stommelen grabbed the lifeline of a Brabham drive after de Adamich's accident at Silverstone in 1973, and was then called up to replace Guy Edwards in the Hill Lola in mid-1974.

Rolf got on well with Hill and secured a seat for 1975, but his first race in the new Hill GH1 at the trouble-torn Spanish GP ended in disaster when a wing stay failed while he was leading the race. The car was pitched into the crowd, killing four spectators and seriously injuring the driver. Happily Rolf soon recovered and returned later in the year, but by that time Tony Brise had emerged as Hill's prize asset.

For 1976 Stommelen returned to sports car racing with Martini Porsche, winning at Enna and Watkins Glen, and this helped him to a couple of rides in the works Brabham that season. The following year he won the Nürburgring 1000 Km for Porsche, and also took the German national touring car title in the Gelo Racing 935 turbo. With Warsteiner backing the Arrows team in 1978, Rolf was given the second seat and a chance to renew his Grand Prix career, but the season was a severe disappointment and Stommelen returned to sports and GT racing, where he was still a competitive runner. In 1980 he won the Daytona 24 Hours and the Nürburgring 1000 Km in a Porsche, and he continued to race for top endurance teams such as Porsche, Lancia and Rondeau, as well as trying his hand at IMSA. It was racing a Porsche 'replica' 935 in this category that he lost his life after crashing in a race at Riverside in April 1983.

STOHR, Siegfried (I) b 10/10/1952

1981

	Race	Circuit	No	Entrant	Car/Engine	Comment
dnq	US GP WEST	Long Beach	30	Arrows Racing Team	3.0 Arrows A3-Cosworth V8	
ret	BRAZILIAN GP	Rio	30	Arrows Racing Team	3.0 Arrows A3-Cosworth V8	collision with Tambay
9	ARGENTINE GP	Buenos Aires	30	Arrows Racing Team	3.0 Arrows A3-Cosworth V8	1 lap behind
dnq	SAN MARINO GP	Imola	30	Arrows Racing Team	3.0 Arrows A3-Cosworth V8	
ret/dns	BELGIAN GP	Zolder	30	Arrows Racing Team	3.0 Arrows A3-Cosworth V8	collision with Patrese in first start
ret	MONACO GP	Monte Carlo	30	Arrows Racing Team	3.0 Arrows A3-Cosworth V8	electrics
ret	SPANISH GP	Jarama	30	Arrows Racing Team	3.0 Arrows A3-Cosworth V8	engine
dnq	FRENCH GP	Dijon	30	Arrows Racing Team	3.0 Arrows A3-Cosworth V8	
ret	BRITISH GP	Silverstone	30	Arrows Racing Team	3.0 Arrows A3-Cosworth V8	collision with Rebaque
12	GERMAN GP	Hockenheim	30	Arrows Racing Team	3.0 Arrows A3-Cosworth V8	
ret	AUSTRIAN GP	Österreichring	30	Arrows Racing Team	3.0 Arrows A3-Cosworth V8	spun off-could not restart
7	DUTCH GP	Zandvoort	30	Arrows Racing Team	3.0 Arrows A3-Cosworth V8	3 laps behind
dnq	ITALIAN GP	Monza	30	Arrows Racing Team	3.0 Arrows A3-Cosworth V8	

GP Starts: 8 (9)   GP Wins: 0   Pole positions: 0   Fastest laps: 0   Points: 0

STOMMELEN, Rolf (D) b 11/7/1943 – d 24/5/1983

1969

	Race	Circuit	No	Entrant	Car/Engine	Comment
8	GERMAN GP (F2)	Nurburging	22	Roy Winkelmann Racing Ltd	1.6 Lotus 59B-Ford 4	4th in F2 class

1970

ret	SOUTH AFRICAN GP	Kyalami	14	Auto Motor Und Sport	3.0 Brabham BT33-Cosworth V8	engine
ret	SPANISH GP	Jarama	24	Auto Motor Und Sport	3.0 Brabham BT33-Cosworth V8	engine
dnq	MONACO GP	Monte Carlo	6	Auto Motor Und Sport	3.0 Brabham BT33-Cosworth V8	
5	BELGIAN GP	Spa	19	Auto Motor Und Sport	3.0 Brabham BT33-Cosworth V8	
dnq	DUTCH GP	Zandvoort	19	Auto Motor Und Sport	3.0 Brabham BT33-Cosworth V8	
7	FRENCH GP	Clermont Ferrand	22	Auto Motor Und Sport	3.0 Brabham BT33-Cosworth V8	
dns	BRITISH GP	Brands Hatch	18	Auto Motor Und Sport	3.0 Brabham BT33-Cosworth V8	accident in practice
5	GERMAN GP	Hockenheim	21	Auto Motor Und Sport	3.0 Brabham BT33-Cosworth V8	1 lap behind
3	AUSTRIAN GP	Österreichring	11	Auto Motor Und Sport	3.0 Brabham BT33-Cosworth V8	
5	ITALIAN GP	Monza	46	Auto Motor Und Sport	3.0 Brabham BT33-Cosworth V8	
ret	CANADIAN GP	St Jovite	12	Auto Motor Und Sport	3.0 Brabham BT33-Cosworth V8	steering
12	US GP	Watkins Glen	16	Auto Motor Und Sport	3.0 Brabham BT33-Cosworth V8	pit stop-brakes/4 laps behind
ret	MEXICAN GP	Mexico City	16	Auto Motor Und Sport	3.0 Brabham BT33-Cosworth V8	fuel system

1971

12	SOUTH AFRICAN GP	Kyalami	21	Auto Motor Und Sport-Team Surtees	3.0 Surtees TS7-Cosworth V8	2 laps behind
ret	SPANISH GP	Montjuich Park	25	Auto Motor Und Sport-Team Surtees	3.0 Surtees TS9-Cosworth V8	fuel pressure release valve
6	MONACO GP	Monte Carlo	24	Auto Motor Und Sport-Team Surtees	3.0 Surtees TS9-Cosworth V8	1 lap behind
dsq	DUTCH GP	Zandvoort	29	Auto Motor Und Sport-Team Surtees	3.0 Surtees TS9-Cosworth V8	spun off-push start
11	FRENCH GP	Paul Ricard	24	Auto Motor Und Sport-Team Surtees	3.0 Surtees TS9-Cosworth V8	2 laps behind
5	BRITISH GP	Silverstone	24	Auto Motor Und Sport-Team Surtees	3.0 Surtees TS9-Cosworth V8	1 las behind
10	GERMAN GP	Nürburgring	12	Auto Motor Und Sport-Team Surtees	3.0 Surtees TS9-Cosworth V8	handling problems/1 lap behind
7	AUSTRIAN GP	Österreichring	24	Auto Motor Und Sport-Team Surtees	3.0 Surtees TS9-Cosworth V8	
dns	ITALIAN GP	Monza	8	Auto Motor Und Sport-Team Surtees	3.0 Surtees TS9-Cosworth V8	accident in practice
ret	CANADIAN GP	Mosport Park	24	Auto Motor Und Sport-Team Surtees	3.0 Surtees TS9-Cosworth V8	oil pressure

1972

13	SOUTH AFRICAN GP	Kyalami	25	Team Eifelland Caravans	3.0 Eifelland March 721-Cosworth V8	2 laps behind
ret	SPANISH GP	Jarama	16	Team Eifelland Caravans	3.0 Eifelland March 721-Cosworth V8	spun-hit barrier
10	MONACO GP	Monte Carlo	27	Team Eifelland Caravans	3.0 Eifelland March 721-Cosworth V8	handling problems in rain/-3 laps
11	BELGIAN GP	Nivelles	6	Team Eifelland Caravans	3.0 Eifelland March 721-Cosworth V8	2 laps behind
16	FRENCH GP	Clermont Ferrand	10	Team Eifelland Caravans	3.0 Eifelland March 721-Cosworth V8	pit stop-puncture/1 lap behind
10	BRITISH GP	Brands Hatch	33	Team Eifelland Caravans	3.0 Eifelland March 721-Cosworth V8	5 laps behind
ret	GERMAN GP	Nürburgring	22	Team Eifelland Caravans	3.0 Eifelland March 721-Cosworth V8	electrics
nc	AUSTRIAN GP	Österreichring	27	Team Eifelland Caravans	3.0 Eifelland March 721-Cosworth V8	p stops-bodywork problems/-6 laps

1973

11	GERMAN GP	Nürburgring	9	Ceramica Pagnossin Team MRD	3.0 Brabham BT42-Cosworth V8	
ret	AUSTRIAN GP	Österreichring	9	Ceramica Pagnossin Team MRD	3.0 Brabham BT42-Cosworth V8	front wheel bearing
12	ITALIAN GP	Monza	9	Ceramica Pagnossin Team MRD	3.0 Brabham BT42-Cosworth V8	
12	CANADIAN GP	Mosport Park	9	Ceramica Pagnossin Team MRD	3.0 Brabham BT42-Cosworth V8	

1974

ret	AUSTRIAN GP	Österreichring	27	Embassy Racing with Graham Hill	3.0 Lola T370-Cosworth V8	tyre punctured-accident
ret	ITALIAN GP	Monza	27	Embassy Racing with Graham Hill	3.0 Lola T370-Cosworth V8	suspension mounting plate
11	CANADIAN GP	Mosport Park	27	Embassy Racing with Graham Hill	3.0 Lola T370-Cosworth V8	2 laps behind
12	US GP	Watkins Glen	27	Embassy Racing with Graham Hill	3.0 Lola T370-Cosworth V8	2 pit stops-tyres/5 laps behind

1975

13	ARGENTINE GP	Buenos Aires	23	Embassy Racing with Graham Hill	3.0 Lola T370-Cosworth V8	pit stop-tyre/2 laps behind
14	BRAZILIAN GP	Interlagos	23	Embassy Racing with Graham Hill	3.0 Lola T370-Cosworth V8	
7	SOUTH AFRICAN GP	Kyalami	23	Embassy Racing with Graham Hill	3.0 Lola T371-Cosworth V8	
ret	SPANISH GP	Montjuich Park	23	Embassy Racing with Graham Hill	3.0 Hill GH1-Cosworth V8	lost rear wing-accident-broken leg
16	AUSTRIAN GP	Österreichring	23	Embassy Racing with Graham Hill	3.0 Hill GH1-Cosworth V8	2 laps behind
ret	ITALIAN GP	Monza	23	Embassy Racing with Graham Hill	3.0 Hill GH1-Cosworth V8	accident at chicane

1976

6	GERMAN GP	Nürburgring	77	Martini Racing	3.0 Brabham BT45-Alfa Romeo F12	
dns	"	"	32	RAM Racing	3.0 Brabham BT44B-Cosworth V8	practice only
12	DUTCH GP	Zandvoort	25	Hesketh Racing with Rizla/Penthouse	3.0 Hesketh 308D-Cosworth V8	
ret	ITALIAN GP	Monza	7	Martini Racing	3.0 Brabham BT45-Alfa Romeo F12	engine

1978

9	SOUTH AFRICAN GP	Kyalami	36	Arrows Racing Team	3.0 Arrows FA1-Cosworth V8	pit stop-fuel/1 lap behind
9	US GP WEST	Long Beach	36	Arrows Racing Team	3.0 Arrows FA1-Cosworth V8	1 lap behind
ret	MONACO GP	Monte Carlo	36	Arrows Racing Team	3.0 Arrows FA1-Cosworth V8	driver unwell-rib injury
ret	BELGIAN GP	Zolder	36	Arrows Racing Team	3.0 Arrows FA1-Cosworth V8	crashed
14	SPANISH GP	Jarama	36	Arrows Racing Team	3.0 Arrows FA1-Cosworth V8	2 pit stops/4 laps behind
14	SWEDISH GP	Anderstorp	36	Arrows Racing Team	3.0 Arrows FA1-Cosworth V8	3 laps behind
15	FRENCH GP	Paul Ricard	36	Arrows Racing Team	3.0 Arrows FA1-Cosworth V8	1 lap behind
dnq	BRITISH GP	Brands Hatch	36	Arrows Racing Team	3.0 Arrows FA1-Cosworth V8	
dsq	GERMAN GP	Hockenheim	36	Arrows Racing Team	3.0 Arrows FA1-Cosworth V8	took back entrance to pits
dnpq	AUSTRIAN GP	Österreichring	36	Arrows Racing Team	3.0 Arrows A1-Cosworth V8	
dnpq	DUTCH GP	Zandvoort	36	Arrows Racing Team	3.0 Arrows A1-Cosworth V8	
dnpq	ITALIAN GP	Monza	36	Arrows Racing Team	3.0 Arrows A1-Cosworth V8	
16	US GP EAST	Watkins Glen	36	Arrows Racing Team	3.0 Arrows A1-Cosworth V8	pit stop-brakes/5 laps behind
dnq	CANADIAN GP	Montreal	36	Arrows Racing Team	3.0 Arrows A1-Cosworth V8	

GP Starts: 54   GP Wins: 0   Pole positions: 0   Fastest laps: 0   Points: 14

STREIFF, Philippe (F) b 26/6/1955

1984

	Race	Circuit	No	Entrant	Car/Engine	Comment
ret	PORTUGUESE GP	Estoril	33	Equipe Renault Elf	1.5 t/c Renault RE50 V6	driveshaft

1985

	Race	Circuit	No	Entrant	Car/Engine	Comment
10	ITALIAN GP	Monza	25	Equipe Ligier Gitanes	1.5 t/c Ligier JS25-Renault V6	2 laps behind
9	BELGIAN GP	Spa	25	Equipe Ligier Gitanes	1.5 t/c Ligier JS25-Renault V6	1 lap behind
8	EUROPEAN GP	Brands Hatch	25	Equipe Ligier Gitanes	1.5 t/c Ligier JS25-Renault V6	2 laps behind
ret	SOUTH AFRICAN GP	Kyalami	4	Tyrrell Racing Organisation	1.5 t/c Tyrrell 014-Renault V6	accident
3	AUSTRALIAN GP	Adelaide	25	Equipe Ligier Gitanes	1.5 t/c Ligier JS25-Renault V6	

1986

	Race	Circuit	No	Entrant	Car/Engine	Comment
7	BRAZILIAN GP	Rio	4	Data General Team Tyrrell	1.5 t/c Tyrrell 014-Renault V6	2 laps behind
ret	SPANISH GP	Jerez	4	Data General Team Tyrrell	1.5 t/c Tyrrell 014-Renault V6	engine-lost oil
ret	SAN MARINO GP	Imola	4	Data General Team Tyrrell	1.5 t/c Tyrrell 014-Renault V6	transmission
11	MONACO GP	Monte Carlo	4	Data General Team Tyrrell	1.5 t/c Tyrrell 015-Renault V6	hit by Jones-spin/4 laps behind
12	BELGIAN GP	Spa	4	Data General Team Tyrrell	1.5 t/c Tyrrell 014-Renault V6	3 laps behind
11	CANADIAN GP	Montreal	4	Data General Team Tyrrell	1.5 t/c Tyrrell 014-Renault V6	4 laps behind
9	US GP (DETROIT)	Detroit	4	Data General Team Tyrrell	1.5 t/c Tyrrell 015-Renault V6	
dns	" "	"	4	Data General Team Tyrrell	1.5 t/c Tyrrell 014-Renault V6	practice only
ret	FRENCH GP	Paul Ricard	4	Data General Team Tyrrell	1.5 t/c Tyrrell 015-Renault V6	fuel leak-fire
6	BRITISH GP	Brands Hatch	4	Data General Team Tyrrell	1.5 t/c Tyrrell 015-Renault V6	3 laps behind
ret	GERMAN GP	Hockenheim	4	Data General Team Tyrrell	1.5 t/c Tyrrell 015-Renault V6	engine
8	HUNGARIAN GP	Hungaroring	4	Data General Team Tyrrell	1.5 t/c Tyrrell 015-Renault V6	2 laps behind
ret	AUSTRIAN GP	Österreichring	4	Data General Team Tyrrell	1.5 t/c Tyrrell 015-Renault V6	engine
9	ITALIAN GP	Monza	4	Data General Team Tyrrell	1.5 t/c Tyrrell 015-Renault V6	2 laps behind
ret	PORTUGUESE GP	Estoril	4	Data General Team Tyrrell	1.5 t/c Tyrrell 015-Renault V6	engine
ret	MEXICAN GP	Mexico City	4	Data General Team Tyrrell	1.5 t/c Tyrrell 015-Renault V6	turbo
5/ret	AUSTRALIAN GP	Adelaide	4	Data General Team Tyrrell	1.5 t/c Tyrrell 015-Renault V6	out of fuel/2 laps behind

1987

	Race	Circuit	No	Entrant	Car/Engine	Comment
11	BRAZILIAN GP	Rio	4	Data General Team Tyrrell	3.5 Tyrrell 016-Cosworth V8	2nd non-turbo/4 laps behind
8	SAN MARINO GP	Imola	4	Data General Team Tyrrell	3.5 Tyrrell 016-Cosworth V8	1st non-turbo/2 laps behind
9	BELGIAN GP	Spa	4	Data General Team Tyrrell	3.5 Tyrrell 016-Cosworth V8	2nd non-turbo
ret	MONACO GP	Monte Carlo	4	Data General Team Tyrrell	3.5 Tyrrell 016-Cosworth V8	hit barrier
ret	US GP (DETROIT)	Detroit	4	Data General Team Tyrrell	3.5 Tyrrell 016-Cosworth V8	lost wheel-hit wall
6	FRENCH GP	Paul Ricard	4	Data General Team Tyrrell	3.5 Tyrrell 016-Cosworth V8	1st non-turbo/4 laps behind
ret	BRITISH GP	Silverstone	4	Data General Team Tyrrell	3.5 Tyrrell 016-Cosworth V8	engine
4	GERMAN GP	Hockenheim	4	Data General Team Tyrrell	3.5 Tyrrell 016-Cosworth V8	1st non-turbo/1 lap behind
9	HUNGARIAN GP	Hungaroring	4	Data General Team Tyrrell	3.5 Tyrrell 016-Cosworth V8	2nd non-turbo/2 laps behind
ret/dns	AUSTRIAN GP	Österreichring	4	Data General Team Tyrrell	3.5 Tyrrell 016-Cosworth V8	accident in first start
12	ITALIAN GP	Monza	4	Data General Team Tyrrell	3.5 Tyrrell 016-Cosworth V8	1st non-turbo/3 laps behind
12	PORTUGUESE GP	Estoril	4	Data General Team Tyrrell	3.5 Tyrrell 016-Cosworth V8	3rd non-turbo/4 laps behind
7	SPANISH GP	Jerez	4	Data General Team Tyrrell	3.5 Tyrrell 016-Cosworth V8	2nd non-turbo/1 lap behind
8	MEXICAN GP	Mexico City	4	Data General Team Tyrrell	3.5 Tyrrell 016-Cosworth V8	3rd non-turbo/3 laps behind
12	JAPANESE GP	Suzuka	4	Data General Team Tyrrell	3.5 Tyrrell 016-Cosworth V8	2nd non-turbo/2 laps behind
ret	AUSTRALIAN GP	Adelaide	4	Data General Team Tyrrell	3.5 Tyrrell 016-Cosworth V8	spun off

1988

	Race	Circuit	No	Entrant	Car/Engine	Comment
ret	BRAZILIAN GP	Rio	14	Automobiles Gonfaronaise Sportive	3.5 AGS JH23-Cosworth V8	spun off
10	SAN MARINO GP	Imola	14	Automobiles Gonfaronaise Sportive	3.5 AGS JH23-Cosworth V8	2 laps behind
ret/dns	MONACO GP	Monte Carlo	14	Automobiles Gonfaronaise Sportive	3.5 AGS JH23-Cosworth V8	throttle cable before start
12	MEXICAN GP	Mexico City	14	Automobiles Gonfaronaise Sportive	3.5 AGS JH23-Cosworth V8	4 laps behind
ret	CANADIAN GP	Monteal	14	Automobiles Gonfaronaise Sportive	3.5 AGS JH23-Cosworth V8	rear suspension
ret	US GP (DETROIT)	Detroit	14	Automobiles Gonfaronaise Sportive	3.5 AGS JH23-Cosworth V8	suspension
ret	FRENCH GP	Paul Ricard	14	Automobiles Gonfaronaise Sportive	3.5 AGS JH23-Cosworth V8	fuel leak
ret	BRITISH GP	Silverstone	14	Automobiles Gonfaronaise Sportive	3.5 AGS JH23-Cosworth V8	broken rear wing
ret	GERMAN GP	Hockenheim	14	Automobiles Gonfaronaise Sportive	3.5 AGS JH23-Cosworth V8	throttle cable
ret	HUNGARIAN GP	Hungaroring	14	Automobiles Gonfaronaise Sportive	3.5 AGS JH23-Cosworth V8	lost wheel
10*	BELGIAN GP	Spa	14	Automobiles Gonfaronaise Sportive	3.5 AGS JH23-Cosworth V8	*3rd & 4th place cars dsq/-1 lap
ret	ITALIAN GP	Monza	14	Automobiles Gonfaronaise Sportive	3.5 AGS JH23-Cosworth V8	gearbox
9	PORTUGUESE GP	Estoril	14	Automobiles Gonfaronaise Sportive	3.5 AGS JH23-Cosworth V8	2 laps behind
ret	SPANISH GP	Jerez	14	Automobiles Gonfaronaise Sportive	3.5 AGS JH23-Cosworth V8	engine
8	JAPANESE GP	Suzuka	14	Automobiles Gonfaronaise Sportive	3.5 AGS JH23-Cosworth V8	1 lap behind
11/ret	AUSTRALIAN GP	Adelaide	14	Automobiles Gonfaronaise Sportive	3.5 AGS JH23-Cosworth V8	electrics

GP Starts: 52 (54) GP Wins: 0 Pole positions: 0 Fastest laps: 0 Points: 11

STUCK, Hans Snr (A) b 27/12/1900 – d 9/2/1978

1951

	Race	Circuit	No	Entrant	Car/Engine	Comment
dns	ITALIAN GP	Monza	32	BRM Ltd	1.5 s/c BRM P15 V12	tried car in practice only

1952

ret	SWISS GP	Bremgarten	2	AFM	2.0 AFM 4-Kuchen V8	engine
dnq	ITALIAN GP	Monza	20	Ecurie Espadon	2.0 Ferrari 212 V12	

1953

ret	GERMAN GP	Nürburgring	21	Hans Stuck	2.0 AFM 4-Bristol 6	
nc	ITALIAN GP	Monza	48	Hans Stuck	2.0 AFM 4-Bristol 6	23 laps behind winner

GP Starts: 3 GP Wins: 0 Pole positions: 0 Fastest laps: 0 Points: 0

PHILIPPE STREIFF

This tall, intense French driver came to the fore in 1980, when an acrimonious Formula 3 season ended with a splendid win at the final European round at Zolder. The following year he concentrated on winning the French F3 championship in his Martini, and took fourth in the European series, joining the two-car AGS Formula 2 team for 1982. Streiff's season was up and down, due in part to the arguments that raged over the technical regulations, but he finished the year strongly to take sixth place in the final standings.

In 1983, AGS and Streiff really got to work, despite the team's chronic shortage of funds, and the Frenchman carried the fight to the dominant Ralts, though he had to wait until the very end of the 1984 season before scoring a long overdue and well earned win. He did, however, have the fillip of a Grand Prix outing for Renault in the 1984 Portuguese GP. His F3000 campaign with AGS in 1985 was well funded yet strewn with mechanical failures, but by now he had been elevated to the Grand Prix ranks, taking over the Ligier of de Cesaris in mid-season and scoring a fine third place in the end-of-year Australian GP. With Ligier missing the South African GP because of the political situation, Philippe drove for Tyrrell, and he joined the Ockham team full time in 1986 to handle their Renault-engined cars. He drove well enough on occasions during the next two seasons, but was generally outpaced by his team-mates Brundle and Palmer, the latter claiming the non-turbo honours after a switch to Cosworth power in 1987.

Streiff was taking a gamble when he joined the tiny AGS GP team for 1988, but at least it was an environment with which the Frenchman was familiar, and early in the season he caught the eye with some spirited performances, most notably at Imola, where he qualified and raced superbly, only for engine problems to intervene. Philippe was looking forward to another season with the team in 1989, but in a pre-season test at Rio he crashed heavily, sustaining serious back injuries which, possibly due to a lack of prompt medical assistance, resulted in the unfortunate driver being left paralysed.

HANS STUCK

Stuck's competition career spanned some 39 years – from 1924 to 1963 – during which he took part in more than 700 events. Most of his success was gained in hill-climbs, of which he became the undisputed master during the 1920s in his Austro-Daimlers and into the early 1930s with a Mercedes SSK sports, by which time he was also winning on the circuits, taking the 1931 Rio de Janeiro GP. In 1934, Stuck joined the Auto Union team to win the German, Swiss and Czech GPs, adding the Italian GP to his tally in 1935, as well as an unending run of hill-climb successes.

After the war, Stuck got back into action with a little 1100 cc Cisitalia, before racing the AFM Formula 2 car, which was fast but fragile. He took a third place in the 1950 Solitude GP, and won a minor race at Grenzlandring in 1951, but on the hills, of course, he was still a regular winner. By the end of the 1952 season the AFM was totally outclassed, and he briefly raced an Ecurie Espadon Ferrari, taking fifth at AVUS, and ninth at Modena.

Stuck later joined BMW and raced their cars successfully in saloon events until the early 1960s.

HANS-JOACHIM STUCK

As the son of the famous pre-war Auto Union ace, it was perhaps natural that Hans Jnr should follow his father into a career in motor racing, especially as he had driven karts and small-capacity BMWs long before he was eligible for a racing licence. After driving a BMW 2002 in national hill-climbs, he graduated to the works European championship touring car team, winning the Nürburgring 24-hour race in 1969. Stuck then took over from Jochen Mass in the Ford Germany Capri in the national series for 1972, and won the Spa 24 Hours with Mass as co-driver.

His single-seater career began properly in 1973 when he raced the works March in Formula 2, graduating to the Grand Prix team the following year, but he proved to be somewhat inconsistent, very quick on some occasions, but mysteriously lacklustre on others. He did well in F2, however, finishing second in the championship with four wins (at Barcelona, Hockenheim, Rouen and Enna). Initially dropped from the March Grand Prix team for 1975, Stuck made a successful sortie into IMSA with BMW, but was then recalled to the Bicester ranks to replace the out-of-favour Lella Lombardi. He remained with the team in 1976, but it was the same infuriating mixture of the brilliant and the banal once more. At Watkins Glen Hans finished fifth, after being 23rd on the first lap, and occasional Formula 2 outings with the 762 produced three wins in only five starts.

Given the chance to race the Brabham-Alfa in 1977 following the death of Carlos Pace in an air crash, Hans scored superb third places in Germany and Austria, and led the US GP at Watkins Glen before blotting his copybook by sliding off the circuit. From then on it was down-hill all the way as far as Formula 1 was concerned, a season with Shadow bringing only one points finish, and an even more dispiriting year with ATS yielding the same return.

Hans then turned his back on F1, but certainly not on motor sport, for he was soon immersed in a huge schedule of sports, GT and touring car racing. He joined the Rothmans Porsche team in 1985, sharing the drivers' crown with Derek Bell in both 1985 and 1986, and won Le Mans with Bell and Holbert in 1986 and '87. Switching to Audi, his presence spiced up IMSA's GTO class in 1989, and back at home he won the 1990 GTCC championship in the awesome 3.6-litre V8 quattro.

STUCK, Hans-Joachim (D) b 1/1/1951

1974

	Race	Circuit	No	Entrant	Car/Engine	Comment
ret	ARGENTINE GP	Buenos Aires	9	March Engineering	3.0 March 741-Cosworth V8	*transmission*
ret	BRAZILIAN GP	Interlagos	9	March Engineering	3.0 March 741-Cosworth V8	*seized constant-velocity joint*
5	SOUTH AFRICAN GP	Kyalami	9	March Engineering	3.0 March 741-Cosworth V8	
4	SPANISH GP	Jarama	9	March Engineering	3.0 March 741-Cosworth V8	*2 laps behind*
ret	BELGIAN GP	Nivelles	9	March Engineering	3.0 March 741-Cosworth V8	*clutch*
ret	MONACO GP	Monte Carlo	9	March Engineering	3.0 March 741-Cosworth V8	*collision with Hunt*
ret	DUTCH GP	Zandvoort	9	March Engineering	3.0 March 741-Cosworth V8	*collision while braking*
dnq	FRENCH GP	Dijon	9	March Engineering	3.0 March 741-Cosworth V8	

ret	BRITISH GP	Brands Hatch	9	March Engineering	3.0 March 741-Cosworth V8	*spun off*
7	GERMAN GP	Nürburgring	9	March Engineering	3.0 March 741-Cosworth V8	
11/ret	AUSTRIAN GP	Österreichring	9	March Engineering	3.0 March 741-Cosworth V8	*broken suspension-spun off/-6 laps*
ret	ITALIAN GP	Monza	9	March Engineering	3.0 March 741-Cosworth V8	*engine mounting bolt*
ret	CANADIAN GP	Mosport Park	9	March Engineering	3.0 March 741-Cosworth V8	*engine*
dnq	US GP	Watkins Glen	9	March Engineering	3.0 March 741-Cosworth V8	

1975

ret	BRITISH GP	Silverstone	10	Lavazza March	3.0 March 751-Cosworth V8	*spun off in rain-hit barrier*
ret	GERMAN GP	Nürburgring	10	Lavazza March	3.0 March 751-Cosworth V8	*engine*
ret	AUSTRIAN GP	Österreichring	10	Lavazza March	3.0 March 751-Cosworth V8	*spun off in rain-hit barrier*
ret	ITALIAN GP	Monza	10	Lavazza March	3.0 March 751-Cosworth V8	*hit chicane*
8	US GP	Watkins Glen	10	Lavazza March	3.0 March 751-Cosworth V8	*took flag in pits-puncture/-1 lap*

1976

4	BRAZILIAN GP	Interlagos	34	March Racing	3.0 March 761-Cosworth V8	
12	SOUTH AFRICAN GP	Kyalami	34	March Racing	3.0 March 761-Cosworth V8	*2 laps behind*
ret	US GP WEST	Long Beach	34	Theodore Racing	3.0 March 761-Cosworth V8	*collision with Fittipaldi*
ret	SPANISH GP	Jarama	34	March Racing	3.0 March 761-Cosworth V8	*gearbox*
ret	BELGIAN GP	Zolder	34	March Racing	3.0 March 761-Cosworth V8	*suspension*
4	MONACO GP	Monte Carlo	34	March Racing	3.0 March 761-Cosworth V8	
ret	SWEDISH GP	Anderstorp	34	March Racing	3.0 March 761-Cosworth V8	*engine*
7	FRENCH GP	Paul Ricard	34	March Racing	3.0 March 761-Cosworth V8	
ret	BRITISH GP	Brands Hatch	34	March Racing	3.0 March 761-Cosworth V8	*collision-Peterson and Depailler*
ret/dns	GERMAN GP	Nürburgring	34	March Racing	3.0 March 761-Cosworth V8	*clutch in first start/did not restart*
ret	AUSTRIAN GP	Österreichring	34	March Racing	3.0 March 761-Cosworth V8	*fuel pressure*
ret	DUTCH GP	Zandvoort	34	March Racing	3.0 March 761-Cosworth V8	*engine*
ret	ITALIAN GP	Monza	34	March Racing	3.0 March 761-Cosworth V8	*collision with Andretti*
ret	CANADIAN GP	Mosport Park	34	March Racing	3.0 March 761-Cosworth V8	*handling*
5	US GP EAST	Watkins Glen	34	March Racing	3.0 March 761-Cosworth V8	
ret	JAPANESE GP	Mount Fuji	34	March Racing	3.0 March 761-Cosworth V8	*electrics*

1977

ret	SOUTH AFRICAN GP	Kyalami	10	Team Rothmans International	3.0 March 761B-Cosworth V8	*engine*
ret	US GP WEST	Long Beach	8	Martini Racing	3.0 Brabham BT45B-Alfa Romeo F12	*brakes*
6	SPANISH GP	Jarama	8	Martini Racing	3.0 Brabham BT45B-Alfa Romeo F12	*1 lap behind*
ret	MONACO GP	Monte Carlo	8	Martini Racing	3.0 Brabham BT45B-Alfa Romeo F12	*fire-electrical fault*
6	BELGIAN GP	Zolder	8	Martini Racing	3.0 Brabham BT45B-Alfa Romeo F12	*1 lap behind*
10	SWEDISH GP	Anderstorp	8	Martini Racing	3.0 Brabham BT45B-Alfa Romeo F12	*1 lap behind*
ret	FRENCH GP	Dijon	8	Martini Racing	3.0 Brabham BT45B-Alfa Romeo F12	*collision with Laffite*
5	BRITISH GP	Silverstone	8	Martini Racing	3.0 Brabham BT45B-Alfa Romeo F12	
3	GERMAN GP	Hockenheim	8	Martini Racing	3.0 Brabham BT45B-Alfa Romeo F12	
3	AUSTRIAN GP	Österreichring	8	Martini Racing	3.0 Brabham BT45B-Alfa Romeo F12	
7	DUTCH GP	Zandvoort	8	Martini Racing	3.0 Brabham BT45B-Alfa Romeo F12	*2 laps behind*
ret	ITALIAN GP	Monza	8	Martini Racing	3.0 Brabham BT45B-Alfa Romeo F12	*engine*
ret	US GP EAST	Watkins Glen	8	Martini Racing	3.0 Brabham BT45B-Alfa Romeo F12	*1st-crashed-car jumped out of gear*
ret	CANADIAN GP	Mosport Park	8	Martini Racing	3.0 Brabham BT45B-Alfa Romeo F12	*engine*
7	JAPANESE GP	Mount Fuji	8	Martini Racing	3.0 Brabham BT45B-Alfa Romeo F12	*1 lap behind*

1978

17	ARGENTINE GP	Buenos Aires	16	Shadow Racing Team	3.0 Shadow DN8-Cosworth V8	*handling problems/2 laps behind*
ret	BRAZILIAN GP	Rio	16	Shadow Racing Team	3.0 Shadow DN8-Cosworth V8	*fuel pump*
dnq	SOUTH AFRICAN GP	Kyalami	16	Shadow Racing Team	3.0 Shadow DN8-Cosworth V8	
dns	US GP WEST	Long Beach	16	Shadow Racing Team	3.0 Shadow DN8-Cosworth V8	*practice accident*
ret	MONACO GP	Monte Carlo	16	Shadow Racing Team	3.0 Shadow DN9-Cosworth V8	*collision-Keegan/steering damage*
ret	BELGIAN GP	Zolder	16	Shadow Racing Team	3.0 Shadow DN9-Cosworth V8	*spun off-stalled*
ret	SPANISH GP	Jarama	16	Shadow Racing Team	3.0 Shadow DN9-Cosworth V8	*broken rear suspension*
11	SWEDISH GP	Anderstorp	16	Shadow Racing Team	3.0 Shadow DN9-Cosworth V8	*2 laps behind*
11	FRENCH GP	Paul Ricard	16	Shadow Racing Team	3.0 Shadow DN9-Cosworth V8	*1 lap behind*
5	BRITISH GP	Brands Hatch	16	Shadow Racing Team	3.0 Shadow DN9-Cosworth V8	*1 lap behind*
ret	GERMAN GP	Hockenheim	16	Shadow Racing Team	3.0 Shadow DN9-Cosworth V8	*collision with Mass*
ret	AUSTRIAN GP	Österreichring	16	Shadow Racing Team	3.0 Shadow DN9-Cosworth V8	*spun off in rain*
ret	DUTCH GP	Zandvoort	16	Shadow Racing Team	3.0 Shadow DN9-Cosworth V8	*differential*
ret/dns	ITALIAN GP	Monza	16	Shadow Racing Team	3.0 Shadow DN9-Cosworth V8	*accident in first start-concussion*
ret	US GP EAST	Watkins Glen	16	Shadow Racing Team	3.0 Shadow DN9-Cosworth V8	*fuel pump*
ret	CANADIAN GP	Montreal	16	Shadow Racing Team	3.0 Shadow DN9-Cosworth V8	*hit by Fittipaldi*

1979

dnq	ARGENTINE GP	Buenos Aires	9	ATS Wheels	3.0 ATS D2-Cosworth V8	
ret	BRAZILIAN GP	Interlagos	9	ATS Wheels	3.0 ATS D2-Cosworth V8	*broken steering wheel*
ret	SOUTH AFRICAN GP	Kyalami	9	ATS Wheels	3.0 ATS D2-Cosworth V8	*spun off*
dsq	US GP WEST	Long Beach	9	ATS Wheels	3.0 ATS D2-Cosworth V8	*push start*
14	SPANISH GP	Jarama	9	ATS Wheels	3.0 ATS D2-Cosworth V8	*2 pit stops-tyres/6 laps behind*
8	BELGIAN GP	Zolder	9	ATS Wheels	3.0 ATS D2-Cosworth V8	*pit stop-puncture/1 lap behind*
ret	MONACO GP	Monte Carlo	9	ATS Wheels	3.0 ATS D2-Cosworth V8	*broken wheel*
dns	FRENCH GP	Dijon	9	ATS Wheels	3.0 ATS D2-Cosworth V8	*withdrawn after practice*
dnq	BRITISH GP	Silverstone	9	ATS Wheels	3.0 ATS D2-Cosworth V8	
ret	GERMAN GP	Hockenheim	9	ATS Wheels	3.0 ATS D2-Cosworth V8	*broken suspension*
ret	AUSTRIAN GP	Österreichring	9	ATS Wheels	3.0 ATS D3-Cosworth V8	*engine*
dns	"	"	9	ATS Wheels	3.0 ATS D3-Cosworth V8	*practice only*
ret	DUTCH GP	Zandvoort	9	ATS Wheels	3.0 ATS D3-Cosworth V8	*driveshaft*
11	ITALIAN GP	Monza	9	ATS Wheels	3.0 ATS D3-Cosworth V8	*1 lap behind*
ret	CANADIAN GP	Montreal	9	ATS Wheels	3.0 ATS D3-Cosworth V8	*accident with Arnoux*
5	US GP	Watkins Glen	9	ATS Wheels	3.0 ATS D3-Cosworth V8	

GP Starts: 72 (74)   GP Wins: 0   Pole positions: 0   Fastest laps: 0   Points: 29

SULLIVAN, Danny (USA) b 9/3/1950

	Race	Circuit	No	Entrant	Car/Engine	Comment
	1983					
11	BRAZILIAN GP	Rio	4	Benetton Tyrrell Team	3.0 Tyrrell 011-Cosworth V8	1 lap behind
8	US GP WEST	Long Beach	4	Benetton Tyrrell Team	3.0 Tyrrell 011-Cosworth V8	severe tyre vibration/2 laps behind
ret	FRENCH GP	Paul Ricard	4	Benetton Tyrrell Team	3.0 Tyrrell 011-Cosworth V8	clutch
ret	SAN MARINO GP	Imola	4	Benetton Tyrrell Team	3.0 Tyrrell 011-Cosworth V8	spun off
5	MONACO GP	Monte Carlo	4	Benetton Tyrrell Team	3.0 Tyrrell 011-Cosworth V8	2 laps behind
12	BELGIAN GP	Spa	4	Benetton Tyrrell Team	3.0 Tyrrell 011-Cosworth V8	1 lap behind
ret	US GP (DETROIT)	Detroit	4	Benetton Tyrrell Team	3.0 Tyrrell 011-Cosworth V8	electrics
dsq*	CANADIAN GP	Montreal	4	Benetton Tyrrell Team	3.0 Tyrrell 011-Cosworth V8	9th on road/*dsq car underweight
14	BRITISH GP	Silverstone	4	Benetton Tyrrell Team	3.0 Tyrrell 011-Cosworth V8	2 laps behind
12	GERMAN GP	Hockenheim	4	Benetton Tyrrell Team	3.0 Tyrrell 011-Cosworth V8	2 laps behind
ret	AUSTRIAN GP	Österreichring	4	Benetton Tyrrell Team	3.0 Tyrrell 011-Cosworth V8	multiple collision on lap 1
ret	DUTCH GP	Zandvoort	4	Benetton Tyrrell Team	3.0 Tyrrell 011-Cosworth V8	engine
ret	ITALIAN GP	Monza	4	Benetton Tyrrell Team	3.0 Tyrrell 011-Cosworth V8	fuel pump drive
ret	EUROPEAN GP	Brands Hatch	4	Benetton Tyrrell Team	3.0 Tyrrell 012-Cosworth V8	fire-broken fuel line
7	SOUTH AFRICAN GP	Kyalami	4	Benetton Tyrrell Team	3.0 Tyrrell 012-Cosworth V8	2 laps behind

GP Starts: 15   GP Wins: 0   Pole positions: 0   Fastest laps: 0   Points: 2

DANNY SULLIVAN

Sullivan is now a multi-millionaire, thanks to his fabulous success in IndyCar racing, but it wasn't always that way, for the Kentucky kid spent a good few hard seasons in England climbing the ladder towards a top-line career. Without any financial help, Danny somehow clung on in various junior formulae, scoring the occasional success, only to be knocked back by some misfortune. Eventually he went back to the States to get his career moving again, making a good impression in Can-Am with an old Lola in 1980, and returned the following year, winning a race at Las Vegas and taking fourth in the championship. Suddenly the momentum was building; an IndyCar debut for Forsythe-Newman at Atlanta brought third place, and after he had been bumped from the team by Rebaque and his bank balance, Danny returned to Can-Am to finish third in the standings.

For 1983 he took the plunge into Formula 1 with Tyrrell, a fifth place at Monaco and second in the Race of Champions showing what he could do, but the lure of a more competitive drive in Indy cars took Danny back across the Atlantic. In Shierson's team he took three wins in 1984, before joning Roger Penske's crack team to win a famous victory at Indy in 1985 which made him a household name in the US. Subsequently he went on to win the IndyCar title in 1988, with four wins and eight pole positions, before joining the ultimately unsuccessful Patrick Racing Alfa Romeo effort. He then moved to the Galles team with substantial backing from Molson, taking his total of wins to 17 by the end of the 1993 season.

MARC SURER

Something of a late starter in motor racing, Surer graduated from karts and Super Vee to the German F3 championship with the KWS team, taking the runner-up slot in 1976. The following year he made the move into Formula 2, gathering valuable experience. He had also been signed by Jochen Neerpasch to race a BMW 320i in the up-to-2-litre division of the German touring car championship for BMW's 'Junior Team', but his season was somewhat overshadowed by a clash with Hans Heyer which saw him suspended for two months.

Despite this unfortunate incident, Marc was promoted to the BMW Team Polifac Formula 2 team for 1978, as number two to Bruno Giacomelli, who went on to dominate proceedings. However, Surer backed his team-mate superbly, taking a clear second place in the championship with six second-place finishes. In 1979 he was promoted to team leader and duly took the honours, but serious doubts over his pedigree were already being voiced, as he seemed unable to dominate proceedings in the manner of true champions. Nevertheless Marc had already been given his Grand Prix baptism by Ensign, and he signed to drive for ATS in 1980, but his season had barely begun when he crashed in practice for the South African GP, sustaining broken ankles, which kept him sidelined until mid-season. For 1981, Surer joined the little Ensign team, and really began to come out of his shell, taking a superb fourth place and fastest lap in Brazil, and sixth at Monaco, before moving to Teddy Yip's Theodore team.

In 1982 his progress was once more halted by injury, when a crash at Kyalami left him with leg injuries which delayed his Arrows debut. Fit again, he was somewhat overshadowed by the emerging Boutsen and his chances to shine were restricted by the late development of the turbo car in 1984. When François Hesnault quit the Brabham team early in 1985, Marc finally got the opportunity to show his ability, and he enjoyed his best-ever season as team-mate to Nelson Piquet. In 1986, Surer was back with Arrows but, taking part in a German rally, he crashed his Ford into a tree, killing his co-driver and sustaining serious injuries and burns himself which ended his competitive racing career.

SURER, Marc (CH) b 18/9/1951

	Race	Circuit	No	Entrant	Car/Engine	Comment
	1979					
dnq	ITALIAN GP	Monza	22	Team Ensign	3.0 Ensign N179-Cosworth V8	
dnq	CANADIAN GP	Montreal	22	Team Ensign	3.0 Ensign N179-Cosworth V8	
ret	US GP EAST	Watkins Glen	22	Team Ensign	3.0 Ensign N179-Cosworth V8	engine
	1980					
ret	ARGENTINE GP	Buenos Aires	9	Team ATS	3.0 ATS D3-Cosworth V8	fire-brake fluid on disc
7	BRAZILIAN GP	Interlagos	9	Team ATS	3.0 ATS D3-Cosworth V8	1 lap behind
dnq	SOUTH AFRICAN GP	Kyalami	9	Team ATS	3.0 ATS D4-Cosworth V8	crashed in practice-broken ankle
ret	FRENCH GP	Paul Ricard	9	Team ATS	3.0 ATS D4-Cosworth V8	gearbox
ret	BRITISH GP	Brands Hatch	9	Team ATS	3.0 ATS D4-Cosworth V8	engine
12	GERMAN GP	Hockenheim	9	Team ATS	3.0 ATS D4-Cosworth V8	1 lap behind
12	AUSTRIAN GP	Österreichring	9	Team ATS	3.0 ATS D4-Cosworth V8	1 lap behind
10	DUTCH GP	Zandvoort	9	Team ATS	3.0 ATS D4-Cosworth V8	pit stop-fuel/3 laps behind
ret	ITALIAN GP	Imola	9	Team ATS	3.0 ATS D4-Cosworth V8	engine
dnq	CANADIAN GP	Montreal	9	Team ATS	3.0 ATS D4-Cosworth V8	
8	US GP EAST	Watkins Glen	9	Team ATS	3.0 ATS D4-Cosworth V8	2 laps behind

1981

ret	US GP WEST	Long Beach	14	Ensign Racing	3.0 Ensign N180B-Cosworth V8	electrics
4	BRAZILIAN GP	Rio	14	Ensign Racing	3.0 Ensign N180B-Cosworth V8	FL
ret	ARGENTINE GP	Buenos Aires	14	Ensign Racing	3.0 Ensign N180B-Cosworth V8	engine
9	SAN MARINO GP	Imola	14	Ensign Racing	3.0 Ensign N180B-Cosworth V8	pit stop-tyres/1 lap behind
11	BELGIAN GP	Zolder	14	Ensign Racing	3.0 Ensign N180B-Cosworth V8	2 laps behind
6	MONACO GP	Monte Carlo	14	Ensign Racing	3.0 Ensign N180B-Cosworth V8	2 laps behind
12	FRENCH GP	Paul Ricard	33	Theodore Racing Team	3.0 Theodore TY01-Cosworth V8	2 laps behind
11/ret	BRITISH GP	Silverstone	33	Theodore Racing Team	3.0 Theodore TY01-Cosworth V8	fuel pressure/7 laps behind
14/ret	GERMAN GP	Hockenheim	33	Theodore Racing Team	3.0 Theodore TY01-Cosworth V8	spun off last corner/2 laps behind
ret	AUSTRIAN GP	Österreichring	33	Theodore Racing Team	3.0 Theodore TY01-Cosworth V8	distributor
8	DUTCH GP	Zandvoort	33	Theodore Racing Team	3.0 Theodore TY01-Cosworth V8	3 laps behind
dnq	ITALIAN GP	Monza	33	Theodore Racing Team	3.0 Theodore TY01-Cosworth V8	
9	CANADIAN GP	Montreal	33	Theodore Racing Team	3.0 Theodore TY01-Cosworth V8	2 laps behind
ret	CAESARS PALACE GP	Las Vegas	33	Theodore Racing Team	3.0 Theodore TY01-Cosworth V8	rear suspension

1982

7*	BELGIAN GP	Zolder	29	Arrows Racing Team	3.0 Arrows A4-Cosworth V8	* 3rd place car dsq/4 laps behind
9	MONACO GP	Monte Carlo	29	Arrows Racing Team	3.0 Arrows A4-Cosworth V8	6 laps behind
8	US GP (DETROIT)	Detroit	29	Arrows Racing Team	3.0 Arrows A4-Cosworth V8	1 lap behind
5	CANADIAN GP	Montreal	29	Arrows Racing Team	3.0 Arrows A4-Cosworth V8	1 lap behind
10	DUTCH GP	Zandvoort	29	Arrows Racing Team	3.0 Arrows A4-Cosworth V8	pit stop-tyres/1 lap behind
ret	BRITISH GP	Brands Hatch	29	Arrows Racing Team	3.0 Arrows A4-Cosworth V8	engine
13	FRENCH GP	Paul Ricard	29	Arrows Racing Team	3.0 Arrows A4-Cosworth V8	2 laps behind
6	GERMAN GP	Hockenheim	29	Arrows Racing Team	3.0 Arrows A4-Cosworth V8	1 lap behind
ret	AUSTRIAN GP	Österreichring	29	Arrows Racing Team	3.0 Arrows A4-Cosworth V8	air lock in fuel system
15	SWISS GP	Dijon	29	Arrows Racing Team	3.0 Arrows A5-Cosworth V8	pit stop-tyres/4 laps behind
ret	ITALIAN GP	Monza	29	Arrows Racing Team	3.0 Arrows A4-Cosworth V8	engine
7	CAESARS PALACE GP	Las Vegas	29	Arrows Racing Team	3.0 Arrows A5-Cosworth V8	1 lap behind

1983

6	BRAZILIAN GP	Rio	29	Arrows Racing Team	3.0 Arrows A6-Cosworth V8	
5	US GP WEST	Long Beach	29	Arrows Racing Team	3.0 Arrows A6-Cosworth V8	1 lap behind
10	FRENCH GP	Paul Ricard	29	Arrows Racing Team	3.0 Arrows A6-Cosworth V8	1 lap behind
6	SAN MARINO GP	Imola	29	Arrows Racing Team	3.0 Arrows A6-Cosworth V8	1 lap behind
ret	MONACO GP	Monte Carlo	29	Arrows Racing Team	3.0 Arrows A6-Cosworth V8	accident with Warwick
11	BELGIAN GP	Spa	29	Arrows Racing Team	3.0 Arrows A6-Cosworth V8	1 lap behind
11	US GP (DETROIT)	Detroit	29	Arrows Racing Team	3.0 Arrows A6-Cosworth V8	2 laps behind
ret	CANADIAN GP	Montreal	29	Arrows Racing Team	3.0 Arrows A6-Cosworth V8	transmission
17	BRITISH GP	Silverstone	29	Arrows Racing Team	3.0 Arrows A6-Cosworth V8	3 laps behind
7	GERMAN GP	Hockenheim	29	Arrows Racing Team	3.0 Arrows A6-Cosworth V8	1 lap behind
ret	AUSTRIAN GP	Österreichring	29	Arrows Racing Team	3.0 Arrows A6-Cosworth V8	accident with Ghinzani and Laffite
8	DUTCH GP	Zandvoort	29	Arrows Racing Team	3.0 Arrows A6-Cosworth V8	2 laps behind
10	ITALIAN GP	Monza	29	Arrows Racing Team	3.0 Arrows A6-Cosworth V8	1 lap behind
ret	EUROPEAN GP	Brands Hatch	29	Arrows Racing Team	3.0 Arrows A6-Cosworth V8	engine
8	SOUTH AFRICAN GP	Kyalami	29	Arrows Racing Team	3.0 Arrows A6-Cosworth V8	2 laps behind

1984

7*	BRAZILIAN GP	Rio	17	Barclay Nordica Arrows BMW	3.0 Arrows A6-Cosworth V8	* 5th place car dsq/2 laps behind
9	SOUTH AFRICAN GP	Kyalami	17	Barclay Nordica Arrows BMW	3.0 Arrows A6-Cosworth V8	4 laps behind
8*	BELGIAN GP	Zolder	17	Barclay Nordica Arrows BMW	3.0 Arrows A6-Cosworth V8	* 6th place car dsq/2 laps behind
ret	SAN MARINO GP	Imola	17	Barclay Nordica Arrows BMW	1.5 t/c Arrows A7-BMW 4	turbo
ret	FRENCH GP	Dijon	17	Barclay Nordica Arrows BMW	3.0 Arrows A6-Cosworth V8	accident with Warwick
dnq	MONACO GP	Monte Carlo	17	Barclay Nordica Arrows BMW	3.0 Arrows A6-Cosworth V8	
ret	CANADIAN GP	Montreal	17	Barclay Nordica Arrows BMW	3.0 Arrows A6-Cosworth V8	engine
ret/dns	US GP (DETROIT)	Detroit	17	Barclay Nordica Arrows BMW	3.0 Arrows A6-Cosworth V8	hit Piquet-1st start/did not restart
ret	US GP (DALLAS)	Dallas	17	Barclay Nordica Arrows BMW	1.5 t/c Arrows A7-BMW 4	hit wall
11	BRITISH GP	Brands Hatch	17	Barclay Nordica Arrows BMW	1.5 t/c Arrows A7-BMW 4	11th place car dsq/4 laps behind
ret	GERMAN GP	Hockenheim	17	Barclay Nordica Arrows BMW	1.5 t/c Arrows A7-BMW 4	turbo
6	AUSTRIAN GP	Österreichring	17	Barclay Nordica Arrows BMW	1.5 t/c Arrows A7-BMW 4	1 lap behind
ret	DUTCH GP	Zandvoort	17	Barclay Nordica Arrows BMW	1.5 t/c Arrows A7-BMW 4	wheel bearing
ret	ITALIAN GP	Monza	17	Barclay Nordica Arrows BMW	1.5 t/c Arrows A7-BMW 4	engine
ret	EUROPEAN GP	Nürburgring	17	Barclay Nordica Arrows BMW	1.5 t/c Arrows A7-BMW 4	accident with Berger, Fabi & Ghinzani
ret	PORTUGUESE GP	Estoril	17	Barclay Nordica Arrows BMW	1.5 t/c Arrows A7-BMW 4	electrics

1985

15	CANADIAN GP	Montreal	8	Motor Racing Developments Ltd	1.5 t/c Brabham BT54-BMW 4	3 laps behind
8	US GP (DETROIT)	Detroit	8	Motor Racing Developments Ltd	1.5 t/c Brabham BT54-BMW 4	1 lap behind
8	FRENCH GP	Paul Ricard	8	Motor Racing Developments Ltd	1.5 t/c Brabham BT54-BMW 4	1 lap behind
6	BRITISH GP	Silverstone	8	Motor Racing Developments Ltd	1.5 t/c Brabham BT54-BMW 4	2 laps behind
ret	GERMAN GP	Nürburgring	8	Motor Racing Developments Ltd	1.5 t/c Brabham BT54-BMW 4	engine
6	AUSTRIAN GP	Österreichring	8	Motor Racing Developments Ltd	1.5 t/c Brabham BT54-BMW 4	1 lap behind
10/ret	DUTCH GP	Zandvoort	8	Motor Racing Developments Ltd	1.5 t/c Brabham BT54-BMW 4	exhaust/5 laps behind
4	ITALIAN GP	Monza	8	Motor Racing Developments Ltd	1.5 t/c Brabham BT54-BMW 4	
8	BELGIAN GP	Spa	8	Motor Racing Developments Ltd	1.5 t/c Brabham BT54-BMW 4	1 lap behind
ret	EUROPEAN GP	Brands Hatch	8	Motor Racing Developments Ltd	1.5 t/c Brabham BT54-BMW 4	turbo
ret	SOUTH AFRICAN GP	Kyalami	8	Motor Racing Developments Ltd	1.5 t/c Brabham BT54-BMW 4	engine
ret	AUSTRALIAN GP	Adelaide	8	Motor Racing Developments Ltd	1.5 t/c Brabham BT54-BMW 4	engine

1986

ret	BRAZILIAN GP	Rio	17	Barclay Arrows BMW	1.5 t/c Arrows A8-BMW 4	engine
ret	SPANISH GP	Jerez	17	Barclay Arrows BMW	1.5 t/c Arrows A8-BMW 4	fuel system
9	SAN MARINO GP	Imola	17	Barclay Arrows BMW	1.5 t/c Arrows A8-BMW 4	3 laps behind
9	MONACO GP	Monte Carlo	17	Barclay Arrows BMW	1.5 t/c Arrows A8-BMW 4	3 laps behind
9	BELGIAN GP	Spa	17	Barclay Arrows BMW	1.5 t/c Arrows A8-BMW 4	2 laps behind

GP Starts: 81 (82)   GP Wins: 0   Pole positions: 0   Fastest laps: 1   Points: 17

JOHN SURTEES

John Surtees is widely honoured as the only World Champion on two wheels and four, a remarkable achievement of which he can justly be proud. But that tag tends to be used so often that it is easy to forget what a brilliant all-round racing driver he really was.

Born into a motor cycling background – his father Jack was an amateur racer – the young Surtees began racing on two wheels seriously in 1951, becoming a star on Nortons through to the mid-fifties when he switched to the Italian MV Agusta concern. From 1956 to 1960 Surtees was the outstanding rider of the day, winning seven world titles in the 350 cc and 500 cc classes. He had some promising trials with both Vanwall and Aston Martin in 1959 and, when his bike commitments allowed, embarked on his car racing career early in 1960. A win first time out at Goodwood in Ken Tyrrell's Cooper Formula Junior marked him down as a special talent. No sooner had he purchased his own F2 Cooper than he received an invitation from Lotus to race their Formula 1 Lotus 18. At this point Colin Chapman was adroitly juggling with a number of drivers, a situation of which John was unaware. Nevertheless he proved staggeringly quick for one so inexperienced. In his second Grand Prix he was second only to Brabham, and he led in Portugal before an error cost him dear. Not so worldly-wise in those early days, John shied away from signing to drive alongside Jim Clark for the 1961 season, unhappy with Chapman's somewhat cavalier attitude towards his contract with Innes Ireland. In the short term at least, it proved to be the wrong decision. Joining the Yeoman Credit-backed team running off-the-shelf Coopers for 1961, Surtees recorded only mediocre results, the sole minor success being a win in the Glover Trophy. Things improved when the team, now under the Bowmaker banner, aligned themselves with Lola, and Surtees, deeply involved in the development of the car, came close to a Grand Prix victory. He did win a non-title race at Mallory Park, but at the end of the year could resist the overtures of Ferrari no longer.

John had a galvanising effect on the team, not only as a driver but also as a source of technical input, particularly in the development of the monocoque chassis. Prior to his arrival at Maranello, Ferrari had completely lost their way but by mid-1963 Surtees had won both the German GP and Mediterranean GP to re-establish the Scuderia as a potent force once more. When the team introduced the 158 V8 engine early in 1964, Surtees at last found the car in which he could make a realistic championship bid. Mid-season victories in Germany and Italy enabled him to travel to the final round in Mexico with a chance of the title, and luck was on his side as his two rivals, Clark and Hill, both hit trouble. It may not have been one of the most convincing championship wins, but in a year when all the cars were evenly matched it was still thoroughly deserved.

The 1965 season found Ferrari bogged down with their flat-12 engine project, and most of Surtees' success came in the older 158 V8 at the beginning of the season. Apart from his sports car commitments, which brought victory in the Nürburgring 1000 Km, John was now running his own Lola T70 on the North American sports car scene, but in practice for a race at Mosport he suffered a massive accident which he was very lucky to survive – as it was he lay in hospital with serious back injuries for many weeks before making a brave comeback the following spring. Ironically 1966 was probably his finest year despite the bitter disagreement which caused him to leave Ferrari in mid-term. Before the split, John had won the Belgian GP, the Syracuse GP and the Monza 1000 Km sports car race, but afterwards he scored victories in the Mexican GP for Cooper and a whole succession of sports car races back in his Lola.

The 1967 season was another busy one. Surtees joined the Honda F1 effort but development proved to be a slow and painful process, though some reward came when the hastily prepared Lola-based 'Hondola' won a sensational Italian GP by a hair's-breadth from Jack Brabham. John's involvement with Lola was deep. Running their Formula 2 car, he broke the Brabham dominance on occasion, which was a not inconsiderable feat, but the Lola-Aston Martin sports car project was best forgotten. Meanwhile his transatlantic journeys to bag some of the lucrative purse-money on offer in Can-Am went on unhindered. With little headway being made during the second year of the Surtees-Honda alliance, the project was abandoned at the end of the season, and for 1969 John joined BRM but it was to become a nightmarish season for both parties. His Can-Am drives for Chaparral that year were also less than satisfactory when the narrow 2H car proved to be the most difficult machine he had ever handled.

The logical decision was to follow the example of his fellow drivers Brabham and McLaren and build his own Formula 1 car. He was obliged to run a McLaren while his own challenger was being prepared, but a superb drive and fastest lap in South Africa proved he could still cut it behind the wheel. There was even a brief and successful return to Ferrari for three sports car races, before development of the Surtees TS7 took over, an aggregate win in the end-of-season Gold Cup race at Oulton Park boosting his morale. The 1971 season proved tougher than expected as the new TS9 made only an occasional impression on the Grand Prix elite. In the less rarefied atmosphere of non-championship races, John scored some useful placings, again winning the Gold Cup, but there was no denying it had been a disappointing season for a man who had been used to much greater things. Mike Hailwood's drive at Monza, coupled with a realisation that he could no longer fulfil all the roles in his team effectively, saw Surtees take a back seat in 1972. His third place in the International Trophy was his last Formula 1 success, while in Formula 2 he signed off his racing career with wins in the Japanese GP at Mount Fuji and the Shell GP at Imola. Thenceforth he concentrated on running his team, with a succession of drivers good, bad and indifferent filling the cockpit depending on the exigencies of the times. Certainly few of them could meet the exacting standards required by this hardest of task masters. When suitable sponsorship dried up and medical problems which had dogged him intermittently as a result of his 1965 Mosport accident resurfaced, he quit the racing scene somewhat disillusioned. Happily, having remarried and become a contented family man, John now enjoys the historic racing scene in both cars and bikes, where he is a major attraction demonstrating many of the machines he handled with such brilliance in the past.

SURTEES, John (GB) b 11/2/1934

1960

	Race	Circuit	No	Entrant	Car/Engine	Comment
ret	MONACO GP	Monte Carlo	26	Team Lotus	2.5 Lotus 18-Climax 4	transmission
2	BRITISH GP	Silverstone	9	Team Lotus	2.5 Lotus 18-Climax 4	
ret	PORTUGUESE GP	Oporto	18	Team Lotus	2.5 Lotus 18-Climax 4	radiator/Pole/FL
ret	US GP	Riverside	11	Team Lotus	2.5 Lotus 18-Climax 4	spun-hit by Clark

1961

	Race	Circuit	No	Entrant	Car/Engine	Comment
ret	MONACO GP	Monte Carlo	22	Yeoman Credit Racing Team	1.5 Cooper T53-Climax 4	head gasket
7	DUTCH GP	Zandvoort	12	Yeoman Credit Racing Team	1.5 Cooper T53-Climax 4	
5	BELGIAN GP	Spa	24	Yeoman Credit Racing Team	1.5 Cooper T53-Climax 4	
ret	FRENCH GP	Reims	40	Yeoman Credit Racing Team	1.5 Cooper T53-Climax 4	suspension
ret	BRITISH GP	Aintree	34	Yeoman Credit Racing Team	1.5 Cooper T53-Climax 4	transmission
5	GERMAN GP	Nürburgring	18	Yeoman Credit Racing Team	1.5 Cooper T53-Climax 4	
ret	ITALIAN GP	Monza	42	Yeoman Credit Racing Team	1.5 Cooper T53-Climax 4	accident

ret	US GP	Watkins Glen	18	Yeoman Credit Racing Team	1.5 Cooper T53-Climax 4	*engine*
dns	"	" "	26	Frank J Harrison	1.5 Lotus 18-Climax 4	*Lloyd Ruby's car-practice only*

1962

ret	DUTCH GP	Zandvoort	19	Bowmaker Racing Team	1.5 Lola 4-Climax V8	*suspension/Pole*
4	MONACO GP	Monte Carlo	28	Bowmaker Racing Team	1.5 Lola 4-Climax V8	*1 lap behind*
5	BELGIAN GP	Spa	5	Bowmaker Racing Team	1.5 Lola 4-Climax V8	*1 lap behind*
5	FRENCH GP	Rouen	18	Bowmaker Racing Team	1.5 Lola 4-Climax V8	*2 laps behind*
2	BRITISH GP	Aintree	24	Bowmaker Racing Team	1.5 Lola 4-Climax V8	
dns	"	"	24	Bowmaker Racing Team	1.5 Lola 4A-Climax V8	*practice only*
2	GERMAN GP	Nürburgring	14	Bowmaker Racing Team	1.5 Lola 4A-Climax V8	
dns	"	"	14	Bowmaker Racing Team	1.5 Lola 4A-Climax V8	*practice only*
ret	ITALIAN GP	Monza	46	Bowmaker Racing Team	1.5 Lola 4A-Climax V8	*engine*
dns	"	"	46	Bowmaker Racing Team	1.5 Lola 4-Climax V8	*practice only*
ret	US GP	Watkins Glen	18	Bowmaker Racing Team	1.5 Lola 4-Climax V8	*crankcase plug*
ret	SOUTH AFRICAN GP	East London	6	Bowmaker Racing Team	1.5 Lola 4-Climax V8	*engine*

1963

4	MONACO GP	Monte Carlo	21	Scuderia Ferrari SpA SEFAC	1.5 Ferrari 156 V6	*FL*
ret	BELGIAN GP	Spa	9	Scuderia Ferrari SpA SEFAC	1.5 Ferrari 156 V6	*fuel injection pipe*
3	DUTCH GP	Zandvoort	2	Scuderia Ferrari SpA SEFAC	1.5 Ferrari 156 V6	*1 lap behind*
ret	FRENCH GP	Reims	16	Scuderia Ferrari SpA SEFAC	1.5 Ferrari 156 V6	*fuel pump*
2	BRITISH GP	Silverstone	10	Scuderia Ferrari SpA SEFAC	1.5 Ferrari 156 V6	*FL*
1	GERMAN GP	Nürburgring	7	Scuderia Ferrari SpA SEFAC	1.5 Ferrari 156 V6	*FL*
ret	ITALIAN GP	Monza	4	Scuderia Ferrari SpA SEFAC	1.5 Ferrari 156 V6	*engine/Pole*
9/ret	US GP	Watkins Glen	23	Scuderia Ferrari SpA SEFAC	1.5 Ferrari 156 V6	*engine-valve spring*
dsq	MEXICAN GP	Mexico City	23	Scuderia Ferrari SpA SEFAC	1.5 Ferrari 156 V6	*push start at pit stop*
ret	SOUTH AFRICAN GP	East London	3	Scuderia Ferrari SpA SEFAC	1.5 Ferrari 156 V6	*engine*

1964 World Champion Driver

ret	MONACO GP	Monte Carlo	21	Scuderia Ferrari SpA SEFAC	1.5 Ferrari 158 V8	*gearbox*
dns	"	" "	21	Scuderia Ferrari SpA SEFAC	1.5 Ferrari 156 V6	*practice only*
2	DUTCH GP	Zandvoort	2	Scuderia Ferrari SpA SEFAC	1.5 Ferrari 158 V8	
ret	BELGIAN GP	Spa	10	Scuderia Ferrari SpA SEFAC	1.5 Ferrari 158 V8	*engine*
ret	FRENCH GP	Rouen	24	Scuderia Ferrari SpA SEFAC	1.5 Ferrari 158 V8	*oil pipe*
3	BRITISH GP	Brands Hatch	7	Scuderia Ferrari SpA SEFAC	1.5 Ferrari 158 V8	
dns	"	" "	7	Scuderia Ferrari SpA SEFAC	1.5 Ferrari 156 V6	*practice only*
1	GERMAN GP	Nürburgring	7	Scuderia Ferrari SpA SEFAC	1.5 Ferrari 158 V8	*Pole/FL*
ret	AUSTRIAN GP	Zeltweg	7	Scuderia Ferrari SpA SEFAC	1.5 Ferrari 158 V8	*rear suspension*
1	ITALIAN GP	Monza	2	Scuderia Ferrari SpA SEFAC	1.5 Ferrari 158 V8	*Pole/FL*
2	US GP	Watkins Glen	7	North American Racing Team	1.5 Ferrari 158 V8	
dns	"	" "	7T	North American Racing Team	1.5 Ferrari 156 V6	*practice only*
dns	"	" "	8T	North American Racing Team	1.5 Ferrari 1512 F12	*practice only*
2	MEXICAN GP	Mexico City	7	North American Racing Team	1.5 Ferrari 158 V8	

1965

2	SOUTH AFRICAN GP	East London	2	Scuderia Ferrari SpA SEFAC	1.5 Ferrari 158 V8	
4/ret	MONACO GP	Monte Carlo	18	Scuderia Ferrari SpA SEFAC	1.5 Ferrari 158 V8	*out of fuel/1 lap behind*
ret	BELGIAN GP	Spa	1	Scuderia Ferrari SpA SEFAC	1.5 Ferrari 158 V8	*engine*
3	FRENCH GP	Clermont Ferrand	2	Scuderia Ferrari SpA SEFAC	1.5 Ferrari 158 V8	
3	BRITISH GP	Silverstone	1	Scuderia Ferrari SpA SEFAC	1.5 Ferrari 1512 F12	
dns	"	"	71	Scuderia Ferrari SpA SEFAC	1.5 Ferrari 158 V8	*practice only*
7	DUTCH GP	Zandvoort	2	Scuderia Ferrari SpA SEFAC	1.5 Ferrari 1512 F12	*1 lap behind*
dns	"	"	2	Scuderia Ferrari SpA SEFAC	1.5 Ferrari 158 V8	*practice only*
ret	GERMAN GP	Nürburgring	7	Scuderia Ferrari SpA SEFAC	1.5 Ferrari 1512 F12	*gearbox*
ret	ITALIAN GP	Monza	8	Scuderia Ferrari SpA SEFAC	1.5 Ferrari 1512 F12	*clutch*

1966

ret	MONACO GP	Monte Carlo	17	Scuderia Ferrari SpA SEFAC	3.0 Ferrari 312/66 V12	*transmission*
1	BELGIAN GP	Spa	6	Scuderia Ferrari SpA SEFAC	3.0 Ferrari 312/66 V12	*Pole/FL*
ret	FRENCH GP	Reims	10	Cooper Car Co	3.0 Cooper T81-Maserati V12	*overheating*
ret	BRITISH GP	Brands Hatch	12	Cooper Car Co	3.0 Cooper T81-Maserati V12	*transmission*
ret	DUTCH GP	Zandvoort	24	Cooper Car Co	3.0 Cooper T81-Maserati V12	*electrics*
2	GERMAN GP	Nürburgring	7	Cooper Car Co	3.0 Cooper T81-Maserati V12	*FL*
ret	ITALIAN GP	Monza	14	Cooper Car Co	3.0 Cooper T81-Maserati V12	*fuel leak*
3	US GP	Watkins Glen	7	Cooper Car Co	3.0 Cooper T81-Maserati V12	*spin-pit stop/FL/1 lap behind*
1	MEXICAN GP	Mexico City	7	Cooper Car Co	3.0 Cooper T81-Maserati V12	*Pole*

1967

3	SOUTH AFRICAN GP	Kyalami	11	Honda Racing	3.0 Honda RA273 V12	*tyre problems/1 lap behind*
ret	MONACO GP	Monte Carlo	7	Honda Racing	3.0 Honda RA273 V12	*engine*
ret	DUTCH GP	Zandvoort	7	Honda Racing	3.0 Honda RA273 V12	*sticking throttle slides*
ret	BELGIAN GP	Spa	7	Honda Racing	3.0 Honda RA273 V12	*engine*
6	BRITISH GP	Silverstone	7	Honda Racing	3.0 Honda RA273 V12	*2 laps behind*
4	GERMAN GP	Nürburgring	7	Honda Racing	3.0 Honda RA273 V12	
1	ITALIAN GP	Monza	14	Honda Racing	3.0 Honda RA300 V12	*Lola developed chassis*
ret	US GP	Watkins Glen	3	Honda Racing	3.0 Honda RA300 V12	*alternator-flat battery*
4	MEXICAN GP	Mexico City	3	Honda Racing	3.0 Honda RA300 V12	*1 lap behind*

1968

8	SOUTH AFRICAN GP	Kyalami	7	Honda Racing	3.0 Honda RA300 V12	*2 pit stops-misfire/5 laps behind*
ret	SPANISH GP	Jarama	7	Honda Racing	3.0 Honda RA301 V12	*gearbox*
ret	MONACO GP	Monte Carlo	8	Honda Racing	3.0 Honda RA301 V12	*gearbox*
ret	BELGIAN GP	Spa	20	Honda Racing	3.0 Honda RA301 V12	*rear suspension/FL*
ret	DUTCH GP	Zandvoort	7	Honda Racing	3.0 Honda RA301 V12	*alternator drive-flat battery*
2	FRENCH GP	Rouen	16	Honda Racing	3.0 Honda RA301 V12	*pit stop-tyres*
5	BRITISH GP	Brands Hatch	7	Honda Racing	3.0 Honda RA301 V12	*rear wing fell off/2 laps behind*

ret	GERMAN GP	Nürburgring	7	Honda Racing	3.0 Honda RA301 V12	*overheating-ignition*
ret	ITALIAN GP	Monza	14	Honda Racing	3.0 Honda RA301 V12	*crashed avoiding Amon/Pole*
ret	CANADIAN GP	St Jovite	8	Honda Racing	3.0 Honda RA301 V12	*transmission*
3	US GP	Watkins Glen	5	Honda Racing	3.0 Honda RA301 V12	*1 lap behind*
ret	MEXICAN GP	Mexico City	5	Honda Racing	3.0 Honda RA301 V12	*overheating*

1969

ret	SOUTH AFRICAN GP	Kyalami	10	Owen Racing Organisation	3.0 BRM P138 V12	*engine*
5	SPANISH GP	Montjuich Park	14	Owen Racing Organisation	3.0 BRM P138 V12	*2 pit stops-fuel metering/-6 laps*
ret	MONACO GP	Monte Carlo	14	Owen Racing Organisation	3.0 BRM P138 V12	*gearbox-accident with Brabham*
9	DUTCH GP	Zandvoort	14	Owen Racing Organisation	3.0 BRM P138 V12	*pit stop-fuel/3 laps behind*
dns	"		14T	Owen Racing Organisation	3.0 BRM P139 V12	*practice only*
ret	BRITISH GP	Silverstone	14	Owen Racing Organisation	3.0 BRM P139 V12	*collapsed front suspension*
dns	GERMAN GP	Nürburgring	14	Owen Racing Organisation	3.0 BRM P139 V12	*suspension problems in practice*
11	ITALIAN GP	Monza	14	Owen Racing Organisation	3.0 BRM P139 V12	*2 pit stops-various/8 laps behind*
ret	CANADIAN GP	Mosport Park	14	Owen Racing Organisation	3.0 BRM P139 V12	*engine*
3	US GP	Watkins Glen	14	Owen Racing Organisation	3.0 BRM P139 V12	*2 laps behind*
ret	MEXICAN GP	Mexico City	14	Owen Racing Organisation	3.0 BRM P139 V12	*gearbox*

1970

ret	SOUTH AFRICAN GP	Kyalami	7	Team Surtees	3.0 McLaren M7C-Cosworth V8	*engine/FL*
ret	SPANISH GP	Jarama	8	Team Surtees	3.0 McLaren M7C-Cosworth V8	*gearbox*
ret	MONACO GP	Monte Carlo	14	Team Surtees	3.0 McLaren M7C-Cosworth V8	*oil pressure*
6	DUTCH GP	Zandvoort	16	Team Surtees	3.0 McLaren M7C-Cosworth V8	*1 lap behind*
ret	BRITISH GP	Brands Hatch	20	Team Surtees	3.0 Surtees TS7-Cosworth V8	*oil pressure*
9/ret	GERMAN GP	Hockenheim	7	Team Surtees	3.0 Surtees TS7-Cosworth V8	*engine/4 laps behind*
ret	AUSTRIAN GP	Österreichring	15	Team Surtees	3.0 Surtees TS7-Cosworth V8	*engine*
ret	ITALIAN GP	Monza	14	Team Surtees	3.0 Surtees TS7-Cosworth V8	*electrics*
5	CANADIAN GP	St Jovite	4	Team Surtees	3.0 Surtees TS7-Cosworth V8	*pit stop-misfire/1 lap behind*
ret	US GP	Watkins Glen	17	Team Surtees	3.0 Surtees TS7-Cosworth V8	*flywheel*
8	MEXICAN GP	Mexico City	17	Team Surtees	3.0 Surtees TS7-Cosworth V8	*1 lap behind*

1971

ret	SOUTH AFRICAN GP	Kyalami	20	Brooke Bond Oxo/Rob Walker/Team Surtees	3.0 Surtees TS9-Cosworth V8	*gearbox*
ret	"	"	20T	Brooke Bond Oxo/Rob Walker/Team Surtees	3.0 Surtees TS7-Cosworth V8	*practice only*
nc	SPANISH GP	Montjuich Park	24	Brooke Bond Oxo/Rob Walker/Team Surtees	3.0 Surtees TS9-Cosworth V8	*2 pit stops-body damage*
7	MONACO GP	Monte Carlo	22	Brooke Bond Oxo/Rob Walker/Team Surtees	3.0 Surtees TS9-Cosworth V8	*1 lap behind*
5	DUTCH GP	Zandvoort	23	Brooke Bond Oxo/Rob Walker/Team Surtees	3.0 Surtees TS9-Cosworth V8	*2 laps behind*
8	FRENCH GP	Paul Ricard	22	Brooke Bond Oxo/Rob Walker/Team Surtees	3.0 Surtees TS9-Cosworth V8	
6	BRITISH GP	Silverstone	23	Brooke Bond Oxo/Rob Walker/Team Surtees	3.0 Surtees TS9-Cosworth V8	*1 lap behind*
7	GERMAN GP	Nürburgring	7	Brooke Bond Oxo/Rob Walker/Team Surtees	3.0 Surtees TS9-Cosworth V8	
ret	AUSTRIAN GP	Österreichring	22	Brooke Bond Oxo/Rob Walker/Team Surtees	3.0 Surtees TS9-Cosworth V8	*engine*
ret	ITALIAN GP	Monza	7	Brooke Bond Oxo/Rob Walker/Team Surtees	3.0 Surtees TS9-Cosworth V8	*engine*
11	CANADIAN GP	Mosport Park	22	Brooke Bond Oxo/Rob Walker/Team Surtees	3.0 Surtees TS9-Cosworth V8	*4 laps behind*
17	US GP	Watkins Glen	18	Brooke Bond Oxo/Rob Walker/Team Surtees	3.0 Surtees TS9-Cosworth V8	*pit stop-ignition/5 laps behind*

1972

ret	ITALIAN GP	Monza	7	Team Surtees	3.0 Surtees TS14-Cosworth V8	*fuel vaporisation*
dns	US GP	Watkins Glen	24	Team Surtees	3.0 Surtees TS14-Cosworth V8	*practice only-engine shortage*

GP Starts: 111 GP Wins: 6 Pole positions: 8 Fastest laps: 11 Points: 180

SUZUKI, Aguri (J) b 8/9/1960

1988

	Race	Circuit	No	Entrant	Car/Engine	Comment
16	JAPANESE GP	Suzuka	29	Larrousse Calmels	3.5 Lola LC88-Cosworth V8	*3 laps behind*

1989

dnpq	BRAZILIAN GP	Rio	35	West Zakspeed Racing	3.5 West Zakspeed 891-Yamaha V8	
dnpq	SAN MARINO GP	Imola	35	West Zakspeed Racing	3.5 West Zakspeed 891-Yamaha V8	
dnpq	MONACO GP	Monte Carlo	35	West Zakspeed Racing	3.5 West Zakspeed 891-Yamaha V8	
dnpq	MEXICAN GP	Mexico City	35	West Zakspeed Racing	3.5 West Zakspeed 891-Yamaha V8	
dnpq	US GP (PHOENIX)	Phoenix	35	West Zakspeed Racing	3.5 West Zakspeed 891-Yamaha V8	
dnpq	CANADIAN GP	Montreal	35	West Zakspeed Racing	3.5 West Zakspeed 891-Yamaha V8	
dnpq	FRENCH GP	Paul Ricard	35	West Zakspeed Racing	3.5 West Zakspeed 891-Yamaha V8	
dnpq	BRITISH GP	Silverstone	35	West Zakspeed Racing	3.5 West Zakspeed 891-Yamaha V8	
dnpq	GERMAN GP	Hockenheim	35	West Zakspeed Racing	3.5 West Zakspeed 891-Yamaha V8	
dnpq	HUNGARIAN GP	Hungaroring	35	West Zakspeed Racing	3.5 West Zakspeed 891-Yamaha V8	
dnpq	BELGIAN GP	Spa	35	West Zakspeed Racing	3.5 West Zakspeed 891-Yamaha V8	
dnpq	ITALIAN GP	Monza	35	West Zakspeed Racing	3.5 West Zakspeed 891-Yamaha V8	
dnpq	PORTUGUESE GP	Estoril	35	West Zakspeed Racing	3.5 West Zakspeed 891-Yamaha V8	
dnpq	SPANISH GP	Jerez	35	West Zakspeed Racing	3.5 West Zakspeed 891-Yamaha V8	
dnpq	JAPANESE GP	Suzuka	35	West Zakspeed Racing	3.5 West Zakspeed 891-Yamaha V8	
dnpq	AUSTRALIAN GP	Adelaide	35	West Zakspeed Racing	3.5 West Zakspeed 891-Yamaha V8	

1990

ret	US GP (PHOENIX)	Phoenix	30	Espo Larrousse F1	3.5 Lola LC89-Lamborghini V12	*brakes*
ret	BRAZILIAN GP	Rio	30	Espo Larrousse F1	3.5 Lola LC89-Lamborghini V12	*suspension*
ret	SAN MARINO GP	Imola	30	Espo Larrousse F1	3.5 Lola LC90-Lamborghini V12	*clutch*
ret	MONACO GP	Monte Carlo	30	Espo Larrousse F1	3.5 Lola LC90-Lamborghini V12	*electrics*
12	CANADIAN GP	Montreal	30	Espo Larrousse F1	3.5 Lola LC90-Lamborghini V12	*collision-Martini pit stop/-4 laps*
ret	MEXICAN GP	Mexico City	30	Espo Larrousse F1	3.5 Lola LC90-Lamborghini V12	*collision with Nakajima*
7	FRENCH GP	Paul Ricard	30	Espo Larrousse F1	3.5 Lola LC90-Lamborghini V12	*1 lap behind*
6	BRITISH GP	Silverstone	30	Espo Larrousse F1	3.5 Lola LC90-Lamborghini V12	*1 lap behind*
ret	GERMAN GP	Hockenheim	30	Espo Larrousse F1	3.5 Lola LC90-Lamborghini V12	*clutch*
ret	HUNGARIAN GP	Hungaroring	30	Espo Larrousse F1	3.5 Lola LC90-Lamborghini V12	*engine*

ret/dns	BELGIAN GP	Spa	30	Espo Larrousse F1	3.5 Lola LC90-Lamborghini V12	accident at first start/did not restart
ret	ITALIAN GP	Monza	30	Espo Larrousse F1	3.5 Lola LC90-Lamborghini V12	electrics
14/ret	PORTUGUESE GP	Estoril	30	Espo Larrousse F1	3.5 Lola LC90-Lamborghini V12	collision with Caffi/3 laps behind
6	SPANISH GP	Jerez	30	Espo Larrousse F1	3.5 Lola LC90-Lamborghini V12	
3	JAPANESE GP	Suzuka	30	Espo Larrousse F1	3.5 Lola LC90-Lamborghini V12	
ret	AUSTRALIAN GP	Adelaide	30	Espo Larrousse F1	3.5 Lola LC90-Lamborghini V12	differential

1991

6	US GP (PHOENIX)	Phoenix	30	Larrousse F1	3.5 Larrousse Lola L91-Cosworth V8	2 laps behind
dns	BRAZILIAN GP	Interlagos	30	Larrousse F1	3.5 Larrousse Lola L91-Cosworth V8	no fuel pressure on dummy grid
ret	SAN MARINO GP	Imola	30	Larrousse F1	3.5 Larrousse Lola L91-Cosworth V8	spun off
ret	MONACO GP	Monte Carlo	30	Larrousse F1	3.5 Larrousse Lola L91-Cosworth V8	brake problems-crashed
ret	CANADIAN GP	Montreal	30	Larrousse F1	3.5 Larrousse Lola L91-Cosworth V8	fire-broken fuel line
ret	MEXICAN GP	Mexico City	30	Larrousse F1	3.5 Larrousse Lola L91-Cosworth V8	gearbox
ret	FRENCH GP	Magny Cours	30	Larrousse F1	3.5 Larrousse Lola L91-Cosworth V8	clutch
ret	BRITISH GP	Silverstone	30	Larrousse F1	3.5 Larrousse Lola L91-Cosworth V8	collision with Alesi
ret	GERMAN GP	Hockenheim	30	Larrousse F1	3.5 Larrousse Lola L91-Cosworth V8	engine
ret	HUNGARIAN GP	Hungaroring	30	Larrousse F1	3.5 Larrousse Lola L91-Cosworth V8	engine
dnq	BELGIAN GP	Spa	30	Larrousse F1	3.5 Larrousse Lola L91-Cosworth V8	
dnq	ITALIAN GP	Monza	30	Larrousse F1	3.5 Larrousse Lola L91-Cosworth V8	
ret	PORTUGUESE GP	Estoril	30	Larrousse F1	3.5 Larrousse Lola L91-Cosworth V8	gearbox
dnq	SPANISH GP	Barcelona	30	Larrousse F1	3.5 Larrousse Lola L91-Cosworth V8	
ret	JAPANESE GP	Suzuka	30	Larrousse F1	3.5 Larrousse Lola L91-Cosworth V8	engine
dnq	AUSTRALIAN GP	Adelaide	30	Larrousse F1	3.5 Larrousse Lola L91-Cosworth V8	

1992

8	SOUTH AFRICAN GP	Kyalami	10	Footwork Mugen Honda	3.5 Footwork FA13-Mugen Honda V10	2 laps behind
dnq	MEXICAN GP	Mexico City	10	Footwork Mugen Honda	3.5 Footwork FA13-Mugen Honda V10	
ret	BRAZILIAN GP	Interlagos	10	Footwork Mugen Honda	3.5 Footwork FA13-Mugen Honda V10	oil system
7	SPANISH GP	Barcelona	10	Footwork Mugen Honda	3.5 Footwork FA13-Mugen Honda V10	2 laps behind
10	SAN MARINO GP	Imola	10	Footwork Mugen Honda	3.5 Footwork FA13-Mugen Honda V10	2 laps behind
11	MONACO GP	Monte Carlo	10	Footwork Mugen Honda	3.5 Footwork FA13-Mugen Honda V10	2 laps behind
dnq	CANADIAN GP	Montreal	10	Footwork Mugen Honda	3.5 Footwork FA13-Mugen Honda V10	
ret	FRENCH GP	Magny Cours	10	Footwork Mugen Honda	3.5 Footwork FA13-Mugen Honda V10	slid off avoiding Grouillard
12	BRITISH GP	Silverstone	10	Footwork Mugen Honda	3.5 Footwork FA13-Mugen Honda V10	2 laps behind
ret	GERMAN GP	Hockenheim	10	Footwork Mugen Honda	3.5 Footwork FA13-Mugen Honda V10	spun off lap 1
ret	HUNGARIAN GP	Hungaroring	10	Footwork Mugen Honda	3.5 Footwork FA13-Mugen Honda V10	collision with Gachot
9	BELGIAN GP	Spa	10	Footwork Mugen Honda	3.5 Footwork FA13-Mugen Honda V10	1 lap behind
ret	ITALIAN GP	Monza	10	Footwork Mugen Honda	3.5 Footwork FA13-Mugen Honda V10	spun off
10	PORTUGUESE GP	Estoril	10	Footwork Mugen Honda	3.5 Footwork FA13-Mugen Honda V10	started from pit lane/3 laps behind
8	JAPANESE GP	Suzuka	10	Footwork Mugen Honda	3.5 Footwork FA13-Mugen Honda V10	1 lap behind
8	AUSTRALIAN GP	Adelaide	10	Footwork Mugen Honda	3.5 Footwork FA13-Mugen Honda V10	2 laps behind

1993

ret	SOUTH AFRICAN GP	Kyalami	10	Footwork Mugen Honda	3.5 Footwork FA13B-Mugen Honda V10	ran into Barbazza-suspension
ret	BRAZILIAN GP	Rio	10	Footwork Mugen Honda	3.5 Footwork FA13B-Mugen Honda V10	crashed in rainstorm
ret	EUROPEAN GP	Donington	10	Footwork Mugen Honda	3.5 Footwork FA14-Mugen Honda V10	gearbox
9	SAN MARINO GP	Imola	10	Footwork Mugen Honda	3.5 Footwork FA14-Mugen Honda V10	stop & go penalty/brakes/-7 laps
10	SPANISH GP	Barcelona	10	Footwork Mugen Honda	3.5 Footwork FA14-Mugen Honda V10	2 laps behind
ret	MONACO GP	Monte Carlo	10	Footwork Mugen Honda	3.5 Footwork FA14-Mugen Honda V10	spun off
13	CANADIAN GP	Montreal	10	Footwork Mugen Honda	3.5 Footwork FA14-Mugen Honda V10	gearbox trouble/spin/-3 laps
12	FRENCH GP	Magny Cours	10	Footwork Mugen Honda	3.5 Footwork FA14-Mugen Honda V10	stalled at pit stop/2 laps behind
ret	BRITISH GP	Silverstone	10	Footwork Mugen Honda	3.5 Footwork FA14-Mugen Honda V10	spun off
ret	GERMAN GP	Hockenheim	10	Footwork Mugen Honda	3.5 Footwork FA14-Mugen Honda V10	spun/stop & go penalty/gearbox
ret	HUNGARIAN GP	Hungaroring	10	Footwork Mugen Honda	3.5 Footwork FA14-Mugen Honda V10	spun off
ret	BELGIAN GP	Spa	10	Footwork Mugen Honda	3.5 Footwork FA14-Mugen Honda V10	hydraulic failure
ret	ITALIAN GP	Monza	10	Footwork Mugen Honda	3.5 Footwork FA14-Mugen Honda V10	collision-Warwick spun off lap 1
ret	PORTUGUESE GP	Estoril	10	Footwork Mugen Honda	3.5 Footwork FA14-Mugen Honda V10	spin/gearbox
ret	JAPANESE GP	Suzuka	10	Footwork Mugen Honda	3.5 Footwork FA14-Mugen Honda V10	spun off
7	AUSTRALIAN GP	Adelaide	10	Footwork Mugen Honda	3.5 Footwork FA14-Mugen Honda V10	1 lap behind

GP Starts: 57 (58)   GP Wins: 0   Pole positions: 0   Fastest laps: 0   Points: 7

SUZUKI, Toshio (J) b 10/3/1955

1993

	Race	Circuit	No	Entrant	Car/Engine	Comment
12	JAPANESE GP	Suzuka	19	Larrousse F1	3.5 Larrousse LH93-Lamborghini V12	spin/2 laps behind
14	AUSTRALIAN GP	Adelaide	19	Larrousse F1	3.5 Larrousse LH93-Lamborghini V12	5 laps behind

GP Starts: 2   GP Wins: 0   Pole positions: 0   Fastest laps: 0   Points: 0

SWATERS, Jacques (B) b 30/10/1926

1951

	Race	Circuit	No	Entrant	Car/Engine	Comment
10	GERMAN GP	Nürburgring	93	Ecurie Belgique	4.5 Lago-Talbot T26C 6	2 laps behind
ret	ITALIAN GP	Monza	28	Ecurie Belgique	4.5 Lago-Talbot T26C 6	overheating

1953

dns	BELGIAN GP	Spa	42	Ecurie Francorchamps	2.0 Ferrari 500 4	practised only
7	GERMAN GP	Nürburgring	18	Ecurie Francorchamps	2.0 Ferrari 500 4	
ret	SWISS GP	Bremgarten	2	Ecurie Francorchamps	2.0 Ferrari 500 4	crashed

1954

ret	BELGIAN GP	Spa	2	Ecurie Francorchamps	2.5 Ferrari 500/625 4	engine
8	SWISS GP	Bremgarten	2	Ecurie Francorchamps	2.5 Ferrari 500/625 4	
ret	SPANISH GP	Pedralbes	30	Ecurie Francorchamps	2.5 Ferrari 500/625 4	engine

GP Starts: 7   GP Wins: 0   Pole positions: 0   Fastest laps: 0   Points: 0

AGURI SUZUKI

To date Suzuki is Japan's most successful Grand Prix contender, and the only one to stand on the podium, courtesy of his excellent third place in the 1990 Japanese GP. His father was the founder of the Japanese karting association, and the young Suzuki naturally became involved in the sport, winning the the title in 1981. He then moved into F3 and finished second in the 1983 championship, which brought an offer to race for Nissan in sports and touring cars, Aguri taking the 1986 Group A championship.

Single-seaters were still his first priority, and in 1987 Suzuki went into the All-Japan F3000 series, finishing runner-up, before finishing the job the following year by taking the title. His eyes were now on Grand Prix racing and he briefly came to Europe to race the Footwork-backed March in the F3000 series, before being given a race in the Japanese GP with the Larrousse teamin place of the indisposed Dalmas. Having previously been associated with Yamaha, Aguri joined the Zakspeed team which was runnning the Japanese manufacturer's engines for 1989, but Suzuki drew a complete blank, failing even to pre-qualify the hopeless device at every one of the 16 Grands Prix.

This could have sunk many a driver's career, but luckily he was able to find a drive with Larrousse in 1990, when he became a points-scorer on three occasions, including his splendid drive at Suzuka, which cemented his future. Unfortunately the precarious financial position at Larrousse, and consequent lack of testing and development, blunted his progress the following year, and for 1992 Aguri joined the Footwork team, which was itself regrouping, but armed with the Mugen-Honda V10. Suzuki's season was disappointing, his form not helped by the problems he had fitting into the cockpit, and he was completely overshadowed by team-mate Michele Alboreto. For 1993, he remained with the team, paired with Derek Warwick, but once again finishes in the points eluded him. The year was punctuated by a worryingly high number of spins and collisions, and apart from sixth place on the grid at Spa, which seemed to suit the Footwork's active suspension system, there precious little to cheer the Japanese driver whose career was seemingly at the crossroads.

TOSHIO SUZUKI

In 1993 Toshio Suzuki took part in a Grand Prix for the first time at the age of 38, having arranged a two-race deal with Larrousse in place of Philippe Alliot. His aim was to finish, and in that he succeeded, but just to compete at this level must have been a source of great satisfaction for this very popular driver, who had been Japanese Formula 3 champion as far back as 1979. He raced in Europe during 1980-81, and has been a leading contender in the Japanese F2 and F3000 series for more than a decade but enjoyed little luck.

It was in sports car racing that Toshio found his greatest success. After driving Toyotas, he joined Nissan to team up with Kazuyoshi Hoshino, the pair becoming a formidable combination not only at home but also on the international stage, their greatest triumph coming in the 1992 Daytona 24 Hours when, with Masahiro Hasemi, they became the first all-Japanese crew to win a major race.

JACQUES SWATERS

A great enthusiast, Swaters made his racing debut in the 1948 Spa 24 Hours in an MG shared with his friend Paul Frère. In 1950, he was one of the founders of Ecurie Belgique and initially handled a Veritas, but when Pilette was injured in the team's Talbot at the 1951 Dutch GP, Jacques stepped in to take his place. For 1952, the team bought a Ferrari T500, which was mainly raced by de Tornaco, but Swaters drove it in two Grands Prix the following year and also won the AVUS F2 race. For 1954, Jacques raced the Ferrari fitted with a 625 engine, but found greater success in sports car events with the team's recently acquired Jaguar C-Type, taking fourth at Le Mans and third in the Reims 12 Hours with Laurent. Swaters then concentrated on sports cars, taking the team's D-Type to third place at Le Mans with Claes in 1955, and finishing fourth in 1956 with the same car, partnered by Rousselle. By this time he was busy with the management of Ecurie Francorchamps, and his thriving Ferrari concession, and retired from racing after a final appearance in the Sarthe classic in 1957.

NORITAKE TAKAHARA

Though not as fast a driver in the seventies as his rivals, Masahiro Hasemi and Kazuyoshi Hoshino, Takahara nevertheless got the results that mattered, winning the Japanese F2 title and the Grand Champion sports car series – for the third time – in 1976.

He began racing in 1969 in a Honda S800 coupé, and was a successful March driver in Japan in the early seventies. In 1973 he appeared very briefly in European Formula 2 with a GRD and the following season saw him race a works March 741 in the International Trophy, where he drove steadily and sensibly into 11th place. His ninth-place finish in a rented Surtees at Fuji in 1976 earned him the distinction of being the first Japanese driver to finish a World Championship Grand Prix. Much to the chagrin of Hasemi, Takahara took over his seat in the Kojima team in 1977, racing in that year's Grand Prix. He was a leading contender in the Japanese Formula 2 series for the rest of the decade, driving Nova, Martini and March chassis, and like his aforementioned rivals continued to race, though much less regularly, throughout the eighties.

TAKAHARA, Noritake (J) b 6/6/1951

	Race	Circuit	No	Entrant	Car/Engine	Comment
	1976					
9	JAPANESE GP	Mount Fuji	18	Team Surtees	3.0 Surtees TS19-Cosworth V8	*3 laps behind*
	1977					
ret	JAPANESE GP	Mount Fuji	51	Kojima Engineering	3.0 Kojima KE009-Cosworth V8	*crashed avoiding Andretti's wheel*
	GP Starts: 2 GP Wins: 0 Pole positions: 0 Fastest laps: 0 Points: 0					

TAKAHASHI, Kunimitsu (J) b 29/1/1940

1977

Race		Circuit	No	Entrant		Car/Engine	Comment
9	JAPANESE GP	Mount Fuji	50	Meiritsu Racing Team	.	3.0 Tyrrell 007-Cosworth V8	2 laps behind

GP Starts: 1   GP Wins: 0   Pole positions: 0   Fastest laps: 0   Points: 0

KUNIMITSU TAKAHASHI

Takahashi began his career on two wheels as a motor cycle racer, gaining the distinction of being the first Japanese rider to win a World Championship Grand Prix on a 250 cc Honda in 1961, when aged just 21. A serious accident in 1962 during the Isle of Man TT races halted his progress and he eventually switched to four wheels. A regular competitor in the Japanese sports car series in the 1970s, he raced the old Tyrrell that had been used by Hoshino the previous year in the 1977 Japanese GP and took a distant ninth place, though satisfyingly he was ahead of the Kojima driven by Hoshino.

He subsequently joined the Kojima team for the domestic Formula 2 series and later also ran a Toleman TG280 with backing from Yokohama tyres.

PATRICK TAMBAY

Easy-going and impeccably mannered, the general consensus is that Patrick was just too nice a guy to succeed in the cut-throat world of Grand Prix racing. Certainly the cosmopolitan Frenchman had a lot of talent, but maybe he lacked the single-minded determination which is a crucial part of any true champion's armoury.

Patrick's career got off to the brightest of starts when he won the Pilote Elf scheme, which was the passport to Formule Renault in 1973. Finishing runner-up in the series, he leap-frogged straight into the European F2 championship with the Elf team for 1974 and won a round at Nogaro to cap a consistent first season at this level. A seat in the Elf-backed works March team the following year should have brought Tambay more success than a singleton victory. Although he scored four second places to take the runner-up position in the series, worryingly he was involved in a series of silly accidents. Competing in the series with Elf backing for a third year in 1976 but this time running a Martini chassis, he once again scored just a single victory – remarkably, like his two previous wins, it came at Nogaro – but finishing third in the championship was regarded as a failure by the French oil company, who dropped him in favour of Didier Pironi.

Tambay's career was in limbo at the start of 1977 until he was offered the Carl Haas/Jim Hall Can-Am car in place of the badly injured Brian Redman. Though the opposition was in the main modest, he made the most of the opportunity and won six of the seven rounds in which he competed to take the championship easily. His luck had turned for the better for, after a fiasco at Dijon where he was dumped into a Surtees at short notice in a desperate attempt to get him into the race, he finally made his Grand Prix debut in Teddy Yip's Ensign at Silverstone. Given the previous poor reliability record of the N177, the inexperienced Tambay did well to score points in three races, and even a massive practice crash at Monza failed to dent the Frenchman's new-found confidence.

Joining the McLaren team in 1978 should have seen Patrick make the big break-through, but unfortunately their star was temporarily on the wane, and although he took five points-scoring finishes that year his second season was something of a disaster. Failing to qualify at both Zolder and Monaco was the nadir of a year in which McLaren plumbed the depths. So in 1980 he was back across 'the pond', making hay in Can-Am once more and taking a second title in the Carl Haas Lola T530.

Teddy Yip still had faith in the Frenchman and signed him for his Theodore F1 outfit for 1981. A sixth place in the US GP first time out was way beyond the little team's expectations, but Patrick performed so well in the car subsequently that he was an obvious candidate to replace Jean-Pierre Jabouille when he decided to retire from Ligier in mid-season. However, Tambay's short stay with the French team was a desperately unhappy one, ending in a string of accidents which could have beached his Grand Prix career for good.

In motor racing one man's misfortune is another's opportunity, however, and in the saddest of circumstances Patrick was brought into the Ferrari line-up in place of the late Gilles Villeneuve. He soon found his feet and after yet another terrible setback for the team at Hockenheim, when Pironi was injured so terribly in practice, he rose to the occasion magnificently by winning the race. For the rest of the season he carried the weight of the team manfully despite a painful back problem which caused him to miss two races. Tambay was joined by René Arnoux for 1983, and the two Frenchmen had the equipment to launch a championship assault. Although Arnoux came closer in terms of results, Patrick's all-round performances were the more convincing, and it was a major surprise when he was the one released at the end of the year to make way for Alboreto.

Moving to Renault for the 1984 season, Tambay failed to find any sort of continuity as minor problems constantly undermined his efforts. This led to an inconsistency which was scarcely helped by the introduction of the disappointing RE60 in 1985. Patrick made a solid start but the car could never be persuaded to offer a truly satisfactory level of performance on a regular basis, which must have driven both Tambay and Warwick to distraction as they gave their all. At the end of the year the Renault factory team closed their doors to lick their wounds, leaving Tambay seeking employment once more. He found it with the Haas Lola team, who were embarking on a full season with the Ford turbo engine. As an exercise in wasting money, this was as good as any, and both Tambay and Alan Jones were forced to spend the season in midfield mediocrity before the team folded.

Subsequently Patrick joined the TWR Jaguar team for the 1989 season, gaining some good placings with Jan Lammers. He now works in Grand Prix racing once more, as a TV commentator.

TAMBAY, Patrick (F) b 25/6/1949

1977

	Race	Circuit	No	Entrant	Car/Engine	Comment
dnq	FRENCH GP	Dijon	18	Team Surtees	3.0 Surtees TS19-Cosworth V8	Ensign not ready/1 session only
ret	BRITISH GP	Silverstone	23	Theodore Racing Hong Kong	3.0 Ensign N177-Cosworth V8	electrics
6	GERMAN GP	Hockenheim	23	Theodore Racing Hong Kong	3.0 Ensign N177-Cosworth V8	
ret	AUSTRIAN GP	Österreichring	23	Theodore Racing Hong Kong	3.0 Ensign N177-Cosworth V8	engine
5	DUTCH GP	Zandvoort	23	Theodore Racing Hong Kong	3.0 Ensign N177-Cosworth V8	out of fuel/2 laps behind
ret	ITALIAN GP	Monza	23	Theodore Racing Hong Kong	3.0 Ensign N177-Cosworth V8	engine
dnq	US GP EAST	Watkins Glen	23	Theodore Racing Hong Kong	3.0 Ensign N177-Cosworth V8	engine problems in practice
5	CANADIAN GP	Mosport Park	23	Theodore Racing Hong Kong	3.0 Ensign N177-Cosworth V8	
ret	JAPANESE GP	Mount Fuji	23	Theodore Racing Hong Kong	3.0 Ensign N177-Cosworth V8	engine

1978

	Race	Circuit	No	Entrant	Car/Engine	Comment
6	ARGENTINE GP	Buenos Aires	8	Marlboro Team McLaren	3.0 McLaren M26-Cosworth V8	
ret	BRAZILIAN GP	Rio	8	Marlboro Team McLaren	3.0 McLaren M26-Cosworth V8	hit by Scheckter-spun off
ret	SOUTH AFRICAN GP	Kyalami	8	Marlboro Team McLaren	3.0 McLaren M26-Cosworth V8	spun-damaged radiator & rear wing
12/ret	US GP WEST	Long Beach	8	Marlboro Team McLaren	3.0 McLaren M26-Cosworth V8	hit by Laffite/6 laps behind
7	MONACO GP	Monte Carlo	8	Marlboro Team McLaren	3.0 McLaren M26-Cosworth V8	1 lap behind
ret	SPANISH GP	Jarama	8	Marlboro Team McLaren	3.0 McLaren M26-Cosworth V8	spun off
4	SWEDISH GP	Anderstorp	8	Marlboro Team McLaren	3.0 McLaren M26-Cosworth V8	1 lap behind
9	FRENCH GP	Paul Ricard	8	Marlboro Team McLaren	3.0 McLaren M26-Cosworth V8	pit stop-rear end problems
6	BRITISH GP	Brands Hatch	8	Marlboro Team McLaren	3.0 McLaren M26-Cosworth V8	1 lap behind
ret	GERMAN GP	Hockenheim	8	Marlboro Team McLaren	3.0 McLaren M26-Cosworth V8	puncture-crashed
ret	AUSTRIAN GP	Österreichring	8	Marlboro Team McLaren	3.0 McLaren M26-Cosworth V8	spun off
9	DUTCH GP	Zandvoort	8	Marlboro Team McLaren	3.0 McLaren M26-Cosworth V8	1 lap behind
5	ITALIAN GP	Monza	8	Marlboro Team McLaren	3.0 McLaren M26-Cosworth V8	
6	US GP EAST	Watkins Glen	8	Marlboro Team McLaren	3.0 McLaren M26-Cosworth V8	
8	CANADIAN GP	Montreal	8	Marlboro Team McLaren	3.0 McLaren M26-Cosworth V8	

1979

	Race	Circuit	No	Entrant	Car/Engine	Comment
ret/dns	ARGENTINE GP	Buenos Aires	8	Marlboro Team McLaren	3.0 McLaren M28-Cosworth V8	accident in first start/did not restart
ret	BRAZILIAN GP	Interlagos	8	Marlboro Team McLaren	3.0 McLaren M26-Cosworth V8	accident with Regazzoni
dns	"	"	8	Marlboro Team McLaren	3.0 McLaren M26-Cosworth V8	crashed in practice
10	SOUTH AFRICAN GP	Kyalami	8	Marlboro Team McLaren	3.0 McLaren M28-Cosworth V8	pit stop-tyres
ret	US GP WEST	Long Beach	8	Löwenbräu Team McLaren	3.0 McLaren M28-Cosworth V8	accident with Lauda
13	SPANISH GP	Jarama	8	Marlboro Team McLaren	3.0 McLaren M28-Cosworth V8	pit stop-fuel/3 laps behind
dnq	BELGIAN GP	Zolder	8	Marlboro Team McLaren	3.0 McLaren M26-Cosworth V8	
dnq	MONACO GP	Monte Carlo	8	Marlboro Team McLaren	3.0 McLaren M28-Cosworth V8	
10	FRENCH GP	Dijon	8	Marlboro Team McLaren	3.0 McLaren M28-Cosworth V8	2 laps behind
7/ret	BRITISH GP	Silverstone	8	Marlboro Team McLaren	3.0 McLaren M28-Cosworth V8	out of fuel/2 laps behind
ret	GERMAN GP	Hockenheim	8	Marlboro Team McLaren	3.0 McLaren M29-Cosworth V8	broken rear suspension
10	AUSTRIAN GP	Österreichring	8	Marlboro Team McLaren	3.0 McLaren M29-Cosworth V8	1 lap behind
ret	DUTCH GP	Zandvoort	8	Marlboro Team McLaren	3.0 McLaren M29-Cosworth V8	engine
ret	ITALIAN GP	Monza	8	Marlboro Team McLaren	3.0 McLaren M29-Cosworth V8	engine
ret	CANADIAN GP	Montreal	8	Marlboro Team McLaren	3.0 McLaren M29-Cosworth V8	engine
ret	US GP EAST	Watkins Glen	8	Marlboro Team McLaren	3.0 McLaren M29-Cosworth V8	engine

1981

	Race	Circuit	No	Entrant	Car/Engine	Comment
6	US GP WEST	Long Beach	33	Theodore Racing Team	3.0 Theodore TY01-Cosworth V8	1 lap behind
10	BRAZILIAN GP	Rio	33	Theodore Racing Team	3.0 Theodore TY01-Cosworth V8	1 lap behind
ret	ARGENTINE GP	Buenos Aires	33	Theodore Racing Team	3.0 Theodore TY01-Cosworth V8	engine-lost oil
11	SAN MARINO GP	Imola	33	Theodore Racing Team	3.0 Theodore TY01-Cosworth V8	pit stop-tyres/2 laps behind
dnq	BELGIAN GP	Zolder	33	Theodore Racing Team	3.0 Theodore TY01-Cosworth V8	
7	MONACO GP	Monte Carlo	33	Theodore Racing Team	3.0 Theodore TY01-Cosworth V8	4 laps behind
13	SPANISH GP	Jarama	33	Theodore Racing Team	3.0 Theodore TY01-Cosworth V8	2 laps behind
ret	FRENCH GP	Dijon	25	Equipe Talbot Gitanes	3.0 Ligier JS17-Matra V12	seized rear wheel bearing
ret	BRITISH GP	Silverstone	25	Equipe Talbot Gitanes	3.0 Ligier JS17-Matra V12	ignition
ret	GERMAN GP	Hockenheim	25	Equipe Talbot Gitanes	3.0 Ligier JS17-Matra V12	rear wheel bearing
ret	AUSTRIAN GP	Österreichring	25	Equipe Talbot Gitanes	3.0 Ligier JS17-Matra V12	engine
ret	DUTCH GP	Zandvoort	25	Equipe Talbot Gitanes	3.0 Ligier JS17-Matra V12	accident with Pironi
ret	ITALIAN GP	Monza	25	Equipe Talbot Gitanes	3.0 Ligier JS17-Matra V12	puncture
ret	CANADIAN GP	Montreal	25	Equipe Talbot Gitanes	3.0 Ligier JS17-Matra V12	spun off
ret	CAESARS PALACE GP	Las Vegas	25	Equipe Talbot Gitanes	3.0 Ligier JS17-Matra V12	crashed

1982

	Race	Circuit	No	Entrant	Car/Engine	Comment
8	DUTCH GP	Zandvoort	27	Scuderia Ferrari SpA SEFAC	1.5 t/c Ferrari 126C2 V6	tyre problems/1 lap behind
3	BRITISH GP	Brands Hatch	27	Scuderia Ferrari SpA SEFAC	1.5 t/c Ferrari 126C2 V6	
4	FRENCH GP	Paul Ricard	27	Scuderia Ferrari SpA SEFAC	1.5 t/c Ferrari 126C2 V6	
1	GERMAN GP	Hockenheim	27	Scuderia Ferrari SpA SEFAC	1.5 t/c Ferrari 126C2 V6	
4	AUSTRIAN GP	Österreichring	27	Scuderia Ferrari SpA SEFAC	1.5 t/c Ferrari 126C2 V6	pit stop-tyre/1 lap behind
dns	SWISS GP	Dijon	27	Scuderia Ferrari SpA SEFAC	1.5 t/c Ferrari 126C2 V6	withdrawn, Sun a.m.-bad back
2	ITALIAN GP	Monza	27	Scuderia Ferrari SpA SEFAC	1.5 t/c Ferrari 126C2 V6	
dns	CAESARS PALACE GP	Las Vegas	27	Scuderia Ferrari SpA SEFAC	1.5 t/c Ferrari 126C2 V6	withdrawn, Sun a.m.-bad back

1983

	Race	Circuit	No	Entrant	Car/Engine	Comment
5	BRAZILIAN GP	Rio	27	Scuderia Ferrari SpA SEFAC	1.5 t/c Ferrari 126C2/B V6	
ret	US GP WEST	Long Beach	27	Scuderia Ferrari SpA SEFAC	1.5 t/c Ferrari 126C2/B V6	accident with Rosberg/Pole
4	FRENCH GP	Paul Ricard	27	Scuderia Ferrari SpA SEFAC	1.5 t/c Ferrari 126C2/B V6	pit stop-tyres
1	SAN MARINO GP	Imola	27	Scuderia Ferrari SpA SEFAC	1.5 t/c Ferrari 126C2/B V6	
4	MONACO GP	Monte Carlo	27	Scuderia Ferrari SpA SEFAC	1.5 t/c Ferrari 126C2/B V6	
2	BELGIAN GP	Spa	27	Scuderia Ferrari SpA SEFAC	1.5 t/c Ferrari 126C2/B V6	
ret	US GP (DETROIT)	Detroit	27	Scuderia Ferrari SpA SEFAC	1.5 t/c Ferrari 126C2/B V6	stalled at start
3	CANADIAN GP	Montreal	27	Scuderia Ferrari SpA SEFAC	1.5 t/c Ferrari 126C2/B V6	FL
3	BRITISH GP	Silverstone	27	Scuderia Ferrari SpA SEFAC	1.5 t/c Ferrari 126C3 V6	
ret	GERMAN GP	Hockenheim	27	Scuderia Ferrari SpA SEFAC	1.5 t/c Ferrari 126C3 V6	engine/Pole

ret	AUSTRIAN GP	Österreichring	27	Scuderia Ferrari SpA SEFAC	1.5 t/c Ferrari 126C3 V6	engine/Pole
2	DUTCH GP	Zandvoort	27	Scuderia Ferrari SpA SEFAC	1.5 t/c Ferrari 126C3 V6	
4	ITALIAN GP	Monza	27	Scuderia Ferrari SpA SEFAC	1.5 t/c Ferrari 126C3 V6	
ret	EUROPEAN GP	Brands Hatch	27	Scuderia Ferrari SpA SEFAC	1.5 t/c Ferrari 126C3 V6	fluid leak, lost brakes-accident
ret	SOUTH AFRICAN GP	Kyalami	27	Scuderia Ferrari SpA SEFAC	1.5 t/c Ferrari 126C3 V6	turbo/Pole

1984

5*/ret	BRAZILIAN GP	Rio	15	Equipe Renault Elf	1.5 t/c Renault RE50 V6	out of fuel/*5th place car dsq
ret	SOUTH AFRICAN GP	Kyalami	15	Equipe Renault Elf	1.5 t/c Renault RE50 V6	fuel metering unit/FL
7*	BELGIAN GP	Zolder	15	Equipe Renault Elf	1.5 t/c Renault RE50 V6	spin/*6th place car dsq/-2 laps
ret	SAN MARINO GP	Imola	15	Equipe Renault Elf	1.5 t/c Renault RE50 V6	hit by Cheever
2	FRENCH GP	Dijon	15	Equipe Renault Elf	1.5 t/c Renault RE50 V6	Pole
ret	MONACO GP	Monte Carlo	15	Equipe Renault Elf	1.5 t/c Renault RE50 V6	collision with Warwick-hurt leg
dns	CANADIAN GP	Montreal	15	Equipe Renault Elf	1.5 t/c Renault RE50 V6	unfit-withdrew after untimed practice
ret	US GP (DETROIT)	Detroit	15	Equipe Renault Elf	1.5 t/c Renault RE50 V6	transmission
ret	US GP (DALLAS)	Dallas	15	Equipe Renault Elf	1.5 t/c Renault RE50 V6	hit wall
8/ret	BRITISH GP	Brands Hatch	15	Equipe Renault Elf	1.5 t/c Renault RE50 V6	turbo
5	GERMAN GP	Hockenheim	15	Equipe Renault Elf	1.5 t/c Renault RE50 V6	
ret	AUSTRIAN GP	Österreichring	15	Equipe Renault Elf	1.5 t/c Renault RE50 V6	engine
6	DUTCH GP	Zandvoort	15	Equipe Renault Elf	1.5 t/c Renault RE50 V6	1 lap behind
ret	ITALIAN GP	Monza	15	Equipe Renault Elf	1.5 t/c Renault RE50 V6	throttle cable
ret	EUROPEAN GP	Nürburgring	15	Equipe Renault Elf	1.5 t/c Renault RE50 V6	fuel feed
7	PORTUGUESE GP	Estoril	15	Equipe Renault Elf	1.5 t/c Renault RE50 V6	1 lap behind

1985

5	BRAZILIAN GP	Rio	15	Equipe Renault Elf	1.5 t/c Renault RE60 V6	2 laps behind
3	PORTUGUESE GP	Estoril	15	Equipe Renault Elf	1.5 t/c Renault RE60 V6	1 lap behind
3	SAN MARINO GP	Imola	15	Equipe Renault Elf	1.5 t/c Renault RE60 V6	1 lap behind
ret	MONACO GP	Monte Carlo	15	Equipe Renault Elf	1.5 t/c Renault RE60 V6	hit Johansson on lap 1
7	CANADIAN GP	Montreal	15	Equipe Renault Elf	1.5 t/c Renault RE60 V6	1 lap behind
ret	US GP (DETROIT)	Detroit	15	Equipe Renault Elf	1.5 t/c Renault RE60 V6	spun off
6	FRENCH GP	Paul Ricard	15	Equipe Renault Elf	1.5 t/c Renault RE60B V6	
ret	BRITISH GP	Silverstone	15	Equipe Renault Elf	1.5 t/c Renault RE60B V6	spun-hit by Johansson
ret	GERMAN GP	Nürburgring	15	Equipe Renault Elf	1.5 t/c Renault RE60B V6	spun off
10/ret	AUSTRIAN GP	Österreichring	15	Equipe Renault Elf	1.5 t/c Renault RE60B V6	engine/6 laps behind
ret	DUTCH GP	Zandvoort	15	Equipe Renault Elf	1.5 t/c Renault RE60B V6	started from pit lane/transmission
7	ITALIAN GP	Monza	15	Equipe Renault Elf	1.5 t/c Renault RE60B V6	1 lap behind
ret	BELGIAN GP	Spa	15	Equipe Renault Elf	1.5 t/c Renault RE60B V6	gearbox
12	EUROPEAN GP	Brands Hatch	15	Equipe Renault Elf	1.5 t/c Renault RE60B V6	3 laps behind
ret	AUSTRALIAN GP	Adelaide	15	Equipe Renault Elf	1.5 t/c Renault RE60B V6	transmission

1986

ret	BRAZILIAN GP	Rio	16	Team Haas (USA) Ltd	1.5 t/c Lola THL1-Hart 4	flat battery
8	SPANISH GP	Jerez	16	Team Haas (USA) Ltd	1.5 t/c Lola THL1-Hart 4	6 laps behind
ret	SAN MARINO GP	Imola	16	Team Haas (USA) Ltd	1.5 t/c Lola THL1-Hart 4	engine
ret	MONACO GP	Monte Carlo	16	Team Haas (USA) Ltd	1.5 t/c Lola THL2-Cosworth V6	accident with Brundle
ret	BELGIAN GP	Spa	16	Team Haas (USA) Ltd	1.5 t/c Lola THL2-Cosworth V6	accident with Fabi
dns	CANADIAN GP	Montreal	16	Team Haas (USA) Ltd	1.5 t/c Lola THL2-Cosworth V6	accident in Sun a.m. warm-up
ret	FRENCH GP	Paul Ricard	16	Team Haas (USA) Ltd	1.5 t/c Lola THL2-Cosworth V6	brakes
ret	BRITISH GP	Brands Hatch	16	Team Haas (USA) Ltd	1.5 t/c Lola THL2-Cosworth V6	gearbox
8	GERMAN GP	Hockenheim	16	Team Haas (USA) Ltd	1.5 t/c Lola THL2-Cosworth V6	1 lap behind
7	HUNGARIAN GP	Hungaroring	16	Team Haas (USA) Ltd	1.5 t/c Lola THL2-Cosworth V6	2 laps behind
5	AUSTRIAN GP	Österreichring	16	Team Haas (USA) Ltd	1.5 t/c Lola THL2-Cosworth V6	2 laps behind
ret	ITALIAN GP	Monza	16	Team Haas (USA) Ltd	1.5 t/c Lola THL2-Cosworth V6	accident with Patrese
nc	PORTUGUESE GP	Estoril	16	Team Haas (USA) Ltd	1.5 t/c Lola THL2-Cosworth V6	3 pit stops-brakes/8 laps behind
ret	MEXICAN GP	Mexico City	16	Team Haas (USA) Ltd	1.5 t/c Lola THL2-Cosworth V6	hit by Arnoux on lap 1
nc	AUSTRALIAN GP	Adelaide	16	Team Haas (USA) Ltd	1.5 t/c Lola THL2-Cosworth V6	collision Dumfries/gearbox/-12 laps

GP Starts: 113 (114)   GP Wins: 2   Pole positions: 5   Fastest laps: 2   Points: 103

GABRIELE TARQUINI

This pleasant and underrated Italian caused quite a stir back in 1985 when, as reigning world karting champion and with almost no Formula 3 experience to speak of, he became an instant front-runner in F3000. He finished his first year a very creditable sixth in the standings, but his 1986 season was less startling as the newly formed Coloni team struggled to find its feet, though he did score third places at Enna and the Österreichring.

Joining Lamberto Leoni's FIRST racing ream for 1987, Gabriele was once again a 'nearly-man' in terms of ultimate success, but he made his Formula 1 debut for Osella at Imola, and then rejoined Enzo Coloni for a testing first Grand Prix season in 1988.

With poor Philippe Streiff gravely injured in a Brazilian testing accident Tarquini came into the AGS line-up for the 1989 San Marino GP, soon gaining a priceless point for the little team in Mexico. Over the next three seasons, the ever-cheerful Italian plugged away against insurmountable odds as the debt-ridden team headed towards extinction, but before the end came he had been allowed to sign for Fondmetal (formerly Osella). With Ford HB engines at his disposal for 1992, Tarquini had easily his best opportunity to shine but the team was hampered by a lack of adequate funding – the Italian was under strict instructions to conserve the car at all costs – and any promise it had possessed soon evaporated, resulting in the outfit's withdrawal before the season was out.

Tarquini then joined the horde of famous names in the Italian touring car championship in 1993, taking third place in the series with his works Alfa Romeo.

TARQUINI, Gabriele (I) b 2/3/1962

1987

	Race	Circuit	No	Entrant	Car/Engine	Comment
ret	SAN MARINO GP	Imola	22	Osella Squadra Corse	1.5 t/c Osella FA1G-Alfa Romeo V8	gearbox

1988

	Race	Circuit	No	Entrant	Car/Engine	Comment
ret	BRAZILIAN GP	Rio	31	Coloni SpA	3.5 Coloni FC188-Cosworth V8	rear upright bearing
ret	SAN MARINO GP	Imola	31	Coloni SpA	3.5 Coloni FC188-Cosworth V8	throttle cable
ret	MONACO GP	Monte Carlo	31	Coloni SpA	3.5 Coloni FC188-Cosworth V8	suspension
14	MEXICAN GP	Mexico City	31	Coloni SpA	3.5 Coloni FC188-Cosworth V8	5 laps behind
8	CANADIAN GP	Montreal	31	Coloni SpA	3.5 Coloni FC188-Cosworth V8	2 laps behind
dnpq	US GP (DETROIT)	Detroit	31	Coloni SpA	3.5 Coloni FC188-Cosworth V8	
dnpq	FRENCH GP	Paul Ricard	31	Coloni SpA	3.5 Coloni FC188-Cosworth V8	
dnpq	BRITISH GP	Silverstone	31	Coloni SpA	3.5 Coloni FC188-Cosworth V8	
dnpq	GERMAN GP	Hockenheim	31	Coloni SpA	3.5 Coloni FC188-Cosworth V8	
13	HUNGARIAN GP	Hungaroring	31	Coloni SpA	3.5 Coloni FC188-Cosworth V8	rear suspension problems/-5 laps
nc	BELGIAN GP	Spa	31	Coloni SpA	3.5 Coloni FC188-Cosworth V8	steering rack problem/-7 laps
dnq	ITALIAN GP	Monza	31	Coloni SpA	3.5 Coloni FC188B-Cosworth V8	
11	PORTUGUESE GP	Estoril	31	Coloni SpA	3.5 Coloni FC188B-Cosworth V8	5 laps behind
dnpq	SPANISH GP	Jerez	31	Coloni SpA	3.5 Coloni FC188B-Cosworth V8	
dnpq	JAPANESE GP	Suzuka	31	Coloni SpA	3.5 Coloni FC188B-Cosworth V8	
dnq	AUSTRALIAN GP	Adelaide	31	Coloni SpA	3.5 Coloni FC188B-Cosworth V8	

1989

	Race	Circuit	No	Entrant	Car/Engine	Comment
8	SAN MARINO GP	Imola	40	Automoblies Gonfaronaise Sportive	3.5 AGS JH23B-Cosworth V8	1 lap behind
ret	MONACO GP	Monte Carlo	40	Automobiles Gonfaronaise Sportive	3.5 AGS JH23B-Cosworth V8	electrics
6	MEXICAN GP	Mexico City	40	Automobiles Gonfaronaise Sportive	3.5 AGS JH23B-Cosworth V8	1 lap behind
7/ret	US GP (PHOENIX)	Phoenix	40	Automobiles Gonfaronaise Sportive	3.5 AGS JH23B-Cosworth V8	engine last lap/2 laps behind
ret	CANADIAN GP	Montreal	40	Automobiles Gonfaronaise Sportive	3.5 AGS JH23B-Cosworth V8	collision with Arnoux
ret	FRENCH GP	Paul Ricard	40	Automobiles Gonfaronaise Sportive	3.5 AGS JH23B-Cosworth V8	engine
dns	"	" "	40	Automobiles Gonfaronaise Sportive	3.5 AGS JH24-Cosworth V8	practice only-new car
dnq	BRITISH GP	Silverstone	40	Automobiles Gonfaronaise Sportive	3.5 AGS JH24-Cosworth V8	
dnpq	GERMAN GP	Hockenheim	40	Automobiles Gonfaronaise Sportive	3.5 AGS JH23B-Cosworth V8	
dnpq	HUNGARIAN GP	Hungaroring	40	Automobiles Gonfaronaise Sportive	3.5 AGS JH24-Cosworth V8	
dnpq	BELGIAN GP	Spa	40	Automobiles Gonfaronaise Sportive	3.5 AGS JH24-Cosworth V8	
dnpq	"	"	40	Automobiles Gonfaronaise Sportive	3.5 AGS JH23B-Cosworth V8	
dnpq	ITALIAN GP	Monza	40	Automobiles Gonfaronaise Sportive	3.5 AGS JH24-Cosworth V8	brake problems
dnpq	PORTUGUESE GP	Estoril	40	Automobiles Gonfaronaise Sportive	3.5 AGS JH24-Cosworth V8	
dnpq	SPANISH GP	Jerez	40	Automobiles Gonfaronaise Sportive	3.5 AGS JH24-Cosworth V8	
dnpq	JAPANESE GP	Suzuka	40	Automobiles Gonfaronaise Sportive	3.5 AGS JH24-Cosworth V8	
dnpq	AUSTRALIAN GP	Adelaide	40	Automobiles Gonfaronaise Sportive	3.5 AGS JH24-Cosworth V8	

1990

	Race	Circuit	No	Entrant	Car/Engine	Comment
dnpq	US GP (PHOENIX)	Phoenix	17	Automobiles Gonfaronaise Sportive	3.5 AGS JH24-Cosworth V8	
dnpq	BRAZILIAN GP	Interlagos	17	Automobiles Gonfaronaise Sportive	3.5 AGS JH24-Cosworth V8	
dnpq	SAN MARINO GP	Imola	17	Automobiles Gonfaronaise Sportive	3.5 AGS JH25-Cosworth V8	no time recorded
dnpq	MONACO GP	Monte Carlo	17	Automobiles Gonfaronaise Sportive	3.5 AGS JH25-Cosworth V8	
dnpq	CANADIAN GP	Montreal	17	Automobiles Gonfaronaise Sportive	3.5 AGS JH25-Cosworth V8	
dnpq	MEXICAN GP	Mexico City	17	Automobiles Gonfaronaise Sportive	3.5 AGS JH25-Cosworth V8	
dnq	FRENCH GP	Paul Ricard	17	Automobiles Gonfaronaise Sportive	3.5 AGS JH25-Cosworth V8	
ret	BRITISH GP	Silverstone	17	Automobiles Gonfaronaise Sportive	3.5 AGS JH25-Cosworth V8	engine
dnpq	GERMAN GP	Hockenheim	17	Automobiles Gonfaronaise Sportive	3.5 AGS JH25-Cosworth V8	
13	HUNGARIAN GP	Hungaroring	17	Automobiles Gonfaronaise Sportive	3.5 AGS JH25-Cosworth V8	pit stop-tyres/3 laps behind
dnq	BELGIAN GP	Spa	17	Automobiles Gonfaronaise Sportive	3.5 AGS JH25-Cosworth V8	
dnq	ITALIAN GP	Monza	17	Automobiles Gonfaronaise Sportive	3.5 AGS JH25-Cosworth V8	
dnq	PORTUGUESE GP	Estoril	17	Automobiles Gonfaronaise Sportive	3.5 AGS JH25-Cosworth V8	
ret	SPANISH GP	Jerez	17	Automobiles Gonfaronaise Sportive	3.5 AGS JH25-Cosworth V8	electrics
dnq	JAPANESE GP	Suzuka	17	Automobiles Gonfaronaise Sportive	3.5 AGS JH25-Cosworth V8	
ret	AUSTRALIAN GP	Adelaide	17	Automobiles Gonfaronaise Sportive	3.5 AGS JH25-Cosworth V8	oil fire

1991

	Race	Circuit	No	Entrant	Car/Engine	Comment
8	US GP (PHOENIX)	Phoenix	17	Automobiles Gonfaronaise Sportive	3.5 AGS JH25-Cosworth V8	pit stop-tyres/misfire/4 laps behind
ret	BRAZILIAN GP	Interlagos	17	Automobiles Gonfaronaise Sportive	3.5 AGS JH25-Cosworth V8	spun off on first lap
dnq	SAN MARINO GP	Imola	17	Automobiles Gonfaronaise Sportive	3.5 AGS JH25-Cosworth V8	
ret	MONACO GP	Monte Carlo	17	Automobiles Gonfaronaise Sportive	3.5 AGS JH25-Cosworth V8	gearbox
dnq	CANADIAN GP	Montreal	17	Automobiles Gonfaronaise Sportive	3.5 AGS JH25-Cosworth V8	
dnq	MEXICAN GP	Mexico City	17	Automobiles Gonfaronaise Sportive	3.5 AGS JH25-Cosworth V8	
dnq	FRENCH GP	Paul Ricard	17	Automobiles Gonfaronaise Sportive	3.5 AGS JH25B-Cosworth V8	
dnq	BRITISH GP	Silverstone	17	Automobiles Gonfaronaise Sportive	3.5 AGS JH25B-Cosworth V8	
dnq	GERMAN GP	Hockenheim	17	Automobiles Gonfaronaise Sportive	3.5 AGS JH25B-Cosworth V8	
dnpq	HUNGARIAN GP	Hungaroring	17	Automobiles Gonfaronaise Sportive	3.5 AGS JH25B-Cosworth V8	
dnpq	BELGIAN GP	Spa	17	Automobiles Gonfaronaise Sportive	3.5 AGS JH25B-Cosworth V8	
dnpq	ITALIAN GP	Monza	17	Automobiles Gonfaronaise Sportive	3.5 AGS JH27-Cosworth V8	
dnpq	"	"	17	Automobiles Gonfaronaise Sportive	3.5 AGS JH25B-Cosworth V8	
dnq	PORTUGUESE GP	Estoril	17	Automobiles Gonfaronaise Sportive	3.5 AGS JH27-Cosworth V8	
12	SPANISH GP	Barcelona	14	Fondmetal F1 SpA	3.5 Fomet F1-Cosworth V8	2 laps behind
11	JAPANESE GP	Suzuka	14	Fondmetal F1 SpA	3.5 Fomet F1-Cosworth V8	2 laps behind
dnpq	AUSTRALIAN GP	Adelaide	14	Fondmetal F1 SpA	3.5 Fomet F1-Cosworth V8	

1992

	Race	Circuit	No	Entrant	Car/Engine	Comment
ret	SOUTH AFRICAN GP	Kyalami	15	Fondmetal F1 SpA	3.5 Fondmetal GR01-Ford HB V8	engine
ret	MEXICAN GP	Mexico City	15	Fondmetal F1 SpA	3.5 Fondmetal GR01-Ford HB V8	clutch
ret	BRAZILIAN GP	Interlagos	15	Fondmetal F1 SpA	3.5 Fondmetal GR01-Ford HB V8	overheating
ret	SPANISH GP	Barcelona	15	Fondmetal F1 SpA	3.5 Fondmetal GR01-Ford HB V8	spun off
ret	SAN MARINO GP	Imola	15	Fondmetal F1 SpA	3.5 Fondmetal GR01-Ford HB V8	overheating
ret	MONACO GP	Monte Carlo	15	Fondmetal F1 SpA	3.5 Fondmetal GR01-Ford HB V8	overheating
ret	CANADIAN GP	Montreal	15	Fondmetal F1 SpA	3.5 Fondmetal GR02-Ford HB V8	gearbox failed at start

ret	FRENCH GP	Magny Cours	15	Fondmetal F1 SpA	3.5 Fondmetal GR02-Ford HB V8	throttle cable
14	BRITISH GP	Silverstone	15	Fondmetal F1 SpA	3.5 Fondmetal GR02-Ford HB V8	2 laps behind
ret	GERMAN GP	Hockenheim	15	Fondmetal F1 SpA	3.5 Fondmetal GR02-Ford HB V8	engine
ret	HUNGARIAN GP	Hungaroring	15	Fondmetal F1 SpA	3.5 Fondmetal GR02-Ford HB V8	collision van de Poele on lap 1
ret	BELGIAN GP	Spa	15	Fondmetal F1 SpA	3.5 Fondmetal GR02-Ford HB V8	engine
ret	ITALIAN GP	Monza	15	Fondmetal F1 SpA	3.5 Fondmetal GR02-Ford HB V8	gearbox

GP Starts: 37   GP Wins: 0   Pole positions: 0   Fastest laps: 0   Points: 1

TARUFFI, Piero (I) b 12/1/1906 – d 12/6/1988

1950

	Race	Circuit	No	Entrant	Car/Engine	Comment
ret	ITALIAN GP	Monza	60	Alfa Romeo SpA	1.5 s/c Alfa Romeo 158 8	engine/Fangio took over

1951

2	SWISS GP	Bremgarten	44	Scuderia Ferrari	4.5 Ferrari 375F1 V12	
ret	BELGIAN GP	Spa	12	Scuderia Ferrari	4.5 Ferrari 375F1 V12	transmission
5	GERMAN GP	Nürburgring	73	Scuderia Ferrari	4.5 Ferrari 375F1 V12	
5	ITALIAN GP	Monza	8	Scuderia Ferrari	4.5 Ferrari 375F1 V12	2 laps behind
ret	SPANISH GP	Pedralbes	8	Scuderia Ferrari	4.5 Ferrari 375F1 V12	lost wheel

1952

1	SWISS GP	Bremgarten	30	Scuderia Ferrari	2.0 Ferrari 500 4	FL
ret	BELGIAN GP	Spa	6	Scuderia Ferrari	2.0 Ferrari 500 4	spun-hit by Behra
3	FRENCH GP	Rouen	12	Scuderia Ferrari	2.0 Ferrari 500 4	1 lap behind
2	BRITISH GP	Silverstone	17	Scuderia Ferrari	2.0 Ferrari 500 4	1 lap behind
4	GERMAN GP	Nürburgring	103	Scuderia Ferrari	2.0 Ferrari 500 4	1 lap behind
7	ITALIAN GP	Monza	14	Scuderia Ferrari	2.0 Ferrari 500 4	3 laps behind

1954

6	GERMAN GP	Nürburgring	4	Scuderia Ferrari	2.5 Ferrari 625 4	1 lap behind

1955

nc*	MONACO GP	Monte Carlo	48	Scuderia Ferrari	2.5 Ferrari 555 4	* Frere took over car/14 laps behind
4	BRITISH GP	Aintree	50	Daimler Benz AG	2.5 Mercedes Benz-W196 8	1 lap behind
2	ITALIAN GP	Monza	14	Daimler Benz AG	2.5 Mercedes Benz-W196 8	

1956

ret	FRENCH GP	Reims	8	Officine Alfieri Maserati	2.5 Maserati 250F 6	mechanical
ret	ITALIAN GP	Monza	16	Vandervell Products Ltd	2.5 Vanwall 4	suspension

GP Starts: 18   GP Wins: 1   Pole positions: 0   Fastest laps: 1   Points: 41

TAYLOR, Henry (GB) b 16/12/1932

1959

	Race	Circuit	No	Entrant	Car/Engine	Comment
11	BRITISH GP (F2)	Aintree	58	R H H Parnell	1.5 Cooper T51-Climax 4	2nd in F2 class

1960

7	DUTCH GP	Zandvoort	10	Yeoman Credit Racing Team	2.5 Cooper T51-Climax 4	5 laps behind
4	FRENCH GP	Reims	46	Yeoman Credit Racing Team	2.5 Cooper T51-Climax 4	1 lap behind
8	BRITISH GP	Silverstone	15	Yeoman Credit Racing Team	2.5 Cooper T51-Climax 4	3 laps behind
dns	PORTUGUESE GP	Oporto	10	Yeoman Credit Racing Team	2.5 Cooper T51-Climax 4	practice accident-injured
14	US GP	Riverside	8	Yeoman Credit Racing Team	2.5 Cooper T51-Climax 4	pit stop/7 laps behind

1961

dnq	MONACO GP	Monte Carlo	34	UDT-Laystall Racing Team	1.5 Lotus 18-Climax 4	
dnp	BELGIAN GP	Spa	16	UDT-Laystall Racing Team	1.5 Lotus 18/21-Climax 4	car crashed by Allison in practice
10	FRENCH GP	Reims	30	UDT-Laystall Racing Team	1.5 Lotus 18/21-Climax 4	3 laps behind
ret	BRITISH GP	Aintree	30	UDT-Laystall Racing Team	1.5 Lotus 18/21-Climax 4	accident in rain
11	ITALIAN GP	Monza	20	UDT-Laystall Racing Team	1.5 Lotus 18/21-Climax 4	4 laps behind

GP Starts: 8   GP Wins: 0   Pole positions: 0   Fastest laps: 0   Points: 3

TAYLOR, John (GB) b 23/3/1933 – d 8/91966

1964

	Race	Circuit	No	Entrant	Car/Engine	Comment
14	BRITISH GP	Brands Hatch	22	Bob Gerard Racing	1.0 Cooper T73-Ford 4	long stop-gearbox/24 laps behind

1966

6	FRENCH GP	Reims	44	David Bridges	2.0 Brabham BT11-BRM V8	3 laps behind
8	BRITISH GP	Brands Hatch	22	David Bridges	2.0 Brabham BT11-BRM V8	4 laps behind
8	DUTCH GP	Zandvoort	38	David Bridges	2.0 Brabham BT11-BRM V8	6 laps behind
ret	GERMAN GP	Nürburgring	16	David Bridges	2.0 Brabham BT11-BRM V8	accident-burns which later proved fatal

GP Starts: 5   GP Wins: 0   Pole positions: 0   Fastest laps: 0   Points: 1

TAYLOR, Mike (GB) b 24/4/1934

1959

	Race	Circuit	No	Entrant	Car/Engine	Comment
ret	BRITISH GP (F2)	Aintree	50	Alan Brown Equipe	1.5 Cooper T45-Climax 4	transmission

1960

dns	BELGIAN GP	Spa	20	Taylor-Crawley Racing Team	2.5 Lotus 18-Climax 4	broken steering in practice-crashed

GP Starts: 1   GP Wins: 0   Pole positions: 0   Fastest laps: 0   Points: 0

PIERO TARUFFI

Originally a successful motor cycle racer, Taruffi first tasted four-wheel competition in the 1930 Mille Miglia, and was soon showing promise with his Itala. That brought him to the attention of Ferrari, who provided him with a 2.3 Alfa Romeo to beat Biondetti in the Coppa Frigo hill-climb. He was still racing on two wheels but took second place in the 1932 Rome GP behind Fagioli in an Alfa Monza, and third in the 1933 Eifelrennen.

By 1934 he was driving works Maseratis but crashed badly at Tripoli, and in 1935 he moved to the Bugatti team, taking a third at Turin. Taruffi was still involved in motor cycling, and though he stopped racing in 1937 he continued to manage the Gilera team both before and after the war.

Between 1947 and 1949, Piero drove Dusio's Cisitalias with great success and, guesting for Alfa Romeo, he took fourth in the Monza GP in 1948. Joining Scuderia Ferrari in 1949, Taruffi took second place in the Rome GP at Caracalla with the Tipo 166. In 1950 he occasionally represented both Alfa Romeo, taking third in the Grand Prix of Nations in Geneva, and Ferrari, his third in the end-of-year Penya Rhin GP at Barcelona bringing an invitation to join the works team on a regular basis in 1951. This was the final year of Alfa's dominance, but Piero finished second in the Swiss GP and third in the non-title Bari GP at Lungomare. In sports cars he took second place in the Tour of Sicily and, sharing a 4.1-litre with Chinetti, won the Carrera Panamericana.

Taruffi enjoyed his finest year in 1952. With the Tipo 500 now the car to beat, he backed the brilliant Ascari superbly, winning the Swiss GP at Bremgarten, and with some other excellent drives finished third in the drivers' championship. In other important single-seater races, Piero won the Paris GP at Montlhéry, and was second at both Syracuse and Naples, while in the big-capacity cars he took second in Turin and won the Libre Silverstone race in Vandervell's Ferrari 'Thinwall Special'. For 1953 he joined the Lancia team, racing their sports cars without great success, though he did finish second in the Carrera Panamericana in a 3.3 Lancia. Things improved in 1954, as victories in the Targa Florio and the Tour of Sicily demonstrate, the latter success being repeated the following year, this time at the wheel of a Ferrari.

Taruffi was still an occasional Grand Prix driver who could be relied upon to do a good job, and Mercedes brought him into their team after Hans Herrmann had put himself out of action, Piero bringing the silver car to excellent finishes in his two outings. For 1956 he joined Maserati's sports car team, sharing the winning car with Moss, Schell and Behra in the Nürburgring 1000 Km, and taking second in the Targa Florio, the Circuit of Sicily and the Pescara GP. His final F1 race came in the 1957 Syracuse GP when, driving a Scuderia Centro Sud Maserati 250F, he finished fourth, despite a broken shock absorber. Soon after, and at his 13th attempt, Taruffi achieved his great ambition, by taking victory in the ill-fated Mille Miglia in a works Ferrari as a late replacement for Musso. With this, he announced his retirement from racing, and set up a racing drivers' school.

HENRY TAYLOR

A farmer, Taylor entered club racing in 1954 with a Cooper-Vincent, taking the Autosport championship the following year. He added to his experience racing a Jaguar D-Type, taking third in the 1957 Belgian sports car GP, but it was 1958 before he began to make his mark in single-seaters, winning the GP de Paris in a Cooper. He continued to make good progress in Formula 2, taking a superb second place at the 1959 Auvergne Trophy, ahead of McLaren's works car, and second in class at the British GP at Aintree.

For 1960 Taylor signed to race Ken Tyrrell's Cooper-Austin in Formula Junior, winning the prestigious Monaco race, and made his debut in the Yeoman Credit Cooper, scoring a morale-boosting fourth place at Reims for a team still reeling from Bristow's fatal accident at Spa. He continued under the UDT Laystall banner in 1961, racing the team's Lotus 18/21 F1 car as well as a Lotus 19 in sports car events. Taylor gained a few minor placings outside Grands Prix, until a nasty crash in the British GP left him injured and trapped in his car. He recovered to compete again at the ill-fated Monza race when, perhaps with the tragic events of the day in mind, he decided to retire from circuit racing to concentrate on farming.

Taylor was soon back in action, rallying for Ford, and became the first man to compete in the Cortina. He later returned to the tracks occasionally in 1963 and 1964, when he finished second at both Zolder and Brands Hatch and third at the Nürburgring in Alan Mann's Lotus-Cortina. After finally retiring in 1966, he became competitions manager at Ford.

JOHN TAYLOR

A protégé of Bob Gerard, Taylor raced extensively in Formula Junior during 1962-63 with the Midlander's Cooper-Ford, gaining quite a bit of success, mainly at club level, and also took part in the British non-championship Formula 1 races of the period. In 1964 John was fifth in the Aintree 200 with a four-cylinder car and seventh in the Mediterranean GP at Enna in Gerard's Cooper-Climax V8, which he drove in three more non-championship races in 1965.

Having finished sixth in the 1966 International Trophy, Taylor took David Bridges' Brabham-BRM to the French GP and, despite his limited experience, scored a priceless point. However, in the German GP, he was involved in a collision with Ickx's F2 Matra. His car crashed off the track and burst into flames, leaving the poor driver badly burned. Though he seemed to be making a slow recovery, he died in hospital a few weeks later.

MIKE TAYLOR

An amateur racer who showed a great deal of skill in the Lotus XI sports car in 1958, winning a number of club races, Taylor continued to race the car in 1959, taking victory in the GP des Frontières at Chimay. He also campaigned a Formula 2 Cooper-Climax and won the BARC 200 at Aintree against moderate opposition, before making his GP debut at the same venue in July. Late in the season, Taylor planned to compete in the US GP, but had to stand down after contracting jaundice.

For the 1960 season, Mike's syndicate bought one of Colin Chapman's latest Lotus 18s, which – after an outing in the International Trophy – he took to Spa for the Belgian GP. In a meeting which saw Moss badly injured and Stacey and Bristow killed, the car careered off the track into the woods during practice after the steering column failed, leaving Taylor with multiple injuries but lucky to have survived. He successfully sued Lotus for damages, but never raced again, instead turning to property speculation.

TREVOR TAYLOR

Even this gritty and determined Yorkshireman was eventually battered into submission by a catalogue of crashes which would have frightened a lesser man from the cockpit of a racing car for ever. As it was, he returned from a bombed-out Formula 1 career to later establish himself as a top-line F5000 campaigner, which says a lot for the qualities he possessed.

The son of a garage proprietor, Trevor was given much encouragement in his early racing days by his father, who bought a Triumph TR2 for him to race in 1955. This was soon replaced by a succession of 500 cc F3 cars, one of them the ex-Lewis-Evans Cooper-Norton. Progress was slow initially, but by 1958 Trevor was good enough to take the British F3 championship. The garage purchased an F2 Cooper for him to race in 1959, but apart from a minor Libre win at Rufforth little of note was achieved. Colin Chapman offered to run Taylor as part of his Junior team in 1960 if he purchased a Lotus 18, and it proved to be a sound decision for both parties. Taylor shared the championship that year with Jim Clark, and was taken into the team proper for 1961, when he again won the title, this time on his own. With Ireland injured at Monaco, Trevor was given his Grand Prix debut at Zandvoort where he finished 13th, and last, in a race unique for its complete lack of a pit stop or retirement.

There were a few other Formula 1 outings that year, his best results being a second place in the Rand GP at Kyalami, followed by a win in the Cape GP at Killarney early in 1962. By this time Chapman had placed his faith in the youngster, putting him into the Formula 1 team at the expense of Innes Ireland. A second place at Zandvoort was a great start, but he was shaken up at Spa when a duel with Willy Mairesse left both cars wrecked and the Belgian in hospital. This was followed by an 80 mph crash-test into the back of Trintignant's stalled car at Rouen which left him bruised from head to foot, and at the Nürburgring he was the victim of an engine malady which sent him through a hedge. His confidence was restored at the end of the year, however, when he shared the winning car in the Mexican GP with Clark and then won the Natal GP at Westmead.

Retained for 1963, Taylor took second places at Pau and Karlskoga, but apart from a single point at Monaco was out of luck in championship events. The Mediterranean GP at Enna supplied perhaps Taylor's most astounding escape, when he was pitched from his Lotus at over 100 mph, rolling some 50 yards down the circuit as his car hurtled to destruction. Amazingly he emerged with just grazes and bruising. With Peter Arundell knocking at the door, Taylor was released to join the BRP team in 1964, but apart from a sixth place at Watkins Glen there was little to enthuse about in the performances of the pale-green cars. Trevor raced a Brabham in Formula 2 during 1965-66, and was briefly involved in the amateurish Shannon project, which represented the nadir of his career. From 1967 he went back to basics, first running a Lotus 47 with encouraging results before moving up to a Lola T70 to win the 1969 Tourist Trophy at Oulton Park. This was the inaugural year of F5000, and Trevor took his Surtees TS5 right to the brink of a championship win before losing out to Peter Gethin after the pair collided in the final round at Brands Hatch. Trevor continued in the formula throughout the next three seasons, always a competitive proposition but never quite the force of that first year. At the end of 1972 he brought the curtain down on a sometimes unlucky career, but the fact that he had emerged intact after some of those early mishaps was probably cause enough for him to count his blessings.

MIKE THACKWELL

In 1980, at the age of 19, Thackwell became the youngest-ever starter in a World Championship Grand Prix, when he left the grid at Montreal only to be involved in a multiple collision which halted the race. Mike's car was *hors de combat* and the race restarted without him. So there's the conundrum: technically, did he start or not? In the event, it was to be nearly four years before another Grand Prix chance came his way, and by that time his career had lost momentum – and the driver, perhaps, the necessary determination.

Mike's early career was meteoric. In 1979, aged just 18, he contested the Vandervell F3 series in a works March, finishing third in the championship with five wins. In 1980 he raced the ICI March 802, putting in some brilliant drives without gaining the reward he deserved, turned down the chance to race the works Ensign, practised an Arrows at Zandvoort, and then joined the Tyrrell team for Montreal.

A hot favourite for the Formula 2 title in 1981, Thackwell started the season with a win at Silverstone, but a heavy crash at Thruxton left him on crutches and his title hopes evaporated. Ron Tauranac, unconvinced about Mike's fitness, dropped him from the F2 team just before the start of the 1982 season, and his confused driver was left in the lurch, eventually scraping a deal together which saw him living from race to race. Fortunately the New Zealander was back in the Ralt fold for 1983, though a slowish start meant he had to play second fiddle to team-mate and champion-elect Palmer. However, 1984 was to be his year and, showing a new resolve, he dominated proceedings, winning seven of the 11 rounds, taking six poles and nine fastest laps, and leading an incredible 408 of the 580 laps run.

Still without a Formula 1 ride, and eyeing IndyCar racing, Thackwell moved somewhat unwillingly into F3000 with Ralt in 1985. Having proved beyond doubt that he was the best driver in the series but failed to clinch the title through sheer bad luck, he understandably felt dissatisfied with his lot and refused to commit himself to a full season in 1986. When he did compete, notably at Pau, he showed what talent was being wasted, subsequently running around – albeit quite successfully – in endurance racing with Sauber and Brun before a brief reunion with Ralt in F3000 in 1988. Disillusioned, he then walked away from the sport before the age of 30.

ERIC THOMPSON

Life as a Lloyds broker left Eric Thompson with less time to race than he would have liked, but he still managed to make his mark as a member of the Aston Martin sports car team between 1949 and 1953. He enjoyed some excellent results with David Brown's *équipe*, finishing third at Le Mans in 1951 with Macklin and second at Dundrod in the 1953 Tourist Trophy, and winning the BARC 9 Hours at Goodwood with Reg Parnell.

His single-seater outings were largely confined to minor Formula Libre events in Rob Walker's Connaught but, given a works machine for the 1952 British GP, Eric did extremely well to bring the car home in fifth place and secure two championship points in his only Grand Prix appearance.

TAYLOR, Trevor (GB) b 26/12/1936

1959

	Race	Circuit	No	Entrant	Car/Engine	Comment
dnq	BRITISH GP (F2)	Aintree	44	Ace Garage (Rotherham)	1.5 Cooper T51-Climax 4	

1961

	Race	Circuit	No	Entrant	Car/Engine	Comment
13	DUTCH GP	Zandvoort	16	Team Lotus	1.5 Lotus 18-Climax 4	2 laps behind

1962

	Race	Circuit	No	Entrant	Car/Engine	Comment
2	DUTCH GP	Zandvoort	5	Team Lotus	1.5 Lotus 24-Climax V8	
dns	"	"	5	Team Lotus	1.5 Lotus 24-Climax 4	practice only
ret	MONACO GP	Monte Carlo	20	Team Lotus	1.5 Lotus 24-Climax V8	oil leak
dns	"	"	20	Team Lotus	1.5 Lotus 24-BRM V8	practice only
ret	BELGIAN GP	Spa	17	Team Lotus	1.5 Lotus 24-Climax V8	accident with Mairesse
8	FRENCH GP	Rouen	14	Team Lotus	1.5 Lotus 25-Climax V8	hit Trintignant at finish/-5 laps
8	BRITISH GP	Aintree	22	Team Lotus	1.5 Lotus 24-Climax V8	1 lap behind
ret	GERMAN GP	Nürburgring	6	Team Lotus	1.5 Lotus 24-Climax V8	engine problems-accident
ret	ITALIAN GP	Monza	22	Team Lotus	1.5 Lotus 25-Climax V8	gearbox
12	US GP	Watkins Glen	9	Team Lotus	1.5 Lotus 25-Climax V8	pit stop-oil pressure/15 laps behind
ret	SOUTH AFRICAN GP	East London	2	Team Lotus	1.5 Lotus 25-Climax V8	gearbox

1963

	Race	Circuit	No	Entrant	Car/Engine	Comment
6	MONACO GP	Monte Carlo	10	Team Lotus	1.5 Lotus 25-Climax V8	gearchange problems
ret	BELGIAN GP	Spa	2	Team Lotus	1.5 Lotus 25-Climax V8	leg injury after practice accident
10	DUTCH GP	Zandvoort	8	Team Lotus	1.5 Lotus 25-Climax V8	pit stop-misfire/14 laps behond
13/ret	FRENCH GP	Reims	20	Team Lotus	1.5 Lotus 25-Climax V8	transmission/12 laps behind
dsq*	BRITISH GP	Silverstone	5	Team Lotus	1.5 Lotus 25-Climax V8	fuel pump/*push start at pit stop
8	GERMAN GP	Nürburgring	4	Team Lotus	1.5 Lotus 25-Climax V8	1 lap behind
ret	US GP	Watkins Glen	9	Team Lotus	1.5 Lotus 25-Climax V8	transistor box
ret	MEXICAN GP	Mexico City	9	Team Lotus	1.5 Lotus 25-Climax V8	engine
8	SOUTH AFRICAN GP	East London	2	Team Lotus	1.5 Lotus 25-Climax V8	spin/p stop-gearchange/4 laps behind

1964

	Race	Circuit	No	Entrant	Car/Engine	Comment
ret	MONACO GP	Monte Carlo	15	British Racing Partnership	1.5 BRP 1-BRM V8	fuel leak
7	BELGIAN GP	Spa	4	British Racing Partnership	1.5 BRP 2-BRM V8	
ret	FRENCH GP	Rouen	18	British Racing Partnership	1.5 BRP 2-BRM V8	brakes-accident
ret	BRITISH GP	Brands Hatch	12	British Racing Partnership	1.5 BRP 2-BRM V8	driver unwell after practice accident
dns	"	" "	12	British Racing Partnership	1.5 BRP 2-BRM V8	practice accident
ret	AUSTRIAN GP	Zeltweg	15	British Racing Partnership	1.5 BRP 1-BRM V8	rear suspension
dnq	ITALIAN GP	Monza	44	British Racing Partnership	1.5 BRP 1-BRM V8	
6	US GP	Watkins Glen	12	British Racing Partnership	1.5 BRP 2-BRM V8	4 laps behind
ret	MEXICAN GP	Mexico City	12	British Racing Partnership	1.5 BRP 2-BRM V8	overheating

1966

	Race	Circuit	No	Entrant	Car/Engine	Comment
ret	BRITISH GP	Brands Hatch	23	Aiden Jones/Paul Emery	3.0 Shannon-Climax Godiva V8	split fuel tank

GP Starts: 27   GP Wins: 0   Pole positions: 0   Fastest laps: 0   Points: 8

TERRA, Max de (B) b 6/10/1918 – d Jan 1983

1952

	Race	Circuit	No	Entrant	Car/Engine	Comment
ret	SWISS GP	Bremgarten	50	Alfred Dattner	1.5 Simca Gordini Type 11 4	magneto

1953

	Race	Circuit	No	Entrant	Car/Engine	Comment
nc	SWISS GP	Bremgarten	40	Ecurie Espadon	2.0 Ferrari 166C V12	17 laps behind

GP Starts: 2   GP Wins: 0   Pole positions: 0   Fastest laps: 0   Points: 0

THACKWELL, Mike (NZ) b 30/3/1961

1980

	Race	Circuit	No	Entrant	Car/Engine	Comment
dnq	DUTCH GP	Zandvoort	30	Warsteiner Arrows Racing Team	3.0 Arrows A3-Cosworth V8	
ret/dns	CANADIAN GP	Montreal	43	Candy Tyrrell Team	3.0 Tyrrell 010-Cosworth V8	accident in first start/did not restart
dnq	US GP EAST	Watkins Glen	43	Candy Tyrrell Team	3.0 Tyrrell 010-Cosworth V8	

1984

	Race	Circuit	No	Entrant	Car/Engine	Comment
ret	CANADIAN GP	Montreal	10	Skoal Bandit Formula 1 Team	1.5 t/c RAM 02-Hart 4	broken wastegate
dnq	GERMAN GP	Hockenheim	4	Tyrrell Racing Organisation	3.0 Tyrrell 012-Cosworth V8	

GP Starts: 1   GP Wins: 0   Pole positions: 0   Fastest laps: 0   Points: 0

THIELE, Alfonse (I/USA) b 1922

1960

	Race	Circuit	No	Entrant	Car/Engine	Comment
ret	ITALIAN GP	Monza	34	Scuderia Centro Sud	2.5 Cooper T51-Maserati 4	gearbox

GP Starts: 1   GP Wins: 0   Pole positions: 0   Fastest laps: 0   Points: 0

THOMPSON, Eric (GB) b 4/11/1919

1952

	Race	Circuit	No	Entrant	Car/Engine	Comment
5	BRITISH GP	Silverstone	5	Connaught Engineering	2.0 Connaught A Type-Lea Francis 4	3 laps behind

GP Starts: 1   GP Wins: 0   Pole positions: 0   Fastest laps: 0   Points: 2

THORNE, Leslie (GB) b 23/6/1916

1954

	Race	Circuit	No	Entrant	Car/Engine	Comment
nc	BRITISH GP	Silverstone	26	Ecurie Ecosse	2.0 Connaught A Type-Lea Francis 4	12 laps behind

GP Starts: 1   GP Wins: 0   Pole positions: 0   Fastest laps: 0   Points: 0

TINGLE, Sam (RSR) b 24/8/1921

1963

	Race	Circuit	No	Entrant	Car/Engine	Comment
ret	SOUTH AFRICAN GP	East London	20	Sam Tingle	1.5 LDS 01-Alfa Romeo 4	driveshaft

1965

13	SOUTH AFRICAN GP	East London	25	Sam Tingle	1.5 LDS 01-Alfa Romeo 4	12 laps behind

1967

ret	SOUTH AFRICAN GP	Kyalami	18	Sam Tingle	2.7 LDS 01-Climax 4	burst tyre-accident

1968

ret	SOUTH AFRICAN GP	Kyalami	18	Team Gunston	3.0 LDS 01-Repco V8	ignition/fuel

1969

8	SOUTH AFRICAN GP	Kyalami	17	Team Gunston	3.0 Brabham BT24-Repco V8	7 laps behind

GP Starts: 5   GP Wins: 0   Pole positions: 0   Fastest laps: 0   Points: 0

TITTERINGTON, Desmond (GB) b 1/5/1928

1956

	Race	Circuit	No	Entrant	Car/Engine	Comment
ret	BRITISH GP	Silverstone	20	Connaught Engineering	2.5 Connaught B Type-Alta 4	engine

GP Starts: 1   GP Wins: 0   Pole positions: 0   Fastest laps: 0   Points: 0

TOMASO, Alessandro de (RA) b 10/7/1928

1957

	Race	Circuit	No	Entrant	Car/Engine	Comment
9	ARGENTINE GP	Buenos Aires	26	Scuderia Centro Sud	2.5 Ferrari 500/625 4	

1959

ret	US GP	Sebring	14	Automobili OSCA	2.0 Cooper T43-OSCA 4	brakes

GP Starts: 2   GP Wins: 0   Pole positions: 0   Fastest laps: 0   Points: 0

TORNACO, Charles de (B) b 7/6/1927 – d 18/9/1953

1952

	Race	Circuit	No	Entrant	Car/Engine	Comment
7	BELGIAN GP	Spa	34	Ecurie Francorchamps	2.0 Ferrari 500 4	3 laps behind
ret	DUTCH GP	Zandvoort	24	Ecurie Francorchamps	2.0 Ferrari 500 4	engine
dnq	ITALIAN GP	Monza	70	Ecurie Francorchamps	2.0 Ferrari 500 4	

1953

dns	BELGIAN GP	Spa	44	Ecurie Francorchamps	2.0 Ferrari 500 4	practice only

GP Starts: 2   GP Wins: 0   Pole positions: 0   Fastest laps: 0   Points: 0

SAM TINGLE

A great enthusiast, this Rhodesian raced in his homeland from 1950, and contested the South African championship with great verve throughout the 1960s in one of Doug Serrurier's LDS-Alfas, scoring his first big win in the 1966 Border Trophy at East London, although he took many other good placings.

By 1968 Sam was perhaps past his prime, but still managed to stay competitive in his final seasons of competition by dint of getting his hands on an ex-works Brabham BT24-Repco.

ALESSANDRO de TOMASO

A useful sports car driver in his native Argentina, first with a Maserati T200S and then the little OSCA, de Tomaso made his GP debut in an old Ferrari in his home event in 1957, before coming to Europe to drive the small-capacity OSCA, winning the Index of Performance at Le Mans in 1958. After racing his Cooper-OSCA hybrid at Sebring in 1959, he retired from racing, subsequently building an unsuccessful Formula 1 car on two occasions (1962 and 1970). However, he did make money from a road car project, which was taken up by Ford in the late sixties.

DESMOND TITTERINGTON

Having gained experience in an Allard, Titterington joined Ecurie Ecosse for the 1953 Tourist Trophy at Dundrod, finishing sixth. The Ulsterman then raced the team's Jaguar, and was second in the BARC 9 Hours at Goodwood in 1955, before joining the full works team, taking third at Reims in 1956. He also raced for Mercedes in the 1955 Targa Florio, finishing fourth with John Fitch.

In Formula 1, he scored a superb third at Oulton Park in 1955 on his debut for Vanwall, and also took third in the 1956 International Trophy for Connaught, for whom he drove in that year's British GP. After a remarkable rise from obscurity, this very talented driver suddenly retired from racing at the end of the 1956 season.

CHARLES de TORNACO

The wealthy son of twenties racer Baron de Tornaco, the young Charles, encouraged by his long-time friend Jacques Swaters, took part in the 1949 Spa 24 Hours with a BMW, and then drove a Veritas in the 1950 event, before helping found Ecurie Belgique. In truth, he was not a talented driver, but his enthusiasm was such that when the team regrouped as Ecurie Francorchamps in 1952, he remained, racing their Ferrari T500, though his best result that year was a fourth place at Chimay in an HWM. He raced less regularly in 1953, but in practice for the Modena GP he rolled the team's Ferrari, fracturing his skull and breaking his neck. Scandalously, there was no proper medical assistance present, and he died on the way to hospital in an ordinary saloon car.

MAURICE TRINTIGNANT

Maurice was the youngest of the five sons of a prosperous vineyard owner and followed three of his brothers into racing. Despite the death of Louis at Péronne in 1933, he could not resist the urge to try his hand at the sport five years later at the wheel of the Bugatti used by his unfortunate sibling. He took it to fifth place in the Pau GP, and won the 1939 GP des Frontières at Chimay before the war caused the cessation of racing activities. When the first post-war motor race was held in the Bois de Boulogne, Trintignant was there with his trusty Bugatti. Unfortunately his car suffered fuel starvation which was later found to have been caused by rat droppings *(les petoules)* left in the tank from its wartime lay-up. This was the cause of much merriment and Maurice was henceforth given the sobriquet *'Le Petoulet'*, which he accepted in fine spirit.

He soon replaced the Bugatti with an Amilcar, winning at Avignon in 1947, and after half a season in the Gersac team's Delage joined the Simca Gordini team. The 1948 season started well with wins at Perpignan and Montlhéry, but he was seriously injured in the tragic Swiss GP at Bremgarten in which three drivers were killed. Maurice was more fortunate. He spun his car and was flung into the middle of the track and only split-second reactions by the approaching Farina, Bira and Manzon enabled them to miss his unconscious body, the three brave pilots eliminating themselves in avoidance. In hospital Maurice's life hung by a thread as he lay in a coma for eight days. At one stage he was pronounced dead, but his pulse returned and a slow recovery began. He was back in action at the beginning of 1949 for Simca, winning the Circuit des Ramparts at Angoulême. Showing no ill-effects from his accident, Trintignant remained with Gordini to the end of the 1953 season, taking the little pale-blue car to victories at Geneva in 1950, Albi and Cadours in 1951 and Cadours again in 1953, the year he was crowned racing champion of France. The Gordinis were, of course, notorious for their fragility, and in World Championship Grands Prix he could achieve no better than three fifth places.

After winning the Buenos Aires GP in Rosier's Ferrari, he joined the works team for the bulk of 1954, which brought an immediate improvement in results. Regularly placing in World Championship events, Trintignant won F1 races at Caen and Rouen and was second at Syracuse and Bari. He also shared the winning 4.9-litre Ferrari with Gonzalez to win the Le Mans 24-hour race. In 1955 a steady drive at Monaco brought him his first-ever World Championship win, and in sports cars he won the Messina 10 Hours with Castellotti. He continued to race the Scuderia's sports cars successfully in 1956, winning the Agadir, Dakar and Swedish GPs. But in Formula 1 the picture was less happy, Trintignant having a dismal time in the Vanwall and the ambitious but ill-fated Bugatti. He drove less frequently in 1957, but won the F2 Coupe de Vitesse at Reims in Ferrari's Dino V6, and took third in the Moroccan GP in BRM's P25.

Maurice was back at the forefront again in 1958 when, with Rob Walker's little Cooper, he won the Monaco GP once more and also took victories at Pau and Clermont Ferrand. He was to enjoy his two-year association with the Walker *équipe* and, despite being 'number two' to Moss, provided them with some excellent Grand Prix results in 1959, as well as another victory at Pau. After finishing second at Le Mans in the Aston Martin that year, Maurice found his outings with David Brown's Formula 1 team in 1960 restricted by the project's myriad problems and he was forced to find rides with Centro Sud. He also ran his own Cooper in Formula 2 that season, plenty of solid placings bringing excellent remuneration. He was also awarded the *Légion d'honneur* for his services to French motor racing, but he had no intention of resting on his laurels. After a thin time in 1961, he was back with Rob Walker in 1962 following the Goodwood accident which was to end the career of Stirling Moss. Though now past his best, Trintignant could still teach Jim Clark a thing or two, as he showed when he took a third win at Pau.

Maurice raced very little in 1963 and retirement seemed imminent, but he purchased a BRM V8 for 1964 and drove exceedingly well in the German GP to be classified fifth, thus taking two championship points at the age of 47. Although this was his final season in Grands Prix, his farewell came at Le Mans in 1965, ending a remarkable career during which – his Bremgarten crash apart – he had perhaps been one of the safest drivers around. Rarely involved in accidents, his mechanical sympathy ensured a great many finishes, which was much appreciated by team managers.

In his final race *'Le Petoulet'* drove a Ford GT, which was quite a long way down the chain of motor racing evolution from a Type 35 GP Bugatti, and the cause of his retirement from the 24 Hours certainly wasn't rat droppings!

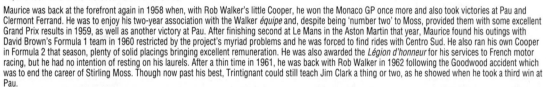

TRINTIGNANT, Maurice (F) b 30/10/1917

1950

	Race	Circuit	No	Entrant	Car/Engine	Comment
ret	MONACO GP	Monte Carlo	12	Equipe Gordini	1.5 s/c Simca Gordini Type 15 4	multiple accident
ret	ITALIAN GP	Monza	42	Equipe Gordini	1.5 s/c Simca Gordini Type 15 4	water pipe

1951

	Race	Circuit	No	Entrant	Car/Engine	Comment
ret	FRENCH GP	Reims	32	Equipe Gordini	1.5 s/c Simca Gordini Type 15 4	engine
ret	GERMAN GP	Nürburgring	81	Equipe Gordini	1.5 s/c Simca Gordini Type 15 4	engine
ret	ITALIAN GP	Monza	50	Equipe Gordini	1.5 s/c Simca Gordini Type 15 4	engine
ret	SPANISH GP	Pedralbes	12	Equipe Gordini	1.5 s/c Simca Gordini Type 15 4	engine

1952

	Race	Circuit	No	Entrant	Car/Engine	Comment
dns	BELGIAN GP	Spa	14	Ecurie Rosier	2.0 Ferrari 166 V12 F2	engine trouble
5	FRENCH GP	Rouen	44	Equipe Gordini	1.5 Simca Gordini Type 15 4	4 laps behind
ret	BRITISH GP	Silverstone	25	Equipe Gordini	2.0 Gordini Type 16 6	gearbox
ret	GERMAN GP	Nürburgring	109	Equipe Gordini	2.0 Gordini Type 16 6	brakes/suspension
6	DUTCH GP	Zandvoort	12	Equipe Gordini	2.0 Gordini Type 16 6	3 laps behind
ret	ITALIAN GP	Monza	4	Equipe Gordini	2.0 Gordini Type 16 6	engine

1953

	Race	Circuit	No	Entrant	Car/Engine	Comment
7*	ARGENTINE GP	Buenos Aires	28	Equipe Gordini	2.0 Gordini Type 16 6	* Schell took over/6 laps behind
6	DUTCH GP	Zandvoort	24	Equipe Gordini	2.0 Gordini Type 16 6	3 laps behind
5	BELGIAN GP	Spa	18	Equipe Gordini	2.0 Gordini Type 16 6	1 lap behind
ret	FRENCH GP	Reims	4	Equipe Gordini	2.0 Gordini Type 16 6	transmission
ret	BRITISH GP	Silverstone	29	Equipe Gordini	2.0 Gordini Type 16 6	transmission
ret	GERMAN GP	Nürburgring	10	Equipe Gordini	2.0 Gordini Type 16 6	differential
ret	SWISS GP	Bremgarten	8	Equipe Gordini	2.0 Gordini Type 16 6	transmission
5	ITALIAN GP	Monza	36	Equipe Gordini	2.0 Gordini Type 16 6	1 lap behind

1954

	Race	Circuit	No	Entrant	Car/Engine	Comment
4	ARGENTINE GP	Buenos Aires	26	Ecurie Rosier	2.5 Ferrari 625 4	1 lap behind
2	BELGIAN GP	Spa	8	Scuderia Ferrari	2.5 Ferrari 625 4	
dns	"	"	8	Scuderia Ferrari	2.5 Ferrari 553 4	practice only
ret	FRENCH GP	Reims	4	Scuderia Ferrari	2.5 Ferrari 625 4	engine
5	BRITISH GP	Silverstone	10	Scuderia Ferrari	2.5 Ferrari 625/555 4	3 laps behind
3	GERMAN GP	Nürburgring	2	Scuderia Ferrari	2.5 Ferrari 625 4	

ret	SWISS GP	Bremgarten	26	Scuderia Ferrari	2.5 Ferrari 625/555 4	engine
5	ITALIAN GP	Monza	30	Scuderia Ferrari	2.5 Ferrari 625/555 4	5 laps behind
ret	SPANISH GP	Pedralbes	40	Scuderia Ferrari	2.5 Ferrari 553/555 4	engine

1955

ret	ARGENTINE GP	Buenos Aires	14	Scuderia Ferrari	2.5 Ferrari 625/555 4	engine
2*	"	" "	12	Scuderia Ferrari	2.5 Ferrari 625/555 4	* Gonzalez/Farina also drove
3*	"	" "	10	Scuderia Ferrari	2.5 Ferrari 625/555 4	* Farina/Maglioli also drove/-2 laps
1	MONACO GP	Monte Carlo	44	Scuderia Ferrari	2.5 Ferrari 625/555 4	
6	BELGIAN GP	Spa	4	Scuderia Ferrari	2.5 Ferrari 555 4	1 lap behind
ret	DUTCH GP	Zandvoort	4	Scuderia Ferrari	2.5 Ferrari 555 4	gearbox
dns	"	"	4	Scuderia Ferrari	2.5 Ferrari 625 4	practice only
ret	BRITISH GP	Aintree	18	Scuderia Ferrari	2.5 Ferrari 625/555 4	overheating
8	ITALIAN GP	Monza	8	Scuderia Ferrari	2.5 Ferrari 555 4	5 laps behind

1956

ret	MONACO GP	Monte Carlo	14	Vandervell Products Ltd	2.5 Vanwall 4	overheating after accident
ret	BELGIAN GP	Spa	12	Vandervell Products Ltd	2.5 Vanwall 4	engine
ret	FRENCH GP	Reims	28	Automobiles Bugatti	2.5 Bugatti 251 8	throttle pedal
ret	BRITISH GP	Silverstone	17	Vandervell Products Ltd	2.5 Vanwall 4	fuel line
ret	ITALIAN GP	Monza	20	Vandervell Products Ltd	2.5 Vanwall 4	rear suspension

1957

5	MONACO GP	Monte Carlo	30	Scuderia Ferrari	2.5 Lancia-Ferrari 801 V8	5 laps behind
ret	FRENCH GP	Rouen	16	Scuderia Ferrari	2.5 Lancia-Ferrari 801 V8	magneto
4	BRITISH GP	Aintree	16	Scuderia Ferrari	2.5 Lancia-Ferrari 801 V8	Collins took over/2 laps behind

1958

1	MONACO GP	Monte Carlo	20	R R C Walker Racing Team	2.0 Cooper T45-Climax 4	
9	DUTCH GP	Zandvoort	9	R R C Walker Racing Team	2.0 Cooper T45-Climax 4	3 laps behind
7	BELGIAN GP	Spa	28	Scuderia Centro Sud	2.5 Maserati 250F 6	1 lap behind
ret	FRENCH GP	Reims	18	Owen Racing Organisation	2.5 BRM P25 4	oil pipe
8	BRITISH GP	Silverstone	4	R R C Walker Racing Team	2.0 Cooper T43-Climax 4	2 laps behind
3	GERMAN GP	Nürburgring	11	R R C Walker Racing Team	2.2 Cooper T45-Climax 4	
8	PORTUGUESE GP	Oporto	12	R R C Walker Racing Team	2.0 Cooper T43-Climax 4	2 laps behind
ret	ITALIAN GP	Monza	2	R R C Walker Racing Team	2.2 Cooper T45-Climax 4	gearbox
dns	"	"	2	R R C Walker Racing Team	2.0 Cooper T43-Climax 4	practice only
ret	MOROCCAN GP	Casablanca	36	R R C Walker Racing Team	2.2 Cooper T45-Climax 4	engine

1959

3	MONACO GP	Monte Carlo	32	R R C Walker Racing Team	2.5 Cooper T51-Climax 4	2 laps behind
8	DUTCH GP	Zandvoort	10	R R C Walker Racing Team	2.5 Cooper T51-Climax 4	2 laps behind
nc	FRENCH GP	Reims	14	R R C Walker Racing Team	2.5 Cooper T51-Climax 4	spun and stalled/14 laps behind
5	BRITISH GP	Aintree	18	R R C Walker Racing Team	2.5 Cooper T51-Climax 4	1 lap behind
4*	GERMAN GP	AVUS	8	R R C Walker Racing Team	2.5 Cooper T51-Climax 4	* agg-6th Heat 1/4th Heat 2/-1 lap
4	PORTUGUESE GP	Monsanto	5	R R C Walker Racing Team	2.5 Cooper T51-Climax 4	2 laps behind
9	ITALIAN GP	Monza	16	R R C Walker Racing Team	2.5 Cooper T51-Climax 4	2 laps behind
2	US GP	Sebring	6	R R C Walker Racing Team	2.5 Cooper T51-Climax 4	FL

1960

3*	ARGENTINE GP	Buenos Aires	38	R R C Walker Racing Team	2.5 Cooper T51-Climax 4	* Moss took over-no points allowed
ret	MONACO GP	Monte Carlo	44	Scuderia Centro Sud	2.5 Cooper T51-Maserati 4	gearbox
ret	DUTCH GP	Zandvoort	18	Scuderia Centro Sud	2.5 Cooper T51-Maserati 4	transmission
ret	FRENCH GP	Reims	38	Scuderia Centro Sud	2.5 Cooper T51-Maserati 4	hit by G Hill on grid
11	BRITISH GP	Silverstone	19	David Brown Corporation	2.5 Aston Martin DBR4/250 6	5 laps behind
15	US GP	Riverside	18	Scuderia Centro Sud	2.5 Cooper T51-Maserati 4	9 laps behind

1961

7	MONACO GP	Monte Carlo	42	Scuderia Serenissima	1.5 Cooper T51-Maserati 4	5 laps behind
ret	BELGIAN GP	Spa	26	Scuderia Serenissima	1.5 Cooper T51-Maserati 4	gearbox
dns	"	"	26	Scuderia Serenissima	1.5 Cooper T43-Climax 4	practice only
13	FRENCH GP	Reims	32	Scuderia Serenissima	1.5 Cooper T51-Maserati 4	10 laps behind
dns	"	"	32	Scuderia Serenissima	1.5 de Tomaso F1-001-OSCA 4	practice only
ret	GERMAN GP	Nürburgring	20	Scuderia Serenissima	1.5 Cooper T51-Maserati 4	engine
9	ITALIAN GP	Monza	48	Scuderia Serenissima	1.5 Cooper T51-Maserati 4	2 laps behind

1962

ret	MONACO GP	Monte Carlo	30	Rob Walker Racing Team	1.5 Lotus 24-Climax V8	first corner accident
8	BELGIAN GP	Spa	18	Rob Walker Racing Team	1.5 Lotus 24-Climax V8	2 laps behind
7	FRENCH GP	Rouen	28	Rob Walker Racing Team	1.5 Lotus 24-Climax V8	hit by T Taylor after finish
ret	GERMAN GP	Nürburgring	17	Rob Walker Racing Team	1.5 Lotus 24-Climax V8	gearbox
ret	ITALIAN GP	Monza	36	Rob Walker Racing Team	1.5 Lotus 24-Climax V8	electrics
ret	US GP	Watkins Glen	6	Rob Walker Racing Team	1.5 Lotus 24-Climax V8	brakes

1963

ret	MONACO GP	Monte Carlo	17	Reg Parnell (Racing)	1.5 Lola 4A-Climax V8	clutch
dns	"	" "	17	Reg Parnell (Racing)	1.5 Lola 4-Climax V8	practice only
8	FRENCH GP	Reims	28	Reg Parnell (Racing)	1.5 Lotus 24-Climax V8	3 laps behind
9	ITALIAN GP	Monza	66	Scuderia Centro Sud	1.5 BRM P57 V8	3 laps behind

1964

ret	MONACO GP	Monte Carlo	4	Maurice Trintignant	1.5 BRM P57 V8	overheating
11	FRENCH GP	Rouen	28	Maurice Trintignant	1.5 BRM P57 V8	5 laps behind
dnq	BRITISH GP	Brands Hatch	25	Maurice Trintignant	1.5 BRM P57 V8	
5/ret	GERMAN GP	Nürburgring	22	Maurice Trintignant	1.5 BRM P57 V8	flat battery/1 lap behind
ret	ITALIAN GP	Monza	48	Maurice Trintignant	1.5 BRM P57 V8	fuel injection

GP Starts: 82   GP Wins: 2   Pole positions: 0   Fastest laps: 1   Points: 72.33

WOLFGANG VON TRIPS

This dashing, handsome and immensely popular German aristocrat stood on the verge of the drivers' World Championship at Monza on a sunny September day in 1961. Everything was going to plan; his red Ferrari sat on pole position at the head of a two-by-two grid, cunningly arranged by the organisers to help reduce the chances of any fast non-Italian machines gaining the all-important tow. However, when the flag dropped Trips was not the quickest away and was enmeshed in the leading bunch which hammered around the banking to complete the first lap. The German was under pressure from the Lotus of Jim Clark and when the young Scot pulled out of the Ferrari's slipstream in an attempt to pass, Trips moved over too. . .

Clipping the front wheel of the Lotus sent the number 4 Ferrari out of control and it crashed up a bank and along a fence packed with spectators before rolling back down to the track. The driver lay on the circuit, flung like a rag doll; Jim Clark was wandering around unhurt but in shock as the cars sped past on their third lap; and one driver and 14 spectators were to pay the sport's ultimate price. The race went on, and team-mate Phil Hill was crowned World Champion, but Wolfgang von Trips was dead. Such were the stark realities of motor racing.

The German had always lived on the edge. His first Grand Prix appearance at Monza was ended by a practice crash when the steering failed, but he escaped serious injury this time around. In 1958 he collided with Schell on the opening lap and ended up with a broken leg. Returning to action at the start of 1959 he spun the works F2 Porsche at Monaco and eliminated the rest of his class. This sorry tally makes him seem a liability, but that was far from the case, for from the earliest days, when he took a third place in the 1955 Tourist Trophy in a Mercedes 300SLR at Dundrod, Trips was a fearless and skilled driver, particularly in sports cars. He was European hill-climb champion in 1958 in a works Porsche RSK, and in 1959 drove a brilliant race in the small-capacity Porsche in the Tourist Trophy at Goodwood to finish second ahead of Brooks' Ferrari.

By 1960 von Trips was emerging as a trusty and reliable single-seater exponent. Apart from his placings in the championship races, he won at Syracuse and Solitude for Ferrari, and took second in the F2 German GP for Porsche. His work with the rear-engined prototype car set him up for the 1961 season, and with the new 156 'sharknose' Ferrari he took his first Grand Prix win at Zandvoort in masterly style. In sports cars, the Targa Florio was won with Gendebien, and then back in F1 he coped with the early wet conditions at Aintree to extend his championship lead. Even a second place behind the genius of Moss in the German Grand Prix seemed to be sufficient, for the next race was at Monza and, surely, the title would be his . . .

TRIPS, Wolfgang von (D) b 4/5/1928 – d 10/9/1961

	Race	Circuit	No	Entrant	Car/Engine	Comment
	1956					
dns	ITALIAN GP	Monza	50	Scuderia Ferrari	2.5 Lancia-Ferrari D50 V8	*accident in practice*
	1957					
6*	ARGENTINE GP	Buenos Aires	18	Scuderia Ferrari	2.5 Lancia-Ferrari D50 V8	** Perdisa & Collins also drove*
ret*	MONACO GP	Monte Carlo	24	Scuderia Ferrari	2.5 Lancia-Ferrari 801 V8	*engine/*Hawthorn drove for 4 laps*
3	ITALIAN GP	Monza	36	Scuderia Ferrari	2.5 Lancia-Ferrari 801 V8	*2 laps behind*
	1958					
ret	MONACO GP	Monte Carlo	40	Scuderia Ferrari	2.4 Ferrari Dino 246 V6	*engine*
3	FRENCH GP	Reims	6	Scuderia Ferrari	2.4 Ferrari Dino 246 V6	
ret	BRITISH GP	Silverstone	3	Scuderia Ferrari	2.4 Ferrari Dino 246 V6	*engine*
4	GERMAN GP	Nürburgring	4	Scuderia Ferrari	2.4 Ferrari Dino 246 V6	
5	PORTUGUESE GP	Oporto	24	Scuderia Ferrari	2.4 Ferrari Dino 246 V6	*1 lap behind*
ret	ITALIAN GP	Monza	16	Scuderia Ferrari	2.4 Ferrari Dino 246 V6	*collision with Schell-broken leg*
	1959					
ret	MONACO GP	Monte Carlo	6	Dr Ing hcf Porsche KG	1.5 Porsche 718 F4	*multiple accident*
dns	GERMAN GP	AVUS	14	Dr Ing hcf Porsche KG	1.5 Porsche 718 F4	*withdawn after Behra's accident*
6	US GP	Sebring	4	Scuderia Ferrari	2.4 Ferrari Dino 246 V6	*4 laps behind*
	1960					
5	ARGENTINE GP	Buenos Aires	30	Scuderia Ferrari	2.4 Ferrari Dino 246 V6	
8/ret	MONACO GP	Monte Carlo	38	Scuderia Ferrari	2.4 Ferrari Dino 246 V6	*clutch/39 laps behind*
5	DUTCH GP	Zandvoort	2	Scuderia Ferrari	2.4 Ferrari Dino 246 V6	
dns	"	"	2	Scuderia Ferrari	2.4 Ferrari Dino 246P V6	*practice only*
ret	BELGIAN GP	Spa	26	Scuderia Ferrari	2.4 Ferrari Dino 246 V6	*transmission*
ret	FRENCH GP	Reims	4	Scuderia Ferrari	2.4 Ferrari Dino 246 V6	*transmission*
6	BRITISH GP	Silverstone	11	Scuderia Ferrari	2.4 Ferrari Dino 246 V6	*2 laps behind*
4	PORTUGUESE GP	Oporto	28	Scuderia Ferrari	2.4 Ferrari Dino 246 V6	
5	ITALIAN GP	Monza	22	Scuderia Ferrari	1.5 Ferrari Dino 246P V6 F2	*2 laps behind*
9	US GP	Riverside	26	Scuderia Centro Sud	2.5 Cooper T51-Maserati 4	*3 laps behind*
	1961					
4/ret	MONACO GP	Monte Carlo	40	Scuderia Ferrari SpA SEFAC	1.5 Ferrari 156 V6	*engine failed-crashed/2 laps behind*
1	DUTCH GP	Zandvoort	3	Scuderia Ferrari Spa SEFAC	1.5 Ferrari 156 V6	
2	BELGIAN GP	Spa	2	Scuderia Ferrari SpA SEFAC	1.5 Ferrari 156 V6	
ret	FRENCH GP	Reims	20	Scuderia Ferrari SpA SEFAC	1.5 Ferrari 156 V6	*engine*
1	BRITISH GP	Aintree	4	Scuderia Ferrari SpA SEFAC	1.5 Ferrari 156 V6	
2	GERMAN GP	Nürburgring	3	Scuderia Ferrari SpA SEFAC	1.5 Ferrari 156 V6	
ret	ITALIAN GP	Monza	4	Scuderia Ferrari SpA SEFAC	1.5 Ferrari 156 V6	*fatal accident/Pole*

GP Starts: 27   GP Wins: 2   Pole positions: 1   Fastest laps: 0   Points: 56

TUNMER, Guy (ZA) b 1/12/1948

1975

	Race	Circuit	No	Entrant	Car/Engine	Comment
11	SOUTH AFRICAN GP	Kyalami	34	Team Gunston	3.0 Lotus 72-Cosworth V8	2 laps behind

GP Starts: 1 GP Wins: 0 Pole positions: 0 Fastest laps: 0 Points: 0

ULMEN, Toni (D) b 12/1/1906 – d 4/11/1976

1952

	Race	Circuit	No	Entrant	Car/Engine	Comment
ret	SWISS GP	Bremgarten	4	Toni Ulmen	2.0 Veritas-Meteor 6 sports	fuel tank
8	GERMAN GP	Nürburgring	125	Toni Ulmen	2.0 Veritas-Meteor 6 sports	2 laps behind

GP Starts: 2 GP Wins: 0 Pole positions: 0 Fastest laps: 0 Points: 0

UNSER, Bobby (USA) b 20/2/1934

1968

	Race	Circuit	No	Entrant	Car/Engine	Comment
dns	ITALIAN GP	Monza	25	Owen Racing Organisation	3.0 BRM P126 V12	racing in USA within 24 hours
ret	US GP	Watkins Glen	9	Owen Racing Organisation	3.0 BRM P138 V12	engine
dns	"	" "	9	Owen Racing Organisation	3.0 BRM P126 V12	accident in practice

GP Starts: 1 GP Wins: 0 Pole positions: 0 Fastest laps: 0 Points: 0

URIA, Alberto (U)

1955

	Race	Circuit	No	Entrant	Car/Engine	Comment
ret	ARGENTINE GP	Buenos Aires	30	Alberto Uria	2.5 Maserati A6GCM/250F 6	fuel starvation

1956

	Race	Circuit	No	Entrant	Car/Engine	Comment
6*	ARGENTINE GP	Buenos Aires	16	Alberto Uria	2.5 Maserati A6GCM/250F 6	* shared with Oscar Gonzalez/-10 laps

GP Starts: 2 GP Wins: 0 Pole positions: 0 Fastest laps: 0 Points: 0

VACCARELLA, Nino (I) b 4/3/1933

1961

	Race	Circuit	No	Entrant	Car/Engine	Comment
ret	ITALIAN GP	Monza	50	Scuderia Serenissima	1.5 de Tomaso F1 003-Alfa Romeo 4	engine

1962

	Race	Circuit	No	Entrant	Car/Engine	Comment
dnq	MONACO GP	Monte Carlo	42	Scuderia SSS Republica di Venezia	1.5 Lotus 18/21-Climax 4	
15	GERMAN GP	Nürburgring	26	Scuderia SSS Republica di Venezia	1.5 Porsche 718 F4	
9	ITALIAN GP	Monza	24	Scuderia SSS Republica di Venezia	1.5 Lotus 24-Climax V8	2 laps behind

1965

	Race	Circuit	No	Entrant	Car/Engine	Comment
12/ret	ITALIAN GP	Monza	6	Scuderia Ferrari SpA SEFAC	1.5 Ferrari 158 V8	engine/8 laps behind

GP Starts: 4 GP Wins: 0 Pole positions: 0 Fastest laps: 0 Points: 0

GUY TUMNER

This South African amateur racer began competing in Minis in the late sixties, racing an Alfa with brother Derek, before turning to single-seaters regularly in 1973 with a March 722. In 1975 he drove for Team Gunston in both the Grand Prix and the local F1 series with their Lotus 72E, winning the False Bay 100 at Killarney. Guy also raced in Europe in John Lepp's March at the Monza 1000 Km. When the premier domestic single-seater class switched to Formula Atlantic, Tumner raced his own front-running Chevron B34 in 1976.

BOBBY UNSER

A legend in USAC/IndyCar racing, twice champion (1968 and 1974) and three times Indianapolis 500 winner (1968, 1975 and 1981) Bobby Unser stands among the all-time greats with a career total of 35 victories to his credit.

His Grand Prix appearance with the BRM could hardly have been less auspicious: not allowed to race at Monza due to clashing race schedules, Unser managed to crash his car in practice at Watkins Glen and also blew a couple of engines. All in all an expensive exercise best forgotten.

TONI ULMEN

The outstanding Veritas driver, Ulmen was the German F2 champion in 1949 and always posed a real threat in his Veritas-Meteor. In 1950 he was third at Erlen, less than ten seconds behind two Ferraris led by Villoresi, second in the Eifelrennen and fourth in the German GP. In 1951 he took second place and fastest lap at AVUS, and third at the ultra-fast Grenzlandring circuit.

For 1952 Toni entered his sports-bodied Veritas in two World Championship events without success, but took a fifth place at the Eifelrennen, and won the Formula 2 high-speed thrash at Grenzlandring and a 2-litre sports car race at the Nürburgring. Despite announcing his retirement in early 1953, he was soon back, albeit briefly, sharing Roosdorp's Jaguar in sports car events and finishing third in the Spa 24 Hours.

NINO VACCARELLA

A Sicilian lawyer, Vaccarella was almost deified by the local fans after some superb drives in the Targa Florio, a race which he won three times – and it could have been more. A top sports car driver from 1962 to 1975, Nino also won Le Mans in 1964 for Ferrari with Guichet, and the 1970 Sebring 12 Hours with Andretti and Giunti. He also scored many other placings, and was a very reliable practitioner, rarely damaging the car and enjoying a remarkable ratio of finishes in this

punishing category. His Formula 1 career started brightly with Scuderia Serenissima in 1961, when he took a third in the Coppa Italia at Vallelunga, and he finished sixth in the 1962 Pau GP, but that was as far as it went, his 'one-off' Ferrari drive at Monza in 1965 being literally just that.

GILLES VILLENEUVE

To this day opinions are sharply divided about Gilles Villeneuve. To many he was simply what motor racing was all about. To the more dispassionate he was an accident waiting to happen, and when the end came, well, they were proved right, weren't they?

In soccer, if the ball goes to a Pele or Best, or now Giggs, there is a collective sense of anticipation, a feeling that something special could be about to happen . . . It was like that with Gilles. As an ordinary punter denied access to the inner sanctum of pit or paddock, you could stand on any corner, at any circuit and wait for his Ferrari to scream into view. Then came the reward. With a glint of wildness in his eyes, and the car at some wicked angle – more often than not at its very limit and then some – Villeneuve would pass and you could sense the thrill.

Gilles raced snowmobiles for several years and tried drag racing before turning to Formula Ford in 1973. Winning seven out of ten races seemed to indicate that a move into Formula Atlantic would be needed to test his powers, but he was soon sidelined, but only for a month, by a fractured leg sustained in an accident at Mosport. Once back in the groove, he started to be noticed, especially after a race at Trois Rivières in 1976 when James Hunt, no less, was soundly thrashed. Typically James told McLaren to sign this man up as soon as possible. The following July, the French-Canadian was in a McLaren – at Silverstone – but for only one race. He was to make the most of it, indulging in countless spins, which to most onlookers seemed to indicate he was in over his head. Gilles knew better; he was just finding the limits in a Grand Prix car and the only way to do that was to go up to and beyond the point of adhesion. Amazingly, Teddy Mayer felt that he could pass on Villeneuve, and so he was picked up by Ferrari. It could all have ended after just two races, for at Fuji he ran into the Tyrrell of Ronnie Peterson and his car somersaulted wildly into a prohibited area, killing two spectators. This time Gilles walked away. . .

He was to be involved in a string of shunts at the start of 1978, some of his own making, some not. But he was undoubtedly quick and as the year wore on he got quicker. At Monza he and Andretti battled for the win, only for both drivers to be penalised for jumping the start. The last race of 1978 was in Canada, and Gilles finally scored his first Grand Prix win, but only after Jarier's Lotus had hit trouble. He felt that his triumph was somehow devalued by that – not having won the race on merit took the gloss off the victory. In statistical terms 1979 was the season he could have won the World Championship, but it went instead to team-mate Jody Scheckter and Gilles supported the South African all the way. There were, of course, the moments of genius, such as his battle with Arnoux at Dijon, or his qualifying performance at Watkins Glen in the rain when he was *eleven* seconds quicker than Scheckter. There was also controversy, with his notorious return to the pits at Zandvoort with the rear wheel hanging off the Ferrari following a blown tyre and spin. Pure Gilles!

In 1980 his efforts were handicapped by the truly awful handling of the Ferrari 312T5, which even the matchless skill of Villeneuve could do little to tame, but the new 126CK V6 car was a different proposition. Sure the chassis still needed to be refined, but the turbo power gave him a chance to compete on more equal terms with the Williamses and Brabhams. He took only two wins that year, but they were both memorable. At Monaco he pounced on Alan Jones' faltering Williams to take an unlikely win when many would have long given up the race for lost. Then came an unforgettable performance at Jarama when he kept the snarling pack of cars in his wake for the bulk of the race to take a win one would not have believed possible.

Certainly the cars of the period did a driver like Villeneuve no favours and by the time the 1982 season came round, he hated ground-effect and all it stood for. But he was being paid to drive and just got on with the job in typical fashion. At Imola, the Ferraris had it all their own way and Gilles had the race under control, until team-mate Pironi 'stole' the victory from him on the last lap. Villeneuve was shocked, outraged and suffered every other conceivable hurt over the Fenchman's underhand tactics. He would not speak to him again – ever.

Two weeks later at Zolder, Gilles was hardly any less anguished. He went out for practice, 100 per cent committed as usual, but this time he was not to return, for having touched the March of Jochen Mass his Ferrari cartwheeled across the track in an accident of sickening ferocity. The hapless driver was thrown from the car, receiving terrible injuries. There was no hope of survival, but while the little man had gone, the legend he left behind would never die.

VILLENEUVE, Gilles (CDN) b 18/1/1950 – d 8/5/1982

1977

	Race	Circuit	No	Entrant	Car/Engine	Comment
11	BRITISH GP	Silverstone	40	Marlboro Team McLaren	3.0 McLaren M23-Cosworth V8	*pit stop-faulty temperature gauge*
12/ret	CANADIAN GP	Mosport Park	21	Scuderia Ferrari SpA SEFAC	3.0 Ferrari 312T2 F12	*driveshaft*
ret	JAPANESE GP	Mount Fuji	11	Scuderia Ferrari SpA SEFAC	3.0 Ferrari 312T2 F12	*accident-hit Peterson and crashed*

1978

	Race	Circuit	No	Entrant	Car/Engine	Comment
8	ARGENTINE GP	Buenos Aires	12	Scuderia Ferrari SpA SEFAC	3.0 Ferrari 312T2 F12	
ret	BRAZILIAN GP	Rio	12	Scuderia Ferrari SpA SEFAC	3.0 Ferrari 312T2 F12	*spun off*
ret	SOUTH AFRICAN GP	Kyalami	12	Scuderia Ferrari SpA SEFAC	3.0 Ferrari 312T3 F12	*oil leak*
ret	US GP WEST	Long Beach	12	Scuderia Ferrari SpA SEFAC	3.0 Ferrari 312T3 F12	*collision with Regazzoni*
ret	MONACO GP	Monte Carlo	12	Scuderia Ferrari SpA SEFAC	3.0 Ferrari 312T3 F12	*tyre failure-accident*
4	BELGIAN GP	Zolder	12	Scuderia Ferrari SpA SEFAC	3.0 Ferrari 312T3 F12	
10	SPANISH GP	Jarama	12	Scuderia Ferrari SpA SEFAC	3.0 Ferrari 312T3 F12	*pit stop-tyres/1 lap behind*
9	SWEDISH GP	Anderstorp	12	Scuderia Ferrari SpA SEFAC	3.0 Ferrari 312T3 F12	*pit stop-tyres/1 lap behind*
12	FRENCH GP	Paul Ricard	12	Scuderia Ferrari SpA SEFAC	3.0 Ferrari 312T3 F12	*pit stops-tyres/1 lap behind*
ret	BRITISH GP	Brands Hatch	12	Scuderia Ferrari SpA SEFAC	3.0 Ferrari 312T3 F12	*driveshaft*
8	GERMAN GP	Hockenheim	12	Scuderia Ferrari SpA SEFAC	3.0 Ferrari 312T3 F12	*pit stop-tyres*
3	AUSTRIAN GP	Österreichring	12	Scuderia Ferrari SpA SEFAC	3.0 Ferrari 312T3 F12	
6	DUTCH GP	Zandvoort	12	Scuderia Ferrari SpA SEFAC	3.0 Ferrari 312T3 F12	
7*	ITALIAN GP	Monza	12	Scuderia Ferrari SpA SEFAC	3.0 Ferrari 312T3 F12	** 2nd on road-1 min pen-jumped start*
ret	US GP EAST	Watkins Glen	12	Scuderia Ferrari SpA SEFAC	3.0 Ferrari 312T3 F12	*engine*
1	CANADIAN GP	Montreal	12	Scuderia Ferrari SpA SEFAC	3.0 Ferrari 312T3 F12	

1979

	Race	Circuit	No	Entrant	Car/Engine	Comment
ret	ARGENTINE GP	Buenos Aires	12	Scuderia Ferrari SpA SEFAC	3.0 Ferrari 312T3 F12	*engine*
5	BRAZILIAN GP	Interlagos	12	Scuderia Ferrari SpA SEFAC	3.0 Ferrari 312T3 F12	*1 lap behind*
1	SOUTH AFRICAN GP	Kyalami	12	Scuderia Ferrari SpA SEFAC	3.0 Ferrari 312T4 F12	*FL*
1	US GP WEST	Long Beach	12	Scuderia Ferrari SpA SEFAC	3.0 Ferrari 312T4 F12	*Pole/FL*

7	SPANISH GP	Jarama	12	Scuderia Ferrari SpA SEFAC	3.0 Ferrari 312T4 F12	pit stop-tyres/FL
7/ret	BELGIAN GP	Zolder	12	Scuderia Ferrari SpA SEFAC	3.0 Ferrari 312T4 F12	accident-p stop/out of fuel/FL/-1 lap
ret	MONACO GP	Monte Carlo	12	Scuderia Ferrari SpA SEFAC	3.0 Ferrari 312T4 F12	transmission
2	FRENCH GP	Dijon	12	Scuderia Ferrari SpA SEFAC	3.0 Ferrari 312T4 F12	
14/ret	BRITISH GP	Silverstone	12	Scuderia Ferrari SpA SEFAC	3.0 Ferrari 312T4 F12	fuel vaporisation
8	GERMAN GP	Hockenheim	12	Scuderia Ferrari SpA SEFAC	3.0 Ferrari 312T4 F12	pit stop-rear wing/FL/-1 lap
2	AUSTRIAN GP	Österreichring	12	Scuderia Ferrari SpA SEFAC	3.0 Ferrari 312T4 F12	
ret	DUTCH GP	Zandvoort	12	Scuderia Ferrari SpA SEFAC	3.0 Ferrari 312T4 F12	blown tyre-suspension damage/FL
2	ITALIAN GP	Monza	12	Scuderia Ferrari SpA SEFAC	3.0 Ferrari 312T4 F12	
2	CANADIAN GP	Montreal	12	Scuderia Ferrari SpA SEFAC	3.0 Ferrari 312T4 F12	
1	US GP EAST	Watkins Glen	12	Scuderia Ferrari SpA SEFAC	3.0 Ferrari 312T4 F12	

1980

ret	ARGENTINE GP	Buenos Aires	2	Scuderia Ferrari SpA SEFAC	3.0 Ferrari 312T5 F12	accident-suspension-steering
16/ret	BRAZILIAN GP	Interlagos	2	Scuderia Ferrari SpA SEFAC	3.0 Ferrari 312T5 F12	jammed throttle/4 laps behind
ret	SOUTH AFRICAN GP	Kyalami	2	Scuderia Ferrari SpA SEFAC	3.0 Ferrari 312T5 F12	transmission
ret	US GP WEST	Long Beach	2	Scuderia Ferrari SpA SEFAC	3.0 Ferrari 312T5 F12	driveshaft
6	BELGIAN GP	Zolder	2	Scuderia Ferrari SpA SEFAC	3.0 Ferrari 312T5 F12	1 lap behind
5	MONACO GP	Monte Carlo	2	Scuderia Ferrari SpA SEFAC	3.0 Ferrari 312T5 F12	pit stop-tyre/1 lap behind
8	FRENCH GP	Paul Ricard	2	Scuderia Ferrari SpA SEFAC	3.0 Ferrari 312T5 F12	pit stop-tyres/1 lap behind
ret	BRITISH GP	Brands Hatch	2	Scuderia Ferrari SpA SEFAC	3.0 Ferrari 312T5 F12	engine
6	GERMAN GP	Hockenheim	2	Scuderia Ferrari SpA SEFAC	3.0 Ferrari 312T5 F12	pit stop-tyres
8	AUSTRIAN GP	Österreichring	2	Scuderia Ferrari SpA SEFAC	3.0 Ferrari 312T5 F12	pit stop-tyres/1 lap behind
7	DUTCH GP	Zandvoort	2	Scuderia Ferrari SpA SEFAC	3.0 Ferrari 312T5 F12	pit stop-tyres/1 lap behind
ret	ITALIAN GP	Imola	2	Scuderia Ferrari SpA SEFAC	3.0 Ferrari 312T5 F12	puncture-accident
5	CANADIAN GP	Montreal	2	Scuderia Ferrari SpA SEFAC	3.0 Ferrari 312T5 F12	
ret	US GP EAST	Watkins Glen	2	Scuderia Ferrari SpA SEFAC	3.0 Ferrari 312T5 F12	hit chicane

1981

ret	US GP WEST	Long Beach	27	Scuderia Ferrari SpA SEFAC	1.5 t/c Ferrari 126CX V6	driveshaft
ret	BRAZILIAN GP	Rio	27	Scuderia Ferrari SpA SEFAC	1.5 t/c Ferrari 126CK V6	turbo
ret	ARGENTINE GP	Buenos Aires	27	Scuderia Ferrari SpA SEFAC	1.5 t/c Ferrari 126CK V6	driveshaft
7	SAN MARINO GP	Imola	27	Scuderia Ferrari SpA SEFAC	1.5 t/c Ferrari 126CK V6	pit stop-tyres/FL
4	BELGIAN GP	Zolder	27	Scuderia Ferrari SpA SEFAC	1.5 t/c Ferrari 126CK V6	
1	MONACO GP	Monte Carlo	27	Scuderia Ferrari SpA SEFAC	1.5 t/c Ferrari 126CK V6	
1	SPANISH GP	Jarama	27	Scuderia Ferrari SpA SEFAC	1.5 t/c Ferrari 126CK V6	
ret	FRENCH GP	Dijon	27	Scuderia Ferrari SpA SEFAC	1.5 t/c Ferrari 126CK V6	electrics
ret	BRITISH GP	Silverstone	27	Scuderia Ferrari SpA SEFAC	1.5 t/c Ferrari 126CK V6	spun off
10	GERMAN GP	Hockenheim	27	Scuderia Ferrari SpA SEFAC	1.5 t/c Ferrari 126CK V6	pit stop-tyres
ret	AUSTRIAN GP	Österreichring	27	Scuderia Ferrari SpA SEFAC	1.5 t/c Ferrari 126CK V6	accident
ret	DUTCH GP	Zandvoort	27	Scuderia Ferrari SpA SEFAC	1.5 t/c Ferrari 126CK V6	accident with Giacomelli &Patrese
ret	ITALIAN GP	Monza	27	Scuderia Ferrari SpA SEFAC	1.5 t/c Ferrari 126CK V6	turbo
3	CANADIAN GP	Montreal	27	Scuderia Ferrari SpA SEFAC	1.5 t/c Ferrari 126CK V6	
dsq	CAESARS PALACE GP	Las Vegas	27	Scuderia Ferrari SpA SEFAC	1.5 t/c Ferrari 126CK V6	started from wrong grid position

1982

ret	SOUTH AFRICAN GP	Kyalami	27	Scuderia Ferrari SpA SEFAC	1.5 t/c Ferrari 126C2 V6	turbo
ret	BRAZILIAN GP	Rio	27	Scuderia Ferrari SpA SEFAC	1.5 t/c Ferrari 126C2 V6	spun off
dsq*	US GP WEST	Long Beach	27	Scuderia Ferrari SpA SEFAC	1.5 t/c Ferrari 126C2 V6	3rd on road/*wing infringement
2	SAN MARINO GP	Imola	27	Scuderia Ferrari SpA SEFAC	1.5 t/c Ferrari 126C2 V6	upset by Pironi's victory
dns	BELGIAN GP	Zolder	27	Scuderia Ferrari SpA SEFAC	1.5 t/c Ferrari 126C2 V6	fatal practice accident

GP Starts: 67   GP Wins: 6   Pole positions: 2   Fastest laps: 8   Points: 107

VILLORESI, Luigi (I) b 16/5/1909

1950

	Race	Circuit	No	Entrant	Car/Engine	Comment
ret	MONACO GP	Monte Carlo	38	Scuderia Ferrari	1.5 s/c Ferrari 125 V12	transmission
ret	SWISS GP	Bremgarten	22	Scuderia Ferrari	1.5 s/c Ferrari 125 V12	transmission
6	BELGIAN GP	Spa	2	Scuderia Ferrari	1.5 s/c Ferrari 125 V12	2 laps behind

1951

ret	SWISS GP	Bremgarten	18	Scuderia Ferrari	4.5 Ferrari 375F1 V12	crashed in rain
3	BELGIAN GP	Spa	10	Scuderia Ferrari	4.5 Ferrari 375F1 V12	
3	FRENCH GP	Reims	10	Scuderia Ferrari	4.5 Ferrari 375F1 V12	3 laps behind
3	BRITISH GP	Silverstone	10	Scuderia Ferrari	4.5 Ferrari 375F1 V12	2 laps behind
4	GERMAN GP	Nürburgring	72	Scuderia Ferrari	4.5 Ferrari 375F1 V12	
4	ITALIAN GP	Monza	4	Scuderia Ferrari	4.5 Ferrari 375F1 V12	1 lap behind
ret	SPANISH GP	Pedralbes	4	Scuderia Ferrari	4.5 Ferrari 375F1 V12	ignition

1952

3	DUTCH GP	Zandvoort	6	Scuderia Ferrari	2.0 Ferrari 500 4	
3	ITALIAN GP	Monza	16	Scuderia Ferrari	2.0 Ferrari 500 4	

1953

2	ARGENTINE GP	Buenos Aires	14	Scuderia Ferrari	2.0 Ferrari 500 4	1 lap behind
ret	DUTCH GP	Zandvoort	4	Scuderia Ferrari	2.0 Ferrari 500 4	throttle cable/FL
2	BELGIAN GP	Spa	8	Scuderia Ferrari	2.0 Ferrari 500 4	
6	FRENCH GP	Reims	12	Scuderia Ferrari	2.0 Ferrari 500 4	
ret	BRITISH GP	Silverstone	7	Scuderia Ferrari	2.0 Ferrari 500 4	transmission
ret*	GERMAN GP	Nürburgring	4	Scuderia Ferrari	2.0 Ferrari 500 4	* Ascari took over/engine
8*	"	"	1	Scuderia Ferrari	2.0 Ferrari 500 4	* took over Ascari's car/-1 lap
6	SWISS GP	Bremgarten	28	Scuderia Ferrari	2.0 Ferrari 500 4	2 laps behind
3	ITALIAN GP	Monza	2	Scuderia Ferrari	2.0 Ferrari 500 4	1 lap behind

1954

5	FRENCH GP	Reims	14	Officine Alfieri Maserati	2.5 Maserati 250F 6	on loan from Lancia/3 laps behind
ret*	BRITISH GP	Silverstone	32	Officine Alfieri Maserati	2.5 Maserati 250F 6	* Ascari took over/oil pressure
dns	GERMAN GP	Nürburgring	5	Officine Alfieri Maserati	2.5 Maserati 250F 6	withdrawn after Marimón's death
ret	ITALIAN GP	Monza	22	Officine Alfieri Maserati	2.5 Maserati 250F 6	clutch
ret	SPANISH GP	Pedralbes	36	Scuderia Lancia	2.5 Lancia D50 V8	brakes

1955

ret	ARGENTINE GP	Buenos Aires	34	Scuderia Lancia	2.5 Lancia D50 V8	accident
ret	"	" "	36	Scuderia Lancia	2.5 Lancia D50 V8	took Castellotti's car-crashed
5	MONACO GP	Monte Carlo	28	Scuderia Lancia	2.5 Lancia D50 V8	1 lap behind
dns	ITALIAN GP	Monza	10	Scuderia Ferrari	2.5 Lancia D50 V8	tyre problems in practice

1956

5	BELGIAN GP	Spa	22	Scuderia Centro Sud	2.5 Maserati 250F 6	2 laps behind
ret	FRENCH GP	Reims	38	Luigi Piotti	2.5 Maserati 250F 6	brakes
6	BRITISH GP	Silverstone	11	Luigi Piotti	2.5 Maserati 250F 6	5 laps behind
ret	GERMAN GP	Nürburgring	18	Luigi Piotti	2.5 Maserati 250F 6	engine
ret*	ITALIAN GP	Monza	34	Officine Alfieri Maserati	2.5 Maserati 250F 6	*Bonnier took over/engine

GP Starts: 31   GP Wins: 0   Pole positions: 0   Fastest laps: 1   Points: 49

LUIGI VILLORESI

Success and tragedy in equal measure marked the 25-year career of 'Gigi' Villoresi, the silver-haired Italian who was at his zenith in the immediate post-war era. He began racing back in 1931 with Fiats before turning to the marque that would make his name: Maserati. That was in 1936, and by then he and his brother Emilio had established a reputation as a pretty wild pair. Nevertheless Luigi won the *voiturette* Brno GP in Czechoslovakia in 1937 to earn promotion to the Maserati Grand Prix team. He became the 1500 cc Italian champion in 1938 and 1939, and took wins in the Albi, Pescara and South African GPs. He also won the Targa Florio in both 1939 and 1940, again in a Maserati, but the period was clouded by the death of Emilio, who was by now racing as a rival in the Alfa Romeo team.

During the war Villoresi was held as a prisoner of war, but upon his release he was immediately looking to race again. He and Farina soon vied for the title of Italy's fastest driver, and with Wimille he was regarded as the world's best. In 1946 he scored victories in Nice and the Circuit of Voghera with his Maserati and took a 3-litre 8CL to Indianapolis, where he finished seventh, and the following season he notched up wins at Buenos Aires, Mar del Plata, Nimes, Nice, Strasbourg and Luxembourg. The 1948 season saw him suffer a major crash at Bremgarten which he was lucky to survive, though he was to triumph as Italian champion for the second successive year. Wins were recorded at Buenos Aires in two races, Comminges, Albi, Silverstone (the first post-war British GP) and Barcelona. After winning the Libre races at Interlagos and Gavea, Villoresi finally forsook his beloved Maserati to join Ferrari along with Ascari, to whom he passed on much of his racecraft. He was soon winning races for the Scuderia at Zandvoort in the super-charged car and in Formula 2 at Brussels, Luxembourg, Rome and Garda.

The 1950 and 1951 seasons were spent chasing the Alfa Romeos, but Villoresi still found success aplenty; wins at Buenos Aires and Rosario were followed by more success at Marseilles, Erlen and Monza in 1950, while the following year saw a very consistent championship campaign with the Type 375, which he took to victory at Syracuse and Pau in non-title events. It was a good year for 'Gigi', for he won the Mille Miglia and was second in the Carrera Panamericana, and shared a Lancia with Ascari to win the Sestrieres Rally. During 1952-53 he was forced sit in the shadow of his brilliant pupil Ascari, but could still do the job when required, taking wins at Turin and Modena.

Villoresi signed for Lancia for the 1954 season along with Ascari, but they were forced to wait for their Formula 1 car, which failed to appear until the last Grand Prix of the season. 'Gigi' raced for Maserati in the interim, but a crash in the Mille Miglia had dulled his edge. He continued with the Lancia concern in 1955 but, after the death of Ascari and the subsequent amalgamation of the team with Ferrari, found himself out of a works drive when the 1956 season began. By now well past his best, he drove privateer Maseratis and the works OSCA in sports car events. It was in this form of racing, driving a Maserati, that he suffered yet another serious injury when he crashed at Castelfusano and broke his leg very badly. Begged by his family to retire, he deferred to their wishes, but couldn't resist taking part in the 1958 Acropolis Rally, which he won in a Lancia.

VILLOTA, Emilio de (E) b 26/7/1946

1976

	Race	Circuit	No	Entrant	Car/Engine	Comment
dnq	SPANISH GP	Jarama	33	RAM Racing	3.0 Brabham BT44B-Cosworth V8	

1977

13	SPANISH GP	Jarama	36	Iberia Airlines	3.0 McLaren M23-Cosworth V8	5 laps behind
dnq	BELGIAN GP	Zolder	36	Iberia Airlines	3.0 McLaren M23-Cosworth V8	
dnq	SWEDISH GP	Anderstorp	36	Iberia Airlines	3.0 McLaren M23-Cosworth V8	
dnq	BRITISH GP	Silverstone	36	Iberia Airlines	3.0 McLaren M23-Cosworth V8	
dnq	GERMAN GP	Hockenheim	36	Iberia Airlines	3.0 McLaren M23-Cosworth V8	
17/ret	AUSTRIAN GP	Österreichring	36	Iberia Airlines	3.0 McLaren M23-Cosworth V8	collision with course car/-4 laps
dnq	ITALIAN GP	Monza	36	Iberia Airlines	3.0 McLaren M23-Cosworth V8	

1978

| dnq | SPANISH GP | Jarama | 28 | Centro Aseguredor F1 | 3.0 McLaren M23-Cosworth V8 | |

1981

| dns | SPANISH GP | Jarama | 37 | Equipe Banco Occidental | 3.0 Williams FW07-Cosworth V8 | wdn-in breach of Concorde Agreement |

1982

dnpq	BELGIAN GP	Zolder	19	LBT Team March	3.0 March 821-Cosworth V8	
dnpq	MONACO GP	Monte Carlo	19	LBT Team March	3.0 March 821-Cosworth V8	
dnq	US GP (DETROIT)	Detroit	19	LBT Team March	3.0 March 821-Cosworth V8	
dnq	CANADIAN GP	Montreal	19	LBT Team March	3.0 March 821-Cosworth V8	
dnpq	DUTCH GP	Zandvoort	19	LBT Team March	3.0 March 821-Cosworth V8	

GP Starts: 2   GP Wins: 0   Pole positions: 0   Fastest laps: 0   Points: 0

VOLONTERIO, Ottorino (CH) b 7/12/1917

1954

	Race	Circuit	No	Entrant	Car/Engine	Comment
ret*	SPANISH GP	Pedralbes	22	Baron de Graffenried	2.5 Maserati A6GCM/250F 6	* took over from de Graffenried/engine

1956

| nc | GERMAN GP | Nürburgring | 22 | Ottorino Volonterio | 2.5 Maserati A6GCM/250F 6 | 6 laps behind |

1957

| nc* | ITALIAN GP | Monza | 28 | Ottorino Volonterio | 2.5 Maserati 250F 6 | * shared with Simon/15 laps behind |

GP Starts: 3   GP Wins: 0   Pole positions: 0   Fastest laps: 0   Points: 0

VONLANTHEN, Jo (CH) b 31/5/1942

1975

	Race	Circuit	No	Entrant	Car/Engine	Comment
ret	AUSTRIAN GP	Österreichring	20	Frank Williams Racing Cars	3.0 Williams FW03-Cosworth V8	engine

GP Starts: 1   GP Wins: 0   Pole positions: 0   Fastest laps: 0   Points: 0

EMILIO de VILLOTA

After contesting the Shellsport championship in 1976 with a Lyncar, de Villota, a bank manager with Banco Iberico, gave up his day job and, with support from his former employers, went Grand Prix racing the following year with a McLaren M23. However, he was out of his depth and settled for a return to the G8 series, where he could shine in a competitive car. In 1978 the Aurora AFX F1 series was inaugurated, and de Villota became a staunch supporter of the championship during its short life. Racing a Lotus 78, he took third place overall in 1979, before clinching the title in 1980 with his RAM Racing Williams FW07.

After the series folded, de Villota – having failed to gain an entry for his home Grand Prix in 1981 – turned briefly to sports cars, winning the Enna 6 Hours and the Flying Tigers 1000 at Brands in a Lola T600 with Guy Edwards, before returning to Formula 1 in 1982 for a completely fruitless spell in the works March run by his old colleagues at RAM.

OTTORINO VOLONTERIO

A lawyer from Locarno, Volonterio raced a Maserati sports car with a modicum of success, taking second place in the Coupe de Paris at Montlhéry in 1955. He shared Baron de Graffenried's Maserati at Pedralbes in 1954, but when he acquired the car for 1955 he was usually slow or hopelessly slow.

In 1957 he purchased a Maserati 250F, but in the main he wisely left it to others to race; Mackay-Fraser practised the car for the GP de Reims, but was killed in the F2 supporting race. Ottorino did make one final appearance, at Monza, where he shared the car with André Simon, the pair finishing 15 laps behind.

JO VONLANTHEN

A car trader from Frauenfeld in Switzerland, Vonlanthen began racing in Formula Vee in 1968 and, driving a Tecno, won the 1972 Swiss F3 championship. He went into Formula 2 in 1973 with a GRD, taking a third place in the Rome GP, but this was easily his best result until he came second in the opening round of the 1975 series at Estoril in a March 742-BMW, when most of the front-runners fell by the wayside.

His brief Formula 1 career lasted just three races in 1975, Jo driving a works Ensign in the International Trophy before switching to Williams for the Swiss GP at Dijon. After taking a distant 14th place in this non-championship race, Vonlanthen made the grid in his Williams for the Austrian GP only because both Henton and Wilson Fittipaldi had practice mishaps. He returned to Formula 2 on an irregular basis in 1976, but never really featured.

FRED WACKER Jnr

An SCCA racer from Chicago who competed regularly at the wheel of an Allard-Cadillac, and a member of the Cunningham team at Le Mans in 1951, Wacker raced for Gordini on a number of occasions, taking a third place at Chimay in 1953 and fourth in the minor Cadours GP the following season. In World Championship Grands Prix, he was extremely lucky to escape with a lightly fractured skull after crashing the Gordini in practice for the 1953 Swiss GP. After his European adventures, he continued racing sports cars in the States.

DAVE WALKER

This rugged Australian trained to be an accountant until a chance meeting with some motor sport enthusiasts took him hill-climbing. Dave came to Britain in 1962 dreaming of emulating the likes of Brabham, but soon realised that he was too inexperienced to make it at this stage and hitch-hiked home to go about racing in a more serious manner. By 1966 he was back to begin an on-off Formula 3 career which saw him slowly climb the ladder. In 1967 he took the European trail in a Merlyn, winning a race at Ojatia, but during 1968-69 Walker was stuck in Formula Ford in the works Alexis. However, he joined the works Lotus F3 team in 1970, winning the Lombank F3 championship, and in 1971 he was back for more, securing both the Shell and Forward Trust titles. Although a Grand Prix outing in the Lotus turbine was unhappy, he was chosen to partner Fittipaldi in 1972, but apart from a fifth place in the non-title Brazilian GP the year was a personal disaster for Walker, while the Brazilian stormed to his first World Championship. Set to race for GRD in Formula 2 in 1973, Dave suffered two separate road accidents, breaking a leg in one and an arm in the other, but came back to race in 2-litre sports car events. He then had a brief stab at F5000 in 1975, before trying his hand at Canadian Formula Atlantic.

PETER WALKER

Walker gained a certain notoriety for his aggressive, sliding style in Peter Whitehead's ERA before the war, and in the late forties became one of the few drivers to glean much success in the E-Type ERA both on the circuits and on the hills, where he put in some stunning performances in 1948. He raced the ERA at the 1950 British GP with Rolt, but it soon failed. He did well to finish the race the following year, however, when he brought the hitherto unreliable BRM into seventh place despite extreme discomfort from a burning-hot exhaust.

Signed by Jaguar in 1951 to race their sports cars, he shared his greatest triumphs with his old friend Peter Whitehead, the pair winning Le Mans and finishing second at Dundrod in the Tourist Trophy. In addition, Walker took second place at Le Mans in 1953, this time with Moss. Moving to Aston Martin, Peter won the Goodwood 9 Hours with Dennis Poore in 1955, and raced single-seaters once more at Zandvoort (for Moss) and Aintree (for Rob Walker). After escaping a nasty accident at Le Mans in 1956 relatively lightly, Walker decided to retire, though he was tempted back one more time, to race Rob Walker's Connaught at Syracuse in 1957.

WACKER (Jnr), Fred (USA) b 10/7/1918

	Race	Circuit	No	Entrant	Car/Engine	Comment
	1953					
dns	DUTCH GP	Zandvoort	40	Equipe Gordini	2.0 Gordini Type 16 6	engine needed by Schell
9	BELGIAN GP	Spa	38	Equipe Gordini	2.0 Gordini Type 16 6	4 laps behind
dns	SWISS GP	Bremgarten	44	Equipe Gordini	2.0 Gordini Type 16 6	practice accident-fractured skull
	1954					
ret	SWISS GP	Bremgarten	14	Equipe Gordini	2.5 Gordini Type 16 6	transmission
6	ITALIAN GP	Monza	42	Equipe Gordini	2.5 Gordini Type 16 6	5 laps behind

GP Starts: 3 GP Wins: 0 Pole positions: 0 Fastest laps: 0 Points: 0

WALKER, Dave (AUS) b 10/6/1941

	Race	Circuit	No	Entrant	Car/Engine	Comment
	1971					
ret	DUTCH GP	Zandvoort	15	Gold Leaf Team Lotus	Turbine Lotus 56B-Pratt & Witney	straight on at Tarzan in the rain
dns	"	"	12	Gold Leaf Team Lotus	3.0 Lotus 72D-Cosworth V8	practice only
	1972					
dsq	ARGENTINE GP	Buenos Aires	12	John Player Team Lotus	3.0 Lotus 72D-Cosworth V8	outside assistance
10	SOUTH AFRICAN GP	Kyalami	9	John Player Team Lotus	3.0 Lotus 72D-Cosworth V8	
9/ret	SPANISH GP	Jarama	21	John Player Team Lotus	3.0 Lotus 72D-Cosworth V8	out of fuel
14	MONACO GP	Monte Carlo	9	John Player Team Lotus	3.0 Lotus 72D-Cosworth V8	pit stop-handling
14	BELGIAN GP	Nivelles	33	John Player Team Lotus	3.0 Lotus 72D-Cosworth V8	2 pit stops-tyres-oil pressure
18/ret	FRENCH GP	Clermont Ferrand	6	John Player Team Lotus	3.0 Lotus 72D-Cosworth V8	gearbox
ret	BRITISH GP	Brands Hatch	9	John Player Team Lotus	3.0 Lotus 72D-Cosworth V8	rear suspension
ret	GERMAN GP	Nürburgring	25	John Player Team Lotus	3.0 Lotus 72D-Cosworth V8	oil tank
ret	AUSTRIAN GP	Österreichring	21	John Player Team Lotus	3.0 Lotus 72D-Cosworth V8	engine
ret	US GP	Watkins Glen	11	John Player Team Lotus	3.0 Lotus 72D-Cosworth V8	engine

GP Starts: 11 GP Wins: 0 Pole positions: 0 Fastest laps: 0 Points: 0

WALKER, Peter (GB) b Oct 1913 – d 1/3/1984

	Race	Circuit	No	Entrant	Car/Engine	Comment
	1950					
ret*	BRITISH GP	Silverstone	9	Peter Walker	1.5 s/c ERA E Type 6	* shared with Rolt/gearbox
	1951					
7	BRITISH GP	Silverstone	7	BRM Ltd	1.5 s/c BRM P15 V16	burnt by exhaust/6 laps behind
	1955					
ret	DUTCH GP	Zandvoort	26	Stirling Moss Ltd	2.5 Maserati 250F 6	wheel
ret	BRITISH GP	Silverstone	36	R R C Walker Racing Team	2.5 Connaught B-Alta 4	* shared with Rolt/throttle cable

GP Starts: 4 GP Wins: 0 Pole positions: 0 Fastest laps: 0 Points: 0

HEINI WALTER

A Swiss amateur who raced Porsche Carrera and RSK models both on the circuits and in hill-climbs, Walter was an extremely able driver who was 1961 European mountain-climb champion and drove the Filipinetti Porsche at the German GP, his only major appearance in a single-seater. He later concentrated on hill-climbs with a Ferrari 250 LM, before returning to a Porsche.

RODGER WARD

Ward perhaps holds the unwanted distinction of having raced the most unsuitable machine ever to appear in a Grand Prix when he ran a Kurtis Midget at Sebring in 1959. After years of trying, he had just won the Indianapolis 500, starting a run of successes at the Brickyard (second/third/first/fourth/second) that extended through to 1964. With 26 USAC career victories, Ward now stands eighth in the sport's all-time winners' rankings.

In 1963 Rodger made another Formula 1 appearance in the US GP, this time with more suitable machinery – a Lotus 24-BRM V8.

DEREK WARWICK

Sometimes there seems to be no justice in motor racing. For a driver as committed and talented as Derek Warwick to have toiled for more than a decade and taken part in nearly 150 Grands Prix without even a single victory must be particularly galling. Yet there is no bitterness from the down-to-earth Hampshireman, who in the early days of his Formula 1 career looked a likelier prospect than Nigel Mansell.

After the hurly-burly of stock car racing, Derek funded his own early career in Formula Ford. He took second place in the 1976 DJM championship in his Hawke, before moving into Formula 3 the following year with a Chevron. In 1978 Warwick became embroiled in a terrific three-way battle with Piquet and Serra, winning the Vandervell F3 championship and emerging as runner-up to Nelson in the BP series. Moving to Formula 2 in 1979 with a Theodore Racing-entered March brought little cheer, but a switch to Toleman for 1980 signalled the start of a great relationship with the emerging team. That first year was in Formula 2, and he won two races (at Silverstone and Monza) as his more experienced team-mate Brian Henton took the coveted European title. Flushed with their success, Toleman made the jump to Formula 1 the following year but it proved to be a tough baptism for Derek, who managed to qualify only at the season's final race.

Things could only get better, and they did. In 1982 and 1983 Warwick battled away in the Pirelli-shod turbo car, scrapping ferociously for every place, no matter how far down the field. This fighting spirit no doubt helped to earn him his chance when the call came from Renault to race for them in 1984. Derek was never to get closer to that elusive Grand Prix win than on his debut for the team at Rio, where he was leading comfortably when the suspension collapsed. Somehow that blow seemed to set the tone for a season which failed to meet expectations of both the car and the driver. Then came the worst decision of Warwick's career – to stay with Renault in 1985. The year was a personal disaster, and the offer of a seat at Williams which he rejected and was taken by Mansell instead must always haunt him. When the French team pulled the plug on their Formula 1 effort, Derek was an out-of-work Grand Prix driver. A Jaguar sports car ride was his only realistic option for 1986 but he did a fine job for the team, missing the drivers' championship by just one point. However, the tragic death of Elio de Angelis found Warwick making a swift return to the Grand Prix scene with the difficult 'lay-down' Brabham BT55, a car with which nobody could have found success.

Warwick then joined Arrows, who, like their new driver, were still looking for their first Grand Prix victory, and this was their tenth season of trying. In the three years he was to stay with the team, a few worthwhile results were achieved, but the cars were mediocrity personified. A switch to the well-funded but disorganised Lotus team in 1990 was probably the bottom of the barrel for poor Derek, who showed incredible bravery at Monza, where he crashed spectacularly at the exit of the Parabolica, only to calmly walk back to the pits to take the spare car for the inevitable restart, and then at Jerez, where he raced despite Donnelly's disturbing accident in practice.

Derek then took another Formula 1 sabbatical to return to sports car racing, first with Jaguar in 1991 and then the following year with Peugeot, with whom he was to enjoy the sweet taste of victory at Le Mans and also share the drivers' championship with team-mate Yannick Dalmas. However, Warwick's cheerful countenance was to be found in the Formula 1 paddocks yet again in 1993, as he teamed up with Jack Oliver once more in the renamed Footwork team. The year was better than the team had experienced for some time but, even with the expensive acquisition of the TAG/McLaren active suspension system, the cars were top-six runners at best. At the time of writing Derek's future plans are unclear. Rightly no longer interested in Formula 1 if he cannot have a competitive car, he has been taking a keen interest in the PPG Indy Car World Series, which could well offer him a rewarding future.

WALTER, Heini (CH) b 28/7/1927

1962

	Race	Circuit	No	Entrant	Car/Engine	Comment
14	GERMAN GP	Nürburgring	32	Ecurie Filipinetti	1.5 Porsche 718 F4	1 lap behind

GP Starts: 1 GP Wins: 0 Pole positions: 0 Fastest laps: 0 Points: 0

WARD, Rodger (USA) b 10/1/1921

1959

	Race	Circuit	No	Entrant	Car/Engine	Comment
ret	US GP	Sebring	1	Leader Cards Incorporated	1.75 Kurtis Kraft-Offenhauser 4	clutch/car completely outclassed

1963

	Race	Circuit	No	Entrant	Car/Engine	Comment
ret	US GP	Watkins Glen	18	Reg Parnell (Racing)	1.5 Lotus 24-BRM V8	gear selection

GP Starts: 2 GP Wins: 0 Pole positions: 0 Fastest laps: 0 Points: 0

WARWICK, Derek (GB) b 27/8/1954

1981

	Race	Circuit	No	Entrant	Car/Engine	Comment
dnq	SAN MARINO GP	Imola	36	Candy Toleman Motorsport	1.5 t/c Toleman TG181-Hart 4	
dnq	BELGIAN GP	Zolder	36	Candy Toleman Motorsport	1.5 t/c Toleman TG181-Hart 4	
dnq	MONACO GP	Monte Carlo	36	Candy Toleman Motorsport	1.5 t/c Toleman TG181-Hart 4	
dnq	SPANISH GP	Jarama	36	Candy Toleman Motorsport	1.5 t/c Toleman TG181-Hart 4	
dnq	FRENCH GP	Dijon	36	Candy Toleman Motorsport	1.5 t/c Toleman TG181-Hart 4	
dnq	BRITISH GP	Silverstone	36	Candy Toleman Motorsport	1.5 t/c Toleman TG181-Hart 4	
dnq	GERMAN GP	Hockenheim	36	Candy Toleman Motorsport	1.5 t/c Toleman TG181-Hart 4	
dnq	AUSTRIAN GP	Österreichring	36	Candy Toleman Motorsport	1.5 t/c Toleman TG181-Hart 4	
dnq	DUTCH GP	Zandvoort	36	Candy Toleman Motorsport	1.5 t/c Toleman TG181-Hart 4	
dnq	ITALIAN GP	Monza	36	Candy Toleman Motorsport	1.5 t/c Toleman TG181-Hart 4	
dnq	CANADIAN GP	Montreal	36	Candy Toleman Motorsport	1.5 t/c Toleman TG181-Hart 4	
ret	CAESARS PALACE GP	Las Vegas	36	Candy Toleman Motorsport	1.5 t/c Toleman TG181-Hart 4	gearbox

1982

	Race	Circuit	No	Entrant	Car/Engine	Comment
ret	SOUTH AFRICAN GP	Kyalami	35	Candy Toleman Motorsport	1.5 t/c Toleman TG181B-Hart 4	accident
dnq	BRAZILIAN GP	Rio	35	Candy Toleman Motorsport	1.5 t/c Toleman TG181B-Hart 4	
dnpq	US GP WEST	Long Beach	35	Candy Toleman Motorsport	1.5 t/c Toleman TG181C-Hart 4	
ret	SAN MARINO GP	Imola	35	Toleman Group Motorsport	1.5 t/c Toleman TG181C-Hart 4	electrics
ret	BELGIAN GP	Zolder	35	Toleman Group Motorsport	1.5 t/c Toleman TG181C-Hart 4	driveshaft
dnq	MONACO GP	Monte Carlo	35	Toleman Group Motorsport	1.5 t/c Toleman TG181C-Hart 4	
ret	DUTCH GP	Zandvoort	35	Toleman Group Motorsport	1.5 t/c Toleman TG181C-Hart 4	engine/FL
ret	BRITISH GP	Brands Hatch	35	Toleman Group Motorsport	1.5 t/c Toleman TG181C-Hart 4	driveshaft-c.v. joint
15	FRENCH GP	Paul Ricard	35	Toleman Group Motorsport	1.5 t/c Toleman TG181C-Hart 4	pit stop/4 laps behind
10	GERMAN GP	Hockenheim	35	Toleman Group Motorsport	1.5 t/c Toleman TG181C-Hart 4	pit stop/2 laps behind
ret	AUSTRIAN GP	Österreichring	35	Toleman Group Motorsport	1.5 t/c Toleman TG181C-Hart 4	rear suspension
ret	SWISS GP	Dijon	35	Toleman Group Motorsport	1.5 t/c Toleman TG181C-Hart 4	engine
ret	ITALIAN GP	Monza	35	Toleman Group Motorsport	1.5 t/c Toleman TG183-Hart 4	spin-hit by Henton
ret	CAESARS PALACE GP	Las Vegas	35	Toleman Group Motorsport	1.5 t/c Toleman TG183-Hart 4	misfire

1983

	Race	Circuit	No	Entrant	Car/Engine	Comment
8	BRAZILIAN GP	Rio	35	Candy Toleman Motorsport	1.5 t/c Toleman TG183B-Hart 4	1 lap behind
ret	US GP WEST	Long Beach	35	Candy Toleman Motorsport	1.5 t/c Toleman TG183B-Hart 4	tyre failure-accident
ret	FRENCH GP	Paul Ricard	35	Candy Toleman Motorsport	1.5 t/c Toleman TG183B-Hart 4	split water pipe-engine
ret	SAN MARINO GP	Imola	35	Candy Toleman Motorsport	1.5 t/c Toleman TG183B-Hart 4	spun off
ret	MONACO GP	Monte Carlo	35	Candy Toleman Motorsport	1.5 t/c Toleman TG183B-Hart 4	accident with Surer
7	BELGIAN GP	Spa	35	Candy Toleman Motorsport	1.5 t/c Toleman TG183B-Hart 4	2 pit stops-tyre-fuel
ret	US GP (DETROIT)	Detroit	35	Candy Toleman Motorsport	1.5 t/c Toleman TG183B-Hart 4	water leak-engine
ret	CANADIAN GP	Montreal	35	Candy Toleman Motorsport	1.5 t/c Toleman TG183B-Hart 4	engine
ret	BRITISH GP	Silverstone	35	Candy Toleman Motorsport	1.5 t/c Toleman TG183B-Hart 4	gearbox
ret	GERMAN GP	Hockenheim	35	Candy Toleman Motorsport	1.5 t/c Toleman TG183B-Hart 4	engine
ret	AUSTRIAN GP	Österreichring	35	Candy Toleman Motorsport	1.5 t/c Toleman TG183B-Hart 4	turbo
4	DUTCH GP	Zandvoort	35	Candy Toleman Motorsport	1.5 t/c Toleman TG183B-Hart 4	pit stop-fuel
6	ITALIAN GP	Monza	35	Candy Toleman Motorsport	1.5 t/c Toleman TG183B-Hart 4	pit stop-fuel
5	EUROPEAN GP	Brands Hatch	35	Candy Toleman Motorsport	1.5 t/c Toleman TG183B-Hart 4	pit stop-fuel
4	SOUTH AFRICAN GP	Kyalami	35	Candy Toleman Motorsport	1.5 t/c Toleman TG183B-Hart 4	pit stop-fuel/1 lap behind

1984

	Race	Circuit	No	Entrant	Car/Engine	Comment
ret	BRAZILIAN GP	Rio	16	Equipe Renault Elf	1.5 t/c Renault RE50 V6	hit by Lauda-suspension
3	SOUTH AFRICAN GP	Kyalami	16	Equipe Renault Elf	1.5 t/c Renault RE50 V6	1 lap behind
2	BELGIAN GP	Zolder	16	Equipe Renault Elf	1.5 t/c Renault RE50 V6	
4	SAN MARINO GP	Imola	16	Equipe Renault Elf	1.5 t/c Renault RE50 V6	1 lap behind
ret	FRENCH GP	Dijon	16	Equipe Renault Elf	1.5 t/c Renault RE50 V6	accident with Surer
ret	MONACO GP	Monte Carlo	16	Equipe Renault Elf	1.5 t/c Renault RE50 V6	accident with Tambay
ret	CANADIAN GP	Montreal	16	Equipe Renault Elf	1.5 t/c Renault RE50 V6	loose underbody
ret	US GP (DETROIT)	Detroit	16	Equipe Renault Elf	1.5 t/c Renault RE50 V6	gearbox/FL
ret	US GP (DALLAS)	Dallas	16	Equipe Renault Elf	1.5 t/c Renault RE50 V6	spun off
2	BRITISH GP	Brands Hatch	16	Equipe Renault Elf	1.5 t/c Renault RE50 V6	
3	GERMAN GP	Hockenheim	16	Equipe Renault Elf	1.5 t/c Renault RE50 V6	
ret	AUSTRIAN GP	Österreichring	16	Equipe Renault Elf	1.5 t/c Renault RE50 V6	engine
ret	DUTCH GP	Zandvoort	16	Equipe Renault Elf	1.5 t/c Renault RE50 V6	spun off on oil
ret	ITALIAN GP	Monza	16	Equipe Renault Elf	1.5 t/c Renault RE50 V6	oil pressure
11/ret	EUROPEAN GP	Nürburgring	16	Equipe Renault Elf	1.5 t/c Renault RE50 V6	engine
ret	PORTUGUESE GP	Estoril	16	Equipe Renault Elf	1.5 t/c Renault RE50 V6	gearbox

1985

	Race	Circuit	No	Entrant	Car/Engine	Comment
10	BRAZILIAN GP	Rio	16	Equipe Renault Elf	1.5 t/c Renault RE60 V6	2 pit stop-plugs-tyres/-4 laps
7	PORTUGUESE GP	Estoril	16	Equipe Renault Elf	1.5 t/c Renault RE60 V6	2 laps behind
10	SAN MARINO GP	Imola	16	Equipe Renault Elf	1.5 t/c Renault RE60 V6	spin/pit stop-electrics/-4 laps
5	MONACO GP	Monte Carlo	16	Equipe Renault Elf	1.5 t/c Renault RE60 V6	1 lap behind
ret	CANADIAN GP	Montreal	16	Equipe Renault Elf	1.5 t/c Renault RE60 V6	accident
ret	US GP (DETROIT)	Detroit	16	Equipe Renault Elf	1.5 t/c Renault RE60 V6	transmission
7	FRENCH GP	Paul Ricard	16	Equipe Renault Elf	1.5 t/c Renault RE60 V6	
5	BRITISH GP	Silverstone	16	Equipe Renault Elf	1.5 t/c Renault RE60B V6	1 lap behind
ret	GERMAN GP	Nürburgring	16	Equipe Renault Elf	1.5 t/c Renault RE60B V6	ignition
ret	AUSTRIAN GP	Österreichring	16	Equipe Renault Elf	1.5 t/c Renault RE60B V6	engine
ret	DUTCH GP	Zandvoort	16	Equipe Renault Elf	1.5 t/c Renault RE60B V6	gearbox
ret	ITALIAN GP	Monza	16	Equipe Renault Elf	1.5 t/c Renault RE60B V6	transmission
6	BELGIAN GP	Spa	16	Equipe Renault Elf	1.5 t/c Renault RE60B V6	1 lap behind
ret	EUROPEAN GP	Brands Hatch	16	Equipe Renault Elf	1.5 t/c Renault RE60B V6	fuel injection
ret	AUSTRALIAN GP	Adelaide	16	Equipe Renault Elf	1.5 t/c Renault RE60B V6	transmission

1986

ret	CANADIAN GP	Montreal	8	Motor Racing Developments Ltd	1.5 t/c Brabham BT55-BMW 4	engine
10	US GP (DETROIT)	Detroit	8	Motor Racing Developments Ltd	1.5 t/c Brabham BT55-BMW 4	pit stop-tyres/3 laps behind
9	FRENCH GP	Paul Ricard	8	Motor Racing Developments Ltd	1.5 t/c Brabham BT55-BMW 4	had to hold car in 4th gear/-3 laps
8	BRITISH GP	Brands Hatch	8	Motor Racing Developments Ltd	1.5 t/c Brabham BT55-BMW 4	2 pit stops-tyres/3 laps behind
7	GERMAN GP	Hockenheim	8	Motor Racing Developments Ltd	1.5 t/c Brabham BT55-BMW 4	1 lap behind
ret	HUNGARIAN GP	Hungaroring	8	Motor Racing Developments Ltd	1.5 t/c Brabham BT55-BMW 4	accident with Alboreto
dns	AUSTRIAN GP	Österreichring	8	Motor Racing Developments Ltd	1.5 t/c Brabham BT55-BMW 4	Patrese drove car
ret	ITALIAN GP	Monza	8	Motor Racing Developments Ltd	1.5 t/c Brabham BT55-BMW 4	spun off
ret	PORTUGUESE GP	Estoril	8	Motor Racing Developments Ltd	1.5 t/c Brabham BT55-BMW 4	electrics
ret	MEXICAN GP	Mexico City	8	Motor Racing Developments Ltd	1.5 t/c Brabham BT55-BMW 4	engine
ret	AUSTRALIAN GP	Adelaide	8	Motor Racing Developments Ltd	1.5 t/c Brabham BT55-BMW 4	brakes

1987

ret	BRAZILIAN GP	Rio	17	USF&G Arrows Megatron	1.5 t/c Arrows A10-Megatron 4	engine
11/ret	SAN MARINO GP	Imola	17	USF&G Arrows Megatron	1.5 t/c Arrows A10-Megatron 4	out of fuel/4 laps behind
ret	BELGIAN GP	Spa	17	USF&G Arrows Megatron	1.5 t/c Arrows A10-Megatron 4	water hose
ret	MONACO GP	Monte Carlo	17	USF&G Arrows Megatron	1.5 t/c Arrows A10-Megatron 4	gear linkage
ret	US GP (DETROIT)	Detroit	17	USF&G Arrows Megatron	1.5 t/c Arrows A10-Megatron 4	hit wall
ret	FRENCH GP	Paul Ricard	17	USF&G Arrows Megatron	1.5 t/c Arrows A10-Megatron 4	turbo
5	BRITISH GP	Silverstone	17	USF&G Arrows Megatron	1.5 t/c Arrows A10-Megatron 4	
ret	GERMAN GP	Hockenheim	17	USF&G Arrows Megatron	1.5 t/c Arrows A10-Megatron 4	turbo
6	HUNGARIAN GP	Hungaroring	17	USF&G Arrows Megatron	1.5 t/c Arrows A10-Megatron 4	2 laps behind
ret	AUSTRIAN GP	Österreichring	17	USF&G Arrows Megatron	1.5 t/c Arrows A10-Megatron 4	engine
ret	ITALIAN GP	Monza	17	USF&G Arrows Megatron	1.5 t/c Arrows A10-Megatron 4	electrics
13	PORTUGUESE GP	Estoril	17	USF&G Arrows Megatron	1.5 t/c Arrows A10-Megatron 4	2 spins/4 laps behind
10	SPANISH GP	Jerez	17	USF&G Arrows Megatron	1.5 t/c Arrows A10-Megatron 4	2 laps behind
ret	MEXICAN GP	Mexico City	17	USF&G Arrows Megatron	1.5 t/c Arrows A10-Megatron 4	hit by Nakajima
10	JAPANESE GP	Suzuka	17	USF&G Arrows Megatron	1.5 t/c Arrows A10-Megatron 4	1 lap behind
ret	AUSTRALIAN GP	Adelaide	17	USF&G Arrows Megatron	1.5 t/c Arrows A10-Megatron 4	transmission

1988

4	BRAZILIAN GP	Rio	17	USF&G Arrows Megatron	1.5 t/c Arrows A10B-Megatron 4	
9	SAN MARINO GP	Imola	17	USF&G Arrows Megatron	1.5 t/c Arrows A10B-Megatron 4	2 laps behind
4	MONACO GP	Monte Carlo	17	USF&G Arrows Megatron	1.5 t/c Arrows A10B-Megatron 4	1 lap behind
5	MEXICAN GP	Mexico City	17	USF&G Arrows Megatron	1.5 t/c Arrows A10B-Megatron 4	1 lap behind
7	CANADIAN GP	Montreal	17	USF&G Arrows Megatron	1.5 t/c Arrows A10B-Megatron 4	2 laps behind
ret	US GP (DETROIT)	Detroit	17	USF&G Arrows Megatron	1.5 t/c Arrows A10B-Megatron 4	stuck throttle-crashed
ret	FRENCH GP	Paul Ricard	17	USF&G Arrows Megatron	1.5 t/c Arrows A10B-Megatron 4	spun off avoiding Nakajima
6	BRITISH GP	Silverstone	17	USF&G Arrows Megatron	1.5 t/c Arrows A10B-Megatron 4	1 lap behind
7	GERMAN GP	Hockenheim	17	USF&G Arrows Megatron	1.5 t/c Arrows A10B-Megatron 4	1 lap behind
ret	HUNGARIAN GP	Hungaroring	17	USF&G Arrows Megatron	1.5 t/c Arrows A10B-Megatron 4	brakes
5*	BELGIAN GP	Spa	17	USF&G Arrows Megatron	1.5 t/c Arrows A10B-Megatron 4	*3rd & 4th place cars disqualified
4	ITALIAN GP	Monza	17	USF&G Arrows Megatron	1.5 t/c Arrows A10B-Megatron 4	
4	PORTUGUESE GP	Estoril	17	USF&G Arrows Megatron	1.5 t/c Arrows A10B-Megatron 4	despite severe vibration problems
ret	SPANISH GP	Jerez	17	USF&G Arrows Megatron	1.5 t/c Arrows A10B-Megatron 4	slid over kerb-chassis damage
ret	JAPANESE GP	Suzuka	17	USF&G Arrows Megatron	1.5 t/c Arrows A10B-Megatron 4	spun off
ret	AUSTRALIAN GP	Adelaide	17	USF&G Arrows Megatron	1.5 t/c Arrows A10B-Megatron 4	engine

1989

5	BRAZILIAN GP	Rio	9	Arrows Grand Prix International	3.5 Arrows A11-Cosworth V8	
5	SAN MARINO GP	Imola	9	Arrows Grand Prix International	3.5 Arrows A11-Cosworth V8	1 lap behind
ret	MONACO GP	Monte Carlo	9	Arrows Grand Prix International	3.5 Arrows A11-Cosworth V8	electrical short-circuit
ret	MEXICAN GP	Mexico City	9	Arrows Grand Prix International	3.5 Arrows A11-Cosworth V8	electrics
ret	US GP (PHOENIX)	Phoenix	9	Arrows Grand Prix International	3.5 Arrows A11-Cosworth V8	ran into de Cesaris-suspension
ret	CANADIAN GP	Montreal	9	Arrows Grand Prix International	3.5 Arrows A11-Cosworth V8	led race briefly on wets/engine
9	BRITISH GP	Silverstone	9	Arrows Grand Prix International	3.5 Arrows A11-Cosworth V8	2 laps behind
6	GERMAN GP	Hockenheim	9	Arrows Grand Prix International	3.5 Arrows A11-Cosworth V8	no clutch/1 lap behind
10	HUNGARIAN GP	Hungaroring	9	Arrows Grand Prix International	3.5 Arrows A11-Cosworth V8	despite collision-Nakajima/-1 lap
6	BELGIAN GP	Spa	9	Arrows Grand Prix International	3.5 Arrows A11-Cosworth V8	
ret	ITALIAN GP	Monza	9	Arrows Grand Prix International	3.5 Arrows A11-Cosworth V8	fuel flow-engine cut out
ret	PORTUGUESE GP	Estoril	9	Arrows Grand Prix International	3.5 Arrows A11-Cosworth V8	accident
9	SPANISH GP	Jerez	9	Arrows Grand Prix International	3.5 Arrows A11-Cosworth V8	despite collisions/2 laps behind
6*	JAPANESE GP	Suzuka	9	Arrows Grand Prix International	3.5 Arrows A11-Cosworth V8	* 1st place car dsq/1 lap behind
ret	AUSTRALIAN GP	Adelaide	9	Arrows Grand Prix International	3.5 Arrows A11-Cosworth V8	engine cut out and in-crashed

1990

ret	US GP (PHOENIX)	Phoenix	11	Camel Team Lotus	3.5 Camel Lotus 102-Lamborghini V12	rear suspension
ret	BRAZILIAN GP	Rio	11	Camel Team Lotus	3.5 Camel Lotus 102-Lamborghini V12	electrics
7	SAN MARINO GP	Imola	11	Camel Team Lotus	3.5 Camel Lotus 102-Lamborghini V12	1 lap behind
ret	MONACO GP	Monte Carlo	11	Camel Team Lotus	3.5 Camel Lotus 102-Lamborghini V12	brakes/spun-stalled
6	CANADIAN GP	Montreal	11	Camel Team Lotus	3.5 Camel Lotus 102-Lamborghini V12	part-detached undertray/-2 laps
10	MEXICAN GP	Mexico City	11	Camel Team Lotus	3.5 Camel Lotus 102-Lamborghini V12	low on revs/1 lap behind
11	FRENCH GP	Paul Ricard	11	Camel Team Lotus	3.5 Camel Lotus 102-Lamborghini V12	1 lap behind
ret	BRITISH GP	Silverstone	11	Camel Team Lotus	3.5 Camel Lotus 102-Lamborghini V12	engine
8	GERMAN GP	Hockenheim	11	Camel Team Lotus	3.5 Camel Lotus 102-Lamborghini V12	severe vibration/1 lap behind
5	HUNGARIAN GP	Hungaroring	11	Camel Team Lotus	3.5 Camel Lotus 102-Lamborghini V12	
11	BELGIAN GP	Spa	11	Camel Team Lotus	3.5 Camel Lotus 102-Lamborghini V12	misfire/1 lap behind
ret	ITALIAN GP	Monza	11	Camel Team Lotus	3.5 Camel Lotus 102-Lamborghini V12	clutch
ret	PORTUGUESE GP	Estoril	11	Camel Team Lotus	3.5 Camel Lotus 102-Lamborghini V12	throttle
ret	SPANISH GP	Jerez	11	Camel Team Lotus	3.5 Camel Lotus 102-Lamborghini V12	gearbox
ret	JAPANESE GP	Suzuka	11	Camel Team Lotus	3.5 Camel Lotus 102-Lamborghini V12	gearbox
ret	AUSTRALIAN GP	Adelaide	11	Camel Team Lotus	3.5 Camel Lotus 102-Lamborghini V12	gearbox

1993

7	SOUTH AFRICAN GP	Kyalami	9	Footwork Mugen Honda	3.5 Footwork FA13B-Mugen Honda V10	spun off/3 laps behind
9	BRAZILIAN GP	Interlagos	9	Footwork Mugen Honda	3.5 Footwork FA13B-Mugen Honda V10	2 laps behind

ret	EUROPEAN GP	Donington	9	Footwork Mugen Honda	3.5 Footwork FA14-Mugen Honda V10	*gearbox*
ret	SAN MARINO GP	Imola	9	Footwork Mugen Honda	3.5 Footwork FA14-Mugen Honda V10	*spun off*
13	SPANISH GP	Barcelona	9	Footwork Mugen Honda	3.5 Footwork FA14-Mugen Honda V10	*2 spins/3 laps behind*
ret	MONACO GP	Monte Carlo	9	Footwork Mugen Honda	3.5 Footwork FA14-Mugen Honda V10	*throttle failure*
16	CANADIAN GP	Montreal	9	Footwork Mugen Honda	3.5 Footwork FA14-Mugen Honda V10	*poor handling/4laps behind*
13	FRENCH GP	Magny Cours	9	Footwork Mugen Honda	3.5 Footwork FA14-Mugen Honda V10	*2 laps behind*
6	BRITISH GP	Silverstone	9	Footwork Mugen Honda	3.5 Footwork FA14-Mugen Honda V10	*1 lap behind*
17	GERMAN GP	Hockenheim	9	Footwork Mugen Honda	3.5 Footwork FA14-Mugen Honda V10	*spin-wing damage/3 laps behind*
4	HUNGARIAN GP	Hungaroring	9	Footwork Mugen Honda	3.5 Footwork FA14-Mugen Honda V10	*1 lap behind*
ret	BELGIAN GP	Spa	9	Footwork Mugen Honda	3.5 Footwork FA14-Mugen Honda V10	*electrical failure*
ret	ITALIAN GP	Monza	9	Footwork Mugen Honda	3.5 Footwork FA14-Mugen Honda V10	*collision with Suzuki on lap 1*
15/ret	PORTUGUESE GP	Estoril	9	Footwork Mugen Honda	3.5 Footwork FA14-Mugen Honda V10	*taken off by Patrese/8 laps behind*
14/ret	JAPANESE GP	Suzuka	9	Footwork Mugen Honda	3.5 Footwork FA14-Mugen Honda V10	*hit by Irvine-spun off/5 laps behind*
10	AUSTRALIAN GP	Adelaide	9	Footwork Mugen Honda	3.5 Footwork FA14-Mugen Honda V10	*driver unwell/spin/2 laps behind*

GP Starts: 147   GP Wins: 0   Pole positions: 0   Fastest laps: 2   Points: 71

JOHN WATSON

'Wattie' has perhaps not been given the credit that is his due, which may sound strange when you consider he holds the MBE. But because his successes in Grand Prix racing were not concentrated into one great spell, his long and in the main very successful career, which spanned more than twenty years, tends to be overlooked.

In fact he started racing way back in 1963-64 in his native Northern Ireland with an Austin Healey Sprite, before graduating to single-seaters. Outstanding in Irish Formula Libre, he soon crossed the water to try his hand against sterner opposition. In 1970 he took his Brabham BT30 into the European F2 championship, but a heavy crash at Rouen left him with a broken arm and leg. Undaunted, he was back the following year and, competing as a privateer in his elderly car, put to shame many more vaunted names. His persistence was about to bring rewards, for in 1972 a sixth place in the John Player Trophy race at Brands Hatch in a March 721, plus some excellent drives in Alan McCall's F2 Tui, caught the eye of both Brabham and Gulf, who were to give the then bearded Ulsterman his first real breaks. The 'luck of the Irish' certainly deserted him when, in the Race of Champions early in 1973, he broke his leg once more after the throttle stuck open on the new Brabham BT42. With typical quiet determination he was back to make his Grand Prix debut at Silverstone, and by the end of the year he had set up a full F1 season with Hexagon Racing's private Brabham. A great drive to sixth place at Monaco was followed by some terrific performances once he had the use of the BT44 chassis, headed by a brilliant drive into fourth in Austria after a pit stop.

Sadly the team were unable to continue in 1975, and Watson, having previously driven in a few Formula 2 races for Surtees, joined 'Big John's' outfit. A second place in the Race of Champions and fourth in the International Trophy were as good as it was going to get in a year fraught with mechanical difficulties. Just before the end of the season Surtees withdrew to regroup his efforts, leaving 'Wattie' unemployed. Fortunately he soon picked up a ride in the Penske team at Watkins Glen and, after taking ninth place with a car not set up for the track, he was offered a contract for the 1976 season. The team were to suffer something of an up-and-down year, but John's magnificent victory in Austria gave him the confidence that comes from being a winner. The only thing he lost that day was his famous beard, as a result of a wager with Roger Penske!

When Penske decided to call it a day at the end of the year, Bernie Ecclestone lost no time in signing John to join Carlos Pace in his Brabham-Alfa team for 1977. Tragically, the Brazilian was soon killed in an air crash, leaving Watson to carry the burden of development in an unproven car. He nearly won at Paul Ricard until fuel pick-up problems took away his last-lap lead. The season ended up as a major disappointment after beginning with so much promise, but things improved in 1978, when at least he was a regular points scorer, although teamed with Niki Lauda his performances seemed a trifle erratic. When James Hunt became disillusioned with McLaren, Watson was the man chosen to take his place. Initially it seemed to be a disastrous move, for the team were at a low ebb under the declining Teddy Mayer regime. The following season was frustrating, with points scraped here and there in a difficult car, and the following year was to bring even less cheer, Watson being out-driven in the early part of the year by newcomer Alain Prost. Some observers were tempted to write him off but John fought back, and his confidence and speed began to return – particularly when he was installed in the John Barnard-designed MP4 under McLaren's new Ron Dennis regime in 1981. He scored a lucky win at Silverstone when Arnoux's Renault faltered, and generally re-established his standing as one of the leading drivers which had seemed under threat.

Joined by Niki Lauda in 1982, Watson answered the Austrian's Long Beach challenge with a well-taken win at Zolder, but overall his season was hampered by unpredictable lapses in form which led to some lacklustre showings. In 1983 he came through the field to take an unexpected win at Long Beach, but was generally handicapped by the lack of turbo power until late in the season. He fully expected to remain paired with Lauda for a third year in 1984, but protracted negotiations worked against him when Alain Prost came onto the scene after be ing released by Renault. With no other options open, 'Wattie' was left to find a seat in sports car racing, driving occasionally for Rothmans Porsche over the next couple of years and taking a win at Fuji in 1984 with Bellof. A last-minute call-up by McLaren to deputise for the injured Lauda in the European GP merely emphasised how two seasons out can take away the edge, and there was to be no more Formula 1.

Instead he returned to endurance racing in the Silk Cut Jaguar and later Toyota teams, before retiring from the track to concentrate on his Silverstone-based Performance Driving school and acting as a commentator for the satellite channel Eurosport.

WATSON, John (GB) b 4/5/1946

	1973					
	Race	Circuit	No	Entrant	Car/Engine	Comment
ret	BRITISH GP	Silverstone	29	Ceramica Pagnossin-Team MRD	3.0 Brabham BT37-Cosworth V8	*seized fuel metering unit*
ret	US GP	Watkins Glen	9	Ceramica Pagnossin-Team MRD	3.0 Brabham BT42-Cosworth V8	*engine*
	1974					
12	ARGENTINE GP	Buenos Aires	28	John Goldie Racing with Hexagon	3.0 Brabham BT42-Cosworth V8	*pit stop-nose cone/-4 laps*
ret	BRAZILIAN GP	Interlagos	28	John Goldie Racing with Hexagon	3.0 Brabham BT42-Cosworth V8	*clutch*

ret	SOUTH AFRICAN GP	Kyalami	28	John Goldie Racing with Hexagon	3.0 Brabham BT42-Cosworth V8	*fuel union*
11	SPANISH GP	Jarama	28	John Goldie Racing with Hexagon	3.0 Brabham BT42-Cosworth V8	*pit stop-tyres/4 laps behind*
11	BELGIAN GP	Nivelles	28	John Goldie Racing with Hexagon	3.0 Brabham BT42-Cosworth V8	*pit stop-tyres/2 laps behind*
6	MONACO GP	Monte Carlo	28	John Goldie Racing with Hexagon	3.0 Brabham BT42-Cosworth V8	*1 lap behind*
11	SWEDISH GP	Anderstorp	28	John Goldie Racing with Hexagon	3.0 Brabham BT42-Cosworth V8	*3 laps behind*
7	DUTCH GP	Zandvoort	28	John Goldie Racing with Hexagon	3.0 Brabham BT42-Cosworth V8	
16	FRENCH GP	Dijon	28	John Goldie Racing with Hexagon	3.0 Brabham BT42-Cosworth V8	*pit stop-exhaust/4 laps behind*
11	BRITISH GP	Brands Hatch	28	Goldie Hexagon Racing	3.0 Brabham BT42-Cosworth V8	*pit stop-puncture/2 laps behind*
ret	GERMAN GP	Nürburgring	28	Goldie Hexagon Racing	3.0 Brabham BT44-Cosworth V8	*accident damage*
dns	"	"	28	Goldie Hexagon Racing	3.0 Brabham BT42-Cosworth V8	*practice only*
4	AUSTRIAN GP	Österreichring	28	Goldie Hexagon Racing	3.0 Brabham BT44-Cosworth V8	
7	ITALIAN GP	Monza	28	Goldie Hexagon Racing	3.0 Brabham BT44-Cosworth V8	*1 lap behind*
ret	CANADIAN GP	Mosport Park	28	Goldie Hexagon Racing	3.0 Brabham BT44-Cosworth V8	*broken suspension-accident*
5	US GP	Watkins Glen	28	Goldie Hexagon Racing	3.0 Brabham BT44-Cosworth V8	

1975

dsq	ARGENTINE GP	Buenos Aires	18	Team Surtees	3.0 Surtees TS16-Cosworth V8	*repairs outside of pit area*
10	BRAZILIAN GP	Interlagos	18	Team Surtees	3.0 Surtees TS16-Cosworth V8	*slow puncture*
ret	SOUTH AFRICAN GP	Kyalamia	18	Team Surtees	3.0 Surtees TS16-Cosworth V8	*clutch*
8	SPANISH GP	Montjuich Park	18	Team Surtees	3.0 Surtees TS16-Cosworth V8	*pit stop-flat spotted tyre/-3 laps*
ret	MONACO GP	Monte Carlo	18	Team Surtees	3.0 Surtees TS16-Cosworth V8	*spun off*
10	BELGIAN GP	Zolder	18	Team Surtees	3.0 Surtees TS16-Cosworth V8	*collision-pstop-nose cone/-2 laps*
16	SWEDISH GP	Anderstorp	18	Team Surtees	3.0 Surtees TS16-Cosworth V8	*3 laps behind*
ret	DUTCH GP	Zandvoort	18	Team Surtees	3.0 Surtees TS16-Cosworth V8	*severe vibration*
13	FRENCH GP	Paul Ricard	18	Team Surtees	3.0 Surtees TS16-Cosworth V8	*1 lap behind*
11/ret	BRITISH GP	Silverstone	18	Team Surtees	3.0 Surtees TS16-Cosworth V8	*spun off in rainstorm/-2 laps*
ret	GERMAN GP	Nürburgring	6	John Player Team Lotus	3.0 Lotus 72E-Cosworth V8	*broken front suspension*
10	AUSTRIAN GP	Österreichring	18	Team Surtees	3.0 Surtees TS16-Cosworth V8	*1 lap behind*
9	US GP	Watkins Glen	28	Penske Cars	3.0 Penske PC1-Cosworth V8	*pit stop-went off at chicane/-2 laps*
dns	"	" "	28	Penske Cars	3.0 Penske PC3-Cosworth V8	*practice only*

1976

ret	BRAZILIAN GP	Interlagos	28	Citibank Team Penske	3.0 Penske PC3-Cosworth V8	*fire-broken fuel line*
5	SOUTH AFRICAN GP	Kyalami	28	Citibank Team Penske	3.0 Penske PC3-Cosworth V8	*1 lap behind*
nc	US GP WEST	Long Beach	28	Citibank Team Penske	3.0 Penske PC3-Cosworth V8	*2 p stops-nose cone-exhaust/-2 laps*
ret	SPANISH GP	Jarama	28	Citibank Team Penske	3.0 Penske PC3-Cosworth V8	*engine*
7	BELGIAN GP	Zolder	28	Citibank Team Penske	3.0 Penske PC3-Cosworth V8	*1 lap behind*
10	MONACO GP	Monte Carlo	28	Citibank Team Penske	3.0 Penske PC3-Cosworth V8	*2 laps behind*
ret	SWEDISH GP	Anderstorp	28	Citibank Team Penske	3.0 Penske PC4-Cosworth V8	*accident-throttle stuck open*
3*	FRENCH GP	Paul Ricard	28	Citibank Team Penske	3.0 Penske PC4-Cosworth V8	**dsq-but reinstared on appeal*
3	BRITISH GP	Brands Hatch	28	Citibank Team Penske	3.0 Penske PC4-Cosworth V8	*1 lap behind*
7	GERMAN GP	Nürburgring	28	Citibank Team Penske	3.0 Penske PC4-Cosworth V8	
1	AUSTRIAN GP	Österreichring	28	Citibank Team Penske	3.0 Penske PC4-Cosworth V8	
ret	DUTCH GP	Zandvoort	28	Citibank Team Penske	3.0 Penske PC4-Cosworth V8	*gearbox*
11	ITALIAN GP	Monza	28	Citibank Team Penske	3.0 Penske PC4-Cosworth V8	*started from back of grid*
10	CANADIAN GP	Mosport Park	28	Citibank Team Penske	3.0 Penske PC4-Cosworth V8	*1 lap behind*
6	US GP EAST	Watkins Glen	28	Citibank Team Penske	3.0 Penske PC4-Cosworth V8	
ret	JAPANESE GP	Mount Fuji	28	Citibank Team Penske	3.0 Penske PC4-Cosworth V8	*engine*

1977

ret	ARGENTINE GP	Buenos Aires	7	Martini Racing	3.0 Brabham BT45-Alfa Romeo F12	*handling-sheared suspension mounting*
ret	BRAZILIAN GP	Interlagos	7	Martini Racing	3.0 Brabham BT45-Alfa Romeo F12	*crashed*
6	SOUTH AFRICAN GP	Kyalami	7	Martini Racing	3.0 Brabham BT45-Alfa Romeo F12	*FL*
dsq	US GP WEST	Long Beach	7	Martini Racing	3.0 Brabham BT45B-Alfa Romeo F12	*outside assistance*
ret	SPANISH GP	Jarama	7	Martini Racing	3.0 Brabham BT45B-Alfa Romeo F12	*fuel metering unit*
ret	MONACO GP	Monte Carlo	7	Martini Racing	3.0 Brabham BT45B-Alfa Romeo F12	*gearbox/Pole*
ret	BELGIAN GP	Zolder	7	Martini Racing	3.0 Brabham BT45B-Alfa Romeo F12	*hit by Andretti*
5	SWEDISH GP	Anderstorp	7	Martini Racing	3.0 Brabham BT45B-Alfa Romeo F12	
2	FRENCH GP	Dijon	7	Martini Racing	3.0 Brabham BT45B-Alfa Romeo F12	*out of fuel on last lap when 1st*
ret	BRITISH GP	Silverstone	7	Martini Racing	3.0 Brabham BT45B-Alfa Romeo F12	*engine-fuel feed*
ret	GERMAN GP	Hockenheim	7	Martini Racing	3.0 Brabham BT45B-Alfa Romeo F12	*engine*
8	AUSTRIAN GP	Österreichring	7	Martini Racing	3.0 Brabham BT45B-Alfa Romeo F12	*FL/1 lap behind*
ret	DUTCH GP	Zandvoort	7	Martini Racing	3.0 Brabham BT45B-Alfa Romeo F12	*engine-lost oil damaged sump*
ret	ITALIAN GP	Monza	7	Martini Racing	3.0 Brabham BT45B-Alfa Romeo F12	*accident-hit kerb*
12	US GP EAST	Watkins Glen	7	Martini Racing	3.0 Brabham BT45B-Alfa Romeo F12	*3 pit stops-tyres/2 laps behind*
ret	CANADIAN GP	Mosport Park	7	Martini Racing	3.0 Brabham BT45B-Alfa Romeo F12	*hit Peterson*
ret	JAPANESE GP	Mount Fuji	7	Martini Racing	3.0 Brabham BT45B-Alfa Romeo F12	*gearbox*

1978

ret	ARGENTINE GP	Buenos Aires	2	Parmalat Racing Team	3.0 Brabham BT45C-Alfa Romeo F12	*engine*
8	BRAZILIAN GP	Rio	2	Parmalat Racing Team	3.0 Brabham BT45C-Alfa Romeo F12	*2 laps behind*
3	SOUTH AFRICAN GP	Kyalami	2	Parmalat Racing Team	3.0 Brabham BT46-Alfa Romeo F12	
dns	"	"	2	Parmalat Racing Team	3.0 Brabham BT45C-Alfa Romeo F12	*practice only*
ret	US GP WEST	Long Beach	2	Parmalat Racing Team	3.0 Brabham BT46-Alfa Romeo F12	*oil tank*
4	MONACO GP	Monte Carlo	2	Parmalat Racing Team	3.0 Brabham BT46-Alfa Romeo F12	
ret	BELGIAN GP	Zolder	2	Parmalat Racing Team	3.0 Brabham BT46-Alfa Romeo F12	*spun and damaged chassis*
5	SPANISH GP	Jarama	2	Parmalat Racing Team	3.0 Brabham BT46-Alfa Romeo F12	
ret	SWEDISH GP	Anderstorp	2	Parmalat Racing Team	3.0 Brabham BT46-Alfa Romeo F12	*stuck throttle after spin/fan car*
4	FRENCH GP	Paul Ricard	2	Parmalat Racing Team	3.0 Brabham BT46-Alfa Romeo F12	*Pole*
3	BRITISH GP	Brands Hatch	2	Parmalat Racing Team	3.0 Brabham BT46-Alfa Romeo F12	
7	GERMAN GP	Hockenheim	2	Parmalat Racing Team	3.0 Brabham BT46-Alfa Romeo F12	
7	AUSTRIAN GP	Österreichring	2	Parmalat Racing Team	3.0 Brabham BT46-Alfa Romeo F12	*pit stop-tyres/1 lap behind*
4	DUTCH GP	Zandvoort	2	Parmalat Racing Team	3.0 Brabham BT46-Alfa Romeo F12	
2*	ITALIAN GP	Monza	2	Parmalat Racing Team	3.0 Brabham BT46-Alfa Romeo F12	** 1st & 2nd cars received 1 min penalty*
ret	US GP EAST	Watkins Glen	2	Parmalat Racing Team	3.0 Brabham BT46-Alfa Romeo F12	*engine2*
ret	CANADIAN GP	Montreal	2	Parmalat Racing Team	3.0 Brabham BT46-Alfa Romeo F12	*collision with Andretti*

1979

3	ARGENTINE GP	Buenos Aires	7	Marlboro Team McLaren	3.0 McLaren M28-Cosworth V8	
8	BRAZILIAN GP	Interlagos	7	Marlboro Team McLaren	3.0 McLaren M28-Cosworth V8	*1 lap behind*
ret	SOUTH AFRICAN GP	Kyalami	7	Marlboro Team McLaren	3.0 McLaren M28-Cosworth V8	*ignition*
ret	US GP WEST	Long Beach	7	Löwenbräu Team McLaren	3.0 McLaren M28-Cosworth V8	*fuel injection unit*
ret	SPANISH GP	Jarama	7	Marlboro Team McLaren	3.0 McLaren M28-Cosworth V8	*engine*
6	BELGIAN GP	Zolder	7	Marlboro Team McLaren	3.0 McLaren M28-Cosworth V8	
4	MONACO GP	Monte Carlo	7	Marlboro Team McLaren	3.0 McLaren M28-Cosworth V8	
11	FRENCH GP	Dijon	7	Marlboro Team McLaren	3.0 McLaren M28-Cosworth V8	*pit stop-tyres/2 laps behind*
4	BRITISH GP	Silverstone	7	Marlboro Team McLaren	3.0 McLaren M29-Cosworth V8	*1 lap behind*
5	GERMAN GP	Hockenheim	7	Marlboro Team McLaren	3.0 McLaren M29-Cosworth V8	
9	AUSTRIAN GP	Österreichring	7	Marlboro Team McLaren	3.0 McLaren M29-Cosworth V8	*1 lap behind*
ret	DUTCH GP	Zandvoort	7	Marlboro Team McLaren	3.0 McLaren M29-Cosworth V8	*engine*
ret	ITALIAN GP	Monza	7	Marlboro Team McLaren	3.0 McLaren M29-Cosworth V8	*accident with Jarier*
6	CANADIAN GP	Montreal	7	Marlboro Team McLaren	3.0 McLaren M29-Cosworth V8	*pit stop-fuel/2 laps behind*
6	US GP EAST	Watkins Glen	7	Marlboro Team McLaren	3.0 McLaren M29-Cosworth V8	*pit stop-tyres/1 lap behind*

1980

ret	ARGENTINE GP	Buenos Aires	7	Marlboro Team McLaren	3.0 McLaren M29-Cosworth V8	*gearbox oil leak*
11	BRAZILIAN GP	Interlagos	7	Marlboro Team McLaren	3.0 McLaren M29-Cosworth V8	*1 lap behind*
11	SOUTH AFRICAN GP	Kyalami	7	Marlboro Team McLaren	3.0 McLaren M29-Cosworth V8	*2 laps behind*
4	US GP WEST	Long Beach	7	Marlboro Team McLaren	3.0 McLaren M29-Cosworth V8	*1 lap behind*
nc	BELGIAN GP	Zolder	7	Marlboro Team McLaren	3.0 McLaren M29-Cosworth V8	*2 pit stops-brakes/11 laps behind*
dnq	MONACO GP	Monte Carlo	7	Marlboro Team McLaren	3.0 McLaren M29-Cosworth V8	
7	FRENCH GP	Paul Ricard	7	Marlboro Team McLaren	3.0 McLaren M29-Cosworth V8	*1 lap behind*
8	BRITISH GP	Brands Hatch	7	Marlboro Team McLaren	3.0 McLaren M29-Cosworth V8	*pit stop-tyres/2 laps behind*
ret	GERMAN GP	Hockenheim	7	Marlboro Team McLaren	3.0 McLaren M29-Cosworth V8	*engine*
ret	AUSTRIAN GP	Österreichring	7	Marlboro Team McLaren	3.0 McLaren M29-Cosworth V8	*engine*
ret	DUTCH GP	Zandvoort	7	Marlboro Team McLaren	3.0 McLaren M29-Cosworth V8	*engine*
ret	ITALIAN GP	Imola	7	Marlboro Team McLaren	3.0 McLaren M29-Cosworth V8	*brakes/wheel bearing*
4	CANADIAN GP	Montreal	7	Marlboro Team McLaren	3.0 McLaren M29-Cosworth V8	
nc	US GP EAST	Watkins Glen	7	Marlboro Team McLaren	3.0 McLaren M29-Cosworth V8	*pit stop-shock absorber/-9 laps*

1981

ret	US GP WEST	Long Beach	7	McLaren International	3.0 McLaren M29F-Cosworth V8	*engine*
8	BRAZILIAN GP	Rio	7	McLaren International	3.0 McLaren M29F-Cosworth V8	*1 lap behind*
ret	ARGENTINE GP	Buenos Aires	7	McLaren International	3.0 McLaren MP4-Cosworth V8	*transmission*
10	SAN MARINO GP	Imola	7	McLaren International	3.0 McLaren MP4-Cosworth V8	*pit stop-hit Arnoux-nose cone/-2 laps*
7	BELGIAN GP	Zolder	7	McLaren International	3.0 McLaren MP4-Cosworth V8	*gearbox problems*
ret	MONACO GP	Monte Carlo	7	McLaren International	3.0 McLaren MP4-Cosworth V8	*engine*
3	SPANISH GP	Jarama	7	McLaren International	3.0 McLaren MP4-Cosworth V8	
2	FRENCH GP	Dijon	7	McLaren International	3.0 McLaren MP4-Cosworth V8	
1	BRITISH GP	Silverstone	7	McLaren International	3.0 McLaren MP4-Cosworth V8	
6	GERMAN GP	Hockenheim	7	McLaren International	3.0 McLaren MP4-Cosworth V8	*1 lap behind*
6	AUSTRIAN GP	Österreichring	7	McLaren International	3.0 McLaren MP4-Cosworth V8	
ret	DUTCH GP	Zandvoort	7	McLaren International	3.0 McLaren MP4-Cosworth V8	*electrics*
ret	ITALIAN GP	Monza	7	McLaren International	3.0 McLaren MP4-Cosworth V8	*crashed*
2	CANADIAN GP	Montreal	7	McLaren International	3.0 McLaren MP4-Cosworth V8	*FL*
7	CAESARS PALACE GP	Las Vegas	7	McLaren International	3.0 McLaren MP4-Cosworth V8	*pit stop-tyres*

1982

6	SOUTH AFRICAN GP	Kyalami	7	Marlboro McLaren International	3.0 McLaren MP4B-Cosworth V8	
2*	BRAZILIAN GP	Rio	7	Marlboro McLaren International	3.0 McLaren MP4B-Cosworth V8	** 1st & 2nd place cars disqualified*
6	US GP WEST	Long Beach	7	Marlboro McLaren International	3.0 McLaren MP4B-Cosworth V8	*1 lap behind*
1	BELGIAN GP	Zolder	7	Marlboro McLaren International	3.0 McLaren MP4B-Cosworth V8	*FL*
ret	MONACO GP	Monte Carlo	7	Marlboro McLaren International	3.0 McLaren MP4B-Cosworth V8	*oil leak/battery*
1	US GP (DETROIT)	Detroit	7	Marlboro McLaren International	3.0 McLaren MP4B-Cosworth V8	
3	CANADIAN GP	Montreal	7	Marlboro McLaren International	3.0 McLaren MP4B-Cosworth V8	
9	DUTCH GP	Zandvoort	7	Marlboro McLaren International	3.0 McLaren MP4B-Cosworth V8	*pit stop-tyres/1 lap behind*
ret	BRITISH GP	Brands Hatch	7	Marlboro McLaren International	3.0 McLaren MP4B-Cosworth V8	*spun off avoiding Jarier/Serra*
ret	FRENCH GP	Paul Ricard	7	Marlboro McLaren International	3.0 McLaren MP4B-Cosworth V8	*battery lead*
ret	GERMAN GP	Hockenheim	7	Marlboro McLaren International	3.0 McLaren MP4B-Cosworth V8	*front suspension*
ret	AUSTRIAN GP	Österreichring	7	Marlboro McLaren International	3.0 McLaren MP4B-Cosworth V8	*engine-split water hose*
13	SWISS GP	Dijon	7	Marlboro McLaren International	3.0 McLaren MP4B-Cosworth V8	*pit stop-broken skirt/-3 laps*
4	ITALIAN GP	Monza	7	Marlboro McLaren International	3.0 McLaren MP4B-Cosworth V8	
2	CAESARS PALACE GP	Las Vegas	7	Marlboro McLaren International	3.0 McLaren MP4B-Cosworth V8	

1983

ret	BRAZILIAN GP	Rio	7	Marlboro McLaren International	3.0 McLaren MP4/1C-Cosworth V8	*engine*
1	US GP WEST	Long Beach	7	Marlboro McLaren International	3.0 McLaren MP4/1C-Cosworth V8	
ret	FRENCH GP	Paul Ricard	7	Marlboro McLaren International	3.0 McLaren MP4/1C-Cosworth V8	*throttle linkage*
5	SAN MARINO GP	Imola	7	Marlboro McLaren International	3.0 McLaren MP4/1C-Cosworth V8	*1 lap behind*
dnq	MONACO GP	Monte Carlo	7	Marlboro McLaren International	3.0 McLaren MP4/1C-Cosworth V8	
ret	BELGIAN GP	Spa	7	Marlboro McLaren International	3.0 McLaren MP4/1C-Cosworth V8	*accident with Jarier*
3	US GP (DETROIT)	Detroit	7	Marlboro McLaren International	3.0 McLaren MP4/1C-Cosworth V8	*FL*
6	CANADIAN GP	Montreal	7	Marlboro McLaren International	3.0 McLaren MP4/1C-Cosworth V8	*pit stop-tyres/1 lap behind*
9	BRITISH GP	Silverstone	7	Marlboro McLaren International	3.0 McLaren MP4/1C-Cosworth V8	*pit stop-tyres/1 lap behind*
5	GERMAN GP	Hockenheim	7	Marlboro McLaren International	3.0 McLaren MP4/1C-Cosworth V8	*pit stop-tyres/1 lap behind*
9	AUSTRIAN GP	Österreichring	7	Marlboro McLaren International	3.0 McLaren MP4/1C-Cosworth V8	*pit stop-tyres/2 laps behind*
3	DUTCH GP	Zandvoort	7	Marlboro McLaren International	3.0 McLaren MP4/1C-Cosworth V8	*pit stop-tyres*
ret	ITALIAN GP	Monza	7	Marlboro McLaren International	1.5 t/c McLaren MP4/1E-TAG V6	*engine*
ret	EUROPEAN GP	Brands Hatch	7	Marlboro McLaren International	1.5 t/c McLaren MP4/1E-TAG V6	*accident-rear wing failure*
dsq	SOUTH AFRICAN GP	Kyalami	7	Marlboro McLaren International	1.5 t/c McLaren MP4/1E-TAG V6	*overtook cars on warm-up lap*

1985

7	EUROPEAN GP	Brands Hatch	1	Marlboro McLaren International	1.5 t/c McLaren MP4/2B-TAG V6	*2 laps behind*

GP Starts: 152   GP Wins: 5   Pole positions: 2   Fastest laps: 5   Points: 169

KARL WENDLINGER

Racing was in Wendlinger's blood, for both his father and grandfather had competed in the past, and naturally Karl followed suit. After some karting experience the Austrian was helped greatly by Gerhard Berger (an old family friend) to get started in FF1600 in 1987.

Assisted by the former Grand Prix driver Dr Helmut Marko, he came to the fore in the 1989 German F3 championship with some excellent drives in a Ralt and took the title, edging out Schumacher and Frentzen after the closest fought of battles.

This trio of young talent was then selected by Mercedes-Benz to to be groomed in their Group C programme as possible candidates for a future Formula 1 return. Paired with Jochen Mass, the best possible tutor, the young Austrian learned quickly and helped the company achieve its goal of winning the teams' championship with a win at Spa and second places at Suzuka and Monza. However, the necessity of have having top-class equipment at his disposal was brought home when he endured a rather lacklustre time in Formula 3000 that year with a Helmut Marko-run Lola, taking only two championship points. The 1991 season saw the two star pupils Wendlinger and Schumacher paired together in the same Mercedes, and they performed splendidly in the somewhat less than previously dominant silver cars. A win at Autopolis was the high point of the season, and Karl was found a place in the Leyton House team for the final two races of the year. All eyes were really opened in South Africa at the beginning of 1992, when he qualified the largely unregarded car in seventh place on the grid. A brilliant fourth place in Canada gave some indication of the driver's potential, but the season was largely inconclusive due to reliability problems with the Ilmor V10. It had been a useful preparatory year for Karl, and for 1993 he moved to the new Sauber team as Mercedes had foreseen. In its first season the Swiss entrant made excellent progress and Wendlinger scored points on four occasions, though he was unfortunately involved in a number of on-track incidents which could damage his reputation if they continue. Through no real fault of his own, Wendlinger has been rather left behind in the race for the championship crown by Michael Schumacher. Karl's hope must be that Sauber, with the vast resources of Mercedes-Benz in the background, can provide him with the car to make his challenge. In the long term, it might be a case of the tortoise and the hare.

PETER WESTBURY

Westbury's career fell neatly into two halves, the first as a top-notch hill-climber, the second as a true circuit racer. He took to the hills in 1962 with a Cooper-Daimler, and when the V8 was dropped into his own Felday chassis in 1963 his first British hill-climb championship was duly attained. For the following year Westbury got his hands on the Ferguson 4WD, which proved almost unbeatable. Although he continued to compete in 1965, Peter was busy building up his Felday Engineering firm, but he made a successful transition to Formula 3 in 1967 with a Brabham BT21. He won races at Silverstone, Chimay and Cermont Ferrand, and took further victories at Chimay again and Reims in 1968. That year saw a couple of Formula 2 drives, before a full season in 1969 with his own Brabham BT30 which yielded second place in the Lottery GP at Monza and fifth in the F2 class of the German GP. Peter was given a chance to try a pukka F1 machine when he joined BRM for the 1970 US GP, but the car suffered a blown engine and the disappointed driver failed to qualify. He was a consistent top-six finisher in Formula 2 during 1970-71 but results sagged the following year, and early in 1973 Westbury announced his retirement.

KEN WHARTON

A Smethwick garage owner, Wharton was a versatile all-rounder who began racing immediately before the war in an Austin Seven special, but it was not until the late forties that he began to make his mark in a number of motor sport arenas. In trials he won successive RAC championships, and his special was much copied by his competitors, while in rallies he campaigned a Ford Pilot, winning the Tulip Rally on three occasions.

In 1950 Wharton won at Zandvoort with a Cooper-JAP, while in 1951 he went hill-climbing, winning the first of four successive championships. Meanwhile he had taken up circuit racing in a big way, initially competing in Grands Prix with a large and old-fashioned Frazer-Nash. It ran reliably on its debut at Bremgarten in 1952, and Wharton took it to fourth place, his best-ever World Championship finish. This car was replaced by a more competitive Cooper-Bristol by the end of the season, but he could gain no major success with it the following season. He was kept busy by BRM, who were still racing their V16 car in Libre events, and joined the Owen team for 1954 to handle their Maserati 250F in Grands Prix and their V16 in Libre races, winning the Glover Trophy.

As if he wasn't already sufficiently stretched by his commitments, Wharton also tried his hand at sports car racing with the works Jaguar, winning the 1954 Reims 12 Hours with Peter Whitehead. For 1955, Ken joined the Vanwall team, suffering a nasty accident in the International Trophy at Silverstone which resulted in burns to his arms and neck. It was generally an unproductive year, and Wharton freelanced in 1956, taking a third place in the Australian Tourist Trophy in Melbourne with a Ferrari Monza. However, early in 1957 he was killed after crashing this car in a sports car race at Ardmore, New Zealand.

WENDLINGER, Karl (A) b 20/12/1968

1991

	Race	Circuit	No	Entrant	Car/Engine	Comment
ret	JAPANESE GP	Suzuka	16	Leyton House Racing	3.5 Leyton House GC911-Ilmor V10	multiple collision lap 1
20	AUSTRALIAN GP	Adelaide	16	Leyton House Racing	3.5 Leyton House GC911-Ilmor V10	rain shortened race/2 laps behind

1992

	Race	Circuit	No	Entrant	Car/Engine	Comment
ret	SOUTH AFRICAN GP	Kyalami	16	March F1	3.5 March CG 911-Ilmor V10	overheating
ret	MEXICAN GP	Mexico City	16	March F1	3.5 March CG 911-Ilmor V10	collision with Capelli on lap 1
ret	BRAZILIAN GP	Interlagos	16	March F1	3.5 March CG 911-Ilmor V10	clutch
8	SPANISH GP	Barcelona	16	March F1	3.5 March CG 911-Ilmor V10	2 laps behind
12	SAN MARINO GP	Imola	16	March F1	3.5 March CG 911-Ilmor V10	3 laps behind
ret	MONACO GP	Monte Carlo	16	March F1	3.5 March CG 911-Ilmor V10	gearbox
4	CANADIAN GP	Montreal	16	March F1	3.5 March CG 911-Ilmor V10	1 lap behind
ret	FRENCH GP	Magny Cours	16	March F1	3.5 March CG 911-Ilmor V10	gearbox
ret	BRITISH GP	Silverstone	16	March F1	3.5 March CG 911-Ilmor V10	gearbox
16	GERMAN GP	Hockenheim	16	March F1	3.5 March CG 911-Ilmor V10	3 laps behind
ret	HUNGARIAN GP	Hungaroring	16	March F1	3.5 March CG 911-Ilmor V10	collision with Grouillard
11	BELGIAN GP	Spa	16	March F1	3.5 March CG 911-Ilmor V10	1 lap behind
10	ITALIAN GP	Monza	16	March F1	3.5 March CG 911-Ilmor V10	3 laps behind
ret	PORTUGUESE GP	Estoril	16	March F1	3.5 March CG 911-Ilmor V10	oil cooler/gearbox

1993

	Race	Circuit	No	Entrant	Car/Engine	Comment
ret	SOUTH AFRICAN GP	Kyalami	29	Sauber	3.5 Sauber C12-Ilmor V10	electronics
ret	BRAZILIAN GP	Interlagos	29	Sauber	3.5 Sauber C12-Ilmor V10	overheating
ret	EUROPEAN GP	Donington	29	Sauber	3.5 Sauber C12-Ilmor V10	hit by Andretti on lap 1
ret	SAN MARINO GP	Imola	29	Sauber	3.5 Sauber C12-Ilmor V10	engine
ret	SPANISH GP	Barcelona	29	Sauber	3.5 Sauber C12-Ilmor V10	engine
13	MONACO GP	Monte Carlo	29	Sauber	3.5 Sauber C12-Ilmor V10	collision-Lehto-p stop/4 laps behind
6	CANADIAN GP	Montreal	29	Sauber	3.5 Sauber C12-Ilmor V10	1 lap behind
ret	FRENCH GP	Magny Cours	29	Sauber	3.5 Sauber C12-Ilmor V10	gearbox
ret	BRITISH GP	Silverstone	29	Sauber	3.5 Sauber C12-Ilmor V10	spun off
9	GERMAN GP	Hockenheim	29	Sauber	3.5 Sauber C12-Ilmor V10	1 lap behind
6	HUNGARIAN GP	Hungaroring	29	Sauber	3.5 Sauber C12-Ilmor V10	1 lap behind
ret	BELGIAN GP	Spa	29	Sauber	3.5 Sauber C12-Ilmor V10	engine
4	ITALIAN GP	Monza	29	Sauber	3.5 Sauber C12-Ilmor V10	1 lap behind
5	PORTUGUESE GP	Estoril	29	Sauber	3.5 Sauber C12-Ilmor V10	1 lap behind
ret	JAPANESE GP	Suzuka	29	Sauber	3.5 Sauber C12-Ilmor V10	stuck throttle
15/ret	AUSTRALIAN GP	Adelaide	29	Sauber	3.5 Sauber C12-Ilmor V10	brake disc-spun off/5 laps behind

GP Starts: 32　GP Wins: 0　Pole positions: 0　Fastest laps: 0　Points: 10

WESTBURY, Peter (GB) b 26/5/1938

1969

	Race	Circuit	No	Entrant	Car/Engine	Comment
9	GERMAN GP (F2)	Nürburgring	31	Felday Engineering Ltd	1.6 Brabham BT30-Cosworth 4	5th in F2 class/1 lap behind

1970

	Race	Circuit	No	Entrant	Car/Engine	Comment
dnq	US GP	Watkins Glen	32	Yardley Team BRM	3.0 BRM P153 V12	

GP Starts: 1　GP Wins: 0　Pole positions: 0　Fastest laps: 0　Points: 0

WHARTON, Ken (GB) b 21/3/1916 – d 12/1/1957

1952

	Race	Circuit	No	Entrant	Car/Engine	Comment
4	SWISS GP	Bremgarten	22	Scuderia Franera	2.0 Frazer Nash FN4B-Bristol 6	2 laps behind
ret	BELGIAN GP	Spa	36	Scuderia Franera	2.0 Frazer Nash FN4B-Bristol 6	spun off
ret	DUTCH GP	Zandvoort	34	Scuderia Franera	2.0 Frazer Nash 421-Bristol 6	transmission
9	ITALIAN GP	Monza	40	Scuderia Franera	2.0 Cooper T20-Bristol 6	4 laps behind

1953

	Race	Circuit	No	Entrant	Car/Engine	Comment
ret	DUTCH GP	Zandvoort	32	Ken Wharton	2.0 Cooper T23-Bristol 6	rear suspension
ret	FRENCH GP	Reims	40	Ken Wharton	2.0 Cooper T23-Bristol 6	engine
8	BRITISH GP	Silverstone	16	Ken Wharton	2.0 Cooper T23-Bristol 6	
7	SWISS GP	Bremgarten	20	Ken Wharton	2.0 Cooper T23-Bristol 6	3 laps behind
nc	ITALIAN GP	Monza	30	Ken Wharton	2.0 Cooper T23-Bristol 6	13 laps behind

1954

	Race	Circuit	No	Entrant	Car/Engine	Comment
ret	FRENCH GP	Reims	42	Owen Racing Organisation	2.5 Maserati 250F 6	transmission
8	BRITISH GP	Silverstone	8	Owen Racing Organisation	2.5 Maserati 250F 6	4 laps behind
dns	GERMAN GP	Nürburgring	17	Owen Racing Organisation	2.5 Maserati 250F 6	withdrawn during practice
6	SWISS GP	Bremgarten	18	Owen Racing Organisation	2.5 Maserati 250F 6	2 laps behind
8	SPANISH GP	Pedralbes	28	Owen Racing Organisation	2.5 Maserati 250F 6	6 laps behind

1955

	Race	Circuit	No	Entrant	Car/Engine	Comment
nc*	BRITISH GP	Aintree	28	Vandervell Products Ltd	2.5 Vanwall 4	* Schell took over car
ret	ITALIAN GP	Monza	44	Vandervell Products Ltd	2.5 Vanwall 4	fuel injection pump mounting

GP Starts: 15　GP Wins: 0　Pole positions: 0　Fastest laps: 0　Points: 3

GRAHAM WHITEHEAD

Graham began racing Peter's ERA in 1951, and then drove his F2 Alta in the 1952 British GP, before a long and generally successful period when he competed in Jaguar and Aston Martin sports cars, often paired with his half-brother. Their greatest success together was second place in the 1958 Le Mans 24 Hours, only weeks before the crash in the Tour de France in which Peter was killed. Graham escaped serious injury and returned to competition racing an Aston Martin and then a Ferrari 250GT until the end of the 1961 season.

PETER WHITEHEAD

A throwback to the age of the truly amateur driver, Whitehead, a wealthy businessman, had the means with which to indulge his passion for motor sport in the best possible fashion. He began racing in 1934 and was soon making a name for himself in an ERA. He took the car to Australia in 1938 and won the Grand Prix at the Bathurst circuit.

His trusty ERA was back in action after the war and took second place in the 1947 British Empire Trophy at the Isle of Man. The following year he was seriously injured – not racing, but in an air crash at Croydon aerodrome when preparing to fly to Milan to arrange the purchase of a Ferrari 125. It was the 1949 season before he was able to put the green-painted machine through its paces in competition. He looked set to win the French GP at Reims, until gearbox problems dropped him to third place, but he did triumph in Czechoslovakia, becoming the first Briton to win a major race abroad since Seaman. His successes with the Ferrari continued into the 1950 season when he took the Jersey Road Race and the Ulster Trophy. Despite his amateur status, Peter was certainly no slouch as a driver and he scored some excellent Continental placings in the 1951 season with the Ferrari, but the highlight of his year was undoubtedly a glorious Le Mans win with Peter Walker for Jaguar.

The 1952 and 1953 seasons saw Whitehead campaigning an Alta and a Cooper-Alta in addition to his Ferrari, but he was now finding it more rewarding to race sports cars, where the chances of success were greater. In 1953, with a D-Type Jaguar, he won the Reims 12 Hours with Moss and the Hyères 12 Hours with Tom Cole. He triumphed again in the Reims 12 Hours the following year, sharing a works Jaguar with Ken Wharton, but after his last British GP appearance, Peter was little seen in Formula 1, preferring to concentrate on his newly acquired Cooper-Jaguar sports car and Libre events with his Ferrari 3-litre – particularly in the Antipodes, where he often raced during the English winter.

His last great performance came in the 1958 Le Mans 24 Hours, when he shared the second-placed Aston Martin with his half-brother Graham. Just a couple of months later Peter lost his life during the Tour de France when the pair's Jaguar, with Graham at the wheel, crashed over a bridge parapet into a ravine, injuring the driver but killing his unfortunate passenger.

WHITEHEAD, Graham (GB) b 15/4/1922 – d 15/1/1981

1952

	Race	Circuit	No	Entrant	Car/Engine	Comment
12	BRITISH GP	Silverstone	1	Peter Whitehead	2.0 Alta F2 4	5 laps behind

GP Starts: 1   GP Wins: 0   Pole positions: 0   Fastest laps: 0   Points: 0

WHITEHEAD, Peter (GB) b 12/11/1914 – d 21/9/1958

1950

	Race	Circuit	No	Entrant	Car/Engine	Comment
dns	MONACO GP	Monte Carlo	28	Peter Whitehead	1.5 s/c Ferrari 125 V12	engine in practice
3	FRENCH GP	Reims	14	Peter Whitehead	1.5 s/c Ferrari 125 V12	3 laps behind
7	ITALIAN GP	Monza	8	Peter Whitehead	1.5 s/c Ferrari 125 V12	8 laps behind

1951

	Race	Circuit	No	Entrant	Car/Engine	Comment
ret	SWISS GP	Bremgarten	16	Scuderia Ferrari	1.5 s/c Ferrari 125 V12	crashed-cut face
ret	FRENCH GP	Reims	24	Graham Whitehead	1.5 s/c Ferrari 125 V12	cylinder head gasket
9	BRITISH GP	Silverstone	14	G A Vandervell	4.5 Thinwall Ferrari 375F1 V12	6 laps behind
ret	ITALIAN GP	Monza	16	Peter Whitehead	1.5 s/c Ferrari 125 V12	engine

1952

	Race	Circuit	No	Entrant	Car/Engine	Comment
ret	FRENCH GP	Rouen	26	Peter Whitehead	2.0 Alta F2 4	clutch
10	BRITISH GP	Silverstone	21	Peter Whitehead	2.0 Ferrari 125/166/F2 V12	4 laps behind
dnq	ITALIAN GP	Monza	68	Peter Whitehead	2.0 Ferrari 125/166/F2 V12	

1953

	Race	Circuit	No	Entrant	Car/Engine	Comment
9	BRITISH GP	Silverstone	20	Atlantic Stable	2.0 Cooper T24-Alta 4	brake problems/12 laps behind

1954

	Race	Circuit	No	Entrant	Car/Engine	Comment
ret	BRITISH GP	Silverstone	21	Peter Whitehead	2.5 Cooper T24-Alta 4	engine

GP Starts: 10   GP Wins: 0   Pole positions: 0   Fastest laps: 0   Points: 4

WHITEHOUSE, Bill (GB) b 1/4/1909 – d 14/7/1957

1954

	Race	Circuit	No	Entrant	Car/Engine	Comment
ret	BRITISH GP	Silverstone	22	Bill Whitehouse	2.0 Connaught A Type-Lea Francis 4	*fuel system*

GP Starts: 1   GP Wins: 0   Pole positions: 0   Fastest laps: 0   Points: 0

WIDDOWS, Robin (GB) b 27/5/1942

1968

	Race	Circuit	No	Entrant	Car/Engine	Comment
ret	BRITISH GP	Brands Hatch	16	Cooper Car Co	3.0 Cooper T86-BRM V12	*ignition*

GP Starts: 1   GP Wins: 0   Pole positions: 0   Fastest laps: 0   Points: 0

WIETZES, Eppie (CDN) b 28/5/1938

1967

	Race	Circuit	No	Entrant	Car/Engine	Comment
ret	CANADIAN GP	Mosport Park	5	Team Lotus/Comstock Racing Team	3.0 Lotus 49-Cosworth V8	*wet ignition*

1974

	Race	Circuit	No	Entrant	Car/Engine	Comment
ret	CANADIAN GP	Mosport Park	50	Team Canada Formula 1 Racing	3.0 Brabham BT42-Cosworth V8	*transmission*

GP Starts: 2   GP Wins: 0   Pole positions: 0   Fastest laps: 0   Points: 0

WILDS, Mike (GB) b 7/1/1946

1974

	Race	Circuit	No	Entrant	Car/Engine	Comment
dnq	BRITISH GP	Brands Hatch	35	Dempster International Racing Team	3.0 March 731-Cosworth V8	
dnq	AUSTRIAN GP	Österreichring	22	Team Ensign	3.0 Ensign N174-Cosworth V8	
dnq	ITALIAN GP	Monza	25	Team Ensign	3.0 Ensign N174-Cosworth V8	
dnq	CANADIAN GP	Mosport Park	22	Team Ensign	3.0 Ensign N174-Cosworth V8	
nc	US GP	Watkins Glen	22	Team Ensign	3.0 Ensign N174-Cosworth V8	*pit stop-fuel pump/9 laps behind*

1975

	Race	Circuit	No	Entrant	Car/Engine	Comment
ret	ARGENTINE GP	Buenos Aires	14	Stanley BRM	3.0 BRM P201 V12	*oil scavenge pump drive belt*
ret	BRAZILIAN GP	Interlagos	14	Stanley BRM	3.0 BRM P201 V12	*electrics-damaged by loose nut*

1976

	Race	Circuit	No	Entrant	Car/Engine	Comment
dnq	BRITISH GP	Brands Hatch	40	Team P R Reilly	3.0 Shadow DN3-Cosworth V8	

GP Starts: 3   GP Wins: 0   Pole positions: 0   Fastest laps: 0   Points: 0

BILL WHITEHOUSE

One of the top 500 cc F3 Cooper drivers in the early 1950s, 'Big Bill' raced Gordon Watson's F2 Alta briefly in 1951 before breaking out of the tiddler class in 1954 with his own F2 Connaught, sensibly keeping to Libre and national events with the exception of the British GP.

After an accident, Bill retired but, once fit, the lure of the track proved too great for this enthusiast. In 1957, he bought an F2 Cooper-Climax, which he raced at Syracuse, and when his car suffered engine trouble at Reims he was delighted to be loaned the works Bob-tail 'streamliner' for the race. Tragically, he was to meet his death when a tyre appeared to burst as he approached Thillois, the car somersaulting and bursting into flames.

MIKE WILDS

A former Firestone employee, Mike spent seven years in club racing before hitting the Formula 3 trail in 1972. With backing from a loyal sponsor in Dempster Developments, Wilds was a leading runner and occasional winner in F3 before opting to race in F5000 in 1974, but in mid-season he was given the chance to race in Formula 1, initially with a March and then with Ensign. Invited to lead the BRM team for 1975, poor Wilds only lasted two races before the Stanley axe fell.

Shortly afterwards Mike split from his long-time sponsor, and rejoined the F5000 trail, racing an ex-works Shadow in 1976. Driving a Ralt, he took the F2 class championship in the 1978 Aurora AFX series, and since then he has been a star of club racing once more, enjoying himself immensely in historic and sports cars.

EPPIE WIETZES

One of Canada's most enduring and successful drivers at national level, Wietzes began racing as far back as 1958, and by the early 1960s was a leading sports and GT contender with such diverse cars as AC Cobras, Ford Mustangs and a Ford GT40.

In 1967 he hired the third works Lotus to race alongside Clark and Hill in the first World Championship Canadian GP. Switching to single-seaters, he was Canadian FA champion with a Lola T142 in 1969, and again the following year, this time with a McLaren M10. Eppie then became one of the leading privateers on the US F5000 circuit in the early seventies. He won a round at Donnybrooke in 1972 in his Lola T300 and drove superbly in 1974, generally being beaten only by Andretti and Redman. Wietzes ran a hired Brabham in the 1974 Grand Prix, without success, and after the demise of F5000 Stateside re-appeared in Trans-Am. In 1981 he took the CRC Championship with some stylish drives in Garretson Enterprises' Chevrolet Corvette.

ROBIN WIDDOWS

An Olympic-standard bobsleigh rider, Robin raced an MG Midget and a Lotus 23, winning the Autosport Class C championship in 1965, before successfully moving up to Formula 3 the following year. A syndicate of friends financed a season of Formula 2 in 1967 in a Brabham BT23, the highlight of which was a surprise win in the Rhine Cup at Hockenheim. For 1968, he joined the Chequered Flag team to drive a McLaren M4A, and took second place at Pau with a superb display.

Cooper gave him his only Grand Prix outing at that year's British GP, and he was back in Formula 2 with Bob Gerard in 1969. He did well once more, winning the Lottery GP and taking second at Reims, and also raced sports cars for Matra, finishing seventh at Le Mans with Galli. In 1970 he raced Alistair Walker's Brabham, again in F2, until suddenly retiring from racing in mid-season.

WILLIAMS. Jonathan (GB) b 26/10/1942

1967

	Race	Circuit	No	Entrant	Car/Engine	Comment
8	MEXICAN GP	Mexico City	12	Scuderia Ferrari SpA SEFAC	3.0 Ferrari 312/67 V12	

GP Starts: 1   GP Wins: 0   Pole positions: 0   Fastest laps: 0   Points: 0

WILLIAMSON, Roger (GB) b 2/2/1948 – d 29/7/1973

1973

	Race	Circuit	No	Entrant	Car/Engine	Comment
ret	BRITISH GP	Silverstone	14	STP March Racing/Wheatcroft Racing	3.0 March 721G/731-Cosworth V8	*multiple accident*
ret	DUTCH GP	Zandvoort	14	STP March Racing Team	3.0 March 721G/731-Cosworth V8	*fatal accident*

GP Starts: 2   GP Wins: 0   Pole positions: 0   Fastest laps: 0   Points: 0

WILSON, Vic (RSR) b 14/4/1931

1960

	Race	Circuit	No	Entrant	Car/Engine	Comment
ret	ITALIAN GP	Monza	30	Equipe Prideaux/Dick Gibson	1.5 Cooper T43-Climax 4	*engine*

1966

dns	BELGIAN GP	Spa	8	Team Chamaco-Collect	2.0 BRM T261-V8	*practice only-Bondurant raced car*

GP Starts: 1   GP Wins: 0   Pole positions: 0   Fastest laps: 0   Points: 0

WINKELHOCK, Manfred (D) b 6/10/1952 – d 12/8/1985

1980

	Race	Circuit	No	Entrant	Car/Engine	Comment
dnq	ITALIAN GP	Imola	30	Warsteiner Arrows Racing Team	3.0 Arrows A3-Cosworth V8	

1982

10	SOUTH AFRICAN GP	Kyalami	9	Team ATS	3.0 ATS D5-Cosworth V8	*2 laps behind*
5*	BRAZILIAN GP	Rio	9	Team ATS	3.0 ATS D5-Cosworth V8	** 1st & 2nd cars dsq/1 lap behind*
ret	US GP WEST	Long Beach	9	Team ATS	3.0 ATS D5-Cosworth V8	*collision with Borgudd*
dsq	SAN MARINO GP	Imola	9	Team ATS	3.0 ATS D5-Cosworth V8	*under weight limit*
ret	BELGIAN GP	Zolder	9	Team ATS	3.0 ATS D5-Cosworth V8	*clutch*
ret .	MONACO GP	Monte Carlo	9	Team ATS	3.0 ATS D5-Cosworth V8	*differential*
ret	US GP (DETROIT)	Detroit	9	Team ATS	3.0 ATS D5-Cosworth V8	*steering arm-accident*
dnq	CANADIAN GP	Montreal	9	Team ATS	3.0 ATS D5-Cosworth V8	
12	DUTCH GP	Zandvoort	9	Team ATS	3.0 ATS D5-Cosworth V8	*delayed start/2 laps behind*
dnq	BRITISH GP	Brands Hatch	9	Team ATS	3.0 ATS D5-Cosworth V8	
11	FRENCH GP	Paul Ricard	9	Team ATS	3.0 ATS D5-Cosworth V8	
ret	GERMAN GP	Hockenheim	9	Team ATS	3.0 ATS D5-Cosworth V8	*clutch/gearbox*
ret	AUSTRIAN GP	Österreichring	9	Team ATS	3.0 ATS D5-Cosworth V8	*spun off*
ret	SWISS GP	Dijon	9	Team ATS	3.0 ATS D5-Cosworth V8	*engine mounting*
dnq	ITALIAN GP	Monza	9	Team ATS	3.0 ATS D5-Cosworth V8	
nc	CAESARS PALACE GP	Las Vegas	9	Team ATS	3.0 ATS D5-Cosworth V8	*2 pit stops-misfire/13 laps behind*

1983

16	BRAZILIAN GP	Rio	9	Team ATS	1.5 t/c ATS D6-BMW 4	*pit stop-fuel feed/4 laps behind*
ret	US GP WEST	Long Beach	9	Team ATS	1.5 t/c ATS D6-BMW 4	*mechanical breakage-hit wall*
ret	FRENCH GP	Paul Ricard	9	Team ATS	1.5 t/c ATS D6-BMW 4	*exhaust-engine*
11	SAN MARINO GP	Imola	9	Team ATS	1.5 t/c ATS D6-BMW 4	*3 laps behind*
ret	MONACO GP	Monte Carlo	9	Team ATS	1.5 t/c ATS D6-BMW 4	*accident with Boesel*
ret	BELGIAN GP	Spa	9	Team ATS	1.5 t/c ATS D6-BMW 4	*lost rear wheel*
ret	US GP (DETROIT)	Detroit	9	Team ATS	1.5 t/c ATS D6-BMW 4	*hit wall*
9*	CANADIAN GP	Montreal	9	Team ATS	1.5 t/c ATS D6-BMW 4	** 9th place car dsq/2 pit stops*
ret	BRITISH GP	Silverstone	9	Team ATS	1.5 t/c ATS D6-BMW 4	*overheating*
dnq	GERMAN GP	Hockenheimq	9	Team ATS	1.5 t/c ATS D6-BMW 4	
ret	AUSTRIAN GP	Österreichring	9	Team ATS	1.5 t/c ATS D6-BMW 4	*overheating*
dsq	DUTCH GP	Zandvoort	9	Team ATS	1.5 t/c ATS D6-BMW 4	*overtook cars on warm-up lap*
ret	ITALIAN GP	Monza	9	Team ATS	1.5 t/c ATS D6-BMW 4	*broken exhaust*
8	EUROPEAN GP	Brands Hatch	9	Team ATS	1.5 t/c ATS D6-BMW 4	*pit stop-tyres*
ret	SOUTH AFRICAN GP	Kyalami	9	Team ATS	1.5 t/c ATS D6-BMW 4	*engine*

1984

dns	BRAZILIAN GP	Rio	14	Team ATS	1.5 t/c ATS D7-BMW 4	*disqualified in practice*
ret	SOUTH AFRICAN GP	Kyalami	14	Team ATS	1.5 t/c ATS D7-BMW 4	*engine*
ret	BELGIAN GP	Zolder	14	Team ATS	1.5 t/c ATS D7-BMW 4	*electrics/exhaust*
ret	SAN MARINO GP	Imola	14	Team ATS	1.5 t/c ATS D7-BMW 4	*turbo*
ret	FRENCH GP	Dijon	14	Team ATS	1.5 t/c ATS D7-BMW 4	*clutch*
ret	MONACO GP	Monte Carlo	14	Team ATS	1.5 t/c ATS D7-BMW 4	*spun off*
8	CANADIAN GP	Montreal	14	Team ATS	1.5 t/c ATS D7-BMW 4	*2 laps behind*
ret	US GP (DETROIT)	Detroit	14	Team ATS	1.5 t/c ATS D7-BMW 4	*accident*
8	US GP (DALLAS)	Dallas	14	Team ATS	1.5 t/c ATS D7-BMW 4	*3 laps behind*
ret	BRITISH GP	Brands Hatch	14	Team ATS	1.5 t/c ATS D7-BMW 4	*spun off*
ret	GERMAN GP	Hockenheim	14	Team ATS	1.5 t/c ATS D7-BMW 4	*turbo boost/gearbox*
dns	AUSTRIAN GP	Österreichring	14	Team ATS	1.5 t/c ATS D7-BMW 4	*gearbox in warm-up*
ret	DUTCH GP	Zandvoort	14	Team ATS	1.5 t/c ATS D7-BMW 4	*spun off*
dns	ITALIAN GP	Monza	14	Team ATS	1.5 t/c ATS D7-BMW 4	*gearbox in warm-up*
10	PORTUGUESE GP	Estoril	2	MRD International	1.5 t/c Brabham BT53-BMW 4	*1 lap behind*

1985

13	BRAZILIAN GP	Rio	9	Skoal Bandit Formula 1 Team	1.5 t/c RAM 03-Hart 4	*4 laps behind*
nc	PORTUGUESE GP	Estoril	9	Skoal Bandit Formula 1 Team	1.5 t/c RAM 03-Hart 4	*tyre problems/17 laps behind*
ret	SAN MARINO GP	Imola	9	Skoal Bandit Formula 1 Team	1.5 t/c RAM 03-Hart 4	*engine*
dnq	MONACO GP	Monte Carlo	9	Skoal Bandit Formula 1 Team	1.5 t/c RAM 03-Hart 4	
ret	CANADIAN GP	Montreal	9	Skoal Bandit Formula 1 Team	1.5 t/c RAM 03-Hart 4	*hit by de Cesaris-hit wall*
ret	US GP (DETROIT)	Detroit	9	Skoal Bandit Formula 1 Team	1.5 t/c RAM 03-Hart 4	*turbo*
12	FRENCH GP	Paul Ricard	9	Skoal Bandit Formula 1 Team	1.5 t/c RAM 03-Hart 4	*3 laps behind*
ret	BRITISH GP	Silverstone	9	Skoal Bandit Formula 1 Team	1.5 t/c RAM 03-Hart 4	*turbo*
ret	GERMAN GP	Nürburgring	9	Skoal Bandit Formula 1 Team	1.5 t/c RAM 03-Hart 4	*engine*

GP Starts: 47   GP Wins: 0   Pole positions: 0   Fastest laps: 0   Points: 2

JONATHAN WILLIAMS

An Englishman abroad. Williams, based in Italy, was plucked from the relative obscurity of the de Sanctis F3 team to join Ferrari in 1967, competing in but one Grand Prix and a single F2 race, in addition to a handful of sports and Can-Am outings, before being discarded as casually as he seemed to have been signed. Certainly Jonathan had been amazingly successful in European F3 in 1965-66, but his sojourn at Maranello did his career prospects no favours. A Formula 1 project for Abarth proved abortive, leaving him scratching for rides thereafter. He did some Formula 2 in 1968, winning the Rhine Cup race for his old F3 racing partner Frank Williams, and then raced the works Serenissima and various other privateer sports cars into the early seventies before retiring.

ROGER WILLIAMSON

Williamson is remembered as a smashing bloke, completely without pretension, and a terrific talent, who was needlessly to pay the ultimate price in front of millions of TV viewers that tragic day at Zandvoort in 1973.

Roger had a successful karting career behind him when, with encouragement from his father, he took up circuit racing in an 850 Mini, winning 14 races in 1968. Deciding to try single-seaters, he purchased a Cooper T71, which was unfortunately burnt out in a garage fire. However, Roger took the engine and fitted it to a Ford Anglia and it proved to be a potent combination. In 1970 he won the 1000 cc class of the Hepolite Glazier championship with ease, and decided to try Formula 3 the following year. Despite his inexperience, he was soon a front-runner, with his spectacular driving in a March 713 catching the eye. He was fortunate at this time to be helped financially by local businessman and racing enthusiast Tom Wheatcroft, and the pair became firm friends, with Tom guiding his rise towards the top.

Having won the Lombank F3 championship, Williamson stayed in the formula for a further year and convincingly took both the major F3 titles that season. His foray into Formula 2 was not so happy, but it was good experience for a planned season in 1973 with GRD. The car turned out to be no match for the dominant March chassis, and Wheatcroft swiftly provided his charge with the equipment he needed. Almost immediately Roger won the Lottery GP at Monza, and would have taken another victory at Misano but for engine problems, establishing himself as a truly serious talent. A season in Formula 1 was the goal in 1974, and to this end Wheatcroft hired an STP March for a couple of races to allow Williamson to become acclimatised. At Silverstone he was eliminated in the now notorious Jody Scheckter-induced carnage, and then came Zandvoort. It is thought a tyre failed, sending his car into an inadequately secured barrier which launched it across the track. The March came to rest upside down and on fire, with poor Roger trapped in the cockpit. Scandalously, nobody came to his help, apart from the brave David Purley, who single-handedly attempted to right the inverted machine. Then the fire caught hold and a truly nightmarish scenario was complete. For poor Williamson it was a cruel and gruesome end.

VIC WILSON

Vic was born in England, but spent his teens living in South Africa. He began racing in Rhodesia in the late fifties, finding success with a variety of MGs and then a Lotus XI. Plans to race a Lotus in England went awry when the car was written off, but he then approached Dick Gibson, who was languishing in hospital after recently crashing his almost new Cooper. Having repaired the machine, Wilson went racing along with Bruce Halford and Keith Ballisat, competing in the boycotted Italian GP of 1960.

Settling in Yorkshire, Vic did not race at all between 1961 and 1963, but at the behest of his wealthy cousin Bernard White he returned late in 1964, before a busy season racing a Lotus 30 and a Ferrari 250LM in 1965. Team Chamaco Collect then planned a full season of Grands Prix in 1966 with a couple of BRMs, but after Vic took a distant fourth at the Syracuse GP and practised briefly at Spa Bob Bondurant became the team's sole driver, leaving Wilson in the cold.

MANFRED WINKELHOCK

Manfred was a likeable man, friendly and unassuming, for whom Formula 1 was not the be-all-and-end-all of his life. He was quite content to enjoy his racing in sports-prototypes and touring cars, happy to be part of the Grand Prix scene while it wanted him. He started racing in the Scirocco Cup in 1976, but soon began a long and happy association with BMW which saw him rapidly progress through their junior team from saloons to Formula 2. He was to spend three seasons in the formula, coming close to victory at Hockenheim in 1981, when his troubled Ralt was overhauled almost within sight of the finish. An abortive drive for Arrows apart, Manfred's Grand Prix career began with the ATS team at the start of 1982. There were those who thought his style harsh and crude, but there was no doubting either his commitment or bravery as he manhandled the cars for all they were worth. Unfortunately, as the statistics show, his Formula 1 efforts were largely frustrated by a catalogue of retirements and he was no doubt glad to be able to go racing properly in the Kremer Porsche – particularly in 1985, when the season had started so brightly with a second place at Mugello and then a win at Monza, teamed with Marc Surer. Tragedy was to strike at Mosport, however, when in an unexplained accident Manfred's Porsche left the track at high speed. The driver was finally freed from the wreckage, and taken to hospital critically injured. Though no bones were broken, his head injuries were severe, and he died some 24 hours later.

REINE WISELL

A contemporary and rival of Ronnie Peterson in Scandinavian Formula 3, Wisell did not quite have the talent to make a top-line career, despite a most promising start in 1970 when, thrust into the Lotus team at Watkins Glen, he took the 72C into third place.

His career had begun as far back as 1962 with an unreliable Mini Cooper and he then switched to an Anglia, which was similarly troublesome, but Reine plugged away, returning to a Mini in 1965 to take the runner-up position in the Swedish Group 5 championship. Early in 1966 he swapped his saloon for a Cooper F3 car and soon began to show a great deal of flair. By the end of that season he had done well enough to progress to a Brabham bought from his experienced rival Picko Troberg, and he was the man to watch in 1967, comfortably taking the Swedish F3 title, but more importantly making an impression in his occasional appearances in European events. It was now time to spread his wings and compete outside Scandinavia on a regular basis. He travelled down to Bologna with Ronnie Peterson and the two Swedes each ordered themselves a new F3 Tecno for the 1968 season. Reine gained valuable experience racing abroad that year and scored 11 wins in total, while his younger rival concentrated on racing at home and took the Swedish crown.

In 1969 Wisell took up an offer to race F3 and GT cars for Chevron, but generally endured a disappointing time. Feeling that he now needed to find a more challenging arena, Reine was persuaded to join Jo Bonnier's sports car team in 1970, and also took over the Sid Taylor F5000 McLaren with great success, winning three of the final four rounds towards the end of the year. Of course, by then his big chance had arrived, his performance and that of Emerson Fittipaldi ensuring their places in the Lotus team for 1971. It was to be a hectic year for the Swede, who did a full Formula 2 programme highlighted by a splendid win in the Pau GP. His performances in Formula 1 were solid but not inspired, and Chapman decided to promote his then current hot-shot Dave Walker into the team for 1972.

Wisell moved to BRM who were running a multi-car squad which spread the available resources too thinly. Nothing worthwhile was achieved and Reine even made a brief return to the Lotus fold in place of the luckless Walker for the Canadian GP. Wisell, no longer considered to have sufficient Grand Prix potential, drifted into other forms of the sport. His superb win in the F2 Eifelrennen was a timely reminder of the talent that still lurked, but his subsequent occasional Grand Prix appearances brought no joy.

After sharing a Gulf/John Wyer GR7 with Vern Schuppan in 1974, but gaining little success, Wisell raced a Porsche Carrera with distinction in 1975 before drifting out of the sport.

ROELOF WUNDERINK

Roelof began his racing career in a Simca in 1970, before progressing to Formula Ford and winning the Dutch championship in 1972. With the benefit of strong sponsorship from HB alarm systems, Wunderink rushed through Formula 3 and F5000 during the next two seasons, and found himself in a works-backed Ensign for 1975 without showing anything like the form to justify such a chance. Nevertheless, he bravely got on with the job, hampered at first by having to make do with the '74 car and then being sidelined with a broken cheekbone and concussion after a testing accident in an F5000 car. At the end of the season, having tried but failed, the quiet Dutchman stepped out of the racing limelight.

ALESSANDRO ZANARDI

This untypically quiet and unassuming Italian spent seven seasons racing karts before taking the Italian Formula 3 trail in 1988. His promise shone through the following year but his Racing for Italy Ralt RT33 was handicapped when a switch to unleaded fuel in mid-season hobbled his Toyota engine and his results inevitably suffered. However, switching to a Dallara chassis in 1990, Alessandro finished second in the championship just three points adrift of Roberto Colciago, winning two of the series' 12 rounds.

Having made an inauspicious debut in F3000 at the tail-end of the 1989 season, nothing much was expected of Zanardi when he took his place in the new Il Barone Rampante team for the start of the 1991 campaign. Extensive pre-season testing gave the Italian an early advantage, but despite victories at Vallelunga and Mugello he eventually lost the championship to the more consistent finishing record of Christian Fittipaldi. Not that it really mattered, for by this time Zanardi had been chosen to fill the Jordan seat vacated by Schumacher for the final three races of the season. His hopes of a place in the Tyrrell line-up for 1992 were dashed when the team opted for de Cesaris, but he secured a testing contract with Benetton and ultimately made three unhappy appearances for Minardi in place of his former F3000 adversary Fittipaldi, who had injured his back.

Alessandro was offered a chance to prove himself in 1993 when Mika Häkkinen left Lotus for McLaren, and Peter Collins was to be pleased with the Italian's early form. He drove a storming race at Monaco, where he was unlucky to miss the points, and his contribution to the development of the team's highly complex active suspension programme drew warm praise, but his season came to a premature end after an extremely violent 150 mph accident at Spa's notorious Eau Rouge which finished with his car destroyed and Zanardi in hospital with severe concussion. Not unnaturally, he took quite some while to recover from this shaking, and was rested in favour of Pedro Lamy for the remaining Grands Prix. Unfortunately there is little room for sentiment in Formula 1, and the Portuguese hot-shot retained the ride for the 1994 season, although Zanardi has been kept on in the role of test driver.

WISELL, Reine (S) b 30/9/1941

1970

	Race	Circuit	No	Entrant	Car/Engine	Comment
3	US GP	Watkins Glen	23	Gold Leaf Team Lotus	3.0 Lotus 72C-Cosworth V8	
10	MEXICAN GP	Mexico City	23	Gold Leaf Team Lotus	3.0 Lotus 72C-Cosworth V8	*3 pit stops-oil line/9 laps behind*

1971

	Race	Circuit	No	Entrant	Car/Engine	Comment
4	SOUTH AFRICAN GP	Kyalami	3	Gold Leaf Team Lotus	3.0 Lotus 72C-Cosworth V8	
12	SPANISH GP	Montjuich Park	3	Gold Leaf Team Lotus	3.0 Lotus 72C-Cosworth V8	*pit stop-gearbox/17 laps behind*
ret	MONACO GP	Monte Carlo	2	Gold Leaf Team Lotus	3.0 Lotus 72C-Cosworth V8	*rear hub bearing*
dsq	DUTCH GP	Zandvoort	14	Gold Leaf Team Lotus	3.0 Lotus 72D-Cosworth V8	*reversed into pits*
6	FRENCH GP	Paul Ricard	2	Gold Leaf Team Lotus	3.0 Lotus 72D-Cosworth V8	
nc	BRITISH GP	Silverstone	3	Gold Leaf Team Lotus	Turbine Lotus 56B-Pratt & Witney	*2 pit stops/11 laps behind*
8	GERMAN GP	Nürburgring	9	Gold Leaf Team Lotus	3.0 Lotus 72D-Cosworth V8	*left on grid-fuel pressure*
4	AUSTRIAN GP	Österreichring	3	Gold Leaf Team Lotus	3.0 Lotus 72D-Cosworth V8	
5	CANADIAN GP	Mosport Park	3	Gold Leaf Team Lotus	3.0 Lotus 72D-Cosworth V8	*1 lap behind*
ret	US GP	Watkins Glen	3	Gold Leaf Team Lotus	3.0 Lotus 72D-Cosworth V8	*brakes-hit barrier*

1972

	Race	Circuit	No	Entrant	Car/Engine	Comment
ret	ARGENTINE GP	Buenos Aires	4	Marlboro BRM	3.0 BRM P153 V12	*water leak*
ret	SPANISH GP	Jarama	10	Austria Marlboro BRM	3.0 BRM P160B V12	*went off at end of main straight*
ret	MONACO GP	Monte Carlo	28	Marlboro BRM	3.0 BRM P160B V12	*engine*
ret	FRENCH GP	Clermont Ferrand	24	Marlboro BRM	3.0 BRM P160B V12	*gear linkage*
ret	GERMAN GP	Nürburgring	18	Marlboro BRM	3.0 BRM P160C V12	*engine seized*
12	ITALIAN GP	Monza	24	Marlboro BRM	3.0 BRM P160C V12	*pit stop-gearbox/4 laps behind*
ret	CANADIAN GP	Mosport Park	6	John Player Team Lotus	3.0 Lotus 72D-Cosworth V8	*engine*
10	US GP	Watkins Glen	12	John Player Team Lotus	3.0 Lotus 72D-Cosworth V8	*2 laps behind*

1973

	Race	Circuit	No	Entrant	Car/Engine	Comment
dns	SWEDISH GP	Anderstorp	27	Team Pierre Robert	3.0 March 731-Cosworth V8	*suspension in warm-up*
ret	FRENCH GP	Paul Ricard	15	Clarke-Mordaunt-Guthrie-Durlacher	3.0 March 721G/731-Cosworth V8	*engine*

1974

	Race	Circuit	No	Entrant	Car/Engine	Comment
ret	SWEDISH GP	Anderstorp	9	March Engineering	3.0 March 741-Cosworth V8	*suspension*

GP Starts: 22   GP Wins: 0   Pole positions: 0   Fastest laps: 0   Points: 13

WUNDERINK, Roelof (NL) b12/12/1948

1975

	Race	Circuit	No	Entrant	Car/Engine	Comment
ret	SPANISH GP	Montjuich Park	31	HB Bewaking Team Ensign	3.0 Ensign N174-Cosworth V8	*driveshaft*
dnq	MONACO GP	Monte Carlo	31	HB Bewaking Team Ensign	3.0 Ensign N174-Cosworth V8	
dnq	BRITISH GP	Silverstone	31	HB Bewaking Team Ensign	3.0 Ensign N175-Cosworth V8	
nc	AUSTRIAN GP	Österreichring	33	HB Bewaking Team Ensign	3.0 Ensign N174-Cosworth V8	*pit stop-tyres/4 laps behind*
dnq	ITALIAN GP	Monza	31	HB Bewaking Team Ensign	3.0 Ensign N174-Cosworth V8	
ret	US GP	Watkins Glen	31	HB Bewaking Team Ensign	3.0 Ensign N175-Cosworth V8	*gearbox*

GP Starts: 3   GP Wins: 0   Pole positions: 0   Fastest laps: 0   Points: 0

ZANARDI, Alessandro (I) b 23/10/1966

1991

	Race	Circuit	No	Entrant	Car/Engine	Comment
9	SPANISH GP	Barcelona	32	Team 7UP Jordan	3.5 Jordan 191-FordHB V8	*1 lap behind*
ret	JAPANESE GP	Suzuka	32	Team 7UP Jordan	3.5 Jordan 191-FordHB V8	*gearbox*
9	AUSTRALIAN GP	Adelaide	32	Team 7UP Jordan	3.5 Jordan 191-FordHB V8	*race stopped after 14 laps-rain*

1992

	Race	Circuit	No	Entrant	Car/Engine	Comment
dnq	BRITISH GP	Silverstone	23	Minardi Team	3.5 Minardi M192-Lamborghini V12	
ret	GERMAN GP	Hockenheim	23	Minardi Team	3.5 Minardi M192-Lamborghini V12	*clutch on first lap*
dnq	HUNGARIAN GP	Hungaroring	23	Minardi Team	3.5 Minardi M192-Lamborghini V12	

1993

	Race	Circuit	No	Entrant	Car/Engine	Comment
ret	SOUTH AFRICAN GP	Kyalami	11	Team Lotus	3.5 Lotus 107B-Ford HB V8	*collision with Hill*
6	BRAZILIAN GP	Interlagos	11	Team Lotus	3.5 Lotus 107B-Ford HB V8	*1 lap behind*
8	EUROPEAN GP	Donington	11	Team Lotus	3.5 Lotus 107B-Ford HB V8	*4 laps behind*
ret	SAN MARINO GP	Imola	11	Team Lotus	3.5 Lotus 107B-Ford HB V8	*spun into wall-lost wheel*
ret	SPANISH GP	Barcelona	11	Team Lotus	3.5 Lotus 107B-Ford HB V8	*engine*
7	MONACO GP	Monte Carlo	11	Team Lotus	3.5 Lotus 107B-Ford HB V8	*2 laps behind*
11	CANADIAN GP	Montreal	11	Team Lotus	3.5 Lotus 107B-Ford HB V8	*spin/2 laps behind*
ret	FRENCH GP	Magny Cours	11	Team Lotus	3.5 Lotus 107B-Ford HB V8	*active suspension failure*
ret	BRITISH GP	Silverstone	11	Team Lotus	3.5 Lotus 107B-Ford HB V8	*lost body panel-spun off*
ret	GERMAN GP	Hockenheim	11	Team Lotus	3.5 Lotus 107B-Ford HB V8	*spun off*
ret	HUNGARIAN GP	Hungaroring	11	Team Lotus	3.5 Lotus 107B-Ford HB V8	*gearbox failure*
dns	BELGIAN GP	Spa	11	Team Lotus	3.5 Lotus 107B-Ford HB V8	*accident in Fri a.m. practice*

GP Starts: 15   GP Wins: 0   Pole positions: 0   Fastest laps: 0   Points: 1

RENZO ZORZI

Zorzi has the same date of birth as Emerson Fittipaldi, but not the same racing pedigree. A graduate of Italian Formula 3 while acting as a test driver at Pirelli, Renzo shot to prominence with a surprise win in the 1975 Monaco F3 support race, after Conny Andersson had been given a one-minute penalty and the other front-runners had eliminated each other.

His immediate reward was a Williams seat for the Italian GP, where he drove sensibly to the finish. Zorzi started the 1976 season in the newly constituted Wolf-Williams *équipe*, but was dropped after just one Grand Prix, being replaced by Michel Leclère. For Zorzi, it was back to F3 in a Modus while he waited for a further opportunity, which came in 1977, when Francesco Ambrosio sponsored his drive in the Shadow team. A sixth place in the Brazilian GP was achieved mainly because of a high rate of attrition, and soon Renzo himself was to become a Formula 1 casualty, losing his drive after falling out with Ambrosio. He reappeared towards the end of the decade in occasional rounds of the World Championship of Makes, and then in the 1980 Aurora AFX Monza Lottery GP in Charles Clowes' Arrows A1B, retiring after a collision.

RICARDO ZUNINO

During two seasons with a March-BMW in Formula 2 (1977-78), this Argentine driver's performances were nothing more than thoroughly ordinary, despite his having access to competitive machinery. A lacklustre start to his third year in the formula convinced him a switch to the less demanding world of the Aurora F1 championship would be beneficial, and he was right. Racing an Arrows in the final nine rounds of the series, Zunino won one race and finished five others in the top six.

Somewhat ambitiously, he managed to step into Grand Prix racing at the end of 1979, when Lauda suddenly quit at Montreal, and he started 1980 still driving the second Brabham BT49, but was eased out of the team in mid-season when Rebaque took his place. Ricardo was back with Brabham at the start of 1981, but only for the non-championship South African GP, in which he finished eighth. He then joined Tyrrell to contest the two South American rounds, before giving way to a shining new talent by the name of Michele Alboreto.

ZORZI, Renzo (I) b 12/12/1946

1975

	Race	Circuit	No	Entrant	Car/Engine	Comment
14	ITALIAN GP	Monza	20	Frank Williams Racing Cars	3.0 Williams FW03-Cosworth V8	6 laps behind
	1976					
9	BRAZILIAN GP	Interlagos	21	Frank Williams Racing Cars	3.0 Williams FW04-Cosworth V8	
	1977					
ret	ARGENTINE GP	Buenos Aires	17	Shadow Racing Team	3.0 Shadow DN5-Cosworth V8	gearbox
6	BRAZILIAN GP	Interlagos	17	Shadow Racing Team	3.0 Shadow DN5-Cosworth V8	1 lap behind
ret	SOUTH AFRICAN GP	Kyalami	17	Shadow Racing Team	3.0 Shadow DN8-Cosworth V8	engine
ret	US GP WEST	Long Beach	16	Shadow Racing Team	3.0 Shadow DN8-Cosworth V8	gearbox
ret	SPANISH GP	Jarama	16	Shadow Racing Team	3.0 Shadow DN8-Cosworth V8	engine

GP Starts: 7   GP Wins: 0   Pole positions: 0   Fastest laps: 0   Points: 1

ZUNINO, Ricardo (RA) b 13/4/1949

1979

	Race	Circuit	No	Entrant	Car/Engine	Comment
7	CANADIAN GP	Montreal	5	Parmalat Racing Team	3.0 Brabham BT49-Cosworth V8	pit stop-gear linkage/4 laps behind
ret	US GP EAST	Watkins Glen	5	Parmalat Racing Team	3.0 Brabham BT49-Cosworth V8	spun off
	1980					
7	ARGENTINE GP	Buenos Aires	6	Parmalat Racing Team	3.0 Brabham BT49-Cosworth V8	2 laps behind
8	BRAZILIAN GP	Interlagos	6	Parmalat Racing Team	3.0 Brabham BT49-Cosworth V8	1 lap behind
10	SOUTH AFRICAN GP	Kyalami	6	Parmalat Racing Team	3.0 Brabham BT49-Cosworth V8	1 lap behind
ret	US GP WEST	Long Beach	6	Parmalat Racing Team	3.0 Brabham BT49-Cosworth V8	hit wall avoiding Mass on lap 1
ret	BELGIAN GP	Zolder	6	Parmalat Racing Team	3.0 Brabham BT49-Cosworth V8	clutch/gearbox
dnq	MONACO GP	Monte Carlo	6	Parmalat Racing Team	3.0 Brabham BT49-Cosworth V8	
ret	FRENCH GP	Paul Ricard	6	Parmalat Racing Team	3.0 Brabham BT49-Cosworth V8	clutch
	1981					
13	BRAZILIAN GP	Rio	4	Tyrrell Racing	3.0 Tyrrell 010-Cosworth V8	5 laps behind
13*	ARGENTINE GP	Buenos Aires	4	Tyrrell Racing	3.0 Tyrrell 010-Cosworth V8	* penalised 1 lap overshot chicane/-2 laps

GP Starts: 10   GP Wins: 0   Pole positions: 0   Fastest laps: 0   Points: 0

NON-STARTERS

DRIVERS WHO ATTEMPTED TO QUALIFY FOR A WORLD CHAMPIONSHIP GRAND PRIX WITHOUT STARTING A RACE

GIOVANNA AMATI   **MICHAEL BARTELS**   **ENRICO BERTAGGIA**   **GARY BRABHAM**   **GIANFRANCO BRANCATELLI**

ALAIN de CHANGY   **PEDRO CHAVES**   **KEVIN COGAN**   **WILLIE FERGUSON**   **HIROSHI FUSHIDA**

DAVINA GALICA   **DAVID KENNEDY**   **NAOKI HATTORI**   **MASAMI KUWASHIMA**   **CLAUDIO LANGES**

GIANCARLO MARTINI   **PERRY McCARTHY**   **JAC NELLEMAN**   **STEPHEN SOUTH**   **OTTO STUPPACHER**

TONY TRIMMER   **JACQUES VILLENEUVE**   **VOLKER WEIDLER**   **DESIRÉ WILSON**   **JOACHIM WINKELHOCK**

AMATI, Giovanna (I) b 20/7/1962

1992

	Race	Circuit	No	Entrant	Car/Engine	Comment
dnq	SOUTH AFRICAN GP	Kyalami	8	Motor Racing Developments Ltd	3.5 Brabham BT60B-Judd V10	
dnq	MEXICAN GP	Mexico City	8	Motor Racing Developments Ltd	3.5 Brabham BT60B-Judd V10	
dnq	BRAZILIAN GP	Interlagos	8	Motor Racing Developments Ltd	3.5 Brabham BT60B-Judd V10	

Lady driver who competed regularly in Italian national racing before reaching the limit of her abilities in F3000

BARTELS, Michael (D) b 8/3/1968

1991

	Race	Circuit	No	Entrant	Car/Engine	Comment
dnq	GERMAN GP	Hockenheim	12	Team Lotus	3.5 Lotus 102B-Judd V8	
dnq	HUNGARIAN GP	Hungaroring	12	Team Lotus	3.5 Lotus 102B-Judd V8	
dnq	ITALIAN GP	Monza	12	Team Lotus	3.5 Lotus 102B-Judd V8	
dnq	SPANISH GP	Barcelona	12	Team Lotus	3.5 Lotus 102B-Judd V8	

Star of German F3 in the late eighties, subsequently left in the shadows of Schumacher and Wendlinger

BAYARDO, Astrubel (BR)

1959

	Race	Circuit	No	Entrant	Car/Engine	Comment
dnq	FRENCH GP	Reims	36	Scuderia Centro Sud	2.5 Maserati 250F 6	*no practice time recorded*

BERTAGGIA, Enrico (I) b 19/9/1964

1989

	Race	Circuit	No	Entrant	Car/Engine	Comment
dnpq	BELGIAN GP	Spa	32	Coloni SpA	3.5 Coloni C3-Cosworth V8	
dnpq	ITALIAN GP	Monza	32	Coloni SpA	3.5 Coloni C3-Cosworth V8	
dnpq	PORTUGUESE GP	Estoril	32	Coloni SpA	3.5 Coloni C3-Cosworth V8	
dnpq	SPANISH GP	Jerez	32	Coloni SpA	3.5 Coloni C3-Cosworth V8	
dnpq	JAPANESE GP	Suzuka	32	Coloni SpA	3.5 Coloni C3-Cosworth V8	*no practice time recorded*
dnpq	AUSTRALIAN GP	Adelaide	32	Coloni SpA	3.5 Coloni C3-Cosworth V8	

1992

	Race	Circuit	No	Entrant	Car/Engine	Comment
dnp	SOUTH AFRICAN GP	Kyalami	35	Andrea Moda Formula	3.5 Coloni C4B-Judd V10	*team excluded from meeting*
dnp	MEXICAN GP	Mexico City	35	Andrea Moda Formula	3.5 Moda S921-Judd V10	*cars not ready-entry withdrawn*

BORDEAU, Jean-Manuel (F)

1961

	Race	Circuit	No	Entrant	Car/Engine	Comment
dnq	FRENCH GP	Reims	28	UDT Laystall Racing Team	1.5 Lotus 18/21-Climax 4	*car raced by Bianchi*

BRABHAM, Gary (AUS) b 29/3/1961

1990

	Race	Circuit	No	Entrant	Car/Engine	Comment
dnpq	US GP (PHOENIX)	Phoenix	39	Life Racing Engines	3.5 Life L190 W12	
dnpq	BRAZILIAN GP	Interlagos	39	Life Racing Engines	3.5 Life L190 W12	

Second son of Sir Jack. After an excellent British F3 record, career in limbo after Life fiasco. Now planning to set up his own team in Indy Lights

BRAMBILLA, Tino (Ernesto) (I)

1963

	Race	Circuit	No	Entrant	Car/Engine	Comment
dnq	ITALIAN GP	Monza	62	Scuderia Centro Sud	1.5 Cooper T53-Maserati 4	

1969

	Race	Circuit	No	Entrant	Car/Engine	Comment
dns	ITALIAN GP	Monza	10	Scuderia Ferrari SpA SEFAC	3.0 Ferrari 312/68/69 V12	*Rodriguez raced car*

Notoriously hard racer and elder brother of Vittorio. Tino raced works Formula 2 Ferraris with some success, but was never given a real F1 chance

BRANCATELLI, Gianfranco (I) b 18/1/1950

1979

	Race	Circuit	No	Entrant	Car/Engine	Comment
dnq	SPANISH GP	Jarama	36	Willi Kauhsen Racing Team	3.0 Kauhsen WK-Cosworth V8	
dnq	BELGIAN GP	Zolder	36	Willi Kauhsen Racing Team	3.0 Kauhsen WK-Cosworth V8	
dnpq	MONACO GP	Monte Carlo	24	Team Merzario	3.0 Merzario A2-Cosworth V8	

1970s Formula Italia and F3 star, who after his unhappy failures in F1 turned to a solid career in touring cars and Group C

CADE, Phil (USA) b 12/7/1916

1959

	Race	Circuit	No	Entrant	Car/Engine	Comment
dns	US GP	Sebring	22	Phil Cade	2.5 Maserati 250F 6	*mechanical problems in practice*

Amateur enthusiast who raced a Chrysler-engined 1936 Maserati in SCCA events during the 1950s

CHAVES Pedro (P) b 27/2/65

1991

	Race	Circuit	No	Entrant	Car/Engine	Comment
dnpq	US GP (PHOENIX)	Phoenix	31	Coloni Racing Srl	3.5 Coloni C4-Cosworth V8	
dnpq	BRAZILIAN GP	Interlagos	31	Coloni Racing Srl	3.5 Coloni C4-Cosworth V8	
dnpq	SAN MARINO GP	Imola	31	Coloni Racing Srl	3.5 Coloni C4-Cosworth V8	
dnpq	MONACO GP	Monte Carlo	31	Coloni Racing Srl	3.5 Coloni C4-Cosworth V8	
dnpq	CANADIAN GP	Montreal	31	Coloni Racing Srl	3.5 Coloni C4-Cosworth V8	
dnpq	MEXICAN GP	Mexico City	31	Coloni Racing Srl	3.5 Coloni C4-Cosworth V8	
dnpq	FRENCH GP	Magny Cours	31	Coloni Racing Srl	3.5 Coloni C4-Cosworth V8	
dnpq	BRITISH GP	Silverstone	31	Coloni Racing Srl	3.5 Coloni C4-Cosworth V8	
dnpq	GERMAN GP	Hockenheim	31	Coloni Racing Srl	3.5 Coloni C4-Cosworth V8	
dnpq	HUNGARIAN GP	Hungaroring	31	Coloni Racing Srl	3.5 Coloni C4-Cosworth V8	
dnpq	BELGIAN GP	Spa	31	Coloni Racing Srl	3.5 Coloni C4-Cosworth V8	
dnpq	ITALIAN GP	Monza	31	Coloni Racing Srl	3.5 Coloni C4-Cosworth V8	
dnpq	PORTUGUESE GP	Estoril	31	Coloni Racing Srl	3.5 Coloni C4-Cosworth V8	

1990 British F3000 champion, now racing in Indy Lights after moribund season with Coloni

CHANGY, Alain de (B)

1959

	Race	Circuit	No	Entrant	Car/Engine	Comment
dnq	MONACO GP	Monte Carlo	12	Equipe Nationale Belge	1.5 Cooper T51-Climax 4	

CHAPMAN, Colin (GB) b 19/5/1928 – d 16/12/1982

1956

	Race	Circuit	No	Entrant	Car/Engine	Comment
dns	FRENCH GP	Reims	26	Vandervell Products Ltd	2.5 Vanwall 4	*practice accident-car damaged*

Founder of Lotus, a true innovator whose designs changed the shape of Formula 1. Also a very good sports car driver, who could mix it with the best

COGAN, Kevin (USA) b 31/3/1956

1980

	Race	Circuit	No	Entrant	Car/Engine	Comment
dnq	CANADIAN GP	Montreal	51	RAM/Rainbow Jeans Racing	3.0 Williams FW07B-Cosworth V8	

1981

	Race	Circuit	No	Entrant	Car/Engine	Comment
dnq	US GP WEST	Long Beach	4	Tyrrell Racing	3.0 Tyrrell 010-Cosworth V8	

One-time IndyCar winner whose later career has been blighted by injury after a succession of major accidents

COLOMBO, Alberto (I) b 23/2/1946

1978

	Race	Circuit	No	Entrant	Car/Engine	Comment
dnq	BELGIAN GP	Zolder	10	ATS Racing Team	3.0 ATS HS1-Cosworth V8	
dnq	SPANISH GP	Jarama	10	ATS Racing Team	3.0 ATS HS1-Cosworth V8	
dnpq	ITALIAN GP	Monza	34	Team Merzario	3.0 Merzario A1-Cosworth V8	

CRESPO, Alberto (I)

1952

	Race	Circuit	No	Entrant	Car/Engine	Comment
dnq	ITALIAN GP	Monza	58	Enrico Platé	2.0 Maserati 4CLT/48-Maserati/Platé 4	

DOCHNAL, Frank J (USA)

	Race	Circuit	No	Entrant	Car/Engine	Comment
dns	MEXICAN GP	Mexico City	20	Frank J Dochnal	1.5 Cooper T53-Climax 4	*crashed in unofficial practice*

Along with Tom Jones, perhaps the most obscure character in this book, whose fleeting appearance above seems to be the sum total of his achievements

DRYVER, Bernard de (B) b 19/9/1952

1977

	Race	Circuit	No	Entrant	Car/Engine	Comment
dnq	BELGIAN GP	Zolder	38	British Formula 1 Racing	3.0 March 761-Cosworth V8	

1977

	Race	Circuit	No	Entrant	Car/Engine	Comment
dnc	BELGIAN GP	Zolder	–	Bernard de Dryver	3.0 Ensign N177-Cosworth V8	*did not qualify for official practice*

DUSIO, Piero (I)

1952

	Race	Circuit	No	Entrant	Car/Engine	Comment
dnq	ITALIAN GP	Monza	44	Piero Dusio	Cisitalia D46	

ECCLESTONE, Bernie (GB) b 28/10/1931

1958

	Race	Circuit	No	Entrant	Car/Engine	Comment
dnq	MONACO GP	Monte Carlo	12	B C Ecclestone	2.5 Connaught B-Alta 4	*not a serious attempt*
dnq	BRITISH GP	Silverstone	14	B C Ecclestone	2.5 Connaught B-Alta 4	*car driven by Fairman*

Subsequently owned Brabham team, and in his capacities with FOCA and the FIA has been the driving force shaping the development of Grand Prix racing

FACETTI, Carlo (I)

1974

	Race	Circuit	No	Entrant	Car/Engine	Comment
dnq	ITALIAN GP	Monza	31	Scuderia Finotto	3.0 Brabham BT42-Cosworth V8	

FERGUSON, Willie (ZA)

1972

	Race	Circuit	No	Entrant	Car/Engine	Comment
dns	SOUTH AFRICAN GP	Kyalami	28	Team Gunston	3.0 Brabham BT33-Cosworth V8	*engine in practice*
dns	" "	"	27T	Team Gunston	3.0 Surtees TS9-Cosworth V8	*car driven by Love in race*

FRANCIA, Giorgio (I) b 8/11/1947

1977

	Race	Circuit	No	Entrant	Car/Engine	Comment
dnq	ITALIAN GP	Monza	21	Martini Racing	3.0 Brabham BT45B-Alfa Romeo F12	*withdrawn after first practice*

1981

	Race	Circuit	No	Entrant	Car/Engine	Comment
dnq	SPANISH GP	Jarama	32	Osella Squadra Corse	3.0 Osella FA1B-Cosworth V8	

Alfa Romeo stalwart, who has raced for over two decades in most categories. Still going strong in 1993 as part of Alfa's GTCC squad

FUSHIDA, Hiroshi (J)

1975

	Race	Circuit	No	Entrant	Car/Engine	Comment
dns	DUTCH GP	Zandvoort	35	Maki Engineering	3.0 Maki F101C-Cosworth V8	*blown engine in practice*
dnq	BRITISH GP	Silverstone	35	Maki Engineering	3.0 Maki F101C-Cosworth V8	

GALICA, Davina (GB) b 13/8/1946

1976

	Race	Circuit	No	Entrant	Car/Engine	Comment
dnq	BRITISH GP	Brands Hatch	13	Shellsport/Whiting	3.0 Surtees TS16-Cosworth V8	

1978

	Race	Circuit	No	Entrant	Car/Engine	Comment
dnq	ARGENTINE GP	Buenos Aires	24	Olympus Cameras with Hesketh	3.0 Hesketh 308E-Cosworth V8	
dnq	BRAZILIAN GP	Rio	24	Olympus Cameras with Hesketh	3.0 Hesketh 308E-Cosworth V8	

Determined lady racer and international skiier who made her mark in the mid-seventies Shellsport G8 series

'GIMAX' (I)

1978

	Race	Circuit	No	Entrant	Car/Engine	Comment
dnq	ITALIAN GP	Monza	18	Team Surtees	3.0 Surtees TS20-Cosworth V8	

GLOCKNER, Helmut (D)

1953

	Race	Circuit	No	Entrant	Car/Engine	Comment
dns	GERMAN GP	Nürburgring	39	Equipe Anglaise	3.0 Cooper T23-Bristol 6	*engine threw rod in practice*

GUBBY, Brian (GB)

1965

	Race	Circuit	No	Entrant	Car/Engine	Comment
dnq	BRITISH GP	Silverstone	26	Brian Gubby	1.5 Lotus 24-Climax V8	

HATTORI, Naoki (J) b 13/6/1966

1991

	Race	Circuit	No	Entrant	Car/Engine	Comment
ret	JAPANESE GP	Suzuka	31	Coloni Racing Srl	3.5 Coloni C4-Cosworth V8	
ret	AUSTRALIAN GP	Adelaide	31	Coloni Racing Srl	3.5 Coloni C4-Cosworth V8	

Motor sport journalist and Japanese F3 champion in 1990. Controversially refused a superlicence to race a Brabham in F1 in 1992

HEYER, Hans (D) *also included in main statistics*

1977

	Race	Circuit	No	Entrant	Car/Engine	Comment
ret	GERMAN GP	Hockenheim	35	ATS Racing Team	3.0 Penske PC4-Cosworth V8	*gear linkage/dnq but started anyway*

JONES, Tom (CDN)

1967

	Race	Circuit	No	Entrant	Car/Engine	Comment
dnq	CANADIAN GP	Mosport Park	41	Tom Jones	2.0 Cooper T82-Climax V8	*too slow*

JOVER, Juan (E)

1951

	Race	Circuit	No	Entrant	Car/Engine	Comment
dns	SPANISH GP	Pedralbes	46	Scuderia Milano	1.5 s/c Maserati 4CLT/48 4	*mechanical trouble in practice*

KAVANAGH, Ken (AUS)

1958

	Race	Circuit	No	Entrant	Car/Engine	Comment
dnq	MONACO GP	Monte Carlo	50	Ken Kavanagh	2.5 Maserati 250F 6	
dns	BELGIAN GP	Spa	34	Ken Kavanagh	2.5 Maserati 250F 6	*engine in practice*

Very successful Norton and Moto-Guzzi motor cycle racer, who dabbled briefly in four-wheeled competition

KENNEDY, David (IRL) b 15/1/1953

1980

	Race	Circuit	No	Entrant	Car/Engine	Comment
dnq	ARGENTINE GP	Buenos Aires	18	Shadow Cars	3.0 Shadow DN11-Cosworth V8	
dnq	BRAZILIAN GP	Interlagos	18	Shadow Cars	3.0 Shadow DN11-Cosworth V8	
dnq	SOUTH AFRICAN GP	Kyalami	18	Shadow Cars	3.0 Shadow DN11-Cosworth V8	
dnq	US GP WEST	Long Beach	18	Shadow Cars	3.0 Shadow DN11-Cosworth V8	
dnq	BELGIAN GP	Zolder	18	Shadow Cars	3.0 Shadow DN11-Cosworth V8	
dnq	MONACO GP	Monte Carlo	18	Theodore Shadow	3.0 Shadow DN11-Cosworth V8	
dnq	FRENCH GP	Paul Ricard	18	Theodore Shadow	3.0 Shadow DN12-Cosworth V8	

Note: qualified and raced in 1980 Spanish GP – subsequently deprived of championship status

1976-77 Formula Ford champion who switched to sports cars after his brief F1 career failed to take off. Raced regularly with Mazda in the late eighties

KESSLER, Bruce (USA)

1958

	Race	Circuit	No	Entrant	Car/Engine	Comment
dnq	MONACO GP	Monte Carlo	12	B C Ecclestone	2.5 Connaught B-Alta 4	

KOZAROWITSKY, Mikko (SF) b 1949

1977

	Race	Circuit	No	Entrant	Car/Engine	Comment
dnq	SWEDISH GP	Anderstorp	32	RAM Racing/F & S Properties	3.0 March 761-Cosworth V8	
dnpq	BRITISH GP	Silverstone	32	RAM Racing/F & S Properties	3.0 March 761-Cosworth V8	

KRAKAU, Willi (D)

1952

	Race	Circuit	No	Entrant	Car/Engine	Comment
dns	GERMAN GP	Nürburgring	133	Willi Krakau	2.0 AFM 6	

KUHNKE, Kurt (D)

1963

	Race	Circuit	No	Entrant	Car/Engine	Comment
dnq	GERMAN GP	Nürburgring	27	Kurt Kuhnke	1.5 BKL Lotus 18-Borgward 4	

KUWASHIMA, Masami (J) b 14/9/1950

1976

	Race	Circuit	No	Entrant	Car/Engine	Comment
dns	JAPANESE GP	Mount Fuji	21	Walter Wolf Racing	3.0 Williams FW05-Cosworth V8	*sponsors withdrew*

LANGES, Claudio (I) b 4/8/1961

1990

	Race	Circuit	No	Entrant	Car/Engine	Comment
dnpq	US GP (PHOENIX)	Phoenix	34	EuroBrun Racing	3.5 EuroBrun ER189-Judd V8	
dnpq	BRAZILIAN GP	Interlagos	34	EuroBrun Racing	3.5 EuroBrun ER189-Judd V8	
dnpq	SAN MARINO GP	Imola	34	EuroBrun Racing	3.5 EuroBrun ER189B-Judd V8	
dnpq	MONACO GP	Monte Carlo	34	EuroBrun Racing	3.5 EuroBrun ER189B-Judd V8	
dnpq	CANADIAN GP	Montreal	34	EuroBrun Racing	3.5 EuroBrun ER189B-Judd V8	
dnpq	MEXICAN GP	Mexico City	34	EuroBrun Racing	3.5 EuroBrun ER189B-Judd V8	
dnpq	FRENCH GP	Paul Ricard	34	EuroBrun Racing	3.5 EuroBrun ER189B-Judd V8	
dnpq	BRITISH GP	Silverstone	34	EuroBrun Racing	3.5 EuroBrun ER189B-Judd V8	
dnpq	GERMAN GP	Hockenheim	34	EuroBrun Racing	3.5 EuroBrun ER189B-Judd V8	
dnpq	HUNGARIAN GP	Hungaroring	34	EuroBrun Racing	3.5 EuroBrun ER189B-Judd V8	
dnpq	BELGIAN GP	Spa	34	EuroBrun Racing	3.5 EuroBrun ER189B-Judd V8	
dnpq	ITALIAN GP	Monza	34	EuroBrun Racing	3.5 EuroBrun ER189B-Judd V8	
dnpq	PORTUGUESE GP	Estoril	34	EuroBrun Racing	3.5 EuroBrun ER189B-Judd V8	
dnpq	SPANISH GP	Jerez	34	EuroBrun Racing	3.5 EuroBrun ER189B-Judd V8	

Gave a number of good performances in junior formulae and F3000, but his task with the EuroBrun was hopeless. Since succesfully raced touring cars

LUCIENBONNET, Jean (F)

1959

	Race	Circuit	No	Entrant	Car/Engine	Comment
dnq	MONACO GP	Monte Carlo	14	Jean Lucienbonnet	2.0 Cooper T45-Climax 4 F2	

McCARTHY, Perry (GB) b 3/3/1963

1992

	Race	Circuit	No	Entrant	Car/Engine	Comment
dnpq	SPANISH GP	Barcelona	35	Andrea Moda Formula	3.5 Moda S921-Judd V10	*did not practise*
dnpq	SAN MARINO GP	Imola	35	Andrea Moda Formula	3.5 Moda S921-Judd V10	
dnpq	MONACO GP	Monte Carlo	35	Andrea Moda Formula	3.5 Moda S921-Judd V10	*did not practise*
dnpq	CANADIAN GP	Montreal	35	Andrea Moda Formula	3.5 Moda S921-Judd V10	*did not practise*
dnpq	BRITISH GP	Silverstone	35	Andrea Moda Formula	3.5 Moda S921-Judd V10	
dsq	GERMAN GP	Hockenheim	35	Andrea Moda Formula	3.5 Moda S921-Judd V10	*missed car weight check*
dnpq	HUNGARIAN GP	Hungaroring	35	Andrea Moda Formula	3.5 Moda S921-Judd V10	*no time recorded*
dnq	BELGIAN GP	Spa	35	Andrea Moda Formula	3.5 Moda S921-Judd V10	

McGUIRE, Brian (AUS) b 13/12/1945 – d 29/8/1977

1976

	Race	Circuit	No	Entrant	Car/Engine	Comment
dnc	BRITISH GP	Brand Hatch	41	Brian McGuire	3.0 Williams FW04-Cosworth V8	*reserve entry-not allowed to compete*

1977

	Race	Circuit	No	Entrant	Car/Engine	Comment
dnpq	BRITISH GP	Silverstone	45	Brian McGuire	McGuire BM1-Cosworth V8	

Travelled over from Oz with Alan Jones to seek fame and fortune. Killed practising his own car during a national meeting at Brands Hatch

MERKEL, Harry (D)

1952

	Race	Circuit	No	Entrant	Car/Engine	Comment
dns	GERMAN GP	Nürburgring	134	Willi Krakau	2.0 BMW-Eigenbau 6	

MOSS, Bill (GB)

1959

	Race	Circuit	No	Entrant	Car/Engine	Comment
dnq	BRITISH GP (F2)	Aintree	56	United Racing Stable	1.5 Cooper T51-Climax 4 F2	

NELLEMAN, Jac (DK)

1976

	Race	Circuit	No	Entrant	Car/Engine	Comment
dnq	SWEDISH GP	Anderstorp	33	RAM Racing	3.0 Brabham BT42-Cosworth V8	
dnq	"	"	33	RAM Racing	3.0 Brabham BT44B-Cosworth V8	

OPPITZHAUSER, Karl (DK)

1976

	Race	Circuit	No	Entrant	Car/Engine	Comment
dnp	AUSTRIAN GP	Österreichring	40	Sports Cars of Austria	3.0 March 761-Cosworth V8	*No F1 experience-not allowed to run*

PIÀN, Alfredo (RA)

1950

	Race	Circuit	No	Entrant	Car/Engine	Comment
dns	MONACO GP	Monte Carlo	4	Scuderia Achille Varzi	1.5 s/c Maserati 4CLT/48 4	*practice accident*

PRINOTH, Ernesto (I)

1962

	Race	Circuit	No	Entrant	Car/Engine	Comment
dnq	ITALIAN GP	Monza	54	Scuderia Jolly Club	1.5 Lotus 18-Climax 4	

RICHARDSON, Ken (GB)

1951

	Race	Circuit	No	Entrant	Car/Engine	Comment
dnq	ITALIAN GP	Monza	32	BRM Ltd	1.5 s/c BRM P15 V16	did not possess correct licence

Test and development driver on the drawn-out and largely unsuccessful BRM V16 project of the early fifties

RIU, Giovanni de (I)

1954

	Race	Circuit	No	Entrant	Car/Engine	Comment
dnq	ITALIAN GP	Monza	2	Giovanni de Riu	2.5 Maserati A6GCM/250F 6	too slow

ROLLINSON, Alan (GB) b 1943

1965

	Race	Circuit	No	Entrant	Car/Engine	Comment
dnq	BRITISH GP	Silverstone	25	Gerard Racing	1.5 Cooper T71/73-Ford 4	

Talented British F5000 runner who never made a Grand Prix start, but enjoyed a long and successful career in other formulae

RUDAZ, Jean-Claude (CH)

1964

	Race	Circuit	No	Entrant	Car/Engine	Comment
dns	ITALIAN GP	Monza	60	Fabre Urbain	1.5 Cooper T60-Climax V8	engine in practice

SEIFFERT Gunther (D)

1962

	Race	Circuit	No	Entrant	Car/Engine	Comment
dnq	GERMAN GP	Nürburgring	34	Autosport Team Wolfgang Seidel	1.5 Lotus 24-BRM V8	shared car with Seidel

SOUTH, Stephen (GB) b 19/2/1952

1980

	Race	Circuit	No	Entrant	Car/Engine	Comment
dnq	US GP WEST	Long Beach	8	Marlboro Team McLaren	3.0 McLaren M29-Cosworth V8	

Looked to have a big future until Can-Am accident in 1980 resulted in the amputation of part of his leg

STUPPACHER, Otto (A)

1976

	Race	Circuit	No	Entrant	Car/Engine	Comment
dnq	ITALIAN GP	Monza	39	OASC Racing Team	3.0 Tyrrell 007-Cosworth V8	
dnq	CANADIAN GP	Mosport Park	39	OASC Racing Team	3.0 Tyrrell 007-Cosworth V8	
dnq	US GP EAST	Watkins Glen	39	OASC Racing Team	3.0 Tyrrell 007-Cosworth V8	

Austrian hill-climber and Porsche sports car exponent of no great pedigree

SUTCLIFFE, Andy (GB) b 9/5/1947

1977

	Race	Circuit	No	Entrant	Car/Engine	Comment
dnpq	BRITISH GP	Silverstone	33	RAM Racing	3.0 March 761-Cosworth V8	

British Formula 3 flyer who failed to meet expectations in Formula 2 with a privateer March

TAYLOR, Dennis (GB) b 12/6/1921 – d 2/6/1962

1959

	Race	Circuit	No	Entrant	Car/Engine	Comment
dnq	BRITISH GP (F2)	Aintree	62	Dennis Taylor	1.5 Lotus 12-Climax 4	

Enthusiastic sports and Formula Junior racer who was killed when he crashed in the Monaco FJ support race in 1962

TESTUT, André (MC)

1958

	Race	Circuit	No	Entrant	Car/Engine	Comment
dnq	MONACO GP	Monte Carlo	56	André Testut	2.5 Maserati 250F 6	

1959

	Race	Circuit	No	Entrant	Car/Engine	Comment
dnq	MONACO GP	Monte Carlo	56	Monte Carlo Auto Sport	2.5 Maserati 250F 6	

TRIMMER, Tony (GB) b 12/6/1921

1975

	Race	Circuit	No	Entrant	Car/Engine	Comment
dnq	GERMAN GP	Nürburgring	35	Maki Engineering	3.0 Maki F101C-Cosworth V8	
dnq	AUSTRIAN GP	Österreichring	35	Maki Engineering	3.0 Maki F101C-Cosworth V8	
dnq	ITALIAN GP	Monza	35	Maki Engineering	3.0 Maki F101C-Cosworth V8	

1976

dnq	JAPANESE GP	Mount Fuji	54	Maki Engineering	3.0 Maki F102A-Cosworth V8	

1977

dnpq	BRITISH GP	Silverstone	44	Melchester Racing	3.0 Surtees TS19-Cosworth V8	

1978

dnq	BRITISH GP	Brands Hatch	40	Melchester Racing	3.0 McLaren M23-Cosworth V8	

Formula Ford star and 1970 British Formula 3 champion, whose career lost its way after he ended up in succession of uncompetitive cars

VILLENEUVE, Jacques (CDN) b 4/11/1955

1981

	Race	Circuit	No	Entrant	Car/Engine	Comment
dnq	CANADIAN GP	Montreal	30	Arrows Racing Team	3.0 Arrows A3-Cosworth V8	
dnq	CAESARS PALACE GP	Las Vegas	30	Arrows Racing Team	3.0 Arrows A3-Cosworth V8	

1983

dnq	CANADIAN GP	Montreal	17	RAM Automotive Team March	3.0 March RAM 01-Cosworth V8	

Older brother of the great Gilles. Jacques' F1 career never took off, but he did win an IndyCar race in 1985

WEIDLER, Volker (D) b 18/3/1962

1989

	Race	Circuit	No	Entrant	Car/Engine	Comment
dnpq	BRAZILIAN GP	Rio	39	Rial Racing	3.5 Rial ARC2-Cosworth V8	
dnpq	SAN MARINO GP	Imola	39	Rial Racing	3.5 Rial ARC2-Cosworth V8	
dnpq	MONACO GP	Monte Carlo	39	Rial Racing	3.5 Rial ARC2-Cosworth V8	
dnpq	MEXICAN GP	Mexico City	39	Rial Racing	3.5 Rial ARC2-Cosworth V8	
dnpq	US GP (PHOENIX)	Phoenix	39	Rial Racing	3.5 Rial ARC2-Cosworth V8	
dnpq	CANADIAN GP	Montreal	39	Rial Racing	3.5 Rial ARC2-Cosworth V8	
dnpq	FRENCH GP	Paul Ricard	39	Rial Racing	3.5 Rial ARC2-Cosworth V8	
dnpq	BRITISH GP	Silverstone	39	Rial Racing	3.5 Rial ARC2-Cosworth V8	
excl	GERMAN GP	Hockenheim	39	Rial Racing	3.5 Rial ARC2-Cosworth V8	*received outside assistance*
dnq	HUNGARIAN GP	Hungaroring	39	Rial Racing	3.5 Rial ARC2-Cosworth V8	

F3000 graduate whose time with Rial put paid to any further F1 chances. Won Le Mans with Mazda in 1991, then went to race in F3000 in Japan

WHITEAWAY, Ted (GB) b 1/11/1928

1955

	Race	Circuit	No	Entrant	Car/Engine	Comment
dnq	MONACO GP	Monte Carlo	24	E N Whiteaway	2.5 HWM-Alta 4	

WILSON, Desiré (ZA) b 26/11/1953

1980

	Race	Circuit	No	Entrant	Car/Engine	Comment
dnq	BRITISH GP	Brands Hatch	43	Brands Hatch Racing	3.0 Williams FW07-Cosworth V8	

South African who became the first woman ever to win a Formula 1 race of any kind at a round of the Aurora F1 series at Brands Hatch in 1980

WINKELHOCK, Joachim (D) b 24/10/1960

1989

	Race	Circuit	No	Entrant	Car/Engine	Comment
dnpq	BRAZILIAN GP	Rio	41	Automobiles Gonfaronaise Sportive	3.5 AGS JH23B-Cosworth V8	
dnpq	SAN MARINO GP	Imola	41	Automobiles Gonfaronaise Sportive	3.5 AGS JH23B-Cosworth V8	
dnpq	MONACO GP	Monte Carlo	41	Automobiles Gonfaronaise Sportive	3.5 AGS JH23B-Cosworth V8	
dnpq	MEXICAN GP	Mexico City	41	Automobiles Gonfaronaise Sportive	3.5 AGS JH23B-Cosworth V8	
dnpq	US GP (PHOENIX)	Phoenix	41	Automobiles Gonfaronaise Sportive	3.5 AGS JH23B-Cosworth V8	
dnpq	CANADIAN GP	Montreal	41	Automobiles Gonfaronaise Sportive	3.5 AGS JH23B-Cosworth V8	
dnpq	FRENCH GP	Paul Ricard	41	Automobiles Gonfaronaise Sportive	3.5 AGS JH23B-Cosworth V8	

1988 German F3 champion who had a disastrous spell with AGS before turning to touring cars with BMW. BTCC champion in 1993

ZAPICO, Emilio (E)

1976

	Race	Circuit	No	Entrant	Car/Engine	Comment
dnq	SPANISH GP	Jarama	25	Mapfre-Williams	3.0 Williams FW04-Cosworth V8	

SELECTED BIBLIOGRAPHY

YEARBOOKS, MAGAZINES & PERIODICALS

AUTOCAR & MOTOR	AUTOCOURSE
AUTOSPORT	THE 'MOTOR' YEARBOOK 1948 to 1960
GRAND PRIX INTERNATIONAL	MARLBORO GRAND PRIX GUIDE 1972 to 1974
MOTORING NEWS	JOHN PLAYER MOTOR SPORT YEAR 1972 to 1976
MOTOR SPORT	INTERNATIONAL MOTOR RACING YEAR 1977 to 1978
ROAD & TRACK	MOTOR RACING AND RALLY DIRECTORY 1957

BOOKS

MICHAEL COOPER-EVANS
ROB WALKER
Hazleton Publishing

ROBERT CUTTER & BOB FENDELL
ENCYCLOPEDIA OF AUTO GREATS
Prentice Hall

ROBERT DALEY
THE CRUEL SPORT
Studio Vista

ROBERT DALEY
CARS AT SPEED
Foulis

LYLE KENYON ENGEL
JACKIE STEWART – WORLD DRIVING CHAMPION
Arco Publishing

JUAN MANUEL FANGIO
FANGIO
Temple Press

EMERSON FITTIPALDI & ELIZABETH HAYWARD
FLYING ON THE GROUND
William Kimber

G N GEORGEANO (Ed)
ENCYCLOPEDIA OF MOTOR RACING
Ebury Press and Michael Joseph

DAVID HAYHOE
GRAND PRIX DATA BOOK
Kimberley

ALAN HENRY
GRAND PRIX – DRIVER BY DRIVER
Crowood Press

ALAN HENRY
MARCH, THE GRAND PRIX & INDY CARS
Hazleton Publishing

DENIS JENKINSON (Ed)
FANGIO
Michael Joseph

DENIS JENKINSON & CYRIL POSTHUMUS
VANWALL
Patrick Stephens

JENKINSON/ROEBUCK/HENRY/HAMILTON
THE GRAND PRIX DRIVERS
Hazleton Publishing

CHRIS JONES
ROAD RACE
George Allen & Unwin

MICHAEL KEYSER
THE SPEED MERCHANTS
Prentice Hall

GORDON KIRBY
EMERSON FITTIPALDI
Hazleton Publishing

RAYMOND MAYS & PETER ROBERTS
BRM
Pan Books

PETER MILLER
MEN AT THE WHEEL
Batsford

PETER MILLER
THE FAST ONES
Stanley Paul

CHRIS NIXON
**RACING WITH THE DAVID BROWN
ASTON MARTINS Vols 1 & 2**
Transport Bookman

DOUG NYE
**THE AUTOCOURSE HISTORY OF THE GRAND PRIX
CAR 1945-65 & 1966-91**
Hazleton Publishing

DOUG NYE
THEME LOTUS 1958-86
MRP

DOUG NYE
DINO – THE LITTLE FERRARI
Osprey

DOUG NYE
**RACERS: THE INSIDE STORY OF WILLIAMS GRAND
PRIX ENGINEERING**
Osprey

DOUG NYE
COOPER CARS
Osprey

DOUG NYE
THE UNITED STATES GRAND PRIX 1908-77
Batsford

DOUG NYE
THE BRITISH GRAND PRIX 1926-76
Batsford

HEINZ PRÜLLER
JOCHEN RINDT
William Kimber

PETER REVSON & LEON MANDEL
**SPEED WITH STYLE – THE AUTOBIOGRAPHY OF
PETER REVSON**
William Kimber

NIGEL ROEBUCK
GRAND PRIX GREATS
Patrick Stephens

Dr K PAUL SHELDON with DUNCAN RABAGLIATI
**A RECORD OF GRAND PRIX AND VOITURETTE
RACING – Volumes 5, 6 & 7**
St Leonard's Press

JOHN SURTEES
JOHN SURTEES – WORLD CHAMPION
Hazleton Publishing

HANS TANNER & DOUG NYE
FERRARI
Haynes

JONATHAN THOMPSON with DUNCAN
RABAGLIATI & Dr K PAUL SHELDON
THE FORMULA ONE RECORD BOOK
Leslie Frewin

THE AUTHOR

Now 'forty-something', Steve Small has been a close follower of motor sport since the mid-sixties, when the likes of Clark, Hill, Rindt and Stewart seemed to be racing almost every weekend across the many categories of the sport.

Having gained a Dip. A.D. and M.A. in Graphic Design, he worked for more than a decade in advertising and design, before moving into the publishing world. The Managing and Art Editor of the prestigious motor sport annual AUTOCOURSE since 1986, he has been involved with many other acclaimed motor sport titles, as well as the successful *'Player by Player'* soccer series recently published by Guinness.